THE EXPOSITOR'S

GREEK TESTAMENT

EDITED BY THE REV.

W. ROBERTSON NICOLL, M.A., LL.D.

EDITOR OF "THE EXPOSITOR," "THE EXPOSITOR'S BIBLE," ETC.

VOLUME IV.

WM. B. EERDMANS PUBLISHING COMPANY

GRANDS RAPIDS, MICHIGAN

U. S. A.

THE EXPOSITOR'S
GREEK TESTAMENT

I
THE FIRST AND SECOND EPISTLES TO THE THESSALONIANS
BY
JAMES MOFFATT, D.D.

II
THE FIRST AND SECOND EPISTLES TO TIMOTHY
AND
THE EPISTLE TO TITUS
BY
NEWPORT J. D. WHITE, D.D.

III
THE EPISTLE TO PHILEMON
BY
W. E. OESTERLEY, M.A., B.D.

IV
THE EPISTLE TO THE HEBREWS
BY
MARCUS DODS, D.D.

V
THE GENERAL EPISTLE OF JAMES
BY
W. E. OESTERLEY, M.A., B.D.

WM. B. EERDMANS PUBLISHING COMPANY
GRANDS RAPIDS, MICHIGAN
U. S. A.

THE FIRST AND SECOND EPISTLES OF
PAUL THE APOSTLE
TO THE
THESSALONIANS

INTRODUCTION.

§ 1. *The Mission to Thessalonica.*—The Christian inhabitants of Thessalonica were mainly Greeks by birth and training (i. 9, *cf.* ii. 14; Acts xiv. 15, xv. 19), who had been won over from paganism by the efforts of Paul, Silvanus (Silas), and Timotheus (Timothy), during an effective campaign which lasted for a month or two. It had opened quietly with a three weeks' mission in the local synagogue. Luke, who by this time had left the trio, enters into no details about its length or methods, adding merely that some of the Jews believed, while a host of devout Greeks and a considerable number of the leading women threw in their lot with the apostles. Luke is seldom interested in the growth or fortunes of individual churches. But, as the subsequent membership of the church, its widespread influence and fame, its inner condition, and the resentment caused by the success of the Pauline mission (continued from the house of Jason, Acts xvii. 5) all imply, a considerable interval must have elapsed before the time when the apostles were forced prematurely to quit the place. Their stay was prolonged to an extent of which Acts gives no idea; for Paul not only supported himself by working at his trade but had time to receive repeated gifts of money[1] from his friends at Philippi, a hundred miles away, as well as to engage perhaps in mission work throughout Macedonia (i. 7) if not as far west as Illyricum (Rom. xv. 19, *cf.* Lightfoot's *Biblical Essays*, 237 f.). Two or three months possibly may be allowed for this fruitful mission at Thessalonica.

When the local πολιτάρχαι, at the instigation of Jews who were nettled at the Christians' success, finally expelled Paul and his companions, the subsequent movements of the latter were governed by a desire to keep in touch with the inexperienced and unconsolidated Christian community which they had left behind them. The summary outline of Acts xvii. 10-15 requires to be supplemented and

---

[1] Probably this was one of the reasons which led to the imputation of mercenary motives (ii. 5, 9).

corrected at this point by the information of 1 Thess. ii. 17-iii. 6.
According to Luke, Silas and Timotheus remained at Beroea, under
orders to rejoin Paul as soon as possible.   They only reached him at
Corinth (Acts xviii. 5), however.   Now since Timotheus, as we know
from Paul, visited Thessalonica in the meantime, we must assume
one of two courses.   (a) Leaving Silas at Beroea, Timotheus hurried on to Paul at Athens, was sent back (with a letter ?) to Thessalonica, and, on his return, picked up Silas at Beroea ; whereupon
both joined their leader, who by this time had moved on suddenly to
Corinth.   This implies that the plural in iii. 1 is the *pluralis majesta-*
ticus or *auctoris* (see on iii. 5), since Silas was not with Paul at
Athens.   But the possibility of that plural meaning both Paul and
Silas, together with the silence of Acts, suggests (b) an alternative
reconstruction of the history, *viz.*, that Timotheus and Silas jour-
neyed together from Beroea to Athens, where they met Paul and
were despatched thence on separate missions, Silas[1] perhaps to
Philippi, Timotheus at an earlier date to Thessalonica, both rejoining
Paul eventually at Corinth.   In any case the natural sense of iii. 1, 2
is that Paul sent Timotheus from Athens, not (so *e.g.*, von Soden,
Studien u. Kritiken, 1885, 291 f.) that he sent directions from Athens
for his colleague to leave Beroea and betake himself to Thessalonica
(*E. Bi.*, 5076, 5077).

From no church did Paul tear himself with such evident reluct-
ance.   His anxiety to get back to it was not simply due to the feeling that he must go on with the Macedonian mission, if at all
possible, but to his deep affection for the local community.   The
Macedonian churches may almost be termed Paul's favourites.
None troubled him less.   None came so near to his heart.   At Thessalonica the exemplary character of the Christians,[2] their rapid growth,

---

[1] This mission, or a mission of Silas (*cf.* iii. 5) after Timotheus to Thessalonica
itself, though passed over both by Luke and Paul, must be assumed, if the statement
of Acts xviii. 5 is held to be historical, since the latter passage implies that Paul was
not accompanied by Silas from Athens to Corinth.   The alternative is to suppose
that he left Silas behind in Athens, as at Beroea.   A comparison of 1 Thess. with
Acts bears out the aphorism of Baronius that *epistolaris historia est optima historia ;*
Luke's narrative is neither clear nor complete.

[2] Renan (*S. Paul,* 135-139) praises the solid, national qualities of the Macedonians, "un peuple de paysans protestants; c'est une belle et forte race, laborieuse,
sédentaire, aimant sons pays, pleine d'avenir".   It was their very warmth of heart
which made them at once so loyal to Paul and his gospel, and also so liable to
unsettlement in view of their friends' death (iv. 15 f.).   Compare the description
of the Macedonian churches in von Dobschütz's *Christ. Life in the Primitive Church,*
pp. 81 f.

their exceptional opportunities,[1] and their widespread reputation, moved him to a pardonable pride. But, as he learnt, they had been suffering persecution since he left, and this awakened sympathy as well as concern for its effects on their faith. Unable to return himself, he had at last sent Timotheus to them; it was the joyful tidings (iii. 6) just brought by him which prompted Paul to send off this informal letter, partly (i.) to reciprocate their warm affection, partly (ii.) to give them some fresh instructions upon their faith and conduct.

§ 2. *The First Epistle.*—This two-fold general object determines the course of the letter, which was written from Corinth[2] (Acts xviii. 11). It begins with a hearty thanksgiving for the success of the mission at Thessalonica (i. 2-10), and this naturally passes into an *apologia pro vita sua* (ii. 1-12) against the insinuations which he had heard that local outsiders were circulating vindictively against the character of the apostles. The Thessalonian church knew better than to believe such sordid calumnies! The second reason for thanksgiving is (ii. 13 f.) the church's brave endurance of hardship at the hands of their townsmen. "Would that we could be at your side! Would that we could uphold you and share the good fight! But we cannot. It is our misfortune, not our fault." Paul now gives a detailed *apologia pro absentia sua* (ii. 17 f.), which ends with praise for the staunchness of his friends during his enforced absence. The latter part of the letter (iv. 1 f.) consists of a series of shrewd, kindly injunctions for the maintenance of their position: περὶ ἁγιασμοῦ (iv. 3-8), περὶ φιλαδελφίας (9 f.) περὶ τῶν κοιμωμένων (13-18), περὶ τῶν χρόνων καὶ τῶν καιρῶν (v. 1-11). With a handful of precepts upon social and religious duties, and an earnest word of prayer, the epistle then closes. Its date depends on the view taken of Pauline chronology in general; that is, it may lie between 48 and

---

[1] "Nature has made it the capital and seaport of a rich and extensive district" (Finlay, *Byzantine Empire*, book ii., chap. i. 2). One of its great streets was part of the famous Via Egnatia, along which Paul and his companions had travelled S.W. from Philippi; thus Thessalonica was linked with the East and with the Adriatic alike (*cf.* i. 7, 8), while its position at the head of the Thermaic Gulf made it a busy trading centre for the Egean. Hence the colony of Jews with their synagogue. It was a populous, predominantly Greek town, of some military importance, with strong commercial interests throughout Macedonia (*cf.* i. 8) and even beyond. On the far horizon, south-west, the cloudy height of Mount Olympus was visible, no longer peopled by the gods, but, as Cicero put it, occupied merely by snow and ice (*cf.* i. 9).

[2] This is proved not by ἐν ᾿Αθήναις (iii. 1, *cf.* 1 Cor. xv. 32, xvi. 8) but by the reference to Achaia in 1 Thess. i. 7, 8.

53 A.D., probably nearer the latter date than the former. The epistle itself contains no reference to any year or contemporary event, which would afford a fixed point of time. An ingenious attempt has been made by Prof. Rendel Harris (*Exp.*[5] viii. 161 f., 401 f. ; *cf.* B. W. Bacon's *Introd. to N.T.*, 73 f. and his *Story of St. Paul*, 235 f.) to show that Timotheus had previously taken a letter from Paul to the church, and that the canonical epistle represents a reply to one sent from the church to Paul ; the hypothesis is tenable, but the evidence is rather elusive. The use of καὶ, *e.g.*, in ii. 13, iii. 5, is not to be pressed into a proof of this : οἴδατε is not an infallible token of such a communication (= "you have admitted in your letter," which Timotheus brought), and ἀπαγγέλλετε [1] is an unsupported conjecture in i. 9.

§ 3. *The Position of the Local Church.*—The occasion and the significance of this epistle to the Christians of Thessalonica thus become fairly clear.

(*a*) Paul and his friends had left them the memory and inspiration of a Christian character. The epistle came to be written because the legacy had been disputed.

The insinuations of some local Jews and pagans [2] against Paul's character were like torches flung at an unpopular figure ; they simply served to light up his grandeur. Had it not been for such attacks, at Thessalonica as at Corinth, we should not have had these passages of indignant and pathetic self-revelation in which Paul opens his very heart and soul. But this is the compensation derived by a cool and later age. At the moment the attack was more than distasteful to Paul himself. He resented it keenly on account of his converts, for his enemies and theirs were trying to strike at these inexperienced Christians through him, not by questioning his apostolic credentials but by calumniating his motives during the mission and his reasons for not returning afterwards. To discredit him was to shake their faith. To stain his character was to upset their religious standing. The passion and persistence with which he finds it needful to repudiate such misconceptions, show that he felt them to be not simply

---

[1] The ordinary reading gives quite a good sense : ἃ γὰρ αὐτοὺς ἐχρῆν παρ' ἡμῶν ἀκούειν, ταῦτα αὐτοὶ προλαβόντες λέγουσι (Chrysostom). It is both arbitrary and fanciful of Zahn (*Einleitung*, § 13) to mould such allusions into a theory that the news had reached Asia, and that Paul was now in personal touch with envoys from the churches of Galatia, to whom he wrote Galatians before Silvanus and Timotheus rejoined him at Athens.

[2] It is unreal to confine the calumnies to the one or to the other, particularly to the pagans (so *e.g.*, von Soden, pp. 306 f. ; Clemen, *Paulus*, ii. 181 f.).

a personal insult but likely to prove a serious menace to the interests of his friends at Thessalonica. The primary charge against the Christian evangelists had been treason or sedition; they were arraigned before the local authorities for setting up βασιλέα ἕτερον (Acts xvii. 6-8). But during his enforced absence (thanks to the success of this manœuvre), further charges against Paul's personal character were disseminated. He was just a sly, unscrupulous, selfish fellow! He left his dupes in the lurch! And so forth. Naturally, when he comes to write, it is the latter innuendoes which occupy his mind. The former charge is barely mentioned (ii. 12, *God's own kingdom*, *cf.* II., i. 5).

Paul's vindication of his character and conduct, which occupies most of the first part of the epistle, is psychologically apt. He was the first Christian the Thessalonians had ever seen. He and his friends practically represented the Christian faith. It had been the duty of the apostles to give not only instruction but a personal example of the new life to these converts; thus their reputation formed a real asset at Thessalonica. καὶ ὑμεῖς μιμηταὶ ἡμῶν ἐγενήθητε καὶ τοῦ κυρίου.[1] If the local Christians were to lose faith in their leaders, then, with little or nothing to fall back upon, their faith in God might go (*cf.* iii. 5). It was this concern on their behalf[2] which led Paul to recall his stay among them and to go over his actions since then, with such anxious care (see notes on i. 4 f., ii. 1-11, 17 f., iii. 1-13).

(*b*) In addition to this, the Thessalonian community possessed definite παραδόσεις, in the shape of injunctions or regulations as to the faith and conduct of the Christian life (ii. 11, iv. 1, 12 ; *cf.* 2 Thess. ii. 5, 15, iii. 6). These were authoritative regulations,[3] as the other epistles indicate (*cf. e.g.*, 1 Cor. iv. 17) which had the sanc-

---

[1] On the ethical function of this self-assertion, as a means of inspiration and education, see *Exp. Ti.*, x. 445 f. The young Italian patriots who died, as they had lived, confessing their faith in "God, Mazzini, and Duty," are a modern case in point. The example of τοῦ κυρίου implies that the Thessalonians were familiar with the earthly trials and temptations of Jesus.

[2] The language of ii. 1-10 must not be taken as if Paul had been blaming himself for having appeared to leave his friends in the lurch. It is not the sensitiveness of an affectionate self-reproach but the indignant repudiation of local slanders which breathes through the passage. The former would be a sadly *post factum* defence.

[3] The epistle itself (*cf.* v. 27) takes its place in the series; this verse (see note) is perfectly intelligible as it stands and need not be suspected as the interpolation of a later reader to emphasise the apostolic authority of the epistle (so Schmiedel and others), much less taken (as *e.g.*, by Baur, van der Vies, 106 f., and Schräder, *der Apostel Paulus*, 36) to discredit the entire epistle. There is no hint of any clerical organisation such as the latter theory involves.

tion of apostolic tradition, and must have been based, in some cases, upon definite sayings of Jesus. It is the Christian halacha of which the later epistles give ample if incidental proof.

This suggests a further question. To what extent do the Thessalonian epistles reveal (c) an acquaintance on the part of Paul and the local church with the sayings of the Lord? The evidence cannot be estimated adequately except in the light of the corroborative facts drawn from an examination of the other epistles, but it is enough to bear the general consideration in mind, that no preoccupation with the risen Christ and his return could have rendered Paul absolutely indifferent to the historical data of the life of Jesus.[1] When he told the Thessalonians that Jesus was the Christ, they could not believe without knowing something of Jesus. The wrath of God they might have reason to fear. But ὁ ῥυόμενος? Who was He to exercise this wonderful function? Where had He lived? Why had He died? Had He risen? And when was He to return? Some historical content[2] had to be put into the name Jesus, if faith was to awaken, especially in people who lived far from Palestine. The Spirit did not work in a mental vacuum, or in a hazy mist of apocalyptic threats and hopes. Hence, a priori, it is natural to assume that such historical allusions to the life and teaching of Jesus may be reflected in Paul's letters, as they must have been present in his preaching. This expectation is justified.

The coincidence of ii. 7 and Luke xxii. 27 is not indeed sufficient to warrant any such inference, while the different meanings of καλεῖν in ii. 12 and in the parable of Luke xiv. 15 f. (cf. ver. 24) prevent any hypothesis of a connection. On the other hand ii. 14-16 certainly contains a reminiscence of the logia preserved in a passage like Luke xi. 48 f. = Matt. xxiii. 32-34 (see the full discussion in Resch's Parallel Texte, ii. 278 f., iii. 209 f.), and, while the thought of iii. 3b-4 (cf. i. 4-6) only resembles that of Luke ix. 22-24, just as iii. 13 may be derived from an O.T. background instead of, necessarily, from synoptic logia like those of Mark viii. 38 = Matt. xvi. 27, a sentence such as that in iv. 8 distinctly echoes the saying in Luke x. 16 (" l'allusion

---

[1] This idea dominates von Soden's brilliant essay in Theol. Abhandlungen C. von Weizsäcker gewidmet (1892), pp. 113-167. More balanced estimates are to be found in Keim's Jesus of Nazara, i., pp. 54 f.; Titius, der Paulinismus unter dem Gesichtspunkt der Seligkeit (1900), pp. 10-18, and M. Goguel, L'Apôtre Paul et Jésus Christus (1904), pp. 67-99. The English reader may consult Sabatier's Paul, pp. 76 f., and Dr. R. J. Knowling's Witness of the Epistles (1892) where, as in his Testimony of St. Paul to Christ (1905), the shallows as well as the depths of the relevant literature are indefatigably dredged.

[2] Cf. Prof. Denney in DCG, ii. 394 f.

est d'une netteté parfaite," M. Goguel, p. 87). The well-known λόγος Κυρίου of iv. 16 f. cannot be adduced in this connection without hesitation (see note). But no possible doubt attaches to the evidence of v. 1-3. The saying of Jesus which is echoed here has been preserved in Luke xii. 39 (ὁ κλέπτης ἔρχεται) [1] and xxi. 34 (μή ποτε . . . ἐπιστῇ ἐφ' ὑμᾶς ἐφνίδιος ἡ ἡμέρα ἐκείνη ὡς παγίς), but the common original seems to have been in Aramaic or Hebrew (so Prof. Marshall, *Exp*.[4] ii. 73 f.), since Paul's ὥσπερ ἡ ὠδίν and Luke's ὡς παγίς must reflect a phrase like חבל(כ), which might be rendered either as חֶבֶל (snare) or as חֵבֶל (travail), the latter echoing the well-known conception of ἀρχὴ ὠδινῶν (*cf*. Mark xiii. 8). A further echo of the primitive evangelic tradition is to be heard possibly in v. 6 (Matt. xxiv. 42), certainly in v. 13 (*cf*. Mark ix. 50). But the connection of v. 21 with the agraphon, γίνεσθε δόκιμοι τραπεζῖται, is curious rather than vital.

In the second epistle, apart from coincidences like i. 5 (= Luke xx. 35) and iii. 3 (= Matt. vi. 13), the allusions to the teaching of Jesus are less numerous, although Resch hears the echo of a logion in iii. 10 (*Paulinismus*, 409 f.), on most inadequate grounds. The apocalyptic passage, ii. 1-10, contains several striking parallels to the language of Matt. xxiv. (*cf*. H. A. A. Kennedy, *St. Paul's Conception of the Last Things*, 55 f., 96 f.), but no literary relationship can be assumed.

(*d*) Finally, before Paul left, he arranged for a kind of informal organisation. An ordination of πρεσβύτεροι is not to be thought of, but probably the earliest converts, or at any rate those who had natural gifts, assumed an unofficial superintendence of the community, arranged for its worship and internal management, and were careful that the sick and poor and young were looked after. Otherwise, the movement might have been dissipated. Wesley, in his journal (Aug., 1763), writes : " I was more convinced than ever that the preaching like an apostle, without joining together those that are awakened, and training them up in the ways of God, is only begetting children for the murderer. How much preaching has there been for these twenty years all over Pembrokeshire ! but no regular societies, no discipline, no order or connection ; and the consequence is, that nine in ten of the once-awakened are now faster asleep than ever." Paul was alive to the same need. He was a practical missionary,

---

[1] With Luke's πίνειν καὶ μεθύσκεσθαι (45) and μέθη (xxi. 34) compare the οἱ μεθυσκόμενοι of 1 Thess. v. 7. Contrast also the ἐκφυγεῖν of xxi. 36 with Paul's οὐ μὴ ἐκφύγωσιν (v. 3). The phrase *sons of light* may well have been common among the early Christians (*cf*. Abbott's *Johannine Vocabulary*, 1782-1783).

and, as these epistles show (*cf.* I., v. 12 f., II., iii. 6 f.), he knew better than to leave his young societies with nothing more than the vague memory of pious preaching. The local organisation was, as yet, primitive, but evidently it was sufficient to maintain itself and carry on the business of the church, when the guiding hand of the missionary was removed (*cf.* Clem. Rom. xlii.), though the authority of the leaders still required upon occasion the support and endorsement of the apostles (see on v. 12).

§ 4. *The Character and Setting of the Second Epistle.*—In the second and shorter epistle, after congratulating the local Christians especially on their patient faith (i. 1-4), Paul explains that the trials and troubles which called this virtue into exercise were but the prelude to a final relief and vindication at the ἀπο-κάλυψις τοῦ κυρίου Ἰησοῦ (4-12). As the ardent expectation of this had, however, produced a morbid excitement in some quarters, he sets himself (ii. 1-12) to weed out such mistakes and mischiefs by reminding the church of his previous warning that the end could not come until the μυστήριον τῆς ἀνομίας attained its climax in a supernatural and personal embodiment of evil, which would vainly challenge the authority and provoke the interposition of the Lord. He then concludes (ii. 13-17) with an expression of confidence in them, an appeal for loyalty to his teaching, and a brief prayer on their behalf. Asking their prayers, in return, for himself, he renews his expression of confidence and interest (iii. 1-5); whereupon, with a word upon the maintenance of discipline and industry, the epistle ends (iii. 6-18).

Assuming both epistles to have come from Paul,[1] we may unhesitatingly place 2 Thess. after 1 Thess. The evidence for the opposite order, advocated by Grotius in his *Annotationes* (ii. 715 f., based on an antiquated chronology), Ewald (*Jahrb. für bibl. Wiss.* 1861, 249 f., *Sendschreiben des Paulus*, 19 f.), Laurent (*Studien u. Kritiken*, 1864, pp. 497 f., *N.T. Studien*, 49 f.), and J. S. Chamberlain (*The Epp. of Paul the Apostle*, 1907, 5 f.), breaks down upon examination. It is unnatural to find a reference to II. iii. 6-16 in I. iv. 10-11; besides, as Bornemann points out (p. 495), if 2 Thess. is held to betray all the characteristics of a first letter (Ewald), what about II. ii. 15? There is no reason why such a criterion of genuineness

---

[1] On the hypothesis that both are post-Pauline, Baur (*Paulus*, Eng. tr., ii. 336 f. and van der Vies (*de beiden brieven aan de Th.*, 1865, pp. 128-164) argue for the priority of 2 Thess., the latter separating the two by the fall of Jerusalem; van Manen (*Onderzoek naar de Echtheid van P. tweeden Brief an die Thess.*, 1865, pp. 11-25) refutes both critics. The arguments for the canonical order are best stated by von Hofmann (365), Lünemann (160 f.), and Bornemann (492 f.) in their editions.

as that of II. iii. 17, should have occurred in the earliest of Paul's letters; in view of ii. 3, its appearance, after the composition of 1 Thess. and even of other letters, is psychologically valid. The comparative absence of allusions in 2 Thess. to 1 Thess. (*cf.* however, II. ii. 1 = I. iv. 17, etc.) is best explained by the fact that in the second letter Paul is going back to elaborate part of his original oral teaching in the light of fresh needs which had emerged since he wrote the first epistle. In this sense, and in this sense only, 2 Thess. anticipates the other letter. Finally, while I. ii. 17-iii. 6 does not absolutely exclude the possibility of a previous letter, it cannot be taken to presuppose one of the character of 2 Thess., least of al when the letter is dated from Beroea (Acts xvii. 10, Ewald and Laurent).

§ 5. *Its Authenticity.*—Since Paul Schmidt's edition (see below) and von Soden's essay (*Studien u. Kritiken*, 1885, pp. 263-310), with which the English reader may compare Jowett's proof (vol. i., pp. 4-17), it is no longer necessary to discuss the authenticity of the first epistle, or even its integrity. Almost the only passage where a marginal gloss may be reasonably conjectured to have crept into the text is ii. 16.[1] The second epistle, however, starts a real problem, both on the score of its resemblance to the first epistle and of its divergence from the style and thought of that or indeed of any other Pauline letter. Paul is still with Silvanus and Timotheus (i. 1) at Corinth (iii. 2, reff.; 1 Thess. ii. 15 f.), writing presumably not long after the despatch of the former epistle (ii. 15). Fresh information has reached him (iii. 11),[2] and his aim is to repudiate further misconceptions of his teaching upon the Last Things, as well as to steady the church amid its more recent anabaptist perils. Hence he writes in substantially the same tone and along the same lines as before; anything he has to communicate is practically a restatement of what he had already taught orally (ii. 5, 15), not a discussion of novel doubts and principles. If any change has taken place in the local situation, it has been in the

---

[1] The *terminus ad quem* for the composition of the epistle, if it is genuine, is his next visit to Thessalonica (Acts xx. 1, 2); most probably it was despatched before Acts xviii. 12. Corinth is the only place where we know the three men were together at this period.

[2] How, we are not told. Possibly Paul had been asked by the local leaders to exert his influence and authority against pietistic developments in the community (iii. 14). The situation demanded an explicit written message; probably no visit of Silvanus or Timotheus would have sufficed, even had they been able to leave Corinth. Spitta's theory (see below) implies that Timotheus had been in Thessalonica since 1 Thess. was written (ἔτι, ii. 5), but of this there is no evidence whatever.

direction of shifting the centre of gravity from fears about the dead to extravagant ideas entertained by the living. Hence, for one thing, the general similarity of structure and atmosphere in both epistles, and, upon the other hand, the sharper emphasis in the second upon Paul's authority.

Both features have raised widespread suspicion and elicited a variety of reconstructions of the epistle's date and object (*cf. Historical New Testament*, 142-146). The common ground of all such theories is the postulate that 2 Thess. is the work of a later Paulinist, during the age of Nero or of Trajan, who has employed 1 Thess. in order to produce a restatement of early Christian eschatology, under the aegis of the apostle, or to claim Paul's sanction for an onslaught upon Gnostic views. This is a fair hypothesis, which at first sight seems to account adequately for several of the variations and resemblances between the two writings. When it is worked out in detail, however, it becomes rather less convincing. Some chastening facts emerge. Why, *e.g.*, should such a writer fix on 1 Thess., and laboriously work on it? Then (i.) one serious preliminary obstacle is that while pseudonymous epistles addressed ostensibly to individuals (*e.g.*, the pastorals) or to Christendom in general (*e.g.*, 2 Peter) are intelligible enough, the issue of such an epistle, addressed to a definite church which had already a genuine letter of the apostle, involves very serious difficulties. These are not eased by the light-hearted explanation (so Schmiedel and Wrede[1]) that the epistle was really meant not for Thessalonica at all, but for some other community! This is to buttress one hypothesis by another. Furthermore (ii.) the style and vocabulary offer no decisive proof of a post-Pauline origin. *Of* the ἄπαξ εὑρημένα, which are comparatively few, one or two, like ἀποστασία (ii. 3), δίκη (= punishment, i. 9, *cf.* Sap. xviii. 11, etc. Jude 7), ἐνδοξάζομαι (i. 10, 12), ἐγκαυχᾶσθαι (i. 4 Pss.), τίνω (i. 9), περιεργάζομαι (iii. 2, *cf.* Sir. iii. 23), σέβασμα (ii. 4, *cf.* Sap. xiv. 20), and σημειοῦσθαι (iii. 14), may be fairly ascribed to the influence of the LXX[2] upon

---

[1] In pp. 38 f. of his able pamphlet on *Die Echtheit des zweiten Th.* (1903). Wrede knocks on the head (pp. 96 f.) the earlier theories (best represented by Schmiedel) which dated the epistle in the seventh decade of the first century, but he does not succeed better than Holtzmann or Hollmann in presenting any very satisfactory theory of its origin *c.* 100 A.D. His essay is carefully reviewed by Wernle (*Gött. Gelehrte Anzeigen*, 1905, 347 f.), who adheres to the Pauline authorship, as does Clemen (*Paulus*, i., pp. 115-122). Klöpper's article in defence of the epistle against the older attacks (*Theol. Studien u. Skizzen aus Ostpreussen*, 1889, viii., pp. 73-140) is almost as difficult to read as it is to refute.

[2] The absence of any explicit quotation from the LXX only throws into relief the extent to which, especially in i. 5 f., O.T. language and ideas have been woven into the tissue of the epistle (Acts xvii. 2, 3, ἀπὸ ·ων γραφῶν).

the writer's mind. Similarly with εἵλατο (ii. 13) and ἰσχύς (i. 9). The occurrence of ἐπιφάνεια (ii. 8), elsewhere only in the pastorals, is certainly striking, and were there more of these words, the case for a later date would be reinforced. But there are not. Besides, the construction of ἐπιφ. here is different from those which occur in the pastorals, and the latter are as likely to have copied 2 Thess. as *vice-versa*, if any literary relationship has to be assumed. The vocabulary thus, as is generally recognised, permits of no more than a *non liquet* verdict. The style, upon the whole, has quite a Pauline ring about it ; and, while this may be due to imitation, it would be uncritical to assume this result without examining (iii.) the internal relation of the two epistles. It is on this aspect of the problem that recent critics are content to rest their case (so *e.g.*, Wrede, 3-36, H. J. Holtzmann, in *Zeitschrift für die neutest. Wissenschaft*, 1901, 97-108, and Hollmann, *ibid.*, 1904, 28-38). The so-called (*a*) discrepancies need not detain us long. The different reasons given by Paul for having supported himself (*cf.* on I. ii. 9 ; II. iii. 7) are not contradictory but correlative ; both are psychologically credible, as expressions of a single experience. Greater difficulty attaches to the apparent change of front towards the second advent. In I. v. 2, the advent is unexpected and sudden ;[1] in II. ii. 3 f., it is the climax of a development. But this discrepancy, such as it is (*cf.* on I. v. 3), attaches to almost all the early Christian views of the end ; to be instantaneous and to be heralded by a historical prelude were traits of the End which were left side by side not only by Jesus (*cf.* Matt. xxiv. 3 f., 23 f., 32 f.)[2] but by later prophets (*cf.* Rev. iii. 3 = vi. 1 f.). In any case, Paul was more concerned about the practical religious needs of his readers than about any strict or verbal consistency in a region of thought where Christian expectation, like the Jewish tradition to which it generally went back, was as yet far from being homogeneous or definite. The inconsistencies of the two Thessalonian epistles are at least as capable of explanation when they are taken to be variations of one man's mind at slightly different periods as when they are

[1] Not simply for unbelievers, but for Christians. It is hardly fair to explain the difference between the two epistles by confining the suddenness of the advent to the former. Hollmann is right in maintaining this against Jülicher and others, but the pseudonymity of 2 Thess. is by no means a necessary inference from it (see note on v. 3).

[2] This argument is not affected by the recognition of a small synoptic apocalypse in this chapter ; even so, the primitive and genuine tradition of the words of Jesus on the end presents the same combination as the Thessalonian letters show. On the general attitude of Paul to the political and retributory elements in the current or traditional apocalyptic, *cf.* Titius, *der Paulinisimus* (1900), pp. 47 f.

held to denote the revision and correction of Paul's ideas by a later
writer who had to reconcile the apparent postponement of the Advent
with the primitive hope. This Baur himself is forward to admit
(*Paulus*, Eng. Tr., ii. 93). "It is perfectly conceivable that one and
the same writer, if he lived so much in the thought of the παρουσία as
the two epistles testify, should have looked at this mysterious subject in different circumstances and from different points of view, and
so expressed himself regarding it in different ways." This verdict
really gives the case away. Such variations are hardly conceivable
if both epistles emanated from a later writer, but they are intelligible,
if Paul, living in the first flush and rush of the early Christian hope
is held to be responsible for them. (*b*) The numerous and detailed
similarities between the two epistles might be explained by the
hypothesis that Paul read over a copy of 1 Thess. before writing
2 Thess., or that his mind was working still along the lines of thought
voiced in the former epistle, when he came to write the latter. The
first hypothesis is not to be dismissed lightly. The second can be
illustrated from any correspondence. It is true that apart from
ii. 1-12 the fresh material of 2 Thess. consists mainly in i. 5-12, ii. 15,
iii. 2, 13, 14 f., and that there is throughout the letter a certain
poverty of expression, a comparative absence of originality, a stiffness
in parts, and a stereotyped adherence to certain forms.[1] But in the
treatment of a subject like this it was inevitable that some phrases of
self-repetition should recur, *e.g.*, the θλῖψις-group (i. 4-6), the πίστις-
group (i. 4, 10, 11, ii. 11-13, iii. 2, 3), ἐργάζεσθαι, etc. Parts of the
letter are unlike Paul. That is practically all we can say. But parts
are fairly characteristic of him, and these not only outweigh the
others, but dovetail into the corresponding data of 1 Thess. Such
incidental agreements are too natural and too numerous to be the
artificial mosaic of a later writer.

The internal evidence of ii. 3-12 is no longer adduced as a crucial
proof of the un-Pauline origin of 2 Thess. Indeed most recent critics
have given up this argument as primary. Fresh investigations into
the origins of gnosticism and of the semi-political variations in
primitive eschatology have undermined the older hypothesis which
relegated this prophecy to the latter part of the first or the opening
part of the second century, and it is only necessary to determine
which of the possible reconstructions is most suitable to the age of
Paul himself. On the whole, no solution of the apocalyptic prophecy

---

[1] The severer tone (iii. 6-15), as well as the more official tinge, of the letter were
as necessary now for the Thessalonians as they were soon to be for the Corinthians
(1 Cor. iv. 21, v. 3-5).

in ii 3 f. fits in with the data so well as the early theory that ὁ κατέχων and τὸ κατέχον denote, not the episcopate as a restraint against gnosticism (Hilgenfeld and others), but the Emperor and imperial power of Rome ("quis nisi Romanus status?" Tertullian, *de Resurr.*, xxiv.). Paul had ample experience of the protection afforded by the polity of the empire against the malevolence of the Jews, and he apparently anticipated that this would continue for a time, until the empire fell. But how could the fall of the empire be expected? The answer lies not so much in any contemporary feelings of panic and dismay, as in the eschatological tradition, derived from a study of Daniel, which was evidently becoming current in certain Jewish and early Christian circles, that the empire represented the penultimate stage in the world's history. "And when Rome falls, the world." Hence the tone of reserve and cryptic ambiguity with which Paul speaks of its collapse, "ne calumniam incurreret, quod Romano imperio male optauerit, cum speraretur aeternum" (Aug., *Civ. Dei.*, xx.; so Jerome on 2 Thess. ii. 6). The idea of Rome's downfall could not be spoken of, or at least written about, openly. All that a Christian prophet could do was to hint that this future Deceiver or pseudo-Messiah would prove too strong even for the Restraining Empire, and that King Jesus would ultimately intervene to meet and to defeat him. An entire change came over the spirit of the dream, when, nearly half a century later the imperial cultus in Asia Minor stirred the prophet John to denounce Rome as the supreme antagonist of God. The empire, on this view, was no providential restraint on τὸ μυστήριον τῆς ἀνομίας, but was herself μυστήριον (Rev. xvii. 5), loathsome and dangerous and doomed. This altered prospect lay far beyond the horizon of Paul. The imperial worship had not yet become formidable, and to him the empire, with its administrative justice, stood for a welcome, even though a temporary, barrier against the antagonistic forces of Judaism. The kingdom of God was not the opponent of the empire, but simply the final conqueror of a foe who would prove too strong even for the restraining control of Roman civilisation.

This interpretation of the restraining power[1] implies that the supernatural antagonist issues from Judaism (so especially Weiss, *N.T. Theologie*, § 63). Here again patristic tradition seems to cor-

---

[1] *Cf.* Neumann's *Hippolytus von Rom* (Leipzig, 1902), pp. 4 f. The κατέχων is not to be associated with any special emperor, not even with Claudius, whose name has a curious resemblance to it. The theories which identify the Restrainer with Vespasian (as a check on Nero Redivivus), Antichrist, or Domitian. depend on *a priori* conceptions of the epistle's origin and aim.

roborate it. Both Irenæus (adv. Haer., v. 25, i. 30, 2) and Hippolytus (de Antichristo, vi., xiv.) expressly state that antichrist is to
be of Jewish descent, and the later echoes of the tradition are as pronounced (cf. Bousset's Antichrist, pp. 24 f., 127 f., 182 f. ; E. Bi.,
179 f.).[1] Antichrist is to set up his kingdom in Judah ; his reign is
from Jerusalem, and the Jews are the dupes of his miraculous influence.[2] The ἀποστασία, which Paul anticipates, implies a relationship to God which could not be postulated of Christians, much less
of pagans in general who, ex hypothesis, "knew not God" (i. 8). The
only deliberate anti-Christian movement, which Paul and his friends
had already experienced (ἤδη ἐνεργεῖται), was Jewish fanaticism ; its
professed zeal for the Law was really ἀνομία, as the apostle puts it
with a touch of scathing irony.

Paul is plainly operating with a Beliar(l)-saga[3] in this passage.
If one could only be certain that Sibyll. iii. 63-73 represented a pre-
Christian Jewish fragment, as its context indicates, or that any
Christian interpolations were confined to minor phrases like ἐκ δὲ
Σεβαστηνῶν, we should have one clear trace of this saga. Belial there
works many signs (as in Sibyll. ii. 37, καὶ βελίαρ θ' ἥξει καὶ σήματα
πολλὰ ποιήσει ἀνθρώποις), seduces many even of elect believers within
Judaism (πολλοὺς πλανήσει, πιστούς τ' ἐκλεκτούς θ' Ἑβραίους, ἀνόμους τε
καὶ ἄλλους ἀνέρας, οἵτινες οὔπω Θεοῦ λόγον εἰσήκουσαν), and is finally
burned up, together with his adherents. The suspicions of this passage's Jewish character seem unjustified ; it may be taken, without much hesitation, as one reflection of the tradition which was in

---

[1] Bousset often exaggerates the independence of patristic eschatological tradition ; he fails to allow enough for the luxuriant fancies of a later age, which applied
the N.T. text arbitrarily to contemporary life. But on this point the evidence is fairly
decisive, viz., that the early fathers were not merely building on the text of 2 Thess.
ii. 3-6, when they spoke of Antichrist being a seducer whose false worship was set up
within a reconstructed temple at Jerusalem.

[2] Professor Warfield (Expos.[3] iv. 40 f.) regards the Jewish state as the divine
restraint upon the revelation of Rome's self-deification. This view is more sensible
than that of the Restrainer as Christianity or the church (cf. Reimpell, Studien u.
Kritiken, 1887, 711-736), but it is difficult to see how Judaism could be said to im-
pose any check upon the imperial cultus ; besides, is it likely that Paul would
have subtly combined a polemic against the obstinate antagonism of the Jews with
a theory of their unconscious protective services to the church ?

[3] See R. H. Charles' edition of Ascensio Isaiae (pp. lxii.-lxiii.) and M. Friedländer's Religiösen Bewegungen innerhalb des Judentums im Zeitalter Jesu (1905,
pp. 50 f.). This would be corroborated if Beliar were shown to be, as the latter
writer argues (in his Der Antichrist, 1901), a pre-Christian embodiment of the Jewish
antinomian sect מינים. For a possible source of such traditions in Paul's case
cf. 2 Tim. iii. 8.

Paul's mind when he wrote 2 Thess. ii. 2 f. Belial is not indeed named here, as he is in 2 Cor. vi. 15. But he is the opponent of Jesus the true messiah. He appears in human form (cf. Asc. Isa., iv. 2 : "Beliar the great ruler, the king of this world will descend . . . in the likeness of a man, a lawless king") as the arch-emissary or agent of Satan. The latter, whom Paul here as elsewhere (in consonance with Jewish tradition) keeps in the background, is the supreme opponent of God ; but as God's representative is the Lord Jesus Christ, so Satan's active representative is this mysterious figure, whose methods are a caricature of the true messiah's (see notes below on the passage). This is borne out by the contemporary sense of Βελίαλ as ἄγγελος τῆς ἀνομίας (Asc. Isa., ii. 4, etc.) or ἀνομία (ἀποστασία) in LXX. The man of lawlessness, whom Paul predicts, is thus one of whom Belial is a prototype. Only, the apostle fuses this παράνομος with the false messiah, originally a different figure, who is represented as the incarnation of Satan, the devil in human embodiment. That he expected this mysterious opponent to rise within Judaism is not surprising under the circumstances. He was in no mood, at this moment of tension, to think hopefully of the Jews. They were a perpetual obstacle and annoyance to him, ἄτοποι καὶ πονηροί. He had already denounced them as θεῷ μὴ ἀρεσκόντων (I., ii. 15), and from this it was but a step to the position, suggested by the tradition perhaps, that their repudiation of God's final revelation in Jesus would culminate in an ἀποστασία, which welcomed the last rival of Jesus as God's messiah. His prophecy thus embodies a retort.[1] "You Jews hate and persecute us as apostates from God ; you denounce our Jesus as a false messiah. But the

---

[1] In Dan. viii. 23 f. when the cup of Israel's guilt is full (πληρουμένων τῶν ἁμαρτιῶν αὐτῶν), the climax of their punishment came in the person of Antiochus Epiphanes, the presumptuous (ἡ καρδία αὐτοῦ ὑψωθήσεται, cf. 2 Thess. ii. 4) and astute (τὸ ψεῦδος ἐν χερσὶν αὐτοῦ . . . καὶ δόλῳ ἀφανιεῖ πολλούς, cf. 2 Thess. i. 9, 11). Paul, like the rest of the early Christians, still looked for some immediate fulfilment of this prophecy. In the contemporary malevolence of the Jews towards the gospel he saw a sign of its realisation, as the allusion in 1 Thess. ii. 16 (εἰς τὸ ἀναπληρῶσαι αὐτῶν τὰς ἁμαρτίας) indicates. The penal consequence of this attitude must have also formed part of his oral teaching at Thessalonica, but he does not mention it till local circumstances drew from him a reminder of the final Deluder who must soon come (2 Thess. ii. 3 f.). It is important to notice this underlying tradition, or application of tradition, in the apostle's mind, on account of its bearing upon the general harmony of the eschatology in the two epistles. Furthermore, since the days of Antiochus Epiphanes, the book of Daniel had made self-deification a note of the final enemy. Any vivid expectation of the End, such as that cherished by a Jewish Christian of Paul's temperament, instinctively seized upon this trait of the false messiah.

false messiah will come from you, and his career will be short-lived
at the hands of our Christ." To the Christian the prophecy brought
an assurance that, while the coldest and darkest hour must precede
the dawn, the dawn was sure to come, and to come soon. Thus
in both epistles, but particularly in the second, the reader can
see the torch of apocalyptic enthusiasm, streaming out with smoke as
well as with red flame, which many early Christians employed to light
up their path amid the dark providences of the age. Paul is prophesying—none the less vividly that he does so ἐκ μέρους.

Attempts have also been made, from various sides, to solve
the literary problem of the writing by finding in it (a) either a Pauline
nucleus which has been worked over, (b) or a Pauline letter which
has either suffered interpolation or (c) incorporated some earlier
apocalyptic fragment, possibly of Jewish origin. (a) According to Paul
Schmidt (*Der erste Thess. nebst einem Excurs über den zweiten gleichn.
Brief*, 1885, pp. 111 f.), a Paulinist in 69 A.D. edited and expanded a
genuine letter = i. 1-4, ii. 1-2a, ii. 13-iii. 18. But, apart from other
reasons, the passages assigned to Paul are not free from the very
feature which Schmidt considers fatal to the others, *viz.*, similarity
to 1 Thess. And the similarities between ii. 3-12 and the apocalypse of John are very slight. The activity assigned to the editor
is too restricted ; besides, ii. 3-12 is so cardinal a feature of the
epistle, that the latter stands or falls with it—so much so that it
would be easier, with Hausrath, to view the whole writing as a scaf-
folding which rose round the original Pauline nucleus of ii. 1-12.
Finally, the literary criteria do not bear out the distinction postulated by both theories. (b) The strongly retributive cast, the
liturgical swing, and the O.T. colouring, of i. 6-10 have suggested the
possibility of interpolation in this passage (McGiffert, *E. Bi.*, 5054,
Findlay, p. lvii.), either as a whole or in part. This is at any rate
more credible than the older idea that ii. 1-12 embodies a Montanist
interpolation (J. E. C. Schmidt, *Bibliothek für Kritik u. Exegese der
N.T.*, 1801, 385 f.) or ii. 1-9 a piece of Jewish Christian apocalyptic
(Michelsen, *Theol., Tijdschrift*, 1876, 213 f.). Finally (c) the large
amount of common ground between the Jewish and the primitive
Christian conceptions of eschatology is enough (see on ii. 5) to invali-
date Spitta's lonely theory (*Offenbarung des Joh.*, 497 f., and *Zur
Gesch. und Litt. des Urchristentums*, i. 139 f.) of a Caligula-apo-
calypse, due in part to Timotheus,[1] in ii. 2-12, or the idea of Pierson

---

[1] *Cf.* Prof. G. G. Findlay's refutation in *Expos.*[6] ii. 255 f., and Bornemann's
paragraphs (pp. 492, 529 f.).

and Naber (*Verisimilia*, 1886, 21 f.) that a pre-Christian apocalypse (i. 5-10, ii. 1-12, iii. 1-6, 14, 15) has been worked up by the unknown Paul of the second century whom the Holland critics find so prolific and indispensable.

The second epistle is inferior, in depth and reach, to the first, whatever view be taken of its origin, but both are especially valuable as indications of the personal tie between Paul and his churches, and as samples of the new literary form which the religious needs of early Christianity created in the epistle. Dryden has hit this off in his well-known lines upon the apostles and their communities :—

> As charity grew cold or faction hot,
> Or long neglect their lessons had forgot,
> For all their wants they wisely did provide,
> And preaching by epistles was supplied.
> So great physicians cannot all attend,
> But some they visit and to some they send.
> Yet all those letters were not sent to all,
> Nor first intended, but occasional—
> Their absent sermons.

The Thessalonian epistles were written to supply the lack of further personal intercourse and to supplement instruction already given. They were not treatises designed to convey the original teaching of the apostles ; they imply that, and they apply it along special lines, but they are not protocols of doctrine (*cf.* note on 1 Thess. iv. 4). At the same time, "occasional" must not be taken to mean casual or off-hand. Paul dictated with some care. His ideas are not impromptu notions, nor are they thrown out off-hand ; they represent a prolonged period of thought and of experience. Even these, the least formal of his letters, though written for the moment's need, reflect a background of wide range and fairly matured beliefs. Nevertheless, they are hardly "absent sermons". " Letters mingle souls," as Donne remarked, and 1 Thessalonians in particular is the unpremeditated outpouring of a strong man's tender, firm, and wise affection for people whom he bore upon his very heart. It is the earliest of Paul's extant letters, and it delivers the simpler truths of the Christian faith to us with all the dew and the bloom of a personal experience which not only enjoined them but lived to impart them. Both epistles show, as Jowett puts it, how Paul was " ever feeling, if haply he may find them, after the hearts of men ". " He is not a bishop administering a regular system, but a person dealing with other persons out of the fulness of his own mind and nature. . . . If they live, he lives ; time and distance never snap the cord of sympathy.   His government of them is a sort of communion with them; a receiving of their feelings and a pouring forth of his own."

§ 6. *External Evidence, Text, and Literature of both Epistles.*— As both epistles are included not only in the Muratorian canon but in Marcion's strictly Pauline collection (Tert. *adv. Marc.* v. 15; Epiph., *Haer.* xlii. 9), they must have been known and circulated by the first quarter of the second century, although quotations (mainly of the eschatological sections) do not emerge till Irenæus and Tertullian.   Both Clement of Alexandria and Origen used them, and other evidence of their existence will be found in any text book of the N.T. Canon.   But the so-called allusions to 1 Thess. in the earlier apostolic fathers are, for the most part, scanty and vague; *e.g.*, of i. 5 and iv. 2 in Clem., Rom. xlii. 3.   Hermas, *Vis.* iii. 9, 10 (εἰρηνεύετε ἐν αὐτοῖς) might go back to Mark as easily as to Paul (*cf.* on v. 13), though there is a similarity of context, while the general correspondence of outline between iv. 14-16 and Did. xvi. 6 (revelation of the Lord, trumpet, resurrection) may imply no more than a common use of tradition, if not of Matt. xxiv.   The use of the epistle in the correspondence of Ignatius is probable, but far from certain; *e.g.*, i. 6 in Eph. x. 3 (μιμηταὶ δὲ τοῦ Κυρίου σπουδάζωμεν εἶναι, different context); ii. 4 in Rom. ii. 1 (οὐ θέλω ὑμᾶς ἀνθρωπαρεσκῆσαι, ἀλλὰ Θεῷ), and v. 17 in Eph. x. 1 (ἀδιαλείπτως προσεύχεσθε, *si vera lectio*).   There is but one parallel in Barnabas, iv. 9 = Barn. xxi. 6 (γένεσθε δὲ θεοδίδακτοι, different context).   This scarcity of allusions is not surprising.   The comparative lack of doctrinal interest in the first epistle, and its personal, intimate contents, would prevent it from being so often read and cited as the other Pauline letters.   The second epistle, however, was evidently known to Justin Martyr (*Dial.* xxxii., cx., cxvi.) as well as to Polycarp who not only alludes to iii. 15 (in xi. 4, " et non sicut inimicos tales existimetis ") but misquotes i. 4 (in quibus laborauit beatus Paulus, qui estis in principio epistulae eius, de uobis enim gloriatur in omnibus ecclesiis) as if it were addressed to the Philippians (*cf.* Wrede, 92 f.); and such data prove the circulation of 1 Thess. as well.   The echoes of 2 Thess. in Barnabas (2 Thess. ii. 6 = Barn. xviii. 2; ii. 8, 12 = xv. 5) indicate rather more than a common basis of oral tradition (so Rauch in *Zeitschrift für die Wissensch. Theologie*, 1895, 458 f.), and, like the apocalypse of John, it appears to have been circulated in Gaul before the end of the second century (*cf.* letter from churches of Lyons and Vienne, Eus. *H. E.*, v. 1).

The text printed in this edition agrees generally with that of most critical editors.   To save space, all textual notes have been cut out, except where a variant reading bears directly on the exposition, or possesses some independent interest. Since Alford published his edition, the chief foreign commentaries have been those of von Hofmann (1869), Reuss (1878-9), Lünemann (Eng. tr., 1880) and Bornemann (1894) in Meyer's series, Schäfer (1890), Zöckler (1894), Zimmer's *Theologischer Commentar* (1891), Schmiedel (*Hand Commentar*, second edition, 1892, incisive and thorough), S. Goebel (second edition, 1897), B. Weiss (second edition, 1902), Wohlenberg (in Zahn's *Kommentar*, 1903; sec. ed. 1908), and Lueken (in *Die Schriften des N.T.*, 1905); in English, those of Eadie (1877), Alexander (*Speaker's Comm.*, 1881), Dr. Marcus Dods (*Schaff's Comm.*, iii., 1882), Dr. John Hutchinson (1884), Dr. J. Drummond (*Internat. Hdbk. to N.T.*, ii., 1899), and Dr. Adeney (*Century Bible*, n. d.), with three recent and able editions of the Greek text by Lightfoot (*Notes on Epp. of St. Paul*, 1895, pp. 1-92), Prof. G. G. Findlay (*Cambridge Greek Testament*, 1904), and Dr. G. Milligan (1908). Of the older works, the editions of L. Pelt (1830), H. O. Schott (1834), and A. Koch (on the first epistle, second edition, Berlin, 1855), in German, together with those of Ellicott (fourth edition, 1880) and Jowett (third edition, 1894), deserve special notice. Dr. Denney's terse exposition (*Expositor's Bible*, 1892), Lightfoot's essay (*Biblical Essays*, 251-269), and E. H. Askwith's *Introduction to the Thessalonian Epistles* (1902), together with the articles of Lock (Hastings' *D.B.*, iv. 743-749) and A. C. McGiffert (*E. Bi.*, 5036-5046), and Dr. W. Gunion Rutherford's translation (1908), will furnish the English student with all necessary material for a general study of the epistles. Zimmer's monograph (*Der Text der Thess. Briefe*, 1893) and article on 2 Thess. (*Zeits. f. wiss. Theol.*, xxxi. 322-342) give a competent survey of the textual data.

The abbreviations are for the most part familiar and obvious; *e.g.*, Blass = *Neutest. Grammatik*, Burton = *Moods and Tenses* (1894), Deissmann = D.'s *Bible Studies* (Eng. tr., Edinburgh, 1901), DCG = Hastings' *Dictionary of Christ and the Gospels* (1907-1908), E. Bi. = *Encyclopædia Biblica*, Field = *Otium Norvicense*, part iii. (1899), Moulton = J. H. Moulton's *Grammar of N.T. Greek*, vol. i. (1906), Viteau = Viteau's *Étude sur le grec du N.T.* (1893, 1896), Win. = Schmiedel's edition of G. B. Winer's *Grammatik* (Göttingen, 1894 f.). With regard to the references to Sap. (*i.e.*, The Wisdom of Solomon), it must be remembered that Paul in all likelihood knew this writing at first hand.

ΠΡΟΣ ΘΕΣΣΑΛΟΝΙΚΕΙΣ Ā.

I. 1. ΠΑΥΛΟΣ καὶ ᵃΣιλουανὸς καὶ Τιμόθεος τῇ ἐκκλησίᾳ Θεσσαλο- ᵃ *Cf.* on 2 Cor. i. 19.
νικέων ἐν ᵇΘεῷ πατρὶ καὶ Κυρίῳ Ἰησοῦ Χριστῷ· ᶜχάρις ὑμῖν καὶ ᵇ On absence of
εἰρήνη. article, see Blass,

2. ᵈΕὐχαριστοῦμεν τῷ Θεῷ ᵉπάντοτε περὶ ᵉπάντων ὑμῶν, ᶠμνείαν §§ 46. 6, 47. 10.
ποιούμενοι ᶠἐπὶ τῶν προσευχῶν ἡμῶν 3. ᵍἀδιαλείπτως, μνημονεύ- ᶜ See on 1 Cor. i. 3 and Eph. i. 2.

d So Col. i. 3.   e Eph. v. 20.   f Eph. i. 16.   g v. 17; Rom. i. 9

Chapter I.—Ver. 1, *Greeting.*—As any trouble at Thessalonica had arisen over Paul's character more than his authority, or rather as his authority had been struck through his character, he does not introduce his own apostolic rank or that of his colleagues (ii. 6) in the forefront of this letter, which is intimate and unofficial throughout. Silvanus is put before Timothy as an older man and colleague, and also as Paul's special coadjutor in the local mission. Acts never mentions Timothy in the Macedonian mission till xvii. 14, where he appears beside Silvanus. This does not mean (Bleek) that Timothy took no part in the work at Thessalonica; his intimate relations with the church forbid this supposition. Probably he is left unnoticed as being a junior subordinate, till the time comes when he can act as an useful agent of his leaders.—ἐκκλ. a pagan term appropriated by Christianity. An implicit contrast lies in the following words (so in ii. 14): there were ἐκκλησίαι at Thessalonica and elsewhere (*cf.* Chrysostom and Orig., *Cels.* III. xxix.-xxx.) which had not their basis and being ἐν . . . Χριστῷ. The latter phrase is a suggestive and characteristic periphrasis for "Christian," and the omission of the ἐν before κυρίῳ, as of τῇ before ἐν, is enough to show that the seven words form a unity instead of a double antithesis to "pagan" and "Jewish" respectively.—κυρίῳ Ἰησοῦ Χριστῷ, a new κύριος (= dominus) for people like the Thessalonians who were hitherto familiar with the title as applied to Claudius (*cf.* Wilcken's *Griechische*

Ostraka, 1899, s.v.) the emperor, or to the God of the Jews (*cf.* Knowling's *Witness of the Epistles,* 260 f.). See the ample discussion in Kattenbusch, *das Apost. Symbol,* ii. 596 f., with his note (pp. 691 f.) on ἐκκλησία. The hope and help of God implied that Christians must hold together, under their κύριος. "No Christian could have fought his way through the great dark night of idolatry and immorality as an isolated unit; the community was here the necessary condition for all permanent life" (Wernle, *Beginnings of Christianity,* i. 189).

Vv. 2-10. *Thanksgiving for the origin and achievements of the church.*—Ver. 2. Whenever Paul was at his prayers, he remembered his friends at Thessalonica; and whenever he recalled them his first feeling was one of gratitude to God (see iii. 9) for the Christian record which, as individuals and as a church (πάντων), they displayed of active faith (i. 4-10, ii. 13-16), industrious love (iv. 9 f.), and tenacious hope (v. 1-11). And not Paul alone. The plural implies that all three missionaries prayed together.—εὐχαριστοῦμεν. The greeting is followed, as in ordinary letters of the period, by a word of gratitude and good wishes. εὐχ. is common in votive inscriptions, in connection with thanksgiving to a god. But while Paul, in dictating his letter, starts with a conventional epistolary form, the phrase immediately expands loosely into μνημ . . . θεοῦ (μνείαν π. as frequently in ethnic phraseology).

Ver. 3. ἀδιαλ. Neither distance nor fresh interests make any difference to his

h See on 2 Cor. ii. 4 and Heb. vi. 10-11.
With gen. as Rom. v. 2;
cf. Win. § 30. 12, e.
i Cf. iii. 9, 13 and other side in II. i. 4.
k Cf. iii. 5.
l II. ii. 13.
See Col. iii. 12

οντες ὑμῶν τοῦ ἔργου τῆς πίστεως καὶ τοῦ κόπου τῆς ʰἀγάπης καὶ τῆς ὑπομονῆς τῆς ʰἐλπίδος τοῦ Κυρίου ἡμῶν Ἰησοῦ Χριστοῦ, ⁱ ἔμπροσθεν τοῦ Θεοῦ καὶ πατρὸς ἡμῶν· 4. ᵏ εἰδότες, ἀδελφοὶ ˡἠγαπημένοι ὑπὸ Θεοῦ, τὴν ἐκλογὴν ὑμῶν· 5. ὅτι τὸ εὐαγγέλιον ἡμῶν οὐκ ᵐἐγενήθη ⁿεἰς ὑμᾶς ἐν °λόγῳ μόνον ἀλλὰ καὶ ἐν °δυνάμει καὶ ᵖἐν Πνεύματι Ἁγίῳ καὶ ᑫπληροφορίᾳ πολλῇ, καθὼς οἴδατε οἷοι ἐγενήθημεν ἐν ὑμῖν δι᾽ ὑμᾶς. 6. καὶ ὑμεῖς ʳμιμηταὶ ἡμῶν ἐγενήθητε ˢκαὶ τοῦ Κυρίου, ʳδεξάμενοι τὸν λόγον ἐν ʳθλίψει πολλῇ μετὰ ᵗχαρᾶς

and Deut. xxxiii. 12.   m Blass, § 20, 1.   n Gal. iii. 14.   o Cf. 1 Cor. ii. 1-4, iv. 19-20.
p "At most of rhetorical value" (Sx. *Lang. N.T.* 158).   q Clem. Rom. xlii. 3.   r Cf. Introd.
§ 1, 1; ii. 13-14, and on 2 Cor. xi. 4.   s 1 Cor. xi. 1.   t Rom. xiv. 17; Gal. v. 22.

affection; his life is bound up with their welfare; his source of happiness is their Christian well-being (cf. ii. 17-20, iii. 7-10). The adverb (a late Greek formation, cf. *Expos.*, 1908, 59) goes equally well with the preceding or with the following words; better with the former, on the whole, as the participles then open the successive clauses in 2, 3 and 4.— ὑμῶν is prefixed for emphasis to the three substantives which it covers, while the closing ἔμπροσθεν . . . ἡμῶν (cf. ii. 19) gathers up the thought of μνημον.— Faith in one sense is a work, but Paul here (as in Gal. v. 6) means faith that does work (*opus opponitur sermoni inani*, Bengel), by producing a change of life and a cheerful courage under trials. It would be no pleasure to recall a merely formal or voluble belief, any more than a display of Christian love (cf. Col. i. 4) which amounted simply to emotions or fitful expressions of goodwill, much less a hope which could not persist in face of delay and discouraging hardships.

Ver. 4. The practical evidence of the Spirit in their lives showed that God had willed to enrol them among His chosen people (note the O.T. associations of *beloved by God* and *election*), just as the same consciousness of possessing the Spirit gave them the sure prospect of final entrance into the Messianic realm— an assurance which (ver. 6) filled them with joy amid all their discomforts. The phenomenon of the Spirit thus threw light backwards on the hidden purpose of God for them, and forwards on their prospect of bliss.—Recollections depend on know'edge; to be satisfied about a person implies settled convictions about his character and position. The apostles feel certain that the Thessalonian Christians had been truly chosen and called by God, owing to (a) the genuineness and

effectiveness of their own ministry at Thessalonica, where they had felt the gospel going home to many of the inhabitants, and (b) the genuine evidence of the Thessalonians' faith; (a) comes first in ver. 5, (b) in vv. 6 f. In ii. 1 f. Paul reverts to (a), while in ii. 13-16 (b) is again before his mind. As the divine ἐκλογή manifested itself in the Christian qualities of ver. 3, Paul goes back to their historical origin.

Ver. 5. ὅτι = "inasmuch as".—τὸ εὐαγγ. ἡμῶν, the gospel of which the apostles, and by which their hearers, were convinced. As the καθὼς clause indicates, πληροφ. must here denote personal conviction and unfaltering confidence on the part of the preachers. The omission of the ἐν before πληρ. throws that word and πνεύματι together into a single conception, complementary to δυνάμει, which here has no specific reference to miracles, but to the apostles' courage (ii. 2), honesty and sincerity (4, 5), devotion (7, 8), earnestness (9), and consistency (10). The effect of the Spirit on the preachers is followed up (in ver. 6) by its effect on the hearers; and this dual aspect recurs in ver. 9 (we and you). ἐν (om. Blass) ὑμῖν="among you".

Ver. 6. θλίψει . . . χαρᾶς, cf. for this paradox of experience, Mazzini's account of his comrades in the Young Italy movement: "We were often in real want, but we were light-hearted in a way and smiling because we believed in the future". The gladness of the primitive Christian lay in the certainty of possessing soon that full salvation of which the Spirit at present was the pledge and foretaste. In view of Ps. li. 13, 14 it is hardly correct to say, with Gunkel (*Wirkungen des heiligen Geistes*, 71), that this connection of joy and the Spirit was entirely foreign to Judaism.

Πνεύματος Ἁγίου, 7. ὥστε γενέσθαι ὑμᾶς [u] τύπον [1] πᾶσι τοῖς πιστεύ- u 1 Pet. v.
3. *Cf.*
ουσιν ἐν τῇ Μακεδονίᾳ καὶ ἐν τῇ Ἀχαΐᾳ. 8. ἀφ' ὑμῶν γὰρ [v] ἐξήχη- Phil. iii.
17.
ται ὁ λόγος τοῦ Κυρίου οὐ μόνον ἐν τῇ Μακεδονίᾳ καὶ Ἀχαΐᾳ [w] ἀλλὰ v ἀπ. λεγ.;
cf. Joel
ἐν [x] παντὶ τόπῳ ἡ [y] πίστις ὑμῶν ἡ πρὸς τὸν Θεὸν ἐξελήλυθεν, ὥστε iii. 14
(LXX);
μὴ [z] χρείαν ἔχειν ἡμᾶς λαλεῖν τι. 9. [a] αὐτοὶ γὰρ περὶ [b] ἡμῶν ἀπ- 3 Macc.
iii. 2.
αγγέλλουσιν ὁποίαν [c] εἴσοδον ἔσχομεν πρὸς ὑμᾶς καὶ πῶς [d] ἐπεστρέψατε w Blass, §
[e] πρὸς τὸν Θεὸν ἀπὸ τῶν εἰδώλων, δουλεύειν Θεῷ [f] ζῶντι καὶ [g] ἀληθινῷ x *Cf.* 1 Cor.
i. 2; Acts
10. καὶ [h] ἀναμένειν τὸν υἱὸν αὐτοῦ [i] ἐκ τῶν οὐρανῶν, ὃν ἤγειρεν ἐκ Rom. i. 8;
τῶν νεκρῶν, Ἰησοῦν, τὸν [k] ῥυόμενον ἡμᾶς ἐκ τῆς [l] ὀργῆς τῆς ἐρχομένης. y Rom. i. 8;
Clem.
Rom.
xxxv. 5.

Philemon 5: = "the fact of your faith in God". z iv. 9, v. 1. a "people, wherever we go".
b *i.e.*, us, apostles. c *Cf.* Ps. cxx. (cxxi.) 8; LXX. d See on Acts xiv. 15. *Cf.* Jer. iii. 22
(LXX). e *Cf.* Eph. ii. 12. f See on Rev. vii. 2. g See on John vi. 57; Rev. iii. 7, etc.
Only here in Paul. h Isa. lix. 11, 20; Æsch., *Eum.*, 243. i Phil. iii. 20. k *Cf.* Burton,
M.T. 429, and on 2 Cor. i. 10. l Rom. v. 9; *cf.* below, v. 9 (negat. side of ἐκλογή).

[1] For τυπους (ℵACGKLP, g, syr.P, Chrys., Theod., etc., Calvin, Schott,
Alexander, Koch, Wohl., Zim.), conformed to υμας, read τυπον with BD* vss.,
edd.

Ver. 8. ἡ πίστις . . . ἐξελ. (Rom. x.
18), by anacoluthon, reiterates for emphasis ἀφ' ὑμῶν . . . κυρίου (ὁ λόγος
τ. Κ. depending for its effectiveness on
the definite testimony of Christians).
Paul is dictating loosely but graphically.
The touch of hyperbole is pardonable
and characteristic (*cf.* Rom. i. 8; 1 Cor.
iv. 17; Col. i. 6); but the geographical
and commercial position of Thessalonica
see Introd., p. 5) must have offered
ample facilities for the rapid dissemination of news and the promulgation of the
faith, north and south, throughout European Greece (*Encycl. Bibl.*, i. 32). The
local Christians had taken full advantage
of their natural opportunities. Through
their imitation of the apostles (see Introd.,
p. 7) and of Christ (here as in 1 Peter
ii. 19-21, in his sufferings), they had become a pattern for others. The ἐν τῇ is
omitted before Ἀχαΐᾳ here because M. and
A. are grouped together, over against
π. τ.—ὥστε . . . γάρ, the reputation of
the apostles rested upon solid evidence.
Ver. 9. The positive and negative aspects of faith : " Videndum est ut ruinam
errorum sequatur aedificium fidei" (Calvin).—ἀληθινῷ = "real" as opposed to
false in the sense of "counterfeit".—
ζῶντι, as opposed to dead idols (see
above, p. 5) impotent to help their
worshippers. Elsewhere the phrase (*cf.*
1 Tim. iii. 15; Heb. iii. 12) "implies a
contrast with the true God made practically a dead deity by a lifeless and
rigid form of religion" (Hort, *Christian
Ecclesia*, 173). Nothing brings home
the reality of God (*i.e.*, as Father, vv. 1-3)

to the Christian at first so much as the
experience of forgiveness.
Ver. 10. In preaching to pagans, the
leaders of the primitive Christian mission
put the wrath and judgment of God
in the forefront (*cf.* Sabatier's *Paul*, 98
f.), making a sharp appeal to the moral
sense, and denouncing idolatry (*cf.* Sap.,
xiv., 12 f., 22 f.). Hence the revival they
set on foot. They sought to set pagans
straight, and to keep them straight, by
means of moral fear as well as of hope.
Paul preached at Thessalonica as he did
at Athens (Acts xvii. 29-31; see Harnack's *Expansion of Christianity*, i. 108 f.)
and the substance of his mission-message
on the wrath of God is preserved in Rom.
i. 18—ii. 16. The *living* God is manifested by His raising of Jesus from the
dead, His awakening of faith in Christians, and His readiness to judge human
sin in the hereafter. Seeberg (*der Katechismus der Urchristenheit*, 82-85) finds
here an echo of some primitive Christian
formula of faith, but his proofs are
very precarious.—τὸν υἱὸν αὐτοῦ. This
marked them out from Jewish proselytes,
who might also be said to have turned
from idols to serve the living God. The
quiet combination of monotheism and a
divine position of Jesus is striking (*cf.*
Kattenbusch, *op. cit.*, ii. 550 f.).—ἐκ τῶν
οὐρανῶν . . . ἐκ τ. νεκρῶν, both the hope
and the historical fact lay outside the
experience of the Thessalonians, but both
were assured to them by their experience
of the Spirit which the risen Jesus had
bestowed, and which guaranteed His final
work. Were it not for touches like the

a = "re- **II. 1.** Αὐτοὶ γὰρ ᵃοἴδατε, ἀδελφοί, τὴν εἴσοδον ἡμῶν τὴν πρὸς ὑμᾶς,
member,"
as 1 Cor. ὅτι ᵇ οὐ κενὴ γέγονεν· **2.** ἀλλὰ προπαθόντες καὶ ὑβρισθέντες, καθὼς
i. 16 (cf.
Field, οἴδατε, ἐν ᶜΦιλίπποις, ᵈἐπαρρησιασάμεθα ἐν τῷ Θεῷ ᵉἡμῶν λαλῆσαι
187).
b Cf. i. 5, πρὸς ὑμᾶς τὸ εὐαγγέλιον τοῦ Θεοῦ ἐν πολλῷ ᶠἀγῶνι. **3.** ἡ γὰρ
and 1
Cor. xv. ᵍπαράκλησις ἡμῶν ʰοὐκ ἐκ πλάνης, οὐδὲ ἐξ ἀκαθαρσίας, οὐδὲ¹ ἐν
10.
c See on δόλῳ, **4.** ἀλλὰ καθὼς ᵏδεδοκιμάσμεθα ὑπὸ τοῦ Θεοῦ ¹πιστευθῆναι
Acts xvi.
19 f.
d See on Eph. vi. 20 and Acts ix. 26; on form cf. Win. § 5. 26 b.   e iii. 9; II. i. 11-12.   f Cf.
Phil. i. 30.   g "appeal" (cf. Polyb. iii. 109, 6).   h Sc. ἐστίν, cf. 2 Cor. vi. 8.   i 2 Cor. iv. 2
and xii. 16.   k 2 Macc. iv. 3.   l Cf. Gal. ii. 7.

---

¹ The second ουδε (אABCD*GP, min., etc., edd.) [cf. II. iii. 7-8] is preferable to
the v. 1. ουτε (Pelt, Hofm., Wohl.); for ακαθαρσιας, Bentl. conj. "forte εξ αν.
αρεσκιας" [i.e. ανθρωπαρεσκιας].

---

deeper sense of δουλεύειν, the celestial
origin of Jesus, and the eschatological
definition of ὀργή, one might be tempted
to trace a specious resemblance between
this two-fold description of Christianity
at Thessalonica and the two cardinal
factors in early Greek religion, viz., the
service of the Olympian deities (θερα-
πεύειν) and the rites of aversion (ἀπο-
πομπαί) which were designed to depre-
cate the dark and hostile powers of evil.
Paul preached like the Baptist judgment
to come. But his gospel embraced One
who baptised with the Spirit and with
the fire of enthusiastic hope (cf. 1 Cor. i. 7).

CHAPTER II.—Vv. 1-12. An apologia
pro vita et labore suo.

Ver. 1. αὐτοί, as opposed to the α.
of i. 9.—γέγονεν κ.τ.λ., our mission was
a vital success, as its results still show.
For its motives and methods were genuine
(2-12).

Ver. 2. "Though we had suffered—aye
and suffered outrage" in one town, yet
on we went to another with the same
errand; a practical illustration of Matt.
x. 23.

Ver. 3. γάρ: Our mission (whatever
that of others may be) is not the
outcome of self-seeking, otherwise it
would readily be checked by such un-
toward circumstances. Our confidence
is in God, not in ourselves; our work is
not self-appointed but a sacred trust or
commission, for which we are responsible to Him (4). Hence, discouragement and hesitation are impossible.
Paul argues that the very fact of their
cheerful perseverance at Thessalonica,
after their bad treatment at Philippi,
points to the divine source and strength
of their mission; what impelled them
was simply a sense of lasting responsibility to God, upon the one hand, and
an overpowering devotion to men upon

the other (cf. the δι' ὑμᾶς of i. 5), for the
gospel's sake. Had the apostles yielded
to feelings of irritation and despondency,
giving up their task in Macedonia, after
the troubles at Philippi, or had they conducted themselves at Thessalonica in such
a way as to secure ease and profit; in
either case, they would have proved their
mission to be ambitious or selfish, and
therefore undivine. As it was, their courage and sincerity were at once the evidence and the outcome of their divine
commission.—πλάνης, "error" (cf. Armitage Robinson on Eph. iv. 14). Their
preaching did not spring from some delusion or mistake. Paul was neither fool
nor knave, neither deceived nor a deceiver
(δόλῳ). Nor was his mission a sordid attempt (ἀκαθαρσίας) to make a good thing
out of preaching, the impure motive being
either to secure money (cf. πλεονεξίας
ver. 5, and ver. 9), or to gain a position
of importance (ver. 6) and popularity.
Cf. Tacit., Annal., vi, 21 (of Tiberius'
attitude to astrologers) "si uanitatis aut
fraudum suspicio incesserat". Both
features were only too familiar in the
contemporary conduct of wandering so-
phists, ἀρεταλόγοι, and thaumaturgists
(e.g., Acts xiii. 10, and Clemen's article
in Neue Kirchl. Zeitschrift, 1896, 151 f.)
whose practices would also explain the
literal interpretation of ἀκ. (= sensuality). But the context favours the associations of greed (cf. Eph. v. 3), as in the
case of πλεονεξία. On the persuasive-
ness of sincerity in a speaker, i.e., the
extent to which his effectiveness depends
upon his hearers' conviction of his own
earnestness and honesty, see Aristotle's
analysis of ἠθικὴ πίστις (Rhet., ii. 1) and
Isocrates' description of εὐνοίας δύναμις
(Orat., xv. 278, 279).

Ver. 4. "As God, who tests our
hearts, has attested our fitness to be

τὸ εὐαγγέλιον, οὕτω λαλοῦμεν, οὐχ ^m ὡς ἀνθρώποις ⁿἀρέσκοντες, ἀλλὰ m Causal
(see Vit-
^o Θεῷ τῷ δοκιμάζοντι τὰς καρδίας ἡμῶν.   5. οὔτε γάρ ποτε ἐν λόγῳ eau, i.
304).
^p κολακείας ἐγενήθημεν, καθὼς οἴδατε, οὔτε ἐν ^qπροφάσει πλεονεξίας · n Gal. i. 10;
for οὐ
Θεὸς μάρτυς · 6. οὔτε ζητοῦντες ἐξ ἀνθρώπων ^r δόξαν, οὔτε ἀφ᾽ ὑμῶν with ptc.
see Moult.
οὔτε ^s ἀπ᾽ ἄλλων, ^t δυνάμενοι ἐν βάρει εἶναι ὡς Χριστοῦ ἀπόστολοι · i. 231.
7. ἀλλ᾽ ἐγενήθημεν ^u ἤπιοι ἐν μέσῳ ὑμῶν, ὡς ^v ἐὰν τροφὸς θάλπῃ τὰ ^o Contrast
ver. 15,
ἑαυτῆς τέκνα · ¹ 8. οὕτως ὁμειρόμενοι ὑμῶν ^w εὐδοκοῦμεν ^x μεταδοῦναι and cf.
Sap. i.
ὑμῖν ^y οὐ μόνον τὸ εὐαγγέλιον τοῦ Θεοῦ ἀλλὰ καὶ τὰς ἑαυτῶν ψυχάς, p Here only
(N.T.),

Win.-Schm. § v. 13c.   q "any pretext', cf. on 2 Cor. xi. 12, ii. 17; 2 Pet. ii. 3.   r Cf. John
viii. 50, v. 41-44.   s e.g. i. 9.   t Cf. 1 Cor. ix. 1 f.   u of a father (ver. 11) in e.g. Hom.
Iliad, xxiv. 770, Odyssey, ii. 234.   v = ὅταν (Viteau, i. 217).   w iii. 1; see on Rom. xv. 26;
= "we were right willing".   x Rom. i. 11.   So. 2 Cor. viii. 5 (force of this example).   y Cf.
Burton, M.T. 481.

¹ The important variant νηπιοι, which is even better attested (cf. WH ii. 128),
and is adopted, e.g., by Bentley, Lachm., Schrader, Jowett, Zimmer, Bisping, WH,
Lgft., and Wohl., probably arose from a not uncommon dittography of the final N in
the preceding word : ηπιος "properly implies the kindness of a superior" (Liddell
and Scott s.v.), whereas νηπιος has usually associations of immaturity in Paul.

entrusted with the gospel," a characteristic play on the word. The definite
commission of the gospel excluded any
weak attempt to flatter men's prejudices
or to adapt oneself to their tastes.
Hence the thought of the following verse.

Ver. 5. "Never did we resort to
words of flattery" (in order to gain
some private end) ; cf. Arist., Eth. Nik.,
iv. 6. As self-interest is more subtle
than the desire to please people (which
may be one form of self-interest), the
appeal is changed significantly from κ. ο.
to θεὸς μάρτυς (Rom. i. 9) : "auaritia aut
ambitio, duo sunt isti fontes ex quibus
manat totius ministerii corruptio" (Calvin). Cf. Introduction, § 1—on θεός and
ὁ θεός, cf. Kattenbusch, das Apost.
Symbol, ii. 515 f.

Ver. 6. To put a full stop after
ἄλλων, and begin a new sentence
with δυνάμενοι (so e.g., Vulgate, Calvin, Koppe, Weizsäcker, H. J. Gibbins,
Exp. Ti., xiv. 527), introduces an awkward asyndeton, makes ἀλλὰ follow a
concessive participle very awkwardly, and
is unnecessary for the sense.

Ver. 7. ἐν βάρει εἶναι = "be men
of weight," or "be a burden" on
your funds. Probably both meanings
are intended, so that the phrase (cf.
Field, 199) resumes the ideas of πλεον.
and ἀνθ. δόξαν (self-interest in its mercenary shape and as the love of reputation)
which are reiterated in vv. 7-12, a defence
of the apostles against the charges, current against them evidently in some
circles (probably pagan) at Thessalonica,

of having given themselves airs and unduly asserted their authority, as well as
of having levied or at any rate accepted
contributions for their own support.—
ἀπόστολοι were known to any of the local
Christians who had been Jews (cf. Harnack's Expansion of Christianity, i. 66 f.,
409 f.), since agents and emissaries (ἀπόστολοι) from Jerusalem went to and fro
throughout the synagogues : but ἀ. Χριστ-
τοῦ was a new conception. The Christian ἀπόστολοι had their commission
from their heavenly messiah.—ἤπιοι (2
Tim ii. 24) ; as Bengel observes, there
was nothing ex cathedra about the
apostles, nothing selfish or crafty or
overbearing. All was tenderness and
devotion, fostering and protecting care,
in their relations to these Thessalonian
Christians who had won their hearts.
To eschew flattery (5) did not mean any
indifference to consideration and gentleness, in their case; they were honest
without being blunt or masterful.—τροφός, a nursing mother (cf. Hor., Ep. i.
4, 8). "In the love of a brave and faithful man there is always a strain of
maternal tenderness ; he gives out again
those beams of protecting fondness which
were shed on him as he lay on his
mother's knee" (George Eliot). Rutherford happily renders : "On the contrary, we carried ourselves among you
with a childish simplicity, as a mother
becomes a child again when she fondles
her children".

Ver. 8. ὁμειρόμενοι (cf. Job iii. 21,
LXX ; Ps. lxii. 2, Symm.) = "yearning

z *Cf.* 1 Cor· διότι ᶻ ἀγαπητοὶ ἡμῖν ἐγενήθητε. 9. μνημονεύετε γὰρ, ἀδελφοί,
xiii. 5.
a *Cf.* II. iii. τὸν ᵃ κόπον ἡμῶν καὶ τὸν ᵃ μόχθον· νυκτὸς καὶ ἡμέρας ᵇ ἐργαζόμενοι
8 and 2
Cor. xi. ᶜ πρὸς τὸ μὴ ᵈ ἐπιβαρῆσαί τινα ὑμῶν, ἐκηρύξαμεν εἰς ὑμᾶς τὸ εὐαγ-
27.
b *Cf.* Acts γέλιον τοῦ Θεοῦ. 10. ὑμεῖς ᵉ μάρτυρες καὶ ὁ Θεός, ὡς ᶠ ὁσίως καὶ
xviii. 3.
c *Cf.* 2 Cor. δικαίως καὶ ᵍ ἀμέμπτως ὑμῖν τοῖς πιστεύουσιν ἐγενήθημεν, 11. καθ-
iii. 13 for
constr. άπερ οἴδατε, ὡς ʰ ἕνα ἕκαστον ὑμῶν, ὡς πατὴρ τέκνα ἑαυτοῦ, ⁱ παρα-
d *Cf.* 2 Cor. καλοῦντες ὑμᾶς καὶ ⁱ παραμυθούμενοι 12. καὶ ᵏ μαρτυρόμενοι ¹ εἰς τὸ
ii. 5.
e 1 Sam. ¹ περιπατεῖν ὑμᾶς ¹ ἀξίως τοῦ Θεοῦ τοῦ ᵐ καλοῦντος ὑμᾶς εἰς τὴν
xii. 3 :
Num. xvi. ἑαυτοῦ βασιλείαν καὶ ⁿ δόξαν.
15 ; Acts
xx. 23. 13. Καὶ διὰ ᵒ τοῦτο καὶ ἡμεῖς εὐχαριστοῦμεν τῷ Θεῷ ᵖ ἀδιαλείπτως,
f Only here
in N.T., ὅτι παραλαβόντες �q λόγον ἀκοῆς παρ' ἡμῶν ʳ τοῦ Θεοῦ ˢ ἐδέξασθε οὐ
="pious-
ly". *Cf.* λόγον ἀνθρώπων ἀλλὰ καθώς ἐστιν ἀληθῶς λόγον Θεοῦ, ᵗ ὃς καὶ
Eph. iv.
24.
g *Cf.* v. 23
(Clem. Rom. xliv. 4). h See on Acts xx. 31. i *Cf.* iv. 1 and on 1 Cor. xiv. 3, with 2 Macc.
xv. 8-9. k Eph. iv. 17; see on Acts xx. 26 and Gal: v. 3. l See on Phil. i. 27; ethnic phrase
(Deissm. 248). m See on Rom. viii. 28. ix. 11 and Gal. v. 8. n *Cf.* II. ii. 14. o As well
as i. 2 f. p i. 3. q *Cf.* Heb. iv. 2. ἀκ. = id quod auditur. r With λόγον, *cf.* Win. § 30. 12d.
s *Cf.* i. 6. t *i.e.* the word.

¹ μαρτυρομενοι (אBDᵇᶜHKL, 17, 47, Chrys., Dam., etc., edd.) is preferable to the
passive variant μαρτυρουμενοι, a corrupt western reading which has been conformed
to παραμ.

for, or, over ". εὐδοκ., for absence of
augment *cf.* W. H., ii. 161, 162.—διότι
causal (" for as much as "), almost = γάρ
(as in Modern Greek).

Ver. 9. " Paul means by the phrase,
night and day, that he started work before dawn ; the usage is regular and frequent. He no doubt began so early in
order to be able to devote some part of
the day to preaching " (Ramsay, *Church
in Roman Empire*, p. 85). Paul, to the
very last (*cf.* Acts xx. 29 f.), seems to
have been sensitive on this point of
independence.

Ver. 10. " We made ourselves yours "
(*cf.* 8), the dative going closely (as Rom.
vii. 3) with the verb, which is qualified
(as in 1 Cor. xvi. 10) by the adverbs ;
so Born., Findlay.- ὑμῖν κ.τ.λ. (dative
of possession). Paul had met other
people at Thessalonica, but only the
Christians could properly judge his real
character and conduct.

Ver. 11. καθάπερ, sharper than καθώς.
Viteau (ii. 111) suggests that κ. ο. is a
parenthesis, and ὡς a causal introductory
particle for the participles (" hearten-
ing," " encouraging," " adjuring ") which
in their turn depend on ὑμῖν . . . ἐγενήθημεν, but the likelihood is that in the
rush of emotion, as he dictates, Paul
leaves the participial clause without a
finite verb (so *e.g.*, 2 Cor. vii. 5).—ὡς

πατήρ κ.τ.λ. (*cf.* ὡς ἐὰν τροφός, 7). The
figure was used by Jewish teachers of
their relationship to their pupils. *Cf.*
e.g., the words of Eleazar b. Azarja in his
dying master, " Thou art more to Israel
than father or mother ; they only bring
men into this world, whereas thou guid-
est us for this world and the next ".
Catullus, lxxii. 4 (dilexi tum te non tantum ut uulgus amicam, sed pater ut
natos diligit et generos).

Ver. 12. ἀξίως in this connection (see
references) was a familiar ethnic phrase.
C. Michel (in his *Recueil d'inscriptions
grecques*, 1900, 266, 413) quotes two pre-
Christian instances with τῶν θεῶν.—εἰς
τὸ, κ.τ.λ., grammatically meaning either
the object or the content of the solemn
charge (*cf.* Moulton, 218 f.). The ethic
is dominated by the eschatology, as in
iii. 13, v. 23.

Vv. 13-16. *Further thanksgiving for
their endurance of trial.*

Ver. 13. " And for this we also render
thanks, *viz.*, that ;" the καί, by a loose but
not unusual (*cf.* iii. 5 ; Rom. iii. 7, v. 3, etc.)
construction, goes not with the pronoun
but with the verb, or simply emphasises
the former (*e.g.*, Soph., *Oed. Col.*, 53,
520, etc.).—τοῦ θεοῦ comes in so awkwardly that one is tempted to regard it,
with Baljon and some other Dutch critics,
as a scribal gloss.

ⁿ ἐνεργεῖται ἐν ὑμῖν τοῖς πιστεύουσιν. 14. ὑμεῖς ᵛ γὰρ μιμηταὶ
ἐγενήθητε, ἀδελφοί, ʷ τῶν ἐκκλησιῶν τοῦ Θεοῦ τῶν οὐσῶν ἐν τῇ
ʷ Ἰουδαίᾳ ἐν Χριστῷ Ἰησοῦ, ὅτι τὰ αὐτὰ ἐπάθετε καὶ ὑμεῖς ὑπὸ τῶν
ἰδίων ˣ συμφυλετῶν, ʸ καθὼς καὶ αὐτοὶ ὑπὸ τῶν Ἰουδαίων, 15. τῶν καὶ
τὸν Κύριον ἀποκτεινάντων Ἰησοῦν καὶ τοὺς ᶻ προφήτας ¹ καὶ ἡμᾶς ᵃ ἐκδιωξάντων καὶ Θεῷ μὴ ᵇ ἀρεσκόντων καὶ πᾶσιν ἀνθρώποις ἐναντίων,
16. ᶜ κωλυόντων ἡμᾶς τοῖς ἔθνεσι λαλῆσαι ᵇ ἵνα σωθῶσιν, ᵈ εἰς τὸ
ᵉ ἀναπληρῶσαι αὐτῶν τὰς ἁμαρτίας πάντοτε[· ᶠ ἔφθασε δὲ ἐπ᾽ αὐτοὺς
ἡ ᵍ ὀργὴ ʰ εἰς τέλος].

17. Ἡμεῖς δέ, ἀδελφοί, ⁱ ἀπορφανισθέντες ἀφ᾽ ὑμῶν πρὸς καιρὸν
ὥρας (ᵏ προσώπῳ οὐ καρδίᾳ) ˡ περισσοτέρως ἐσπουδάσαμεν τὸ πρόσ-

u "Is made
operative" (cf.
Robin-
son's
Ephes.
pp. 241 f.).
v Proof and
result of
ἐνεργεῖ-
ται.
w Gal. i. 22;
2 Cor. i. 1.
x Only here
in N.T.,
= "com-
patriots"
y = ἅπερ.
z Matt. v.
12, xxiii.
34, etc.
a So Lk. xi.
c Lk. xi. 52;
e 2 Macc. vi.
Cf. Sap.
Cf. on Rom. i. 18.
"to the bitter end"

49 (Acts xvii. 5-14). Cf. 2 Cor. xi. 24, 26. b 1 Cor. x. 33. Cf. on Eph. ii. 12.
Acts xvii. 5, xxii. 22. d Cf. Burton, M.T. 411 and Moult. i. 219. e 2 Macc. vi. 14. Cf. Sap.
xii. 27 and Gen. xv. 16. f Cf. Phil. iii. 16, etc. g Lk. xiv. 21, xxi. 23. Cf. on Rom. i. 18.
h "Utterly, completely" (Ps. Sol. i. 1, ii. 5; Joseph. B. J. vii. 8, 1), alm. = "to the bitter end"
(Abbott, Joh. Gramm. 2322). i Here only (N.T.): = "bereft," cf. Field 199 f. k 1 Cor. v.
3; 2 Cor. v. 12. l Gal. i. 14; 2 Cor. i. 12.

¹ Om. the Syrian interpolation ιδιους with אABD*GP (min.), sah., cop., arm.,
aeth., Orig., Euth., edd., as an insertion by Marcion (Tert., cf. Nestle's Einf. 253)
before προφητας.

Ver. 14. μιμηταί, and soon helpers
(Rom. xv. 26). The fact that they
were exposed to persecution, and bore
it manfully, proved that the gospel was
a power in their lives, and also that
they were in the legitimate succession
of the churches. Such obstacles would
as little thwart their course as they
had thwarted that of Jesus or of his
immediate followers. συμφ. might include Jews (Acts xvii. 6), but Gentiles
predominate in the writer's mind.—The
καί after καθώς simply emphasises the
comparison (as in iv. 5, 13). As Calvin
suggests, the Thessalonians may have
wondered why, if this was the true religion, it should be persecuted by the
Jews, who had been God's people. σ.
is racial rather than local, but the local
persecution may have still been due in
part to Jews (cf. Zimmer, pp. 16 f.).
Ver. 15. "The Lord, even Jesus" (cf.
Acts ii. 36). προφ. may go either with
ἀποκτ. or with ἐκδιωξάντων.
Ver. 16. κωλυόντων κ.τ.λ., defining
(Luke xi. 52) from the Christian standpoint that general and familiar charge
of hatred to the human race (ἐναντίων
κ.τ.λ.) which was started by the exclu-
siveness of the ghetto and the synagogue.
—ἔφθασε κ.τ.λ., "the Wrath has come
upon them," apparently a reminiscence
of Test. Levi. vi. 11. This curt and
sharp verdict on the Jews sprang from
Paul's irritation at the moment. The
apostle was in no mood to be concilia-

tory. He was suffering at Corinth from
persistent Jewish attempts to wreck the
Christian propaganda, and he flashes
out in these stern sentences of anger.
Later on (Rom. ix.-xi.) he took a kinder
and more hopeful view, though even this
did not represent his final outlook on the
prospects of Judaism. Consequently, it
is arbitrary to suspect vv. 14 (15)-16 as a
later interpolation, written after 70 A.D.
(cf. the present writer's Hist. New Testament, pp. 625, 626). But the closing sentence of ver. 16 has all the appearance of
a marginal gloss, written after the tragic
days of the siege in 70 A.D. (so e.g.,
Spitta, Pfleiderer, Primitive Christianity,
i. 128, 129, Schmiedel, Teichmann, die
Paul. Vorstellungen von Auferstehung
u. Gericht, 83, Drummond, etc.). The
Jews, no doubt, had recently suffered,
and were suffering, as a nation in a way
which might seem to Paul, in a moment
of vehement feeling, a clear proof of con-
dign punishment (so e.g., Schmidt, 86-
90). But neither the edict of Claudius
nor the bloody feuds in Palestine quite
bear out the language of this verse. And
ὀργή is surely more than judicial hardening (cf. Dante's Paradiso, vi. 88-93);
its eschatological significance points to
a more definite interpretation.
Ver. 17-CHAPTER III. Ver. 13. Paul's
apologia pro absentia suâ.
Ver. 17. πρὸς κ. ὥ., as we both expected, but, as it turned out, for much
longer. προσ. οὐ κ., "not where I

ωπον ὑμῶν ἰδεῖν ἐν πολλῇ ἐπιθυμίᾳ. 18. [m] διότι ἠθελήσαμεν ἐλθεῖν
πρὸς ὑμᾶς, ἐγὼ [n] μὲν Παῦλος καὶ [o] ἅπαξ καὶ [o] δίς, καὶ [p] ἐνέκοψεν
ἡμᾶς ὁ Σατανᾶς. 19. τίς γὰρ ἡμῶν ἐλπὶς ἢ [q] χαρὰ ἢ [q] στέφανος
[r] καυχήσεως [s] (ἢ οὐχὶ καὶ ὑμεῖς) ἔμπροσθεν τοῦ [t] Κυρίου ἡμῶν [t] Ἰησοῦ
ἐν τῇ αὐτοῦ παρουσίᾳ; 20. ὑμεῖς γάρ ἐστε [u] ἡ [v] δόξα ἡμῶν καὶ ἡ
χαρά.

m Win. § 5, 7, d, *cf.* on ii. 8. n = "For my part"; on absence of δέ, *cf.* Blass, § 77, 12. o = "More than once" (Phil. iv. 16). p *Cf.* Gal. v. 7; Rom. xv. 22. q Phil. iv. 1. r *Cf.* Prov. xvi. 31 (LXX). s Blass, § 77, 11. t *Cf.* Kattenbusch: *das Apost. Symbol*, ii. 597 f. u Win. § 18, 8, d. v 2 Cor. viii. 23, *cf.* 2 Cor. i. 14.

breathe; but where I love, I live" (Southwell, the Elizabethan Jesuit poet, echoing Augustine's remark that the soul lives where it loves, not where it exists); *cf.* Eurip., *Ion*, 251. The next paragraph, ii. 17-iii. 13, starts from a fresh imputation against the apostles' honour. Paul, it was more than hinted by calumniators at Thessalonica, had left his converts in the lurch (*cf.* 18); with him, out of sight was out of mind; fresh scenes and new interests in the South had supplanted them in his affections, and his failure to return was interpreted as a fickle indifference to their concerns. The reply is three-fold. (*a*) Paul's continued absence had been unavoidable (17 f.); he had often tried to get back. In proof of this anxiety (*b*) he had spared Timothy from his side for a visit to them (iii. 1-5), and (*c*) Timothy's report, he adds (iii. 6 f.) had relieved a hearty concern on his part for their welfare; he thus lets them see how much they were to him, and still prays for a chance of re-visiting them (11). He was not to blame for the separation; and, so far from blunting his affection, it had only whetted (**περισσοτέρως**) his eagerness to get back.

Ver. 18. "We did crave to reach you," **διότι** (= because) not being required with the English stress on *did*. The whole verse is parenthetical, syntactically.—**καὶ . . . Σατανᾶς.** The mysterious obstacle, which Paul traced back to the ultimate malice of Satan, may have been either (*a*) an illness (*cf.* 2 Cor. xii. 7, so Simon, *die Psychologie des Apostels Paulus*, 63, 64), (*b*) local troubles, (*c*) the exigencies of his mission at the time being (Grotius), or (*d*) a move on the part of the Thessalonian politarchs who may have bound over Jason and other leading Christians to keep the peace by pledging themselves to prevent Paul's return (Ramsay's *St. Paul the Traveller*, 230 f., Woodhouse, *E. Bi.*, 5047, Findlay). Early Christian thought referred all such hindrances to the devil as the opponent of God and of God's cause. The words **ἐν Ἀθήναις** (iii. 1) rule out Zimmer's application of (*b*) to the emergency at Corinth, while the silence of Acts makes any of the other hypotheses quite possible, though (*d*) hardly fits in with the ordinary view of the Empire in II. ii. 2 f. and renders it difficult to see why the Thessalonians did not understand at once how Paul could not return. The choice really lies between (*a*) and (*c*). Kabisch (27-29), by a forced exegesis, takes ver. 20 as the explanation of this satanic manœuvre. Satan prevented us from coming, in order to rob us of our glory and praise on the last day, by wrecking your Christian faith; he was jealous of our success among you.

Ver. 19. Of course we wanted to come back, for (**γάρ**), etc. The touch of fine exaggeration which follows is true to the situation. Paul's absence from the young church was being misinterpreted in a sinister way, as if it implied that the Achaian Christians had ousted the Thessalonians from his affections. *You it is*, he protests, *who but you* (**καὶ** superfluous after **ἢ**, as in Epict. i. 6, 39; Rom. xiv. 10, but really heightening the following word, as in Rom. v. 7; almost = "indeed" or "even")—*you are my pride and delight!*—**στέφανος**, of a public honour granted (as to Demosthenes and Zeno) for distinguished public service. The metaphor occurs often in the inscriptions (*cf.* also Pirke Aboth, iv. 9). Paul coveted no higher distinction at the arrival of the Lord than the glory of having won over the Thessalonian church. *Cf.* Crashaw's lines to St. Teresa in heaven:

"Thou shalt look round about, and see
Thousands of crown'd souls throng to be
Themselves thy crown".

Παρουσία = royal visit (*cf.* Wilcken's *Griech. Ostraka*, i. 274 f.), and hence applied (*cf.* Matt. xxiv.) to the arrival of the messiah, though the evidence for the

III. 1. Διὸ μηκέτι στέγοντες, [a]ηὐδοκήσαμεν [b]καταλειφθῆναι ἐν a *i.e.* Paul
Ἀθήναις μόνοι 2. καὶ ἐπέμψαμεν Τιμόθεον τὸν ἀδελφὸν ἡμῶν καὶ and Silvanus, *cf.* ii.
[c]συνεργὸν [c]τοῦ Θεοῦ [1] ἐν τῷ εὐαγγελίῳ τοῦ Χριστοῦ, εἰς τὸ [d]στηρίξαι b 8. Acts xxv,
ὑμᾶς καὶ [d]παρακαλέσαι [e]ὑπὲρ τῆς πίστεως ὑμῶν, 3. [f]τὸ μηδένα c 14. 2 Macc.
[g]σαίνεσθαι [2] ἐν ταῖς θλίψεσι ταύταις · αὐτοὶ γὰρ οἴδατε ὅτι εἰς [h]τοῦτο viii. 7, etc.,1 Cor.
[i]κείμεθα · 4. καὶ γὰρ ὅτε [k]πρὸς ὑμᾶς ἦμεν, προελέγομεν ὑμῖν ὅτι d iii. 9. II. ii. 17;
[l]μέλλομεν θλίβεσθαι, καθὼς καὶ ἐγένετο καὶ οἴδατε · 5. διὰ τοῦτο *cf.* below, ver. 13.
[m]κἀγὼ μηκέτι στέγων ἔπεμψα [n]εἰς τὸ γνῶναι τὴν πίστιν ὑμῶν, μή e =περὶ (*cf.*
πως [o]ἐπείρασεν ὑμᾶς ὁ πειράζων καὶ [p]εἰς κενὸν [q]γένηται ὁ κόπος II. ii. 1; Rom. i. 8; Plato's *Apol.* xxxix. e).

f *Cf.* Viteau, i. 272; Blass, § 71, 2, opposition to preceding clause (*cf.* iv. 6).   g Here only (N.T.),
= "allured, beguiled" or "disturbed" (Diog. Laert. viii. 43: οἱ δὲ σαινόμενοι τοῖς λεγομένοις ἐδάκρυον).
h *i.e.* τὸ θλίβεσθαι, *cf.* i. 6, II. i. 5.   i Phil. i. 16.   k = "with" II. iii. 1, 10, etc.   l "We
Christians."   m *Cf.* on ii. 13.   n *Cf.* on ii. 16.   o Unrealised purpose, see Gal. ii. 2,
iv. 11, for mood; also Burton, M.T. 227.   p Win. § 29, 2, b.   q deliberative conjunctive.

[1] For ημων και διακονον τ.θ. και συνεργον ημων (DcKL, syr.sch, Chrys., Theod.,
Dam., etc.), or ημων και δ.τ.θ. (ℵAP, min., vg., cop., syr.ptxt, arm., aeth., Euth.,
etc., Ti., Tr., Bj., Zim.) read the original and harder Western text ημων και συνεργον
τ.θ. (D*, d, e, 17, Amb. [B om. τ.θ. so Weiss, Findlay], Lach., Al., Ell., WH
marg., Born., Schm., Wohl., Feine), from which the variants seem to have sprung.
Later scribes are more likely to have stumbled at τ.θ. after συνεργον than to have
inserted it by a reminiscence of 1 Cor. iii. 9.

[2] For μ. σαινεσθαι (*cf.* Zahn, *Einl.* § 14, 2), Lach., Ernesti, and Verschuis (so
Alexander) conj. μηδεν ασαινεσθαι (= χαλεπῶς φέρειν), a more than dubious passive
form of ασαω, Beza and Bentley μηδενα σαλενεσθαι (v.l. σενεσθαι, Bentl.), and
Holwerda μηδεν αναινεσθαι (= repent or be ashamed of); if any change is required
(but *cf.* Koch's full note, 233-237), it would be in the direction of σιεινεσθαι
(=σιαινεσθαι, to be disheartened, unnerved), the attractive reading of FG which is
preferred by Sophocles (Lex., s.v.), Reiske, and Nestle (*Exp. Ti.* xviii. 479, Preuschen's
Zeitschrift, vii. 361-62, *cf.* Mercati, *ibid.* viii. 242).   G elsewhere (*cf.* Rom. xi. 26,
xii. 17) confuses ει and αι.

use of the term in pre-Christian Judaism
is scanty (Test. Jud. xxii. 3; Test. Levi.
viii. 15; for the idea of the divine "coming" *cf.* *Slav. En.*, xxxii. 1, xlii. 5). This
is the first time the term is used by Paul,
but it was evidently familiar to the
readers. Later on, possibly through
Paul's influence, it became an accepted
word for the second advent in early
Christianity.
    CHAPTER III.—Ver. 1. μηκ., instead
of οὐκ., to bring out the personal motive.
—στέγοντες "able to bear" (*cf.* Philo,
Flacc., § 9, μηκέτι στέγειν δυνάμενοι τὰς
ἐνδείας), sc. the anxiety of ii. 11 f.—ἐν
Ἀ. μόνοι. Paul shrank from loneliness,
especially where there was little or no
Christian fellowship; but he would not
gratify himself at the expense of the
Thessalonians. Their need of Timothy
must take precedence of his.
    Ver. 3. *Cf.* Artemid., *Oneirocritica* ii.
11, ἀλλότριοι δὲ κύνες σαίνοντες μὲν
δόλους καὶ ἐνέδρας ὑπὸ πονηρῶν ἀνδρῶν
[*cf.* 2 Thess. iii. 2] ἢ γυναικῶν [*cf.* Acts
xvii. 4] σημαίνουσιν.

Ver. 4. *Cf.* Acts xvii. 3, 6, 13 f.
    Ver. 5. Resuming the thought of iii.
1-3a, after the parenthetical digression
of 3b, 4, but adding a fresh reason for the
mission of Timothy, *viz.*, the apostle's
desire to have his personal anxiety about
the Thessalonians relieved. It is needless to suppose (with Hofmann and
Spitta) that iii. 5 refers to a fresh messenger or a letter (Wohl.) despatched by
Paul on his own account. As in ii. 18,
Paul passes to the singular, to emphasise
his personal interest in the matter; the
change of number, especially after the
generic use of the plural in 3, 4, does not
necessarily prove that the plural of ver.
1 means Paul alone. The dominating
anxiety of Paul was about their faith (5-
10). He was overjoyed to hear that they
retained "a kindly remembrance" of
himself, and he reciprocates their desire
for another meeting; but, while this undoubtedly entered into their general
Christian position, it is the former on
which unselfishly he dwells (*cf.* the
transition in 10a and 10b).—πίστιν

ἡμῶν. 6. [r] ἄρτι δὲ ἐλθόντος Τιμοθέου πρὸς ἡμᾶς ἀφ᾽ ὑμῶν καὶ
[s] εὐαγγελισαμένου ἡμῖν τὴν πίστιν καὶ τὴν ἀγάπην ὑμῶν καὶ ὅτι
ἔχετε μνείαν ἡμῶν ἀγαθὴν πάντοτε, ἐπιποθοῦντες ἡμᾶς ἰδεῖν, [t] καθάπερ καὶ ἡμεῖς ὑμᾶς, 7. [u] διὰ τοῦτο παρεκλήθημεν, ἀδελφοί, [v] ἐφ᾽
ὑμῖν ἐπὶ πάσῃ [w] τῇ ἀνάγκῃ καὶ [w] θλίψει ἡμῶν διὰ τῆς ὑμῶν πίστ-
εως· 8. ὅτι νῦν [x] ζῶμεν, [y] ἐὰν ὑμεῖς [z] στήκετε ἐν Κυρίῳ. 9. τίνα
γὰρ [a] εὐχαριστίαν δυνάμεθα τῷ Θεῷ ἀνταποδοῦναι περὶ ὑμῶν, ἐπὶ
πάσῃ τῇ χαρᾷ ᾗ χαίρομεν δι᾽ ὑμᾶς ἔμπροσθεν τοῦ Θεοῦ ἡμῶν, 10.
νυκτὸς καὶ ἡμέρας [b] ὑπερεκπερισσοῦ δεόμενοι [c] εἰς τὸ ἰδεῖν [d] ὑμῶν
τὸ πρόσωπον καὶ καταρτίσαι τὰ ὑστερήματα τῆς πίστεως ὑμῶν; 11.
[e] Αὐτὸς δὲ [f] ὁ Θεὸς καὶ πατὴρ ἡμῶν καὶ ὁ Κύριος ἡμῶν Ἰησοῦς [g] κατευθύναι τὴν ὁδὸν ἡμῶν πρὸς ὑμᾶς· 12. ὑμᾶς δὲ ὁ Κύριος [h] πλεονάσαι
καὶ [i] περισσεύσαι τῇ ἀγάπῃ εἰς ἀλλήλους καὶ εἰς πάντας (καθάπερ
καὶ ἡμεῖς [k] εἰς ὑμᾶς) 13. εἰς τὸ [l] στηρίξαι [m] ὑμῶν τὰς καρδίας [n] ἀμέμ-
πτους ἐν [o] ἁγιωσύνῃ, ἔμπροσθεν τοῦ Θεοῦ καὶ πατρὸς ἡμῶν ἐν τῇ
παρουσίᾳ τοῦ Κυρίου ἡμῶν Ἰησοῦ μετὰ [p] πάντων τῶν [q] ἁγίων αὐτοῦ.

r = "A moment ago," "just".
s *Cf.* Lk. i. 19; in untechnical classical sense of "bringing good news".
t *Cf.* ii. 11, 17.
u resumptive = "by this good news".
v *Cf.* 2 Cor. vii. 7.
w Job xv. 24 (LXX), "we were suffering (*cf.* ver. 3.) as well as you".
x Intensive (*cf.* 2 Cor. vi. 9, xiii. 4: "uiuimus, hoc est recte ualemus" (Calvin).
y = *ὅταν*, ii. 7.
z II. ii. 15, late form, *cf.* Blass § 65, 4; Win. § 5, 19; Burton, *M.T.* 247, and Moult. i. 168.
a *Cf.* on Acts xxiv. 3.
b *Cf.* Dan. iii. 23 (Theod.) and v. 13 below.
c II. ii. 2; constr. as in ii. 12.
d See note on v. 23.
e *Cf.* iv. 16, and contrast ii. 18.
f *Cf.* Win. § 18, 7, Moult. i. 179.
g II. iii. 5, Lk. i. 79.
h Transit. as Num. xxvi. 54 (LXX), etc.
i Transit. as 2 Cor. ix. 8; *cf.* for thought Phil. i. 9.
k *Sc.* "abound in love".
l *Cf.* above, ver. 2.
m See note on v. 23.
n Proleptic (*cf.* Viteau, II. 275), as v. 23; *cf.* Phil. ii. 15, Clem. Rom. xliv. 6, Sap. ii. 22.
o *Cf.* 2 Cor. vii. 1.
p *Cf.* iv. 17, ἡμεῖς . . . *σὺν αὐτοῖς*.
q Jude 14, *cf.* Everling: *die paul. Angelologie* (78-79).

κ.τ.λ. "Initium omnium malarum tentationum inconstantia animi est et parua ad Deum confidentia" (*De Imit. Christi*, i. 13, 5).—**ἐπείρασεν,** with success, it is implied.

Ver. 8. The news put life and spirit into him.—**στήκετε,** for construction *cf.* Mark xi. 25 and Abbott's *Johan. Gramm.*, 2515 (i).

Ver. 10. Another adaptation of ethnic phraseology, *cf. Griechische Urkunden*, i. 246, 12, **νυκτὸς καὶ ἡμέρας ἐντυγχάνω τῷ θεῷ ὑπὲρ ὑμῶν** (a pagan papyrus from second or third century, A.D.). The connection of **δεόμενοι κ.τ.λ.** with the foregoing words is loose, but probably may be found in the vivid realisation of the Thessalonians called up before his mind as he praised God for their constancy. Timothy had told him of their loyalty, but had evidently acquainted him also with some less promising tendencies and shortcomings in the church; possibly the Thessalonians had even asked for guidance on certain matters of belief and practice (see below). Hence Paul's eagerness to be on the spot again, not merely for the sake of happy fellowship (Rom. i. 11), but to educate and guide his friends, supplying what was defective in their faith. As this was impracticable in the meantime, he proceeds to write down some kindly admonitions. Thus 10*b* forms the transition to the second part of the letter; Paul, as usual, is wise enough to convey any correction or remonstrance on the back of hearty commendation. In the prayer which immediately follows, 10*a* is echoed in 11, 10*b* in 12, 13, for the maturing of the Thessalonian's faith does not depend on the presence of their apostles. Whatever be the answer to the prayer of 11, the prayer of 12, 13 can be accomplished.

Ver. 11. **κατευθύναι** (optative), as already (Acts xvi. 8-10, xvii. 1). The singular (*cf.* II., ii. 16, 17) implies that God and Jesus count as one in this connection. The verb is common (*e.g.*, Ep. Arist., 18, etc.) in this sense of providence directing human actions.

Vv. 12, 13. The security and purity of the Christian life are rested upon its brotherly love (so Ep. Arist., 229); all breaches or defects of **ἁγιωσύνη,** it is implied, are due to failures there (*cf.* iv. 3, 6); even sensuality becomes a form of selfishness, on this view, as much as impatience or resentment. This profound **ἀγάπη** "is an ever-fixed mark That looks

IV. 1. ᵃ Λοιπὸν οὖν, ἀδελφοί, ᵇ ἐρωτῶμεν ὑμᾶς καὶ παρακαλοῦμεν
ἐν Κυρίῳ Ἰησοῦ, ἵνα καθὼς παρελάβετε παρ' ἡμῶν ᶜτὸ πῶς δεῖ ὑμᾶς
περιπατεῖν ᵈ καὶ ᵉ ἀρέσκειν Θεῷ, καθὼς καὶ περιπατεῖτε, ἵνα περισ-
σεύητε μᾶλλον· 2. οἴδατε γὰρ τίνας παραγγελίας ἐδώκαμεν ὑμῖν
διὰ τοῦ Κυρίου Ἰησοῦ. 3. ᶠτοῦτο γάρ ἐστι ᶠθέλημα τοῦ Θεοῦ, ὁ

a "Locutio
proper-
antis ad
finem"
(Grotius),
Test.
Reub. v.
5; cf. on
2 Cor.
xiii. 11,
and Jan-

naris in *Exp.*ᵇ viii. 429 f.   b Phil. iv. 3.   c On article in indir. questions, see Blass, § 47.
5, Viteau, I. 132, Win. § 18, 2.   d And so (result).   e Contr. ii. 15.   f v. 18, Ps. xxix. 5, etc.

on tempests and is never shaken;" it
fixes the believing man's life in the very
life of God, by deepening its vital powers
of growth; no form of ἁγιωσύνη which
sits loose to the endless obligations
of this ἀγάπη will stand the strain
of this life or the scrutiny of God's
tribunal at the end.—ὑμᾶς δὲ, what
ever becomes of us.—ἁγίων, either (*a*)
"saints" (as II., i. 10, De Wette, Hofmann, Zimmer, Schmidt, Everling, Kabisch, Findlay, Wohl.), or (*b*) "angels"
(Ex. i. 9; Ps. Sol. xvii. 49, etc. Hühn,
Weiss, Schrader, Titius, Schmiedel,
Lueken), or (*c*) both (*cf.* 4 Esd. vii. 28,
xiv. 9; Bengel, Alford, Wohl., Askwith,
Ellicott, Lightfoot, Milligan). The reminiscence of Zech. xiv. 5 (LXX) is almost decisive for (*b*), though Paul may have put
another content into the term; πάντων must not be pressed to support (*c*).
In any case, the phrase goes closely with
παρουσίᾳ. The ἅγιοι are a retinue.

CHAPTER IV.-Ver. 1-CHAPTER V.-Ver.
11. *Special instructions (iv. 1-12) on
chastity, etc.*

Ver. 1. Resuming the thought of ii.
11, 12 as well as of iii. 10-13. *Cf.* a pre-
Christian letter in Oxyrh. Papyri, iv. 294
(13 ἐρωτῶ σε οὖν ἵνα μὴ, 6 f. ἐρωτῶ σε
καὶ παρακαλῶ σε). The ἵνα, repeated
often for the sake of clearness, is sub-final
(so II., iii. 12) = infinitive, *cf.* Moulton,
i. 206 f. Paul meant to write οὕτως καὶ
περιπατῆτε, but the parenthesis of praise
(κ. καὶ π.) leads him to assume that and
to plead for fresh progress along the
lines already laid down by himself.

Ver. 2. Almost a parenthesis, as
Bahnsen points out in his study of 1-12
(*Zeitschrift f. wiss. Theol.*, 1904, 332-358).
The injunctions (παραγγελίαι in semi-
military sense, as 1 Tim. i. 18) relate to
chastity (3-8) and charity, (9, 10), with a
postscript against excitement and idle-
ness (11, 12).—παραγγ. for the cognate
use of this term (*cf.* ver. 8) in the inscriptions of Dionysopolis (παραγγέλλω πᾶσιν
μὴ καταφρονεῖν τοῦ θεοῦ) *cf. Exp. Ti.*,
x. 159.—διὰ κ.τ.λ., the change from the
ἐν of ver. 1 does not mean that the Thes-

salonians before their conversion got such
injunctions from Paul on the authority
of Christ, while afterwards they simply
needed to be reminded of the obligations
of their union (ἐν) with the Lord. No
strict difference can be drawn between
both phrases (*cf.* Heitmüller's *Im Namen
Jesu*, 71 f.), though the διά lays rather
more stress on the authority. For Jesus
to command διά the apostles seems to
us more natural than to say that the
apostles issue commands διὰ τοῦ Κυρίου,
but the sense is really the same. The
apostles give their orders on the authority
of their commission and revelations from
the Lord whom they interpret to His followers (*cf.* Rom. xv. 30, xii. 2). But this
interpretation must have appealed to
the sayings of Jesus which formed part
of the παράδοσις (*cf.* Weizsäcker's
Apostolic Age, i. 97, 120, ii. 39). Thus
8a is an echo of the saying preserved in
Luke x. 16.

Ver. 3. ἁγιασμός (in apposition to
τοῦτο, θέλημα without the article being
the predicate) = the moral issue of a life
related to the Ἅγιος (*cf.* ver. 8), viewed
here in its special and negative aspect of
freedom from sexual impurity. The
gospel of Jesus, unlike some pagan cults,
e.g., that of the Cabiri at Thessalonica
(*cf.* Lightfoot's *Biblical Essays*, pp.
257 f.), did not tolerate, much less foster,
licentiousness among its worshippers.
At Thessalonica as at Corinth Paul found
his converts exposed to the penetrating
taint of life in a large seaport. As the
context indicates, ἁγ. ὑμῶν = "the perfecting of you in holiness" (ἁγ. in its
active sense, ὑμῶν genitive objective: so
Lünemann, Ellicott, Bahnsen). The absence of any reference to δικαιοσύνη is
remarkable. But Paul's dialectic on justification was occasioned by controversies
about ὁ νόμος which were not felt at
Thessalonica. Besides, the "justified"
standing of the believer, even in that
synthesis of doctrine, amounted practically to the position assured by the possession of the Spirit to the Christian. In his
uncontroversial and eschatological mo-

g Acts xv.   ἁγιασμὸς ὑμῶν, ᵍ ἀπέχεσθαι ὑμᾶς ἀπὸ τῆς ᶠπορνείας· 4. ᵍ εἰδέναι
20; infin.
of apposi- ἕκαστον ὑμῶν τὸ ἑαυτοῦ ʰ σκεῦος κτᾶσθαι ἐν ¹ ἁγιασμῷ καὶ ᵏ τιμῇ,
tion, as
Acts xv.   5. μὴ ἐν ¹πάθει ᵏ ἐπιθυμίας, καθάπερ ᵐ καὶ τὰ ἔθνη ⁿτὰ μὴ εἰδότα
28; Sap.
ii. 16.   τὸν Θεόν· 6. ᵒτὸ ᵖμὴ ὑπερβαίνειν καὶ πλεονεκτεῖν ᵠἐν τῷ ᵠπράγματι
h 1 Pet. iii.
7.   τὸν ἀδελφὸν αὐτοῦ· διότι ʳἔκδικος Κύριος περὶ πάντων τούτων,
i See Tob.
viii. 4-9,
and 1 Cor. vii. 39.   k See Heb. xiii. 4 and Ignat. *ad Polyk.* v. 2.   l 4 Macc. 1. 35.   m *Cf.*
on ii. 14.   n From Jer. x. 25; *cf.* II. i. 8: "whose characteristic is ignorance of God" (Win.
§ 20, 3 b).   o *sc. τινα* from ἕκαστον (4).   p *Cf.* iii. 3, for the accus. infin. with neg. to denote
purpose.   q *Cf.* on 2 Cor. vii. 11.   r Ps. xciv. 1, *cf.* Sir. v. 3; Rom. xii. 19, and xiii. 4.

ments, Paul taught as here that the experience of the Spirit guaranteed the believer's vindication at the end (*cf.* i. 9, 10) and also implied his ethical behaviour during the interval. The comparative lack of any allusion to the forgiveness of sins (*cf. e.g.*, iii. 5, 10, 13) does not mean that Paul thought the Thessalonians would be kept sinless during the brief interval till the parousia (so Wernle, *der Christ u. die Sünde bei Paulus*, 25-32); probably no occasion had called for any explicit teaching on this commonplace of faith (1 Cor. xv. 3, 11).

Ver. 4. Paul demands chastity from men; it is not simply a feminine virtue. Contemporary ethics, in the Roman and Greek world, was often disposed to condone marital unfaithfulness on the part of husbands, and to view prenuptial unchastity as ἀδιάφορον or at least as a comparatively venial offence, particularly in men (*cf.* Lecky's *History of European Morals*, i. 104 f., ii. 314 f.). The strict purity of Christ's gospel had to be learnt (εἰδέναι). — σκεῦος (lit. "vessel") = "wife;" the rendering "body" (*cf.* Barn. vii. 3) conflicts with the normal meaning of κτᾶσθαι ("get," "acquire;" of marriage, LXX. Ruth iv. 10; Sir. xxxvi. 29, Xen., *Symp.*, ii. 10). Paul views marriage on much the same level as he does in 1 Cor. vii. 2, 9; in its chaste and religious form, it is a remedy against sensual passion, not a gratification of that passion. Each of you (he is addressing men) must learn (εἰδέναι = know [how] to, *cf.* Phil. iv. 12) to get a wife of his own (when marriage is in question), but you must marry ἐν ἁγιασμῷ (as a Christian duty and vocation) καὶ τιμῇ (with a corresponding sense of the moral dignity of the relationship). The two latter words tend to raise the current estimate, presupposed here and in ver. 6, of a wife as the σκεῦος of her husband; this in its turn views adultery primarily as an infringement of the husband's rights or an attack on his personal pro-

perty. Paul, however, closes with an emphatic word on the religious aspect (6-8) of the question; besides, as Dr. Drummond remarks, "is it not part of his greatness that, in spite of his own somewhat ascetic temperament, he was not blind to social and physiological facts?" It is noticeable that his eschatology has less effect on his view of marriage here than in 1 Cor. vii. Even were κτᾶσθαι taken as = "possess," a usage not quite impossible for later Greek (*cf.* Field, 72), it would only extend the idea to the duties of a Christian husband. The alternative rendering ("acquire mastery of," Luke xxi. 19) does not justify the "body" sense of σκεῦος.

Ver. 6. Compare the saying of rabbi Simon ben Zoma (on Deut. xxiii. 25): "Look not on thy neighbour's vineyard. If thou hast looked, enter not; if thou hast entered, regard not the fruits; if thou hast regarded them, touch them not; if thou hast touched them, eat them not. But if thou hast eaten, then thou dost eject thyself from the life of this world and of that which is to come" (quoted in Bacher's *Agada der Tannaiten*, 2nd ed., 1903, i. 430). There is no change of subject, from licentiousness to dishonesty. The asyndeton and the euphemistic ἐν τῷ πράγματι (not τῷ = τινί, Win. § 6 4*d*) show that Paul is still dealing with the immorality of men, but now as a form of social dishonesty and fraud. The metaphors are drawn from trade, perhaps as appropriate to a trading community. While ὑπερβαίνειν may be intransitive (in its classical sense of "transgress"), it probably governs ἀδελφόν in the sense of "get the better of," or "overreach;" πλεονεκτεῖν similarly = "overreach," "defraud," "take advantage of" (2 Cor. ii. 2, xii. 17, 18; Xen., *Mem.*, iii. 5, 2; Herod. viii. 112). Compare ἀκαθαρσίας πάσης ἐν πλεονεξίᾳ (Eph. iv. 19). The passage (with ver. 8) sounds almost like a vague reminiscence of Test. Asher, ii. 6: ὁ πλεονεκτῶν τὸν

καθὼς καὶ *προείπαμεν ὑμῖν καὶ ᵗδιεμαρτυράμεθα. 7. οὐ γὰρ ˢ
ἐκάλεσεν ἡμᾶς ὁ Θεὸς ᵘἐπὶ ᵛἀκαθαρσίᾳ ἀλλ' ʷἐν ἁγιασμῷ. 8. ˣτοι-
γαροῦν ὁ ἀθετῶν οὐκ ἄνθρωπον ἀθετεῖ ἀλλὰ τὸν Θεὸν τὸν διδόντα τὸ
Πνεῦμα αὐτοῦ τὸ Ἅγιον ʸεἰς ὑμᾶς. 9. περὶ δὲ τῆς ˣφιλαδελφίας
οὐ ᵃχρείαν ἔχετε ᵃγράφειν ὑμῖν· ¹ αὐτοὶ γὰρ ὑμεῖς ᵇθεοδίδακτοί ἐστε
ᶜεἰς τὸ ἀγαπᾶν ἀλλήλους· 10. καὶ γὰρ ποιεῖτε αὐτὸ εἰς πάντας τοὺς
ἀδελφοὺς ᵈἐν ὅλῃ τῇ Μακεδονίᾳ. παρακαλοῦμεν δὲ ὑμᾶς, ἀδελφοί,
*περισσεύειν μᾶλλον 11. καὶ ᶠφιλοτιμεῖσθαι ᵍἡσυχάζειν καὶ ᵇπράσ-

Cf. Win. § 13, 13. = "Solemnly testified" (cf. 1 Tim. v. 21). "With a view to" (cf. Eph. ii. 10): object and terms. "Sexual vice" (as

Col. iii. 5, Eph. v. 3), Test. Jos. iv. 6.   w = εἰς (1 Cor. vii. 15; Eph. iv. 4; Win. § 50, 5).
x Heb. xii. 1.   y As in Ezek. xxxvii. 14 (LXX).   z See on Rom. xii. 10.   a Blass, § 69, 5;
2 Cor. ix. 1; Heb. v. 12.   b Elaborated in Rom. v. 5; 2 Cor. v. 14, cf. Barn. xxi. 6; Isa. liv.
13; Ps. Sol. xvii. 35.   c Epexegetic infinitive, (Moult. 218-219) of object.   d Philippi,
Berea, etc.   e Active side of iii. 12.   f See on 2 Cor. v. 9 and Rom. xv. 20 = "be distinguished for a quiet life," "strive to be quiet".   g Cf. II. iii. 12.   h = "attend to your own
business," cf. Dem. Olynth. ii. 16.

¹ ου χ. εχετε γραφειν υμιν (א*ADc, etc., edd.), an irregular but not uncommon
turn ("you have no need of anyone to write you"), corrected in אᶜD*G, vg., Chrys.,
etc., to εχομεν κ.τ.λ. (so Lünem., Lachm., Blass, cf. i. 8), and in B to ειχομεν κ.τ.λ.
(Weiss, Bahnsen), as in H to γραφεσθαί κ.τ.λ. (from v. 1).

πλησίον παροργίζει τὸν Θεόν . . . τὸν
ἐντολέα τοῦ νόμου Κύριον ἀθετεῖ. Only
τὸν ἀνθ. here is not the wronged party
but the apostles who convey God's
orders.—διότι κ.τ.λ. = "since (cf. ii. 8)
the Lord is the avenger (from Deut. xxxii.
35; cf. Sap. xii. 12; Sir. xxx. 6; 1 Macc.
xiii. 6, ἐκδικήσω περὶ; 4 Macc. xv. 29) in
all these matters" (of impurity). How,
Paul does not explain (cf. Col. iii. 5, 6).
By a premature death (1 Cor. xi. 30)?
Or, at the last judgment (i. 10)? not in
the sense of Sap. iii. 16, iv. 6 (illegitimate
children evidence at last day against their
parents) at any rate.

Ver. 8. Elsewhere (i. 5, 6) ἅγιον simply
denotes the divine quality of πνεῦμα as
operating in the chosen ἅγιοι of God,
but here the context lends it a specific
value. Impurity is a violation of the
relationship established by the holy God
between Himself and Christians at baptism, when the holy Spirit is bestowed
upon them for the purpose of consecrating them to live His life (cf. 1 Cor. iii.
16, vi. 19). The gift of the Spirit here
is not regarded as the earnest of the
future kingdom (for which immorality
will disqualify) so much as the motive and
power of the new life.—διδόντα = "the
giver of," not implying continuous or
successive impartation; present as in ch.
v. 24; Gal. v. 8. He not only calls, but
supplies the atmosphere and energy requisite for the task.—ἀθετῶν κ.τ.λ. (cf.
ii. 13) = contemns by ignoring such injunctions (2-6) in practical life, deliberately sets aside their authority. Cf. Isa.
xxiv. 16, 17 f., οὐαὶ τοῖς ἀθετοῦσιν· οἱ

ἀθετοῦντες τὸν νόμον, φόβος καὶ βόθυνος
καὶ παγὶς ἐφ' ὑμᾶς (nor shall any escape:
cf. below on v. 3). In 2 Sam. xii. 9 f.
Nathan fixes on the selfishness of David's
adultery and charges him especially with
despising the commandment of the Lord.

Vv. 9-10. περὶ φιλαδελφίας. One
might have expected that adultery,
especially when viewed as selfish greed
(cf. ver. 6), would have come under
φ., but the latter bears mainly here on
charity and liberality, a Christian impulse
or instinct which seems to have come
more naturally to the Thessalonians than
ethical purity. "A new creed, like a new
country, is an unhomely place of sojourn,
but it makes men lean on one another
and join hands" (R. L. Stevenson).

Ver 10. Their ἀγάπη was no parochial affection, but neither was it to be
fussy or showy, much less to be made an
excuse for neglecting their ordinary business (11, 12); this would discredit them
in the eyes of the busy outside public
(πρὸς = in intercourse or relations with)
and sap their own independence. Such
seems the least violent way of explaining
the transition in καὶ φιλοτιμεῖσθαι κ.τ.λ.
The church was apparently composed, for
the most part, of tradesmen and working
people (χερσὶν ὑμῶν, cf. Renan's S. Paul,
246 f.) with their families, but there may
have been some wealthier members,
whose charity was in danger of being
abused. Cf. Demos., Olynth., iii. 35: οὐκ
ἔστιν ὅπου μηδὲν ἐγὼ ποιοῦσιν τὰ τῶν
ποιούντων εἶπον ὡς δεῖ νέμειν, οὐδ' αὐτοὺς μὲν ἀργεῖν καὶ σχολάζειν καὶ ἀπορεῖν.

Ver. 11. φιλοτ. ἡσυχάζειν (οχυ-

i See on
1 Cor.
xiv. 40.
k See on
1 Cor. v.
12.
Neuter
(Heb. v.
12, etc.).
m Cf. note
on ii. 14.
n i.e. pa-
gans as in
Eph. ii. 3, cf. Sap. ii. 1 f.   o Cf. Theogn. 567, Iph. Aul. 1250, Sap. ii. 22, iii. 18.   p i.e.
"then it follows that".

σειν τὰ ἴδια καὶ ἐργάζεσθαι ταῖς χερσὶν ὑμῶν, καθὼς ὑμῖν παρηγγεί-
λαμεν· 12. ἵνα περιπατῆτε ¹ εὐσχημόνως πρὸς ᵏ τοὺς ἔξω καὶ ¹ μη-
δενὸς χρείαν ἔχητε.

13. οὐ θέλομεν δὲ ὑμᾶς ἀγνοεῖν, ἀδελφοί, περὶ τῶν κοιμωμένων,
ἵνα μὴ λυπῆσθε καθὼς ᵐκαὶ οἱ ⁿλοιποὶ °οἱ μὴ ἔχοντες ἐλπίδα. 14.
εἰ γὰρ πιστεύομεν ὅτι Ἰησοῦς ἀπέθανε καὶ ἀνέστη, ᴾ οὕτω καὶ ὁ Θεὸς

moron). The prospect of the second advent (iv. 13 f., v. 1-10) seems to have
made some local enthusiasts feel that
it was superfluous for them to go on
working, if the world was to be broken
up immediately. This feverish symptom
occupies Paul more in the diagnosis of
his second letter, but it may have been
present to his mind here. For instances
of this common phase in unbalanced
minds compare the story of Hippolytus
(*Comm. Dan.*, iv. 19) about a Pontic bishop
in the second century who misled his
people by prophesying the advent within
six months, and also a recent outburst of
the same superstition in Tripoli (*Westminster Gazette*, Nov., 1899) where "the
report that the end of the world will
come on November 13" produced "an
amazing state of affairs. The Israelites
are sending their wives to pray in the
synagogues, and most workmen have
ceased work. Debtors refuse to pay their
debts, so that trade is almost paralysed."
—καὶ πράσσειν τὰ ἴδια. Plato uses a
similar expression in his *Republic*, 496 D
(ἡσυχίαν ἔχων καὶ τὰ αὐτοῦ πράττων) ;
but of the philosopher who withdraws in
despair from the lawlessness of a world
which he is impotent to help (see also
Thompson's note on *Gorg.*, 526c).

Vv. 13-18. περὶ τῶν κοιμωμένων.

Ver. 13. δὲ, after οὐ θέλομεν as a
single expression.—Affection for the living has another side, *viz.*, unselfish solici-
tude for the dead. Since Paul left,
some of the Thessalonian Christians had
died, and the survivors were distressed by
the fear that these would have to occupy
a position secondary to those who lived
until the advent of the Lord, or even that
they had passed beyond any such participation at all. At Corinth some of
the local Christians felt this anguish so
keenly, on behalf of friends and relatives
who had died outside the church, that
they were in the habit of being baptised
as their representatives, to ensure their
final bliss (1 Cor. xv. 29). The concern

of the Thessalonians, however, was for
their fellow-Christians, in the intermediate state of Hades. As the problem had
not arisen during Paul's stay at Thessalonica, he now offers the church a reasonable solution of the difficulty (13-18).—
οὐ θέλομεν δὲ ὑμᾶς ἀγνοεῖν, contrast the
οἴδατε of iv. 2, v. 2, and compare the
ordinary epistolary phrases of the papyri
(*Expos.*, 1908, 55) such as γεινώσκειν σε
θέλω (commonly at the beginning of a
letter, *cf.* Col. ii. 1 ; Phil. i. 12 ; 2 Cor.
i. 8, and with ὅτι, but here, as in 1 Cor.
xii. 1, with περί).—τῶν κοιμωμένων =
the dead in Christ (16), a favourite Jewish euphemism (Kennedy, *St. Paul's Conc.
of Last Things*, 247 f., and *cf.* Fries in
Zeitschrift für neutest. Wiss. i. 306 f.),
not unknown to Greek and Roman literature.—οἱ λοιποί, κ.τ.λ., *cf.* Butcher's
Some Aspects of the Greek Genius, pp.
153 f., 159 f. Hope is the distinguishing
note of Christians here as in Eph. ii. 12 ;
Col. i. 22, etc.

Ver. 14. Unlike some of the Corinthians (1 Cor. xv. 17, 18), the Thessalonians did not doubt the fact of Christ's
resurrection (εἰ of course implies no
uncertainty). Paul assumes their faith
in it and argues from it. Their vivid and
naïve belief in Christ's advent within
their own lifetime was the very source
of their distress. Paul still shares that
belief (17).—διὰ τοῦ Ἰησοῦ is an unusual
expression which might, so far as grammar is concerned, go either with τ. κ.
(so. *e.g.*, Ellic., Alford, Kabisch, Lightfoot, Findlay, Milligan) or ἄξει. The
latter is the preferable construction (so
most editors). The phrase is not needed
(*cf.* 15) to limit τ. κ. to Christians (so
Chrys., Calvin), for the unbelieving dead
are not before the writer's mind, and,
even so, ἐν would have been the natural
preposition (*cf.* 16) ; nor does it mean
martyrdom. In the light of v. 9 (*cf.*
Rom. v. 9 ; 1 Cor. xv. 21), it seems to
connect less awkwardly with ἄξει, though
not = "at the intercession of Jesus"

^q τοὺς κοιμηθέντας διὰ τοῦ Ἰησοῦ ^r ἄξει σὺν αὐτῷ. 15. τοῦτο γὰρ ^q = "those
ὑμῖν λέγομεν ^s ἐν λόγῳ ^s Κυρίου, ὅτι ἡμεῖς οἱ ζῶντες οἱ ^t περιλειπό- fallen
μενοι εἰς τὴν παρουσίαν τοῦ Κυρίου ^u οὐ μὴ ^v φθάσωμεν τοὺς κοιμη- (Moult. i.
162).
r Cf. Heb.
i. 6 and Asc. Isa. iv. 16.　　s LXX of 1 Kings xx. 35, "Domini nomine et quasi eo loquente"
(Beza).　t 2 Macc. i. 31, viii. 14, etc.　u "by no means" (cf. 1 Cor. viii. 13).　v Sap. vi. 13, etc.

(Rutherford). Jesus is God's agent in
the final act, commissioned to raise and
muster the dead (cf. Stähelin, Jahrb. f.
deut. Theol., 1874, 189 f., and Schettler,
Die paul. Formel "Durch Christus," 1907,
57 f.). The divine mission of the Christ,
which is to form the climax of things,
involves the resurrection of the dead
who are His (v. 10). Any general resurrection is out of the question (so Did.,
xvi. 6: ἀνάστασις νεκρῶν· οὐ πάντων
δὲ, ἀλλ' ὡς ἐρρέθη, ἥξει ὁ Κύριος καὶ
πάντες οἱ ἅγιοι μετ' αὐτοῦ).
Ver. 15. κυρίου. On the tendency of
the N.T. writers to reserve κύριος, with
its O.T. predicates of divine authority, for
Jesus, cf. Kattenbusch, op. cit., ii. 522.
Paul's use of the term goes back to
Christ's own claim to κύριος in the higher
sense of Mark xii. 35 f.—λέγομεν. Contrast the οἴδατε of v. 2 and the language
of iv. 1. Evidently Paul had not had
time or occasion to speak of such a contingency, when he was with them.—ἐν
λόγῳ κυρίου may mean either (a) a quotation (like Acts xx. 35) from the sayings of
Jesus, or (b) a prophetic revelation vouchsafed to Paul himself, or to Silvanus (cf.
Acts xv. 32). In the former case (so,
among modern editors, Schott, Ewald,
Drummond, Wohl.), an ἄγραφον is cited
(Calvin, Koch, Weizsäcker, Resch, Paulinismus, 238 f.; Ropes, die Sprüche Jesu,
153 f.; M. Goguel; van der Vies, 15-17;
O. Holtzmann, Life of Jesus, 10; von
Soden) but it is evidently given in a free
form, and the precise words cannot (even
in ver. 16) be disentangled. Besides we
should expect τινι to be added. Unless,
therefore, we are to think of a primitive
collection (Lake, Amer. Journ. Theol.,
1906, 108 f.) or of some oral tradition,
(b) is preferable. The contents of Matt.
xxiv. 31 (part of the small apocalypse)
are too dissimilar to favour the conjecture
(Pelt, Zimmer, Weiss) that Paul was
thinking of this saying as current perhaps in oral tradition, and the O.T. analogy of λόγος Κυρίου (= God's prophetic word), together with the internal
probabilities of the case (Paul does not
remind them of it, as elsewhere in the
epistle) make it on the whole more likely

that Paul is repeating words heard in a
vision (cf. 2 Cor. xii. 9; so Chryst.,
Theod., etc., followed by Alford, de
Wette, Ellicott, Dods, Lünemann, Godet, Paret: Paulus und Jesus, 53 f.,
Simon: die Psychologie des Ap. Paulus,
100, Findlay, Lightfoot, Milligan, Lueken). Cf. the discussion in Knowling's
Witness of the Epistles, 408 f., and Feine's
Jesus Christus u. Paulus, 178, 179. Later
in the century a similar difficulty vexed
the pious Jew who wrote Fourth Esdras
(v. 41, 42 : I said, But lo, O Lord, thou
hast made the promise to those who shall
be in the end: and what shall they do
that have been before us . . .? And He
said to me, I will liken my judgment to a
ring ; as there is no slackness of those
who are last, so shall there be no swiftness
of those who are first). His theory
is that the previous generations of Israel
will be as well off as their posterity in the
latter days. Further on (xiii. 14 f.) he
raises and answers the question whether
it was better to die before the last days
or to live until they came (the phrase,
those that are left, "qui relicti sunt," vii.
28 = Paul's οἱ περιλειπόμενοι). His
solution (which Steck, in Jahrb. für
prot. Theol., 1883, 509-524, oddly regards
as the λόγος κ. of 1 Thess. iv. 15 ; see
Schmidt's refutation, pp. 107-110) is the
opposite of Paul's : those who are left are
more blessed than those who have died.
If this difficulty was felt in Jewish circles
during the first half of the century, it
may have affected those of the Thessalonian Christians who had been formerly
connected with the synagogue, but the
likelihood is that Paul's language is
coloured by his own Jewish training (cf.
Charles on Asc. Isa., iv. 15). The misunderstanding of the Thessalonians,
which had led to their sorrow and perplexity, was evidently due to the fact
that, for some reason or another, Paul
had not mentioned the possibility of any
Christians dying before the second advent (so sure was he that all would soon
survive it), coupled with the fact that
Greeks found it hard to grasp what exactly resurrection meant (cf. Acts xvii.
32) for Christians.

w *Cf.* iii.
11; not
angels as
in Mt.
xxiv. 31.
x Jude 9:
to sum-
mon the
angels?
(iii. 13).
y 1 Cor. xv.
52, from
Joel ii. 1
(LXX); *cf.* 4 Esd. vi. 23, etc.   z 1 Cor. xv. 15.   a Blass, § 47, 7.   b 1 Cor. xv.7, 23.
c v. 10, II. i. 7 ; 2 Cor. iv. 14.   d Post-classical form, Win. § 13, 10   *cf.* Sap. iv. 10.   e Genitive
as in Mt. xxv. 1.   f Burton, M.T. 237.   g v. 11., ii. 11.   h Instrumental, as 1 Cor. iv.
21, etc.   i *i.e.* 15-17.

θέντας · 16. ὅτι ᵂαὐτὸς ὁ Κύριος ἐν κελεύσματι, ἐν φωνῇ ˣἀρχαγγέλου καὶ ἐν ʸσάλπιγγι Θεοῦ, καταβήσεται ἀπ᾽ οὐρανοῦ, καὶ ᶻοἱ νεκροὶ ᵃἐν Χριστῷ ἀναστήσονται πρῶτον · 17. ᵇἔπειτα ἡμεῖς οἱ ζῶντες, οἱ περιλειπόμενοι, ᶜἅμα σὺν αὐτοῖς ᵈἁρπαγησόμεθα ἐν νεφέλαις εἰς ἀπάντησιν ᵉτοῦ Κυρίου εἰς ἀέρα, καὶ οὕτω πάντοτε σὺν Κυρίῳ ἐσό- μεθα. 18. ᶠὥστε ᵍπαρακαλεῖτε ἀλλήλους ʰἐν τοῖς λόγοις ⁱτούτοις.

Ver. 16. **κελεύσματι** = the loud sum-mons which was to muster the saints (so in Philo, *De praem. et poen.*, 19 : **καθάπερ οὖν ἀνθρώπους ἐν ἐσχατιαῖς ἀπῳκισμένους ῥᾳδίως ἑνὶ κελεύσματι συναγάγοι ὁ θεὸς ἀπὸ περάτων εἰς ὅ τι ἂν θελήσῃ χωρίον**), forms, as its lack of any genitive shows, one conception with the **φ. α.** and the **σ. θ.** (*cf. DCG*, ii. 766). The archangel is Michael, who in Jewish tradition not only summoned the angels but sounded a trumpet to herald God's approach for judgment (*e.g.*, in *Apoc. Mosis*, xxii.). With such scenic and real-istic details, drawn from the heterogene-ous eschatology of the later Judaism, Paul seeks to make intelligible to his own mind and to that of his readers, in quite an original fashion (*cf.* Stähelin, *Jahrb. f. deut. Theol.*, 1874, pp. 199-218), the profound truth that neither death nor any cosmic crisis in the future will make any essential difference to the close relation between the Christian and his Lord. **Οὕτω πάντοτε σὺν κυρίῳ ἐσόμεθα** (*cf.* v. 11; 2 Cor. v. 8; Phil. i. 20) : this is all that remains to us, in our truer view of the universe, from the naïve **λόγος κυρίου** of the apostle, but it is everything. Note that Paul says nothing here about any change of the body (Teichmann, 35 f.), or about the embodiment of the risen life in its celestial **δόξα**. See *Asc. Isa.*, iv. 14-15 : "And the Lord will come with His holy angels and with the armies of the holy ones from the seventh heaven . . . and He will give rest to the godly whom He shall find in the body in this world."

Ver. 17. **ἐν νεφέλαις**, the ordinary method of sudden rapture or ascension to heaven (Acts i. 9, 11; Rev. xi. 12; Slav. En. iii. 1, 2).—**ἁρπαγησόμεθα**. So in Sap. iv. 11, the righteous man, **εὐάρεστος τῷ θεῷ** (1 Thess. iv. 1) **γενόμενος ἠγαπήθη** (1 Thess. i. 4), is caught up (**ἡρπάγη**).—**ἅμα σὺν αὐτοῖς . . . σὺν Κυρίῳ**, the future bliss is a re-union of

Christians not only with Christ but with one another.—**εἰς ἀπάντησιν**, a pre-Christian phrase of the *koinê* (*cf. e.g.*, *Tebtunis Papyri*, 1902, pt. i., n. 43, 7, **παρεγενήθημεν εἰς ἀπάντησιν, κ.τ.λ.**, and Moulton, i. 14), implying welcome of a great person on his arrival. What fur-ther functions are assigned to the saints, thus incorporated in the retinue of the Lord (iii. 13; *cf.* 2 Thess. i. 10),—whether, *e.g.*, they are to sit as assessors at the judgment (Sap. iii. 8; 1 Cor. vi. 2, 3 ; Luke xxii. 30)—Paul does not stop to state here. His aim is to reassure the Thessalonians about the prospects of their dead in relation to the Lord, not to give any complete programme of the future (so Matt. xxiv. 31; Did. x., xvi.). Plainly, however, the saints do not rise at once to heaven, but return with the Lord to the scene of his final manifesta-tion on earth (so Chrysost., Aug., etc.). They simply *meet* the Lord in the air, on his way to judgment—a trait for which no Jewish parallel can be found.—**καὶ οὕτως πάντοτε σὺν κυρίῳ ἐσόμεθα** (no more sleeping in him or waiting for him).

Ver. 18. **ἐν τοῖς λόγοις τούτοις**. Paul had an intelligible word upon the future, unlike the Hellenic mysteries which usually made religion a matter of feel-ing rather than of definite teaching (Hardie's *Lect. on Classical Subjects*, pp. 53 f.). A pagan letter of consolation has been preserved from the second century (*Oxyrh. Papyri*, i. 115) : "Eirene to Taonnophris and Philon good cheer ! I was as grieved and wept as much over Eumoiros as over Didymas, and I did all that was fitting, as did all my family. . . . But still we can do nothing in such a case. So comfort yourselves. Good-bye." One of Cicero's pathetic letters (*ad. Fam.*, xiv. 2), written from Thessa-lonica, speaks doubtfully of any re-union after death ("haec non sunt in manu nostra").

V. 1. Περὶ δὲ τῶν [a]χρόνων καὶ τῶν [a]καιρῶν, ἀδελφοί, οὐ [b]χρείαν a See on
ἔχετε ὑμῖν γράφεσθαι · 2. [b]αὐτοὶ γὰρ [c]ἀκριβῶς οἴδατε ὅτι [d]ἡμέρα b Cf. iv. 9.
Κυρίου [e]ὡς κλέπτης ἐν νυκτὶ οὕτως ἔρχεται · 3. [f]ὅταν [1] λέγωσιν,
"[g]Εἰρήνη καὶ ἀσφάλεια," [f]τότε [h]αἰφνίδιος αὐτοῖς [i]ἐπίσταται [k]ὄλε-
θρος [l]ὥσπερ ἡ [m]ὠδὶν τῇ ἐν γαστρὶ ἐχούσῃ, καὶ [n]οὐ μὴ ἐκφύγωσιν.
4. ὑμεῖς δὲ, ἀδελφοί, οὐκ ἐστὲ ἐν [o]σκότει [p]ἵνα ἡ ἡμέρα [q]ὑμᾶς ὡς
κλέπτας [2] καταλάβῃ · 5. πάντες γὰρ ὑμεῖς [r]υἱοὶ φωτός ἐστε καὶ υἱοὶ

c Cf. on
Acts xviii.
25.
d Without
article as
in Phil. i.
6, 10, ii.
16.
e Remini-
scence of
saying in
Lk. xii.

39; cf. Rev. iii. 3, xvi. 15.　f Cf. 1 Cor. xv. 54.　g Ezek. xiii. 10.　h Lk. xxi. 34.　i Win.
§ 5, 10, c.; Sap. vi. 5.　k "Destruction" (II. i. 9).　l Cf. En. lxii. 4.　m On form, cf.
Win. § 9, 10.　n iv. 15; cf. Ps. Sol. xv. 9, and above on iv. 8.　o Rom. ii. 19; cf. Hom.
Iliad, iii. 10, κλέπτῃ δέ τε νυκτὸς ἀμείνω.　p Conceived result (cf. Burton, M.T., 218-219) = "so
that".　q Emphatic.　r From Lk. xvi. 8 (cf. En. cviii. 11)?

[1] To the original asyndeton of οταν (א*AG, 17, 44, 47, 179, d, e, f, g, Syr.sch,
arm., aeth., Tert., Cyp., Jer, Orig., etc.; so edd.), either γαρ (KLP, vg. Euthal.,
Dam.), or δε (אcBD, cop., Syr.P, Eus., Chrys., Theod., Schott, Findlay, WH marg.)
has been subsequently added.　For ωσπερ η ωδιν, Bentl. conj. ωσπερει ωδινες.

[2] κλεπτας (AB cop., so Bentl., Grot., Koch, Ewald, Renan, Jowett, Rutherford,
Lach., WH, Lgft.), seems to be smoothed away in the strongly attested variant and
correction κλεπτης (from ver. 2). Field (200-201) cites instances from Plutarch (e.g.,
Vit. Crassi, xxix., τον δε Κρασσον ημερα κατελαβεν) and Pausanias, to illustrate
nocturnal operations being surprised by the advent of the dawn. "The echo of the
word (κλεπτης) is still in his ears; to avoid repetition, he changes its use. Lastly,
the reading κλεπτας gives a point to υιοι φωτος (Jowett). For another instance of
AB preserving the original reading, cf. Eph. i. 20.

CHAPTER V.—Vv. 1-11. περὶ τῶν
χρόνων καὶ τῶν καιρῶν.

Ver. 1. The *times and periods* are not
"simply the broad course of time, of
which the ἡμέρα Κυρίου constitutes the
closing scene" (Baur); καιρός denotes
a section of time more definitely than
χρόνος, in Greek usage. "No nation
has distinguished so subtly the different
forms under which time can be logically
conceived. Χρόνος is time viewed in its
extension, as a succession of moments,
the external framework of action. . . .
Καιρός, a word, which has, I believe,
no single or precise eqivalent in any
other language . . . is that immediate
present which is what we make it; time
charged with opportunity" (Butcher,
Harvard Lect. on Gk. Subjects, pp. 117-
119). In the plural, especially in this
eschatological outlook, the phrase is little
more, however, than a periphrasis for
"when exactly things are to happen".
Paul thought he needed to do no more
than reiterate the suddenness of the Last
Day. But, not long afterwards, he found
that the Thessalonians did require to have
the χρόνοι καὶ καιροί explained to them
in outline (II., ii. 2 f.).

Ver. 2. οἴδατε, referring to the teaching of Jesus on this crucial point, which
Paul had transmitted to them (see Introduction).

Ver. 3. ὅταν, κ.τ.λ., when the very
words, "All's well," "It is all right," are
on their lips.—ἐπίσταται, of an enemy
suddenly appear ng (Isocrat., *Evag.*,
§ 58 ἐπὶ τὸ βασίλειον ἐπιστάς, Herod.
iv. 203).—αὐτοῖς, *i.e.*, while the Day
comes suddenly to Christians and unbelievers alike, only the latter are surprised by it. Christians are on the alert,
open-eyed; they do not know when it
is to come, but they are alive to any
signs of its coming. Thus there is no
incompatibility between this emphasis
on the instantaneous character of the
advent and the emphasis, in II., ii. 3 f.,
on the preliminary conditions.

Ver. 4. From the sudden and unexpected nature of the Last Day, Paul
passes, by a characteristic inversion of
metaphor in κλέπτας, to a play of thought
upon the day as light. A double symbolism of ἡμέρα, as of κοιμᾶσθαι, thus
pervades 4-8. Lightfoot cites a very
striking parallel from Eur., *Iph. Taur.*,
1025-1026.

Ver. 5. The present age is utter night
(שֶׁכֻּלּוֹ לַיְלָה), as contemporary
rabbis taught; the age to come is all day.
Meantime faith is to be held fast through
this night (cf. passages quoted in Schlat-
ter's *die Sprache u. Heimat des vierten
Evangelisten*, 17, 18). υἱοὶ φ. καὶ υ.

s ii. 3,
t Cf. II. ii.
15; cf. 1
Rom. v.
18, etc.
u Cf. on
Eph. v. 14.
v iv. 13.
w Cf. on 1
Cor. xvi.
13; Mt.
xxiv. 42.
x See on 1
Pet. v. 8.
y Win. §
15.
z Eph. vi.
14, 17;
Rom. xiii.
11 f.
a Constr.;

ἡμέρας· οὐκ ἐσμὲν νυκτὸς ^sοὐδὲ σκότους. 6 Ἄρα ^tοὖν μὴ ^uκαθ-
εύδωμεν ὡς οἱ ^vλοιποί ἀλλά ^wγρηγορῶμεν καὶ ^xνήφωμεν. 7. οἱ
γὰρ καθεύδοντες νυκτὸς καθεύδουσι· καὶ οἱ ^yμεθυσκόμενοι νυκτὸς
μεθύουσιν· 8. ^zἡμεῖς δὲ ^aἡμέρας ὄντες νήφωμεν, ^bἐνδυσάμενοι
^cθώρακα πίστεως καὶ ἀγάπης καὶ περικεφαλαίαν ἐλπίδα σωτηρίας·
9. ὅτι οὐκ ^dἔθετο ^eἡμᾶς ὁ Θεὸς εἰς ^fὀργήν ἀλλ᾽ εἰς ^gπεριποίησιν
σωτηρίας διὰ τοῦ Κυρίου ἡμῶν Ἰησοῦ Χριστοῦ, 10. τοῦ ἀποθαν-
όντος ὑπὲρ ἡμῶν, ἵνα ^hεἴτε γρηγορῶμεν, εἴτε καθευδωμεν, ⁱἅμα σὺν
αὐτῷ ζήσωμεν. 11. διὸ ^kπαρακαλεῖτε ἀλλήλους καὶ οἰκοδομεῖτε
^lεἰς τὸν ἕνα, καθὼς καὶ ποιεῖτε.

cf. Win. § 30, 11, b.   b Isa. lix. 17.   c Cf. on Eph. vi. 14="coat of mail".   d 1 Pet. ii. 8.
e Emphatic, as opposed to οἱ λοιποί.   f i. 10,   g Cf. on Eph. i. 14; here active (= possess.)
as in II. ii. 14. Heb. x. 39.   h Cf. for syntax, Rom. xiv. 8; Burton, M.T., 252-253.   i iv. 17.
k iv. 18.   l unclassical, Blass, § 45, 2; cf. 1 Cor. v. 6.

ἡμέρας is a stronger and Semitic way of
expressing the thought of "belonging
to" (cf. ver. 8).

Ver. 6. To be alert, in one's sober
senses (νήφειν), is more than to be
merely awake. Here, as in verse 8, the
Christians are summoned to live up to
their privileges and position towards the
Lord. "There are few of us who are
not rather ashamed of our sins and follies
as we look out on the blessed morning
sunlight, which comes to us like a bright-
winged angel beckoning us to quit the
old path of vanity that stretches its
dreary length behind us" (George Eliot).
In one of the Zoroastrian scriptures
(Vendidad, xviii. 23-25) the cock, as the
bird of the dawn, is inspired to cry, "Arise,
O men! . . . Lo here is Bushyasta coming down upon you, who lulls to sleep
again the whole living world as soon as
it has awoke, saying, 'Sleep, sleep on,
O man [and live in sin, Yasht, xxii. 41]!
The time is not yet come.'"

Ver. 7. Cf. Plutarch, De Iside, vi.,
Οἶνον δὲ οἱ μὲν ἐν Ἥλιου πόλει θερα-
πεύοντες τὸν θεὸν οὐκ εἰσφέρουσιν τοπα-
ράπαν εἰς τὸ ἱερόν, ὡς οὐ προσῆκον ἡμέρας πίνειν, τοῦ κυρίου καὶ βασιλέως
ἐφορῶντος.

Ver. 8. ἐνδυσάμενοι θώρακα κ.τ.λ.,
the thought of ii. 12, 13; the mutual love
of Christians, which forms the practical
expression of their faith in God, is their
true fitness and equipment for the second
advent. Faith and love are a unity;
where the one goes the other follows.
They are also not merely their own coat
of mail, requiring no extraneous protection, but the sole protection of life against
indolence, indifference and indulgence.
They need simply to be used. If they

are not used, they are lost, and with them
the Christian himself. The transition to
the military metaphor is mediated (as in
Rom. xiii. 12, 13) by the idea of the
sentry's typical vigilance.

Ver. 9. The mention of the future
σωτηρία starts Paul off, for a moment,
on what it involves (9, 10).

Ver. 10. Life or death makes no difference to the Christian's union and
fellowship with Jesus Christ, whose death
was in our eternal interests (cf. Rom. xiv.
7-9). For this metaphorical use of γρηγ.
εἴτε καθ. (different from that in 6), Wohl.
cites Plato, Symp., 203a : διὰ τούτου (i.e.
Eros) πᾶσα ἐστιν ἡ ὁμιλία καὶ ἡ διά-
λεκτος θεοῖς πρὸς ἀνθρώπους, καὶ ἐγρη-
γορόσι καὶ καθεύδουσιν, as a possible
basis.

Ver. 11. The modification in the
primitive attitude of Christians to the
Parousia of Jesus is significant. Instead
of all expecting to be alive at that blessed
crisis, the inroads of death had now forced
men to the higher consolation that "it
did not make the least difference whether
one became partaker of the blessings of
that event in the ranks of the dead or of
the living. The question whether the
Parousia was to happen sooner or later
was no longer of paramount importance.
The important thing was to cultivate
that attitude of mind which the writer
of this epistle recommended" (Baur).—
οἰκοδομεῖτε, the term sums up all the
support and guidance that a Christian
receives from the fellowship of the church
(cf. Beyschlag's N.T. Theology, ii. 232).
—καθὼς καὶ ποιεῖτε, another instance
(cf. iv. 1, 10) of Paul's fine courtesy
and tact. He is careful to recognise the Thessalonians' attainments,

12. ^mἘρωτῶμεν δὲ ὑμᾶς, ἀδελφοί, ⁿεἰδέναι τοὺς ^oκοπιῶντας ἐν
ὑμῖν καὶ ^pπροϊσταμένους ὑμῶν ἐν Κυρίῳ καὶ ^qνουθετοῦντας ὑμᾶς, 13.
καὶ ^rἡγεῖσθαι αὐτοὺς ὑπερεκπερισσῶς ἐν ἀγάπῃ διὰ τὸ ἔργον αὐτῶν.
^sεἰρηνεύετε ἐν ^tἑαυτοῖς. 14. ^uπαρακαλοῦμεν δὲ ὑμᾶς, ἀδελφοί,
νουθετεῖτε τοὺς ^vἀτάκτους, ^wπαραμυθεῖσθε τοὺς ^xὀλιγοψύχους, ἀντέ-
χεσθε τῶν ἀσθενῶν, ^yμακροθυμεῖτε πρὸς πάντας. 15. ὁρᾶτε ^zμή
τις ^aκακὸν ἀντὶ κακοῦ τινὶ ἀποδῷ· ἀλλὰ πάντοτε τὸ ^bἀγαθὸν διώκετε εἰς ἀλλήλους καὶ εἰς πάντας. 16. πάντοτε ^cχαίρετε, 17. ^dἀδια-

m iv. 1, II
ii. 2.
n Cf. Ps.
cxliv. 3
r Cor.
xvi. 18
Ign.
Smyrn. ix.
o Gal. iv.
11 ; 1 Cor.
xv. 10.
p Cf. on
Rom.
xii. 8.
q See on
Acts xx.
31 ; 1 Cor.

iv. 14.   r Phil. ii. 3; cf. Thuc. iv. 5, etc.   s Mk. ix. 50; 2 Cor. xiii. 11.   t = ἀλλήλοις.
(so Plato, Gorg. 465 c).   u Cf. ii. 11.   v Xen. Mem. III. i. 7.   w ii. 11; Joh. xi. 19. 31.
x Exod. vi. 9; Isa. lvii. 15; Sir. vii. 10, and Ps. Sol. xvi. 11.   y See on 1 Cor. xiii. 4.   z Object.
clause (Burton, M.T. 209).   a Prov. xx. 22 (Matt. v. 44); Rom. xii. 17.   b = "What is kind
and helpful."   c Paul's practice, 2 Cor. vi. 10; cf. Phil. iv. 4; Rom. xii. 12, and Col. i. 11.
d i. 3; cf. Ign. Eph. x.; Herm. Sim. ix. 11, 7; Ep. Arist. 226 (τὸν Θεὸν ἐπικαλοῦ διαπαντός).

even while stirring them up to further
efforts.

Vv. 12-22.   General instructions for
the church.

Ver. 12.   These προϊστάμενοι are not
officials but simply local Christians like
Jason, Secundus, and perhaps Demas (in
whose houses the Christians met), who,
on account of their capacities or position,
had informally taken the lead and made
themselves responsible for the welfare
and worship of the new society. The
organisation is quite primitive, and the
triple description of these men's functions
is too general to permit any precise delineation of their duties (cf. Lindsay's
The Church and the Ministry in the Early
Centuries, pp. 122 f.). κοπιῶντας denotes
the energy and practical interest of these
people, which is further defined by προϊ-
στάμενους (a term with technical associations, to which ἐν κυρίῳ is added in order
to show that their authority rests on religious services) and νουθετοῦντας (= the
moral discipline, perhaps of catechists,
teachers and prophets). An instinct of
rebellion against authority is not confined
to any one class, but artisans and tradesmen are notorious for a tendency to suspect
or depreciate any control exercised over
them in politics or in religion, especially
when it is exercised by some who have
risen from their own ranks. The community at Thessalonica was largely re-
cruited from this class, and Paul, with
characteristic penetration, appeals for
respect and generous appreciation towards
the local leaders.

Ver. 13.   "Regard them with a very
special love for their works' sake" (so
thorough and important it is). "Be at
peace among yourselves" (instead of
introducing divisions and disorder by any
insubordination or carping).

Ver. 14.   The particular form of insubordination at Thessalonica was idle-
ness (for the contemporary use of ἀτ. in
this sense, see Oxyrh. Papyri, ii. 1901,
p. 275). Similarly, in Olynth. iii. 11,
Demosthenes denounces all efforts made
to shield from punishment τοὺς ἀτακ-
τοῦντας, i.e., those citizens who shirk active service and evade the State's call for
troops.—ὀλιγοψύχους = "faint-hearted"
(under trial, i. 6, see references), ἀντέ-
χεσθε (cleave to, put your arm round),
ἀσθενῶν (i.e., not in health only but
in faith or position, Acts xx. 35), μακ.
π. πάντας = do not lose temper or
patience with any (of the foregoing
classes) however unreasonable and exacting they may be (cf. Prov. xviii. 14, LXX):
The mutual services of the community
are evidently not to be left to the προϊστάμενοι, for Paul here urges on the rank
and file the same kind of social duties as
he implies were incumbent upon their
leaders (cf. νουθετ. 12, 14). If ἀδελφοί
here meant the προϊστάμενοι, it would
have been more specificially defined.
An antithesis between 12 and 14 would
be credible in a speech, not in a letter.

Ver. 15.   The special circumstances
which called for forbearance (ver. 14) were
likely to develop a disposition to retaliate
upon those who displayed an ungenerous
and insubordinate spirit (e.g., the ἀτα-
κτοι) ; but the injunction has a wider
range (εἰς πάντας, including their fellow-
countrymen, ii. 14).

Ver. 16.   To comment adequately upon
these diamond drops (16-18) would be to
outline a history of the Christian experience in its higher levels. π. χαίρετε, cf.
Epict., i. 16 (" Had we understanding,
ought we to do anything but sing hymns
and bless the Deity and tell of His benefits ? . . . What else can I do, a lame

λείπτως προσεύχεσθε,
18. [e] ἐν παντὶ [f] εὐχαριστεῖτε· [g] τοῦτο γὰρ [g] θέλημα Θεοῦ ἐν Χριστῷ Ἰησοῦ [h] εἰς ὑμᾶς.
19. τὸ πνεῦμα [i] μὴ [k] σβέννυτε,
20. προφητείας μὴ ἐξουθενεῖτε·
21. πάντα [1] δὲ [1] δοκιμάζετε, τὸ [m] καλὸν κατέχετε·
22. [n] ἀπὸ παντὸς [o] εἴδους πονηροῦ [p] ἀπέχεσθε.
23. [q] Αὐτὸς δὲ ὁ Θεὸς τῆς εἰρήνης ἁγιάσαι ὑμᾶς [r] ὁλοτελεῖς· καὶ

e *Cf.* on 2 Cor. iv. 8. 2 Cor. vi. 10; Phil. iv. 6; Clem. Rom. xxx.-viii. 4.
g iv. 3.
h For absence of article in this constr. see Field, 59-60 on the similar usage in Lk. vii. 30.
i "Give over": *μὴ* with pres. imper. implies action already begun Moult. i. 122 f.
k Contrast 2 Tim. i. 5, and *cf.* 1 Cor. xiv. 1.
l ii. 4; 1 Jo. iv. 1.
m 2 Cor. xiii. 7; Phil. i. 10.
n Like Job (Job i. 1, 8, ii. 3).
o = "form" or "sort" (so Jos. *Ant.* x. 3).
p iv. 3; *cf.* Did. iii. 1.
q iii. 11, iv. 16.
r Only here (N.T.), = ὅλους (through and through).

[1] After **παντα** edd. add the disjunctive **δε** (with almost all MSS. and vss., also Clem., Alex., *Paed.* iii. 12, 95, exc. ℵ*A, cop., syr.sch), which became absorbed by the first syllable of the following word. Blass (after K, min., etc.) **δοκιμαζοντες.**

old man, than sing hymns to God? . . . I exhort you to join in this same song.") There is a thread of connection with the foregoing counsel. The unswerving aim of being good and doing good to all men, is bound up with that faith in God's unfailing goodness to men which enables the Christian cheerfully to accept the disappointments and sufferings of social life. This faith can only be held by prayer, *i.e.*, a constant reference of all life's course to God, and such prayer must be more than mere resignation; it implies a spirit of unfailing gratitude to God, instead of any suspicious or rebellious attitude.

Ver. 17. "*Pray always*, says the Apostle; that is, have the habit of prayer, turning your thoughts into acts by connecting them with the idea of the redeeming God" (Coleridge, *Notes on the Book of Common Prayer*), cp. iii. 11, v. 23.

Ver. 18. Chrysostom, who wrote: **τὸ ἀεὶ δηλονότι εὐχαριστεῖν, τοῦτο φιλοσόφου ψυχῆς,** gave a practical illustration of this heroic temper by repeating, as he died in the extreme hardships of an enforced and painful exile, **δόξα τῷ θεῷ πάντων ἕνεκα.** For thanksgiving even in bereavement, *cf.* Aug., *Conf.*, ix. 12; and further, *ibid.*, ix. 7 (tunc hymni et psalmi ut canerentur, secundum morem Orientalium partium, ne populus maeroris taedio contabesceret, institutum est).

Ver. 19. **τοῦτο κ.τ.λ.** The primary reference is to **εὐχαριστεῖτε,** but the preceding imperatives are so closely bound up with this, that it is needless to exclude them from the scope of the **θέλημα.—ἐν Χ. Ἰ.** This glad acceptance of life's rain and sunshine alike as from the hand of God, Jesus not only exemplified (*cf.* context of **μιμηταὶ . . . τοῦ Κυρίου,** i. 6) but also enabled all who keep in touch with him to realise. The basis of it is the Christian revelation and experience; apart from the living Lord it is neither conceivable nor practicable (*cf.* R. H. Hutton's *Modern Guides of English Thought*, pp. 122 f.).

Ver. 20. As **εὐχαριστεῖν** was a special function of the prophets in early Christian worship (*cf.* Did. x. 7), the transition is natural. The local abuses of ecstatic prophecy in prediction (2 Thess. ii. 2) or what seem to be exaggerated counsels of perfection (ver. 16 f.) must not be allowed to provoke any reaction which would depreciate and extinguish this vital gift or function of the faith. Paul, with characteristic sanity, holds the balance even. Such enthusiastic outbursts are neither to be despised as silly vapouring nor to be accepted blindly as infallible revelations. The true criticism of **προφητεία** comes (ver. 21) from the Christian conscience which is sensitive to the **καλόν,** the **συμφέρον,** the **οἰκοδομή,** or the **ἀναλογία τῆς πίστεως** (*cf.* Weizsäcker's *Apost. Age*, ii. 270 f.). But this criticism must be positive. In applying the standard of spiritual discernment, it must sift, not for the mere pleasure of rejecting the erroneous but with the object of retaining what is genuine.

Ver. 22. A further general precept, added to bring out the negative side of **κατέχετε, κ.τ.λ.—πονηροῦ** neut. abstract = "of wickedness," as Gen. ii. 9 (**τοῦ εἰδέναι γνωστὸν καλοῦ καὶ πονηροῦ**).—**παντὸς κ.τ.λ.**, perhaps an allusion to the manifold ways of going wrong (Arist., *Nik. Eth.*, ii. 6 14, **τὸ μὲν ἁμαρτάνειν πολλαχῶς ἐστίν . . . τὸ δὲ κατορθοῦν μοναχῶς**).

Ver. 23. **εἰρήνης,** with a special allusion to the breaches of harmony and charity produced by vice (*cf.* connection of iii. 12, 13 and iv. 3 f.), indolence, impatience of authority or of defects in one

ᵉ ὁλόκληρον ὑμῶν τὸ πνεῦμα καὶ ἡ ψυχὴ καὶ τὸ ᵗ σῶμα ἀμέμπτως ἐν ˢ τῇ παρουσίᾳ τοῦ Κυρίου ἡμῶν Ἰησοῦ Χριστοῦ τηρηθείη. 24. ᵘ πιστὸς ὁ ᵛ καλῶν ὑμᾶς, ὃς καὶ ᵂ ποιήσει.

25. Ἀδελφοί, ˣ προσεύχεσθε περὶ ἡμῶν. 26. ἀσπάσασθε τοὺς ἀδελφοὺς πάντας ἐν ʸ φιλήματι ᶻ ἁγίῳ.

27. ἐνορκίζω¹ ὑμᾶς ᵃ τὸν Κύριον, ᵇ ἀναγνωσθῆναι τὴν ᶜ ἐπιστολὴν ᵘ πᾶσι τοῖς ἀδελφοῖς.

28. ἡ χάρις τοῦ Κυρίου ἡμῶν Ἰησοῦ Χριστοῦ μεθ' ὑμῶν.

Right margin notes:
s Adj. put first for emphasis agreeing with first of subst. which it precedes.
t Cf. Phil. iii. 21.
u See above on iii. 13, and ii. 10.
v See on 1 Cor. i. 9.

w As Num. xxiii. 19; Ps. xxxvii. 5 (LXX).   x Ver. 17, II. iii. 1.   y See on Rom. xvi. 16;
1 Cor. xvi. 20; and Justin's Apol. i. 65.   z Clem. Alex. Paed. III. ii. 81.   a For constr. cf.
Acts xix. 13.   b Lk. iv. 16; Acts xv. 21; 2 Cor. iii. 15; Col. iv. 16.   c II. ii. 15.

¹ Read ἐνορκιζω [only here N.T., = "adjure," strengthened form of ὁρκίζω] with ABD*, min., Euth., Dam. (edd.). But om. αγιοις before αδελφοις with א*BDG, min., d, e, f, g, aeth., Euth., Amb., Cassiod. (edd., exc. de Wette, Koch, Ellic., Weiss); the addition of αγιοις, like the omission of πασι, "entspringt vielleicht dem hierarchischen Interesse, die Bibel nicht Allen zugänglich zu machen" (Zimmer).

another (v. 13 f.), retaliation (v. 15), and differences of opinion (v. 19 f.) Such faults affect the σῶμα, the ψυχή and the πνεῦμα respectively, as the sphere of that pure and holy consciousness whose outcome is εἰρήνη.—ὑμῶν, unemphatic genitive (as in iii. 10, 13, cf. Abbott's Johannine Grammar, 2559a) throwing the emphasis on the following word or words. πνεῦμα is put first, as the element in human nature which Paul held to be most directly allied to God, while ψυχή denotes as usual the individual life. The collocation of these terms is unusual but of course quite untechnical.—ἀμέμπτως has almost a proleptic tinge = "preserved entire, (so as to be) blameless at the arrival of," which has led to the substitution, in some inferior MSS., of εὑρεθείη for τηρηθείη (cf. textual discussion in Amer. Jour. Theol., 1903, 453 f.). The construction is rather awkward, but the general sense is clear. With the thought of the whole verse compare Ps. Sol. xviii. 6: καθαρίσαι ὁ θεὸς Ἰσραὴλ . . . εἰς ἡμέραν ἐκλογῆς ἐν ἀνάξει Χριστοῦ αὐτοῦ, also the description of Abraham being preserved by the divine σοφία in Sap. x. 5 (ἐτήρησεν αὐτὸν ἄμεμπτον θεῷ).

Ver. 24. The call implies that God will faithfully carry out the process of ἁγιάζεσθαι and τηρεῖσθαι (cf. Phil. i. 6), which is the divine side of the human endeavour outlined in the preceding verse.

Vv. 25-27. Closing words of counsel and prayer.

Ver. 26. Neither here, nor above at ver. 14, is there any reason to suppose that Paul turns to address the leaders of the local church (so e.g., Bornemann, Ellicott, Alford, Askwith, Zimmer, Light-

foot, Weiss, Findlay) as though they were, in the name of the apostle(s), to convey the holy (i.e. not of convention or human passion) kiss, which betokened mutual affection (cf. Renan's S. Paul, 262, DCG. i. 935, and E. Bi. 4254) in the early Christian worship. This greeting by proxy is not so natural as the ordinary sense of the words; the substitution of τ. ἁ. π. for the more common ἀλλήλους is intelligible in the light, e.g., cf. Phil. iv. 21; and it would be harsh to postulate so sharp a transition from the general reference of v. 25 and v. 28. Even in ver. 27 it is not necessary to think of the local leaders. While the epistle would naturally be handed to some of them in the first instance, it was addressed to the church; the church owned it and was held responsible for its public reading at the weekly worship.—πᾶσιν, like the πάντας of ver. 26, simply shows Paul's desire to prevent the church from becoming, on any pretext, a clique or coterie. But the remarkable emphasis of the injunction points to a period when such public reading of an apostolic epistle was not yet a recognised feature in the worship of the churches. Paul lays stress upon the proper use of his epistle, as being meant not for a special set, but for the entire brotherhood (i.e., at Thessalonica, not, as Flatt thinks, in Macedonia). See that every member gets a hearing of it at some meeting or other (ἀναγ., timeless aor.), and thus knows exactly what has been said. So Apoc. Bar. lxxxvi.: "when therefore ye receive this my epistle, read it in your congregations with care. And meditate thereon, above all on the days of your fasts."

I. 1. ᵃΠΑΥΛΟΣ καὶ Σιλουανὸς καὶ Τιμόθεος τῇ ἐκκλησίᾳ Θεσσαλο-
νικέων ἐν Θεῷ πατρὶ ἡμῶν καὶ Κυρίῳ Ἰησοῦ Χριστῷ · 2. χάρις ὑμῖν
καὶ ᵃεἰρήνη ᵇἀπὸ Θεοῦ πατρὸς ¹ καὶ Κυρίου Ἰησοῦ ᵇΧριστοῦ.

3. ᶜεὐχαριστεῖν ᶜὀφείλομεν τῷ Θεῷ πάντοτε περὶ ὑμῶν, ἀδελφοί,
(καθὼς ᵈἄξιόν ἐστιν) ὅτι ᵉὑπεραυξάνει ἡ πίστις ὑμῶν καὶ ᶠπλεονάζει
ἡ ᵍἀγάπη ἑνὸς ἑκάστου πάντων ὑμῶν εἰς ἀλλήλους · 4. ὥστε αὐτοὺς
ʰἡμᾶς ἐν ὑμῖν ⁱἐγκαυχᾶσθαι ἐν ταῖς ᵏἐκκλησίαις τοῦ Θεοῦ, ὑπὲρ
τῆς ὑπομονῆς ὑμῶν καὶ πίστεως ἐν πᾶσι τοῖς διωγμοῖς ὑμῶν καὶ

a Cf. I. i. 1.
b Cf. 1 Cor.
i. 3, etc.
c ii. 13;
Clem.
Rom.
xxxviii.
4. Cf.
1 John
iii. 16, iv.
11.
d See on 1
Cor. xvi.
4 and
Phil. i. 7.
e Only here
in N.T.
f 2 Pet. i. 8.   g In answer to prayer of I. iii. 12, iv. 9-10.   h As well as others (I. i. 8); ὥστε
with inf. as in I. i. 7.   i See 2 Cor. ix. 2.   k i.e. of Achaia, etc. Cf. I. i. 3.

¹ Om. ημων after πατρος with BDP, 17, 49, 71, d, e, Theoph., Pelag. (Al., Lachm.,
WH, Findlay, Milligan, etc.), as a scribal addition from ver. 1.

CHAPTER I.—Vv. 1-8. The address
(i. 1, 2) is followed first by a thanksgiving
(3-10) which passes into a prophetic piece
of consolation, and then by a brief
prayer (11, 12).

Ver. 3. περὶ ὑμῶν : Your thankless
situation. (4 f.) only throws into more
brilliant relief your personal character
and bearing under adverse circumstances.
ὅτι is best represented by our colloquial
"because," which includes both the
causal and the objective senses of the
word ; what forms matter for thanksgiving is naturally the reason for thanksgiving. ἀγάπη κ.τ.λ., a period of strain
tires mutual gentleness (see on Rev. ii. 4)
as well as patience towards God (ver. 4),
since irritation and lack of unselfish consideration for others (cf. iii. 6 f.) may be
as readily produced by a time of tension
and severe anxiety as an impatient
temper of faith. Paul is glad and grate-
ful that suffering was drawing his friends
together and binding them more closely
to their Lord, instead of stunting the
growth of their faith and drying up
the flow of their mutual charity. Praise
comes as usual before blame. Paul is
proud of his friends, because suffering
has not spoiled their characters, as suffer-

ing, especially when due to oppression
and injustice, is too apt to do.—ὀφείλομεν
(so Cic. ad. Fam., xiv. 2, gratiasque
egi, ut debui ; Barn. v. 3, vii. 1), the
phrase is unexampled in Paul, but not
unnatural (cf. Rom. xv. 1, etc.) ; "the
form of duty is one which all thoughts
naturally take in his mind" (Jowett).

Ver. 4. The single article groups
ὑπομονὴ and πίστις as a single conception = faith in its special aspect of
patient endurance (cf. on Rev. xiii. 10),
faithful tenacity of purpose. M. Geb-
hardt, in his L'Italie Mystique (pp. 318 f.),
observes that "the final word of Dante's
belief, of that 'religion of the heart'
which he mentions in the Convito, is given
in the 24th canto of the Paradiso. He
comes back to the very simple symbol of
Paul, faith, hope and love ; for him as for
the apostle faith is at bottom simply
hope." Faith is more than that to Paul,
but sometimes hardly more. The Thessalonians are not to fear that they are holding a forlorn outpost. Neither man nor
God overlooks their courage (cf. Plato's
Theaet., xxv., ἀνδρικῶς ὑπομεῖναι καὶ μὴ
ἀνάνδρως φεύγειν). Their founders and
friends at a distance are watching with
pride their resolute faith ; while in God's

ταὶς θλίψεσιν αἷς ἀνέχεσθε, 5. [m] ἔνδειγμα τῆς δικαίας κρίσεως τοῦ
Θεοῦ, [n] εἰς τὸ [o] καταξιωθῆναι ὑμᾶς τῆς βασιλείας τοῦ Θεοῦ, ὑπὲρ ἧς
καὶ πάσχετε· 6. [p] εἴπερ [q] δίκαιον παρὰ Θεῷ [r] ἀνταποδοῦναι τοῖς
θλίβουσιν ὑμᾶς θλῖψιν 7. καὶ ὑμῖν τοῖς θλιβομένοις [s] ἄνεσιν [t] μεθ᾽
ἡμῶν ἐν τῇ [u] ἀποκαλύψει τοῦ Κυρίου Ἰησοῦ ἀπ᾽ οὐρανοῦ μετ᾽ ἀγγέλων
δυνάμεως αὐτοῦ 8. [v] ἐν πυρὶ φλογός, διδόντος [w] ἐκδίκησιν [x] τοῖς μὴ
εἰδόσι Θεὸν καὶ τοῖς μὴ [y] ὑπακούουσι τῷ [y] εὐαγγελίῳ τοῦ Κυρίου

l Attract. fr ἅς or ὧν (Win. § 24, 4e).
m Only here in N.T.; for idea, see Phil. i. 27-28 and Sap. iii. 3 f.
n *Cf.* I. ii. 12.
o See on Acts v. 41 and xiv. 22.
p See on Rom. iii. 30, viii. 9, 17 = "since".
q Exod. xxiii. 22; see on Rom. ii. 5-6, 9, viii. 17; 2 Cor. iv. 17 f.
r From Isa. lxvi. 2 (LXX).
s *Cf.* 2 Cor. ii. 13; Asc. Isa. iv. 15 (quoted on I. iv. 16).
t 1 Thess. ii. 15; see below, iii. 2. "We need it too, God knows!"
u 1 Cor. i. 7; Rom. ii. 5.
v *Cf.* LXX of Exod. iii. 2; Isa. xxix. 6, lxvi. 6, 15 f. and on 1 Cor. iii. 13. A Hebraism.
w Ezek. xxv. 14 (LXX); Jer. xxv. 12; Deut. vii. 9.
x *Cf.* I. iv. 5 (Jer. x. 25; Ps. lxxviii. 6).
y *Cf.* Rom. x. 16. Acts vi. 7; Clem. Rom. xlii. 4.

sure process of providence that faith has a destiny of its own, since it is bound up with His eternal designs. Hope is only mentioned once (ii. 16, *cf.* iii. 5) in this epistle, for all its preoccupation with the future. Faith covers almost all its contents here.—**θλίψεσιν** more general than **διωγμοῖς.**—**ὑπὲρ,** as in I., iii. 2, is equivalent to **περί,** with a touch of personal interest (Abbott's *Johannine Grammar*, p. 559; Meisterhans, *Gramm. d. attischen Inschriften*, 182).

Ver. 5. **ἔνδειγμα,** in apposition to the general thought of the preceding clause; it does not matter to the sense whether the word is taken as an elliptic nominative or an appositional accusative. "All this is really a clear proof of (or points to) the equity of God's judgment," which will right the present inequalities of life (Dante, *Purg.*, x. 109 f.). **Δικαία κρίσις** is the future and final judgment of 6-10, whose principle is recompense (Luke xvi. 25); there is a divine law of compensation which will operate. This throws back light upon the present sufferings of the righteous. These trials, it is assumed, are due to loyalty and innocence of life; hence, in their divine aspect (ver. 5), they are the necessary qualification or discipline for securing entrance into the realm of God. They are significant, not casual. Paul begins by arguing that their very infliction or permission proves that God must be contemplating a suitable reward and destiny for those who endured them in the right spirit. **εἰς τὸ κ.τ.λ.,** is thus a loose expansion (from the common rabbinic phrase, *cf.* Dalman's *Worte Jesu*, 97 f.; E. Tr., 119) of one side of the **δικ. κρίσις.** The other side, the human aspect of **θλῖψις,** then emerges in ver. 6. Since the Thessalonians were suffering at the hands of men (**τοὺς θλίβοντας,** Isa. xix. 20), the two-handed engine of retribution (so Lam. iii. 64 f.; Obad. 15; Isa. lix. 18, for **ἀνταποδ.**) must in all fairness punish the persecutors (*cf.* Sap. xi. 9, 10). This is the only passage in which Paul welcomes God's vengeance on the enemies of the church as an element in the recompense of Christians.—**ὑπὲρ ἧς καὶ πάσχετε:** to see an intelligible purpose in suffering, or to connect it with some larger movement and hope, is always a moral stay. "God gave three choice gifts to Israel—the Torah, the Land of Promise, and Eternal Life, and each was won by suffering" (*Berachoth*, 5*a*).

Ver. 7. After noting the principle of recompence (5-7*a*), Paul proceeds (7*b*-10) to dwell on its time and setting, especially in its punitive aspect. He consoles the Thessalonians by depicting the doom of their opponents rather than (9*c*, 10) their own positive relief and reward. The entire passage breathes the hot air of the later Judaism, with its apocalyptic anticipation of the *jus talionis* applied by God to the enemies of His people; only, Paul identifies that people not with Israel but with believers in Christ Jesus. He appropriates Israel's promises for men and women whom Israel expelled and persecuted.—The **ἄγγελοι** are the manifestation of Christ's **δύναμις,** as the **ἅγιοι** (saints not angels) are of his **δόξα** (ver. 10); the position of **ἀγγ.** (*cf.* Win., § 80, 12*b*) tells against Hofmann's interpretation of **δυν.** = "host" (צָבָא, so LXX). Here and in the following verses the divine prerogatives (*e.g.*, fiery manifestation and judicial authority) are carried over to Jesus.

Ver. 8. *Those who know not God* are of course not pagans as such but immoral pagans, in the sense of Rom. i. 28 f. *Those who refuse obedience to the*

z 4 Macc. ἡμῶν Ἰησοῦ · 9. οἵτινες δίκην τίσουσιν, ᶻ ὄλεθρον ᵃαἰώνιον, ᵃ ἀπὸ
x. 15.

a From Isa. προσώπου τοῦ Κυρίου καὶ ἀπὸ τῆς δόξης τῆς ἰσχύος αὐτοῦ, 10. ὅταν
ii. 10, 19,
21 (LXX). ᵇ ἔλθῃ ᶜ ἐνδοξασθῆναι ἐν τοῖς ἁγίοις αὐτοῦ καὶ ᵈ θαυμασθῆναι ἐν πᾶσι
Cf. Ps. li.
11; Lk. τοῖς πιστεύσασιν (ὅτι ἐπιστώθη ¹ τὸ ᵉ μαρτύριον ἡμῶν ἐφ᾽ ὑμᾶς) ᶠ ἐν
xiii. 27,
etc. τῇ ἡμέρᾳ ἐκείνῃ. 11. ᵍ εἰς ὃ καὶ προσευχόμεθα πάντοτε περὶ ὑμῶν,
b = fut.
perf. ʰ ἵνα ὑμᾶς ἀξιώσῃ τῆς κλήσεως ὁ Θεὸς ἡμῶν καὶ πληρώσῃ πᾶσαν
(Moult.
186).

c Only here in N.T., cf. Ex. xiv. 4; Sir. xxxviii. 6, etc.; Isa. iv. 2 f., xlix. 3.   d Reminiscence
of Ps. lxviii. 36; lxxxix. 8 (LXX). Cf. Sir. xxxviii. 3; 4 Macc. xviii. 3.   e Cf. 1 Cor. i. 6.   f From
Isa. ii. 11 (17).   g Cf. Col. i. 29. "It is to this our thoughts turn as we pray, etc." (Rutherford).   h Equivalent, as e.g. in LXX of Exod. ix. 16.

¹ For επιστευθη Markland and Hort conj. επιστωθη (so 31, 112), as if "the
Christian testimony (vv. 4-5) of suffering for the faith had been confirmed and sealed
upon the Thessalonians" (cf. Ps. xcii. 4 f, LXX, θαυμαστος εν υψηλοις ο κυριος · τα
μαρτυρια σου επιστωθησαν σφοδρα). πιστωθητω is used (as here with επι) of the
divine word in 1 Chron. xvii. 23 (cf. 2 Chron. ii. 9). The MSS. reading throws
επιστευθη to the front for emphasis, but it must go with εφ ημας. The point of the
sentence, as Lgft. admits, leads us to expect "a direct connexion between the
Thessalonians and a belief in the gospel rather than between the Thess. and the
preaching of the gospel," so that μαρτυριον is less vital to εφ ημας. No satisfactory
parallel can be quoted for either construction of επιστευθη, however, and the likelihood
upon the whole is that it represents a primitive and natural corruption of επιστωθη.

gospel are, as the repetition of the article
suggests, a different class of people, perhaps drawn both from Jews and pagans.
But as Paul never seems to contemplate
the idea of any Jew failing to hear the
gospel (cf. Rom. x. 16 f.), the description
here applies principally to them.—ἐν πυρὶ
φλογός, one of the most favourite real-
istic traits of the last judgment, in
apocalyptic Judaism (cf. passages in
Volz's Jüdische Eschatologie, 285, 286);
here it is simply a descriptive touch,
which Paul does not pause to elaborate
(cf. 1 Cor. iii. 13). The rather "broad
and inflated" language (Weizsäcker) of
the whole passage is probably due to the
subject, more than to Paul's employment of Silvanus, himself a prophet (cf.
Acts xv. 32 and 1 Thess. ii. 12-16), as his
amanuensis.

Ver. 9. The overwhelming manifestation of the divine glory sweeps from before it (pregnant ἀπὸ) into endless ruin
the disobedient (Ps. lxxvi. 7) men who
(see Moulton, 91 f.) shall pay the penalty
of (see Prov. xxvii. 12, LXX) eternal destruction (the common apocalyptic belief,
see Volz, Jüd. Eschat., 286 f.).

Ver. 10. ἐπιστώθη, like the variant
ἐπιστεύθη, is suggested by πιστεύουσιν
(cf. a similar instance in iii. 3). The
abrupt parenthesis ("you included—for")
shows how Paul was thinking of the
Thessalonians especially, while he depicted the bliss of the saints in general.—
ἔνδοξ., in one sense they were to be a
credit and honour to their apostles
(I., ii. 19 f.); in another, they were a
glory to Christ Himself, by their ripened
character—a Johannine touch (cf. John
xvii. 10, and ver. 12 of this chapter; the
parallel between ἔργον πίστεως and John
vi. 29 is verbal).—θαυμ. = to be wondered
at (by whom? cf. Ezek. xxxix. 21, Eph.
iii. 10?) in (i.e., by reason of, on account
of) believers; for a partial parallel to the
phrase see Isa. lxii. 6 (καὶ ἐν τῷ πλούτῳ
αὐτῶν θαυμασθήσεσθε). If ὅτι . . .
ὑμᾶς had been meant to give the reason
for θαυμασθῆναι (so Zimmer, Wohl.),
Paul would probably have put God's witness instead of our witness, and expressed
the idea unambiguously; the transition
from the πᾶσιν to the special case of the
Thessalonians becomes, on this construction, an anti-climax. The rhythmical
swing of 7b-10 suggests a reminiscence
or quotation of some early Christian liturgical hymn, perhaps one of the prophetic ψαλμοί which he had heard at
Corinth (1 Cor. xiv. 15, 26).

Ver. 11. καὶ κ.τ.λ., we pray as well
as render thanks (ver. 3) for you. Unable any longer to give the Thessalonians
their personal example and instructions—
the time for that had passed (ἐπιστώθη)—
Paul and his colleagues can still pray for
them. The duties of a preacher or
evangelist do not cease with the utterance of his message. ἀξιώσῃ : one
proof that God deemed them worthy of
His kingdom lay in the discipline of

[i] εὐδοκίαν [k] ἀγαθωσύνης καὶ ἔργον πίστεως [l] ἐν δυνάμει · 12. [h] ὅπως
[m] ἐνδοξασθῇ τὸ [n] ὄνομα τοῦ Κυρίου ἡμῶν Ἰησοῦ ἐν ὑμῖν, [o] καὶ ὑμεῖς ἐν
[o] αὐτῷ, κατὰ τὴν χάριν [p] τοῦ Θεοῦ [p] ἡμῶν καὶ [q] Κυρίου Ἰησοῦ Χριστοῦ.

II. 1. Ἐρωτῶμεν δὲ ὑμᾶς, ἀδελφοί, [a] ὑπὲρ τῆς παρουσίας τοῦ
Κυρίου [1] Ἰησοῦ Χριστοῦ καὶ [b] ἡμῶν [c] ἐπισυναγωγῆς ἐπ' αὐτόν, 2. [d] εἰς
τὸ μὴ [e] ταχέως [f] σαλευθῆναι ὑμᾶς ἀπὸ τοῦ νοὸς μηδὲ [g] θροεῖσθαι,
μήτε διὰ πνεύματος, μήτε διὰ λόγου, μήτε δι' [h] ἐπιστολῆς (ὡς [i] δι'

i Contrast
ii. 12; cf.
on Rom.
x. 1; Eph.
i. 5.
k See on
Rom. xv.
14 and
Eph. v. 9.
l Col. i. 29.
m Cf. LXX;
of Isa.
xxiv. 15,
lxvi. 5;
Mal. i. 11;

Ezek. xxxix. 21.   n = Person or character (cf. on Phil. ii. 9-10).   o John xvii. 1, 10, 21 f.
p So ver. 11.   q For κ. without article, cf. Win. § 19. 13 d, § 18. 7.   a "with regard to," =
περί (an Ionism, cf. Meisterhans, Gramm. d. attisch. Inschrift. 182).   b See on i. 7.   c Cf. Matt.
xxiv. 31; 2 Macc. ii. 7, etc.   d I. iii. 10.   e Gal. i. 6 = "hastily".   f See Acts xvii. 13;
Sap. iv. 4.   g Elsewhere in N.T., only in Matt. xxiv. 6 (= Mk. xiii. 7).   h Forged? cf.
Jos. Vit. xi., xxxv.   i Sc. γεγραμμένης.

[1] Om. ημων after Κυριου, with B, syr. (WH, Weiss, Findlay).

suffering by means of which He developed their patient faith (4, 5), but Paul here finds another proof of it in their broader development of moral character and vital religion (cf. 10). πᾶσαν includes ἔργον as well as εὐδοκίαν; the prayer is for success to every practical enterprise of faith as well as for the satisfaction of every aspiration and desire after moral excellence. Compare Dante's Paradiso, xviii. 58-60. κλῆσις is "the position you are called to occupy," "your vocation," as heirs of this splendid future—a not unnatural extension (cf. Phil. iii. 14) of its ordinary use (= 1 Cor. i. 26, etc.). This implies that a certain period of moral ripening must precede the final crisis. In ii. 1-iii. 5, Paul proceeds to elaborate this, in order to allay the feverish excitement at Thessalonica, while in iii. 6 f., he discusses the further ethical disorders caused by the church's too ardent hope. The heightened misery of the present situation must neither break down their patience (4 f.), nor on the other hand must it be taken as a proof that the end was imminent.

Ver. 12. Here at any rate it is impossible to take χάριν in a universalistic sense (so Robinson, Ephesians, pp. 225 f.), as though it implied that Christians were put on the same level as O.T. saints. The idea is the merciful favour of God, to the exclusion of human merit. The main topic of the letter is now brought forward; ii. 1-2 gives the occasion for the λόγος παρακλήσεως (3-12) which follows.

CHAPTER II.—Ver. 1. ἐπισυν., a term whose verb was already in use for the muster of saints to the messianic reign. —σαλ. "get unsettled". Epictetus uses ἀποσαλεύεσθαι for the unsettling of the mind by sophistries (iii. 25), and the

nearest equivalent for νοῦς here is our "mind". This mental agitation (aor.) results in θροεῖσθαι = nervous fear (Wrede, 48 f.) in prospect of the imminent end.

Ver. 2. ὡς δι' ἡμῶν, "purporting to come from us," goes with ἐπιστολῆς alone, for, while λόγος (Lünemann) might be grouped under it, πνεῦμα cannot. A visionary would claim personal, not borrowed, authority for his revelation. If ὡς δ. ἡ. went with the preceding verbs (so Dods, Askwith, 92 f., Wohl. = "we are the true interpreters of Paul's meaning"), an active (as in ver. 3) not a passive turn might have been expected to the sentence.—ἐνέστηκεν = "were already present". The cry was, ὁ κύριος πάρεστι. The final period had already begun, and the Thessalonians were probably referred to their sufferings as a proof of this. Paul could only guess the various channels along which such a misconception had flowed into the local church: either, e.g., πνεύματος, the hallucination of some early Christian prophet at Thessalonica; or λόγου, oral statement, based in part perhaps on some calculation of contemporary history or on certain logia of Jesus; or ἐπιστολῆς, i.e., the misinterpretation of some passage in 1 Thess. or in some lost letter of Paul. Possibly Paul imagined an epistle had been forged purporting to come from him or his companions, but we have no means of knowing whether his suspicion was well-founded or not. In any case the allusion is quite credible within his lifetime. Such expectations may have been excited in a more or less innocent fashion, but Paul peremptorily (ver. 3) ranks them all as dishonest; he is concerned not with their origin but with their mis-

k *Cf.* 2 Cor. ἡμῶν),¹ ᵏ ὡς ᵏ ὅτι ¹ ἐνέστηκεν ἡ ἡμέρα τοῦ Κυρίου.   3. Μή τις ὑμᾶς
xi. 21, "to
the effect ᵐ ἐξαπατήσῃ κατὰ μηδένα τρόπον · ὅτι ⁿ ἐὰν μὴ ἔλθῃ ° ἡ ἀποστασία
that ".
l Rom. viii, ᵖ πρῶτον καὶ �q ἀποκαλυφθῇ ὁ ἄνθρωπος τῆς ἀνομίας,² ὁ υἱὸς ʳ τῆς
38, etc.
m Aor.conj. ἀπωλείας,   4. ὁ ἀντικείμενος καὶ ὑπεραιρόμενος ἐπὶ ˢ πάντα λεγό-
as in 2
Cor. xi.   μενον ³ ˢ θεὸν ἢ ᵗ σέβασμα, ὥστε αὐτὸν ᵘ εἰς τὸν ναὸν τοῦ θεοῦ καθίσαι,
16; 1 Cor.
xvi. 11.   ᵛ ἀποδεικνύντα ἑαυτὸν ὅτι ἐστὶ θεός.   5. οὐ μνημονεύετε ὅτι ἔτι ὢν
n Sc. "it
shall not
come" (ellipsis, as in. ver. 7).   o "The well known."   p = πρότερον (I. iv. 16).   q Matt·
xxiv. 12.   r Win. § 30, 6, b; *cf.* Deissm. 163; Jub. x. 3.   s 1 Cor.viii. 5.   t Elsewhere
in N.T., only in Acts xvii. 23 (Sap. xv. 17).   u Matt. xxiv. 15.   v By deeds as well as words,
cf. Acts ii. 22; here = " proclaim ".

¹ On ὡς δι ημων Field (202) writes: " Perhaps the apostle wrote ὡς δη ημων, as
pretending to be ours," adding instances from Ast. *Lex. Plat.* to justify the latter's
statement that " cum irrisione quadam plerumque ponitur ὡς δη ".

² The ανομιας of אB min., cop., arm., Euth., Dam., Tert., Amb. (Ti., Tr., WH,
Zim., Bj., Findlay, Lgft.), is preferable to the Western paraphrastic αμαρτιας (Alford,
Ellic., Wohl., Weiss).

³ Bentl. conj. επι παν το λεγομενον.

chievous effects upon the church (*cf.*
Matt. xxiv. 4). Probably his suspicions
of misinterpretation were due to his
recent experiences in Galatia, though
the Macedonian churches seem to have
escaped any infusion of the anti-Pauline
propaganda which soured Corinth not
long afterwards.

Ver. 3. καὶ ἀποκ., the apostasy and
the appearance (so of Beliar, *Asc. Isa.*, iv.
18) of the personal anti-Christ or pseudo-
Christ form a single phenomenon. From
the use of ἡ ἀποστασία as a Greek
equivalent for Belial (LXX of 1 Kings
xxi. 13, A, and Aquila), this eschatological application of the term would naturally flow, especially as איש בליעל
might well be represented by ὁ ἄνθρωπος
τῆς ἀνομίας on the analogy of 2 Sam.
xxii. 5 (LXX) = Ps. xvii. (xviii.).   4.
Lawlessness was a cardinal trait in the
Jewish figure of Belial, as was persecution of the righteous (i. 4, ii. 7, see *Asc.
Isa.*, ii. 5, etc.). The very order of the
following description (ἀπωλείας set between ἀνομίας and ὁ ἀντικείμενος, etc.,
unchronologically, but dramatically) suggests that this incarnation of lawlessness
was a doomed figure, although he chal-
lenged and usurped divine prerogatives.
He is another Antiochus Epiphanes
(Dan. xi. 36, καὶ ὑψωθήσεται ἐπὶ πάντα
θεὸν καὶ ἐπὶ τὸν θεὸν τῶν θεῶν ἔξαλλα
λαλήσει, though Paul carefully safe-
guards himself against misconception by
inserting λεγόμενον in his quotation of
the words). This conception of a supernatural antagonist to Jesus Christ at the
end is the chief element of novelty introduced by Paul, from Jewish traditions,
into the primitive Christian eschatology.
The recent attempt of Caligula to erect a
statue of himself in the Temple at Jerusalem may have furnished a trait for
Paul's delineation of the future Deceiver ;
the fearful impiety of this outburst had
sent a profound shock through Judaism,
which would be felt by Jewish Christians
as well. But Paul does not identify the
final Deception with the Imperial cultus,
which was far from a prominent feature
when he wrote. His point is that the
last pseudo-Messiah or anti-Christ will
embody all that is profane and blasphem-
ous, every conceivable element of impiety ; and that, instead of being repudiated, he will be welcomed by Jews as
well as pagans (*cf.* Acts xii. 21, 22).

Ver. 5. It was no after-thought, on
Paul's part (the singular rules out
Spitta's idea that Timothy wrote this
apocalyptic piece). Nor was it an idio-
syncrasy of his teaching. Especially
since the days of Antiochus Ep phanes
(Dan. vii., xi. ; *cf.* Gunkel's *Schöpfung u.
Chaos*, 221 f.), a more or less esoteric
and varied Jewish tradition had pervaded
pious circles, that the last days would be
heralded by a proud uprising against
God. The champion of this movement
was no longer the Dragon or cosmic opponent of God, as in the older mythology
(though traces of this belief still linger),
but an individual (ὁ ἄνομος) who incor-
porates human wickedness (τὸ μυστήριον
τῆς ἀνομίας) and infernal cunning in his
own person, and who essays to supplant
and suppress the worship of the true God,
by claiming divine honours for himself.

πρὸς ὑμᾶς, ταῦτα ἔλεγον ὑμῖν; 6. καὶ νῦν τὸ ʷκατέχον ˣοἴδατε εἰς w = κωλύον (Chrys.).
τὸ ἀποκαλυφθῆναι αὐτὸν ἐν τῷ αὐτοῦ ʸκαιρῷ. 7. τὸ γὰρ μυστήριον x Matt.xiii.
ἤδη ἐνεργεῖται ᶻτῆς ἀνομίας, ᵃμόνον ὁ κατέχων ἄρτι ἕως ἐκ μέσου y "Ap 11, etc.
γένηται· 8. ᵇκαὶ τότε ἀποκαλυφθήσεται ὁ ἄνομος, ὃν ὁ Κύριος (as Dan.
Ἰησοῦς ᶜἀνελεῖ ᵈτῷ πνεύματι τοῦ στόματος ᵈ αὐτοῦ καὶ ᵉ καταργήσει xi. 29, 35).
τῇ ἐπιφανείᾳ τῆς παρουσίας αὐτοῦ· 9. οὗ ἐστιν ἡ παρουσία κατ᾽ z Epexeg.
ἐνέργειαν τοῦ Σατανᾶ ἐν πάσῃ δυνάμει καὶ ᶠσημείοις καὶ τέρασι ᶠψεύ- a Gal. ii. 10.
δους 10. καὶ ἐν πάσῃ ἀπάτῃ ᵍἀδικίας ʰτοῖς ⁱἀπολλυμένοις, eschat.
ᵏἀνθ᾽ ὧν τὴν ἀγάπην τῆς ἀληθείας οὐκ ˡἐδέξαντο εἰς τὸ σωθῆναι formula
(cf. 1 Cor.
iv. 5, etc.).
c Post-

classical, Win. § 13, 5.   d From Isa. xi. 4 (LXX), copied in Ps. Sol. xvii. 27, 41; cf. Job iv. 9, 4 Esd. xiii. 38.   e See on 1 Cor. i. 28.   f Cf. on 2 Cor. xii. 12; Matt. xxiv. 24.   g Gen. of origin.   h Dat. incommodi (Blass, § 37, 2), as in 1 Cor. i. 18; cf. Moulton, 114-115 ("strongly durative though the verb is, we see perfectivity in the fact that the goal is ideally reached"). i Cf. on 2 Cor. ii.15.   k See on Acts xii. 23.   l Contrast I. i. 6, ii. 13.

He is Satan's messiah, an infernal caricature of the true messiah. Cf. Asc. Isa., iv. 6, where it is said that Belial "will do and speak like the Beloved and he will say, I am God and before me there has been none".

Ver. 6. Well now, you know what restrains him from being manifested (coming fully into play and sight) before his appointed season. Νῦν probably goes with οἴδατε, not with τὸ κατέχον (as e.g., in John iv. 18, so Olshausen, Bisping, Wieseler, Zahn, Wrede), and καὶ νῦν is not temporal, but "a mere adverb of passage" (Lünemann, Alford) in the argument (so with οἶδα in Acts iii. 17). Were νῦν temporal, it would mean (a) that during the interval between Paul's teaching and the arrival of this letter fresh circumstances (so Zimmer) had arisen to throw light on the thwarting of the adversary. But of this there is no hint whatsoever in the context. Or (b), preferably, it would contrast with the following ἐν τῷ αὐτοῦ καιρῷ, as an equivalent for "already" (Hofmann, Wohl., Milligan, etc.).

Ver. 7. γὰρ, explaining οἴδατε. The κατέχων is a fact of present experience and observation, which accounts for the ἀνομία being as yet a μυστήριον, operating secretly, and not an ἀποκάλυψις. Paul does not say by whom (the ἄνομος himself?) the restraint is removed.— μόνον, the hiatus must be filled up with some phrase like "it cannot be manifested". Its real character and full scope are not yet disclosed. For ἄρτι = νῦν, cf. Nägeli's note in der Wortschätz des Apostels Paulus (36, 37), and for omission of ἄν, Blass, § 65, 10.

Ver. 8. ὃν, κ.τ.λ., his career is short and tragic. The apparition (cf. 1 Tim.

vi. 14, etc., Thieme, Die Inschriften von Magnesia, 34 f.) of Jesus heralds his overthrow.—ἐπιφανείᾳ = sudden appearance of a deity at some crisis (cf. Diod., Sicul., i. 25), as the god in 2 Macc. ii. 21, iii. 24, etc. "In hieratic inscriptions the appearing of the god in visible form to men is commonly expressed by the same word" (Ramsay, Exp. Ti., x. 208). This passage, with its fierce messianic anticipation of the adversary's doom interrupts the description of his mission which is resumed (in ver. 9) with an account of the inspiration (κατὰ), method (ἐν) and results (ver. 10), of this evil advent. Galen (de facult. nat., i. 2, 4-5) physiologically defines ἐνέργεια as the process of activity whose product is ἔργον. The impulse to ἐνέργεια is δύναμις. The δύναμις of this supernatural delusion is specially manifested in signs and wonders. The power of working miracles in order to deceive people (ver. 11) was an accepted trait in the Jewish and early Christian ideas of such eschatological opponents of God (cf. on Rev. xiii. 13, and Friedländer's Geschichte d. jüd. Apolog., 493 f.).

Ver. 10. ἀγάπη (cf. ver. 12) here, as Luke xi. 42, with obj. gen. Cf. Asc. Isa., iv. 15, 16: "And He will give rest [above, ch. i. 7] to the godly whom He shall find in the body in this world, and to all who because of their faith in Him have execrated Beliar and his kings". ἀλήθεια, not = "truth" in the general sense of the term (Lünemann, Lightfoot, Zimmer) but = "the truth of the gospel" (as usual in Paul) as against ἀδικία and ψεῦδος (Rom. i. 15 f., ii. 8). The apostle holds that the refusal to open one's mind and heart to the gospel leaves life a prey to moral delusion; judicial infatua-

m See
Ezek. xx.
24-25, and
Rom. i.
24, 26, 28,
etc.

n Sap. v.
6-7.

o = κατακρ.
(as Heb.
xiii. 4,
etc.).

p See on
Rom.i.18,
and 1 Cor.
xiii. 6.

q Contrast
i. 11.

αὐτούς· 11. καὶ διὰ τοῦτο ᵐπέμπει αὐτοῖς ὁ Θεὸς ἐνέργειαν ⁿπλάνης,
εἰς τὸ πιστεῦσαι αὐτοὺς τῷ ψεύδει   12. ἵνα ᵒκριθῶσι πάντες οἱ μὴ
πιστεύσαντες τῇ ᵖἀληθείᾳ ἀλλ' ᑫεὐδοκήσαντες τῇ ᵖἀδικίᾳ.   13.
ʰἩμεῖς δὲ ʳὀφείλομεν εὐχαριστεῖν τῷ Θεῷ πάντοτε περὶ ὑμῶν, ˢἀδελ-
φοὶ ἠγαπημένοι ὑπὸ Κυρίου, ὅτι ᵗεἵλατο ὑμᾶς ὁ Θεὸς ᵘἀπαρχὴν ¹ εἰς
σωτηρίαν ἐν ᵛἁγιασμῷ ᵛπνεύματος καὶ πίστει ἀληθείας, 14. εἰς ʷὃ
ἐκάλεσεν ὑμᾶς διὰ τοῦ ˣεὐαγγελίου ˣἡμῶν, εἰς ʸπεριποίησιν δόξης
τοῦ Κυρίου ἡμῶν Ἰησοῦ Χριστοῦ.   15. ᶻἆρα οὖν, ἀδελφοί, ᵃστήκετε
καὶ κρατεῖτε τὰς ᵇπαραδόσεις ἃς ἐδιδάχθητε, εἴτε διὰ λόγου εἴτε δι',

r i. 3.   s Cf. I. i. 4 (in similar connexion).   t Alexandrian form (Win. § 13, 13); cf. Deut.
xxvi. 18.   u Rom. xi. 16, xvi. 5; 1 Cor. xv. 20, etc.;   v I. iv. 7-8.   w i.e., general
position reflected in ver. 13.   x Cf. 2 Cor. iv. 3.   y Cf. I. v. 9.   z Cf. I. v. 6; resumes
thought of ii. 1-2.   a Cf. I. iii. 8 and 1 Cor. xvi. 13.   b See iii. 6 and 1 Cor. xi. 2.

¹ The singular variant απαρχην, adopted by Lach., WH marg., Weiss (Lgft.?)
from BGgrP, min., f. vg., syr.P, Euth., Dam., etc., is preferable to the strongly
supported απ αρχης (Pauline απ. ευρ., in historical sense of Phil. iv. 15, Ac. xv. 7,
etc.). The Thessalonians or Macedonians are *first-fruits*, as contrasted with others
yet to follow (cf. iii. 1, and i. 4).

tion is the penalty of disobedience to the
truth of God in Christ.

Ver. 11. An echo of the primitive
Semitic view (still extant, cf. Curtis's
Prim. Sem. Religion To-Day, pp. 69 f.),
that God may deliberately lead men
astray, or permit them to be fatally in-
fatuated, as a penal discipline (cf. Ps.
Sol. viii. 15; Test. XII. Patr. Dan. ix.).
A modern would view the same phenomenon as wilful scepticism issuing in
superstition, or in inability to distinguish
truth from falsehood. Delusions of this
kind cannot befall believers (cf. Mark xiii.
22; Test. Issach. iii.). In Test. Napht.
iii. 3, idols are πνεύματα πλάνης (cf.
Test. Levi. iii. 3, etc.).

Ver. 12. Like the prophet John half
a century later (xiii. 2 f.), Paul distinguishes his anti-Christ or antitheistic
hero from the Satan whose campaign he
executes; but, unlike John, the apostle
has nothing to say about the fate of
Satan. The tools and the victims of
Satan are destroyed, and they alone.—
εὐδοκ. not with ἐν as usual, but with the
less common (cf. e.g., 1 Macc. i. 43, καὶ
πολλοὶ ἀπὸ Ἰσραὴλ ηὐδόκησαν τῇ λατ-
ρίᾳ αὐτοῦ dative. "And the greater
number of those who shall have been
associated together in order to receive
the Beloved he [i.e., Beliar] will turn
aside after him" (Asc. Isa., iv. 9).

Ver. 13-CHAPTER III.-Ver. 5. Thanks,
prayers and counsels.

Ver. 13. God has chosen you (εἵλατο,
another LXX expression, implying that
Christians had now succeeded to the
cherished priviliges of God's people) to

be saved, instead of visiting you with a
deadly delusion (10, 11) which ends in
judgment (12); your discipline is of sanctification (contrast 12b) and belief in what
is true (contrast 11, 12a), these forming
the sphere and the scope (cf. 1 Tim. ii.
15, and for ἐν ἁγιασμῷ in this sense Ps.
Sol. xvii. 33) for salvation being realised.
Those who are sanctified and who truly
believe shall be saved. Cf. ver. 14 and
Apoc. Bar., liv. 21: "in fine enim saeculi
uindicta erit de iis qui improbe egerunt,
iuxta improbitatem eorum, et glorificabis
fideles iuxta fidem eorum".—πνεύματος
may be either (a) = "wrought by the
(holy) Spirit" (cf. 1 Peter i. 2), the divine
side of the human πίστει, or (b) = "of
the spirit" (cf. I. v. 23; 2 Cor. vii. 1), as
of the heart (I., iii. 13). The absence of
the article is not decisive against the
former rendering, but the latter is the
more probable in view of the context;
the process of ἁγιασμός involves a love of
the truth and a belief in it (i.e., in the
true gospel) which is opposed to religious
delusions cf. ii. 2).

Ver. 14. To be saved ultimately (12)
is to possess or rather to share the glory
of Christ (cf. I., ii. 12).

Ver. 15. The divine purpose does not
work automatically, but implies the co-
operation of Christians—in this case, a
resolute stedfastness resting on loyalty to
the apostolic gospel. In view of passages like 1 Cor. xi. 23, xv. 5, it is gratui-
tous to read any second-century passion
for oral apostolic tradition into these
words or into those of iii. 6.

^cἐπιστολῆς ἡμῶν. 16. ^dαὐτὸς δὲ ὁ Κύριος ἡμῶν Ἰησοῦς Χριστὸς
καὶ ^dὁ Θεὸς ὁ πατὴρ ἡμῶν, ὁ ἀγαπήσας ἡμᾶς ^eκαὶ δοὺς ^fπαράκλησιν
^gαἰωνίαν καὶ ἐλπίδα ἀγαθὴν ^hἐν χάριτι, 17. ⁱπαρακαλέσαι ὑμῶν
τὰς καρδίας καὶ ⁱστηρίξαι ^kἐν παντὶ ἔργῳ καὶ ^lλόγῳ ^lἀγαθῷ.

III. 1. ^aΤὸ λοιπὸν, ^bπροσεύχεσθε, ἀδελφοί, περὶ ^bἡμῶν, ἵνα ^cὁ
λόγος τοῦ ^cΚυρίου ^dτρέχῃ καὶ ^eδοξάζηται καθὼς καὶ ^fπρὸς ὑμᾶς, 2.
καὶ ἵνα ^gῥυσθῶμεν ἀπὸ τῶν ^hἀτόπων καὶ ^hπονηρῶν ⁱἀνθρώπων· ^kοὐ
γὰρ πάντων ἡ πίστις. 3. ^lπιστὸς δέ ἐστιν ὁ Κύριος, ὃς ^mστηρίξει
ὑμᾶς καὶ ⁿφυλάξει ἀπὸ τοῦ πονηροῦ. 4. ^oπεποίθαμεν δὲ ἐν Κυρίῳ
^oἐφ’ ὑμᾶς, ὅτι ἃ παραγγέλλομεν ποιεῖτε ^pκαὶ ποιήσετε. 5. ὁ δὲ

c I. v. 27.
d For order,
cf. 2 Cor.
xiii. 13.
e Cf. Rom.
v. 5, 8.
f See on 2
Cor. i.
3·7.
g Contrast
i. 9.
h = ' gra-
ciously."
i Cf. I. iii.
11, 13.
k 1 Cor. i. 5.
l Cf. Lk.
xxiv. 19;
Thuc. i.
139, 4 ;
Test.

Gad, vi. 1. a I. iv. 1; Eph. vi. 10. b I. v. 25. c I. i. 8. d Ps. cxlvii. 15, etc. (LXX),
contrast 2 Tim. ii. 9. e In sense of Acts xiii. 48. f I. iii. 4. g Cf. Rom. xv. 31; 2 Ti. iv. 17;
Ps. Sol. iv. 27. h See on Acts xxviii. 6; Isa. xxv. 4 (LXX); and on I. lii. 3, "misguided and
unprincipled" Rutherford. i e.g., in Corinth; cf. Acts xviii. 6 f. 2 Ti. iii. 13. k Cf. Rom.
x. 16 with Acts xvii. 12, 34. l Cf. i. 10, Acts xviii. 9 f. m ii. 17. n 2 Ti. iv. 18. o 2 Co.
ii. 3. p Cf. I. iv. 10.

Ver. 16. αὐτὸς δὲ, perhaps with a
slight implicit apposition to the *you* or
we of the previous sentence.—ἀγαπήσας
καὶ δοὺς, κ.τ.λ., connecion as in John
iii. 16.—παράκλησιν for this world,
ἐλπίδα for the world to come ; all hope
is encouragement, but not vice-versa.

Ver. 17, in contrast to the disquiet and
confusion of ii. 2. ἔργῳ as in i. 11, iii. 4,
7 f., λόγῳ as iii. 1, 15 ; I., i. 8. See the
fulsome pagan inscription of Halicar-
nassus, which after giving thanks for the
birth of Augustus, σωτῆρα τοῦ κοινοῦ
τῶν ἀνθρώπων γένους, declares that men
now are full of ἐλπίδων μὲν χρηστῶν
πρὸς τὸ μέλλον, εὐθυμίας δὲ εἰς τὸ παρόν.
Contrast also the κενὴ ἐλπίς of the impious in Sap. iiⁱ. 11.

CHAPTER III.—Ver. 1. In addition to
offering prayers on their behalf, Paul asks
them to pray for the continued success of
the gospel ("may others be as blest as
we are "!) and (ver. 2), for its agents'
safety (Isa. xxv. 4, LXX, a reminiscence
of). The opponents here are evidently
(ii. 10 f.) beyond hope of conversion ;
preservation from their wiles is all that
can be expected. For a speedy answer
to this prayer, see Acts xviii. 9 f. The
repeated use of ὁ Κύριος in vv. 1-5, brings
out the control of God amid the plots and
passions of mankind. — ἀτόπων. The
general sense of the term is given by
Ph lo in his queer allegorising of Gen. iii.
9 (*Leg. Alleg.*, iii. 17, ἄτοπος λέγεται
εἶναι ὁ φαῦλος) ; commonly it is used, as
elsewhere in the N.T., of things, but here
of persons, either as = "ill-disposed," or,
in a less general and derivative sense =
"perverse" (*cf.* Nägeli, *der Wortschatz*

des Paulus, p. 37), or "froward". The
general aim of the passage is to widen
the horizon of the Thessalonians, by en-
listing their sympathy and interest on
behalf of the apostles. They are not the
only sufferers, or the only people who
need prayer and help.—οὐ παντὸς ἀνθρὸς
εἰς Κόρινθόν ἐσθ’ ὁ πλοῦς, so ran the
ancient proverb. Paul writes from Corinth that while everyone has the chance,
not all have the desire, to arrive at the
faith. ἡ πίστις is the faith of the gospel,
or Christianity. By a characteristic play
upon the word, Paul (ver. 3), hurries on
to add, "but the Lord is faithful '. ὑμᾶς
(for which Bentley and Baljon plausibly
conjecture ἡμᾶς) shows how lightly his
mind rests on thoughts of his own peril
as compared with the need of others. It
is imposs ble to decide, either from the
grammar or from the context, whether
τοῦ πονηροῦ is neuter or masculine.
Either sense would suit, though, if there
is a reminiscence here of the Lord's
prayer (so Feine, *Jesus Christus u.
Paulus*, 252 f., and Chase, *Texts and
Studies*, i. 3. 112 f.), the masculine would
be inevitable, as is indeed more probable
for general reasons (so *e.g.*, Hofmann,
Everling, Ellicott, etc.)

Ver. 4. πεποίθαμεν (= we have faith),
still playing on the notion of πίστις.
Paul rallies the Thessalonians by reminding them, not only of God's faithfulness,
but of their friends' belief in them.

Ver. 5. κατευθύναι, κ.τ.λ. Paul no
longer (I., iii. 11) entertains the hope of
revisiting tnem soon. "God's love and
Christ's patient endurance" (*i.e.*, the
ὑπομονή which Christ inspires and re-

q 1 Chron. Κύριος ᑫ κατευθύναι ὑμῶν τὰς καρδίας εἰς τὴν ʳ ἀγάπην τοῦ Θεοῦ καὶ
xxix. 18
(LXX).   εἰς ὑπομονὴν τοῦ Χριστοῦ.
Ps. Sol.
xii. 6, etc.   6. ᵃΠαραγγέλλομεν δὲ ὑμῖν, ἀδελφοί, ᵗ ἐν ὀνόματι τοῦ Κυρίου
ʳ Cf. ii. 16;
cf. Abbott, Ἰησοῦ Χριστοῦ, ᵘ στέλλεσθαι ὑμᾶς ἀπὸ παντὸς ἀδελφοῦ ᵛ ἀτάκτως
Joh.
Gramm.   περιπατοῦντος καὶ μὴ κατὰ τὴν παράδοσιν ἣν παρελάβετε¹ παρ' ἡμῶν.
2033 b.
s Cf. Ignat. 7. αὐτοὶ γὰρ οἴδατε πῶς δεῖ ʷ μιμεῖσθαι ἡμᾶς· ὅτι οὐκ ἠτακτήσαμεν
ad Polyk. ἐν ὑμῖν, 8. ˣ οὐδὲ δωρεὰν ἄρτον ἐφάγομεν παρά τινος, ἀλλ' ʸ ἐν κόπῳ
5.
t See on καὶ μόχθῳ νυκτὸς καὶ ἡμέρας ἐργαζόμενοι πρὸς τὸ μὴ ᶻ ἐπιβαρῆσαί
1 Cor. i.
10.   τινα ὑμῶν· 9. ᵃ οὐχ ὅτι οὐκ ἔχομεν ἐξουσίαν, ἀλλ' ἵνα ἑαυτοὺς
u See on 2
Cor. viii. ᵇ τύπον δῶμεν ὑμῖν εἰς τὸ ᵇ μιμεῖσθαι ἡμᾶς. 10. καὶ γὰρ ὅτε ἦμεν
20.
v Cf. I. v. πρὸς ὑμᾶς, τοῦτο παρηγγέλλομεν ὑμῖν, ὅτι ᶜ εἴ τις οὐ θέλει ἐργάζ-
14, "a
loafer"
(Ruther:ord).   w Cf. I. i. 6, ii. 14, and on 1 Cor. iv. 16.   x I. ii. 3, v. 5.   y Cf. I. ii.
9, 2 Cor. xi. 27, Herm. Sim. v. 6, 2, etc., "toiling and moiling" (Rutherford).   z I. ii. 9 (with a
different motive).   a See on 1 Cor. ix. 3-18, and 2 Cor. i. 24.   b See on Phil. iii. 17.   c Did.
xii. 3.

¹ Read παρελαβετε, with BG, 43, 73, 80, g, goth., syr.P, arm., etc. (so Lach., Tr.,
WH, Bj., Weiss), or παρελαβοσαν (ελαβοσαν D*) with א_*A, d, e, 17, etc. (Ti.,
Al., Zim., Lgft., Wohl., Findlay [Tr., WH, Lach., all in marg.]).

quires, cf. Ignat. ad. Rom., last words)
correspond to the double experience of
love and hope in ii. 16. It is by the
sense of God's love alone, not by any
mere acquiescence in His will or stoical
endurance of it, that the patience and
courage of the Christian are sustained.
Cf. Ep. Arist., 195, ἐπὶ τῶν καλλίστων
πράξεων οὐκ αὐτοὶ κατευθύνομεν τὰ
βουλευθέντα· θεὸς δὲ τελεοῖ τὰ πάντων.
Connect with ver. 3 and cf. Mrs. Browning's line, "I waited with patience, which
means almost power".

Vv. 6-16. Injunctions upon church-
life and order.

Ver. 6. How necessary it was to promote ὑπομονή with its attendant virtues
of diligence and order at Thessalonica, is
evident from the authoritative (ἐν ὀν. τ.
Κυρίου) tone and the crisp detail of the
following paragraph. Παραγγ., like ἀτάκτως, has a military tinge (cf. on I. iv. 2,
and Dante's Paradiso, xii. 37-45). στελλ.,
for his own sake (ver. 14) as well as for
yours: a service as well as a precaution. The collective action of his fellow-
Christians, besides preserving (1 Cor. v.
6) themselves from infection—and nothing is so infectious as an insubordinate,
indolent, interfering spirit—will bring
home to him a sense of his fault. Lightfoot aptly cites the παράγγελμα of Ger-
manicus to his mutinous troops : " dis-
cedite a contactu, ac diuidite turbidos : id
stabile ad paenitentiam, id fidei uinculum
erit " (Tacit. Annal., i. 43).—The ἄτακτοι
of 6-12 are excitable members who " break

the ranks " by stopping work in view of
the near advent, and thus not only dis-
organise social life but burden the church
with their maintenance. The apostles
had not been idle or hare-brained enthusiasts, and their example of an orderly,
self-supporting life is held up as a pattern.
Insubordination of this kind is a breach
of the apostolic standard of the Christian
life, and Paul deals sharply with the first
symptoms of it. He will not listen to
any pious pleas for this kind of conduct.

Ver. 8. Paul's practice of a trade and
emphasis upon the moral discipline of
work are quite in keeping with the best
Jewish traditions of the period. Compare
e.g., the saying of Gamaliel II. (Kiddusch.
i. 11) : " He who possesses a trade is
like a fenced vineyard, into which no
cattle can enter, etc."—δωρεάν = " for
nothing, gratis ".

Ver. 9. The apostles had the right to
be maintained by the church, but in this
case they had refused to avail themselves
of it. The Thessalonians are not to mis-
construe their action.

Ver. 10. Precept as well as example
(DCG, ii. 2). As is perhaps implied in
ὅτι, εἰ . . . ἐσθιέτω is a maxim quoted
by the apostle, not from some unwritten
saying of Jesus (Resch) but from the
Jewish counterparts, based on Gen. iii.
19, which are cited by Wetstein, especially Beresch. rabba, xiv. 12 : " ut, si non
laborat, non manducet ". Cf. Carlyle's
Chartism, chap. iii (" In all ways it needs,
especially in these times, to be proclaimed

εσθαι, μηδὲ ἐσθιέτω.   11. ᵈἀκούομεν γάρ τινας περιπατοῦντας ἐν ᵈ "We are
ὑμῖν ἀτάκτως, μηδὲν᾿ ἐργαζομένους ἀλλὰ °περιεργαζομένους.   12. informed"
τοῖς δὲ τοιούτοις παραγγέλλομεν καὶ ᶠπαρακαλοῦμεν ἐν Κυρίῳ Ἰησοῦ ᵉ For the
Χριστῷ ᵍἵνα μετὰ ʰἡσυχίας ἐργαζόμενοι τὸν ἑαυτῶν ἄρτον ἐσθίωσιν. Blass, §
13. ὑμεῖς δὲ, ἀδελφοί, μὴ ᶦἐγκακήσητε ᵏκαλοποιοῦντες.   14. εἰ δέ 82, 4, and
τις οὐχ ὑπακούει τῷ λόγῳ ἡμῶν διὰ ˡτῆς ἐπιστολῆς, τοῦτον ᵐσημει- 225.
οῦσθε, μὴ ⁿσυναναμίγνυσθαι αὐτῷ, ἵνα °ἐντραπῇ· 15. καὶ μὴ ὡς ᵍ Cf. on I.
ἐχθρὸν ᵖἡγεῖσθε, ἀλλὰ ᑫνουθετεῖτε ὡς ἀδελφόν.   16. αὐτὸς δὲ ὁ ʰ Cf. on
Κύριος τῆς εἰρήνης ʳδῴη ὑμῖν τὴν εἰρήνην ˢδιὰ παντὸς ἐν παντὶ 18.
τρόπῳ.   ᶦ Cf. on
                                                                          Gal. vi. 9;
                                                                          Eph. iii.
                                                                          3.
k Only here in N.T.   l i.e., not 1 Thess.(so Lünemann, Schmiedel, Schäfer) but (so Pelt, Lgft.,
Findlay, etc.) the present, Win. § 18, 4.   m Only here in N.T.   n Cf. 1 Cor. v. 9 f.   o Cf.
Tit. ii. 8.   p Cf. Job xix. 11 (LXX).   q f. I. v. 14, 1 Cor. iv. 14, and 2 Cor. ii. 7.   r Opt.
without ἄν, as in 1 Peter i. 2; Hellenistic opt., Win. § 14, 10.   s = "continually" Lk. xxiv.
53, Ps. Sol. ii. 40, etc.

aloud that for the idle man there is no place in this England . . . he that will not work according to his faculty, let him perish according to his necessity "). The use of ἐν Κυρίῳ here and in 1 Cor. xi. 11 (cf. Matt. xix. 4 f.) proves, as Titius argues (der Paulinismus unter dem Gesichtspunkt der Seligkeit, 1900, p. 105), that the original divine ideas of the Creation are fulfilled and realised in the light of Christ's gospel; the entire process of human life culminates in the faith of Christ, and therefore no unqualified antithesis can be drawn between ordinary life and Christian conduct.

Ver. 11. The γάρ goes back to ver. 6. " Whereas I am told that some of your number are behaving in a disorderly fashion, not busy but busybodies," fussy and officious, doing anything but attending to their daily trade. "Ab otio ualde procliue est hominum ingenium ad curiositatem" (Bengel). The first persecution at Thessalonica had been fostered by a number of fanatical loungers (Acts xvii. 5). On the sensible attitude of the primitive church to labour, see Harnack's Expansion, i. 215 f. M. Aurelius (iii. 4) warns people against idle, fussy habits, but especially against τὸ περίεργον καὶ κακόηθες, and an apt parallel to this use of ἀτάκτως lies in Dem. Olynth., iii. 34: ὅσα (funds or food) οὗτος ἀτάκτως νῦν λαμβάνων (i.e., takes without rendering personal service in the field) οὐκ ὠφελεῖ, ταῦτ' ἐν ἴσῃ τάξει λαμβανέτω.

Ver. 12. They are not directly addressed (contrast 6, 13).—μετὰ ἡσυχίας, in the homely sphere of work. The three causes of disquiet at Thessalonica are (a) the disturbing effect of persecution, (b) the tension produced by the thought of the advent of Christ, and (c), as an outcome of the latter, irregularity and social disorganisation in the community.

Ver. 13. ὑμεῖς δέ, whoever else drops out of the ranks of industrious, steady Christians.—μὴ ἐγκ., implying that they had not begun to grow slack (Moulton, 122 f.). Perhaps with a special allusion to the presence of people who abused charity; generous Christians must not forego liberality and help, arguing that it is no use to succour any because some will take advantage of the church's largess.

Ver. 14. διὰ τ. ἐπ., implying that the matter ends with this letter (Weiss); Paul has spoken his last word on the subject. With this and the following verse, cf. Did. xv. 3 (ἐλέγχετε δὲ ἀλλήλους μὴ ἐν ὀργῇ ἀλλ' ἐν εἰρήνῃ, ὡς ἔχετε ἐν τῷ εὐαγγελίῳ· καὶ παντὶ ἀστοχοῦντι κατὰ τοῦ ἑτέρου μηδεὶς λαλείτω μηδὲ παρ' ὑμῶν ἀκουέτω, ἕως οὗ μετανοήσῃ).—ἐντραπῇ, "be ashamed" (= αἰδεῖσθαι as often).

Ver. 15. Disapproval, as a means of moral discipline, loses all its effect if the offender does not realise its object and reason (νουθετεῖτε), or if it is tainted with personal hostility.—ὡς ἀδελφόν. Compare the fine saying of Rabbi Chanina ben Gamaliel on Deut. xxv. 3, that after the punishment the offender is expressly called brother, not sinner.

Ver. 16. εἰρήνην, as opposed to these fears and troubles of the church. Κύριος is probably, in accordance with Paul's usual practice, to be taken as = Jesus Christ, but the language of ver. 5 and of

‹ Emphatic: ὁ Κύριος μετὰ ᵗ πάντων ὑμῶν.
the cen-
sured as   17. ὁ ᵘ ἀσπασμὸς τῇ ἐμῇ χειρὶ Παύλου, ὅ ἐστι σημεῖον ἐν πάσῃ
well as
the steady ἐπιστολῇ · ᵛ οὕτω γράφω.
members.

ᵘ Cf. on 1   18. ἡ χάρις τοῦ Κυρίου ἡμῶν Ἰησοῦ Χριστοῦ μετὰ ᵗ πάντων ὑμῶν.
Cor. xvi.
21, and 2
Cor. xiii. 13.   v Autograph as means of recognising authenticity, cf. Abbott, Joh. Gram.
2691, and Cicero's Catil. iii. 5, Plautus, Bacch. iv. 4, 78, etc.

I., v. 23, makes the reference to God quite possible.

Vv. 17, 18. Conclusion. Paul now takes the pen from his amanuensis, to add the salutation in his own handwriting or the purpose of authenticating the epistle (otherwise in 1 Cor. xvi. 21). This, he observes, is the sign-manual of his letters (cf. ii. 2), i.e., the fact of a personal written greeting at the close, not any form of words (like ver. 18), or the use of the word " grace," or " certum quendam nexum literarium " (Grotius).

The precaution is natural, in view of his suspicion about unauthorised communications. Compare "the σεσημείωμαι (generally contracted into σεση) with which so many of the Egyptan papyrus-letters and ostraca close " (Milligan, p. 130), or the postscript in one's own handwriting (ξύμβολον) which guaranteed an ancient letter (Deissmann : Licht vom Osten, 105). μετά (cf. ver. 16), the divine presence is realised through the experience of Christ's grace.

INTRODUCTION TO THE PASTORAL
EPISTLES.

INTRODUCTION TO THE PASTORAL EPISTLES.

PRELIMINARY.

THOSE who propose to read this exposition of the Pastoral Epistles may find it convenient to be apprised at the outset of the conclusions assumed in it concerning the genuineness and integrity of the Letters. After a careful review of the arguments adduced by the traditionalists and the anti-traditionalists, and after the devotion of considerable thought to a minute study of the Epistles themselves, the present writer finds it easier to believe that St. Paul was the author of them, as they have come down to us, than that a Paulinist (assuming that there ever was a special school of Pauline thought), sometime between 90 and 120 A.D., worked up a few fragments of genuine letters of his master into 2 Timothy and Titus, and then composed 1 Timothy in imitation of his own style. This second alternative represents, broadly speaking, the theory of the anti-traditional school of critics.

The only serious difficulties which preclude an unhesitating acceptance of these letters, as they stand, as the composition of St. Paul, lie in (1), the style, which, although fundamentally not un-Pauline, presents undeniably certain obvious peculiarities which are not found in any of the ten other Pauline letters, and (2) in the writer's outlook on religion—in particular, the relations of God and Christ respectively to man's salvation, and the place of faith and works in the spiritual life—which seems to be that of one who had travelled on the Pauline road (assuming that there was a public highway that could be so described), further than we should have deemed it possible in the years—few at most—which separate the close of St. Paul's life from the date of the Epistles of the first Roman captivity. The main features of the landscape are the same, but the distances are different.

On the other hand, this altered theological outlook, as well as the writer's concern about Church institutions, is responsible for the peculiar religious phraseology in so far as it does indeed differ from features common to the earlier groups of letters ; so that whatever considerations help us to account for the former change will also aid in the solution of the problem of style and vocabulary.

The other arguments against the Pauline authorship, based on : (3) the impossibility of fitting into the Acts of the Apostles the personal and local references in the Pastorals, (4) the all ged marks of the second century in the heresy which is combated, and (5) the allegation that the details of Church organisation reflect the policy of the dominant party of the early second century—are, it is believed, assumptions for which there is no foundation. And, in fact, (4) and (5) are not now insisted on by many of the anti-traditional school, and will not be dealt with in this introduction.

Before passing on to a brief discussion of the style and the historical setting of the Epistles, it will not be amiss to suggest some considerations which may help, not indeed to solve the problem before us, but to enable us to believe that it would not be a problem at all could we only know a little more about the personal history of St. Paul, and of the inner life of the Christian Church in the first century. In the first place, we must remember that it was a period of intensely vigorous and rapidly developing Church life. We are so much accustomed to regard as normal Christian communities in which nine-tenths of the professed adherents are spiritually only half alive, that we find it difficult to realise what manner of thing Church life was when every one took a keen interest in his religion, and the spiritual life of every Church member was full and strong, even if not always consistent. The years that elapsed between Pentecost and 100 A.D. represent the infancy of the Church ; and we all know how momentous in their after consequences are a child's experiences during the first five or six years of its life. But the first century was even more significant for the subsequent history of the Church than is infancy in the case of a human being. The development of the Church, as we experience it, at least in Europe, is slow ; looking back thirty years we can indeed perceive some change ; but in the first century a year wrought what it now takes a generation to effect. What we know of the rapid development in applied science in our own day supplies us with an experience somewhat analogous to the growth of the Christian Church— doctrinally and institutionally—in the first century. We have seen in the space of ten, or even five, years a complete revolution in men's notions as to what is possible and reasonable in the rate of travel on the high road or in the air.

It was while the Church was thus rapidly taking shape that St. Paul came into it; and, if we may judge from the extant evidence, he quickly became the most powerful constructive force in it. But there were other agencies at work, human, as well as Divine and divinely inspired, and St. Paul was himself wrought on and shaped as much, or more, than he shaped others. Always a student but never a recluse, he shared to the full the common life of the un-exclusive early Church. He did not "dwell apart," though always conscious that his innermost life was "hid with Christ in God". And not only did his life move with the Church's life, but it was brought into close touch with every possible human experience—except those of domestic life—to a degree rarely equalled by any other man. The label that correctly describes the contents of a given human personality to-day may be, in some cases, not misleading five or ten years hence; but St. Paul was not one of these constant quantities. His personality was not that of a Milton, self-determining, holding on its course "like a star," unaffected by the storms of the lower atmosphere; he was as sympathetic, and therefore open to impressions from without, as if he had been a weak man. Of this impressionableness and craving for sympathy we have abundant evidence in the Epistles that are universally acknowledged to be genuine. Such a man is likely to undergo changes in mental outlook, to become possessed by fresh ideals and conceptions, so as to be-wilder less agile minds; and, of course, new thoughts require for their expression words and phrases for which the man had no use before. In the case of St. Paul, this is no imaginary supposition. The difference between the Paul of Philippians and the Paul of 1 Timothy is not greater than, perhaps not as great as, between the Paul of Thessalonians and the Paul of Ephesians. The fact just noticed should put us on our guard against the easy assumption that the normal Pauline presentation of the relations between God and man is that found in the central group of his Epistles: Romans, 1 Corinthians, 2 Corinthians, Galatians.

There is, however, a difference between the Pastorals and the earlier letters for which the lapse of time alone cannot account, and that is a diminution in force. The letters to Timothy and Titus are certainly of apostolic quality; the ordinary reader, and still more the student, who compares them with the best of the sub-apostolic literature, can at once perceive the difference between what is inspired and what is merely interesting, edifying, and even noble. Neverthe-less, we miss in the Pastorals the exuberant vigour, the reserved strength of the earlier letters. The explanation of this may well be that before St. Paul wrote these letters he had ceased to be an elderly, and had, perhaps rapidly, become an old man. There is nothing impossible in this supposition. The surprising thing is that it has not been more generally recognised as a probable factor in the solution of the problem presented by the Pastorals. When we think of the intensity with which St. Paul had lived his life—always at high pressure—and what a hard life it had been, it would be a marvel indeed if old age with its diminished powers had not come suddenly upon him.

We hold then that the author of the Pastorals was Paul; but "Paul the aged"; much more aged, and more truly so, than when he penned his note to Philemon. We may observe, as a sign of old age, a certain inertia which makes him satisfied to express his meaning in habitual, almost stereotyped, words and phrases; words and phrases which are only open to the objection—in itself unreasonable—that we have heard them quite recently. The brain no longer responds to the will to utter "words that burn"; and it seems as fitful in the origination of "thoughts that breathe". It is not that St. Paul is not truly inspired in the Pastorals. These letters satisfy the practical test of inspiration, *viz.*, their yield of matter for thought is never exhausted by study. There are, moreover, several passages in them that have touched the hearts of Christians in every age as nearly as anything the apostle ever wrote. But even in these, perhaps more in these than in less striking paragraphs—for ordinary details of Church life must be dealt with in ordinary language—we detect a failing of power in comparison with the Paul of the earlier letters: the inspiration is as true, but it is not as strong; the heart and arteries and veins do their duty, but the blood does not course so quickly as in the days of youth. To put it quite plainly: the difficulties that meet the student of the Pastoral Epistles lie rather in the logical connexion of the paragraphs than in the profundity of the thoughts expressed in them; and whatever obscurity there may be in some of the expressions used is due in nearly every case to the meagreness of our information concerning the circumstances of the writer and of the Church.

In the earlier epistles, on the contrary, it often happens that the apostle's thoughts and conceptions are too great for expression. He does not, indeed cannot, formulate them precisely; he gives them the most adequate expression he can; and the Holy Spirit has ever since been leading the Church to a constantly increasing comprehension of them. But in the Pastorals we do not meet any such struggles between thought and language. We are never conscious that we are present at the birth of some mighty principle which can reach maturity only at the end of time. Great theological statements concerning man's salvation—not of the relation of Christ to the universe—are formulated, not daringly sketched; the conceptions of the mutual relations of God and man which are involved in these statements are not new to the author; he has mastered them completely, and presents them with a finished expression which leaves the reader satisfied. Take, for example, the statement of the wideness of God's saving purposes in 1 Tim. ii. 4-6; the summary of the working out of the Incarnation in 2 Tim. i. 9, 10; the analysis of the saving process in Tit. iii. 4-7. Here we have theological principles in their classical expression; they do not need exegesis, they only demand to be " marked, learned, and inwardly digested '.

Again, the apostle, in these letters is not only not creative; he is displayed to us as receptive of the thoughts of other makers of Christian theology, his contemporaries. When St. Paul wrote the Pastoral Epistles, his own work as an originating constructive theologian had come to an end; and there comes into clear view— what had been hitherto veiled—the effect on him of the action of the religious life of the communities in which he lived. It is a truth, obvious when stated, yet sometimes ignored, that the thoughts about religion current in the Christian Society of the first century, had not been generated only by St. Paul, but by St. John and St. Peter and others whose names and achievements we can only conjecture. When we were young, we used to picture the Palestine of the patriarchs as a land in which no person or thing except Abraham, Isaac, and Jacob and their flocks were of any significance; they dominated the landscape as do the saints in medieval pictures. When we grew older, it was almost disturbing to one's faith to realise that to the busy merchants and peasants of Palestine, Abraham, Isaac and Jacob were not persons of unusual importance. Yet, as always happens, the truer account, unpalatable at first, is found to be more suggestive and helpful than the older fancy. In like manner, a realisation that St. Paul did not dominate the Church of his time, as his history in the Acts and his epistles so largely dominate the New Testament, will be found a helpful consideration.

The Church is a greater thing than the greatest saint or theologian in it; and St. Paul could not have helped, even if he would, being influenced by the Christianity, as actually lived, of the men and women around him; and that in three ways at least. (1) His own theology came back to him not quite the same as it had come from his brain. It is not only the elements of matter that are subject to reaction in consequence of fusion; the same natural law operates in the interaction of the thoughts of a thoughtmaker with the minds of those to whom his thoughts are communicated. And, if we may carry on the same analogy, the Church of St Paul's time was unable to take up, to hold in solution, the whole of the Pauline theology; a considerable amount of it was held in suspension to be absorbed gradually by the Church in the course of the ages. (2) Again, as has just been pointed out, the religious thought of the Christian Society in which St. Paul lived was fed and stirred by other apostles, of whom we can name St. John and St. Peter. It is surely not unreasonable to suppose that these apostles spoke before they wrote, that what they published was the most perfect expression attainable by them of what they had been speaking about during the whole of their ministry; that, in fact, Johannine literature was, for the Church of the first century, the final presentation, not the origination, of Johannine thought and expression. Is it too much to expect that those who study the writings contained in the New Testament should cease to think of the authors of them as solitaries who had no other means but books of acquiring ideas or a vocabulary, and who, in turn, only influenced the thought and phraseology of the men of their time by books or treatises composed at the close of their lives. It is strange that men cannot see the Church, the Society which conditioned, was not conditioned by, St. Paul, St. John and St. Peter. This consideration is intended to prepare the reader to be not astonished or perplexed by the occasional Johannine turns of phrase that occur in the Pastorals, and which are noted in the course of the exposition. (3) Furthermore, it must not be thought strange that the Providence of God, the Holy Spirit Who guides the Church, should have called the apostle Paul almost wholly away from thoughts of the Church's place in history and in the universe to the administration of, and provision for, the daily needs of the Church as actually experienced by man. Our own generation has not been without examples of men summoned from the library of the "great house" into less obviously inspiring chambers, which serve the more material, but not less necessary, needs of the household. Christians who think of the Church as a visible Divine Society with a life on earth continuous to the end of time, cannot think that St. Paul as reflected in the Pastorals is less worthy of admiration than St. Paul as reflected in Romans. Nor will they be offended if they find that his new preoccupation with ordinary Church life has left a trace on his idiom; if, it may be, he has caught some of the current phrases of ordinary religious society. He is not less intelligible to Timothy, or less truly himself.

THE STYLE OF THE LETTERS.

It was noticed in the beginning of this Introduction that the consideration of most weight against the Pauline authorship of the Pastoral Epistles is the style of the composition, which differs from that of any of the groups of the other ten Pauline letters—the genuineness of which is here assumed—by (a) the recurrence in them of certain, almost stereotyped, forms of expression, (b) by a general difference in the structure of sentences, and (c) by the absence from them of alleged characteristic Pauline words. These three sorts of variation are here enumerated in the order of their importance. No fair-minded traditionalist will be disposed to minimise the gravity of the problem presented by these indisputable facts. On the other hand, these acknowledged peculiarities must not be allowed to obscure the equally undoubted fact that the Epistles present not only as many characteristic Pauline words as the writer had use for, but that, in the more significant matter of turns of expression, the style of the letters is, as has been stated before, fundamentally Pauline. This will be evident from an inspection of the references. Perhaps it is true to say that the positive stylistic peculiarities of the letters—the large number of unusual words,[1] the recurrent phraseology—deprive of its just weight the counter argument based on its admittedly Pauline element, just because this is normal, and does not strike the eye. It is at least a strong argument on the traditionalist side, that the un-Pauline style of the Pastorals was not commented on by the early Greek Christian critics, as was the un-Pauline style of Hebrews, and the un-Johannine style of the Apocalypse. On the other hand, the peculiarities of expression are not such as a clever imitator of St. Paul's style would introduce.

Taking up, in the first place, the recurrent words, terms and phrases, it will be convenient to divide them into three categories.

A. Terms, or phrases, of the religious life of the Christian Society.
B. Polemical phraseology in reference to false teaching.
C. Favourite terms, or expressions, of the author's.

It is not pretended that this classification can be carried out consistently ; but it seemed to be worth attempting. In particular it

---

[1] Dean Bernard, *Past. Epp.*, p. xxxvi., notes that the ἄπαξ λεγόμενα amount to 176, a number " proportionately twice as great as in any other of St. Paul's letters."

may deserve consideration whether we have not presented to us, in the style of the Pastorals, a new, but not the less true, aspect of St. Paul as a writer, no longer creating a Christian terminology, but freely making use of the phraseology he heard around him, towards the formation of which he had been a principal, but not the only, contributor. On the other hand, in so far as this supposition is true it precludes our making use of the occurrence of certain phrases and words in extant early writings, as proofs that the authors of those writings had read the Pastoral Epistles.

In the following list of terms and phrases, a = 1 Timothy; b = 2 Timothy; c = Titus; the numbers indicate the number of occurrences of the term or phrase in the epistle. When the term or phrase is not peculiar to the Pastorals, a reference is given to its occurrence elsewhere, or "etc." is added.

TERMINOLOGY OF THE CHRISTIAN SOCIETY.

a, b, c.

ἡ ἀλήθεια, in a technical sense : a, 3 ; b, 4 ; c (2 Cor. iv. 2, etc.).

ἡ διδασκαλία : A, The body of doctrine ; absolutely, or with epithets (see ὑγιαίνουσα) : a, 4 ; b, 2 ; c, 3.

ἡ διδασκαλία : B, The act of teaching : a, 3 ; b, c (Rom. xii. 7).

ἡ πίστις, *fides quae creditur* : a, 8 ; b, 2 ; c, 3.

πίστις [κ.] ἀγάπη : a, 4 ; b, 2 ; c (1 Thess. iii. 6, v. 8).

πίστις, ἀγάπη, ὑπομονή : a, [b], c.

ἡ ὑγιαίνουσα διδασκαλία : a, b, c, 2. ὑγιαίνοντες λόγοι : a, b. ὑγιαίνειν τῇ πίστει : c, 2. λόγος ὑγιής : c. *Cf.* νοσῶν : a ; γάγγραινα : b.

ἐπίγνωσις ἀληθείας and ἐπιγινώσκειν τ. ἀλήθειαν : a, 2 ; b, 2 ; c. (Heb. x. 26 ; *cf.* Philem. 6).

[ἡ] εὐσέβεια : a, 7 ; b. κατ᾽ εὐσέβειαν : a, c. εὐσεβῶς ζῆν : b, c. εὐσεβεῖν : a (Acts, 4 ; 2 Pet. 5).

σώφρων : a, c, 3. σωφρονεῖν : c (Mark v. 15 ; Rom. xii. 3 ; 2 Cor. v. 13). σωφρονισμός : b. σωφρονίζειν : c. σωφρόνως : c. σωφροσύνη : a, 2 (Acts xxvi. 25).

ὁ νῦν αἰών : a, b, c.

ἐπιφάνεια : a, b, 3 ; c (2 Thess. ii. 8) (ἐπιφαίνειν : c, 2 ; Luke i. 79 ; Acts xxvii. 20 ; *cf.* Acts ii. 20).

ὠφέλιμος : a, 2 ; b, c.

διάβολοι, adj. : a, b, c.

ἀρνεῖσθαι : a, b, 4 ; c, 2, etc., but not Paul.

a, b.

συνείδησις καθαρά : a, b (συνείδ. ἀγαθή : a, 2 ; Acts xxiii. 1 ; 1 Pet. iii. 16, 21).

καθαρὰ καρδία : a, b.

πίστις ἀνυπόκριτος : a, b.

πίστις κ. ἀγάπη ἡ ἐν Χριστῷ Ἰησοῦ : a, b.

πίστις ἡ ἐν Χριστῷ Ἰησοῦ : a, b ; etc.

καλός : qualifying adj. (not incl. καλὸν ἔργον): a, 9 ; b, 3 (esp. καλὴ στρατεία, a, or στρατιώτης, b, καλὸς ἀγών, a, b) ; etc., but not Paul.

παγὶς : a ; τοῦ διαβόλου : a, b.

φεῦγε · δίωκε δὲ δικαιοσύνην . . . πίστιν ἀγάπην : a, b. ⁓

ἀγωνίζομαι τὸν καλὸν ἀγῶνα : a, b.

παραθήκην φυλάσσειν : a, b, 2.

παρακολουθεῖν διδασκαλίᾳ : a, b.

ἄνθρωπος [τ.] Θεοῦ : a, b.

a, c.

καλὸν ἔργον, καλὰ ἔργα : a, 4 ; c, 4 ; etc., but not Paul.

σεμνός : a, 2 ; c (Phil. iv. 8) ; or σεμνότης : a, 2 ; c.

σωτήρ (of God the Father, not incl. Tit. ii. 13) : a, 3 ; c, 3.

b, c.

εἰς πᾶν ἔργον ἀγαθὸν ἡτοιμασμένον : b.

πρὸς „   „   „   ἐξηρτισμένος : b.

„   „   „   „   ἀδόκιμοι : c.

„   „   „   „   ἑτοίμους : c.

Peculiar to *one* Letter.

ἀπόδεκτον ἐνώπιον τ. Θεοῦ : a, 2.

μιᾶς γυναικὸς ἀνήρ : a, 2 (ἑνὸς ἀνδρὸς γυνή : a,).

ἐπιλαβέσθαι τῆς ζωῆς : a, 2.

μακάριος (of God) : a, 2.

τὸ μυστήριον τῆς πίστεως, or τῆς εὐσεβείας : a, 2.

πίστις κ. ἀγάπη κ. ἁγιασμός, or ἁγνεία : a, 2.

ἐπαισχύνεσθαι τί or τινά : b, 3 (Rom. i. 16, and five other ins.).

ἐκείνη ἡ ἡμέρα (Last Day) : b, 3 (Matt. 2 ; Luke, 3 ; 2 Thess. 1).

καλῶν ἔργων προΐστασθαι : c, 2.

Polemical Phraseology.

ἀληθεία : ἀπεστερημένων τῆς ἀληθείας : a. περὶ τὴν ἀλήθειαν ἠστόχησαν : b. μετάνοιαν εἰς ἐπίγνωσιν ἀληθείας : b. μηδέποτε εἰς ἐπίγνωσιν ἀληθ. ἐλθεῖν δυνάμενα : b. ἀνθίστανται τῇ ἀληθείᾳ : b. ἀπὸ τῆς ἀληθείας τ. ἀκοὴν ἀποστρέψουσιν : b. ἀποστρεφομένων τὴν ἀλήθειαν : c.

νοῦς: διεφθαρμένων . . . τ. νοῦν: a.   κατεφθαρμένοι τ. νοῦν: b. μεμίανται αὐτῶν . . . ὁ νοῦς: c.

πίστις: περὶ τ. πίστιν ἐναυάγησαν: a.   περὶ τ. πίστιν ἠστόχησαν: a. ἀδόκιμοι περὶ τ. πίστιν: b.   ἀποστήσονταί τινες τ. πίστεως: a.   ἀπεπλανή-θησαν ἀπὸ τ. πίστεως: a.   Cf. 1 Tim. i. 5, 19.

συνείδησις: κεκαυστηριασμένων τὴν ἰδίαν συνείδησιν: a.   μεμίανται αὐτῶν . . . ἡ συνείδησις: c.   Cf. 1 Tim. i. 5, 19.

ἀστοχεῖν: a, 2; b.   See ἀλήθεια and πίστις.

ἀνατρέπουσιν τήν τινων πίστιν: b. ὅλους οἴκους ἀνατρέπουσιν: c.   Cf. ἐπὶ καταστροφῇ τῶν ἀκουόντων, b.

βέβηλος: a, 3; b (Heb. xii. 16).   (βέβηλοι κενοφωνίαι: a, b).

γενεαλογίαι: a, c.

ἐκζητήσεις or ζητήσεις: a, 2; b, c.   (μωραὶ ζητήσεις: b, c.)

λογομαχεῖν and λογομαχία: a, b.

ματαιολογία and ματαιολόγος: a, c.   Cf. ζητήσεις . . . μάταιοι, c.

ἔρις: a, c.

μάχη: b, c.

μῦθος: a, 2; b, c (2 Pet. i. 16).

νόμος: a, 2; νομικός: c; νομοδιδάσκαλος: a.

ἐπὶ πλεῖον προκόψουσιν ἀσεβείας: b.   οὐ προκόψουσιν ἐπὶ πλεῖον: b. προκόψουσιν ἐπὶ τὸ χεῖρον: b.

AUTHOR'S FAVOURITE TERMS.

a, b, c.

πιστὸς ὁ λόγος: a, b, c.

πιστὸς ὁ λόγος κ. πάσης ἀποδοχῆς ἄξιος: a, 2.

παραιτοῦ: a, 2; b, c.

οἶκος (household): a, 5; b, 2; c (1 Cor. i. 16, etc.).

περί with accusative: a, 3; b, 2; c (Phil. ii. 23, etc.).

a, b.

χάριν ἔχω; a, b (Luke xvii. 9; Heb. xii. 28).

διαμαρτύρομαι ἐνώπιον τ. Θεοῦ, or τ. Κυρίου: a; b, 2.

εἰς ὃ ἐτέθην ἐγὼ κῆρυξ κ. ἀπόστολος . . . διδάσκαλος: a, b.

χάρις, ἔλεος, εἰρήνη: a, b.

ὧν ἐστίν: a; b, 2.

a, c.

ὡσαύτως: a, 4; c, 2.

ὃ ἐπιστεύθην ἐγώ: a, c.

καιροῖς ἰδίοις: a, 2; c.

διαβεβαιοῦσθαι περί τινος: a, c.

προσέχειν: a, 5; c.   (προσέχειν μύθοις: a, c.)

b, c.

σπούδασον : b, 3 ; c. (σπούδασον ἐλθεῖν : b, 2 ; c.)

περιίστασο : b, c.

δι' ἣν αἰτίαν : b, 2 ; c (Luke viii. 47 ; Acts xxii. 24 ; Heb. ii. 11).

b.

συνκακοπάθησον : b, 2.

The second difference in style by which the Pastoral Epistles are marked off from the earlier letters may be given in the words of Lightfoot.

The Syntax.

(a) "It is stiffer and more regular than in the earlier Epistles, more jointed and less flowing. The clauses are marshalled together, and there is a tendency to parallelism."

e.g., 1 Tim. i. 9, ii. 1, 2, iii. 16, iv. 12, 13, 15, v. 10, vi. 9, 11, 12, 13, 15, 18 ; 2 Tim. ii. 11, 12, iii. 1-8, 10-13, 16, iv. 2, 4, 5, 7 ; Tit. i. 7, 8, 9, ii. 7, 12, iii. 1-3.

(b) "There is a greater sententiousness, an abruptness and positiveness of form. Imperative clauses are frequent.

e.g., 1 Tim. iv. 11, 15, 16, v. 7, 8, 22-25, vi. 2, 6, 11, 20 ; 2 Tim. i. 13, 14, ii. 1, 3, 7, 8, 14, 19, 22, 23, iii. 1, 5, 12, 16."

(*Biblical Essays*, p. 402.)

These differences in syntax are not unconnected with the small variety and paucity of particles which are a negative feature of the Pastorals. But neither characteristic is very astonishing, since in point of fact, the Epistles are of the nature of episcopal charges, authoritative, not argumentative ; enforcing disciplinary regulations, not unfolding theological conceptions, or vindicating personal claims.

We come, in the last place, to state and consider the problem presented by the purely negative characteristic of the style of the Pastoral Epistles, the fact that we do not find in them certain alleged characteristic Pauline words. Those who urge this as a serious argument against the traditional belief as to the authorship of these letters do not seem to make allowance for the fact that they are *ex hypothesi* dealing with a real man—not a machine; a man who had travelled much, and had read much ; who was constantly coming into contact with fresh people, constantly confronted with fresh problems of practical life. The vocabulary of such a man is not likely to remain unaffected in its contents or use. Add to this, that each of the other letters which are ascribed to him arose out of special circumstances, and deals almost exclusively with those special circumstances, and that the circumstances which called forth the letters to Timothy and Titus were, confessedly, quite different from those out of which any of the other Pauline letters arose. When these obvious facts are considered, it is difficult to treat seriously an argument which assumes that St. Paul was provided with only one set of words and terms; unalterable, no matter to whom, or on what subject, he was writing.

It is not thus that non-Biblical compositions are critically examined. We do not demand that Shakespeare's *Sonnets* or *Cymbeline* should exhibit a certain percentage of *Hamlet* words. And the argument becomes all the more unreasonable when one thinks how very small in extent is the extant literary work of St. Paul: less than 150 small octavo pages in Westcott and Hort's edition, and of these the Pastorals occupy only fifteen. If we had been privileged to hear St. Paul's sermons, or to listen to his conversation, how many Pauline words, as shown in a concordance, should we have heard?

Antecedently, we should not expect that an author's favourite expressions would be distributed over the pages of his book like the spots on a wall-paper pattern; nor is this notion confirmed when we examine the list of Pauline words missing from the Pastorals, as given by Holtzmann (*Pastoralbriefe*, p. 98, *sqq.*) and less fully by von Soden (*Hand-Commentar*, p. 177 *sqq.*).

In the complete list of verbs, nouns, adjectives and adverbs, fifty in all, as printed below, each group of cognate words, bracketed together, is for argument's sake, treated as a unit. And the numbers indicate the number of times the word occurs in St. Paul's Epistles. The words that are spaced are those, which after an examination of a concordance, can be plausibly claimed as characteristically Pauline; that is to say, they are of comparative frequent occurrence, and are found in at least three groups of his Epistles. It must be allowed that the absence of all of these is surprising. The simplest explanation is that some of them had passed out of St. Paul's ordinary vocabulary; and that, in the case of others, the subject matter of the Pastorals did not demand their use. Some of them, obviously, belong to the vocabulary of certain theological conceptions, others to that of a writer's temperament and temper.

For the purpose of analysis, it will be convenient to think of the other ten epistles of St. Paul as falling into four groups, *viz.*:—

(i.) 1 and 2 Thessalonians.

(ii.) Rom., 1 Cor., 2 Cor., Gal.

(iii.) Eph., Col., Philem.

(iv.) Philippians, which though it is one of group iii., as being one of the epistles of the first Roman captivity, yet inasmuch as it was written somewhat later, may be considered apart.

ἄδικος, 3, ἀκαθαρσία, 9, ἀκροβυστία, 19, (ἀποκαλύπτειν, 13, ἀποκάλυψις, 13), ἀπολύτρωσις, 7, γνωρίζειν, 18, διαθήκη, 9 (δικαιοῦν, 27, δικαίωμα, 5), δικαιοσύνη Θεοῦ, 9, δοκεῖν, 18, ἕκαστος, 42, (ἐλευθερία, 7, ἐλεύθερος, 16, ἐλευθεροῦν, 5), (ἐνέργεια, 8, ἐνεργεῖν, 17, ἐνέργημα, 2, ἐνεργής, 2), ἔξεστιν, 5, ἔργα νόμου, 9, κἀγώ, 27, καταργεῖν, 25, κατεργάζεσθαι, 20, (καυχᾶσθαι, 35, καύχημα, 10, καύχησις, 10), κρείσσων, 4, μείζων, 4, μικρός, 4, μωρία, 5, (ὁμοιοῦν, 1, ὁμοίωμα, 5), ὁμοίως, 4, ὁρᾶν, 10, οὐρανός, 21, παράδοσις, 5, παραλαμβάνειν, 11, πατὴρ ἡμῶν, 7, outside salutations, πείθειν, 2, (περισσεία, 3, περισσεύειν, 26, περίσσευμα, 2, περισσός, 2, περισσότερος, 6), περιπατεῖν, 32, (πεποιθέναι, 12, πεποίθησις, 6), πλεονάζειν, 8, (πλεονεκτεῖν, 5, πλεονέκτης, 4, πλεονεξία, 6), οἱ πολλοί, 8, (πρᾶγμα, 4, πρᾶξις, 3, πράσσειν, 18), σπλάγχνα, 8, (συνεργεῖν, 3, συνεργός, 12), σῶμα, 91, (ταπεινός, 3, ταπεινοῦν, 4), (τέλειος, 8, τελειότης, 1, τελειοῦν, 1), υἱοθεσία, 5, υἱὸς τ. Θεοῦ, 17, (ὑπακοή, 11, ὑπακούειν, 11), (φρονεῖν, 24, φρόνημα, 4, φρόνησις, 1, φρόνιμος, 5), φύσις, 11, χαρίζεσθαι, 16, χρηστός, 3.

Of the fifty characteristically Pauline words no less than eleven do not occur in groups i., iii., iv., *viz.*, ἄδικος, δικαιοῦν, δικαιοσύνη Θεοῦ, ἔξεστιν, ἔργα νόμου, μείζων, μικρός, μωρία, ὁμοίως, πείθειν, οἱ πολλοί. Of these, ἄδικος is not found in 2 Cor. or Gal.; δικαιοῦν not in 2 Cor. though twice in the Pastorals; while δικαίωμα only occurs in Rom.; δικαιοσύνη Θεοῦ not in 1 Cor. or Gal.; ἔξεστιν not in Rom. or Gal.; ἔργα νόμου not in 1 Cor. or 2 Cor.; μείζων not in 2 Cor. or Gal.; μικρός not in Rom.; μωρία only in 1 Cor. (while μωρός, also in 1 Cor. (4), occurs in the Pastorals twice); ὁμοίως not in 2 Cor. or Gal.; πείθειν not in Rom. or 1 Cor.; οἱ πολλοί not in Gal., but five times in Rom. It is obvious, from these facts, that these eleven words are not characteristically Pauline.

Of the others, four do not occur in groups i. and iii., *viz.*, δοκεῖν, κρείσσων, ὁμοιοῦν, ταπεινός. Of these, δοκεῖν not in Rom.; κρείσσων not in Rom., 2 Cor. or Gal.; ὁμοιοῦν not in 1 Cor., 2 Cor. or Gal.; and ταπεινός not in 1 Cor. or Gal.

Seven do not occur in groups i. and iv., *viz.*, ἀκροβυστία, ἀπολύτρωσις, διαθήκη, ἐλευθερία, υἱοθεσία, φύσις, χρηστός. Of these, ἀκροβυστία not in 2 Cor.; ἀπολύτρωσις not in 2 Cor. or Gal. Of the ἐλευθερία group, ἐλεύθερος and ἐλευθεροῦν are not in 2 Cor., and ἐλευθεροῦν is not in 1 Cor. υἱοθεσία not in 1 Cor. or 2 Cor.; φύσις not in 2 Cor.; χρηστός not in 2 Cor. or Gal.; leaving διαθήκη (once in iii.) and ἐλευθερία (twice in iii.) as the only words that are evenly distributed in group ii.

Among those which do not occur in group i., *viz.*, γνωρίζειν, κατεργάζεσθαι, σπλάγχνα, τέλειος, φρονεῖν, χαρίζεσθαι, we notice that of the twenty instances of κατεργάζεσθαι seventeen occur in Rom. and 2 Cor.; σπλάγχνα, not found in Rom., 1 Cor. or Gal., occurs three times in Philem.; none of the τέλειος group is found in 2 Cor. or Gal., while τελειοῦν and τελειότης are absent from Rom. and 1 Cor. Of the thirty-four instances of the φρονεῖν group, one of which is 1 Tim. vi. 17, Rom. and Phil. account for twenty-five; φρόνημα is only found in Rom., φρόνησις only in Eph., φρόνιμος only in Rom., 1 Cor., and 2 Cor.; leaving γνωρίζειν and χαρίζεσθαι fairly representative words.

It remains to notice a few of these characteristically Pauline words which are not found in Philippians, *viz.*: ἀκαθαρσία, καταργεῖν, ὁρᾶν, παράδοσις, πλεονεκτεῖν, and υἱὸς τ. Θεοῦ. ἀκαθαρσία is not found in 1 Cor.; καταργεῖν does, in point of fact, occur in 2 Tim.; ὁρᾶν, found in 1 Tim. iii. 16, does not occur in 2 Cor. or Gal., παράδοσις not in Rom. or 2 Cor.; none of the πλεονεκτεῖν group is found in Gal., while πλεονεκτεῖν and πλεονεξία are both absent from 1 Cor., and πλεονέκτης from 2 Cor. Of the seventeen places where our Lord is called υἱὸς [τ. Θεοῦ,] eleven are found in Rom. and Gal.

In the whole list, then, there are twenty-seven words, or more than half, the absence of which from the Pastorals obviously need call for no remark. The following facts with regard to the distribution of some of the others are suggestive; and diminish, if they do not wholly remove, the difficulty of the problem before us. ἕκαστος (42) occurs twenty-two times in 1 Cor.; of the ἐνέργεια group (29) three members are not found in Rom., 2 Cor., or Gal., *i.e.*, ἐνέργεια, ἐνέργημα, ἐνεργής; neither is ἐνέργεια found in 1 Cor. Of the twenty-seven occurrences of κἀγώ, more than half, nineteen, are found in 1 Cor. and 2 Cor. Of the καυχᾶσθαι group (55) more than half, twenty-nine, occur in 2 Cor; παραλαμβάνειν (11) is not found in Rom. or 2 Cor. πατὴρ ἡμῶν, apart from its common use in salutations, is found three times in 1 Thess., twice in 2 Thess., and once each in Gal. and Phil. Of the περισσεία group (39), none is found in Gal.; three not in 1 Cor., *i.e.*, περισσεία, περισσός and περίσσευμα; two not in Rom., *i.e.*, περίσσευμα and περισσότερος. On the other hand, nearly half, seventeen, of the total is found in 2 Cor. (which has also περισσοτέρως seven times), seven occur in 1 Cor. and five in Phil. Neither πεποιθέναι nor πεποίθησις occurs in 1 Cor.; πεποίθησις not in Rom. or Gal. Here again seven cases belong to 2 Cor. and seven to Phil. Of the πρᾶγμα group (25), thirteen belong to Rom., which has ten out of the eighteen occurrences of πράσσειν. Neither of the συνεργεῖν group (15) occurs in Gal.; yet its distribution is otherwise fairly even. The distribution of σῶμα (91) is remarkable. Just more than half, forty-six, of its occurrences are found in 1 Cor.; chap. vi. having eight, chap. xii., eighteen, chap. xv., nine. Neither ὑπακοή nor ὑπακούειν occur in 1 Cor. or Gal.; ὑπακούειν not in 2 Cor.

An analysis of the list of Pauline particles that are not found in the Pastoral Epistles yields the same general result; that is to say, the great majority of them are confined to group ii. of the Epistles; and that is explained by the fact that that group is the most argu-mentative and controversial, and the subject matter demands the employment of inferential and similar particles. Thus ἄρα (15), ἕνεκεν (6), ἴδε (1) ἰδού (9, of which 6 are in 2 Cor.), ποῦ (10, 8 of which are in 1 Cor.), παρά, acc. (14), are not found outside group ii.; ἔπειτα (11, 7 of which are in 1 Cor.), μήπως (10), οὔτε (34, of which 22 are in 4 verses), are only in group ii. and in 1 Thess. The following also do not occur in groups i and iii.: ἄχρι (ii. 12, iv. 2), οὔπω (ii. 2, iv. 1) πάλιν (ii. 25, iv. 3). The following do not occur in group iii. διότι (10: i. 3, ii. 6, iv. 1), ἔμπροσθεν (7: i. 4, ii. 2, iv. 1), ἔτι (15: i. 1, ii. 13, iv. 1). The distribution of the others is as follows: ἀντί (5: i, 2, ii. 2, iii. 1), ἄρα οὖν (12: i. 2, ii. 9, iii, 1), διό (27, i. 2, ii. 18, iii. 6, iv. 1), ὅπως (9: i. 1, ii. 7, iii. 1), οὐκέτι (15: ii. 13, iii. 2), ἐν παντί (16: i. 1, ii. 11, of which 10 are in 2 Cor.; iii. 2, iv. 2), ποτέ (does occur in Tit., otherwise 19: i. 1, ii. 8, iii. 9, iv. 1), ὥσπερ (14: i. 1 ii. 13), σύν (38: i. 4, ii. 21, iii. 9, iv. 4). There are twenty-four char-acteristically Pauline particles in the above enumeration. Of these, ten are not found in group i., fifteen are not found in group iii., and in fact, in the epistles of the first Roman captivity (groups iii. and iv.), which are about half as long again as the Pastoral Epistles, particles are very sparingly used; διό, ἐν παντί and σύν alone being at all common. It may be proper to note here in connexion with the absence of σύν from the Pastorals, that twice, in 2 Tim. iv. 11 and Tit. iii. 15, μετά is used where the other Pauline letters have σύν; other-wise the usage of μετά in the Pastorals does not differ from that of St. Paul elsewhere. Another noteworthy feature in the Pastorals is the absence of the article, especially before common Christian terms. This peculiarity, and also the deficiency in particles, may be possibly due to the amanuensis employed by St. Paul at this time. See Dean Bernard, *Past. Epp.* p. xli., and Milligan, *Thessalonians*, p. 126.

Historical Setting of the Epistles.

It is altogether unneccessary for any one now to restate the arguments which prove that the references to persons and places in the Pastorals cannot be accommodated to the history of St. Paul and of his companions as given in the Acts. The "historical contradictions" are marshalled with crushing force by Lightfoot in his *Biblical Essays*, p. 403 *sqq.* Critics of the anti-traditional school who accept, as genuine Pauline fragments, those sections of the Pastorals in which the personal and local references occur are obliged to allocate these references to different parts of the Acts ; and, even so, the explanations given are forced and unconvincing. It must then be clearly understood that our claim of the Pastorals for St. Paul is based on the assumption that his ministry was prolonged for at least two years beyond the date of the close of the Acts. If St. Paul was martyred immediately, or very soon, after the expiration of the two years' confinement mentioned in Acts xxviii. 30, then he did not write the Pastoral Epistles or any portion of them. This is a vital point ; and demands at least a brief discussion of the main arguments in favour of the traditional opinion. Supposing that the Pastorals were not in our hands, and the question were asked, Was the two years' confinement in Rome mentioned in Acts xxviii. 30, followed by St. Paul's execution, or by his release ?—the answer must be that all the *positive* evidence available is in favour of the latter alternative. There are three lines of argument : (1) the way in which the Acts ends ; (2) the evidence of the epistles written during, or towards the end, of those two years ; (3) external testimony.

(1) It ought to be unnecessary to observe that the author of the Acts knew what happened at the end of those two years. We can only guess why he stopped where he did ; yet some guesses have more probability than others. There were limits to the size of books in those days. On the supposition that St. Luke knew of a subsequent ministry of his master's, the close of the Roman captivity would be a suitable point at which to bring vol. i. of the Acts to a conclusion, whether regard be had to considerations of space, or of literary fitness ; the arrival at Rome being the fulfilment of the apostle's intention announced in Acts xix. 21. On the other hand, if St. Luke knew that St. Paul's two years' confinement had been followed at once by his execution, the historian's omission to mention

it cannot be accounted for. A brief record would have been all that was necessary, and this would not have added unduly to the length of the book.

Salmon's explanation (*Introduction*, p. 312) that "why St. Luke has told us no more is, that he knew no more ; and that he knew no more, because at the time nothing more had happened—in other words, that the book of the Acts was written a little more than two years after Paul's arrival at Rome," will not commend itself to many scholars. It seems more natural to suppose that both the Gospel and the Acts were published after St. Paul's death. Literary men do not always succeed in completing their designs before they die ; and the later the date we assign to Acts, the greater is the probability that St. Luke died before he had reduced to literary form his memories of the Apostle's post-Roman-captivity history.

Passing now to an examination on this point of the third group of St. Paul's Epistles, the evidence afforded by them is distinctly favourable to the supposition that St. Paul was released after the two years of Acts xxviii. 30. We must of course avoid the error into which some fall, of imagining that every foreboding or declared intention recorded in a narrative, or preserved in a published letter, would have been suppressed by the editor if it had not been realised. And accordingly we can only infer from the tone of Philippians and Philemon that, in St. Paul's judgment, when he wrote these letters, the prospect of his release was favourable. No other inference can be drawn from " I know that I shall abide, yea, and abide with you all, for your progress and joy in the faith " (Phil. i. 25) ; " I trust in the Lord that I myself also shall come shortly " (ii. 24) ; " Prepare me also a lodging : for I hope that through your prayers I shall be granted unto you " (Philem. 22). Contrast with these passages the tone of 2 Timothy, which is that of a man who knew that his days were numbered, and that the end was not far off.

What seems to be a natural conclusion from the internal evidence of Acts xxviii. and of Philippians and Philemon is confirmed by the tradition of the early Church as it is expressed by Eusebius, *H. E.*, ii., 22 : "Paul is said (λόγος ἔχει), after having defended himself to have set forth again upon the ministry of preaching, and to have entered the same city a second time, and to have there ended his life by martyrdom. Whilst then a prisoner, he wrote the Second Epistle to Timothy, in which he both mentions his first defence, and his impending death." It is to be noted that there is no contrary tradition ; nor is it easy to see what end could have been served by the invention of this one.

There are two passages in earlier writers which are adduced as proof that St. Paul at one time visited Spain. Since it is impossible to find room for such a journey within the period covered by the Acts, these passages, if accepted as proofs of the expedition to Spain, are therefore proofs of a missionary activity of St. Paul subsequent to the date of the close of the Acts. In the Letter of Clement of Rome to the Corinthians, § 5, the writer speaks of Peter and Paul as contemporary martyrs ; and Paul he describes as κῆρυξ γενόμενος ἔν τε τῇ ἀνατολῇ καὶ ἐν τῇ δύσει . . . δικαιοσύνην διδάξας ὅλον τὸν κόσμον καὶ ἐπὶ τὸ τέρμα τῆς δύσεως ἐλθών.

It is difficult to believe that a native of Rome, writing from Rome, would speak of the world's capital as ἡ δύσις or τὸ τέρμα τῆς δύσεως ; nor did Corinth lie so far to the east of Rome as to justify such a rhetorical expression (see Lightfoot's note *in loc.*). Nor can we argue from the opening of the following chapter—" Unto these men of holy lives was gathered (συνηθροίσθη) a vast multitude "—that Clement meant to date the fury of Neronic persecution as subsequent to the martyrdom of St. Paul. Writing about thirty years after " the great tribulation," he mentions the martyrs in order of dignity. In any case, he mentions Peter's death before that of Paul ; yet this was never considered an argument against the tradition that the two apostles were martyred together ; nor would it be felt as a serious objection to the recent theory that St. Peter outlived St. Paul by many years.

The following passage from the Muratorian Canon, in its obscure simplicity, reads like a fragment of a genuine tradition rather than a literary figment based on Rom. xv. 28 : " Acta autem omnium apostolorum sub uno libro scripta sunt. Lucas optime Theophilo comprendit, quia sub praesentia eius singula gerebantur, sicuti et semote passionem [*perh.* semota passione] Petri euidenter declarat, sed et *profectionem* [*perh.* profectione] *Pauli ab urbe ad Spaniam proficiscentis* " (text as given by Westcott, *Canon. N.T.*, p. 535). The argument is unaffected even if the words from " passionem " be derived from the early second century *Actus Petri cum Simone.* See James, *Apocrypha Anecdota*, ii., xi., and Dean Bernard, *Pastoral Epp.*, p. xxx. These considerations force us to the conclusion that the assumption that St. Paul's life ended where St. Luke's history terminates is arbitrary, and contrary to the evidence that is available. It remains to present to the reader a conjectural outline (based on Lightfoot's *Biblical Essays*, p. 223) of St. Paul's movements between his release and his second Roman imprisonment.

(1) A journey from Rome to Asia Minor. It is natural to suppose

that he visited Philippi and Colossæ, in accordance with the intimations cited above from Phil. and Philem. Perhaps he now visited Crete.

(2) A journey to Spain; perhaps passing through Dalmatia and Gaul (?) (2 Tim. iv. 10). Possibly on this journey he became aware of the convenience of Nicopolis in Epirus as a centre for work.

(3) Last journey Eastward. Visits Ephesus (1 Tim. i. 3). The dispute with Hymenæus and Alexander the smith, and the services of Onesiphorus (1 Tim. i. 20; 2 Tim. i. 18, iv. 14) perhaps now took place. Leaves Timothy in charge of the Church at Ephesus. Visits Macedonia (1 Tim. i. 3).

[1 Timothy.]

Visits Crete; leaves Titus in charge; returns to Asia (as hoped in 1 Tim. iii. 14, iv. 13).

[Titus.]

Passes through Miletus (2 Tim. iv. 20), Troas (2 Tim. iv. 13), where perhaps he was arrested, Corinth (2 Tim. iv. 20). In any case he never reached Nicopolis as anticipated in Tit. iii. 12. It is here assumed that the winter mentioned in 2 Tim. iv. 21, is the same as that of Tit. iii. 12.

[2 Timothy.]

EXTERNAL EVIDENCE.

With regard to the external attestation to the Pastoral Epistles, it must be acknowledged that some early heretics, who acknowledged the genuineness of the other letters attributed to St. Paul, rejected these. Basilides, who flourished in the reign of Hadrian (117-138 A.D.), is the first who is said to have done so. Clement Al. (*Strom.* ii. 11) states that some, Gnostics apparently, were actuated in this decision by dislike of the expression ἡ ψευδώνυμος γνῶσις in 1 Tim. vi. 20: ὑπὸ ταύτης ἐλεγχόμενοι τῆς φωνῆς οἱ ἀπὸ τῶν αἱρέσεων τὰς πρὸς Τιμόθεον ἀθετοῦσιν ἐπιστολάς. On the other hand, the extant fragments of another Gnostic, Heracleon, contain an allusion to 2 Tim. ii. 13: ἀρνήσασθαι ἑαυτὸν οὐδέποτε δύναται (Clem. Al., *Strom.* iv. 9). The Canon of Marcion, which contained only his own edition of the Gospel according to St. Luke and ten of St. Paul's epistles, of course did not include the Pastorals; but Tatian (died about 170) did not wholly follow him in this, since he regarded Titus as certainly genuine. "Hanc vel maxime Apostoli pronuntiandam credidit, parvi pendens Marcionis, et aliorum qui cum eo in hac parte consentiunt, assertionem" (Jerome, *Prol. in Tit.*). In the same context, St.

Jerome declares that these adverse judgments were not critical in any true sense, but merely arbitrary : "cum haeretica auctoritate pronuntient et dicant, Illa epistola Pauli est, haec non est". However that may be, there is at least no trace in the writings of the Church controversialists of arguments of a critical nature; whereas in the dispute as to the authorship of Hebrews, Clement Al. and Origen were compelled to discuss the problem presented by its un-Pauline style. In any case, the fact that the rejection of the Pastorals by some heretics was noted amounts to a positive testimony in their favour by the contemporary Church.

From the time of Irenæus, Clement Al. and Tertullian [1]—that is, practically from the time that N.T. books are quoted by their author's names—until the year 1804, when Schmidt in his *Introduction* denied the genuineness of 1 Timothy, no one, Christian or non-Christian, doubted that the Pastoral Epistles were genuine letters of the Apostle Paul. They are included in all MSS., Versions and Lists of the Pauline Epistles without exception, and in the same order (*i.e.*, 1 Tim., 2 Tim., Tit.). An interesting exception as regards the order meets us in the Muratorian Fragment : "Uerum ad Philemonem unam, et ad Titum unam, et ad Timotheum duas pro affectu et dilectione ; in honore tamen ecclesiae catholicae in ordinatione ecclesiasticae disciplinae sanctificatae sunt". The composer of this catalogue here arranges the groups of four personal letters of St. Paul in rough chronological order. As 2 Tim. was obviously the last letter that St. Paul wrote, the two to Timothy are placed last, Titus being joined to them as evidently dealing with kindred topics.

It remains that the reader should have placed before him the traces, more or less distinct, of the Pastoral Epistles in the writings of the Apostolic Fathers, and of the pre-Irenæus period.

CLEMENT OF ROME. *Ad Cor.* 1. (A.D. 95.)

§ 1 (1 Tim. vi. 1). ὥστε τὸ . . . ὄνομα ὑμῶν μεγάλως βλασφημηθῆναι.

§ 1 (1 Tim. v. 17). τιμὴν τὴν καθήκουσαν ἀπονέμοντες τοῖς . . . πρεσβυτέροις.

§ 1 (1 Tim. ii. 9, 11 ; Tit. ii. 4). γυναιξίν . . . στεργούσας καθηκόντως τοὺς ἄνδρας ἑαυτῶν ἔν τε τῷ κανόνι τῆς ὑποταγῆς ὑπαρχούσας τὰ κατὰ τὸν οἶκον σεμνῶς οἰκουργεῖν ἐδιδάσκετε, πάνυ σωφρονούσας.

---

[1] *e.g.*, Irenæus, *Haer*. Praef. ; i. 16, 3 ; ii. 14, 7 ; iii. 3, 3 ; iii. 3, 4 ; iv. 16, 3. Clem. Al., *Strom*. i. p. 350. Tert., *de Praescr*. 6, 25. *Adv. Marcion*. v. 21.

§ 2 (1 Tim. vi. 8). τοῖς ἐφοδίοις τοῦ Θεοῦ ἀρκούμενοι.

* § 2 (Tit. iii. 1). ἕτοιμοι εἰς πᾶν ἔργον ἀγαθόν.

§ 7 (1 Tim. vi. 12 ; 2 Tim. iv. 7). ὁ αὐτὸς ἡμῖν ἀγὼν ἐπίκειται.

§ 7 (1 Tim. ii. 3, v. 4). ἴδωμεν . . . τὶ προσδεκτὸν ἐνώπιον τοῦ ποιήσαντος ἡμᾶς.

* § 26 (Tit. ii. 10). αὐτῷ δουλευσάντων ἐν πεποιθήσει πίστεως ἀγαθῆς.

§ 29 (1 Tim. ii. 8). προσέλθωμεν οὖν αὐτῷ ἐν ὁσιότητι ψυχῆς, ἁγνὰς καὶ ἀμιάντους χεῖρας αἴροντες πρὸς αὐτόν.

* § 32 (Tit. iii. 5-7). πάντες οὖν ἐδοξάσθησαν . . . οὐ δι' αὐτῶν ἢ τῶν ἔργων αὐτῶν ἢ τῆς δικαιοπραγίας ἧς κατειργάσαντο, ἀλλὰ διὰ τοῦ θελήματος αὐτοῦ.

* § 37 (1 Tim. i. 18). στρατευσώμεθα οὖν . . . ἐν τοῖς ἀμώμοις προστάγμασιν αὐτοῦ.

§ 42 (1 Tim. iii. 10). καθίστανον τὰς ἀπαρχὰς αὐτῶν, δοκιμάσαντες τῷ πνεύματι, εἰς ἐπισκόπους καὶ διακόνους.

* § 45 (2 Tim. i. 3). τῶν ἐν καθαρᾷ συνειδήσει λατρευόντων.

§ 47 (1 Tim. vi. 1). ὥστε καὶ βλασφημίας ἐπιφέρεσθαι τῷ ὀνόματι Κυρίου.

§ 55 (2 Tim. ii. 1). γυναῖκες ἐνδυναμωθεῖσαι διὰ τῆς χάριτος τοῦ Θεοῦ.

§ 55 (1 Tim. i. 17). Θεὸν τῶν αἰώνων.

§ 61 (1 Tim. i. 17). βασιλεῦ τῶν αἰώνων.

To these we may add, perhaps, the prayer for Kings in §§ 60, 61, in conformity with the direction given in 1 Tim. ii. 2; Tit. iii 2, and in those places only of the N.T.

On a review of these passages, it must in candour be admitted that those marked with an asterisk seem to be the only ones that suggest a literary dependence on the Pastorals. The others, it may be plausibly maintained, are simply illustrations of that current religious phraseology which the Pastorals themselves reflect. Taken all together, they prove that Clement's mind was at home in the religious world to which the Pastorals belong; but while the present writer believes that Clement was as familiar with these letters as he was with 1 Cor., he cannot affirm such a position to be wholly free from uncertainty.

IGNATIUS (circ. A.D. 110).

* *Magn.* § 8 (Tit. i. 14, iii. 9). μὴ πλανᾶσθε ταῖς ἑτεροδοξίαις μηδὲ μυθεύμασιν τοῖς παλαιοῖς ἀνωφελέσιν οὖσιν· εἰ γὰρ μέχρι νῦν κατὰ ἰουδαϊσμὸν ζῶμεν, ὁμολογοῦμεν χάριν μὴ εἰληφέναι.

§ 11 (1 Tim. i. 1). πεπληροφόρησθε ἐν τῇ γεννήσει κ. τ. πάθει κ. τ. ἀναστάσει τῇ γενομένῃ ἐν καιρῷ τῆς ἡγεμονίας Ποντίου Πιλάτου · πραχθέντα ἀληθῶς κ. βεβαίως ὑπὸ Ἰησοῦ Χριστοῦ, τῆς ἐλπίδος ἡμῶν.

Trall. Inscr. and § 2 have also *Jesus Christ our hope.*

Polyc. § 2 (2 Tim. ii. 25). τοὺς λοιμοτέρους ἐν πραΰτητι ὑπό- τασσε.

*§ 2 (2 Tim. iv. 5; ii. 5; i. 10; i. 5, 12). νῆφε, ὡς Θεοῦ ἀθλητής · τὸ θέμα ἀφθαρσία καὶ ζωὴ αἰώνιος, περὶ ἧς καὶ σὺ πέπεισαι.

§ 3 (1 Tim. i. 3, vi. 3). ἑτεροδιδασκαλοῦντες μή σε κατα- πλησσέτωσαν.

*§ 3 (2 Tim. ii. 12). ἕνεκεν Θεοῦ πάντα ὑπομένειν ἡμᾶς δεῖ, ἵνα καὶ αὐτὸς ἡμᾶς ὑπομείνῃ.

§ 3 (1 Tim. i. 17). τὸν ἀόρατον.

*§ 4 (1 Tim. vi. 1, 2). δούλους καὶ δούλας μὴ ὑπερηφάνει · ἀλλὰ μηδὲ αὐτοὶ φυσιούσθωσαν, ἀλλ᾽ εἰς δόξαν Θεοῦ πλέον δουλευ- έτωσαν.

*§ 6 (2 Tim. ii. 4). ἀρέσκετε ᾧ στρατεύεσθε, ἀφ᾽ οὗ καὶ τὰ ὀψώνια κομίζεσθε.

§ 7 (Tit. iii. 1; 2 Tim. ii. 21). ἕτοιμοί ἐστε εἰς εὐποιίαν Θεῷ ἀνήκουσαν.

The echoes of the Pastorals are especially remarkable in the Epistle to Polycarp; and it is peculiarly worthy of remark that in this letter, which was admittedly a personal communication from Ignatius to Polycarp, the writer passes from exhortations to Polycarp himself—and those too of a very delicate nature—to general ex- hortations addressed to the whole Church. Contrast *e.g.* § 5 with § 6; and in the middle of a section addressed to the whole Church he interposes a personal appeal to Polycarp. This illustrates admir- ably a feature in the Pastorals which has been alleged as a serious objection to their acceptation as genuine letters; *i.e.* the interming- ling of personal matter with directions and exhortations addressed to the Church.

POLYCARP. *Ad Phil. (circ.* A.D. 110).

*§ 4 (1 Tim. vi. 10, 7). ἀρχὴ δὲ πάντων χαλεπῶν φιλαρ- γυρία. εἰδότες οὖν ὅτι οὐδὲν εἰσηνέγκαμεν εἰς τὸν κόσμον, ἀλλ᾽ οὐδὲ ἐξενεγκεῖν τι ἔχομεν.

§ 5 (2 Tim. ii. 12). ἐὰν πολιτευσώμεθα ἀξίως αὐτοῦ, καὶ συμβασ- ιλεύσομεν αὐτῷ.

§ 8 (1 Tim. i. 1). προσκαρτερῶμεν τῇ ἐλπίδι ἡμῶν . . . ὅς ἐστι Χριστὸς Ἰησοῦς.

* § 9 (2 Tim. iv. 10).   οὐ γὰρ τὸν νῦν ἠγάπησαν αἰῶνα.

* § 12 (1 Tim. ii. 2, iv. 15).   *Orate* etiam *pro regibus et potestatibus et principibus* . . . ut fructus vester *manifestus sit in omnibus.*

THE ACTS OF MARTYRDOM OF POLYCARP (A.D. 155 OR 156).

§ 10 (1 Tim. ii. 2; Tit. iii. 1).   δεδιδάγμεθα γὰρ ἀρχαῖς καὶ ἐξουσίαις ὑπὸ Θεοῦ τεταγμέναις τιμὴν . . . ἀπονέμειν.

There can be no question that in the Letter of Polycarp to the Philippians we have express citations from 1 and 2 Timothy. It is, to say the least, difficult to believe that a man like Polycarp, who had been a disciple of the Apostle John, and who, when he wrote this letter, was bishop of Smyrna and in full vigour of life, would have made such honourable use of letters which had been compiled by an unknown Paulinist a few years before. We regard the evidence of Polycarp as a fact of capital importance; for it removes any possible doubt that may hang over inferences drawn from Ignatius; and it supports us in our belief that the Pastoral Epistles were also known to Clement of Rome. For the sake of completeness, we may add echoes of the Letters in other extant second century Christian Literature. The three passages cited from the Epistle of Barnabas are not of necessity based on our Letters; and the same may be said of the four quotations from Justin Martyr, with the possible exception of that from *Dial.* § 47.

THE SO-CALLED SECOND EPISTLE OF CLEMENT OF ROME
(circ. 120-140 A.D.).

§ 7 (2 Tim. ii. 4, 5).   ἀγωνισώμεθα, εἰδότες ὅτι . . . οὐ πάντες στεφανοῦνται, εἰ μὴ οἱ πολλὰ κοπιάσαντες καὶ καλῶς ἀγωνισάμενοι . . . ὁ τὸν φθαρτὸν ἀγῶνα ἀγωνιζόμενος, ἐὰν εὑρεθῇ φθείρων . . . ἔξω βάλλεται τοῦ σταδίου.

§ 8 (1 Tim. vi. 14, 12).   τηρήσατε τὴν σάρκα ἁγνὴν καὶ τὴν σφραγῖδα ἄσπιλον, ἵνα τὴν ζωὴν ἀπολάβωμεν.

§ 17 (Tit. ii. 12).   μὴ ἀντιπαρελκώμεθα ἀπὸ τῶν κοσμικῶν ἐπιθυμιῶν.

§ 20 (1 Tim. i. 17).   τῷ μόνῳ Θεῷ ἀοράτῳ . . . ἡ δόξα κ.τ.λ.

THE SO-CALLED EPISTLE OF BARNABAS (A.D. 70-132).

§ 7 (2 Tim. iv. 1).   εἰ οὖν ὁ υἱὸς τοῦ Θεοῦ, ὢν Κύριος καὶ μέλλων κρίνειν ζῶντας καὶ νεκρούς, ἔπαθεν.

§ 12 (1 Tim. iii. 14).   ἡ παράβασις διὰ τοῦ ὄφεως ἐν Εὖᾳ ἐγένετο.

§ 12 (1 Tim. iii. 16).   υἱὸς τοῦ Θεοῦ . . . ἐν σαρκὶ φανερωθείς·

The Epistle to Diognetus (circ. A.D. 150).

* § 4 (1 Tim. iii. 16). τὸ δὲ τῆς ἰδίας αὐτῶν θ ε ο σ ε β ε ί α ς μ υ σ-
τ ή ρ ι ο ν μὴ προσδοκήσῃς δύνασθαι παρὰ ἀνθρώπου μαθεῖν.

* § 9 (Tit. iii. 4). ἦλθε δὲ ὁ καιρὸς ὃν Θεὸς προέθετο λοιπὸν φανερῶσαι
τὴν ἑαυτοῦ χ ρ η σ τ ό τ η τ α καὶ δύναμιν (ὦ τῆς ὑπερβαλλούσης φ ι λ α ν θ ρ ω-
π ί α ς καὶ ἀγάπης τοῦ Θεοῦ), οὐκ ἐμίσησεν ἡμᾶς . . . ἐ λ ε ῶ ν αὐτὸς τὰς
ἡμετέρας ἁμαρτίας ἀνεδέξατο, αὐτὸς τὸν ἴδιον υἱὸν ἀπέδοτο λύτρον ὑπὲρ ἡμῶν.

§ 11 (1 Tim. iii. 16). [μαθηταῖς] οἷς ἐφανέρωσεν ὁ Λόγος φανείς.
This and the following section do not really belong to the Epistle.

Justin Martyr (circ. 140 A.D.).

Dial. § 7 (1 Tim. iv. 1). τ ὰ τ ῆ ς π λ ά ν η ς π ν ε ύ μ α τ α καὶ
δ α ι μ ό ν ι α δοξολογοῦσιν.

§ 35 (1 Tim. iv. 1). ἐκ τοῦ τοιούτους εἶναι ἄνδρας, ὁμολογοῦντας ἑαυτοὺς
εἶναι Χριστιανοὺς καὶ . . . Ἰησοῦν ὁμολογεῖν . . . Χριστόν, καὶ μὴ τὰ ἐκείνου
διδάγματα διδάσκοντας ἀλλὰ τὰ ἀπὸ τ ῶ ν τ ῆ ς π λ ά ν η ς π ν ε υ μ ά τ ω ν.

* § 47 (Tit. iii. 4). ἡ γὰρ χ ρ η σ τ ό τ η ς καὶ ἡ φ ι λ α ν θ ρ ω π ί α τοῦ
Θεοῦ καὶ τὸ ἄμετρον τοῦ πλούτου αὐτοῦ τὸν μετανοοῦντα . . . ὡς δίκαιον
. . . ἔχει.

§ 118 (2 Tim. iv. 1). ὅτι κριτὴς ζώντων καὶ νεκρῶν ἁπάντων αὐτὸς
οὗτος ὁ Χριστός, εἶπον ἐν πολλοῖς.

The Acts of Paul and Thecla (not later than 170 A.D.).

* § 14 (2 Tim. ii. 18). λέγει οὗτος ἀνάστασιν γενέσθαι, ὅτι ἤδη
γέγονεν ἐφ᾽ οἷς ἔχομεν τέκνοις. Note also the use in this work of the
names Demas and Hermogenes as ὑποκρίσεως γέμοντες, § 1, and Onesiphorus as seeking Paul, § 2.

Athenagoras (circ. 176).

Legatio, 16 (1 Tim. vi. 16). πάντα γὰρ ὁ Θεός ἐστιν αὐτὸς αὑτῷ, φ ῶ ς
ἀ π ρ ό σ ι τ ο ν.

* 37 (1 Tim. ii. 2). τοῦτο δ᾽ ἐστὶ καὶ πρὸς ἡμῶν, ὅπως ἤ ρ ε μ ο ν κ α ὶ
ἡ σ ύ χ ι ο ν β ί ο ν δ ι ά γ ο ι μ ε ν.

Theodotus (Excerpta ex Scriptis Theodoti, Clem. Al. p. 350).

(1 Tim. vi. 16). καὶ ὁ μὲν φ ῶ ς ἀ π ρ ό σ ι τ ο ν εἴρηται.

The Epistle of the Churches of Vienne and Lyons (circ.180).

* Euseb. H.E. v. i. (1 Tim. iii. 15). ἐνέσκηψεν ἡ ὀργὴ . . . εἰς
Ἄτταλον Περγαμηνὸν τῷ γένει, σ τ ύ λ ο ν κ α ὶ ἑ δ ρ α ί ω μ α τῶν ἐνταῦθα
ἀεὶ γεγονότα.

* (1 Tim. vi. 13). ὁ δὲ . . . Ποθεινὸς . . . ἐπὶ τὸ βῆμα ἐσύρετο
. . . ὡς αὐτοῦ ὄντος τοῦ Χριστοῦ, ἀπεδίδου τήν καλὴν μαρτυρίαν.

Euseb. *H.E.* v. 3 (1 Tim. iv. 3, 4). ὁ Ἀλκιβιάδης, μὴ χρώμενος
τοῖς κτίσμασι τοῦ Θεοῦ . . . πεισθεὶς δὲ ὁ Ἀλκιβιάδης πάντων
ἀνέδην μετελάμβανε καὶ ηὐχαρίστει τῷ Θεῷ.

Theophilus of Antioch (*circ.* 181).

* *ad Autol.* i. 1 (2 Tim. iii. 8). φράσις εὐεπὴς τέρψιν παρέχει . . .
ἀνθρώποις ἔχουσι τὸν νοῦν κατεφθαρμένον.

* *ad Autol.* ii. 16 (Tit. iii. 5; 1 Tim. ii. 4 (?)). ἔτι μὴν καὶ εὐλογήθη
ὑπὸ τοῦ Θεοῦ τὰ ἐκ τῶν ὑδάτων γενόμενα, ὅπως ᾖ καὶ τοῦτο εἰς δεῖγμα τοῦ
μέλλειν λαμβάνειν τοὺς ἀνθρώπους μετάνοιαν καὶ ἄφεσιν ἁμαρτιῶν διὰ ὕδατος
καὶ λουτροῦ παλιγγενεσίας πάντας τοὺς προσιόντας τῇ
ἀληθείᾳ.

ad Autol. iii. 14 (Tit. iii. 1; Tim. ii. 2). ἔτι μὴν καὶ περὶ τοῦ ὑποτάσσεσθαι ἀρχαῖς καὶ ἐξουσίαις, καὶ εὔχεσθαι ὑπὲρ αὐτῶν κελεύει
ἡμᾶς ὁ Θεῖος λόγος, ὅπως ἤρεμον καὶ ἡσύχιον βίον διάγωμεν.

The Integrity of the Letters.

It is scarcely too much to say that but for the difficulty presented
by their style, and the assumption that St. Paul never left Rome
alive, no one would have suspected these letters of being a compilation. But inasmuch as no one has been found to deny the
bona fide Pauline character of some sections of them—at least in 2
Timothy—those who impugn the genuineness of the letters as they
have come down to us have been compelled to exercise much
ingenuity in attempts to apportion the matter of the letters between
St. Paul and the compiler or compilers. For an account of their
schemes the student is referred to the articles on these epistles in
Hastings *D. B.*, and the *Encyclopædia Biblica*, and for a fuller
account, to Moffatt's *Historical N. T.*

To those who agree that the problem presented by the style and
the historical setting of the Pastorals is unsolved, but not insoluble,
all attempts to decompose these letters will seem unprofitable.
There is sound sense in the old scholastic maxim: "Entia non sunt
multiplicanda praeter necessitatem". The case of the Pastorals is
not like that of 2 Corinthians, in which plausible reasons may be
alleged for theories of dislocation. There is no difficulty in presenting
such an outline of 1 Tim or 2 Tim. or Tit. as will show it to be a
single letter, with as much unity of purpose as a *bona fide* letter—
not a college essay—can be expected to have.

But even were we to grant, one moment, that the style and historical considerations must preclude a Pauline authorship for them, yet, the next moment, we find ourselves confronted by more serious objections to the theory of compilation. To begin with, the historical difficulty presented by the personal and local references in the admittedly Pauline sections is insurmountable, on the hypothesis that the whole of St. Paul's history is contained in the Acts.

Again, without using violent language about "forgery," it is not easy to explain why the alleged compiler should pretend to be St. Paul. The ascription of a book to an honoured name was not a precedent condition to its acceptance or acceptability in the primitive Church. Hebrews, and the so-called Epistle of Barnabas, and the Epistle to Diognetus do not claim anyone as their authors. Whoever it was that produced the Pastorals, he was just as good a practical Christian as St. Paul himself; and he had no compelling reason to hide his identity. The case of 2 Peter is different. That epistle, whoever wrote it, was always reckoned a disputed book.

Again, how are we to explain the honourable use, certainly by Polycarp, and probably by Clement of Rome and Ignatius, not to mention other later second century writers, of a work which only appeared, *ex hypothesi*, not earlier than 90 A.D.? And, further, if these epistles are due to a compiler, he must have been an extraordinarily clever man, and quite capable not only of supplementing the Pauline fragments, but of editing them. Now by the year 90 A.D. Timothy's name had become venerated in the Church. Is it likely that a Churchman of that time, writing too, as is alleged, with an ecclesiastical bias, would have permitted the publication of letters which certainly give the impression of Timothy as a not very heroic person? The treatment of Linus (2 Tim. iv. 21) raises a similar question. A tradition, which no one has ever questioned, names Linus as the first bishop of Rome; the subordinate position he occupies in this letter is, as Salmon has noted (*Introd. N.T.* p. 411), quite intelligible if St. Paul was the author of it. It is, on the other hand, extremely unlikely that an editor of the year 90 A.D., who had no scruple in writing in St. Paul's name, would not have given Linus a more prominent place.

These are a few of the difficulties which may be urged on the traditional side in this "contest of opposite improbabilities".

ANALYSIS OF 1 TIMOTHY.

"*Guard the Deposit.*"

A. i. 1, 2. Salutation.

B. i. 3-20: The Crisis, and the Men—Paul and Timothy.

(*a*) The Crisis: 3-11.

(1) 3-7. The motive of the letter is to provide Timothy with a memorandum of previous oral instructions for the combating of those who mischievously and ignorantly endeavour to oppose the Law to the Gospel.

(2) 8-11. This opposition is really factitious; inasmuch as the Law and the Gospel are, both of them, workings of law, God's law, the final cause of which is right conduct.

(*b*) The Men : 12-20.

(1) 12-17. Paul's own spiritual history illustrates the fundamentally identical moral basis of the Law and the Gospel. Paul had been "faithful," trustworthy, while under the Law; therefore Christ pardoned his violent opposition to the Gospel, because it was due to ignorance, though a sinful ignorance. Moreover, this whole transaction—the triumph of Christ's long-suffering over Paul's sinful antagonism—has an enduring value. It is an object lesson to encourage to repentance sinners to the end of time. Glory be to God!

(2) 18-20. The present charge to Timothy, although its immediate exciting cause is the recent action of Hymenæus and Alexander and their followers, ought not to be new in its substance to Timothy. It is practically identical with what the prophets gave utterance to at his ordination.

C. ii., iii. The foundations of Sound Doctrine. *contradicts 1:3*

False teaching is most effectually combated indirectly; not by controversy, with its negations, but by quiet, positive foundation work on which true views about God and Man can be based. We begin then with :—

(*a*) ii. 1—iii. 1 *a*. Public Prayer.

(1) ii. 1-7. Its universal scope; and the Divine sanction for catholicity in human sympathy.

(2) ii. 8—iii. 1 *a*. The Ministers of Public Prayer: men, not women; with a judgment as to the true function of Woman in the Church and in Society.

(*b*) iii. 1 *b*-16. The Ministry of the Divine Society.

(1) 1 *b*-7. The qualifications of the episcopus.

(2) 8-10, 12, 13. The qualifications of the deacons.

(3) 11. The qualifications of women Church-workers.

(4) 14-16. Caution to Timothy lest he should be tempted to think these details trivial, in comparison with more obviously spiritual things. The importance of rules depends on the importance of that with which they are concerned. The Church, for whose ministers rules have been just laid down, is the greatest Society in the world: human, yet divinely originated and inspired; the House of God; an extension of the Incarnation.

D. iv.A fresh word of prophecy (see i. 18) addressed to Timothy in his present office.

(a) 1-5.The false teaching more clearly defined as a spurious asceticism. This is condemned, *a priori*, by considerations (1) of the declared character and object of the material creation, and (2) of the purifying effect of benedictions.

(b) 6-16.The spurious asceticism, however, as it manifests itself in practice, is best combated (1), 6-10, by the Church teacher showing an example in his own person of genuine holiness, and (2), 11-16, by active pastoral care, courageous outspokenness and the diligent cultivation of all God-given ministerial graces.

E. v. 1—vi. 19.This naturally suggests the specification of directions for administration of the Church by a Father in God.

(a) v. 1, 2.He must not deal with his people *en masse*, but individually. He cannot treat alike old men and young men, elder women and younger women.

(b) v. 3-16.There is one class of the laity in particular which, because they have a special claim on the Church, need a discriminating care : the widows. The Church cannot afford to support all widows, nor would it be right to relieve their relatives, if they have any, of responsibility for them. Consequently, none can be entered on the list for relief but those over a certain age, and who have a good record for consistent Christian lives. Young widows had better marry again.

(c) v. 17-25.The questions of Church finance and discipline, as they concern widows, suggest recommendations on the same subjects, as they concern the presbyters : (1) 17, 18, finance ; (2) 19-25, discipline, with, 23, a parenthetical personal counsel to Timothy, suggested by the word *pure* in 22.

(d) vi. 1, 2.Ruling principles for the conduct of Christians who are slaves, towards heathen and Christian masters respectively.

(e) vi. 3-19.A right judgment in all these matters which affect our daily life depends on right basal convictions as to the true values of things material and spiritual.

(1) 3-10.The false teachers reverse the true order : they regard religion as a sub-section of the world ; whereas the world has its own place— an honourable place—as subordinate to religion.

(2) 11-16.A solemn adjuration to Timothy to adhere to the principles just laid down ; and

(3) 17-19.to urge the observance of them upon the well-to-do members of the Christian Society.

F. vi. 20-21.Final appeal, summing up the perennial antagonism between character (the natural fruit of the faith) and mere intellectualism.

ANALYSIS OF 2 TIMOTHY.

Sursum Corda.

A. i. 1, 2.Salutation.

B. i. 3—ii. 13.Considerations which should strengthen Timothy's moral courage (*a, b, c, d, e*), interspersed with appeals to his loyalty (α, β, γ, δ, ε).

(*a*) 3-5. Paul's thoughts of, and prayers for, him; and Paul's recognition of Timothy's faith.

(*b*) 6, 7. An objective fact in Timothy's own spiritual history: his ordination; since when there is available for his use, Power, Love, and Discipline, the gifts of God.

(α) 8-10. An appeal based on thoughts of the Gospel, as the power of God.

(*c*) 11, 12. Paul's own steadfastness.

(β, γ) 13, 14. Appeals based on loyalty to the human teacher, and to the Divine Spirit.

(*d*) 15. The deterrent example of the disloyal of Asia.

(*e*) 16-18. The stimulating example of Onesiphorus.

(δ) ii. 1, 2. An appeal for the provision of a succession of loyal teachers.

(ε) ii. 3-13. An appeal based on "the Word of the Cross"; *i.e.*, Suffering is the precedent condition of glory. This is exemplified in the earthly analogies of the soldier, the athlete, and the field-labourer; in the actual experiences of Jesus Christ Himself, and of Paul.

C. ii. 14-26. General exhortations to Timothy as a Church teacher, as regards (*a*) 14-18, the positive and negative subject-matter of his instructions; (*b*) 19-21, the true and optimistic conception of the Church in relation to all teachers, true and false; (*c*) 22-26, the personal equipment of the true teacher, and his treatment of the erring.

D. iii. 1—iv. 8. A word of prophecy setting forth—

(*a*) iii. 1-9. The practical shortcomings of the false teachers.

(*b*) iii. 10-17. A recalling of Timothy's past spiritual history: (1) 10-13, the conditions under which his discipleship began; (2) 14-17, the holy persons by whom, and the sacred writings on which, his youth had been nourished.

(*c*) iv. 1-8. A concluding solemn adjuration to play the man while there is time. As for Paul, the contest is over, the crown is in sight; there is a crown for Timothy, too, if he takes Paul's place.

E. iv. 9-22. Personal details: Instructions, 9, 11, 13, 21; News about other members of the Pauline comradeship. 10, 11, 12, 20; A warning, 14, 15; A reminiscence and a confident hope, 16-18; Salutations and greetings, 19, 21; Final benediction, 22.

ANALYSIS OF TITUS.

"*Maintain Good Works.*"

A. i. 1-4. Salutation.

B. i. 5-16. The position of affairs in Crete, which (*a*), 5-9, necessitates that the foundation of Church organisation—the presbyterate—be well and truly laid; in view of (*b*), 10-16, the natural unruliness and bad character of the people, aggravated by Jewish immoral sophistries.

C. ii. 1—iii. 11. Heads of necessary elementary moral instruction for the Cretan folk.

(*a*) ii. 1-10. For aged men and aged women; for young women and young men—and what is said about these latter applies also to Titus—and slaves.

(*b*) ii. 11-15. The eternal sanction for this insistence on the practice of elementary virtues is the all-embracing scope of the Gospel of God's Grace;
which has been visibly manifested, with its call to repentance, its assurance of help, and its certain hope.

(*c*) iii. 1, 2. Obedience to the civil authority is also a Gospel virtue.

(*d*) iii. 3-7. These instructions are not given in a spirit of superiority. We
ourselves were once in as bad moral condition as are the Cretans, if
not worse, until we came to know, and test the love of God, unmerited
and saving.

(*e*) iii. 8-11. In conclusion, the sum of all is: Let the people maintain good
works, and shun useless speculations. Let Titus not be lax in dealing
with leaders of the false teaching.

D. iii. 12, 13. Personal instructions.

E. iii. 14. Concluding summary, repeating the teaching of 8-11.

F. iii. 15. Final salutation.

The Text.

The text which is printed above the exposition is in the main
that of Westcott and Hort.   In a very few cases other readings have
been adopted in this text (see *e.g.* 1 Tim. ii. 8; Tit. ii. 4, iii. 9); and
in some places their punctuation has been modified.

The *apparatus criticus* is based on that of Tischendorf's eighth
edition. The readings of the Old Latin fragments, r, Cod. Frisingensis, have been added, and the references to m (*Speculum*) have
been given according to the edition by Weihrich in the Vienna
Corpus Script. Eccles. Lat. Of the uncial MSS. cited by Tisch., E$_3$
(Cod. Petropolitanus, or Sangermanensis, ix. or x.) has not been
noted, since it is merely a transcript of D$_2$. On the other hand, it
has been thought best to cite both F$_2$ and G$_3$, since it is not certain
that the latter is a copy of the former, though both are derived from
one exemplar.

Only the most important cursives are mentioned in these notes.
The reader will understand that the attestation of KLP carries with
it, in most cases, that of the great bulk of the cursive MSS. Neither
has it been thought advisable to cite the more obscure versions.
Even if their readings were critically ascertained they would not
carry much weight. For a similar reason patristic citations are
sparingly used. Subjoined is a list of the authorities cited in the
critical notes.

א, Cod. Sinaiticus, iv. St Petersburg.

A, Cod. Alexandrinus, v. London.

C, Cod. Ephraemi rescriptus, v. Paris. It does not contain 1
Tim. i. 1-iii. 9, μυστη | ριον.

D (D$_2$), Cod. Claromontanus, vi. Paris.

F (F$_2$), Cod. Augiensis, ix.   Trinity College, Cambridge.

G (G$_3$), Cod. Boernerianus, ix.   Dresden.

H (H$_3$), Cod. Coislinianus, vi.   Fragments.   Those that contain portions of the Pastorals are in Paris and Turin.   It only contains: 1 Tim. iii. 7-13, vi. 9-13 ; 2 Tim. ii. 1-9 ; Tit. i. 1-3, 15— ii. 5, iii, 13-15.

I (I^2), Cod. Tischendorfianus (Petropolitanus, Tisch.), v.   St. Petersburg.   Contains only Tit. i. 1-13.

K (K$_2$) Cod. Mosquensis, ix.   Moscow.

L (L$_2$), Cod. Bibliothecae Angelicae, ix.   Rome.

P (P$_2$), Cod. Porphyrianus, ix.   St. Petersburg.

Of the Old Latin MSS. cited, d, e, f, g are the Latin portions of the bilingual uncials, D$_2$, E$_3$, F$_2$ and G$_3$ respectively.   m is the treatise entitled *Speculum*, practically a catena of texts or *testimonia*, formerly ascribed to St Augustine.   r is the Cod. Frisingensis, v. or vi. (Munich) fragments, containing *inter alia*, 1 Tim. i. 12—ii. 15 ; v. 18—vi. 13.

The only MSS. of the Vulgate cited are Cod. Amiatinus (am.), A.D. 716, Florence, and Cod. Fuldensis (fuld.) A.D. 541-546, Fulda in Germany.

The other versions are indicated as follows :—

syr^{pesh} (Tisch., syr^{sch}) = Peshitto Syriac.

syr^{hcl} (Tisch., syr^p) = Harkleian Syriac.

syrr = both Syriac Versions.

boh (Tisch., cop.)   = Bohairic Egyptian.

sah = Sahidic Egyptian.

arm = Armenian.

go = Gothic.

For a complete bibliography of the Pastoral Epistles the reader is referred to the articles, "Timothy, Epistle to," and "Titus, Epistle to," by W. Lock, in Hastings' *D.B.*, vol. iv., pp. 775, 785, and the articles "Timothy and Titus (Epistles)," by J. Moffatt, in the *Encyclopædia Biblica*.   To the articles themselves—the former temperately conservative, the latter, uncompromisingly anti-traditional—the present writer is much indebted.   Diligent use has also been made of the labours of the following commentators on the continuous text: St. Chrysostom's Homilies, full of good sense and practical wisdom ; Bengel, pithy, direct and spiritual ; Ellicott, a sound grammarian from the classical Greek standpoint, and therefore useful as a warning against possible pitfalls, but very dry ; Alford, still most serviceable as the variorum edition of A.D. 1865 ; J. H. Bernard (*Cambridge Greek Testament*) whose notes on the ethical language of the Epistles are most illuminating, and H. von Soden, in the *Hand-Commentar*, remarkable for subtle verbal analysis ; but his exegesis is vitiated by his critical position as to the authorship and date of the letters. Suspicion and half-heartedness do not make for profound exposition.

Plummer's large treatment of certain sections, in the *Expositor's Bible*, has been found helpful and suggestive.   Field's *Notes* (alas, too few!) *on Trans. N.T.* are indispensable ; and H. P. Liddon's analysis of 1 Timothy is masterly.

On the general subject of the Epistles, Salmon's *Introduction N.T.* (p. 397 *sqq.*), Lightfoot's *Biblical Essays* (xi., xii.), Wace's Introduction in the *Speaker's Commentary*, J. H. Bernard's Introduction (*Cambridge Greek Testament*), Holtzmann, *Die Pastoralbriefe*, and Hort's *Judaistic Chistianity* and *Christian Ecclesia* have been largely made use of.   It has not, however, been thought necessary, especially when space had to be considered, to specify in every case the authority for the sentiment expressed, or the explanation adopted. In any case, the Church, in the long run, acts on the counsel of Thomas à Kempis : " Non quaeras quis hoc dixerit : sed quid dicatur attende " (*De Imit. Christi*, i. 5).

September, 1909.

ΠΡΟΣ ΤΙΜΟΘΕΟΝ Ā

I. 1. ΠΑΥΛΟΣ ^aἀπόστολος ^aΧριστοῦ ^a'Ιησοῦ ¹ ^bκατ' ^bἐπιταγὴν ²   a 2 Cor. i. 1, Eph. i. 1, ^cΘεοῦ ^cσωτῆρος ^cἡμῶν καὶ ³ Χριστοῦ 'Ιησοῦ ⁴ τῆς ἐλπίδος ἡμῶν,   Col. i. 1, 2 Tim. i. 1, cf. 1

Cor. i. 1, Tit. i. 1.   b Rom. xvi. 26, Tit. i. 3.   c Jude 25, cf. 1 Tim. ii. 3, iv. 10, Tit. i. 3, ii. 10, iii. 4.

¹ So ℵDFGP, 80, one other, d, f, g, fuld., boh., syr^{hcl}; 'Ιησ. Χριστ. AKL, am., syr^{pesh}, arm.

² ἐπαγγελίαν ℵ.

³ Ins. Κυρίου ℵD^cKL; om. AD*FGP, 17, 31, seven others, d, f, g, vg., go., syrr., sah., boh., arm.

⁴ So AD*FGP, 17, five others, d, f, g, am., fuld., go., sah., syrr.; 'Ιησ. Χριστ. ℵD^cKL, boh., arm.

Chapter I.—Vv. 1-2. Salutation.—
Ver. 1. ἀπόστολος Χρ. 'Ιησ. The use of this official title is an indication that the Pastoral Epistles were not merely private letters (ctr. Παῦλος δέσμιος Χρ. 'Ιησ., Philem. 1), but were intended to be read to the Churches committed to the charge of Timothy and Titus respectively. The phrase means simply one *sent by* Christ, not primarily one *belonging to* Christ. Cf. Phil. ii. 25, where Epaphroditus is spoken of as ὑμῶν ἀπόστ., and 2 Cor. viii. 23, ἀπόστ. ἐκκλησιῶν. ἀπόστ. Χρ. 'Ιησ. is also found in 2 Cor. i. 1, Eph. i. 1, Col. i. 1, 2 Tim. i. 1; ἀπόστ. 'Ιησ. Χρ. in 1 Cor. i. 1, Tit. i. 1. The difference in the use *Jesus Christ* and *Christ Jesus* seems to be this: in each case the first member of the compound name indicates whether the historical or the notional idea of the Person is chiefly in the writer's mind. *Jesus Christ* briefly expresses the proposition, "Jesus is the Christ"; it embodies the first theological assertion concerning Jesus; it represents the conception of the historical Jesus in the minds of those who had seen Him. St. John, St. Peter and St. James employ this name when speaking of our Lord. But in *Christ Jesus*, on the other hand, the theological conception of *the Christ* predominates over that of the actual *Jesus* Who had been seen, felt and

heard by human senses. Accordingly we find *Christ Jesus* in every stage of the Pauline Epistles; and, as we should expect, more frequently in the later than in the earlier letters. In almost every instance of the occurrence of *Jesus Christ* in the Pastoral Epistles the thought of the passage concerns the humanity, or historical aspect, of our Lord. Thus in Tit. i. 1, "a servant of God and an apostle of Jesus Christ," we could not substitute *Christ Jesus* without weakening the antithesis. See note there. St. Paul, here as elsewhere, claims to have been as truly *sent* by Christ as were those who were apostles before him.

κατ' ἐπιταγήν: *in obedience to the command.* The full phrase κατ' ἐπιτ. θ. σ. ἡμῶν occurs again (τοῦ σωτ. ἡμ. θεοῦ) in a similar context in Tit. i. 3; κατ' ἐπιτ. τοῦ αἰωνίου θ. in Rom. xvi. 26. In 1 Cor. vii. 6, 2 Cor. viii. 8, κατ' ἐπιτ. is used in a different sense.

St. Paul more commonly refers the originating cause of his mission to the *will of God* (1 Cor. i. 1; 2 Cor. i. 1; Eph. i. 1; Col. i. 1; 2 Tim. i. 1). He would hardly say *through the will of Christ,* θέλημα being used of the eternal counsel of the Godhead; but inasmuch as the *command* is the consequent of the *will,* he can speak of his apostleship as being due to the *command*

d Phil. iv. 3, 2. Τιμοθέῳ ^d γνησίῳ ^e τέκνῳ ^f ἐν ^f πίστει · χάρις, ^g ἔλεος, εἰρήνη ἀπὸ
Tit. i. 4,
cf. 2 Cor. Θεοῦ Πατρὸς ¹ καὶ Χριστοῦ Ἰησοῦ τοῦ Κυρίου ἡμῶν. 3. Καθὼς
viii. 8,
Phil. ii.
20, Ecclus. vii. 18.   e 1 Cor. iv. 17, ver. 18, 2 Tim. i. 2, ii. 1, Tit. i. 4. Philem. 10, 3 John 4.
f Ver. 4, 1 Tim. ii. 7, Tit. iii. 15.   g 2 Tim. i. 2, 2 John 3, Jude 2.

¹ Ins. ἡμῶν אcDcKLP, syrr., sah.

of Christ Jesus, as well as of God the
Father. In this matter Jesus Christ is
co-ordinated with God the Father in
Gal. i. 1; while in Rom. i. 4, 5. Paul's
apostleship is "through Jesus Christ
our Lord" only. On the other hand, in
Tit. i. 3, St. Paul says he was intrusted
with the message "according to the
commandment of God our Saviour".
Here it is to be noted that the *command*
proceeds equally from God and Christ
Jesus. This language could hardly have
been used if St. Paul conceived of Christ
Jesus as a creature. Moulton and Milligan (*Expositor*, vii., vii. 379) compare St. Paul's use of ἐπιταγή as a
Divine command with its technical use
in heathen dedicatory inscriptions. We
cannot, with Chrys., narrow the "commandment of God" to the specific date
of St. Paul's commission by the Church,
whether in Acts xiii. 2 or on an earlier
occasion. St. Paul claimed that he had
been "separated from his mother's
womb" (Gal. i. 15).

θεοῦ σωτῆρος ἡμῶν: Westcott on 1
John iv. 14 has an instructive note on
the Biblical use of the term σωτήρ.
"The title is confined (with the exception of the writings of St. Luke) to the
later writings of the N.T., and is not
found in the central group of St. Paul's
Epistles." It may be added that in the
Lucan references (Luke i. 47, of God ;
ii. 11, Acts v. 31, xiii. 23, of Christ) the
term σωτήρ has not primarily its full
later evangelical import, and would be
best rendered *deliverer*, as in the constant O.T. application of the term to
God. Perhaps the same is true of Phil.
iii. 20, and Eph. v. 23, where it is used
of Christ. On the other hand, apart
from ὁ σωτὴρ τ. κόσμου (John iv. 42 ; 1
John iv. 14), the conventional evangelical use is found : of God the Father in
(a) 1 Tim. i. 1, Jude 25, θεὸς σωτὴρ
ἡμῶν ; (b) 1 Tim. ii. 3, Tit. i. 3, ii. 10,
iii. 4, ὁ σωτὴρ ἡμῶν θεός ; (c) 1 Tim. iv.
10, σωτήρ in apposition to θεός in the
preceding clause ; of Christ, in (a) 2
Tim. i. 10, ὁ σωτὴρ ἡμῶν Χριστὸς
Ἰησοῦς ; (b) Tit. i. 4, iii. 6, Χρ. Ἰησ. ὁ
σωτὴρ ἡμῶν ; (c) 2 Pet. i. 11, ii. 20, iii.
18, ὁ Κύριος ἡμῶν καὶ σωτὴρ Ἰησ. Χρ. ;

(d) 2 Pet. iii. 2, ὁ Κύριος καὶ σωτήρ.
To the (c) class belong, perhaps, Tit. ii.
13, 2 Pet. i. 1, ὁ [μέγας] θεὸς [ἡμῶν] καὶ
σωτὴρ [ἡμῶν] Ἰησ. Χρ. ; but see note on
Tit. ii. 13.

In the text, there is an antithesis between the offices of God as *our Saviour*
and of Christ Jesus as *our hope*. The
one points to the past, at least chiefly,
and the other to the future. In speaking
of the saving action of God, St. Paul
uses the aorist 2 Tim. i. 9, Tit. ii. 11,
iii. 4, 5. He *saved* us, potentially. See
further on ch. ii. 3. God, as the Council
of Trent says (Sess. vi. cap. 7), is *the
efficient cause* of our justification, while
Jesus, "our righteousness," besides
being *the meritorious cause,* may be
said to be *the formal cause ;* for "the
righteousness of God by which He
maketh us righteous" is embodied in
Jesus, Who "was made unto us . . .
righteousness and sanctification" (1
Cor. i. 30). We advance from salvation
to sanctification ; and accordingly we
must not narrow down the conception
Christ Jesus our hope to mean "the
hope of Israel" (Acts xxiii. 6, xxviii. 20) ;
but rather the historical manifestation of
the Son of God as Christ Jesus is the
ground of our "hope of glory" (Col. i.
27). Our hope is that "the body of our
humiliation will be conformed to the
body of His glory" (Phil. iii 20, 21).
See also Eph. iv. 13. Our hope is that
"we shall be like Him" (1 John iii. 2,
3). See also Tit. ii. 13, προσδεχόμενοι
τὴν μακαρίαν ἐλπίδα. For this vivid
use of an abstract noun compare Eph.
ii. 14, αὐτὸς γάρ ἐστιν ἡ εἰρήνη ἡμῶν.

Ignatius borrows this noble appella-
tion : *Magn.* 11 ; *Trall.* inscr., "Jesus
Christ Who is our hope through our
resurrection unto Him" ; *Trall.* 2,
"Jesus Christ our hope ; for if we live
in Him, we shall also be found in Him".
See also Polycarp, 8.

Ver. 2. γνησίῳ qualifies the compound
τέκνῳ ἐν πίστει, just as in Tit. i. 4 it
qualifies τέκνῳ κατὰ κοινὴν πίστιν. As
in the relation of the heavenly Father to
those who are His children by adoption
and grace, some are "led by the Spirit
of God," and so are genuine sons of

^h παρεκάλεσά σε ⁱ προσμεῖναι ἐν Ἐφέσῳ, πορευόμενος εἰς Μακε- h 1 Cor. xvi.
δονίαν, ἵνα ^k παραγγείλῃς τισὶν μὴ ^l ἑτεροδιδασκαλεῖν, 4. μηδὲ 12, 2 Cor.
viii. 6, ix.
5, xii. 18.
i Matt. xv.
32 = Mark viii. 2, Acts xviii. 18.   k 1 Cor. vii. 10, xi. 17, 1 Thess. iv. 11, 2 Thess. iii. 4, 6, 10,
12, 1 Tim. iv. 11, v. 7, vi. 13, 17.   l 1 Tim. vi. 3 only, not LXX.

God, so in the filial relationships of earth—physical, spiritual, or intellectual —some sons realise their vocation, others fail to do so. γνήσιος (and γνησίως, Phil. ii. 20) is only found in the N.T. in Paul. See reff. It might be rendered *lawful, legitimate*, as γυνή γνησία means "lawful wife" (Moulton and Milligan, *Expositor*, vii., vi. 382). Dean Bernard (*comm. in loc.*) cites an interesting parallel from Philo (*de Vit. Cont.* p. 482, ed. Mangey), where "the young men among the Therapeutae are described as ministering to their elders καθάπερ υἱοὶ γνήσιοι." τέκνῳ ἐν πίστει: The parallel from Tit. i. 4 quoted above proves that πίστις here is *the* faith, as A.V. Absence of the article before familiar Christian terms is a characteristic of the Pastorals. *Cf.* 1 Cor. iv. 15, "In Christ Jesus I begat you through the gospel". See also Gal. iv. 19, Philem. 10; and, for the term τέκνον as applied to Timothy, see reff. St. Paul "begat him through the gospel" on the first missionary journey. He was already a disciple in Acts xvi. 1. Nothing can be safely inferred from the variation ἀγαπητῷ in 2 Tim. i. 2 for γνησίῳ. The selection from among these semi-conventional terms of address is influenced by passing moods of which the writer is not wholly conscious; but a pseudepigraphic author would be careful to observe uniformity.

ἔλεος as an element in the salutation in addition to χάρις and εἰρήνη is only found, in the Pauline Epistles, in 1 and 2 Timothy. See reff. "Mercy" is used in an informal benediction, Gal. vi. 16, "Peace be upon them, and mercy". Bengel notes that personal experience of the mercy of God makes a man a more efficient minister of the Gospel. See vv. 13, 16, 1 Cor. vii. 25, 2 Cor. iv. 1, Heb. ii. 17. See also Tobit vii. 12 (ℵ) ὁ κύριος . . . ποιήσαι ἐφ' ὑμᾶς ἔλεος κ. εἰρήνην and Wisd. iii. 9, iv. 15, χάρις κ. ἔλεος τοῖς ἐκλεκτοῖς αὐτοῦ. If one may hazard a conjecture as to what prompted St. Paul to wish *mercy* to Timothy rather than to Titus, it may be a subtle indication of the apostle's anxiety as to Timothy's administrative capacity. Another variation in the salutation in Titus is the substitution of *Saviour* for *Lord*. This calls for no comment.

Note the anarthrous θεὸς πατήρ as in all the Pauline salutations, with the exception of 1 Thess., where we have simply χάρις ὑμῖν κ. εἰρήνη. In Colossians the blessing is only from God the Father. ἡμῶν is added to πατρὸς except in 2 Thess. and the Pastorals.

Vv. 3-7. THE MOTIVE OF THIS LETTER: to provide Timothy with a written memorandum of previous verbal instructions, especially with a view to novel speculations about the Law which sap the vitality of the Gospel; the root of which is sincerity, and its fruit, love.

Ver. 3. καθώς: The apodosis supplied at the end of ver. 4 in the R.V., *so do I now*, is feebler than the *so do* of the A.V. We need something more vigorous. St. Paul was more anxious that Timothy should *charge some*, etc., than that he should merely *abide at Ephesus*. This is implied in the A.V., in which *so do* = *stay there and be a strong ruler*.

An exact parallel occurs in Mark i. 2. Similar anacolutha are found in Rom. v. 12, Gal. ii. 4, 5, 6, Eph. iii. 1.

παρεκάλεσά σε: It is far-fetched to regard this word as specially expressive of a *mild* command, as Chrys. suggests. παρακαλεῖν constantly occurs, and with very varying meanings, in the Pauline Epistles. διεταξάμην is used in the corresponding place in Tit. i. 5, because there the charge concerns a series of injunctions.

προσμεῖναι: *ut remaneres* (Vulg.). The word (see Acts xviii. 18) naturally implies that St. Paul and Timothy had been together at Ephesus, and that St. Paul left Timothy there as vicar apostolic.

πορευόμενος refers to St. Paul, not to Timothy, as De Wette alleged. The grammatical proof of this is fully gone into by Winer-Moulton, *Gram.* p. 404, "If the subject of the infinitive is the same as that of the finite verb, any attributes which it may have are put in the nominative".

It is unnecessary here to prove that it is impossible to fit this journey of St. Paul to Macedonia, and Timothy's stay at Ephesus connected therewith, into the period covered by the Acts.

τισίν: τινες is intentionally vague. The writer has definite persons in his mind, but for some reason he does not

m Acts viii. ¹¹¹ προσέχειν ⁿ μύθοις καὶ ᵒ γενεαλογίαις ᵖ ἀπεράντοις, αἵτινες ᵠ ἐκ-
6, 10, 11,
xvi. 14, 1   ζητήσεις ¹ ʳ παρέχουσι μᾶλλον ἢ ˢ οἰκονομίαν ² Θεοῦ τὴν ᵗ ἐν ᵗ πίστει.
Tim. iii.
8, iv. 1, 13.

Tit. i. 14, Heb. ii. 1, vii. 13, 2 Peter i. 19.   n 1 Tim. iv. 7, 2 Tim. iv. 4, Tit. i. 14, 2 Pet. i. 16,
Wisd. xvii. 4, Ecclus. xx. 19.   o Tit. iii. 9 only, not LXX.   p Here only, N.T., Job xxxvi. 26, 3
Macc. ii. 9.   q Here only, not LXX, see 1 Tim. vi. 4.   r 1 Tim. vi. 17, Tit. ii. 7, etc,
s 1 Cor. ix. 17, Eph. i. 10, iii. 2, 9, Col. i. 25.   t See ver. 1,

¹ So אA, 17, three others; ζητήσεις DFGKLP.

² So אAFGKLP, boh., syrʰᶜˡ-txt, arm.; οἰκοδομίαν Dᶜ, 192, Dam. txt; οἰκοδομήν
D*, Iren., go., syrpesh and ʰᶜˡ-mg; aedificationem d, f, g, m⁵⁰, vg. See Eph. iv. 29.

choose to specify them. To do so, in this case, would have had a tendency to harden them in their heresy, "render them more shameless" (Chrys.). The introduction of the personal element into controversy has a curiously irritating effect. For this use of τινες see 1 Cor. iv. 18, 2 Cor. iii. 1, x. 2, Gal. i. 7, ii. 12, 1 Tim. i. 6, 19, v. 15, vi. 10, 21, 2 Tim. ii. 18.

μὴ ἑτεροδιδασκαλεῖν: This compound occurs again in 1 Tim. vi. 3, and means to teach a gospel or doctrine different from that which I have taught. ἕτερος certainly seems to connote difference in kind. Gal. i. 6, ἕτερον εὐαγγέλιον, ὃ οὐκ ἔστιν ἄλλο, and 2 Cor. xi. 4, illustrate St. Paul's language here. The heresy may have been of recent origin, and not yet completely systematised—heresy of course does not aim at finality—but St. Paul does not mean to deal gently with it. It was to him false and accursed (cf. Gal. i. 8, 9). His forebodings for the church in Ephesus (Acts xx. 29, 30) were being fulfilled now. Hort (Judaistic Christianity, p. 134) compares the διδαχαῖς ποικίλαις καὶ ξέναις of Heb. xiii. 9.

St. Paul elsewhere uses compounds with ἑτερο, e.g., 2 Cor. vi. 14, ἑτεροζυγεῖν; and more remarkably still, when quoting Isa. xxviii. 11 in 1 Cor. xiv. 21, he substitutes ἐν ἑτερογλώσσοις for διὰ γλώσσης ἑτέρας of the LXX. The word is found in Ignat. ad Polyc. 3, οἱ δοκοῦντες ἀξιόπιστοι εἶναι καὶ ἑτεροδιδασκαλοῦντες.

Ver. 4. μηδὲ προσέχειν: nor to pay attention to. This perhaps refers primarily to the hearers of the ἑτεροδιδάσκαλοι rather than to the false teachers themselves. See reff.

μύθοις καὶ γενεαλογίαις ἀπεράντοις: " Polybius uses both terms in similarly close connection, Hist. ix. 2, 1 " (Ell.). Two aspects of, or elements in, the one aberration from sound doctrine.

Some light is thrown upon this clause by other passages in this group of letters

(1 Tim. i. 6, 7, iv. 7, vi. 4, 20; 2 Tim. ii. 14, 16, 23, iv. 4; Tit. i. 10, 14, iii. 9). The myths are expressly called Jewish (Tit. i. 14), and this affords a good argument that νομοδιδάσκαλοι and νόμος, in 1 Tim. i. 7, 8 and Tit. iii. 9, refer to the Mosaic Law, not restricting the term Law to the Pentateuch. Now a considerable and important part of the Mosaic legislation has relation only to Palestine and Jerusalem; it had no practical significance for the devotional life of the Jews of the Dispersion, with the exception of the community that worshipped at Hierapolis in Egypt. There is a strong temptation to mystics to justify to themselves the continued use of an antiquated sacred book by a mystical interpretation of whatever in it has ceased to apply to daily life. Thus Philo (De Vit. Contempl. § 3) says of the Therapeutae, "They read the holy Scriptures, and explain the philosophy of their fathers in an allegorical manner, regarding the written words as symbols of hidden truth which is communicated in obscure figures". Those with whom St. Paul deals in the Pastoral Epistles were not the old-fashioned conservative Judaisers whom we meet in the Acts and in the earlier Epistles; but rather the promoters of an eclectic synthesis of the then fashionable Gentile philosophy and of the forms of the Mosaic Law. μύθοι, then, here and elsewhere in the Pastorals (see reff.), would refer, not to the stories and narrative of the O.T. taken in their plain straightforward meaning, but to the arbitrary allegorical treatment of them.

γενεαλογίαι may similarly refer to the genealogical matter in the O.T. which is usually skipped by the modern reader; but which by a mystical explanation of the derivations of the nomenclature could be made to justify their inclusion in a sacred book, every syllable of which might be supposed antecedently to contain edification. This general interpretation, which is that of Weiss, is

5. Τὸ δὲ τέλος τῆς ᵘπαραγγελίας ἐστὶν ἀγάπη ἐκ ᵛκαθαρᾶς ᵂκαρ- ^u Acts v. 28,
δίας καὶ ᵂσυνειδήσεως ᵂἀγαθῆς καὶ ˣπίστεως ˣ ʸἀνυποκρίτου· 6. ὧν
τινὲς ᶻἀστοχήσαντες ᵃἐξετράπησαν εἰς ᵇματαιολογίαν, 7. θέλοντες

u Acts v. 28, xvi. 24, 1 Thess. iv. 2, ver. 18, not LXX.
v Ps. l. (li.) 12, Matt.

v. 8, 2 Tim. ii. 22.   w Acts xxiii. 1, 1 Tim. i. 19, 1 Pet. iii. 16, 21.   x 2 Tim. i. 5.   y Rom. xii. 9, 2 Cor. vi. 6, Jas. iii. 17, 1 Pet. i. 22.   z 1 Tim. vi. 21, 2 Tim. ii. 18 only, N.T., Ecclus. vii. 19, viii. 9.   a 1 Tim. v. 15, vi. 20, 2 Tim. iv. 4, Heb. xii. 13.   b Here only, not LXX. cf Tit. i. 10.

supported by Ignat. *Magn.* 8, "Be not seduced by strange doctrines nor by antiquated fables (ἑτεροδοξίαις μηδὲ μυθεύμασιν τοῖς παλαιοῖς), which are profitless. For if even unto this day we live after the manner of Judaism (κατὰ ἰουδαϊσμὸν ζῶμεν), we avow that we have not received grace." Hort maintains that γενεαλογίαι here has a derived meaning, "all the early tales adherent, as it were, to the births of founders" (see *Judaistic Christianity*, p. 135 *sqq.*). On the other hand, Irenæus (*Haer.* Praef. 1 and Tertullian (*adv. Valentin.* 3; *de Praescript.* 33) suppose that the Gnostic groupings of *aeons* in genealogical relationships are here alluded to. It was natural that they should read the N.T. in the light of controversies in which they themselves were engaged.

ἀπεράντοις: *endless, interminatis* (Vulg.), *infinitis* (m.), because leading to no certain conclusion. Discussions which do not concern realities are interminable, not from their profundity, as the ocean is popularly speaking unfathomable in parts, but because they lead to no convincing end. One end or conclusion is as good as another. The choice between them is a matter of taste.

αἵτινες: qualitative, *they are of such a kind as, the which* (R.V.).

ἐκζητήσεις: *Questionings* to which no answer can be given, which are not worth answering. See reff. on vi. 4. Their unpractical nature is implied by their being contrasted with οἰκονομία θεοῦ. Life is a trust, a stewardship, committed to us by God. Anything that claims to belong to religion, and at the same time is prejudicial to the effectual discharge of this trust is self-condemned.

παρέχουσι: παρέχω is used here as in the phrase κόπους παρέχω.

It will be observed that οἰκονομία is here taken subjectively and actively (*the performance of the duty of an* οἰκονόμος entrusted to a man by God; so also in Col. i. 25); not objectively and passively (*the dispensation of God, i.e.*, the Divine plan of salvation). The Western reading οἰκοδομήν or οἰκοδομίαν, *aedificationem*, is easier; but the text gives a deeper meaning.

τὴν ἐν πίστει: This is best taken as in *the* faith; *cf.* ver. 2, ii. 7, Tit. iii. 15. The trust committed to us by God is exercised in the sphere of the faith.

The aposiopesis at the end of ver. 4 is due to an imperative need felt by St. Paul to explain at once, and develop the thought of, οἰκονομία θεοῦ. The true teaching—that of the apostle and of Timothy—would be the consequence of the charge given by Timothy and would issue in, be productive of, an οἰκονομία θεοῦ. This οἰκονομ. θ. is *the object aimed at*, τέλος, *of the charge;* and is further defined as *love*, etc.

This is the only place in Paul in which τέλος means *the final cause*. In every other instance it means *termination, result, i.e. consequence.* 1 Peter i. 9 is perhaps an instance of a similar use.

The charge is referred to again in ver. 18. See also 1 Thess. iv. 2. The expressed object of the charge being the comprehensive virtue, love, it is strange that Ellicott should characterise this exegesis as "too narrow and exclusive". Bengel acutely observes that St. Paul does not furnish Timothy with profound arguments with which to refute the heretics, because the special duty of a church ruler is concerned with what is positively necessary. The love here spoken of is that which is "the fulfilment of the law" (Rom. xiii. 10); and its nature is further defined by its threefold source. Heart, conscience, faith, mark stages in the evolution of the inner life of a man. Heart, or disposition, is earlier in development than conscience; and faith, in the case of those who have it, is later than conscience.

καθαρὰ καρδία is an O.T. phrase. See reff. συνείδησις is καθαρά in 1 Tim. iii. 9, 2 Tim. i. 3; it is ἀγαθή in reff.; καλή in Heb. xiii. 18; it occnrs without any epithet in 1 Tim. iv. 2, Tit. i. 15. πίστις ἀννπόκριτος occurs again 2 Tim. i. 5; and the adj. is applied to ἀγάπη, Rom. xii. 9, 2 Cor. vi. 6. See other reff. It is evident that no stress can be laid on the choice of epithets in any particular passage.

Ver. 6. ὧν: *i.e.*, the disposition, con-

c Luke v. 17,
Acts v. 34,
not LXX.
d Tit. iii. 8,
not LXX.
e 2 Tim. ii.
5, 4 Macc, vi. 18 only.

εἶναι ᶜνομοδιδάσκαλοι, μὴ νοοῦντες μήτε ἃ λέγουσιν, μήτε περὶ τίνων ᵈδιαβεβαιοῦνται. 8. Οἴδαμεν δὲ ὅτι καλὸς ὁ νόμος ἐάν τις αὐτῷ ᵉνομίμως χρῆται¹· 9. εἰδὼς τοῦτο, ὅτι δικαίῳ νόμος οὐ

¹ So ℵDFGKL; χρήσηται AP, 73.

science, and faith as qualified. τινὲς : see note on ver. 3. ἀστοχήσαντες : (aberrantes, Vulg.; recedentes, m⁷; excedentes, m⁵⁰). In the other passages where this word occurs the A.V. and R.V. have erred ; here swerved. They missed the mark in point of fact. It may be questioned whether they really had aimed at a pure heart, etc. But having missed, being in fact "corrupted in mind" vi. 5; "branded in their conscience," iv. 2; and "reprobate concerning the faith," 2 Tim. iii. 8, they did not secure as their own love, practical beneficence, but its exact opposite, empty talking, vaniloquium, Tit. i. 10. The content of this empty talking is analysed in Tit. iii. 9.

It is more natural to suppose that ὧν is governed by ἀστοχήσαντες (Huther, Grimm, Alf.) than by ἐξετράπησαν (Ellicott). ἀστοχεῖν is used absolutely with περί elsewhere in the Pastorals ; but in Ecclus. it governs a genitive directly. ἐκτρέπεσθαι governs both gen. and acc.; the latter in vi. 20.

Moulton and Milligan, Expositor, vii., vii. 373, quote examples of ἀστοχέω from papyri (ii. B.C. ii. A.D.) in the sense "fail" or "forget," e.g., ἀστοχήσαντες τοῦ καλῶς ἔχοντος. ἐξετράπησαν introduces a new metaphor : they had turned aside out of the right path.—ματαιολογία : Here only ; but ματαιολόγοι occurs, Tit. i. 10. See vi. 20 : "Vanitas maxima, ubi de rebus divinis non vere disseritur, Rom. i. 21" (Bengel).

Ver. 7. νομοδιδάσκαλοι : The Mosaic or Jewish law is meant. See Tit. iii. 9. The term is used seriously, of official teachers of the law, in reff.

μὴ νοοῦντες, κ.τ.λ. : Though they understand neither, etc. The participle is concessive, and μὲ is here subjective, as usual, expressing St. Paul's opinion about them. For the sentiment cf. vi. 4, I Cor. viii. 2. λέγουσιν refers to the substance of their assertions, while διαβεβαιοῦνται (affirmant, see Tit. iii. 8) is expressive of the confident manner (R.V.) in which they made them. They did not grasp the force either of their own propositions (hence resulted βέβηλοι κενοφωνίαι), or the nature of the great

topics—Law, Philosophy, etc.—on which they dogmatised, hence their inconsistencies, ἀντιθέσεις τοῦ ψευδωνύμου γνώσεως (vi. 20). On the combination of the relative and interrogative pronouns in one sentence, see Winer-Moulton, Grammar, p. 211.

Vv. 8-11.. And yet this alleged antagonism of the Law to the Gospel is factitious : the Law on which they insist is part of law in general ; so is the Gospel with which I was entrusted. The intention of both is to a large extent identical : to promote right conduct.

Ver. 8. οἴδαμεν, as in Rom. vii. 14. I Cor. viii. 1, 4, introduces a concession in the argument. καλὸς ὁ νόμος was a concession made by St. Paul, Rom. vii. 16, also Rom. vii. 12, ὁ μὲν νόμος ἅγιος. It is possible that it had been objected that his language was inconsistent with his policy. It may be questioned whether καλός, in St. Paul's use of it, differs from ἀγαθός, as meaning good in appearance as well as in reality. For the use of καλός in the Pastorals, see notes on i. 18 and iii. 1. τις has no special reference to the teacher as distinct from the learner. The law is καλός in its own sphere ; but Corruptio optimi pessima ; "Sweetest things turn sourest by their deeds". νομίμως here means in accordance with the spirit in which the law was enacted. It does not mean lawfully in the usual acceptation of that term. St. Paul impresses the word into his service, and does it violence in order to give an epigrammatic turn to the sentence. In 2 Tim. ii. 5, νομίμως has its ordinary meaning in accordance with the rules of the game. χρῆται : In Euripides, Hipp. 98 νόμοις χρῆσθαι means "to live under laws".

Ver. 9. εἰδώς refers to τις, as knowing this (R.V.). For the expression cf. οἶδας τοῦτο, 2 Tim. i. 15 and Eph. v. 5. νόμος : Although νόμος when anarthrous may mean the Mosaic Law, the statement here is perfectly general (so R.V.). The Mosaic Law does not differ in the range of its application, though it may in the details of its enactments, from law in general, of which it is a subdivision. Law is not enacted for

κεῖται, ⁱἀνόμοις δὲ καὶ ᵍἀνυποτάκτοις, ʰἀσεβέσι ʰκαὶ ʰἁμαρτωλοῖς, f Mark xv.
ⁱἀνοσίοις καὶ ᵏβεβήλοις, ˡπατρολῴαις καὶ ᵐμητρολῴαις, ⁿἀνδρο-
φόνοις, ɪο. πόρνοις, ᵒἀρσενοκοίταις, ᵖἀνδραποδισταῖς, ۹ψεύσταις,
ʳἐπιόρκοις, καὶ εἴ τι ἕτερον τῇ ˢὑγιαινούσῃ ˢδιδασκαλίᾳ ἀντίκειται,

Mark xv.
28 (?) =
Luke
xxii. 37 =
Is. liii. 12,
Acts ii. 23,
1 Cor. ix.
21 (4), 2
Thess. ii.

8, 2 Pet. ii. 8.   g Tit. i. 6, 10, Heb. ii. 8, not LXX.   h Prov. xi. 31, 1 Pet. iv. 18.   i 2 Tim.
iii. 2, only, N.T.   k 1 Tim. iv. 7, vi. 20, 2 Tim. ii. 16, Heb. xii. 6 only, N.T.   l Here only,
not LXX.   m Here only, not LXX.   n Here only N.T., 2 Macc. ix. 28.   o 1 Cor. vi. 9,
not LXX.   p Here only, not LXX.   q Rom. iii. 4, Tit. i. 12, Rev. xxi. 8? John (2), 1 John (5).
r Here only N.T., cf. Matt. v. 33.   s 2 Tim. iv. 3, Tit. i. 9, ii. 1, cf. 1 Tim. vi. 3, 2 Tim. i. 13,
Tit. ii. 8, Tit. i. 13, ii. 2.

a *naturally law-abiding man* (dative of reference). δίκαιος is used here in the popular sense, as in "I came not to call the righteous". It is unnecessary to suppose that St. Paul had his theory of justification in his mind when writing this; though of course those who "are led by the Spirit" are δίκαιοι of the highest quality, κατὰ τῶν τοιούτων οὐκ ἔστιν νόμος (Gal. v. 18 sqq., 23). The enumeration of those whom legislators have in view when enacting laws naturally begins with ἄνομοι, of whom the ἀνυπότακτοι, *unruly*, those who deliberately rebel against restriction of any kind, are the extreme type. There is no special class or quality of crime involved in the terms ἄνομος and ἀνυπότακτος. As the series advances, the adjectives indicate more definite and restricted aspects of lawlessness: the first three pairs represent states of mind; then follow examples of violations of specific enactments. Since St. Paul is here dealing with the law of natural religion, it is not safe to deepen the shade of ἀσεβής, κ.τ.λ. by looking at the conceptions they express in the light of the Lord.

ὁ ἀσεβὴς καὶ ἁμαρτωλός is a pair of epithets familiar from its occurrence in Prov. xi. 31 (quoted 1 Pet. iv. 18. See also Jude 15). The ἀσεβής is one whose mental attitude towards God Himself is that of deliberate irreverence; the βέβηλος acts contumeliously towards recognised expressions or forms of reverence to God.

Alford and Ellicott, following a hint from Bengel, suppose that in the series commencing πατρολῴαις St. Paul is going through the second table of the Decalogue. It is an argument against this that when St, Paul is unquestionably enumerating the Commandments, Rom. xiii. 9, he places the command against adultery before that against murder (so Luke xviii. 20; Jas ii. 11; Philo, *De Decalogo*, xxiv. and xxxii.; Tert. *de Pudic*, v., all following LXX (B)

of Deut. chap. v.). There is therefore no necessity to give πατρολῴας the weak rendering *smiter of a father* (R.V. m.) in order to make the word refer to normal breaches of the Fifth Commandment, It can, of course, both by derivation and use, be so rendered, The Greek word, like *parricide* in Latin and English, may be applied to any unnatural treatment of a parent.

The apostle is here purposely specifying the most extreme violations of law, as samples (καὶ εἴ τι ἕτερον) of what disregard of law may lead to. The healthy, wholesome teaching of Christ is of course in opposition to such enormities; it is also in opposition to the false teachers; these teachers have failed to attain to a pure heart, etc. Consequently, although professing to teach the Law, they find themselves in opposition to the essential spirit of law. Let them, and those who listen to them, take care lest their teaching inevitably issue in similar enormities.

Ver. 10. ἀνδραποδισταῖς, *plagiariis* (Vulg.), includes all who exploit other men and women for their own selfish ends; as πόρνοις and ἀρσενοκοίταις include all improper use of sexual relations.

διδασκαλία means *the body of doctrine*, the apostolic *Summa Theologiæ*. The noun is used absolutely, 1 Tim. vi. 1, or with varying epithets : ὑγιαίνουσα, *sana* (here, 2 Tim. iv. 3; Tit. i. 9, ii. 1); καλή, *bona* (1 Tim. iv. 6); κατ᾽ εὐσέβειαν, *secundum pietatem* (1 Tim. vi. 3); μου (2 Tim. iii. 10); τοῦ σωτῆρος ἡμῶν θεοῦ (Tit. ii. 10).

It means *the act of teaching* in Rom. xii. 7, xv. 4, 1 Tim. iv. 13, 16, v. 17, 2 Tim. iii. 16, Tit. ii. 7. The term occurs fifteen times in the Pastoral Epistles in a technical Christian sense. This is in the writer's mind even in 1 Tim. iv. 1, διδασκαλίαις δαιμονίων. It is found four times in the other Pauline Epistles. Of these Rom. xii. 7 is the nearest approach to the special connotation here. With ὑγιαίνουσα (see reff.) compare

t 1 Tim. vi. 11. κατὰ τὸ εὐαγγέλιον τῆς δόξης τοῦ ᵗμακαρίου Θεοῦ, ὃ ᵘἐπι-
15.
u Rom. iii. στεύθην ἐγώ. 12. ¹ᵛΧάριν ᵛἔχω τῷ ʷἐνδυναμώσαντί² με Χριστῷ
2, 1 Cor.
ix.17,Gal. Ἰησοῦ τῷ Κυρίῳ ἡμῶν, ὅτι ˣπιστόν με ˣἡγήσατο, θέμενος εἰς
ii. 7, 1
Thess. ii.
4, Tit. i. 3.   v Luke xvii. 9, 2 Tim. i. 3, Heb. xii. 28.   w Acts ix. 22, Rom. iv. 20, Eph. vi. 10,
Phil. iv. 13, 2 Tim. ii. 1, 2 Tim. iv. 17.   x Heb. xi. 11, ef. Acts xxvi. 2, Phil. ii. 3, 1 Thess. v. 13,
2 Thess. iii. 15.

¹ Ins. καὶ DKL, d, go., syrr.; om. καὶ ℵAFGP, 17, 31, 67**, 80, 238, five others,
f, g, vg., boh., arm.

² ἐνδυναμοῦντι ℵ*, 2, 17, three others, Thphyl.

ὑγιαίνοντες λόγοι (1 Tim. vi. 3; 2 Tim.
i. 13), λόγος ὑγιής (Tit. ii. 8), and
ὑγιαίνειν (ἐν) τῇ πίστει (Tit. i. 13, ii. 2).
The image is peculiar to the Pastoral
Epistles; but it is not therefore un-
Pauline, unless on the assumption that
a writer never enlarges his vocabulary
or ideas. *Healthy, wholesome* admirably
describes Christian teaching, as St. Paul
conceived it, in its complete freedom
from casuistry or quibbles in its theory,
and from arbitrary or unnatural restrictions in its practice. The terms νοσῶν
as applied to false teaching (1 Tim. vi.
4), and possibly γάγγραινα (2 Tim. ii. 17)
were suggested by contrast. See Dean
Bernard's note on this verse.

Ver. 11. κατὰ τὸ εὐαγγέλιον, κ.τ.λ.,
refers to the whole preceding sentence
and is not to be connected with διδασκαλίᾳ only, which would necessitate τῇ
κατά, κ.τ.λ. This reading is actually
found in D,* d, f, g, Vg., Arm., *quae est
secundum*, etc. Von Soden connects
with δικαίῳ νόμος οὐ κεῖται.
Inasmuch as unsound teaching had
claimed to be a εὐαγγέλιον (Gal. i. 6),
St. Paul finds it necessary to recharge
the word with its old force by distinguishing epithets. εὐαγγέλιον had become
impoverished by heterodox associations.
The gospel with which St. Paul had
been entrusted was *the gospel of the
glory of the blessed God. Cf.* "the
gospel of the glory of Christ," 2 Cor. iv.
4. *The gospel concerning the glory*, etc.,
which reveals the glory. And this glory,
although primarily an attribute of God,
is here and elsewhere treated as a blessed
state to which those who obey the gospel may attain, and which it is possible
to miss (Rom. iii. 23, v. 2, xv. 7. See
Sanday and Headlam on Rom. iii. 23).
The phrase is not, as in A.V., an expansion of "The gospel of God," Mark i.
14, etc., "the gospel of which God is the
author," τῆς δόξης being a genitive of
quality=*glorious*. (Compare Rom. viii.
21, 2 Cor. iv. 6; Eph. i. 6, 18; Col. i. 11,
27; Tit. ii. 13).

μακαρίου: *Blessed* as an epithet of
God is only found here and in vi. 15,
where see note. Grimm compares the
μάκαρες θεοί of Homer and Hesiod. But
the notion here is much loftier. We
may call God *blessed*, but not *happy;*
since happiness is only predicated of
those whom it is possible to conceive of
as unhappy.

ὃ ἐπιστεύθην ἐγώ: This phrase occurs
again Tit. i. 3. *Cf.* Rom. iii. 2, 1 Cor.
ix. 17, Gal. ii. 7, 1 Thess. ii. 4. St.
Paul does not here allude to his particular presentation of the gospel, as in Gal.
ii. 7; nor is he thinking specially of
God's goodness to him in making him a
minister, as in Rom. xv. 16, Eph. iii. 8,
Col. i. 25; he is merely asserting his
consistency, and repudiating the charge
of antinomianism which had been brought
against him.

Vv. 12-14. I cannot mention my part
in the furtherance of the gospel without
expressing my gratitude to our Lord for
His forgiveness of my errors and His
confidence in my natural trustworthiness, and His grace which gave me
strength to serve Him.

Ver. 12. This parenthetical thanksgiving, which is quite in St. Paul's
manner, is suggested by ὃ ἐπιστεύθην
ἐγώ. *Cf.* 1 Cor. xv. 9 *sqq.*, Eph. iii. 8.

χάριν ἔχω: see note on 2 Tim. i. 3.
ἐνδυναμώσαντι: The aor. is used because the writer's thoughts pass back to
the particular time when he received
inward strength increasingly, Acts ix.
22. In Phil. iv. 13 the present participle
is appropriate, because he is describing
his present state. The word ἐν-
δυναμοῦσθαι is only found in N.T. in
Paul and Acts ix. 22. Is it fanciful to
suppose that Luke's use of it in Acts
was suggested by his master's account
of that crisis? ὅτι: *because*.

πιστόν: *trustworthy*, as a steward is
expected to be, 1 Cor. iv. 2. See ref.
There is, as Bengel remarks, a touch of
ἀνθρωποπάθεια, of anthropomorphism or
accommodation, in πιστόν με ἡγήσατο.

διακονίαν, 13. τὸ¹ πρότερον ὄντα²ʸ βλάσφημον καὶ ᶻ διώκτην καὶ yʸ 2 Tim. iii.
ᵃ ὑβριστήν· ἀλλὰ ἠλεήθην, ὅτι ἀγνοῶν ἐποίησα ἐν ἀπιστίᾳ· 14. zᶻ Here only
ᵇ ὑπερεπλεόνασεν δὲ ἡ χάρις ᶜ τοῦ ᶜ Κυρίου ᶜ ἡμῶν μετὰ ᵈᵉ πίστεως xv. 9, Gal.
ᵈᵉ καὶ ᵈ ἀγάπης ᵈ τῆς ᵈ ἐν ˣ Χριστῷ ᵈ Ἰησοῦ. 15. ᶠ Πιστὸς³ ᶠ ὁ Phil. iii.,

a Rom. i. 30 only (N.T.).   b Here only, not LXX.   c 2 Tim. i. 8, Heb. vii. 14, 2 Pet. iii. 15,
Rev. xi. 15.   d 2 Tim. i. 13.   e Col. i. 4, 1 Thess. iii. 6, v. 8, 1 Tim. ii. 15, vi. 11, 2 Tim. ii. 22,
Tit. ii. 2, cf. Gal. v. 6, Eph. vi. 23, 1 Tim. iv. 12, Rev. ii. 19.   f 1 Tim. iii. 1, iv. 9, 2 Tim. ii. 11, Tit.
iii. 8, cf. Tit. i. 9, Rev. xxi. 5, xxii. 6.

¹ So אAD*FGP, 17, 47, 67**, 80, three others; τὸν DᶜKL.
² Ins. με A, 73, g.
³ *Humanus* 1, Latin MSS. known to Jerome, Ambrst., Julian pel., Aug.

The Divine Master *knew* that His
steward Paul would be trustworthy.
Paul, not unnaturally, speaks as if God's
apprehension of him were of the same
relative nature as his own *hope* of final
perseverance.

θέμενος εἰς διακονίαν: The fact that
Christ employed Paul in His service was
a sufficient proof of His estimate of him.
διάκονος and διακονία are used in a general sense of St. Paul's ministry also in
Rom. xi. 13, 1 Cor. iii. 5, 2 Cor. iii. 6, iv.
1, v. 18, vi. 3, Eph. iii. 7, Col. i. 23, 25.
Cf. 1 Tim. iv. 6, 2 Tim. iv. 5, 11. The
nature of it is exactly defined in Acts xx.
24, "to testify the gospel of the grace
of God".

Ver. 13. ὄντα: concessive: "*though I
was*," etc. βλάσφημον: *a blasphemer*.
The context alone can decide whether
βλασφημεῖν is to be rendered *rail* or
blaspheme. It was against Jesus personally that Paul had acted (Acts ix. 5,
xxii. 7, xxvi. 14). This brings into
stronger relief the kindness of Jesus to
Paul. ὑβριστής, rendered *insolent* (R.V.),
Rom. i. 30, covers both words and deeds
of despitefulness. *Injurious* is sufficiently
comprehensive, but, in modern English,
is not sufficiently vigorous.

ἀλλὰ ἠλεήθην: *Obtaining mercy* does
not in this case mean the pardon which
implies merely exemption from punishment; no self-respecting man would value
such a relationship with God. Rather St.
Paul has in his mind what he has expressed elsewhere as the issue of having
received mercy, *viz.*, to have been granted
an opportunity of serving Him whom he
had injured. *Cf.* 1 Cor. vii. 25, xv. 10,
2 Cor. iv. 1.

ἀγνοῶν ἐποίησα: A possible echo of
the Saying from the Cross recorded in
Luke xxiii. 34, οὐ γὰρ οἴδασιν τί ποιοῦσιν.
See also John xv. 21, xvi. 3, Acts iii. 17,
xiii. 27, 1 Cor. ii. 8. There is a remarkable parallel in *The Testaments of the*

Twelve Patriarchs (Judah xix. 3, ἠλέησέ
με ὅτι ἐν ἀγνωσίᾳ τοῦτο ἐποίησα) dated
by Charles between 109-106 B.C.

ἐν ἀπιστίᾳ does not so much qualify
ἀγνοῶν, as correct a possible notion that
all ignorance must be excusable. St.
Paul declares, on the contrary, that his
was a positive act of sinful disbelief;
but "where sin abounded, grace did
abound more exceedingly," ὑπερεπερίσ-
σευσεν ἡ χάρις, Rom. v. 20.

Ver. 14. ὑπερπλεονάζειν only occurs
here in N.T.; but St. Paul constantly
uses compounds with ὑπέρ. The comparative force of the ὑπέρ—grace out-
weighing sin—is brought out in Rom. v.
15 *sqq.* In these passages at least it is not
true, as Ellicott maintains, that ὑπέρ has
a superlative (*abound exceedingly*) force.

τοῦ κυρίου ἡμῶν: The expression *our
Lord* (without the addition of *Jesus*
or *Jesus Christ*), common in modern
times, is rare in N.T. See reff. In 2
Peter iii. 15 it is not certain if the refe-
rence is to Christ, the Judge, or to the
Father who determines the moment of
His coming. In Rev. xi. 15 God the
Father is meant.

*Faith and love which is in Christ
Jesus* occurs again in 2 Tim. i. 13. In
both places the singular relative is im-
properly used for the plural. It is one
of the writer's habitual phrases; and
therefore we cannot suppose any special
relevance to the context in either of its
constituent parts, though here Bengel
contrasts *faith* with the *unbelief*; and
love with the *blasphemer*, etc., of ver. 13.
Faith and love, are the inward and
outward manifestations respectively of
the bestowal and realisation of grace.

πίστις ἐν Χρ. Ἰησ. occurs Gal. iii. 26,
1 Tim. iii. 13, 2 Tim. iii. 15. πίστις and
ἀγάπη are also associated (in this order)
in the first six reff.

Vv. 15-17. The dealings of Christ with
me, of course, are not unique. My ex-

g 1 Tim. iv. ᶠλόγος καὶ πάσης ᵍ ἀποδοχῆς ἄξιος, ὅτι Χριστὸς Ἰησοῦς ʰ ἦλθεν ʰ εἰς
9 only,
not LXX. ʰ τὸν ʰ κόσμον ἁμαρτωλοὺς σῶσαι· ὧν πρῶτός εἰμι ἐγώ.   16. ἀλλὰ
h John i. 9.
iii. 19, vi.
14, ix. 39, xi. 27, xii.|46, xvi. 28, xviii. 37.

perience is the same in kind, though not in degree, as that of all saved sinners. Christ's longsuffering will never undergo a more severe test than it did in my case, so that no sinner need ever despair. Let us giorify God therefor.

Ver. 15. πιστὸς ὁ λόγος: The complete phrase, πιστὸς . . . ἄξιος recurs in 1 Tim. iv. 9; and πιστὸς ὁ λόγος in 1 Tim. iii. 1, 2 Tim. ii. 11, Tit. iii. 8.

The only other places in the N.T. in which πιστὸς is applied to λόγος in the sense of *that can be relied on* are Tit. i. 9, ἀντεχόμενον τοῦ κατὰ τὴν διδαχὴν πιστοῦ λόγου; Rev. xxi. 5, xxii. 6, οὗτοι οἱ λόγοι πιστοὶ καὶ ἀληθινοί.

In Tit. i. 9 the πιστὸς λόγος cannot mean an isolated saying, but rather the totality of the revelation given in Christ. Of the other five places in which the phrase occurs there are not more than two in which it is possible to say with confidence that a definite saying is referred to, *i.e.*, here, and perhaps 2 Tim. ii. 11. In the other passages, the expression seems to be a brief parenthetical formula, affirmative of the truth of the general doctrine with which the writer happens to be dealing. See notes in each place.

πάσης ἀποδοχῆς ἄξιος: Field (*Notes on Trans. N.T.* p. 203) shows by many examples from Diodorus Siculus and Diog. Laert. that this phrase was a common one in later Greek. He would render ἀποδοχή by *approbation* or *admiration*. See also Moulton and Milligan, *Expositor*, vii., vi. 185. ἀπόδεκτος occurs 1 Tim. ii. 3, v. 4; ἀποδέχεσθαι in Luke and Acts.

Other examples in the Pastorals of the use of πᾶς (=*summus*) with abstract nouns (besides ch. iv. 9) are 1 Tim. ii. 2, 11, iii. 4, v. 2, vi. 1, 2 Tim. iv. 2, Tit. ii. 10, 15, iii. 2.

Χρ. Ἰησ. ἦλθεν—σῶσαι: This is quite evidently a saying in which the apostolic church summed up its practical belief in the Incarnation. ἔρχεσθαι εἰς τὸν κόσμον, as used of Christ, is an expression of the Johannine theology; see reff. It is the converse of another Johannine expression, ἀπέστειλεν ὁ θεὸς . . . (or ὁ πατὴρ) εἰς τὸν κόσμον: John iii. 17, x. 36, xvii. 18, 1 John iv. 9. εἰσερχόμενος εἰς τὸν κόσμον is used in the same asso-

ciation, Heb. x. 5. εἰσέρχεσθαι εἰς τὸν κόσμον is used of sin, Rom. v. 12; ἐξέρχεσθαι εἰς τ. κ. of false prophets in 1 John iv. 1, 2 John 7.

When we say that this is a Johannine expression, we do not mean that the writer of this epistle was influenced by the Johannine *literature*. But until it has been proved that John the son of Zebedee did not write the Gospel which bears his name, and that the discourses contained in it are wholly unhistorical, we are entitled, indeed compelled, to assume that what we may for convenience call Johannine theology, and the familiar expression of it, was known wherever John preached.

With ἦλθεν . . . σῶσαι *cf.* Luke xix. 10, ἦλθεν . . . σῶσαι τὸ ἀπολωλός. For the notion expressed in ἁμαρτωλοὺς σῶσαι *cf.* Matt. i. 21, ix. 13; see also John xii. 47, ἦλθον . . . ἵνα σώσω τὸν κόσμον; John i. 29, ὁ αἴρων τὴν ἁμαρτίαν τοῦ κόσμου; and 1 John ii. 2.

The pre-existence of Christ, as well as His resistless power to save, is of course assumed in this noble summary of the gospel.

ὧν πρῶτός εἰμι ἐγώ: In the experiences of personal religion each individual man is alone with God. He sees nought but the Holy One and his own sinful self (*cf.* Luke xviii. 13, μοι τῷ ἁμαρτωλῷ). And the more familiar a man becomes with the meeting of God face to face the less likely is he to be deceived as to the gulf which parts him, limited, finite, defective, from the Infinite and Perfect. It is not easy to think of anyone but St. Paul as penning these words; although his expressions of self-depreciation elsewhere (1 Cor. xv. 9, Eph. iii. 8) are quite differently worded. In each case the form in which they are couched arises naturally out of the context. The sincerity of St. Paul's humility is proved by the fact that he had no mock modesty; when the occasion compelled it, he could appraise himself; *e.g.*, Acts xxiii. 1, xxiv. 16, 2 Cor. xi. 5, xii. 11, Gal. ii. 6.

Ver. 16. ἀλλά: This is not adversative, but rather continues from ver. 13, and develops the expression of self-depreciation. The connexion is: "I was such a sinner that antecedently one might doubt

διὰ τοῦτο ἠλεήθην, ἵνα ἐν ἐμοὶ πρώτῳ [1] ἐνδείξηται Χριστὸς Ἰησοῦς [1] i (of God)
τὴν [k] ἅπασαν [k] μακροθυμίαν, πρὸς [l] ὑποτύπωσιν τῶν μελλόντων
πιστεύειν ἐπ᾽ αὐτῷ εἰς [m] ζωὴν [m] αἰώνιον. 17. τῷ δὲ [n] βασιλεῖ [n] τῶν k
[n] αἰώνων, [o] ἀφθάρτῳ,[2] [p] ἀοράτῳ, [q] μόνῳ [3] θεῷ, τιμὴ καὶ δόξα εἰς τοὺς

Rom. ix.
17, 22.
Eph. ii. 7.
2 Tim. iv.
2, cf. Col.
i. 11, see
2 Tim. iii.
10.

2 Tim. i. 13 only, not LXX.   m John iv. 14, 36, vi. 27, xii. 25, Acts xiii. 48, Rom. v.
vi. 12, Tit i. 2, iii. 7, etc.   n Tob. xiii. 6, 10, Enoch ix. 4, Rev. xv. 3, cf. 1 Tim. vi. 15.
xii. 1, xviii. 4, Rom. i. 23.   p Col. i. 15, Heb. xi. 27.   q John v. 44, Jude 25.

21, 1 Tim.
o Wisd.

[1] So AD, 17, 47, 80, six others, d, f, r, vg., go., sah. ; Ἰησ. Χριστ. ℵKLP, 37,
syrr., boh., arm.

[2] ἀθανάτῳ D*, inmortali d, f, r, vg., go., syrhcl-mg ; FG, g, r (incorruptibili) add
ἀθανάτῳ after ἀοράτῳ.

[3] Ins. σοφῷ ℵcDbcKLP, go., syrhcl (from Rom. xvi. 27) ; om. σοφῷ ℵ*AD*FG,
17, 37, one other, Latt., sah., boh., syrpesh.

whether I could be saved or was worth saving. But Christ had a special object in view in extending to me His mercy."

διὰ τοῦτο, followed by ἵνα and referring to what follows, occurs in Rom. iv. 16, 2 Cor. xiii. 10, Eph. vi. 13, 2 Thess. ii. 11, Philem. 15. See also Rom. xiii. 6. ἐν ἐμοί is used as in Gal. i. 16, 24, and as ἐν ἡμῖν in 1 Cor. iv. 6. I was an object lesson in which Christ displayed the extent of His longsuffering.

πρώτῳ: Alford correctly says that the foll. μελλόντων proves that St. Paul here combines the senses first (A.V.) and as chief (R.V.).

τὴν ἅπασαν μακροθυμίαν: the utmost longsuffering which he has (Blass, Grammar, p. 162). Here r renders μακροθ. longanimitatem. Chrys., followed by Alf. and Ell., explains, "Greater longsuffering He could not show in any case than in mine, nor find a sinner that so required all His longsuffering ; not a part only". If there had been only one soul of sinful man to save, it would have needed the Incarnation to save that soul. In St. Paul's case, conversion had been preceded by a long internal struggle on his part, and patience on Christ's part : " It is hard for thee to kick against the goad ". ἅπαξ only occurs in the Pauline epistles again in Eph. vi. 13. Its use " is confined principally to literary documents " (Moulton and Milligan, Expositor, vii. vi. 88).

πρὸς ὑποτύπωσιν τῶν μελλόντων: The use of the genitive here is paralleled exactly in 2 Peter ii 6, ὑπόδειγμα μελλόντων ἀσεβεῖν, " an example unto those that should live ungodly " ; and 1 Cor. x. 6, ταῦτα δὲ τύποι ἡμῶν ἐγενήθησαν ; also 1 Tim. iv. 12, where see reff. It does not mean as R.V. (an ensample of them), that St. Paul was the first speci-

men of Jesus' work of grace, but rather as A.V. (a pattern to them), that no one who ever afterwards hears the gracious invitation of Christ need hang back from accepting it by reason of the greatness of his sin, when he has the example of St. Paul before him (so Chrys.). The ὑποτύπωσις, of course, is the whole transaction of St. Paul's conversion in all its bearings, ad informationem eorum qui credituri sunt illi (Vulg.). Bengel compares Ps. xxxii. 5, 6, " Thou forgavest the iniquity of my sin. For this let every one that is godly pray unto thee," etc.

πιστεύειν ἐπ᾽ αὐτῷ : πιστεύειν is usually followed by εἰς and the acc., or the simple dat. But ἐπί with acc., and ἐν are also found. The construction in the text is due to an unconscious recollection of Isaiah xxviii. 16 (also quoted Rom. ix. 33, x. 11, 1 Peter ii. 6) ; and no other explanation need be sought. The only other certain instance of the same construction is Luke xxiv. 25. The critical editors reject it in Matt. xxvii. 42.

Ver. 17. This noble doxology might be one used by St. Paul himself in one of his eucharistic prayers. It is significant that in the Jewish forms of thanksgiving מֶלֶךְ הָעוֹלָם is of constant occurrence. See reff., and θεὸς τῶν αἰ. in Ecclus. xxxvi. 22. Bengel's suggestion (on ch. i. 4) that there is a polemical reference to the aeons of Gnosticism is fanciful and unnecessary. βασιλεύς, as a title of God the Father, is found in vi. 15 and Rev. xv. 3, a passage of which Swete says (comm. in loc.), "The thought as well as the phraseology of the Song is strangely Hebraic ". Cf. Ps. ix. 37 (x. 16).

ἀφθάρτῳ: The three adjectives ἀφθά-

¹ See ver. 5. αἰῶνας τῶν αἰώνων · ἀμήν.   18. Ταύτην τὴν ʳ παραγγελίαν ˢ παρα-
ˢ Luke xii.
48, xxiii. τίθεμαί σοι, ᵗ τέκνον Τιμόθεε, κατὰ τὰς ᵘ προαγούσας ἐπὶ σὲ προφη-
46, Acts
xiv. 23,
xx. 32, 2 Tim. ii. 2, 1 Pet. iv. 19.   t See ver. 2.   u 1 Tim. v. 24.

ρτῳ, ἀοράτῳ, μόνῳ are co-ordinate epithets of θεῷ, to God immortal, invisible, unique.

ἄφθαρτος, immortal, as an epithet of God, occurs Rom. i. 23 (cf. Wisd. xii. 1, τὸ γὰρ ἄφθαρτόν σου . . . πνεῦμά ἐστιν ἐν πᾶσιν, and Moulton and Milligan, Expositor, vii., vi. 376). It is expanded in vi. 15 sq., who only hath immortality, just as ἀοράτῳ becomes whom no man hath seen, nor can see (for the thought, see John i. 18, Col. i. 15, Heb. xi. 27, 1 John iv. 12), and μόνῳ becomes the blessed and only potentate. For the epithet μόνος, used absolutely, see reff. and also Ps. lxxxvi. 10, John xvii. 3, Rom. xvi. 27.

τιμὴ καὶ δόξα: This combination in a doxology is found Rev. iv. 9, δώσουσιν . . . δόξαν καὶ τιμὴν; v. 13, ἡ τιμὴ καὶ ἡ δόξα. In St. Paul's other doxologies (Gal. i. 5, Rom. xi. 36, xvi. 27, Phil. iv. 20, Eph. iii. 21, 1 Tim. vi. 16, 2 Tim. iv. 18), with the exception of 1 Tim. vi. 16 (τιμὴ καὶ κράτος), τιμή is not found; and he always has ἡ δόξα (see Westcott, Additional Note on Heb. xiii. 21).

Vv. 18-20. The charge that I am giving you now is in harmony with what you heard from the prophets at your ordination. It only emphasises the fundamental moral relations of man to things unseen and seen. The rejection of these principles of natural religion naturally issues in a perversion of revealed religion, such as caused the excommunication of Hymenaeus and Alexander.

Ver. 18. ταύτην τὴν παραγγελίαν is partly resumptive of ver. 3; it is the positive aspect of what is there negatively expressed; but as it concerns Timothy directly, it has a reference forward to ἵνα στρατεύῃ, κ.τ.λ., and to the general contents of the epistle. Bengel refers it to παραγγελίας, ver. 5. Peile to πιστὸς ὁ λόγος, κ.τ.λ.

παρατίθεμαί σοι: The use of this word, as in Luke xii. 48, 2 Tim. ii. 2, suggests that the παραγγελία is more than an injunction of temporary urgency, that it is connected with, if not the same as, the παραθήκη (depositum) of 1 Tim. vi. 20, etc.

τέκνον Τιμόθεε: There is a peculiar affectionate earnestness in this use of the personal name, here and in the con-

clusion of the letter (vi. 20). Cf. Luke x. 41, Martha, Martha; xxii. 34, Peter; John xiv. 9, Philip; xx. 16, Mary. For τέκνον see note on ver. 2.

κατὰ τὰς . . . προφητείας, κ.τ.λ.: By the prophecies, etc., are meant the utterances of the prophets, such as Silas (and not excluding St. Paul himself) who were with St. Paul when the ordination of Timothy became possible; utterances which pointed out the young man as a person suitable for the ministry, led the way to him (R.V.m.). So Chrys. There is no need to suppose that any long interval of time elapsed between the first prophetical utterances and the laying on of hands. In any case, similar prophecies accompanied the act of ordination. This explanation agrees best with the order of the words, and is in harmony with earlier and later references to the extraordinary function of prophets in relation to the ministry in the apostolic church. Thus in Acts xiii. 1, 2, the imposition of hands on Paul and Barnabas—whether for a special mission or to a distinct order it matters not—was at the dictation of prophets. And Clem. Alex. (Quis Dives, 42) speaks of the Apostle John, κλήρῳ ἕνα γέ τινα κληρώσων τῶν ὑπὸ τοῦ Πνεύματος σημαινομένων. In the same sense may be understood Clem. Rom. ad Cor. i. 42: οἱ ἀπόστολοι . . . καθίστανον τὰς ἀπαρχὰς αὐτῶν, δοκιμάσαντες τῷ πνεύματι, εἰς ἐπισκόπους καὶ διακόνους.

It is evident from iv. 14 that the prophecy accompanying the laying-on of hands was considered at least contributory to the bestowal of the charisma; it is natural to suppose that it was of the nature of a charge to the candidate. St. Paul here says that his present charge to Timothy is in accordance with, in the spirit of, and also in reinforcement of (ἵνα στρατεύῃ ἐν αὐταῖς) the charge he had originally received on an occasion of peculiar solemnity. This is a stimulating appeal like that of 2 Tim. iii. 14, "knowing of whom thou hast learned them ".

Ellicott disconnects προαγούσας from ἐπὶ σέ; but "forerunning, precursory," is pointless as an epithet of predictions, though quite appropriate [as applied to ἐντολή in Heb. vii. 18; and the notion

τείας, ἵνα ᵛστρατεύῃ ¹ ἐν αὐταῖς τὴν καλὴν ᵂστρατείαν, 19. ἔχων ᵛ ¹ Cor. ix.
7, 2 Cor.
πίστιν καὶ ˣἀγαθὴν ˣσυνείδησιν, ἥν τινες ᵞἀπωσάμενοι ᵃπερὶ ᵗτὴν x. 3, 2
Tim. ii. 4.
ᶻπίστιν ᵃἐναυάγησαν· 20. ὧν ἐστὶν Ὑμέναιος καὶ Ἀλέξανδρος, οὓς w 2 Cor. x.
4.
ᵇπαρέδωκα ᵇτῷ ᵇΣατανᾷ ἵνα ᶜπαιδευθῶσι μὴ ᵈβλασφημεῖν.   x See ver. 5.
y Acts xiii.
46.

z 1 Tim. vi. 21, 2 Tim. iii. 8.   a 2 Cor. xi. 25 only, not LXX.   b 1 Cor. v. 5.   c Acts vii.
22, xxii. 3, 1 Cor. xi. 32, 2 Cor. vi. 9, 2 Tim. ii. 25, Tit. ii. 12.   d Matt. ix. 3=Mark ii. 7, Matt.
xxvi. 65, John x. 36, Acts xiii. 45, xviii. 6, xxvi. 11.

¹ στρατεύσῃ ℵ*D*.

of "prophecies uttered over Timothy at
his ordination . . . foretelling his future
zeal and success " is unnatural.

ἵνα στρατεύῃ . . . τὴν καλὴν στρατείαν : The ministry is spoken of as a
warfare, militia, " the service of a
στρατιώτης in all its details and particulars " (Ell.). See reff., and an interesting parallel in 4 Macc. ix. 23, ἱερὰν
κ. εὐγενῆ στρατείαν στρατεύσασθε περὶ
τῆς εὐσεβείας.

ἐν αὐταῖς: in them, as 'in defensive
armour. (Winer Moulton, Grammar, p.
484). Cf. Eph. vi. 14, 16, for a similar
use of ἐν.

καλός is characteristic of the Pastorals,
in which it occurs twenty-four times as
against sixteen times in the other
Pauline Epistles. It has a special
Christian reference in such phrases as
the present, and as qualifying στρατιώτης, 2 Tim. ii. 3 ; ἀγών, 1 Tim. vi.
12, 2 Tim. iv. 7 ; διδασκαλία, 1 Tim. iv.
6 ; ὁμολογία, 1 Tim. vi. 12, 13 : παραθήκη, 2 Tim. i. 14 ; διάκονος, 1 Tim. iv.
6. Moreover, the use of the word in
these epistles is also different from that
found in the earlier epistles : (a) it is
used as a qualifying adjective twelve times
in the Pastorals (excluding καλὸν ἔργον,
καλὰ ἔργα) viz., in addition to the reff.
already given, 1 Tim. iii. 7, 13, vi. 19.
This use is not found in the other Pauline
Epistles. (b) As a predicate it occurs twice,
viz., 1 Tim. i. 8, iv. 4, as against once
elsewhere in Paul, Rom. vii. 16. On the
other hand, τὸ καλόν is not found in the
Pastorals, though five times elsewhere
(Rom. vii. 18, 21 ; 2 Cor. xiii. 7; Gal. vi.
9 ; 1 Thess. v. 21) ; nor καλά (Rom. xii.
17 ; 2 Cor. viii. 21) ; nor καλόν (Rom. xiv.
21 ; 1 Cor. v. 6, vii. 1, 8, 26, ix. 15 ;
Gal. iv. 18) ; but τοῦτο καλόν occurs
chap. ii. 3 (Tit. iii. 8) as well as in 1
Cor. vii. 26. See also note on chap. iii.
1.

Ver. 19. ἔχων: It is best perhaps to
suppose that the metaphor of warfare is
not continued beyond στρατείαν ; else
we might render, holding faith, as a

shield, cf. Eph. vi. 16. But ἐν αὐταῖς
implies that the prophecies included
every piece of defensive armour. So
ἔχων here simply means possessing, as
in 1 Tim. iii. 9, 2 Tim. i. 13, iii. 5,
Rom. ii. 20, 1 Cor. xv. 34, 1 Pet. iii. 16.
συνείδησιν: see note on ver. 5.
τινες : see note on ver. 3.
ἀπωσάμενοι : The indictment against
the moral standard of the false teachers
is here expressed more severely than
above in ver. 6. There they are said to
have " missed " or " neglected " faith,
etc.; but here that they thrust it from
them (R.V., cf. Acts xiii. 46) when it im-
portuned for admittance into their hearts.
" Recedit invita. Semper dicit, Noli me
laedere " (Bengel).
περὶ τὴν πίστιν ἐναυάγησαν : Another
change of metaphor : they suffered moral
shipwreck, so far as the faith is concerned. "When the life is corrupt, it
engenders a doctrine congenial to it "
(Chrys.). We are not justified in interpreting suffered shipwreck as though it
meant that they were lost beyond hope
of recovery. St. Paul himself had suffered shipwreck at least four times (2
Cor. xi. 25) when he wrote this epistle.
He had on each occasion lost everything
except himself. For the construction,
cf. περὶ τὴν πίστιν [ἀλήθειαν] ἠστόχησαν, 1 Tim. vi. 21, 2 Tim. ii. 18 ;
ἀδόκιμοι περὶ τὴν πίστιν, 2 Tim. iii. 8.
περί with acc. is used in a somewhat
similar sense in Mark iv. 19, Luke x. 40,
41, Acts xix. 25, Phil. ii. 23 (the only instance in Paul outside the Pastorals) 1
Tim. vi. 4, Tit. ii. 7.
Hymenaeus and Alexander were the
ringleaders of those who had suffered shipwreck. There is no sufficient reason to
suppose that this Hymenaeus is different
from the heretic of the same name in 2
Tim. ii. 17, where his error is more precisely defined. The identification of
Alexander with Alexander the smith of
2 Tim. iv. 14 is more precarious.
Ver. 20. οὓς παρέδωκα τῷ Σατανᾷ:
I have delivered (A.V.) expresses more

a Rom. xii.
1, 1 Cor.
iv. 16,
Eph. iv. 1.
b Luke v. 33,
Phil. i. 4.

II. 1. ᵃΠαρακαλῶ ¹ ᵃοὖν πρῶτον πάντων ᵇποιεῖσθαι ᵇδεήσεις, προσευχάς, ᶜἐντεύξεις, ᵈεὐχαριστίας, ὑπὲρ πάντων ἀνθρώπων·—

c 2 Macc. iv. 8, 1 Tim. iv. 5.   d 1 Cor. xiv. 16, Phil. iv. 6.

¹ παρακάλει, obsecra, D*FgrG, d, g (not r), sah.

accurately than I delivered (R.V.) the force of the aorist followed by the subjunctive: they were still under sentence of excommunication (see Field in loc.). The theory of the relation of the Church to non-Christians which underlies this phrase is expressed in 1 John v. 19, ἐκ τοῦ θεοῦ ἐσμεν, καὶ ὁ κόσμος ὅλος ἐν τῷ πονηρῷ κεῖται. The ἐξουσία τοῦ Σατανᾶ was "the darkness" over against "the light" of the Kingdom of God (Acts xxvi. 18). The conception is not popular among modern Christians. The two kingdoms, if there are two, have interpenetrated each other. The phraseology, here and in the parallel, 1 Cor. v. 5, is based on Job ii. 6, ἰδοὺ παραδίδωμί σοι αὐτόν. The name Σατανᾶς also occurs in chap. v. 15 and in eight other places in the Pauline Epistles.

ἵνα παιδευθῶσι: The apostolic severity was not merely punitive; it was also corrective. The intention, at least, of excommunication was ἵνα τὸ πνεῦμα σωθῇ, 1 Cor. v. 5. So Chrys. We must not therefore render here, sarcastically, that they may learn, A.V., but that they might be taught or instructed. At the same time, it is unnatural to assume with Bengel that the παιδεία was intended to keep them from blaspheming at all; St. Paul hoped that it might prevent a repetition of the sin. The term has more of the association of discipline here and in 1 Cor. xi. 32, 2 Cor. vi. 9, than in the other references.

βλασφημεῖν: It is absurd to suppose that St. Paul here refers to a railing disparagement of his own apostolic claims.

CHAPTER II.—Vv. 1-7. In the first place, let me remind you that the Church's public prayers must be made expressly for all men, from the Emperor downwards. This care for all becomes those who know that they are children of a Father who wishes the best for all His children. He is one and the same to all, and the salvation He has provided in the Atonement is available for all. My own work among the Gentiles is one instance of God's fetching home again His banished ones.

Ver. 1. παρακαλῶ οὖν: This is resumptive of, and a further development of the παραγγελία of i. 18. See reff. St. Paul here at last begins the subject matter of the letter. The object of παρακαλῶ is not expressed; it is the Church, through Timothy.

πρῶτον πάντων is to be connected with παρακαλῶ: The most important point in my exhortation concerns the universal scope of public prayer. The A.V. connects πρῶτ. πάντ. with ποιεῖσθαι, as though the framing of a liturgy were in question.

ποιεῖσθαι is mid. The mid. of ποιεῖν is not of frequent occurrence in N.T.; it is found chiefly in Luke and Paul. For the actual expression δεήσεις ποιεῖσται, see reff., and Winer-Moulton, Grammar, p. 320, note, and Deissmann, Bible Studies, trans. p. 250.

There is of course a distinction in meaning between δεήσεις, προσευχάς, ἐντεύξεις, supplications (in special crises) prayers, petitions; that is to say, they cannot be used interchangeably on every occasion; but here the nuances of meaning are not present to St. Paul's mind: his object in the enumeration is simply to cover every possible variety of public prayer. This is proved conclusively by the addition εὐχαριστίας, which of course could not be, in any natural sense, for all men. But every kind of prayer must be accompanied by thanksgiving, Phil. iv. 6, Col. iv. 2. On ἔντευξις, see Moulton and Milligan, Expositor, vii., vii. 284, and Deissmann, Bible Studies, trans. p. 121. The retention of thanksgivings in the reference to this verse in the opening of the Anglican prayer For the whole state of Christ's Church is scarcely justified by referring it to God's triumphs of grace in the lives of the faithful departed. Less unnatural is the explanation of Chrysostom, that "we must give thanks to God for the good that befals others".

προσευχή and δέησις (in this order) are combined, Eph. vi. 18, Phil iv. 6; and in chap. v. 5 in the same order as here.

ὑπὲρ πάντων ἀνθρώπων: The blessed effects of intercessory prayer on those who pray and on those for whom prayer

2. ὑπὲρ βασιλέων καὶ πάντων τῶν ἐν ᵉ ὑπεροχῇ ὄντων, ἵνα ᶠ ἥρεμον ᵉ 2 Macc. iii.
καὶ ᵍ ἡσύχιον ʰ βίον ⁱ διάγωμεν ἐν πάσῃ ᵏ εὐσεβείᾳ καὶ ˡ σεμνότητι · ii. 1.
f Es. iii. 13
only.

g 1 Pet. iii. 4.   h Luke viii. 14, 2 Tim. ii. 4, 1 John ii. 16.   i Ecclus. xxxviii. 27, 2 Macc. xii.
38, 3 Macc. ii. 3, iv. 8, vi. 35, Tit. iii. 3.   k Acts iii. 12, 1 Tim. iii. 16, iv. 7, 8, vi. 3, 5, 6, 11,
2 Tim. iii. 5, Tit. i. 1, 2 Pet. i. 3, 6, 7, iii. 11.   l 2 Macc. iii. 12, 1 Tim. iii. 4, Tit. ii. 7.

is made is urged with special reference to the circumstances of the early Church by Polycarp, *Phil.* 12; Tert. *Apol.* § 30; *ad Scapulam*, § 2; Justin Martyr, *Apol.* i. 17; *Dial.* 35. "No one can feel hatred towards those for whom he prays. . . . Nothing is so apt to draw men under teaching, as to love and be loved" (Chrys.).

Ver. 2. ὑπὲρ βασιλέων: Prayer for all men must be given intensity and directness by analysis into prayer for each and every sort and condition of men. St. Paul begins such an analytical enumeration with *kings and all that are in high place*; but he does not proceed with it. This verse 2 is in fact an explanatory parenthesis, exemplifying how the prayer "for all men" is to begin. The plural *kings* has occasioned some difficulty; since in St. Paul's time, Timothy and the Ephesian Church were concerned with one king only, the Emperor. Consequently those who deny the Pauline authorship of the Pastorals suppose that the writer here betrays his consciousness of the associated emperors under the Antonines. But, in the first place, he would have written τῶν βασιλέων: and again, the sentiment was intended as a perfectly general one, applicable to all lands. St. Paul knew of kingdoms outside the Roman empire to which, no doubt, he was sure the Gospel would spread; and even within the Roman empire there were honorary βασιλεῖς whose characters could seriously affect those about them. The plural is similarly used in Matt. x. 18 and parallels.

On the duty of prayer for kings see Jer. xxix. 7, Ezra vi. 10, Bar. i. 11, 1 Macc. vii. 33, Rom. xiii. 1, Tit. iii. 1, 1 Pet. ii. 13.

Such prayer was a prominent feature in the Christian liturgy from the earliest times to which we can trace it (*e.g.*, Clem. Rom. *ad Cor.* i. 61). It is specially noted in the Apologies as a proof of the loyalty of Christians to the Government, *e.g.*, Justin Martyr, *Apol.* i. 17; Tert. *Apol.* 30, 31, 39; Athenagoras, *Legatio*, p. 39. Origen, *Cont. Cels.* viii. 12.

ἐν ὑπεροχῇ: *in high place* (R.V.). The noun occurs in an abstract sense,

καθ᾽ ὑπεροχὴν λόγου ἢ σοφίας, 1 Cor. ii. 1; but the verb is found in this association: Rom. xiii. 1, ἐξουσίαις ὑπερεχούσαις; 1 Pet. ii. 13, βασιλεῖ ὡς ὑπερέχοντι. The actual phrase τῶν ἐν ὑπεροχῇ ὄντων is found in an inscription at Pergamum "after 133 B.C." (Deissmann, *Bible Studies*, trans. p. 255).

ἵνα ἥρεμον: This expresses not the reason why prayer was to be made for kings, but the purport of the prayer itself. *Cf.* Tert. *Apol.* 39, "Oramus etiam pro imperatoribus, pro ministeriis eorum ac potestatibus, pro statu seculi, pro rerum quiete". So Clem. Rom. *ad Cor.* i. 60, δὸς ὁμόνοιαν καὶ εἰρήνην ἡμῖν . . . [ὥστε σώζεσθαι ἡμᾶς] ὑπηκόους γινομένους . . . τοῖς ἄρχουσιν καὶ ἡγουμένοις ἡμῶν ἐπὶ τῆς γῆς, and esp. § 61. Von Soden connects ἵνα, κ.τ.λ. with παρακαλῶ.

ἥρεμος and ἡσύχιος, *tranquil and quiet* (R.V.), perhaps refer to inward and outward peace respectively. See Bengel, on 1 Pet. iii. 4. ἡσυχία also has an external reference where it occurs in N.T., Acts xxii. 2, 2 Thess. iii. 12, 1 Tim. ii. 11, 12. ἠρεμέω is found in a papyrus of ii. A.D. cited by Moulton and Milligan, *Expositor*, vii., vii. 471.

διάγω is used in the sense of *passing one's life*, absolutely, without βίον expressed, in Tit. iii. 3.

ἐν πάσῃ εὐσεβείᾳ κ. σεμνότητι: *with as much piety and earnestness or seriousness as is possible*. This clause, as Chrys. points out, qualifies the prayer for a tranquil and quiet life. εὐσέβεια and σεμνότης, *piety and seriousness*, belong to the vocabulary of the Pastoral Epistles, though εὐσ. occurs elsewhere; see reff. In the Pastorals εὐσέβεια is almost a technical term for *the Christian religion as expressed in daily life*. It is used with a more general application, *religious conduct*, in 1 Tim. vi. 11 and in 2 Peter. It and its cognates were "familiar terms in the religious language of the Imperial period" (Deissmann, *Bible Studies*, trans. p. 364). σεμνότης is rather *gravitas*, as Vulg. renders it in Tit. ii. 7, than *castitas* (Vulg. here and 1 Tim. iii. 4) just as σεμνός is a wider term than *pudicus* as Vulg. always renders it (Phil. iv. 8; 1 Tim. iii. 8, 11; Tit. ii. 2). The

—3. [m] τοῦτο [1] [m] καλὸν καὶ [n] ἀπόδεκτον [o] ἐνώπιον [o] τοῦ [p] σωτῆρος
[p] ἡμῶν [o] [p] Θεοῦ, 4. ὃς πάντας ἀνθρώπους θέλει σωθῆναι καὶ εἰς
[q] ἐπίγνωσιν [q] ἀληθείας ἐλθεῖν. 5. Εἷς γὰρ Θεός, εἷς καὶ [r] μεσίτης

m 1 Cor. vii. 26, *cf.* Tit. iii. 8. n 1 Tim. v. 4 only, not LXX. o Rom. xiv. 22, 1 Cor. i. 29, 2 Cor. iv. 2, vii. 12, Gal. i. 20, 1 Tim. v. 4, 21, vi. 13, 2 Tim. ii. 14, iv. 1, *cf.* Rom. iii 20, 2 Cor. viii. 21. p See 1 Tim. i. 1. q 2 Tim. ii. 25, iii. 7, Tit. i. 1, Heb. x. 26, *cf.* 1 Tim. iv. 3. r Gal. iii. 19, 20, Heb. viii. 6, ix. 15, xii. 24.

[1] Ins. γὰρ ℵcDFGKLP, d, f, g, m101, r, vg. (*enim*), go., syrr., arm.; om. γὰρ ℵ*A, 17, 67**, boh., sah.

A.V. *honesty* is an older English equivalent for *seemliness.* σεμνός and σεμνότης connote gravity which compels genuine respect.

Ver. 3. τοῦτο: *i.e.*, prayer for all men.

καλόν: not to be joined with ἐνώπιον, but taken by itself, as in reff. See note on i. 18. ἀπόδεκτον ἐνώπιον τοῦ θεοῦ occurs again, v. 4. *Prayer for all men approves itself to the natural conscience, and it is also in accordance with the revealed will of God.*

θεοῦ is almost epexegetical of σωτῆρος ἡμῶν. *Our Saviour*, if it stood alone, might mean Christ; but it is God the Father that is the originating cause of salvation. See note on i. 1.

Ver. 4. "The grace of God hath appeared, bringing salvation to all men" (Tit. ii. 11) as was foreshadowed in the O.T.; *e.g.* Ps. lxvii. 2, "Thy saving health among all nations". God is, so far as His inclination or will is concerned, "the Saviour of all men," but actually, so far as we can affirm with certainty, "of them that believe" (1 Tim. iv. 10). These *He saved*, ἔσωσεν (2 Tim. i. 9; Tit. iii. 5), *i.e.*, *placed in a state of being saved.* But here St. Paul does not say θέλει σῶσαι, but θέλει σωθῆναι; for by His own limitation of His powers, so far as they are perceived by us, the salvation of men does not depend on God alone. It depends on the exercise of the free will of each individual in the acceptance or rejection of salvation (so Wiesinger, quoted by Alf.; and, as Bengel notes on ἐλθεῖν, *non coguntur*), as well as on the co-operation of those who pray for all men; and, by so doing, generate a spiritual atmosphere in which the designs of God may grow.

It is also to be observed that since *salvation* means *a state of being saved*, there is no difficulty in *the knowledge of the truth* following it in the sentence, as though it were a consequence rather than a precedent condition. This is indeed the order indicated in the Last Commission: "baptising them . . . teaching them" (Matt. xxviii. 19, 20). So that there is no need to suppose with Ell., that καὶ εἰς . . . ἐλθεῖν was "suggested by . . . the enunciation of the great truth which is contained in the following verse".

εἰς ἐπίγνωσιν ἀληθείας ἐλθεῖν: This whole phrase recurs in 2 Tim. iii. 7. For ἐπίγνωσις ἀληθείας see reff. In Heb. x. 26 both words have the article. It has been shown by Dean Armitage Robinson (*Ephesians*, p. 248 *sqq.*) that ἐπίγνωσις is not *maior exactiorque cognitio;* but, as distinguished from γνῶσις "which is the wider word and expresses 'knowledge' in the fullest sense, ἐπίγνωσις is knowledge directed towards a particular object, perceiving, discerning, recognising". *Cf.* 2 Macc. ix. 11, ἤρξατο . . . εἰς ἐπίγνωσιν ἔρχεσθαι. ἀληθεία occurs fourteen times in the Pastorals; and often with a special Christian reference, like ὁδός and εὐσέβεια. See *e.g.* in addition to this place, 1 Tim. iii. 15, iv. 3, vi. 5, 2 Tim. ii. 15, 18, iii. 8, iv. 4, Tit. i. 14. It is a term that belongs to the Johannine theology as well as to the Pauline.

Ver. 5. This emphatic statement as to the unity of the Godhead is suggested by the singular σωτῆρος just preceding. The εἷς neither affirms nor denies anything as to the complexity of the nature of the Godhead; it has no bearing on the Christian doctrine of the Trinity; it simply is intended to emphasise the uniqueness of the relations of God to man. The use of *one*, with this intention, is well illustrated by Eph. iv. 4-6, ἓν σῶμα, κ.τ.λ. The current thought of the time was conscious of many σωτῆρες. In contrast to these, St. Paul emphasises the uniqueness of the σωτήρ and θεός worshipped by Christians. The contrast is exactly parallel to that in 1 Cor. viii. 6, εἰσὶν θεοὶ πολλοί, καὶ κύριοι πολλοί· ἀλλ' ἡμῖν εἷς θεὸς ὁ πατήρ . . . καὶ εἷς κύριος Ἰησ. Χρ. The question as to the

Θεοῦ καὶ ἀνθρώπων, ἄνθρωπος Χριστὸς Ἰησοῦς, 6. ὁ ˢ δοὺς ˢ ἑαυτὸν ˢ Gal. i. 4,
ᵗ ἀντίλυτρον ὑπὲρ πάντων, τὸ ᵘ μαρτύριον ¹ ᵛ καιροῖς ᵛ ἰδίοις, 7. ʷ εἰς ᵗ Here only.

Tit. ii. 14,
not LXX
u Acts iv.

33, 1 Cor. i. 6, ii. 1, 2 Thess. i. 10, 2 Tim. i. 8. v 1 Tim. vi. 15, Tit. i. 3. w 2 Tim. i. 11,
cf. 1 Pet. ii. 8.

¹ Om. τὸ μαρτύριον A; καὶ μαρτ. ℵ*; οὗ τὸ μαρτ. καιρ. ἰδ. ἐδόθη D*FgᵣG, d,
g, Ambrst., datum est; 67**, 80, 115 ins. οὗ. [Lucas Brug.: "Testimonium
temporibus suis. His verbis nec praeponendum est cuius, nec postponendum confirmatum est : haec enim consulto a patribus omissa sunt ". One at least of MSS.
of vg. reads confirmatum est.]

mutual relations of the Persons of the
Godhead had not arisen among Christians, and was not present to the writer's
mind. Indeed if it had been we could
not regard the epistle as a portion of
revealed theology. Revealed theology
is unconscious. The prima facie distinction here drawn between εἰς θεός and εἰς
μεσίτης would have been impossible in a
sub-apostolic orthodox writer.

Again, the oneness of God has a bearing on the practical question of man's
salvation. It is possible for all men to
be saved, because over them there are
not many Gods that can exercise possibly conflicting will-power towards
them, but one only. See also Rom. iii.
30. One Godhead stands over against
one humanity ; and the Infinite and the
finite can enter into relations one with
the other, since they are linked by a
μεσίτης who is both God and man.
It is noteworthy that μεσίτης θεοῦ κ.
ἀνθρώπων is applied to the archangel
Michael in The Test. of the Twelve
Patriarchs, Dan. vi. 2.

ἄνθρωπος explains how Christ Jesus
could be a mediator. He can only be an
adequate mediator whose sympathy with,
and understanding of, both parties is
cognisable by, and patent to, both.
Now, although God's love for man is
boundless, yet without the revelation of
it by Christ it would not be certainly
patent to man; not to add that one of
two contending parties cannot be the
mediator of the differences (Gal. iii. 20).
See also Rom. v. 15. Again, we must
note that ἄνθρωπος (himself man, R.V.,
not the man, A.V.) in this emphatic
position suggests that the verity of our
Lord's manhood was in danger of being
ignored or forgotten.

Ver. 6. ὁ δοὺς ἑαυτόν : The Evangelists record our Lord's own declarations
that His death was a spontaneous and
voluntary sacrifice on His part, Matt.
xx. 28 = Mark x. 45, δοῦναι τὴν ψυχὴν
αὐτοῦ λύτρον ἀντὶ πολλῶν. Cf. John
x. 18; and St. Paul affirms it, Gal. i. 4,

τοῦ δόντος ἑαυτὸν ὑπὲρ τῶν ἁμαρτιῶν
ἡμῶν; Tit. ii. 14, ὃς ἔδωκεν ἑαυτὸν ὑπὲρ
ἡμῶν κ.τ.λ. (παραδίδωμι is used in Gal.
ii. 20, Eph. v. 2, 25). We may note that
this statement necessarily implies not
only the pre-existence of our Lord, but
also His co-operation in the eternal
counsels and purpose of the Father as
regards the salvation of man.

Alford is probably right in saying that
δοῦναι ἑαυτόν, as St. Paul expresses it,
suggests more than δοῦναι τὴν ψυχὴν
αὐτοῦ. The latter might naturally be
limited to the sacrifice of His death ; the
former connotes the sacrifice of His lifetime, the whole of the humiliation and
self-emptying of the Incarnation. The
soundness of this exegesis is not im-
paired by the probability that τὴν ψυχὴν
αὐτοῦ may be nothing more than a
Semitic periphrasis for ἑαυτόν. See
J. H. Moulton, Grammar, vol. i. p. 87,
who compares Mark viii. 36, ζημιωθῆναι
τὴν ψυχὴν αὐτοῦ, with Luke ix. 25,
ἑαυτὸν δὲ ἀπολέσας ἢ ζημιωθείς.

ἀντίλυτρον ὑπὲρ πάντων: If we are
to see any special force in the ἀντί, we
may say that it expresses that the λύτρον
is equivalent in value to the thing pro-
cured by means of it. But perhaps St.
Paul's use of the word, if he did not coin
it, is due to his desire to reaffirm our
Lord's well-known declaration in the
most emphatic way possible. λύτρον
ἀντὶ merely implies an exchange; ἀντίλυτρον ὑπέρ implies that the exchange
is decidedly a benefit to those on whose
behalf it is made. As far as the suggestion of vicariousness is concerned, there
does not seem to be much difference
between the two phrases.

τὸ μαρτύριον, as Ellicott says, "is an
accusative in apposition to the preceding
sentence," or rather clause, ὁ δοὺς . . .
πάντων. So R.V. Bengel compares
ἔνδειγμα, 2 Thess. i. 5; cf. also Rom.
xii. 1. The great act of self-sacrifice is
timeless ; but as historically apprehended
by us, the testimony concerning it must
be made during a particular and suitable

x 2 Tim. i.   ʷδ ʷ ἐτέθην ἐγὼ ˣ κῆρυξ καὶ ἀπόστολος——ʸ ἀλήθειαν ʸ λέγω,¹ ᶻ οὐ
11, 2 Pet.
ii. 5.   ʸψεύδομαι——ᵃ διδάσκαλος ἐθνῶν ᵇ ἐν ᵇ πίστει καὶ ἀληθείᾳ.   8. ᶜΒού-
y John viii.
45, 46,
Rom. ix. 1, cf. 2 Cor. xii. 6.   z Rom. ix. 1, 2 Cor. xi. 31, Gal. i. 20.   a 2 Tim. i. 11.   b See
1 Tim. i. 2.   c 2 Cor. i. :7, Phil. i. 12, 1 Tim. v. 14, Tit. iii. 8.

¹ Add ἐν Χριστῷ (from Rom. ix. 1) א*DᶜKL, 17, 37, many others, go., arm.

period of history, i.e., from the descent
of the Holy Spirit upon the apostolic
company (Acts i. 8) until the Second
Coming (2 Thess. i. 10). The temporal
mission of the Son of God took place
"when the fulness of the time came"
(Gal. iv. 4); it was an οἰκονομία τοῦ
πληρώματος τῶν καιρῶν (Eph. i. 10).
The testimony is of course borne by God
(1 John v. 9-11), but He uses human
agency, the preachers of the Gospel.

καιροῖς ἰδίοις: See reff. The analogy
of Gal. vi. 9, καιρῷ γὰρ ἰδίῳ θερίσομεν,
suggests that we should render it always
in due season. The plural expresses
the fact that the bearing of testimony
extends over many seasons; but each
man reaps his own harvest only once.
In any case, the seasons relate both to
the Witness and that whereof He is a
witness: "his own times" and "its own
times" (R.V.).

The dative is that "of the time wherein the action takes place," Ell., who
compares Rom. xvi. 25, χρόνοις αἰωνίοις
σεσιγημένου.

Ver. 7. εἰς δ: scil. τὸ μαρτύριον, or
τὸ εὐαγγέλιον, as in the parallel passage,
2 Tim. i. 11.

The phrase εἰς δ ἐτέθην ἐγὼ κῆρυξ κ.
ἀπόστολος [καὶ] διδάσκαλος is repeated
in 2 Tim. i. 11, as ἀλήθειαν . . . ψεύδομαι
occurs again Rom. ix. 1; but there we
have the significant addition [λέγω] ἐν
Χριστῷ. For similar asseverations of
the writer's truthfulness see Rom. i. 9,
2 Cor. xi. 10, xii. 19, Gal. i. 20.

There is nothing derogatory from the
apostle in supposing that the personal
struggle in which he had been for years
engaged with those who opposed his
gospel made him always feel on the
defensive, and that his self-vindication
came to be expressed in stereotyped
phrases which rose to his mind whenever the subject came before him, even
in a letter to a loyal disciple.

κῆρυξ is used in the N.T. of a preacher
here, and twice elsewhere; see reff.
But κήρυγμα and κηρύσσω are constantly used of Christian preaching. Cf.
esp. Rom. x. 15, πῶς δὲ κηρύξωσιν ἐὰν
μὴ ἀποσταλῶσιν; Bengel takes it in the
sense of ambassador; cf. 2 Cor. v. 20.

διδάσκαλος: διδάσκαλοι, in the technical Christian sense, are mentioned in
Acts xiii. 1, 1 Cor. xii. 28, 29, Eph. iv. 11.
Here and in 2 Tim. i. 11 the term is used
in a general signification. St. Paul does
use διδάσκειν of his own ministerial functions: 1 Cor. iv. 17, Col. i. 28, 2 Thess.
ii. 15.

ἐν πίστει καὶ ἀληθείᾳ: It is best to
take both these words in connexion with
διδάσκαλος, and objectively, in the faith
and the truth (see on ch. i. 2). It is
no objection to this view that the article
is not expressed; the anarthrousness of
common Christian terms is a feature of
these epistles. Others, with Chrys., take
both terms subjectively, faithfully and
truly. Ellicott "refers πίστις to the
subjective faith of the apostle, ἀλήθ. to
the objective truth of the doctrine he
delivered". This does not yield a natural
sense.

Harnack notes that the collocation of
ἀπόστολος, διδάσκαλος is peculiar to
the Pastorals and Hermas (Sim. ix. 15,
16, 25; Vis. iii. 5, "The apostles and
bishops and teachers and deacons").
Harnack opines that "Hermas passed
over the prophets because he reckoned
himself one of them". But the opinion
of Lietzmann, which he quotes, seems
sounder: Hermas "conceives this προφ-
ητεύειν as a private activity which God's
equipment renders possible, but which
lacks any official character" (Mission
and Expansion of Christianity, trans.
vol. i. p. 340).

Vv. 8—iii. 1a. The ministers of public
prayer must be the men of the congregation, not the women. A woman's
positive duty is to make herself conspicuous by good works, not by personal display. Her place in relation to
man is one of subordination. This is
one of the lessons of the inspired narra-
tives of the Creation and of the Fall.
Nevertheless this does not affect her eternal position. Salvation is the goal alike
of man and woman. They both attain
supreme blessedness in the working out
of the primal penalty imposed on Adam
and Eve.

Ver. 8. βούλομαι οὖν: οὖν is resumptive
of the general topic of public worship

λομαι οὖν [d] προσεύχεσθαι τοὺς ἄνδρας [e] ἐν [o] παντὶ [o] τόπῳ, [f] ἐπαίροντας [d] 1 Cor. xi.
[g] ὁσίους [f] χεῖρας [h] χωρὶς [i] ὀργῆς καὶ [k] διαλογισμοῦ,[1] 9. [l] ὡσαύτως [2 3]
γυναῖκας ἐν [m] καταστολῇ [n] κοσμίῳ [4] μετὰ [o] αἰδοῦς καὶ [p] σωφροσύνης

4, 5, 13,
e 1 Cor. i. 2.
xiv. 14, 15,
14, 1
2 Cor. ii.
Thess. i. 8

f Luke xxiv. 50.   g Tit. i. 8, Heb. vii. 26, Rev. xv. 4, xvi. 5.   h Phil. ii. 14, 1 Tim. v. 21.
Mark iii. 5, Rom. xii. 19, xiii. 4, 5, Eph. iv. 31, Col. iii. 8, Jas. i. 19, 20.   k Rom. xiv. 1, Phil.
ii. 14.   l 1 Tim. iii. 8, 11, v. 25, Tit. ii. 3, 6.   m Here only N.T., Isa. lxi. 3.   n Eccles.
xii. 9, 1 Tim. iii. 2.   o Here only N.T., 3 Macc. i. 19, iv. 5.   p Acts xxvi. 25, ver. 15.

[1] So א*ADKLP, d, f, m25,81, r, vg., go., sah., arm.; διαλογισμῶν אcFgrG,
17, 47, 67**, 80, nineteen others, g, boh., syrr.

[2] Ins. καὶ אcDFGKL, d, f, g, m81, r (autem et), vg., go., sah., boh., syrr., arm.;
om καὶ א*AP, 17, 71.

[3] Ins. τὰς DbcKL.   [4] κοσμίως אcDgr*FG, 17.

from which the writer has digressed in
vv. 3-7. βούλομαι οὖν is found again in
v. 14. In both places, βούλομαι has the
force of a practical direction issued after
deliberation. See also reff. On the contrary, θέλω δέ is used only in reference to
abstract subjects. See Rom. xvi. 19, 1
Cor. vii. 7, 32, xi. 3, xiv. 5. προσεύχεσθαι τοὺς ἄνδρας: that the men should
conduct public worship. Perhaps Bengel
is right in understanding 1 Peter iii. 7
in the same sense. See reff. for προσεύχεσθαι in this special signification.
τοὺς ἄνδρας: the men of the community
as opposed to the women, ver. 9 (R.V.).
There is no specific restriction of the
conduct of worship to a clergy.

ἐν παντὶ τόπῳ: to be connected with
what precedes: the directions are to
apply to every Church without exception; no allowance is to be made for
conditions peculiar to any locality; as it
is expressed in 1 Cor. xiv. 33, 34, ὡς ἐν
πάσαις ταῖς ἐκκλησίαις τῶν ἁγίων, αἱ
γυναῖκες ἐν ταῖς ἐκκλησίαις σιγάτωσαν.
The words do not mean in any place,
as though fixed places for worship were
a matter of indifference; neither is there
any allusion, as Chrys. explain it, to the
abolition by Christ of the restriction of
worship to one place, Jerusalem, as in
John iv. 21. ἐπαίροντας ὁσίους χεῖρας:
This is not directly intended to enjoin a
particular gesture appropriate to prayer,
but merely avoids the repetition of
προσεύχεσθαι. To uplift the hands in
prayer was customary: 1 Kings viii. 22,
Ps. xxviii., 2 etc., Isa. i. 15, Clem. Rom.
ad Cor. i. 29. The men that are to have
the conduct of the public worship of the
Church must be upright men who have
clean hands, hands that are holy (Job.
xvii. 9; Ps. xxiii. (xxiv.) 4; Jas. iv. 8).
For ὅσιος as an adj. of two terminations,
compare Luke ii. 13, Rev. iv. 3. See
Winer Moulton, Grammar, p. 80.

χωρὶς ὀργῆς καὶ διαλογισμοῦ: This
indicates the two conditions necessary to
effectual prayer: freedom from irritation
towards our fellow-men (Matt. vi. 14,
15, Mark xi. 25), and confidence towards
God (Jas. i. 6; Luke xii. 29). διαλογισμός
has the sense of doubt in Rom. xiv. 1.
This sense (A.V. doubting) is that given
to the term here by Chrysostom (ἀμφι-
βολία) and Theodoret (πιστεύων ὅτι
λήψῃ). The rendering disputing (R.V.)
disceptatio (Vulg.) merely enlarges the
notion conveyed in ὀργή. The reff. to
ὀργή are places where it is spoken of as
a human affection.

Ver. 9. Having assigned to the men
the prominent duties of the Church, St.
Paul proceeds to render impossible any
misconception of his views on this subject by forbidding women to teach in
public. But he begins by emphasising
what is their characteristic and proper
glory, the beauty of personality which
results from active beneficence.

The essential parts of the sentence are
ὡσαύτως γυναῖκας . . . κοσμεῖν ἑαυτάς
. . . δι᾽ ἔργων ἀγαθῶν. Both προσεύχεσθαι and κοσμεῖν ἑαυτάς depend on
βούλομαι, as does ὡσαύτως, which introduces another regulation laid down by
the apostle. In the Christian Society,
it was St. Paul's deliberate wish that
the men should conduct public worship,
and that the women should adorn the
Society and themselves by good works.
This verse has no reference to the demeanour of women while in Church. It
is inconsistent with the whole context
to supply προσεύχεσθαι after γυναῖκας.

The connexion of ἐν καταστολῇ—
σωφροσύνης has been disputed. Ellicott
takes it as "a kind of adjectival predica-
tion to be appended to γυναῖκας," stating
what is the normal condition of women,
who are to superadd the adornment of
good works. But it is more natural to

q Tit. ii. 10, ^q κοσμεῖν ἑαυτάς, μὴ ἐν ^r πλέγμασιν καὶ ¹ ^s χρυσίῳ ² ἢ μαργαρίταις ἢ
1 Pet. iii.
5.   ^t ἱματισμῷ ^u πολυτελεῖ, 10. ἀλλ'—ὃ ^v πρέπει γυναιξὶν ^w ἐπαγγελλο-
r Here only,
not LXX μέναις ^x θεοσέβειαν—δι' ^y ἔργων ^z ἀγαθῶν. 11. Γυνὴ ἐν ^α ἡσυχίᾳ
s 1 Pet. iii.
3, Rev.   ^a μανθανέτω ἐν πάσῃ ^b ὑποταγῇ. 12. διδάσκειν δὲ γυναικὶ ³ οὐκ
xvii. 4.
t Luke vii.

25, ix. 29, John xix. 24, Acts xx. 33.   u Mark xiv. 3, 1 Pet. iii. 4.   v Eph. v. 3, Tit. ii. 1,
Heb. ii. 10, vii. 26.   w 1 Tim. vi. 21, Tit. i. 2.   x Here only N.T., cf. John ix. 31.   y 1 Tim. v.
10, 2 Tim. ii. 21, iii. 17, Tit. i. 16, iii. 1.   z Acts xxii. 2, 2 Thess. iii. 12.   a 1 Cor. xiv. 35.
b Wisd. xviii. 16, 2 Cor. ix. 13, Gal. ii. 5, 1 Tim. iii. 4.

¹ ἢ DcKL, f, m81, r, vg., go., sah., syrhcl.
² So AFGP, 17, 31, 47, 80, a few others; χρυσῷ ℵDKL.
³ γυν. δὲ διδάσκ. KL.

connect it directly with κοσμεῖν, with
which ἐν πλέγμασιν, κ.τ.λ. is also connected as well as δι' ἔργων ἀγαθῶν; the
change of preposition being due to the
distinction between the means employed for adornment and the resultant
expression of it. The effect of the practice of good works is seen in an *orderly
appearance*, etc.

ὡσαύτως is a word of frequent occurrence in the Pastorals. See reff. Except
in v. 25, it is used as a connecting link
between items in a series of regulations.
The use of it in Rom. viii. 26, 1 Cor. xi.
25 is different.

καταστολή, as Ellicott says, "conveys
the idea of external appearance as *principally* exhibited in dress". It is "*deportment*, as exhibited externally, whether
in look, manner or dress". The commentators cite in illustration Josephus,
Bell. Jud. ii. 8, 4, where the καταστολὴ
κ. σχῆμα σώματος of the Essenes is described in detail. The Latin *habitus* is
a good rendering, if we do not restrict
that term to dress, as the Vulg. here,
habitu ornato, seems to do. But *ordinato*
(r) hits the meaning better.

κόσμιος is applied to the episcopus in
iii. 2. It means *orderly*, as opposed to
disorderliness in appearance. κοσμίως
(see *apparat. crit.*) would be a ἅπαξ λεγ.
both in Old and New Testament. μετὰ
αἰδοῦς: *with shamefastness and self-
control* or *discreetness:* the inward characteristic, and the external indication or
evidence of it.

For σωφροσύνη, see Trench, *Synonyms*,
N.T. The cognate words σωφρονίζειν,
Tit. ii. 4; σωφρονισμός, 2 Tim. i. 7;
σωφρόνως, Tit. ii. 12; σώφρων, 1 Tim.
iii. 2, Tit. i. 8, ii. 2, 5, are in N.T. peculiar to the Pastoral Epistles; but σωφρονεῖν, Tit. ii. 6, is found also in Mark,
Luke, Rom., 2 Cor. and 1 Pet. See Dean
Bernard's note here.

ἐν πλέγμασιν, κ.τ.λ.: The parallel in
1 Pet. iii. 3, ὁ ἔξωθεν ἐμπλοκῆς τριχῶν
καὶ περιθέσεως χρυσίων, ἢ ἐνδύσεως
ἱματίων κόσμος, is only a parallel. The
two passages are quite independent. The
vanities of dress—of men and women—is
common topic.

Ver. 10. ἀλλ' ὃ πρέπει: It has been
assumed above that δι' ἔργων ἀγαθῶν is
to be connected with κοσμεῖν. In this
case ὃ πρέπει—θεοσέβειαν is a parenthetical clause in apposition to the sentence.
It is, however, possible, though not so
natural, to connect δι' ἔργων ἀγαθῶν with
ἐπαγγ. θεοσ. So Vulg., *promittentes
pietatem per bona opera.* Then ὃ would
mean καθ' ὃ, or ἐν τούτῳ ὃ (Math.), and
the whole clause, ἀλλ' ὃ—ἀγαθῶν, would
be an awkward periphrasis for, and repetition of, ἐν καταστολῇ—σωφροσύνης.

ἐπαγγέλλεσθαι usually means *to promise* as in Tit. i. 2; but here and in vi.
21 *to profess.*

θεοσέβεια: ἅπ. λεγ., but the adj. θεοσε-
βής occurs John ix. 31.

διά is instrumental, as in iv. 5, 2 Tim.
i. 6, 10, 14, 15, iv. 17, Tit. iii. 5, 6,
not of accompanying circumstances, as
in 1 Tim. ii. 15, iv. 14, 2 Tim. ii. 2.

ἔργων ἀγαθῶν: see note on chap. iii. 1.

Ver. 11 *sqq.* With these directions
compare those in 1 Cor. xiv. 33-35.

ἐν πάσῃ ὑποταγῇ: *with complete subjection* [to their husbands]. *Cf.* Tit. ii. 5.

Ver. 12. διδάσκειν: This refers of
course only to public teaching, or to a
wife's teaching her husband. In Tit. ii. 3
St. Paul indicates the natural sphere for
woman's teaching. In 1 Cor. women are
forbidden λαλεῖν in the Church. The
choice of terms is appropriate in each
case.

αὐθεντεῖν ἀνδρός: *dominari in vir-
um, to have dominion over* (R.V.). "The
adj. αὐθεντικός is very well established
in the vernacular. See Nägeli, p. 49

ἐπιτρέπω, οὐδὲ ᶜαὐθεντεῖν ἀνδρός, ἀλλ' εἶναι ἐν ˣἡσυχίᾳ.   13. c Here only not LXX
Ἀδὰμ γὰρ πρῶτος ᵈἐπλάσθη, εἶτα Εὖα·   14. καὶ Ἀδὰμ οὐκ d Gen. ii. 7, Rom. ix.
ἠπατήθη, ἡ δὲ γυνὴ ᶠἐξαπατηθεῖσα¹ ἐν ᵍπαραβάσει γέγονεν.   15.   20.
                                                          e Eph. v. 6, Jas. i. 26.

f Rom. vii. 11, xvi. 18, 1 Cor. iii. 18, 2 Cor. xi. 3, 2 Thess. ii. 3.   g Rom. ii. 23, iv. 15, v. 14, Gal iii. 19, Heb. ii. 2, ix. 15.

¹ ἀπατηθεῖσα אᶜDᵇ﹖ᶜKL.

... the Atticist warns his pupil to use αὐτοδικεῖν because αὐθεντεῖν was vulgar (κοινότερον) ... αὐθέντης is properly one who acts on his own authority, hence in this context an autocrat" (Moulton and Milligan, *Expositor*, vii., vi. 374).

ἀλλ' εἶναι: dependent on some such verb as βούλομαι implied, as opposed to οὐκ ἐπιτρέπω.

Ver. 13. It would not be fair to say that St. Paul's judgment about the relative functions of men and women in the church depended on his belief as to the historicity of the Biblical story of the Creation. He certainly uses this account in support of his conclusions; yet supposing the literal truth of the early chapters of Genesis, it would be possible to draw quite other inferences from it. The first specimen produced of a series is not always the most perfect. The point in which Adam's superiority over Eve comes out in the narrative of the Fall is his greater strength of intellect; therefore men are better fitted for the work of public instruction. "The woman taught once, and ruined all" (Chrys.). Eve's reasoning faculty was at once overcome by the allegation of jealousy felt by God, an allegation plausible to a nature swayed by emotion rather than by reflection. The Tempter's statement seemed to be supported by the appearance of the fruit, as it was rendered attractive by hopes of vanity to be gratified. Adam's better judgment was overcome by personal influence (Gen. iii. 17, "Thou hast hearkened unto the voice of thy wife"); he was not deceived. But the intellectual superior who sins against light may be morally inferior to him who stumbles in the dusk.

Ἀδὰμ πρῶτος ἐπλάσθη: The elder should rule. A more profound statement of this fact is found in 1 Cor. xi 9, οὐκ ἐκτίσθη ἀνὴρ διὰ τὴν γυναῖκα, ἀλλὰ γυνὴ διὰ τὸν ἄνδρα.

πλάσσειν is the term used in Gen. ii. 7 and expresses the notion of God as a potter, Rom. ix. 20. (*am* here has *figuratus*.)

Ver. 14. ἡ δὲ γυνή: St. Paul says ἡ γυνή rather than Εὖα, emphasing the sex rather than the individual, because he desires to gives the incident its general application, especially in view of what follows. So Chrys.

ἐξαπατηθεῖσα: It is doubtful if we are entitled to render this, as Ell. does, *being completely deceived*. In 2 Cor. xi. 3 St. Paul says ὁ ὄφις ἐξηπάτησεν Εὖαν, where there is no reason why he should not have used the simple verb. St. Paul uses the compound verb in five other places, the simple verb only once (see reff.). So that the simplest account that we can give of his variation here, and in 2 Cor. xi. 3, from the ὁ ὄφις ἠπάτησέν με of Gen. iii. 13, is that the compound verb came naturally to his mind.

ἐν παραβάσει γέγονεν: Inasmuch as παράβασις is used of Adam's transgression in Rom. v. 14, it may be asked, What is the force of St. Paul's apparent restriction here of the phrase to Eve? Might it not be said of Adam as well, that he ἐν παραβ. γέγονεν? To which St. Paul would perhaps have replied that he meant that it was woman who *first* transgressed, in consequence of having been deceived. ἀπὸ γυναικὸς ἀρχὴ ἁμαρτίας, καὶ δι' αὐτὴν ἀποθνήσκομεν πάντες. Ecclus. xxv. 24. This notion of *coming into a state of sin at a definite point of time* is well expressed by γέγονεν. For γίνεσθαι ἐν cf. ἡ διακονία ... ἐγενήθη ἐν δόξῃ (2 Cor. iii. 7); ἐν λόγῳ κολακίας ἐγενήθημεν (1 Thess. ii. 5).

Ver. 15. σωθήσεται δὲ διὰ τῆς τεκνογονίας: The penalty for transgression, so far as woman is concerned, was expressed in the words, "I will greatly multiply thy sorrow and thy conception; in sorrow thou shalt bring forth children" (Gen. iii. 16). But just as in the case of man, the world being as it is, the sentence has proved a blessing, so it is in the case of woman. "In the sweat of thy face shalt thou eat bread" expresses man's necessity, duty, privilege, dignity. If the necessity of work be "a stumbling-block," man can "make it a stepping-stone" (Browning, *The Ring and the*

h Here
only, not
LXX, cf.
1 Tim. v.
14.
i John viii.
31, xv. 9,

σωθήσεται δὲ διὰ τῆς ʰτεκνογονίας, ἐὰν ⁱμείνωσιν ⁱἐν ᵏπίστει.ᵏ καὶ
ᵏἀγάπῃ καὶ ˡἁγιασμῷ μετὰ ᵐσωφροσύνης· III. 1. ᵃΠιστὸς¹ ὁ
ᵃλόγος.

10, 2 Tim. iii. 14, 1 John iv. 16, 2 John 9.   k See 1 Tim. i. 14.   l Rom. vi. 19, 22, 1 Cor. i. 30,
1 Thess. iv. 3, 4, 7, 2 Thess. ii. 13, Heb. xii. 14, 1 Pet. i. 2.   m Ver. 9.   a See 1 Tim i. 15.

¹ ἀνθρώπινος D*, humanus d, m47, g (humanus t fidelis), Ambrst., Sedul. Similarly humanus is the rendering in chap. i. 15 in r, Aug., Julianᴘᵉˡᵃᵍ apud Aug.
Jerome comments adversely on this rendering (Ep. 24 ad Marcell.).

Book, The Pope, 413), Nay, it is the only
stepping-stone available to him.   If St.
Paul's argument had led him to emphasise the man's part in the first transgression, he might have said, " He shall be
saved in his toil," his overcoming the
obstacles of nature.

So St. Paul, taking the common-sense
view that childbearing, rather than public
teaching or the direction of affairs, is
woman's primary function, duty, privilege
and dignity, reminds Timothy and his
readers that there was another aspect
of the story in Genesis besides that of
woman's taking the initiative in transgression : the pains of childbirth were her
sentence, yet in undergoing these she
finds her salvation. She shall be saved
in her childbearing (R.V.m. nearly).
That is her normal and natural duty;
and in the discharge of our normal and
natural duties we all, men and women
alike, as far as our individual efforts can
contribute to it, "work out our own
salvation".

This explanation gives an adequate
force to σωθήσεται, and preserves the
natural and obvious meaning of τεκνογονία, and gives its force to τῆς. διά
here has hardly an instrumental force
(as Vulg. per filiorum generationem) ; it
is rather the διά of accompanying circumstances, as in 1 Cor. iii. 15.
σωθήσεται . . . διὰ πυρός. It remains
to note three other explanations :—
   (1) She shall be "preserved in the
great danger of child-birth ".
   (2) Women shall be saved if they bring
up their children well, as if τεκνογονία =
τεκνοτροφία.   So Chrys.
   (3) She shall be saved by means of
the Childbearing "of Mary, which gave
to the world the Author of our Salvation"
(Liddon).   "The peculiar function of
her sex (from its relation to her Saviour)
shall be the medium of her salvation"
(Ellicott).   The R.V., saved through the
childbearing, is possibly patient of this
interpretation.   No doubt it was the

privilege of woman alone to be the
medium of the Incarnation.   This miraculous fact justifies us perhaps in pressing
the language of Gen. iii. 15, " thy seed,"
and in finding an allusion (though this is
uncertain) in Gal. iv. 4, γενόμενον ἐκ
γυναικός ; but woman cannot be said to
be saved by means of a historic privilege,
even with the added qualification, "if
they continue," etc.   See Luke xi. 27,
28, " Blessed is the womb that bare
thee. . . . Yea, rather, blessed are they
that hear the word of God," etc.

ἐὰν μείνωσιν : This use of μένειν with
ἐν and an abstract noun is chiefly Johannine, as the reff. show.

The subject of μείνωσιν is usually
taken to be γυναῖκες ; but inasmuch as
St. Paul has been speaking of women
in the marriage relation, it seems better
to understand the plural of the woman
and her husband.   Compare 1 Cor. vii.
36 where γαμείτωσαν refers to the παρ-
θένος and her betrothed, whose existence
is implied in the question of her marriage.
If this view be accepted, then πίστις,
ἀγάπη, and ἁγιασμός refer respectively
to the duties of the man and wife to God,
to society, and to each other : faith towards God, love to the community, and
sanctification in their marital relations.
See chap. iv. 12 where these three
virtues are again combined.   See ver.
9 for σωφροσύνη.

CHAPTER III.—Ver. 1.   πιστὸς ὁ
λόγος : This refers to the exegesis of
Genesis which has preceded.   (So
Chrys.).   We may compare Barnabas,
§ 9, where, after an allegorical explanation of Abraham's 318 servants, the
writer exclaims, οὐδεὶς γνησιώτερον
ἔμαθεν ἀπ' ἐμοῦ λόγον· ἀλλὰ οἶδα ὅτι
ἄξιοί ἐστε ὑμεῖς.   See note on i. 15.

Vv. 1 b-13.   The qualifications of the
men who are to be ministers ; and first
(a) of the episcopus (1 b-7) secondly (b)
of the deacons (8-13) with a parenthetical instruction respecting women church-
workers (11).

Εἴ τις ἐπισκοπῆς °ὀρέγεται, ᵈκαλοῦ ᵈἔργου °ἐπιθυμεῖ. 2. ᶠδεῖ ᶠοὖν b Here only
in this
τὸν ἐπίσκοπον ᵉἀνεπίλημπτον εἶναι, ʰ μιᾶς ʰ γυναικὸς ʰ ἄνδρα, ⁱνηφά-   sense,
Acts i. 20.
c 1 Tim. vi.

10, Heb. xi. 16.   d 1 Tim. v. 10, 25, vi. 18, Tit. ii. 7, 14, iii. 8, 14.   e Here only in Pastorals.
f Acts i. 21.   g 1 Tim. v. 7, vi. 14, not LXX.   h Ver. 12, Tit. i. 6.   i 1 Tim. iii. 11, Tit
ii. 2, not LXX.

εἴ τις ἐπισκοπῆς, κ.τ.λ.: Having given
elementary directions concerning the
scope of public prayer, and the ministers
thereof, St. Paul now takes up the
matter of Church organisation. He
begins with the office of the episcopus,
or presbyter, because that is of the very
essence of Church order. On the question as to the terms presbyter and
episcopus, it is sufficient here to state
my own conclusion, that they represent
slightly different aspects of the same
office, pastoral and official; aspects which
came naturally into prominence in the
Jewish and Greek societies respectively
which gave birth to the names. This
seems the obvious conclusion from a
comparison of Acts xx. 17, 28 ; Phil. i. 1 ;
Tit. i. 5, 7 ; 1 Tim. iii. 1, 2, 4, 5, v. 17 ;
1 Pet. v. 1, 2 ; Clem. Rom. 1 Cor. 44 ;
Polycarp, 5 ; Clem. Al. Quis Dives, § 42.
ὀρέγεται . . . ἐπιθυμεῖ: The R.V.
(seeketh . . . desireth) indicates to the
English reader that two distinct Greek
words are used ; a fact which is concealed in the A.V. (desire . . . desireth).
So Vulg. has desiderat in both places;
but m⁴⁷, cupit . . . desiderat. ὀρέγεσθαι,
which occurs again in vi. 10 of reaching
after money, is not used in any depreca-
tory sense. Field (in loc.) notes that
"it has a special application to such
objects as a man is commonly said to
aspire to". The sanity of St. Paul's
judgment is nowhere better seen than in
his commendation of lawful ambition.
A man may be actuated by a variety of
motives ; yet it is not inevitable that
those that are lower should impair the
quality of the higher ; they need not in-
terpenetrate each other. In any case,
St. Paul credits the aspirant with the
noblest ideal : He who aspires to be an
episcopus desires to perform a good work,
"Est opus ; negotium, non otium. Acts
xv. 38, Phil. ii. 30 " (Bengel).
καλοῦ ἔργου : καλὸν ἔργον and καλὰ
ἔργα (see reff.) are not peculiar to the
Pastorals (Matt. v. 16, xxvi. 10 = Mark
xiv. 6 ; John x. 32, 33) ; but, as the references show, the phrase is found in
them only of the Pauline Epistles. On
the other hand, ἔργα ἀγαθά occurs six
times in the Pastorals. See reff. on
chap. ii. 10. We perceive in the use
of it a qualification of the earlier de-

preciation of the works of the Law,
induced by a natural reaction from the
abuse of that teaching.
Ver. 2. With the qualifications of the
episcopus as given here should be compared those of the deacons, ver. 8 sqq.,
and those of the episcopus in Tit. i.
6 sqq.
δεῖ οὖν . . . ἀνεπίλημπτον εἶναι. The
ἐπισκοπή being essentially a good work,
" bonum negotium bonis committendum "
(Bengel). The episcopus is the persona
of the Church. It is not enough for
him to be not criminal ; he must be one
against whom it is impossible to bring
any charge of wrong doing such as could
stand impartial examination. (See
Theodoret, cited by Alf.). He must be
without reproach (R.V.), irreprehensible
(Trench), a term which involves a less
exacting test than blameless (A.V.) ; the
deacon (and the Cretan episcopus) must
be ἀνέγκλητος, one against whom no
charge has, in point of fact, been brought.
No argument can be based on the
singular τὸν ἐπίσκοπον, here or in Tit.
i. 7, in favour either of the monarchical
episcopate or as indications of the late
date of the epistle ; it is used generically
as ἡ χήρα, ch. v. 5 ; δοῦλον Κυρίου, 2
Tim. ii. 24.
The better to ensure that the episcopus
be without reproach, his leading characteristic must be self-control. In the first
place—and this has special force in the
East—he must be a man who has—
natural or acquired—a high conception
of the relations of the sexes : a married
man, who, if his wife dies, does not
marry again. Men whose position is less
open to criticism may do this without
discredit, but the episcopus must hold up
a high ideal. Second marriage, which
is mentioned as a familiar practice (Rom.
vii. 2, 3), is expressly permitted to Christian women in 1 Cor. vii. 39, and even
recommended to, or rather enjoined upon,
young widows in 1 Tim. v. 14.
μιᾶς γυναικὸς ἄνδρα, of course, does
not mean that the episcopus must be, or
have been, married. What is here forbidden is digamy under any circumstances. This view is supported (a) by
the general drift of the qualities required
here in a bishop ; self-control or temperance, in his use of food and drink, pos-

λιον, [k] σώφρονα, [l] κόσμιον, [m] φιλόξενον, [n] διδακτικόν, 3. μὴ [o] πάροινον,
μὴ [o] πλήκτην,[1] ἀλλὰ [p] ἐπιεικῆ, [q] ἄμαχον, [r] ἀφιλάργυρον, 4. τοῦ ἰδίου
οἴκου [s] καλῶς [t] προϊστάμενον, τέκνα ἔχοντα ἐν [u] ὑποταγῇ μετὰ πάσης

k Tit. i. 8, ii. 2, 5. l See 1 Tim. ii. 9. m Tit. i. 8, 1 Pet. iv. 9, not LXX, *cf.* Rom. xii. 13, Heb. xiii. 2. n 2 Tim. ii. 24, not LXX. o Tit. i. 7, not LXX. p Phil iv. 5, Tit. iii, 2, Jas. iii. 17, 1 Pet. ii. 18. q Tit. iii. 2, not LXX. r Heb. xiii. 5, not LXX. s Ver. 12, 1 Tim. v. 17. t Rom. xii. 8, 1 Thess. v. 12, 1 Tim. iii. 12, v. 17, *cf.* Tit iii. 8, 14. u See 1 Tim. ii. 11.

[1] Ins. μὴ αἰσχροκερδῆ 37, very many others.

sessions, gifts, temper; (*b*) by the corresponding requirement in a church widow, v. 9, **ἑνὸς ἀνδρὸς γυνή**, and (*c*) by the practice of the early church (Apostolic Constitutions, vi. 17; Apostolic Canons, 16 (17); Tertullian, *ad Uxorem*, i. 7: *de Monogam.* 12; *de Exhort. Castitatis*, cc. 7, 13; Athenagoras, *Legat.* 33; Origen, *in Lucam*, xvii. p. 953, and the Canons of the councils, *e.g.*, Neocaesarea (A.D. 314) can. 7. Quinisext. can. 3).

On the other hand, it must be conceded that the patristic commentators on the passage (with the partial exception of Chrysostom)—Theodore Mops. Theodoret, Theophylact, Oecumenius, Jerome—suppose that it is bigamy or polygamy that is here forbidden. But commentators are prone to go too far in the emancipation of their judgments from the prejudices or convictions of their contemporaries. In some matters "the common sense of most" is a safer guide than the irresponsible conjectures of a conscientious student.

νηφάλιον: *temperate* (R.V.). A.V. has *vigilant* here, following Chrys.; *sober* in ver. 11, and Tit. ii. 2, with *vigilant* in margin. As this quality is required also in women officials, ver. 11, and in aged men, Tit. ii. 2, it has in all probability a reference to moderate use of wine, etc., and so would be equivalent to the **μὴ οἴνῳ πολλῷ προσέχοντας** of the diaconal qualifications, ver. 8. **ἐγκρατῆ** is the corresponding term in Tit. i. 8. The adj. only occurs in these three places; but the verb **νήφειν** six times; in 1 Thess. v. 6, 8, and in 1 Peter iv. 7, it is used of the moderate use of strong drink.

σώφρονα: *soberminded* (R.V.), *serious, earnest*. See note on ii. 9. Vulg., *prudentem* here and in Tit. ii. 2, 5; but *sobrium* in Tit. i. 8. Perhaps **σεμνός** (ver. 8) is the quality in deacons that corresponds to **σώφρων** and **κόσμιος** in the episcopus.

κόσμιον: *orderly* (R.V.), perhaps *dignified* in the best sense of the term. *ordinatum* (m[47]). "Quod **σώφρων** est intus, id **κόσμιος** est extra" (Bengel). The word is not found in *Titus*.

φιλόξενον: This virtue is required in the episcopus also in Tit. i. 8, but not of the deacons, below; of Christians generally, 1 Peter iv. 9, 1 Tim. v. 10 (*q.v.*), Rom. xii. 13, Heb. vi. 10, xiii. 2, 3 John 5. See Hermas, *Sim.* ix. 27 ("Bishops, hospitable persons (**φιλόξενοι**), who gladly received into their houses at all times the servants of God without hypocrisy"). This duty, in episcopi, "was closely connected with the maintenance of external relations," which was their special function. See Ramsay, *Church in the Roman Empire*, p. 368.

διδακτικόν, as a moral quality would involve not merely the ability, but also the willingness, to teach, such as ought to characterise a servant of the Lord, 2 Tim. ii. 24. The notion is expanded in Tit. i. 9. The deacon's relation to theology is passive, ver. 9.

Ver. 3. **μὴ πάροινον** (*no brawler*, R.V., *quarrelsome over wine*, R.V.m.), and **μὴ πλήκτην** are similarly coupled together in Tit. i. 7. **παροινία** means *violent temper*, not specially excited by overindulgence in strong drink. In the time of Chrysostom and Theodoret manners had so far softened that it was felt necessary to explain the term **πλήκτης** figuratively, of "some who unseasonably smite the consciences of their brethren". But see 2 Cor. xi. 20.

ἀλλ' ἐπιεικῆ, ἄμαχον: *gentle, not contentious*. This pair, again, of cognate adjectives is repeated in the general directions as to Christian conduct, Tit. iii. 2. Compare 2 Tim. ii. 24 (of the servant of the Lord). The corresponding episcopal virtues in *Titus* (i. 7) are **μὴ αὐθάδη, μὴ ὀργίλον**.

ἀφιλάργυρον: In *Titus* the corresponding episcopal virtue is **μὴ αἰσχροκερδῆ**. See note on ver. 8 and Tit. i. 7.

Ver. 4. **τοῦ ἰδίου οἴκου**: Although **ἴδιος** commonly retains in the N.T. the emphatic sense *own*, yet there can be no doubt that examples occur of the later weakened sense in which it means simply **αὐτοῦ**, *e.g.*, 1 Cor. vii. 2. We are not therefore justified in insisting on the emphatic sense, *own*, here or in ver. 12.

^v σεμνότητος,—5. εἰ δέ τις τοῦ ἰδίου οἴκου ^t προστῆναι οὐκ οἶδεν, πῶς _{v See 1}

Tim. ii. 2

^w ἐκκλησίας ^w Θεοῦ ^x ἐπιμελήσεται ;—6. μὴ ^y νεόφυτον, ἵνα μὴ ^z τυφω- _{w Ver. 15,}

see note
here.

x Luke x. 34, 35.   y Here only, N.T.   z 1 Tim. vi. 4, 2 Tim. iii. 4, not LXX.

vi. 1, Tit. ii. 5, 9. See J. H. Moulton *Grammar*, vol. i. p. 87 *sqq.*, and *Expositor*, vi., iii. 277, and Dei smann, *Bible Studies*, trans. p. 123 *sq.* οἶκος also means *house-hold*, 1 Cor. i. 16 and in the Pastorals.

προϊστάμενον: προΐστασθαι is per-haps used, here and in ver. 12, because it would naturally suggest church govern-ment. See reff., and Hermas, *Vis.* ii. 4; Justin Martyr, *Apol.* i. 65. A different use is found in Tit. iii. 8, 14, καλῶν ἔργων προΐστασθαι, where see note. The domestic qualification, as we may call it, of the episcopus, also applies to deacons (ver. 12) and to the Cretan episcopus (Tit. i. 6).

τέκνα ἔχοντα : Alford cannot be right in supposing that τέκνα is emphatic. It would be absurd to suppose that a man otherwise suited to the office of an epis-copus would be disqualified because of childlessness. The clause is parallel to μιᾶς γυναικὸς ἄνδρα : if the episcopus be a married man, he must not be a diga-mist ; if he have children, they must be ἐν ὑποταγῇ.

ἐν ὑποταγῇ—σεμνότητος : *with the strictest regard to propriety*, see note on chap. ii. 2. Most commentators join these words closely together. The σεμνότης of the children in their extra-family relations being the outward and visible expression of the ὑποταγή to which they are subject in domestic life. This is a more natural reference of σεμνότ. than to the general household arrangements, "*ut absit luxuria*" (Ben-gel). On the other hand there is much force in Dean Bernard's remark that "σεμνότης is hardly a grace of child-hood." He connects ἔχοντα μετὰ πασ. σεμν. This seems to be supported by ver. 8, διακόνους ὡσαύτως σεμνούς and ver. 11. Von Soden takes a similar view.

Ver. 5. The argument is akin to that stated by our Lord, Luke xvi. 10. "He that is faithful in a very little is faithful also in much, etc." It is all the more cogent inasmuch as the Church is the house of God. The point is resumed in ver. 15. Alf. quotes a sentence from Plato in which both προστῆναι and ἐπιμελεῖσθαι are used of the government of a family ; nevertheless it is not fanciful to suppose that we have here a deliberate interchange of terms,

προστῆναι being, as we have seen above, almost a technical term to express Church government ; while ἐπιμελ. ex-presses the personal care and attention of a father for his family. See the use of the verb in Luke x. 34, 35, and of ἐπιμέλεια in Acts xxvii. 3.

ἐκκλησία θεοῦ is also found in ver. 15. ἐκκλησία τοῦ θεοῦ occurs nine times in Paul (1 Thess. ; 2 Thess. ; 1 Cor. ; 2 Cor. ; Gal.). The omission of the article before θεοῦ is characteristic of the Pas-torals The phrase is found also in St. Paul's apostolic charge to the episcopi of Ephesus in Acts xx. 28.

Ver. 6. Verses 6 and 7 have nothing corresponding to them in *Titus*, or in the qualifications for the diaconate in this chapter.

μὴ νεόφυτον κ.τ.λ. : *not a recent con-vert*. νεόφυτος in O.T. is used literally of a young plant (Job xiv. 9; Ps. cxxvii. (cxxviii.) 3 ; cxliii. (cxliv.) 12 ; Isa. v. 7). For its use in secular literature, see Deissmann, *Bible Studies*, trans. p. 220.

The significance of this qualification is apparent from its absence in the parallel passage in *Titus*. It is evident that Church organisation in Crete was in a very much less advanced state than in Ephesus. On the first introduction of the Gospel into a country, the apostles naturally " appointed their first fruits to be bishops and deacons " (Clem. Rom. i. § 42 ; Acts xiv. 23), because no others were available; and men appointed in such circumstances would have no temptation to be puffed up any more than would the leaders of a forlorn hope. But as soon as there came to be a Christian community of such a size as to supply a considerable number of men from whom leaders could be selected, and in which office might be a natural object of ambition, the moral risk to νεόφυτοι of early advancement would be a real danger. It is difficult to avoid at least a passing attack of τύφωσις, if you are promoted when young.

τυφωθείς : τυφόω comes from τῦφος, the primary meaning of which is *smoke* or *vapour*, then *conceit* or *vanity* which befogs a man's judgment in matters in which he himself is concerned. The R.V. always renders it *puffed up*. Vulg. here, *in superbiam elatus*.

a 1 Tim. vi θεὶς εἰς κρίμα ª ἐμπέσῃ τοῦ ᵇ διαβόλου.   7. δεῖ δὲ ¹ καὶ ᶜ μαρτυρίαν
9. Heb. x.
3¹. καλὴν ἔχειν ἀπὸ ᵈ τῶν ᵈ ἔξωθεν, ἵνα μὴ εἰς ᵉ ὀνειδισμὸν ª ἐμπέσῃ καὶ
b Eph.iv.27,
vi. 11, 1 ᶠᵍ παγίδα ᵍ τοῦ ᵇᵍ διαβόλου.   8. Διακόνους ʰ ὡσαύτως ¹ σεμνούς,²
Tim. iii.7,
2 Tim. ii.
26.   c Tit. i. 13 only, in Paul.   d Mark iv. 11, 1 Cor. v. 12, 13, Col. iv. 5, 1 Thess. iv. 12.
e Rom. xv. 3 (Ps. lxix 10), Heb. x. 33, xi. 26, xiii. 13.   f Rom. xi. 9 (Ps. lxix. 23), 1 Tim. vi. 9.
g 2 Tim. ii. 26.   h See 1 Tim. ii. 9.   i Phil. iv. 8, 1 Tim. iii. 11, Tit. ii. 2.

¹ Ins. αὐτὸν DKLP, d, f, m47, vg.   ² Om. σεμνούς ℵ*, three cursives.

κρίμα ἐμπέσῃ τοῦ διαβόλου : κρίμα is best taken in the sig. *condemnation*, as in Rom. iii. 8, Rev. xvii. 1, and τοῦ διαβόλου as objective genitive : "*Lest he be involved in the condemnation.which the devil incurred*," or, *the judgment pronounced on the devil*, whose sin was, and is, pride. See Ecclus. x. 13, 2 Pet. ii. 4. So most commentators, especially the ancients. On the other hand, τοῦ διαβόλου in ver. 7 is the subjective genitive, *a snare laid by the devil* ; and it is possible to render κρίμα τ. διαβ. *the accusation brought by the devil*, or *a judgment effected by the devil*, who may succeed in this case, though he failed in that of Job. This is however not a natural translation ; and it is to be observed that ἐμπίπτειν in reff. expresses a final doom, not a trial, such as that of temptation or probation. Dean Bernard takes τοῦ διαβόλου as subjective genitive in both verses ; and in the sense of *slanderer : the judgment passed by the slanderer ; the snare prepared by the slanderer.*

τοῦ διαβόλου : St. Paul uses this name for the Evil Spirit three times in the Pastorals and twice in Eph. (see reff.) ; ὁ πονηρός in Eph. vi. 16; ὁ Σατανᾶς elsewhere eight times. διάβολος, without the article, means *slanderer* in ver. 11 and reff. there.

Ver. 7. τῶν ἔξωθεν : οἱ ἔξω in Mark iv. 11 (ἔξωθεν, W.H. m.) means those who came into contact—more or less close—with Jesus, but who were not His disciples. In the Pauline use (see reff.) it means the non-Christian Society in which the Church lives. St. Paul's attitude towards *them that without* is one of the many proofs of his sanity of judgment. On the one hand, they are emphatically outside the Church ; they have no *locus standi* in it, no right to interfere. On the other hand, they have the law of God written in their hearts ; and, up to a certain point, their moral instincts are sound and their moral judgments worthy of respect. In the passage before us, indeed, St. Paul may

be understood to imply that the opinion of "those without" might usefully balance or correct that of the Church. There is something blameworthy in a man's character if the consensus of outside opinion be unfavourable to him; no matter how much he may be admired and respected by his own party. The *vox populi*, then, is in some sort a *vox Dei ;* and one cannot safely assume, when we are in antagonism to it, that, because we are Christians, we are absolutely in the right and the world wholly in the wrong. Thus to defy public opinion in a superior spirit may not only bring *discredit*, ὀνειδισμός, on oneself and on the Church, but also catch us in the devil's snare, *viz.*, a supposition that because the world condemns a certain course of action, the action is therefore right and the world's verdict may be safely set aside.

We cannot infer with Alford and von Soden, from the absence of another preposition before παγίδα, that ὀνειδισμόν also depends on τοῦ διαβόλου. It would not be easy to explain satisfactorily ὀνειδ. τ. διαβόλου.

Ver. 8. διακόνους ὡσαύτως : *s.c.* δεῖ εἶναι.

For ὡσαύτως, see on ii. 9.

σεμνούς : *grave*. "The word we want is one in which the sense of gravity and dignity, and of these as inviting reverence, is combined" (Trench). See note on ver. 2. The term is used in reference to women workers and old men.

μὴ διλόγους : Persons who are in an intermediate position, having in the same department chiefs and subordinates, are exposed to a temptation to speak of the same matter in different tones and manner, according as their interlocutor is above or below them. So Theodoret, ἕτερα μὲν τούτῳ ἕτερα δὲ ἐκείνῳ λέγοντες. Polycarp (§ 5) has the same phrase of deacons. Lightfoot there suggests the rendering *tale-bearers*. Perhaps *insincere*. *Cf.* δίγλωσσος, Prov xi. 13, etc.

μὴ ᵏδιλόγους, μὴ ˡοἴνῳ ˡπολλῷ ᵐπροσέχοντας, μὴ ⁿαἰσχροκερδεῖς, kHere only,
not LXX
9. ἔχοντας τὸ ᵒμυστήριον τῆς πίστεως ἐν ᵖκαθαρᾷ ᵖσυνειδήσει. 10. ˡTit. ii. 3,
cf. 1 Tim.
καὶ οὗτοι δὲ ᑫδοκιμαζέσθωσαν πρῶτον, εἶτα ʳδιακονείτωσαν, ˢἀνέγ- v. 23.
m See 1
κλητοι ὄντες. 11. γυναῖκας ʰὡσαύτως ⁱσεμνάς, μὴ ᵗδιαβόλους, Tim. i. 4.
n Tit. i, 7,
not LXX,

cf. Tit. i. 11, 1 Pet. v. 2. o Ver. 16, 1 Cor. ii. 17, iv. 1, Eph. vi. 19, Col. i. 26, 27, ii. 2, iv. 3.
p 2 Tim. i. 3. q 1 Cor. xi. 28, xvi. 3, 2 Cor. viii. 22, xiii. 5, 1 Thess. ii. 4. r Acts xix. 22, ver.
13, 1 Pet. iv. 11, not LXX. s 3 Macc. v. 31, 1 Cor. i. 8, Col. i. 22, Tit. i. 6, 7. t 2 Tim. iii.
3, Tit. ii. 3.

μὴ οἴνῳ πολλῷ προσέχοντας: Less ambiguously expressed than νηφάλιος in the case of the episcopus. A similar direction is given about women, Tit. ii. 3, μὴ οἴν. πολ. δεδουλωμένας.

μὴ αἰσχροκερδεῖς: This negative qualification is demanded of the episcopus in Tit. i. 7. See reff. The rendering *not greedy of filthy lucre* is unnecessarily strong; the αἰσχρότης consists, not in the source whence the gain comes, but in the setting of gain before one as an object in entering the ministry. *Not greedy of gain* expresses the writer's meaning. The κέρδος becomes αἰσχρόν when a man makes the acquisition of it, rather than the glory of God, his prime object. On the other hand, the special work of deacons was Church finance; and no doubt they had to support themselves by engaging in some secular occupation. They would thus be exposed to temptations to mis-appropriate Church funds, or to adopt questionable means of livelihood. If such circumstances were contemplated, *not greedy of filthy lucre* might be an allowable rendering. In Crete, the episcopus would seem to have also performed the duties of the deacon; consequently he is required to be μή αἰσχροκερδής.

ἔχοντας: See note on chap. i. 19.

Ver. 9. τὸ μυστήριον τῆς πίστεως: *the faith as revealed*, is the same as τὸ τῆς εὐσεβείας μυστήριον, ver. 16. In the earlier epistles of St. Paul τὸ μυστήριον is *a revealed secret*, in particular, the purpose of God that Jew and Gentile should unite in one Church. The notion of *a secret* is still prominent, because the revelation of it was recent; but just as *revelation* passes from a phase of usage in which the wonderful fact and manner of the disclosure is prominent to a stage in which the content or substance of what has been revealed is alone thought of, so it was with μυστήριον; in the Pastorals it means *the revelation given in Christ*, the Christian creed in fact. See Dean Armitage Robinson, *Ephesians*, p. 234 *sqq.*, and Lightfoot on Col. i. 26.

It was not the function of a deacon to teach or preach; it was sufficient if he were a firm believer. ἐν. καθ. συνειδ. is connected with ἔχοντας. Hort (*Christian Ecclesia*, p. 201) approves of the expl. given by Weiss of τὸ μυστ. τ. πίστ., "the secret constituted by their own inner faith". This seems unnatural.

Ver. 10. δοκιμαζέσθωσαν: Chrys. notes that this corresponds to the provision μὴ νεόφυτον in the case of the episcopus. This testing of fitness for the office of deacon may have been effected either by (*a*) a period of probationary training,—if the injunction in v. 22, "Lay hands hastily on no man," has reference to ordination, it is another way of saying δοκιμαζέσθωσαν πρῶτον,—or by (*b*) the candidates producing what we should call testimonials of character. Such testimonials would attest that a man was ἀνέγκλητος, *i.e.*, that no specific charge of wrong-doing had been laid against him (*unblamed* is Hort's rendering). Until a man has proved his suitability for a post by administering it, this is the most that can be demanded. Each step subjects a man's character to a fresh strain. If he comes out of the trial unscathed, he is entitled to be called ἀνεπίλημπτος. It is sign ficant that in Tit. i. 6, 7, where the ordination of presbyters, or episcopi, with no antecedent diaconate is contemplated, this elementary and superficial test, that they should be ἀνέγκλητοι, is mentioned. See note on ver. 2. In a normal condition of the Church, episcopi are chosen from those whose fitness is matter of common knowledge.

διακονείτωσαν: For instances of this absolute technical sense of the word see reff.

Ver. 11. γυναῖκας: Sc. δεῖ εἶναι, not governed by ἔχοντας (ver. 9). These are *the deaconesses, ministrae* (Pliny, *Ep.* x. 97) of whom Phoebe (Rom. xvi. 1) is an undoubted example. They performed for the women of the early Church the same sort of ministrations that the deacons did for the men. In confirmation of this

u See ver. 2. ^u νηφαλίους, πιστὰς ἐν πᾶσιν. 12. διάκονοι ἔστωσαν ^v μιᾶς ^v γυναικὸς
v Ver. 2,
Tit. i. 6. ^v ἄνδρες, τέκνων ^w καλῶς ^w προϊστάμενοι καὶ τῶν ἰδίων οἴκων · 13. οἱ
w See ver. 4.
x See ver. γὰρ καλῶς ^x διακονήσαντες ^y βαθμὸν ἑαυτοῖς καλὸν ^z περιποιοῦνται
10.
y Here only,
N.T. z Luke xvii. 33, Acts xx. 28, 1 Macc. vi. 44, etc.

view it should be noted that ὡσαύτως is used in introducing a second or third member of a series. See on ii. 9. The series here is of Church officials. Again, the four qualifications which follow correspond, with appropriate variations, to the first four required in deacons, as regards demeanour, government of the tongue, use of wine, and trustworthiness. And further, this is a section dealing wholly with Church officials. These considerations exclude the view that *women in general*, as R.V. apparently, are spoken of. If *the wives of the deacons* or of the clergy were meant, as A.V., it would be natural to have it unambiguously expressed, *e.g.*, by the addition of αὐτῶν.

διαβόλους: *slanderers*. While men are more prone than women to be δίλογοι, double-tongued, women are more prone than men to be slanderers. See Tit. ii. 3. The term is predicated in 2 Tim. iii. 3, not of *men*, but as characterising the human race, ἄνθρωποι, in the last days.

νηφαλίους: see note on ver. 2.

πιστὰς ἐν πᾶσιν: It may be that, as Ell. suggests, this has a reference to the function of deaconesses as almoners, a possible inference from *Constt. Apost.* iii. 16. But more probably it is a comprehensive summary with a general reference, like πᾶσαν πίστιν ἐνδεικνυμένους ἀγαθήν, Tit. ii. 10.

Ver. 12. As the episcopi were naturally drawn from the ranks of the deacons, the diaconate was a probation time, in the course of which the personal moral qualifications for the ἐπισκοπή might be acquired. See notes on vv. 2 and 4.

Ver. 13. From what has been noted above on St. Paul's teaching in relation to men's lawful aspirations, it will appear that it is not necessary to explain away the obvious meaning of this clause in accordance with a false spirituality which affects to depreciate the inducements of earthly rewards. The parable of the talents (Matt. xxv. 21), implies Christ's approval of reasonable ambition. Nor is this to be answered by a statement that "the recompense of reward" to which we are permitted to look is heavenly and spiritual. For the Christian, there can

be no gulf fixed between the earthly and the heavenly; at least in the category of things which are open to him, as a Christian, to desire. The drawing of such distinctions is akin to the Manichaean disparagement of matter.

The βαθμὸν καλόν which the man may acquire who has served well as a deacon is *advancement* to the presbyterate or episcopate. So Chrys. The R.V., *gain to themselves a good standing*, does not necessarily imply an advance in rank, but an assured position in the esteem of their fellow-Christians. We know that among the many who possess the same rank, whether in church or state, some from their character and abilities gain a standing that others do not.

Some modern commentators follow Theodoret in giving a purely spiritual force to βαθμόν, i.e., ἐν τῷ μέλλοντι βίῳ, "a good standing place, viz., at the Great Day" (Alf.); "the step or degree which a faithful discharge of the διακονία would gain in the eyes of God" (Ell.). Alf. lays emphasis on the aor. part. as viewing the διακονία from the standpoint of the Day of Judgment; but it is equally suitable if the standpoint be that of the day on which they receive their advancement. There is more force in his emphasis on the present, περιποιοῦνται, *they are acquiring*. This interpretation does not seem to be in harmony with the context. The qualifications that are noted in ver. 12 have relation to the effectual administration of the Church on earth. It would be harsh to affirm that one who was a digamist and who could not keep his household in order would suffer for it in the Day of Judgment, however unsuitable he might be for office in the church.

πολλὴν παρρησίαν: a Pauline phrase. See reff. In these passages παρρ. means *confidence*, without reference to *speech*.

Although Ell. renders the clause "great boldness in the faith that is in Christ Jesus," he explains the boldness as resting on faith in Christ Jesus, and as descriptive of the believer's attitude in regard to, and at, the Day of Judgment. See 1 John iv. 17. If we reject his explanation of βαθμόν, it would be natural to interpret παρρ., κ.τ.λ., of a

καὶ ^aπολλὴν ^aπαρρησίαν ἐν ^bπίστει ^bτῇ ^bἐν ^bΧριστῷ ^bἸησοῦ. 14 ^a 2 Cor. iii.
12, vii. 4,
Ταῦτά σοι γράφω, ἐλπίζων ἐλθεῖν πρὸς σὲ ¹ ^cἐν ^cτάχει,² 15. ἐὰν δὲ ^b Philem. 8
2 Tim. iii
^dβραδύνω, ἵνα εἰδῇς πῶς δεῖ ³ ἐν οἴκῳ Θεοῦ ^eἀναστρέφεσθαι, ἥτις 15, cf. 2
Tim. i. 13
ἐστὶν ^fἐκκλησία ^fΘεοῦ ζῶντος, στύλος καὶ ^gἑδραίωμα τῆς ἀληθείας. ^c Rom. xvi
20, Luke
xviii. 8,

Acts xii. 7, xxii. 18, xxv. 4, Rev. i. 1, xxii. 6.   d 2 Pet. iii. 9 only, N.T.   e 2 Cor. i. 12
Eph. ii. 3, Heb. x. 33, xiii. 18, 1 Pet. i. 17, 2 Pet. ii. 18.   f See ver. 5.   g Here on.y, not LXX
cf. 1 Cor. vii. 37, xv. 58, Col. i. 23.

1 Om. πρὸς σὲ FgrGgr, 67**, two others, arm ; f, g ins. after *cito*.

2 ἐν τάχει ACD*P, 17, two others ; τάχιον אDᶜFGKL.

3 Ins. σε D*, d, f, vg., arm.

confident public expression of the faith, such as would belong to an experienced Christian who had gained a good standing, and had, in consequence, no temptation to be δίλογος. Von Soden connects ἐν πίστει with περιποιοῦνται, *cf.* 2 Tim. i. 13.

Vv. 14-16. These general directions will serve you as a guide in the administration of the Church until you see me. Your charge is one of transcendent importance. The Church is no human institution : it is the household of God, and also the means whereby the power of the Incarnation is available for man's use.

Ver. 14. This verse makes it clear that Timothy's position was a temporary one ; he was acting as St. Paul's representative at Ephesus to "put them in remembrance of his ways which be in Christ" (1 Cor. iv. 17).

ταῦτα has a primary reference to the preceding directions regarding public prayers and Church officers ; but it naturally includes the following supplementary remarks. For this use of γράφω, in place of the epistolary aorist, see especially 2 Cor. xiii. 10, also 1 Cor. xiv. 37, 2 Cor. i. 13, Gal. i. 20.

ἐλπίζων . . . βραδύνω is parenthetical ; and expresses at once an excuse for the brevity and incompleteness, from one point of view, of the directions, and also an expectation that they are sufficient to serve their temporary purpose.

ἐν τάχει : τάχιον, which is read by Tisch., is, according to Blass (*Grammar*, pp. 33, 141, 142), an instance of the intensive or elative use of the comparative : *cf.* βέλτιον 2 Tim. i. 18. This view is rejected by Winer-Moulton (*Grammar*, p. 304) and Ellicott ; but their explanations are far-fetched : "More quickly, sooner, than thou wilt need these instructions," "sooner than I anticipate". See also J. H. Moulton, *Grammar*, vol. i. pp. 78, 79, 236.

Ver. 15. ἵνα εἰδῇς . . . ἀναστρέφεσθαι : It is a matter of indifference whether we render *how men ought to behave themselves* (R.V.), or *how thou oughtest to behave thyself* (A.V. ; R.V. m.). It was Timothy's duty to carry out the apostle's directions, directions relating to the life, ἀναστροφή, of the Church. His ἀναστροφή would necessarily react on that of the Church. See the Western interpolation in *apparat. crit.*

οἴκῳ θεοῦ : *the household*, perhaps, rather than *the house, of God*. In view of the prevailing paucity of articles in these Epistles, one cannot lay stress on the absence of τῷ before οἴκῳ, so as to render, *a house of God such as is the Church*, etc. οἶκος τοῦ θεοῦ is always found elsewhere. The Church is God's οἶκος, Heb. iii. 6 ; God's κατοικητήριον, Eph. ii. 22 ; a ναὸς ἅγιος, Eph. ii. 21 ; ναὸς θεοῦ, 1 Cor. iii. 16, 2 Cor. vi. 16 ; a μεγάλη οἰκία, of which God is the δεσπότης, 2 Tim. ii. 20 ; an οἶκος πνευματικός, 1 Pet. ii. 5.

The body of the Church, τὸ σῶμα ὑμῶν, is a ναὸς ἁγίου πνεύματος (1 Cor. vi. 19) ; and the human body of Jesus was a ναός (John ii. 21) ; but it is not in accordance with Scriptural language so to describe the body of any individual Christian.

οἴκῳ . . . ἥτις : "The noun which forms the predicate in a relative sentence, annexed for the purpose of explanation (ὃς . . . ἐστίν), sometimes gives its own gender and number to the relative, by a kind of attraction" (Winer-Moulton, *Grammar*, p. 206).

θεοῦ ζῶντος : A constant phrase, occurring again iv. 10.

στύλος καὶ ἑδραίωμα κ.τ.λ. : The view of Gregory Nyssen and Greg. Naz. that στύλος here refers to Timothy does not need refutation, although an early reference to this passage in the Letter of the Churches of Lyons and Vienne (Eus.

h Here only, 16. καὶ ʰ ὁμολογουμένως μέγα ἐστὶν τὸ τῆς ⁱ εὐσεβείας ᵏ μυστήριον ·
N.T., 4
Macc. (3). ὃς ¹ ¹ ἐφανερώθη ἐν σαρκί, ᵐ ἐδικαιώθη ἐν πνεύματι, ⁿ ὤφθη ἀγγέλοις,
i See 1
Tim. ii. 2.
k See note.   1 John i. 31. Heb. ix. 26, 1 Pet. i. 20, 1 John i. 2, iii. 5, 8.   m Ps. l. (li.) 6, Matt.
xi. 19 = Luke vii. 35, Luke vii. 29.   n Luke xxiv. 34, Acts ix. 17, xiii. 31, xxvi. 16, 1 Cor. xv. 5,
6, 7, 8, Heb. ix. 28.

¹ So א*cA*C*FgrGgr, 17, 73, 181, sah., boh., syrhcl-mg, go., Or.int, Epiph., Theod.
Mops., Cyr. Al.   Liberatus Diaconus (circ. 560 A.D.), *Breviarium causae Nest. et
Eutych.*, 19, says, " Hoc tempore Macedonius Constantinopolitanus episcopus, ab
imperatore Anastasio dicitur expulsus, tanquam evangelia falsasset, & maxime
illud apostoli dictum : *qui apparuit in carne, justificatus est in spiritu.*   Hunc enim
immutasse, ubi habet ὅς, id est, *qui*, monosyllabum graecum, littera mutata Ο in
Θ vertisse, & fecisse, ΘC, id est *deus*, ut esset *Deus apparuit per carnem*" ; a
relative is found in syrpesh, syrhcl-txt, arm., all Latin Fathers ; ὃ D*, *quod*, d, f, g,
vg. ; θεὸς אe(xii/)CcDcKLP, Chrys., Thdrt., Euthalius, Damasc., Thphl., Oec.,
Didymus, Greg. Nyss.

H. E. v. 1) applies στύλος καὶ ἑδραίωμα
to the martyr Attalus. στύλος has of
course a personal reference in Gal. ii. 9 ;
cf. also Rev. iii. 12 ; but it is childish to
suppose that metaphors have a constant
value in the Bible.   Holtzmann's suggestion that στύλος is in apposition to
θεοῦ is rightly rejected by von Soden.

The clause is, of course, in apposition
to ἐκκλησία which is by a kindred metaphor called in 2 Tim. ii. 19 ὁ στερεὸς
θεμέλιος τοῦ θεοῦ.   This latter passage
suggests that we should here render
ἑδραίωμα *ground* or *basis* rather than
stay (R.V. m.).   ἑδραῖος is rendered
steadfast elsewhere.   See reff. and especially Col. i. 23 (τεθεμελιωμένοι καὶ
ἑδραῖοι), *ctr.* Hort, *Christian Ecclesia*,
p. 174.

The truth, ἡ ἀλήθεια, has, as has been
already stated, a technical Christian connotation in the Pastorals, and has not a
wider reference than the Christian revelation, which is the 'truth in so far as
it has been revealed.   The Church, of
the old covenant or of the new, is the
divinely constituted human Society by
which the support and maintenance in
the world of revealed truth is conditioned.
Truth if revealed to isolated individuals,
no matter how numerous, would be dissipated in the world.   But the Divine
Society, in which it is given an objective
existence, at once compels the world to
take knowledge of it, and assures those
who receive the revelation that it is independent of, and external to, themselves,
and not a mere fancy of their own.

Bengel puts a full stop at ζῶντος and
removes it after ἀληθείας, making τὸ . . .
μυστήριον the subject of the sentence,
and στύλος . . . μέγα the predicate,
The mystery, etc., is the pillar, etc.,
and confessedly great," μέγα being used

as in 1 Cor. ix. 11, 2 Cor. xi. 15, the whole
expression being equivalent to πιστὸς ὁ
λόγος καὶ πάσης ἀποδοχῆς ἄξιος.   He
quotes from Rabbi Levi Barcelonita and
Maimonides parallel expressions concerning precepts of the Law, "*fundamentum magnum et columna valida
legis,*" and a striking phrase from Irenæus, *Haer.* iii. 11, 8, *Columna autem
et firmamentum ecclesiae est evangelium,*
στύλος δὲ καὶ στήριγμα ἐκκλησίας τὸ
εὐαγγέλιον.

Ver. 16.   The connexion of thought
lies in a feeling that the lofty terms in
which the Church has been just spoken
of may demand a justification. *The
truth* of which the Church is στύλος καὶ
ἑδραίωμα is not a light thing nor an in-
substantial fabric ; *the truth* is, more
expressly, τὸ τῆς εὐσεβείας μυστήριον,
*the revelation to man of practical reli-
gion ;* and, beyond yea or nay, this
truth, this revelation, is great.   Whether
you believe it or not, you cannot deny
that the claims of Christianity are
tremendous.

μέγας is rare in Paul : (Rom. ix. 2 ; 1
Cor. ix. 11, xvi. 9 ; 2 Cor. xi. 15 ; Eph. v.
32 ; 1 Tim. vi. 6 ; 2 Tim. ii. 20 ; Tit. ii. 13).
The nearest parallel to the present passage is Eph. v. 32, τὸ μυστήριον τοῦτο
μέγα ἐστίν.   See note on ver. 9.   On
εὐσέβεια, see chap. ii. 2.

If we assume that ὅς is the right reading, it is difficult to avoid the conclusion
that what follows is a quotation by St.
Paul from a primitive creed or summary
of the chief facts to be believed about
Jesus Christ.   And one is tempted to
conjecture that another fragment of the
same summary is quoted in 1 Pet. iii. 18,
θανατωθεὶς μὲν σαρκὶ ζωοποιηθεὶς δὲ
πνεύματι. ὅς, then, does not form part of
the quotation at all ; it is simply intro-

° ἐκηρύχθη ° ἐν ° ἔθνεσιν, ἐπιστεύθη ἐν κόσμῳ, ᵖ ἀνελήμφθη ᑫ ἐν ο Gal. ii. 2, cf. 2 Cor. i. 19, Col.

i. 23. p Mark xvi. 19, Acts i. 2, 11, 22. q Luke ix. 31, 1 Cor. xv. 43, Phil. iv. 19, Col. iii. 4.

ductory, and relative to the subject, Jesus Christ, whose personality was, in some terms, expressed in an antecedent sentence which St. Paul has not quoted.

As the passage stands, there are three pairs of antithetic thoughts: (1) (a) the flesh and (b) the spirit of Christ, (2) (a) angels and (b) Gentiles—the two extremes of the rational creation, (3) (a) the world and (b) glory. In another point of view, there is a connexion between 2 a and 3 b, and between 2 b and 3 a. Again, we may say that we have here set forth (1) the Incarnation in itself, (2) its manifestation, (3) its consequence or result, as affecting man and God.

The antithesis between the σάρξ and πνεῦμα of Christ is drawn, in addition to 1 Pet. iii. 18, also in Rom. i. 3, 4. τοῦ γενομένου ἐκ σπέρματος Δαυεὶδ κατὰ σάρκα, τοῦ ὁρισθέντος υἱοῦ θεοῦ ἐν δυνάμει κατὰ πνεῦμα ἁγιωσύνης. We cannot leave out of account in discussing these passages the parallel in 1 Pet. iv. 6, εἰς τοῦτο γὰρ καὶ νεκροῖς εὐηγγελίσθη ἵνα κριθῶσι μὲν κατὰ ἀνθρώπους σαρκί ζῶσι δὲ κατὰ θεὸν πνεύματι. The πνεῦμα of Christ, as man, in these passages means His human spirit, the naturally permanent spiritual part of a human personality. See also 1 Cor. v. 5.

ἐφανερώθη ἐν σαρκί: He who had been from all eternity "in the form of God" became cognisable by the limited senses of human beings, ἐν ὁμοιώματι σαρκὸς ἁμαρτίας (Rom. viii. 3), became manifest in the flesh, σὰρξ ἐγένετο (John i. 14). φανεροῦν is used in connexion with Christ in four associations in the N.T. :—

(1) as here, of the objective fact of the Incarnation: John i. 31 (?), Heb. ix. 26, 1 Pet. i. 20, 1 John i. 2 (bis), iii. 5, 8.

(2) of the revelation involved in the Incarnation: Rom. xvi. 26, Col. i. 26, iv. 4, 2 Tim. i. 10, Tit. i. 3. N.B. in Rom. and Col. the verb is used of a μυστήριον.

(3) of the post-resurrection appearances of Christ, which were, in a sense, repetitions of the marvel of the Incarnation, as being manifestations of the unseen: Mark xvi. 12, 14, John xxi. 1 (bis), 14.

(4) of the Second Coming, which will be, as far as man can tell, His final manifestation: Col. iii. 4, 1 Pet. v. 4, 1 John ii. 28, iii. 2.

ἐδικαιώθη ἐν πνεύματι: proved or pronounced to be righteous in His higher nature. The best parallel to this use of δικαιοῦν is Ps. l. (li.) 6, ὅπως ἂν δικαιωθῆς ἐν τοῖς λόγοις σου, also Matt. xi. 19 = Luke vii. 35. We are not entitled to assume that the ἐν has the same force before πνεύματι that it has before σαρκί; the repetition of the preposition is due to a felt need of rhythmic effect. If we are asked, When did this δικαίωσις take place? we reply that it was on a review of the whole of the Incarnate Life. The heavenly voice, ἐν σοὶ εὐδόκησα, heard by human ears at the Baptism and at the Transfiguration, might have been heard at any moment during the course of those "sinless years". He was emphatically ὁ δίκαιος (Acts iii. 14, xxii. 14; 1 John ii. 1. See also Matt. iii. 15; John xvi. 10.) It is enough to mention without discussion the opinions that πνεύματι refers (a) to the Holy Spirit, or (b) to the Divine Personality of Christ.

ὤφθη ἀγγέλοις: Ellicott points out that in these three pairs of clauses, the first member of each group points to earthly relations, the second to heavenly. So that these words ὤφθη ἀγγέλοις refer to the fact that the Incarnation was "a spectacle to angels" as well as "to men"; or rather, as Dean Bernard notes (Comm. in loc.), ὤφθη and ἐκηρύχθη mark the difference in the communication of the Christian Revelation to angels—the rational creatures nearest to God—and to the Gentiles—farthest from God. "The revelation to Gentiles is mediate, by preaching . . . ; the revelation to the higher orders of created intelligences is immediate, by vision." It was as much a source of wonderment to the latter as to the former. See 1 Pet. i. 12. The angels who greeted the Birth (Luke ii. 13), who ministered at the temptations (Matt. iv. 11, Mark i. 13), strengthened Him in His agony (Luke xxii. 43), proclaimed His Resurrection and stood by at the Ascension, are only glimpses to us of "a cloud of witnesses" of whose presence Jesus was always conscious (Matt. xxvi. 53).

ὤφθη is usually used of the post-resurrection appearances of Christ to men. See reff.

ἐπιστεύθη ἐν κόσμῳ: This was in itself a miracle. See 2 Thess. i. 10, John xvii. 21.

a Here only, q δόξῃ.   IV. 1. Τὸ δὲ Πνεῦμα ᵃῥητῶς λέγει ὅτι ἐν ᵇὑστέροις καιροῖς
not LXX.
b Matt. xxi. ᶜἀποστήσονταί τινες τῆς πίστεως, ᵈπροσέχοντες πνεύμασι ᵉπλάνοις ¹
31 only,
N.T.   καὶ διδασκαλίαις δαιμονίων 2. ἐν ᶠὑποκρίσει ᵍψευδολόγων, ʰκεκαυ-
c Luke viii.
13, 2 Tim.
ii. 19, Heb. iii. 12.   d See 1 Tim. i. 4.   e Here only as adj., cf. 2 John 7, Eph. iv. 14,
2 Thess. ii. 11.   f 2 Macc. vi. 25, Gal. ii. 13, Matt. xxiii. 28, Mark xii. 15, Luke xii. 1, 1 Pet. ii. 1·
g Here only, not LXX.   h Here only, not LXX.

¹ πλάνης P, 31, 37, twenty-four others, vg. (erroris), go., arm.

Winer-Moulton notes (Grammar, p. 326) that ἐπιστεύθη cannot be referred to πιστεύειν Χῷ but presupposes the phrase πιστ. Χόν. Cf. 2 Thess. i. 10.

ἀνελήμφθη ἐν δόξῃ: This is the verb used of the Ascension. See reff. Cf. ἀνάλημψις Luke ix. 51.

ἐν δόξῃ: ἐν has, in this case,, a pregnant sense, εἰς δόξαν καὶ ἐστὶν ἐν δόξῃ (Ell.). See also reff., in which ἐν δόξῃ is a personal attribute of the glory that surrounds and transfigures a glorified spiritual person; but in this place δόξα means the place or state of glory; cf. Luke xxiv. 26, ἔδει . . . τὸν Χριστόν . . . εἰσελθεῖν εἰς τὴν δόξαν αὐτοῦ.

CHAPTER IV.—Vv. 1-5. Over against the future triumph of the truth, assured to us by the finished work of Christ, we must set the opposition, grievous at present, of the force of error. His attacks have been foreseen by the Spirit of holiness. They are just now expressed in a false spirituality which condemns God's good creatures of marriage and food.

Ver. 1. τὸ δὲ πνεῦμα: The Apostle here passes to another theme, the manifestation of religion in daily life. The connexion between this section and the last is as indicated above. There is a slightly adversative force in the connecting δέ.

The Spirit is the Holy Spirit Who speaks through the prophets of the New Dispensation, of whom St. Paul was one. Here, if the following prophetical utterance be his own, he speaks as if Paul under the prophetic influence had an activity independent of Paul the apostle.

ἐν ὑστέροις καιροῖς: The latter times, of course, may be said to come before the last days, ἔσχαται ἡμέραι (Isa. ii. 2, ₑActs ii. 17, Jas. v. 3, 2 Pet. iii. 3; καιρὸς ἔσχατος, 1 Pet. i.5; ἔσχ. χρόνος, Jude 18). But a comparison with 2 Tim. iii. 1, a passage very similar in tone to this, favours the opinion that the terms were not so distinguished by the writers of the N.T. In this sort of prophetical warning or denunciation, we are not in-

tended to take the future tense too strictly. Although the prophet intends to utter a warning concerning the future, yet we know that what he declares will be hereafter he believes to be already in active operation. It is a convention of prophetical utterance to denounce sins and sinners of one's own time (τινες) under the form of a predictive warning. Cf. 2 Tim. iv. 3, ἔσται γὰρ καιρὸς, κ.τ.λ. It gives an additional impressiveness to the arraignment, to state that the guilty persons are partners in the great apostacy, the culmination of the world's revolt from God.

τινες is intentionally vague. See note on 1 Tim. i. 3. It is not used, as in Rom. iii. 3, of an indefinite number.

πνεύμασι πλάνοις: As the Church is guided aright by the Spirit of truth, He is opposed in His beneficent ministrations by the Spirit of error, τὸ πνεῦμα τῆς πλάνης (1 John iv. 6), who is τὸ πνεῦμα τοῦ κόσμου, whose agents work through individuals, the "many false prophets who have gone out into the world" (1 John iv. 1).

διδασκαλίαις δαιμονίων must be, in this context, doctrines taught by demons, a σοφία δαιμονιώδης (Jas. iii. 15). See Tert. de Praescr. Haeret. 7. The phrase does not here mean doctrines about demons, demonology. Still less are heresiarchs here called demons. This is the only occurrence of δαιμόνιον in the Pastorals. In Acts xvii. 18 the word has its neutral classical meaning, "a divine being," see also ver. 22; but elsewhere in the N.T. it has the LXX reference to evil spirits. For διδασκ. see note on chap. i. 10.

Ver. 2. ἐν ὑποκρίσει ψευδολόγων: The three genitives ψευδολ. κεκαυστ. κωλ. are coordinate, and refer to the human agents of the seducing spirits and demons. ἐν ὑποκρίσει depends on πνεύμασι and διδασκαλίαις. The spirits work, and the teachings are exhibited, in the hypocrisy of them that speak lies; and this hypocrisy finds detailed expression in regulations suggested by a false asceticism.

στηριασμένων τὴν ἰδίαν συνείδησιν, 3. κωλυόντων γαμεῖν, ¹ ἀπέχεσθαι i Acts xv.
20, 29, 1
ᵏ βρωμάτων ἃ ὁ Θεὸς ἔκτισεν εἰς ¹ μετάλημψιν μετὰ εὐχαριστίας τοῖς Thess. iv
3, 1 Pet.
ii. 11.

k Rom. xiv. 15, 20, 1 Cor. viii. 8, 13, Heb. xiii. 9. l Here only, not LXX.

Although the ψευδολόγοι are included
in the τινες . . . προσέχοντες, yet there
is a large class of persons who are merely
deceived; who are not actively deceiving
others, and who have not taken the initiative in deceit.   These latter are the
ψευδολόγοι.   For this reason it is better
to connect ἐν ὑποκρίσει with προσέχοντες
(Ell., von Soden) rather than with
ἀποστήσονται (Bengel, Alf.), though no
doubt both verbs refer to the same class.

ἐν ὑποκρίσει of course is not adverbial
as A.V., *speaking lies in hypocrisy*. This
could only be justified if ψευδολόγων
referred to δαιμονίων.   The absence of
an article before ὑποκρίσει need cause
no astonishment.

ψευδολόγων: This word expresses perhaps more than ψεύστης the notion of
definite false statements.   A man might
be on some occasions and on special
points a ψευδολόγος, *a speaker of that
which is not true*, and yet not deserve to
be classed as a ψεύστης, *a liar*.

κεκαυστηριασμένων τὴν ἰδίαν συνείδησιν: These speakers of falsehood are
radically unsound.   They are in worse
case than the unsophisticated heathen
whose conscience bears witness with the
law of God (Rom. ii. 15).   The conscience of these men is perverted.
κεκαυστ. may mean that they are *past
feeling*, ἀπηλγηκότες (Eph. iv. 19), that
their conscience is callous from constant
violation, as skin grows hard from sear-
ing (A.V., R.V. m., so Theodoret); or it
may mean that these men *bore branded
on their conscience the ownership marks
of the Spirit of evil*, the devil's seal (ctr.
2 Tim. ii. 19), so perhaps R.V.; as St.
Paul "bore branded on his body the
marks of Jesus" (Gal. vi. 17), as "Christ's
bondservant" (1 Cor. vii. 22).   (So
Theophylact.   Either of these interpretations is more attractive than that of
Bengel, followed by Alford, who takes it
to mean that *the marks of crime are
burnt into them*, so that they are self-
condemned.   See Tit. i. 15, iii. 11.

There is no special force in ἰδίαν (see
on chap. iii. 4), as though a course of
deceiving others should, by a righteous
judgment, result in a loss to themselves
of moral sensitiveness.

Ver. 3. κωλυόντων γαμεῖν: Spurious
asceticism, in this and other departments
of life, characterised the Essenes (Joseph.

Bell. Jud. ii. 8, 2) and the Therapeutae
(Philo *Vit. Contempl.* § 4), and all the
other false spiritualists of the East; so
that this feature does not supply a safe
ground for fixing the date of the epistle.
At the same time, it is not likely that this
particular heresy was present to St. Paul's
mind when he was writing 1 Cor. vii.
25-40; see especially 38, ὁ μὴ γαμίζων
κρεῖσσον ποιήσει; but similar views are
condemned in Col., see especially Col. ii.
16, 21, 22.   See also Heb. xiii., iv.   St.
Paul had come to realise how tyrannous
the weak brother could be; and he had
become less tolerant of him.

ἀπέχεσθαι: The positive κελευόντων,
commanding, must be supplied from the
negative κελευόντων μή, *commanding not*
= κωλυόντων.

d. f. g. Vulg. preserve the awkwardness of the Greek, *prohibentium nubere,
abstinere a cibis*.   But Faustus read
abstinentes, and Origen int. *et abstinentes
se a cibis*.   Epiphanius inserts παραγ-
γέλλουσιν after βρωμ., and Isidore inserts καὶ κελευόντων before ἀπεχ., which
was also suggested by Bentley.   Theophylact inserts similarly συμβουλευόντων.
Hort conjectures that ἀπέχεσθαι is a
primitive corruption for ἢ ἅπτεσθαι or
καὶ γεύεσθαι.   He maintains that "no
Greek usage will justify or explain this
combination of two infinitives, adverse
to each other in the tenor of their sense,
under the one verb κωλυόντων; and their
juxtaposition without a conjunction in a
sentence of this kind is at least strange".
Blass, however (*Grammar*, p. 291) alleges
as a parallel κωλύσει ἐνεργεῖν καὶ [*sc.*
ποιήσει] ζημιοῦν from Lucian, *Charon*,
§ 2.   Another instance of zeugma, though
not so startling as this, is in ii. 12, οὐκ
ἐπιτρέπω . . . εἶναι ἐν ἡσυχίᾳ.   See
also τ Cor. x. 24, xiv. 34 (T.R.).   For
ἀπέχεσθαι, as used in this connexion, see
reff.

ἃ ὁ Θεὸς ἔκτισεν, κ.τ.λ.: It has been
asked why St. Paul does not justify by
specific reasons the use of marriage, as
he does the use of food.   The answer
seems to be that the same general argument applies to both.   The final cause
of both is the same, *i.e.*, to keep the race
alive; and man is not entitled to place
restrictions on the use of either, other
than those which can be shown to be in
accordance with God's law.

m *Cf.* i Tim. πιστοῖς καὶ ᵐ ἐπεγνωκόσι ᵐ τὴν ᵐ ἀλήθειαν.   4.   ὅτι πᾶν ⁿ κτίσμα
ii. 4.
n Jas. i. 18. Θεοῦ καλόν, καὶ οὐδὲν ᵒ ἀπόβλητον μετὰ εὐχαριστίας ᵖ λαμβανόμενον ·
Rev. v. 13,
viii. 9.   5. ἁγιάζεται γὰρ διὰ λόγου Θεοῦ καὶ �q ἐντεύξεως.   6. Ταῦτα
o Here only,
not LXX.
p Mark xv. 23, John xiii. 30, xix. 30, Acts ix. 19, Rev. xxii. 17.   q See i Tim. ii. 1.

μετάλημψιν μετὰ εὐχαριστίας is one
complex conception. This expresses the
ideal use, truly dignified and human, of
food. See Rom. xiv. 6, ὁ ἐσθίων κυρίῳ
ἐσθίει, εὐχαριστεῖ γὰρ τῷ θεῷ; and i Cor.
x. 30, εἰ ἐγὼ χάριτι μετέχω, τί βλασφη-
μοῦμαι ὑπὲρ οὗ ἐγὼ εὐχαριστῶ; St.
Paul of course does not mean that
believers only are intended by God to
partake of food. His argument is an
à *fortiori* one. "Those that believe,"
etc., are certainly included in God's intention. He who makes His sun to rise
on the evil is certainly well pleased to
make it rise on the good.

Again, St. Paul does not merely desire
to vindicate the use of some of God's
creatures for them that believe, but the
use of *all* of God's creatures, so far as
they are not physically injurious. "God
saw *every thing* that he had made, and
behold, it was very good," καλὰ λίαν
(Gen. i. 31).

For the association of μετάλημψις
compare the phrase μεταλαμβάνειν τροφῆς, Acts ii. 46, and reff. on 2 Tim. ii. 6.
τοῖς πιστοῖς: *dat. commodi*, as in Tit.
i. 15, where see note.

τὴν ἀλήθειαν means, as elsewhere in
these epistles, the Gospel truth in general, not the truth of the following statement, πᾶν κτίσμα, κ.τ.λ.

Ver. 4. ὅτι πᾶν κτίσμα: This is the
proof of the preceding statement, consisting of (*a*) a plain reference to Gen. i.
31, (*b*) a no less clear echo of our Lord's
teaching, Mark vii. 15 (Acts x. 15), also
re-echoed in Rom. xiv. 14, Tit. i. 15.

λαμβανόμενον: This verb is used of
taking food into one's hand before eating (in the accounts of the feeding of the
multitudes, Matt. xiv. 19 = Mark vi. 41;
Matt. xv. 36 = Mark viii. 6, also Luke xxiv.
30, 43) as well as of eating and drinking.
See reff. Perhaps it is not fanciful to
note its special use in connexion with
the Eucharist (i Cor. xi. 23; Matt. xxvi.
26 (bis) 27; Mark xiv. 22, 23; Luke xxii.
19).

καὶ οὐδὲν ἀπόβλητον: The statement
of Gen. i. 31 which is summed up in
Every creature of God is good might be
met by the objection that nevertheless
certain kinds of food were, in point of
fact, to be *rejected* by the express com-

mand of the Mosaic Law. St. Paul
replies that *thanksgiving* disannuls the
Law in each particular case. Nothing
over which thanksgiving can be pronounced is any longer included in the
category of things tabooed. It is evident,
from the repetition of the condition, μετὰ
εὐχαριστίας λαμβ., that St. Paul regarded that as the only restriction on
Christian liberty in the use of God's
creatures. Is it a thing of such a kind
that I can, without incongruity, give
thanks for it ?

Field regards οὐδὲν ἀπόβλητον here
as a proverbial adaptation of Homer's
saying (*Il.* Γ. 65): οὔτοι ἀπόβλητ' ἐστὶ
θεῶν ἐρικυδέα δῶρα.

For κτίσμα see reff. κτίσις is found
in Rom. (7), 2 Cor. (1), Gal. (1), Col. (2);
but in these places *creation* is the best
or a possible rendering. κτίσμα means
unambiguously *thing created*.

Ver. 5. ἁγιάζεται: The use of the present tense here supports the explanation
given of ver. 4, and helps to determine
the sense in which λόγος θεοῦ is used.
The food lying before me at this moment,
which to some is ἀπόβλητος, is sanctified
here and now by the εὐχαριστία. See
i Cor. x. 30.

λόγος θεοῦ and ἔντευξις (see note
on ii. 1) are in some sense co-ordinate
(almost a hendiadys), and together form
elements in a εὐχαριστία. If St. Paul
had meant by λόγος θεοῦ, the general
teaching of Scripture, or the particular
text, Gen. i. 31, he must have said
ἡγίασται. At the same time, the written
word was an element in the notion of
the writer. λόγος θεοῦ has not here
merely its general sense, a divine communication to man ; it rather determines
the quality of the ἔντευξις, as *a scriptural
prayer; a prayer in harmony with God s
revealed truth.* The examples that have
come down to us of grace before meat
are, as Dean Bernard notes here, "packed
with scriptural phrases ".

The best commentary on this verse
is the action of St. Paul himself on the
ship, when, having "taken bread, he
gave thanks to God in the presence of
all; and he brake it, and began to eat"
(Acts xxvii. 35).

Although there is not here any direct

ʳ ὑποτιθέμενος τοῖς ἀδελφοῖς καλὸς ἔσῃ διάκονος Χριστοῦ Ἰησοῦ,¹ r Here only
(N.T.) in
ˢ ἐντρεφόμενος τοῖς λόγοις τῆς πίστεως καὶ τῆς καλῆς διδασκαλίας this
sense.
ᾗ² ᵗ παρηκολούθηκας.³   7. τοὺς δὲ ᵘ βεβήλους καὶ ᵛ γραώδεις s Here only,
not LXX.
t Luke i. 3,

2 Tim. iii. 10.   u See 1 Tim. i. 9.   v Here only, not LXX

¹ Ἰησ. Χριστ. Dᶜ, 17, 31, 47, many others, am., syrᵖᵉˢʰ.
² ἧς A, 80, one other.
³ So ℵADKLP; παρηκολούθησας CFG.

reference to the Sacrament of the Eucharist, it is probable that thoughts about it
have influenced the language; for the
Eucharist is the supreme example of
all benedictions and consecrations of
material things. And if this be so, the
passage has light thrown on it by the
language of Justin Martyr and Irenæus
about the Prayer of Consecration; *e.g.*,
Justin, *Apol.* i. 66. "As Jesus Christ
our Saviour, by the word of God (διὰ
λόγου θεοῦ) made flesh, had both flesh
and blood for our salvation, so we have
been taught that *the food over which
thanks have been given by the word of
prayer which comes from him* (τὴν δι᾽
εὐχῆς λόγου τοῦ παρ᾽ αὐτοῦ εὐχαριστη-
θεῖσαν τροφήν)—that food from which
our blood and flesh are by assimilation
nourished—is both the flesh and the
blood of that Jesus who was made flesh".
Similarly Irenæus (*Haer.* v. 2, 3), "Both
the mingled cup, and the bread which
has been made, receives upon itself *the
word of God*, and the Eucharist becomes
the body of Christ" (ἐπιδέχεται τὸν
λόγον τοῦ θεοῦ, καὶ γίνεται ἡ εὐχαριστία
σῶμα Χριστοῦ). Perhaps by *the word
of prayer which comes from him* Justin
means a formula authorised by Christ.
It must be added that the Prayer Book
of Serapion, bishop of Thmuis in Egypt,
circ. A.D. 380, contains an *epiclesis* in
which we read, "O God of truth, let thy
holy Word come to sojourn on this bread,
that the bread may become Body of the
Word, and on this cup, that the cup may
become Blood of the Truth" (Bishop
J. Wordsworth's trans.).

A comparison of these passages suggests an association in the thought of
the primitive Church of the Holy Spirit
and the λόγος τοῦ θεοῦ.

Vv. 6-10. The spread of these mischievous notions among the brethren is
most effectively discouraged by a demon-
stration in the person of the minister
himself of the positive teaching of the
Gospel as to practical life. We are assured, and declare our confidence by our

lives, that Christianity differs essentially
from theosophy in that it has respect to
the eternal future, as well as to the passing present.

Ver. 6. ταῦτα: repeated in ver. 11,
refers to all the preceding directions, but
more especially to the warnings against
false asceticism.

ὑποτιθέμενος: (*remind, suggest*) is a
somewhat mild term, as Chrys. points
out; but in some circumstances suggestion is more effectual than direct exhortation.

διάκονος Χρ. Ἰησ. seems emphatic, a
deacon, not of the Church, but of Christ
Jesus, who is the Chief Pastor.

ἐντρεφόμενος: The present tense is
significant, "meaning to imply constancy
in application to these things" (Chrys.),
"ever training thyself" (Alf.). "The
present . . . marks a continuous and
permanent nutrition" (Ell.). The process begun from his earliest years, 2
Tim. i. 5, iii. 15, was still maintained.

ἡ πίστις and ἡ διδασκαλία denote
respectively the sum total of Christian
belief, conceived as an ideal entity, and
the same as imparted little by little to
the faithful. See note on i. 10.

ᾗ παρηκολούθηκας: There is a similar
use of this verb in 2 Tim. iii. 10, where
see note. Alford attempts to give the
word here the same force as in Luke i. 3,
by rendering *the course of which thou
hast followed*. The A.V., *whereunto
thou hast attained*, expresses also the
sense of achievement which we find in
Luke *l.c.* It seems better, however, to
associate the word with the notion of
discipleship; so R.V., *doctrine which
thou hast followed until now*.

Ver. 7. W. H. place a comma after
παρηκολούθηκος and a full stop after
παραιτοῦ; so R.V. nearly. But as
παραιτοῦ is an imperative, as in reff. in
Pastorals, it is best taken as antithetic
to γύμναζε.

γραώδεις: The μῦθοι, in addition to
their profane nature, as impeaching the

w See 1 Tim. i. 4.
x 1 Tim. v. 11, 2 Tim. ii. 23, Tit. iii. 10, Heb. xii.
y 2 Macc. x. 15, Heb. v. 14, xii.

ʷ μύθους ˣ παραιτοῦ, ʸ γύμναζε δὲ σεαυτὸν πρὸς ᵃ εὐσέβειαν · 8. ἡ
γὰρ ᵃ σωματικὴ ᵇ γυμνασία ᶜ πρὸς ᶜ ὀλίγον ἐστὶν ᵈ ὠφέλιμος · ἡ δὲ
ᶻ εὐσέβεια πρὸς πάντα ᵈ ὠφέλιμός ἐστιν, ᵉ ᶠ ἐπαγγελίαν ᵉ ἔχουσα
ᶠ ζωῆς τῆς νῦν καὶ τῆς μελλούσης. 9. ᵍ πιστὸς ᵍ ὁ ᵍ λόγος ᵍ καὶ
ᵍ πάσης ᵍ ἀποδοχῆς ᵍ ἄξιος. 10. εἰς τοῦτο γὰρ ¹ ʰ κοπιῶμεν καὶ

11, 2 Pet. ii. 14.   z See 1 Tim. ii. 2.   a 4 Macc. i. 32, iii. 1, Luke iii. 22.   b 4 Macc. xi. 20
only.   c Jas. iv. 14.   d 2 Tim. iii. 16, Tit. iii. 8, not LXX.   e Cf. Different use in 2 Cor.
vii. 1, Heb. vii. 6.   f 2 Tim. i. 1.   g See 1 Tim. i. 15.   h Matt. xi. 28, Col. i. 29, Phil.
ii. 16, cf. 1 Tim. v. 17.

¹ Ins. καὶ FgʳGKL.

goodness of the Creator, were absurd, unworthy of a grown man's consideration. See note on chap. i. 4. Hort's view (*Judaistic Christianity*, p. 138) that βέβηλους here merely means "the absence of any divine or sacred character" does not seem reasonable.

παραιτοῦ: *refuse, turn away from*, as n Heb. xii. 25. Alf. renders *excuse thyself from*, as in Luke xiv. 18 (bis), 19. *Decline* would be a better rendering. In addition to the reff. given above, παραιτέομαι occurs in Mark xv. 6, Acts xxv. 11 (a speech of St. Paul's), Heb. xii. 19.

γύμναζε: There is here an intentional paradox. Timothy is to meet the spurious asceticism of the heretics by *exercising himself in the practical piety of the Christian life*. See chap. ii. 2. The paradox is comparable to φιλοτιμεῖσθαι ἡσυχάζειν of 1 Thess. iv. 11. The true Christian asceticism is not essentially σωματική, although the body is the means by which the spiritual nature is affected and influenced. Although it brings the body into subjection (1 Cor. ix. 27), this is a means, not an end in itself.

Ver. 8. σωματικὴ γυμνασία: The parallel cited by Lightfoot (*Philippians*, p. 290) from Seneca (*Ep. Mor.* xv. 2, 5) renders it almost certain that the primary reference is to gymnastic exercises (as Chrys., etc., take it); but there is as certainly in σωματικὴ γυμνασία a connotation of ascetic practices as the outward expression of the theories underlying the fables of ver. 7. παραιτοῦ elsewhere in the Pastorals is followed by reasons why the particular thing or person should be avoided. The teaching is identical with that in Col. ii. 23. St. Paul makes his case all the stronger by conceding that an asceticism which terminates in the body is of some use. The contrast then is not so much between *bodily exercise*, commonly so called, and *piety*, as between *piety* (which includes a

discipline of the body) and an absurd and profane theosophy of which discipline of the body was the chief or only practical expression.

πρὸς ὀλίγον: *to a slight extent;* as contrasted with πρὸς πάντα. πρὸς ὀλίγον means *for a little while* in Jas. iv. 14. This notion is included in the other. The R.V., *for a little* is ambiguous; perhaps intentionally so. In view of the genuine asceticism of St. Paul himself, not to mention other examples, it is unreasonable to think him inconsistent in making this concession.

ἐπαγγελίαν ἔχουσα ζωῆς; If we take ἐπαγγελία to signify *the thing promised* (as in Luke xxiv. 49, Acts i. 4, xiii. 32), rather than *a promise*, we can give an appropriate force to the rest of the sentence. A consistent Christian walk possesses, does not forfeit, that which this life promises; in a very real sense "it makes the best of both worlds". ἔχω will then have its usual meaning; and ζωῆς is the genitive of possession, as in Luke xxiv. 49, Acts i. 4 (ἐπ. τοῦ πατρός). It is not the genitive of apposition, *piety promises life*. That which is given by life to Christians is the best thing that life has to give. Von Soden compares πάντα ὑμῶν, 1 Cor. iii. 21 sq. Bacon's saying "Prosperity is the blessing of the Old Testament; Adversity is the blessing of the New" is only half a truth. If religion does not make us happy in this life, we have needlessly missed our inheritance (see Matt. vi. 33; Mark x. 30). On the other hand, though piety does bring happiness in this life, the exercise of it deliberately with that end in view is impious; as Whately said, "Honesty is the best policy, but the man who is honest for that reason is not honest".

Ver. 9. πιστός—ἄξιος: This is parenthetical and retrospective. The teaching of ver. 8 is the λόγος. So Chrys.

Ver. 10. γὰρ, as in the parallel 2

ⁱ ἀγωνιζόμεθα,¹ ὅτι ^kἠλπίκαμεν² ἐπὶ Θεῷ ζῶντι, ὅς ἐστιν ^lσωτὴρ i 1 Cor. ix.
25, Col. i.
πάντων ἀνθρώπων, μάλιστα πιστῶν. 11. ^mΠαράγγελλε ταῦτα καὶ 29, 1 Tim.
vi. 12, 2
δίδασκε. 12. μηδείς σου τῆς νεότητος καταφρονείτω, ἀλλὰ ⁿτύπος Tim. iv. 7.
k John v. 45,
2 Cor. i.

10, 1 Tim. v. 5, vi. 17.　　l See 1 Tim. i. 1.　　m See 1 Tim. i. 3.　　n 1 Cor. x. 6, Phil. iii. 17,
1 Thess. i. 7, 2 Thess. iii. 9, Tit. ii. 7, 1 Pet. v. 3.

¹ So ℵ*ACFgrGgrK, 17, 31, 47, five others; ὀνειδιζόμεθα ℵcDLP, d, f, g, vg., go.,
syrr., boh., arm.

² ἠλπίσαμεν D*, 17.

Tim. ii. 11, introduces a statement in support of the judgment, πιστὸς ὁ λόγος.

εἰς τοῦτο: *i.e.* with a view to the obtaining the promised blessings of life. The best commentary on this is what St. Paul said in an earlier epistle, "As sorrowful, yet alway rejoicing; as poor, yet making many rich; as having nothing, and yet possessing all things" (2 Cor. vi. 10).

κοπιῶμεν καὶ ἀγωνιζόμεθα express St. Paul's personal experience of what the profession of Christianity involved. It was then an almost universal experience, see Acts xiv. 22; but is not of necessity a concomitant of the exercising of oneself to godliness. The two words are similarly combined Col. i. 29, εἰς ὃ καὶ κοπιῶ ἀγωνιζόμενος. κοπιᾶν is usually used by St. Paul of ministerial labours: his own, 1 Cor. xv. 10, Gal. iv. 11, and those of others, Rom. xvi. 12, 1 Cor. xvi. 16, 1 Thess. v. 12, 1 Tim. v. 17; but this restriction is not necessary, nor would it be suitable here. See reff.

For ὀνειδιζόμεθα (var. lect.) *cf.* Matt. v. 11 = Luke vi. 22; 1 Pet. iv. 14.

ὅτι ἠλπίκαμεν, κ.τ.λ.: This was at once an incentive to exertion, and thus correlative to ἐπαγγελία ζωῆς, and in itself a part of the thing promised, the ἐπαγγελία. A consciousness that we are in an harmonious personal relation with the living God lifts us into a sphere in which labour and striving have no power to distress us.

ἠλπίκαμεν: *we have our hope set on* (R.V.). The same use of the perfect of this verb, "expressing the continuance and permanence of the ἐλπίς" (Ell.), is found in the reff. In addition, ἐλπίζω is also followed by ἐπί with the dat. in Rom. xv. 12 (Isa. xi. 10) and 1 Tim. vi. 17; by ἐπί with the acc. in 1 Tim. v. 5, 1 Pet. i. 13; by εἰς with an acc. in John v. 45, 2 Cor. i. 10, 1 Pet. iii. 5; and by ἐν followed by the dat. in 1 Cor. xv. 19.

Θεῷ ζῶντι: As indicated above, this is said in relation to ἐπαγγελίαν ζωῆς. To know the living God is life eternal (John xvii. 3).

ὅς ἐστιν σωτὴρ πάντων, κ.τ.λ.: *Saviour of all* (τὸν πάντων σωτῆρα) occurs in Wisd. xvi. 7. *Cf. Saviour of the world*, John iv. 42.

The *prima facie* force of μάλιστα certainly is that all men share in some degree in that salvation which the πιστοί enjoy in the highest degree. Compare the force of μάλιστα in Acts xxv. 26, Gal. vi. 10, Phil. iv. 22, 1 Tim. v. 8, 17, 2 Tim. iv. 13; Tit. i. 10.

The statement is more unreservedly universalist in tone than chap. ii. 4 and Tit. ii. 11; and perhaps must be qualified by saying that while God is potentially Saviour of all, He is actually Saviour of the πιστοί. It is an argument *a minori ad majus* (as Bengel says); and the unqualified assertion is suitable. If all men can be saved, surely the πιστοί are saved, in whose number we are included. It is better to qualify the statement thus than, with Chrys. and Bengel, to give to σωτὴρ a material sense of God's relation to all men, as the God of nature; but a spiritual sense of His relation to them that believe, as the God of grace. See notes on ch. i. 1; ii. 4.

Vv. 11-16. Silent example or mild suggestion will not do in every case. There are many occasions when it will be necessary for you to speak out, with the authority given to you at your ordination. At the same time, do not forget that the charismatic gift will die if it be neglected. Give yourself wholly to the cultivation of your character; so will you save yourself and those committed to your charge.

Ver. 11. παράγγελλε: In point of time, *teaching* precedes *commanding*. The tone of command can only be used in relation to fundamentals which have been accepted, but are in danger of being forgotten. Similar directions recur in v. 7 and vi. 3.

Ver. 12. μηδείς—καταφρονείτω ("*Libenter id faciunt senes inanes*," Ben-

o Gal. i. 13, γίνου τῶν πιστῶν ἐν λόγῳ, ἐν °ἀναστροφῇ, ἐν ᵖἀγάπῃ,¹ ἐν ᵖ πίστει,
Eph. iv.
22, Heb. ἐν ᑫἁγνίᾳ. 13. ἕως ἔρχομαι ʳπρόσεχε τῇ ˢἀναγνώσει, τῇ παρα-
xiii. 7,
Jas. iii.13, κλήσει, τῇ διδασκαλίᾳ. 14. μὴ ᵗἀμέλει τοῦ ἐν σοὶ ᵘχαρίσματος, ὃ
1 Pet. (6),
2 Pet. (2).

p See 1 Tim. i. 14.   q 1 Tim. v. 2 only, N.T.   r See 1 Tim. i. 4.   s Acts xiii. 15, 2 Cor. iii. 14.
t Heb. ii. 3.   u Rom. i. 11, xii. 6, 1 Cor. i. 7, vii. 7, xii. 4, 9, 28, 30, 31, 2 Tim. i. 6, 1 Pet. iv. 10.

¹ Add ἐν πνεύματι KLP.   See 2 Cor. vi. 6.

gel). Many, probably, of the Ephesian presbyters were older than Timothy. For **μηδείς** in this position, cf. 1 Cor. iii. 18, x. 24; Eph. v. 6; Col. ii. 18; Tit. ii. 15; Jas. i. 13. **καταφρονέω** connotes that the contempt felt in the mind is displayed in injurious action. (See Moulton and Milligan, *Expositor*, vi., viii. 432). The meaning of this direction is qualified by the following **ἀλλὰ τύπος γίνου, κ.τ.λ.** It means, *Assert the dignity of your office even though men may think you young to hold it. Let no one push you aside as a boy.* Compare the corresponding direction Tit. ii. 15, **μηδείς σου περιφρονείτω**. On the other hand, St. Paul shows Timothy "a more excellent way" than self-assertion for the keeping up of his dignity : Give no one any ground by any fault of character for despising thy youth.

σου depends on **τῆς νεότητος**. Field supports this by an exact parallel from Diodorus Siculus. The two genitives do not, in strict grammar, depend on **καταφρον.**, *despise thee for thy youth*.

τῆς νεότητος : St. Paul had met Timothy on the second missionary journey, dated by Harnack in A.D. 47, and by Lightfoot in A.D. 51. About the year 57, St. Paul says of Timothy, "Let no man despise him" (1 Cor. xvi. 11). 1 Tim. may be dated not more than a year before St. Paul's martyrdom, which Harnack fixes in A.D. 64, and Lightfoot in A.D. 67. The question arises, Could Timothy's **νεότης** have lasted all that time, about fifteen or sixteen years? We must remember that we have no information about Timothy's age when he joined St. Paul's company. But if he had been then fifteen or sixteen, or even seventeen, **νεότης** here need cause no difficulty. Lightfoot (*Apostolic Fathers*, Part II. vol. i. p. 448) adduces evidence from Polybius and Galen to show that a man might be called **νέος** up to the age of thirty-four or thirty-five. In any case, the terms "young" and "old" are used relatively to the average age at which men attain to positions in the world.

Forty is reckoned old for a captain in the army, young for a bishop, very young for a Prime Minister. In an instructive parallel passage, Ignatius commends the Magnesians (§ 3) and their presbyters for not presuming upon the youth of their bishop. For Timothy's comparative youth, cf. 2 Tim. ii. 22, **τὰς δὲ νεωτερικὰς ἐπιθυμίας φεῦγε**.

τύπος γίνου : For the sentiment, compare reff. and 1 Cor. iv. 16, Phil. iv. 9.

τύπος is followed by the genitive of the person for whose edification the **τύπος** exists in 1 Cor. x. 6, 1 Pet. v. 3.

In the following enumeration, **λόγος** is coupled with **ἀναστροφή** as *words* with *deeds* (Rom. xv. 18; Col. iii. 17). These refer to Timothy's public life; while *love*, *faith* and *purity* refer to his private life, in reference to which they are found in conjunction in ii. 15.

Ver. 13. **ἕως ἔρχομαι** : For **ἕως** with present indic. instead of fut. see Winer-Moulton, *Grammar*, p. 370. Cf. Luke xix. 13, John xxi. 22, 23.

ἀνάγνωσις, παράκλησις, διδασκαλία are the three elements in the ministry of the word: (*a*) *reading aloud* of Scripture (Luke iv. 16; Acts xiii. 15; 2 Cor. iii. 14, see Moulton and Milligan, *Expositor*, vii., v. 262); (*b*) *exhortation* based on the reading, and appealing to the moral sense (2 Tim. iv. 2; Justin Martyr, *Apol.* i. 67); (*c*) *teaching*, appealing to the intellect, see note on chap. i. 10. Exhortation and teaching are similarly joined in Rom. xii. 7, 8, and 1 Tim. vi. 2.

Ver. 14. **μὴ ἀμέλει** : J. H. Moulton (*Grammar*, vol. i. p. 122 *sqq.*), distinguishes (*a*) **μή** with the pres. imperat, "Do not go on doing so and so," *e.g.*, 1 Tim. v. 22, 23, from (*b*) **μή** with the aor. subjunctive, "Do not begin to do it" (1 Tim. v. 1; 2 Tim. i. 8). In this case, **μὴ ἀμέλει** is equivalent to **πάντοτε μελέτα**. Timothy's **χάρισμα** lay in his commission to rule and in his powers as a preacher. The **χάρισμα** was given by God; in this particular case the formal and solemn assumption of its use was accompanied by the indication of prophecy addressed to the ear, and by the

ἐδόθη σοι διὰ προφητείας μετὰ ᵛἐπιθέσεως ᵛτῶν ᵛχειρῶν τοῦ
ᵂπρεσβυτερίου. 15. ταῦτα ˣμελέτα, ἐν τούτοις ἴσθι, ἵνα σου ἡ
ʸπροκοπὴ ᶻφανερὰ ᶻῇ¹ πᾶσιν. 16. ᵃἔπεχε σεαυτῷ καὶ τῇ διδασ-
καλίᾳ· ᵇἐπίμενε αὐτοῖς· τοῦτο γὰρ ποιῶν καὶ σεαυτὸν σώσεις καὶ
τοὺς ἀκούοντάς σου.

V. 1. Πρεσβυτέρῳ μὴ ᵃἐπιπλήξῃς, ἀλλὰ παρακάλει ὡς πατέρα,

v Acts viii.
18, 2 Tim.
i. 6. Heb.
vi. 2.
w Here only
in this
sense.
x Acts iv. 25
(Ps. ii. 1).
y Phil. i. 12,
25.
z Rom. i. 19,
Gal. v. 19,

1 John iii. 10.   a Luke xiv. 7, Acts iii. 5, xix. 22.   b Acts xiii. 43 (T.R.), Rom. vi. 1, xi. 22, 23,
Col. i. 23.   a Here only, not LXX.

¹ Ins. ἐν DᶜKLP.

laying on of hands addressed to the eye. See Acts xiii. 1-3.

Winer-Moulton notes, p. 471, that the *instrument*, as such, is never expressed by μετά in good prose. Here, *with*, amid *imposition of hands* (conjointly with the act of imposition). μετά is here equivalent to διά in the sense given above, *i.e.*, of accompanying circumstances.

2 Tim. i. 6 is usually reconciled with this passage by saying that the body of presbyters was associated with St. Paul in the laying on of hands. But there is no reason to suppose that the same transaction is referred to in both places. Here the charismata refer to preaching and teaching; but in 2 Tim., to the administrative duties committed to Timothy, as it is reasonable to suppose, by St. Paul alone, when he appointed him his representative. Note that διά is used of St. Paul's imposition of hands (2 Tim. i. 6), μετά of that of the presbyters, here. This suggests that it was the imposition of hands by St. Paul that was the instrument used by God in the communication of the charisma to Timothy.

πρεσβυτέριον: elsewhere in N.T. (Luke xxii. 66; Acts xxii. 5) means the Jewish Sanhedrin; but Ignatius uses the term, as here, to indicate the presbyters in a local Church (*Trall.* 7, 13; *Philadelph.* 7, etc.).

Ver. 15. ταῦτα: *i.e.*, reading, exhortation, teaching. μελέτα: *practise, exercise thyself in*, rather than *meditari*. So R.V., *Be diligent in*. (Bengel compares γύμναζε ver. 7.) *Cf.* Psal. i. 2, ἐν τῷ νόμῳ αὐτοῦ μελετήσει, "In his law will he exercise himself," P.B.V., quoted by Prof. Scholefield.

ἐν τούτοις ἴσθι: To the parallels cited by Wettstein, ἐν τούτοις ὁ Καῖσαρ . . . ἦν (Plut. *Pomp.* p. 656 *b*), "Omnis in hoc sum" (Horace *Epistles*, i. 1, 11) and Alford: "Totus in illis" (Horace, *Sat.* i. 9, 2), we may add ἐν φόβῳ Κυρίου ἴσθι,

Prov. xxiii. 17. Timothy's progress manifest to all would secure his youth from being despised: *cf.* Matt. v. 16.

φανερὰ ῇ: This expression is quite Pauline; see reff.; but St. Paul more frequently has φανερὸς γενέσθαι, 1 Cor. iii. 13, xi. 19, xiv. 25, Phil. i. 13.

Ver. 16. ἔπεχε σεαυτῷ, κ.τ.λ.: The teacher must needs prepare himself before he prepares his lesson. A similar thought is conveyed by the order of the words in Gen. iv. 4, "The Lord had respect unto Abel and to his offering". ἐπέχειν (see reff. and Moulton and Milligan, *Expositor*, vii., vii. 377) has a quite different signification in Phil. ii. 16. *Cf.* Acts xx. 28, προσέχετε ἑαυτοῖς.

τῇ διδασκαλίᾳ: *Thy teaching* (R.V.). *The doctrine* (A.V.) can take care of itself. See note on i. 10. αὐτοῖς is neuter, referring to the same things as ταῦτα; not masc., "Remain with the Ephesians," as Grotius supposed, a view tolerated by Bengel.

σεαυτὸν σώσεις: *cf.* Ezek. xxxiii. 9.

CHAPTER V.—Vv. 1-16. The wise Church ruler must understand how to deal with his people individually. Each age and condition needs separate treatment: old men, young men; old women, young women. Widows in particular need discriminating care; since some of them may have to be supported by the Church; and we must not let the Church be imposed on, nor give occasion for scandal. Accordingly Church widows must be at least sixty years old, and be of good character.

Ver. 1. πρεσβυτέρῳ is best taken as a term of age, *seniorem* (Vulg.). This view is supported by the ὡς πατέρα, πρεσβυτέρας, νεωτέρας. The term νεωτέρους might possibly refer to a subordinate Church officer. In Acts v. 6 it is susceptible of that meaning; but in the subsequent narrative (Acts v. 10) οἱ νεώτεροι who are in attendance on the Apostles are merely νεανίσκοι.

b Here only, νεωτέρους ὡς ἀδελφούς, 2. ᵇ πρεσβυτέρας ὡς μητέρας, νεωτέρας ὡς
N.T.
c See 1 Tim. ἀδελφὰς ἐν πάσῃ ᶜ ἁγνείᾳ. 3. Χήρας τίμα τὰς ᵈ ὄντως χήρας. 4.
iv. 12.
ᵈ Mark xi. εἰ δέ τις χήρα τέκνα ἢ ᵉ ἔκγονα ἔχει, μανθανέτωσαν ¹ πρῶτον τὸν
32, 1 Tim.
v. 5, 16, ἴδιον οἶκον ᶠ εὐσεβεῖν καὶ ᵍ ἀμοιβὰς ἀποδιδόναι τοῖς ʰ προγόνοις·
vi. 19.
e Here only, τοῦτο γὰρ ἐστιν ² ⁱ ἀπόδεκτον ᵏ ἐνώπιον ᵏ τοῦ ᵏ Θεοῦ. 5. ἡ δὲ ¹ ὄντως
N.T.
f 4 Macc.
(5), Sus. 64, Acts xvii. 23.   g Here only, N.T., not LXX.   h 2 Tim. i. 3 only, N.T.   i 1 Tim.
ii. 3.   k See 1 Tim. ii. 3.   l See ver. 3.

¹ μανθανέτω two cursives, d, f, m82, vg. (except am* = discant).
² Ins. καλὸν καὶ 37, many others, boh., go., arm.   See chap. ii. 3.

ἐπιπλήξῃς : *Treat harshly.* The more
usual ἐπιτιμᾶν occurs 2 Tim. iv. 2.
παρακάλει ὡς πατέρα : Respect for age
must temper the expression of reproof of
an old man's misdemeanours. νεωτέρους
and the following accusatives in ver. 2
are governed by some such verb as *treat,
behave towards, deal with,* implied in
ἐπιπλήξῃς and παρακάλει.

Ver. 2. ἐν πάσῃ ἁγνίᾳ : *with the
strictest regard to purity,* or perhaps
propriety. Christians, Athenagoras tells
us (*Legat.* 32), considered other Christians, according to their age, as sons and
daughters; brothers and sisters; fathers
and mothers. Ellicott quotes Jerome's
maxim, "Omnes puellas et virgines
Christi aut aequaliter ignora aut aequaliter dilige" (Epist. 52, 5, p. 259). Compare *de Imitatione Christi,* i. 8, "Be not
a friend to any one woman, but recommend all good women in general to God".

Ver. 3. τίμα : It is difficult to fix precisely the force of τιμάω in this connexion. On the one hand, the passage
(vv. 3-8) is a part of the general directions as to Timothy's personal relations
to his flock. *Respect, honour,* would,
then, render the word adequately. On
the other hand, vv. 4 and 8 show that
the question of widows' maintenance,
as a problem of Church finance, was
in the apostle's mind; and he goes on,
in ver. 9, to lay down regulations for
the admission of widows to the number
of those who were entered on the Church
register for support. Perhaps *respect*
was first in the writer's mind, while the
term used, τίμα, easily lent itself to the
expression of the notion of *support,* which
immediately suggested itself. Similarly
Chrys. (τῆς τῶν ἀναγκαίων τροφῆς),
comparing ver. 17, where τιμή has the
sense of *pay, cf.* Ecclus. xxxviii. 1, Matt.
xv. 4-6, Acts xxviii. 10. *Honora beneficiis*
is Bengel's comment.

τὰς ὄντως : Those who really deserve
the name of widows are (1) those who
have no younger relatives on whom they

have a claim for support, (2) those who
conform to certain moral and spiritual
requirements detailed below.

Ver. 4. ἔκγονα : *offspring* ought to be
the best rendering of this. It has a
wider connotation than *children* and
narrower than *descendants.*

μανθανέτωσαν : It ought not to be
necessary to say that the subject of this
verb is τέκνα ἢ ἔκγονα, only that Chrys.
Theod. Vulg. and d agree in referring it
to the class χῆραι. ('Requite them in
their descendants, repay the debt through
the children," Chrys.; "*Discat primum
domum suam regere.*" See critical note.)
Similarly Augustine says of his mother
Monica, "Fuerat enim unius viri uxor,
mutuam vicem parentibus reddiderat,
domum suam pie tractaverat" (*Confes-
siones,* ix. 9). This can only be regarded
as a curiosity in exegesis.

πρῶτον : The first duty of children is
filial piety. οἶκον, which is usually correlative to parents rather than children,
is used here "to mark the duty as an act
of family feeling and family honour"
(De Wette, quoted by Ell.).

εὐσεβεῖν (*domum pie tractare,* m82)
with a direct accusative is also found in
reff. Ellicott supplies an appropriate
illustration from Philo, *de Decalogo,* § 23,
"where storks are similarly said εὐσεβεῖν
and γηροτροφεῖν".

προγόνοις : When the term occurs
again, 2 Tim. i. 3, it has its usual meaning *forefather.* It is usually applied to
forbears that are dead. Here it means
parents, grandparents, or great-grand-
parents that are living; and this use of
it was probably suggested by ἔκγονα, a
term of equally vague reference. Plato,
Laws, xi. p. 932, is quoted for a similar
application of the word to the living.

τοῦτο γάρ, κ.τ.λ. : Besides being enjoined in the O.T., our Lord taught the
same duty, Mark vii. 16-13 = Matt. xv.
4-6. See also Eph. vi. 1, 2.

Ver. 5. ἤλπικεν ἐπί : *hath her hope set
on.* See on iv. 10, the analogy of

χήρα καὶ ^m μεμονωμένη ⁿ ἤλπικεν ἐπὶ ¹ Θεὸν ² καὶ ^o προσμένει ταῖς
δεήσεσιν καὶ ταῖς προσευχαῖς νυκτὸς καὶ ἡμέρας· 6. ἡ δὲ ^p σπατα-
λῶσα ζῶσα τέθνηκεν. 7. καὶ ταῦτα ^q παράγγελλε, ἵνα ^r ἀνεπίλημπτοι
ὦσιν. 8. εἰ δέ τις ^s τῶν ^s ἰδίων καὶ μάλιστα ³ ^t οἰκείων οὐ ^u προνοεῖ,⁴ τὴν ^v πίστιν ^{v w} ἤρνηται καὶ ἔστιν ἀπίστου χείρων. 9. Χήρα
^x καταλεγέσθω μὴ ἔλαττον ἐτῶν ἐξήκοντα γεγονυῖα, ἑνὸς ἀνδρὸς

m Here only, not LXX.
n See 1 Tim. iv. 10.
o Wisd. iii.
p Ecclus. xxi. 15, Ezek. xvi. 49, Jas. v. 5.

q See 1 Tim. 1 3.   r See 1 Tim. iii. 2.   s John i. 11, xiii. 1, Acts iv. 23.   t Gal. vi. 10, Eph.
ii. 19.   u Rom. xii. 17, 2 Cor. viii. 21.   v Rev. ii. 13.   w 2 Tim. iii. 5, Tit. ii. 12, cf. also
2 Tim. ii. 12, 13, Tit. i. 16.   x Here only, N.T.

¹ Ins. τὸν אcADKL ; om. τὸν א*CFGP.

² So אcACKLP, d, e, f, m25, 82, 110, vg. ; Κύριον א*Dgr*.

³ Ins. τῶν CDbcKLP.

⁴ So אcACDcLP ; προνοεῖται א*D*FGK, one cursive.

which favours the omission of the article here.

προσμένει : She is like Anna, νηστεί-αις καὶ δεήσεσιν λατρεύουσα νύκτα καὶ ἡμέραν (Luke ii. 37). προσκαρτερεῖν is more usual in this connexion, e.g., Rom. xii. 12, Col. iv. 2.

Ell. notes that Paul always has the order νυκτ. καὶ ἡμ. as here. Luke has also this order, with the acc., but ἡμ. καὶ νυκτ. with the gen. In Rev. the order is ἡμ. καὶ νυκτός.

Ver. 6. σπαταλῶσα : The modern term fast, in which the notion of prodigality and wastefulness is more prominent than that of sensual indulgence, exactly expresses the significance of this word. The R.V., she that giveth herself to pleasure, is stronger than the A.V. A somewhat darker force is given to it here by the associated verb in ver. 11, καταστρηνιά-σωσιν. The Vulg. is felicitous, Quae in deliciis est, vivens mortua est. The expression is more terse than in Rev. iii. 1, "Thou hast a name that thou livest and thou art dead". Cf. Rom. vii. 10, 24, Eph. iv. 18. Wetstein quotes in illustration from Stobaeus (238), as descriptive of a poor man's life of anxiety, πένης ἀποθανὼν φροντίδων ἀπηλλάγη, ζῶν γὰρ τέθνηκε.

Ver. 7. ταῦτα is best referred to ver. 4, with its implied injunctions to the younger generation to support their widows.

ἀνεπίλημπτοι : i.e., all Christians whom it concerns, not widows only.

Ver. 8. The Christian faith includes the law of love. The moral teaching of Christianity recognises the divine origin of all natural and innocent human affections. The unbeliever, i.e., the born heathen, possesses natural family affec-

tion ; and though these feelings may be stunted by savagery, the heathen are not likely to be sophisticated by human perversions of religion, such as those denounced by Jesus in Mark vii. Ell. says. "It is worthy of notice that the Essenes were not permitted to give relief to their relatives without leave from their ἐπί-τροποι, though they might freely do so to others in need ; see Joseph. Bell. Jud. ii. 8, 6."

The Christian who falls below the best heathen standard of family affection is the more blameworthy, since he has, what the heathen has not, the supreme example of love in Jesus Christ. We may add that Jesus Himself gave an example of providing for one's own, when He provided a home for His mother with the beloved disciple.

οἱ ἴδιοι are near relatives : οἱ οἰκεῖοι, members of one's household. One of the most subtle temptations of the Devil is his suggestion that we can best comply with the demands of duty in some place far away from our home. Jesus always says, Do the next thing ; "Begin from Jerusalem", The path of duty begins from within our own house, and we must walk it on our own feet.

οἰκείων : The omission of the article in the true text before οἰκείων precludes the possibility of taking the word here in the allegorical sense in which it is used in Gal. and Eph. : "the household of the faith" ; "the household of God".

προνοεῖ : This verb is only found elsewhere in N.T. in the phrase προνοεῖσθαι καλά, Rom. xii. 17, 2 Cor. viii. 21 (from Prov. iii. 4, προνοοῦ καλὰ ἐνώπιον Κυρίου καὶ ἀνθρώπων).

Ver. 9. καταλεγέσθω : St. Paul passes naturally from remarks about the duty of

y Acts vi. 3. γυνή, 10. ᵞ ἐν ˣ ἔργοις ˣ καλοῖς ᵞ μαρτυρουμένη, εἰ ᵃ ἐτεκνοτρόφησεν,
x. 22, xxii.
12, Heb. εἰ ᵇ ἐξενοδόχησεν, εἰ ἁγίων πόδας ἔνιψεν, εἰ ᵉ θλιβομένοις ᵈ ἐπήρκεσεν,
xi. 2, 39.
z See 1 Tim.

iii. 1.   a Here only, not LXX.   b Here only, not LXX.   c 2 Cor. i. 6, iv. 8, vii. 5, 1 Thess.
iii. 4, 2 Thess. i. 6, 7, Heb. xi. 37.   d 1 Macc. (2), ver. 16 only.

Church members to their widowed relatives to specific rules about the admission of widows to the roll of Church
widows (see Acts vi. 1). The χήρα of
this ver. is ἡ ὄντως χήρα of vv. 3 and 5,
who was to receive consideration and
official recognition. These widows had
no doubt a ministry to fulfil—a ministry
of love, prayer, intercession, and giving
of thanks (Polycarp, 4) ; but it is difficult
to suppose that St. Paul, or any other
practically minded administrator, would
contemplate a presbyteral order of widows, the members of which would enter
on their duties at the age of 60, an age
relatively more advanced in the East
and in the first century than in the West
and in our own time. We may add that
the general topic of widows' maintenance
is resumed and concluded in ver. 16.

In the references to widows in the
earliest Christian literature outside the
N.T. (with the exception of Ignatius
Smyrn. 13) they are mentioned as objects
of charity along with orphans, etc. (Ignatius, Smyrn. 6, Polyc. 4; Polycarp,
4; Hermas, Vis. ii. 4, Mand. viii., Sim.
i. v. 3, ix. 26, 27; Justin, Apol. i. 67).
None of these places hints at an order of
widows. The subject cannot be further
discussed here; but the evidence seems
to point to the conclusion that the later
institution of widows as an order with
official duties was suggested by this passage. The history of Christianity affords
other examples of supposed revivals of
apostolic institutions.

Ell., who follows Grotius in seeing
in this verse regulations respecting an
ecclesiastical or presbyteral widow, objects to the view taken above that it is
"highly improbable that when criteria
had been given, ver. 4 sq., fresh should
be added, and those of so very exclusive
a nature: would the Church thus limit
her alms ? "

But ver. 4 sq. does not give the criteria,
or qualifications of an official widow;
but only describes the dominant characteristic of the life of the "widow indeed,"
viz., devotion; and again, the Church of
every age, the apostolic not less than
any other, has financial problems to deal
with. Charity may be indiscriminating,
but there are only a limited number of

widows for whose whole support the
Church can make itself responsible ; and
this is why the limit of age is here so
high. At a much younger age than 60
a woman would cease to have any temptation to marry again.

Lightfoot has important notes on the
subject in his commentary on Ignatius,
Smyrn. §§ 6, 13 (Apost. Fathers, part ii.
vol. ii. pp. 304, 322). See also, on the
deaconess widow, Harnack, Mission and
Expansion of Christianity, trans. vol. i.
p. 122. The opinion of Schleiermacher
that deaconesses are referred to here is
refuted (1) by the provision of age, and
(2) by the fact that they have been dealt
with before, iii. 11.

According to Bengel, the gen. ἐτῶν
depends on χήρα, μὴ ἔλαττον being an
adverb, "of 60 years, not less ".

γεγονυῖα: It is best to connect this
with the preceding words, as in Luke ii.
42, καὶ ὅτε ἐγένετο ἐτῶν δώδεκα. In
favour of this connexion is the consideration that in the parallel, iii. 2, μιᾶς
γυναικὸς ἄνδρα stands alone, and that if
γεγονυῖα were to be joined with what
follows, it would most naturally follow
γυνή. As a matter of fact, this trans-
position is found in P.; and this connexion is suggested in D, two cursives,
d, f, g, m¹⁴¹, Vulg. (quae fuerit (g fuerat)
unius viri uxor) go, boh, syrr, Theodore
Mops., Theodoret, and Origen.

ἑνὸς ἀνδρὸς γυνή : The Church widows
must conform to the same ideal of the
married life as the episcopi. See Tert.
ad uxorem, i. 7, "Quantum fidei de-
trahant, quantum obstrepant sanctitati
nuptiae secundae, disciplina ecclesiae et
praescriptio apostoli declarat, cum diga-
mos non sinit praesidere, cum viduam
allegi in ordinem [al. ordinationem], nisi
univiram, non concedit."

Ver. 10. ἐν ἔργοις καλοῖς μαρτυρουμένη:
ἐν with μαρτυρεῖσθαι means in respect
of. See reff. and Moulton and Milligan,
Expositor, vii., vii., 562.

It is characteristic of the sanity of
apostolic Christianity that as typical examples of "good works," St. Paul instances the discharge of commonplace
duties, "the daily round, the common
task ". For ἔργα καλά see on chap. iii. 1.

εἰ ἐτεκνοτρόφησεν: As has been just

εἰ παντὶ ° ἔργῳ ° ἀγαθῷ ᶠ ἐπηκολούθησεν. 11. νεωτέρας δὲ χήρας e See 1 Tim-
ᵍ παραιτοῦ· ὅταν γὰρ ʰ καταστρηνιάσωσιν ¹ τοῦ Χριστοῦ, γαμεῖν f Josh. xiv.
14.
iv. 7.   h Here only, not LXX.
ii. 10.
g See 1 Tim.

¹ So אCDKL; καταστρηνιάσουσιν AFGP, 31.

explained, the εἰ is not so much dependent on καταλεγέσθω as explanatory of
ἐν ἔργοις καλ. μαρτ. The rendering of
the Vulg., d, f, g, Amb., *filios educavit*,
is better than that of m¹⁴¹, *nutrivit*, or
Ambrst. *enutrivit*. It is not child-birth
so much as the "Christianly and virtu-
ously bringing up of children," her own
or those entrusted to her charge, that St.
Paul has in his mind. Tert. *de Virg. vel.*
9, alluding to this passage, says, "Non
tantum univirae, id est nuptae, aliquando
eliguntur, sed et matres et quidem edu-
catrices filiorum, scilicet ut experimentis
omnium affectuum structae facile norint
ceteras et consilio et solatio iuvare, et ut
nihilominus ea decucurrerint, per quae
femina probari potest". The later Church
widows, among other duties, had the
care of the Church orphans (*cf*, Hermas
Mand. viii.; Lucian, *de morte Peregrini*,
12).

ἐξενοδόχησεν: Hospitality is a virtue
especially demanded in a condition of
society in which there is much going to
and fro, and no satisfactory hotel accommodation. The episcopus must be
φιλόξενος (iii. 2, where see note).

εἰ ἁγίων πόδας ἔνιψεν: If the strangers
were also "saints," members of the
Christian Society, they would naturally
receive special attention. The mistress
of the house would act as servant of the
servants of God (*cf*. Gen. xviii. 6; 1 Sam.
xxv. 41). Unless we assume the unhistorical character of St. John's Gospel,
it is natural to suppose that the story
told in John xiii. 5-14, and the Master's
command to do as He had done, was
known to St. Paul and Timothy. The
absence of an article before πόδας "is
due to assimilation to ἁγίων" (Blass,
Grammar, p. 151, note 2).

εἰ παντὶ—ἐπηκολούθησεν cuts short
any further enumeration of details, *if
in short, she has devoted herself to good
works of every kind*. There is an exact
parallel to this use of ἐπακολουθέω in Josh.
xiv. 14, διὰ τὸ αὐτὸν [Caleb] ἐπακολου-
θῆσαι τῷ προστάγματι Κυρίου θεοῦ Ἰσραήλ. The word also means to "check"
or "verify" an account. In Mark xvi. 20,
"the signs 'endorse' the word" (Moulton and Milligan, *Expositor*, vii., vii. 376).

So here it may connote sympathy with,
and interest in, good works, without
actual personal labour in them.

Ver. 11. There are two main factors
in the interpretation of this verse: (1) a
general Church regulation—not laid
down by St. Paul but found in existence
by him—that a widow in receipt of
relief should be ἑνὸς ἀνδρὸς γυνή; and
(2) his determination to make provision
that no scandal should arise from broken
vows. The notion was that there was
a marriage tie between Christ and the
Church widow. This would be *her first
faith, her earliest and still valid plighted
troth*. *Cf.* Rev. ii. 4, τὴν ἀγάπην σου
τὴν πρώτην ἀφῆκες (of the Church at
Ephesus).

νεωτέρας may be rendered positively,
young.

παραιτοῦ: *reject*. This verb is used
of "profane and old wives' fables" (iv.
7), of "foolish and ignorant questionings" (2 Tim. ii. 23), of "a man that is
heretical" (Tit. iii. 10); so that, at first
sight, it seems a harsh term to use in
reference to "young widows". But the
harshness is explained when we remember that St. Paul is speaking, not of the
widows in themselves, but as applicants
for admission to the roll of specially
privileged Church widows. In a Church
still immature as to its organisation and
morale the authorities would be only
courting disaster were they to assume
the control of young widows, a class
whose condition gave them independence in the heathen society around them.

καταστρηνιάσωσιν: *Cum enim
luxuriatae fuerint [in deliciis egerint,
m ¹¹⁰] in Christo* (Vulg.).

The word denotes the particular character of their restiveness. It was understood with this sexual reference in Pseud.
Ignat. *ad Antioch.* 11, αἱ χῆραι μὴ
σπαταλάτωσαν, ἵνα μὴ καταστρηνιάσωσι
τοῦ λόγου. στρῆνος (over-strength),
wantonness or *luxury* occurs Rev. xviii.
3; στρηνιάω, Rev. xviii. 7, 9, to *wax
wanton, live wantonly*, or *luxuriously*.
The preposition κατά, with the genitive,
has the sense *against*, of opposition, as
in καταβραβεύω, καταγελάω, καταδικάζω,
κατακαυχάομαι, κατακρίνω, etc.

Mark vii. θέλουσιν, 12. ἔχουσαι κρίμα ὅτι τὴν πρώτην πίστιν [1] ἠθέτησαν.
9, Luke
vii. 30. 13. [k] ἄμα [k] δὲ [k] καὶ [l] ἀργαὶ μανθάνουσιν, [m] περιερχόμεναι τὰς οἰκίας,
Gal. ii. 21,
iii. 15, οὐ μόνον δὲ ἀργαὶ ἀλλὰ καὶ [n] φλύαροι καὶ [o] περίεργοι, λαλοῦσαι [p] τὰ
Heb. x. 28.
k Acts xxiv.
26, Col. iv. 3, Philem. 22.   l Matt. xii. 36, xx. 3, 6, Tit. i. 12, Jas. ii. 20, 2 Pet. i. 8.   m Acts
xix. 13, Heb. xi. 37.   n Here only, N.T.; see note.   o Not LXX; see note.   p Tit. i. 11.

For ὅταν with the subjunctive or in-dicative, see Winer Moulton, *Grammar*, p. 388. The subjunctive, as in the text, is the normally correct way of expressing a contemplated contingency.

τοῦ Χριστοῦ: Here only in the Pas-torals.

γαμεῖν θέλουσι: θέλειν has here an emphatic sense, as in John vii. 17; and its association here supports the view that it "designates the will which pro-ceeds from inclination," as contrasted with βούλομαι, "the will which follows deliberation" (Thayer's Grimm, *s.v.*). γαμεῖν is used of the woman also, ver. 14, Mark x. 12; 1 Cor. vii. 28, 34.

Ver. 12. ἔχουσαι κρίμα: *deserving censure*. There is no special force in ἔχουσαι, as Ell. explains, "bearing about with them a judgment, *viz*., that they broke their first faith". This seems forced and unnatural. ἔχειν κρίμα is correlative to λαμβάνεσθαι κρίμα (Mark xii. 40; Luke xx. 47; Rom. xiii. 2; Jas. iii. 1). They *have condemnation be-cause, etc., habentes damnationem quia* (Vulg. m). κρίμα of course by itself means *judgment*; but where the context, as here, implies that the judgment is a sentence of guiltiness, it is reasonable so to translate it.

τὴν πρώτην πίστιν: This has been already explained. On the use of πρῶτος for πρότερος see Blass, *Gram.* p. 34.

ἠθέτησαν: *annulled, irritam fecerunt* (Vulg. m).

Ver. 13. ἄμα δὲ καί is Pauline. See reff.

It is best to assume an omission of εἶναι, not necessarily through corruption of the text, as Blass supposes (*Gram.* p. 247). On the example cited by Winer-Moulton, *Gram.* p. 437 from Plato, *Euthyd.* p. 276 *b*, οἱ ἀμαθεῖς ἄρα σοφοὶ μανθάνουσιν, and Dio. Chrys. lv. 558, Field notes, "Although the reading in Plato may be doubtful, there is no doubt of the agreement of St. Paul's construc-tion with *later* usage". Field adds two from St. Chrysostom T. vii. p. 699 *a* : τί οὖν; ἂν παλαιστὴς μανθάνῃς; T. ix. p. 259 *b* : εἰ ἰατρὸς μέλλοις μανθάνειν. He notes that the correlative phraseology, διδάξαι (or διδάξασθαι) τινὰ τεκτόνα,

χαλκέα, ἱππέα, ῥήτορα, is to be found in the best writers.

It is impossible to connect μανθ. περιερχ. as Vulg., *discunt circuire domos*; for, as Alf. says, "μανθάνω with a parti-ciple always means *to be aware of, take notice of*, the act implied in the verb". Here, *e.g.*, the meaning would be "they learn that they are going about," which is absurd. Bengel's view, that μανθάνουσι is to be taken absolutely, is equally im-possible: "being idle, they are learners," the nature of the things they learn to be inferred from the way they spend their time. Von Soden connects μανθ. with τὰ μὴ δέοντα; suggesting that they learnt in the houses referred to in 2 Tim. iii. 6 what was taught there (ἃ μὴ δεῖ, Tit. i. 11).

περιερχόμεναι τὰς οἰκίας: These last words may possibly refer to the house to house visitation, *going about* (R.V.), which might be part of the necessary duty of the Church widows; but which would be a source of temptation to young women, and would degenerate into *wandering* (A.V.).

οὐ μόνον δὲ . . . ἀλλὰ καί is a Pauline use of constant occurrence. See Rom. v. 3, 11, viii. 23, ix. 10; 2 Cor. vii. 7, viii. 19; Phil. ii. 27 [οὐ . . . δὲ μόνον]; 2 Tim. iv. 8. Also in Acts xix. 27, 3 Macc. iii. 23.

ἀργαί, φλύαροι, περίεργοι: A series of natural causes and consequences. The social intercourse of idle people is naturally characterised by silly chatter which does not merely affect the under-standing of those who indulge in it, but leads them on tô mischievous interfer-ence in other people's affairs.

φλύαροι: φλυαρεῖν is found in 3 John 10, *prating*. φλύαρος is an epithet of φιλοσοφία in 4 Macc. v. 10; and in Prov. xxiii. 29 (א[e]) φλυαρίαι ὁμιλίαι ἐνφιλόνικοι are among the consequences of excessive wine-drinking.

περίεργοι: See 2 Thess. iii. 11, μηδὲν ἐργαζομένους ἀλλὰ περιεργαζομένους. In Acts xix. 19 τὰ περίεργα, *curious arts*, means the arts of those who are curious about, and pry into, matters concealed from human knowledge, *impertinent* to man's lawful needs.

ᴾμὴ ᴾδέοντα. 14. ꟼβούλομαι οὖν νεωτέρας γαμεῖν, ʳτεκνογονεῖν, ꟼSee 1 Tim.
ii. 8.
ˢοἰκοδεσποτεῖν, μηδεμίαν ᵗᵘἀφορμὴν ᵘ διδόναι τῷ ᵛἀντικειμένῳ ᵂλοι- ʳHere only,
not LXX,
δορίας ˣχάριν· 15. ἤδη γάρ τινες ʸἐξετράπησαν ¹ὀπίσω τοῦ Σατανᾶ· cf. 1 Tim:
ii. 15.
16. εἴ τις ² πιστὴ ἔχει χήρας ᶻἐπαρκείτω ³ αὐταῖς, καὶ μὴ ᵃβαρείσθω sHere only,
not LXX.
ἡ ἐκκλησία, ἵνα ταῖς ᵇὄντως χήραις ἐπαρκέσῃ. tLuke xi.
54, Rom.
vii. 8, 11,

2 Cor. xi. 12, Gal. v. 13.   u 2 Cor. v. 12.   v 2 Thess. ii. 4, cf. Luke xiii. 17, xxi. 15, 1 Cor. xvi.
9, Phil. i. 28.   w 1 Pet. iii. 9 only, N.T.   x Luke vii. 47, Gal. iii. 19, Eph. iii. 1, 14, Tit. i.
5, 11, 1 John iii. 12, Jude 16.   y See 1 Tim. i. 6.   z See ver. 10.   a See note.   b See ver. 3.

¹ ἐξετράπ. τινες AFgrG, g.
² Ins. πιστὸς ἢ DKL, d, fuld., syrr.
³ So CDKLP; ἐπαρκείσθω ℵA[FG], 17.

λαλοῦσαι τὰ μὴ δέοντα expresses the
positively mischievous activity of the
φλύαροι, as περίεργοι. Compare Tit.
i. 11, διδάσκοντες ἃ μὴ δεῖ. In both
passages μή is expressive of the impro-
priety, in the writer's opinion, of whatever
might conceivably be spoken and taught;
whereas τὰ οὐ δέοντα would express
the notion that certain specific improper
things had, as a matter of fact, been
spoken. See Winer-Moulton, Gram. p.
603.

Ver. 14. βούλομαι οὖν: See note on
1 Tim. ii. 8.

νεωτέρας: The insertion of χήρας before νεωτέρας in about 30 cursives, Chrys.
Theodoret, John Damasc., Jerome, is a
correct gloss (so R.V.). The whole
context deals with widows, not with
women in general, as A.V. and von
Soden.

γαμεῖν: There is nothing really inconsistent between this deliberate injunction that young widows should marry
again, and the counsel in 1 Cor. vii. 8,
that widows should remain unmarried.
The widows here spoken of would come
under the class of those who "have not
continency"; not to mention that the
whole world-position of the Church had
altered considerably since St. Paul had
written 1 Cor.

οἰκοδεσποτεῖν: well rendered in Vulg.,
matres-familias esse. The verb is only
found here in the Greek Bible, but οἰκο-
δεσπότης frequently occurs in the Synoptists. It is the equivalent of οἰκουργούς,
Tit. ii. 5.

τῷ ἀντικειμένῳ: The singular (see ref.)
does not refer to Satan, but is used generically for human adversaries. The
plural is more usual, as in the other reff.
Cf. ὁ ἐξ ἐναντίας, Tit. ii. 8.

λοιδορίας χάριν is connected of course
with ἀφορμήν, not with βούλομαι, as
Mack suggests, "I will . . . on account

of the reproach which might otherwise
come on the Church".

For the sentiment cf. vi. 1, Tit. ii. 5, 8,
1 Peter ii. 12, iii. 16. In all these places
the responsibility of guarding against
scandal is laid on the members of the
Church generally, not specially on the
Church rulers. The construction of
χάριν here is not quite the same as in
Gal. iii. 19, Tit. i. 11, Jude 16. Here it
is an appendage to the sentence, explanatory of ἀφορμὴν διδόναι.

Ver. 15. τινες: See note on i. 3.

ἐξετράπησαν ὀπίσω τοῦ Σ.: This is a
pregnant phrase, meaning They have
turned out of the way [of life and light]
and have followed after Satan". "The
prepositional use of ὀπίσω, which is
foreign to profane writers, takes its origin
from the LXX (Hebr. אַחֲרֵי)" (Blass,
Gram. p. 129). The primary phrase is
ἔρχεσθαι [also ἀκολουθεῖν or πορεύεσθαι]
ὀπίσω τινός. For ὀπίσω in an unfavourable sense cf. Luke xxi. 8, John xii. 19,
Acts v. 37, xx. 30, 2 Peter ii. 10, Jude 7,
Rev. xiii. 3. The phrase, no doubt, refers
to something worse than a second marriage.

Ver. 16. εἴ τις πιστή: This is one of
those difficulties that prove the bona fide
character of the letter. We may explain
it in either of two ways: (1) It not un-
frequently happens that the language in
which we express a general statement is
unconsciously coloured by a particular
instance of which we are thinking at the
moment. St. Paul has some definite
case in his mind, of a Christian woman
who had a widow depending on her, of
whose support she wishes the Church to
relieve her, or (2) the verse may be an
afterthought to avoid the possibility of
the ruling given in vv. 4, 7, 8 being supposed to refer to men only. Von Soden
explains it by the independent position

c See 1 Tim.   17. Οἱ ᶜκαλῶς ᶜπροεστῶτες πρεσβύτεροι διπλῆς τιμῆς ᵈἀξιού-
iii. 4.
d Heb. iii. 3, σθωσαν, μάλιστα οἱ ᵉκοπιῶντες ἐν λόγῳ καὶ διδασκαλίᾳ · 18. ᶠλέγει
x. 29.
e See note
on 1 Tim. iv. 10.   f Rom. ix. 17, x. 11, cf. Mark xv. 28.

of married women indicated in ver. 14
and Tit. ii. 5. The phrase ἔχει χήρας
may be intended to include dependent
widowed relatives, aunts or cousins, who
could not be called προγόνοι.

βαρείσθω. Compare the use of βάρος,
1 Thess. ii. 6, δυνάμενοι ἐν βάρει εἶναι;
of ἐπιβαρέω, 1 Thess. ii. 9, 2 Thess. iii.
8; καταβαρέω, 2 Cor. xii. 16; ἀβαρής,
2 Cor. xi. 9.

This verse proves that the κατάλογος
of widows here in view was primarily at
least for poor relief.

Vv. 17-25. What I have been saying
about the support of widows reminds me
of another question of Church finance:
the payment of presbyters. Equity and
scriptural principles suggest that they
should be remunerated in proportion to
their usefulness. You are the judge of
the presbyters; in the discharge of this
office be cautious in accusing, and bold
in rebuking. I adjure you to be impartial. Do not absolve without deliberate consideration. A lax disciplinarian
is partner in the guilt of those whom he
encourages to sin. Keep yourself pure.
I do not mean this in the ascetic sense;
on the contrary, your continual delicacy
demands a stimulant. But, to resume
about your duties as a judge, you need
not distress yourself by misgivings; you
will find that your judgments about men,
even when only instinctive, are generally
correct.

Ver. 17. The natural and obvious
meaning of the verse is that while all
presbyters discharge administrative functions, well or indifferently, they are not
all engaged in preaching and teaching.
We distinguish then in this passage
three grades of presbyters: (1) ordinary
presbyters with a living wage; (2) efficient presbyters (κοπιῶντες, 1 Thess. v.
12); (3) presbyters who were also
preachers and teachers. Cf. Cyprian
(Epist. 29), presbyteri doctores. It must
be added that Hort rejects the distinction
between (2) and (3) (Christian Ecclesia,
p. 196).

ὁ διδάσκων and ὁ παρακαλῶν were
possessors of distinct and recognised
charismata (Rom. xii. 7; 1 Cor. xii. 8,
28, 29, xiv. 6).

προεστῶτες: See note on 1 Tim. iii. 4.

διπλῆς τιμῆς: Remuneration is a
better rendering of τιμή than pay, as

less directly expressive of merely mone-
tary reward. Liddon suggests the
rendering honorarium. On the one
hand, διπλῆς certainly warrants us
in concluding that presbyters that
ruled well were better paid than those
that performed their duties perfunctorily.
Bengel justifies the better pay given to
those that "laboured in the word, etc.,"
on the ground that persons so fully occupied would have less time to earn their
livelihood in secular occupations. On
the other hand, we must not press the
term double too strictly (cf. Rev. xviii.
6, διπλώσατε τὰ διπλᾶ). πλείονος
τιμῆς (Theod.) is nearer the meaning
than "double that of the widows, or of
the deacons, or simply, liberal support "
(Chrys.). The phrase is based, according
to Grotius, on Deut. xxi. 17; in the
division of an inheritance the first-born
received two shares, cf. 2 Kings ii. 9.
The custom of setting a double share of
provisions before presbyters at the love
feasts (Constt. Ap. ii. 28) must have
been, as De Wette says, based on a misunderstanding of this passage.

ἀξιούσθωσαν implies that what they
were deemed worthy of they received.

κοπιῶντες: There is no special stress
to be laid on this, as though some
preachers and teachers worked harder in
the exercise of their gift than others.

λόγῳ: The omission of the article,
characteristic of the Pastorals, obscures
the reference here to the constant phrase
speak, or preach the word, or the word
of God.

διδασκαλίᾳ: See note on chap. i. 10.

Ver. 18. If this verse is read without
critical prejudice, it implies that in the
writer's judgment a quotation from Deut.
xxv. 4 and the Saying, ἄξιος, κ.τ.λ.
might be coordinated as ἡ γραφή; just
as in Mark vii. 10, Acts i. 20, and Heb. i.
10, two O.T. quotations are coupled by
a καί. For this formula of quotation, in
addition to the reff., see John xix. 37;
Rom. iv. 3, xi. 2; Gal. iv. 30; Jas. ii.
23, iv. 5.

The question then arises, Is ἄξιος,
κ.τ.λ. a proverbial saying carelessly or
mistakenly quoted by St. Paul as ἡ
γραφή? or, Was St. Paul familiar with
its presence in a written document, an
early gospel, the subject of which was so
sacred as to entitle it to be called ἡ

γὰρ [f] ἡ [f] γραφή, Βοῦν ἀλοῶντα οὐ [g] φιμώσεις [1] · καὶ, Ἄξιος ὁ ἐργάτης g *Cf.* Matt.
τοῦ μισθοῦ αὐτοῦ. 19. κατὰ πρεσβυτέρου [h] κατηγορίαν μὴ [i] παρα-

xxii. 12,
34, Mark
i. 25, iv.
39, Luke

iv. 35, 1 Pet. ii. 15.   h John xviii. 29, Tit. i. 6, not LXX.   i Acts xxii. 18

[1] οὐ φιμ. βοῦν ἀλο. ACP, 17, 37, 80, five others, f, vg., boh., syrpesh, arm.

γραφή? The question has been pre-judged by supposed necessary limitations as to the earliest possible date for a gospel; and many have thought it safest to adopt Stier's statement that ἄξιος, κ.τ.λ. was a common proverb made use of both by our Lord (Luke x. 7; Matt. x. 10), and by St. Paul. In that case, it is difficult to avoid the conclusion that St. Paul forgot that it was not ἡ γραφή; for here it is not natural to take ἄξιος, κ.τ.λ., as a supplementary or confirmatory statement by the writer in the words of a well-known proverb. The proverb, if it be such, is rather the second item in ἡ γραφή, just as in 2 Tim. ii. 19, the "seal" consists of (a) "The Lord knoweth them that are his," and (b) "Let every one that nameth," etc. Our Lord no doubt employed proverbs that were current in His time, e.g., Luke iv. 23, John iv. 37. In both these cases He intimates that He is doing so; but He does not do so in Matt. x. 10, or Luke x. 7. Besides, while the variation here between Matt. (τῆς τροφῆς) and Luke (τοῦ μισθοῦ) is of the same degree as in other cases of varying reports of Sayings from Q common to Matthew and Luke, yet such variation in wording is not likely in the case of a well-known proverb. We may add that it is difficult to know to what ruling of Christ reference is made in 1 Cor. ix. 14 if it be not this Saying. Critical opinion has recently grown inclined to believe that much of the gospel material which underlies the Synoptists was put into writing before our Lord's earthly ministry closed. (See Sanday, *The Life of Christ in Recent Research*, p. 172.) The only question, therefore, is not, Could St. Paul have read the Evangelic narrative? but, Could he have co-ordinated a gospel document with the written oracles of God, venerated by every Hebrew as having a sanctity all their own? The question cannot be considered apart from what we know to have been St. Paul's conception of the person of Jesus Christ. We may readily grant that it would be a surprising thing if St. Paul thought of the writings of any contemporary apostle as "Scripture," as 2 Pet. iii. 16 does; but since he believed that Christ was "the end of the

Law" (Rom. x. 4), it would be surprising were he not to have esteemed His words to be at least as authoritative as the Law which He superseded.

The order in Deut. xxv. 4 is οὐ φιμ. βοῦν ἀλο. The same text is quoted, 1 Cor. ix. 9 in the form οὐ κημώσεις βοῦν ἀλο. (B*D*FG). St. Paul's treatment of the command, as pointing to an analogy in the life of human beings, does not need any defence. Our just repudiation of the spirit in which he asks in 1 Cor., "Is it for the oxen that God careth?" must not blind us to the large element of truth in his answer, "Yea, for our sake it was written".

Ver. 19. The mention of καλῶς προεστῶτες πρεσβύτεροι, and of what was due to them, naturally suggests by contrast the consideration of unsatisfactory presbyters. Yet even these were to be protected against the possibility of arbitrary dismissal. They were to have a fair trial in accordance with the provisions of the Old Law, Deut. xix. 15 (see also Deut. xvii. 6, Num. xxxv. 30. This requirement of two or three witnesses is used allegorically in 2 Cor. xiii. 1. *Cf.* John viii. 17, Heb. x. 28.) It has been asked, Why should this, the ordinary rule, be mentioned at all? The solution is to be found in a consideration of the private, unofficial, character of the Christian Church when this epistle was written. The Church was altogether a voluntary society, unrecognised by the state. The crimes of which its governors could take cognisance were spiritual; or if they were such as were punishable by the ordinary state law, the Church was concerned only with the spiritual and moral aspect of them, that is to say, so far as they affected Church life. There were then no spiritual courts, in the later sense of the term. No Church officer could enforce any but spiritual punishments. In these circumstances, the observance of legal regulations would not be a matter of necessity. Indeed a superintendent who was jealous for the purity of the Church might feel himself justified in acting even on suspicion, when the question arose as to the dismissal of a presbyter.

ἐκτὸς εἰ μή: This phrase arises from a

k 1 Cor. xiv. δέχου, ᵏ ἐκτὸς ᵏ εἰ ᵏμὴ ἐπὶ δύο ἢ τριῶν μαρτύρων.¹ 20. τοὺς²
5, xv. 2.
l Acts xix. ἁμαρτάνοντας ¹ἐνώπιον ¹πάντων ἔλεγχε, ἵνα καὶ οἱ λοιποὶ φόβον
19, xxvii.
35. ἔχωσιν. 21. ᵐΔιαμαρτύρομαι ⁿ ἐνώπιον ⁿ τοῦ ⁿ Θεοῦ καὶ³ Χριστοῦ
m 2 Tim. ii.,
14, iv. 1. Ἰησοῦ⁴ καὶ τῶν ᵒἐκλεκτῶν ἀγγέλων, ἵνα ταῦτα ᵖφυλάξῃς ᑫχωρὶς
n See 1 Tim.
ii. 3.
o 1 Pet. i. 1, ii. 6, 9, 2 John i. 13.   p Matt. xix. 20 (= Mark x. 20 = Luke xviii. 21), Luke xi. 28, John
xii. 47, Acts vii. 53, xvi. 4, xxi. 24, Rom. ii. 26, Gal. vi. 13, 1 Tim. vi. 20, 2 Tim. i. 14.   q Phil.
ii. 14, 1 Tim. ii. 8.

¹ Om. ἐκτὸς-μαρτύρων Latin MSS. known to Jerome, also apparently Cyp. and
Ambrst.

² Ins. δὲ AD*, d, f, g, autem (not r), go. ; ins. δὲ after ἁμαρτ. FG.

³ Ins. Κυρίου DᶜKLP, go., syrr.   ⁴ Ἰησ. Χριστ. DᶜFKLP, go., syrr., arm.

blend of εἰ μή and ἐκτὸς εἰ. Examples of
its use are cited from Lucian. Alford
notes that similar "pleonastic expressions such as χωρὶς εἰ, or εἰ μή, are
found in later writers such as Plutarch,
Dio Cassius, etc.". Deissmann cites an
instructive example for its use in the
Cilician Paul from an inscription of Mops-
uestia in Cilicia of the Imperial period
(Bible Studies, trans. p. 118). See reff.
ἐπὶ . . . μαρτύρων: This seems an
abbreviation for ἐπὶ στόματος μαρτ.
So R.V. Cf. 2 Cor. xiii. 1, Hebr.
עַל־פִּי עֵד. It is a different use from
ἐπὶ in the sense of before (a judge),
Mark xiii. 9, Acts xxv. 9, 10. See Blass,
Gram. p. 137.
Ver. 20. τοὺς ἁμαρτάνοντας: It
cannot be certainly determined whether
this refers to offending presbyters only or
to sinners in general. In favour of the
first alternative, is the consideration that
it seems to be a suitable conclusion to
ver. 19; and the vehemence of the adjuration in ver. 21 receives thus a justification. It demands greater moral courage
to deal judicially with subordinate officials than with the rank and file of a
society.
On the other hand, the sequence of
thought in these concluding verses of the
chapter is not formal and deliberate. Although it has been shown above that vv.
17-25 form one section, marked by one
prominent topic, the relation of Timothy
to presbyters, it cannot be maintained
that the connexion is indisputably obvious;
and the use of the present participle suggests that habitual sinners are under discussion. One is reluctant to suppose
that such men would be found amongst
the presbyters of the Church.
ἐνώπιον πάντων: At first sight this
seems opposed to the directions given by
our Lord, Matt. xviii. 15, "Shew him

his fault between thee and him alone";
but the cases are quite different : Christ
is there speaking of the mutual relations
of one Christian with another, as brothers
in the household of God; here St. Paul
is giving directions to a father in God, a
Christian ruler, as in 2 Tim. iv. 2, Tit. i.
13, ii. 15. Moreover, as Ell. points
out, Christ is speaking of checking the
beginning of a sinful state, St. Paul is
speaking of persistent sinners.
ἵνα καὶ οἱ λοιποί, κ.τ.λ.: Cf. Deut.
xiii. 11.
Ver. 21. διαμαρτύρομαι: It is easy to
see that St. Paul had not perfect confidence in the moral courage of Timothy.
He interjects similar adjurations, vi. 13,
2 Tim. iv. 1. In 1 Thess. iv. 6 we can
understand διεμαρτυράμεθα to mean that
purity had been the subject of a strong
adjuration addressed by the apostle to
his converts.
τῶν ἐκλεκτῶν ἀγγέλων: The epithet
elect has probably the same force as
holy in our common phrase, The holy
angels. Compare the remarkable parallel, cited by Otto and Krebs, from
Josephus, B. J. ii. 16, 4, μαρτύρομαι δὲ
ἐγὼ μὲν ὑμῶν τὰ ἅγια καὶ τοὺς ἱεροὺς
ἀγγέλους τοῦ θεοῦ καὶ πατρίδα τὴν
κοινήν, and Testament of Levi, xix. 3,
μάρτυς ἐστι κύριος, κ. μάρτυρες οἱ
ἄγγελοι αὐτοῦ, κ. μάρτυρες ὑμεῖς. The
references to angels in St. Paul's
speeches and letters suggest that he had
an unquestioning belief in their beneficent ministrations; though he may not
have attached any importance to speculations as to their various grades.
We are safe in saying that the elect
angels are identical with "the angels
which kept their own principality" (Jude
6), "that did not sin" (2 Pet. ii. 4).
Ellicott follows Bp. Bull in giving
ἐνώπιον a future reference to the Day of
Judgment, when the Lord will be at-

ʳ προκρίματος, μηδὲν ποιῶν κατὰ ˢ πρόσκλισιν.¹ 22. Χεῖρας ᵗ ταχέως r Here only,
not LXX.

μηδενὶ ἐπιτίθει, μηδὲ ᵘ κοινώνει ἁμαρτίαις ᵛ ἀλλοτρίαις· σεαυτὸν s Here only,
not LXX.

t 2 Thess.

ii. 2.   u 2 John 11.   v Rom. xiv. 4, xv. 20, 2 Cor. x. 15, 16, Heb. ix. 25.

¹ So אFGK, 47**, 67**, many others, d, f, g, r, vg.; πρόσκλησιν ADLP, 17, 31, 37, 47*, 80, more than fifty-four others.

tended by "ten thousands of His holy ones" (Jude 14). But this seems an evasion due to modern prejudice. ἐνώπιον implies that the solemnity of the charge or adjuration is heightened by its being uttered in the actual presence of God, Christ, and the angels. Perhaps one may venture to suppose that these are thought of as in three varying degrees of remoteness from human beings, with our present powers of perception. God the Father, though indeed "He is not far from each one of us," "dwells in light unapproachable"; Christ Jesus, though in one sense He dwells in us and we in Him, is for the most part thought of as having His special presence at the right hand of the Majesty in the heavens; but the angels, though spiritual beings, are akin to ourselves, creatures as we are, powers with whom we are in immediate and almost sensible contact, *media* perhaps through which the influences of the Holy Spirit are communicated to us. ταῦτα refers to all the preceding disciplinary instructions.

προκρίματος: *dislike, praejudicium.*

πρόσκλισιν: *partiality (nihil faciens in aliam partem declinando,* Vulg.).

Clem. Rom., *ad Cor.* 21, has the phrase κατὰ προσκλίσεις. The reading πρόσκλησιν is almost certainly due to itacism. It could only mean "*by invitation, i.e.,* the invitation or summons of those who seek to draw you over to their side" (Thayer's Grimm).

Ver. 22. Our best guide to the meaning of χεῖρας . . . ἐπιτίθει is the context, and more especially the following clause, μηδὲ . . . ἀλλοτρίαις. μηδέ constantly introduces an extension or development of what has immediately preceded; it never begins a new topic. Now the injunction *Be not partaker of other men's sins* is certainly connected with the disciplinary rebuke of sin, and refers of course to definite acts of sin committed in the past, as well as to their consequences or continuation. The whole procedure is outlined: we have the accusation in ver. 19, the conviction and sentence in ver. 20, and—in the true Pauline spirit—repentance and reconciliation in

this verse; and the topic of ministerial treatment of sin is resumed and continued in ver. 24 *sq.* We can hardly doubt that St. Paul had in his mind Lev. xix. 17, "Thou shalt surely rebuke thy neighbour and not bear sin because of him," καὶ οὐ λήμψῃ δι' αὐτὸν ἁμαρτίαν. To witness in silence an act of wrong-doing is to connive at it. If this is true in the case of private persons, how much more serious an offence is it in the case of those to whom government is committed? See 2 John 11, ὁ λέγων γὰρ αὐτῷ χαίρειν κοινωνεῖ τοῖς ἔργοις αὐτοῦ τοῖς πονηροῖς.

χεῖρας . . . ἐπιτίθει is then best referred to imposition of hands on reconciled offenders, on their re-admission to Church communion. Eusebius (*H. E.,* vii. 2), speaking of reconciled heretics, says, "The ancient custom prevailed with regard to such that they should receive only the laying on of hands with prayers," μόνῃ χρῆσθαι τῇ διὰ χειρῶν ἐπιθέσεως εὐχῇ. See Council of Nicea, can. 8, according to one explanation of χειροθετουμένους, and Council of Arles, can. 8.

This was used in the case of penitents generally. So Pope Stephen (ap. Cyprian, *Ep.* 74), "Si qui ergo a quacunque haeresi venient ad vos, nihil innovetur nisi quod traditum est, ut manus illis imponatur in paenitentiam". See Bingham, *Antiquities,* xviii. 2, 1, where the 15th Canon of the Council of Agde (A.D. 506) is cited: "Poenitentes tempore quo poenitentiam petunt, impositionem manuum et cilicium super caput a sacerdote consequantur." The antiquity of the custom may be argued from the consideration that imposition of hands was so prominent a feature in ordination, that it is not likely that its use would have been extended to anything else if such extension could not have claimed unquestioned antiquity in its favour. If the explanation of this verse given above—which is that of Hammond, De Wette, Ellicott, and Hort—be accepted, we have here the first distinct allusion to the custom of receiving back penitents by imposition of hands.

w 2 Cor. xi. ἁγνὸν ^wτήρει. 23. μηκέτι ^xὑδροπότει, ἀλλὰ οἴνῳ ὀλίγῳ ^yχρῶ διὰ
9, Jas. i.
27, cf. 1 τὸν ^zστόμαχον¹ καὶ τὰς ^aπυκνάς σου ^bἀσθενείας. 24. τινῶν
Tim. vi.
14, 2 Tim. ἀνθρώπων αἱ ἁμαρτίαι ^cπρόδηλοί εἰσιν, ^dπροάγουσαι εἰς κρίσιν,
iv. 7.
x Here only
N.T., Dan. i. 12, LXX.   y Here only (N.T.) of food.   z Here only, not LXX.   a Here
only, N.T., as adj.   b Matt. viii. 17, Luke v. 15, viii. 2, xiii. 11, 12, John v. 5, xi. 4, Acts xxviii. 9,
1 Cor. ii. 3, Gal. iv. 13.   c Vv. 24, 25, Heb. vii. 14, Judith viii. 29, 2 Macc. iii. 17, xiv. 39.
d 1 Tim. i. 18.

¹ Ins. σου DcFGKL, f, g, vg., go., sah., boh., syrr., arm.; om. σου ℵAD*P, 17,
d, r.

Timothy is bidden to restrain by deliberate prudence the impulses of mere pity. A hasty reconciliation tempts the offender to suppose that his offence cannot have been so very serious after all; and smoothes the way to a repetition of the sin. "Good-natured easy men" cannot escape responsibility for the disastrous consequences of their lax administration of the law. They have a share in the sins of those whom they have encouraged to sin. Those who give letters of recommendation with too great facility fall under the apostolic condemnation.

On the other hand, the ancient commentators — Chrys., Theod., Theoph., Oecumen.—refer χεῖρας ἐπιτίθει to hasty ordinations; and in support of this, the generally adopted view, it must be granted that ἐπίθεσις χειρῶν undoubtedly refers to ordination in iv. 14, 2 Tim. i. 6. If we assume the same reference here, the intention of the warning would be that Timothy will best avoid clerical scandals by being cautious at the outset as to the character of those whom he ordains. The clause in iii. 10, καὶ οὗτοι δὲ δοκιμαζέσθωσαν πρῶτον, would, in this case, have the same reference; and we should explain ἁμαρτίαι ἀλλότριαι as possible future sins, for the commission of which a man's advancement may give him facilities, and responsibility for which attaches, in various degrees of blameworthiness, to those who have rendered it possible for him to commit them.

σεαυτόν is emphatic, repeating in brief the warning of the previous clause.

ἁγνόν: The context demands that the meaning should not be chaste (castum Vulg.), as in Tit. ii. 5, 2 Cor. xi. 2; but pure in the sense of upright, honourable, as in 2 Cor. vii. 11, Phil. iv. 8, Jas. iii. 17.

Ver. 23. μηκέτι ὑδροπότει: An adequate explanation of this seemingly irrelevant direction is that since there is a certain degree of ambiguity in ἁγνός, St. Paul thought it necessary to guard against any possible misunderstanding of Keep thyself pure: "I do not mean you to practice a rigid asceticism; on the contrary, I think that you are likely to injure your health by your complete abstinence from wine; so, be no longer a water-drinker, etc." So Hort, who thinks that this is "not merely a sanitary but quite as much a moral precept" (Judaistic Christianity, p. 144). This explanation is preferable to that of Paley who regards this as an example of "the negligence of real correspondence . . . when a man writes as he remembers: when he puts down an article that occurs the moment it occurs, lest he should afterwards forget it" (Horae Paulinae). Similarly Calvin suggested that σεαυτὸν —ἀσθενείας was a marginal note by St. Paul himself. Alford's view has not much to commend it, viz., that Timothy's weakness of character was connected with his constant ill health, and that St. Paul hoped to brace his deputy's will by a tonic.

For this position of μηκέτι cf. Mark ix. 25, xi. 14, Luke viii. 49, John v. 14, viii. 11, Rom. xiv. 13, Eph. iv. 28; and see note on chap. iv. 14.

διὰ τὸ στόμαχον: Wetstein's happy quotation from Libanius, Epist. 1578 must not be omitted: πέπτωκε καὶ ἡμῖν ὁ στόμαχος ταῖς συνεχέσιν ὑδροποσίαις.

Ver. 24. The connexion of this general statement is especially with ver. 22. The solemn warning against the awful consequences of an ill-considered moral judgment on those condemned was calculated to overwhelm a weak man with anxiety. Here the apostle assures Timothy that in actual practical experience the moral diagnosis of men's characters is not so perplexing as might be supposed antecedently. The exegesis of προάγουσαι and ἐπακολουθοῦσιν depends on the view we take of κρίσις; viz., whether it refers to a judgment passed by man in this world, or to the final doom pronounced by God in the next. κρίσις is used of such a judgment as man may pass, in John viii. 16, 2 Peter ii. 11, Jude 9; though the

τισὶν δὲ καὶ ᵉἐπακολουθοῦσιν· 25. ᶠὡσαύτως¹ καὶ τὰ ᵍἔργα ᵍτὰ e Mark xvi.
ᵍκαλὰ² ᶜπρόδηλα,³ καὶ τὰ ʰἄλλως ἔχοντα κρυβῆναι οὐ δύνανται.⁴   20, 1 Pet.
                                                                   ii. 21, cf.
                                                                   ver. 10.
VI. 1. Ὅσοι εἰσὶν ªὑπὸ ªζυγὸν δοῦλοι τοὺς ἰδίους ᵇ˙ⁿ δεσπόταςf See 1 Tim.
                                                                   ii. 9.
πάσης τιμῆς ἀξίους ᶜἡγείσθωσαν, ᵈἵνα ᵈμὴ τὸ ὄνομα τοῦ Θεοῦ καὶgSee 1 Tim.
                                                                   iii. 1.
                                                                   h Hereonly,
N.T.   a Ecclus. li. 26, Zech. iii. 9, Jer. xxxiv. (xxvii.) 8, 11.   b Luke ii. 29, 1 Tim. vi. 1,
2, 2 Tim. ii. 21, Tit. ii. 9, 1 Pet. ii. 18, 2 Pet. ii. 1.   c See 1 Tim. i. 12.   d Tit. ii. 5, Rom. ii.
24 (Isa. lii. 5).

¹ Ins. δὲ AFG, f, g, go.   ² τὰ καλὰ ἔργα KL.
³ Add ἐστι KL; add εἰσὶ DFGP, 17, 67*, five others.
⁴ So ADP, 17, 47, 67, more than thirty-five others; δύναται ℵFGKL.

word is more frequently used of the Great final Judgment. If, as is generally allowed, these verses, 24 and 25, are resumptive of ver. 22, the κρίσις here indicated is that of the Church ruler, Timothy in this case, deciding for or against the admission of men to communion (or to ordination). It is evident that the final Judgment of God, which no one can certainly forecast, cannot help or hinder a decision made in this life by one man about another. The meaning, then, of the clause is as follows: In the case of some men, you have no hesitation as to your verdict; their sins are notorious and force you to an adverse judgment. With regard to others, your suspicions, your instinctive feeling of moral disapproval, comes to be confirmed and justified by subsequent revelation of sins that had been concealed. This is, in the main, the explanation adopted by Alford.

πρόδηλοι: Not *open beforehand* (A.V.), but *evident* (R.V.), *manifesta sunt* (Vulg.) as in Heb. vii. 14 (neut.). The προ is not indicative of antecedence in time, but of publicity, as in προεγράφη, Gal. iii. 1.

προάγουσαι: It is best to take this in a transitive sense, as in Acts xii. 1, xvii. 5, xxv. 26, of bringing a prisoner forth to trial. Here the object of the verb is understood out of τινῶν ἀνθρώπων. The men are in the custody of their sins, which also testify against them. In the other case, the witnesses—the sins—do not appear until the persons on trial have had sentence pronounced on them. We supply εἰς κρίσιν after ἐπακολουθοῦσιν.

Ver. 25. ὡσαύτως here, as in chap. ii. 9, naturally introduces an antithesis to what has gone before; and this determines the meaning of τὰ ἄλλως ἔχοντα; not as ἔργα which are not καλά, but as ἔργα καλά which are not πρόδηλα; and justifies the R.V. rendering, *There are good works that are evident*. The next clause is parallel to the corresponding part of ver. 24: Sins and good works alike cannot be successfully and indefinitely concealed; they follow—are disclosed some time or other in justification of—the κρίσις of men. The literal rendering in R.V. m., *The works that are good are evident*, could only be defended by laying emphasis on καλά, "good in appearance as well as in reality"; but καλὰ ἔργα is of frequent occurrence in these epistles without any such special signification; see on iii. 1; and this rendering deprives ὡσαύτως of any force. Von Soden thinks that we have here a reference to the sayings in Matt. v. 14-16.

CHAPTER VI.—Vv. 1-2. The duty of Christian slaves to heathen and Christian masters respectively.

Ver. 1. The politico-social problem of the first ages of Christianity was the relation of freemen to slaves, just as the corresponding problem before the Church in our own day is the relation of the white to the coloured races. The grand truth of the brotherhood of man is the revolutionary fire which Christ came to cast upon earth. Fire, if it is to minister to civilisation, must be so controlled as to be directed. So with the social ethics of Christianity; the extent to which their logical consequences are pressed must be calculated by common sense. One of the great dangers to the interests of the Church in early times was the teaching of the gospel on liberty and equality, crude and unqualified by consideration of the other natural social conditions, also divinely ordered, which Christianity was called to leaven, not wholly to displace.

The slave problem also meets us in Eph. vi. 5, Col. iii. 22, Tit. ii. 9, Philem. 1 Pet. ii. 18. In each place it is dealt with consistently, practically, Christianly. The difficulty in this verse is ὑπὸ

e Ps. lxxvii. ἡ διδασκαλία ᵈ βλασφημῆται.   2. οἱ δὲ πιστοὺς ἔχοντες ᵇ δεσπότας
(lxxviii.)
11, Wisd. μὴ καταφρονείτωσαν, ὅτι ἀδελφοί εἰσιν · ἀλλὰ μᾶλλον δουλευέτωσαν,
xvi. 11, 24,
2 Macc. ὅτι πιστοί εἰσιν καὶ ἀγαπητοὶ οἱ τῆς ᵉ εὐεργεσίας ᶠ ἀντιλαμβανόμενοι.
vi. 13, ix.
26, 4
Macc. viii. 17, Acts iv. 9.   f 1 Macc. ii. 48, 2 Macc. xiv. 15, Luke i. 54, Acts xx. 35.

ζυγόν. The contrast in ver. 2, οἱ δὲ πιστ.
ἔχ. δεσπ. seems to prove that a δοῦλος
ὑπὸ ζυγόν is one that belongs to a heathen
master. The R.V. is consistent with
this view, *Let as many as are servants
under the yoke*. The heathen estimate
of a slave differed in degree, not in kind,
from their estimate of cattle ; a Christian
master could not regard his slaves as ὑπὸ
ζυγόν.

τοὺς ἰδίους δεσπότας : The force of
ἴδιος was so much weakened in later
Greek that it is doubtful if it amounts
here to more than αὐτῶν. See on iii. 4.

δεσπότης is more strictly the correlative of δοῦλος than is κύριος, and is used
in this sense in reff. except Luke ii. 29.
St. Paul has κύριος in his other epistles
(Rom. xiv. 4 ; Gal. iv. 1 ; Eph. vi. 5, 9 ;
Col. iii. 22, iv. 1) ; but, as Wace acutely
remarks, in all these passages there is a
reference to the Divine κύριος which
gives the term a special appropriateness.

πάσης τιμῆς ἀξίους, *worthy of the
greatest respect*.

ἵνα μὴ—βλασφημῆται : The phrase
"blaspheme the name of God" comes
from Isa. lii. 5 (*cf.* Ezek. xxxvi. 20-23).
See Rom. ii. 24, 2 Pet. ii. 2. See note
on v. 14. The corresponding passage in
Tit. ii. 10, ἵνα τὴν διδασκαλίαν τὴν τοῦ
σωτῆρος ἡμῶν θεοῦ κοσμῶσιν, supports
Alford's contention that the article here is
equivalent to a possessive pronoun, *His
doctrine*. On the other hand, the phrase
does not need any explanation ; *the doctrine* would be quite analogous to St.
Paul's use elsewhere when speaking of
the Christian faith. For διδασκαλία, see
note on i. 10.

Ver. 2. A Christian slave would be
more likely to presume on his newly
acquired theory of liberty, equality and
fraternity in relation to a Christian
master than in relation to one that was
a heathen. The position of a Christian
master must have been a difficult one,
distracted between the principles of a
faith which he shared with his slave, and
the laws of a social state which he felt
were not wholly wrong. 1 Cor. vii. 22
and Philem. 16 illustrate the position.

μᾶλλον δουλευέτωσαν : *serve them all
the more, magis serviant* (Vulg.).

For this use of μᾶλλον *cf.* Rom. xiv.

13, 1 Cor. v. 2, vi. 7, 9, Eph. iv. 28, v.
11. Ignat. *Polyc.* 4 says of Christian
slaves, μηδὲ αὐτοὶ φυσιούσθωσαν, ἀλλ'
εἰς δόξαν θεοῦ πλέον δουλευέτωσαν.

ὅτι πιστοί, κ.τ.λ.: The Christian
slave is to remember that the fact of his
master being a Christian, *believing and
beloved*, entitles him to service better,
if possible, than that due to a heathen
master. The slave is under a moral obligation to render faithful service to any
master. If the spiritual status of the
master be raised, it is reasonable that the
quality of the service rendered be not
lowered, but rather idealised. "*The
benefit* is the improved quality of the service, and *they that partake of or enjoy it
are the masters*" (Field *in loc.*). So
Vulg., *qui beneficii participes sunt*.

εὐεργεσία has its usual non-religious
signification, as in Acts iv. 9. It does
not indicate the goodness of God in
redemption, as suggested in A.V., influenced no doubt directly by Calvin and
Beza, though the explanation is as old
as Ambr., *because they are faithful and
beloved, partakers of the benefit*. On
the other hand, it is more natural to use
εὐεργεσία of the kindness of an employer
to a servant or employee, than of the advantage gained by the employer from his
servant's good-will. Accordingly Chrysostom takes it here in the former sense,
the whole clause referring to the slaves.
Von Soden, taking εὐεργεσία similarly,
renders, *as those who occupy themselves
in doing good*. No doubt the best reward
of faithful service is the acquisition of a
character of trustworthiness and the grate-
ful love of the master to whom you are
invaluable ; but it is rather far-fetched to
read this subtle meaning into the passage
before us. In support of the view taken
above, Alford quotes from Seneca, *De
Beneficiis*, iii. 18, a discussion of the query,
"An beneficium dare servus domino possit ?" which Seneca answers in the
affirmative, adding further : "Quidquid
est quod servilis officii formulam excedit,
quod non ex imperio sed ex voluntate
praestatur, beneficium est". See Lightfoot, *Philippians*, 270 *sqq.*, *St. Paul and
Seneca*.

ἀντιλαμβανόμενοι : ἀντιλαμβάνεσθαι
properly means *to lay hold of*, hence

Ταῦτα δίδασκε καὶ παρακάλει. 3. εἴ τις [g]ἑτεροδιδασκαλεῖ καὶ μὴ
[h]προσέρχεται [1] [i]ὑγιαίνουσι [i]λόγοις, τοῖς τοῦ Κυρίου ἡμῶν Ἰησοῦ
Χριστοῦ, καὶ [k]τῇ [k]κατ᾽ [k][l]εὐσέβειαν διδασκαλίᾳ, 4. [m]τετύφωται,
μηδὲν [n]ἐπιστάμενος, ἀλλὰ [o]νοσῶν περὶ [p]ζητήσεις καὶ [q]λογομαχίας,

g See 1 Tim. i. 3. h See note. i 2 Tim. i. Tim. i. 10. k Tit. i. 1. l See 1 Tim. ii. 2.

m See 1 Tim. iii. 6.   n Mark xiv. 68, Acts (9), Heb. xi. 8, Jas. iv. 14, Jude 10.   o Wisd. xvii. 8 (bis) only.   p John iii. 25, Acts xv. 2, 7, xxv. 20, 2 Tim. ii. 23, Tit. iii. 9, not LXX.   q Here only, not LXX, cf. 2 Tim. ii. 14.

[1] προσέχεται א*.   So Bentley conj. from Latin adquiescit.

to help, as in reff.; and the Harclean Syriac gives that sense here. Like our English word apprehend, it passes from an association with the sense of touch to an association with the other senses or faculties which connect us with things about us. Field (in loc.) gives examples of the use of ἀντιλαμβάνεσθαι as expressive of a person being sensible of anything which acts upon the senses, e.g., the smell of a rose. The Peshitta agrees with this. Alford renders mutually receive, by which he seems to intend the same thing as Ell., who suggests that ἀντί has "a formal reference to the reciprocal relation between master and servant". Field rejects this because "receive in exchange" is ἀντιλαμβάνειν, and the examples cited by Alf. are middle only in form.

δίδασκε καὶ παρακάλει : See note on iv. 13.

Vv. 3-21. Thoughts about the right use of wealth are suggested by the slave problem, a mischievous attitude towards which is associated with false doctrine. If a man possesses himself, he has enough. This possession is eternal as well as temporal. This is my lesson for the poor, for you as a man of God (and I solemnly adjure you to learn and teach it), and for the rich.

Ver. 3. ἑτεροδιδασκαλεῖ : See note on i. 3.

καὶ μή : Blass (Gramm. p. 514) notes this case of μή following εἰ with the indicative (supposed reality) as an abnormal conformity to classical use. The usual N.T. use, εἰ . . . οὐ, appears in 1 Tim. iii. 5, v. 8. In these examples, however, the οὐ is in the same clause as εἰ, not separated from it, as here, by a καί.

προσέρχεται : assents to. The noun προσήλυτος, proselyte, "one who has come over," might alone render this use of προσέρχομαι defensible. But Ell. gives examples of this verb from Irenæus and Philo; and Alf. from Origen, which completely justify it. The reading προ-

σέχεται, which seems to derive support from the use of προσέχειν, i. 4, Tit. i. 14, has not exactly the same force ; "to give heed," or "attend to," a doctrine falls short of giving in one's adhesion to it.

ὑγιαίνουσι λόγοις : See on i. 10.

τοῖς τοῦ Κυρίου : This is in harmony with St. Paul's teaching elsewhere, that the words spoken through the prophets of the Lord are the Lord's own words. It is thus we are to understand Acts xvi. 7, "The Spirit of Jesus suffered them not," and 1 Cor. xi. 23, "I received of the Lord," etc. The words of Jesus, "He that heareth you heareth me" (Luke x. 16) have a wider reference than was seen at first.

τῇ κατ᾽ εὐσέβειαν διδασκαλίᾳ : See ref. and notes on i. 10, ii. 2.

Ver. 4. τετύφωται : inflatus est (d, m⁵⁰, r) ; superbus est (Vulg.). See on iii. 6. νοσῶν : morbidly busy (Liddon), languens (Vulg.), aegrotans (m⁵⁰). His disease is intellectual curiosity about trifles. Both doting and mad after (Alf.) as translations of νοσῶν, err by excess of vigour. The idea is a simple one of sickness as opposed to health. See on i. 10.

περί : For this use of περί see on i. 19.

ζητήσεις : See on i. 4.

λογομαχίας : It is not clear whether what is meant are wordy quarrels or quarrels about words. The latter seems the more likely. There is here the usual antithesis of words to deeds. The heretic spoken of is a theorist merely ; he wastes time in academic disputes ; he does not take account of things as they actually are. On the other hand, it is interesting and suggestive that to the heathen, the controversy between Christianity and Judaism seemed to be of this futile nature (see Acts xviii. 15, xxiii. 29, xxv. 19).

φθόνος, ἔρις are similarly juxtaposed Rom. i. 29, Gal. v. 20, 21, Phil. i. 15. The plural ἔρεις is a well-supported variant in Rom. xiii. 13, Gal. v. 20. In Tit. iii. 9 it is the true reading ; but in other lists of vices (1 Cor. iii. 3,

r Here only, ἐξ ὧν γίνεται φθόνος, ἔρις,[1] βλασφημίαι, ʳὑπόνοιαι πονηραί, 5.
N.T.
s Here only, ˢ διαπαρατριβαὶ[2] ᵗ διεφθαρμένων ἀνθρώπων τὸν νοῦν καὶ ᵘ ἀπεστερη-
not LXX.
t Here only μένων τῆς ἀληθείας, ᵛ νομιζόντων ᵂ πορισμὸν εἶναι τὴν ¹ εὐσέβειαν.³
metaph.,
cf. Luke 6. ˣἘστιν δὲ ˣ πορισμὸς μέγας ἡ ʸ εὐσέβεια μετὰ ᶻ αὐταρκείας · 7.
xii. 33, 2
Cor. iv.
16, Rev. viii. 9, xi. ː8.   u Mark x. 19, 1 Cor. vi. 7, 8, vii. 5, Jas. v. 4 (?).   v Matt. (3), Luke
(2), Acts (7), 1 Cor. vii. 26, 36.   w Wisd. xiii. 19, xiv. 2 only; verb, Wisd. xv. 12 only.   x See
ver. 5.   y See 1 Tim. ii. 2.   z 2 Cor. ix. 8, cf. Phil. iv. 11.

¹ So ℵAKᵉⁱˡP, 17, many others, syrᵖᵉˢʰ, sah., boh., arm.; ἔρεις DFGL, 47, some
others, d, f, g, m⁵⁰, r, vg., go., syrʰᶜˡ.

² παραδιατριβαὶ a few cursives.

³ Add ἀφίστασο ἀπὸ τῶν τοιούτων Dgr ᶜKLP, m⁵⁰, Discede ab eiusmodi, syrr.,
arm.

2 Cor. xii. 20, Phil. i. 15) the singular is
found.

βλασφημία also occurs in a list of sins,
Eph. iv. 31, Col. iii. 8.

ὑπόνοιαι πονηραί: ὑπόνοια (only here
in N.T., but ὑπονοέω in Acts xiii. 25,
xxv. 18, xxvii. 27, all in neutral sense, to
suppose) has sometimes the sense of suspicion. See examples given by Ell. The
phrase here does not mean wicked or unworthy thoughts of God—the class of
mind here spoken of does not usually
think about God directly, though an unworthy opinion about Him underlies their
life—but malicious suspicions as to the
honesty of those who differ from them.

Ver. 5. διαπαρατριβαί: The force of
the διά is expressed in the R.V., wrang-
lings, which denotes protracted quarrel-
lings, perconfricationes (r), conflictationes
(d, Vulg.).   Field (in loc.) comparing
διαμάχεσθαι, διαφιλοτιμεῖσθαι, etc.,
prefers the sense of reciprocity, mutual
irritations, gallings one of another
(A.V.m.), "as infected sheep by contact
communicate disease to the sound"
(Chrys.). παραδιατριβαί (T.R.), perverse
disputings, is given a milder sense by
Winer-Moulton, Gram. p. 126, "mis-
placed diligence or useless disputing".

διεφθαρμένων τὸν νοῦν: cf. κατεφθαρμένοι τὸν νοῦν, 2 Tim. iii. 8, the acc.
being that of the remoter object. Cf., for
the notion, τὸν παλαιὸν ἄνθρωπον τὸν
φθειρόμενον κατὰ τὰς ἐπιθυμίας τῆς
ἀπάτης, Eph. iv. 22, also 1 Cor. xv. 33,
2 Cor. xi. 3, Jude 10.

ἀπεστερημένων: privati. ἀποστερέω
conveys the notion of a person being
deprived of a thing to which he has a
right. See reff. This is expressed in
R.V., bereft of. The truth was once
theirs; they have disinherited themselves.
The A.V., destitute of, does not assume
that they ever had it.

νομιζόντων, κ.τ.λ.: since they suppose. For this use of the participle
Bengel compares Rom. ii. 18, 20, 2 Tim.
ii. 21, Heb. vi. 6.

πορισμόν: a means of gain, quaestus.
The commentators quote Plutarch, Cato
Major, § 25, δυσὶ κεχρῆσθαι μόνοις
πορισμοῖς, γεωργίᾳ καὶ φειδοῖ.

τὴν εὐσέβειαν: not godliness in general, pietatem (Vulg.), but the profession of
Christianity, culturam Dei (m⁵⁰). See
ii. 2. Allusions elsewhere to those who
supposed that the gospel was a means
of making money have usually reference
to self-interested and grasping teachers
(2 Cor. xi. 12, xii. 17, 18; Tit. i. 11; 2
Pet. ii. 3). Here the significance of the
clause may be that the false teachers de-
moralised slaves, suggesting to slaves
who were converts, or possible converts,
that the profession of Christianity involved an improvement in social position
and worldly prospects. The article before εὐσεβ. shews that the A.V. is wrong,
supposing that gain is godliness.

Ver. 6. The repetition of πορισμός in
a fresh idealised sense is parallel to the
transfigured sense in which νομίμως is
used in i. 8.

αὐταρκείας: not here sufficientia
(Vulg.), though that is an adequate rendering in 2 Cor. ix. 8. St. Paul did not
mean to express the sentiment of the
A.V. of Eccles. vii. 11, "Wisdom is good
with an inheritance". Contentment does
not even give his meaning. Contentment
is relative to one's lot; αὐτάρκεια is
more profound, and denotes independence of, and indifference to, any lot; a
man's finding not only his resources in
himself, but being indifferent to everything else besides. This was St. Paul's
condition when he had learnt to be
αὐτάρκης, Phil. iv. 11. "Lord of himself, though not of lands" (Sir. H. Wot-

οὐδὲν γὰρ εἰσηνέγκαμεν εἰς τὸν κόσμον,[1] ὅτι οὐδὲ ἐξενεγκεῖν τι ᵃ
δυνάμεθα· 8. ἔχοντες δὲ ᵃ διατροφὰς [2] καὶ ᵇ σκεπάσματα, τούτοις ᵇ
ᵉ ἀρκεσθησόμεθα. 9. οἱ δὲ βουλόμενοι πλουτεῖν ᵈ ἐμπίπτουσιν εἰς ᶜ
πειρασμὸν καὶ ᵉ παγίδα [3] καὶ ἐπιθυμίας πολλὰς ᶠ ἀνοήτους [4] καὶ
ᵍ βλαβεράς, αἵτινες ʰ βυθίζουσι τοὺς ἀνθρώπους εἰς ⁱ ὄλεθρον καὶ

a 1 Macc.vi.
49 only.
b Here only,
not LXX.
c Luke iii.
14, Heb.
xiii. 5.
d See 1 Tim.
iii. 6.
e 1 Tim. iii.
7, 2 Tim.

ii. 26.　f Luke xxiv. 25, Rom. i. 14, Gal. iii. 1, 3, Tit. iii. 3.　　g Prov. x. 26 only.　h 2 Macc.
xii. 4, Luke v. 7 only.　　i 1 Cor. v. 5, 1 Thess. v. 3, 2 Thess. i. 9 only, N.T.

[1] Ins. δῆλον ℵcDbcKLP; ins. ἀληθὲς D*, verum (quoniam) d, verum (quia) m98,
haud dubium (quia) f, vg., [h]aut dubium, verum tamen fuld., verum Cyp., go., syrr.;
om. δῆλον ℵ*AFG, 17, g, r, vgsome MSS, sah., boh., arm.

[2] So ℵAL, f, vg.; διατροφὴν DFGKP, d, g, m98, r (victum).

[3] Ins. τοῦ διαβόλου D*FG, 37mg, 238, d, f, g, m98 (not r), vg. (not am.), go.

[4] ἀνόνητος 2, two others, d, f, g, vg., Cyp., Ambrst. (inutilia) m98 (quae nihil
prosunt) r (stulta).

ton). See chap. iv. 8. The popular as
opposed to the philosophical use of
αὐτάρκεια, as evidenced by the papyri,
is simply *enough*. See Moulton and
Milligan, *Expositor*, vii., vi. 375.

Ver. 7. The reasoning of this clause
depends on the evident truth that since a
man comes naked into this world (Job. i.
21), and when he leaves it can "take
nothing for his labour, which he may
carry away in his hand" (Eccles. v. 15;
Ps. xlix. 17), nothing the world can give
is any addition to the man himself. He is
a complete man, though naked (Matt. vi.
25; Luke xii. 15; Seneca, *Ep. Mor.* lii. 25,
"Non licet plus efferre quam intuleris").

Field is right in supposing that if
δῆλον, as read in the Received Text, is
spurious, yet "there is an ellipsis of
δῆλον, or that ὅτι is for δῆλον ὅτι. L.
Bos adduces but one example of this
ellipsis, 1 John iii. 20: ὅτι ἐὰν κατα-
γινώσκῃ ἡμῶν ἡ καρδία, ὅτι μείζων ἐστὶν
ὁ θεὸς τῆς καρδίας ἡμῶν; in which, if an
ellipsis of δῆλον before the second ὅτι
were admissible, it would seem to offer
an easy explanation of that difficult text."
Field adds two examples from St. Chrysostom. Hort's conjecture that "ὅτι is
no more than an accidental repetition of
the last two letters of κόσμον, ON being
read as OTI" is almost certainly right.

Ver. 8. ἔχοντες δέ: The δέ has a
slightly adversative force, guarding against
a too literal conclusion from ver. 7. It is
true that "unaccommodated man" (*Lear*,
iii. 4) is "a man for a' that," yet he has
wants while alive, though his real wants
are few.

σκεπάσματα: may include clothes
and shelter, *covering* (R.V.), *tegumen-
tum* (r), *quibus tegamur*, as the Vulg. well

puts it; but the word is used of clothing
only in Josephus (*B. J.* ii. 8. 5; *Ant.* xv.
9, 2). So A.V., *raiment*, d, *vestitum* (so
Chrys.).

Jacob specifies only "bread to eat and
raiment to put on" (Gen. xxviii. 20);
but the Son of Sirach is more indulgent
to the natural man (Ecclus. xxix. 21,
xxxix. 26, 27).

ἀρκεσθησόμεθα: This future is impera-
tival, or authoritative, as Alf. calls it.
He cites in illustration, Matt. v. 48,
ἔσεσθε οὖν ὑμεῖς τέλειοι. From this
point of view, the R.V., *We shall be
therewith content, cf.* reff., is preferable
to his rendering (which is equivalent to
R.V. m.), *With these we shall be sufficiently provided* (*cf.* Matt. xxv. 9; John
vi. 7; 2 Cor. xii. 9).

Ver. 9. οἱ δὲ βουλόμενοι: St. Chrysostom calls attention to the fact that
St. Paul does not say, *They that are
rich*, but *They that desire to be rich*
(R.V.), they that make the acquisition of
riches their aim. The warning applies to
all grades of wealth: all come under it
whose ambition is to have more money
than that which satisfies their accustomed
needs. We are also to note that what is
here condemned is not an ambition to
excel in some lawful department of human
activity, which though it may bring an
increase in riches, develops character,
but the having a single eye to the accumulation of money by any means.
This distinction is drawn in Prov. xxviii.
20: "A faithful man shall abound with
blessings: But he that maketh haste to
be rich shall not be unpunished".

ἐμπίπτουσιν. Wetstein notes the
close parallel in the words of Seneca:
"Dum divitias consequi volumus in mala

k Matt. vii. ᵏ ἀπώλειαν.   10. ῥίζα γὰρ πάντων τῶν κακῶν ἐστὶν ἡ ¹φιλαργυρία·
13, Acts
viii. 20,   ἧς τινὲς ᵐ ὀρεγόμενοι ⁿ ἀπεπλανήθησαν ἀπὸ τῆς πίστεως καὶ ἑαυτοὺς
Rom. lx.
22, Heb.   ᵒ περιέπειραν ᵖ ὀδύναις πολλαῖς.   11. ᑫ Σὺ ᑫ δέ, ὦ ἄνθρωπε ¹ Θεοῦ,
x. 39, Rev.
xvii. 8, 11
(all with εἰς).   l 4 Macc. i. 26, ii. 15 (?), cf. 2 Tim. iii. 2.   m See 1 Tim. iii. 1.   n Mark.
xiii. 22.   o Here only, not LXX.   p Rom. ix. 2 only, N.T.   q Rom. xi. 17, 20, xiv. 10,
2 Tim. iii. 10, 14, iv. 5, Tit. ii. 1.

¹ Ins. τοῦ all except אּ*A, 17.

multa incidimus" (Ep. 87). Cf. also
Jas. i. 2, πειρασμοῖς περιπέσητε
ποικίλοις. πειρασμόν refers rather to
the consequencess of one's money-grub-
bing spirit on others, παγίδα to its
disastrous effect on one's own character.
ἀνοήτους καὶ βλαβεράς: The desires
in question are foolish, because they cannot be logically defended; they are hurtful, because they hinder true happiness.
See Prov. xxiii. 4, "Weary not thyself to
be rich".
αἵτινες: qualitative, such as.
βυθίζουσιν: The word is found in its
literal signification in Luke v. 7. Moulton and Milligan (Expositor, vii., vi. 381)
illustrate its use here from a papyrus of
cent. 1 B.C., συνεχέσι πολέμοις κατα-
βυθισθεῖ[σαν] τὴν πόλιν. Bengel notes
on ἐμπίπτ. βυθίζ., "incidunt: mergunt.
Tristis gradatio." We must not lose sight
of εἰς. Destruction and perdition are not,
strictly speaking, the gulf in which the
men are drowned.   The lusts, etc., overwhelm them; and the issue is destruction,
etc.   See reff. on ἀπώλειαν.
Ver. 10. ῥίζα, κ.τ.λ.: The root of all
evils. The R.V., a root of all kinds of
evil is not satisfactory. The position of
ῥίζα in the sentence shows that it is emphatic.   Field (in loc.) cites similar examples of the absence of the article
collected by Wetstein from Athenæus,
vii. p. 280 A (ἀρχὴ καὶ ῥίζα παντὸς
ἀγαθοῦ ἡ τῆς γαστρὸς ἡδονή), and Diog.
Laërt. vi. 50; and adds five others from
his own observation. It is, besides, unreasonable in the highest degree to expect
that, on the ground of his inspiration, St.
Paul's ethical statements in a letter should
be expressed with the precision of a text
book.   When one is dealing with a de-
grading vice of any kind, the interests of
virtue are not served by qualified assertions.
φιλαργυρία: avaritia (r) rather than
cupiditas (d, m, Vulg.).   The use of this
word supports the exposition given above
of ver. 9.   Love of money, meanness
and covert dishonesty where money is
concerned, is the basest species of the
genus πλεονεξία.

ἧς: In sense the relative refers to
ἀργύριον, understood out of φιλαργυρία,
with which it agrees in grammar. The
meaning is clear enough; but the expression of it is inaccurate. This occurs
when a man's power of grammatical expression cannot keep pace with his
thought. Alf. cites as parallels, Rom.
viii. 24, ἐλπὶς βλεπομένη, and Acts xxiv.
15, ἐλπίδα . . . ἣν καὶ αὐτοὶ οὗτοι
προσδέχονται.
τινες: See note on ch. i. 3.
ὀρεγόμενοι: reaching after (R.V.) expresses the most defensible aspect of
coveting (A.V.).
ἀπεπλανήθησαν: peregrinati sunt (r)
erraverunt (d, Vulg.).   The faith is a
very practical matter. Have been led
astray (R.V.) continues the description
of the man who allows himself to be the
passive subject of temptation. Chrys.
illustrates the use of this word here from
an absent-minded man's passing his destination without knowing it.
περιέπειραν: inseruerunt se. The
force of περί in this compound is intensive, as in περιάπτω, περικαλύπτω, πε-
ρικρατής, περικρύπτω, περίλυπος.
ὀδύναις πολλαῖς: There is a touch of
pity in this clause, so poignantly descriptive of a worldling's disillusionment.
Vv. 11-16 are a digression into a personal appeal. Cf. 2 Tim. ii. 1, iii. 10,
14, iv. 5.
Ver. 11. ὦ ἄνθρωπε θεοῦ: It argues
a very inadequate appreciation of the
fervour of the writer to suppose, as
Theod. does, that this is an official title.
The apostrophe is a personal appeal,
arising out of the topic of other-worldliness
which begins in ver. 5. Timothy, as a
Christian man, had been called to a
heavenly citizenship.   He was a man of
God, i.e., a man belonging to the spiritual
order of things with which that which is
merely temporal, transitory and perishing
can have no permanent relationship.
The term occurs again, with an admittedly general reference, in 2 Tim. iii. 17.
In any case Man of God, as an official
title, belonged to prophets, the prophets
of the Old Covenant; and we have no

ταῦτα ʳ φεῦγε · ˢ δίωκε δὲ δικαιοσύνην, ᵗ εὐσέβειαν, ᵘ πίστιν, ᵘ ἀγάπην, ʳ 1 Cor. vi. 18, x. 14.
ᵛ ὑπομονήν, ʷ πραϋπάθιαν.¹ 12. ˣ ἀγωνίζου ʸ τὸν ʸ καλὸν ʸ ἀγῶνα 2 Tim. ii. 22.
τῆς πίστεως · ᶻ ἐπιλαβοῦ τῆς ᵃ αἰωνίου ᵃ ζωῆς, εἰς ἣν ² ἐκλήθης, καὶ ˢ Rom. ix. 30, 31, xii.
ᵇ ὡμολόγησας τὴν καλὴν ᶜ ὁμολογίαν ἐνώπιον πολλῶν μαρτύρων. 13, xiv. 19, 1 Cor. xiv. 1, 1 Thess

v. 15, 2 Tim. ii. 22, Heb. xii. 14, 1 Pet. iii. 11.   t See 1 Tim. ii. 2.   u See 1 Tim. i. 14.
v Rom. v. 3, 2 Cor. vi. 4, xii. 12, Col. i. 11, 2 Tim. iii. 10, Tit. ii. 2, 2 Pet. i. 6, etc.   w Here only,
not LXX.   x See 1 Tim. iv. 10.   y 2 Tim. iv. 7, cf. Phil. iii. 12, 1 Thess. ii. 2, Heb.
xii. 1.   z 1 Tim. vi. 19.   a See 1 Tim. i. 16.   b John i. 20, ix. 22, xii. 42, Acts xxiii. 8,
Rom. x. 9, 10, Tit. i. 16, Heb. xi. 13, xiii. 15, etc.   c Heb. iii. 1, iv. 14, x. 23.

¹ So ℵ*AFG[P]; πραότητα [ℵcD*] DcKL, [31].
² Ins. καὶ 37, some others, syrʰᶜˡ c.*

proof that Timothy was a prophet of the New Covenant, though he was an evangelist (2 Tim. iv. 5), and possibly an apostle (1 Thess. ii. 6).

ταῦτα: i.e., φιλαργυρία and its attendant evils. Love of money in ministers of religion does more to discredit religion in the eyes of ordinary people than would indulgence in many grosser vices.

It is to be noted that φεῦγε · δίωκε δὲ δικαιοσύνην, πίστιν, ἀγάπην recurs in 2 Tim. ii. 22. The phraseology is based on Prov. xv. 9, διώκοντας δὲ δικαιοσύνην ἀγαπᾷ, and is thoroughly Pauline, as the reff. prove. The six virtues fall perhaps into three pairs, as Ell. suggests: "δικαιοσ. and εὐσέβ. have the widest relations, pointing to general conformity to God's law and practical piety [cf. σωφρόνως κ. δικαίως κ. εὐσεβῶς, Tit. ii. 12]; πίστις and ἀγάπη are the fundamental principles of Christianity; ὑπομ. and πραϋπ. the principles on which a Christian ought to act towards his gainsayers and opponents". As a group, they are contrasted with the group of vices in vv. 4 and 5; but we cannot arrange them in pairs of opposites. We may add that πίστις results in ὑπομονή (Jas. i. 3; Rom. v. 3; 2 Thess. i. 4; 2 Tim. iii. 10; Tit. ii. 2; Heb. xii. 1), as ἀγάπη does in πραϋπάθεια. ὑπομονή is sustinentia (r here, and Vulg. in 1 Thess. i. 3) rather than patientia (d and Vulg. here).

πίστις, ἀγάπη, and ὑπομονή are also combined in Tit. ii. 2; cf. 2 Tim. iii. 10, also 2 Pet. i. 5-7, where εὐσέβεια, with other virtues, forms part of the group.

Ver. 12. ἀγωνίζου . . . ἀγῶνα: There is evidence that ἀγωνίζομαι ἀγῶνα had become a stereotyped expression, perhaps from the line of Euripides: καίτοι καλόν γ' ἂν τόνδ' ἀγῶν' ἠγωνίσω (Alcestis, 648 or 664). See an Athenian inscription quoted by Moulton and Milligan, Ex-

positor, vii., vi. 370. Nevertheless the metaphor has its full force here, and in 2 Tim. iv. 7: Engage in the contest which profession of the faith entails; it is a noble one. Allusions to the public games are notoriously Pauline (1 Cor. ix. 24; Phil. iii. 12). The present imperative indicates the continuous nature of the ἀγών, while the aor. ἐπιλαβοῦ expresses the single act of laying hold of the prize (so ver. 19). It does not seem an insuperable objection to this view that καταλαμβάνω is the word used in 1 Cor. ix. 24, Phil. iii. 12. On the other hand, Winer-Moulton (Gram., p. 392) argues from the asyndeton (cf. Mark iv. 39) that ἐπιλαβοῦ, κ.τ.λ. forms one notion with ἀγωνίζου; that "it is not the result of the contest, but itself the substance of the striving". Yet in ver. 19 (ἵνα ἐπιλάβωνται τῆς ὄντως ζωῆς) there is nothing in the context suggestive of struggle.

εἰς ἣν ἐκλήθης: We are called to eternal life (1 Cor. i. 9; 1 Pet. v. 10); it is placed well within our reach; but it is not put into our hands; each man must grasp it for himself.

καὶ ὡμολόγησας, κ.τ.λ.: This clause has no syntactical connexion with what has preceded. It refers to ἀγῶνα, the contest on which Timothy entered at his baptism, when he was called, enrolled as a soldier in the army of Jesus Christ (2 Tim. ii. 4; 1 Cor. ix. 7), and professed fidelity to his new Leader (his response to the divine call) before many witnesses. ὁμολογία is perhaps best referred to a formal profession of faith, here as in the reff. Cyril Jer., when recalling the baptismal ceremonies to the newly baptised, says in reference to their profession of belief in the Trinity, ὡμολογήσατε τὴν σωτήριον ὁμολογίαν (Cat. xx. 4).

In the primitive Church the baptism of an individual was a matter in which the Church generally took an interest and part. The rule laid down in The Didache,

d See 1 Tim. 13. ᵈ Παραγγέλλω σοι ¹ ᵉ ἐνώπιον ᵉ τοῦ ² ᵉ Θεοῦ τοῦ ᶠ ζωογονοῦντος ³
i. 3.
e See 1 Tim. τὰ πάντα καὶ Χριστοῦ Ἰησοῦ ⁴ τοῦ ᵍ μαρτυρήσαντος ἐπὶ Ποντίου
ii. 3.
1 Sam. ii.
6, Luke xvii. 33, Acts vii. 19.   g John v. 32, 1 John v. 10, with acc.

¹ Om. σοι א*FG, 17 [g, praecipio tibi t contestor].   ² Om. τοῦ א.

³ So ADFGP, 17, 31, four others; ζωοποιοῦντος אKL.

⁴ So ADKLP, 17, 31, 37, many others, d, vg., go., syrhcl, armcodd; Ἰησ. Χριστ.
אFG, more than five cursives, f, g, syrpesh, sah., boh., armed.

7, shows this: "Before the baptism let him that baptizeth and him that is baptized fast, and any others also who are able". Also Justin Martyr, *Apol.* i. 61, ἡμῶν συνευχομένων καὶ συννηστευόντων αὐτοῖς. These passages explain "the many witnesses" of Timothy's good confession. It is not so natural to refer *the good confession* to a crisis of persecution, or to his ordination. The epithet καλήν here and in the following verse does not characterise the particular act of confession made by Timothy or by Christ, but refers to the class of confession, its import, as Ell. says.

Ver. 13. παραγγέλλω σοι: St. Paul passes in thought from the past epoch in Timothy's life, with its human witnesses, among whom was the apostle himself, to the present probation of Timothy, St. Paul far away; and he feels impelled to remind his lieutenant that there are Witnesses of his conduct whose real though unseen presence is an encouragement as well as a check. See on v. 21.

ζωογονοῦντος: This word has the sense *preserve alive*, as R.V. m. See reff. A good example from O.T. is 1 Sam. ii. 6, Κύριος θανατοῖ καὶ ζωογονεῖ. The word has here a special appropriateness. Timothy is stimulated to exhibit moral courage by an assurance that he is in the hands of One whose protective power is universal, and by the example of One who, as Man, put that protective power to a successful test, and was "saved out of death" (Heb. v. 7).

τὴν καλὴν ὁμολογίαν must have the same reference here as in the preceding verse. We have seen that in the case of Timothy, it means his baptismal profession of faith in God as revealed by Jesus Christ. In the case of Jesus Himself it is best understood of His habitual sense of His heavenly Father's presence and protection, which found its supreme expression on the Cross (Luke xxiv. 46).

μαρτυρήσαντος: Although Jesus, as Man, and His followers make the same ὁμολογία, yet their respective relations to it are different. μαρτυρέω indicates a

power of origination and authentication which ὁμολογέω does not. The utterances and acts of Jesus, as Man, are human; yet He spoke and acted as no other man ever did. Matt. xvii. 27 ("That take, and give unto them for *me and thee*," not "for *us*") and John xx. 17 ("I ascend unto *my* Father *and your* Father," etc. not *our* Father or *our* God) illustrate very well this difference between Jesus and His brethren in relations which they share alike. This is why St. Paul does not here use ὁμολογέω ὁμολογίαν of Christ, but employs instead the unusual μαρτυρέω ὁμολογίαν. Jesus is ὁ μάρτυς ὁ πιστός, Rev. i. 5, ὁ μαρτ. ὁ πιστ. καὶ ἀληθινός, Rev. iii. 14. Bengel suggests that the two verbs indicate the attitudes of the bystanders in each case: "*confessus est*, cum assensione testium: *testatus est*, non assentiente Pilato". The Vulg. treats τὴν καλ. ὁμολ. as an acc. of closer specification, *qui testimonium reddidit sub Pontio Pilato, bonam confessionem.*

ἐπὶ Ποντίου Πειλάτου: With the explanation of the ὁμολογία of Jesus which has just been given, it would be natural to render this, with the Vulg., *under Pontius Pilate*; and this view is favoured by the change from ἐνώπιον, ver. 12, to ἐπί, and by the likelihood that this is a fragment of a creed. Yet the rendering *before Pontius Pilate* (Chrys., etc.), is not inconsistent with the notion that the ὁμολογία in one sense was made all during our Lord's ministry; for undoubtedly from one point of view it was when Jesus' life was hanging in the balance, depending on the decision of Pontius Pilate, that His trust in the protective love of His Father was most tried. His calm repose of soul on the assurance of God's wise and good disposition of events is well illustrated by His words as recorded in John xix. 11, "Thou wouldest have no power against me, except it were given thee from above". Until it has b..en been proved that the Fourth Gospel is not a record of facts, it is reasonable to suppose that St. Paul and his contem-

Πειλάτου τὴν καλὴν [h]ὁμολογίαν, 14. [i]τηρῆσαί σε τὴν ἐντολὴν [h] See ver.
[k]ἄσπιλον [l]ἀνεπίλημπτον μέχρι τῆς [m]ἐπιφανείας τοῦ Κυρίου ἡμῶν [i] 2 Tim. iv.
7, see
Ἰησοῦ Χριστοῦ· 15. ἣν [n]καιροῖς [n]ἰδίοις δείξει ὁ [o]μακάριος καὶ note.
[k] Jas. i. 27,
1 Pet. i.

19, 2 Pet. iii. 14, not LXX.   l See 1 Tim. iii. 2.   m 2 Thess. ii. 8, 2 Tim. i. 10, iv. 1, 8, Tit,
ii. 13.   n See 1 Tim. ii. 6.   o 1 Tim. i. 11.

poraries were acquainted with the general
account of the trial of Jesus as therein
described.

Ver. 14. τηρῆσαι κ.τ.λ.: The phrase
τηρεῖν τὴν ἐντολήν, τὰς ἐντολάς or τὸν
λόγον, τοὺς λόγους is a common one;
found in Matt. xix. 17, and especially in
the Johannine writings; but wherever it
occurs it means to obey or observe a
command or a saying; whereas here
it means to preserve intact. Perhaps
the two meanings were present to the
apostle's mind; and no doubt in actual
experience they merge one into the other;
for a tradition is only preserved by obedience to the demand which it makes for
observance. This use of the verb and the
similar τὴν πίστιν τετήρηκα, 2 Tim. iv.
7, mutually illustrate each other. τὴν
ἐντολὴν τηρεῖν is probably equivalent to
τὴν παραθήκην φυλάσσειν, understanding the tradition or deposit in the most
comprehensive moral and spiritual sense,
in which it is nothing else than "the law
of the Gospel (cf. ἡ παραγγελία, i. 5),
the Gospel viewed as a rule of life" (so
Ell. and Alf.). St. Paul would not have
distinguished this from the charge given
to Timothy at his baptism. Cyril Jer.
(Cat. v. 13), in quoting this passage, substitutes ταύτην τὴν παραδεδομένην πίστιν
for ἐντολήν. This interpretation is permissible so long as we do not divorce
creed from character.

ἄσπιλον ἀνεπίλημπτον: These epithets
present a difficulty somewhat similar to
that presented by τηρῆσαι. ἄσπιλος is
a personal epithet (though applied to
οὐρανός, Job. xv. 15, Symm.); and so is
ἀνεπίλημπτος. See reff. on both. Alford shows, after De Wette, by examples
from Philo and Plato, that ἀνεπίλ. may
be applied to impersonal objects, such as
τέχνη, τὸ λεγόμενον. Nevertheless although it would be intolerably awkward
to refer the adjectives to σε—the ordinary
construction with τηρεῖν being that the
qualifying adj. should belong to its object, e.g., 1 Tim. v. 22; Jas. i. 27; 2 Cor.
xi. 9 (Alf.)—yet St. Paul had the personal
reference to Timothy chiefly in his mind
when he chose these words as qualifying
ἐντολήν; and the R.V., which places a
comma after commandment, possibly is

intended to suggest a similar view. The
man and the word are similarly identified
in the parable of the Sower (Matt. xiii.
19, etc.). If Timothy "keeps himself un-
spotted" (Jas. i. 27) and "without reproach," the ἐντολή, so far as he is
concerned, will be maintained flawless.

The Ancient Homily which used to be
attributed to Clem. Rom. contains a sentence written in a similar tone (§ 8),
τηρήσατε τὴν σάρκα ἁγνὴν καὶ τὴν
σφραγῖδα ἄσπιλον, ἵνα τὴν ζωὴν ἀπολάβωμεν.

μέχρι τῆς ἐπιφανείας, κ.τ.λ.: Death
may mark the close of our probation
state; but we shall not render the account of our stewardship until the
ἐπιφάνεια. When the Pastorals were
written the ἐπιφάνεια had in men's
thoughts of it receded beyond each man's
death. At an earlier period Christians
set it before them as men now set death.
In 2 Thess. ii. 8 the compound phrase
occurs ἐπιφάν. τῆς παρουσίας αὐτοῦ.
ἐπιφάνεια is the term used in the Pastoral Epistles (see reff.); but the Second
Coming of Christ is called παρουσία in
1 Cor. xv. 23; 1 Thess. ii. 19, iii. 13, iv.
15, v. 23, 2 Thess. ii. 1. In 2 Tim. i.
19, ἐπιφάνεια includes the first manifestation of Christ in the flesh; and this application of the term is in exact
correspondence with its use in heathen
sacred associations, where it denoted "a
conspicuous appearance or intervention
of the higher powers on behalf of their
worshippers". The title ἐπιφανής, assumed by the Seleucidæ, meant a claim
to be worshipped as an incarnation of
Zeus or Apollo, as the case might be (see
Moulton and Milligan, Expositor, vii.,
vii. 380).

Ver. 15. καιροῖς ἰδίοις: See note on ii.
6. In due season may refer primarily
either to the appropriateness of the occasion of the ἐπιφάνεια or to the supreme
will of the δυνάστης. The wording of
the discouragement given by Jesus, in
Acts i. 7, to those who would pry into
the future makes it natural to suppose
that this latter notion chiefly was in St.
Paul's mind here (καιροὺς οὓς ὁ πατὴρ
ἔθετο ἐν τῇ ἰδίᾳ ἐξουσίᾳ). We may perhaps put it thus: A devout mind recog-

Eccius. μόνος ᴾΔυνάστης, ὁ ᑫΒασιλεὺς τῶν βασιλευόντων καὶ Κύριος τῶν
xlvi. 5, 16,
2 Macc. ʳκυριευόντων, 16. ὁ μόνος ἔχων ˢἀθανασίαν, φῶς ᵗοἰκῶν ᵘἀπρόσιτον,
(8), 3
Macc. (4). ὃν εἶδεν οὐδεὶς ἀνθρώπων οὐδὲ ἰδεῖν δύναται· ᾧ τιμὴ καὶ ᵛκράτος
q Cf. 1 Tim.
i. 17. αἰώνιον· ἀμήν.
r Luke xxii.
25. 17. Τοῖς πλουσίοις ἐν ᵂτῷ ᵂνῦν ᵂαἰῶνι παράγγελλε μὴ ʸὑψη-
s Here only
N.T.,

Wisd. (5), 4 Macc. (2).   t Rom. (4), 1 Cor. (3).   u Here only, not LXX.   v 1 Pet. iv. 11
v. 11, Jude 25, Rev. i. 6, v. 13.   w 2 Tim. iv. 10, Tit. ii. 12.   x See 1 Tim. i. 3.   y Here
only, not LXX, cf. Rom. xi. 20, xii. 16.

nises the providential ordering of past events as having taken place at the time best fitted for them, and shrinks from the presumption of guessing the appropriate time for future events. Thus there is no presumption in saying "When the fulness of the time came, God sent forth his Son"; and when the time is ripe, He will send Him again (Acts iii. 20).

δείξει: Ell. well explains the force of this verb from John ii. 18, τί σημεῖον δεικνύεις ἡμῖν; The last ἐπιφάνεια will be the final *proof* offered by God to the human race.

The terms of this magnificent characterisation of God are an expansion of the epithets in the doxology in i. 17 *q.v.*

μακάριος: See on i. 11. Philo (*de Sacrific. Abelis et Caini*, p. 147) has the remarkable parallel, περὶ θεοῦ τοῦ ἀγεννήτου, καὶ ἀφθάρτου, καὶ ἀτρέπτου, καὶ ἁγίου, καὶ μόνου μακαρίου.

δυνάστης is found as a title of God in the Apocrypha. See reff., esp. 2 Macc. iii. 24, ὁ . . . δυνάστης ἐπιφανίαν μεγάλην ἐποίησεν. It occurs in the ordinary sense, Luke i. 52, Acts viii. 27. The choice of the phrase μόνος δυν. here was perhaps suggested by the thought of His absolute and irresponsible power in arranging the times and seasons for the affairs of men. It is unnecessary to seek any special polemical object in μόνος, as exclusive of dualism. As has been already suggested (on i. 17), the predications of glory to God that occur in these epistles are probably repeated from eucharistic prayers uttered by St. Paul in the discharge of his prophetic liturgical functions.

ὁ βασιλεύς, κ.τ.λ.: The Vulg. renders rather inconsistently, *Rex regum et Dominus dominantium*. So also in Rev. xix. 16. It is not quite obvious why the phrase is varied from the usual βασιλεὺς βασιλέων (2 Macc. xiii. 4; Rev. xvii. 14, xix. 16) and Κύριος [τῶν] Κυρίων (Deut. x. 17; Ps. cxxxvi. 3; Enoch ix. 4). Perhaps the participle gives new vigour to a phrase that had lost its freshness.

Ver. 16. **ὁ μόνος ἔχων ἀθανασίαν**: God the Father is the subject of this whole attribution; and it is the Catholic doctrine that He alone has endless existence as His *essential* property. (οὐσίᾳ ἀθάνατος οὐ μετουσίᾳ, Theod. *Dial.* iii. p. 145, quoted by Ell.). God the Son and God the Holy Spirit are co-eternal with the Father; but Their life is derived from and dependent on His. This is expressly declared by Christ of Himself, "As the Father hath life in himself, even so gave he to the Son also to have life in himself" (John v. 26). On this Westcott notes: "The Son has not life only as given, but life *in Himself* as being a spring of life. . . . The tense (*gave*) carries us back beyond time". Accordingly, the creed of Cæsarea, which formed the basis of that adopted at Nicea, spoke of the Son as Ζωὴν ἐκ Ζωῆς; a doctrine sufficiently expressed in the other phrase, Φῶς ἐκ Φωτός, which has survived.

φῶς οἰκῶν ἀπρόσιτον: This is a grander conception than that in Ps. civ. 2, "Who coverest thyself with light as with a garment". Here, if one may venture so to express it, the Person of God is wholly concealed by His dwelling, which is light; and this dwelling is itself unapproachable. Josephus, *Ant.* iii. 5. 1, says that God was thought to dwell in Mount Sinai, φοβερὸν καὶ ἀπρόσιτον. (See also Philo, *de Vita Mosis*, ii. [iii.] 2 cited by Dean Bernard).

ὃν εἶδεν οὐδεὶς ἀνθρώπων: None *of men*; only the Son (John i. 18; Matt. xi. 27, etc.).

κράτος: For this word in doxologies see reff.

Ver. 17. **ἐν τῷ νῦν αἰῶνι**: It is the present contrast, not that between riches in this world and riches in the world to come (as Chrys.), that the apostle has in mind. Those who have money may, as well as those "that are poor as to the world," be "rich in faith, and heirs of the kingdom, etc." (Jas. ii. 5). The passage indicates that the Church had affected Society more widely in Ephesus than it

λοφρονεῖν,[1] μηδὲ ²ἠλπικέναι ἐπὶ πλούτου ªἀδηλότητι, ἀλλ' ἐπὶ²³ z See 1 Tim.
Θεῷ⁴ τῷ ᵇπαρέχοντι ἡμῖν ⁵πάντα ᶜπλουσίως⁶ εἰς ᵈἀπόλαυσιν, 18. ᵃ iv. 10.
ᵉἀγαθοεργεῖν, πλουτεῖν ἐν ᶠἔργοις ᵍκαλοῖς, ᵍεὐμεταδότους εἶναι, b 1 Tim. i.
ʰκοινωνικούς, 19. ⁱἀποθησαυρίζοντας ἑαυτοῖς ᵏθεμέλιον καλὸν ˡεἰς
τὸ ˡμέλλον, ἵνα ᵐἐπιλάβωνται τῆς ⁿὄντως⁷ ζωῆς.

not LXX
4, Luke
vii. 4,
Acts
xxviii. 2,
Col. iv. 1.
c Col. iii. 16,
Tit. iii. 6, 2 Pet. i. 11, not LXX.   d 3 Macc. vii. 16, Heb. xi. 25 only.   e Acts xiv. 17, not
LXX.   f See 1 Tim. iii. 1.   g Here only, not LXX.   h Here only, not LXX.   i Ecclus.
iii. 4 only.   k Rom. xv. 20, 1 Cor. iii. 10, 11, 12, Eph. ii. 20, 2 Tim. ii. 19, Heb. vi. 1.   l Luke
xiii. 9.   m 1 Tim. vi. 12.   n See 1 Tim. v. 3.

¹ ὑψηλὰ φρονεῖν ℵ.   ²ἐν DcKL.
³ Ins. τῷ ADcKLP ; om. τῷ ℵD*FG, three cursives arm.
⁴ Ins. [τῷ]ζῶντι DKL, d, e, m22, vg. (am. not fuld*), syrr.
⁵ Ins. τὰ A, 37, a few others.
⁶ πλουσίως πάντα a few cursives.   ⁷ αἰωνίου DcKLP.

had at Corinth when St. Paul wrote,
"Not many mighty, not many noble, are
called" (1 Cor. i. 26). It is to be observed that the expression ὁ νῦν αἰών is
only found in N.T. in the Pastoral
Epistles (see reff.). ὁ αἰὼν οὗτος is the
expression elsewhere in N.T. (Matt. xii.
32; Luke xvi. 8, xx. 34); Rom. xii. 2; 1
Cor. i. 20, ii. 6 (bis), 8, iii. 18; 2 Cor. iv.
4; Eph. i. 21). Both represent the Rabbinic עוֹלָם הַזֶּה, the present age, as
contrasted with עוֹלָם הַבָּא, the age
to come. St. Paul also has ὁ κόσμος
οὗτος in 1 Cor. iii. 19, v. 10, vii. 31, and
ὁ νῦν καιρός in Rom. iii. 26, viii. 18, xi.
5, 2 Cor. viii. 14. See Dean Armitage
Robinson's note on Eph. i. 21. It does
not follow that because these are renderings of the same Hebrew expression,
they meant the same to a Greek ear. In
the three places in which ὁ νῦν αἰών
occurs it has a definite material physical
sense; whereas ὁ αἰὼν οὗτος has a more
notional ethical force.

ἠλπικέναι ἐπί: have their hope set on.
See note on iv. 10. For the thought
compare Job. xxxi. 24, Ps. xlix. 6, lii. 7,
Prov. xi. 28, Mark x. 24.

ἠλπικ. ἐπὶ πλούτου ἀδηλότητι: This
vigorous oxymoron is not quite parallel
in form to ἐν καινότητι ζωῆς, Rom. vi. 4,
as Ell. suggests. There ζωῆς is a further
definition of the καινότης, the prominent
notion. This is a rhetorical intensifying
of riches which are uncertain; πλούτου
is the prominent word. "When the
genitive stands before the governing noun,
it is emphatic" (Winer-Moulton, Gram.
p. 240). For the thought cf. Prov. xxiii.
5, xxvii. 24.

ἀλλ' ἐπὶ θεῷ: God who cannot change,
who abides faithful, is contrasted with the
uncertainty of riches which are unreal.

τῷ παρέχ. πάντα πλουσίως: cf. Acts
xiv. 17.

εἰς ἀπόλαυσιν: This is a greater concession to the sensuous view of life than
the εἰς μετάλημψιν of iv. 3. It approaches the declaration of the Preacher
that for a man to "eat and drink, and
make his soul enjoy good in his labour
. . . is from the hand of God" (Eccles.
ii. 24), "the gift of God" (Eccles. iii. 13,
v. 19). No good purpose is served by
pretending that God did not intend us to
enjoy the pleasurable sensations of physical life. After all, things that have
been enjoyed have served their purpose;
they have "perished," yet "with the
using" (Col. ii. 22). Obviously, they
cannot take God's place as an object of
hope.

Ver. 18. ἀγαθοεργεῖν: corrects any
possible misunderstanding of εἰς ἀπόλαυσιν. πλουτεῖν ἐν ἔργοις καλοῖς: see
note on iii. 1. Cf. εἰς θεὸν πλουτῶν,
Luke xii. 21.

εὐμεταδότους: facile tribuere (Vulg.),
ready to impart (cf. the use of
μεταδίδωμι in Luke iii. 11; Rom. i. 11,
xii. 8; Eph. iv. 28; 1 Thess. ii. 8).

κοινωνικούς: This does not mean soci-
able (A.V. m.), ready to sympathise (R.V.
m.), as Chrys., and Thdrt. explain it, but
ταῖς χρείαις τῶν ἁγίων κοινωνοῦντες,
Rom. xii. 13 (cf. Gal. vi. 6; Phil. iv.
15). A good illustration of the general
sentiment is Heb. xiii. 16, τῆς δὲ
εὐποιΐας καὶ κοινωνίας μὴ ἐπιλανθάνεσθε.
Von Soden notes that the thought in
εὐμεταδ. is of the needs of others, in
κοινων. of the imparting of one's own.

Ver. 19. ἀποθησαυρίζοντας: The true
hoarding produces, as its first result, a
good foundation, which will entitle a
man to grasp the prize, which is true
life, the only life worth talking about.

o 2 Tim. i. 12, 14, *cf.* Lev. vi. 2, 4, Tob. x. 13, 2 Macc. iii. 10, 15. p See 1 Tim. v. 21. q See 1 Tim. i. 6. r See 1 Tim. i. 9. s 2 Tim. ii. 16. t 2 Tim. ii. 16, not LXX. u Here only, not LXX. v Here only, not LXX.

20. ᾿Ω Τιμόθεε, τὴν [o] παραθήκην [1] [o p] φύλαξον, [q] ἐκτρεπόμενος τὰς [r s] βεβήλους [s t] κενοφωνίας [2] καὶ [u] ἀντιθέσεις τῆς [v] ψευδωνύμου

[1] παρακαταθήκην many cursives.

[2] καινοφωνίας FG, a few cursives, d, e, f, g, m50, vg. (*vocum novitates*).

Stability is the essential characteristic of a foundation. There is a contrast implied between the shifting uncertainty of riches, as a ground of hope, and the firm and permanent foundation of a Christian character. (So, nearly, Theod.)

Ingenious conjectures have been suggested for θεμέλιον; but it is safe to say that the mixture of metaphors—due to the condensation of language—does not distress those who read in a devout rather than in a critical spirit. For the sentiment *cf.* Matt. vi. 19, 20. There is some support given to the conjecture of Lamb-Bos, θέμα λίαν, by the parallel from Tobit iv. 8 *sq.* cited by Bengel, μὴ φοβοῦ ποιεῖν ἐλεημοσύνην· θέμα γὰρ ἀγαθὸν θησαυρίζεις σεαυτῷ εἰς ἡμέραν ἀνάγκης. See, on the other hand, what Ecclus. i. 15 says of Wisdom, μετὰ ἀνθρώπων θεμέλιον αἰῶνος ἐνόσσευσεν. θεμέλιος is used metaphorically also in reff. It is to be observed that in 2 Tim. ii. 19 there is again a confusion of imagery: the foundation has a seal.

εἰς τὸ μέλλον is found in a slightly different sense (*thenceforth*), Luke xiii. 9.

ἐπιλάβωνται: See on ver. 12.

τῆς ὄντως ζωῆς: *the life which is life indeed*, an expression which is one of the precious things of the R.V. It is "the life which is in Christ Jesus" (2 Tim. i. 1). For ὄντως see v. 3.

Ver. 20. As Ell. points out, this concluding apostrophe, like the last paragraph in 2 Cor. (xiii. 11 *sqq*.), is a summary of the whole epistle.

On the intensity of the appeal in the use of the personal name see on i. 18.

τὴν παραθήκην: *depositum*. The term occurs in a similar connexion with φυλάσσω, 2 Tim. i. 14, and also in 2 Tim. i. 12, where see note. Here, and in 2 Tim. i. 14, it means, as Chrys. explains, ἡ πίστις, τὸ κήρυγμα; so Vincent of Lerins, from whose *Commonitorium* (c. 22) Alf. quotes. "Quid est *depositum*? id est, quod tibi creditum est, non quod a te inventum; quod accepisti, non quod excogitasti; rem non ingenii, sed doctrinae; non usurpationis privatae, sed publicae traditionis . . . catholicae fidei talentum inviolatum illibatumque conserva. . . . Aurum accepisti, aurum redde: nolo mihi pro aliis alia subjicias: nolo pro auro aut impudenter plumbum, aut fraudulenter aeramenta supponas." That the "deposit" is practically identical with the "charge," ch. i. 5, 18, "the sound doctrine," i. 10, "the commandment," vi. 14, is indicated by the use of the cognate verb παρατίθεμαι in i. 18, 2 Tim. ii. 2, and the correlative παρέλαβες, Col. iv. 17, and even more by the contrast here between it and "the knowledge falsely so called".

ἐκτρεπόμενος: *turning away from, devitans.*

τὰς βεβήλους κενοφωνίας: In 2 Tim. ii. 16 the Vulg. has *vaniloquia*. The rendering *vocum novitates* found here in Vulg. and O.L. represents the variant καινοφωνίας. The term does not differ much from ματαιολογία, i. 6, which is also rendered *vaniloquium.*

ἀντιθέσεις: In face of the general anarthrous character of the Greek of these epistles it is not certain that the absence of an article before ἀντιθ. proves that it is qualified by βεβήλους. The meaning of ἀντιθ. is partly fixed by κενοφωνίας, to which it is in some sort an explanatory appendix; but it must finally depend upon the signification we attach to τῆς ψευδωνύμου γνώσεως. The epithet ψευδων. is sufficient to prove that γνῶσις was specially claimed by the heretics whom St. Paul has in his mind. That it should be so is in harmony with the other notices which we find in these epistles suggestive of a puerile and profitless intellectual subtlety, as opposed to the practical moral character of Christianity. We are reminded of the contrast in 1 Cor. viii. 1, "Knowledge puffeth up, but love buildeth up". Hort (*Judaistic Christianity*, p. 139 *sqq.*) proves that γνῶσις here and elsewhere in N.T. (Luke xi. 52; Rom. ii. 20 *sq.*) refers to the special lore of those who interpreted mystically the O.T., especially the Law. Knowledge which is merely theoretical. the knowledge of God professed by those who "by their works deny Him" (Tit. i.

γνώσεως, 21. ἥν τινες ᵂ ἐπαγγελλόμενοι ˣ περὶ ˣ τὴν ˣ πίστιν ʸ ἠστό- w 1 Tim. ii.
χησαν.

'Η χάρις μεθ' ὑμῶν.¹

10.
x 1 Tim. i.
19, 2 Tim.
iii. 8.
y See 1 Tim.
i. 6.

¹ So אAFgᵣGP, 17, g (*vobiscum t tecum*) boh.; μετὰ σοῦ DKL, d, e, f, vg., syrr., arm.; sah. om. ἡ χάρ.—ὑμῶν; add ἀμήν אᶜDᵇᶜKLP, e, f, vg., syrr., boh.

א, 17 add πρὸς Τιμόθεον ā. To this D adds, ἐπληρώθη · ἄρχεται πρὸς Τιμόθεον β, similarly FG. A, etc., have πρὸς Τιμόθεον ā ἐγράφη ἀπὸ Λαοδικείας; to which K adds, ἥτις ἐστὶ μητρόπολις Φρυγίας τῆς Πακατιανῆς, similarly L. P has a subscription like that of A, substituting Νικοπόλεως for Λαοδικείας.

16), is not real knowledge. The ἀντιθέσεις then of this spurious knowledge would be the dialectical distinctions and niceties of the false teachers. Perhaps *inconsistencies* is what is meant. For an example of ἀντίθετος in this sense, see Moulton and Milligan, *Expositor*, vii., v. 275. Something more definite than (*a*) *oppositions*, *i.e.*, *objections* of opponents (so Chrys. Theoph. and von Soden, who compares ἀντιδιατιθεμένους, 2 Tim. ii. 25) is implied; but certainly not (*b*) the formal categorical oppositions between the Law and the Gospel alleged by Marcion.

Ver. 21. τινες: See note on i. 3.

ἐπαγγελλόμενοι: See note on ii. 10.

περὶ τὴν πίστιν ἠστόχησαν: See notes on i. 6, 19, and reff.

μεθ' ὑμῶν: An argument in support of the μετὰ σοῦ of the Received Text is that μεθ' ὑμῶν is indisputably the right reading in the corresponding place in 2 Tim. and 'Tit., and might have crept in here by assimilation. Ell. has reason on his side when he maintains that the plural here is not sufficient to prove that the epistle as a whole was intended for the Church. "The study of papyri letters will show that the singular and the plural alternated in the same document with apparently no distinction of meaning" (Moulton, *Expositor*, vi., vii. 107). The colophon in the T.R., "The First to Timothy was written from Laodicea, which is the chiefest city of Phrygia Pacatiana," has a double interest: as an echo of the notion that this is the Epistle from Laodicea (Col. iv. 16), a notion sanctioned by Theophyl.; and the mention of Phrygia Pacatiana proves that the author of the note lived after the fourth century, towards the close of which that name for Phrygia Prima came into use.

a See 1 Tim. I. 1. ΠΑΥΛΟΣ ᵃἀπόστολος ᵃΧριστοῦ ᵃʼΙησοῦ¹ ᵇδιὰ ᵇθελήματος
i. 1.
b Rom. xv. ᵇΘεοῦ κατ' ᶜἐπαγγελίαν ᶜᵈζωῆς τῆς ᵈἐν ᵈΧριστῷ ᵈʼΙησοῦ 2. Τιμοθέῳ
32, 1 Cor.
i. 1, 2 Cor. ᵉἀγαπητῷ ᵉτέκνῳ· χάρις, ᶠἔλεος, εἰρήνη ἀπὸ Θεοῦ Πατρὸς καὶ
i. 1, viii.
5, Eph. Χριστοῦ ʼΙησοῦ² τοῦ Κυρίου ἡμῶν.
i. 1, Col.
i. 1.   3. ᵍΧάριν ᵍἔχω τῷ Θεῷ,³ ᾧ ʰλατρεύω ἀπὸ ¹προγόνων ἐν ᵏκαθαρᾷ
c 1 Tim. iv.
8.
d Rom. viii. 2.   e 1 Cor. iv. 14, 17, Eph. v. 1, see 1 Tim. i. 2.   f See 1 Tim. i. 2.   g See 1 Tim·
i. 12.   h Acts xxiv. 14, xxvii. 23, Rom. i. 9, Phil. iii. 3.   i See 1 Tim. v. 4.   k 1 Tim. iii. 9·

¹ ʼΙησ. Χριστ. AL, 37, most others, vg., go., syrʰᶜˡ, arm.

² So אᶜADFGKL, d, f, g, vg., go., sah., boh., syrʰᶜˡ, arm.; Κυρίου ʼΙησ. Χριστ.
א*, 17, 37 (so also two cursives, syrᵖᵉˢʰ, which om. foll. τοῦ Κυρίου ἡμῶν).

³ Add μου D*, 17, one other, d, e, fuld., go., sah.

CHAPTER I.—Vv. 1, 2. Salutation.

Ver. 1. ἀπόστολος Χρ. ʼΙησ. See note on 1 Tim. i. 1.

διὰ θελήματος Θεοῦ: This formula is found also in 1 and 2 Cor. Eph. and Col. See note on 1 Tim. i. 1, where it is pointed out that while the same ἐπιταγή may be said to be issued by God the Father and God the Son, θέλημα is always used of the Father's eternal purpose as regards the salvation of man (Rom. ii. 18, xii. 2; 2 Cor. viii. 5; Gal. i. 4; Eph. i. 5, 9, 11; Col. i. 9, iv. 12; 1 Thess. iv. 3, v. 18, etc.). St. Paul believed that his own commission as an apostle was a part of God's arrangements to this end, one of the ways in which the Will manifested itself.

κατ' ἐπαγγελίαν ζωῆς, κ.τ.λ.: To be connected with ἀπόστολος. His apostleship was *for the accomplishment of the promise*, etc. See Rom. i. 5, ἐλάβομεν . . . ἀποστολὴν εἰς ὑπακοὴν πίστεως ἐν πᾶσιν τοῖς ἔθνεσιν. For the force of κατά with acc. see Winer-Moulton, *Gram.* p. 502. The notion is more largely expressed in the corresponding passage of Tit. (i. 2), ἐπ' ἐλπίδι ζωῆς αἰωνίου ἣν ἐπηγγείλατο . . . θεός. We must not suppose that there is any limitation in the reference of the expression here. The mention of "the promise of the life which is in Christ Jesus" (Gal. ii. 19,

20) is not intended as a consolation to Timothy (as Chrys., Bengel), nor was it even specially suggested by his own near approaching death. The preciousness of that promise is never wholly absent from the minds of Christians; though of course it comes to the surface of our consciousness at crises when death is, or seems to be, imminent.

Ver. 2. ἀγαπητῷ: On the variation here from γνησίῳ, which occurs in 1 Tim. i. 2 and Tit. i. 4, see the note in the former place. Ver. 5 ("the unfeigned faith that is in thee") proves that St. Paul did not wish to hint that Timothy had ceased to be his γνήσιον τέκνον. Timothy is St. Paul's τέκνον ἀγαπητόν also in 1 Cor. iv. 17. ἀγαπητός is complete in itself: it does not require the explanatory addition, ἐν πίστει, or κατὰ κοινὴν πίστιν.

χάρις, κ.τ.λ.: See note on 1 Tim. i. 2.

Vv. 3-7. I know that your weak point is deficiency in moral courage. Be braced, therefore, by the assurance that I am constantly thinking with thankfulness and prayer about your genuine and inborn faith; and by the fact that the gift of the Holy Spirit which you received at ordination was that of power and love and discipline.

Ver. 3. χάριν ἔχω: The expression of thanksgiving in the exordium of an

ᵏ συνειδήσει, ὡς ¹ ἀδιάλειπτον ᵐ ἔχω τὴν περὶ σοῦ ᵐ ⁿ μνείαν ἐν ταῖς ¹ Rom. ix. 2, not LXX.
δεήσεσίν μου νυκτὸς καὶ ἡμέρας, 4. ° ἐπιποθῶν ° σε ° ἰδεῖν, ᵖ μεμνη- m 1 Thess. iii. 6.
μένος σου τῶν δακρύων, ἵνα χαρᾶς ᑫ πληρωθῶ, 5. ʳ ὑπόμνησιν λαβὼν ¹ n Rom. i. 9. Eph. i. 16, Phil. i. 3;

1 Thess. i. 2, iii. 6, Philem. 4.　　o Rom. i. 11, Phil. ii. 26, 1 Thess. iii. 6.　　p 1 Cor. xi. 2, Matt.
(3), Luke (6), John (3), Acts (2), Heb. (4, of which 3 are O.T.), 2 Pet. (1), Jude (1), Rev. (1).　　q Here
only in Pastorals.　　r Ps. lxx. (lxxi.) 6, Wisd. xvi. 11, 2 Macc. vi. 17, 2 Pet. i. 13, iii. 1 only.

¹ λαμβάνων ℵᶜDKL.

---

epistle is usually prefaced by St. Paul with εὐχαριστῶ (Rom. i. 8, 1 Cor. i. 4, Phil. i. 3, Philem. 4; εὐχαριστοῦμεν Col. i. 3, 1 Thess. i. 2; οὐ παύομαι εὐχαριστῶν, Eph. i. 16; εὐχαριστεῖν ὀφείλομεν, 2 Thess. i. 3). A comparison of these passages makes it evident that χάριν ἔχω is to be connected with ὑπόμνησιν λαβών, κ.τ.λ.; ὡς ἀδιάλειπτον—πληρωθῶ being a parenthetical account of St. Paul's state of mind about his absent friend, while μεμνημένος—δακρύων is also a parenthetical clause. The thanksgiving is for the grace of God given to Timothy (cf. esp. 1 Cor. i. 4; 1 Thess. i. 2; 2 Thess. i. 3); and the expression of thankfulness is called forth whenever St. Paul calls him to mind, unceasingly in fact.　The use of χάριν ἔχω in 1 Tim. i. 12 is not a parallel case to this.　The phrase is quoted from the papyri by Dean Armitage Robinson, *Ephesians*, p. 283.

ᾦ λατρεύω ἀπὸ προγόνων κ.τ.λ.: Two thoughts are in St. Paul's mind: (a) the inheritance of his religious consciousness from his forefathers, and (b) the continuity of the revelation of God; the same light in the New Covenant as in the Old, only far brighter.

If St. Paul had been asked, When did you first serve God? he would have answered, Even before God separated me from my mother's womb for His service. St. Paul was conscious that he was the result of generations of God-fearing people.　His inborn, natural instincts were all towards the service of God.　(See Acts xxii. 3, xxiv. 14; Rom. xi. 1; 2 Cor. xi. 22; Phil. iii. 5).

Moreover St. Paul always maintained that the Gospel was the divinely ordained sequel of Judaism; not a new religion, but the fulfilment of "the promise made of God unto our fathers" (Acts xxvi. 6; see also xxiii. 6, xxiv. 14).

ἐν καθαρᾷ συνειδήσει: Compare the claim he makes, Acts xxiii. 1, xxiv. 16; 1 Cor. iv. 4; 2 Cor. i. 12; 1 Thess. ii. 10; and for the language here see note on 1 Tim. i. 5.　ὡς is best rendered *as*

(Winer-Moulton, *Gram.* p. 561, where Matt. vi. 12, Gal. vi. 10 are cited in illustration).　The ʳR.V. *how* (so Alf.) implies that the cause for thankfulness is the unceasing nature of St. Paul's remembrance of Timothy; the A.V. *that* (*quod*, Vulg.) refers the cause to the remembrance itself. Rom. i. 9 is not a parallel instance of ὡς.

ἀδιάλειπτον—δεήσεσίν μου: A regular epistolary formula, as is evidenced by the papyri; though no doubt in St. Paul's case it corresponded to reality. See his use of it in reff. and Dean Armitage Robinson, *Ephesians*, pp. 37 *sq.*, 275 *sqq.* esp. p. 279, *sq.* on the formula μνείαν ποιεῖσθαι, from which this passage is a remarkable variation.

νυκτὸς καὶ ἡμέρας is connected by the R.V. with ἐπιποθῶν.　In 1 Thess. ii. 9, iii. 10, the phrase unquestionably is connected with what follows.　On the other hand, in 1 Tim. v. 5 it comes at the end of a clause; and in this place the A.V. connects it with ταῖς δεήσεσίν μου. This is certainly right, on the analogy of 1 Thess. iii. 10, where see Milligan's note. Alf. and Ell. connect it with ἀδιάλειπτον ἔχω.

ἐπιποθῶν σε ἰδεῖν: a Pauline expression.　See reff. ἰδεῖν is not expressed in 2 Cor. ix. 14, Phil. i. 8, ii. 26.

Ver. 4.　μεμνημένος—δακρύων: Parenthetical.　St. Paul's longing was made keener by his recollection of the tears Timothy had shed at their last parting. So Chrys. fixes the occasion.　We are reminded of the scene at Miletus, Acts xx. 37.　Bengel, comparing Acts xx. 19, thinks that reference is rather made to an habitual manifestation of strong emotion. At that time, and in that society, tears were allowed as a manifestation of emotion more freely than amongst modern men of the West.

χαρᾶς πληρωθῶ: For πληρόω with a genitive, cf. Rom. xv. 13, 14.　It takes a dat., Rom. i. 29, 2 Cor. vii. 4, cf. Eph. v. 18; an acc., Phil. i. 11, Col. i. 9.

Ver. 5. ὑπόμνησιν λαβών: *Having been reminded.* Not to be connected

s See 1 Tim. τῆς ἐν σοὶ ˢἀνυποκρίτου πίστεως, ἥτις ᵗἐνῴκησεν πρῶτον ἐν τῇ
i. 5.
t See note. ᵘμάμμη σου Λωΐδι καὶ τῇ μητρί σου Εὐνίκῃ, ᵛπέπεισμαι δὲ ὅτι καὶ
u 4 Macc.
xvi. 9   ἐν σοί. 6. ʷδι' ʷἣν ʷαἰτίαν ˣἀναμιμνήσκω σε ʸἀναζωπυρεῖν τὸ
only.
v Rom. viii.
    38, xiv. 14, xv. 14, ver. 12.   w Luke viii. 47, Acts xxii. 24, 2 Tim. i. 12, Tit. i. 13, Heb. ii. 11.
    x 1 Cor. iv. 17.   y Gen. xlv. 27, 1 Macc. xiii. 7 only.

with the clause immediately preceding,
as R.V.m. ὑπόμνησις, a *reminder, i.e.*,
an act of recollection specially excited
by a particular person or thing, thus
differs from ἀνάμνησις, which is self-
originated (so Ammonius Grammaticus,
quoted by Bengel). Ell. compares for
the thought Eph. i. 15. For this use of
λαμβάνω, *cf.* Rom. vii. 8, 11 (ἀφορμὴν
λ.), Heb. ii. 3 (ἀρχὴν λ.), xi. 29, 36
(πεῖραν λ.), 2 Pet. i. 9 (λήθην λ.). The
fact that St. Paul received this reminder
of Timothy's faith suggests that there
were other aspects of his conduct—possibly as an administrator—which were
not wholly satisfactory. His unfeigned
faith made up for much.

ἥτις ἐνῴκησεν κ.τ.λ.: ἐνοικέω is used
in Rom. viii. 11 and 2 Tim. i. 14 of the
indwelling of the Holy Spirit; and in
Col. iii. 16 of the Word of Christ. In 2
Cor. vi. 16, ἐνοικήσω is added in the
quotation from Lev. xxvi. 12 to ἐνπερι-
πατήσω. Tisch. and W.H. read
ἐνοικοῦσα for οἰκοῦσα in Rom. vii. 17.
Timothy's faith was hereditary as St.
Paul's was. πρῶτον does not mean
that Lois was the first of her family to
have faith, but that it dwelt in her, to St.
Paul's knowledge, before it dwelt in
Timothy. It is to be observed that it is
implied that the faith of God's people before Christ came is not different in kind
from faith after Christ has come.

μάμμη: an infantile equivalent in
early Greek for μήτηρ, is used in later
Greek for τήθη, *grandmother*. It occurs,
e.g., in 4 Macc. xvi. 9, οὐκ ὄψομαι ὑμῶν
τέκνα, οὐδὲ μάμμη κληθεῖσα μακαρισθή-
σομαι. See also Moulton and Milligan,
Expositor, vii., vii. 561.

Λωΐδι: Since Timothy's father was a
Greek, and his mother a Jewess (Acts
xvi. 1), we may conclude that Lois was
the mother of Eunice (see art. in Hastings' *D. B.*).

Εὐνίκῃ: See art. in Hastings' *D. B.*,
where Lock notes that the curious reading of cursive 25 in Acts xvi. 1, υἱὸς
γυναικός τινος Ἰουδαίας χήρας, and the
substitution of χήρας for Ἰουδαίας in
Gig., fuld. "may embody a tradition of
her widowhood".

πέπεισμαι: The other examples of St.

Paul's use of this word (see reff.) give no
support to the notion of Thdrt. (followed
by Alf.) that πέπεισμαι here has the
force of our *I am sure, I am certain*,
when we wish to hint gently that we
desire reassurance on the point about
which we express our certainty. In all
the places in which St. Paul uses
πέπεισμαι he is anxious to leave no
doubt as to his own certitude. Nevertheless, in this case, it was quite possible
for him to be perfectly certain that unfeigned faith animated Timothy, and at
the same time to have misgivings (ver. 7)
as to Timothy's moral courage in dealing with men. We supply ἐνοικεῖ after
σοί.

Ver. 6. δι' ἣν αἰτίαν: not so much
"because I am persuaded of thine unfeigned faith" (Theoph., Thdrt.), as,
"because this faith does of a surety
dwell in thee". We are most fruitfully
stimulated to noble action, not when we
know other people think well of us, but
when their good opinion makes us recognise the gifts to us of God's grace. Faith,
as well as salvation, is the gift of God,
Eph. ii. 8. Except in this phrase (see
reff. and Acts xxviii. 20), αἰτία is not
found elsewhere in Paul. It is common
in Matt., Mark, John, and Acts.

ἀναζωπυρεῖν: In both places cited
in reff.—the only occurrences in the
Greek Bible—the verb is intransitive:
his, or *their, spirit revived*. Chrys. well
compares with the image suggested by
ἀναζωπυρεῖν ("stir into flame,") "quench
not the Spirit," 1 Thess. v. 19, where by
"the Spirit" is meant His charismatic
manifestations of every kind. It is interesting to note in this connexion that
ἀναζωπυρεῖν φαντασίας is opposed to
σβεννύναι in M. Antoninus, vii. 2 (quoted
by Wetstein).

τὸ χάρισμα τοῦ θεοῦ: This expression
refers to the salvation of the soul by
God's grace, in Rom. vi. 23, xi. 29. The
narrower signification, as here, of a gift
given to us to use to God's glory is χάρισμα ἐκ θεοῦ, 1 Cor. vii. 7, or more usually
simply χάρισμα. The particular nature
of the gift must be determined by the
context. In this case it was a charisma
that was exercised in a spirit not of fear-

ᵃχάρισμα ᵃτοῦ ᵃΘεοῦ ὅ ἐστιν ἐν σοὶ διὰ τῆς ᵃἐπιθέσεως ᵃτῶν z See 1 Tim.
ᵃχειρῶν μου· 7. οὐ γὰρ ἔδωκεν ἡμῖν ὁ Θεὸς πνεῦμα ᵇδειλίας,¹ ἀλλὰ
δυνάμεως καὶ ἀγάπης καὶ ᶜσωφρονισμοῦ. 8. Μὴ οὖν ᵈἐπαισχυνθῇς
τὸ ᵉμαρτύριον ᶠτοῦ ᶠΚυρίου ᶠἡμῶν μηδὲ ἐμὲ τὸν ᵍδέσμιον αὐτοῦ·

iv. 14, and
note here.
a See 1 Tim.
iv. 14.
b Here only,
N.T.
c Here only,
not LXX,

d Mark viii. 38=Luke ix. 26, Rom. i. 16, 2 Tim. i. 16, Heb. xi. 16, cf. ver. 12.   e See 1 Tim. ii. 6.
See 1 Tim. i. 14.   g See note.

¹ δουλείας 238, two others, Didymus, Clem. Al., Chrys., by a confused recollection of Rom. viii. 15.

fulness. We can scarcely be wrong,
then, if we suppose the charisma of
administration and rule to be in St.
Paul's mind rather than "the work of an
evangelist" (ch. iv. 5). So Chrys., "for
presiding over the Church, for the working of miracles, and for every service".

διὰ τῆς ἐπιθέσεως—μου: See note on
1 Tim. iv. 14, where it is pointed out
that we have no right to assume that
hands were laid on Timothy once only.
Thus Acts ix. 17 and xiii. 3 are two such
occasions in St. Paul's spiritual life.
There may have been others.

Ver. 7. οὐ γὰρ ἔδωκεν ἡμῖν: The γὰρ
connects this statement with the exhortation preceding in such a way as to suggest that God's gift "to us" of a spirit
of power is in the same order of being
as the charisma imparted to Timothy by
the laying on of St. Paul's hands. The
question is, then, To whom is reference
made in ἡμῖν? We can only reply, The
Christian Society, represented by the
apostles on the Day of Pentecost. (The
aor. ἔδωκεν points to a definite occasion).
Then it was that the Church began to
receive the power, δύναμις, which had
been promised (Luke xxiv. 49; Acts i. 8)
by the Lord, and realised by the apostles
collectively (Acts iv. 33 ; 1 Cor. iv. 20, v.
4), and individually (Acts vi. 8 ; 1 Cor. ii.
4 ; 2 Cor. vi. 7, xii. 9). Whatever special
charismata are bestowed on the ministers
of the Church at ordination, they are a
part of the general stream of the Pentecostal gift which is always being poured
out by the ascended Lord.

πνεῦμα δειλίας: It is simplest to take
πνεῦμα here as a comprehensive equivalent to χάρισμα, as in 1 Cor. xiv. 12,
ζηλωταί ἐστε πνευμάτων. God did not
infuse into us fearfulness, etc. The gen.
after πνεῦμα, in this and similar cases,
Rom. viii. 15 (δουλείας, υἱοθεσίας), xi. 8
(κατανύξεως), 1 Cor. iv. 21, Gal. vi. 1
(πραΰτητος), 2 Cor. iv. 13 (πίστεως),
Eph. i. 17 (σοφίας, κ.τ.λ.), expresses the
prominent idea, the term πνεῦμα adds
the notion that the quality spoken of is

not self-originated. The personal Holy
Spirit is not meant unless the context
names Him unambiguously, as in Eph.
i. 13.

δειλία: fearfulness, timidity, timor.
This is the right word here, as δουλείας is
the right word in Rom.viii.15. It is curious
that in Lev. xxvi. 36, where B has δουλείαν
A &c. have δειλίαν. See apparat. crit.
There was an element of δειλία in
Timothy's natural disposition which must
have been prejudicial to his efficiency as
a Church ruler. For that position is
needed (a) force of character, which if
not natural may be inspired by consciousness of a divine appointment, (b) love,
which is not softness, and (c) self-disci-
pline, which is opposed to all easy self-
indulgence which issues in laxity of
administration. σωφρονισμοῦ:sobrietatis.
Better active, as R.V., discipline, first of
self, then of others. See Blass, Grammar, p. 61.

Vv. 8–ii. 2. The leading thoughts in
this section are (a) the Day of reward
and judgment which is surely coming
(12, 18), (b) the unreasonableness therefore of cowardly shame (8, 12, 16), and
(c) the necessity that Timothy should
guard the deposit and hand it on (14-
ii. 2).

Be not ashamed, therefore, of the Gospel to which our Lord was not ashamed
to testify; nor be ashamed of me, who
am in prison because of testimony borne
to Him and it. Share our sufferings in
the strength given by God, whose power
is displayed in the Gospel of life of which
I was appointed a preacher. This is the
direct cause of my present lot; but I am
not ashamed; for I know the power of
Him to whom I have committed myself
in trust. Do you imitate His faithfulness:
guard the deposit committed to you. I
am not asking you to do more than some
others have done. You know Onesiphorus and his work as well as I do.
When all turned their backs on me, he
was not ashamed to make inquiries for
me; and, finding me in prison, he con-

h 2 Tim. ii. 3, not LXX.
i Rom. viii. 28, ix. 11, Eph. i. 11, iii. 11.

ἀλλὰ ʰσυνκακοπάθησον τῷ εὐαγγελίῳ κατὰ δύναμιν Θεοῦ, 9. τοῦ
σώσαντος ἡμᾶς καὶ καλέσαντος κλήσει ἁγίᾳ, οὐ κατὰ τὰ ἔργα ἡμῶν,
ἀλλὰ κατὰ ἰδίαν ˡπρόθεσιν καὶ χάριν τὴν δοθεῖσαν ἡμῖν ἐν Χριστῷ

stantly cheered me by his visits. May God bless him and his! Do you, then, welcome the strengthening grace of Christ, and provide for a succession of faithful teachers to preserve intact the sacred deposit of the faith.

Ver. 8. μὴ οὖν ἐπαισχυνθῇς: The Saying of Jesus (Mark viii. 38 = Luke ix. 26) was probably in St. Paul's mind. He alludes to it again, ii. 12. The aor. subj. with μὴ forbids the supposition that Timothy had actually done what St. Paul warns him against doing (Winer-Moulton, *Grammar*, p. 628, and J. H. Moulton, *Grammar*, vol. i. p. 122 *sq.*). See note on 1 Tim. iv. 14. Personal appeals are a feature of this epistle *cf.* ver. 13, ii. 3, 15, iii. 14, iv. 1, 2, 5.

τὸ μαρτύριον τ. Κυρίου: *Testimony borne by our Lord*, His words, His ethical and spiritual teaching, by which Christianity has influenced the ideals and practice of society. The gen. after μαρτύριον is best taken as subjective. See 1 Cor. i. 6, ii. 1; 2 Thess. i. 10.

τοῦ Κυρίου ἡμῶν: See note on 1 Tim. i. 14.

ἐμὲ τὸν δέσμιον αὐτοῦ: This does not mean *one made prisoner by the Lord*, but *one who belongs to the Lord and is a prisoner for His sake*. There is nothing figurative about δέσμιος. St. Paul calls himself ὁ δέσμ. τ. Χρ. Ἰησ. in Eph. iii. 1, δέσμ. Χρ. Ἰησ. Philem. 1 and 9. The idea is more clearly expressed in ὁ δέσμ. ἐν Κυρίῳ Eph. iv. 1. He is a prisoner; he is also "in Christ". The expression also suggests the thought that his earthly imprisonment is ordered by the Lord, not by man. The present captivity is alluded to again in ver. 16 and ii. 9. It is not the same figure as in 2 Cor. ii. 14, "God which always leadeth us in triumph in Christ" as His captives. See Lightfoot on Col. ii. 15.

συνκακοπάθησον τῷ εὐαγγελίῳ: *Join us [the Lord and me] in our sufferings for the Gospel's sake.* More than once in this epistle St. Paul declares that he is suffering (πάσχω, ver. 12; κακοπαθῶ, ii. 9). He has said, "Be not ashamed . . . of me"; but he has just coupled the testimony of the Lord with his own; and further on (ii. 8) Jesus Christ is noted as the great illustration of the law, "No cross, no crown". See note there.

best then to give a wider reference than μοι to the συν in συνκακοπάθ. The R.V., *Suffer hardship with the gospel* is needlessly harsh. The dat. τῷ εὐαγγελίῳ is the *dativus commodi*.

κατὰ δύναμιν Θεοῦ must be connected with συνκακοπάθ.; and this suggests that the power of God here means *power given by God*, as in 2 Cor. vi. 7, 1 Pet. i. 5, "the power that worketh in us" (Eph. iii. 20), the assured possession of which would brace Timothy to suffer hardship. Alf. and Ell., following Bengel, take it subjectively: *the power of God displayed in our salvation* (as in Rom. i. 16; 1 Cor. i. 18, 24, ii. 5; 2 Cor. xiii. 4). But St. Paul could scarcely exhort Timothy to display a degree of fortitude comparable to God's active power. The next verse, τοῦ σώσαντος, κ.τ.λ., is not a detailed description of God's power to save, but a recalling of the fact that Timothy had actually experienced God's saving grace in the past. This consideration would stimulate Timothy to play the man.

Ver. 9. τοῦ σώσαντος, κ.τ.λ.: The connexion, as has been just remarked, is that our recognition at our baptism of God's saving and calling grace—He saved us and called us at a definite point of time (aor.)—ought to strengthen our faith in the continuance in the future of His gifts of power to us. On the insistence in this group of epistles on God's saving grace, see notes on 1 Tim. i. 1, ii. 4.

καλέσαντος κλήσει ἁγίᾳ: *To a holy calling, i.e.*, to a life of holiness, is less ambiguous than *with a holy calling*, which might mean "a calling uttered by a Holy One," or "in holy language". κλῆσις does not here mean *the invitation* (as in Rom. xi. 29), but, when qualified as here by an adj., it means the condition into which, or the purpose for which, we have been called (so ἡ ἄνω κλ., Phil. iii. 14, ἐπουράνιος κλ., Heb. iii. 1; and *cf.* 1 Cor. vii. 20). We have been "called to be saints," Rom. i. 7, "called into the fellowship of God's Son," 1 Cor. i. 9.

οὐ κατὰ τὰ ἔργα: The sentiment is more clearly expressed in Tit. iii. 5, οὐκ ἐξ ἔργων . . . ἃ ἐποιήσαμεν ἡμεῖς. There is an echo in both places of the controversy, now over, concerning works and grace. Perhaps κατά is used in this

Ἰησοῦ [k]πρὸ [k]χρόνων [k]αἰωνίων, 10. [l]φανερωθεῖσαν δὲ νῦν διὰ τῆς [m]ἐπιφανείας [n]τοῦ [n]σωτῆρος [n]ἡμῶν [n]Χριστοῦ [n]Ἰησοῦ,[1] [o]καταργήσαντος μὲν τὸν [o]θάνατον [p]φωτίσαντος δὲ ζωὴν καὶ [q]ἀφθαρσίαν διὰ τοῦ εὐαγγελίου, 11. [r]εἰς [s]ὃ [s]ἐτέθην [s]ἐγὼ [s]κῆρυξ [r]καὶ ἀπόστολος καὶ [r]διδάσκαλος.[2] 12. [t]δι᾽ [u]ἣν [u]αἰτίαν καὶ ταῦτα [t]πάσχω· ἀλλ᾽ οὐκ [u]ἐπαισχύνομαι· οἶδα γὰρ ᾧ πεπίστευκα, καὶ [v]πέπεισμαι ὅτι [w]δυνατός [w]ἐστιν τὴν [x]παραθήκην μου [x]φυλάξαι εἰς [y]ἐκείνην [y]τὴν

k Tit. i. 2, cf. Rom. xvi. 25.
l See note on 1 Tim. iii. 16.
m See 1 Tim. vi. 14.
n Tit. i. 4, ii. 13, iii. 6 (?).
o 1 Cor. xv. 26, Heb. ii. 14.

p 1 Cor. iv. 5, Eph. iii. 9.   q Wisd. (2), 4 Macc. (2), Rom. ii. 7, 1 Cor. xv. 42, 50, 53, 54, Eph. vi. 24.
r See 1 Tim. ii. 7.   s See ver. 6.   t Here only in Pastorals.   u Ps. cxviii. (cxix.) 6, cf. ver. 8.
v See ver. 5.   w Luke xiv. 31, Rom. iv. 21, xi. 23, Tit. i. 9, cf. Heb. xi. 19, Jas. iii. 2.   x See
1 Tim. vi. 20.   y 2 Thess. i. 10, 2 Tim. i. 18, iv. 8.

[1] So אֿ*AD*, d, e, sah.; Ἰησ. Χριστ. אֿcCDcFGKLP, all cursives, f, g, vg., go., boh., syrr., arm.

[2] Add ἐθνῶν (from 1 Tim. ii. 7), all except אֿ*A, 17.

clause to mark more vividly the antithesis to the next, κατὰ ἰδ. πρόθ., in which its use is more normal. See Eph. ii. 8, οὐκ ἐξ ὑμῶν, θεοῦ τὸ δῶρον.

ἀλλὰ κατὰ ἰδίαν πρόθεσιν, κ.τ.λ.: The grace in which the divine purpose for man expresses itself was given to mankind before times eternal; mankind, sons of God, being summed up, concentrated, in the Son of God, whom we know now as Christ Jesus. In Him was present, germ-wise, redeemed humanity, to be realised in races and individuals in succeeding ages.

We have here the same teaching about the Church and Christ as is more fully given in Ephesians and Colossians (see especially Eph. i. 4). In Rom. xvi. 25 the antithesis between a reality veiled in the past and now unveiled, or manifested, is expressed in language very similar to that of the passage before us: κατὰ ἀποκάλυψιν μυστηρίου χρόνοις αἰωνίοις σεσιγημένου φανερωθέντος δὲ νῦν.

πρὸ χρόνων αἰωνίων: expresses the notion of that which is anterior to the most remote period in the past conceivable by any imagination that man knows of.

Ver. 10. φανερωθεῖσαν: See note on 1 Tim. iii. 16. Bengel calls attention to the fit juxtaposition of illustria verba: φανερωθεῖσαν, ἐπιφανείας, φωτίσαντος.

διὰ τῆς ἐπιφανείας, κ.τ.λ.: See on 1 Tim. vi. 14. The ἐπιφάνεια here must not be referred to the Incarnation, considered as having taken place at a particular moment in time. It includes it; the ἐπιφάνεια began then; and will be continued, becoming ever brighter and clearer, until its consummation, to which the term ἐπιφάνεια is elsewhere restricted.

καταργήσαντος: We cannot, because of the absence of an article before the participles, safely translate, when he brought to nought, rather than, who brought to nought. Abolished does not express the truth. Christians all "taste of death" as their Master did (John viii. 52, Heb. ii. 9), though they do not "see" it; and they are confident that they too will be "saved out of death" (Heb. v. 7). Death for them has lost its sting (Heb. ii. 14, 15). It need not cause any difficulty that here the undoing of death is spoken of as past, whereas in 1 Cor. xv. 26, 54, it is "the last enemy that shall be abolished" (see Rev. xx. 14). We have a parallel in John xvi. 11, "The prince of this world hath been judged".

τὸν θάνατον: Alf., following Bengel, sees a special force in the art.—"as if he had said Orcum illum".

φωτίσαντος: To be connected with διὰ τοῦ εὐαγγελίου. The Gospel is that by which the presence of Christ, the light, is apprehended. That light does not create life and incorruption: it displays them.

ζωὴν καὶ ἀφθαρσίαν: Immortality or Incorruption defines the life more clearly.

Ver. 11. εἰς ὃ ἐτέθην, κ.τ.λ.: See 1 Tim. ii. 7, where these words are also found, and the note on 1 Tim. i. 11.

Ver. 12. δι᾽ ἣν αἰτίαν: i.e., because I am a preacher of the Gospel. Cf. Gal. v. 11.

οὐκ ἐπαισχύνομαι: Non confundor. I am not disappointed of my hope, as in ref.

πεπίστευκα . . . πέπεισμαι: The perfects have their usual force. For πέπεισμαι see Rom. viii. 38 and note on ver. 5.

τὴν παραθήκην μου is best taken as that which I have deposited for safe

z See 1 Tim. ^y ἡμέραν.   13.   ^{z z}Ὑποτύπωσιν ἔχε ^aὑγιαινόντων ^aλόγων ὧν παρ'
i. 16.
a See 1 Tim. ἐμοῦ ἤκουσας ἐν ^bπίστει ^bκαὶ ^bἀγάπῃ ^bτῇ ^bἐν ^bΧριστῷ ^bἸησοῦ.
vi. 3.
b 1 Tim. i.   14.   τὴν καλὴν ^cπαραθήκην ¹ ^{c d}φύλαξον διὰ Πνεύματος Ἁγίου τοῦ
14.
c See 1 Tim. ^eἐνοικοῦντος ἐν ἡμῖν.   15.   Οἶδας τοῦτο ὅτι ^fἀπεστράφησάν με
vi. 20.
d See 1 Tim.
v. 21.   e Rom. viii. 11.   f Matt. v. 42, 2 Tim. iv. 4, Tit. i. 14, Heb. xii. 25.

¹ παρακαταθήκην 47, many others.

keeping. Cf. the story of St. John and
the robber from Clem. Alex. *Quis Dives,*
§ 42, quoted by Eus. *H. E.* iii. 23, τὴν
παρακαταθήκην ἀπόδος ἡμῖν. Here it
means "my soul" or "myself," *cf.* Ps.
xxx. (xxxi.) 6, εἰς χεῖράς σου παραθήσο-
μαι τὸ πνεῦμά μου, Luke xxiii. 46, 1 Pet.
iv. 19, 1 Thess. v. 23. This explanation of παραθήκην harmonises best with
ἐπαισχύνομαι, πεπίστευκα, and φυλάξαι.
The whole verse has a purely personal
reference. Nothing but a desire to give
παραθήκη the same meaning wherever
it occurs (1 Tim. vi. 20, *q.v.*; 2 Tim. i. 14)
could have made Chrys. explain it here
as "the faith, the preaching of the Gospel". So R.V.m., *that which he hath
committed unto me.* "Paulus, decessui
proximus, duo deposita habebat : alterum
Domino, alterum Timotheo committendum," Bengel. This exegesis compels
us to refer ᾧ to God the Father.
εἰς ἐκείνην τὴν ἡμέραν: The day of
judgment and award, 1 Cor. iii. 13.
Ver. 13. ὑποτύπωσιν ἔχε: A resumption of the exhortation which was broken
off in ver. 9. This command is strictly
parallel to that which follows : ὑποτ.
ὑγιαιν.—ἤκουσας corresponds to, and
is the external expression of, τὴν καλ.
παραθήκην; ἔχε corresponds to φύλαξον;
and ἐν πίστει—'Ιησοῦ to διὰ—ἡμῖν.
ὑποτύπωσιν ὑγιαινόντων λόγων: The
gen. is that of apposition : *a pattern,
sc.* of faith, *expressed in sound words.*
The phrase marks an advance on the
μόρφωσις τῆς γνώσεως (Rom. ii. 20) or
μόρφ. εὐσεβείας (2 Tim. iii. 5). It happily suggests the power of expansion
latent in the simplest and most primitive
dogmatic formulas of the Christian faith.
ἔχε has the same strengthened signification as in 1 Tim. i. 19, where see note.
ὑγιαινόντων λόγων: See note on 1
Tim. i. 10.
ὧν . . . ἤκουσας: Alf. notes that the
use of ὧν rather than ἣν shows that
ὑγιαιν. λόγ. and not ὑποτύπ. is the chief
thing in St. Paul's mind. It is obvious
that Timothy could not have *heard* the
ὑποτύπωσις, which is a concept of the

mind expressed in many sound words
heard on various occasions. As to the
translation, von Soden agrees with Hort,
who insists on "the order, the absence
of τὴν, and the use of ἔχε" as compelling
us to render, "Hold as a pattern," etc.
This rendering would favour Hort's conjecture that "ΩΝ is a primitive corruption for ΟΝ," *i.e.*, "Hold as a pattern
of sound words the word which thou hast
heard," etc. But the absence of the
article is such a marked feature in the
Pastorals that no argument can be based
on it here.
Bengel calls attention to the change
in order in ii. 2. Here, παρ' ἐμοῦ ἤκουσας, the emphasis being on St. Paul's
personal authority; there, ἤκουσας παρ'
ἐμοῦ, because of the antithesis between
ἤκουσας and παράθου.
ἐν πίστει, κ.τ.λ.: See note on 1 Tim.
i. 14. This clause must be joined with
ἔχε, not with ἤκουσας, nor with ὑγιαιν.
λόγ. only : *as given in faith,* etc. (von
Soden),
Ver. 14. τὴν καλὴν παραθήκην: The
faith, which is a ὑποτύπωσις in relation
to the growing apprehension of it by the
Church, is a παραθήκη, *deposit,* in the
case of each individual. On the constant
epithet καλός see 1 Tim. i. 18, and on
παραθήκη 1 Tim. vi. 20. There is a
special force in καλήν here, as distinguishing the precious faith from τὴν
παραθήκην μου of ver. 12.
φύλαξον διὰ Πνεύματος Ἁγίου: φυλάσσειν is more than ἔχειν: it implies here
final perseverance; and that can only be
attained through the Holy Spirit. God
must co-operate with man, if man's
efforts are to be successful. *Cf.* "Work
out your own salvation . . . for it is God
which worketh in you" (Phil. ii. 12, 13).
Πνεύματος Ἁγίου: This verse and Tit.
iii. 5 are the only places in the Pastorals
in which the Holy Spirit is mentioned.
Ver. 15. οἶδας τοῦτο: There is a personal appeal for loyalty in this reminder.
The whole paragraph, with its examples
cited of disloyalty and loyalty, was intended as an object lesson to Timothy.

πάντες οἱ ἐν τῇ Ἀσίᾳ· ὧν ἐστιν Φύγελος καὶ Ἑρμογένης.   16. ᵍδώῃ g Deut. xiii.
17 (18),
ᵍ ἔλεος ὁ Κύριος τῷ Ὀνησιφόρου οἴκῳ· ὅτι πολλάκις με ʰ ἀνέψυξεν Josh. xi.
20, Isa.
καὶ τὴν ¹ἀλυσίν μου οὐκ ᵏἐπαισχύνθη,¹ 17. ἀλλὰ γενόμενος ἐν xlvii. 6,
Jer. xvi.
Ῥώμῃ ¹σπουδαίως² ἐζήτησέν με καὶ εὗρεν——18. δώῃ αὐτῷ ὁ 13, xlix.
(xlii.) 12,
Mic.

vii. 20.   h Here only, N.T.   i Eph. vi. 20.   k See ver. 8.   l Luke vii. 4, Phil. ii. 28, Tit. iii. 13.

¹ ἐπησχύνθη ℵ*K.   ² σπουδαιότερον DᶜKL; σπουδαιότερως A, two cursives.

ἀπεστράφησάν με: The reff., with the exception of chap. iv. 4, are parallel to this use of the verb.

πάντες must not be pressed: it is the sweeping assertion of depression. If it had been even approximately true, Timothy would have had no church to administer. On the other hand, something less serious than apostasy from the faith may be alluded to, such as personal neglect of the apostle (cf. iv. 16, πάντες με ἐγκατέλειπον, and the contrast of Onesiphorus' conduct with theirs in the next verse), a thing which to us who see St. Paul through the halo of centuries of veneration seems painfully hard to understand. But it is abundantly plain that apostles did not during their lifetime receive that universal and unquestioning reverence from their fellow-Christians which we would have antecedently supposed could not have been withheld from them. Cf. 3 John 9.

οἱ ἐν τῇ Ἀσίᾳ: Asia means the Roman province, which included Mysia, Lydia, Caria, great part of Phrygia, the Troad, and the islands off the coast.

This statement is most naturally explained of a defection in Asia of natives of Asia.. Plummer conjectures that St. Paul had applied by letter from Rome for help to some leading Asiatic Christians, and had been refused. Of course it is possible that St. Paul refers to something that had taken place in Rome (so Bengel, who compares chap. iv. 16). But all who are in Asia would be a strange way of referring to some Asiatics who had been in Rome and had returned to Asia; and though οἶδας τοῦτο is naturally understood as mentioning something of which Timothy had knowledge only by report, we cannot be sure that St. Paul is not here to distinguish οἶδας from γινώσκεις. Perhaps the defection had taken place during an absence of Timothy from Asia. Nothing else is known certainly of Phygelus and Hermogenes.

Ver. 16. δώῃ ἔλεος, κ.τ.λ.: δίδωμι ἔλεος, like εὑρίσκω ἔλεος, is a Hebraism. See reff. The correlative, λαμβάνω ἔλεος

occurs Heb. iv. 6. ποιεῖν ἔλεος μετά τινος (Luke i. 72, x. 37; Jas. ii. 13) is a similar phrase. Here, we should say, May God bless so and so. Ἔλεος does not correspond to any special sin.

τῷ Ὀν. οἴκῳ: This household is saluted in iv. 19. It is most natural to suppose that Onesiphorus himself was dead, both from this expression and from the pious wish in ver. 18. Prayer for living friends is normally and naturally in regard to objects which will be realised here in earth. The evidence of 2 Macc. xii. 44, 45, proves that an orthodox Jew of our Lord's time could have prayed for the dead. A full discussion of the question must embrace a consideration of the final cause of prayer, and of the nature of that which we call death. See reff. to recent literature on this subject in Milligan's art. Onesiphorus in Hastings' D. B.

ἀνέψυξεν: The comprehensive term refresh expresses the notion admirably. They are "the blessed of God the Father" to whom the King shall say, "I was in prison, and ye came unto me" (Matt. xxv. 36. See Heb. x. 34, xiii. 3). For St. Paul's appreciation of the pleasures of friendly intercourse, see Rom. xv. 32, 1 Cor. xvi. 18, 2 Cor. vii. 13, Philem. 7, 20.

ἐπαισχύνθη: For other examples of the absence of the temporal augment cf. Luke xiii. 13 (ἀνορθώθη A B D, etc.); xxiv. 27, John vi. 18, Acts ii. 25, Rom. ix. 29 (ὁμοιώθημεν A F G L P).

Ver. 17. γενόμενος ἐν Ῥώμῃ: The reference is most likely to the apostle's first Roman imprisonment, Eph. vi. 20. Whichever it was, πολλάκις implies that it had lasted some time.

Ver. 18. It is immaterial whether we explain ὁ Κύριος, in this verse, of God the Father, the source of judgment, or of God the Son, the instrument of judgment. It is far-fetched to suppose that the repeated Κύριος . . . Κυρίου refer to different divine Persons. Huther's expl., followed by Alf., seems the best, that δώῃ ὁ Κύριος had become so completely a for-

m Gen. xix. Κύριος ᵐ εὑρεῖν ᵐ ἔλεος παρὰ Κυρίου¹ ἐν ⁿ ἐκείνῃ ⁿ τῇ ⁿ ἡμέρᾳ—καὶ
19, Num.
xi. 15, ὅσα ἐν Ἐφέσῳ ° διηκόνησεν, βέλτιον σὺ γινώσκεις.
Judg. vi.
17, Dan.   II. 1. Σὺ οὖν, ᵃ τέκνον μου, ᵇ ἐνδυναμοῦ ἐν τῇ χάριτι τῇ ἐν
LXX, iii.
39 (TH. Χριστῷ Ἰησοῦ· 2. καὶ ἃ ἤκουσας παρ' ἐμοῦ διὰ πολλῶν μαρτύρων
iii. 38), ix.
3. ταῦτα ᶜ παράθου πιστοῖς ἀνθρώποις οἵτινες ᵈ ἱκανοὶ ἔσονται καὶ
n See ver.
12.

o 1 Pet. i. 12, iv. 10, with acc.   a See 1 Tim. i. 2.   b See 1 Tim. i. 12.   c See 1 Tim. i. 18.
d 1 Cor. xv. 9, 2 Cor. ii. 16, iii. 5.

¹ θεῷ D*, d, e.

mula that the recurrence did not seem harsh.

καὶ ὅσα κ.τ.λ.: This clause is an afterthought.

διηκόνησεν: The verb is used with a perfectly general reference here, as in Heb. vi. 10.

βέλτιον: The comparative here is intensive or elative. See Blass, *Grammar*, pp. 33, 141, 142. Other examples are in 1 Tim. iii. 14 (Tisch.) and in the Received Text of ver. 17 of this chapter.

CHAPTER II.—Ver. 1. σύ: emphatic, as in 1 Tim. vi. 11 and ch. iii. 10; but the appeal is not primarily that Timothy should imitate Onesiphorus, or learn by the example of Phygelus and Hermogenes, but rather marks the intensity of the apostle's anxiety for the future conduct of Timothy in the Church; and similarly οὖν is resumptive of all the considerations and appeals for loyalty in chap. i.

τέκνον: See note on 1 Tim. i. 2.

ἐνδυναμοῦ ἐν, κ.τ.λ.: The thought is resumed from i. 8, 9, and expanded in vv. 3-13. The closest parallel is that in Eph. vi. 10, ἐνδυναμοῦσθε ἐν Κυρίῳ, κ.τ.λ. See note on 1 Tim. i. 12 and reff., esp. Rom. iv. 20, Phil. iv. 13. Although the verb is passive, as indicated in the R.V., those who are, or who are exhorted to be, strengthened are not merely passive recipients of an influence from without. The act of reception involves man's co-operation with God. Compare "Abide in me, and I in you" (John xv. 4). The perfection of God's power is conditioned by the weakness of man (2 Cor. xii. 9).

τῇ χάριτι τῇ ἐν Χρ. Ἰησ.: The two passages, 2 Cor. xii. 9, and Eph. vi. 10, alluded to in the last note, explain this. *Grace* here has its simplest theological meaning, as the divine help, the unmerited gift of assistance that comes from God.

Ver. 2. St. Paul is here contemplating an apostolical succession in respect of

teaching rather than of administration. It is natural that in the circumstances of the primitive Church the building up of converts in the faith should have occupied a larger place in the Christian consciousness than the functions of an official ministry; but the historical continuity of the ministry of order is of course involved in the direction here. St. Paul would have been surprised if any other conclusion had been drawn from his words. In any case, the Providence of God sees further than do His servants.

ἃ ἤκουσας παρ' ἐμοῦ: See note on i. 13.

διὰ πολλῶν μαρτύρων: not *per multos testes* (Vulg.), but *coram multis testibus* (Tert. *de Praescript.* 25). The usual Greek for "in the presence of witnesses" is ἐπὶ μαρτύρων; but διὰ θεῶν μαρτύρων is quoted from Plutarch (see Field, *in loc.*).

The διὰ is that of accompanying circumstances. The reference is to a solemn *traditio* of the essentials of the faith on the occasion of Timothy's ordination, rather than his baptism. The former reference seems clear from the parallel drawn between St. Paul's committal of the faith to Timothy and Timothy's committal of it to others. On the other hand, a comparison of 1 Tim. vi. 12 favours the view that this refers to a formal public instruction at baptism. Reasons have been already suggested against the identification of the laying-on of hands of 1 Tim. iv. 14 with that of 2 Tim. i. 6. Otherwise it would be natural to suppose that the *many witnesses* were the members of the presbytery who were joined with St. Paul in the ordination of Timothy. But there is no reason why the reference should be thus restricted. The action was a public one, "in the face of the Church". So Chrys., "Thou hast not heard in secret, nor apart, but in the presence of many, with all openness of speech". The view of Clem. Alex.

ἑτέρους διδάξαι. 3. ᵉΣυνκακοπάθησον¹ ὡς καλὸς ᶠστρατιώτης e See 2 Tim.
i. 8.
Χριστοῦ Ἰησοῦ.² 4. οὐδεὶς ᵍστρατευόμενος ʰἐμπλέκεται ταῖς τοῦ f Here only
in Paul.
ⁱβίου ᵏπραγματίαις, ἵνα τῷ ˡστρατολογήσαντι ἀρέσῃ. 5. ἐὰν δὲ g See 1 Tim.
i. 18.
καὶ ᵐἀθλῇ τις, οὐ ⁿστεφανοῦται ἐὰν μὴ °νομίμως ᵐἀθλήσῃ. 6. h 2 Pet. ii.
20 only,
τὸν κϙπιῶντα γεωργὸν δεῖ πρῶτον τῶν καρπῶν ᵖμεταλαμβάνειν. N.T.
i See 1 Tim.
ii. 2.

k Here only, N.T.   l Here only, not LXX.   m Here only, not LXX, cf. Heb. x. 32.   n Heb.
ii. 7, 9 only, N.T.   o See 1 Tim. i. 8.   p Acts. ii. 26, xxvii. 33, 34, Heb. vi. 7, xii. 10.

¹ σὺ οὖν κακοπάθ. CcDcKL, syrhcl-txt, go.   ² Ἰησ. Χριστ. DcKL, syrpesh.

(*Hypot.* vii. ed. Potter, ii. p. 1015) that the πολλοὶ μάρτυρες mean testimonies from the Law and the Prophets is only a curiosity of exegesis.

παράθου : See note on 1 Tim. 18.

πιστοῖς : *trustworthy*, carries on the figure of the faith as a deposit. It is possible, as Bengel suggests, that the injunctions in vv. 14-21 have reference to these ministers.

ἱκανοί : *qualified*. See reff. δυνατός, in Tit. i. 9, expresses capability as proved by experience.

Vv. 3-13. The condition of all success is toil; toil which may involve pain. Think of the price of a soldier's victory, the conditions of an athlete's crown, of a field-labourer's wage. Our Lord Jesus Himself, as man, is the great Exemplar of this law. I am another. This is a faithful saying; and therefore we sing, "We shall live with Him because we died with Him, etc.".

Ver. 3. συνκακοπάθησον : *Take thy part in suffering hardship* (R.V.m.). This general reference is better than to supply μοι, as R.V. See note on i. 8. στρατιώτης : *cf.* συνστρατιώτης, Phil. ii. 25, Philem. 2.

Ver. 4. στρατευόμενος : *militans Deo* (Vulg.). *Soldier*, in the sense of a person belonging to the army, not *soldier on service*, as R.V., which makes the same error in Luke iii. 14 marg. (See *Expositor*, vi., vii. 120).

ἐμπλέκεται : *implicat se* (Vulg.). The verb is used in a similar metaphor, 2 Pet. ii. 20, but in a more adverse sense than here. A soldier, who is bound to go anywhere and do any thing at the bidding of his captain, must have no ties of home or business. The implied counsel is the same as that given in 1 Cor. vii. 26-34, with its warnings against distraction between the possibly conflicting interests of the Lord and of this life. Note the use of ἀρέσκω in 1 Cor. vii. 32-34.

ἀρέσῃ : *that he may be of use to* (see Milligan on 1 Thess. ii. 4).

Ver. 5. The sequence of images here—the soldier, the athlete, the field-labourer—affords an interesting illustration of repetition due to association of ideas. The soldier and the field-labourer are combined in 1 Cor. ix. 7-10; the athlete appears in 1 Cor. ix. 24 *sqq.* And the present passage has light thrown upon it from the earlier epistle, in which the various figures are more fully developed.

The connexion between the thought of the soldier and the athlete lies in the word νομίμως (see note on 1 Tim. i. 8); and the exact force of νομίμως will appear from a reference to 1 Cor. ix. 25, "Every man that striveth in the games is temperate in all things". No one can be said to comply with the rules of the contest who has not undergone the usual preliminary training. One illustration from those cited by Wetstein will suffice, that from Galen, *comm. in Hippocr.* i. 15: οἱ γυμνασταὶ καὶ οἱ νομίμως ἀθλοῦντες, ἐπὶ μὲν τοῦ ἀρίστου τὸν ἄρτον μόνον ἐσθίουσιν, ἐπὶ δὲ τοῦ δείπνου τὸ κρέας.

Ver. 6. The difficulty in this verse is that the principle here laid down seems to be employed in 1 Cor. ix, 7, 9, as an argument from analogy in support of the liberty of Christian ministers to enjoy some temporal profit from their spiritual labours ; whereas here St. Paul is urging a temper of other-worldliness. It is sufficient to say that there is no practical inconsistency between the two passages ; "each man hath his own gift from God, one after this manner, and another after that ". There is a time to insist on one's liberty to "use the world," and there is a time to warn ourselves and others that self-repression is necessary to keep ourselves from "using it to the full". The main connexion here lies in the word κοπιῶντα, which is emphatic ; while πρῶτον,

q Mark xii. 7. νόει δ¹ λέγω· δώσει² γάρ σοι ὁ Κύριος �q σύνεσιν ἐν
33, Luke
ii. 47, 1   πᾶσιν. 8. ʳμνημόνευε Ἰησοῦν Χριστὸν ἐγηγερμένον ἐκ νεκρῶν, ἐκ
Cor. i. 19,
Eph.iii.4, σπέρματος Δαυείδ, ˢκατὰ ˢτὸ ˢεὐαγγέλιόν ˢμου· 9. ἐν ᾧ ᵗκακοπαθῶ
Col. i. 9,
ii. 2.   μέχρι ᵘδεσμῶν ὡς ᵛκακοῦργος· ἀλλὰ ὁ λόγος τοῦ Θεοῦ οὐ δέδεται.
r Matt. xvi.
9, 1 Thess.
ii. 9, Rev. xviii. 5 (with acc.).   s Rom. ii. 16, xvi. 25.   t Jonah iv. 10, 2 Tim. iv. 5, Jas. v. 13, only.
u Acts xx. 23, xxvi. 29, Phil. i. 7, 13, 14, 17, Col. iv. 18, Philem. 10, 13.   v Luke xxiii. 32, 33, 39.

¹ So ℵ*ACFgrGP, 17, g go., syrpesh; ἃ ℵcDKL, d, e, f, vg., boh., syrhcl, arm.
² δῴη CcKLP.

which is also emphatic, expresses in the illustration from the γεωργός the idea corresponding to τῷ στρατ. ἀρέσῃ, and to
στεφανοῦται in the others respectively.
The labourer receives his hire, no matter
how poor the crop may be : his wages are
the first charge on the field. *Cf.* γῆ . . .
τίκτουσα βοτάνην εὔθετον ἐκείνοις δι'
οὓς καὶ γεωργεῖται (Heb. vi. 7); his
reward is sure, but then he must really
labour. "The fruits" are the reward of
faithful labour in the Lord's vineyard,
the "well done!" heard from the Captain's lips, "the crown of glory that
fadeth not away". We must not press
all the details of an allegory.

Ver. 7. νόει δ λέγω: *Intellige quae dico*
(Vulg.), *Grasp the meaning*, cautionary
and encouraging, of these three similes.
Cf. "I speak as to wise men ; judge ye
what I say" (1 Cor. x. 15), and the use
of the verb in 1 Tim. i. 7.

δώσει, κ.τ.λ.: If you have not sufficient wisdom to follow my argument,
"ask of God, who giveth to all men liber-
ally" (Jas. i. 5).

μνημόνευε Ἰησοῦν Χριστὸν—Δαυείδ:
These words form rather the conclusion
of the preceding paragraph than the beginning of a new one. St. Paul in pressing home his lesson, passes from figures
of speech to the great concrete example
of suffering followed by glory. And as
he has, immediately before, been laying
stress on the certainty of reward, he gives
a prominent place to ἐγηγερμένον ἐκ
νεκρῶν. Jesus Christ, of the seed of
David, "Himself man" (1 Tim. ii. 5),
is the ideal soldier, athlete, and field-
labourer ; yet One who can be an example to us. It is not the resurrection
as a doctrinal fact (A.V.) that St. Paul
has in mind, but the resurrection as a
personal experience of Jesus Christ, the
reward He received, His being "crowned
with glory and honour, because of the
suffering of death" (Heb. ii. 9). It is
not τὸν Ἰησοῦν καὶ τὴν ἀνάστασιν (Acts
xvii. 18), but Ἰησοῦν ἐγηγερμένον, the

perfect (as in 1 Cor. xv. 4, 12, 13, 14, 16
17, 20) preserving the notion of the permanent significance of that personal experience of Jesus. In the other passage,
Rom. i. 3, in which St. Paul distinctly
alludes to our Lord's human ancestry,
the phrase τοῦ γενομένου ἐκ σπέρματος
Δαυείδ has a directly historical and polemical intention, as expressing and emphasising the human nature of Christ in
antithesis to His Divinity. Here ἐκ
σπερμ. Δ. merely expresses the fact of
His humanity. We cannot affirm with
certainty that the phrase has the Messianic import that *Son of David* has in
the Gospels.

κατὰ τὸ εὐαγγέλιόν μου: *The Gospel
preached by me.* See reff., and τὸ εὐ. τὸ
εὐαγγελισθὲν ὑπ' ἐμοῦ (Gal. i. 11 ; 1 Cor.
xv. 1). which of course is identical in
substance with τὸ εὐ. . . . ὃ ἐπιστεύθην
ἐγώ (1 Tim. i. 11). The verity both of
Christ's humanity and of His resurrection
was emphasised in the Gospel preached
by St. Paul. This is brought out by the
punctuation of R.V.

Ver. 9. ἐν ᾧ κακοπαθῶ: *in which
sphere of action, cf.* Rom. i. 9, 2 Cor. x.
14, Phil. iv. 2. The connexion seems to
be that St. Paul is now indicating that
he himself, in his degree, is an imitator
of Jesus Christ.

ὡς κακοῦργος (see reff.) : *malefactor*
(R.V.). *Evil doer* (A.V.) does not so
vividly express the notion of criminality
implied in the word. Ramsay notes that
the use of this word here marks "exactly
the tone of the Neronian period, and . . .
refers expressly to the *flagitia*, for which
the Christians were condemned under
Nero, and for which they were no longer
condemned in A.D. 112" (*Church in the
Roman Empire*, p. 249). Compare 1 Pet.
iv. 15.

ἀλλὰ—οὐ δέδεται: We have the same
contrast between the apostle's own restricted liberty and the unconfinable
range of the Gospel in Phil. i. 12, 14, and
2 Tim. iv. 17. There is no reference, as

10. διὰ τοῦτο πάντα ὑπομένω διὰ τοὺς ʷἐκλεκτούς, ἵνα καὶ αὐτοὶ ʷ See note.
σωτηρίας ˣτύχωσιν τῆς ἐν Χριστῷ Ἰησοῦ μετὰ ʸδόξης ʸ αἰωνίου.¹
11. ᶻπιστὸς ᶻὁ ᶻλόγος· εἰ γὰρ ᵃσυναπεθάνομεν, καὶ ᵇσυνζήσομεν·
12. εἰ ὑπομένομεν, καὶ ᶜσυνβασιλεύσομεν· εἰ ᵈἀρνησόμεθα,² κἀκεῖνος

x Luke xx.
35, Acts
xxiv. 3,
xxvi. 22,
xxvii. 3,
Heb. viii.
6, xi. 35.
y 1 Pet. v. 10.

z See 1 Tim. i. 15.   a Ecclus. xix. 10, Mark xiv. 31, 2 Cor. vii. 3 only.   b Rom. vi. 8,
2 Cor. vii. 3, not LXX.   c 1 Esd. viii. 26, 1 Cor. iv. 8 only.   d See 1 Tim. v. 8.

¹ οὐρανίου f, vg., syrhcl-mg, arm.   ² ἀρνούμεθα אcDKLP, d, e.

Chrys. supposes, to the liberty permitted to St. Paul to preach the kingdom of God in his prison, as during the first imprisonment (Acts xxviii. 30, 31). The clause here is a natural reflective parenthetical remark.

Ver. 10. διὰ τοῦτο: The knowledge that others had been, and were being, saved through his ministry was regarded by St. Paul as no small part of his reward. Thus, the Churches of Macedonia were his "crown," as well as his "joy" (Phil. iv. 1, 1 Thess. ii. 19). He had already in sight his "crown of righteousness". This consideration suggests that we should refer διὰ τοῦτο to what follows rather than to what immediately precedes (ὁ λόγος . . . δέδεται). So Alf., who cites in illustration Rom. iv. 16, 2 Cor. xiii. 10, 1 Tim. i. 16, Philem 15. On this view, we have completely displayed the conformity of Jesus Christ and of St. Paul to the conditions of success exemplified in the soldier, the athlete, and the field-labourer.

πάντα ὑπομένω: as Love does, 1 Cor. xiii. 7. Ellicott rightly points out that Christian endurance is active, not passive: pain is felt as pain, but is recognised as having a moral and spiritual purpose.

διὰ τοὺς ἐκλεκτούς: St. Paul was much sustained by the thought that his labours and sufferings were, in the providence of God, beneficial to others (2 Cor. i. 6, xii. 15; Eph. iii. 1, 13; Phil. ii. 17; Col. i. 24; Tit. i. 1). "The elect" are those who, in the providence of God's grace, are selected for spiritual privileges with a view directly to the salvation of others, as well as of themselves. The absolute phrase as here is found in Matt. xxiv. 22, 24 = Mark xiii. 20, 22; οἱ ἐκλεκτοὶ αὐτοῦ in Matt. xxiv. 31 = Mark xiii. 27 (?), Luke xviii. 7; ἐκλεκτοὶ θεοῦ in Rom. viii. 33, Col. iii. 12, Tit. i. 1; ὁ ἐκλεκτὸς ἐν Κυρίῳ in Rom. xvi. 13.

καὶ αὐτοί: they also (as well as I). It would be no Paradise to St. Paul "to live in Paradise alone". Compare his supreme expression of selflessness in Rom. ix. 3.

σωτηρίας μετὰ δόξης αἰωνίου: Salvation may be enjoyed in part in this life; it will be consummated in eternal glory. See ref., and 2 Cor. iv. 17.

Ver. 11. πιστὸς ὁ λόγος: The teaching or saying referred to is "the word of the cross" as set forth by simile and living example in the preceding verses, 4-11. So R.V.m. This is an exactly parallel case to 1 Tim. iv. 9. Here, as there, γάρ introduces a reinforcement of the teaching.

εἰ γὰρ συναπεθάνομεν, κ.τ.λ.: The presence of γάρ does not militate against the supposition that we have here a fragment of a Christian hymn. A quotation adduced in the course of an argument must be introduced by some inferential particle; see on 1 Tim. iv. 10. On the other hand, it is questionable if εἰ ἀρνησόμεθα, κ.τ.λ. is suitable in tone to a hymn; and St. Paul's prose constantly rises to rhythmical cadences, e.g., Rom. viii. 33 sqq., 1 Cor. xiii. We have here contrasted two crises, and two states in the spiritual life: συναπεθάνομεν and ἀρνησόμεθα point to definite acts at definite times; while ὑπομένομεν and ἀπιστοῦμεν indicate states of being, more or less prolonged.

εἰ συναπεθάνομεν καὶ συνζήσομεν: The two verbs are coupled also in 2 Cor. vii. 3; but the actual parallel in thought is found in Rom. vi. 4, 5, 8. We died (aor., R.V.) with Christ at our baptism (Rom. vi. 8; Col. iii. 3), which, as normally administered by immersion, symbolises our burial with Christ and our rising again with Him to newness of life (Rom. vi. 4; Col. ii. 12). The future, συνζήσομεν, must not be projected altogether into the resurrection life; it includes and is completed by that; and no doubt the prominent notion here is of the life to come; but here, and in Rom. vi. 8, it is implied that there is a beginning of eternal life even while we are in the flesh, viz. in that newness of life to which we are called, and for which we are enabled, in our baptism.

Ver. 12. εἰ ὑπομένομεν καὶ συνβασι-

e Tit. iii. 1,   ^d ἀρνήσεται ἡμᾶς · 13. εἰ ἀπιστοῦμεν, ἐκεῖνος πιστὸς μένει · ἀρνή-
John xiv.
26, 2 Pet.   σασθαι γὰρ ¹ ἑαυτὸν οὐ δύναται.
i. 12, Jude
5.   14. Ταῦτα ^e ὑπομίμνησκε, ^f διαμαρτυρόμενος ^g ἐνώπιον ^g τοῦ ^g Θεοῦ,²
f See 1 Tim.
v. 21.   μὴ ^h λογομαχεῖν,³ ἐπ' ⁴ οὐδὲν ⁱ χρήσιμον, ἐπὶ ^k καταστροφῇ τῶν
g See 1 Tim.
ii. 3.
h Here only, not LXX, cf. 1 Tim. vi. 4.   i Here only, N.T.   k 2 Pet. ii. 6 only, N.T.

¹ Om. γὰρ א^cK, d, e, vg., go., syrhcl, arm.

² So אCFG, 37, 67*, 80, 238, and about thirteen other cursives, f, g, boh., syrhcl-mg, arm.-ap.-Gb., Chrys., Thphyl., Amb., Pelag.; Κυρίου ADKLP, most cursives, d, e, vg., go., syrpesh et hcl-txt, arm.-ap.-Treg., Chrys., Euthal., Thdrt., Dam., Thphyl., Ambrst., Prim.

³ λογομάχει AC*, d, e, f, g, vg.   ⁴ εἰς א^cDKL.

λεύσομεν: See Matt. xxv. 34; Luke xxii. 28, 29; Acts xiv. 22; Rom. viii. 17; 2 Thess. i. 5; Rev. i. 6, xx. 4.

εἰ ἀρνησόμεθα, κ.τ.λ.: An echo of our Lord's teaching, Matt. x. 33. See also 2 Pet. ii. 1; Jude 4. "The *future* conveys the ethical possibility of the action" (Ell.)

Ver. 13. εἰ ἀπιστοῦμεν: It is reasonable to hold that the sense of ἀπιστέω in this place must be determined by the antithesis of πιστὸς μένει. Now πιστός, as applied to God, must mean *faithful* (Deut. vii. 9); one who "keepeth truth for ever" (Ps. cxlvi. 6; 2 Cor. i. 18; 1 Thess. v. 24; 2 Thess. iii. 3; Heb. x. 23, xi. 11). There is the same contrast in Rom. iii. 3, "Shall their want of faith (ἀπιστία) make of none effect the faithfulness (πίστιν) of God?" But while we render ἀπιστοῦμεν, with R.V., *are faithless*, we must remember that unreliability and disbelief in the truth were closely allied in St. Paul's conception of them.

ἀρνήσασθαι γὰρ—οὐ δύναται: Being essentially the unchangeable Truth, He cannot be false to His own nature, as we, when ἀπιστοῦμεν, are false to our better nature which has affinity with the Eternal. A lie in word, or unfaithfulness in act, is confessedly only an expedient to meet a temporary difficulty; it involves a disregard of the permanent element in our personality. The more a man realises the transitory nature of created things, and his own kinship with the Eternal, the more unnatural and unnecessary does falsity in word or deed appear to him. It is therefore inconceivable that God should lie (Num. xxiii. 19; 1 Sam. xv. 29; Mal. iii. 6; Tit. i. 2; Heb. vi. 18). The application of the clause here is not that "He will not break faith with us" (Alf.), but that the consideration of our powerlessness to affect the constancy

of God our Father should brace us up to exhibit moral courage, as being His "true children".

Vv. 14-26. Discourage the new false teaching by precept and example. There is no need, however, that you should despair of the Church. It is founded upon a rock, in spite of appearances. Take a broad view of the case: the Church is not the special apartment of the Master from which things unseemly are banished; it is a great House with places and utensils for every need of life. This great House differs from those of earth in that provision is made for the promotion of the utensils from the basest use to the Master's personal service.

Ver. 14. ταῦτα has special reference to the issues of life and death set out in vv. 11-13. There is no such prophylactic against striving about words as a serious endeavour to realise the relative importance of time and of eternity. "He to whom the eternal Word speaks is set at liberty from a multitude of opinions" (*De Imitatione Christi*, i. 3).

ὑπομίμνησκε: sc. αὐτούς, as in Tit. iii. 1.

διαμαρτυρόμενος: See on 1 Tim. v. 21.

ἐνώπιον τοῦ θεοῦ: It is an argument in favour of this reading that ἐνώπιον Κυρίου only occurs once in Paul (in a quotation), in 2 Cor. viii. 21.

λογομαχεῖν: See on 1 Tim. vi. 4.

ἐπ' οὐδὲν χρήσιμον and ἐπὶ καταστροφῇ τῶν ἀκουόντων are coordinate, and describe the negative and the positive results of λογομαχία. The subject of this λογομαχία is probably identical with that of the μάχαι νομικαί of Tit. iii. 9, which were "unprofitable and vain".

ἐπὶ καταστροφῇ, κ.τ.λ.: contrast λόγος ... ἀγαθὸς πρὸς οἰκοδομὴν τῆς χρείας, Eph. iv. 29; and compare the antithesis

ἀκουόντων. 15. [l]σπούδασον σεαυτὸν [m]δόκιμον [n]παραστῆσαι τῷ
Θεῷ, ἐργάτην [o]ἀνεπαίσχυντον, [p]ὀρθοτομοῦντα τὸν λόγον τῆς ἀληθείας.
16. τὰς δὲ [q]βεβήλους [q]κενοφωνίας [1] [r]περιίστασο· [st]ἐπὶ [st]πλεῖον

l 2 Tim iv. 9, 21, Tit. iii. 12, verb also Gal. (1), Eph. (1), 1 Thess. (1), Heb. (1), 2 Pet. (3). m Rom. xiv. 18, xvi. 10, 1 Cor. xi. 19, 2 Cor. x. 18, xiii. 7, Jas. i. 12. n Matt. xxvi. 53, Luke ii. 22, Acts i. 3, ix. 41, xxiii. 33, Rom. vi. 13, 16, 19, xii. 1, 1 Cor. viii. 8, 2 Cor. iv. 14, xi. 2, Eph. v. 27, Col. i. 22, 28. o Here only, not LXX. p Prov. iii. 6, xi. 5 only. q 1 Tim. vi. 20, see 1 Tim. i. 9. r Tit. iii. 9. s Acts iv. 17, xx. 9, xxiv. 4. t 2 Tim. iii. 9.

[1] **καινοφωνίας** FG, *novitates vocum* or *verborum* d, e, g, m50. See 1 Tim. vi. 20.

between **καθαίρεσις** and **οἰκοδομή** in 2 Cor. xiii. 10.

It should be added that **ἐπ' οὐδὲν χρήσιμον** is connected closely with **λογομαχεῖν** (or **λογομάχει**) by Cyr. Alex., Clem. Alex., and the Bohairic version. The Clementine Vulg. renders unambiguously, *ad nihil enim utile est;* so F.G. add **γάρ**.

In addition to the weight of adverse textual evidence against the reading **λογομάχει,** it is open to the objections that **ταῦτα—θεοῦ,** disconnected with what follows, is a feeble sentence; and that **μαρτύρομαι** and **διαμαρτύρομαι** in Paul are always followed and completed by an exhortation, *e.g.*, Eph. iv. 17; 1 Tim. v. 21; 2 Tim. iv. 1.

Ver. 15. **σπούδασον**: *Give diligence to present thyself* (as well as thy work) *to God, approved.*

ἀνεπαίσχυντον: Chrys. takes this to mean *a workman that does not scorn to put his hand to anything;* but it is better explained as *a workman who has no cause for shame when his work is being inspected.* In any case, the word must be so explained as to qualify **ἐργάτης** naturally; and therefore it cannot be interpreted by a reference to i. 8 (**μὴ ἐπαισχυνθῇς**), of the shame that may deter a man from confessing Christ.

ὀρθοτομοῦντα: **ὀρθοτομέω** is found in reff. as the translation of יִשֵּׁר (Piel) *direct, make straight, make plain.* "He shall direct thy paths," "The righteousness of the perfect shall direct his way". This use of the word suggests that the metaphor passes from the general idea of a workman to the particular notion of the minister as one who "makes straight paths" (**τροχιὰς ὀρθάς**) for the feet of his people to tread in (Heb. xii. 13). *The word of truth* is "The Way" (Acts ix. 2, etc.). Theodoret explains it of a ploughman who drives a straight furrow. Similarly R.V. m. (1), *Holding a straight course in the word of truth.* Chrys., of cutting away what is spurious or bad. Alf. follows Huther in supposing that the idea of cutting has passed out of this word, as it has out of **καινοτομεῖν,** and renders, *rightly administering*, as opposed to "adulterating the word of God" (2 Cor. ii. 17). Other examples of words which have wholly lost their derivational meaning are **πρόσφατος** and **συκοφαντέω.** The imagery underlying the A.V., R.V.m. (2), *rightly dividing*, is either that of the correct cutting up of a Levitical victim (Beza), or a father (Calvin), or steward (Vitringa), cutting portions for the food of the household. The R.V., *handling aright*, follows the Vulg., *recte tractantem*, and gives the general sense well enough. The use of **ὀρθοτομία** in the sense of *orthodoxy*, in Clem. Al. *Strom.* vii. xvi., and Eus. *H. E.* iv. 3, is probably based on this passage.

Ver. 16. **κενοφωνίας**: See on 1 Tim. vi. 20. Here, as Bengel suggests, **κενο-** is contrasted with **ἀληθείας, φωνίας** with **λόγον.**

περιίστασο: *shun*, *devita*, "*Give them a wide berth*" (Plummer), also in Tit. iii. 9. In these places **περιίστασθαι** has the same meaning as **ἐκτρέπεσθαι,** 1 Tim. vi. 20. In fact Ell. cites from Lucian, *Hermot.* § 86, **ἐκτραπήσομαι καὶ περιστήσομαι,** where the two verbs are evidently used as indifferent alternatives. Where **περιίστημι** elsewhere occurs (N.T.), *viz.*, John xi. 42, Acts xxv. 7, it means "to stand around".

ἐπὶ πλεῖον, κ.τ.λ.: Those who utter "babblings" (subject of **προκόψουσιν**) are not, as is sometimes supposed, merely negatively useless; they are positively and increasingly mischievous. In iii. 9, **οὐ προκόψουσιν ἐπὶ πλεῖον,** the situation is different. When a man's **ἄνοια** has become manifest to all, he has lost his power to do mischief to others; on the other hand there is no limit to the deterioration of "evil men and impostors" in themselves, **προκόψουσιν ἐπὶ τὸ χεῖρον** (iii. 13).

ἀσεβείας: genitive after **ἐπὶ πλεῖον.** The commentators compare Joseph. *Bell. Jud.* vi. 2, 3. **προὔκοψαν εἰς τοσοῦτον**

u Luke ii. γὰρ ^tᵘπροκόψουσιν ᵛἀσεβείας · 17. καὶ ὁ λόγος αὐτῶν ὡς ʷγάγγραινα
52, Rom.
xiii. 12, ˣνομὴν ἕξει· ὧν ἐστὶν Ὑμέναιος καὶ Φιλητός, 18. οἵτινες περὶ τὴνʸ
Gal. i. 14,
2 Tim.iii. ἀλήθειαν ʸἠστόχησαν, λέγοντες¹ ἀνάστασιν ἤδη γεγονέναι, καὶ
9, 13, not z
LXX. ἀνατρέπουσιν τὴν τινων πίστιν. 19. ὁ ᵃμέντοι ᵇστερεὸς ᶜθεμέλιος
v Rom. i. 18,
xi. 26, Tit. τοῦ Θεοῦ ἕστηκεν, ἔχων τὴν ᵈσφραγῖδα ταύτην, Ἔγνω Κύριος τοὺς
ii. 12, Jude
15, 18.
w Here only, not LXX.   x John x. 9 only, N.T.   y See 1 Tim. i. 6.   z John ii. 15, Tit.
i. 11 only, N.T.   a John (5), Jas. ii. 8. Jude 8.   b Heb. v. 12, 14, 1 Pet. v. 9.   c See 1 Tim.
vi. 19.   d Rom. iv. 11, 1 Cor. ix. 2, Rev. ix. 4, etc.

¹ Ins. τὴν ACDKLP, and almost all other authorities ; om. τὴν אFG, 17.

παρανομίας. Charles thinks προκόψουσιν ἐπὶ κακῷ ἐν πλεονεξίᾳ, *Test. of Twelve Patriarchs*, Judah, xxi. 8, the source of this phrase ; but it is merely a parallel.

Ver. 17. ὡς γάγγραινα νομὴν ἕξει: *spread*, R.V.m., *ut cancer serpit*, Vulg. Ell. compares Ovid. *Metam.* ii. 825, "solet immedicabile cancer Serpere, et illaesas vitiatis addere partes". Alf. supplies many illustrations of νομή as "the medical term for the consuming progress of mortifying disease".

Harnack (*Mission*, vol. i., pp. 114, 115) illustrates copiously this conception of moral evil from the writings of the early fathers.

Ὑμέναιος καὶ Φιλητός. This Hymenaeus is perhaps the same as he who is mentioned in 1 Tim. i. 20. Of Philetus nothing is known from other sources.

Ver. 18. οἵτινες implies that Hymenaeus and Philetus were only the more conspicuous members of a class of false teachers.

περὶ—ἠστόχησαν: See notes on 1 Tim. i. 6, 19.

λέγοντες, κ.τ.λ.: There can be little doubt that the false teaching here alluded to was akin to, if not the same as, that of some in Corinth a few years earlier who said, "There is no resurrection of the dead" (1 Cor. xv. 12). What these persons meant was that the language of Jesus about eternal life and a resurrection received its complete fulfilment in our present conditions of existence, through the acquisition of that more elevated knowledge of God and man and morality and spiritual existence generally which Christ and His coming had imparted to mankind. This subimest knowledge of things divine is, they said, a resurrection, and the only resurrection that men can attain unto. These false teachers combined a plausible but false spirituality, or sentimentality, with an invincible materialism ; and they attempted to find support for their materialistic disbelief in the resurrection of the body in a perverse misunderstanding of the Christian language about "newness of life" (Rom. vi. 4; Col. ii. 12, iii. 1). "Esse resurrectionem a mortuis, agnitionem ejus quae ab ipsis dicitur veritatis" (Irenæus, *Haer.* ii. 31, 2; *cf.* Tert. *de Resurr.* 19); an achieved moral experience, in fact; not a future hope. The heresy of Marcion, on the other hand, while denying the future resurrection of the body, affirmed positively the immortality of the soul; *cf.* Justin Martyr, *Dial.* 80. "Marcion enim in totum carnis resurrectionem non admittens, et soli animae salutem repromittens, non qualitatis sed substantiae facit quaestionem" (Tert. *adv. Marcionem*, v. 10).

τινων: See note on 1 Tim. i. 3.

Ver. 19. "We will not fear. The city of God . . . shall not be moved" (Ps. xlvi. 2, 4; *cf.* Heb. xii. 28). The Church of the New Covenant is like the Church of the Old Covenant: it has an ideal integrity unaffected by the defection of some who had seemed to belong to it. "They are not all Israel, which are of Israel. . . . All Israel shall be saved" (Rom. ix. 6, xi. 26). "They went out from us, but they were not of us; for if they had been of us, they would have continued with us" (1 John ii. 19). The Church, as existing in the Divine Knowledge, not as apprehended by man's intellect, is *the firm foundation of God* (R.V.), *i.e.*, that which God has firmly founded. It is called here θεμέλιος τοῦ θεοῦ rather than οἶκος τ. θεοῦ, so as to express the better its immobility, unaffected by those who ἀνατρέπουσι, κ.τ.λ.; *cf.* στύλος καὶ ἑδραίωμα τῆς ἀληθείας (1 Tim. iii. 15). There can hardly be an allusion to the parable with which the Sermon on the Mount closes, Luke vi. 48, 49. With στερεός compare the use of στερεόω, Acts x. 1. 5, and of στερέωμα, Col. ii. 5.

ἔχων τὴν σφραγῖδα: It was noted on

ὄντας αὐτοῦ, καὶ °ʼΑποστήτω ἀπὸ ἀδικίας πᾶς ὁ ᶠὀνομάζων τὸ ᶠὄνομα e See 1 Tim.
iv. 1.
Κυρίου.¹ 20. ἐν μεγάλῃ δὲ οἰκίᾳ οὐκ ἐστιν μόνον σκεύη χρυσᾶ καὶ f Acts xix.
13, Rom.
ἀργυρᾶ ἀλλὰ καὶ ᵍ ξύλινα καὶ ʰ ὀστράκινα, καὶ ἃ μὲν εἰς τιμὴν ἃ δὲ xv. 20,
Eph. i. 21.
g Rev. ix.20
h 2 Cor. iv.
7.

¹ Χριστοῦ a few cursives.

1 Tim. vi. 19 that in the two places in
which θεμέλιος occurs in the Pastorals,
there is a condensation of expression
resulting in a confusion of metaphor.
Here the apostle passes rapidly from the
notion of the Church collectively as a
foundation, or a building well founded,
to that of the men and women of whom it
is composed, and who have been sealed
by God (see reff. and also Ezek. ix. 4;
John vi. 27; 2 Cor. i. 22; Eph. i. 13,
iv. 30; Rev. vii. 3, 4, 5-8). They are
marked by God so as to be recognised
by Him as His; and this mark also serves
as a perpetual reminder to them that
"they are not their own," and of their
consequent obligation to holiness of life
(1 Cor. vi. 19, 20). There is no allusion
to the practice of carving inscriptions
over doors and on pillars and foundation
stones (Deut. vi. 9, xi. 20; Rev. xxi. 14).
The one seal bears two inscriptions, two
mutually complementary parts or aspects:
(a) The objective fact of God's superin-
tending knowledge of His chosen; (b)
the recognition by the consciousness of
each individual of the relation in which
he stands to God, with its imperative call
to holiness.

Ἔγνω Κύριος κ.τ.λ.: The words are
taken from Num. xvi. 5, ἐπέσκεπται καὶ
ἔγνω ὁ θεὸς τοὺς ὄντας αὐτοῦ, "In the
morning the Lord will shew who are
His". The intensive use of know is
lilustrated by Gen. xviii. 19, Ex. xxxiii.
12, 17, Nah. i. 7, John x. 14, 27, 1 Cor.
viii. 3, xiii. 12, xiv. 38, R.V.m., Gal. iv. 9.
Ἀποστήτω κ.τ.λ.: The language is
perhaps another echo of the story of
Korah: Ἀποσχίσθητε ἀπὸ τῶν σκηνῶν
τῶν ἀνθρώπων τῶν σκληρῶν τούτων . . .
μὴ συναπόλησθε ἐν πάσῃ τῇ ἁμαρτίᾳ
αὐτῶν. καὶ ἀπέστησαν ἀπὸ τῆς σκηνῆς
Κόρε (Num. xvi. 26, 27). But Isa. lii. 11
is nearer in sentiment, ἀπόστητε ἀπόστητε, ἐξέλθατε ἐκεῖθεν καὶ ἀκαθάρτου
μὴ ἅψησθε, . . . οἱ φέροντες τὰ σκεύη
Κυρίου, cf. Luke xiii. 27. Also Isa. xxvi.
13, Κύριε, ἐκτὸς σοῦ ἄλλον οὐκ οἴδαμεν,
τὸ ὀνομά σου ὀνομάζομεν. The spiritual
logic of the appeal is the same as that of
Gal. v. 25, "If we live by the Spirit, by the
Spirit let us also walk". Bengel thinks
that ἀπὸ ἀδικίας is equivalent to ἀπὸ

ἀδίκων, the abstract for the concrete; cf.
ver. 21, "purge himself from these".
Ver. 20. Although the notional Church,
the corpus Christi verum, is unaffected
by the vacillation and disloyalty of its
members, nevertheless (δὲ) the Church
as we experience it contains many unworthy persons, the recognition of whom
as members of the Church is a trial
to faith. The notional Church is best
figured as a foundation, which is out of
sight. But the idea of the superstructure
must be added in order to shadow forth
the Church as it meets the eye. It is a
house, a Great House too, the House of
God (1 Tim. iii. 15), and therefore containing a great variety of kinds and quality of furniture and utensils. On οἰκίᾳ,
a whole house, as distinguished from
οἶκος, which might mean a set of rooms
only, a dwelling, see Moulton in Expositor, vi., vii. 117. There are two
thoughts in the apostle's mind, thoughts
which logically are conflicting, but which
balance each other in practice. These
are: (1) the reality of the ideal Church,
and (2) the providential ordering of the
actual Church. Until the drag-net is full,
and drawn up on the beach, the bad fish
in it cannot be cast away (Matt. xiii. 47,
48). This is the view of the passage
taken by the Latin expositors, e.g., Cyprian, Ep. lv. 25. The explanation of the
Greek commentators, that by the "great
house" is meant the world at large, is
out of harmony with the context. It
is to be observed that St. Paul expresses
here a milder and more hopeful view of
the unworthy elements in the Church
than he does in the parallel passage in
Rom. ix. 21, 22. There "the vessels unto dishonour" are "vessels of wrath
fitted unto destruction". Here they are
all at least in the Great House, and all
for some use, even if for less honourable
purposes than those served by the vessels
of gold and silver; and the next verse
suggests that it is perhaps possible for
that which had been a "vessel unto dishonour" to become fit for honourable use
in the Master's personal service. We
are reminded of the various qualities of
superstructure mentioned in 1 Cor. iii. 12,
"gold, silver, costly stones, wood, hay,

ⁱ ¹ Cor. v. 7. **εἰς ἀτιμίαν.**　21. **ἐὰν οὖν τις** ¹**ἐκκαθάρῃ ἑαυτὸν ἀπὸ τούτων, ἔσται**
k Prov.
xxxi. 13, **σκεῦος εἰς τιμήν, ἡγιασμένον,**¹ k **εὔχρηστον τῷ** ¹**δεσπότῃ, εἰς** m **πᾶν**
Wisd.
xiii. 13, 2 m **ἔργον** m **ἀγαθὸν** n **ἡτοιμασμένον.**　22. **τὰς δὲ** º **νεωτερικὰς ἐπιθυμίας**
Tim. iv.
11, p **φεῦγε·** p **δίωκε δὲ δικαιοσύνην,** q **πίστιν,** q **ἀγάπην, εἰρήνην μετὰ** ²
Philem.
11 only. **τῶν** r **ἐπικαλουμένων τὸν Κύριον ἐκ** s **καθαρᾶς** s **καρδίας.**　23. **τὰς δὲ**
1 See 1 Tim.
vi. 1. t **μωρὰς καὶ** u **ἀπαιδεύτους** t v **ζητήσεις** w **παραιτοῦ, εἰδὼς ὅτι γεννῶσι**
m 2 Tim. iii.
17, Tit. i.
16, iii. 1, see 1 Tim. ii. 10.　　n Rev. ix. 7, 15, with εἰς; cf. Tit. iii. 1.　　o 3 Macc. iv. 8 only.
p See 1 Tim. vi. 11.　　q See 1 Tim. i. 14.　　r Acts vii. 59, ii. 21, ix. 14, 21, xxii. 16, Rom. x. 12,
13, 14, 1 Cor. i. 2, 1 Pet. i. 17.　　s See 1 Tim. i. 5.　　t Tit. iii. 9.　　u Here only, N.T.
v See 1 Tim. vi. 4.　　w See 1 Tim. iv. 7.

¹ Ins. **καὶ** אcC*DbcKLP, f, vg., sah., syrhcl, arm.

² Ins. **πάντων** ACFgrG, 17, 31, 73, three others (FG, 73 om. foll. **τῶν**), g, sah.,
syrhcl.　See 1 Cor. i. 2.

stubble ". See also Wisd. xv. 7. Field,
Notes, in loc., suggests that **δεσπότης**
here is best rendered *the owner.* See
notes on 1 Tim. iii. 15 and vi. 1.

Ver. 21. St. Paul drops the metaphor.
The general meaning is clear enough,
that a man may become "heaven's consummate cup," **σκεῦος ἐκλογῆς** (Acts ix.
15), if he "mistake not his end, to slake
the thirst of God". When we endue
the vessels with consciousness, it is seen
that they may "rise on stepping-stones
of their dead selves to higher things".
The **τις** has been, it is implied, among
the "vessels unto dishonour". " Paul
was an earthen vessel, and became a
golden one. Judas was a golden vessel,
and became an earthen one " (Chrys.).
Bengel supposes that the **ἐάν τις** is an
exhortation to Timothy himself. This is
suggested in R.V. of ver. 22, " But flee,"
etc. The reference in **τούτων** is not
quite clear. It is best perhaps to explain it of the false teachers themselves,
"vessels unto dishonour," rather than of
their teaching or immoral characteristics,
though of course this is implied. The
thoroughness of the separation from the
corrupting environment of evil company
is expressed by the **ἐκ-** and **ἀπό.** Where
ἐκκαθαίρω occurs again, 1 Cor. v. 7, the
metaphor (leaven) also refers to the removal of a corrupting personal element.
There the person is to be expelled; here
the persons are to be forsaken. **ἡγια-**
σμένον is the equivalent in actual experience of the simile **σκεῦος εἰς τιμήν,** as
εἰς πᾶν—ἡτοιμασμένον is of **εὔχρηστον**
τῷ δεσπότῃ. Compare 1 Cor. vi. 11, "And
such were some of you : but ye were
washed [lit. washed yourselves], but ye
were sanctified " (**ἡγιάσθητε**).

ἡτοιμασμένον : " Even though he do
not do it, he is fit for it, and has a capa-

city for it " (Chrys.). *Cf.* Eph. ii. 10,
κτισθέντες. . . ἐπὶ ἔργοις ἀγαθοῖς οἷς
προητοίμασεν ὁ θεὸς ἵνα ἐν αὐτοῖς περι-
πατήσωμεν, and reff.

Ver. 22. **νεωτερικὰς ἐπιθυμίας** :
"Every inordinate desire is a youthful
lust. Let the aged learn that they ought
not to do the deeds of the youthful ".
(Chrys.). This is sound exegesis ; yet it is
reasonable to suppose that Timothy was
still of an age to need the warning in its
natural sense. See 1 Tim. iv. 12. He
has just been cautioned against errors of
the intellect; he must be warned also
(**δὲ**) against vices of the blood.

φεῦγε· δίωκε δὲ, κ.τ.λ. : See note on 1
Tim. vi. 11.

εἰρήνην : to be joined closely with the
following words, *cf.* Heb. xii. 14. While
avoiding the company of evil men, he is
to cultivate friendly relations with those
who are sincere worshippers of the same
God as himself. **οἱ ἐπικαλούμενοι τὸν**
Κύριον, *i.e.,* Christ, is almost a technical
term for Christians. See reff. It comes
ultimately from Joel ii. 32 (iii. 5).

ἐκ καθαρᾶς καρδίας is emphatic. See
Tit. i. 15, 16.

Ver. 23. **ἀπαιδεύτους** : *ignorant.* An
ignorant question is one that arises from
a misunderstanding of the matter in dispute. Misunderstandings are a fruitful
source of strife. *Cf.* 1 Tim. vi. 4.

παραιτοῦ : *refuse, i.e.,* Such questions
will be brought before you : refuse to
discuss them. The A.V., *avoid* might
mean merely, Evade the necessity of
meeting them.

γεννῶσι : There is no other instance
of the metaphorical use of this word in
the N.T.

μάχας : in the weaker sense of *conten-*
tion, quarrel, as in 2 Cor. vii. 5, Tit. iii.
9; but not Jas. iv. 1.

ˣ μάχας. 24. δοῦλον δὲ Κυρίου οὐ δεῖ μάχεσθαι, ἀλλὰ ʸ ἤπιον εἶναι
πρὸς πάντας, ᶻ διδακτικόν, ᵃ ἀνεξίκακον, 25. ἐν ᵇ πραΰτητι ᶜ παιδεύοντα
τοὺς ᵈ ἀντιδιατιθεμένους, μή ποτε δώῃ ¹ αὐτοῖς ὁ Θεὸς ᵉ μετάνοιαν
ᶠ εἰς ᶠ ἐπίγνωσιν ᶠ ἀληθείας, 26. καὶ ᵍ ἀνανήψωσιν ἐκ τῆς ʰ τοῦ ʰ διαβόλου ʰ παγίδος, ⁱ ἐζωγρημένοι ὑπ᾽ αὐτοῦ εἰς τὸ ἐκείνου θέλημα.

III. 1. Τοῦτο δὲ γίνωσκε ² ὅτι ἐν ᵃ ἐσχάταις ᵃ ἡμέραις ᵇ ἐνστήσονται

x 2 Cor. vii.
5, Tit. iii.
y Jas. iv.
1.
y 1 Thess.
ii. 7, not
LXX.
z 1 Tim. iii.
2, not
LXX.
a Here only,
not LXX,
cf. Wisd.

ii. 19.   b 1 Cor. iv. 21, 2 Cor. x. 1, Gal. v. 23, vi. 1, Eph. iv. 2, Col. iii. 12, Tit. iii. 2, Jas. i. 21,
iii. 13, 1 Pet. iii. 15.   c See 1 Tim. i. 20.   d Here only, not LXX.   e Rom. ii. 4, 2 Cor.
vii. 9, 10 (Paul).   f See 1 Tim. ii. 4.   g Here only, not LXX.   h 1 Tim. iii. 7.   i Luke
v. 10 only, N.T.   a Acts ii. 17 (Joel iii. 1), Jas. v. 3, 2 Pet. iii. 3.   b 2 Thess. ii. 2, cf. Rom.
viii. 38, 1 Cor. iii. 22, vii. 26, Gal. i. 4, Heb. ix. 9.

¹ δ ῷℵᶜDᶜKLP, 17, many others.

² γινώσκετε A [FgᵣG, 17, one other γινώσκεται], 238, two others, g.

Ver. 24. δοῦλον δὲ Κυρίου: here is
used in its special application to the
ministers of the Church. On the general
teaching, see 1 Thess. ii. 7, 1 Tim. iii. 3,
Tit. iii. 2.

ἤπιος, as Ell. notes, implies gentleness
in demeanour, πραΰτης meekness of disposition. "Gentle unto all men, so he
will be apt to teach; forbearing towards
opponents, so he will be able to correct"
(Bengel).

Ver. 25. τοὺς ἀντιδιατιθεμένους: They
who err from right thinking are to be
dealt with as tenderly and considerately
as they who err from right living. Cf.
Gal. vi. 1, καταρτίζετε τὸν τοιοῦτον ἐν
πνεύματι πραΰτητος. See also chap. iv.
2, and reff. Field takes ἀντιδιατίθεσθαι
as equivalent to ἐναντίως διατίθεσθαι,
"to be contrariwise or adversely affected". Similarly Ambrosiaster, eos
qui diversa sentiunt. Field notes that
"the only other example of the compound
verb is to be found in Longinus περὶ
ὕψους, xvii. 1". The A.V. and R.V. take
the word here as middle, them that oppose
themselves, eos qui resistunt [veritati]
(Vulg.). von Soden finds in this word the
key to the meaning of ἀντιθέσεις, 1 Tim.
vi. 20.

μήποτε (not elsewhere in Paul) =
εἴποτε.

δώῃ: The subjunctive seems a syn-
tactical necessity. See J. H. Moulton,
Grammar, vol. i. pp. 55, 193, 194, Blass,
Grammar, p. 213. On the other hand, W.
H. text, and Winer-Moulton, Grammar, p.
374, read δῴη, optative.

μετάνοιαν: It is certainly implied
that false theories in religion are not unconnected with moral obliquity and faulty
practice. See Tit. i. 15, 16, iii. 11.

Ver. 26. ἀνανήψωσιν is to be connected with εἰς τὸ ἐκείνου θέλημα. Com-

pare ἐκνήψατε δικαίως, 1 Cor. xv. 34.
ἐκείνου then refers to ὁ θεός, and θέλημα
will have its usual force as the Will of
God (see 1 Pet. iv. 2): That they who
had been taken captive by the devil may
recover themselves (respiscant, Vulg.) out
of his snare, so as to serve the will of
God. This is Beza's explanation and
that of von Soden (nearly), who compares αἰχμαλωτίζοντες, 2 Cor. x. 5. It
has the advantage of giving a natural
reference to αὐτοῦ and ἐκείνου respectively, which are employed accurately in
iii. 9. The paradoxical use of ζωγρέω in
Luke v. 10 must not be taken as determining the use of the word elsewhere.
Of the other explanations, that of the
A.V. and Vulg., which supposes an in-
elegant but not impossible reference of
both αὐτοῦ and ἐκείνου to τοῦ διαβόλου,
is preferable to the R.V., following Wetstein and Bengel, which refers αὐτοῦ
back to δοῦλον Κυρίου, and dissociates
ἐζωγρημένοι from παγίδος, with which it
is naturally connected. The reference of
αὐτοῦ and ἐκείνου to the same subject, as
given in the A.V., is paralleled by Wisd.
i. 16, συνθήκην ἔθεντο πρὸς αὐτόν, ὅτι
ἄξιοί εἰσιν τῆς ἐκείνου μερίδος εἶναι.

CHAPTER III.—Vv. 1-9. Evil times
are upon us; we have indeed amongst
us specimens of the perennial impostor,
worthy successors of Jannes and Jambres. The shortlived nature of their
success, will be, however, patent to all.

Ver. 1. ἐν ἐσχάταις ἡμέραις ἐνστήσονται: Although St. Paul had abandoned
his once confident expectation that the
Lord would come again during his own
lifetime, it is plain that here, as in 1
Tim. iv. 1, he regards the time now present as part of the last days. See ἀπο-
τρέπου . . . εἰσιν οἱ ἐνδύνοντες, vv. 5, 6.
The prophetical form of the sentence is a

c Matt. viii. καιροὶ ^cχαλεποί · 2. ἔσονται γὰρ οἱ ἄνθρωποι ^dφίλαυτοι, ^eφιλάρ-
28 only,
N.T., γυροι, ^fἀλαζόνες, ^gὑπερήφανοι, ^hβλάσφημοι, γονεῦσιν ⁱἀπειθεῖς,
Wisd. iii.
19, xvii. ^kἀχάριστοι, ^lἀνόσιοι, 3. ^mἄστοργοι, ⁿἄσπονδοι, ^oδιάβολοι, ^pἀκρα-
11, xix.13,
Isa. xviii. τεῖς, ^qἀνήμεροι, ^rἀφιλάγαθοι, 4. ^sπροδόται, ^tπροπετεῖς, ^uτετυφω-
2, 2 Macc.
(3), 4 μένοι, ^vφιλήδονοι μᾶλλον ἢ ^wφιλόθεοι, 5. ἔχοντες ^xμόρφωσιν
Macc. (3).

d Here only,
not LXX.   e Luke xvi. 14, 4 Macc. ii. 8 only.   f Rom. i. 30 only, N.T.   g Luke i. 51,
Rom. i. 30, Jas. iv. 6 = 1 Pet. v. 5 (Prov. iii. 4).   h 1 Tim. i. 13.   i Rom. i. 30, cf. Tit. i. 16,
iii. 3.   k Luke vi. 35, Wisd. (1), Ecclus. (2), 4 Macc. (1).   l See 1 Tim. i. 9.   m Rom. i.
31, not LXX.   n Here only, not LXX.   o See 1 Tim. iii. 11.   p Prov. xxvii. 20 only.
q Here only, not LXX.   r Here only, not LXX, cf. Tit. i. 8.   s Luke vi. 16, Acts vii. 52.
t Acts xix. 36, Prov. x. 14, xiii. 3, Ecclus. ix. 18.   u See 1 Tim. iii. 6.   v Here only, not LXX.
w Here only, not LXX.   x Rom. ii. 20 only, not LXX.

rhetorical way of saying that things are
going from bad to worse. The same account is to be given of 2 Pet. iii. 3 ; Jude
18. St. John says plainly, "It is the last
hour" (1 John ii. 18). See note on 1
Tim. iv. 1.

ἐνστήσονται : will be upon us, insta-
bunt (Vulg.).

χαλεποί : grievous (R.V.); but not
necessarily perilous (A.V.) to those who
feel their grievousness.

Ver. 2. οἱ ἄνθρωποι : mankind in general, not οἱ ἄνδρες. This list of human
vices should be compared with that given
in Rom. i. 29 sqq.; ἀλαζόνες, ὑπερήφανοι,
γονεῦσιν ἀπειθεῖς, ἄστοργοι are common
to both passages. φίλαυτοι appropriately heads the array, egoism or self-
centredness being the root of almost
every sin, just as love which "seeketh
not its own" (1 Cor. xiii. 5) is "the
fulfilment of the law" (Rom. xiii. 10).
φιλαυτία is used favourably by Aristotle in the sense of self-respect (Nic.
Eth. ix. 8. 7). But "once the sense of
sin is truly felt, self-respect becomes an
inadequate basis for moral theory. So
Philo (de Prof. 15) speaks of those who
are φίλαυτοι δὴ μᾶλλον ἢ φιλόθεοι"
(Dean Bernard, in loc).

φιλάργυροι : covetousness (πλεονεξία,
Rom. i. 29) naturally springs from, or is
one form of, selfishness ; but we cannot
suppose with Chrys. that there is a similar sequence intended all through.

Other compounds of φιλ.- in the Pastorals, besides the five that occur here,
are φιλάγαθος, Tit. i. 8, φίλανδρος,
φιλότεκνος, Tit. ii. 4, φιλανθρωπία, Tit.
iii. 4, φιλόξενος, 1 Tim. iii. 2, Tit. i. 8.

ἀλαζόνες, ὑπερήφανοι : elati, superbi.
The ἀλαζών, boastful, betrays his character by his words; the ὑπερήφανος,
haughty, more usually by his demeanour
and expression.

βλάσφημοι : abusive, railers (R.V.);
not necessarily blasphemers (A.V.).

γονεῦσιν ἀπειθεῖς and ἀχάριστοι naturally go together ; since, as Bengel observes, gratitude springs from filial duty.

Ver. 3. ἄστοργοι : without natural
affection, sine affectione. This and the
three preceding adjectives appear to have
reference to domestic relations.

ἄσπονδοι : implacable, sine pace (ab-
sque foedere, Rom. i. 31); not truce-
breakers (A.V.), which would be ἀσύν-
θετοι, Rom. i. 31; the ἄσπονδος refuses
to treat with his foe at all.

διάβολοι : A.V.m. here and in Tit. ii. 3,
has makebates. See note on 1 Tim. iii.
11.

ἀκρατεῖς : without self-control (R.V.)
rather than incontinent (A.V.). The
latter word has a purely sexual reference, whereas ἀκρατεῖς, as Chrys. notes,
is used "with respect both to their
tongue, and their appetite, and everything
else". It is naturally coupled with
ἀνήμεροι, fierce, immites. "Simul et
molles et duri" (Bengel).

ἀφιλάγαθοι : No lovers of good
(R.V.), the good being "things true,
honourable, just, pure, lovely, and of
good report" (Phil. iv. 8). The positive
φιλάγαθος, Tit. i. 8, has the same reference. It is a characteristic of the heavenly Wisdom (Wisd. vii. 22). The
A.V. in both places narrows the reference
to persons : Despisers of those that are
good ; A lover of good men. The
Vulg. sine benignitate, benignum, does
not express the active positive force of
the Greek. φιλάγαθος and ἀφιλάργυρος
are applied to the Emperor Antoninus in
a papyrus of ii. A.D. which also uses the
term ἀφιλοκαγαθία (perh. = ἀφιλοκαλο-
καγαθία) of Marcus Aurelius (Moulton
and Milligan, Expositor, vii., vi. 376).

Ver. 4. προδόται : has no special reference to persecution of Christians.

τετυφωμένοι : See note on 1 Tim. iii.
6.

Ver. 5. ἔχοντες (see note on 1 Tim. i.

εὐσεβείας τὴν δὲ ᵡδύναμιν αὐτῆς ᵃἠρνημένοι· καὶ τούτους ᵇἀπο-
τρέπου. 6. ἐκ τούτων γάρ εἰσιν οἱ °ἐνδύνοντες εἰς τὰς οἰκίας καὶ
ᵈαἰχμαλωτίζοντες ¹ °γυναικάρια ᶠσεσωρευμένα ἁμαρτίαις, ᵍἀγόμενα
ʰἐπιθυμίαις ʰⁱποικίλαις, 7. πάντοτε μανθάνοντα καὶ μηδέποτε ᵏεἰς
ᵏἐπίγνωσιν ᵏἀληθείας ᵏἐλθεῖν δυνάμενα. 8. ὃν τρόπον δὲ 'Ιαννῆς

y See 1 Tim.
 ii. 2.
z 1 Cor. ii.
 5, iv. 19,
 20, 1
 Thess. i.
 5, Heb.
 vii. 16.
a See 1 Tim.
 v. 8.
b Here only,

N.T., 4 Macc. i. 33, etc.　　c Here only, N.T.　　d Luke xxi. 24, Rom. vii. 23, 2 Cor. x. 5.
e Here only, not LXX.　　f Prov. xxv. 22, Judith xv. 11, Rom. xii. 20.　　g Rom. ii. 4, viii. 14,
 1 Cor. xii. 2, Gal. v. 18.　　h Tit. iii. 3.　　i Matt. iv. 24 (π. νόσοις) = Mark i. 34 = Luke iv.
 40, Heb. ii. 4, xiii. 9, Jas. i. 2, 1 Pet. i. 6, iv. 10.　　k See 1 Tim. ii. 4.

¹ αἰχμαλωτεύοντες [Eph. iv. 8] DᶜKL; add τὰ a few cursives.

19) μόρφωσιν, κ.τ.λ.: *Habentes speciem quidem pietatis.* We have an exact parallel in Tit. i. 16, θεὸν ὁμολογοῦσιν εἰδέναι, τοῖς δὲ ἔργοις ἀρνοῦνται. They were professing Christians, but nothing more; genuine Christians must also be professing Christians. This considera- tion removes any difficulty that may be felt by a comparison of this passage with Rom. ii. 20, where it is implied that it is a point in the Jew's favour that he has τὴν μόρφωσιν τῆς γνώσεως καὶ τῆς ἀληθείας ἐν τῷ νόμῳ. The μόρφωσις, embodiment, is external in both cases, but not unreal as far as it goes. The ineffectiveness of it arises from the co- existence in the mind of him who "holds" it of some other quality that neutralises the advantage naturally derivable from the possession of the μόρφωσις in question. In this case, it was that they of whom St. Paul is speaking had a purely theoretical, academic apprehen- sion of practical Christianity (εὐσέβεια, see 1 Tim. ii. 2), but a positive disbelief in the Gospel as a regenerating force. Com- pare what St. John says of the rulers who believed on Jesus but did not con- fess Him (John xii. 42, 43). They too were φιλήδονοι μᾶλλον ἢ φιλόθεοι. In *Romans* the case is similar: the posses- sion of an admirable moral code did not make the Jew's moral practice better than that of the Gentile (see Sanday and Headlam on Rom. ii. 20). There is therefore no necessity to suppose with Lightfoot that " the termination -ωσις denotes the aiming after or affecting the μορφή " (*Journal of Class. and Sacr. Philol.* (1857), iii. 115).

δύναμιν: the opposition between μόρφωσις and δύναμις here is the same as that between δύναμις and σοφία in 1 Cor. ii. 5, or λόγος, 1 Cor. iv. 19, 20, 1 Thess. i. 5; see also Heb. vii. 16.

ἠρνημένοι: *To deny a thing* or *a per- son* involves always more than an act of

the mind; it means carrying the negation into practice. See on 1 Tim. v. 8.

καί: perhaps refers back to ii. 22, 23.

Ver. 6. ἐνδύνοντες: *who insinuate themselves into houses* [which they over- throw], Tit. i. 11. " Observe how he shows their impudence by this expres- sion, their dishonourable ways, their deceitfulness " (Chrys.). παρεισέδυησαν (Jude 4) and παρεισῆλθον (Gal. ii. 4) are similar expressions.

γυναικάρια: *Mulierculas.* Chrys. acutely implies that the victims of the crafty heretics were " silly women " of both sexes: " He who is easy to be deceived is a silly woman, and nothing like a man; for to be deceived is the part of silly women ". St. Paul, how- ever, refers to women only.

σεσωρευμένα ἁμαρτίαις. *overwhelmed*, rather than *burdened* (βεβαρημένα) (Field). Is there any contrast implied between the diminutive, indicating the insignificance of the women, and the load of sins which they carry? De Wette (quoted by Alf.), notes that a sin-laden conscience is easily tempted to seek the easiest method of relief.

ποικίλαις: There is no great dif- ficulty in diverting them from the right path, for they are inconstant even in vice.

Ver. 7. πάντοτε μανθάνοντα: They have never concentrated their attention on any spiritual truth so as to have learnt it and assimilated it. They are always being attracted by " some newer thing," τι καινότερον (Acts xvii. 21), and thus their power of comprehension be- comes atrophied.

μηδέποτε: For negatives with the participle, see Blass, *Grammar*, p. 255.

εἰς ἐπίγνωσιν ἀληθείας: See on 1 Tim. ii. 4.

Ver. 8. The apostle now returns from the γυναικάρια to their seducers, whom he compares to the magicians who withstood Moses and Aaron, both

1 Acts xiii. καὶ ᾿Ιαμβρῆς [1] [1]ἀντέστησαν Μωυσεῖ, οὕτως καὶ οὗτοι [1]ἀνθίστανται
8, etc.,
Rom. ix. τῇ ἀληθείᾳ, ἄνθρωποι [m]κατεφθαρμένοι τὸν νοῦν, [n]ἀδόκιμοι [o]περὶ
19. xiii. 2,
Gal. ii. 11, [o]τὴν [o]πίστιν. 9. ἀλλ᾽ οὐ [p]προκόψουσιν [p]ἐπὶ [p]πλεῖον, ἡ γὰρ
Eph. vi.
13, 2 Tim. [q]ἄνοια αὐτῶν [r]ἔκδηλος ἔσται πᾶσιν, ὡς καὶ ἡ ἐκείνων ἐγένετο.
iv. 15, etc.
m Here 10. [s]Σὺ [s]δὲ [t]παρηκολούθησάς [2] μου τῇ διδασκαλίᾳ, τῇ [u]ἀγωγῇ,
only,
N.T., cf.
1 Tim. vi. 5.   n Rom. i. 28, 1 Cor. ix. 27, 2 Cor. xiii. 5, 6, 7, Tit. i. 16, Heb. vi. 8.   o 1 Tim. i.
19, vi. 21.   p See 2 Tim. ii. 16.   q Wisd. xv. 18, xix. 3, etc., Luke vi. 11 only, N.T.   r 3 Macc.
iii. 19, vi. 5 only.   s See 1 Tim. vi. 11.   t See 1 Tim. iv. 6.   u Here only, N.T., Esth.
(2), 2 Macc. (3), 3 Macc. (1).

[1] Μαμβρῆς FG, d, e, f, g, m50, vg., go.

[2] So אAC [FG, ἠκολούθησας], 17; παρηκολούθηκας DKLP. See 1 Tim. iv. 6.

in their hostility to the truth and in their subsequent fate. St. Paul is the earliest extant authority for the names; but of course he derived them from some source, written (Origen), or unwritten (Theodoret), it is immaterial which. But the former theory is the more probable. The book is called by Origen (in Matt. p. 916, on Matt. xxvii. 8), Jannes et Mambres liber, and is perhaps identical with Pœnitentia Jamnis et Mambrae condemned in the Decretum Gelasii. Pliny, whose Natural History appeared in A.D. 77, mentions Jannes along with Moses and Lotapis (or Jotapis) as Jewish Magi posterior to Zoroastes (Hist. Nat. xxx. 1). He is followed by Apuleius, Apol. c. 90. Numenius (quoted by Eusebius (Prep. Ev. ix. 8) mentions Jannes and Jambres as magicians who resisted Moses. In the Targ. of Jonathan on Ex. vii. 11, the names are given as יונים וימברים, Janis and Jamberes; but in the Talmud as יחנא וממרא, Jochana and Mamre. It is generally agreed that Jannes is a form of Jochanan (Johannes), and that Jambres is from the Hiphil of מרה to rebel. For the legends associated with these names, see art. in Hastings' D. B.

ἀντέστησαν: The same word is used of Elymas the Sorcerer, Acts xiii. 8. The οὕτως refers rather to the degree of their hostility than to the manner in which it was expressed, i.e., by magical arts. At the same time, it is possible that magic was practised by the false teachers; they are styled impostors, γόητες, in ver. 13; and Ephesus was a home of magic. See Acts xix. 19.

κατεφθαρμένοι τὸν νοῦν: cf. 1 Tim. vi. 5, διεφθαρμ. τὸν νοῦν. This is the Pauline equivalent for the Platonic "lie in the soul". κατεφθ. is not coordinate with ἀδόκ.; the latter is the exemplification of the former.

ἀδόκιμοι: reprobate. The A.V.m. gives the word here, and in Tit. i. 16, an active force, of no judgment, void of judgment. For περὶ with the acc. see on 1 Tim. i. 19.

Ver. 9. οὐ προκόψουσιν ἐπὶ πλεῖον. There is only a verbal inconsistency between this statement and those in ii. 16 and iii. 13, where see notes. The meaning here is that there will be a limit to the success of the false teachers. They will be exposed, found out; those to whom that fact is apparent will not be imposed on any more. In ii. 16, the increasing impiety of the teachers and the cancerous growth of their teaching is alleged as a reason why Timothy should avoid them. In ver. 13, προκόψουσιν ἐπὶ τὸ χεῖρον does not indicate success in gaining adherents, but simply advance in degradation. "Saepe malitia, quum late non potest, profundius proficit" (Bengel).

ἄνοια: dementia (m50) is nearer the mark than insipientia (Vulg.).

ὡς καὶ ἡ ἐκείνων ἐγένετο: "Aaron's rod swallowed up their rods" (Ex. vii. 12); they failed to produce lice (vii. 18). "And the magicians could not stand before Moses because of the boils; for the boils were upon the magicians" (ix. 11). During the plague of darkness, "they lay helpless, made the sport of magic art, and a shameful rebuke of their vaunts of understanding" (Wisd. xvii. 7).

Vv. 10-17. I am not really uneasy about your steadfastness. You joined me as a disciple from spiritual and moral inducements only. The persecutions you saw me endure you knew to be typical of the conditions of a life of godliness. Stand in the old paths. Knowledge of the Holy Scriptures on which your growing mind was fed is never out of date as an equipment for the man of God.

Ver. 10: παρηκολούθησας: See on 1 Tim. iv. 6. Thou didst follow (R.V.)

τῇ ᵛπροθέσει, τῇ πίστει, τῇ ᵂμακροθυμίᾳ, τῇ ἀγάπῃ, τῇ ˣὑπομονῇ, 11. τοῖς ʸδιωγμοῖς, τοῖς παθήμασιν, οἷά μοι ἐγένετο ἐν Ἀντιοχείᾳ, ἐν Ἰκονίῳ, ἐν Λύστροις, οἵους ʸδιωγμοὺς ᵃὑπήνεγκα· καὶ ἐκ πάντων με ᵇἐρύσατο ὁ Κύριος. 12. καὶ πάντες δὲ οἱ θέλοντες ᶜᵉζῆν ᶜᵈεὐσεβῶς¹ ᵉἐν ᵉΧριστῷ ᵉ¹Ἰησοῦ ᶠδιωχθήσονται. 13. πονηροὶ δὲ ἄνθρωποι καὶ ᵍγόητες ʰπροκόψουσιν ἐπὶ τὸ χεῖρον, ⁱπλανῶντες καὶ ᵏπλανώμενοι. 14. ¹σὺ ¹δὲ ᵐμένε ᵐἐν οἷς ἔμαθες καὶ ⁿἐπιστώθης,

v Acts xi. 23, xxvii. 13.
w See 1 Tim. i. 16, 2 Cor. vi.
6, Gal. v. 22, Eph. iv. 2, Col. i. 11, iii. 12, 2 Tim iv,2, Heb. vi. 12, Jas. v. 10 (of man).

x See 1 Tim. vi. 11.   y Acts xiii. 50, Rom. viii. 35, 2 Cor. xii. 10, 2 Thess. i.4.   z Rom. viii. 18, 2 Cor. i. 5, 6, 7, Phil. iii. 10, Col. i. 24, Heb. ii. 10, x. 32, 1 Pet. iv. 13, v. 9, etc , not LXX. a 1 Cor. x. 13, 1 Pet. ii. 19, only, N.T.   b Matt. vi. 13, Rom. xv. 31, 2 Cor. i. 10, 2 Thess. iii. 2, 2 Tim. iv. 17, 18, 2 Pet. ii. 7, 9.   c Tit. ii. 12.   d 4 Macc. vii. 21 only.   e Rom. vi. 11, cf. Gal. ii. 20.   f Matt. v. 10, 11, John xv. 20, 1 Cor. iv. 12, 2 Cor. iv. 9, Gal. v. 11, etc.   g Here only, not LXX.   h See 2 Tim. ii. 16.   i Matt. xxiv. 4, 5, 11, 24 (= Mark xiii. 5, 6), 1 John i. 8, ii. 26, iii. 7, Rev. (7), etc.   k Matt. xviii. 12, Tit. iii. 3, Heb v. 2, 1 Pet. ii. 25, etc.   l See 1 Tim. vi. 11.   m See 1 Tim. ii. 15.   n Here only, N.T.

¹ So אAP, 17, 37, two others; εὐσεβῶς ζῆν CDFGKL.

's susceptible of the meaning "Thou wert attracted as a disciple to me on account of". It is not necessarily implied that Timothy had copied his master in all these respects. The A.V., *Thou hast fully known*, follows the A.V. of Luke i. 3. This translation fails to bring out the appeal to Timothy s loyalty which underlies the passage. The aorist is appropriate here, because St. Paul is recalling to Timothy's recollection the definite occasion in the past when the youth cast in his lot with him. He is not thinking, as in 1 Tim. iv. 6, of Timothy's consistent discipleship up to the moment of writing. Bengel quotes aptly 2 Macc. ix. 27, παρακολουθοῦντα τῇ ἐμῇ προαιρέσει. (So cod. Venetus: A has συνσταθέντα for παρακολ.) This limitation of the reference explains why St. Paul mentions only the places in which he suffered on his first missionary journey.

διδασκαλίᾳ: See note on 1 Tim. i. 10.

ἀγωγῇ: *conduct* (R.V.). The A.V., *manner of life* has perhaps reference to guiding principles of conduct rather than to the external expression of them, which is meant here.

προθέσει: For πρόθεσις in this sense of human purpose see reff. Here it means what St. Paul had set before himself as the aim of his life. In Rom. viii. 28, ix. 11, Eph. i. 11, iii. 11, 2 Tim. i. 9 the word is used of God's eternal purpose for man.

ὑπομονῇ: See on 1 Tim. vi. 11.

Ver. 11. Ἀντιοχείᾳ: Acts xiii. 14, 45, 50; Ἰκονίῳ: Acts xiv. 1, 2, 5; Λύστροις: Acts xiv. 6, 19.

οἵους διωγμούς: There is no necessity to supply, with Alf., "Thou sawest".

καί: *and yet.* The verse is an echo

of Ps. xxxiii. (xxxiv.) 18, ὁ Κύριος . . . ἐκ πασῶν τῶν θλίψεων αὐτῶν ἐρύσατο αὐτούς. See also reff.

Ver. 12. This verse is an interesting example of the effect of association of ideas. St. Paul's teaching after his persecutions at Antioch, etc., had strongly emphasised this topic. St. Luke (Ac's xiv. 22) actually repeats the very words used by the preachers, "Through many tribulations we must enter into the kingdom of God". Consistency in the life in Christ must necessarily be always opposed by the world. θέλοντες is emphatic, as Ell. notes, "whose will is". Cf. Luke xiv. 28, John vii. 17.

εὐσεβῶς of course qualifies ζῆν, as in Tit. ii. 12. There is a similar extension of thought, from self to all, in iv. 8.

Ver. 13. πονηροὶ δὲ: The antithesis seems to be between the apparent discomfiture of those who wish to live in Christ (their persecution being after all almost a means conditional to their at. taining their desire), and the paradoxical success of evil men; they advance indeed; but only in degradation; *proficient in peius* (Vulg.). See notes on ver. 9 and ii. 16.

γόητες, *impostors* (R.V.), *seductores*, exactly expresses the term. γοητεία occurs 2 Macc. xii. 24, where it means *trickery*.

πλανώμενοι: cf. Tit. iii. 3. Those who deceive others impair, in so doing, their sense of the distinction between truth and falsehood, and thus weaken their power of resistance to self-deceit, and to imposition by others.

προκόψουσιν ἐπὶ τὸ χεῖρον: See on ver. 9.

Ver. 14. σὺ δὲ μένε: Both σύ and μένε are in strong contrast to the πονηροὶ

o Ecclus. εἰδὼς παρὰ τίνων[1] ἔμαθες, 15. καὶ ὅτι ἀπὸ °βρέφους [2]ᵖ ἱερὰ
(1), 1
Macc. (1), �q γράμματα οἶδας τὰ δυνάμενά σε ʳ σοφίσαι ˢ εἰς ˢ σωτηρίαν διὰ
2 Macc.
(1), 3 ᵗ πίστεως ᵗ τῆς ᵗ ἐν ᵗ Χριστῷ ᵗ Ἰησοῦ. 16. πᾶσα γραφὴ ᵘθεόπνευστος
Macc. (1),
4 Macc.
(1), Luke (5), Acts vii. 19, 1 Pet. ii. 2.   p 1 Cor. ix. 13 only, N.T.   q John vii. 15, Acts xxvi. 24.
r Ps. xviii. (xix.) 7, civ. (cv.) 22, cxviii. (cxix.) 98.   s Phil. i. 19, 2 Thess. ii. 13, 1 Pet. i. 5, ii. 2, *cf.*
Rom. i. 16, x. 1, 10, 2 Cor. vii. 10, Heb. ix. 28, xi. 7.   t 1 Tim. iii. 13.   u Here only, not LXX.

[1] So ℵAC*FgʳGP, 17, one other, d, e, g; τίνος CᶜDKL, f, vg., go., boh., syrr.,
arm.

[2] Ins. τὰ AC*DᶜKLP; om. τὰ ℵCᵇD*FG, 17, arm.

ἄνθρωποι and προκόψουσιν of ver. 13.
The exhortation is illustrated by 2 John
9, πᾶς ὁ προάγων, καὶ μὴ μένων ἐν
τῇ διδαχῇ τοῦ Χριστοῦ θεὸν οὐκ ἔχει.
The conservatism here enjoined concerns
more especially the fundamental ethical
teaching common to the Old Covenant
and the New. For the idiom, see note
on 1 Tim. ii. 15.

ἐν οἷς ἔμαθες καὶ ἐπιστώθης: ἃ, supplied out of ἐν οἷς, is the direct object of
ἔμαθες, and remoter object of ἐπιστώθης.

ἐπιστώθης: The Latin versions blun-
der here, *quae . . . credita sunt tibi.*
This would be the translation of ἐπιστ-
εύθης. πιστόομαί τι means *to have received confirmation of the truth of a
thing.* Bengel, rendering "fidelis et
firmus es redditus," compares Ps. lxxvii.
(lxxviii.) 8, οὐκ ἐπιστώθη μετὰ τοῦ
θεοῦ τὸ πνεῦμα αὐτῆς, and 37, οὐδὲ ἐπισ-
τώθησαν ἐν τῇ διαθήκῃ αὐτοῦ.

εἰδὼς παρὰ τίνων ἔμαθες: It has to be
remembered that St. Paul is speaking of
moral, not intellectual, authority. The
truths for which St. Paul is contending
were commended to Timothy by the
sanction of the best and noblest personalities whom he had ever known or heard
of. The characters of Timothy's revered
parent and teachers—of Eunice, Lois,
the prophets, and Paul, to enumerate
them in the order in which they had
touched his life—had been moulded in a
certain school of morals. Their characters had admittedly stood the test of life.
What more cogent argument could Timothy have for the truth and reasonableness of their moral teaching?

Ver. 15. καὶ ὅτι: dependent on εἰδώς.
For the change of construction, von Soden
compares Rom. ix. 22, 23; 1 Cor. xiv. 5.
Timothy's knowledge of things divine
was derived not merely from persons, but
from sacred writings; and, perhaps, as
Theophylact notes, the two points are
emphasised: (*a*) that the persons were of
no ordinary merit, and (*b*) that his knowledge of Scripture was conterminous with

the whole of his conscious existence.
He could not recall a period when he had
not known sacred writings. This is the
force of the hyperbolic ἀπὸ βρέφους.

ἱερὰ γράμματα: *sacras litteras, sacred
writings* (R.V.). For this use of γράμματα see John vii. 15, and Moulton and
Milligan, *Expositor,* vii., vi. 383. The
force of this peculiar phrase is that
Timothy's A B C lessons had been of
a sacred nature. The usual N.T. equivalent for *the Holy Scriptures* (A.V.)
is αἱ γραφαί or ἡ γραφή (once γραφαὶ
ἅγιαι, Rom. i. 2); but St. Paul here deliberately uses an ambiguous term in order
to express vigorously the notion that
Timothy's first lessons were in Holy
Scripture. τὰ ἱερὰ γράμματα is found
in Josephus, *Antiq.* Prooem 3 and x. 10,
4, and elsewhere. *Cf.* παραναγνοὺς τὴν
ἱερὰν βίβλον (2 Macc. viii. 23). There
may be also an allusion to γράμματα of
the false teachers which were not ἱερά.
See on next verse.

σοφίσαι: *instruere, cf.* Ps. xviii. (xix.)
8, ἡ μαρτυρία Κυρίου πιστή, σοφίζουσα
νήπια. Also Ps. civ. (cv.) 22, cxviii.
(cxix.) 98. The word is chosen for its
O.T. reference, and also because of its
strictly *educational* association.

εἰς σωτηρίαν: a constant Pauline
phrase. See reff.

διὰ πίστεως: to be joined closely with
σοφίσαι. *Cf. de Imitatione Christi,*
iii. 2, "Let not Moses nor any prophet
speak to me; but speak thou rather, O
Lord God, who art the inspirer and en-
lightener of all the prophets; for thou
alone without them canst perfectly instruct me, but they without thee will
avail nothing. They may indeed sound
forth words, but they do not add to them
the Spirit. . . . They shew the way, but
thou givest strength to walk in it," etc.

Ver. 16. In the absence of any extant
Greek MS. authority for the omission of
καί before ὠφέλιμος, we may assume
that the early writers who ignored it did
so from carelessness. The sentence then

καὶ [1] ᵛὠφέλιμος πρὸς διδασκαλίαν, πρὸς ᵂἐλεγμόν,[2] πρὸς ˣἐπανόρ- v See 1
θωσιν, πρὸς ʸπαιδείαν ˣτὴν ˣἐν ˣδικαιοσύνῃ· 17. ἵνα ᵃἄρτιος ᾖ ὁ Tim.iv.8.
τοῦ Θεοῦ ἄνθρωπος, ᵇπρὸς ᵇπᾶν ᵇἔργον ᵇἀγαθὸν ᶜἐξηρτισμένος.   w Here only.
N.T.
IV. I. ᵃΔιαμαρτύρομαι [3] ᵇἐνώπιον ᵇτοῦ ᵇΘεοῦ καὶ [4] Χριστοῦ Ἰησοῦ,[5]   x I Esd.
viii. 52, 1
Macc.xiv.
34 only.

y Eph. vi. 4, Heb. xii. 5, 7, 8, 11.   z Tit. iii. 5, cf. Eph. iv. 24.   a Here only, not LXX.   b See
2 im. ii. 21 and 1 Tim. ii. 10.   c Exod. xxviii. 7, Acts xxi. 5 only.   a See 1 Tim. v. 21.
b See 1 Tim. ii. 3.

[1] Om. καί bef. ὠφέλιμος f, vg^cle. boh., syrpesh.
[2] So אACFG, 31, 80, two others; ἔλεγχον DKLP.
[3] Ins. οὖν ἐγὼ DcKL, syrhcl.
[4] Ins. τοῦ Κυρίου DcKL, go., syrpesh and syrhcl c.*
[5] Ἰησ. Χριστ. DcKL, vg^cle, syrr., arm.

is best taken as a repetition and expansion of that which has just preceded; θεόπνευστος corresponding to ἱερά, and ὠφέλιμος, κ.τ.λ., τα σοφίσαι, κ.τ.λ.: *Every writing which is inspired by God is also profitable.* γραφή of course has exclusive reference to the definite collection of writings which St. Paul usually designates as ἡ γραφή or αἱ γραφαί; but it is used here in a partitive, not in a collective sense. A parallel case is John xix. 36, 37, ἡ γραφή . . . ἑτέρα γραφή. Hence the rendering *writing* or *passage* is less free from ambiguity than *scripture* (R.V.). The nearest parallel to this *ascensive* use of καί, as Ellicott terms it, is Gal. iv. 7, εἰ δὲ υἱός, καὶ κληρονόμος. See also Luke i. 36, Acts xxvi. 26, xxviii. 28, Rom. viii. 29.

θεόπνευστος: If there is any polemical force in this adj., it is in reference to heretical writings, the contents of which were merely intellectual, not edifying. In any case, the greatest stress is laid on ὠφέλιμος. St. Paul would imply that the best test of a γραφή being θεόπνευστος would be its proved serviceableness for the moral and spiritual needs of man. See Rom. xv. 4, 2 Pet. i. 20, 21. This, the R.V. explanation of the passage is that given by Origen, Chrys., Thdrt., syrr., the Clementine Vulg., *Omnis scriptura divinitus inspirata utilis est ad docendum etc.* [The true Vulg. text, however, is *insp. div. et utilis ad doc.*] The other view (A.V., R.V.m.), which takes καί as a simple copula, *Every Scripture is inspired and profitable*, is open to the objection that neither in the antecedent nor in the following context is there any suggestion that the inspiration of Scripture was being called in question; the theme of the passage being the moral equipment of the man of God. For this view are cited Greg.

Naz., Ath. It is to be added that it is possible to render πᾶσα γραφή, *the whole of Scripture*, on the analogy of Matt. ii. 3, πᾶσα Ἱερόσολυμα (Eph. ii. 21 cannot be safely adduced as a case in point); but it is unnecessary and unnatural.

διδασκαλίαν (see notes on 1 Tim. i. 10) and ἐλεγμόν represent respectively positive and negative teaching. Similarly ἐπανόρθωσιν and παιδείαν have relation respectively to "the raising up of them that fall," and the disciplining the unruly; *ad corrigendum, ad erudiendum* (Vulg.).

τὴν ἐν δικαιοσύνῃ: a παιδεία which *is exercised in righteousness.* Compare the dissertation on the παιδεία Κυρίου, Heb. xii. 5 sqq. παιδεία in reff. is used in relation to children only.

Ver. 17. ἄρτιος: *perfectus*, completely equipped for his work as a Man of God. τέλειος would have reference to his performance of it.

ὁ τοῦ Θεοῦ ἄνθρωπος: see on 1 Tim. vi. 11. *The Man of God* has here a primary reference to the minister of the Gospel.

πρὸς πᾶν, κ.τ.λ.: see ii. 21; and, for this use of πρός, 1 Pet. iii. 15, 2 Cor. ii. 16, x. 4, Eph. iv. 29, Heb. v. 14 and on ἐξαρτίζω, Moulton and Milligan, *Expositor*, vii., vii. 285.

Cf. the use of καταρτίζω, Luke vi. 40, 2 Cor. xiii. 11, Heb. xiii. 21, 1 Pet. v. 10.

CHAPTER IV.—Vv. 1-8. I solemnly charge you, in view of the coming judgment, to be zealous in the exercise of your ministry while the opportunity lasts, while people are willing to listen to your admonitions. Soon the craze for novelty will draw men away from sober truth to fantastic figments. Do you stand your ground. Fill the place which my death will leave vacant. My course is run, my crown is awaiting me. "My crown" did

c See 1 Tim. τοῦ μέλλοντος κρίνειν¹ ζῶντας καὶ νεκρούς, καὶ² τὴν ᵉἐπιφάνειαν
vi. 14.
d Luke (7), αὐτοῦ καὶ τὴν βασιλείαν αὐτοῦ· 2. κήρυξον τὸν λόγον, ᵈἐπίστηθι
Acts (11),
1 Thess. ᵉεὐκαίρως ᶠἀκαίρως, ἔλεγξον, ᵍἐπιτίμησον, παρακάλεσον,³ ἐν ʰπάσῃ
v. 3, 2
Tim. iv. 6. ʰμακροθυμίᾳ καὶ διδαχῇ. 3. ἔσται γὰρ καιρὸς ὅτε τῆς ⁱὑγιαινούσης
e Ecclus.
xviii. 22,
Mark xiv. 11 only, cf. 1 Cor. xvi. 12.   f Ecclus. xxxv. (xxxii.) 4, only. cf. Phil. iv. 10.   g Matt.
(7), Mark (9), Luke (12), Jude 9.   h See 1 Tim. i. 16 and 2 Tim. iii. 10.   i 1 Tim. i. 10 (q.v.),
Tit. i 9 ii. 1.

¹ κρῖναι FG, 17, 67**, six others.   ² κατὰ ℵcDcKLP, vgcle, go., syrr., arm.

³ ἐπιτίμ. παρακάλ. ℵcACDgrKLP, syrhcl, arm.; παρακάλ. ἐπιτίμ. ℵ*FG, 37,
one other, d, e, f, g, vg., go., boh.; om. παρακάλ. syrpesh.

I say? Nay, there is a crown for you, too, and for all who live in the loving longing for the coming of their Lord.

Ver. 1. Διαμαρτύρομαι: See on 1 Tim. v. 21. As the adjuration follows immediately on warnings against a moral degeneration which had already set in and would increase, it is appropriate that it should contain a solemn assurance of judgment to come.

Χριστοῦ Ἰησοῦ, τοῦ μέλλοντος κρίνειν: This was a prominent topic in St. Paul's preaching (Acts xvii. 31; Rom. iii. 16; 1 Cor. iv. 5). κρῖναι is the tense used in the Creeds, as in 1 Pet. iv. 5. (Tisch. R.V.). See apparat. crit.

ζῶντας καὶ νεκρούς: To be understood literally. See 1 Thess. iv. 16, 17.

τὴν ἐπιφάνειαν: per adventum ipsius (Vulg.). The acc. is that of the thing by which a person adjures, as in the case of ὁρκίζω (Mark v. 7; Acts xix. 13; cf. 1 Thess. v. 27). The use of διαμαρτύρομαι with an acc. in Deut. iv. 26, xxxi. 28, is different, διαμαρτ. ὑμῖν σήμερον τόν τε οὐρανὸν καὶ τὴν γῆν. "I call heaven and earth to witness against you." Heaven and earth can be conceived as personalities, cf. Ps. l. 4; not so the appearance or kingdom of Christ. On ἐπιφάνεια see note on 1 Tim. vi. 14.

βασιλείαν: The perfected kingdom, the manifestation of which will follow the second ἐπιφάνεια.

Ver. 2. κήρυξον: In 1 Tim. v. 21 διαμαρτ. is followed by ἵνα with the subj.; in 2 Tim. ii. 14 by the inf. Here the adjuration is more impassioned; hence the abruptness; this is heightened also by the aorists.

ἐπίστηθι: Insta, Be at hand, or Be ready to act. ἐπίστ. εὐκ. ἀκ. qualifies adverbially κήρυξον; while the following imperatives, ἔλεγξον, κ.τ.λ., are various departments of "preaching the word".

εὐκαίρως ἀκαίρως: opportune, impor-

tune (Vulg.). So few καιροί remain available (see next verse), that you must use them all. Do not ask yourself, "Is this a suitable occasion for preaching?" Ask rather, "Why should not this be a suitable occasion?" "Have not any limited season; let it always be thy season, not only in peace and security and when sitting in the Church" (Chrys.).

Similar expressions are cited by Bengel, e.g., digna indigna; praesens absens; nolens volens. We need not ask whether the reasonableness, etc., has reference to the preacher or the hearers. The direction is to disregard the inclinations of both.

ἔλεγξον: Taking this in the sense convict, Chrys. comments thus on the three imperatives, "After the manner of physicians, having shown the wound, he gives the incision, he applies the plaister".

ἐπιτίμησον: "The strict meaning of the word is 'to mete out due measure,' but in the N.T. it is used only of censure". So Swete (on Mark i. 25), who also notes that with the exceptions of this place and Jude 9, it is limited to the Synoptists.

παρακάλεσον: See on 1 Tim. iv. 13.

ἐν πάσῃ μακροθυμίᾳ καὶ διδαχῇ: This qualifies each of the three preceding imperatives; and πάσῃ belongs to διδαχῇ as well as to μακρ., with the utmost patience and the most painstaking instruction.

διδαχῇ: "(teaching) seems to point more to the act, διδασκαλία (doctrine) to the substance or result of teaching" (Ell.). In the only other occurrence of διδαχή in the Pastorals, Tit. i. 9, it means doctrine.

Ver. 3. ὑγιαινούσης διδασκαλίας: See note on 1 Tim. i. 10.

ἰδίας: ἴδιος here, as constantly, has merely the force of a possessive pronoun. See on 1 Tim. iii. 4.

[i] διδασκαλίας οὐκ [k] ἀνέξονται, ἀλλὰ κατὰ τὰς ἰδίας ἐπιθυμίας[1]
ἑαυτοῖς [l] ἐπισωρεύσουσιν διδασκάλους [m] κνηθόμενοι τὴν [n] ἀκοήν, 4.
καὶ ἀπὸ μὲν τῆς ἀληθείας τὴν [n] ἀκοὴν [o] ἀποστρέψουσιν, ἐπὶ δὲ τοὺς
[p] μύθους [q] ἐκτραπήσονται. 5. [r] σὺ [r] δὲ [s] νῆφε ἐν πᾶσιν, [t] κακοπάθη-
σον, ἔργον ποίησον [u] εὐαγγελιστοῦ, τὴν διακονίαν σου [v] πληροφόρησον.
6. ἐγὼ γὰρ ἤδη [w] σπένδομαι, καὶ ὁ καιρὸς τῆς [x] ἀναλύσεώς μου[2]

k Heb. xiii. 22, etc.
l Here only, not LXX.
m Here only, not LXX.
n Matt. xiii. 14 = Acts xxviii. 26 (Isa. vi. 9), 1 Cor. xii. 17, 1 Thess. ii. 13, Heb. iv. 2, v. 11, 2 Pet. ii. 8.
o See 2 Tim. i. 15.
p See 1 Tim. i. 4.
q See 1 Tim. i. 6.
r See 1 Tim. vi. 11.
s 1 Thess. v. 6, 8, 1 Pet. i. 13, iv. 7, v. 8, not LXX.
t See 2 Tim. ii. 9.
u Acts xxi. 8, Eph. iv. 11 only, not LXX.
v Luke i. 1, 2 Tim. iv. 17.
w Phil. ii. 17 only, N.T.
x Here only, not LXX.

[1] **ἐπιθυμίας τὰς ἰδίας** KL. [2] **ἐμῆς ἀναλύσεως** DKL.

ἐπισωρεύσουσιν: *coacervabunt* (Vulg.). "He shews the indiscriminate multitude of the teachers, as also their being elected by their disciples" (Chrys.).

κνηθόμενοι τὴν ἀκοήν: *prurientes auribus* (Vulg.). The same general idea is expressed in **πάντοτε μανθάνοντα** (iii. 7). Their notion of a teacher was not one who should instruct their mind or guide their conduct, but one who should gratify their æsthetic sense. *Cf.* Ezek. xxxiii. 32, "Thou art unto them as a very lovely song of one that hath a pleasant voice, &c." The desire for pleasure is insatiable, and is increased or aggravated by indulgence; hence the heaping up of those who may minister to it. Ell. quotes appropriately from Philo, *Quod Det. Pot.* 21, **ἀποκναίουσι γοῦν [οἱ σοφισταὶ] ἡμῶν τὰ ὦτα.**

Ver. 4. The ears serve as a passage through which the truth may reach the understanding and the heart. Those who starve their understanding and heart have no use for the truth, and do not, as they would say, waste hearing power on it.

μύθους: See note on 1 Tim. i. 4.

Ver. 5. **νῆφε**: *Be sober* (R.V.). *Sobrius esto* (d). *vigila* (Vulg.) [but Vulg. Clem. inserts *sobrius esto* at end of verse]. So A.V., *watch*, and Chrys. *Sober* is certainly right in 1 Thess. v. 6, 8; but in 1 Pet. i. 13, iv. 7, and perhaps v. 8, *to be watchful* or *alert* seems more appropriate.

ἔργον εὐαγγελιστοῦ: The office of evangelist is mentioned Acts xxi. 8, Eph. iv. 11. The evangelist was an itinerant preacher who had not the supervising functions of an apostle, nor the inspiration of a prophet; though both apostle and prophet did, *inter alia*, the work of evangelist. This was in all likelihood the work to which Timothy had originally been called. St. Paul here reminds him that in the faithful performance of what might seem to be subordinate duties lies the best preservative of the Church from error. Note, that the office of an episcopus is also an **ἔργον**, 1 Tim. iii. 1, *cf.* 1 Cor. xvi. 10, Phil. ii. 30, Eph. iv. 12, 1 Thess. v. 13.

τὴν διακονίαν σου πληροφόρησον: *fulfil*. According to Chrys., this does not differ from **πλήρωσον.** See Col. iv. 17, Acts xii. 25. For **διακονία**, *ministry* or service in general, see 1 Tim. i. 12.

Ver. 6. The connexion from ver. 3 seems to be this: The dangers to the Church are pressing and instant; they can only be met by watchfulness, self-sacrifice, and devotion to duty on the part of the leaders of the Church, of whom thou art one. As for me, I have done my best. My King is calling me from the field of action to wait for my reward; thou canst no longer look to me to take initiative in action. This seems to be the force of the emphatic **ἐγώ** and the connecting **γάρ.**

ἤδη σπένδομαι: *jam delibor* (Vulg.). The analogy of Phil. ii. 17, **σπένδ. ἐπὶ τῇ θυσίᾳ καὶ λειτουργίᾳ** (where see Lightfoot's note), is sufficient to prove that St. Paul did not regard his own death as a sacrifice. There the **θυσία** is the persons of the Philippian converts (*cf.* Rom. xii. 1, xv. 16) rendered acceptable by faith, and offered up by their faith. Here the nature of the **θυσία** is not determined, possibly not thought of, by the writer. The reason alleged by Chrys. for the absence here of the term **θυσία** is ingenious: "For the whole of the sacrifice was not offered to God, but the whole of the drink-offering was." It is immaterial to decide whether the imagery is drawn from the Jewish drink-offerings, or heathen libations. Lightfoot quotes interesting parallels from the dying words of Seneca: "stagnum calidae aquae introiit resper-

¹ ἀγῶνα τὸν καλὸν DKLP.

gens proximos servorum, addita voce, libare se liquorem illum Jovi Liberatori" (Tac. Ann. xv. 64), and from Ignatius, "Grant me nothing more than that I be poured out a libation (σπονδισθῆναι) to God, while there is yet an altar ready" (Rom. 2).

τῆς ἀναλύσεως: There is no figure of speech, such as that of striking a tent or unmooring a ship, suggested by ἀνάλυσις. It was as common a euphemism for death as is our word departure. See the verb in Phil. i. 23, and, besides the usual references given by the commentators, see examples supplied by Moulton and Milligan, Expositor, vii., v. 266. The Vulg. resolutionis is wrong. Dean Bernard calls attention to the "verbal similarities of expression" between this letter to Timothy and Philippians, written when Timothy was with St. Paul, viz., σπένδομαι, ἀνάλυσις here and ἀναλῦσαι, Phil. i. 23, and the image of the race; there (Phil. iii. 13, 14) not completed, here finished, v. 7.

ἐφέστηκεν: instat (Vulg.), is come (R.V.), is already present, rather than is at hand (A.V.), which implies a postponement. For similar prescience of approaching death compare 2 Pet. i. 14.

Ver. 7. τὸν καλὸν ἀγῶνα ἠγώνισμαι: See note on 1 Tim. vi. 12. The following τὸν δρόμον, κ.τ.λ., makes this reference to the games hardly doubtful.

τὸν δρόμον τετέλεκα: cursum consummavi (Vulg.). What had been a purpose (Acts xx. 24) was now a retrospect. To say "My race is run," is not to boast, but merely to state a fact. The figure is also found in 1 Cor. ix. 24, Phil. iii. 12. The course is the race of life; we must not narrow it, as Chrys. does, to St. Paul's missionary travels.

τὴν πίστιν τετήρηκα: As in ii. 21, St. Paul passes from the metaphor to the reality. For the force of τηρέω here, see note on 1 Tim. vi. 14; and cf. Rev.

xiv. 12, οἱ τηροῦντες τὰς ἐντολὰς τοῦ θεοῦ καὶ τὴν πίστιν Ἰησοῦ. The faith is a deposit, παραθήκη, a trust which the Apostle is now ready to render up to Him who entrusted it to him. There is no real inconsistency between the tone of this passage and that of some in earlier epistles, e.g., Phil. iii. 12, sqq. St. Paul is merely stating what the grace of God had done for him. A man does well to be distrustful as regards his use of the years of life that may remain to him; but when the life that he has lived has been admittedly lived "in the faith which is in the Son of God" (Gal. ii. 20), mock modesty becomes mischievous ingratitude.

Ver. 8. λοιπόν: For what remains. The R.V. renders it besides in 1 Cor. i. 16, moreover in 1 Cor. iv. 2. The notion of duration of future time is not in the word any more than in the French du reste. St. Paul means here "I have nothing more to do than to receive the crown". λοιπόν has the sense of in conclusion in 2 Cor. xiii. 11, 1 Thess. iv. 1, and does not differ from τὸ λοιπὸν as used in Phil. iii. 1, iv. 8, 2 Thess. iii. 1; or τοῦ λοιποῦ as used in Gal. vi. 17, Eph. vi. 10. The meaning of τὸ λοιπόν in 1 Cor. vii. 29, Heb. x. 13 is henceforth.

ἀπόκειται: reposita est (Vulg.). Cf. Col. i. 5, διὰ τὴν ἐλπίδα τὴν ἀποκειμένην ὑμῖν ἐν τοῖς οὐρανοῖς, and, for the sentiment, 1 Pet. i. 4.

ὁ τῆς δικαιοσύνης στέφανος: The whole context demands that this should be the possessive genitive, The crown which belongs to, or is the due reward of, righteousness, the incorruptible crown of 1 Cor. ix. 25. The verbal analogies of στέφ. τῆς ζωῆς, James i. 12, Rev. ii. 10, and στέφ. τῆς δόξης, 1 Pet. v. 4, support the view that it is the gen. of apposition; but it is difficult on this supposition to give the phrase an intelligible meaning. "Good works, which are the

9. [1m]Σπούδασον [m]ἐλθεῖν [m]πρός [m]με ταχέως· 10. Δημᾶς γάρ | See 2 Tim.
με [n]ἐγκατέλιπεν[1] ἀγαπήσας [o]τὸν [o]νῦν [o]αἰῶνα, καὶ ἐπορεύθη εἰς   ii. 15.
                                             m Tit. iii.
Θεσσαλονίκην, Κρήσκης εἰς Γαλατίαν,[2] Τίτος εἰς Δαλματίαν[3]· 11.   12.
                                               n Josh. i. 5,
                                                Ps. xv.
                                                (xvi.) 10,
    xxi. (xxii.) 1, Isa. i. 4, 2 Cor. iv. 9, Heb. x. 25, 2 Tim. iv. 16.   o See I. Tim. vi. 17.

---

[1] So א[D*] Ksil. most cursives; ἐγκατέλειπεν ACDᵇᶜFGLP, 17, 47*, one other.

[2] Γαλλίαν אC, 23, 31, 39, 73, 80, am*, Eus., H. E. iii. 4, 8.

[3] Δελματίαν C, 2, 67**, eleven others; Δερματίαν A.

---

fruits of Faith and follow after Justification . . . are pleasing and acceptable to God in Christ" (Art. xii.). It is to be noted that στεφ. τῆς δικ. is applied to the golden fillet worn by the high priest in the *Tests. of Twelve Patriarchs*, Levi, viii. 2.

ἀποδώσει : *reddet* (Vulg.). As long as we agree to the statement that Moses ἀπέβλεπεν εἰς τὴν μισθαποδοσίαν (Heb. xi. 26), it seems trifling to dispute the retributive force of ἀπο- in this word. Of course "the reward is not reckoned as of debt, but as of grace". St. Paul could say, "It is a righteous thing with God to recompense (ἀνταποδοῦναι) . . . to you that are afflicted rest with us" (2 Thess. i. 6, 7), see also Rom. ii. 6.

ἐν ἐκείνῃ τῇ ἡμέρᾳ : see on i. 12.

ὁ δίκαιος κριτής : The notion expressed in this phrase goes back to Gen. xviii. 25. For the actual words, see reff.

οὐ μόνον δὲ . . . ἀλλὰ καί : see on 1 Tim. v. 13.

τοῖς ἠγαπηκόσι τὴν ἐπιφάνειαν αὐτοῦ : The ἐπιφάνεια here meant is the Second Coming of Christ. Those who love it do not fear it, for "there is no fear in love" (1 John iv. 18); they endeavour to make themselves increasingly ready and fit for it (1 John iii. 3); when they hear the Lord say, "I come quickly," their hearts respond, "Amen; come, Lord Jesus" (Rev. xxii. 20). The perfect tense is used because their love will have continued up to the moment of their receiving the crown, or because St. Paul is thinking of them from the standpoint of the day of crowning.

Vv. 9-12. Come to me as speedily as you can. I am almost alone. Some of my company have forsaken me; others I have despatched on business. Bring Mark with you. I have use for him.

Ver. 9. ταχέως : more definitely expressed in ver. 21, "before winter".

Ver. 10. Demas had been a loyal fellow-worker of the apostle (Philem. 24; Col. iv. 14). Chrys. supposes that Thessalonica was his home. It is futile to discuss the reality or the degree of his blameworthiness. Possibly he alleged a call to Thessalonica. All we know is that St. Paul singles him out among the absent ones for condemnation.

ἐγκατέλιπεν : *dereliquit* (Vulg.), *forsook*, not merely *left*. See reff. The aorist points to a definite past occasion now in St. Paul's mind.

ἀγαπήσας τὸν νῦν αἰῶνα : See 1 Tim. vi. 17. It is just possible that Bengel is right in seeing an intentional deplorable contrast ("luctuosum vide antitheton") between this expression and ver. 8.

εἰς Θεσσαλονίκην : Lightfoot (*Biblical Essays*, p. 247) alleges other reasons for the supposition that Demas hailed from Thessalonica, *viz.*, He "is mentioned next to Aristarchus, the Thessalonian in Philem. 24, and . . . the name Demetrius, of which Demas is a contract form, occurs twice among the list of politarchs of that city".

Κρήσκης εἰς Γαλατίαν : sc. ἐπορεύθη. Crescens and Titus are not reproached for their absence. This passage, with the variant Γαλλίαν (see *apparat. crit.*), is the source of all that is said about Crescens by later writers.

Γαλατίαν : That this means the Roman province, or the region in Asia Minor (so *Const. Apost.* vii. 46) is favoured by the consideration that all the other places mentioned in this context are east of Rome. On the other hand, if we assume that St. Paul had recently visited Spain (Clem. Rom. 1 *Cor.* 5; Muratorian Canon), it would naturally follow that he had visited Southern Gaul *en route;* and Crescens might plausibly be supposed to have gone to confirm the Churches there. So Euseb. *H. E.* iii. 4, Epiph. *Haeres.* li. 11, Theodore and Theodoret, h. l.

Τίτος εἰς Δαλματίαν : This statement suggests that Titus had only been a temporary deputy for St. Paul in Crete. On the spelling of the name Dalmatia in *apparat. crit.*, see Deissmann, *Bible Studies*, trans. p. 182.

Ver. 11. Λουκᾶς : Nothing can be more natural than that "the beloved

Λουκᾶς ἐστὶν μόνος μετ' ἐμοῦ. Μᾶρκον [p]ἀναλαβὼν ἄγε[1] μετὰ σεαυτοῦ· ἔστιν γάρ μοι [q]εὔχρηστος εἰς διακονίαν. 12. Τυχικὸν δὲ ἀπέστειλα εἰς Ἔφεσον. 13. τὸν [r]φελόνην ὃν [s]ἀπέλιπον[2] ἐν Τρῳάδι παρὰ Κάρπῳ ἐρχόμενος φέρε, καὶ τὰ [t]βιβλία, μάλιστα τὰς [u]μεμ-

p Acts xx. 13, 14, xxiii. 31.
q See 2 Tim. ii. 21.
r Here only, not LXX.
s 2 Tim. iv. 20, Tit. i. 5, Jude 6.
t Luke iv. 17, 20, John xx. 30, xxi. 25, Gal. iii. 10, etc.
u Here only, not LXX.

[1] ἄγαγε A, 31, 47, 238, five others.

[2] So ℵDK sil., many cursives; ἀπέλειπον ACFGLP.

physician" and historian should feel that he of all men was in his place beside St. Paul when the end was so nearly approaching. The **μόνος** is relative to fellow-labourers in the gospel. St. Paul had many friends in Rome (ver. 21).

Μᾶρκον: St. Paul was now completely reconciled to John Mark who had, before Col. iv. 10 was written, vindicated and justified the risk Barnabas had run in giving him a chance of recovering his character (see Acts xiii. 13, xv. 38). **ἀναλαβών**: *assume* (Vulg.). *Take up on your way*. *Assumere* is also the Latin in Acts xx. 14, xxiii. 31, but *suscipere* in xx. 13. It is implied that Mark was somewhere on the line of route between Ephesus and Rome; but we do not know the precise place.

ἄγε μετὰ σεαυτοῦ: This phrase is illustrated from the papyri by Moulton and Milligan, *Expositor*, vii., v. 57.

εὔχρηστος εἰς διακονίαν: As Mark was the **ἑρμηνευτής** of St. Peter, rendering his Aramaic into Greek, so he may have helped St. Paul by a knowledge of Latin. **διακονία**, however, does not necessarily include preaching. It is characteristic of St. Paul that he should not regard "the ministry which he had received from the Lord Jesus" as "accomplished" so long as he had breath to "testify the gospel of the grace of God" (Acts xx. 24).

Ver. 12. **Τυχικὸν δέ, κ.τ.λ.**: The **δέ** does not involve a comparison of Tychicus with Mark, as both **εὔχρηστοι** (so Ell.); but rather distinguishes the cause of Tychicus' absence from that of the others. Demas had *forsaken* the apostle; and Crescens and Titus had *gone*, perhaps on their own initiative; Tychicus had been *sent away* by St. Paul himself. For Tychicus, see Acts xx. 4, Eph. vi. 21, 22, Col. iv. 7, 8, Tit. iii. 12; and the art. in Hastings' *D. B.*

εἰς Ἔφεσον: If the emphasis in the clause lies on **ἀπέστειλα**, as has been just suggested, the difficulty of harmonising **εἰς Ἔφεσον** with the common belief that Timothy was himself in chief authority in the Church at Ephesus is somewhat mitigated. St. Paul had mentioned the places to which Demas, etc., had gone; and even on the supposition that St. Paul knew that Tychicus was with Timothy, he could not say, "I sent away Tychicus" without completing the sentence by adding the destination. This explanation must be adopted, if we suppose with Ell. that Tychicus was the bearer of *First Timothy*. If he were the bearer of *Second Timothy*, **ἀπέστειλα** can be plausibly explained as the epistolary aorist. On the other hand, there is no reason why we should assume that Timothy was at Ephesus at this time. Other local references, *e.g.*, i. 15, 18, and iv. 13 are quite consistent with a belief that he was not actually in that city. Perhaps "Do the work of an evangelist" (iv. 5) is an indication that he was itinerating.

Ver. 13. I want my warm winter cloak and my books.

τὸν φελόνην: The **φελόνης**, or **φαιλόνης**, by metathesis for **φαινόλης**, was the same as the Latin *paenula*, from which it is derived, a circular cape which fell down below the knees, with an opening for the head in the centre. (So Chrys. on Phil. ii. 30; Tert. *De orat.* xii.). The Syriac here renders it *a case for writings, a portfolio*, an explanation noted by Chrys., **τὸ γλωσσόκομον ἔνθα τὰ βιβλία ἔκειτο**. But this is merely a guess suggested by its being coupled with **βιβλία** and **μεμβράνας**.

Τρῳάδι: Even if Timothy was not in Ephesus, he was in Asia, and travellers thence to Rome usually passed through Troas. Perhaps St. Paul had been arrested at Troas, and had not been allowed to take his cloak, etc. This is a more plausible supposition than that he was making a hurried flight from Alexander, as Lock conjectures, Hastings' *D. B.*, iv. 775, *a*.

Κάρπῳ: See art. in Hastings' *D. B.*

τὰ βιβλία would be papyrus rolls in use for ordinary purposes, while the

βράνας.   14. Ἀλέξανδρος ὁ ᵛχαλκεὺς πολλά μοι κακὰ ᵂἐνεδείξατο · vHereonly,
N.T.
—ἀποδώσει ¹ αὐτῷ ὁ Κύριος κατὰ τὰ ἔργα αὐτοῦ ·—15. ὃν καὶ σὺ wGen.l.15,
17, etc., 2
ˣφυλάσσου, ʸλίαν γὰρ ᶻἀντέστη ² τοῖς ἡμετέροις λόγοις.   16. Ἐν Cor. viii.
24, Tit. ii.
τῇ πρώτῃ μου ᵃἀπολογίᾳ οὐδείς μοι ᵇπαρεγένετο,³ ἀλλὰ πάντες 10, iii. 2,
Heb. vi.
10, 11.

x Luke xii. 15, Acts xxi. 25, 2 Pet. iii. 17.   y Matt. (4), Mark (4), Luke (1), 2 John 4, 3 John 3.
z See 2 Tim. iii. 8.   a Acts xxii. 1, xxv. 16, 1 Cor. ix. 3, 2 Cor. vii. 11, Phil. i. 7, 16, 1 Pet. iii, 15.
b Acts v. 21, xxi. 18, xxiii. 35, xxiv. 24, xxv. 7.

¹ So ℵACDFG, 17, 31, 37, 67**, 80, 108, nine others, f, g, vgᶜˡᵉᵐ., go., syrᵖᵉˢʰ,
boh. arm. ; ἀποδῴη DᶜK(δωει)L, most cursives, d, e, am., fuld.

² ἀνθέστηκε ℵᶜDᶜKLP.   ³ συμπαρεγένετο ℵᶜDKLP.

more costly μεμβράναι contained, in all
likelihood, portions of the Hebrew Scriptures, hence μάλιστα (see Kenyon,
Textual Crit. of N. T. p. 22). We
know that St. Paul employed in study the
enforced leisure of prison (Acts xxvi. 24).
We may note that, like Browning's
Grammarian, he did not allow his normal
strenuous life to be affected or diverted
by the known near approach of death.

Vv. 14, 15. Beware of Alexander the
smith.

Ver. 14. Ἀλέξανδρος ὁ χαλκεύς: It
is probable that this is the Alexander
mentioned in 1 Tim. i. 20, and it is possible that he may be the Jew of that
name who was unwillingly prominent in
the riot at Ephesus (Acts xix. 33, 34).

χαλκεύς: does not mean that he
worked only in copper. The term came
to be used of workers in any kind of
metal (see Gen. iv. 22, LXX).

πολλά μοι κακὰ ἐνεδείξατο: Multa
mala mihi ostendit (Vulg.). His odium
theologicum expressed itself in deeds as
well as in words. For this use of ἐν-
δείκνυμαι, compare reff. Moulton and
Milligan (Expositor, vii., vii. 282) cite
from a papyrus of ii. A.D. πᾶσαν πίστιν
μοι ἐνδεικνυμένη.

ἀποδώσει: The future indic. is certainly attested by a greater weight of
external evidence than the optative.
The moral question raised by the clause
is quite independent of the mood and
tense used: it is, Was the future punishment of Alexander, which St. Paul considered equitable, a matter of more
satisfaction than distress to the apostle?
The answer would seem to be, Yes. And,
provided that no element of personal
spite intrudes, such a feeling cannot be
logically condemned. If God is a moral
governor ; if sin is a reality ; those who
know themselves to be on God's side
cannot help a feeling of joy in knowing
that evil will not always triumph over

good. The sentiment comes from Deut.
xxxii. 35, as quoted in Rom. xii. 19, ἐγὼ
ἀνταποδώσω. The exact wording is
found in Ps. lxi. (lxii.) 13, σὺ ἀποδώσεις
ἑκάστῳ κατὰ τὰ ἔργα αὐτοῦ. Cf. Ps.
xxvii. (xxviii.) 4 ; Prov. xxiv. 12.

Ver. 15. φυλάσσου: For this sense
of φυλάσσω with a direct object, see reff.
We infer that Alexander was in Timothy's
vicinity.

ἡμετέροις λόγοις: The λόγοι were
expressions of doctrine common to all
Christians with St. Paul ; hence ἡμετέροις.

Vv. 16-18. I have spoken of my present loneliness. Yet I have no justification for depression ; for since I came to
Rome I have had experience, at my preliminary trial, that God is a loyal protec-
tor when earthly friends fail. And so I
have good hope that He will bring me
safe through every danger to His heavenly kingdom.

Ver. 16. The reference in my first
defence seems at first sight somewhat
uncertain, since ver. 17 states the issue of
that "defence" to have been that "the
message was fully proclaimed, and all the
Gentiles heard it ". This would agree
with the circumstances of the trials before
Felix and Festus, a direct result of which
was that Paul was enabled to "bear witness also at Rome" (Acts xxiii. 11). On
this view, the apostle would be recalling
a signal past instance in which God had
overruled evil for good. On the other
hand, it is a fatal objection to this reference of the phrase that when he was at
Cæsarea he seems to have been kindly
treated by his friends as well as by the
officials. And, moreover, the sentence
reads like a piece of fresh information.
This latter consideration is also an argument against referring it to the first
Roman imprisonment (as Euseb. H. E.
ii. 22), though the very similar sentiments
of Phil. i. 12, 13, render the identification

c See ver. 10.
d Rom. ii.
26, iv.
passim., 2
Cor. v. 19,
Gen. xv.
6, Ps.
xxxi.
(xxxii.) 2.
e Acts xxvii. 23, Rom. xvi. 2.

με ^cἐγκατέλιπον¹·—μὴ αὐτοῖς ^dλογισθείη.—17. ὁ δὲ Κύριός μοι ^eπαρέστη καὶ ^fἐνεδυνάμωσέν με, ἵνα δι᾽ ἐμοῦ ^gτὸ ^gκήρυγμα ^hπληρο-φορηθῇ καὶ ἀκούσωσιν² πάντα τὰ ἔθνη· καὶ ⁱἐρύσθην ἐκ στόματος λέοντος.³ 18. ῥύσεταί με ὁ Κύριος ἀπὸ παντὸς ^kἔργου ^kπονηροῦ

f See 1 Tim. i. 12.   g 1 Cor. i. 21, Tit. i. 3.   h See ver.
i See 2 Tim. iii. 11.   k John iii. 19, vii. 7, Col. i. 21, 1 John iii. 12.

¹ So אD*Ksil., most cursives; ἐγκατέλειπον ACDbcFGLP.
² ἀκούσῃ KL.   ³ Ins. καὶ DcFgrGKLP, g, syrr.

plausible. But in this latter case again the language of *Philippians* has no traces of forsakenness. We decide therefore that St. Paul is here referring to the preliminary investigation (*prima actio*) which he underwent after he arrived at Rome a prisoner for the second time, and which resulted in his remand. He was now writing to Timothy during the interval between his remand and the second, and final, trial. But if we thus explain "my first defence," how are we to interpret ἵνα δι᾽ ἐμοῦ, κ.τ.λ.? The explanation will be suggested by a comparison of such passages as Rom. xv. 19, "From Jerusalem, and round about even unto Illyricum, I have fully preached the gospel of Christ"; Col. i. 23, "The gospel which . . . was preached in all creation". We annex a territory by the mere act of planting our country's flag on a small portion of its soil; so in St. Paul's thought a single proclamation of the gospel might have a spiritual, almost a prophetical, significance, immeasurably greater than could be imagined by one who heard it. "Una sæpe occasio maximi est momenti" (Bengel). It is to be noted too that παρέστη and ἐνεδυνάμωσεν refer to the occasion of the "first defence," and St. Paul does not say that the Lord set him free; so that we are obliged to explain ἵνα δι᾽ ἐμοῦ, κ.τ.λ. of St. Paul's bold assertion of his faith in Christ on that occasion, which however was a public one, not like his previous private teaching to those who came to him "in his own hired dwelling" (Acts xxviii. 30).

παρεγένετο: *adfuit* (Vulg.), *supported me as* "*advocatus*". The verb is used of appearing in a court of justice in reff. It simply means *to come* or *arrive* in 1 Cor. xvi. 3. This complaint is difficult to reconcile with ver 21. Perhaps here St. Paul is referring to old friends on whom he had a special claim.

Ver. 17. παρέστη: *The Lord was my* "*patronus*," *cf.* Rom. xvi. 2. But the word is used in a purely local sense of the felt presence of a Divine Being in reff. in Acts.

ἐνεδυνάμωσεν: See note on 1 Tim. i. 12.

πληροφορηθῇ: *impleatur* (Vulg.). As long as there had been no public proclamation of the gospel by Paul himself in Rome, the function of κῆρυξ had not been completely fulfilled by him.

ἐρύσθην ἐκ στόματος λέοντος: This is most naturally understood as an echo of Ps. xxi.(xxii.) 22, σῶσόν με ἐκ στόματος λέοντος. ῥῦσαι occurs in the verse preceding. And what follows in the LXX seems to point to the most satisfactory explanation of the apostle's meaning, καὶ ἀπὸ κεράτων μονοκερώτων τὴν ταπείνωσίν μου. διηγήσομαι τὸ ὄνομα σου τοῖς ἀδελφοῖς μου, κ.τ.λ. If St. Paul had not been strengthened to complete his κήρυγμα, his failure would have been his ταπείνωσις. As it was, he was delivered from that calamity, and enabled to declare God's name to the Gentiles. It is impossible, in view of ἤδη σπένδομαι (ver. 6), to suppose that delivery from death is implied. πρώτη (ver. 16) proves that the apostle was aware that a second trial was awaiting him, the issue of which he knew would be his execution. It is still more impossible to suppose that literal wild beasts are meant. Paul's Roman citizenship secured him from that degradation. The Greek commentators take "the lion" to mean Nero, "from his ferocity" (Chrys.). *Cf.* Esth. xiv. 13, of Ahasuerus; Joseph. *Antiq.* xviii. 6, 10, of Tiberius. It is no objection to this exegesis that the article is omitted before λέοντος, since, as we have seen, there is none in the Psalm. But deliverance from that lion's mouth would be equivalent to acquittal by the Roman government; and it is evident that St. Paul was well aware that his sentence had been only deferred.

Ver. 18. ἔργου πονηροῦ: The form of the clause may be modelled on the peti-

καὶ σώσει εἰς τὴν βασιλείαν αὐτοῦ τὴν ἐπουράνιον· ᾧ ἡ δόξα εἰς l See ver. 13.
m See 2
Tim. ii. 15. τοὺς αἰῶνας τῶν αἰώνων· ἀμήν.

19. Ἄσπασαι Πρίσκαν καὶ Ἀκύλαν καὶ τὸν Ὀνησιφόρου οἶκον.
20. Ἔραστος ἔμεινεν ἐν Κορίνθῳ· Τρόφιμον δὲ ¹ἀπέλιπον¹ ἐν Μιλήτῳ ἀσθενοῦντα. 21. ᵐσπούδασον πρὸ χειμῶνος ἐλθεῖν.

¹ So אDFGKsil., most cursives; ἀπέλειπον CLP, 17, 31, 47*, one other.

tion in the Lord's Prayer, ῥῦσαι ἡμᾶς ἀπὸ τοῦ πονηροῦ; but the addition of ἔργου proves that the deliverance spoken of is not from an external Evil Personality, but from a possible evil deed of the apostle's own doing. The expression has always a subjective reference. See reff. This exegesis is in harmony with the view taken above of "the mouth of the lion". Failure to be receptive of the strengthening grace of the Lord would have been, in St. Paul's judgment, an "evil deed," though others might easily find excuses for it. Chrys. takes a similar view of ἔργου πονηροῦ, but gives it a wider application: "He will yet again deliver me from every sin, that is, He will not suffer me to depart with condemnation". This view is also supported by what follows, σώσει, κ.τ.λ. At one moment the apostle sees the crown of righteousness just within his grasp, at another, while no less confident, he acknowledges that he could not yet be said "to have apprehended".

σώσει εἰς: shall bring me safely to, salvum faciet (Vulg.). "Dominus est et Liberator, 1 Thess. i. 10, et Salvator, Phil. iii. 20" (Bengel).

βασιλείαν . . . ἐπουράνιον: That the Father's kingdom is also the Son's is Pauline doctrine. ἐπουράνιος became a necessary addition to βασιλεία as it became increasingly evident that the kingdom of heaven which we see is very different from the kingdom of heaven to be consummated hereafter. It is difficult not to see a connexion between this passage and the doxology appended in primitive times to the Lord's Prayer, ὅτι σοῦ ἐστιν ἡ βασιλεία καὶ ἡ δύναμις καὶ ἡ δόξα εἰς τοὺς αἰῶνας.

ᾧ ἡ δόξα: The doxology, unmistakably addressed to Christ, need only cause a difficulty to those who maintain that "God blessed for ever" in Rom. ix. 5 cannot refer to Christ, because St. Paul was an Arian. Yet Rom. xvi. 27, 1 Pet. iv. 11, not to mention 2 Pet. iii. 18, Rev. i. 6. v. 13, are other examples of doxologies to the Son.

Vv. 19-22. Final salutations.
Ver. 19. Πρίσκαν καὶ Ἀκύλαν: The same unusual order, the wife before the husband, is found in Rom. xvi. 3, Acts xviii. 18, 26, but not in Acts xviii. 2, 1 Cor. xvi. 19. "Probably Prisca was of higher rank than her husband, for her name is that of a good old Roman family [the Acilian gens]. Aquila was probably a freedman. The name does indeed occur as cognomen in some Roman families; but it was also a slave name, for a freedman of Maecenas was called (C. Cilnius) Aquila" (Ramsay, St. Paul the Traveller, pp. 268, 269; see also Sanday and Headlam, Romans, p. 118 sqq.).

τὸν Ὀνησιφόρου οἶκον: Their names are inserted after Ἀκύλαν from the Acts of Paul and Thecla, by the cursives 46 and 109: Λέκτραν τὴν γυναῖκα αὐτοῦ καὶ Σιμαίαν καὶ Ζήνωνα τοὺς υἱοὺς αὐτοῦ.

Ver. 20. Ἔραστος ἔμεινεν: The name Erastus is too common to make probable the identification of this companion of St. Paul's and the οἰκονόμος, treasurer, of Corinth, who joins in the apostle's salutation in Rom. xvi. 23. It is not antecedently likely that a city official could travel about as a missionary. On the other hand, it is probable that this Erastus is the same as the companion of Timothy mentioned in Acts xix. 22. It is to be observed that St. Paul here resumes from ver. 12 his explanation of the absence from Rome of members of his company whose presence with their master at this crisis would have been natural. It is possible that Erastus and Trophimus were with St. Paul when he was arrested the second time, and that they remained in his company as far as Miletus and Corinth respectively.

Τρόφιμον: See Acts xx. 4, xxi. 29, and the art. in Hastings' D. B.

ἀσθενοῦντα: Paley's remark is never out of date, "Forgery, upon such an occasion, would not have spared a miracle" (Horae Paul. Philippians 2). Chrys. notes, "The apostles could not do everything, or they did not dispense miraculous gifts upon all occasions, lest more should be ascribed to them than was right".

Ver. 21. πρὸ χειμῶνος: "That thou

Ἀσπάζεταί σε Εὔβουλος καὶ Πούδης καὶ Λίνος καὶ Κλαυδία καὶ οἱ
ἀδελφοὶ πάντες.[1] 22. Ὁ Κύριος[2] μετὰ τοῦ πνεύματός σου. ἡ
χάρις μεθ' ὑμῶν.[3]

[1] Om. πάντες ℵ*, 17.

[2] So, ὁ Κύριος, ℵ*FgrG, 17, one other, g; ins. Ἰησοῦς A, 31, one other; ins.
Ἰησοῦς Χριστὸς ℵcCDKLP, d, e, f, vg., syrr., boh., arm.

[3] Ins. ἀμήν ℵcDKLP, d, e, vg., syrr.; add πρὸς Τιμόθεον ℵC, 17; πρὸς Τ.
β' ἐπληρώθη D; ἐτελέσθη πρ. Τ. β' FG; πρ. Τ. β' ἐγράφη ἀπὸ Λαοδικείας A; πρ.
Τ. β' ἐγράφει ἀπὸ Ῥώμης P; πρ. Τ. δευτέρα· τῆς Ἐφεσίων ἐκκλησίας ἐπίσκοπον
χειροτονηθέντα· ἐγράφη ἀπὸ Ῥώμης, ὅτε ἐκ δευτέρου παρέστη Παῦλος τῷ Καίσαρι
Ῥώμης Νέρωνι K, many cursives, similarly L.

be not detained," sc. by storm (Chrys.).
This seems less urgent than ταχέως of
ver. 9, and we may infer that St. Paul
did not expect his final trial to take place
for some months.

Εὔβουλος : Nothing else is known of
this good man.

Πούδης καὶ Λίνος καὶ Κλαυδία : Lightfoot (*Apostolic Fathers*, part i. vol. i.
pp. 76-79) has an exhaustive discussion
of the various ingenious theories which,
starting with the assumption that Pudens
and Claudia were man and wife—a supposition opposed by the order of the
names—have identified them with (1)
Martial's congenial friend Aulus Pudens,
to whom the poet casually "imputes the
foulest vices of heathenism," and his
bride Claudia Rufina, a girl of British
race (*Epigr.* iv. 13, xi. 53), (2) "a doubtful Pudens and imaginary Claudia " who
have been evolved out of a fragmentary
inscription found at Chichester in 1722.
This appears to record the erection of a
temple by a Pudens with the sanction of
Claudius Cogidubnus, who is probably

a British king who might have had a
daughter, whom he might have named
Claudia, and who might have taken the
name Rufina from Pomponia, the wife
of Aulus Plautius, the Roman commander
in Britain. This last supposition would
identify (1) and (2). It should be added
that in *Const. Apost.* vii. 46 she is mother
of Linus. See also arts. *Claudia* and
Pudens in Hastings' *D. B.*

Linus is identified by Irenæus with
the Linus whom SS. Peter and Paul
consecrated first Bishop of Rome (*Haer.*
iii. 3). See also art. in Hastings' *D. B.*

Ver. 22. μετὰ τοῦ πνεύματός σου:
This expression, with ὑμῶν for σου,
occurs in Gal. vi. 18, Philem. 25 ; but in
both those places it is " The grace of our
Lord Jesus Christ be with," etc. Here a
very close personal association between
the Lord and Timothy is prayed for. Dean
Bernard compares the conclusion of the
Epistle of Barnabas, ὁ κύριος τῆς δόξης
καὶ πάσης χάριτος μετὰ τοῦ πνεύματος
ὑμῶν.

μεθ' ὑμῶν: See note on 1 Tim. vi. 21.

ΠΡΟΣ ΤΙΤΟΝ

I. 1. ΠΑΥΛΟΣ δοῦλος Θεοῦ, ᵃἀπόστολος δὲ ᵃ'Ιησοῦ ᵃΧριστοῦ [1] a See 1 Tim
κατὰ πίστιν ᵇἐκλεκτῶν ᵇΘεοῦ καὶ ᶜἐπίγνωσιν ᶜἀληθείας ᵈτῆς ᵈκατ' b Rom. viii.
ᵈᵉεὐσέβειαν 2. ἐπ' ᶠἐλπίδι ᶠᵍζωῆς ᶠᵍαἰωνίου, ἣν ἐπηγγείλατο ὁ iii. 12.

i. 1.
33, Col.
c See 1 Tim.
ii. 4.
d 1 Tim. vi. 3.   e See 1 Tim. ii. 2.   f Tit. iii. 7.   g See 1 Tim. i. 16.

[1] Χριστ. Ἰησ. A, 108, two others, fuld., boh., syrʰᶜˡ; om. Ἰησοῦ Dgr*.

CHAPTER I.—Vv. 1-4. Salutation, in which the place of the Gospel in eternity and in time is largely expressed.

Ver. 1. δοῦλος θεοῦ: The only parallel to this phrase in the opening formula of any other epistle in the N.T. is James i. 1; but there it is, "James, a servant of God and of the Lord Jesus Christ." It is no less obvious than necessary to note that this variation from St. Paul's formula δοῦλος Ἰησ. Χρ. (Rom. i. 1; Phil. i. 1) would not be likely in a pseudepigraphic writing.

ἀπόστολος δὲ Ἰησοῦ Χριστοῦ: See note on 1 Tim. i. 1. The δέ is not merely copulative, as in Jude 1; but marks the antithesis between the two aspects of Paul's relationship to the Supreme: between God as known to his fathers, and as recently manifested in the sphere of history.

κατὰ πίστιν κ.τ.λ.: to be connected with ἀπόστολος only. It is natural to suppose that κατά has the same force here as in 2 Tim. i. 1, κατ' ἐπαγγελίαν ζωῆς, where see note. His apostleship was *for the confirmation of the faith of God's elect, and for the spreading of the knowledge*, etc., etc. We take κατά as = *for* or *in regard to*; and expand it according to the exigencies of the context. Here *God's elect* does not mean those whom God intends to select; but those who have been externally selected, and who consequently possess faith. See reff. and Acts xiii. 48. They do not need that it should be generated in them, but that it should be fostered. See note on 2 Tim. ii. 10. Contrast ἀποστολὴν εἰς ὑπακοὴν πίστεως ἐν

πᾶσιν τοῖς ἔθνεσιν, Rom. i. 5, where the Gospel-propagation function of his apostleship is indicated.

The rendering here of the Vulg. and of the English versions, *according to the faith*, etc., *secundum fidem*, preserves the common meaning of κατά, but does not stand examination. St. Paul's office as apostle was not dependent in any way on the faith or knowledge of human beings, as it was on the will or command of God or Christ. The final cause of it was the faith and knowledge of men.

ἐπίγνωσιν ἀληθείας: See on 1 Tim. ii. 4.

εὐσέβειαν: See on 1 Tim. ii. 2.

Ver. 2. ἐπ' ἐλπίδι κ.τ.λ.: This is best taken in connexion with the preceding clause, κατὰ πίστιν ... εὐσέβειαν. The faith and the knowledge there spoken of have as their basis of action, or energy, the hope of eternal life. Cf. 1 Tim. i. 16. Compare the use of ἐπ' ἐλπίδι in Acts xxvi. 6; Rom. iv. 18, viii. 20; 1 Cor. ix. 10. On the other hand, we must not exclude a remoter connexion with ἀπόστολος. A comparison of the parallel passage in 2 Tim. i. 1 suggests that the succession of clauses here, κατὰ πίστιν ... κηρύγματι, is a full and detailed expansion of κατ' ἐπαγγελίαν ... ἐν Χρ. Ἰησ.

ἀψευδής: *qui non mentitur*. See note on 2 Tim. ii. 13.

ἐπηγγείλατο: See Rom. i. 1, iv. 21; Gal. iii. 19.

ἐπηγγείλατο ... πρὸ χρόνων αἰωνίων, ἐφανέρωσεν δέ: The same antithesis is expressed in 2 Tim. i. 9, 10 (*q.v.*); Rom.

h Wisd. vii. ^h ἀψευδὴς Θεὸς ⁱ πρὸ ⁱ χρόνων ⁱ αἰωνίων, 3. ^k ἐφανέρωσεν δὲ ^l καιροῖς
17 only.
i See 2 Tim. ^l ἰδίοις τὸν λόγον αὐτοῦ ἐν ^m κηρύγματι δ ⁿ ἐπιστεύθην ἐγὼ ^o κατ'
i. 9.
k Rom. xvi. ^o ἐπιταγὴν τοῦ ^p σωτῆρος ^p ἡμῶν ^p Θεοῦ, 4. Τίτῳ ^q γνησίῳ ^r τέκνῳ
26, Col. i.
26, 2 Tim. κατὰ κοινὴν πίστιν· χάρις καὶ ^l εἰρήνη ἀπὸ Θεοῦ Πατρὸς καὶ
i. 10, see
1 Tim. iii. ^s Χριστοῦ ^s Ἰησοῦ ^{2 s} τοῦ ^s σωτῆρος ^s ἡμῶν.
16 note.
l See 1 Tim. 5. ^t Τούτου ^t χάριν ^u ἀπέλιπόν ³ σε ἐν Κρήτῃ, ἵνα τὰ ^v λείποντα
ii. 6.
m See 2
Tim. iv. 17. n See 1 Tim. i. 11. o See 1 Tim. i. 1. p See 1 Tim. i. 1. q See 1 Tim.
i. 2. r See 1 Tim. i. 2. s See 2 Tim. i. 10. t Eph. iii. 1, 14, see 1 Tim. v. 14. u See
2 Tim. iv. 13. v Luke xviii. 22, Tit. iii. 13, Jas. i. 4, 5, ii. 15.

¹ ἔλεος ACbKL, syrhcl. ² Κυρίου Ἰησ. Χριστ. DcFGKLP, f, g, syrr.

³ κατέλιπόν ℵcDcK[LP, κατέλειπον].

xvi. 25; Col. i. 26. From different points of view, one may say that eternal life was promised, and given, to man in Christ before times eternal; though the revelation of this purpose and grace could not be made until man was prepared to receive it, καιροῖς, at seasons, occasions, epochs of time as relative to man's comprehension.

Ver. 3. ἐφανέρωσεν τὸν λόγον: For φανερόω see note on 1 Tim. iii. 16. We must observe that no N.T. writer speaks of a manifestation of the *gift* of eternal life (1 John i. 2 refers to the *personal* Incarnate Life). God's message concerning it, which is the revelation of a divine secret purpose, is manifested. See Col. iv. 4 in addition to the last reff. given on ἐπηγγείλατο. περὶ ἧς may be supplied bef. ἐφανέρωσεν (von Soden).

καιροῖς ἰδίοις: See on 1 Tim. ii. 6 and vi. 15. The rendering *his own seasons* suits the context here.

τὸν λόγον αὐτοῦ ἐν κηρύγματι: Note the distinction here indicated between the substance of the revelation (λόγος) given by God, and the form of it as expressible (κήρυγμα) by the human preacher. It is parallel to the use of λόγος and λαλία in John viii. 43.

ὃ ἐπιστεύθην ἐγώ has τὸ εὐαγγέλιον κ.τ.λ. as its antecedent in 1 Tim. i. 11, where see note.

κατ' ἐπιταγὴν τοῦ σωτῆρος ἡμῶν θεοῦ: See note on 1 Tim. i. 1. There the order is θεοῦ σωτῆρος ἡμῶν. Here θεοῦ is epexegetical of σωτῆρος ἡμῶν, as Χριστοῦ Ἰησοῦ is in chap. ii. 13. κατ' ἐπιταγὴν is to be taken with ὃ ἐπιστεύθην ἐγώ, which is another way of expressing the notion of ἀπόστολος. On σωτήρ as a title of God, see notes on 1 Tim. i. 1, ii. 4.

Ver. 4. γνησίῳ τέκνῳ: See note on 1 Tim. i. 2.

κατὰ κοινὴν πίστιν, like ἐν πίστει in 1 Tim. i. 2, qualifies τέκνῳ, but is less ambiguous than ἐν πίστει. It must not be restricted to a faith shared only by St. Paul and Titus; but, like the κοινὴ σωτηρία (Jude 3), it is common to all Christians who "have obtained a like precious faith with us" (2 Pet. i. 1).

χάρις κ.τ.λ.: See on 1 Tim. i. 2.

σωτῆρος: for the more usual κυρίου, 1 Tim. i. 2, 2 Tim. i. 2. The Father and the Son are here co-ordinated as Saviours.

Vv. 5-9. As I left you in Crete to carry out completely the arrangements for the organisation of the Church there, which I set before you in detail, let me remind you of the necessary qualifications of presbyters [since the presbyter is the basal element in the Church Society].

Ver. 5. ἀπέλιπον: The force of ἀπολείπω here will be apparent if we compare 2 Tim. iv. 13, 20. It means to *leave behind temporarily* something or someone; καταλείπω is often used of a permanent leaving behind. St. Paul's language favours the supposition that the commission given to Titus was that of a temporary apostolic legate rather than of a permanent local president.

ἐπιδιορθώσῃ: It is possible that ἐπί has here its original force, so as to imply that St. Paul had begun the correction of deficiencies in the Cretan Church, and that Titus was to carry it still further. (So Bengel.) It seems to have been taken in this sense by A.V.m., which renders τὰ λείποντα *things that are left undone*. If we may judge from this letter, Christianity was at this time in a very disorganised state in Crete. Titus is to ordain presbyters, as the foundation of a ministry; whereas the task committed to Timothy at Ephesus was to

^wἐπιδιορθώσῃ,¹ καὶ ^xκαταστήσῃς ^yκατὰ ^yπόλιν πρεσβυτέρους, ὡς
ἐγώ σοι ^zδιεταξάμην· 6. εἴ τίς ἐστιν ^aἀνέγκλητος, ^bμιᾶς ^bγυναικὸς
^bἀνήρ, τέκνα ἔχων πιστὰ μὴ ἐν ^cκατηγορίᾳ ^dἀσωτίας ἢ ^eἀνυπότακτα.
7. δεῖ γὰρ τὸν ἐπίσκοπον ^aἀνέγκλητον εἶναι ὡς Θεοῦ ^fοἰκονόμον,
μὴ ^gαὐθάδη, μὴ ^hὀργίλον, μὴ ⁱπάροινον, μὴ ⁱπλήκτην, μὴ ^kαἰσχρο-
κερδῆ, 8. ἀλλὰ ^lφιλόξενον, ^mφιλάγαθον, ⁿσώφρονα, δίκαιον, ^oὅσιον,

w Here only, not LXX.
x Matt. xxiv. 45, 47 (=
Luke xii. 42, 44),
xxv. 21, 23, Acts
vi. 3, Heb. v. 1, vii. 28, viii. 3.

y Luke viii. 1, 4, Acts xv. 21, xx. 23. z 1 Cor. vii. 17, ix. 14, xi. 34, xvi. 1. a See 1 Tim. iii. 10.
b 1 Tim. iii. 2, 12. c See 1 Tim. v. 19. d Eph. v. 18, 1 Pet. iv. 4, cf. Luke xv. 13. e See
1 Tim. i. 9. f 1 Cor. iv. 1, 2, 1 Pet. iv. 10. g 2 Pet. ii. 10 only, N.T. h Here only, N.T.
i See 1 Tim. iii. 3. k See 1 Tim. iii. 8. l See 1 Tim. iii. 2. m Wisd. vii. 22 only, cf. 2 Tim.
iii. 3. n See 1 Tim. iii. 2. o See 1 Tim. ii. 8.

¹ ἐπιδιορθώσῃς AD*FG (D* ἐπανορθωσῃς; FG δειορθωσῃς).

continue the organisation of presbyters (*episcopi*) and deacons which was already in full working order. It is significant that καθίστημι is used of the institution of a new order of ministry in Acts vi. 3. καί introduces the chief point in the ἐπιδιόρθωσις.

κατὰ πόλιν: *in every city*. See reff. The number of presbyters is not specified; the meaning is that the order of presbyters should be established all over the island.

σοι διεταξάμην: *disposui tibi* (Vulg.), appropriately used of a number of specific directions on one general subject. Compare Acts xxiv. 23, where the verb is used in reference to three distinct instructions given to the centurion in reference to Paul.

Ver. 6. ἀνέγκλητος: See notes on 1 Tim. iii. 2, 10.

μιᾶς γυναικὸς ἀνήρ: See on 1 Tim. iii. 2.

τέκνα πιστά: It must be supposed that a Christian father who has unbelieving children is himself a recent convert, or a very careless Christian. The fact that St. Paul did not think it necessary to warn Timothy that such men were not eligible for the presbyterate is a proof that Christianity was at this time more firmly established in Ephesus than in Crete.

μὴ ἐν κατηγορίᾳ ἀσωτίας ἢ ἀνυπό-τακτα: It is significant that the moral requirements of the pastor's children are more mildly expressed in 1 Tim. iii. 4, 5, 12. There it is the father's power to keep order in his own house that is emphasised; here the submission of the children to discipline and restraint.

Ver. 7. τὸν ἐπίσκοπον: On the use of the singular as a generic term see on 1 Tim. iii. 2. Here, where the thought is of the various official functions of the minister, the official title is appropriate.

ἀνέγκλητον: See notes on 1 Tim. iii. 2, 10.

θεοῦ οἰκονόμον: a steward appointed by God (Luke xii. 42; 1 Cor. ix. 17), in the house of God (1 Tim. iii. 15), to dispense His mysteries and manifold grace (1 Cor. iv. 1; 1 Pet. iv. 10). θεοῦ is emphatic, suggesting that the steward of such a Lord should conform to the highest ideal of moral and spiritual qualifications.

αὐθάδη: *self - assertive, arrogant*. Vulg. has here *superbum*, but more accurately in 2 Pet. ii. 10, *sibi placentes*.

ὀργίλον: *passionate, iracundum* (Vulg.). The ὀργίλος is one who has not his passion of anger under control.

πάροινον, πλήκτην: See on 1 Tim. iii. 3.

μὴ αἰσχροκερδῆ: This negative quality is required in deacons, 1 Tim. iii. 8. Persons who are concerned in the administration of small sums must be such as are above the commission of petty thefts. There are no regulations here laid down for deacons; so we are entitled to conclude that in Crete, at this time, presbyters performed the duties of every Church office. Hence they should have the appropriate diaconal virtue. See note on 1 Tim. iii. 8. On the other hand, it may be objected against this inference that in 1 Pet. v. 2 μὴ αἰσχρο-κερδῶς is used of the spirit of the ideal presbyter.

Ver. 8. φιλόξενον: See on 1 Tim. iii. 2.

φιλάγαθον: In Wisd. vii. 22, the πνεῦμα which is in σοφία is φιλάγαθον, *loving what is good*. The epithets which immediately precede and follow φιλά-γαθον in Wisd. have no reference to persons, with the exception of φιλάνθ-ρωπον. It seems best, with the R.V., to give the words as wide a reference as possible; see on ἀφιλάγαθοι, 2 Tim. iii. 3.

[p] ἐγκρατῆ, 9. [q] ἀντεχόμενον τοῦ κατὰ τὴν διδαχὴν [r] πιστοῦ [r] λόγου, ἵνα [s] δυνατὸς [s] ᾖ καὶ παρακαλεῖν ἐν τῇ [t] διδασκαλίᾳ τῇ [t] ὑγιαινούσῃ καὶ τοὺς [u] ἀντιλέγοντας ἐλέγχειν. 10. Εἰσὶν γὰρ πολλοὶ [1] [v] ἀνυπότακτοι, [w] ματαιολόγοι καὶ [x] φρεναπάται, μάλιστα [2] [y] οἱ [y] ἐκ [y] τῆς [3] [y] περιτομῆς, 11. οὓς δεῖ [z] ἐπιστομίζειν, οἵτινες ὅλους οἴκους [a] ἀνα-

p Here only, N.T., *cf.* Acts xxiv. 25, Gal. v. 23, 2 Pet. i. 6, 1 Cor. vii. 9, ix. 25.
q Matt. vi. 24 = Luke xvi. 13, 1 Thess. v. 14, Isa. lvi. 4.
r See 1 Tim. i. 15.
s See 2 Tim. i. 12.
t 1 Tim. i. 10 (*q.v.*), 2 Tim. iv. 3, Tit. ii. 1.
u Acts xiii. 45, xxviii. 19, 22, Tit. ii. 9.
v See 1 Tim. i. 9.
w Here only, not LXX, *cf.* 1 Tim. i. 6.
x Here only, not LXX, but *cf.* Gal. vi. 3.
y Acts x. 45, xi. 2, Gal. ii. 12, Col. iv. 11.
z Here only, not LXX.
a See 2 Tim. ii. 18.

[1] Ins. **καὶ** DFGKL, d, e, f, g, vg. [2] Ins. **δὲ** CDgr.
[3] So ℵCD*, 1, 17, one other; om. **τῆς** ADcFGKLP.

σώφρονα: See notes on 1 Tim. ii. 9 and iii. 2.

ἐγκρατῆ: The noun **ἐγκράτεια** occurs Acts xxiv. 25; Gal. v. 23; 2 Pet. i. 6, where to the rendering *temperance* the R.V.m. gives the alternative *self-control.* The verb **ἐγκρατεύομαι** in 1 Cor. vii. 9 is *to have continency*, but in 1 Cor. ix. 25 *to be temperate* generally. The word differs from **σώφρων** as having a reference to bodily appetites, while **σώφρων** has reference also to the desires of the mind. **ἐγκράτ.** concerns action, **σωφρ.** thought.

Ver. 9. **ἀντεχόμενον**: *holding firmly to.* **ἀντέχομαι** is stronger than **ἔχειν**, as used in a similar connexion, 1 Tim. i. 19, etc., etc. The R.V. *holding to* correctly suggests the notion of withstanding opposition, which is not so clearly felt in the A.V. *holding fast.* "Having care of it, making it his business" (Chrys.).

δυνατός: See note on 2 Tim. ii. 2.

τοῦ κατὰ τὴν διδαχὴν πιστοῦ λόγου: *the faithful word which is in accordance with the teaching.* It is indicative of the weakening of the phrase **πιστὸς λόγος** that St. Paul strengthens and defines it here by **κατὰ τὴν διδαχήν.** It was noted on 1 Tim. i. 15 that **πιστὸς λόγος** here means the totality of the revelation given in Christ; and **ἡ διδαχή** is to be taken passively, as equivalent to **ἡ διδασκαλία,** as employed in these epistles. It is tautological to take it actively, *the word which is faithful as regards the teaching of others;* for that is expressed in what follows.

παρακαλεῖν—ἐλέγχειν: *Cf.* 2 Tim iv. 2 for this combination. The shepherd must be able to tend the sheep, and to drive away wolves.

ὑγιαινούσῃ: See on 1 Tim. i. 10. **διδασκαλία** here, as frequently, is a body of doctrine. So R.V., *in the sound doctrine.* The A.V., *by sound doctrine*, would refer to the faith as applied in its various parts to particular needs.

τοὺς ἀντιλέγοντας: It is only a coincidence that where this word occurs in Acts it is in reference to *Jewish* opponents of the Gospel.

Vv. 10-16. I have just mentioned rebuke as a necessary element in a presbyter's teaching. This is especially needful in dealing with Cretan heretics, in whom the Jewish strain is disagreeably prominent. Alike in their new-fangled philosophy of purity, and in their pretensions to orthodoxy, they ring false. Purity of life can only spring from a pure mind; and knowledge is alleged in vain, if it is contradicted by practice.

Ver. 10. The persons spoken of here were Christian Jews. **οἱ ἐκ περιτομῆς** (without **τῆς**, see crit. note) has this meaning in reff. (in Acts x. 45 it is qualified by the addition of **πιστοί**). Rom. iv. 12, is not really an instance of the phrase. That they were at least nominally Christians is also implied by the epithet **ἀνυπότακτοι.** We cannot call those persons *unruly* on whose obedience we have no claim.

ματαιολόγοι: **ματαιολογία** occurs in 1 Tim. i. 6.

φρεναπάται: *seductores.* The verb occurs in Gal. vi. 3.

μάλιστα: it is probable that there were very few false teachers who were not "of the circumcision".

Ver. 11. **οὓς δεῖ ἐπιστομίζειν**: *quos oportet redargui, whose mouths must be stopped* by the unanswerable arguments of the orthodox controversialist. This is the result hoped for from the "conviction," of ver. 9.

ὅλους οἴκους ἀνατρέπουσιν: *pervert whole families* (Alf.); Moulton and Milligan give an apt illustration from a papyrus of second cent. B.C., **τῆς πατ-**

τρέπουσιν διδάσκοντες ᵇἃ ᵇμὴ ᵇδεῖ ᶜαἰσχροῦ ᵈκέρδους ᵉχάριν. b 1 Tim. v.
12. εἶπέν ¹ τις ἐξ αὐτῶν, ᶠἴδιος ᶠαὐτῶν προφήτης, Κρῆτες ἀεὶ c 1 Cor. xi.
ᵍψεῦσται, κακὰ θηρία, γαστέρες ʰἀργαί. 13. ἡ ¹μαρτυρία αὕτη Eph. v.
ἐστὶν ἀληθής. ᵏδι᾽ ᵏἣν ᵏαἰτίαν ἔλεγχε αὐτοὺς ¹ἀποτόμως, ἵνα Tim. iii.
ᵐὑγιαίνωσιν ᵐἐν ² ᵐτῇ ᵐπίστει, 14. μὴ ⁿπροσέχοντες Ἰουδαϊκοῖς 2.

13.
6, xiv. 35,
12, cf. 1
8, 1 Pet. v.
d Phil. i. 21,
iii. 7.

e See 1 Tim. v. 14.　f Mark xv. 20 (Tisch.), 2 Pet. iii. 3.　g See 1 Tim. i. 10.　h See 1 Tim.
v. 13.　i See 1 Tim. iii. 7.　k See 2 Tim. i. 6.　l Wisd. v. 22, 2 Cor. xiii. 10, cf. Rom.
xi. 22 only.　m Tit. ii. 2, see 1 Tim. i. 10.　n See 1 Tim. i. 4.

¹ Ins. δὲ ℵ*G, f, g, boh ; ins. γὰρ 115.　　²·Om. ἐν ℵ*, 47, one other.

ρικῆς οἰκίας . . . ἔτι ἔνπροσθεν ἄρδην
[ἀ]νατετραμμένης δι᾽ ἀσ[ω]τίας (Expositor, vii., v. 269). This suggests the
rendering *upset*. The whole family
would be upset by the perversion of one
member of it.

ἃ μὴ δεῖ: Normally, οὐ is used in relative sentences with the indicative. Other
exceptions will be found in 2 Pet. i. 9, 1
John iv. 3 (T.R.). It is possible that
the force of μή here is given by translating, *which (we think) they ought not*.
If the teaching had been absolutely in-
defensible by any one, he would have
said, ἃ οὐ δεῖ. See Blass, *Grammar*, p.
254.

αἰσχροῦ κέρδους χάριν: The three reff.
on αἰσχροῦ, the only other occurrences in
N.T. of this adj., are instances of the
phrase αἰσχρόν ἐστι. The reference is to
the claim to support made by itinerating
or vagrant prophets and apostles such as
are referred to in the *Didache*, cc. 11, 12,
and alluded to in 2 Cor. xi. 9-13. All such
abuses would exist in an aggravated form
in Crete, the natives of which had an evil
reputation for αἰσχροκέρδεια, according to
Polybius, ὥστε παρὰ μόνοις Κρηταιεῦσι
τῶν ἁπάντων ἀνθρώπων μηδὲν αἰσχρὸν
νομίζεσθαι κέρδος. (*Hist.* vi. 46. 3, cited
by Ell.). They get a bad character also
from Livy (xliv. 45), and Plutarch (*Paul.
Aemil.* 23). The Cretans, Cappadocians,
and Cilicians were τρία κάππα κάκιστα.

Ver. 12. προφήτης: It is possible
that St. Paul applies this title to the
author of the following hexameter line
because the Cretan false teachers were
self-styled prophets. There was a
Cretan prophet once who told plain
truths to his countrymen. The whole
line occurs, according to Jerome, in the
περὶ χρησμῶν of Epimenides, a native of
Cnossus in Crete. The first three words
are also found in the Hymn to Zeus by
Callimachus, where the prophet meant
according to Theodoret ; and the rest has
a parallel in Hesiod, *Theogon.* 26, ποιμένες

ἄγραυλοι, κάκ᾽ ἐλέγχεα, γαστέρες οἶον.
It is generally agreed that St. Paul was
referring to Epimenides. This is the
view of Chrys. and Epiph., as well as of
Jerome. It was Epimenides at whose
suggestion the Athenians are said to
have erected the "anonymous altars,"
i.e., Ἀγνώστῳ Θεῷ (Acts xvii. 23), in the
course of the purification of their city
from the pollution caused by Cylon, 596
B.C. He is reckoned a prophet, or pre-
dictor of the future, by Cicero, *de Divin.*
i. 18, and Apuleius, *Florid.* ii. 15, 4.
Plato calls him θεῖος ἀνήρ (*Legg.* i. p.
642 D).

ψεῦσται: The particular lie which
provoked the poet's ire was the claim
made by the Cretans that the tomb of
Zeus was on their island. Here, the
term has reference to ματαιολόγοι, etc.

γαστέρες ἀργαί: The R.V., *idle glut-
tons*, is more intelligible English than
the A.V., *slow bellies*, but does not so
adequately represent the poet's meaning. He has in his mind the belly, as it
obtrudes itself on the beholder and is a
burden to the possessor, not as a recep-
tacle for food. Alf. quotes aptly Juvenal,
Sat. iv. 107, "Montani quoque *venter*
adest, abdomine tardus ".

Ver. 13. δι᾽ ἣν αἰτίαν: See on 2 Tim.
i. 6.

ἀποτόμως: *severely*. The noun ἀπο-
τομία, *severitas*, occurs Rom. xi. 22.
See Moulton and Milligan, *Expositor*,
vii., vi. 192.

ἵνα ὑγιαίνωσιν: See note on 1 Tim. i.
10. The intention of the reproof was
not merely the securing of a controversial
triumph, but "to bring into the way of
truth all such as have erred, and are
deceived". ἵνα expresses the object
aimed at in the reproof, not the substance
of it.

Ver. 14. προσέχοντες: see on 1 Tim.
i. 4. The word implies the giving one's
consent, as well as one's attention.

Ἰουδαϊκοῖς: This determines the

[o] μύθοις καὶ ἐντολαῖς ἀνθρώπων [p] ἀποστρεφομένων τὴν ἀλήθειαν.
15. [q] πάντα [1] [q] καθαρὰ τοῖς καθαροῖς· τοῖς δε [r] μεμιαμμένοις καὶ
ἀπίστοις οὐδὲν καθαρόν, ἀλλὰ [r] μεμίανται αὐτῶν καὶ ὁ νοῦς καὶ
ἡ συνείδησις. 16. Θεὸν [s] ὁμολογοῦσιν εἰδέναι, τοῖς δὲ ἔργοις
[t] ἀρνοῦνται, [u] βδελυκτοὶ ὄντες καὶ [v] ἀπειθεῖς καὶ πρὸς [w] πᾶν [w] ἔργον
[w] ἀγαθὸν [w] [x] ἀδόκιμοι.

o 1 Tim. i. 4.
p See 2 Tim. i. 15.
q Luke xi. 41, Rom. xiv. 20.
r John xviii. 28, Heb. xii. 15, Jude 8.
s See 1 Tim. vi. 12.
t See 1 Tim. v. 8. iii. 3.
u Prov. xvii. 15, Ecclus. xli. 5, 2 Macc. i. 27 only.
v Luke i. 17, 2 Tim. iii. 2, Tit. iii. 3.
w See 2 Tim. ii. 21 and 1 Tim. ii. 10.
x See 2 Tim. iii. 8.

[1] Ins. μὲν ℵcDcKL, syrhcl; ins. γὰρ boh, syrpesh.

nature of the μῦθοι referred to in these epistles. See on 1 Tim. i. 4.

ἐντολαῖς ἀνθρώπων ἀποστρεφομένων: We are naturally reminded of Mark vii. 7, 8, with its antithesis between the ἐντάλματα ἀνθρώπων and ἐντολὴν τοῦ θεοῦ, and Col. ii. 22, where the same passage of Isaiah (xxix. 13) is echoed. But here the antithesis is not so strongly marked. The commandments are depreciated, not because their authors are men, but because they are *men who turn away from the truth*, impure men (In 1 Tim. iv. 3 "they that believe and know the truth" are men whose thoughts are pure). *The truth* here, as elsewhere in the Pastorals, is almost a Christian technical term. It can hardly be doubted that the ἐντολαί referred to were of the same nature as those noted in Col. ii. 22, arbitrary ascetic prohibitions.

Ver. 15. πάντα καθαρὰ κ.τ.λ.: This is best understood as a maxim of the Judaic Gnostics, based on a perversion of the Saying πάντα καθαρὰ ὑμῖν ἐστιν (Luke xi. 41. *Cf.* Rom. xiv. 20; Mark vii. 18.). St. Paul accepts it as a truth, but not in the intention of the speaker; and answers, τοῖς δὲ μεμιαμμένοις κ.τ.λ. The passage is thus, as regards its form, parallel to 1 Cor. vi. 12 *sqq.*, where St. Paul cites, and shows the irrelevancy of, two pleas for licence: "All things are lawful for me," and "Meats for the belly, and the belly for meats". τοῖς καθαροῖς is of course the *dat. commodi*, *for the use of the pure*, *in their case*, as in the parallels, Luke xi. 41, 1 Tim. iv. 3; not *in the judgment of the pure*, as in Rom. xiv. 14.

τοῖς δὲ μεμιαμμένοις, κ.τ.λ.: The order of the words is to be noted: their moral obliquity is more characteristic of them than their intellectual perversion. The satisfaction of natural bodily desires (for it is these that are in question) is, when lawful, a pure thing, not merely innocent, in the case of the pure; it is an impure thing, even when lawful, in the case of "them that are defiled". And for this reason: their intellectual apprehension (νοῦς) of these things is perverted by defiling associations; "the light that is in them is darkness;" and their conscience has, from a similar cause, lost its sense of discrimination between what is innocent and criminal. That any action with which they themselves are familiar could be pure is inconceivable to them. "When the soul is unclean, it thinks all things unclean" (Chrys.). The statement that the conscience can be defiled is significant. While conscientious scruples are to be respected, yet, if the conscience be defiled, its dictates and instincts are unreliable, false as are the song-efforts of one who has no ear for music.

Ver. 16. θεὸν ὁμολογοῦσιν εἰδέναι: "*We know God*"; that was their profession of faith. They "gloried in God," Rom. ii. 17. This is an allusion to the Jewish pride of religious privilege. Weiss points out that this phrase alone is sufficient to prove that the heretics in question are not the Gnostics of the second century (Hort, *Judaistic Christianity*, p. 133). See the use of the phrase in Gal. iv. 8, 1 Thess. iv. 5. Compare 2 Tim. iii. 5, "Holding a form of godliness, but having denied the power thereof"; also 1 John ii. 4. There is here the constant antithesis between words and deeds.

τοῖς δὲ ἔργοις ἀρνοῦνται: Their lives give the lie to their professions; "They acted as if this Supreme Being was a mere metaphysical abstraction, out of all moral relation to human life, as if He were neither Saviour nor Judge" (J. H. Bernard *comm. in loc.*).

πρὸς πᾶν ἔργον ἀγαθόν: See note on 2 Tim. iii. 17.

ἀδόκιμοι: *worthless*, *unfit*. See note on 2 Tim. iii. 8.

[handwritten: But thou speak, things, become sound teaching]

II. 1. ᵃΣὺ ᵃδὲ λάλει ἃ ᵇπρέπει τῇ ᶜὑγιαινούσῃ ᶜδιδασκαλίᾳ. 2. ᵈπρεσβύτας ᵉνηφαλίους εἶναι, ᶠσεμνούς, ᵍσώφρονας· ʰ ὑγιαίνον-τας ʰτῇ ʰπίστει, τῇ ἀγάπῃ, τῇ ὑπομονῇ. 3. ᵏπρεσβύτιδας ˡὡσαύτως ἐν ᵐκαταστήματι ⁿἱεροπρεπεῖς,¹ μὴ ᵒδιαβόλους, μηδὲ² ᵖοίνῳ ᵖπολλῷ ᑫδεδουλωμένας, ʳκαλοδιδασκάλους, 4. ἵνα ˢσωφρο-

Margin references:
a See 1 Tim. vi. 11.
b See 1 Tim. ii. 10.
c 1 Tim. i. 10 (q.v.), 2 Tim. iv. 3, Tit. i. 9.
d Luke i. 18, Philem. 9.
e See 1 Tim.

iii. 2. f See 1 Tim. iii. 8.   g See 1 Tim. iii. 2.   h Tit. i. 13, see 1 Tim. i. 10.   i See 1 Tim. vi. 11.   k 4 Macc. xvi. 11 only.   l See 1 Tim. ii. 9.   m 3 Macc. v. 45 only.   n 4 Macc. ix. 25, xi. 20 only.   o See 1 Tim. iii. 11.   p See 1 Tim. iii. 8.   q Rom. vi. 18, 22, 1 Cor. vii. 15, ix. 19, Gal. iv. 3, 2 Pet. ii. 19.   r Here only, not LXX.   s Here only, not LXX.

¹ ἱεροπρεπεῖ CH**, 17, 31, 37, two others, d, e, f, g, m81, vg. (in habitu sancto), boh., syrr. (but not syrhcl-mg), arm.

² So א*AC, 73 ; μὴ אᶜDFGHKLP, vg.   See 1 Tim. iii. 8.

CHAPTER II.—Vv. 1-10. In the face of this immoral teaching, do you constantly impress the moral duties of the Gospel on your people of every age and class. There is an ideal of conduct appropriate to old men and old women respectively—the latter have moreover special duties in the training of the young women—and young men. Enforce your words by personal example. Slaves, too, must be taught that they share in responsibility for the good name of the Gospel.

Ver. 1. σὺ δὲ: See reff., and note on 1 Tim. vi. 11. Titus is to be as active in teaching positive truth as the heretics were in teaching evil.

λάλει: emphasises the importance of oral teaching.

τῇ ὑγιαινούσῃ διδασκαλίᾳ: See on 1 Tim. i. 10.

Ver. 2. The heads of moral instruction which begin here are more unmistakably intended for the laity than are the similar passages in Tim. That it should devolve on the apostle's legate to give popular moral instruction is perhaps another indication of the less-developed state of the Church in Crete than in Ephesus and its neighbourhood.

πρεσβύτας: senes; sc. παρακάλει (ver. 6).

νηφαλίους: sober, sobrii; temperate (R.V.) in respect of their use of strong drink. Chrys. explains it to be vigilant, as does the Syriac, and A.V. m. ; but the homely warning seems more appropriate. See note on 1 Tim. iii. 2.

σεμνούς: see note on 1 Tim. iii. 8.

σώφρονας: see notes on 1 Tim. ii. 9, and iii. 2. For ὑγιαίνειν followed by dat. see i. 13. πίστις, ἀγάπη, ὑπομονή are constantly grouped together (see on 1 Tim. vi. 11) ; and this suggests that πίστις here is subjective, not objective,

as in the similar phrase i. 13. See note on 1 Tim. i. 10.

Ver. 3. πρεσβύτιδας: correlative to πρεσβύτας, as πρεσβυτέρας is to πρεσβυτέρῳ in 1 Tim. v. 1, 2.

ὡσαύτως: See on 1 Tim. ii. 9.

ἐν καταστήματι ἱεροπρεπεῖς: reverent in demeanour, R.V. καταστολή in 1 Tim. ii. 9 has an almost exclusive reference to dress. Demeanour (R.V.) is better than behaviour (A.V.), which has a wide reference to conduct, in all respects and on all occasions. Deportment, which includes a slight reference to dress, would be the best rendering, only that the word has become depreciated.

ἱεροπρεπεῖς perhaps = ὃ πρέπει γυναιξὶν ἐπαγγελλομέναις θεοσέβειαν (1 Tim. ii. 10) ; but in itself the word does not guarantee more than the appearance of reverence. Wetstein gives, among other illustrations, one from Josephus (Ant. xi. 8, 5), describing how Jaddua, the high priest, went out in procession from Jerusalem to meet Alexander the Great, ἱεροπρεπῆ καὶ διαφέρουσαν τῶν ἄλλων ἐθνῶν ποιούμενος τὴν ὑπάντησιν.

μὴ διαβόλους: See on 1 Tim. iii. 11, and 2 Tim. iii. 3.

δεδουλωμένας: The A.V., not given to much wine, makes no difference between this and προσέχοντας, which is the verb in the corresponding phrase, in the list of moral qualifications of deacons, 1 Tim. iii. 8. It is proved by experience that the reclamation of a woman drunkard is almost impossible. The best parallel to this use of δουλόω is 2 Pet. ii. 19, ᾧ γάρ τις ἥττηται, τούτῳ δεδούλωται. Cf. also the other reff.

καλοδιδασκάλους: Not only "by discourse at home," as Chrys. explains, but by example.

Ver. 4. σωφρονίζουσιν. The only other examples of ἵνα with a pres. indic.

t Positive here only in this sense.   νίζουσιν¹ τὰς ᵗ νέας ᵘ φιλάνδρους εἶναι, ᵛ φιλοτέκνους, 5. ᵍ σώφρονας, ἁγνάς, ʷ οἰκουργούς,² ˣ ἀγαθάς, ʸ ὑποτασσομένας ʸ τοῖς ʸ ἰδίοις ʸ ἀν-

u Here only, not LXX.   δράσιν, ᶻ ἵνα ᶻ μὴ ὁ λόγος τοῦ Θεοῦ ᶻ βλασφημῆται. 6. τοὺς νεω-

v 4 Macc. xv. 4, 5, 6, φιλοτεκ- νία also 4 Macc. (5) only.   τέρους ᵃ ὡσαύτως παρακάλει ᵇ σωφρονεῖν· 7. περὶ πάντα σεαυτὸν ᶜ παρεχόμενος ᵈ τύπον ᵉ καλῶν ᵉ ἔργων, ἐν τῇ διδασκαλίᾳ ᶠ ἀφθορίαν,³

w Here only, not LXX.   x Matt. xx. 15, Rom. v. 7, 1 Pet. ii. 18.   y Eph. v. 22, Col. iii. 18, 1 Pet. iii. 1, 5, *cf.* 1 Cor. xiv. 34, Eph. v. 24.   z See 1 Tim. vi. 1.   a See 1 Tim. ii. 9. b Mark v. 15 (=Luke viii. 35), Rom. xii. 3, 2 Cor. v. 13, 1 Pet. iv. 7, not LXX.   c See 1 Tim. i. 4, also Acts xvii. 31, xxii. 2, xxviii. 2.   d See 1 Tim. iv. 12.   e See 1 Tim. iii. 1.   f Haggai ii. 18 (17) only.

¹ So ℵ*AFGHP, two cursives; σωφρονίζωσι ℵᶜCDKL.

² So ℵ*ACD*FG; οἰκουρούς ℵᶜDᶜHKLP, syrhcl-mg-gr.

³ ἀδιαφθορίαν ℵᶜDᶜL, syrhcl-mg-gr; ἀφθονίαν FG.

in Paul are 1 Cor. iv. 6 (φυσιοῦσθε) and Gal. iv. 17 (ζηλοῦτε). These may be cases of an unusual formation of the subj., both being verbs in -όω. γινώσ- κομεν, 1 John v. 20, is another instance. *Train* is the excellent rendering of the R.V. The A.V., *teach . . . to be sober*, although an adequate rendering elsewhere, leaves φιλάνδρους εἶναι dis- connected. Timothy is bidden (1 Tim. v. 2) παρακαλεῖν . . . νεωτέρας himself; but this refers to pastoral public moni- tions, not to private training in domestic virtues and duties, as here.

τὰς νέας: There is no other instance in the Greek Bible of νέος, in the posi- tive, being applied to a young person; though it is common in secular litera- ture. There is possibly a certain fit- ness in the word as applied here to recently married women, whom the apostle has perhaps exclusively in view.

φιλάνδρους: "This is the chief point of all that is good in a household" (Chrys.). One of the three things in which Wisdom "was beautified" is "a woman and her husband that walk to- gether in agreement" (Ecclus. xxv. 1).

φιλοτέκνους: "She who loves the root will much more love the fruit" (Chrys.). φιλάνδρῳ καὶ φιλοτέκνῳ is cited from an "epitaph from Pergamum about the time of Hadrian" by Deiss- mann, who gives other references to secular literature. (*Bible Studies*, trans. p. 255 *sq.*).

Ver. 5. οἰκουργούς: *workers at home.* Field says that "the only authority for this word is Soranus of Ephesus, a medical writer, not earlier than the second century," οἰκουργὸν καὶ καθέδριον διάγειν βίον; but the verb is found in Clem. Rom., *ad Cor.* i. 1, γυναιξίν . . . τὰ κατὰ τὸν οἶκον σεμνῶς οἰκουργεῖν

ἐδιδάσκετε. οἰκουρούς, *keepers at home, domum custodientes* (d m⁸¹) *domus curam habentes* (Vulg.), though constantly found in descriptions of virtuous women, is a less obviously stimulating epithet. Mothers who work at home usually find it a more absorbing pleasure than "going about from house to house" (1 Tim. v. 13). But the "worker at home" is under a temptation to be as unsparing of her household as of herself; and so St. Paul adds ἀγαθάς, *benignas, kind* (R.V.), rather than *good* (A.V.). For this force of ἀγαθός, see reff.

ἰδίοις: ἴδιος (see on 1 Tim. iii. 4) is not emphatic: it is simply, *their hus- bands.* The ἴδιος merely differentiates *husband* from *man.*

ἵνα μὴ ὁ λόγος τοῦ Θεοῦ βλασφημῆ- ται: For λόγος, as used here, the more usual word is ὄνομα (from Isa. lii. 5). See reff. on 1 Tim. vi. 1; and also Jas. ii. 7, Rev. xiii. 6, xvi. 9. ἡ ὁδὸς τῆς ἀλη- θείας, in 2 Peter ii. 2, is equivalent to ὁ λόγος τοῦ θεοῦ here. The practical worth of a religion is not unfairly estimated by its effects on the lives of those who pro- fess it. If the observed effect of the Gospel were to make women worse wives, it would not commend it to the heathen; "for the Greeks judge not of doctrines by the doctrine itself, but they make the life and conduct the test of the doctrines" (Chrys.). See note on 1 Tim. v. 14.

Ver. 6. ὡσαύτως: see on 1 Tim. ii. 9.

Ver. 7. περὶ πάντα is joined with the preceding words by Jerome and Lucifer (*ut pudici* [*sobrii*] *sint in omnibus*), fol- lowed by Tischendorf and von Soden. For this use of περί, see on 1 Tim. i. 19. St. Paul's usual phrase is ἐν παντί (fifteen times in all; ten times in 2 Cor.; not in Pastorals), or ἐν πᾶσιν (ten times, five of which are in the Pastorals: 1 Tim. iii.

[g] σεμνότητα,[1] 8. λόγον [h] ὑγιῆ [i] ἀκατάγνωστον, ἵνα ὁ [k] ἐξ [k] ἐναντίας
ἐντραπῇ μηδὲν ἔχων λέγειν[2] περὶ ἡμῶν[3] [m] φαῦλον. 9. δούλους
ἰδίοις [n] δεσπόταις[4] ὑποτάσσεσθαι ἐν πᾶσιν, [o] εὐαρέστους εἶναι, μὴ
[p] ἀντιλέγοντας, 10. μὴ[5] [q] νοσφιζομένους, ἀλλὰ [r] πᾶσαν [r] πίστιν[6]

g See 1 Tim. ii. 2. h See 1 Tim. i. 10. i 2 Macc. iv. 47 only. k Mark xv. 39 (different application). l 2 Thess. iii. 14. m John iii. 20, v. 29, Rom. ix. 11, 2 Cor. v. 10, Jas. iii. 16. n See 1 Tim. vi. 1. o Rom. xiv. 18, 2 Cor. v. 9. p See Tit. i. 9. q Acts v. 2, 3. r 1 Cor. xiii. 2.

[1] Ins. **ἀφθαρσίαν** D^{c}KL, 37, more than thirty others, syr$^{hcl\text{-}mg\ gr}$, arm; ins. **ἁγνείαν** C, 80, three others, syr^{hcl}, arm.

[2] **λέγειν** bef. **φαῦλον** KL. [3] **ὑμῶν** A, many cursives, boh.

[4] **δεσπ. ἰδ.** ADP, 238, four others, d, e, f, vg. [5] **μηδὲ** C^{b}D^{gr*}F^{gr}G^{gr}, 17.

[6] **πίστ. πᾶσ.** KL; **πᾶσ. ἐνδεικ. πίστ.** F^{gr}G g; om. **πίστιν** ℵ*, 17.

11; 2 Tim. ii. 7, iv. 5; Tit. ii. 9, 10); also **εἰς πάντα**, 2 Cor. ii. 9; **κατὰ πάντα**, Col. iii. 20, 22.

σεαυτὸν παρεχόμενος τύπον: The middle is appropriate with **σεαυτὸν**; see reff. given by Deissmann, *Bible Studies*, trans. p. 254; but with **ἀφθορίαν**, etc., the active would seem more natural, as in reff. For **τύπον**, see 1 Tim. iv. 12, and for **καλὰ ἔργα**, see 1 Tim. iii. 1. This exhortation, following **νεωτέρους κ.τ.λ.**, and also ver. 15, suggest that Titus was comparatively young.

διδασκαλίᾳ here is not *doctrine* (A.V.), but *teaching; thy doctrine* (R.V.), including the person of the teacher as well as what he says. See note on 1 Tim. i. 10.

ἀφθορίαν, σεμνότητα, *sincerity . . . impressiveness, integritatem . . . gravitatem.* See on 1 Tim. ii. 2. These refer respectively to the principles and the manner of the teacher, while **λόγον, κ.τ.λ.**, describes the matter of his teaching.

Ver. 8. **ἀκατάγνωστον**: *to which no exception can be taken.* See Deissmann, *Bible Studies*, Trans. p. 200. **ὑγιῆ** implies the conformity of the doctrine taught with the Church's standard (see note on 1 Tim. i. 10), while **ἀκατάγνωστον** has reference to the manner of its presentation to the hearer.

ὁ ἐξ ἐναντίας: The heathen opponent, official or unofficial, **ὁ ἀντικείμενος** (1 Tim. v. 14), **οἱ ἀντιδιατιθέμενοι** (2 Tim. ii. 25), not the Devil himself (Chrys.).

ἐντραπῇ: *vercatur* (Vulg.); but *confundatur*, as in 2 Thess. iii. 14, would be a better rendering here. An antagonist who finds that he has no case "looks foolish," as we say.

φαῦλον: usually applied to actions. See reff. The clause means *having nothing evil to report concerning us*: not, as the English versions, *having no evil thing to say*, which might be explained as, "being unable to abuse us".

Ver. 9. **δούλους**: sc. **παρακάλει**, ver. 6. For the general topic, and the term **δεσπότης**, *cf.* 1 Tim. vi. 1.

ἐν πᾶσιν: joined as in text by Jerome, Ambrosiaster and m[93] with **ὑποτάσσ.** It is in favour of this that **ἐν πᾶσιν** elsewhere in the Pastorals (see note on ver. 7) is at the end of a clause; also that in similar contexts we have **ἐν παντί** (Eph. v. 24) and **κατὰ πάντα** (Col. iii. 22) joined with **ὑποτάσσω** and **ὑπακούω.**

εὐαρέστους: A Pauline word. Alf. notes that it is a servant's phrase, like the English "to give satisfaction". This acute remark brings the present passage into harmony with St. Paul's usage in the reff., in which it is used of persons, of men in their relation to God. **εὐάρεστον** is used of a sacrifice, "acceptable," in Rom. xii. 1, Phil. iv. 18; *cf.* Heb. xii. 28; **τὸ εὐάρεστον**, "that which is well pleasing," in Rom. xii. 2, Eph. v. 10, Col. iii. 20, Heb. xiii. 21. Jerome's view that **εὐαρ.** is passive, "contented with their lot," is not satisfactory.

μὴ ἀντιλέγοντας; *non contradicentes* (Vulg.). Ell. thinks that more is implied than pert answers (A.V. *answering again*); rather "thwarting their masters' plans, wishes, or orders". See ch. i. 9. This is the connotation of *gainsaying* (R.V., A.V.m.).

Ver. 10. **μὴ νοσφιζομένους**: *non fraudantes* (Vulg.), *not purloining.* The particular form of theft implied is the abstraction or retention for oneself, of a part of something entrusted to one's care.

πᾶσαν πίστιν ἐνδεικνυμένους ἀγαθήν: *displaying the utmost trustworthiness.* There is a similar phrase in ch. iii. 2,

s See 2 Tim. *ἐνδεικνυμένους ἀγαθήν,*[1] *ἵνα τὴν διδασκαλίαν τὴν*[2] *τοῦ* [t] *σωτῆρος*
iv. 14.
t See 1 Tim. [t] *ἡμῶν* [t] *Θεοῦ* [u] *κοσμῶσιν ἐν πᾶσιν.*
i. 1.
u See 1 Tim.   11. [v]*Ἐπεφάνη γὰρ ἡ* [w]*χάρις τοῦ Θεοῦ*[3] [x]*σωτήριος*[4] *πᾶσιν*
ii. 9.
v Luke i. 79, *ἀνθρώποις* 12. [y]*παιδεύουσα ἡμᾶς, ἵνα* [z]*ἀρνησάμενοι τὴν* [a]*ἀσέβειαν*
Acts
xxvii. 20, *καὶ τὰς* [b]*κοσμικὰς ἐπιθυμίας* [c]*σωφρόνως καὶ δικαίως καὶ* [d]*εὐσεβῶς*
Tit. iii. 4.
w 2 Cor.
viii. 9.   x Here only, N.T., Am. v. 22, Wisd. i. 14, 3 Macc. (2), 4 Macc. (2) only.   y See 1 Tim.
i. 20.   z See 1 Tim. v. 8.   a See 2 Tim. ii. 16.   b Heb. ix. 1, not LXX.   c Wisd. ix. 11
only.   d See 2 Tim. iii. 12.

---

[1] *πᾶσαν ἐνδεικ. ἀγαθην* ℵ* ; *πᾶσ. ἐνδεικ. ἀγάπην* 17.
[2] Om. *τὴν* KLP.   [3] Ins. *ἡ* C^cD^{bc}KLP.
[4] *σωτῆρος* ℵ*, *τοῦ σωτῆρος ἡμῶν* FG, f, g, vg. (am. om. *ἡμῶν*), boh.

πᾶσαν ἐνδεικ. πραΰτητα. See note on 2
Tim. iv. 14. On this use of *πᾶς*, see on
1 Tim. i. 15. *πίστιν* has a qualifying
adj. elsewhere, *e.g.*, *ἀνυπόκριτος* (1 Tim.
i. 5 ; 2 Tim. i. 5. *Cf.* ch. i. 4. 2 Pet. i. ;
Jude 20), but the addition of another adj.
after *πᾶς* is unusual. In Clem. Rom.
1 *Cor.* 26 *πίστις ἀγαθή* is rendered by
Lightfoot *honest faith ;* but *honest fidelity*
would be an odd expression. Von Soden
would give *ἀγαθή* here the sense of *kind,
wishing well,* as in ver. 5, and as a contrast to *ἀντιλεγ.*, as *πίστιν* is to *νοσφ.*
W.H. suggest that the original reading
here was *πᾶσαν ἐνδεικνυμένους ἀγάπην.*
See apparat. crit.

διδασκαλίαν : See note on 1 Tim. i. 10.
Θεοῦ refers to God the Father. See
i. 3. Von Soden takes it here as objective
genitive ; the *διδασκαλία* being set forth
in vv. 11-14.

κοσμῶσιν : cf. 1 Tim. ii. 9, *κοσμεῖν
ἑαυτάς . . . δι' ἔργων ἀγαθῶν.* The
διδασκαλία, though really practical, can
be plausibly alleged to be mere theory ;
it must then, by good works, be rendered
attractive to them that are without. *Cf.*
Matt. v. 16, Phil. ii. 15.

Vv. 11-15. The justification of this insistence on the universal necessity for
right conduct is the all-embracing scope
of the saving grace of God, which has
visibly appeared as a call to repentance,
a help to amendment of life, and a stimu-
lus to hope. Christ's gift of Himself
for us constrains us to give ourselves
wholly to Him. Insist on these things,
as authoritatively as possible, in every
department of your teaching.

Ver. 11. The emphatic word is *πᾶσιν.*
The connexion is with what has immediately preceded. No rank or class or type
of mankind is outside the saving influence
of God's grace. Chrys. concludes a
striking picture of the adverse moral

environment of slaves with, "It is a
difficult and surprising thing that there
should ever be a good slave".

ἐπεφάνη : See note on 1 Tim. vi. 14.
The grace of God (also iii. 7) is His
kindness and love of man (iii. 4). It
appeared (iii. 4) (*a*) as a revelation, in
the Incarnation, and also (*b*) in its visible
results ; and so it is both *heard* and
recognised (Col. i. 6). Accordingly
Barnabas could *see* it at Antioch (Acts
xi. 23). It is possible to *stand fast in it*
(1 Pet. v. 12), and to *continue in it* (Acts
xiii. 43). It is *given* to men, to be dispensed by them to others (Rom. i. 5,
Eph. iii. 2. 7) ; and if men do not respond
to it, they are said to *fall short of it*
(Heb. xii. 15). Here it is described in
its essential power and range, *σωτήριος
πᾶσιν ἀνθρ., . . . appeared, bringing
salvation to all men* (so R.V. ; A.V.m).
This connexion of the words is favoured
by the fact that *ἐπεφάνη* is used absolutely in iii. 4.

Ver. 12. *παιδεύουσα. erudiens* (Vulg.),
corripiens (d). Grace is potentially
σωτήριος as regards all men ; actually
its efficacy is seen in the disciplining of
individuals one by one ; *ἡμᾶς*, to begin
with. See notes on 1 Tim. i. 1, ii. 4, iv.
10. So Chrys. makes *ἵνα* depend on
ἐπεφάνη more directly than on *παιδεύουσα :* "Christ came that we should
deny ungodliness." The connexion,
then, is *ἐπεφάνη . . . ἵνα . . . ζήσωμεν.*
"The final cause of the Revelation in
Christ is not *creed,* but *character*" (J. H.
Bernard). It is of course possible (and
this is the view usually held) to join
παιδεύουσα ἵνα ; the *ἵνα* introducing the
object (*instructing us, to the intent that,
denying,* etc., R.V.), not the content
(*teaching us that denying,* etc., A.V.)
of the *παιδεία.*

ἀρνησάμενοι . . . ζήσωμεν . . . προσ-

ᵈ ζήσωμεν ἐν °τῷ °νῦν °αἰῶνι, 13. ᶠπροσδεχόμενοι τὴν μακαρίαν e See 1 Tim.
vi. 17.
ἐλπίδα καὶ ᵍἐπιφάνειαν τῆς δόξης τοῦ μεγάλου Θεοῦ καὶ ʰσωτῆρος f Mark xv.
43, Luke
ii. 25, 38,

xii. 36, xxiii. 51, Acts xxiii. 21, xxiv. 15, Heb. xi. 35, Jude 21.   (It means *receive* in Luke xv. 2,
Rom. xvi. 2, Phil. ii. 29, Heb. x. 34.)   g See 1 Tim. vi. 14.   h See 2 Tim. i. 10.

δεχόμενοι represent three successive
stages in the Christian life. The force
of the aorist participle must not be lost
sight of, though it may be pedantic to
mark it in translation. ἀρνησάμενοι
κ.τ.λ., synchronises with the "death
unto sin" which precedes the definite
entry on newness of life, while προσδεχόμενοι expresses the constant mental
attitude of those who are living that new
life.

ἀρνησάμενοι: This indicates the renunciation of the Devil, of the vanity of
this world, and of all the sinful lusts of
the flesh. ἀρνέομαι means here *to repudiate, renounce all connexion with.*
Cf. ἀποθέμενοι, 1 Pet. ii. 1. See on i
Tim . v. 8.

τὴν ἀσέβειαν: εὐσέβεια being Christian practice (see below, εὐσεβῶς ζήσωμεν), ἀσέβεια is heathen practice, the
non-moral life.

τὰς κοσμικὰς ἐπιθυμίας: *saecularia
desideria* (Vulg.), "the desires of the
flesh and of the mind" (Eph. ii. 3),
"the lusts of men" (1 Pet. iv. 2); opposed to σωφρ. καὶ δικαίως; such as
have relation to no higher sphere than
that of the visible world. They are
analysed in 1 John ii. 16.

σωφρόνως: The reference of the three
adverbs is well explained by St. Bernard:
"*sobrie* erga nos ; *juste* erga proximos ;
pie erga Deum".

Ver. 13. προσδεχόμενοι κ.τ.λ., as already stated, describes the glad expect-
ancy which is the ruling and prevailing
thought in the lives of men looking for
their Lord's return (Luke xii. 36), προσδεχόμενοι τὸ ἔλεος τοῦ Κυρίου ἡμῶν
Ἰησοῦ Χριστοῦ (Jude 21). Cf. Rom. viii.
19; 1 Cor. i. 7; Phil. iii. 20; 1 Thess.
i. 10; Heb. ix. ?8; 2 Pet. iii. 12. Isa.
xxv. 9 is the basal passage. Cf. Acts
xxiv. 15, ἐλπίδα ἔχων εἰς τὸν Θεόν, ἣν
καὶ αὐτοὶ οὗτοι προσδέχονται. In this
quotation ἐλπίδα is the mental act,
while the relative ἥν is the realisation of
the hope. ἐλπίς is also passive—the
thing hoped for—in Gal. v. 5 ; Col. i. 5 ;
1 Tim. i. 1.

ἐπιφάνειαν τῆς δόξης: The Second
Coming of Christ will be, as we are as-
sured by Himself, "in the glory of His
Father" (Matt. xvi. 27 ; Mark viii. 38).

"We rejoice in the hope of the glory of
God" (Rom. v. 2, a passage which supports the view that δόξης here is dependent on ἐλπίδα as well as on ἐπιφάνειαν).
von Soden takes ἐπιφάνειαν as epexegetical of ἐλπίδα. The Second Coming of
Christ may, therefore, be regarded as an
ἐπιφάνεια τῆς δόξης Θεοῦ, even though
we should not speak of an ἐπιφάνεια τοῦ
Πατρός, while ἐπιφάνεια Ἰησοῦ Χριστοῦ
is normal and natural (see on 1 Tim. vi.
14). τῆς δόξης having then an intelligible meaning, we are not entitled to treat
it as merely adjectival, *the glorious appearing* (A.V.). The genitival relation
does not differ in this case from τῇ
ἐπιφανείᾳ τῆς παρουσίας αὐτοῦ in 2
Thess. ii. 8. See also note on 1 Tim.
i. 11. Again, there does not seem any
reason why τοῦ σωτῆρος, κ.τ.λ., here
should not depend on ἐπιφάνειαν, on the
analogy of 2 Tim. i. 10. This may be
thought too remote. In any case, the
conception of the Second Coming as an
occasion of manifestation of two δόξαι,
that of the Father and of the Son, is
familiar from Luke ix. 26, ὅταν ἔλθῃ ἐν
τῇ δόξῃ αὐτοῦ καὶ τοῦ πατρὸς, κ.τ.λ.
On the whole, then, we decide in favour
of the R.V.m. in the rendering of this
passage, *appearing of the glory of the
great God and our Saviour Jesus Christ.*
The grammatical argument—"the identity of reference of two substantives
when under the vinculum of a common
article"—is too slender to bear much
weight, especially when we take into
consideration not only the general neglect of the article in these epistles but
the omission of it before σωτήρ in 1
Tim. i. 1, iv. 10. Ellicott says that
"μεγάλου would seem uncalled for if applied to the Father". To this it may
be answered that (*a*) the epithet is not
otiose here; as marking the majesty of
God the Father it is parallel to the ὃς
ἔδωκεν ἑαυτὸν, κ.τ.λ., which recalls the
self-sacrificing love of the Son; both
constituting the double appeal—to fear
and to love—of the Judgment to come.
(*b*) Again, St. Paul is nowhere more
emphatic in his lofty language about
God the Father than in these epistles ;
see 1 Tim. i. 17, vi. 15, 16.
This is the only place in the N.T. in

i See 1 Tim.   ^h ἡμῶν   ^h Χριστοῦ   ^h Ἰησοῦ,¹   14.   ὃς ⁱ ἔδωκεν ⁱ ἑαυτὸν ὑπὲρ ἡμῶν, ἵνα
ii. 6.
k Luke   ^k λυτρώσηται ἡμᾶς ἀπὸ πάσης ἀνομίας, καὶ ¹ καθαρίσῃ ἑαυτῷ λαὸν
xxiv. 21,
1 Pet. i.
18.   l Acts xv. 9, 2 Cor. vii. 1, Eph. v. 26 Heb. ix. 14, Jas. iv. 8, 1 John i. 7, 9.

¹ So ℵ*FgrG, g, boh.; Ἰησ. Χριστ. ℵcACDKLP, all cursives, d, e, f, vg., syrr. arm.

which **μέγας** is applied to the true God, although it is a constant predicate of heathen gods and goddesses, *e.g.*, Acts xix. 28. (See Moulton and Milligan, *Expositor*, vii., vii. 563). In view of the fact that the most probable exegesis of Rom. ix. 5 is that ὁ ὢν ἐπὶ πάντων, Θεὸς εὐλογητὸς, κ.τ.λ. refers to Christ, it cannot be said that ὁ μέγας Θεός, as applied to Him, is un-Pauline. But the proofs that St. Paul held Christ to be God Incarnate do not lie in a few disputable texts, but in the whole attitude of his soul towards Christ, and in the doctrine of the relation of Christ to mankind which is set forth in his epistles. St. Paul's "declarations of the divinity of the Eternal Son" are not *studied*, as Ellicott admits that this would be if the R.V. rendering (*our great God and Saviour, Jesus Christ*) be adopted. To this it may be added that the Versions, with the exception of the Aethiopic, agree with R.V.m. Ell. cites on the other side, of ante-Nicene writers, Clem. Alex., *Protrept.* §7, and Hippolytus, —quoted by Wordsworth—besides the great bulk of the post-Nicene fathers. The text is one which would strike the eye of a reader to whose consciousness the Arian controversy was present; but it is safe to say that if it had read τοῦ σωτῆρος, the μεγάλου would have excited no comment. Consequently the papyri (all vii. A.D.) cited by J. H. Moulton (*Grammar*, vol. i. p. 84) "which attest the translation *our great God and Saviour* as current among Greek-speaking Christians" are too late as guides to St. Paul's meaning here. The similar problem in 2 Peter i. 1 must be discussed independently. At least, even if it be granted that the R.V. there is correct, and that 2 Peter i. 1 is an example of the transference to Christ of the language used of deified kings "in the papyri and inscriptions of Ptolemaic and Imperial times," it does not follow that the same account must be given of Tit. ii. 13.

Ver. 14. ὃς ἔδωκεν ἑαυτὸν κ.τ.λ.: see note on 1 Tim. ii. 6. As already observed, this is an appeal from the constraining love of Christ to the responding love of man.

λυτρώσηται : *deliver.* The language is borrowed from Psalm cxxix. (cxxx). 8 αὐτὸς λυτρώσεται τὸν Ἰσραὴλ ἐκ πασῶν τῶν ἀνομιῶν αὐτοῦ. The material supplied by this passage for a discussion of the Atonement is contained in ἔδωκεν . . . ἡμῶν, not in λυτρώσηται. See Dean Armitage Robinson's note on Eph. i. 14.

ἀνομίας : *Lawlessness* is the essence of sin (1 John iii. 4), self-assertion as opposed to self-sacrifice which is love. Love, which is self-sacrifice, is a dissolvent of self-assertion or sin. And to what degree soever we allow the love of Christ to operate as a controlling principle in our lives, to that degree we are delivered from ἀνομία, as an opposing controlling principle.

καθαρίσῃ ἑαυτῷ λαόν : This is a pregnant expression for "purify and so make them fit to be his people". St. Paul has in mind Ezek. xxxvii. 23, "I will save them out of all their dwelling places, wherein they have sinned, and will cleanse them : so shall they be my people, and I will be their God", ῥύσομαι αὐτοὺς ἀπὸ πασῶν τῶν ἀνομιῶν αὐτῶν ὧν ἡμάρτοσαν ἐν αὐταῖς, καὶ καθαριῶ αὐτοὺς καὶ ἔσονταί μοι εἰς λαόν, κ.τ.λ. There is in καθαρίσῃ an allusion to Holy Baptism, which is explicit in iii. 5. *Cf.* Eph. v. 26, ἵνα αὐτὴν ἁγιάσῃ καθαρίσας τῷ λουτρῷ τοῦ ὕδατος ἐν ῥήματι.

λαὸν περιούσιον : *populum acceptabilem* (Vulg.). *A people for his own possession* (R.V.) is the modern equivalent of *a peculiar people* (A.V.). λαὸς περιούσιος is the LXX for עַם סְגֻלָה. סְגֻלָה means "a valued property, a peculiar treasure" (*peculium*), and occurs first in Exodus xix. 5, "Ye shall be a peculiar treasure unto me." Here the LXX inserts λαός, possibly from the references in Deut., in which the combination סְגֻלָה עַם is found. סְגֻלָה alone occurs in Malachi iii. 17 (εἰς περιποίησιν) and in Ps. cxxxv. 4 (εἰς περιουσιασμόν). The LXX of Mal. iii. 17 is echoed in Eph. i. 14, εἰς ἀπολύτρωσιν τῆς περιποιήσεως, (where see Dean Armitage Robinson's note) and 1 Pet. ii. 9, λαὸς εἰς περιποίησιν, in which λαός is a reminiscence of the

[m] περιούσιον, [n] ζηλωτὴν [o] καλῶν [o] ἔργων. 15. ταῦτα λάλει καὶ
παρακάλει καὶ ἔλεγχε μετὰ πάσης [p] ἐπιταγῆς· μηδείς σου [q] περιφρονείτω.

III. 1. [a] Ὑπομίμνησκε αὐτοὺς [b] ἀρχαῖς[1] [b c] ἐξουσίαις ὑποτάσσεσθαι, [d] πειθαρχεῖν, [e f] πρὸς [e] πᾶν [e g] ἔργον [e g] ἀγαθὸν [f] ἑτοίμους εἶναι,
2. μηδένα βλασφημεῖν, [h] ἀμάχους εἶναι, [h] ἐπιεικεῖς, πᾶσαν [i] ἐνδεικνυμένους [k] πραΰτητα πρὸς πάντας ἀνθρώπους. 3. Ἦμεν γάρ ποτε
καὶ ἡμεῖς [l] ἀνόητοι, [m] ἀπειθεῖς, [n] πλανώμενοι, [o] δουλεύοντες [p] ἐπιθυ-

m Exod. xix. 5, xxiii. 22, Deut. vii. 6, xiv. 2, xxvi. 18.
n Acts xxi. 20, xxii. 3, 1 Cor. xiv. 12, Gal. i. 14, 1 Pet. iii. 13.
o See 1 Tim iii. 1.
p 1 Cor. vii. 6, 2 Cor. viii. 8.
q 4 Macc. vi. 9, xiv. 1 only. a See 2 Tim. ii. 14. b Luke xii. 11, xx. 20. c Luke xxiii. 7, Rom. xiii. 1, 2, 3. d Acts v. 29, 32, xxvii. 21. e See 2 Tim. ii. 21. f 1 Pet. iii. 15. g See 1 Tim. ii. 10. h See 1 Tim. iii. 3. i See 2 Tim. iv. 14. k See 2 Tim. ii. 25. l See 1 Tim. vi. 9. m 2 Tim. iii. 2, Tit. i. 16, etc. n See 2 Tim. iii. 13. o Rom. vi. 6. p 2 Tim. iii. 6.

[1] Ins. **καὶ** D^cKLP, d, e, f, m94, vg., syrr., boh., arm.

LXX of the passages in Exod. and Deut. Perhaps **περιούσιος** refers to the treasure as laid up, while **περιποίησις** refers to it as acquired.

ζηλωτὴν καλῶν ἔργων: See Eph. ii. 10; 1 Pet. i. 15; Heb. x. 24.

Ver. 15. See on 1 Tim. iv. 12.

ταῦτα is best connected with **λάλει** only, and referred to the positive instructions of chap. ii., "the things which befit the sound doctrine"; while **παρακάλει** and **ἔλεγχε** represent the two main functions of the pastor. See i. 9.

ἐπιταγῆς: *authority*, *imperio*; **πάσης ἐπιτ·**: *in the most authoritative manner possible*; not to be connected with **ἔλεγχε** only.

μηδείς σου περιφρονείτω: another way of saying **μετὰ πάσης ἐπιταγῆς**. *Do not permit thine authority to be despised*, *Be consistent*. See 1 Tim. iv. 12.

Chapter III.—Vv. 1-2. As your Cretan folk are naturally intractable, be careful to insist on obedience to the constituted authorities, and on the maintenance of friendly relations with non-Christians.

Ver. 1. With these instructions as to duty towards civil authority, compare Rom. xiii. 1 *sqq.*, 1 Pet. ii. 13 *sqq.* It is perhaps significant of the difference between Crete and the province of Asia, as regards respect for law, that in 1 Tim. ii. 1-3, reasons are given why we should pray for rulers, while here the more elementary duty of obedience is enjoined. Polybius (vi. 46. 9) remarks on the seditious character of the Cretans.

ὑπομίμνησκε: See note on 2 Tim. ii. 14.

ἀρχαῖς: **ἀρχαί** and **ἐξουσίαι** are coupled in this sense in Luke xii. 11; **ἀρχή** and **ἐξουσία** in the abstract, Luke xx. 20. The two words are coupled together as names for ranks of angels in Eph. iii. 10, vi. 12, Col. i. 16, ii. 10, 15; with **δύναμις**, 1 Cor. xv. 24, Eph. i. 31; **ἀρχαί**, alone, Rom. viii. 38.

πειθαρχεῖν: (*dicto obedire*) is best taken absolutely, and with a wider reference than the preceding clause: *i.e.*, as R.V., *to be obedient*, rather than merely *to obey magistrates* (A.V.).

πρὸς πᾶν ἔργον ἀγαθόν. See reff.

Ver. 2. **ἀμάχους . . . ἐπιεικεῖς**: coupled as qualifications of the episcopus, 1 Tim. iii. 3.

πᾶσαν πραΰτητα: *the greatest possible meekness*. Compare Eph. iv. 2; 1 Pet. iii. 15.

Vv. 3-7. Cretans who hear this epistle need not feel hurt as though I were thinking of them with exceptional severity. We were such ourselves until we came to know the love of God, unmerited and saving and sanctifying and perfecting.

Ver. 3. **ἦμεν γάρ ποτε καὶ ἡμεῖς**: The connexion is: you need not suppose that it is hopeless to imagine that these wild Cretan folk can be reclaimed. We ourselves are a living proof of the power of God's grace. Eph. ii. 3 *sqq.* is an exact parallel. *Cf.* also 1 Cor. vi. 11, Eph. v. 8, Col. iii. 7, 1 Pet. iv. 3.

ἀνόητοι: *insipientes*, *foolish*, in the sense in which the word is used in Proverbs (*e.g.* xvii. 28), *without understanding of spiritual things.*

πλανώμενοι: The analogy of 2 Tim. iii. 13 suggests that this is passive, *deceived*, not neuter, *errantes* (Vulg.), though of course there are many ex-

q Luke viii. μίαις καὶ ^qἡδοναῖς ^pποικίλαις· ἐν ^rκακίᾳ καὶ ^rφθόνῳ ^sδιάγοντες,
14, Jas.iv.
1, 3, 2   ^tστυγητοί, ^uμισοῦντες ^uἀλλήλους. 4. ὅτε δὲ ἡ ^rχρηστότης καὶ ἡ
Pet. ii. 13.
r Rom. i. 29, ^wφιλανθρωπία ^xἐπεφάνη τοῦ ^yσωτῆρος ^yἡμῶν ^yΘεοῦ, 5. οὐκ ἐξ ἔργων
  1 Pet. ii. 1.
s See 1 Tim. τῶν ἐν δικαιοσύνῃ ἃ¹ ἐποιήσαμεν ἡμεῖς ἀλλὰ ^zκατὰ ^zτὸ ^zαὐτοῦ
  ii. 2.
t Here only, ^zἔλεος ² ἔσωσεν ἡμᾶς διὰ ^{3 a}λουτροῦ ^bπαλιγγενεσίας καὶ ^cἀνακαι-
  not LXX.
u Matt.xxiv.
  10.   v Rom. ii. 4, xi. 22 *ter*., Eph. ii. 7 (Paul elsewhere 4 times).   w Acts xxviii. 2 only,
N.T., Esth. (1). 2 Macc. (2), 3 Macc. (2).   x See Tit. ii. 11.   y See 1 Tim. i. 1.   z 1 Pet.
i. 3.   a Eph. v. 26 only, N.T., Cant. iv. 2, vi. 5, Ecclus. xxxi. (xxxiv.) 25.   b Matt. xix. 28
only, not LXX.   c Rom. xii. 2 only, not LXX, *cf.* 2 Cor. iv. 16, Col. iii. 10.

¹ ὧν CbDcKLP.   ² τὸν . . . ἔλεον DbcKL.   ³ Ins. τοῦ A.

amples of this latter sense in the N.T.

ποικίλαις: See note on 2 Tim. iii. 6.

διάγοντες: *sc* βίον, as in 1 Tim. ii. 2.

στυγητοί κ.τ.λ.: *odibiles, odientes invicem* (Vulg.). This marks the stage of degradation, before it becomes hopeless : when vice becomes odious to the vicious, stands a self-confessed failure to produce happiness.

Ver. 4. **χρηστότης καὶ φιλανθρωπία**: (*benignitas . . . humanitas*) is a constant combination in Greek. See many examples supplied by Field. Here it expresses the notion of John iii. 16, **οὕτως γὰρ ἠγάπησεν ὁ θεὸς τὸν κόσμον κ.τ.λ.** and of Eph. ii. 4-6. Perhaps also, as von Soden suggests, the kindness of God is here contrasted with the unkindness of men to each other ; *cf.* Eph. iv. 31, 32.

χρηστότης is a Pauline word, used of God also in reff. **φιλανθρωπία** is especially used of the beneficent feelings of divine beings towards men ; more rarely of the relations between man and man, as in Acts xxviii. 2. Diogenes Laert., quoted by Alf., distinguishes three kinds of **φιλανθρ.** (1) geniality of manner, (2) helpfulness, (3) sociability.

ἐπεφάνη: See note on 1 Tim. vi. 14.

τοῦ σωτῆρος ἡμῶν θεοῦ: θεοῦ, as in i. 3, ii. 10, is epexegetical of **σωτῆρος**.

Ver. 5. The **ἡμεῖς** and **ἡμᾶς** refer to the same persons as those mentioned in verse 3, *i.e.*, the apostles and those who have had a similar experience. The verse may be paraphrased as a statement of fact thus :—God saved us by Baptism, which involves two complementary processes, (*a*) the ceremony itself which marks the actual moment in time of the new birth, and (*b*) the daily, hourly, momently renewing of the Holy Spirit, by which the spiritual life is supported and fostered and increased. And the moving cause of this exceeding kindness of God was not any merits of our own, but His mercy

οὐκ ἐξ ἔργων: ἐκ here, as in Rom iii. 30, expresses the source. See also the emphatic repetition in Gal. ii. 16 of **οὐκ ἐξ ἔργων νόμου**. The **δικαιοσύνη** here is that which we can call our own, **ἡ ἐκ νόμου** (Phil. iii. 9). Its existence as **δικαιοσύνη** must not be denied ; but it does not pass as current coin in the kingdom of God. It has indeed no saving value whatever. Accordingly there is no question here as to whether we did, or did not do, works which are **ἐν δικαιοσύνῃ**. "Not the labours of my hands can fulfil *Thy* law's demands." See note on 2 Tim. i. 9.

Bengel, comparing Deut. ix. 5, refers the negative to each term in the clause : we had not been **ἐν δικ.** ; we had not done **ἔργα ἐν δικ.** ; we had no works through which we could be saved. But this exegesis is too much affected by the controversies of the sixteenth century. The A.V., *which we have done*, confuses the thought by a suggestion that the works referred to are those "after justification".

τῶν ἐν δικαιοσύνῃ: **δικαιοσύνη** is the sphere in which the works were done, and to which they are related.

κατὰ . . . ἔλεος: The phraseology is borrowed from Ps. cviii. (cix.) 26, **σῶσόν με κατὰ τὸ μέγα ἔλεός σου**. A remarkable parallel is furnished by 1 Pet. i. 3, **ὁ κατὰ τὸ πολὺ αὐτοῦ ἔλεος ἀναγεννήσας ἡμᾶς** ; and also by 2 Esdr. viii. 32, "For if thou hast a desire to have mercy upon us, then shalt thou be called merciful, to us, namely, that have no works of righteousness ".

ἔσωσεν ἡμᾶς: The N.T. seldom diverts attention from the main lesson to be taught from time to time by noting qualifications, even necessary ones. Here St. Paul is speaking only about the efficient and instrumental and formal causes of salvation, without any thought of man's part in co-operation with God. It is as when teaching the principles of

νώσεως ¹ Πνεύματος Ἁγίου, 6. οὗ ᵈ ἐξέχεεν ἐφ᾽ ἡμᾶς ᵉ πλουσίως διὰ d Acts ii. 17,
᠎   ᠎   ᠎   ᠎   ᠎   ᠎   ᠎   ᠎   ᠎   18, 33
ᶠ Ἰησοῦ ᶠ Χριστοῦ ᶠ τοῦ ᶠ σωτῆρος ἡμῶν, 7. ἵνα ᵍ δικαιωθέντες ᵍ τῇ (=Joel
᠎   ᠎   ᠎   ᠎   ᠎   ᠎   ᠎   ᠎   iii. 1).
ᵍ ἐκείνου ᵍ χάριτι ʰ κληρονόμοι γενηθῶμεν ² κατ᾽ ¹ ἐλπίδα ¹ ᵏ ζωῆς e See 1 Tim.
᠎   ᠎   ᠎   ᠎   ᠎   ᠎   ᠎   ᠎   vi. 17.
¹ ᵏ αἰωνίου. 8. ¹ Πιστὸς ¹ ὁ ¹ λόγος · καὶ περὶ τούτων ᵐ βούλομαί σε f See 2 Tim.
᠎   ᠎   ᠎   ᠎   ᠎   ᠎   ᠎   ᠎   i. 10.
᠎   ᠎   ᠎   ᠎   ᠎   ᠎   ᠎   ᠎   g Rom.

iii. 24.   h Rom. iv. 14, viii. 17, Gal. iii. 29, iv. 7, Heb. vi. 17, Jas. ii. 5.   i Tit. i. 2.   k See
1 Tim. i. 16.   l See 1 Tim. i. 15.   m See 1 Tim. ii. 8.

¹ Ins. διὰ D*FG, d e, g.   ² γενώμεθα ℵcDcKL.

mechanics, we do not confuse the beginner's mind by making allowances for friction, etc. Here, as in Rom. vi. and 1 Pet. iii. 21, it is assumed that man co-operates with God in the work of his own salvation. On the force of the aorist, ἔσωσεν, see note on 1 Tim. ii. 4.

διὰ λουτροῦ : the washing. λουτρόν may mean the water used for washing, or the process itself of washing. The R.V.m. laver would be λουτήρ. See Dean Armitage Robinson's note on Eph. v. 26.

παλινγενεσίας : This defines the nature of the λουτρόν which God employs as His instrument in effecting the salvation of man ; not any λουτρόν whatever, but that of new birth. It is sufficient to observe here that much of the controversy about regeneration might have been avoided had men kept before them the analogy of natural birth, followed as it is immediately, not by vigorous manhood, but by infancy and childhood and youth.

ἀνακαινώσεως : The genitive ἀνακαινώσεως depends on διὰ (which is actually inserted in the Harclean Syriac; so R.V.m., and through renewing), not on λουτροῦ, as apparently Vulg., per lavacrum regenerationis et renovationis Spiritus Sancti, f. Boh. Ạrm., followed by R.V. The λουτρόν, the washing, secures a claim on the Holy Spirit for renewing, just as birth gives a child a claim on society for food and shelter ; but unless we are compelled to do otherwise, it is best to keep the two notions distinct. Birth, natural or spiritual, must be a definite fact taking place at a particular moment ; whereas renewing is necessarily a subsequent process, constantly operating. Without this renewing the life received at birth is at best in a state of suspension. The references to ἀνακαίνωσις and ἀνακαινοῦν, and the similar passage, Eph. iv. 23, show that the terms are always used of those who are actually living the Christian life.

Ver. 6. οὗ ἐξέχεεν : Joel iii. 1 (ii. 28) is the passage alluded to. Cf. in addition

to reff. given above, Acts x. 45, Rom. v. 5, Gal. iv. 6. The οὗ refers of course to πνεύματ. ἁγ. by attraction, not to ἀνακαινώσεως. All gifts of the Holy Spirit that come through Jesus Christ are a continuation of the Pentecostal out-pouring. The aorist is due to the Apostle's thought of that occasion, although the ἡμᾶς shows that the immediate reference is to the experience of St. Paul and other Christians.

διὰ Ἰησοῦ Χριστοῦ : to be connected with ἐξέχεεν. See John xv. 26, Acts ii. 33. The finished work of Jesus Christ was the necessary pre-condition to His effusion of the Holy Spirit.

Ver. 7. ἵνα, κ.τ.λ.: It is not quite certain, whether this expresses the object of ἐξέχεεν or of ἔσωσεν. The former connexion brings out best the climax of the passage. κληρονόμοι marks the highest point to which man can attain in this life. See reff. The two preceding stages are marked by λουτρὸν παλινγενεσίας and ἀνακαίνωσις, while δικαιωθέντες . . . χάριτι is an expression in theological language of the simpler κατὰ τὸ αὐτοῦ ἔλεος ἔσωσεν ἡμᾶς. The grace by which man is justified is usually spoken of as that of God the Father, Rom. iii. 24 ; and so ἐκείνου, not αὐτοῦ, is used as referring to the remoter antecedent.

κληρονόμοι : According to the analogy of the other passages where it occurs, this word is best taken absolutely ; or, if the notion must be completed, we may understand θεοῦ. The term would not need any elucidation to one of St. Paul's company. It is also an argument against connecting κληρ. ζωῆς αἰωνίου (R.V.m) that ἐλπὶς ζωῆς αἰωνίου occurs in i. 2; and Gal. iii. 29, κατ᾽ ἐπαγγελίαν κληρ., is parallel.

Vv. 8-11. To sum up what I have been saying : Belief in God is not a matter of theory or of speculation, but of practice ; it must be accompanied by good works. This true religion unites the beautiful and the profitable. On the other hand, foolish speculations and controversies about the law are profitless

[n] διαβεβαιοῦσθαι, ἵνα [o] φροντίζωσιν [p] καλῶν [p] ἔργων [p] προΐστασθαι οἱ
[q] [r] πεπιστευκότες[1] [r] Θεῷ. [s] ταῦτά ἐστιν[2] [s] καλὰ καὶ [t] ὠφέλιμα τοῖς
ἀνθρώποις. 9. [u] μωρὰς δὲ [u] [v] ζητήσεις καὶ [w] γενεαλογίας καὶ ἔρεις[3]
καὶ [x] μάχας [y] νομικὰς [z] περιΐστασο, εἰσὶν γὰρ [a] ἀνωφελεῖς καὶ μάταιοι.
10. [b] αἱρετικὸν ἄνθρωπον μετὰ μίαν καὶ δευτέραν [c] νουθεσίαν[4]

n 1 Tim. i. 7, not LXX.
o Here only, N.T.
p Tit. iii. 14, see 1 Tim. iii. 1.
q Acts xv. 5, xviii. 27, xix. 18, xxi. 20, 25.
r Gen. xv. 6 (Rom. iv. 3, Gal. iii. 6, Jas. ii. 23), 1 John v. 10. s *Cf.* 1 Tim. ii. 3. t See 1 Tim. iv. 8. u 2 Tim. ii. 23. v See 1 Tim. vi. 4. w See 1 Tim. i. 4. x See 2 Tim. ii. 23. y Here only in this sense (see ver. 13), not LXX. z See 2 Tim. ii. 16. a Heb. vii. 18, Prov xxviii. 3, Wisd. i. 11, Isa. xliv. 10, Jer. ii. 8 only. b Here only, not LXX. c 1 Cor. x. 11, Eph. vi. 4, Wisd. xvi. 6 only.

1 Ins. τῷ most cursives. 2 Ins. τὰ DcKLP.

3 So ℵcACKLP, d, e, f, g, m50, vg, boh, syrr, arm; ἔριν ℵ* [DgrFgrGgr, ερειν], Jerome once.

4 μίαν νουθ. καὶ[ἢ] δευτ. DcFgrG [D*, d, e, καὶ δύο], g; om. καὶ δευτέραν MSS. known to Jerome, m50, Iren. lat., Pamph. lat., Ruf., Tert., Cyp., Lucif., Aug., Amb., Ambrst.

and unpractical. Do not parley long with a confirmed schismatic. If he does not yield to one or two admonitions, reject him altogether. It is beyond your power to set him right.

Ver. 8. **πιστὸς ὁ λόγος.** Here it is evident that **ὁ λόγος** does not refer to any isolated Saying, but to the doctrinal statement contained in verses 4-7 regarded as a single concept—as we, when we speak of *The Incarnation*, sum up in one term a whole system of theology—while **τούτων** refers to the various topics indicated in that statement, not to the practical teaching of ii. 1—iii. 7.

βούλομαι: see note on 1 Tim. ii. 8.

διαβεβαιοῦσθαι: Here the Vulg. has *confirmare*; d has *affirmare*, as in 1 Tim. i. 7, where see note.

ἵνα: It is most significant and suggestive that the apostle held that good works were most certainly assured by a theology which gives special prominence to the free unmerited grace of God. This is made plainer in the R.V. (*to the end that*), than in the A.V. (*that*).

φροντίζωσιν: *curent* (am.), *curam habeant* (fuld).

καλῶν ἔργων προΐστασθαι: *occupy themselves in good works, bonis operibus praeesse* (Vulg.). *Prostare* would have been a better translation, since the **πρό** in this use of **προΐστασθαι** is derived from bodily posture rather than from superiority in station. "From the practice of the workman or tradesman *standing before* his shop for the purpose of soliciting customers . . . we arrive at the general meaning of *conducting* or *managing any matter of business.*" So Field, who also points out that the R.V. m., *profess honest occupations* (similarly A.V.m on ver. 14) is open to the serious objection that **καλὰ ἔργα** everywhere else in N.T., as well as in secular authors, means "good works" in the religious or moral sense.

οἱ πεπιστευκότες θεῷ: This simple phrase is used designedly in order to express the notion that profession of the recently revealed Gospel is indeed merely a logical consequence and natural development of the older simple belief in God.

ταῦτα: The antithesis in the following **μωρὰς δὲ ζητήσεις** proves that *these things* refers to the subject-matter of Titus' pronouncements (**διαβεβαιοῦσθαι**), and means *this enforcement of practical religion.*

καλά: is to be taken absolutely, as in the parallel 1 Tim. ii. 3, and is not to be connected with **τοῖς ἀνθρώποις.**

Ver. 9. **ζητήσεις** and **γενεαλογίαι** are associated together in 1 Tim. i. 4 (where see notes). Here they are co-ordinated; there the **γενεαλογίαι** are one of the sources whence **ζητήσεις** originate. The nature of the **ἔρεις** here deprecated is determined by the context. **ἔρεις** indicate the spirit of contentiousness; **μάχαι** the conflicts as heard and seen. On **μάχαι,** see 2 Tim. ii. 23. The **μάχαι νομικαί** are no doubt the same as the **λογομαχίαι** of 1 Tim. vi. 4. Speaking broadly, the controversy turned on the attempt to give a fictitious permanence to the essentially transient elements in the Mosaical Law.

περιΐστασο: See note on 2 Tim. ii. 16.

μάταιοι: Here, and in James i. 26, **μάταιος** is an adjective of two terminations; yet **ματαία** occurs 1 Cor. xv. 17; **ματαίας,** 1 Peter i. 18.

Ver. 10. **αἱρετικὸν ἄνθρωπον**: St.

ᵈπαραιτοῦ, 11. εἰδὼς ὅτι ᵉἐξέστραπται ὁ τοιοῦτος καὶ ἁμαρτάνει,   d See 1 Tim·
ὢν ᶠαὐτοκατάκριτος.   iv. 7.
                                                                   e Deut.
                                                                   xxxii. 20,
12. Ὅταν πέμψω Ἀρτεμᾶν πρός σε ἢ Τυχικόν, ᵍσπούδασον ἐλθεῖν   etc., heie
                                                                   only, N.T
πρός με εἰς Νικόπολιν· ἐκεῖ γὰρ ʰκέκρικα ⁱπαραχειμάσαι.   13.   f Here only,
                                                                   not LXX.
                                                                   g See 2 Tim.
ii. 15.   h Acts iii. 13, xx. 16, xxv. 25, xxvii. 1, 1 Cor. ii. 2, vii. 37, 2 Cor. ii. 1.   i Acts xxvii.
12, xxviii. 11, 1 Cor. xvi. 6, not LXX.

Paul passes from the reprehensible
opinions to the man who propagates
them. He is the same kind of man
as the φιλόνεικος of 1 Cor. xi. 16; or
"he that refuseth to hear the church"
of Matt. xviii. 17; he is of "them which
cause divisions and occasions of stumbling," Rom. xvi. 17. The term αἵρεσις
is applied in a non-offensive sense to
the sects of Judaism, Acts v. 17, xv.
5, xxvi. 5. St. Luke represents the
Jews as so speaking of the Christian
Church (Acts xxiv. 5, xxviii. 22), and St.
Paul as resenting this application of the
term (Acts xxiv. 14). The Apostle himself uses the word in an unfavourable
sense (1 Cor. xi. 19; Gal. v. 20), as does
2 Pet. ii. 1. A comparison of 1 Cor. xi.
19 with 1 John ii. 19 suggests that
αἵρεσις involved the formation of a separate society (so R.V.m. here, factious),
not merely the holding of aberrant
opinions, or the favouring a policy different from that of the Church rulers.
The νουθεσία addressed to a member of
such a αἵρεσις would be of the nature
of a verbal remonstrance, pointing out
the essentially unchristian character of
needless separation. It is evident that
the αἱρετικὸς ἄνθρωπος would be beyond
any Church discipline. The permission
of a second attempt at reconciliation is
probably not unconnected with our
Lord's counsel, Matt. xviii. 15.

παραιτοῦ: Have nothing to do with
him. See note on 1 Tim. iv. 7. The word
does not necessarily imply any formal
excommunication. Such procedure
would be unnecessary. Excommunication has no terrors for those who deliberately separate themselves. "Monere
desine. quid enim iuvat? laterem la-
vares" (Bengel).

Ver. 11. εἰδώς: since thou mayest know.
ἐξέστραπται: subversus est. Argument with a man whose basal mental
convictions differ from your own, or
whose mind has had a twist, is mere
waste of breath.

αὐτοκατάκριτος: proprio iudicio con-
demnatus (Vulg.). He is self-condemned
because his separation from the Church
is due to his own acknowledged act. He

cannot deny that his views are antagonistic to those which he once accepted as
true; he is condemned by his former,
and, as St. Paul would say, his more
enlightened self.

Vv. 12-14. Come to me, as soon as
you can be spared. Forward Zenas and
Apollos. Let our friends in Crete remember that fruitfulness in good works
is the one thing needful for them.

Ver. 12. ὅταν πέμψω πρός σε: It is
natural to suppose that Artemas or
Tychicus would take the place of Titus
as apostolic legate in Crete. This temporary exercise of apostolic superintendence marks a stage in the development
of monarchical local episcopacy in the
later sense.

Ἀρτεμᾶν: The name is "Greek,
formed from Ἄρτεμις perhaps by con-
traction from Artemidorus, a name common in Asia Minor" (W. Lock, art. in
Hastings' D. B.).

Τυχικόν: See note on 2 Tim. iv. 12.

Νικόπολιν: The subscription in the
later MSS. at the end of the epistle,
ἐγράφη ἀπὸ Νικοπόλεως τῆς Μακεδονίας,
follows the Greek commentators (Chrys.,
Theod., etc.), in identifying this Nicopolis with that in Thrace, on the Nestus ;
but makes a stupid mistake in not perceiving that ἐκεῖ proves that St. Paul
was not at Nicopolis when the letter was
written. If we suppose that the situation
of St. Paul, when writing 2 Tim., must
have been somewhere between Dalmatia,
Thessalonica, Corinth, Miletus, Ephesus
and Troas, then Nicopolis ad Nestum
would meet the needs of the case. But
the more important Nicopolis in Epirus
has found more favour with modern
scholars (see art. by W. M. Ramsay in
Hastings' D.B.).

παραχειμάσαι: It is possible that the
winter is that mentioned in 2 Tim. iv.
21. The apostle was not always permitted to exercise the gift of prophecy, in
the sense of being able to foretell future
events. From this point of view, There
I have determined to winter may be compared with the earlier I know that ye all
. . . shall see my face no more (Acts xx. 25).

Ver. 13. νομικόν: In the absence of

k Matt. xxii.
35, Luke
(7), cf.
ver. 9.
l See 2 Tim.
i. 17.
m Acts xv.
3, xx. 38,
xxi. 5,
Rom. xv.
24, 1 Cor.
xvi. 6, 11,
2 Cor. i.
16, 3 John 6.

Ζηνᾶν τὸν ᵏνομικὸν καὶ ᾽Απολλὼν ¹ ˡσπουδαίως ᵐπρόπεμψον, ἵνα μηδὲν αὐτοῖς ⁿλείπῃ.² 14. μανθανέτωσαν δὲ καὶ ᵒοἱ ᵒἡμέτεροι ᵖᑫκαλῶν ᵖᑫἔργων ᵖπροΐστασθαι εἰς τὰς ʳἀναγκαίας ˢχρείας, ἵνα μὴ ὦσιν ᵗἄκαρποι. 15. ᾽Ασπάζονταί σε οἱ μετ᾽ ἐμοῦ πάντες· ἄσπασαι τοὺς ᵘφιλοῦντας ἡμᾶς ᵛἐν ᵛπίστει. Ἡ χάρις μετὰ πάντων ὑμῶν.³

n See Tit. i. 5.   o Here only.   p Ver. 8.   ꞯ See 1 Tim. iii. 1.   r Acts
x. 24, 1 Cor. xii. 22.   s Acts vi. 3, xx. 34, xxviii. 10, Rom. xii. 13, Eph. iv. 29, Phil. ii. 25, iv. 16, 19,
t 2 Pet. i. 8, Matt. xiii. 22 (= Mark iv. 19), 1 Cor. xiv. 14, Eph. v. 11, Jude 12.   u Matt. (5), Mark.
(1), Luke (2), John (13), 1 Cor. xvi. 22, Rev. (2).   v See 1 Tim. i. 2.

¹ So ℵ*DbH* one cursive; ᾽Απολλῶνα FG ; g (apollo t apollonem) ; ᾽Απολλώ
CD*cH**KLP, d, e, f, vg.

² λίπῃ ℵD*, 37, 47*, about thirteen others.

³ Ins. ἀμήν ℵcDbcFGHKLP, e, f, g, vg. (not fuld.), syrr.

Add πρὸς Τίτον ℵC, 17, to which D adds ἐπληρώθη ; AP add ἐγράφη ἀπὸ
Νικοπόλεως ; FG have ἐτελέσθη ἐπιστολὴ πρὸς Τίτον ; K has πρὸς Τίτον τῆς
Κρητῶν ἐκκλησίας πρῶτον ἐπίσκοπον χειροτονηθέντα, ἐγράφη ἀπὸ Νικοπόλεως τῆς
Μακεδονίας. Similarly HL.

any example of this word being used as the equivalent of *legisperitus* (Vulg.), *jurisconsultus* or *jurisperitus*, it seems best to assume that Zenas was a νομικός in the usual N.T. sense, an expert in the Mosaic Law.

᾽Απολλὼν: For Apollos, see article in Hastings' *D. B.*

πρόπεμψον: *set forward on their journey, praemitte*; but *deduco* is the rendering where the word occurs elsewhere. See reff.

Ver. 14. The δέ does not mark an antithesis between οἱ ἡμέτεροι and the persons who have just been mentioned, but is rather resumptive of verse 8: repeating and emphasising at the close of the letter that which St. Paul had most at heart, the changed lives of the Cretan converts. οἱ ἡμέτεροι of course means *those of our faith* in Crete.

καλῶν ἔργων προΐστασθαι: See on verse 8.

εἰς τὰς ἀναγκαίας χρείας: The best commentary on this expression is 1 Thess. iv. 9-12. Although καλῶν ἔργων προΐστασθαι does not mean *to profess honest occupations*, yet it is plain from St. Paul's letters that he would regard the earning one's own bread respectably as a condition precedent to the doing of good works. The *necessary wants*

to which allusion is made are the maintenance of oneself and family, and helping brethren who are unable to help themselves (Acts xx. 35; Rom. xii. 13; Eph. iv. 28). This view is borne out by the reason which follows, ἵνα μὴ ὦσιν ἄκαρποι. See John xv. 2, Phil. iv. 17, Col. i. 10, 2 Pet. i. 8.

Ver. 15. Final Salutation.

οἱ μετ᾽ ἐμοῦ: The preposition is different elsewhere in Paul: οἱ σὺν ἐμοὶ πάντες ἀδελφοί, Gal. i. 2; οἱ σὺν ἐμοὶ ἀδελφοί, Phil. iv. 21. οἱ μετ᾽ αὐτοῦ is a constant phrase in the Synoptists. There is a similar use of μετά in Acts xx. 34 (a speech of St. Paul's), and in 2 Tim. iv. 11.

τοὺς φιλοῦντας ἡμᾶς ἐν πίστει: *The faith* (see note on 1 Tim. i. 2) is that which binds Christians together more or less closely. Timothy and Titus were St. Paul's τέκνα ἐν πίστει; others were more distantly related to him, though of the same family, "the household of faith".

Dean Armitage Robinson (*Ephesians*, p. 281) gives several examples from papyri of similar formulas of closing, especially two, which read, ἀσπάζου . . . τοὺς φιλοῦντες σε (or ἡμᾶς) πρὸς ἀληθίαν. This suggests the rendering here, *those who love us truly*.

THE EPISTLE OF PAUL

TO

PHILEMON

INTRODUCTION.

§ I. *Authorship, Place and Date.*—The external evidence for the authenticity of this Epistle is sufficiently strong; it is included among the Pauline writings in the collection of Marcion; Tertullian mentions this in his *Adv. Marc.* v. 42. It is also mentioned, in connexion with the Pastoral Epistles, in the Muratorian Fragment. Origen ascribes it to St. Paul (*Hom. in Matth.* xxxiii., xxxiv.); Eusebius reckons it among the ὁμολογούμενα (*H. E.* iii. 25); Jerome, in his commentary on the Epistle, mentions the fact that its genuineness was disputed by some because it did not treat of doctrinal matters; he holds that it would not have been received by the Church from the beginning unless it had been St. Paul's. The fact that it is not mentioned in the sub-apostolic literature cannot excite suspicion, for its shortness and the character of its contents sufficiently account for this non-mention. The internal evidence is equally strong; the Epistle bears the impress of the Pauline spirit throughout; and one has only to compare the vocabulary and style with those of the other Pauline Epistles to be convinced at once that St. Paul wrote it. Very few among modern scholars reject its Pauline authorship; van Manen, for example, finds a difficulty in the " surprising mixture of singular and plural both in the persons speaking and in the persons addressed. This double form points at once to some peculiarity in the composition of the Epistle. It is not a style that is natural to any one who is writing freely and untrammelled, whether to one person or many " (*Encycl. Bibl.* col. 3695). Such a futile objection is self-condemnatory; but he continues: " Here, as throughout the discussion, the constantly recurring questions as to the reason for the selection of the forms, words, expressions adopted, find their answer in the observation that the Epistle was written under the influence of a perusal of 'Pauline' epistles, especially of those to the Ephesians and Colossians " (*ibid.*). That is as much as to say that the fact that a writer is writing in his usual style is presumptive evidence that his style is being imitated by someone else! The minute verbal comparisons which van Manen tabulates between this and the other

Pauline (he would write 'Pauline') Epistles constitutes a strong proof of identity of authorship between them. Objectors like the writer mentioned are, of course, exceptional; as Jülicher says, "the all but universal judgment is that Philemon belongs to the least doubtful part of the Apostle's work" (*Intr. to the N. T.* p. 127).

The *Place* of writing and the *Date* of the Epistle are mutually determining; St. Paul was in prison when he wrote it, therefore the Epistle must have come either from Cæsarea (Acts xxiv.-xxvi.), or from Rome (Acts xxviii. 30); the time of these two imprisonments was A.D. 58-63; the vast majority of writers are agreed that the group of Epistles to the Philippians, Colossians, Ephesians and to Philemon were written from Rome (see, for the reasons for this view, Lightfoot's *Philippians*, pp. 30 ff.); this would narrow the date of our Epistle down to somewhere between A.D. 60-63. As to the question whether Philemon was written early or late within this period, this depends upon the answer to the question as to whether the Epistle to the Philippians should be placed early in the Roman captivity and the three other Epistles later, or *vice versa*, for it is generally allowed that the Epistle to the Philippians stands alone, the other three were written and despatched at or about the same time. For a full discussion of these questions reference must be made to Lightfoot's *Philippians*, pp. 30-46; here it will have to suffice to say that the most probable year for the date of *Philemon* is A.D. 62.

§ II. *Occasion and Contents.*—Although the Epistle is not the only one of St. Paul's addressed to an individual which has come down to us, it is the only one of a, mainly, *private* character; for although in the opening salutation Apphia, Archippus and the Church in Philemon's house are addressed as well as Philemon himself, nevertheless the contents of the Epistle deal with a personal matter. The nearest parallel in the N.T. is 3 John, addressed to "Gaius the beloved". The Epistle is an appeal made by St. Paul to Philemon on behalf of the runaway slave, Onesimus. Philemon was a citizen of Colossæ (*cf.* Col. iv. 17, Philem. 2, 10-12, and see Col. iv. 9); the Word was most likely preached here during the period which St. Paul spent at Ephesus, from which centre his influence extended widely (see Acts xix. 26, 1 Cor. xvi. 19); Philemon was among the converts made by St. Paul himself (see Philem. 19), and he evidently became a zealous worker, since St. Paul applies the title συνεργός to him; that he was loving and hospitable is clear from vv. 5-7.

Onesimus, the immediate cause of the Epistle, who had run away from his master, also became a convert of St. Paul's (ver. 10); from ver. 18 it would almost seem as though he had committed a theft;

if so, the reason of his having run away would have been fear of punishment. St. Paul's influence upon him must have been strong to have induced him to return. The name Onesimus, like Philemon, is Phrygian; for some reason or other Phrygian slaves were regarded with contempt : Φρὺξ ἀνὴρ πληγεὶς ἄμεινον καὶ διακονέστερος (mentioned by Vincent as being quoted by Wallon, *Hist. de l'esclavage dans l'antiquité*, ii. 61, 62). The name was very commonly given to slaves, and appears over and over again on inscriptions as the name of a slave or a freedman.

The letter in which St. Paul intercedes for Onesimus was sent by Tychicus, who was going to Colossæ and Laodicæa with other letters from him to the churches there. Nothing could exceed the affectionate tactfulness displayed in the Epistle; the delicate way in which St. Paul combines the appeal to all that is best in Philemon with a gentle, yet distinct assertion of his own authority (see vv. 8, 9, 21) is very striking. The Epistle is a witness to the high demands which Christianity makes upon men; and the way in which it teaches the universal brotherhood of man together with the eternal truth that one man is better than another—or worse— and that therefore class distinctions lie within the nature of things; this is another side of its permanent value. The power of the Gospel and the noble character of St. Paul are the two notes sounded throughout; or, as Lightfoot so well expresses it, the special value of the Epistle lies in the fact that "nowhere is the social influence of the Gospel more strikingly exerted, nowhere does the nobility of the Apostle's character receive a more vivid illustration than in this accidental pleading on behalf of a runaway slave".

§ III. *Slavery, Jewish and Roman.*—The question of slavery so obviously suggests itself in connexion with this Epistle that a short section on the subject seems called for. It is not enough to refer only to Roman slavery, although Onesimus was a slave and Philemon a master under the Roman *régime ;* for St. Paul was a Hebrew, and the Hebrew conception of slavery must, therefore, be taken into account as well. "Slavery was practised by the Hebrews under the sanction of the Mosaic law, not less than by the Greeks and Romans. But though the same in name, it was in its actual working"—and, we may add, in its whole theory and conception—"something wholly different" (Lightfoot, *Philemon*, p. 319). The Hebrew laws regarding slavery were exceedingly humane, for Hebrew slaves belonged to the Covenant people, for which reason also they were regarded as members of their owner's family; they therefore had their social, as well as their religious rights. A Hebrew slave could not be kept as such for more than six years at the outside, unless he himself wished it ; the laws concerning the redemption of a slave are very explicit. But owing to the conditions of society in ancient times there can be no doubt that a slave was, as a rule, much better off in a servile condition than if he were free ; it was for this reason that the Hebrews had a special law laying down the procedure in the case of those who desired to continue bondmen "for ever". According to Jer. xxxiv. 8-24, however, permanent enslavement of Hebrew men and women is strongly denounced as a sin which will bring about national disaster. According to Lev. xxv. 45, 46, the Hebrew was permitted to buy Gentile slaves, who became personal property and were inherited by the owner's children. But the owner's power over his slaves was strictly limited by the law ; if he punished a slave in such a way as to cause permanent bodily injury the slave gained his freedom as compensation ; if a master chastised his slave so as to cause his death, he was treated as a murderer. Then, again, according to Hebrew law, a slave who had escaped was not to be delivered up again to his master. St. Paul cannot, of course, be accused of having broken this law in the case of Onesimus, since the latter returned voluntarily ; but it is, however, possible that when St. Paul wrote, " For perhaps he was therefore parted from thee for a season, that thou shouldest have him for ever," he had in mind the law of the slave's voluntary return to his master in order to remain his "bondman for ever" (Deut. xv. 16, 17), and thought of how that law had been "fulfilled" by the teaching of Christ (see Matt. v. 17).

Much ancient traditional matter is contained in Talmudical writings ; it is, therefore, interesting to note one or two *data* in these on the subject of slaves ; it is said, for example, that the master of a Hebrew slave (man or woman) must place him on an equality with himself " in meat and drink, in lodging and bed-clothes, and must act towards him in a brotherly manner," so that a saying is preserved in *Kiddushin*, 20a that, " whosoever buys a Hebrew slave buys a master for himself ". Again, the law concerning the escaped slave, referred to above, is in the Talmud construed as applying to one who flees from a place outside the Holy Land into it ; but the slave must give the master from whom he has fled a bond for his value ; if the master refuses to manumit the slave by deed, the court protects the former bondman in his refusal to serve further (*Gittin*, 45a). According to Rabbinical teaching a runaway slave who is recaptured must make good the time of his absence ; if this is traditional and ancient law, which is very probable, it throws an interesting side-light upon our Epistle ; in the first place, it may, in part, have been the reason for St. Paul's insistence on the return of Onesimus to his master; and in the second place, it may have some bearing on the words in vv. 18, 19 " But if he hath wronged thee at all, or oweth thee aught, put that to mine account; I Paul write it with mine own hand, I will repay it"; these last words are perhaps meant literally, the reference being to manual labour, or the like, which St. Paul was prepared to undertake in order to make up for the time lost by Onesimus, this lost time having presumably occasioned loss to Philemon. For the above see further Exod. xxi. 2-11, Lev. xxv. 39-54, Deut. xv. 12-18, xxiii. 16, 17 (15, 16 R.V.); Hamburger, *Real-Encycl. des Judenthums* i. p. 947; *Jewish Encycl.* xi. 404 ff.

These few *data* are sufficient to show the spirit of mercy and fellow-feeling which characterised Jewish slavery.

Utterly different from this was the Roman system; this is well described in Lighfoot's *Colossians and Philemon*, pp. 320 ff., and with great minuteness in Wallon's *Hist. de l'esclavage dans l'antiquité* (2nd ed.), which is the chief authority on the subject. For details concerning slavery in the Roman empire recourse must be had to these works; and for a description of the appalling moral effects of the institution upon both masters and slaves, see Vincent's *Commentary*, pp. 163 ff. While there were undoubtedly exceptions, cp., *e.g.*, the letter written by the younger Pliny (Ep. ix. 21), quoted by Lightfoot, *op. cit.* p. 316, the general rule was that the Roman system was, practically, the antithesis of the Jewish.

St. Paul's attitude towards slavery must be understood in the light of the Jewish system; this contained within itself the germs of the Christian conception of man, which was bound sooner or later to prove fatal to slavery. "When the Gospel taught that God had made all men and women upon earth of one family; that all alike were His sons and His daughters; that, whatever conventional distinctions human society might set up, the supreme King of Heaven refused to acknowledge any; that the slave, notwithstanding his slavery, was Christ's freedman, and the free, notwithstanding his liberty, was Christ's slave; when the Church carried out this principle by admitting the slave to her highest privileges, inviting him to kneel side by side with his master at the same holy table; when, in short, the Apostolic precept that 'in Christ Jesus is neither bond nor free' was not only recognised, but acted upon, then slavery was doomed" (Lightfoot, *op. cit.* p. 325).

§ IV. *Literature* :—

Lightfoot, *Colossians and Philemon*, 1884.

Von Soden, " Philemon," in Holtzmann's *Hand Kommentar*, 1891.

Vincent, " Philemon," in the *International Critical Commentary*, 1897.

The articles on Philemon in Hastings' *Dict. of the Bible* and Cheyne's *Encycl. Biblica*.

For the abbreviations in the Apparatus Criticus see the Intro duction to *St. James*. The Greek text is that published by Nestle, 1907.

ΠΡΟΣ ΦΙΛΗΜΟΝΑ[1]

1. ΠΑΥΛΟΣ [a]δέσμιος[2] Χριστοῦ Ἰησοῦ καὶ Τιμόθεος ὁ [b]ἀδελφὸς
Φιλήμονι τῷ [c]ἀγαπητῷ[3] καὶ [d]συνεργῷ ἡμῶν, 2. καὶ Ἀπφίᾳ τῇ
ἀδελφῇ[4] καὶ [f]Ἀρχίππῳ τῷ [g]συνστρατιώτῃ ἡμῶν καὶ [h]τῇ κατ'

a Acts
xxiii. 18,
Eph. iii.
1.
b Col. i. 1.
c Acts xv.
25, Rom.
xvi. 9.   d Rom. xvi. 3, 9, 21, Phil   ii. 25, Col. iv. 11, 3 John 8.   e Rom. xvi. 1 Cor. vii. 15,
ix. 5.   f Col. iv. 9, 17, 2 Tim. ii. 3.   g Phil. ii. 25, cf. 2 Tim. ii. 3.   h Col. iv. 15.

[1] επιστολη πρ. φιλ. KL.   [2] αποστολος D*E* ; δουλος 33[a].
[3] + αδελφω D*E.
[4] αγαπητη DKL, rec. ; + charissimae Vulg., Pesh., Syr[hark], Chrys., Theod.,
Dam.

Ver. 1. δέσμιος Χρ. Ἰησ. : to
St. Paul an even more precious title than
the usual official ἀπόστολος Χρ. Ἰησ.;
cf. v. 13, ἐν τοῖς δεσμοῖς τοῦ εὐαγγ.,
"they were not shackles which self had
riveted, but a chain with which Christ
had invested him ; thus they were a
badge of office . . . " (Lightfoot) This
title of honour is chosen, and placed in
the forefront of the Epistle, not with the
idea of touching the heart of Philemon,
but rather to proclaim the bondage in
which every true Christian must be,
and therefore also the " beloved fellow-
worker " Philemon. The title is meant,
in view of what follows in the Epistle, to
touch the conscience rather than the
heart.—Τιμόθεος : associated with
St. Paul in Acts xix. 22, 2 Cor. i. 1, Phil.
i. 1, Col. i. 1 ; his mention here points
to his personal friendship with Philemon.—ὁ ἀδελφός : often used by the
Apostle when he desires to be especially
sympathetic ; here, therefore, the emphasis is intended to be upon the thought
of the brotherhood of all Christians ;
this is significant in view of the object of
the Epistle.—Φιλήμονι : See Intr., § II.
—συνεργῷ : when they had worked
together cannot be said with certainty ;
perhaps in Ephesus or Colossae. Probably what is meant is the idea of all
Christians being fellow-workers.
Ver. 2. Ἀπφίᾳ τῇ ἀδελφῇ : A
Phrygian name, often occurring on Phrygian inscriptions. It is most natural to
suppose that she was the wife of Philemon;
but she must have occupied also, most
likely, a quasi-official position in the
Church ; τῇ ἀδελφῇ, coming between
συνεργῷ and συνστρατιώτῃ, suggests
this, especially when one remembers the
important part the ministry of women
played in the early Church, cf. the
labours, e.g., of Mary, Tryphaena and
Tryphosa, Persis, in connexion with
whom the semi-technical term κοπιᾶν is
used (see 1 Thess. v. 12, 1 Tim. v. 17,
for the use of this word), and Prisca ; on
the whole subject see . Harnack, The
Mission and Expansion of Christianity,
i., pp. 122 f., 161 f., 363 f. (1908).—
Ἀρχίππῳ : there is nothing to show
that he was the son of Philemon, rather
the contrary, for why should the son be
addressed in a letter which dealt with
one of his father's slaves ? The inclusion of his name must be due to the fact
that he occupied an important position
in the local church (cf. the words which
follow in the text), which was thus, in a
certain sense, included in the responsibility with regard to Onesimus. Archippus occupied, apparently, a more important position than Philemon (see Col. iv.
17, βλέπε τὴν διακονίαν ἣν παρέλαβες ἐν
Κυρίῳ, ἵνα αὐτὴν πληροῖς,—if Philemon
had occupied any such official position
mention would certainly have been made
of it), but this would be most unlikely to
have been the case if the latter had been
the father of the former. It is more

i Rom. i. 18, οἶκόν σου ἐκκλησίᾳ ʰ · 3. χάρις ὑμῖν καὶ εἰρήνη ἀπὸ Θεοῦ πατρὸς
1 Cor. i. 4,
Phil. i. 3, ἡμῶν ¹ καὶ Κυρίου Ἰησοῦ Χριστοῦ. 4. ⁱ Εὐχαριστῶ τῷ Θεῷ μου ⁱ
1 Thess. i.
2, 2 Thess. πάντοτε ᵏ μνείαν σου ποιούμενος ἐπὶ τῶν προσευχῶν μου,ᵏ 5. ἀκούων
i. 3.
k Rom. i. 10, σου τὴν ¹ ἀγάπην καὶ ᵐ τὴν πίστιν ἣν ἔχεις ᵐ ⁿ πρὸς ² τὸν κύριον
Eph. i. 16,
1 Thess.
i. 2.   l Phil. i. 9.   m 1 Tim. i. 19.   n Cf. 1 Thess. i. 8.

¹ Om. אֵל¹.   ² εἰς ACD*, WH.

natural to regard him as the head of the local Church, who lived in the house where the members met for worship (cf. Theodoret's words, quoted by Lightfoot: ὁ δὲ Ἀρχιππος τὴν διδασκαλίαν αὐτῶν ἐπεπίστευτο). — συνστρατιώτῃ : only elsewhere in N.T., Phil. ii. 25, but for the metaphor cf. 2 Cor. x. 3, 4, 1 Tim. i. 18, 2 Tim. ii. 3, 4,—καὶ τῇ κατ' οἶκον . . . : Cf. Acts xii. 12, Rom. xvi. 5, 1 Cor. xvi. 19, Col. iv. 15. Up to the third century we have no certain evidence of the existence of church buildings for the purposes of worship; all references point to private houses for this. In Rome several of the oldest churches appear to have been built on the sites of houses used for Christian worship ; see Sanday and Headlam, Romans, p. 421, who quote this interesting passage from the Acta Justini Martyris, § 2 (Ruinart) : " Quaesivit Praefectus, quem in locum Christiani convenirent. Cui respondit Justinus, eo unumquemque convenire quo vellet ac posset. An, inquit, existimas omnes nos in eundem locum convenire solitos ? Minime res ita se habet . . . Tunc Praefectus : Age, inquit, dicas, quem in locum conveniatis, et discipulos tuos congreges. Respondit Justinus : Ego prope domum Martini cuiusdam, ad balneum cognomento Timiotinum, hactenus mansi."

Ver. 3. χάρις . . . εἰρήνη: Cf. Rom. i. 7, the usual Pauline greeting (exc. I. 2 Tim.) ; it is a combination of the Greek salutation, χαίρειν, and the Hebrew one, שׁלום. In the N.T. the word εἰρήνη expresses the spiritual state, which is the result of a right relationship between God and man. According to Jewish belief, the establishment of peace, in this sense, was one of the main functions of the Messiah (cf. Luke ii. 14), it was herein that His mediatorial work was to be accomplished. —πατρὸς : see note on Jas. iii. 9. The phrase ἀπὸ Θεοῦ . . . Χριστοῦ expresses the essence of Judaism and Christianity.

Ver. 4. πάντοτε: belongs to εὐχαριστῶ, cf. Eph. i. 16, Phil. i. 3, Col. i. 3, 4. Ver. 5. ἀκούων: probably from Epaphras, see Col. i. 7, 8, iv. 12 (Lightfoot). —τὴν ἀγάπην . . . : i.e., the faith which thou hast towards the Lord Jesus Christ, and the love which thou showest to all the saints. "The logical order," says Lightfoot, "is violated, and the clauses are inverted in the second part of the sentence, thus producing an example of the figure called chiasm ; see Gal. iv. 4, 5. This results here from the apostle's setting down the thoughts in the sequence in which they occur to him, without paying regard to symmetrical arrangement. The first and prominent thought is Philemon's love. This suggests the mention of his faith, as the source from which it springs. This again requires a reference to the object of faith. And then, at length, comes the deferred sequel to the first thought—the range and comprehensiveness of his love."—πίστιν: not "faithfulness," but "faith" (belief), cf. 1 Cor. xiii. 13, Gal. v. 6, 1 Thess. i. 3.—πρὸς . . . εἰς: the difference in these propositions is noteworthy, πρὸς refers to the "faith" to Christ-ward (cf. 1 Thess. i. 8), εἰς to the love to the saints; both are developed in vv. 6, 7.—τοὺς ἁγίους: St. Paul intends Onesimus to be thought of here. The original significance of the title ἅγιος, as applied to men, may be seen in such a phrase as, "Ye shall be holy, for I, the Lord your God, am holy" (Lev. xix. 2). To the Jew, like St. Paul, the corresponding root in Hebrew connoted the idea of something set apart, i.e., consecrated to the service of God (cf. e.g., Exod. xxii. 31 [29]). The ἅγιοι constituted originally the ἐκκλησία; and just as, according to the meaning underlying the Hebrew equivalent of the word ἅγιος, separation for God's service was the main conception, so, according to the root-meaning of ἐκκλησία, it connoted the idea of the body of those "called out," and thus separated from the world.

Ἰησοῦν[n1] καὶ εἰς πάντας τοὺς [o]ἁγίους, 6. ὅπως ἡ [p]κοινωνία τῆς
πίστεώς σου [q]ἐνεργὴς γένηται ἐν [r]ἐπιγνώσει παντὸς[2] ἀγαθοῦ τοῦ[3]
ἐν ἡμῖν[4] εἰς Χριστόν·[5]   7. χαρὰν[6] γὰρ [7]πολλὴν ἔσχον[7] καὶ
[s]παράκλησιν ἐπὶ τῇ ἀγάπῃ σου, ὅτι τὰ [t]σπλάγχνα τῶν ἁγίων
[u]ἀναπέπαυται διὰ σοῦ, [v]ἀδελφέ. 8. Διό, πολλὴν ἐν Χριστῷ
[w]παρρησίαν ἔχων[8] [x]ἐπιτάσσειν σοι τὸ [y]ἀνῆκον. 9. διὰ τὴν
ἀγάπην[9] μᾶλλον [z]παρακαλῶ, τοιοῦτος ὢν ὡς Παῦλος [a]πρεσβύτης,

o Eph. i. 1, etc.
p Phil. ii. 1.
q 1 Cor. xvi. 3, 9, Gal. v. 6, Heb. iv. 12.
r 1 Cor. i. 6, Eph. i. 17, Col. i. 29.
s 2 Cor. vii. 4, 2 Thess. ii. 6.
t 1 Cor. xvi. v Gal. y Eph.

8, 2 Cor. vi. 12, vii. 13, 15, Phil. i. 8.   u Matt. xi. 28, 1 Cor. xvi. 18, 2 Cor. vii. 13.   v Gal.
vi. 18.   w 2 Cor. iii. 12, Eph. iii. 12, Phil. i. 20.   x Mk. i. 27, vi. 27, 39, ix. 25.   y Eph.
v. 4, Col. iii. 18.   z Eph. iv. 1.   a Luke i. 18, Tit. ii. 2.

[1] + χριστον D[1], aeth.   [2] + εργου FG, a, c, e, g, Vulg.   [4] Om. AC.
[4] υμιν אFGP, curss., Syrr., Vulg^A, rec.   [5] + Ιησουν א^cDFGKLP, m, Vulg.
[6] χαριν KL, a, Vulg^F, rec., Chrys., Theod., Dam., Thl.
[7-7] εχομεν πολλεν DCKL, a, m, Pesh., Syr^hark, Vulg^F, rec.; πολλεν εχω a.
[8] Habentes Vulg^F1.   [9] αναγκην A.

Ver. 6. ὅπως: belongs to μνείαν
σου ποιούμενος . . . v. 5 is, as it were, in
brackets. It would be more usual to have
ἵνα here.—κοινωνία: the reference is
to identity of faith; the fellowship among
the saints, cf. Phil. i. 5. The word is
used of a collection of money in Rom.
xv. 26, 2 Cor. viii. 4, ix. 13; cf. Heb.
xiii. 16.—ἐν: see 2 Cor. i. 6, Col. i. 29.
—ἐπιγνώσει: the force of this word is
seen in Phil. i. 9.—παντὸς ἀγαθοῦ:
cf. Rom. xii. 2, xvi. 19, Col. i. 9.—ἐν ἡμ.
εἰς Χρ.: it is not only a ques ion of
men who benefit by "every good thing,"
but also of the relationship to Christ;
cf. Col. iii. 23.
Ver. 7. ἔσχον: the aorist expresses
forcibly the moment of joy which
St. Paul experienced when he heard
this good news about Philemon.—τὰ
σπλάγχνα: regarded as the seat of
the emotions.—ἀναπέπαυται: the
compound "expresses a temporary relief,
the simple παύεσθαι expresses a final
cessation" (Lightfoot).—ἀδελφέ: the
place of the word here makes it emphatic,
cf. Gal. vi. 18, Phil. iv. 1.
Ver. 8. Διό: i.e., because of the good
that he has heard concerning Philemon;
he must keep up his reputation.—ἐπι-
τάσσειν: "to enjoin," or "command";
the word is used "rather of commanding
which attaches to a definite office and
relates to permanent obligations under
the office, than of special injunctions
for particular occasions" (Vincent).—τὸ
ἀνῆκον: the primary meaning of the
verb is that of "having arrived at," or
"reached"; and, ultimately, that of fulfilling a moral obligation. The word occurs

elsewhere in the N.T. only in Ephes. v.
4, Col. iii. 18.
Ver. 9. τοιοῦτος ὢν ὡς: "τοιοῦτος can be defined only by a following
adjective, or by οἷος, ὅς, ὅσος, or ὥστε
with the infinitive; never by ὡς" (Vincent). It seems, therefore, best to take
τοιοῦτος ὢν as referring to . . . μᾶλλον
παρακλῶ, which is taken up again in the
next verse; ὡς Παῦλος . . . Ἰησοῦ must be
regarded as though in brackets; τοιοῦτος
ὢν would then mean "one who beseeches".
—πρεσβύτης: this can scarcely be in
reference to age, for which γέρων would
be more likely to have been used; besides,
in Acts vii. 58, at the martyrdom of St.
Stephen, the term νεανίας is applied to
St. Paul. Lightfoot in his interesting
note on this verse, says: "There is reason for thinking that in the common
dialect πρεσβύτης may have been written
indifferently for πρεσβευτής in St. Paul's
time; and if so, the form here may be
due, not to some comparatively late
scribe, but to the original autograph
itself or to an immediate transcript";
and he gives a number of instances of
the form πρεσβύτης being used for πρεσβευτής. If, as seems very likely, we
should translate the word "ambassador"
here, then we have the striking parallel
in the contemporary epistle to the
Ephesians, vi. 20, ὑπὲρ οὗ πρεσβεύω ἐν
ἁλύσει. Deissmann (Licht vom Osten,
p. 273) points out that both the verb
πρεσβεύω, and the substantive πρεσβευτής, were used in the Greek Orient
for expressing the title of the Legatus of
the emperor. Accepting the meaning
"ambassador" here, the significance of

b 1 Cor. iv.
14, Gal
iv. 19, 1
Tim. i. 2.
c 1 Cor. iv.
15, Gal.
iv. 19.
d Phil. i. 7.
e Col. iv. 9.
f Gal. i. 13.
g Col. i. 21.
h 2 Tim. ii. 21.   i Luke xxiii. 11.   k Luke iv. 22.

νυνὶ δὲ καὶ δέσμιος Χριστ ᷉ Ἰησοῦ,¹ 10. παρακαλῶ σε περὶ τοῦ ἐμοῦ ᵇτέκνου, ὃν ᶜἐγέννησα² ἐν τοῖς ᵈδεσμοῖς,³ ᵉὈνήσιμον, 11. τὸν ᶠποτέ σοι ἄχρηστον ᵍνυνὶ δὲ καὶ⁴ σοὶ καὶ ἐμοὶ ʰεὔχρηστον, 12. ὃν ¹⁵ἀνέπεμψά σοι, αὐτόν,⁵ ⁶τοῦτ᾽ ἔστιν⁶ τὰ ἐμὰ σπλάγχνα·⁷ 13. ὃν ἐγὼ ἐβουλόμην πρὸς ἐμαυτὸν ᵏκατέχειν, ἵνα ὑπὲρ σοῦ μοι

¹ Om. Ιησου D¹; Ιησου χριστου rec.   ² Pr. εγω A, m.

³ + μου אᶜCDEKLP, a, Syrr., rec.

⁴ Om. και AKCDKLP, Pesh., rec., WH.

⁵⁻⁵ ανεπεμψα· συ δε αυτον DE, a, rec.; remisi tibi. Tu autem illum Vulg.

⁶⁻⁶ Ut Vulgᴬ; id est Vulgᶠ.

⁷ + προσλαβου CD, a, rec. (cf. v. 17); + suscipe Vulg.; the Pesh. reads "my son" for τα εμα σπλ.

the passage is much increased; for Christ's ambassador had the right to command, but in merely exhorting he throws so much more responsibility on Philemon. The word "ambassador" would be at least as strong an assertion of authority as "apostle"; to a Greek, indeed, more so.—δέσμιος: perhaps mentioned for the purpose of hinting that in respect of bondage his position was not unlike that of him for whom he is about to plead; cf. the way in which St. Paul identifies himself with Onesimus in vv. 12 . . . αὐτόν, τοῦτ᾽ ἔστιν τὰ ἐμὰ σπλάγχνα, and 17 . . . ὡς ἐμέ.—Χριστου Ἰησοῦ: belongs both to πρεσβύτης and to δέσμιος, cf. v. 1, Eph. iii. 1, iv. 1, 2 Tim. i. 8.

Ver. 10. ὃν ἐγέννησα: cf. Sanhedrin, xix. 2 (Jer. Talm.), "If one teaches the son of his neighbour the Law, the Scripture reckons this the same as if he had begotten him" (quoted by Vincent).—Ὀνήσιμον: one would expect Ὀνησίμου it is attracted to ὃν . . . instead of agreeing with τοῦ ἐμοῦ τέκνου. He is to be ὀνήσιμος in future, no longer ἀνόνητος.—ἄχρηστον: ἅπ. λεγ. in N.T., but used in the Septuagint, Hos. viii. 8, 2 Macc. vii. 5, Wisd. ii. 11, iii. 11, Sir. xvi. 1, xxvii. 19. As applied to Onesimus the reference must be to something wrong done by him; the fear of being punished for this was presumably his reason for running away from his master.—νυνὶ δὲ: a thoroughly Pauline expression, cf. v. 9, Rom. vi. 22, vii. 6, 17, xv. 23, 25, 1 Cor. v. 11, etc.—εὔχρηστον: only elsewhere in N.T. in 2 Tim. ii. 21, iv. 11.

Ver. 12. ὃν ἀνέπεμψά σοι: the aorist, in accordance with the epistolary style. It is clear from these words that

Onesimus himself was the bearer of the letter, cf. Col. iv. 7-9. On St. Paul's insistence that Onesimus should return to his master, see Intr. § III.—αὐτόν: note the emphatic position of this word, cf. Eph. i. 22.—ἐμὰ: again emphatic in thus preceding the noun.

Ver. 13. ἐγὼ: a further emphatic mode of expression.—ἐβουλόμην: βούλεσθαι connotes the idea of purpose, θέλειν simply that of willing. The differences between the tenses—ἐβουλόμην and ἐθέλησα (ver. 14)—is significant; "the imperfect implies a tentative, inchoate process; while the aorist describes a definite complete act. The will stepped in and put an end to the inclinations of the mind" (Lightfoot).—κατέχειν: "to detain," directly opposed to ἀπέχῃς in ver. 15. Deissmann (Op cit., p. 222) points out that κατέχω is often used in papyri and on ostraka of binding, though in a magical sense.—ὑπὲρ σοῦ: "in thy stead," the implication being that Philemon is placed under an obligation to his slave; for the force of ὑπὲρ as illustrated on the papyri, etc., see Deissmann's important remarks on pp. 105, 241 ff. of his work already quoted.—διακονῇ: used in the Pauline Epistles both of Christian ministration generally (Rom. xi. 13; 1 Cor. xii. 5; Eph. iv. 12) and in special reference to bodily wants, such as alms can supply (1 Cor. xvi. 15; 2 Cor. viii. 4).—ἐν τοῖς δεσμ. τοῦ εὐαγγ.: i.e., the bonds which the Gospel had tied, and which necessitated his being ministered unto.—τοῦ εὐαγγελίου: see Mark i. 14, 15 and cf. Matt. iv. 23; Christ uses the word often in reference to the Messianic Era. "The earliest instances of the use of εὐαγγέλιον in the sense of a book would be: Did. 8, 11, 15 bis; Ign.

¹διακονῇ ἐν τοῖς δεσμοῖς τοῦ εὐαγγελίου, 14. χωρὶς δὲ τῆς σῆς ᴹ Matt.
xxvii. 55,
ᵐγνώμης οὐδὲν ἠθέλησα ποιῆσαι, ἵνα μὴ ὡς κατὰ ⁿἀνάγκην τὸ Acts xix.
22, Rom.
ἀγαθόν σου ᾖ ἀλλὰ κατὰ ¹ ἑκούσιον. 15. °τάχα γὰρ διὰ τοῦτο xv. 25,
Heb. vi.
ᵖἐχωρίσθη πρὸς ὥραν, ἵνα αἰώνιον αὐτὸν ᑫἀπέχῃς, 16. οὐκέτι ὡς 10.
ᴹ Acts xx.
δοῦλον ²ἀλλὰ ὑπὲρ δοῦλον,² ʳἀδελφὸν ³ ἀγαπητόν, ˢμάλιστα ἐμοί, 3.
ⁿ 2 Cor. ix.
ᵗπόσῳ δὲ μᾶλλον σοὶ καὶ ᵘἐν σαρκὶ καὶ ᵛἐν κυρίῳ. 17. εἰ οὖν με 7, Heb.
vii. 12.
ἔχεις ʷκοινωνόν, ˣπροσλαβοῦ αὐτὸν ὡς ἐμέ. 18. εἰ δὲ τι ʸἠδίκησέν ₒ Rom. v. 7.
ᵖ 1 Cor. vii.
σε ἢ ᶻὀφείλει, τοῦτο ἐμοὶ ᵃἐλλόγα·⁴ 19. ᵇἐγὼ Παῦλος ἔγραψα τῇ 11, 15.
ᑫ Matt. v.
16, vi. 2,
Phil. iv. 18.   r Eph. vi. 21, Col. iv. 7, 9.   s 1 Tim. iv. 10.   t Rom. xi. 12, 24.   u 1 Tim.
iii. 16.   v Rom. xvi. 2, Phil. ii. 29.   w 1 Cor. x. 18, 20.   x Acts xxviii. 2, Rom. xiv. 1,
3, xv. 7.   y Matt. xx. 13, 1 Cor. vi. 8.   z Matt. xviii. 28.   a Rom. v. 13.   b Gal. vi.
11, 2 Thess. iii. 17.

---

¹ Om. D.   ²⁻² Om. F.   ³ Om. Ͱ¹.   ⁴ ελλογει KL, rec.

Philad. 5, 8 (Sanday, *Bampton Lectures,* p. 319).

Ver. 14. With the thought of this verse *cf.* 2 Cor. ix. 7, 1 Peter v. 2.—ὡς κατὰ ἀνάγκην: "St. Paul does not say κατὰ ἀνάγκην but ὡς κατὰ ἀνάγκην. He will not suppose that it would really be constraint; but it must not even wear the *appearance* (ὡς) of being so. *cf.* 2 Cor. xi. 17, ὡς ἐν ἀφροσύνη" (Lightfoot).

Ver. 15. ἐχωρίσθη: a very delicate way of putting it.—πρὸς ὥραν: *cf.* 2 Cor. vii. 8, Gal. ii. 5.—αἰώνιον: there is no reason why this should not be taken in a literal sense, the reference being to Onesimus as ἀδελφὸν ἀγαπητόν, not as δοῦλον.—ἀπέχῃς: *cf.* Phil. iv. 18, although the idea of restitution is prominent here, that of complete possession seems also to be present in view of αἰώνιον and ἀδελφὸν ἀγαπ., but see further Intr., § III.

Ver. 16. οὐκέτι ὡς δοῦλον: no longer in the character of a slave, according to the world's acceptation of the term, though still a slave (see, however, the note on v. 21); but the relationship between slave and master were in this instance to become altered.—πόσῳ δὲ μᾶλλον . . . : *i.e.*, more than most of all (which he had been to St. Paul) to thee.—With the thought of the verse *cf.* 1 Tim. vi. 2.

Ver. 17. ἔχεις . . . : for this use of ἔχω *cf.* Luke xiv. 18, Phil. ii. 29.— κοινωνόν: for the idea see Rom. xii. 13, xv. 26 f., 2 Cor. viii. 4, ix. 13, Gal. vi. 6, Phil. iv. 15, 1 Tim. vi. 18, Heb. xiii. 16. —προσλαβοῦ αὐτὸν ὡς ἐμέ: *cf.* τὰ ἐμὰ σπλάγχνα in v. 12. An interesting parallel given by Deissmann, *op. cit.* pp. 128 f.) occurs in a papyrus of the second century, written in Latin by a

freedman, Aurelius Archelaus, to the military tribune, Julius Domitius: "Already once before have I commended unto thee my friend Theon. And now again, I pray thee, my lord, that he may be in thy sight as I myself" (ut eum ant' oculos habeas tanquam me).

Ver. 18. εἰ δέ τι: as Lightfoot says, the case is stated hypothetically, but the words doubtless describe the actual offence of Onesimus.—ἐλλόγα: only elsewhere in N.T. in Rom. v. 13; it occurs on the papyri (Deissmann, *op. cit.*, p. 52), "to reckon unto"; here, in the sense: "put it down to my account".

Ver. 19. ἐγὼ Παῦλος: "The introduction of his own name gives it the character of a formal and binding signature, *cf.* 1 Cor. xvi. 21, Col. iv. 18, 2 Thess. iii. 17" (Lightfoot).—ἔγραψα τῇ ἐμῇ χειρὶ ἀποτίσω: ἔγρ. epistolary aorist, *cf.* 1 Pet. v. 12, 1 John ii. 14, 21, 26. Deissmann (*op. cit.*, p. 239) calls attention to the large number of papyri which are acknowledgments of debt (Schuldhandschrift); a stereotyped phrase which these contain is, "I will repay," usually expressed by ἀποδώσω; in case the debtor is unable to write a representative who can do so expressly adds, "I have written this for him". The following is an example: " . . . which we also will repay . . . besides whatever else there is (ἄλλων ὧν) which we owe over and above . . . I, Papos, write it for him, because he cannot write". See also Deissmann's *Neue Bibelstudien*, p. 67, under χειρόγραφον. It seems certain from the words ἔγραψα . . . (*cf.* also v. 21) that St. Paul wrote the whole of this epistle himself; this was quite exceptional, as he usually employed an

c 2 Cor. ix. ἐμῇ χειρί, [b] ἀποτίσω · [c] ἵνα μὴ λέγω [c] σοι ὅτι καὶ σεαυτόν μοι προσο-
4.
d Phil. iv. 3. φείλεις.[1] 20. [d] ναί, ἀδελφέ, ἐγώ σου [e] ὀναίμην ἐν κυρίῳ · ἀνάπαυ-
e Cf. Sir.
xxx. 2. σόν μου τὰ σπλάγχνα [f] ἐν Χριστῷ.[2] 21. [g] Πεποιθὼς τῇ [h] ὑπακοῇ
f Rom. xvi.
7, 9. σου ἔγραψά σοι, εἰδὼς ὅτι καὶ ὑπὲρ ἃ [3] λέγω ποιήσεις. 22. ἅμα
g Phil. i. 14.
h Rom. i. 5. δὲ καὶ [h] ἑτοίμαζέ μοι [k] ξενίαν · ἐλπιζω γὰρ ὅτι [l] διὰ τῶν προσευχῶν
i Cor. vii.
15. x. 5, 6, ὑμῶν [m] χαρισθήσομαι ὑμῖν. 23. Ἀσπάζεταί [4] σε [n] Ἐπαφρᾶς ὁ
Heb. v. 8,
i Pet. i. 2, συναιχμάλωτός μου ἐν Χριστῷ Ἰησοῦ, 24. [p] Μάρκος, [q] Ἀρίσταρχος,
14, 22.
i 2 Tim. ii.
21, 1 Cor. ii. 9, Heb. xi. 16.   k Acts xxviii. 23.   l Rom. xii. 3, Gal. i. 18, Phil. i. 19.   m Acts
iii. 14, xxvii. 24, 1 Cor. ii. 12.   n Col. i. 7, iv. 12.   o Rom. xvi. 7, Col. iv. 10.   p Col
iv. 10.   q Acts xxvii. 2.

[1] + ἐν κυριω D*E*.   [2] κυριω EK, a, rec.
[3] ο DE, a, rec.   [4] ασπαζονται KL, a, rec.

amanuensis ; the quasi-private character
of the letter would account for this. See,
further, Lightfoot's note on Gal. vi. 11.
—ἀποτίσω : a stronger form than the
more usual ἀποδώσω. As a matter of
fact St. Paul, in a large measure, had
repaid whatever was due to Philemon
by being the means whereby the latter
received his slave back, but see Intr. § III.
—ἵνα μὴ λέγω σοι : a kind of men-
tal ejaculation, as though St. Paul were
speaking to himself ; the σοι does not
properly belong to the phrase ; cf. 2 Cor.
ix. 4.—καὶ σεαυτόν : the reference is
to Philemon's conversion, either directly
due to St. Paul, or else indirectly
through the mission into Asia Minor,
which had been the means whereby
Philemon had become a Christian ; in
either case St. Paul could claim Philemon as his spiritual child in the sense
that he did in the case of Onesimus
(see v. 10).—μοι προσοφείλεις :
"thou owest me over and above ". See
further, on ὀφειλή, Deissmann, Neue
Bibelst., p. 48, Licht vom Osten, pp.
46, 239.
Ver. 20. ναί : cf. Phil. iv. 3, ναὶ
ἐρωτῶ καὶ σέ.—ἀδελφέ : an affectionate
appeal, cf. Gal. iii. 15, vi. 1-18.—ἐγώ :
"The emphatic ἐγώ identifies the cause
of Onesimus with his own" (Lightfoot).
—σου ὀναίμην : ἅπ. λεγ. in N.T.,
it occurs once in the Septuagint (Ecclus.
xxx. 2), and several times in the Igna-
tian Epp. (Eph. ii. 2, Magn. ii. 12, Rom.
v. 2, Pol. i. 1, vi. 2). Ὄν. is a play on
the name Onesimus, lit., "May I have
profit of thee" ; Lightfoot says that the
common use of the word ὀναίμην would
suggest the thought of filial offices, and
gives a number of instances of its use.
It is the only proper optative in the
N.T. which is not in the third person
(Moulton, Grammar of N.T. Greek, p.

195).—ἀνάπαυσον : see note on v. 7.
—ἐν Χριστῷ : St. Paul refers to the
real source from which the ἀναπαύειν
gets its strength
Ver. 21. τῇ ὑπακοῇ σου : a hint
regarding the authority which St. Paul
has a right to wield.—ἔγραψα : see
note on v. 19.—ὑπὲρ ἅ : as it stands this
is quite indefinite, but there is much point
in Lightfoot's supposition that the
thought of the manumission of Philemon was in St. Paul's mind ; "throughout this epistle the idea would seem to
be present to his thoughts, though the
word never passes his lips. This reserve is eminently characteristic of the
Gospel. Slavery is never directly attacked as such, but principles are incul-
cated which must prove fatal to it."—
λέγω : note the tense here, a very vivid
touch after ἔγραψα.
Ver. 22. ἅμα . . . i.e., at the same
time that he does what he is going to do
for Onesimus. ἑτοίμαζέ μοι : Lightfoot's remark that "there is a gentle com-
pulsion in this mention of a personal visit
to Colossae," does not seem justified in
view of the stress that St. Paul lays on
Philemon's action being wholly voluntary,
see vv. 10, 14 ; it is more probable that
this is merely an incidental mention of
what had been planned some time before,
namely another missionary journey to
Asia Minor and Greece (see Phil. ii. 24),
without any thought of influencing
Philemon's action thereby.—ξενίαν :
only here and in Acts xxviii. 23, in the
N.T.
Ver. 23. συναιχμάλωτος : lit.
"a prisoner of war," used metaphorically
like συνστρατιώτης, see note on ver. 2 ;
cf. Rom. xvi. 7, where the word is used
in reference to Andronicus and Junius.
Ver. 24. Μάρκος : i.e., John Mark,
cf. Acts xii. 25, xv. 37, Phil. iv. 10 ; he

ʳ Δημᾶς, ʳ Λουκᾶς, οἱ ˢσυνεργοί μου. 25. Ἡ ᵗχάρις τοῦ ᵗκυρίου ¹ r Col. iv. 14.
s Rom. xvi.
ˈΙησοῦ Χριστοῦ μετὰ τοῦ ᵘπνεύματος ὑμῶν.²
3, 9, 21,
1 Cor. iii.
9.

t Col. iv. 18.   u Gal. vi. 18, Phil. iv. 23, 2 Tim. iv. 22.

¹ + ημων Vulg., rec.   ² + αμην אC, m, Vulg., rec.

Subscr.: προς Φιλημονα (και Απφιαν δεσποτας Ονησιμου και προς Αρχιππον
το νδιακονον της εν Κολοσσαις εκκλησιας) εγραφη απο Ρωμης (δια Ονησιμου
οικετου). [Αλλα δη και μαρτυς Χριστου γεγενηται ο μακαριος Ονησιμος εν τη
Ρωμαιων πολει επι Τερτουλλου τηνικαυτα την επαρχικην εξουσιαν διεποντος τη
των σκελων κλασει την ψηφον υπομεινας του μαρτυριον].

and Aristarchus were Jewish-Christians
(Col. iv. 11).—Δ η μ ᾶ ς, Λ ο υ κ ᾶ ς: Gentile Christians (cf. Acts xvi. 10, xx. 5, 6,
xxi. 15, xxvii. 2); the former name is a con-
traction of Δημήτριος (Col. iv. 14; 2 Tim.
iv. 10).
Ver. 25. Ἡ χ ά ρ ι ς: cf. Gal. vi. 18,

2 Tim. iv. 22.—ὑ μ ῶ ν: the reference is
both to those addressed by name in the
opening of the Epistle, as well as to the
members of the local Church, see verse
2. This final verse is a reiteration of
the grace pronounced in verse 3.

THE EPISTLE

TO THE

HEBREWS

INTRODUCTION.

HISTORY OF THE EPISTLE. The early history of this Epistle has already been so fully narrated in various accessible volumes, that a bare outline may here suffice. Its chief interest is the illustration it gives of the difficulties which an anonymous book had to overcome before it won for itself a place in the Canon. The significance of the story of its fortunes may be gathered from the statement of Eusebius:[1] "Paul's fourteen Epistles are well known and undisputed. It is not indeed right to overlook the fact that some have rejected the Epistle to the Hebrews, saying that it is disputed by the Church of Rome on the ground that it was not written by Paul." The Church, that is to say, looked with suspicion, or at any rate hesitation, on any candidate for canonical honours which had not the authentication of apostolic authorship. And although the Epistle to the Hebrews *really* won for itself a place in the Canon by its intrinsic merit, by its cardinal importance as the final adjustment of the Jewish and Christian dispensations, as well as by its marked ability and felicitous style, yet it had to steal into its place under the cloak of an apostle, and it is doubtful whether it would have won universal acceptance had it not been attached, loosely enough it is true, to the collection of Paul's Epistles. Even though there was no certainty regarding its authorship in any part of the church, and in some parts a distinct and expressed conviction that it was not from the hand of Paul, yet obviously it was too rich a treasure to lose ; and because it was not unworthy of the great apostle nor wholly alien from his way of thinking, it was allowed to attach itself to his Epistles, and so, happily, found a place in the Canon.

The difficulty to which Eusebius alludes, as experienced by the Western or Latin Church, was of ancient date. For although the earliest traces of the use of the Epistle are found in Clement of Rome (*c*. 96 A.D.) who betrays familiarity with it, yet no Western writer of the second century acknowledges it as canonical. It was not included in the collection of Pauline Epistles which Marcion

[1] *H. E.*, iii. 3.

formed in the first half of that century, and Tertullian, though object-
ing to his omission of the Pastoral Epistles, makes no remark upon
his rejection of Hebrews. In the latter half of the century Roman
opinion is represented by the Muratorian canon, which makes no
mention of the Epistle at all, unless, as some have fancied, it is
alluded to as that " ad Alexandrinos ".[1] The prevalent Roman
opinion is represented by the presbyter Caius who did not accept the
Epistle as Pauline.[2] According to Photius, Hippolytus also denied
the Pauline authorship; and in the earliest Old Latin Version the
Epistle was omitted.

In the North African branch of the Latin Church not only was
the Pauline authorship denied, but the Epistle was definitely ascribed
to Barnabas. Tertullian (De Pudic., c. 20) in citing Hebrews vi. 4-8
claims for the Epistle only a subordinate authority [" idoneum con-
firmandi de proximo jure disciplinam magistrorum "] because it was
written not by an apostle, but by a "comes apostolorum," whom he
unhesitatingly speaks of as Barnabas.

Meanwhile, however, in the Eastern Church the Pauline authorship was maintained. The Syrian Church accepted the Epistle into
its earliest canon ; and even if translated by a different and later
hand than the other Epistles, this cannot be ascribed to any reluct-
ance to receive it as canonical.[3] In Alexandria towards the close of
the second century it is accepted as Pauline by Pantaenus and
Clement.[4] But as criticism was cultivated with some diligence in
this Church, it could not escape notice that both in its anonymity
and in its style this Epistle differed from those of Paul. The absence
of the usual Pauline address Pantaenus explained as due to the
modesty of the Apostle, who would not even seem to usurp the place
which belonged to the Lord Himself as Apostle of the Hebrews.[5]
Clement accounted for the difference in style by the supposition that
the Epistle was originally written by Paul in Hebrew and afterwards
translated by Luke, while the absence of signature is referred to the
natural fear lest the name of the Apostle of the Gentiles might repel
Hebrew readers. The opinion in which the Church of Alexandria
in general rested may be gathered from the words of Origen :[6] " If I

[1] " Fertur etiam ad Laodicenses, alia ad Alexandrinos Pauli nomine fictae
ad haeresem Marcionis, et alia plura, quae in catholicam ecclesiam recipi non
potest ; fel enim cum melle misceri non congruit."

[2] Euseb., H. E., vi. 20. Jerome, De Vir. Ill., c. 59.

[3] Dr. Bewer (A. J. T., April, 1900, p. 358) dates its introduction to the Syrian
canon in the third century.

[4] Euseb., H. E., vi. 14.   [5] Adopted by Jerome, Ep. ad Gal.

[6] Euseb., H. E., vi. 25.

gave my opinion, I should say that the thoughts are those of the Apostle, but the phrasing and composition are those of some one who remembered what the teacher had said. If then any church holds this Epistle to be Paul's, let it be commended for this. For not without reason (εἰκῇ) have our predecessors (οἱ ἀρχαῖοι ἄνδρες) handed it down as Paul's. But who wrote the Epistle, in truth God knows. The account that has reached us is, that some say it was written by Clement who became bishop of the Romans, while others ascribed it to Luke, the author of the Gospel and Acts."

Unsatisfactory as such a decision was, the idea that the Epistle was Paul's generally [1] prevailed over the whole Church, so that from the fifth century to the reformation, there were few who took the trouble to inquire. The conversion of the Latin Church to this opinion was mainly due to the influence of Augustine and Jerome. The formulæ under which the latter writer cited the Epistle reveal his personal dubiety. "The Epistle which, under the name of Paul, is written to the Hebrews." "He who writes to the Hebrews." "The Apostle Paul, or whoever else wrote the Epistle to the Hebrews." "The Apostle Paul in the Epistle to Hebrews, which the Latin custom does not receive." He mentions that the Greek writers accept it as Paul's, although many ascribe it either to Barnabas or Clement. [2] It would apparently, have taken little to persuade Jerome that the latter opinion was well-grounded, for he had himself noticed a striking similarity between the Epistle of Clement and that to the Hebrews. [3] In short, we find that Jerome acted in regard to this Epistle on the principle he carried through his formation of the Vulgate canon, the principle that it was better to include than to exclude a good book and that prevalent opinion must be allowed a great weight.

Instructive also is Augustine's treatment of the Epistle. Sometimes he reckons it among Paul's, sometimes he cites it anonymously ["epistola quae ad Hebraeos inscribitur," or "est"]; sometimes he calls attention to the doubts entertained regarding it by others, but professes that for his part he is moved by the authority of the Eastern Churches. The facile and uncritical spirit of the time is conspicuous in the manner in which the councils of North Africa dealt with this

[1] For exceptions in the Western Church, see Westcott On the Canon, p. 401.
[2] "Licet plerique eam vel Barnabae vel Clementis arbitrentur," Ep. ad. Dardanum.
[3] "Clemens scripsit . . . utilem epistolam . . . quae mihi videtur characteri epistolae, quae sub Pauli nomine ad Hebraeos fertur, convenire," De Vir. Illus., c. 15.

Epistle. In the council of Hippo in 393, while Augustine was still a presbyter, and in the third council of Carthage, held in 398, the prevalent dubiety regarding the authorship of Hebrews found expression in the enumeration of the New Testament books, "of the Apostle Paul, thirteen Epistles, of the same to the Hebrews, one". But in the fifth council of Carthage, in 419, where Augustine was also present, this feeble and meaningless distinction is abandoned and the enumeration boldly runs, "of the Epistles of Paul in number fourteen".

It is not easy to determine how much or how little we are justified in concluding from these early opinions and traditions. That the ecclesiastical voice gradually settled upon the great name of Paul, if it does not do much credit to the critical sagacity of the Early Church, at least shows that no other name was satisfactory. That Clement should have been mentioned as a possible author, naturally results from the abundant and free use he makes of the Epistle, as well as from his friendship with Paul, and his position as a writer of repute. That Paul's still more prominent ally, Barnabas, should have been credited with the Epistle was possibly the result of its quite superficial resemblance to the well-known and widely-read but spurious *Epistle of Barnabas*. Evidently, however, it is the Epistle itself which must divulge the secret of its authorship if we are at all to ascertain it.

Authorship. The bare reading of the Epistle suffices to convince us that the Pauline authorship may be set aside as incredible. The style is not Paul's, and this Apostle although using an amanuensis, undoubtedly dictated all his letters. The Epistle to the Hebrews reveals a literary felicity not found elsewhere in the New Testament. The writer is master of his words, and perfectly understands how to arrange each clause so that every word shall play its full part in conveying with precision the meaning intended. He knows how to build up his sentences into concise paragraphs, each of which carries the argument one stage nearer to its conclusion. He avoids all irrelevant digressions. His earnestness of purpose never betrays him into carelessness of language, but only serves to give edge and point to its exact use. In all this he markedly and widely differs from the tempestuousness of Paul. As Farrar says: "The writer cites differently from St. Paul; he writes differently; he argues differently; he thinks differently; he declaims differently; he constructs and connects his sentences differently; he builds up his paragraphs on a wholly different model. St. Paul is constantly mingling two constructions, leaving sentences unfinished, breaking into personal allusions, substituting the syllogism of passion for the syllogism of logic. This writer is never ungrammatical, he is never irregular, he is never personal, he never struggles for expression; he never loses himself in a parenthesis; he is never hurried into an anacoluthon. His style is the style of a man who thinks as well as writes in Greek; whereas St. Paul wrote in Greek but thought in Syriac." The same difference was felt by those who themselves used the Greek language. Thus Origen[1] says: "That the verbal style of the Epistle entitled 'to the Hebrews' is not rude like the language of the Apostle who acknowledged himself 'rude in speech,' that is, in expression; but that its diction is purer Greek, any one who has the power to discern differences of phraseology will acknowledge."[2]

But if the style puts it beyond question that Paul cannot have been the immediate author of the Epistle is it not possible to believe with Origen that "the thoughts are those of the Apostle"? This also must be answered in the negative. There is in the Epistle nothing discordant with Pauline doctrine, but its argument moves on different lines and in a different atmosphere from those with which the Apostle to the Gentiles makes us familiar. This is most readily discerned when we consider the attitude held by the two authors respectively to the fundamental idea of Jewish religion, the Law. Paul views the Mosaic economy mainly as a law commanding and threatening. The writer to the Hebrews views it rather as a vast congeries of institutions, observances and promises. To the one writer the Law is mainly juridical; to the other it is ceremonial. To the ardent spirit of Paul athirst for righteousness, the Law with its impracticable precepts had become a nightmare, the embodiment of all that barred access to God and life. The grace of Christianity throwing open the gates of righteousness was the antithesis and

---

[1] Euseb., *H. E.*, vi. 25.

[2] "Diversity of style is more easily felt by the reader than expressed by the critic, without at least a tedious analysis of language; one simple and tangible test presents itself, however, in the use of connecting particles, inasmuch as these determine the structure of sentences. A minute comparison of these possesses therefore real importance in the differentiation of language. Now in the Epistles of St. Paul εἴ τις occurs fifty times, εἴτε sixty-three, ποτε (in affimative clauses) nineteen, εἶτα (in enumerations) six, εἰ δὲ καὶ, four, εἴπερ five, ἐκτὸς εἰ μὴ three, εἴγε four, μήπως twelve, μηκέτι ten, μενοῦνγε three, ἐάν eighty-eight times, while none of them are found in the Epistle except ἐάν and that only once (or twice), except in quotations. On the other hand, ὅθεν which occurs six times and ἐάνπερ which occurs three times in the Epistle are never used by St. Paul." Rendall's *Theol. of Hebrew Christianity*, p. 27.

abolition of the law. But to this writer, brought up in a more latitudinarian school and of a quieter temperament, the law was not this inexorable taskmaster, but rather a system of type and symbol foreshadowing the perfect fellowship with God secured by Christianity and revealed in Him. Both writers have the same question before them : What gives Christianity its power to bring men into harmony with God and thus constitutes it the universal, permanent religion ? What precisely is the relation of this new form of religion to that out of which it sprang and which it supersedes? Paul boldly enounces the incompatibility of faith and works, of grace and merit, of Christianity and the Law. This writer, adopting a method and a view more likely to conciliate the Jew, aims at exhibiting the work of Christianity as that towards which the previous economy had been striving, that the two are essentially connected, and that without Christianity Judaism remains imperfect.[1]

So that Pfleiderer's remark is justified, when he says, "this is a thoroughly original attempt to establish the most essential results of Paulinism upon new presuppositions and in an entirely independent way—a way which proceeds upon lines of thought regarding the constitution of the universe which were widely spread amongst the educated people of that time, and which necessarily had far greater power of diffusing enlightenment than the dialectic of the old Pauline system which was so highly wrought up to an individual standpoint."[2]

Here and there the ideas and expressions of Paul seem to be coloured by the Alexandrian system and manner of thought, which, as Pfleiderer says, influenced the entire educated world of the time ; but in the mind of Paul there lay a deeper soil in which had been sown the governing ideas of Palestinian or Pharisaic theology. The work and person of Christ are presented under different categories by the two writers : the priestly function, which is absent or almost so from the letters of Paul, dominates the thought of the Epistle to the Hebrews. In keeping with this, the idea of sacrifice which colours the whole of the latter Epistle, only occasionally emerges in the Pauline writings. So too it is the kingly state of the risen Christ which occupies the one writer, while in the mind of the other it is a priestly exaltation that is conspicuous. And thus the δικαιοῦν of Paul becomes in Hebrews ἁγιάζειν, or καθαρίζειν or τελειοῦν ; and the leading religious terms "faith" "grace" and so forth have

[1] Cf. Ménégoz (Théol. de l'ep. aux Heb., 190) " L'un abolit la Loi, l'autre la transfigure "; and p. 197, the one was revolutionist, the other evolutionist. See also Holtzmann, N.T. Theol., ii., p. 286 ff. Verhältniss zum Paulinismus.

[2] Paulinism, E. Tr., ii., 53.

one meaning in Paul and another in this Epistle. Evidently the suggestion that Luke was on this occasion Paul's interpreter is quite insufficient to satisfy the conditions.[1]

If the Epistle cannot be ascribed to Paul, must we fall back upon Tertullian's statement,[2] and accept Barnabas as the author? This solution cannot be said to have ever been prevalent in the early Church, notwithstanding the meagre references unearthed by Prof. Bartlet and Mr. Ayles. Over against these references may be set the significant words of Jerome, who designates this ascription of authorship as "juxta Tertullianum," apparently implying that in all his vast store of information he had found no one else holding this opinion. Origen, too, knows nothing of such a tradition. It was, however, revived in the seventeenth century by the Scottish scholar, Cameron, and in more recent times has found supporters in Ritschl, Weiss, Renan, Salmon and Vernon Bartlet.[3] Zahn, who formerly advocated the same authorship, is now less certain. The claims of Barnabas are also urged with fulness and force by Mr. Ayles in an essay devoted to this object.[4] There can be no doubt that Barnabas answers many of the requirements which must be met by any presumed author of the Epistle. He belonged to the circle of Paul and was a man of character and of capacity; he was a Levite and as such predisposed to consider the Christ and His work in its bearing on the Old Testament ritual;[5] he was a native of Cyprus where good Greek was spoken, and at the same time was well known and influential in the Church at Jerusalem. The tradition that Mark, his nephew, introduced the Gospel into Alexandria, might be pressed to indicate some connection with that centre of thought. This, however, tells also against his authorship, for it is unaccountable that Barnabas' name should have been lost in the Church where his nephew presided. It must also be kept in view that the association

---

[1] The similarities to the usage of Luke in the vocabulary of the Epistle have been examined with final thoroughness by Prof. Frederic Gardiner in the *Journal of Soc. of Bibl. Lit. and Exegesis* for June 1887. See also Alexander's *Leading Ideas of the Gospels*, 3rd ed., pp. 302-324; and W. H. Simcox in the *Expositor* for 1888.

[2] *De Pudicitia*, c. 20. "Extat enim et Barnabae titulus ad Hebraeos, adeo satis auctoritati viri, ut quem Paulus juxta se constituerit in abstinentiae tenore (1 Cor. ix. 6); et utique receptior apud ecclesias epistola Barnabae illo apocrypho Pastore moechorum."

[3] *Expositor*, 1902.

[4] *Destination, Date and Authorship of Ep. to Heb.* (Cambridge, 1899).

[5] For supposed mistakes regarding the Temple and its service, *cf.* Zahn, ii., 55,156.

of Barnabas with the Church at Jerusalem only tells in his favour if that be considered the destination of the Epistle. It is, of course, a mere accident that his designation, υἱὸς παρακλήσεως (Acts iv. 36) should correspond with the description of this Epistle as a λόγος παρακλήσεως (Heb. xiii. 22).

Harnack, who had previously[1] considered it probable that Barnabas was the author, has recently[2] in a forcible and brilliant manner urged the claims of Prisca and Aquila. In their favour are such points as these : that the letter proceeds from a highly cultured teacher, answering to the description given in Acts xviii. 26 of Aquila and Prisca ; that it was written by one who belonged to the Pauline circle, as there is no doubt that this couple did (Rom. xvi. 3 συνεργοί) ; that the writer was associated with Timothy, as Aquila and Prisca were for eighteen months in Corinth as well as in Ephesus (cf. 2 Tim. iv. 19) ; that he belonged to one of the house-churches in Rome (to which presumably the Epistle was addressed) and that he had taught there—which corresponds with what we know of Aquila and Prisca (see Acts xviii. 2, Rom. xvi. 3) ; that behind the writer of the Epistle there is some one or more with whom he associates himself in a common " we," for in the letter there are not merely the literary " we " and the " we " which includes writer and readers, but a third use of the pronoun embracing some unnamed person or persons as uniting with the writer in what he says. " If on the ground of these arguments it be considered probable that the Epistle to the Hebrews is to be referred to this couple, it may then be asked whether Prisca or Aquila wrote it. And if the predominant position of the woman, witnessed by both Paul and Luke, be considered, as well as the in- contestable fact that she was foremost in winning Apollos, the balance must incline in favour of her authorship." It is thus he accounts for the most paradoxical feature in the history of the Epistle, the loss of the author's name. This disappearance is at once accounted for, if Prisca was even partly the author, for Paul's prohibition of female teaching in the Church had taken deep root.

That there is in these arguments not merely ingenuity, but much that deserves consideration, will not be denied. Indeed, so careful and sound a scholar as Bleek almost convinced himself that Aquila was the author of the Epistle, and expresses surprise that his claims should not have been urged.[3] But there are grave difficulties in the

---

[1] Chronologie, p. 477-479.

[2] Preuschen's Zeitschrift, vol. i., 16-41.

[3] Hebräer-brief, i., 421, 422. Harnack's claim to originality [niemand an sie gedacht hat] is valid only so far as Prisca is concerned.

double, predominantly feminine authorship advocated by Harnack. A single authorship is unquestionably demanded by certain expressions in the Epistle, as τί ἔτι λέγω, xi. 32; ἵνα τάχιον ἀποκατασταθῶ ὑμῖν, xiii. 19; and the singulars in xiii. 22, 23. It is not possible to construe these singulars as referring to more than one writer: but it is quite possible to construe the plurals of the Epistle as referring to the single writer or to the writer uniting himself with his readers. And that this one writer should have been Prisca is certainly improbable, both on account of Paul's prohibition which so good a friend as Prisca would observe, and because the writer seems to have been one of the ἡγούμενοι, which Prisca could not have been. The impression made by the Epistle is that it proceeds from a masculine mind; and if the Epistle is due to either we should suppose Aquila was more likely to undertake such a task. The familiarity which existed between this couple and Apollos might be supposed to account for the Alexandrian colouring of the Epistle.

The name of Apollos was suggested by Luther[1] who apparently had either heard or read that this authorship had been advocated by others. It has received the suffrages of scholars so competent as Bleek, Tholuck, Hilgenfeld, Lünemann, Reuss, Pfleiderer, Alford, Farrar and Plumptre. In Acts xviii. 24 Apollos is described as an Alexandrian Jew, a learned man, mighty in the Scriptures, who had been instructed in the way of the Lord and who spoke and taught with accuracy the things concerning Jesus. Passing from Ephesus, where he first appears in Christian history, to Achaia " he helped them much who had believed through grace, and powerfully confuted the Jews, and that publicly, showing by the Scriptures that Jesus was the Christ ". Paul also testifies to his influence as a teacher and probably indicates that his special function was that of carrying to maturity those who had already received the truth. The words " Paul planted, Apollos watered " bear this interpretation, and agree with what is said in Acts of his peculiar work. Certainly all this remarkably corresponds with the characteristics of the writer to the Hebrews, who certainly was a Jew of the Alexandrian school, a man of marked ability and culture, whose special training fitted him to build up in the faith and to find in the Scriptures

---

[1] "Autor Epistolae ad Hebraeos, quisquis est, sive Paulus, sive, ut ego arbitror, Apollo" (*Com. on Gen.*); and in his sermon on 1 Cor iii. 4 "the Ep. Heb. is certainly his" [Apollos']. In another sermon he says "Some suppose the Epistle to be Luke's, some refer it to Apollos " ["etliche meinen, sie sei S. Lucas, etliche S. Apollo"]. The most thorough presentation of the claim of Apollos is that by Plumptre in the first vol. of the *Expositor*.

proof that Jesus was the Christ. This, plainly, does not prove
that Apollos was the author, but it lends plausibility to the hypothesis.

Destination. Here, again, however, we find the authorship implicated with the destination of the Epistle. The only places with
which we know Apollos to have been connected are Ephesus, Corinth
and Crete. The first named city was swarming with Jews and was
also impregnated|with Alexandrianism. Corinth resembled it in the
former'and[3] possibly also in the latter characteristic, for the preaching of Apollos had certainly found in that city a very responsive hearing; and it is the only place in which we have any positive reason
to believe that he resided for any length of time. But evidently he
was a man who moved about (Tit. iii. 13); and it is not improbable
that he may have visited Rome. Evidently, however, if we are to
come any nearer to a determination of the authorship, we must first
of all try to ascertain the destination of the letter.

We may put aside the idea that it was not addressed to any
particular Church but was a homily written for all whom it might
concern. This idea has been plausibly stated by Reuss. "The
Epistle to the Hebrews," he says, "is not a letter properly so called
written in view of a local necessity; and the few personal and cir-
cumstantial details added on the last page were certainly not the
reasons which prompted the author to write. This book may have
been already penned and actually concluded when occasion offered
to make it useful to a particular circle of Christians and in reference
to whom he may have added the 13th chapter. The 'Hebrews'
whose name is inserted by the care of a later reader (also truly inspired) are not, as has been imagined, the members of some isolated
community, as *e.g.*, the Church at Jerusalem; they are Jewish
Christians in general, considered from a theoretical point of view."
This view has been adopted by Lipsius and others, and at the first
blush it may seem to have something to say for itself, for letters do
not usually begin without giving the name of the writer and of his
correspondents. But the idea that the entire document is a treatise
written in the study without definite reference to any particular group
of Christians, is contradicted not merely by the personal references
of the 13th chapter, but by the occurrence throughout the Epistle
of expressions which have no meaning if not so addressed. Indeed,
no Epistle more exclusively concentrates itself upon a definite and
actual condition, nor more definitely recognises that its readers have
passed through and are passing through well-marked experiences.

The writer's references in v. 12; vi. 9; x. 32; xii. 4; could only have been made to a definite group of Christians.[1]

This consideration is sufficient to prove that the title πρὸς Ἑβραίους without further designation is too indefinite to have been affixed to his letter by the author himself. Weizsäcker, indeed, is extravagant when he brands the inscription as "the unhappy conjecture of a later time," but we may unhesitatingly adopt Robertson Smith's language, and say that it is "hardly more than a reflection of the impression produced on an early copyist". The suggestion of Prof. Nestle[2] that it may indicate that the Epistle was addressed to the συναγωγὴ Αἰβρέων or Ἐβρέων in Rome is interesting, but obviously if the writer of the Epistle had himself addressed it to a synagogue of Jewish Christians in Rome, he could not have written merely "to Hebrews," but must have more definitely identified them by some further designation. In short, we cannot from this address derive any assistance in determining the Church to which the Epistle was addressed.

But that the inscription is right in so far as it declares that the letter was destined for Hebrew Christians has generally, though not universally, been acknowledged. The scope of the Epistle presupposes a profound attachment to the Mosaic dispensation. Not only is the Old Testament the common ground from which material can be drawn and on which the discussion can proceed, but the argument is one which can scarcely be conceived as addressed to Gentiles. It may almost be said with Dr. Bruce: "If the readers were indeed Gentiles, they were Gentiles so completely disguised in Jewish ideas and wearing a mask with so pronounced Jewish features that the true nationality has been successfully hidden for nineteen centuries". Or more summarily we may say with Reuss: "For this writer there are no Gentiles". To Gentile ears some of the expressions used in the Epistle would be unintelligible, others would be offensive. To the former class belong such exhortations as, "Let us go forth unto Him without the camp"; to the latter, "Not of angels doth He take hold, but of the seed of Abraham He taketh hold".

In spite of this, however, many eminent critics in recent times have reached the persuasion that the letter was addressed not to Hebrew, but to Gentile Christians. Schürer, Weizsäcker, von Soden, Jülicher, McGiffert are of this opinion. They are chiefly influenced by the consideration that the list of rudimentary doctrines

[1] See Burggaller's criticism of Wrede's "Das literarische Rätsel des Hebräerbriefes" in Preuschen's *Zeitschrift* for 1908.

[2] *Expository Times* for June, 1899.

given in chap. vi. are such as would rather be taught to Gentile catechumens than to Jewish converts. No doubt the doctrines there mentioned would be taught to Gentiles, but surely the contrast between faith in God and faith in dead works is peculiarly appropriate to Jews; and it was also the Jew rather than the Gentile who required explanation regarding the relation of Christian baptism to other lustrations. Besides, it must not be overlooked that the doctrines here enumerated are the " rudiments of Christ," and therefore nothing specifically Jewish could be mentioned. They are that common ground or " foundation " which underlay the specially Christian teaching.

Difficulty has also been found in the phrase ἀποστῆναι ἀπὸ θεοῦ ζῶντος (iii. 12). This expression, it is felt, is more appropriate to a relapse to idolatry than to Judaism. But the very point of the whole Epistle is that an abandonment of Christianity is an abandonment of God; that in it God has finally spoken and that to neglect this revelation is to neglect God. In using this particular phrase the writer has not in view the end to which unbelief may lead them, but the fact that unbelief is apostasy from the living God, whether the unbeliever be Jew or Gentile.

These difficulties then are not insuperable, although they are possibly too cavalierly treated by Westcott, who pronounces that " the argument of von Soden, who endeavours to show that the Epistle was written to Gentiles, cannot be regarded as more than an ingenious paradox by any one who regards the general teaching of the Epistle in connection with the forms of thought in the Apostolic age ".

Where, then, were these Jewish Christians resident ? The places most generally approved are Jerusalem, Antioch, Cæsarea, Rome. In favour of the Jewish metropolis there is not much to be urged. To no Church on earth would it be so inappropriate to say that they had received the Gospel at second-hand (ii. 3). Many of its members must have been in direct communication with the Lord. Neither could it with any truth be said of the Church of Jerusalem that she had not been instrumental in teaching others (v. 12). This Church was also a poor community which itself required rather than afforded aid: whereas the society addressed in the Epistle had been conspicuous for charity (vi. 10; x. 34). It also seems most unlikely that if the Church at Jerusalem was addressed, no allusion should be made to the Temple. Neither is it probable that any one, himself a member of the Church at Jerusalem, should prefer Greek to Aramaic as his medium of communication.

As Antioch was the scene of a considerable part of the labours of

Barnabas it naturally suggests itself as the destination in connection with his supposed authorship of the Epistle. The Hebrew Christians in that city must have been very much in his care, and certainly they required some such exposition as is given in the Epistle, of the relation of Judaism to Christianity. And some critics, even while dismissing the claims of Barnabas, are inclined to find in Antioch the group of Jewish Christians to which the Epistle was addressed. Thus Mr Rendall[1] sums up his inquiry in the following terms : "To one of these great Syrian cities, perhaps to Antioch itself, I conceive the Epistle to have been addressed ; for there alone existed flourishing Christian Churches, founded by the earliest missionaries of the Gospel, animated with Jewish sympathies, full of interest in the Mosaic worship, and glorying in the name of Hebrews ; who nevertheless spoke the Greek language, used the Greek version of the Scriptures and numbered amongst their members converts who had, like the author, combined the highest advantages of Greek culture with careful study of the Old Testament and especially of the sacrificial Law." But could a Church which had actually started the great mission of Paul and Barnabas and in which other teachers abounded be open to the rebuke of chap. v. 11 ff. ?

Recently critical opinion has decidedly veered towards Rome as the only possible destination. First suggested by Wetstein it is now advocated by Alford, Holtzmann, Zahn and many others. The clause in the Epistle which inevitably suggests this destination is the greeting in xiii. 24, ἀσπάζονται ὑμᾶς οἱ ἀπὸ τῆς Ἰταλίας "they of Italy (the Italians) salute you ". This clause shows that the Epistle was either written from or to Italy. But it is difficult to believe that the words were intended to convey a greeting from Italians in their own country to the writer's correspondents. For if the writer was in Italy, he was in some particular locality, and this place he would more naturally have named instead of using the general term " Italy ". Certainly the more natural and satisfactory interpretation of the words is that which supposes that the writer who himself is a member of the Church he addresses is surrounded by those who also recognise Italy as their home and who seek to send greetings to their friends in Rome.

Nor does anything in the Epistle contradict this idea. That there was a large Jewish element in the Roman Church appears both from Acts and Romans, and is not denied. It has sometimes been thought that Jewish Christians in Rome could not be expected

[1] *Epistle to Hebrews*, p. 69.

to take so much interest in the Temple-worship or be so concerned about its observance as this Epistle requires ; but, as Principal Fairbairn long ago pointed out, colonists idealise the institutions of their mother-country more than its resident population, and it is an idealised, not an actual worship that is here described. It is also to be considered that it was in Rome both in the time of Paul and in the second century that in many subtle ways Judaism sought to assert itself and to absorb or expunge Christianity. The fact too that it is in Rome we find the first traces of the use of the Epistle (by Clement) has some weight.

Zahn still further narrows the destination and identifies the recipients of the letter as a small circle of Christians in a large city, a house-church alongside of which there was another or several other such churches in the same city. They have an assembly of their own (x. 25), perhaps also rulers of their own (xiii. 17), although the rulers of the whole Church of the city are also their rulers, and therefore greetings are sent to *all* the rulers and to *all* the Saints (xiii. 24). He is not aware of any place which so well answers to these requirements as one of the house-churches in Rome mentioned in the Epistle of Paul to that Church (chap. xvi). To one of these, possibly to that mentioned in Romans xvi. 14, this Epistle was probably addressed.

The Roman destination may seem to carry with it the authorship of Aquila, for this Jew who was himself so well instructed that he was able to instruct Apollos was intimately associated with Rome and with one of the house-churches there (Romans xvi. 3-5). And indeed all that we know of Aquila seems to fit the conditions as well as any other name that has been suggested.

It is impossible then to dogmatise regarding the authorship of this Epistle, and at present it is best frankly to confess our ignorance. But we may adopt the language of Prof. Rhys Roberts in dealing with the similar case of *Longinus on the Sublime* and say that "while it is good science to refuse to hazard any conjecture which our information does not warrant, it is good science also to decline to follow some critics in abandoning all hope of ever seeing a solution of this knotty problem. Let us rather recognise that we are confronted with one of those stimulating and fruitful uncertainties which classical research so often presents to its votaries— uncertainties which are stimulating because there is some possibility of removing them, and fruitful because in any case they lead to the more thorough investigation of the obscurer bye-ways of history and literature." Or we may adopt the words of Dr. Davidson in dealing

with the similar problem of the authorship of the Book of Job:
"There are some minds that cannot put up with uncertainty, and
are under the necessity of deluding themselves into quietude by
fixing on some known name. There are others to whom it is a
comfort to think that in this omniscient age a few things still
remain mysterious. Uncertainty is to them more suggestive than
exact knowledge. No literature has so many great anonymous
works as that of Israel. The religious life of this people was at
certain periods very intense, and at these periods the spiritual energy
of the nation expressed itself almost impersonally, through men who
forgot themselves and were speedily forgotten in name by others."
And if we cannot name, we can at least partially describe the author.
For his letter reveals a man who was not an Apostle but a scholar
of the Apostles; a man of the second Christian generation (genea-
logisch nicht chronologisch, as Harnack says); a Hellenist yet a
member and teacher of a Jewish Christian church; a Paulinist with
some tincture of Alexandrian culture, though his treatment of
Scripture differs *toto coelo* from Philo's; a friend of Timothy and
at the time of writing in the company of Italian Christians.

Aim. But it is not the locality so much as the condition of the
readers that chiefly concerns us. And as we read the Epistle it becomes apparent that the danger which roused the writer to inter-
pose was not such definite and grave heresy as evoked the Epistle to
the Galatians or that to the Colossians, nor such entangling heathen
vices and difficult questions of casuistry as imperilled the Corinthian
Church, but rather a gradual, almost unconscious admission of
doubt which dulled hope and slackened energy. They had professed
Christianity for some time (v. 12); and the sincerity of their profession had been proved by the manner in which they had borne severe
persecution (x. 33, 34). They had taken joyfully the spoiling of
their possessions; they had endured a great conflict of sufferings.
But they found the long-sustained conflict with sin (xii. 4) and the
day-by-day contempt and derision they experienced as Christians
(xiii. 13), more wearing to the spirit than sharper persecution.
Consequently their knees had become feeble to pursue the path of
righteous endurance and activity, their hands hung limply by their
side as if they were defeated men (xii. 12). They had ceased to make
progress and were in danger of falling away (vi. 1-4, iii. 12) and were
allowing an evil heart of unbelief to grow in them. No doubt this
listless, semi-believing condition laid them open to the incursion of
"divers and strange teachings" (xiii. 9) and in itself was full of peril.
To restore in them the freshness of faith the writer at every

part of the Epistle exhorts them to steadfastness and perseverance. " Let us hold fast the profession of our faith without wavering" (xi. 23). " Cast not away your confidence" (x. 35). " If any man draw back, my soul shall have no pleasure in him" (x. 38). Or, what may be taken as the hortatory motto of the Epistle, " We are become partakers of Christ, if we hold fast the beginning of our confidence firm unto the end" (iii. 14). That they may have encouragement to do so, he shows them at large the good ground they have for confidence. The fruits of faith in their fathers are recapitulated in the eloquent eleventh chapter. But especially is Jesus exhibited as the great leader in faith. " Consider Him lest ye be weary and faint in your souls" (xii. 3). His supremacy and trustworthiness are expounded in detail, and especially the eternal sufficiency of His sacrifice and intercession is dwelt upon.

Evidently, then, the persons addressed were in the mental and spiritual condition common in every age of the Christian Church, a condition of languor and weariness, of disappointed expectations, deferred hopes, conscious failure and practical unbelief. They were Christians but had slender appreciation of the glory of their calling, misconstrued their experience, and had allowed themselves to drift away from boldness of hope and intensity of faith. Dr. Bruce describes them as persons who never had " insight into the essential nature and distinctive features of the Christian religion "; and if by " insight " he means such perception of the greatness of Christ as causes men to rejoice in serving and suffering for Him, his description is correct. But he seems less exact when he goes on to say " No greater mistake, I believe, can be committed (though it is a common fault of commentators) than to assume that the first readers were in the main in sympathy with the doctrinal views of the writer ". Some points, no doubt, which the writer adduces were new to the readers. The manner in which the paragraph regarding Melchisedec is introduced proves this. But we cannot therefore conclude that the whole conception of Christ as Priest was new to them; nor can we suppose that they had never thought of Christ as the Son through whom the final revelation was made and the eternal covenant mediated. Rather they had failed *to consider what these great truths involved.* Hence the writer bids them give "the *more earnest* heed to the things they have heard" (ii. 1), and throughout the Epistle he returns to his favourite admonition " Consider Him," let your minds penetrate more deeply into His significance. They had ceased to have that keen interest in truth which prompts contemplation and inquiry, and they now held what they had been taught so externally that they were in danger of wholly losing their faith and becoming practical apostates. They had fallen under the power of the present and visible, and were giving to appearance and shadow the value that belonged only to the eternal reality.

The aim of the writer then was to open up the true significance of Christ and His work, and thus to remove the scruples, hesitations and suspicions which haunted the mind of the Jewish Christian embarrassing his faith, lessening his enjoyment, and lowering his vitality. The Jew who accepted Jesus as the Christ had problems to solve and difficulties to overcome of which the Gentile knew nothing. A transition of equal moment and encompassed by so much obscurity men have rarely, if ever, been summoned to make. It is easy for those who look back upon it as an accomplished fact to see that there was no real breach of continuity between the old religion and the new; but that was not readily perceived by those whose whole life and experience were marked by the turmoil and instability which accompanied the abandonment of old forms, the acceptance of new ideas, the building on other foundations. Brought up in a religion which he was persuaded was of Divine authority the Jew was now required to consider a large part of his belief and worship as antiquated. Accustomed to pride himself on a history marked at various stages by angelic visits, Divine voices, and miraculous interventions, he is now invited to shift his faith from institutions and venerable customs to a Person, and this a Person in whom earthly glory is suggested only by its absence and in whom those *apparently* most qualified to judge could discover nothing but imposture which merited a malefactor's death. Cherishing with extraordinary enthusiasm, as his exclusive heritage, the Temple with all its hallowed associations, its indwelling God, its altar, its august priesthood, its complete array of ordinances, he is yet haunted by the Christian new-born instinct that there is an essential lacking in all these arrangements and that for him they are irrelevant and obsolete. A blight has suddenly fallen on what was brightest in his religion, a blight he can neither dissipate nor perfectly justify.

For the Jewish Christian must have found it quite beyond his power to understand the relation of the old to the new. Already indeed it had become apparent that in Jesus prophecy had been fulfilled. He had been accepted as the predicted Messiah partly because it was beyond dispute that in Him a correspondence was found to the figure more or less clearly defined in the Old Testament. This no doubt hinted that there was some strong and vital connection between the two faiths. But what relation did this Messiah hold to the Mosaic institutions? That was a more difficult problem. The difficulty of it is appreciated when we consider that a large section of the Christian Church judged the old to be irreconcilable with the new, and went so far as to maintain that the God of the Old Testament was antagonistic to the God who revealed Himself in Christ. And even the more moderate section of the Church found difficulty in answering the questions: What was to be thought of the Jewish ordinances and of the Jewish Scriptures which enjoined them? If the ordinances were set aside, could the Scriptures which contained them be retained? In what sense had Christ fulfilled the law, the ceremonial? He had not been a Priest. He had not assumed the Priest's function, but the Rabbi's. He had not been born in a priestly family. A sacrifice, perhaps, in some sense, He had been.

To the Jew, in short, Christ must have created as many problems as He solved. The unquestioning faith that is guided by healthy instincts and can relegate to the future all intellectual explanations and reconcilements is not given to every one; and many a Jewish Christian must have passed those first days in painful unrest, drawn to trust Jesus by all that He knew of His holiness and truth and yet sorely perplexed and hindered from perfect trust by the unexpected spirituality of the new religion, by the contempt of his old co-religionists, by the enforced relinquishment of all outward garnishing and glory, and by the apparent impossibility of fitting the gorgeousness of the old and the bareness of the new into one consistent whole. To this miserable and weakening condition of spirit the writer appeals and aims at removing it by giving them a fuller insight into the relation of Christianity to Mosaism, and especially by illustrating the unique supremacy of Christ and the finality of His work. He makes it his aim to show that every name, every institution, every privilege, which had existed under the old economy survived in the new, but invested with a higher meaning and a truer glory—a meaning and a glory, new indeed in themselves, but yet for the first time fulfilling the great purpose of God which from the first had been dimly shadowed forth. "The first was taken away only in order that the second might be introduced."[1]

To this task he necessarily brought his own philosophical presuppositions. Trained in Alexandrian thought he cherished the Platonic[2] conception of the relation of the seen to the unseen. It

---

"[1] Das Christenthum bringt nichts, was nicht schon im A. T. angelegt, verheissen und vorgebildet gewesen wäre" (Holtzmann, *N. T. Theol.*, ii., 287).

[2] *Timaeus*, 28 C.; *Rep.* 597; Philo, *Mundi Op.*, 4; *De Vita Mosis*, p. 146.

was his inalienable conviction that the visible world is merely phenomenal, the temporary form or manifestation of the invisible, arche-
typal world which alone is real and eternal. In the Epistle these
two worlds are continually related by contrast. The unseen world
[πράγματα οὐ βλεπόμενα xi. 1] is the eternal counterpart of this
present order of things [αὕτη ἡ κτίσις ix. 11] ; the reality, of which
earthly things are but the shadow [σκία viii. 5]. The visible
heaven and earth are one day to pass away, " as things that have
been made " [ὡς πεποιημένων xii. 27], but this only in order that the
eternal things which cannot be removed may remain alone existent.

On this broad philosophical basis, itself unshakable as the eternal
things, the writer builds his argument. Here he finds the key to the
essential distinction between Mosaism and Christianity, as well as
the proof of the superiority and finality of the latter. The Mosaic
dispensation belongs to the seen and temporal, the Christian to the
unseen and eternal. In the one there is a tabernacle "made with
hands " ; a sanctuary of *this world*, equipped and furnished with
material objects ; the sacrifices are of bulls and goats ; the rest appointed cannot be eternal, because it is in a visible earthly land ; their
holy city is one which can be profaned by Roman armies ; above all,
their priesthood is dependent on the flesh. How manifest that all
these things belong to the earthly temporal order. The whole dispensation is involved with things visible, tangible, material, evanescent.

But Mosaism was not wholly useless. It was a shadow of the
good things to come : and to these real, eternal things Christ introduces men. Christ Himself, being Son of God, belongs to the
eternal order. In Him we have throughout to do not with external
ceremonies and temporal arrangements, but with what is spiritual ;
in Him we come into touch not with imperfect revelations of God
made through symbol and human medium, but with the very image
of God. He mediates between God and man in virtue of His connection with both. He leads men into the true relation to God by
Himself perfectly fulfilling the human life of obedience to God's will.
His priesthood or power to carry His human brethren with Him into
the heavenly life, springs out of His personal worth wrought by
discipline to a perfected condition. He is priest in virtue not of
what is of the flesh, not by inherited office, but by virtue of His
sympathy with men and His personal stainlessness. He enters the
presence of God not in an earthly tabernacle nor with the blood of
bulls and goats but with His own blood, bringing men and God
together by the pure and perfect surrender of Himself to God. This
sacrifice though made on earth was yet made in the eternal order,

because made in spirit, in a spirit which necessarily belongs not to this visible and transitory order of things but to the eternal and real, or as the writer says, "through eternal spirit".

That which this writer finds common to the new and the old forms of religion is the purpose of God to bring men into fellowship with Himself, or, in other words, the covenant idea. With this writer religion is the harmony of God and man. He thinks of God, not like Paul, as a Judge before whose bar man must somehow be cleared of guilt, but as entering into covenant with man and providing for the maintenance of this covenant by sacrifice. In history he sees two great epochs in the promotion of this fellowship distinguished by the efficacy with which it is effected. For the covenant being between the holy, heavenly God and His unholy creature, it will not be quite easy to form or to maintain. It involves at any rate two things, that the will of God in the matter be made known, and that man be separated from his sin. It involves, that is to say, that the covenant be effectively mediated and especially in this respect that it be secured that man shall be cleansed from his sin and fitted for true and lasting fellowship with God. So essential is this, that each form of the covenant may be judged by the efficiency with which it accomplishes this. If the arrangements for bringing man into real and abiding union with God are imperfect, then this colours with imperfection the covenant to which these arrangements belong ; if, on the other hand, such arrangements are made as actually cleanse the conscience and renew the character then this determines the perfectness of the covenant in which these arrangements are comprised.

Hence the importance which this writer attaches to priesthood and sacrifice. It is by these the nature and efficacy of every covenant between God and man must be determined. If one covenant only provides for a ceremonial purification and a symbolic introduction to God, this of itself stamps that covenant as inferior to one which provides for a spiritual cleansing and a real union If with one of the covenants there is identified a priesthood which is merely hereditary and therefore fleshly and professional, while the other rests on a natural and spiritual priesthood that offers a real spiritual sacrifice, the sacrifice of self, in contrast with the sacrifice of bulls and goats, there can be little hesitation in determining whether of these two is the eternal covenant. It is the writer's aim to exhibit this distinction. He knows that if only his readers can once see the real glory of Christ and His religion all their doubts will vanish, and accordingly he proceeds to send them such an exposition of that glory as is in point of fact a magnificent apologetic for Christianity from the Jewish point of view.

The relation thus established between the former and the latter dispensation may tend to an undervaluing of the old, and lead to the idea that "the Jew was simply the keeper of a casket which he could not unlock, an actor in a symbolical representation which to him conveyed little or no meaning". It must be borne in mind, therefore, that the arrangements of the Old Testament were primarily for the religious use of the Jews themselves. Their religion was not devised for the intellectual employment or diversion of persons who can now look back upon it, nor altogether for the religious edification of such persons, but primarily for the religious edification of the Jews themselves. They needed a religion as much as we do. They needed assurance of God and His favour, and some means of access to Him and this they found in their religion of type and symbol. To them as to us a gospel was preached (iv. 2). Through the symbolic arrangements of their earthly tabernacle they learned real truth and were brought into fellowship with the eternal. Not that they understood what the physical arrangements of their religion *typified*, but that they did understand what they *symbolised*. The Old Testament ritual was instructive not in so far as it was typical, but in so far as it was symbolical. A symbol is an embodied idea, or what we nowadays call an "object lesson"; an idea rendered visible in a material sign or in an external action. A type not only expresses an idea, but looks forward to a time when this idea shall receive its perfect expression. As Mr. Litton[1] defines it "a type is a prophetic symbol". "Every true type is necessarily a symbol, that is, it embodies and represents the ideas which find their fulfilment in the antitype; but every symbol is not necessarily a type; a symbol may terminate in itself, and point to nothing future; it may even refer to something past." Now it cannot be supposed that the contemporaries of Moses or Moses himself understood what was prefigured by their ritual. But if they did not understand their ritual as a collection of types, they certainly did understand it as a system of symbols. The tabernacle itself was both a symbol and a type. It was a symbol that God dwelt with men, ever in their midst, sharing their fortunes, forgiving their sin, and bestowing blessing. This symbol every child could read. But it was also a type, a symbol with a prophecy wrapped up in it, a symbol giving promise that the truth taught in it would one day find its perfect, eternal manifestation. This could at the best be but imperfectly understood.

[1] Bampton Lectures, p. 82.

But the writer to the Hebrews looking back upon the preparation for Christ can see how this and that prefigured Him who was to come. Every Old Testament institution, ceremony, person or thing in which a principle or idea was embodied which was afterwards embodied in Christ and His Kingdom may legitimately be called "typical". To the Jews themselves these types were helpful not because they threw light upon the person and work of Christ, but because they then and there communicated those very ideas which were subsequently expressed in their reality in Jesus. The institution of sacrifice, *e.g.*, was useful to them not because it taught them to look for a Messiah who should die for their sins—for it had no such effect—but because it then and there communicated the very ideas and the very hopes which the death of Christ expressed—in a dim and unsatisfactory way no doubt, as this writer is careful to show, but still adequately as a first lesson in the holiness and forgiveness of God.

Keeping in view the aim of the writer to convince his readers that the new Christian order of things is an advance on the old Mosaic order, and is indeed the final and universal form of religion, the course of thought is easily followed. The Mediator of the new covenant is first of all compared with the Mediators of the old, with prophets, angels, Moses, Joshua, Aaron, and this comparison occupies the first seven chapters. The writer then proceeds to exhibit the evanescence of the old covenant and the superiority of the new (viii. 6-13), and of the true God-pitched tabernacle and its sacrifice to the first man-made tabernacle with its arrangements and offerings (ix. 1-x. 18). On this demonstrated superiority and finality of the covenant which Christ has mediated the writer founds a forcible appeal and exhorts his readers to hold fast their profession and to use the access to God provided for them (x. 19-25). This exhortation he enforces by warnings (x. 26-31), by awakening remembrances of better times (32-39), by the rapid, sugggestive and eloquent presentation of their predecessors in faith (xi.), and especially of Him whose example in faith and endurance is perfect (xii. 1-4), and by illustrating the reasonableness of hopefully submitting to present trouble as discipline sent by the heavenly Father (xii. 5-13). They are further urged to diligence in sanctification by the consideration that awful as were the sanctions of the old law, those of the new covenant are immensely more awful, that indeed our God is a consuming fire (xii. 14-29). The closing chapter contains miscellaneous but relevant admonitions.

Date. The chief index to the date of the Epistle is its relation to the destruction of the Temple. The impression one receives from its perusal is that the sacrifices and other services of the Temple were still being performed. If particular passages are examined, this impression is deepened. It is quite true that the use of the present tense (as in Heb. ix. 6, viii. 4, etc.) does not always imply an actual present. The use of this tense by Clement (*Ep.* c. 41) in describing ordinances which in his day were certainly obsolete puts this beyond question. But of course the use of the present generally implies the existence of the object spoken of at the time of the speaker; and it is not easy to suppose that if the Temple and its worship had already been abolished, this writer could use such language as we find in c. x. 1, 2; "they can never with the same sacrifices year by year which they offer continually make perfect them that draw nigh. *Else would they not have ceased to be offered?*" And as Ménégoz [1] says : " C'est précisément l'existence du culte levitique qui offrait des dangers pour la fidelité des chretiens. Après la destruction du Temple ce danger avait disparu, du moins en majeure partie." Besides, it is impossible to suppose that a writer wishing to demonstrate the evanescent nature of the Levitical dispensation, and writing after the Temple services had been discontinued, should not have pointed to that event as strengthening his argument. It would appear, then, that the Epistle must have been written while the Temple was yet standing, that is, prior to the year A.D. 70.

Accordingly Salmon dates the Epistle in 63; Ménégoz places it in 64-67. The year 66 or thereabouts is adopted by Riehm, Lünemann, Hilgenfeld, Weiss, Beyschlag, Schürer, Godet, Westcott. Bleek prefers the year 68 or 69. Harnack, Pfleiderer, von Soden, Holtzmann and McGiffert bring it down to some date between A.D. 81 and 96.

Commentaries. Full lists of commentaries on the Epistle are easily accessible in Bible Dictionaries or in Delitzsch's Commentary. A selection is given by von Soden in the *Hand-commentar.* Here it must suffice to name the most outstanding. Among the patristic commentators Chrysostom is unquestionably the most valuable, always sensible and well expressed. Of mediæval writers Primasius, Atto Vercellensis and Herveius may be consulted with advantage.[2] Calvin, Erasmus, Beza, Grotius, Bengel will inevitably be used in the study of this Epistle, as of any part of the New

[1] *La Theol. de l'ep.* etc., p. 40.

[2] On these and others see Riggenbach's *Die ältesten lateinischen Komm : Zum Hebräerbrief* in Zahn's *Forschungen.*

Testament. At the foundation of all more recent elucidation of the Epistle lies Bleek's great work, *Der Brief an die Hebräer erläutert* (1828-1840), the most comprehensive and scholarly, and in all respects one of the best commentaries on any book of the New Testament. Of almost equal value is Weiss' contribution to the revised Meyer. Delitzsch though not so exact is generally suggestive and always rich in material, while his knowledge of the Old Testament enables him to enter into the author's point of view. Westcott, largely indebted to Bleek, is, as always, full and accurate. Vaughan is of great use for ascertaining the precise meaning and biblical usage of words. Davidson (Clark's Bible-class Hand-books) penetrates to the meaning of the writer better than any other commentator. Peake (Jack's *Century Bible*) rivals him in this and has a rare gift of compact lucidity. No better book could be conceived or is needed for English readers. Nothing better has been written on the Epistle than his chapter on its teaching.

Other works such as those by Owen, Peirce, Moses Stuart, Tholuck, Hofmann, McCaul, Lowrie and von Soden will be found helpful, and each has a merit of its own. And naturally the great collectors of illustrative material, Wetstein and Schoettgen, Kypke, Elsner and Raphel will be used. The parallels from Philo have been carefully collected by Carpzov. Where Anz is named, the reference is to his *Subsidia ad cognoscendum Graecorum sermonem vulgarem e Pentateuchi versione Alexandrina repetita* in the Dissertationes Philologicae Halenses, vol. xii., part ii. (1884).

Riehm's *Lehrbegriff des Hebräerbriefes* is a classic, a monument of German industry and comprehensiveness, full of detail but never wearisome, always lighting up old meanings with fresh flashes of insight. Bruce's presentation of the substance of the Epistle (*The Ep. to the Hebrews*, Clark) is characteristically vigorous and full of elevated thought and enriching ideas. An excellent book on *The Theology of the Epistle* has also been issued by Dr. George Milligan. And quite indispensable to the student is *La Theologie de l'Epitre aux Hebreux*, by Eugène Ménégoz.

AUTHORITIES FOR THE TEXT.

I. Greek Uncials.

א Sinaiticus Petropolitanus, Saec. iv. Complete.

A Alexandrinus Londinensis, Saec. v. Complete.

B Vaticanus Romanus, Saec. iv. Defective from ix. 14—end. ["Manus multo recentior supplevit, Heb. ix. 14-xiii. 25, quae Mico Italus ipsius codicis conlator Bentleio jubente contulit et Tischendorfius aliquoties notavit siglo b." Gregory's *Prolegomena*, p. 418.]

C Ephraemi Parisiensis, Saec. v. Wants i. 1 πολυμερως—πνευματος αγιου ii. 4. vii. 26 αμιαντος—μεσιτης ix. 15. x. 24 πης και καλων—μιανθωσιν πολλοι xii. 15.

D Claromontanus Parisiensis Nationalis 107, Graeco-Latinus. ["Latina inprimis in epistula ad Hebraeos errores multos praebent" Gregory.] Saec. vi. Heb. xiii. 21-23 is lost. Beza, to whom we owe the earliest notice of this Codex describes it as of equal antiquity with his copy (D) of the Gospels, and tells us it was found at Clermont, near Beauvais. Many hands have revised it.

E Petropolitanus, Graeco-Latinus, Saec. ix. Wants Heb. xii. 8 παντες—υμων, xiii. 25. A faulty copy of D after it had been more than once corrected.

Fa Coislinianus Parisiensis, Saec. vii. Contains x. 26.

H Coislinianus Parisiensis nationalis 202, Saec. vi. The leaves of this MS. are still scattered, some at Paris, some at Moscow, some at St. Petersburg, some at Mt. Athos, others elsewhere. It contains of Hebrews, chapters ii., iii., iv., x.

K Moscuensis, Saec. ix. Complete.

L Angelicus Romanus, Saec. ix. Complete to xiii. 10 εξουσιαν.

M Londin, Hamburg (Scrivener's *Codex Ruber*, so called from beautifully bright red colour of the ink), Saec. ix. Contains i. 1-iv. 3, and xii. 20-xiii. 25. "Textu ad optimos testes hic codex accedit." Gregory, *cf.* Scrivener, p. 184-85.

N Petropolitanus, Saec. ix. Contains v. 8-vi. 10.

O Fragmenta Mosquensia, Saec vi. (?) Contains x. 1-3, 3-7, 32-34, 35-38. Scrivener.

P Porfirianus Chiovensis, Saec. ix. Complete. xii. 9, 10 illegible.

The first verse of the Epistle has been edited by Messrs. Grenfell & Hunt from a fragment in Lord Amherst's collection of papyri. It is in a small uncial hand of the early fourth century. It reads ἡμῶν after πατράσιν.

II. Greek Cursives.

Of the large number of cursives cited by Tischendorf, it may suffice to mention the Codex Colbertinus of the Imperial Library of Paris, collated by Tregelles, and cited as 17 [33 of the Gospels]. It belongs to the eleventh century, and is of great value. Another MS. which was collated by Tregelles and highly valued by him is the Codex Leicestrensis of the fourteenth century, and cited under the sign 37. Gregory also marks 47, Oxon. Bodl. Roe, as "bonae notae". It also was collated by Tregelles.

III. Versions.

The Old Latin and the Vulgate, the Peshitto and Harklean Syriac, the Coptic and fragments of the Sahidic and Bashmuric versions, together with the Armenian and Æthiopic are available for the ascertainment of the text of the Epistle. [For remarks on these versions, see Westcott's *Com.*, Introduction.]

I. 1. [a]**ΠΟΛΥΜΕΡΩΣ** καὶ πολυτρόπως πάλαι ὁ Θεὸς λαλήσας τοῖς a Num. xii.
πατράσιν ἐν τοῖς προφήταις, ἐπ' ἐσχάτων [2] τῶν ἡμερῶν τούτων ἐλά- 6, 8; Eph. i. 10; Gal. iv. 4.

[1] The title should be simply **ΠΡΟΣ ΕΒΡΑΙΟΥΣ.** See Introd.
[2] T.R. with 47, and some versions; εσχατου with אABDEKLMP, 17, etc.

CHAPTER I.—Vv. 1-3. The aim of the writer is to prove that the old Covenant through which God had dealt with the Hebrews is superseded by the New; and this aim he accomplishes in the first place by exhibiting the superiority of the mediator of the new Covenant to all previous mediators. The Epistle holds in literature the place which the Transfiguration holds in the life of Christ. Former mediators give place and Christ is left alone under the voice "Hear ye Him". With this writer, Jesus is before all else the Mediator of a better Covenant, viii. 6. But 'Mediator' involves the arranging and accomplishing of everything required for the efficacy of the Covenant; the perfect knowledge of the person and purposes of Him who makes the Covenant with men and the communication of this knowledge to them; together with the removal of all obstacles to man's entrance into the fellowship with God implied by the Covenant. This twofold function is in these first three verses shown to be discharged by Christ. He as Son speaks to men for God and thus supersedes all previous revelations; while, instead of appointing a priest who can only picture a cleansing, and accomplish a ceremonial purity, He becomes Priest and actually cleanses men from sin, and so effects their actual fellowship with God.

Ver. 1. In sonorous and dignified terms the writer abruptly makes his first great affirmation: "God having spoken . . . spoke". ὁ Θεὸς λαλήσας . . . ἐλά-

λησεν, for, however contrasted, previous revelations proceeded from the same source and are one in design and in general character with that which is final. In the N.T. λαλεῖν is not used in a disparaging sense, but, especially in this Epistle, is used of God making known His will. See ii. 2, iii. 5, v. 5, etc. God spoke, desired to be understood, to come into communication with men and therefore uttered Himself in intelligible forms, and succeeded, all through the past, in making Himself and His will known to men. He had not kept silence, allowing men to feel after Him if haply they might find Him. He had met the outstretched hand and guided the seeker. And this "speaking" in the past was preparatory to the final speaking in Christ; "God having spoken . . . spoke". The earlier revelations were the preparation for the later but were distinguished from it in four particulars—in the time, in the recipients, in the agents, in the manner.

πολυμερῶς καὶ πολυτρόπως "in many parts and in many ways". The alliteration is characteristic of the author, cf. v. 8, v. 14, vii. 3, ix. 10, etc. For the use of the words in Greek authors see Wetstein. πολυμερῶς points to the fragmentary character of former revelations. They were given piece-meal, bit by bit, part by part, as the people needed and were able to receive them. The revelation of God was essentially progressive; all was not disclosed at once, because all could not at once be understood. One aspect of God's nature, one element in His purposes, reflected from the conditions of their time, the prophets could know ; but in the nature of things it was impossible they should know the whole. They were like men listening to a clock striking, always getting nearer the truth but obliged to wait till the whole was heard. Man can only know in part, ἐκ μέρους, 1 Cor. xiii. [A fine illustration will be found in Browning's *Cleon*, in lines beginning: " those divine men of old time have reached, thou sayest well, each *at one point* the outside verge," etc..] The " speaking " of God to the fathers was conditioned by the capacity of the prophets. His speaking was also πολυτρόπως [*cf. Odyss.* i. 1. Ἄνδρα μοι ἔννεπε, Μοῦσα, πολύτροπον] not in one stereotyped manner but in modes varying with the message, the messenger, and those to whom the word is sent. Sometimes, therefore, God spoke by an institution, sometimes by parable, sometimes in a psalm, sometimes in an act of righteous indignation. For, as Peake says, " the author is speaking not of the forms in which God spoke *to* the prophets, but of the modes in which He spoke *through* them to the fathers. The message took the form of law or prophecy, of history or psalm ; now it was given in signs, now in types." So Hofmann. These features of previous revelations, so prominently set and expressed so grandiloquently, cannot have been meant to disparage them, rather to bring into view their affluence and pliability and many-sided application to the growing receptivity and varying needs of men. He wins his readers by suggesting the grandeur of past revelations. But it is at the same time true, as Calvin remarks, " varietatem fuisse imperfectionis notam ". So Bengel, " Ipsa prophetarum multitudo indicat, eos ex parte prophetasse ". These characteristics, while they encouragingly disclosed God's purpose to find His way to men, did yet discredit, as inadequate for perfect achievement, each method that was tried. The contrast in the new revelation is implied in the word ἐκάθισεν, indicating that the work was once for all accomplished.

The next note of previous revelations is found in πάλαι " of old," not merely " in time past " as A.V. ; marking the time referred to in λαλήσας as contrasted with the writer's present, and gently suggesting that other methods of speaking might now be appropriate. Already

in 2 Cor. iii. 14 the Mosaic covenant is spoken of as ἡ παλαιὰ διαθήκη *cf.* viii. 13. Here πάλαι is contrasted with ἐπ' ἐσχάτου τῶν ἡμερῶν τούτων, " at the last of these days," [" Aufs Ende dieser Tage," Weizsäcker], *i.e.*, in the Messianic time at the close of the period known to the Jews as " this present time or age ". The expression is used in the LXX indifferently with ἐπ' ἐσχάτων τ. ἡμερῶν or ἐν ταῖς ἐσχάταις ἡμέραις to translate בְּאַחֲרִית הַיָּמִים (see Isa. ii. 2; Gen. xlix. 1 ; Num. xxiv. 14), which was used to denote either the future indefinitely or the Messianic period, " the latter days " in which all prophecy was to find its fulfilment. Bleek quotes Kimchi as saying: " Ubicunque leguntur ' Beaharith Hayamim ' ibi sermo est de diebus Messiae ". And Wetstein quotes R. Nachman : " *Extremum dierum* consensu omnium doctorum sunt Dies Messiae ". It was this Jewish usage which the N.T. writers followed in speaking of their own times as " the last days ;" ἐπ' ἐσχάτου τ. χρόνου (Jude 18); ἐπ' ἐσχάτων τ. ἡμερῶν (2 Pet. iii. 3); ἐπ' ἐσχάτου τ. χρόνων (1 Pet. i. 20); and in this Epistle, ix. 26, Christ is said to have appeared ἐπὶ συντελείᾳ τῶν αἰώνων. The first Advent as terminating the old world and introducing the Messianic reign was considered the consummation. The introduction of the word τούτων is suggested by the Jewish division of the world's course into two periods : " This Age " (Ha-Olam Hazzeh) and The Coming Age (Ha-Olam Habbah). The end of " this age " or " these days " was signalised by the coming of the Messiah, the new revelation in Christ. More effectually than the Jews themselves expected has the Advent of the Messiah antiquated the old world and opened a new period.

The temporal contrast is further marked by the words τοῖς πατράσιν (ver. 1) and ἡμῖν (ver. 2). Former revelations had been made to " the fathers," *i.e.*, of the Jewish people, as in John vii. 22; Rom. ix. 5, xv. 8 ; 2 Pet. iii. 4. More frequently " our " " your " " their " is added, as in Acts iii. 13, 25 ; Luke vi. 53. But it is idle to urge, with von Soden, the absence of the pronoun as weighing against the restriction of the term in this place to the Jewish fathers. ἡμῖν " to us " of these last days, of the Christian dispensation.

The determining contrast between the

λησεν ἡμῖν ἐν υἱῷ, 2. ᵇ ὃν ἔθηκε κληρονόμον πάντων, δι' οὗ καὶ τοὺς ᵇ Ps. ii. 8;
αἰῶνας ἐποίησεν,[1] 3. ᶜ ὃς ὢν ἀπαύγασμα τῆς δόξης καὶ χαρακτὴρ

Matt. xxi.
38; Joan.
i. 3; Eph.
iii. 9; Col.
i. 16.   c viii. 1 et ix. 12, etc., et xii. 2; Ps. cx. 1; Sap. vii. 26; Joan. i. 4, et xiv. 9; 2 Cor. iv.4;
Col. i. 15, 7; Phil. ii. 6; Apoc. iv. 11.

[1] T.R. in DbKLP with other MSS. and versions; καὶ εποιησεν τ. αιωνας in ‭ABD*, etc., E, etc.

two revelations is found in this, that in the one God spoke ἐν τοῖς προφήταις, while in the other He spoke ἐν υἱῷ. "The prophets" stand here, not for the prophetic writings as in Jo. vi. 45; Acts xiii. 40, etc.; but for all those who had spoken for God, and especially for that great series of men from Abraham and Moses onwards who had been the organs of revelation and were identified with it (cf. the Parable of the Wicked Husbandmen). The prep. ἐν is not used in its instrumental sense (cf. Habak. ii. 1), nor is it = διά, it brings God closer to the hearers of the prophetic word, and implies that what the prophets spoke, God spoke. So Hofmann and Weiss. ["Ipse in cordibus eorum dixit quicquid illi foras vel dictis vel factis locuti sunt hominibus," Herveius.] The full significance of ἐν is seen in ἐν υἱῷ. ἐν υἱῷ without the article must be translated "in a son" or "in one who is a son," indicating the nature of the person through whom this final revelation was made. The revelation now consisted not merely in what was said [προφήταις] but in what He was [υἱός]. This revelation was final because made by one who in all He is and does, reveals the Father. By uttering Himself He expresses God. A Son who can be characteristically designated a son, carries in Himself the Father's nature and does not need to be instructed in purposes which are also and already His own, nor to be officially commissioned and empowered to do what He cannot help doing. "No man knoweth the Son but the Father; neither knoweth any man the Father save the Son, and he to whomsoever the Son will reveal Him" (cf. John i. 18). The whole section on "The Son of God" in Dalman's Die Worte Jesu should be read in this connection. "Son" is here used in its Messianic reference, as the quotations cited in vv. 5, 6 prove. The attributes ascribed to the Son are at the same time Divine attributes. [So Baur and Pfleiderer. Ménégoz denies this]. The writer apparently experiences no difficulty in attaching to one and the same personality the

creating of the world and the dying to cleanse sin.

The Son is described in six particulars which illustrate His supremacy and His fitness to reveal the Father: (1) His destination to universal lordship (ὃν ἔθηκεν κληρονόμον πάντων); (2) His agency in creation (δι' οὗ ἐποίησεν τ. αἰῶνας); (3) His likeness to God (ὢν ἀπαύγασμα κ.τ.λ.); (4) His relation to the world) φέρων τὰ πάντα); (5) His redemptive work (καθαρισμὸν . . . ποιησάμενος); (6) His exaltation (ἐκάθισεν ἐν δεξιᾷ κ.τ.λ.). Cf. Vaughan. ὃν ἔθηκεν κληρονόμον πάντων "whom He appointed heir of all". Davidson, Weiss and others understand this of the actual elevation of Christ, on His ascension, to the Lordship of all. [" Dass der Verfasser bei diesen Worten an den erhöhten Christus gedacht habe, halten wir für unzweifelhaft," Riehm, p. 295]. But the position of the clause in the verse and the subsequent mention of the exaltation in ver. 3 rather indicate that ἔθηκεν has here its ordinary meaning (see Elsner and Bleek) of "appointed," and that the reference is to Ps. ii. 8 δώσω σοι ἔθνη τὴν κληρονομίαν σου κ.τ.λ., so Hofmann. Through this Son God is to accomplish His purpose. The Son is to reign over all. The writer lifts the thought of the despondent to Christ's triumph and Lordship. In the Parable of the Wicked Husbandmen Christ speaks of Himself as Heir. It is involved in the Sonship; Gal. iv. 7. It is not simply possessor but possessor because of a relation to the Supreme. The Father could not be called κληρονόμος. Dalman shows that the 2nd Psalm "deduces from the filial relation of the King of Zion to God, that universal dominion, originally proper to God, is bequeathed to the Son as an inheritance," Worte Jesu, p. 220, E. Tr. 268. Cf. also Matt. xi. 27, πάντα μοι παρεδόθη ὑπὸ τοῦ πατρός μου. [Chrysostom says the use of the term brings out two points τὸ τῆς υἱότητος γνήσιον, καὶ τὸ τῆς κυριότητος ἀναπόσπαστον.] The inheritance is not fully entered upon, until it can be said

τῆς ὑποστάσεως αὐτοῦ, φέρων τε τὰ πάντα τῷ ῥήματι τῆς δυνάμεως
αὐτοῦ, δι' ἑαυτοῦ [1] καθαρισμὸν ποιησάμενος τῶν ἁμαρτιῶν ἡμῶν, [2]

[1] T.R. in DcEKLM al pler, d, e, Syrutr ; omit δι εαυτου with ℵABDbP, 17, 46*,
47.

[2] Omit ημων with ℵ*ABD*E*MP.

that " the kingdom of the world is become
the Kingdom of our Lord and of His
Christ," Rev. xi. 15. *Cf.* Heb. ii. 8.
But by His incarnation He came into
touch with men and poured His life into
human history, at once claiming and
securing His great inheritance.

δι' οὗ καὶ ἐποίησεν τοὺς αἰῶνας 'through whom also He made the
world," "per quem fecit et secula " (Vulg.),
" durch Welchen er auch die Weltzeiten
gemacht hat" (Weizsäcker). " Secula et
omnia in iis decurrentia " (Bengel). Weiss
thinks it quite improbable that so pure a
Greek writer should use αἰῶνας in the
rabbinical sense as = " world," and he
believes that the Greek interpreters are
right in retaining the meaning " world-
periods ". But in xi. 3 it becomes
obvious that this writer could use the
word as virtually = κόσμος. " The
thought of duration is never wholly lost
in the Scripture use of αἰών, though in
this place, and in xi. 3 it is all but
effaced " (Vaughan). *Cf.* Schoettgen
and McCaul. The writer perhaps has it
in his mind that the significant element
in creation is not the mass or magnifi-
cence of the material spheres but the
evolution of God's purposes through the
ages. The mind staggers in endeavouring to grasp the vastness of the physical
universe but much more overwhelming is
the thought of those times and ages and
aeons through which the purpose of God
is gradually unfolding, unhasting and
unresting, in the boundless life He has
called into being. He who is the end and
aim, the heir, of all things is also their
creator. The καὶ brings out the propriety
of committing all things to the hand that
brought them into being. The revealer
is the creator, Jo. i. 1-5. He only can
guide the universe to its fit end who at
first, presumably with wisdom equal to
His power, brought it into being. [" Cette
idée d'un être céleste chargé de réaliser la
pensée créatrice de Dieu est une idée
philonienne ; elle a pénétré dans le
Judaisme sous l'influence de la philosophie
grecque " (Ménégoz). It is true that
this is a Philonic idea (see numerous
passages in Carpzov, Bleek, McCaul and
Drummond) but we may also say with

Weiss " Die philonischen Aussagen . . .
gehören gar nicht hierher ". Certainly
Philo never claimed for a definite historical person the attributes here enumerated.] For the Son's agency in Creation
see John i. 2; Col. i. 15. Grotius' rendering " propter Messiam conditum esse
mundum " is interesting as illustrating
his standpoint, but would require δι' ὅν.
Ver. 3. ὃς ὢν ἀπαύγασμα. . . .
" Who being effulgence of His glory and
express image of His nature." The
relative ὃς finds its antecedent in υἱῷ,
its verb in ἐκάθισεν ; and the interposed
participles prepare for the statement of the
main verb by disclosing the fitness of
Christ to be the revealer of God, and
to make atonement. The two clauses,
ὢν . . . φέρων τε, are closely bound together and seem intended to convey the
impression that during Christ's redemptive activity on earth there was no ken-
osis, but that these Divine attributes lent
efficacy to His whole work. [On the
difficulty of this conception see Gore's
Bampton Lec., p. 266, and Carpenter's
Essex Hall Lec., p. 87.] ἀπαύγασμα
τῆς δόξης . . . ἀπαύγασμα may mean
either what is flashed forth, or what is
flashed back : either " ray" or " reflection".
Calvin, Beza, Thayer, Ménégoz prefer
the latter meaning. Thus Grotius has,
" repercussus divinae majestatis, qualis
est solis in nube ". The Greek fathers,
on the other hand, uniformly adopt the
meaning " effulgence ". Thus Theodoret
τὸ γὰρ ἀπαύγασμα καὶ ἐκ τοῦ πυρός
ἐστι, καὶ σὺν τῷ πυρί ἐστι· καὶ αἴτιον
μὲν ἔχει τὸ πῦρ, ἀχώριστον δέ ἐστι τοῦ
πυρός . . . καὶ τῷ πυρὶ δὲ ὁμοφυὲς τὸ
ἀπαύγασμα : οὐκοῦν καὶ ὁ ,υἱὸς τῷ
πατρί. So in the Nicene Creed φῶς ἐκ
φωτός. " The word ' effulgence' seems
to mean not rays of light streaming from
a body in their connection with that
body or as part of it, still less the reflection of these rays caused by their falling
upon another body, but rather rays of
light coming out from the original body
and forming a similar light-body themselves " (Davidson). So Weiss, who says
that the " Strahlenglanz ein zweites
Wesen erzeugt ". Philo's use of the
word lends colour to this meaning when

he says of the human soul breathed into man by God that it was ἅτε τῆς μακαρίας καὶ τρισμακαρίας φύσεως ἀπαύγασμα. So in India, Chaitanya taught that the human soul was like a ray from the Divine Being; God like a blazing fire and the souls like sparks that spring out of it. In the Arian contro versy this designation of the Son was appealed to as proving that He is eternally generated and exists not by an act of the Father's will but essentially. See Suicer, s.v. As the sun cannot exist or a lamp burn without radiating light, so God is essentially Father and Son. τῆς δόξης αὐτοῦ. God's glory is all that belongs to him as God, and the Son is the effulgence of God's glory, not only a single ray but as Origen says: ὅλης τῆς δόξης. Therefore the Son cannot but reveal the Father. Calvin says: "Dum igitur audis filium esse splendorem Paternae gloriae, sic apud te cogita, gloriam Patris esse invisibilem, donec in Christo refulgeat". As completing the thought of these words and bringing out still more emphatically the fitness of the Son to reveal, it is added καὶ χαρακτὴρ τῆς ὑποστάσεως αὐτοῦ. χαρακτήρ, as its form indicates, originally meant the cutting agent [χαράσσειν], the tool or person who engraved. In common use, however, it usurped the place of χάραγμα and denoted the impress or mark made by the graving tool, especially the mark upon a coin which determined its value; hence, any distinguishing mark, identifying a thing or person, *character*. "Express image" translates it well. The mark left on wax or metal is the "express image" of the seal or stamp. It is a reproduction of each characteristic feature of the original. ὑποστάσεως rendered "person" in A.V.; "substance," the strict etymological equivalent, in R.V. To the English ear, perhaps, "nature" or "essence" better conveys the meaning. It has not the strict meaning it afterwards acquired in Christian theology, but denotes all that from which the glory springs and with which indeed it is identical. [We must not confound the δόξα with the ἀπαύγασμα as Hofmann and others do. The ὑπόστασις is the nature, the δόξα its quality, the ἀπαύγασμα its manifestation.] There is in the Father nothing which is not reproduced in the Son, save the relation of Father to Son. Ménégoz objects that though a mirror perfectly reflects the object before it and the wax bears the very image of

the seal, the mirror and the wax have not the same nature as that which they represent. And Philo more than once speaks of man's rational nature as τύπος τις καὶ χαρακτὴρ θείας δυνάμεως, and the ἀπαύγασμα of that blessed nature, see *Quod deter. insid.*, c. xxiii.; *De Opif. Mundi*, c. li. All that he means by this is, that man is made in God's image. But while no doubt the primary significance of the terms used by the writer to the Hebrews is to affirm the fitness of Christ to reveal God, the accompanying expressions, in which Divine attributes are ascribed to Him, prove that this fitness to reveal was based upon community of nature. The two clauses, ὃς to αὐτοῦ, have frequently been accepted as exhibiting the Trinitarian *versus* the Arian and Sabellian positions; the Sabellians accepting the ἀπαύγασμα as representing their view of the modal manifestation of Godhead, the Arians finding it possible to accept the second clause, but neither party willing to accept both clauses—separate or individual existence of the Son being found in the figure of the seal, while identity of nature seemed to be affirmed in ἀπαύγασμα. [ὑπόστασις was derived from the Stoics who used it as the equivalent of οὐσία, that which formed the essential substratum, τὸ ὑποκείμενον, of all qualities. The Greek fathers, however, understood by it what they termed πρόσωπον ὁμοούσιον and affirmed that there were in the Godhead three ὑποστάσεις. The Latin fathers trans'ating ὑπόστασις by *substantia* could not make this affirmation. Hence arose confusion until Gregory Nazianzen pointed out that the difference was one of words not of ideas, and that it was due to the poverty of the Latin language. See Suicer, s.v.; Bleek in *loc.*; Bigg's *Christian Platonists*, p. 164-5; Dean Strong's *Articles* in *J.T.S.* for 1901 on the History of the Theological term Substance; Calvin *Inst.*, i, 13, 2; Loofs' *Leitfaden*, p. 109 note and p. 134.]

φέρων τε τὰ πάντα ... "and upholding all things by the word of His power". The meaning of φέρων is seen in such expressions as that of Moses in Num. xi. 14 οὐ δυνήσομαι ἐγὼ μόνος φέρειν πάντα τὸν λαὸν τοῦτον, where the idea of being responsible for their government and guidance is involved. So in Plutarch's *Lucullus*, 6, φέρειν τὴν πόλιν of governing the city. In Latin Cicero (*pro Flac.*, 37) reminds his judges "sustinetis rempublicam humeris vestris". See Bleek. In Rabbinic literature, as

d Eph. i. 21;
Phil. ii. 9,
10.
ἐκάθισεν ἐν δεξιᾷ τῆς μεγαλωσύνης ἐν ὑψηλοῖς, 4. ᵈ τοσούτῳ κρείττων γενόμενος τῶν ἀγγέλων, ὅσῳ διαφορώτερον παρ᾽ αὐτοὺς κεκληρο-

Schoettgen shows, God is commonly spoken of as "portans mundum," the Hebrew word being סָבַל In Philo, the Logos is the helmsman and pilot of all things (*De Cherub.*) τῷ ῥήματι, by the expression of His power, by making His will felt in all created nature. The present, φέρων, seems necessarily to involve that during the whole of His earthly career, this function of upholding nature was being discharged. Probably the clause is inserted not merely to illustrate the dignity of the Son, but to suggest that the whole course of nature and history, when rightly interpreted, reveals the Son and therefore the Father. The responsibility of bringing the world to a praiseworthy issue depends upon Christ, and as contributing to this work His earthly ministry was undertaken. For the notable thing He accomplished as God's Son, the use He made of His dignity and power, is expressed in the words, καθαρισμὸν τ. ἁμαρτιῶν ποιησάμενος "having accomplished purification of the sins". This was as essential to the formation of the covenant as the ability rightly to represent God's mind and will. This itself was the supreme revelation of God, and it was only after accomplishing this He could sit down at God's right hand as one who had finished the work of mediating the eternal covenant. ποιησάμενος, the mid. voice, supersedes the necessity of δι᾽ ἑαυτοῦ. The aorist part. implies that the cleansing referred to was a single definite act performed before He sat down, and in some way preparatory to that Exaltation. The word receives explanation in subsequent passages of the Ep. vii. 27, ix. 12-14. καθαρισμός as used in LXX suggests that the cleansing referred to means the removal of guilt and its consciousness. The worshippers were fitted by cleansing to appear before God.

ἐκάθισεν ἐν δεξιᾷ... "sat down at the right hand of the Majesty on high". ἐκάθισεν seems to denote that the work undertaken by the Son was satisfactorily accomplished; while the sitting down ἐν δεξιᾷ κ.τ.λ. denotes entrance upon a reign. The source of the expression is in Ps. cx. 1 (cited v. 13) where the Lord says to Messiah κάθου ἐκ δεξιῶν μου, and this not only as introducing Him to the place of security and favour, but also of dignity and power. "The King's right hand was the place of power and dignity, belonging to the minister of his authority and his justice, and the channel of his mercy, the Mediator in short between him and his people" (Rendall). *Cf.* Ps. lxxx. 17. In contrast to the ever-growing and never complete revelation to the fathers, which kept the race always waiting for something more suffecing, there came at last that revelation which contained all and achieved all. But the expression not only looks backward in approval of the work done by the Son, but forward to the result of this work in His supremacy over all human affairs. μεγαλωσύνη is ascribed to God in Jude 25 and in Deut. xxxii. 3 δότε μεγαλωσύνην τῷ Θεῷ ἡμῶν. *Cf.* also Clem., *Ep.*, xvi. Here it is used to denote the sovereign majesty inherent in God (*cf.* xii. 2; Mk. xiv. 62). The words ἐν ὑψηλοῖς are connected by Westcott and Vaughan with ἐκάθισεν. It is better, with Beza and Bleek, to connect them with μεγαλωσύνης, for while in x. 12 and xii. 2, where it is said He sat down on the throne *of God*, no further designation is needed; in viii. 1, as here, where it is said that He sat down on the right hand of the Majesty, it is felt that some further designation is needed and ἐν τοῖς οὐρανοῖς is added. No local region is intended, but supreme spiritual influence, mediation between God, the ultimate love, wisdom and sovereignty, and this world. This writer and his contemporary fellow-Christians, had reached the conviction here expressed, partly from Christ's words and partly from their own experience of His power.

Vv. 4—ii. 18. *The Son and the Angels.* Ver. 4, although forming part of the sentence 1-3, introduces a subject which continues to be more or less in view throughout chaps. i. and ii. The exaltation of the Mediator to the right hand of Sovereignty is in keeping with His designation as Son, a designation which marked Him out as superior to the angels. Proof is adduced from the O.T. To this proof, in accordance with the writer's manner, a resulting admonition is attached, ii. 1-4. And the remainder of chap. ii. is occupied with an explanation of the reasonableness of the

νόμηκεν ὄνομα. 5. °Τίνι γὰρ εἶπέ ποτε τῶν ἀγγέλων, "Υἱός μου εἶ e v. 5 ; 2
σὺ, ἐγὼ σήμερον γεγέννηκά σε ; " καὶ πάλιν, "Ἐγὼ ἔσομαι αὐτῷ

e v. 5 ; 2
Sam. vii.
14 ; 1 Par.
xxii. 10 et
xxviii. 6 ;
Ps. ii. 7 ; Acts xiii. 33.

incarnation and the suffering it involved ; or, in other words, it is explained why if Christ is really greater than the angels, He had to be made a little lower than they.

τοσούτῳ κρείττων γενόμενος . . . "having become as much superior to the angels as He has obtained a more excellent name than they ". The form of comparison here used, τοσ. . . . ὅσῳ is found also, vii. 20-22, viii. 6,x. 25 ; also in Philo. κρείττων is one of the words most necessary in an Epistle in which comparison is never out of sight. The Son *became* (γενόμενος) greater than the angels in virtue of taking His seat at God's right hand. This exaltation was the result of His earthly work. It is as Mediator of the new revelation, who has cleansed the sinful by His death, that He assumes supremacy. And this is in keeping with and in fulfilment of His obtaining the name of Son. This name κεκληρονόμηκεν, He has obtained, not " von Anfang an " as Bleek and others say, but as Riehm points out, in the O.T. The Messiah, then future, was spoken of as Son ; and therefore to the O.T. reference is at once made in proof. The Messianic Sonship no doubt rests upon the Eternal Sonship, but it is not the latter but the former that is here in view.

In support of this statement the writer adduces an abundance of evidence, no fewer than seven passages being cited from the O.T. Before considering these, two preliminary objections may first be removed. (1) To us nothing may seem less in need of proof than that Christ who has indelibly impressed Himself on mankind is superior to the angels who are little more than a picturesque adornment of earthly life. But when this writer lived the angels may be said to have been in possession, whereas Christ had yet to win His inheritance. Moreover, as Schoettgen shows (p. 905) it was usual and needful to make good the proposition, " Messias major est Patriarchis, Mose, et Angelis ministerialibus ". Prof. Odgers, too, has shown (*Proceedings of Soc. of Hist. Theol.*, 1895-6) that quite possibly the writer had in view some Jewish Gnostics who believed that Christ Himself belonged to the angelic creation and had, with the angels, a fluid personality

and no proper human nature. In any case it was worth the writer's while to carry home to the conviction of his contemporaries that a mediation accomplished by one who was tempted and suffered and wrought righteousness, a mediation of an ethical and spiritual kind, must supersede a mediation accomplished by physical marvels and angelic ministries. (2) The passages cited from the Old Testament in proof of Christ's superiority although their immediate historical application is disregarded, are confidently adduced in accordance with the universal use of Scripture in the writer's time. But it must not be supposed that these passages are culled at random. With all his contemporaries this writer believed that where statements were made of an Israelitish king or other official in an ideal form not presently realised in those directly addressed or spoken of, these were considered to be Messianic, that is to say, destined to find their fulfilment and realisation in the Messiah. These interpretations of Scripture were the inevitable result of faith in God. The people were sure that God would somehow and at some time fulfil the utmost of His promise.

The first two quotations (ver. 5) illustrate the giving of the more excellent name ; the remaining quotations exhibit the superiority of the Son to angels, or more definitely the supreme rule and imperishable nature of the Son, in contrast to the perishable nature and servile function of the angels.

Ver. 5. τίνι γὰρ εἶπέν ποτε τῶν ἀγγέλων . . . " For to which of the angels did he ever say My Son art Thou, I this day have begotten Thee ?" τίνι to what individual ; ποτε in the whole course of history. The angels as a class are called " Sons of Elohim " in the O.T. (Gen. vi. 2 ; Ps. xxix. 1, lxxxix. 7; Job i. 6). But this was not used in its strict sense but merely as expressive of indefinite greatness, nor was it addressed to any individual. εἶπεν, the subject unexpressed, as is common in citing Scripture (2 Cor. vi. 2 ; Gal. iii. 16 ; Eph. iv. 8, etc.). Winer and Blass supply ὁ θεός, others ἡ γραφή. Warfield, who gives the fullest treatment of the subjectless use of λέγει, φησί, and such words

f Ps. xcvii. εἰς πατέρα, καὶ αὐτὸς ἔσται μοι εἰς υἱόν ; " 6. ᵍ ὅταν δὲ πάλιν εἰσ-
7; Rom.
viii. 29 ; αγάγῃ τὸν πρωτότοκον εἰς τὴν οἰκουμένην, λέγει, "Καὶ προσκυνη-
Col. i. 18.

(*Presb. and Ref. Rev.*, July, 1899) holds that either subject may be supplied, because "under the force of their conception of Scripture as an oracular book it was all one to the N.T. writers whether they said 'God says' or 'Scripture says'." Here, however, the connection involves that the subject is **ὁ θεός.** The words cited are from Ps. ii. 7 and are in verbal agreement with the LXX, which again accurately represents the Hebrew. The psalm was written to celebrate the accession of a King, Solomon or some other ; but the writer, seeing in his mind's eye the ideal King, clothes the new monarch in his robes. The King was called God's Son on the basis of the promise made to David (2 Sam. vii. 14) and quoted in the following clauses : The words ἐγὼ σήμερον γεγέννηκά σε do not seem to add much to the foregoing words, except by emphasising them, according to the ordinary method of Hebrew poetry. σήμερον is evidently intended to mark a special occasion or crisis and cannot allude to the eternal generation of the Son. In its original reference it meant "I have begotten Thee to the kingly dignity". It is not the beginning of life, but the entrance on office that is indicated by γεγέννηκα, and it is as King the person addressed is God's Son. Thus Paul, in his address to the Pisidians (Acts xiii. 33), applies it to the Resurrection of Christ ; *cf.* Rom. i. 4. The words, then, find their fulfilment in Christ's Resurrection and Ascension and sitting down at God's right hand as Messiah. He was thus proclaimed King, begotten to the royal dignity, and in this sense certainly no angel was ever called God's Son.

This is more fully illustrated by another passage introduced by the usual καὶ πάλιν (see x. 30, and Longinus, *De Subl.*, chap. iv, etc.). Ἐγὼ ἔσομαι αὐτῷ εἰς πατέρα . . ., words spoken in God's name by Nathan in reference to David's seed, and conveying to him the assurance that the kings of his dynasty should ever enjoy the favour and protection and inspiration enabling them to rule as God's representatives. This promise is prior in history to the previous quotation, and is its source ; see 2 Sam. vii. 14. ἔσομαι εἰς is Hellenistic after a Hebrew model. See Blass, *Gram.*, p. 85.

Ver. 6. ὅταν δὲ πάλιν εἰσαγάγῃ . . .

"And when He shall again have brought the first-begotten into the world [of men], He says, "And let all God's angels worship Him". Having shown that "Son" is a designation reserved for the Messiah and not given to any of the angels, the writer now advances a step and adduces a Scripture which shows that the relation of angels to the Messiah is one of worship. It is not easy to determine whether πάλιν merely indicates a fresh quotation (so Bleek, Bruce, etc.) as in ver. 5 ; or should be construed with εἰσαγάγῃ. On the whole, the latter is preferable. Both the position of πάλιν and the tense of εἰσαγ. seem to make for this construction. The "bringing in" is still future. Apparently it is to the second Advent reference is made ; *cf.* ix. 28. To refer εἰσαγ. to the incarnation, with Chrysostom, Calvin, Bengel, Bruce (see esp. Schoettgen) ; or to the resurrection with Grotius ; or to an imagined introduction of the Son to created beings at some past period, with Bleek, is, as Weiss says, "sprachwidrig". Rendall remarks : " The words *bring in* have here a legal significance ; they denote the introduction of an heir into his inheritance, and are used by the LXX with reference to putting Israel in possession of his own land both in the time of Joshua and at the Restoration (Exod. vi. 8, xv. 17 ; Deut. xxx. 5)." This throws light not only on εἰσαγ. but also on πρωτότοκον and οἰκουμένην, and confirms the interpretation of the clause as referring to the induction of the first-born into His inheritance, the world of men. πρωτότ. is used of Christ (1) in relation to the other children of Mary (Luke ii. 7 ; Matt. i. 25) ; (2) in relation to other men (Rom. viii. 29 ; Col. i. 18) ; (3) in relation to creation (Col. i. 15). Nowhere else in N.T. is it used absolutely ; but *cf.* Ps. lxxxix. 27. "I will make him first-born," *i.e.*, superior in dignity and closer in intimacy. λέγει, the present is used because the words recorded in Scripture and still unfulfilled are meant. These words, καὶ προσκυνησάτωσαν . . . occur verbatim in Moses' song (Deut. xxxii. 43). In the Alexandrian text, from which this writer usually quotes, we find υἱοὶ Θεοῦ (*v.* Swete's LXX), but in a copy of the song subjoined to the Psalter this MS. itself has ἄγγελοι. The words are not represented in the Hebrew, and

σάτωσαν αὐτῷ πάντες ἄγγελοι Θεοῦ ". 7. ᵍΚαὶ πρὸς μὲν τοὺς g Ps. civ. 4.
ἀγγέλους λέγει, " Ὁ ποιῶν τοὺς ἀγγέλους αὐτοῦ πνεύματα, καὶ
τοὺς λειτουργοὺς αὐτοῦ πυρὸς φλόγα ". 8. ʰπρὸς δὲ τὸν υἱὸν, " Ὁ h Ps. xlv. 6.

are supposed by Delitzsch to have been
added in the liturgical use of Moses'
song. The part of the song to which
they are attached represents the coming
of God to judgment, a fact which further
favours the view that it is the second
Advent our author has in view.
Ver. 7. καὶ πρὸς μὲν τοὺς ἀγγέλους
λέγει. . . . The πρὸς μὲν of this verse is
balanced by πρὸς δὲ in ver. 8 ; and in both
πρός is to be rendered " with reference
to," or " of " as in Luke xx. 19 ; Rom. x.
21 ; Xen., Mem., iv. 2-15. Cf. Winer,
p. 505 : and our own expression " speak
to such and such a point ". ὁ ποιῶν
κ.τ.λ. cited from Ps. civ. 4, Lünemann
and others hold that the Hebrew is
wrongly rendered and means " who
maketh winds his messengers " not " who
maketh His angels winds ". Calvin, too,
finds no reference to angels in the words.
He believes that in this Hymn of Creation
the Psalmist, to illustrate how God is in
all nature, says " who maketh the winds
his messengers," i.e., uses for his purposes
the apparently wildest of natural forces,
and " flaming fire his ministers," the
most rapid, resistless and devouring
of agents controlled by the Divine hand.
Cf. Shakespeare, " thought-executing
fires ". The writer accepts the LXX
translation and it serves his purpose of
exhibiting that the characteristic function
of angels is service, and that their form
and appearance depend upon the will of
God. This was the current Jewish view.
Many of the sayings quoted by Schoettgen and· Weber suggest that with some
of the Rabbis the belief in angels was
little more than a way of expressing
their faith in a spiritual, personal power
behind the forces of nature. " When they
are sent on a mission to earth, they are
wind: when they stand before God they
are fire." The angel said to Manoah,
" I know not after what image I am
made, for God changes us every hour ;
why, then, dost thou ask after my name ?
Sometimes He makes us fire, at others
wind ; sometimes men, at other times
angels." Sometimes they appear to
have no individual existence at all, but
are merely the light-radiance or halo of
God's glory. " No choir of angels sings
God's praises twice, for each day God
creates new hosts which sing His praises
and then vanish into the stream of fire

from under the throne of His glory whence
they came." Cf. also the Book of
Jubilees, ii. 2. " On the first day He
created the heavens which are above and
the earth and the waters and all the
spirits which serve before Him—the
angels of the presence, and the angels of
sanctification, and the angels of the
spirit of the winds, and the angels of the
spirit of the clouds, and of darkness, and
of snow and of hail, and of hoar frost,
and the angels of the voices of the
thunder and of the lightning, and the
angels of the spirits of cold and of heat,
and of winter and of spring, and of
autumn and of summer, and of all the
spirits of His creatures which are in the
heavens and on the earth, the abysses
and the darkness, eventide and the light,
dawn and day which He hath prepared
in the knowledge of His heart." One
thing all these citations serve to bring
out is that the angels were merely
servants ; like the physical forces of
nature they were dependent and perishable. In contrast to these qualities
are those ascribed to the Son.
Ver. 8. πρὸς δὲ τὸν υἱόν . . .,
the quotation being from Ps. xlv. in which
the King in God's kingdom is described
ideally. The points in the quotation which
make it relevant to the writer's purpose are
the ascription of dominion and perpetuity
to the Son. The emphatic words, therefore, are θρόνος, εἰς τὸν αἰῶνα, ῥάβδος,
and παρὰ τοὺς μετόχους σου. It does not
matter, therefore, whether we translate
" Thy throne is God " or " Thy throne, O
God," for the point here to be affirmed is
not that the Messiah is Divine, but that
He has a throne and everlasting dominion. Westcott adopts the rendering
" God is thy throne," and compares Ps.
lxxi. 3 ; Isa. xxvi. 4 ; Ps. xc. 1, xci. 1, 2 ;
Deut. xxx. 27. He thinks it scarcely
possible that " God " can be addressed to
the King. Vaughan, on the other hand,
says : " Evidently a vocative. God is
thy throne might possibly have been said
(Ps. xlvi. 1) : thy throne is God seems an
unnatural phrase. And even in its first
(human) application the vocative would
cause no difficulty (Ps. lxxxii. 6 ; John x.
34, 35)." Weiss strongly advocates this
construction, and speaks of the other as
quite given up. εἰς τὸν αἰῶνα τ.
αἰῶνος, " to the age of the age," " for

θρόνος σου, ὁ Θεός, εἰς τὸν αἰῶνα τοῦ αἰῶνος[1] · ῥάβδος εὐθύτητος ἡ

i Acts x. 38. ῥάβδος[2] τῆς βασιλείας σου.[3] 9. [i]ἠγάπησας δικαιοσύνην, καὶ

ἐμίσησας ἀνομίαν· διὰ τοῦτο ἔχρισέ σε ὁ Θεός, ὁ Θεός σου, ἔλαιον

k Ps. cii. 25. ἀγαλλιάσεως παρὰ τοὺς μετόχους σου." 10. [k]Καί, "Σὺ κατ' ἀρχὰς,

---

[1] Insert καὶ with ℵABD*E*M, 17.

[2] T.R. in DEKLP al fere omn ; η ραβδος ευθ. ραβδος with ℵABM.

[3] αυτου in ℵB ; σου in ADEKLMP.

---

ever and ever," "to all eternity." *Cf.* Eph. iii. 21, εἰς πάσας τ. γενεὰς τοῦ αἰῶνος τ. αἰώνων, and the frequent εἰς τ. αἰῶνας τ. αἰώνων. See others in Vaughan or Concordance. "The aim of all these varieties of expression is the same; to heap up masses of time as an approximation to the conception of eternity" (Vaughan). καὶ ἡ ῥάβδος τῆς εὐθύτητος ῥάβδος τ. βασιλείας σου. The less strongly attested reading [see notes] gives the better sense : The sceptre of thy kingdom is a sceptre of uprightness. The well-attested reading gives the sense : "The sceptre of uprightness is the sceptre of thy kingdom". The everlasting dominion affirmed in the former clause is now declared to be a righteous rule. An assurance of this is given in the the further statement. Ver. 9. ἠγάπησας δικαιοσύνην . . . "Thou lovedst righteousness and didst hate lawlessness, therefore God, thy God, anointed thee with oil of gladness above thy fellows." The quotation is verbatim from LXX of Ps. xlv. 8 [the Alexand. text reads ἀδικίαν in place of ἀνομίαν, so that the author used a text not precisely in agreement with that of Cod : Alex. *v.* Weiss]. The anointing as King is here said to have been the result [διὰ τοῦτο] of his manifestation of qualities fitting him to rule as God's representative, namely, love of right and hatred of iniquity. [ἀνομία is used in 1 John iii. 4, as the synonym and definition of ἁμαρτία. ἡ ἁμαρτία ἐστὶν ἡ ἀνομία. It is contrasted with δικαιοσύνη in 2 Cor. vi, 14, τίς γὰρ μετοχὴ δικαιοσύνη καὶ ἀνομίᾳ ;] It is the Messiah's love of righteousness as manifested in His earthly life which entitles Him to sovereignty. ὁ Θεός is taken as a vocative here, as in ver. 8, by Lünemann, Weiss and others; and ὁ Θεός σου as the direct nom. to ἔχρισε. Westcott thinks that the ἔλαιον ἀγαλλ. refers "not to the solemn anointing to royal dignity but to the festive anointing

on occasions of rejoicing ". So Alford. Davidson, on the other hand, says : "As Kings were anointed when called to the throne, the phrase means made King". So, too, Weiss and von Soden. But the psalm is not a coronation ode, but an epithalamium ; the epithalamium, indeed, of the ideal King, but still a festive marriage song (vv. 10-17), to which the festal ἔλαιον ἀγαλ. is appropriate. The oil of exultation is the oil expressive of intense joy (*cf.* ver. 15 of the psalm). The only objection to this view is that God is said to be the anointer, but this has its parallel in Ps. xxiii. 5.; and throughout Ps. xlv. God is considered the originator of the happiness depicted (*cf.* ver. 2). Whether the marriage rejoicings are here to be applied to the Messiah in terms of vv. 16 and 17 of the psalm is doubtful. The verse is cited probably for the sake of the note of superiority contained in παρὰ τοὺς μετόχους σου. In the psalm the μέτοχοι are hardly other Kings ; rather the companions and counsellors of the young King. In the Messianic application they are supposed by Bleek, Pierce, Alford, Davidson, Peake, etc., to be the angels. It seems preferable to keep the term indefinite as indicating generally the supremacy of Christ (*cf.* Ps. xlv. 2). —[παρά "From the sense of (1) *beside, parallel to,* comes that of (2) *in comparison with ;* and so (3) in *advantageous* comparison with, *more than, beyond*". Vaughan]. Ver. 10. In vv. 10-12 the writer introduces another quotation from Ps. 102 (in LXX 101, 25-7). The quotation is verbatim from the LXX except that σὺ is lifted from the fifth to the first place in the sentence, for emphasis, and that a second ὡς ἱμάτιον is inserted after αὐτούς in ver. 12. With the introductory καὶ Weiss understands πρὸς τὸν υἱὸν λέγει, as in ver. 8. He is also of opinion that the writer considers that the words were spoken by Jehovah and that κύριε, therefore, must be the Messiah.

Κύριε, τὴν γῆν ἐθεμελίωσας, καὶ ἔργα τῶν χειρῶν σου εἰσὶν οἱ 1 Esa. li. 6;
2 Peter iii.
οὐρανοί· 11. ¹αὐτοὶ ἀπολοῦνται, σὺ δὲ διαμένεις· καὶ πάντες ὡς 7, 10.
ἱμάτιον παλαιωθήσονται, 12. καὶ ὡσεὶ περιβόλαιον ἑλίξεις¹ αὐτοὺς² m x. 12, 13,
et xii. 2;
καὶ ἀλλαγήσονται· σὺ δὲ ὁ αὐτὸς εἶ, καὶ τὰ ἔτη σου οὐκ ἐκλείψουσι ". Ps. cx. 1;
Matt.xxii.
13. ᵐ Πρὸς τίνα δὲ τῶν ἀγγέλων εἴρηκέ ποτε, "Κάθου ἐκ δεξιῶν μου, 44; Marc.
xii. 36 :
ἕως ἂν θῶ τοὺς ἐχθρούς σου ὑποπόδιον τῶν ποδῶν σου ;" 14. ⁿοὐχὶ 42 ; Acts
42 ; Acts
πάντες εἰσὶ λειτουργικὰ πνεύματα, εἰς διακονίαν ἀποστελλόμενα διὰ Cor. xv.
25 ; Eph.
i. 20.

n Ps. xxxiv. 7, et xci. 11.

¹ ἑλίξεις ABDᶜKLMP, Vulg., WH ; αλλαξεις ℵ*D* 43, Tisch.
² Insert ως ιματιον with ℵABD*, d, e. Tisch. with KLMP omits as a gloss. It has the appearance of a homoioteleuton.

This is possible, but it is not necessary for the justification of the Messianic reference. This follows from the character of the psalm, which predicts the manifestation of Jehovah as the Saviour of His people, even though this may only be in the far future (see ver. 13 : " Thou shalt arise and have mercy upon Zion. . . . So the heathen shall fear the name of the Lord, etc.") Prof. B. W. Bacon of Yale has investigated this matter afresh and finds that, so far from the application of these verses to the Messiah being an audacious innovation, or even achieved, as Calvin says, " pia deflectione," " the psalm itself was a favourite resort of those who sought in even pre-Christian times for proof-texts of Messianic eschatology"; also that " we have specific evidence of the application of vv. 23, 24 to the Messiah by those who employed the Hebrew or some equivalent text" and finally that by the rendering of ענה in ver. 24 (English ver. 23) by respondit or ἀπεκρίθη " we have the explanation of how, in Christian circles at least, the accepted Messianic passage could be made to prove the doctrine that the Messiah is none other than the pre-existent wisdom of Prov. viii. 22-31, "through whom,"according to our author, ver. 2, " God made the worlds." Indeed, we shall not be going too far if with Bruce we say : " It is possible that the writer (of Heb.) regarded this text (Ps. cii. 25-27) as Messianic because in his mind creation was the work of the pre-existent Christ. But it is equally possible that he ascribed creative agency to Christ out of rega d to this and other similar texts believed to be Messianic on other grounds." See Preuschen's Zeitschrift für N. T. Wissenschaft, 1902, p. 280.

In vv. 13 and 14, we have the final contrast between the place of the Son and that of the angels in human redemptive history. This contrast is connected by the form of its statement with ver. 5 (" to which of the angels, etc."). There it was the greater name that was in question, here it is the higher station and function. πρὸς τίνα δὲ κ.τ.λ. " But to which of the angels has He at any time said . . . ?" implying that to the Son He has said it, as is proved by the citation from Ps. cx. On this psalm (see note on ver. 9). δὲ connects this ver. with ver. 8, and stands in the third place as frequently in classics when a preposition begins the sentence (Herod., viii., 68, 2 ; Thuc., i., 6 ; Soph., Philoct., 764. See examples in Klotz' Devarius, p. 379). κάθου ἐκ δεξιῶν μου, see ver. 3 ; ἐκ δεξ. is not classical, but frequent in Hellenistic Greek, see references. ἕως ἂν θῶ. . . . " Until I set thine enemies as a footstool for thy feet." ὑποπόδιον is a later Greek word used in LXX and N.T. The figure arose from the custom of conquerors referred to in Josh. x. 24. Here it points to the complete supremacy of Christ. This attained sovereignty is the gauge of the World's consummation. The horizon of human history is the perfected rule of Jesus Christ. It is the end for which all things are now making. Whereas the angels are but the agents whose instrumentality is used by God for the furtherance of this end. οὐχὶ πάντες εἰσὶ λειτουργικὰ πνεύματα. . . . " Are they not all ministering spirits sent forth to serve for the sake of those who are to obtain salvation ?" They have no function of rule, but are directed by a higher will to promote the interests of those who are to form Christ's kingdom. This is true of all of them [πάντες] whatever hierarchies there be among them. λειτουργικὰ, cf. v. 5. λειτουργός

τοὺς μέλλοντας κληρονομεῖν σωτηρίαν; II. 1. Διὰ τοῦτο δεῖ
περισσοτέρως ἡμᾶς προσέχειν τοῖς ἀκουσθεῖσι, μή ποτε παρα-

with its cognates has come to play a
large part in ecclesiastical language.
It is originally "a public servant"; from
λεῖτος, an unused adjective connected with
λαός, meaning "what belongs to the
people" and ἔργον. It occurs frequently
in LXX, sometimes denoting the official
who attends on a king (Josh. i. 1), sometimes angels (Ps. ciii. 21), commonly the
priests and Levites (Neh. x. 39), οἱ ἱερεῖς
οἱ λειτουργοί, and Is. lxi. 6. In N.T.
it is used of those who render service to
God or to Christ or to men (cf. Lepine's
Ministers of Jesus Christ, p. 126). εἰς
διακονίαν ἀποστελλόμενα, present part., denoting continuous action.
"Sent forth"; therefore as servants by
a higher power (cf. Acts i. 25, διακονίας
ταύτης κ. ἀποστολῆς). Διακονία originally means the ministry of a body servant
or table servant (cf. Luke iv. 39; Mark
i. 13, οἱ ἄγγελοι διηκόνουν αὐτῷ) and
is used throughout N.T. for ministry
in spiritual things. μέλλοντας
might almost be rendered "destined"
as in Matt. iii. 7, xi, 14, xvi. 27, xvii. 12,
etc. κληρονομεῖν, see on ver. 4.
σωτηρίαν in the classics means either
preservation or deliverance. In N.T. the
word naturally came to be used as the
semi-technical term for the deliverance
from sin and entrance into permanent
wellbeing effected by Christ. See Luke i.
71, 77; John iv. 22; Acts iv. 12, xvi. 17;
Rom. i. 16, etc. In ii. 3 the salvation
referred to is termed τηλικαύτη. Cf.
Hooker's outburst, Eccles. Pol., i., iv., 1,
and Sir Oliver Lodge (Hibbert Journal,
Jan., 1903, p. 223): "If we are open to influence from each other by non-corporeal
methods, may we not be open to influence
from beings in another region or of another order? And if so, may we not be
aided, inspired, guided by a cloud of witnesses—not witnesses only, but helpers,
agents like ourselves of the immanent
God?" On guardian angels, see Charles'
Book of Jubilees, Moulton in J. T. S.,
August 1902, and Rogers' edition of
Aristoph., Eccles., 999, and the Orphic
Fragment quoted by Clement (Strom., v.)
Σῷ δὲ θρόνῳ πυρόεντι παρεστᾶσιν πολυ-
μόχθοι Ἄγγελοι οἷσι μέμηλε βροτοῖς ὡς
πάντα τελεῖται. Cf. Shakespeare's
"Angels and ministers of grace defend
us".

CHAPTER II.—Vv. 1-4. From this
proved superiority of the Son to the

angels the writer deduces the warning
that neglect of the salvation proclaimed
by the Lord Himself and attested by
God in miracles and gifts of the Holy
Ghost will incur heavier punishment
than that which was inflicted upon
those who neglected the word spoken
by angels.

Ver. 1. Διὰ τοῦτο: "on this account," because God has now spoken
not through prophets or angels, but
through a Son. δεῖ . . . ἡμᾶς: "we
must give more excessive heed".
"Alibi utitur verbo ὀφείλειν debere: hic
δεῖ oportet. Illud dicit obligationem:
hoc, urgens periculum"; Bengel, who
also remarks on 1 Cor. xi. 10, ὀφείλει
notat obligationem: δεῖ necessitatem;
illud morale est, hoc quasi physicum;
ut in vernaculâ, wir sollen und müssen".
Here then it is the logical necessity that
is prominent. περισσοτέρως is to
be joined not with δεῖ as in Vulg. (and
Bengel), "abundantius oportet obser-
vare," but with προσέχειν. The adverb
occurs in xiii. 19 and six times in 2 Cor.;
the adj. frequently in N.T. περισσοτέρως
[περιττοτέρως] occurs in Diod. Sic.,
xiii. 108, τὰ περ. εἰργασμένα; also in
Athenaeus, v., p. 192 F. κλισμὸς περιτ.
κεκόσμηται. The comparative is here
used with reference to the greater attention due to the revelation than if it
had been delivered by one of less position. Atto Vercell. suggestively, "Quare
abundantius . . . Nonne et illa Dei
sunt et ista?" His answer being that
those who had been brought up to
reverence the O.T. might be apt to despise the new revelation. προσέχειν
never in N.T. and only once in LXX
(Job vii. 17) has the added τὸν νοῦν
usual in classics. As προσέχειν is commonly used of bringing a ship to land,
this sense may have suggested the
παραρρυῶμεν. ἡμᾶς, including himself, but meaning to indicate all who
in these last days had heard the revelation of Christ. τοῖς ἀκουσθεῖσιν:
"the things heard," the great salvation
first preached by the Lord, ver. 3; cf. Acts
viii. 6, xvi. 14. He means to disclose the
significance of what they have already
heard, rather than to bring forward new
truth. μὴ ποτε παραρρυῶμεν:
"lest haply we drift away". μή ποτε,
as Hoogeveen shows, occurs in N.T. as
= ne quando and also as = ne forte; but

ρρυῶμεν.[1]   2. ᵃεἰ γὰρ ὁ δι' ἀγγέλων λαληθεὶς λόγος ἐγένετο ᵃ Deut.
xxvii. 26;
βέβαιος, καὶ πᾶσα παράβασις καὶ παρακοὴ ἔλαβεν ἔνδικον μισθα- Acts vii.
38, 53;
ποδοσίαν, 3. ᵇπῶς ἡμεῖς ἐκφευξόμεθα τηλικαύτης ἀμελήσαντες Gal. iii.19.
σωτηρίας ; ἥτις ἀρχὴν λαβοῦσα λαλεῖσθαι διὰ τοῦ Κυρίου, ὑπὸ τῶν ᵇ xii. 25 ;
Matt. iv.
17; Marc.
i. 14.

[1] παραρυωμεν with ℵAB*D*LP, 17, 47, 115.   Bleek favours the T.R.   See also
the forms given by Veitch.

in clauses expressing apprehension, as
here, it can always be rendered "lest
perchance". ["In Hellenistic Greek
μήποτε in a principal clause means
'perhaps,' in a dependent clause 'if
perchance,' 'if possibly,'" Blass, p. 212.]
παραρρυῶμεν is 2nd aor. subj. pass.
(with neuter meaning) of παραρρέω, I
flow beside or past; as in Xen., *Cyrop.*,
iv. 52, πιεῖν ἀπὸ τοῦ παραρρέοντος
ποταμοῦ. Hence, to slip aside; as in
Soph., *Philoct.*, 653, of an arrow slipping
from the quiver; in Xen., *Anab.*, iv. 4, of
snow slipping off; Ælian, *V. H.*, iii. 30,
of a coarse story unseasonably slipping
into a discreet conversation; and in
medical writers, frequently of food slipping aside into the windpipe. Origen
(*Contra Celsum*, 393) says the multitude
need fixed holy days, ἵνα μὴ τέλεον
παραρρυῇ, "that they may not quite
drift away". See also Prov. iii. 21, υἱὲ,
μὴ παραρρυῇς, τήρησον δὲ ἐμὴν βουλήν.
Ver. 2. εἰ γὰρ ὁ δι' ἀγγέλων λαληθεὶς
λόγος. . . . An *a fortiori* argument derived from the notoriously inevitable
character of the punishment which over-
took those who disregarded the Law.
"The word spoken through angels" is
the Law, the characteristic and fundamental form under which the old revelation had been made. The belief
that angels mediated the Law is found
in Deut. xxxiii. 2; Acts vii. 53; Gal. iii.
19; Josephus, *Ant.*, xv. 53. ἐγένετο
βέβαιος: "proved steadfast," inviolable, held good; as in Rom. iv. 16, of
the promise εἰς τὸ εἶναι βεβαίαν τὴν
ἐπαγγελίαν. The sanctions of the law
were not a mere *brutum fulmen*. This
appeared in the fact that πᾶσα
παράβασις . . . "every transgression and disobedience". παράβασις is
transgression of a positive command:
παρακοή is neglect to obey. Grotius
renders παρακ. by "contumacia" which
may be involved; but Böhme is right
in his note "non commissa solum, sed
omissa etiam". The inflictions, whether
on individuals, as Achan, or on the
whole people, as in the wilderness-

generation, were "a just recompense,"
not an arbitrary, or excessive punishment. For μισθαποδοσία classical
writers use μισθοδοσία.
Ver. 3. πῶς ἡμεῖς. . . . "How shall
we"—to whom God has spoken through
the Son, i. 2—"escape (ἔνδικον μισθ.
prob. in final judgment, as in x. 27) if we
have neglected (the aorist ἀμελήσαντες
suggesting that life is looked at as a
whole) so great a salvation ?"—the salvation which formed the main theme of
the new revelation. The meaning of
ἀμελήσαντες is best illustrated by Matt.
xxii. 5, where it is used of those who disregarded, or treated with contempt, the
invitation to the marriage-supper. The
guilt and danger of so doing are in proportion to the greatness of the announcement, and this is no longer of law but of
life, *cf.* 2 Cor. iii. The word now spoken
is vastly more glorious and more fully
expressive of its Author than the Law,
"Non erat *tanta* salus in V.T., quanta
est in gratia quam Dei filius nobis
attulit" (Atto Vercell:). The "greatness" of the salvation is involved in the
greatness of Him who mediates it (i. 4),
of the method employed (ii. 10), of the
results, *many* sons being brought to *glory*
(ii. 10). But one relevant aspect of its
greatness, the source and guaranteed
truth of its proclamation is introduced
by ἥτις, which here retains its proper
qualitative sense and may be rendered
"inasmuch as it...". "Its object is to
introduce the mention of a characteristic
quality, which explains or emphasises
the thing in question" (Vaughan). It
was the trustworthiness of the new revelation of salvation which the Hebrews
were beginning to question. The law
had proved its validity by punishing trans-
gressors but the majesty and certainty
of the recent proclamation were doubtful.
Therefore the writer insists that it is
"very great," and illustrates its trustworthiness by adducing these three features : (1) its original proclamation by
the Lord, (2) its confirmation by those
who heard Him, (3) its miraculous certi-

c Marc. xvi.
20; Acts
ii. 22, et
xiv. 3, et
xix. 11;
1 Cor. xii.
4, 7, 11.

ἀκουσάντων εἰς ἡμᾶς ἐβεβαιώθη,   4. °συνεπιμαρτυροῦντος τοῦ Θεοῦ
σημείοις τε καὶ τέρασι καὶ ποικίλαις δυνάμεσι, καὶ Πνεύματος Ἁγίου
μερισμοῖς, κατὰ τὴν αὐτοῦ θέλησιν.

fication by God. [This is not contradicted by Bleek's " Das τηλικ., tantae
talisque salutis, verweist an sich wohl
nicht auf den nachfolgenden relativen
Satz," nor by Weiss' " Das ἥτις hängt
weder sprachlich noch sachlich mit τηλικ.
zusammen."]   ἀρχὴν λαβοῦσα
λαλεῖσθαι, lit.: "having received a
beginning to be spoken" = "having begun to be spoken," or "which was first
proclaimed". ἀρχὴν λαβ., a common
phrase in later Greek, see Stephanus and
Wetstein.   In Polybius of a war "taking
its rise".   In Ælian, V. H., ii. 28. πόθεν
τὴν ἀρχὴν ἔλαβεν ὅδε ὁ νόμος, ἐρῶ. It is
used here to indicate with precision the
origin of the proclamation of the revelation about which they are feeling uncertain. λαλεῖσθαι refers back to ver.
2 and also to i. 1.   διὰ to be connected
with ἀρχὴν λαβ.; it is used instead of
ὑπὸ because God is throughout viewed
as the ultimate source of revelation.
τοῦ Κυρίου, "the Lord" supreme
over angels, and whose present exaltation
reflects dignity and trustworthiness on
the revelation He made while on earth.
The salvation which they are tempted to
neglect was at first proclaimed not by
angels sent out to minister, not by servants or delegates who might possibly
misapprehend the message, but by the
Lord Himself, the Supreme.   The source
then is unquestionably pure.   Has the
stream been contaminated ? God testifies
to its purity.   There is only one link between the Lord and you, they that heard
Him delivered the message to you, and
God by witnessing with them certifies its
truth.   The main verb is ἐβεβαιώθη
which looks back to βέβαιος of ver. 2,
and compares the inviolability of the one
word or revelation with that of the other.
We must not, he argues, neglect a gospel
of whose veracity and importance we
have assurance in this, that it was first
proclaimed by the Lord Himself and that
we have it on the authority of those who
themselves heard Him, and who therefore were first-hand witnesses who had
also made experimental verification of its
validity.   For ἀκουσάντων though without an object expressed, plainly means
those who heard the Lord, cf. Luke i. 1.
εἰς ἡμᾶς is rendered by Theophylact διεπορθμεύθη εἰς ἡμᾶς βεβαίως, it

has been conveyed to us in a trustworthy
manner. To their testimony was added
the all-convincing witness borne by God,
συνεπιμαρτυροῦντος τοῦ θεοῦ.
The word is found in Aristotle, Philo and
Polybius, xxvi. 9, 4, παρόντων δὲ τῶν
Θετταλῶν καὶ συνεπιμαρτυρούντων τοῖς
Δαρδανίοις. Also in Clement, Ep., c.
xxiii., συνεπιμαρτυρούσης τῆς γραφῆς;
but only here in N.T., cf. 1 Pet. v. 12;
Rom. ii. 15, viii. 16, ix. 1.   The sense is
found in Mark xvi. 20, ἐκήρυξαν παντα-
χοῦ, τοῦ Κυρίου συνεργοῦντος καὶ τὸν
λόγον βεβαιοῦντος διὰ τῶν ἐπακολουθ-
ούντων σημείων. This witness was borne
σημείοις τε καὶ τέρασιν "by
signs and wonders," the two words referring to the same manifestations (τε
καὶ closely uniting the words), which in
one aspect were "signs" suggesting a
Divine presence or a spirtual truth, and
in another aspect "wonders" calculated
to arrest attention. [The words are
similarly conjoined in Polybius, Plutarch, Ælian, Philo and Josephus.] καὶ
ποικίλαις δυνάμεσιν "and various
miracles," lit. powers, as in Matt. xi. 21,
καὶ οὐκ ἐποίησεν ἐκεῖ δυνάμεις πολλάς.
Bleek thinks it is not the outward manifestations but the powers themselves that
are here meant. This, he thinks, is suggested by the connexion of the word with
πνεύματος ἁγίου μερισμοῖς, "distributions of the Holy Spirit".   The genitive
is genitive objective, "distributions consisting of the Holy Spirit".   The remarkable character of the Charismata and the
testimony they bore to a Divine presence
and power are frequently alluded to in the
N.T. and are enlarged upon in 1 Cor.
xii. 14.   Paul uses the same argument as
this writer in Gal. iii. 1-4.   The article
is wanting before πνεύματος in accordance with the usage noted by Vaughan,
that it is generally omitted when the
communication of the Spirit is spoken of,
cf. Luke ii. 25, John vii. 39, with John
xiv. 26, Acts xix. 2 with 6. μερισμός
only here and in a different sense in iv.
12; the verb is common. St. Paul uses
it in connection with the distribution of
spiritual gifts in Rom. xii. 3, 1 Cor. vii.
17. No one thought himself possessed
of the fulness of the Spirit, only a μέρος.
These distributions or apportionings,
being of the Spirit of God, are necessarily

5. ᵈ Οὐ γὰρ ἀγγέλοις ὑπέταξε τὴν οἰκουμένην τὴν μέλλουσαν, ᵈ i. 2, 4, 8; 2 Peter
περὶ ἧς λαλοῦμεν. 6. ᵉ διεμαρτύρατο δέ πού τις λέγων, "Τί ἐστιν iii. 13.
e Ps. viii. 4.
et cxliv. 3.

made κατὰ τὴν αὐτοῦ θέλησιν "according to His [God's] will". In 1 Cor. xii.
11 the will is that of the Spirit. "Non
omnibus omnia dabat Deus, sed quae et
quantum et quibus vellet, Eph. iv. 7"
(Grotius). [θέλησις only here in N.T.,
but ten times in LXX. Pollux calls it a
"vulgarism" ἰδιωτικόν. On the substitution of nouns in -μα for nouns in -σις,
see Jannaris' *Hist. Gram.*, p. 1024, and
cf. x. 7, ix. 36, xiii. 21, so that in the present passage the choice of the active form
is deliberate.] The clause is added to
enforce the writer's contention that all
the Charismata with which his readers
were familiar were not mere fruits of
excitement or in any way casual, but
were the result of a Divine intention
to bear witness to the truth of the gospel.

Vv. 5-18. Having sufficiently brought
out the permanence and sovereignty of
the Son by contrasting them with the
fleeting personality and ministerial function of angels, the author now proceeds
to bring the supremacy of the Son into
direct relation to the Messianic administration of "the world to come," the
ideal condition of human affairs; and to
explain why for the purposes of this administration it was needful and seemly
that "the Lord" should for a season appear in a form "a little lower than the
angels". The world of men as it was
destined to be [ἡ οἰκουμένη ἡ μέλλουσα]
was a condition of things in which man
was to be supreme, not subject to any
kind of slavery or oppression. And if
the Jew asked why, in order to bring this
about, the appearance of the Son in so
apparently inglorious a form was necessary; if he asked why suffering and
death on His part were necessary, the
answer is, that it was God's purpose to
bring, not angels, but many human sons
to glory and that as there is but one path,
and that a path of suffering, by which
men can reach their destiny, it was becoming that their leader should act as
pioneer in this path. His path to glory
must be a path in which men can follow
Him; because it is from the human level
and as man that He wins to glory. More
particularly His sufferings accomplish
two objects: they produce in Him the
sympathy which qualifies Him as High
Priest, while His death breaks the power
which kept them enslaved and in fear.
[On this section Robertson Smith's papers

in the *Expositor*, 1881-2, should be consulted.]
Ver. 5. Οὐ γὰρ ἀγγέλοις. . . . "For
not to angels". With γὰρ the writer proceeds to clinch the exhortation contained
in vv. 1-4, by exhibiting the ground of
it. Under the old Covenant angels had
been God's messengers, but this mode of
mediation has passed away. The οἰκουμένη μέλλουσα is not subject to them.
It is the Son as man who now rules
and to whom attention must be given.
ὑπέταξεν . . . "did He"—that is God
—subject the world to come of which we
are speaking, ἡ οἰκουμένη, not κόσμος,
but the inhabited world. So used in
Diod. Sic., i. 8 καθ' ἅπασαν τ. οἰκουμένην, wherever there were men.
From the O.T. point of view "the
world to come" meant the world under
Messianic rule, but in this Epistle the
Messianic Kingdom is viewed as not yet
fully realised. The world to come is
therefore the eternal order of human
affairs already introduced and rendering
obsolete the temporary and symbolic
dispensation. Calvin accurately defines
it thus: "Non vocari orbem futurum
duntaxat, qualem e resurrectione spera-
mus, sed qui coepit ab exordio regni
Christi. Complementum vero suum habe-
bit in ultima redemptione." It is the
present number of men regenerated, death
and all that is inimical to human progress abolished; a condition in which all
things are subjected to man. The repudiation of angels as lords of the world
to come implies the admission that the
obsolescent dispensation had been subject to them. So in Deut. xxxii. 8:
ἔστησεν ὅρια ἐθνῶν κατὰ ἀριθμὸν ἀγγέλων θεοῦ, *cf*. Dan. x. 13-21 and *Book of
Jubilees*, xv. 31. *Cf*. the pages in which
Robertson Smith expands the remark
that "to be subordinated" to the angelic
dispensation is the same thing as to be
"made under the law" (*Expositor*, 1881,
p. 144 ff.). Hermas (*Vis.*, iii. 4, 1) represents the Church as being built by six
angels whom he describes as being the first
created οἷς παρέδωκεν ὁ Κύριος πᾶσαν
τὴν κτίσιν αὐτοῦ, αὔξειν καὶ οἰκοδομεῖν
καὶ δεσπόζειν τῆς κτίσεως πάσης.
Ver 6. διεμαρτύρατο δὲ πού τις λέγων:
"but some one in a certain place solemnly
testifies, saying". The indefinite formula
of quotation is used not because doubt
existed regarding the authorship of the
psalm, nor because the writer was citing

ἄνθρωπος, ὅτι μιμνήσκῃ αὐτοῦ· ἢ υἱὸς ἀνθρώπου, ὅτι ἐπισκέπτῃ
αὐτόν; 7. ἠλάττωσας αὐτὸν βραχύ τι παρ᾽ ἀγγέλους· δόξῃ καὶ
τιμῇ ἐστεφάνωσας αὐτόν, καὶ κατέστησας αὐτὸν ἐπὶ τὰ ἔργα τῶν
χειρῶν σου¹· 8. ¹πάντα ὑπέταξας ὑποκάτω τῶν ποδῶν αὐτοῦ."

Ps. viii. 6;
Matt.
xxviii. 18;
1 Cor. xv.
25, 27;
Eph. i. 22.

¹ This clause καὶ κατέστησας is omitted from B, and the sense favours the
omission.

from memory, but rather as a rhetorical
mode of suggesting that his readers
knew the passage well enough. So
Chrysostom : δεικνύντος ἐστίν, αὐτοὺς
σφόδρα ἐμπείρους εἶναι τῶν γραφῶν.
Philo frequently uses an indefinite form of
quotation : this identical form in De
Ebriet., 14 (Wendland, ii. 181) εἶπε γάρ
πού τις. Cf. Longinus, De Sub., ix. 2
γέγραφά που. Here only in the Epistle
is a quotation from Scripture referred to
its human author. τί ἐστιν ἄνθρωπος. . . . The quotation is from Ps.
viii. and extends to ποδῶν αὐτοῦ in
ver. 8. It illustrates the greatness of man
in three particulars.

1. ἠλάττωσας αὐτὸν βραχύ τι παρ᾽
ἀγγέλους.
2. δόξῃ καὶ τιμῇ ἐστεφάνωσας αὐτόν.
3. πάντα ὑπέταξας ὑποκάτω τῶν
ποδῶν αὐτοῦ.

And the author goes on to say that in
Jesus the two former elements of man's
greatness are seen to be fulfilled (He is
made a little lower than the angels, and
He is crowned with glory and honour),
while the third is guaranteed because
Jesus has tasted death for every man
and so subdued even it, the last enemy,
and therefore all things, under his feet.
In Ps. viii. as in so many other
poets and prose writers (see Pascal's
chapter on The Greatness and Littleness
of Man, A. R. Wallace's Man's Place in
the Universe and Fisk's Destiny of Man),
it is the dignity put upon man which fills
the writer with astonishment. When
Sophocles in the Antigone celebrates
man's greatness, πολλὰ τὰ δεινὰ κοὐδὲν
ἀνθρώπου δεινότερον πέλει, he excepts
death from subjection to man, Ἅιδα
μόνον φεῦξιν οὐκ ἐπάξεται. Here the
Hebrew poet excepts nothing. But
only by Christ was he justified. Man's
real place is first won by Christ. μιμνήσκῃ αὐτοῦ "Thou art mindful of him"
for good as in xiii. 3. Man, the subject
of satire and self-contempt, is the object
of God's thought. υἱὸς ἀνθρώπου
= ἄνθρωπος of the first clause. In
the Heb. אֱנוֹשׁ and בֶּן־אָדָם· ἐπισκ-

ἐπτῃ "visit," generally as a friend (Mat.
xxv. 36, James i. 27) frequently of physician visiting sick ; in judgment, Jer. v.
9, 29. "The day of visitation," ἡμέρα
ἐπισκοπῆς, in good sense, Luke xix. 44 ;
for chastisement, Isa. x. 3 ; cf. 1 Pet. ii. 12.
In Jer. xv. 15 we have the two words
μνήσθητί μου καὶ ἐπίσκεψαί με.
Ver. 7. That God has been mindful
of man and visited him is apparent in
the three particulars now mentioned.
βραχύ τι is "a little," either in material,
or in space, or in time. In 1 Sam. xiv.
29, ἐγευσάμην βραχύ τι τ. μέλιτος. In
Isa. lvii. 17, of time, δι᾽ ἁμαρτίαν βραχύ
τι ἐλύπησα αὐτον. So in N.T., of at-
erial, Jo. vi. 7 ; of space, Acts xxvii. 28 ;
of time Acts, v. 34. So in classics, v.
Bleek. The original of the psalm points
to the translation : "Thou didst make him
little lower than the angels" [in the Heb.

מֵאֱלֹהִים "than God"]. There
seems no reason to depart from this
meaning either in this verse or in ver. 9.
So Alford and Westcott, but Davidson
and Weiss and several others are of
opinion that as the words are in ver. 9
applied to the Messiah, whose superiority
has been so insisted upon, an allusion to
His inferiority would be out of place ;
"and that the phrase should be used of
degree in one place and time in another,
when the point of the passage lies in the
identity of the Son's history with that
of man, is an idea only puerile"
(Davidson). But on any rendering the
inferiority of Jesus to angels so far as
dying goes is granted, and there is no
reason why the sense of degree should
not be kept in both clauses. δόξῃ καὶ
τιμῇ frequently conjoined, Rev. xxi. 26 ;
1 Tim. i. 17; Thucyd., iv. 86; Plut.,
Num., 51 ; Lucian Somn., 13.
Ver. 8. πάντα ὑπέταξας. . . . "Thou
didst put all things under his feet." In
the psalm "all things" are defined as
"all sheep and oxen, yea and the beasts of
the field, the fowl of the air, and the
fish of the sea, and whatsoever passes
through the paths of the sea". But to
our author the scope of the "all" has

Ἐν γὰρ τῷ ὑποτάξαι αὐτῷ τὰ πάντα, οὐδὲν ἀφῆκεν αὐτῷ
ἀνυπότακτον· νῦν δὲ οὔπω ὁρῶμεν αὐτῷ τὰ πάντα ὑποτεταγ-
μένα. 9. ᵍ τὸν δὲ βραχύ τι παρ᾽ ἀγγέλους ἠλαττωμένον βλέπομεν   g Acts ii. 33;
Ἰησοῦν, διὰ τὸ πάθημα τοῦ θανάτου, δόξῃ καὶ τιμῇ ἐστεφανωμένον,   Phil. ii. 7,
                                                                   8, 9.

been enlarged by the event. His argument requires an absolutely universal
subjection, so that everything obstructive
of man's "glory" may be subdued. And
having seen this achieved by Christ, he
is emboldened to give to "all" this
fullest content. The one point he seeks
to make good is that "in subjecting all
things to him, he has left nothing, *and
therefore not the* οἰκουμένη μέλλουσα, unsubjected to him". The
"world to come" is under human dominion and administration. The angels
are left behind; there is no room for
angelic government. But this very sovereignty of man is precisely that which
we do not see visibly fulfilled: "for the
present (νῦν) we do not yet see all
things subjected to him". True, says
the author, but we do see Jesus who for
the suffering of death (or that He might
suffer death) has been made a little lower
than angels, crowned with glory and
honour that by God's grace He might
taste death for every man. In other
words, we see the first two items of man's
supremacy, as given in the psalm, fulfilled,
and the third guaranteed. Jesus was (1)
made a little lower than angels; (2) was
crowned with glory and honour; and
(3) by dying for every man has removed
that last obstacle, the fear of death
which kept men in δουλεία and hindered
them from supreme dominion over all
things. The construction of the sentence
is much debated. But it must be admitted that any construction which makes
the coronation subsequent to the tasting
death for every man, is unnatural; the
ὅπως depends upon ἐστεφανωμένον.
And the difficulty which has been felt in
giving its natural sense to this clause has
been introduced by supposing that δόξῃ
καὶ τιμῇ ἐστεφ. refers to the heavenly
state of Jesus. On this understanding it is
of course difficult to see how it could be
said that Jesus was crowned in order to
taste death. But as undoubtedly the
first clause, ἠλαττουμένον βλέπομεν,
refers to the earthly life of Jesus, it is
natural to suppose that the second clause,
which speaks of his being crowned, also
refers to that life. The tenses are the
same. But if so, what was the crowning
here referred to? It was His recognition

as Messiah, as the true Head and King
of men. He was thus recognised by
God at His baptism and at the Transfiguration [in connection with which the
same words δόξῃ κ. τιμῇ are used, 2 Pet.
i. 16-18] as well as by His disciples at
Caesarea Philippi. It was this crowning
alone which enabled Him to die a
representative death, the King or Head
for His people ; it was this which fitted
Him to taste death for *every* man. He
was made a little lower than the angels
that He might suffer death ; but He was
crowned with glory and honour that
this very death might bring all men to
the glory of supremacy which was theirs
when the fear of death was removed ;
see v. 14, 15. For a fuller exposition of
this view of the verse, see *Expository
Times*, April, 1896. χάριτι θεοῦ, "by
God's grace," to men, not directly to
Jesus. It is remarkable that Weiss, an
expert in textual criticism, should adopt
the reading χωρὶς θεοῦ "apart from God"
finding in these words a reference to the
cry on the cross "My God, My God, etc.".
The other meaning put upon the words,
"except God," needs no comment. The
Nestorians used the reading to prove
that Christ suffered apart from His
Divinity ("divinitate tantisper deposita
οὐ συνὴν ἡ θεότης") but such a meaning
can hardly be found in the words.
ὑπὲρ παντός, these are the emphatic
words, bringing out the writer's point
that Christ's victory and supremacy were
not for Himself alone, but for men.
[Chrysostom strikingly says : οὐχὶ τῶν
πιστῶν μόνον, ἀλλὰ καὶ τῆς οἰκουμένης
ἁπάσης· αὐτὸς μὲν γὰρ ὑπὲρ πάντων
ἀπέθανεν· τί δὲ, εἰ μὴ πάντες ἐπίστευ-
σαν; αὐτὸς τὸ ἑαυτοῦ πεπλήρωκε.]
γεύσηται θανάτου "he might taste
death," *i.e.*, actually experience death's
bitterness. The Greek commentators
suppose the word is chosen to bring out
the shortness of our Lord's experience
of death, μικρὸν ἐν αὐτῷ ποιήσας
διάστημα. This seems incorrect. [The
rule, sometimes laid down,, that γεύεσθαι
followed by an accusative means to
partake freely, and by a genitive sparingly, cannot be universally applied. The
ordinary distinction observed in the use
of verbs of sense that they take the

h v. 9. et xii.
2; Luc.
xxiv. 26,
46; Acts
iii. 15, et
v. 31; Rom. ii. 36; Phil. ii. 8, 9.
ὅπως χάριτι Θεοῦ ὑπέρ¹ παντὸς γεύσηται θανάτου.²　10.　h ᾽Έπρεπε
γὰρ αὐτῷ, δι᾽ ὃν τὰ πάντα καὶ δι᾽ οὗ τὰ πάντα, πολλοὺς υἱοὺς εἰς

¹ T.R. is read in almost all the MSS. and versions and adopted by all editors.
But χωρὶς Θεου is found in M, 67**, Origen.

² "Hic versus multas difficultates interpretationi affert. Fortasse v. 9b (οπως . . .
θανατου) corruptus vel interpolatus est" (Baljon).

accusative of the nearer, the genitive of the remoter source of the sensation is much safer.] The expression γεύεσθαι θανάτου does not occur in the classics, although we find γευ. μόχθον in Soph., *Trachin.*, 1103, where the Scholiast renders by ἐπειράθην, in *Antig.*, 1005, where Jebb renders "proceeded to make trial of," in Eurip., *Hecuba*, 375, with κακῶν and in Plato, *Rep.*, 475 with πάντος μαθήματος.

Vv. 10-18. The humiliation of tbe Son justified; "a condensed and pregnant view of the theory of the whole work of Christ, which subsequent chapters develop, elucidate, and justify dialectically, in contrast or comparison with the O.T. . . . The ultimate source of all doubt whether the new dispensation is superior to the old is nothing else than want of clear insight into the work of Christ, and especially into the significance of His passion, which, to the Jews, from whom the Hebrew Christians of our Epistle were drawn, was the chief stumbling-block in Christianity. Here, therefore, the writer has at length got into the heart of his subject, and, leaving the contrast between Christ and the angels, urges the positive doctrine of the identification of Jesus with those that are his—his brethren, the Sons of God whom He sanctifies—as the best key to that connection between the passion and glorification of Chr st which forms the cardinal point of N.T. revelation" (Robertson Smith). To this it may only be added that in order to prove man's supremacy and justify Psalm viii., it was essential that the writer should show that Christ was man, identified with humanity.

In justification then (justification introduced by γὰρ) of the subjection of Jesus to the πάθημα θανάτου, the writer proceeds to say ἔπρεπεν αὐτῷ "it befitted Him". The expression, says Carpzov, is "frequentissima Philoni phrasis"; but in Scripture, at least in this sense, it stands alone: *cf.* Jer. x. 7; Ps. lxv. 1. Aristotle (*Nic. Eth.*, iv. 2-2 : Burnet, p. 173) says that what is befitting is rela-

tive to the person, the circumstances and the object [τὸ πρέπον δὴ πρὸς αὐτὸν, καὶ ἐν ᾧ καὶ περὶ ὅ]. The object here in view, the "bringing many sons to glory," needs no justification. As Tertullian (*adv. Marcion*, ii. 27) says : "nihil tam dignum Deo, quam salus hominis". But that the means used by God to accomplish this end was not only fit to bring it about but was also πρέπον θεῷ, in other words, that Christ's humiliation and death were in accordance with the Divine nature, is the point the writer wishes to make good. "The whole course of nature and grace must find its explanation in God, and not merely in an abstract Divine *arbitrium*, but in that which befits the Divine nature". This matter of Christ's suffering has not been isolated in God's government but is of a piece with all He is and has done; it has not been handed over to chance, accident, or malevolent powers, but is part of the Divine rule and providence; it is not exceptional, unaccountable, arbitrary, but has its root and origin in the very nature of God. God acted freely in the matter, governed only by His own nature. "Man has not wholly lost the intuitive power by which the fitness of the Divine action, its correspondence to the idea standard of right which his conscience certifies and his reason approves, may be recognised" (Henson, *Disc. and Law*, p. 56). "It is worth noting that the chief value of Anselm's view of the Atonement lies in the introduction into theology of the idea of what befits God— the idea, as he puts it, of God's honour. Anselm fails, however, by thinking rather of what God's honour must receive as its due than of what it is seemly for God in His grace to do, and thus his theory becomes shallow and inadequate" (Robertson Smith). The writer does not say ἔπρεπεν θεῷ but ἔπρεπεν αὐτῷ δι᾽ ὃν τὰ πάντα καὶ δι᾽ οὗ τὰ πάντα "Him on account of whom are all things and through whom are all things," who is the reason and the cause of all existence; in whom, there-

δόξαν ἀγαγόντα, τὸν ἀρχηγὸν τῆς σωτηρίας αὐτῶν διὰ παθημάτων i x. 10, 14;
τελειῶσαι. 11. ¹ὅ τε γὰρ ἁγιάζων καὶ οἱ ἁγιαζόμενοι, ἐξ ἑνὸς πάν- 26.

Acts xvii.

fore, everything must find its reason and justification. " Denn wenn um seinetwillen das All ist, also Alles seinen Zwecken dienen muss, und durch ihn das All ist, also nichts ohne sein Zuthun zu Stande kommt, so muss man bei Allem, was geschieht, und somit auch bei dem Todesleiden fragen, wiefern es ihm angemessen ist" (Weiss). The purpose of God is expressed in the words: πολλοὺς υἱοὺς εἰς δόξαν ἀγαγόντα "in bringing many sons to glory". The accusative ἀγαγ. (although referring to αὐτῷ) does not require us to construe it with ἀρχηγόν. That is a possible but clumsy construction. The use of υἱοὺς implies that the Father is the subject and leads us to expect that the action of God will be mentioned. And this construction, in which the dative of the subject becomes an accusative when an infinitive follows, is not unknown, but is merely a species of attraction—the infinitive drawing the noun into the case appropriate. Cf. Acts xi. 12, xv. 22 ; Luke i. 74. Examples from the classics in Matthiae, 535. The aorist participle has led the Vulgate to translate " qui multos filios in gloriam adduxerat," needlessly, for "the aorist participle is sometimes used adverbially in reference to an action evidently in a general way coincident in time with the action of the verb, yet not identical with it. The choice of the aorist participle rather than the present in such cases is due to the fact that the action is thought of, not as in progress, but as a simple event or fact (Burton, M. and T., 149). πολλοὺς υἱοὺς "many" is not used with any reference to the population of the world, or to the proportion of the saved, but to the one Son already celebrated. It was God's purpose not only to have one Son in glory, but to bring many to be partakers with Him. Hence the difficulty ; hence the need of the suffering of Christ. But it is not merely πολλοὺς but πολλοὺς υἱοὺς suggesting the relationship dwelt upon in the succeeding verses. τὸν ἀρχηγὸν τ. σωτηρίας . . . the author [pioneer] of their salvation indicating that feature of Christ's relation to the saved which determined His experience, " the Captain of their salvation ". R.V. has " author " following Vulg. Chrysostom has ἀρχηγὸν τουτέστι τὸν αἴτιον, and so Robertson

Smith, " it is hardly necessary to put more meaning into the phrase than is contained in the parallel expression of v. 9". So Bleek, Kübel and von Soden. But the word is select, and why select, if not to bring out precisely this, that in the present case the cause is also the leader, " that the Son goes before the saved in the same path ". He is the strong swimmer who carries the rope ashore and so not only secures His own position but makes rescue for all who will follow. " The ἀρχηγός himself first takes part in that which he establishes" (Westcott). One of the chief points in the Epistle is that the Saviour is also ἀρχηγός. The word is commonly used of founders of tribes, rulers and commanders, persons who begin anything in become the source of anything, but or this Epistle (xii. 2) it has over and above the sense of " pioneer ". διὰ παθημάτων τελειῶσαι, "to perfect through sufferings". τελειῶσαι is to make τέλειον, to bring a person or thing to the appropriate τέλος, to complete, perfect, consummate. In the Pentateuch it is regularly used to denote the consecration of the priests. In the N.T. this consecration is no formal setting apart to office, but a preparation involving ethical fitness. So that here the word directly denotes making perfect as leader of salvation, but indirectly and by implication making morally perfect. And this moral perfection, requisite in one who was to cleanse sinners (note σωτηρίας) and lead the way to glory, could only be proved and acquired through the sufferings involved in living as man, tempted and with death to face. Therefore διὰ παθημάτων, " a plurality of sufferings " not merely as in ver. 9 τὸ πάθημα τοῦ θανάτου. Cf. ver. 18. The glory indeed to which this captain of salvation leads is the glory of triumph over temptation and all that tends to terrify and enslave men.

Ver. 11. In the eleventh verse the writer proceeds to explain wherein consisted the fittingness (τὸ πρέπον) of perfecting the ἀρχηγόν through sufferings. It lies in the fact that He and those He leads are brothers. In vv. 11-13 it is shown that this is so, and in the succeeding verses the writer points out what is involved in this brotherhood. ὁ ἁγιάζων and οἱ ἁγιαζόμενοι are to be

k Ps. xxii. τες· δι' ἥν αἰτίαν οὐκ ἐπαισχύνεται ἀδελφοὺς αὐτοὺς καλεῖν, 12.
22, 25; 2
Sam.xxii. k λέγων, "'Απαγγελῶ τὸ ὄνομά σου τοῖς ἀδελφοῖς μου, ἐν μέσῳ ἐκ-
3; Ps.
xviii. 2. κλησίας ὑμνήσω σε". Καὶ πάλιν, "'Εγὼ ἔσομαι πεποιθὼς ἐπ'

taken as present participles, so usually are, in the timeless substantlve sense. ἁγιάζειν means (1) to set apart as belonging to God, in contradistinction to κοινός, belonging to every one. So in Gen. ii. 3, of the seventh day, and in Exodus of the mountain, the tent, the altar. It is especially used of persons set apart to the priesthood or to any special work (Exod. xxx. 30; Jer. i. 5; John x. 36). Through the O.T. ceremonial the whole people were thus ἡγιασμένοι, set apart to God, admitted to His worship. In this Epistle the word is used with much of the O.T. idea cleaving to it, and is often rather equivalent to what we understand by "justify" than to "sanctify". Cf. x. 10. It signifies that which enables men to approach God. But (2) it is in N.T. more and more felt that it is only by purification of character men can be set apart for God, so that this higher meaning also attaches to the word. In the present verse ἁγιάζων introduces the priestly idea, enlarged upon in ver. 17. ἐξ ἑνὸς πάντες "all of one". There is much to be said for Calvin's interpretation "of one nature," or Cappellus' "of one common mass". Certainly Bleek's reason for rejecting such renderings—that ἐξ can only signify origin, is incorrect. "Greek often uses the prepositions of origin (ἐκ, ἀπό) when we prefer those of position or direction, as in ἐξ ἀπροσδοκήτου, on a sudden, ἐξ ἀφανοῦς, in a doubt, ἐκ μιᾶς χειρός, with one hand" (Verrall on Choeph., line 70). In N.T. ἐκ frequently expresses the party or class to which one belongs (Jo. iii. 31). And cf. 1 Cor. x. 17. It might be urged from xi. 12 that this writer had he meant parentage would have said ἀφ' ἑνός. Nevertheless the meaning seems to be "of one father". The πολλοὺς υἱοὺς of ver. 10, and the δι' ἥν αἰτίαν which follows make for this sense. And the argument of ver. 14, that because Christ was brother to men He therefore took flesh, proves that ἐξ ἑνὸς cannot mean "of one nature'. The fact that He and they are ἐξ ἑνὸς is the ground of His incarnation. He was Son and Brother before appearing on earth. The words then can only mean that the "many sons" who are to be brought to glory and the "Son" who leads them are of one parentage. The sonship in both

cases looks to the same Father, and depends on Him and is subject to the same laws of obedience and development. But what Father is meant? Not Adam (Beza, Hofmann, etc.); Weiss argues strongly for Abraham, appealing to ver. 16 and other considerations; but the fact that in ver. 14 the incarnation is treated as a result of the brotherhood, seems to involve that we must understand that God is meant; that before the incarnation Christ recognised His brotherhood. "On this account," because His parentage is the same, "He is not ashamed to call them brothers". He might have been expected to shrink from those who had so belied their high origin, or at the best to move among them with the kindly superior professionalism of a surgeon who enters the ward of an hospital solely to heal, not to live there; but He claims men as his kin and on this bases His action (cf. xi. 16).

Ver. 12. In proof that He is not ashamed to take his place among men as a brother three passages are adduced from the O.T. in which this relationship is implied. These passages are so confidently assumed to be Messianic that they are quoted as spoken by Christ Himself, λέγων. The fact that words of Jesus spoken while He lived on earth are not quoted can scarcely be accepted as proof that the Gospels were not in existence when this Epistle was written, for even after the middle of the second century, the O.T. was still the "Scripture" of the Christian Church. The first quotation is from the twenty-second Psalm applied to Himself by our Lord on the cross. The LXX διηγήσομαι is altered to ἀπαγγελῶ. The significant words in the first clause are τοῖς ἀδελφοῖς μου; and the significance of the second clause consists in the representation of the Messiah as taking part in the worship of God in the congregation. This is one particular form in which His brotherhood manifests itself. For the passages cited not merely affirm the brotherhood, but also exhibit its reality in the participation by the Messiah of human conditions.

Ver. 13. The two quotations cited in the thirteenth verse are from Isa. viii. 17, 18. There they are continuous, here they are separately introduced, each by the

αὐτῷ". 13. ¹Καὶ πάλιν, "Ἰδοὺ ἐγὼ καὶ τὰ παιδία ἅ μοι ἔδωκεν **| Esa. viii.**
ὁ Θεός". 14. ᵐἘπεὶ οὖν τὰ παιδία κεκοινώνηκε σαρκὸς καὶ
αἵματος,¹ καὶ αὐτὸς παραπλησίως μετέσχε τῶν αὐτῶν, ἵνα διὰ
τοῦ θανάτου καταργήσῃ τὸν τὸ κράτος ἔχοντα τοῦ θανάτου, τουτ-

| 18; Joan.
x. 29, et
xvii. 6, 9,
11, 12.
m Esa. xxv.
8; Ose.
xiii. 14;
Joan. i.

14; 1 Cor. xv. 54, 55; Phil. ii. 7; 2 Tim. i. 10.

¹ T.R. in KL, f, vgᶜˡᵉ; αιματ. κ. σαρκος in ℵBCDEMP, 17, 37, 47, 137.

usual καὶ πάλιν, because they serve to bring out two distinct points. In the first, the Messiah utters his trust in God, and thereby illustrates His sonship and brotherhood with man. Like all men He is dependent on God. As Calvin says: "since He depends on the aid of God His condition has community with ours". In the second part, ἰδοὺ ἐγὼ not only calls attention to Himself as closely associated with the παιδία; but also, as Weiss thinks, intimates His readiness to obey, as if "Here am I". This obedience He shares with those whom God has committed to His care, God's παιδία and His brothers. Cf. Jo. vi. 37, 39, xvii. 11.

Vv. 14-16. This saving brotherhood involved incarnation and death. For, as it has ever been the common lot of the παιδία to live under the conditions imposed by flesh and blood, subject to inevitable dissolution and the shrinkings and weaknesses consequent, He also, this Son of God, Himself (καὶ αὐτὸς) shared with them in their identical nature, thus making Himself liable to death; His intention being that by dying He might render harmless him that used death as a terror, and thus deliver from slavery those who had suffered death to rule their life and lived in perpetual dread. κεκοινώνηκεν . . . μετέσχεν perf. and aor.; the one pointing to the common lot which the παιδία have always shared, αἵματος καὶ σαρκός, usually (but not always, Eph. vi. 12) inverted and denoting human nature in its weakness and liability to decay (Gal. i. 16, etc., and especially 1 Cor. xv. 50); the other, expressing the one act of Christ by which He became a sharer with men in this weak condition. He partook, but does not now partake. [Wetstein quotes from Polyaenus that Chabrias enjoined upon his soldiers when about to engage in battle to think of the enemy as ἀνθρώποις αἷμα καὶ σάρκα ἔχουσιν καὶ τῆς αὐτῆς φύσεως ἡμῖν κεκοινωνηκόσι.] This human nature Christ assumed παραπλησίως, which

Chrysostom interprets, οὐ φαντασίᾳ οὐδὲ εἰκόνι ἀλλ' ἀληθείᾳ. It means not merely "in like manner," but "in absolutely the same manner"; as in Arrian vii. 1, 9, σὺ δὲ ἄνθρωπος ὤν, παραπλήσιος τοῖς ἄλλοις, Herod. iii. 104, σχεδὸν παραπλησίως "almost identical"; see also Diod. Sic., v. 45. τῶν αὐτῶν, i.e., blood and flesh. The purpose of the incarnation is expressed in the words ἵνα διὰ τοῦ θανάτου . . . ἦσαν δουλίας. He took flesh that He might die, and so destroy not death but him that had the power of death, and deliver, etc. The double object may be considered as one, the defeat of the devil involving the deliverance of those in bondage. The means He used to accomplish this object was His dying (διὰ τ. θανάτου). How the death of Christ had the result here ascribed to it, we are left to conjecture; for nowhere else in the Epistle is the deliverance of man by Christ's death stated in analogous terms. We must first endeavour to understand the terms here employed. καταργήσῃ: "might render inoperative" (ἄεργον), "bring to nought". Sometimes "destroy" or "put an end to" as in 1 Cor. xv. 26 ἔσχατος ἐχθρὸς καταργεῖται ὁ θάνατος. τὸν τὸ κράτος ἔχοντα τοῦ θανάτου, "him who has the power of death, that is, the devil," τὸν διάβολον (διαβάλλω, I set asunder, put at variance) used by LXX to render שָׂטָן in Job i. ii. and Zach. iii., etc.; Σατάν is used in 1 Kings xi. In N.T. both designations occur frequently. But the significance for our present passage lies in the description "him who has the power of death". ἔχειν τὸ κράτος is classical, and κράτος with the genitive denotes the realm within which or over which the rule is exercised, as Herod., iii. 142, τῆς Σάμου τ. κράτος. In connection with this universal human experience of death he uses his malign influence, and the striking vision of Zech. iii. shows us how he does

n Luc. i. 74: ἔστι, τὸν διάβολον, 15. " καὶ ἀπαλλάξῃ τούτους, ὅσοι φόβῳ θανάτου
Rom. viii.
15. διὰ παντὸς τοῦ ζῆν ἔνοχοι ἦσαν δουλείας.[1] 16. οὐ γὰρ δήπου ἀγ-

¹ δουλιας in אD*E*HP; δουλειας in ABCDb, etc., E**KLM.

so. He brings sins to remembrance, he
appears as the accuser of the brethren, as
the counsel for the prosecution. Thus
he creates a fear of death, a fear which
is one of the most marked features of
O.T. experience. Both Schoettgen and
Weber produce rabbinical sayings which
illustrate the power of a legal religion to
produce servility and fear, so that the
natural expression of the Jew was, "In
this life death will not suffer a man to be
glad". Life, in short, with sin unac-
counted for, and with death viewed as
the punishment of sin to look forward to,
is a δουλεία unworthy of God's sons.
This indeed is expressly stated in ver. 15.
The δουλεία which contradicts the idea of
sonship and prevents men from entering
upon their destiny of dominion over all
things is occasioned by their fear of
death (φόβῳ, the dative of cause) as that
which implies rejection by God. [Among
the races whose conscience was not educated by the law, views of death varied
greatly. These will be found in Geddes'
Phaedo, pp. 217, 223 ; and *cf.* the opening paragraphs of the third Book of the
Republic, as well as pp. 330 and 486 B.
Aristotle with his usual straightforward
frankness pronounces death φοβερώτατον.
On the other hand, many believed
τεθνάμεναι βέλτιον ἢ βίοτος ; Hegesias
was styled ὁ πεισιθάνατος, and by his
persuasions and otherwise suicide became
popular ; and death was no longer
reckoned an everlasting ill, but " portum
potius paratum nobis et perfugium ".
Wholly applicable to the present passage
is Spinoza's " homo *liber* de nihilo minus
quam de morte cogitat". *Cf.* Philo,
Omn. sap. liber, who quotes Eurip.,
τίς ἐστι δοῦλος τοῦ θανεῖν ἄφροντις
ὤν ;] This then was the bondage which
characterised the life (διὰ παντὸς τοῦ ζῆν)
of those under the old dispensation ; the
bondage in which they were held (ἔνοχοι
=ἐνεχόμενοι, "held" or "bound," "subject to." see Thayer, s.v.), and from
which Christ delivered τούτους ὅσοι, not
as if it were a restricted number who
were delivered, but on the contrary to
mark that the deliverance was coexten-
sive with the bondage. ἀπαλλάξῃ, used
especially of freeing from slavery [exx.
from Philo in Carpzov, and *cf.* Isocrates
οὗτος ἀπήλλαξεν αὐτοὺς τοῦ δέους

τούτου. In the *Phaedo* frequently of
soul emancipated from the body.] How
the Son wrought this deliverance διὰ
τοῦ θανάτου can now be answered ; and
it cannot be better answered than in the
words of Robertson Smith : "To break
this sway, Jesus takes upon Himself that
mortal flesh and blood to whose infirmities the fear of death under the O.T.
attaches. But while He passes through
all the weakness of fleshly life, and,.
finally, through death itself, He, unlike
all others, proves Himself not only
exempt from the fear of death, but
victorious over the accuser. To Him,
who in His sinlessness experienced every
weakness of mortality, without diminution of his unbroken strength of fellowship with God, death is not the dreaded
sign of separation from God's grace (*cf.*
ver. 7), but a step in his divinely appointed
career ; not something inflicted on Him
against His will, but a means whereby
(διὰ with genitive) He consciously and
designedly accomplishes His vocation as
Saviour. For this victory of Jesus over
the devil, or, which is the same thing,
the fear of death, must be taken, like
every other part of His work, in connection with the idea of His vocation as
Head and Leader of His people." In
short, we see now what is meant by
His tasting death "*for every man*," and
how this death guarantees the perfect
dominion and glory depicted in Psalm
viii. All the humiliation and death
are justified by the necessities of the
case, he concludes, "For, as I need
scarcely say, it is not angels (presumably
sinless and spiritual beings, πνεύματα,
i. 14) He is taking in hand, but He is
taking in hand Abraham's seed (the
dying children of a dead father ; 'also
dergleichen sterbliche und durch Todes-
furcht in Knechtschaft befangene Wesen,'
Bleek). δήπου : frequently in classics,
as Plato, *Protagoras*, 309 C. οὐ γὰρ
δήπου ἐνέτυχες, "for I may take it for
granted you have not met" (*Apol.*, 21 B).
τί ποτε λέγει ὁ θεός . . . φάσκων ἐμὲ
σοφώτατον εἶναι ; οὐ γὰρ δήπου ψεύδεταί
γε, "for, at any rate, as need hardly be
said, he is not saying what is untrue".
ἐπιλαμβάνεται : "lays hold to help" or
simply " succours," with the idea of taking a person up to see him through. *Cf.*

γέλων ἐπιλαμβάνεται, ἀλλὰ σπέρματος Ἀβραὰμ ἐπιλαμβάνεται.　17.

ºὅθεν ὤφειλε κατὰ πάντα τοῖς ἀδελφοῖς ὁμοιωθῆναι, ἵνα ἐλεήμων o iv. 15, et

v. 2 ; Phil.

γένηται καὶ πιστὸς ἀρχιερεὺς τὰ πρὸς τὸν Θεόν, εἰς τὸ ἱλάσκεσθαι　ii. 7.

Sir.,iv. 11. ἡ σοφία . . . ἐπιλαμβάνεται τῶν ζητούντων αὐτήν, and the Scholiast on Aesch., *Pers.*, 742, ὅταν σπεύδῃ τις εἰς καλὰ ἢ εἰς κακά, ὁ θεὸς αὐτοῦ ἐπιλαμβάνεται. Castellio was the first to propose the meaning "help" in place of "assume the nature of," and Beza having urged the latter rendering as being that of the Greek fathers, goes on to say, "quo magis est execranda Castellionis audacia qui ἐπιλαμ. convertit *opitulatur*,' non modo falsa, sed etiam inepta interpretatione, etc.". It has been suggested that θάνατος might be the nominative which would give quite a good sense, but as Christ is the subject both of the foregoing and of the succeeding clause it is more likely that this affirmation also is made of Him. It is certainly remarkable that instead of saying "He lays hold of man to help him," the writer should give the restricted σπέρματος Ἀβ. Von Soden, who supposes the Epistle is addressed to Gentiles, thinks the writer intends to prepare the way for his introducing the priesthood of Christ, and to exhibit the claim of Christians to the fulfilment of the prophecies made to Abraham (*cf.* Robertson Smith), but this Weiss brands as "eine leere Ausflucht". Perhaps we cannot get further than Estius (cited by Bleek): "gentium vocationem tota hac epistola prudenter dissimulat, sive quod illius mentio Hebraeis parum grata esset, sive quod instituto suo non necessaria". Or, as Bleek says, "es erklärt sich aus dem Zwecke des Briefes".

Ver. 17. ὅθεν [six times in this Epistle; not used by Paul, but *cf.* Acts xxvi. 19] 'wherefore," because He makes the seed of Abraham the object of His saving work, ὤφειλεν, "He was under obligation". ὀφείλω is "used of a necessity imposed either by law and duty, or by reason, or by the times, or by the nature of the matter under consideration" (Thayer). Here it was the nature of the case which imposed the obligation κατὰ πάντα τοῖς ἀδελφοῖς ὁμοιωθῆναι "to be made like His brothers in all respects," and therefore, as Chrysostom says, ἐτέχθη, ἐτράφη, ηὐξήθη, ἔπαθε πάντα ἄπερ ἐχρῆν, τέλος ἀπέθανεν. He must be a real man, and not merely have the appearance of one. He must enter into

the necessary human experiences, look at things from the human point of view, take His place in the crowd amidst the ordinary elements of life. ἵνα introduces one purpose which this thorough incarnation was to serve. It would put Christ in a position to sympathise with the tempted and thus incline Him to make propitiation for the sins of the people. [τοῦ λαοῦ, also a restricted Jewish designation.] The High-Priesthood is here first mentioned, and it is mentioned as an office with which the readers were familiar. The writer does not now enlarge upon the office or work of the Priest, but merely points to one radical necessity imposed by priesthood, "making propitiation for the sins of the people"; and he affirms that in order to do this (εἰς τὸ) he must be merciful and faithful. ἐλεήμων as well as πιστὸς is naturally construed with ἀρχιερεύς, and has its root in Exod. xxii. 27, ἐλεήμων γάρ εἰμι, the priest must represent the Divine mercy; he must also be πιστὸς, primarily to God, as in iii. 2, but thereby faithful to men and to be trusted by them in the region in which he exercises his function, τὰ πρὸς τὸν θεόν, the whole Godward relations of men. The expression is directly connected with ἀρχιερεύς, by implication with πιστὸς, and it is found in Exod. xviii. 19, γίνου σὺ τῷ λαῷ τὰ πρὸς τὸν θεόν. For neat analogies *cf.* Wetstein. εἰς τὸ ἱλάσκεσθαι, "for the purpose of making propitiatio ,'' εἰς indicating the special purpose to be served by Christ's becoming Priest. ἱλάσκομαι (ἱλόσκω is not met with), from ἵλαος, Attic ἵλεως "propitious," "merciful," means "I render propitious to myself". In the classics it is followed by the accusative of the person propitiated, sometimes of the anger felt. In the LXX it occurs twelve times, thrice as the translation of כָּפֶר. The only instance in which it is followed by an accusative of the sin, as here, is Ps. lxiv. (lxv.) 3, τὰς ἀσεβείας ἡμῶν σὺ ἱλάσῃ. In the N.T., besides the present passage, it only occurs in Luke xviii. 13, in the passive form ἱλάσθητί μοι τῷ ἁμαρτωλῷ, *cf.* 2 Kings v. 18. The compound form ἐξιλάσκομαι, although it does not occur in N.T., is more frequently used in the LXX than the simple

p iv. 15, 16.
a iv. 14, et
vi. 20, et
viii. 1, et
ix. 11;
Rom. xv.
8; Phil.
iii. 14.

τὰς ἁμαρτίας τοῦ λαοῦ.　18. ᴾἐν ᾧ γὰρ πέπονθεν αὐτὸς πειρασθείς, δύναται τοῖς πειραζομένοις βοηθῆσαι.

III. 1. ᵃὍΘΕΝ, ἀδελφοὶ ἅγιοι, κλήσεως ἐπουρανίου μέτοχοι,
κατανοήσατε τὸν ἀπόστολον καὶ ἀρχιερέα τῆς ὁμολογίας ἡμῶν Χρισ-

verb, and from its construction something may be learnt. As in profane
Greek, it is followed by an accusative of
the person propitiated, as in Gen. xxxii.
20, where Jacob says of Esau ἐξιλάσομαι
τὸ πρόσωπον αὐτοῦ ἐν τοῖς δώροις
κ.τ.λ.; Zech. vii. 2, ἐξιλάσασθαι τὸν
Κύριον, and viii. 22, τὸ πρόσωπον
Κυρίου, also Matt. i. 9. It is however
also followed by an accusative of the
thing on account of which propitiation
is needed or which requires by some rite
or process to be rendered acceptable to
God, as in Ecclus. iii. 3, iii. 30, v. 6, xx.
28, etc., where it is followed by ἀδικίαν,
and ἁμαρτίας; and in Lev. xvi. 16, 20,
33, where it is followed by τὸ ἅγιον,
τὸ θυσιαστήριον, and in Ezek. xlv. 20
by τὸν οἶκον. At least thirty-two times
in Leviticus alone it is followed by περί,
defining the persons for whom propitiation is made, περὶ αὐτοῦ ἐξιλάσεται ὁ
ἱερεύς or περὶ πάσης συναγωγῆς, or περὶ
τῆς ἁμαρτίας ὑμῶν. In this usage there
is apparent a transition from the idea of
propitiating God (which still survives in
the passive ἱλάσθητι) to the idea of
exerting some influence on that which
was offensive to God and which must be
removed or cleansed in order to complete entrance into His favour. In the
present passage it is τὰς ἁμαρτίας τοῦ
λαοῦ which stand in the way of the full
expression of God's favour, and upon
those therefore the propitiatory influence
of Christ is to be exerted. In what
manner precisely this is to be accomplished is not yet said. "The present
infinitive ἱλάσκεσθαι must be noticed.
The one (eternal) act of Christ (c. x. 12
—14) is here regarded in its continuous
present application to men (cf. c. v. 1, 2),"
Westcott. (See further on ἱλάσκεσθαι
in Blass, *Gram.*, p. 88; Deissmann's *Neue
Bibelstud.*, p. 52; and Westcott's *Epistle
of St. John*, pp. 83-85.) τοῦ λαοῦ the
historical people of God, Abraham's
seed; cf. Matt. i. 21; Heb. iv. 9, xiii. 12.
Ver. 18. ἐν ᾧ γὰρ πέπονθεν. . . . He
concludes this part of his argument by
explaining the process by which Christ's
becoming man has answered the purpose of making Him a merciful and
faithful High Priest. The explanation
is "non ignara mali miseris succurrere

disco". ἐν ᾧ is by some interpreters
resolved into ἐν τούτῳ ὅτι = whereas; by
others into ἐν τούτῳ ὅ = wherein; the second construction has certainly the ampler
warrant, see 1 Pet. ii. 12; Gal. i. 8; Rom.
xiv. 22; but the former gives the better
sense. It is also contested whether the
words mean, that Christ suffered by
being tempted, or that He was tempted
by His sufferings. Both statements of
course are true; but it is not easy to
determine which is here intended. Are
the temptations the cause of the sufferings, or the sufferings the cause of the
temptations? The A.V. and the R.V.,
also Westcott and others, prefer the
former; and from the relation of the
participial πειρασθείς to the main verb
πέπονθεν, which naturally indicates the
suffering as the result of the temptation,
this would seem to be the correct interpretation. Bleek, Delitzsch, Alford
and Davidson, however, prefer the other
sense, Alford translating: "For He
Himself, having been tempted, in that
which He hath suffered, He is able to
succour them that are (now) tempted".
Davidson says: "These sufferings at
every point crossed the innocent human
instinct to evade them; but being laid
on Him by the will of God and in pur-
suance of His high vocation, they thus
became temptations". Dr. Bruce says:
"Christ, having experienced temptation
to be unfaithful to His vocation in connection with the sufferings arising out
of it, is able to succour those who, like
the Hebrew Christians, were tempted
in similar ways to be unfaithful to their
Christian calling". The interpretation
has much to recommend it, but as it
limits the temptations of Christ to those
which arose out of His sufferings, it
seems scarcely to fall in so thoroughly
with the course of thought, especially
with v. 17. δύναται, cf. iv. 15, v. 2.
CHAPTER III. 1.-CHAPTER IV. 13.—
Chapters iii. and iv. as far as ver. 13, form
one paragraph. The purpose of the writer
in this passage, as in the whole Epistle, is
to encourage his readers in their allegiance
to Christ and to save them from apostasy
by exhibiting Christ as the final mediator.
This purpose he has in the first two
chapters sought to achieve by compar-

ing Christ with those who previously mediated between God and man,—the prophets who spoke to the fathers, and the angels who mediated the law and were supposed even to regulate nature. He now proceeds to compare Jesus with him round whose name gathered all that revelation and legislation in which the Jew trusted. Moses was the ideal mediator, faithful in *all* God's house. Underlying even the priesthood of Aaron was the word of God to Moses. And yet, free channel of God's will as Moses had been, he was but a servant and in the nature of things could not so perfectly sympathise with and interpret the will of Him whose house and affairs he administered as the Son who Himself was lord of the house.

He therefore bids his readers encourage themselves by the consideration of His trustworthiness, His competence to accomplish all God's will with them and bring them to their appointed rest. But this suggests to him the memorable breakdown of faith in the wilderness generation of Israelites. And he forthwith strengthens his admonition to trust Christ by adding the warning which was so legibly written in the fate of those who left Egypt under the leadership of Moses, but whose faith failed through the greatness of the way. It was not owing to any incompetence or faithlessness in Moses that they died in the wilderness and failed to reach the promised land. It was "because of their unbelief" (iii. 19). Moses was faithful in all God's house, in everything required for the guidance and government of God's people and for the fulfilment of all God's purpose with them : but even with the most trustworthy leader much depends on the follower, and entrance to the fulness of God's blessing may be barred by the unbelief of those who have heard the promise. The promise was not mixed with faith in them to whom it came. But what of those who were led in by Joshua ? Even they did not enter into God's rest. That is certain, for long after Joshua's time God renewed His promise, saying "To-day if ye hear His voice, harden not your hearts". Entrance into the land, then, did not exhaust the promise of God ; there remains over and above that entrance, a rest for the people of God, for "without us," *i.e.*, without the revelation of Christ the fathers were not perfect, their best blessings, such as their land, being but types of better things to come. Therefore let us give diligence to enter

into that rest, for the word of God's promise is searching ; and, by offering us the best things in fellowship with God, it discloses our real disposition and affinities.

The passage falls into two parts, the former (iii. 1-6) exhibiting the trustworthiness of Christ, the latter (iii. 7-iv. 13) emphasising the unbelief and doom of the wilderness generation.

Ver. 1. Ὅθεν, "wherefore," if through Jesus God has spoken His final and saving word (i. 1), thus becoming the Apostle of God, and if the high priest I speak of is so sympathetic and faithful that for the sake of cleansing the people He became man and suffered, then "consider, etc.". The πιστός of ver. 17 strikes the keynote of this paragraph. Here for the first time the writer designates his readers, and he does so in a form peculiar to himself (the reading in 1 Thess. v. 27 being doubtful) ἀδελφοὶ ἅγιοι, "Christian brethren," literally "brethren consecrated," separated from the world and dedicated to God. Bleek quotes from Primasius : "Fratres eos vocat tam carne quam spiritu qui ex eodem genere erant". But there is no reason to assign to ἀδελφοὶ any other meaning than its usual N.T. sense of "fellow-Christians," *cf.* Matt. xxiii. 8. But there is further significance in the additional κλήσεως ἐπουρανίου μέτοχοι, "partakers of a heavenly calling" (*cf.* οἱ κεκλημένοι τῆς αἰωνίου κληρονομίας, ix. 15) suggested by the latent comparison in the writer's mind between the Israelites called to earthly advantages, a land, etc., and his readers whose hopes were fixed on things above. "In the word 'heavenly' there is struck for the first time, in words at least, an antithesis of great importance in the Epistle, that of this world and heaven, in other words, that of the merely material and transient, and the ideal and abiding. The things of the world are material, unreal, transient : those of heaven are ideal, true, eternal. Heaven is the world of realities, of things themselves (ix. 23) of which the things here are but 'copies'" (Davidson). κατανοήσατε, "consider," "bring your mind to bear upon," "observe so as to see the significance," as in Luke xii. 24, κατανοήσατε τοὺς κόρακας, though it is sometimes, as in Acts xi. 6, xxvii. 39, used in its classical sense "perceive". A "confession" does not always involve that its significance is seen. *Consider* then τὸν ... Ἰησοῦν" the Apostle and high priest of our confession, Jesus," the

b ver. 5;   τὸν¹ Ἰησοῦν·   2.   ᵇπιστὸν ὄντα τῷ ποιήσαντι αὐτόν, ὡς καὶ Μωσῆς²
Num. xii.
7.   ἐν ὅλῳ τῷ οἴκῳ αὐτοῦ.   3. *Πλείονος γὰρ δόξης οὗτος³ παρὰ Μωσῆν
c Zach. vi.
12; Matt. ἠξίωται, καθ᾽ ὅσον πλείονα τιμὴν ἔχει τοῦ οἴκου ὁ κατασκευάσας
xvi. 18.

¹ Delete Χριστον with ℵABC*D*MP, 17, 34, 47.
² Μωσης in ℵABDEM ; Μωυσης in CKLP, 17.
³ ουτος δοξης in ℵABCDEP ; δοξης ουτος KLM.

single article brackets the two designations and Bengel gives their sense : " τὸν
ἀποστ. eum qui Dei causam apud nos
agit. τὸν ἀρχ. qui causam nostram apud
Deum agit ". These two functions embrace not the whole of Christ's work,
but all that He did on earth (cf. i. 1-4).
The frequent use of ἀποστέλλειν by our
Lord to denote the Father's mission of
the Son authorises the present application
of ἀπόστολος. It is through Him God
has spoken (i. 1). Moses is never called
ἀπόστολος (a word indeed which occurs
only once in LXX) though in Exod. iii.
10 God says ἀποστείλω σε πρὸς Φαραώ.
Schoettgen quotes passages from the
Talmud in which the high priest is termed
the Apostle or messenger of God and of
the Sanhedrim, but this is here irrelevant.
καὶ ἀρχιερέα, a title which, as applicable to Jesus, the writer explains in
chaps. v.-viii. τῆς ὁμολογίας ἡμῶν,
" of our confession," or, whom we, in
distinction from men of other faiths,
confess ; chiefly no doubt in distinction
from the non-Christian Jews. ὁμολογία,
as the etymology shows, means " of one
speech with," hence that in which men
agree as their common creed, their confession, see ref. As Peake remarks : " If
this means profession of faith, then ' the
readers already confess Jesus as high
priest, and this is not a truth taught
them in this Epistle for the first time '."
[Carpzov quotes from Philo (De Somn.) :
ὁ μὲν δὴ μέγας Ἀρχιερεὺς τῆς ὁμολογίας,
but here another sense is intended.]
Ἰησοῦν is added to preclude the possibility of error. Ἰησοῦς occurs in this
Epistle nine times by itself, thrice with
Χριστός.
Ver. 2. The characteristic, or particular, qualification of Jesus which is to
hold their attention is His trustworthiness or fidelity. πιστὸν ὄντα might
be rendered " as being faithful ". The
fidelity here in view, though indirectly
to men and encouraging them to trust, is
directly to Him who made Him, sc.,
Apostle and High Priest. τῷ ποιήσαντι αὐτόν. The objection urged
by Bleek, Lünemann and Alford that

ποιεῖν can mean "appoint" only when
followed by two accusatives is not valid.
The second accusative may be understood ; and in 1 Sam. xii. 6 we find
Κύριος ὁ ποιήσας τὸν Μωυσῆν καὶ τὸν
Ἀαρών, words which may have been in
the writer's mind. The Arian translation, " to Him that created Him," is out
of place. Appointment to office finds
its correlative in faithfulness, creation
scarcely suggests that idea. The fidelity
of Jesus is illustrated not by incidents
from His life nor by the crowning proof
given in His death, nor is it argued from
the admitted perfections of His character,
but in accordance with the plan of the
Epistle it is merely compared to that of
Moses, and its superiority is implied in
the superiority of the Son to the servant.
He was faithful "as also Moses in all
His house," this being the crowning instance of fidelity testified to by God
Himself, ὁ θεράπων μου Μωυσῆς ἐν ὅλῳ
τῷ οἴκῳ μου πιστός ἐστι (Num. xii. 7),
where the context throws the emphasis
on ὅλῳ. " The 'house of God' is the
organised society in which He dwells "
(Westcott), cf. 1 Tim. iii. 15. Weiss
says that the words ἐν ὅλῳ τῷ οἴκῳ αὐτοῦ
" necessarily belong " to πιστὸν ὄντα.
This is questionable, because the writer's
point is that Jesus is faithful not " in "
but " over " the house of God (ver. 6).
Ver. 3. The reason is now assigned
why Jesus and His fidelity should eclipse
in their consideration that of Moses. The
reason is that " this man " (οὗτος, " the
person who is the subject of our consideration ") " has been and is deemed
worthy of greater glory ('amplioris
gloriae,' Vulg. πλείονος, qualitative as in
xi. 4) than Moses, in proportion as he
that built the house has more honour
than the house." The genitive follows the
comparative πλείονα. The " greater
glory" is seen in the more important
place occupied by Him in the fulfilment
of God's purpose of salvation. This glory
of Jesus is as much greater than that of
Moses, as the cause is greater than the
effect, the builder than the house. [The
principle is stated by Philo (De Plant.,

αὐτόν · 4. ᵈπᾶς γὰρ οἶκος κατασκευάζεται ὑπό τινος · ὁ δὲ τὰ πάντα   d 2 Cor. v.
17; Eph.
κατασκευάσας, Θεός. 5. ᵉκαὶ Μωσῆς μὲν πιστὸς ἐν ὅλῳ τῷ οἴκῳ   ii. 10.
e ver. 2;
Deut. xviii. 15, 18.

c. 16. In Wendland's ed., ii. 147) ὁ κτησάμενος τὸ κτῆμα τοῦ κτήματος ἀμείνων καὶ τὸ πεποιηκὸς τοῦ γεγονότος, and by Menander and other comic poets as quoted by Justin (*Apol.*, i. 20) μείζονα τὸν δημιουργὸν τοῦ σκευαζομένου. Weiss, however, is of opinion that it is not a general principle that is being stated, but that τοῦ οἴκου refers directly to the house of God.] ὁ κατασκευάσας includes all that belongs to the completion of a house, from its inception and plan in the mind of the architect to its building and furnishing and filling with a household. Originally the word means to equip or furnish, κατασκευάζειν τὴν οἰκίαν τοῖς σκεύεσιν, Diog. L. v. 14. So συμπόσιον κατασ. Plato, *Rep.*, 363 C. σκεύεσιν ἰδίοις τὴν ναῦν κατεσκεύασα, Demosth. *Polyc.*, 1208. Thence, like our word "furnish" or "prepare," it took the wider meaning of "making" or "building" or "providing". Thus the shipbuilder κατασκ. the ship; the mason κατασ. the tower. So in Heb. xi. 7 κατεσκεύασε κιβωτόν, *cf.* 1 Peter iii. 20. (Further, see Stephanus and Bleek). In the present verse it has its most comprehensive meaning, and includes the planning, building, and filling of the house with furniture and with a household. The household is more directly in view than the house. The argument involves that Jesus is identified with the builder of the house, while Moses is considered a part of the house. It is the Son (who in those last Days has spoken God's word to men through the lips of Jesus), who in former times also fulfilled God's purpose by building His house and creating for Him a people. And lest the readers of the epistle should object that Moses was as much the builder of the old as Jesus of the new, the writer lifts their mind from the management of the system or Church to the creation of it.

Ver. 4. πᾶς γὰρ οἶκος . . . θεός. "For every house *is built* by someone, but he that built all is God." Over and above the right conduct of the house there is a builder. No house, no religious system, grows of itself; it has a cause in the will of one who is greater than it. There is a "someone" at the root of all that appears in history. And He who planned and brought into being πάντα,

"all," whether old or new, is God. The present development of this divine house as well as its past condition and equipment is of God. And Christ, the Son, naturally and perfectly representing God or the builder, and by whose agency God created all things (i. 2) is therefore worthy of more honour than Moses. The argument is not so much elliptical as incomplete, waiting to be supplemented by the following verses in which the relation of Jesus to God and the relation of Moses to the house are exhibited. " It is argued that a household must be established by a householder ; now God established the universe, and therefore he is the supreme householder of the universal household or Church of God, and in that household Jesus, as His perfect representative, is entitled to receive glory corresponding " (Rendall).

Ver. 5. καὶ Μωϋσῆς. . . . Another reason for expecting to find fidelity in Jesus and for ascribing to Him greater glory. Moses was faithful as a servant *in* the house (ἐν), Christ as a Son *over* (ἐπὶ) his house. θεράπων denotes a free servant in an honourable position and is the word applied to Moses in Num. xii. 7. [" Apud Homerum nomen est non servile sed ministros significat voluntarios, nec raro de viris dicitur nobili genere natis " (Stephanus). It is especially used of those who serve the gods. See Pindar *Olymp.* iii. 29.] Both the fidelity and the inferior position of Moses are indicated in the words which occur like a refrain in Exodus : " According to all that the Lord commanded, so did he ". Nothing was left to his own initiative ; he had to be instructed and commanded ; but all that was entrusted to him, he executed with absolute exactness. The crowning proof of his fidelity was given in the extraordinary scene (Exod. xxxvii.), where Moses refused to be "made a great nation" in room of Israel. He is said to have been faithful εἰς μαρτύριον τῶν λαληθησομένων. The meaning is, the testimony to his faithfulness which God had pronounced was the guarantee of the trustworthiness of the report he gave of what the Lord afterwards spoke to him. This meaning seems to be determined by the context in Numbers xii. " My servant Moses

f Matt. xxiv.
13; 1 Cor.
iii. 16, et
vi. 19; 2
Cor. vi.
16; Eph.
ii. 21, 22.
1 Tim.
iii. 15; 1
Peter ii. 5.

αὐτοῦ, ὡς θεράπων, εἰς μαρτύριον τῶν λαληθησομένων· 6. ᵗ Χριστὸς
δὲ, ὡς υἱὸς ἐπὶ τὸν οἶκον αὐτοῦ, οὗ ¹ οἶκός ἐσμεν ἡμεῖς, ἐάνπερ ² τὴν
παρρησίαν καὶ τὸ καύχημα τῆς ἐλπίδος μέχρι τέλους βεβαίαν ³
κατάσχωμεν. 7. ᵍ Διὸ, καθὼς λέγει τὸ Πνεῦμα τὸ Ἅγιον, "Σήμερον

g ver. 15, et iv. 7; Ps. xlv. 7.

¹ T.R. in אABC; ος in D*M, 6, 67** d, e, f, Vulg. (quae domus sumus nos).
² T.R. in אcACDcE**KL; εαν in א*BDE*MP, 17, d, e, f, Vulg.
³ WH bracket μεχρι τελους βεβαιαν and Weiss rejects the words with B. All
the other great uncials insert the words. Bleek thinks them genuine.

. . . is faithful in all my house. I *will
speak to him* mouth to mouth, apparently
and not in dark speeches." Grotius
says "ut pronuntiaret populo ea quae
Deus ei dicenda quoquo tempore man-
dabat". Bleek and Davidson refer the
μαρτύριον to Moses not to God. "He
was a servant *for a testimony*, *i.e.*, to bear
testimony of those things which were to
be spoken, *i.e.*, from time to time revealed.
Reference might be made to Barnabas
viii. 3, εἰς μαρτ. τῶν φυλῶν. The
meaning advocated by Calvin, Delitzsch,
Westcott and others is attractive. They
understand the words as referring to the
things which were to be spoken by Christ,
and that the whole of Moses' work was
for a testimony of those things. Thus
Westcott translates "for a testimony of
the things which should be spoken by
God through the prophets and finally
through Christ". This gives a fine
range to the words, but the context in
Numbers is decisively against it. The
idea seems to be that Moses being but
a θεράπων needed a testimonial to his
fidelity that the people might trust him;
and also that he had no initiative but
could only report to the people the words
that God might speak to him. In contrast to this position of Moses, Χριστὸς
ὡς υἱὸς ἐπὶ τὸν οἶκον αὐτοῦ,
Christ's fidelity was that of "a Son
over his house". It was not the fidelity
which exactly performs what another
commands and faithfully enters into and
fulfils His will. It is the fidelity of one
who himself is possessed by the same
love and conceives the same purposes as
the Father. The interests of the house
and the family are the Son's interests.
"We are His house" and in Christ we
see that the interests of God and man, of
the Father and the family are one. [Gro-
tius quotes the jurisconsults: " etiam
vivente patre filium quodam modo dominum esse rerum paternarum".] But
this house so faithfully administered by

the Son Himself is the body of Christian
people, οὗ οἶκός ἐσμεν ἡμεῖς, we are
those on whom this fidelity is spent.
The relative finds its antecedent in
αὐτοῦ. The "house of God" is, in the
Gospels, the Temple; but in 1 Pet. iv.
17 and 1 Tim. iii. 15 it has the same
meaning as here, the people or Church
of God. "Whose house are we," but
with a condition ἐὰν τὴν παρρησίαν . . . κατάσχωμεν, "if we
shall have held fast our confidence and
the glorying of our hope firm to the
end". For, as throughout the Epistle,
so here, all turns on perseverance. παρρησία originally "frank speech," hence
the boldness which prompts it. *Cf.* iv.
16, x. 19, 35; so in Paul and John.
καύχημα, not as the form of the word
might indicate, "the object of boasting," but the disposition as in 1 Cor. v. 6:
οὐ καλὸν τὸ καύχημα ὑμῶν and 2 Cor.
v. 12: ἀφορμὴν διδόντες ὑμῖν καυχή-
ματος. [*Cf.* the interchange of βρῶσις
and βρῶμα in Jo. iv. 32, 34, and Jannaris, *Hist. Gk. Gram.*, 1021 and 1155.]
Whether ἐλπίδος belongs to both substantives is doubtful. The Christian's
hope of a heavenly inheritance (ver. 1), of
perfected fellowship with God, should be
so sure that it confidently proclaims
itself, and instead of being shamefaced
glories in the future it anticipates. And
this attitude must be maintained μέχρι
τέλους βεβαίαν, until difficulty and trial
are past and hope has become possession.
βεβαίαν In agreement with the remoter
substantive, which might give some
colour to the idea that the expression
was lifted from ver. 14 and inserted here;
but Bleek shows by several instances
that the construction is legitimate.

CHAPTER III. 7—IV. 13. The great
instance in history of the disaster which
attends failure of faith is adduced as a
warning to the faltering Hebrews.

Διὸ, "wherefore," since it is only by
holding fast our confidence to the end,

ἐὰν τῆς φωνῆς αὐτοῦ ἀκούσητε, 8. ʰ μὴ σκληρύνητε τὰς καρδίας ʰ Exod.
ὑμῶν, ὡς ἐν τῷ παραπικρασμῷ, κατὰ τὴν ἡμέραν τοῦ πειρασμοῦ ἐν xvii. 2;
τῇ ἐρήμῳ, 9. οὗ ἐπείρασάν με οἱ πατέρες ὑμῶν, ἐδοκίμασάν με,¹ καὶ 13.

¹ T.R.ℵcDcKL al pler, f, vg. ; εν δοκιμασια with ℵ*ABCD*EMP, 17, 73, 137.

that we continue to be the house of
Christ and enjoy His faithful oversight,
cf. ver. 14. Διὸ was probably intended to
be immediately followed by βλέπετε (ver.
12) "wherefore take heed," but a
quotation is introduced from Ps. xcv.
which powerfully enforces the βλέπετε.
Or it may be that διὸ connects with μὴ
σκληρύνητε, but the judicious bracketing
of the quotation by the A.V. is to be
preferred. The quotation is introduced
by words which lend weight to it, καθὼς
λέγει τὸ Πνεῦμα τὸ ἅγιον, a form of
citation not found elsewhere in exactly
the same terms, but in x. 15 we find the
similar form μαρτυρεῖ δὲ ἡμῖν τὸ πνεῦμα
τὸ ἅγ. Cf. also ix. 8. Agabus uses it of
his own words (Acts xxi. 11). In 1 Tim.
iv. 1 we have τὸ δὲ Πνεῦμα ῥητῶς λέγει
cf. Rev. ii.-iii. "It is characteristic of
the Epistle that the words of Holy
Scripture are referred to the Divine
Author, not to the human instrument"
(Westcott). The Psalm (95) is ascribed
to David in iv. 7 as in the LXX it is
called αἶνος ᾠδῆς τῷ Δαυίδ, although
in the Hebrew it is not so ascribed. The
quotation contains vv. 7-11.

Σήμερον, "to-day" is in the first
instance, the "to-day" present to the
writer of the psalm, and expresses the
thought that God's offers had not been
withdrawn although rejected by those to
whom they had long ago been made.
But Delitzsch adduces passages which
show that σήμερον in this psalm was
understood by the synagogue to refer to
the second great day of redemption.
"The history of redemption knows but
of two great turning points, that of the
first covenant and that of the new"
(Davidson). And what the writer to the
Hebrews fears is that the second
announcement of promise may be disregarded as the first. Force is lent to
his fears by the fact that the forty years
of the Messiah's waiting from 30-70 A.D.,
when Jerusalem was to be destroyed,
were fast running out. The fate of the
exasperating Israelites in the wilderness
received an ominous significance in
presence of the obduracy of the generation which had heard the voice of Christ
Himself.

ἐὰν τῆς φωνῆς αὐτοῦ ἀκούσ-

ητε, "if ye shall hear His voice" (R.V.,
Vaughan); not "if ye will hearken to
His voice." The sense is, "If God
should be pleased, after so much in-
attention on our part, to speak again,
see that ye give heed to Him".
Ver. 8. μὴ σκληρύνητε, the pro-
hibitory subjunctive, v. Burton, p. 162.
"The figure is from the stiffening by
cold or disease, of what ought to be
supple and pliable" (Vaughan). [The
verb occurs first in Hippocrates, cf. Anz.
342.] It is ascribed to τὸν τράχηλον
(Deut. x. 16), τὸν νῶτον (2 Kings xvii.
14), τὴν καρδίαν (Exod. iv. 21), τὸ
πνεῦμα (Deut. ii. 30). Sometimes the
hardening is referred to the man, sometimes it is God who inflicts the hardening
as a punishment. Here the possible
hardening is spoken of as if the human
subject could prevent it. τὰς καρδίας,
the whole inner man. ὡς ἐν τῷ . .
ἐρήμῳ. This stands in the psalm as the
translation of the Hebrew which might be
rendered: ["Harden not your hearts]as at
Meribah, as on the day of Massah in the
wilderness," Meribah being represented by
παραπικρασμός and Massah by πειρασμός. The tempting of God by Israel in
the wilderness is recorded in Exod. xvii.
1-7, where the place is called "Massah
and Meribah". This occurred in the
first year of the wanderings. παραπικρασμός is found only in this psalm (although
παραπικραίνειν is frequent) its place
being taken by λοιδόρησις in Exod. xvii.
7 and by ἀντιλογία in Num. xx. 12. It
means "embitterment," "exacerbation,"
"exasperation". κατὰ τὴν ἡμέραν
is rendered by the Vulgate "secundum
diem," rightly. It means 'after the
manner of the day". Westcott, however,
prefers the temporal sense.
Ver. 9. οὗ ἐπείρασάν με . . .
"where your fathers tempted me," i.e., in
the wilderness. Others take οὗ as =
"with which," attracted into genitive by
πειρασμοῦ. ἐν δοκιμασίᾳ, "in
putting me to the proof". καὶ εἶδον
. . . ἔτη, "and saw my works forty
years," the wonders of mercy and of
judgment. In the psalm τεσσ. ἔτη are
joined to προσώχθισα, διὸ being omitted.
The same connection is adopted in
ver. 17.

εἶδον τὰ ἔργα μου τεσσαράκοντα ἔτη· 10. διὸ προσώχθισα τῇ
γενεᾷ ἐκείνῃ, καὶ εἶπον, Ἀεὶ πλανῶνται τῇ καρδίᾳ· αὐτοὶ δὲ οὐκ
ἔγνωσαν τὰς ὁδούς μου· 11. ¹ ὡς ὤμοσα ἐν τῇ ὀργῇ μου, Εἰ εἰσελεύσονται εἰς τὴν κατάπαυσίν μου." 12. βλέπετε, ἀδελφοὶ, μή ποτε
ἔσται ἔν τινι ὑμῶν καρδία πονηρὰ ἀπιστίας, ἐν τῷ ἀποστῆναι ἀπὸ
Θεοῦ ζῶντος· 13. ἀλλὰ παρακαλεῖτε ἑαυτοὺς καθ' ἑκάστην ἡμέραν,

i Num. xiv.
21; Deut.
i. 34.

Ver. 10. δ ι ὸ π ρ ο σ ώ χ θ ι σ α,
"wherefore I was greatly displeased".
In the psalm the Hebrew verb means
"I loathed," elsewhere in the LXX it
translates verbs meaning " I am disgusted
with," " I spue out," " I abhor," cf. Lev.
xxvi. 30, [from ὄχθη a bank, as if from a
river chafing with its banks; or related
to ἄχθος and ἄχθομαι as if " burdened ".]
αὐτοὶ δὲ. . . . The insertion of αὐτοὶ
δὲ shows that this clause is not under
εἶπον, but is joined with the preceding
προσώχθ. "I was highly displeased,—
but yet they did not recognise my ways."
Ver. 11. ὡς ὤμοσα. "As I sware,"
i.e., justifying my oath to exclude them
from the land. εἰ εἰσελεύσονται,
the common form of oath with εἰ which
supposes that some such words as "God
do so to me and more also" have
preceded the " if". The oath quoted in
Ps. xcv. is recorded in Num. xiv. 21-23.
εἰς τὴν κατάπαυσίν μου, "into
my rest," primarily, the rest in Canaan,
but see on chap. iv.
Ver. 12. Βλέπετε ἀδελφοὶ μήπ-
οτε. . . . "Take heed lest haply " as in
xii. 25, Col. ii. 8, for the more classical
ὁρᾶτε μὴ. It is here followed by a
future indicative as sometimes in classics.
ἔν τινι ὑμῶν, the individualising, as
in ver. 13 indicates the writer's earnestness,
whether, as Bleek supposes, it means
that the whole Christian community of
the place is to be watchful for the
individual, may be doubted; although
this idea is confirmed by the παρακαλεῖτε
ἑαυτοὺς of ver. 13. What they are to be
on their guard against is the emergence
of καρδία πονηρὰ ἀπιστίας ἐν
. . . ζῶντος, a wicked heart of unbelief
manifesting itself in departing from Him
who is a living God. ἀπιστίας is
the genitive of quality = a bad, unbelieving heart ; whether the wickedness proceeds from the unbelief, or the unbelief
from the wickedness, is not determined.
Although, from the next verse it might
be gathered that unbelief is considered
the result of allowed sin : i.e., it is when
the heart is hardened through sin, it
becomes unbelieving, so that the psycho-

logical order might be stated thus : sin,
a deceived mind, a hardened heart,
unbelief, apostasy. The main idea in
the writer's mind is that unbelief in God's
renewed offer of salvation is accompanied
by and means apostasy from the living
God. In the O.T. Jehovah is called
"the living God" in contrast to lifeless
impotent idols, and the designation is
suggestive of His power to observe,
visit, judge and succour His people. In
this Epistle it occurs, ix. 14, x. 31, xii. 22.
To object that the apostasy of Jews from
Christianity could not be called "apostasy
from God" is to mistake. The very
point the writer wishes to make is just
this: Remember that to apostatize from
Christ in whom you have found God, is
to apostatize from God. It is one of the
ominous facts of Christian experience that
any falling away from high attainment
sinks us much deeper than our original
starting point.
Ver. 13. To avoid this, π α ρ α κ α λ ε ῖ
τ ε ἑ α υ τ ο ὺ ς κ α θ' ἑ κ ά σ τ η ν
ἡ μ έ ρ α ν, "Exhort one another daily".
ἑαυτούς is equivalent to ἀλλήλους,
see Eph. iv. 32 ; Col. iii. 13. ἄχρις
οὗ τὸ Σήμερον καλεῖται, "as long
as that period endures which can be
called 'to-day'". ἄχρις denotes a
point up to which something is done ;
hence, the term during which something
is done as here. τὸ σήμερον = the
word "to-day". Bengel says, "Dum
Psalmus iste auditur et legitur"; but
this is less likely. The meaning is, So
long as opportunity is given to hear
God's call. ἵνα μὴ . . . ἁμαρτίας,
"lest any of you be rendered rebellious
through sin's deceit"; perhaps the meaning would be better brought out by translating "lest any of you be rendered rebellious by sin's deceit". [On sin's deceit
cf. " Nemo repente pessimus evasit" ; and
the striking motto to the 35th chap.
of The Fortunes of Nigel.] Sin in heart
or life blinds a man to the significance
and attractiveness of God's offer.
Ver. 14. μ έ τ ο χ ο ι γ ά ρ. . . . In ver. 6
the writer had adduced as the reason of
his warning (βλέπετε) that participation

ἄχρις οὗ τὸ σήμερον καλεῖται, ἵνα μὴ σκληρυνθῇ τις ἐξ ὑμῶν ἀπάτῃ
τῆς ἁμαρτίας· 14. ᵏμέτοχοι γὰρ γεγόναμεν τοῦ Χριστοῦ, ἐάνπερ ᵏ Rom. viii
τὴν ἀρχὴν τῆς ὑποστάσεως μέχρι τέλους βεβαίαν κατάσχωμεν, 15. ¹⁷·
ˡἐν τῷ λέγεσθαι, "Σήμερον ἐὰν τῆς φωνῆς αὐτοῦ ἀκούσητε, μὴ σκλη-ˡ ver. 7.
ρύνητε τὰς καρδίας ὑμῶν, ὡς ἐν τῷ παραπικρασμῷ". 16. Τινὲς¹ γὰρ
ἀκούσαντες παρεπίκραναν, ἀλλ' οὐ πάντες οἱ ἐξελθόντες ἐξ Αἰγύπτου

¹ T.R. with LMP, 37; τίνες in agreement with τίσι of vv. 17, 18; and with the
sense. See Bengel in loc.

in the salvation of Christ depended on
continuance in the confident expectation
that their heavenly calling would be
fulfilled; and so impressed is he with
the difficulty of thus continuing that he
now returns to the same thought, and
once again assigns the same reason for
his warning: "For we are become partakers of Christ, if we hold the beginning
of our confidence firm to the end".
Delitzsch, Rendall, Bruce and others
understand by μέτοχοι, "partners" or
"fellows" of Christ, as if the faithful
were not only the house of Christ (ver. 6)
but shared His joy in the house. It may
be objected that μέτοχοι in this Epistle
(ii. 14, iii. 1, v. 13, vi. 4, vii. 13, xii. 8)
is regularly used of participators in
something, not of participators with
someone. In i. 9, however, it is not so
used. The idea of participating with
Christ finds frequent expression in Scripture. See Matt. xxv. 21; Rev. iii. 21.
τοῦ Χριστοῦ, the article may link
this mention of Christ's name with that
in ver. 6; and, if so, μέτοχοι will naturally
refer to companionship with Christ in
His house. This companionship we
have entered into and continue to enjoy
[γεγόναμεν] on the same condition as
above (ver. 6) ἐάνπερ τὴν ἀρχὴν...
"if at least we maintain the beginning of
our confidence firm to the end". ὑποστάσεως is used by LXX twenty times
and represents twelve different Hebrew
words [Hatch in Essays in Bibl. Greek
says eighteen times representing fifteen
different words, but cf. Concordance].
In Ruth i. 12, Ps. xxxix. 8, Ezek. xix. 5
it means "ground of hope" [its primary
meaning being that on which anything is
based], hence it takes the sense, "hope"
or "confidence". Bleek gives examples of
its use in later Greek, Polyb., iv. 50, οἱ
δὲ Ῥόδιοι θεωροῦντες τὴν τῶν Βυζαν-
τίων ὑπόστασιν, so vi. 55 of Horatius
guarding the bridge. It also occurs in
the sense of "fortitude," bearing up
against pain, v. Diod. Sic., De Virt.,

p. 557, and Josephus, Ant., xviii. 1. Confidence the Hebrews already possessed
[ἀρχὴν]; their test was its maintenance
to the end [τέλους], i.e., till it was
beyond trial, finally triumphant, in Christ's
presence.
Ver. 15. ἐν τῷ λέγεσθαι. . . .
"While it is said to-day, etc." The
construction of these words is debated.
Bleek, Delitzsch, von Soden and others
construe them with what follows, beginning at this point a fresh paragraph.
The meaning would thus be: "Since it
is said, 'To-day if ye hear his voice,
harden not, etc.,' who are meant, who
were they who heard and provoked?"
This is inviting but the γὰρ of ver. 16 is
decidedly against it. Davidson connects ἐν τῷ λεγ. with what immediately
precedes: "'if we hold fast . . . unto
the end, while it is said,' i.e., not during
the time that it is said, but in the presence and consciousness of the saying,
Harden not, etc. . . . with this divine
warning always in the ears". Similarly
Weiss. Westcott connects the words
with ver. 13, making 14 parenthetical.
Either of these constructions is feasible.
It is also possible to let the sentence
stand by itself as introductory to what
follows, taking μὴ σκληρ. as directly
addressed to the Hebrews, not as merely
completing the quotation: "While it is
being said To-day if ye hear his voice,
harden not your hearts as in the provoca-
tion". The λέγεσθαι thus contains only
the clause ending with ἀκούσητε.
Ver. 16. τίνες γὰρ ἀκούσαντες
παρεπίκραναν: "For who were they
who after hearing provoked?" He proceeds further to enforce his warning that
confidence begun is not enough, by showing that they who provoked God and fell
in the wilderness had begun a life of
faith and begun it well. For the answer
to his question is "Nay did not all who
came out of Egypt with Moses?" They
were not exceptional sinners who fell
away, but all who came out of Egypt,

m Num.
xiv. 22,
37, et
xxvi. 65.
Ps. cvi.
26; 1 Cor.
x. 5, etc.,
Judæ v.
n Num. xiv.
30, Deut.
i. 34, 35.

διὰ Μωσέως. 17. ᵐτίσι δὲ προσώχθισε τεσσαράκοντα ἔτη; οὐχὶ τοῖς ἁμαρτήσασιν, ὧν τὰ κῶλα ἔπεσεν ἐν τῇ ἐρήμῳ; 18. ⁿτίσι δὲ ὤμοσε μὴ εἰσελεύσεσθαι εἰς τὴν κατάπαυσιν αὐτοῦ, εἰ μὴ τοῖς ἀπειθήσασι; 19. καὶ βλέπομεν ὅτι οὐκ ἠδυνήθησαν εἰσελθεῖν δι' ἀπιστίαν. IV. 1. Φοβηθῶμεν οὖν μή ποτε καταλειπομένης ¹ ἐπαγγελίας εἰσελθεῖν εἰς τὴν κατάπαυσιν αὐτοῦ, δοκῇ τις ἐξ ὑμῶν

¹ T.R. ABCDᶜKLMP; καταλιπομενης אD*.

the whole mass of the gloriously rescued people whose faith had carried them through between the threatening walls of water and over whom Miriam sang her triumphal ode. ἀλλά adds force to the answer, as if it were said, It is asked *who* provoked, as though it were some only, *but* was it not *all?* πάντες, for it is needless excepting Joshua and Caleb. Ver. 17. τίσι δὲ προσώχθισε. . . . "And with whom was He angry forty years?" taking up the next clause of the Psalm, v. 10. Again the question is answered by another "Was it not with them that sinned?" [ἁμαρτήσασιν: "This is the only form of the aorist participle in N.T. In the moods the form of ἥμαρτον is always used except Matt. xviii. 15, Luke xvii. 4, ἁμαρτήσῃ: Rom. vi. 15." Westcott, cf. Blass, p. 43.] It was not caprice on God's part, nor inability to carry them to the promised land. It was because they sinned [see esp. Num. xxxii. 23] that their "carcases fell in the wilderness". ὧν τὰ κῶλα ἔπεσεν ἐν τῇ ἐρήμῳ. These words are taken from Num. xiv. 29, 32, where God utters the doom of the wilderness generation. κῶλον, a limb or member of the body [Æsch., *Prom.*, 81; Soph., *O.C.*, 19, etc.]; hence a clause of a sentence (and in English, the point which marks it). Used by the LXX to translate פֶּגֶר, cadaver. Setting out from Egypt with the utmost confidence, they left their bones in the desert in unnamed and forgotten graves; not because of their weakness nor because God had failed them but because of their sin. Ver. 18. τίσι δὲ ὤμοσε. . . . "And to whom swore He that they should not enter into His rest, but to them that obeyed not?" The real cause of their exclusion from the rest prepared for them was their disobedience. *Cf.* especially the scene recorded in Num. xiv. where Moses declares that as ἀπειθοῦντες Κυρίῳ they were excluded from the land. At the root of their disobedience was unbelief.

Ver. 19. They did not believe God could bring them into the promised land in the face of powerful oppositin and so they would not attempt its conquest when commanded to go forward. They were rendered weak by their unbelief. This is pointed out in the concluding words καὶ βλέπομεν . . . where the emphasis is on οὐκ ἠδυνήθησαν, they were not able to enter in, the reason being given in the words δι' ἀπιστίαν. The application to the Hebrew Christians was sufficiently obvious. They were in danger of shrinking from further conflict and so losing all they had won. They had begun well but were now being weakened and prevented from completing their victory; and this weakness was the result of their not trusting God and their leader.

Between chapters iii. and iv. there is no break. The unbelief of the wilderness generation is held up as a warning, and its use in this respect is justified by the fact that the promise made to them is still made, and is a "living" word which reveals the inmost purposes of the heart and is inevitable in its judgment. Ver. 1. φοβηθῶμεν οὖν, "let us then fear," the writer speaks in the name of the living generation, "lest haply, there being left behind and still remaining a promise to enter [ἐπαγγελίας εἰσελθεῖν; cf. ὥρα ἀπιέναι, Plato, *Apol.*, p. 42] into His (*i.e.*, God's) rest, any of you (not ἡμῶν) should fancy that he has come too late for it; δοκῇ ὑστερηκέναι. Of these words there are three linguistically possible translations.

1. Should seem to have fallen short.
2. Should be judged to have fallen short.
3. Should think that he has fallen short or come too late.
The argument of the passage favours the third reading, for it aims at strengthening the belief that the promise does remain and that the readers are not born too late to enjoy it. "Gloomy imaginations of failure were rife among the Hebrews" (Rendall). These perse-

ὑστερηκέναι. 2. καὶ γάρ ἐσμεν εὐηγγελισμένοι, καθάπερ κἀκεῖνοι·
ἀλλ᾽ οὐκ ὠφέλησεν ὁ λόγος τῆς ἀκοῆς ἐκείνους, μὴ συγκεκραμένος[1]
τῇ πίστει τοῖς ἀκούσασιν. 3. ᵃ εἰσερχόμεθα[2] γὰρ εἰς τὴν κατά- a Ps. xcv.
παυσιν οἱ πιστεύσαντες, καθὼς εἴρηκεν, " Ὡς ὤμοσα ἐν τῇ ὀργῇ μου, 11.
Εἰ εἰσελεύσονται εἰς τὴν κατάπαυσίν μου," καίτοι τῶν ἔργων ἀπὸ
καταβολῆς κόσμου γενηθέντων. 4. ᵇ Εἴρηκε γάρ που περὶ τῆς b Gen. ii.2;
ἑβδόμης οὕτω, " Καὶ κατέπαυσεν ὁ Θεὸς ἐν τῇ ἡμέρᾳ τῇ ἑβδόμῃ ἀπὸ Exod. xx.
πάντων τῶν ἔργων αὐτοῦ"· 5. καὶ ἐν τούτῳ πάλιν, " Εἰ εἰσελεύσονται xxxi. 17.
εἰς τὴν κατάπαυσίν μου". 6. Ἐπεὶ οὖν ἀπολείπεταί τινας εἰσελθεῖν
εἰς αὐτήν, καὶ οἱ πρότερον εὐαγγελισθέντες οὐκ εἰσῆλθον δι᾽ ἀπείθειαν,

---

[1] T.R. 31, 41, 114, d, e, vg.cle [συγκεκερασμενος in ℵ exegetisch allein haltbar
(Weiss)]; συγκεκερασμενους in ABCD*M, Theod. - Mops.; συγκεκραμενους
DcEKLP.

[2] T.R. in ℵBDEKLMP, d, e; εισερχωμεθα in AC, 17, 37* f, vg., Primas.

cuted Christians who had expected to
find the fulfilment of all promise in
Christ, found it hard to believe that
"rest" was attainable in Him. The
writer proceeds therefore to prove that
this promise is left and is still open.
καὶ γάρ ἐσμεν εὐηγγελισμένοι. . . . "For
indeed we, even as also they, have had
a gospel preached to us." We should
have expected an expressed ἡμεῖς, but its
suppression shows us that the writer
wishes to emphasise εὐηγγελ. To us as
to them it is a gospel that is preached;
and the καθάπερ κἀκεῖνοι, " even as they
also had," brings out the fact that under
the promise of a land in which to rest,
the Israelites who came out of Egypt
were brought in contact with the redeeming grace and favour of God. The
expression reflects significant light on
the inner meaning of all God's guidance
of Israel's history. They received this
rich promise laden with God's intention
to bless them, "but the word which they
heard did them no good, because in
those who heard, it was not mixed with
faith". [For συγκεκ. see the Phaedo,
p. 95A. The accusative is best attested
(see critical note), but the sense " not
mixed by faith with those who heard,"
i.e.. Caleb and Joshua, is most improbable.] Belief, then, is everything.
In proof of which our own experience
may be cited: " For we are entering
into the rest, we who have believed ".
This clause confirms both the statements of the previous verse: " we have
the promise as well as they," for we are
entering into the rest [note the emphatic
position of εἰσερχόμεθα]; and " the
word failed them because of their lack of

faith," for it is our faith [οἱ πιστεύσαντες]
which is carrying us into the rest. This
fact that we are entering in by faith is
in accordance with the utterance quoted
already in iii. 11, καθὼς εἴρηκεν, Ὡς
ὤμοσα . . . " I sware in my wrath, they
shall not enter into my rest, although
the works were finished from the foundation of the world ". This quotation
confirms the first clause of the verse,
because it proves two things: first, that
God had a rest, and second, that He
intended that man should rest with Him,
because it was "in His wrath," justly
excited against the unbelieving (cf. iii.
9, 10), that He sware they should not
enter in. Had it not been God's original
purpose and desire that men should
enter into His rest, it could not be said
that "in wrath" He excluded some.
Their failure to secure rest was not due
to the non-existence of any rest, for
God's works were finished when the
world was founded. This again is confirmed by Scripture, εἴρηκεν γάρ
που, viz., in Gen. ii. 2 (cf. Exod. xx. 11,
xxxi. 17), where it is said that after the
six days of creation God rested on the
seventh day from all His works. That
God has a rest is also stated in the
ninety-fifth Psalm, for these words " they
shall not enter into my rest " prove that
God had a rest. The emphasis in this
second quotation (ver. 5) is on the word
μοι.

Ver. 6. The writer now, in vv. 6-9,
gathers up the argument, and reaches his
conclusion that a Sabbatism remains for
God's people. The argument briefly is,
God has provided a rest for men and has
promised it to them. This promise was

7. °πάλιν τινὰ ὁρίζει ἡμέραν, "Σήμερον," ἐν Δαβὶδ λέγων, μετὰ τοσοῦτον χρόνον· καθὼς εἴρηται,[1] "Σήμερον ἐὰν τῆς φωνῆς αὐτοῦ ἀκούσητε, μὴ σκληρύνητε τὰς καρδίας ὑμῶν". 8. Εἰ γὰρ αὐτοὺς Ἰησοῦς
κατέπαυσεν, οὐκ ἂν περὶ ἄλλης ἐλάλει μετὰ ταῦτα ἡμέρας· 9.
ἄρα ἀπολείπεται σαββατισμὸς τῷ λαῷ τοῦ Θεοῦ. 10. ὁ γὰρ εἰσελθὼν εἰς τὴν κατάπαυσιν αὐτοῦ, καὶ αὐτὸς κατέπαυσεν ἀπὸ τῶν

[1] προειρηται in אACD*E*P, d, e, f, vg., Copt., Arm. ; ειρηται in DcE**KL.

not believed by those who formerly heard
it, neither was it exhausted in the bringing in of the people to Canaan. For had
it been so, it could not have been renewed
long after, as it was. It remains, therefore, to be now enjoyed. " Since, therefore, it remains that some enter into it
and those who formerly heard the good
news of the promise did not enter, owing
to disobedience." ἀπολείπεται, there
remains over as not yet fulfilled. In v. 9.
σαββατ. is the nominative, here τινας
εἰσελθεῖν might be considered a nominative but it is better, with Viteau (256), to
construe it as an impersonal verb followed by an infinitive. From the fact
that the offer of the rest had been made,
or the promise given, " it remains " that
some (must) enter in. But a second fact
also forms a premiss in the argument.
viz. : that those to whom the promise
had formerly been made did not enter in ;
therefore, over and above and long after
(μετὰ τοσ. χρόνον) the original proclamation of this gospel of rest, even in
David's time, again (πάλιν), God appoints or specifies a certain day (τινὰ
ὁρίζει ἡμέραν) saying "To-day". This
proves that the offer is yet open, that the
promise holds good in David's time.
The words already quoted (καθὼς
προείρηται) from the 95th Psalm prove
this, for they run, " To-day, if ye hear
His voice," etc. They prove at any
rate that the gospel of rest was not exhausted by the entrance into Canaan
under Joshua, " for if Joshua had given
them rest, God would not after this speak
of another day". The writer takes for
granted that the "To-day" of the Psalm
extends to Christian times, whether be
cause of the life (ver. 12) that is in the
word of promise, or because the reference in the Psalm is Messianic. " This
' voice' of God which is ' heard' is His
voice speaking to us in His Son (i. 1)
and this ' To-day' is ' the end of these
days' in which He has spoken to us in
Him, on to the time when He shall come
again (iii. 13). In effect God has been

' heard' speaking only twice, to Israel
and to us, and what He has spoken to
both has been the same,—the promise of
entering into His rest. Israel came short
of it through unbelief ; we do enter into
the rest who believe (iv. 3) " (Davidson).
At all events, the conclusion unhesitatingly follows : " Therefore there remains
a Sabbath-Rest for the people of God ".
ἄρα though often standing first in a sentence in N.T. cannot in classical Greek
occupy that place. Σαββατισμός, though
found here only in Biblical Greek, occurs
in Plutarch (De Superstit, c. 3). The
verb σαββατίζειν occurs in Exod. xvi. 30
and other places. The word is here employed in preference to κατάπαυσις in
order to identify the rest promised to
God's people with the rest enjoyed by
God Himself on the Sabbath or Seventh
Day. [So Theophylact, ἑρμηνεύει πῶς
σαββατ. ὠνόμασε τὴν τοιαύτην κατά-
παυσιν· διότι, φησί, καταπαύομεν καὶ
ἡμεῖς ἀπὸ τῶν ἔργων τῶν ἡμετέρων,
ὥσπερ καὶ ὁ θεός, καταπαύσας ἀπὸ τῶν
ἔργων τῶν εἰς σύστασιν τοῦ κόσμου,
σάββατον τὴν ἡμέραν ὠνόμασεν.] To
explain and justify the introduction of
this word, the writer adds ὁ γὰρ εἰσελθὼν
. . . as if he said, I call it a Sabbatism,
because it is not an ordinary rest, but
one which finds its ideal and actual fulfilment in God's own rest on the Seventh
Day. It is a Sabbatism because in it
God's people reach a definite stage of
attainment, of satisfactorily accomplished
purpose, as God Himself did when creation was finished. ὁ γὰρ εἰσελθὼν, whoever has entered, not to be restricted to
Jesus, as by Alford, εἰς τ. κατάπαυσιν
αὐτοῦ, into God's rest, καὶ αὐτὸς κ.τ.λ.
himself also rested from his (the man's)
works as God from His."
The salvation which the writer has
previously referred to as a glorious dominion is here spoken of as a Rest. The
significance lies in its being God's rest
which man is to share. It is the rest
which God has enjoyed since the creation.
From all His creative work God could

ἔργων αὐτοῦ, ὥσπερ ἀπὸ τῶν ἰδίων ὁ Θεός. 11. Σπουδάσωμεν οὖν
εἰσελθεῖν εἰς ἐκείνην τὴν κατάπαυσιν, ἵνα μὴ ἐν τῷ αὐτῷ τις ὑποδείγματι πέσῃ τῆς ἀπειθείας. 12. ᵈζῶν γὰρ ὁ λόγος τοῦ Θεοῦ, καὶ
ἐνεργὴς,[1] καὶ τομώτερος ὑπὲρ πᾶσαν μάχαιραν δίστομον, καὶ διϊκνούμενος ἄχρι μερισμοῦ ψυχῆς τε[2] καὶ πνεύματος, ἁρμῶν τε καὶ

d Eccl. xii.
11; Esa.
xix.2; Jer.
xxiii. 29;
1 Cor.xiv.
24, 25; 2
Cor. x. 4,
5; Eph.
vi. 17.

[1] T.R. in ℵACDEHKLP; εναργης in B.
[2] ℵABCHLP omit τε.

not be said to rest till, after what cannot
but appear to us a million of hazards, man
appeared, a creature in whose history
God Himself could find a worthy history,
whose moral and spiritual needs would
elicit the Divine resources and exercise
what is deepest in God. When man
appears God is satisfied, for here is one
in His own image. But from this bare
statement of the meaning of God's rest it
is obvious that God's people must share
it with Him. God's rest is satisfaction
in man; but this satisfaction can be perfected only when man is in perfect harmony with Him. His rest is not perfect
till they rest in Him. This highly
spiritual conception of salvation is involved in our Author's argument. *Cf.*
the grand passage on God's Rest in Philo,
De Cherubim, c. xxvi., and also Barnabas
xv., see also Hughes' *The Sabbatical
Rest of God and Man*.

Ver. 11. The exhortation follows
naturally, "Let us then earnestly strive
to enter into that rest, lest anyone fall
in the same example of disobedience".
The example of disobedience was that
given by the wilderness generation and
they are warned not to fall in the same
way. πέσῃ ἐν is commonly construed
"fall into," but it seems preferable to
render "fall by" or "in"; πέσῃ being
used absolutely as in Rom. xiv. 4, στήκει
ἢ πίπτει. Vaughan has "lest anyone
fall [by placing his foot] in the mark
left by the Exodus generation". ὑπόδειγμα is condemned by Phrynichus who
says : οὐδὲ τοῦτο ὀρθῶς λέγεται·
παράδειγμα λέγε. "In Attic ὑποδείκνυμι was never used except in its
natural sense of *show by implication;*
but in Herodotus and Xenophon it signifies *to mark out, set a pattern.*" Rutherford's *Phryn.*, p. 62. *Cf.* viii. 5 of this
Epistle with John xiii. 15 for both meanings. It is used in James v. 10 with
genitive of the thing to be imitated.

In vv. 12 and 13 another reason is
added for dealing sincerely and stren-
uously with God's promises and especially

with this offer of rest. ζῶν γὰρ ὁ
λόγος τοῦ θεοῦ, "for the word of
God is living," that word of revelation
which from the first verse of the Epistle
has been in the writer's mind and which
he has in chaps, iii., iv. exhibited as a word
of promise of entrance into God's rest.
Evidently, therefore, ὁ λόγος τοῦ θεοῦ is
not, as Origen and other interpreters have
suppo ed, the Personal Word incarnate
in Christ, but God's offers and promises.
Not only is the γάρ, linking this clause
to the promise of rest, decisive for this
interpretation ; but the mention of ὁ
λόγος τῆς ἀκοῆς in ver. 2 and the prominence given in the context to God's
promise make it impossible to think of
anything else. To enforce the admonition to believe and obey the word of God,
five epithets are added, which, says
Westcott, "mark with increasing clearness its power to deal with the individual
soul. There is a passage step by step
from that which is most general to that
which is most personal." It is, first,
ζῶν, "living" or, as A.V. has it, "quick".
Cf. 1 Pet. i. 23, ἀναγεγεννημένοι . . .
διὰ λόγου ζῶντος Θεοῦ καὶ μένοντος, and
ver. 24 τὸ ῥῆμα Κυρίου μένει εἰς τὸν
αἰῶνα. The meaning is that the word remains efficacious, valid and operative, as
it was when it came from the will of God.
"It is living as being instinct with the
life of its source" (Delitzsch). It is also
ἐνεργὴς, active, effective, still doing the
work it was intended to do, *cf.* Isa. 55·11.
τομώτερος ὑπὲρ πᾶσαν μάχαιραν δίστομον, "sharper than any two-edged
sword". τομ. ὑπὲρ is a more forcible
comparative than the genitive; *cf.* Luke
xvi. 8; 2 Cor. xii. 13. The positive
τομός is found in Plato *Tim.* 61 E. and
elsewhere. δίστομος double-mouthed, *i.e.*,
double-edged, the sword being considered
as a devouring beast, see 2 Sam. xi. 25,
καταφάγεται ἡ μάχαιρα. A double-edged
sword is not only a more formidable
weapon than a single-edged, offering less
resistance and therefore cutting deeper
(see Judges iii. 16 where Ehud made for

e Ps. xxxiii.
13, 14, 15,
et xxxiv.
15, et xc.
8, et
cxxxix.
11, 12;
Ecclus. xv. 19.

μυελῶν, καὶ κριτικὸς ἐνθυμήσεων καὶ ἐννοιῶν καρδίας · 13. °καὶ οὐκ
ἔστι κτίσις ἀφανὴς ἐνώπιον αὐτοῦ, πάντα δὲ γυμνὰ καὶ τετραχηλισμένα τοῖς ὀφθαλμοῖς αὐτοῦ, πρὸς ὃν ἡμῖν ὁ λόγος.

himself μάχαιραν δίστομον a span long,
and cf. Eurip., Helena, 983), but it was a
common simile for sharpness as in Prov.
v. 4, ἠκονημένον μᾶλλον μαχαίρας δισ-
τόμου, whetted more than a two-edged
sword; and Rev. i. 16, ῥομφαία δίστομος
ὀξεῖα. The same comparison is used by
Isaiah (xlix. 2) and by St. Paul (Eph. vi.
17); but especially in Wisdom xviii. 15,
"Thine Almighty Word leaped down
from heaven . . . and brought thine unfeigned commandment as a sharp sword.
This sharpness is illustrated by its action,
διϊκνούμενος ἄχρι μερισμοῦ
ψυχῆς καὶ πνεύματος, ἁρμῶντε
καὶ μυελῶν, an expression which does
not mean that the word divides the soul
from the spirit, the joints from the mar-
row, but that it pierces through all that
is in man to that which lies deepest in
his nature. "It is obvious that the
writer does not mean anything very
specific by each term of the enumeration,
which produces its effect by the rhetorical
fullness of the expressions" (Farrar). For
the expression cf. Eurip., Hippol., 255
πρὸς ἄκρον μυελὸν ψυχῆς. But it is in
the succeeding clause that the significance
of his description appears; the word is
Κριτικὸς ἐνθυμήσεων καὶ ἐνν-
οιῶν καρδίας "judging the conceptions and ideas of the heart". The word
of God coming to men in the offer of
good of the highest kind tests their real
desires and inmost intentions. When
fellowship with God is made possible
through His gracious offer, the inmost
heart of man is sifted; and it is infallibly
discovered and determined whether he
truly loves the good and seeks it, or
shrinks from accepting it as his eternal
heritage. The terms in which this is
conveyed find a striking analogy in Philo
(Quis. Rer. Div. Haer., p. 491) where
he speaks of God by His Word "cutting
asunder the constituent parts of all
bodies and objects that seem to be
coherent and united. Which [the word]
being whetted to the keenest possible
edge, never ceases to pierce all sensible
objects, and when it has passed through
them to the things that are called atoms
and indivisible, then again this cutting
instrument begins to divide those things
which are contemplated by reason into

untold and indescribable portions." Cf.
p. 506. In addition to this (καὶ), the
inward operation of the word finds its
counterpart in the searching, inevitable
inquisition of God Himself with whom
we have to do. "No created thing is
hidden before Him (God) but all things
are naked and exposed to the eyes of
Him with whom we have to do."
τετραχηλισμένα has created difficulty. τραχηλίζω is a word of the games,
meaning "to bend back the neck" and
so "to overcome". In this sense of
overmastering it was in very common
use. In Philo, e.g., men are spoken of as
τετραχηλισμένοι ταῖς ἐπιθυμίαις. This
meaning, however, gives a poor sense in
our passage where it is followed by τοῖς
ὀφθαλμοῖς. Chrysostom says the word
is derived from the skinning of animals,
and Theophylact, enlarging upon this
interpretation, explains that when the
victims had their throats cut, the skin
was dragged off from the neck downwards
exposing the carcase. No confirmation
of this use of the word is given. Perizonius in a note on Ælian, Var., Hist., xii.
58, refers to Suetonius, Vitell., 17, where
Vitellius is described as being dragged
into the forum, half-naked, with his hands
tied behind his back, a rope round his
neck and his dress torn; and we are further
told that they dragged back his head by
his hair, and even pricked him under the
chin with the point of a sword as they
are wont to do to criminals, that he
might let his face be seen and not hang
his head. [So, too, Elsner, who refers to
Perizonius and agrees that the word
means resupīnata, manifesta, eorum
quasi cervice ac facie reflexa, atque
adeo intuentium oculis exposita, genere
loquendi ab iis petito, quorum capita
reclinantur, ne intuentium oculos fugiant
et lateant; quod hominibus qui ad
supplicium ducebantur, usu olim accid-
ebat." Cf. "Sic fatus galeam laeva
tenet, atque reflexa Cervice orantis
capulo tenus applicat ensem. Virgil, Æn.
x. 535.] Certainly this bending back of
the head to expose the face gives an
excellent and relevant sense here. The reason for thus emphasising the penetrating
and inscrutable gaze of God is given in
the description appended in the relative

14. ᶠἜχοντες οὖν ἀρχιερέα μέγαν, διεληλυθότα τοὺς οὐρανούς, ^{f iii. 1, et}
Ἰησοῦν τὸν υἱὸν τοῦ Θεοῦ, κρατῶμεν τῆς ὁμολογίας. 15. ᵍΟὐ γὰρ
ἔχομεν ἀρχιερέα μὴ δυνάμενον συμπαθῆσαι ¹ ταῖς ἀσθενείαις ἡμῶν,

f iii. 1, et
vi. 20, et
vii. 26, et
viii. 1, et
ix. 11, 24,
et x. 23.
g ii. 17;

Esa. liii. 9; Luc. xxii. 28; 2 Cor. v. 21; Phil. ii. 7; 1 Peter ii. 22; 1 Joan. iii. 5.

¹ συμπαθ, in BᶜDᶜEKLP; συνπαθ, in אAB*CD*H.

clause; it is He **πρὸς ὃν ἡμῖν ὁ λόγος**, which, so far as the mere words go, might mean " of whom we speak " (*cf.* i. 7 and v. 11), but which obviously must here be rendered, as in A.V., " with whom we have to do," or "with whom is our reckoning," *cf.* xiii. 17.

From iv. 14 to x. 15 the writer treats of the Priesthood of the Son. The first paragraph extends from iv. 14-v. 10, and in this it is shown that Jesus has the qualifications of a priest, a call from God, and the sympathy which makes intercession hearty and real. The writer's purpose is to encourage his readers to use the intercession of Christ with confidence, notwithstanding their sense of sinfulness. And he does so by reminding them that all High priests are appointed for the very purpose of offering sacrifice for sin, and that this office has not been assumed by them at their own instance but at the call of God. It is because God desires that sinful men be brought near to Him that priests hold office. And those are called to office, who by virtue of their own experience are prepared to enter into cordial sympathy with the sinner and heartily seek to intercede for him. All this holds true of Christ. He is Priest in obedience to God's call. The office, as He had to fill it, involved much that was repugnant. With strong crying and tears He shrank from the death that was necessary to the fulfilment of His function. But His godly caution prompted as His ultimate prayer, that the will of the Father and not His own might be done. Thus by the things He suffered He learned obedience, and being thus perfected became the author of eternal salvation to all that obey Him, greeted and proclaimed High Priest for ever after the order of Melchizedek.

Ver. 14. Ἔχοντες οὖν . . . " Having then a great high priest who has passed through the heavens, Jesus the Son of God, let us hold fast our confession." οὖν resumes the train of thought started at iii. 1, where the readers were enjoined to consider the High Priest of their confession. But *cf.* Weiss and Kübel. μέγαν is now added, as in x. 21, xiii. 20,

that they may the rather hold fast the confession they were in danger of letting go. The μέγαν is explained and justified by two features of this Priest: (1) He has passed through the heavens and entered thus the very presence of God. For διεληλ. τ. οὐρανούς cannot mean, as Calvin renders " qui coelos ingressus est ". As the Aaronic High Priest passed through the veil, or, as Grotius and Carpzov suggest, through the various fore courts, into the Holiest place, so this great High Priest had passed through the heavens and appeared among eternal realities. So that the very absence of the High Priest which depressed them, was itself fitted to strengthen faith. He was absent, because dealing with the living God in their behalf. (2) The second mark of His greatness is indicated in His designation Ἰησοῦν τὸν υἱὸν τ. Θεοῦ, the human name suggesting perfect understanding and sympathy, the Divine Sonship acceptance with the Father and pre-eminent dignity. κρατῶμεν τ. ὁμολογίας. " Our confession " primarily of this great High Priest, but by implication, our Christian confession, *cf.* iii. 1.

Ver. 15. Confirmation both of the encouragement of ver. 14 and of the fact on which that encouragement is founded is given in the further idea: οὐ γὰρ ἔχομεν . . . " for we have not a high priest that cannot be touched with the feeling of our infirmities, but has been tempted in all points like us, without sin ". He repels an idea which might have found entrance into their minds, that an absent, heavenly priest might not be able to sympathise. Συνπαθέω [to be distinguished from συνπάσχω which occurs in Rom. viii. 17 and 1 Cor. xii. 26, and means to suffer along with one, to suffer the same ills as another] means to feel for, or sympathise with, and occurs also in x. 34, and is peculiar in N.T. to this writer but found in Aristotle, Isocrates and Plutarch, and in the touching expression of *Acts of Paul and Thekla*, 17, ὃς μόνος συνεπάθησεν πλανωμένῳ κόσμῳ. Jesus is able to sympathise with ταῖς ἀσθενείαις ἡμῶν " our

h x.19, etc. ; πεπειρασμένον δὲ κατὰ πάντα καθ' ὁμοιότητα, χωρὶς ἁμαρτίας.　16.
Rom. v.
2, 25; h προσερχώμεθα οὖν μετὰ παρρησίας τῷ θρόνῳ τῆς χάριτος, ἵνα λά-
Eph. ii.
18, et iii. 12.

infirmities," the weaknesses which under-
mine our resistance to temptation and
make it difficult to hold fast our confession : moral weaknesses, therefore,
though often implicated with physical
weaknesses. Jesus can feel for these
because πεπειρασμένον κατὰ πάντα καθ'
ὁμοιότητα, He has been tempted in
all respects as we are. κατὰ πάντα,
classical, " in all respects," cf. Wetstein
on Acts xvii. 22; and Evagrius, v. 4, of
Christ incarnate, ὁμοιοπαθῆ κατὰ πάντα
χωρὶς ἁμαρτίας, cf. ii. 17. καθ' ὁμοιότητα
may either mean " according to the likeness of our temptations," or, " in accordance with His likeness to us". The
latter is preferable, being most in agreement with ii. 17. So Theophylact,
καθ' ὁμοιότητα τὴν ἡμετέραν, τουτέστι
παραπλησίως ἡμῖν, cf. Gen. i. 11, 12;
and Philo, De Profug., c. 9, κατὰ τὴν
πρὸς τἆλλα ὁμοιότητα. The writer
wishes to preclude the common fancy
that there was some peculiarity in Jesus
which made His temptation wholly
different from ours, that He was a
mailed champion exposed to toy arrows.
On the contrary, He has felt in His own
consciousness the difficulty of being
righteous in this world ; has felt pressing
upon Himself the reasons and inducements that incline men to choose sin
that they may escape suffering and
death ; in every part of His human constitution has known the pain and conflict
with which alone temptation can be
overcome ; has been so tempted that
had He sinned, He would have had a
thousandfold better excuse than ever·
man had. Even though His divinity
may have ensured His triumph, His
temptation was true and could only be
overcome by means that are open to all.
The one difference between our temptations and those of Jesus is that His were
χωρὶς ἁμαρτίας. Riehm thinks this expression is not exhausted by declaring
the fact that in Christ's case temptation
never resulted in sin. It means, he
thinks, further, and rather, that temptation never in Christ's case sprang from
any sinful desire in Himself. So also
Delitzsch, Weiss, Westcott, etc. But if
Theophylact is right in his indication of
the motive of the writer in introducing
the words, then it is Christ's successful
resistance of temptation which is in the

foreground ; ὥστε δύνασθε καὶ ὑμεῖς ἐν
ταῖς θλίψεσιν χωρὶς ἁμαρτίας διαγε-
νέσθαι.

Ver. 16. προσερχώμεθα οὖν....
" Let us, therefore [i.e., seeing that we
have this sympathetic and victorious
High Priest] with confidence approach
the throne of grace ". προσέρχεσθαι is
used in a semi-technical sense for the
approach of a worshipper to God, as in
LXX frequently. Thus in Lev. xxi. 17
it is said of any blemished son of Aaron
οὐ προσελεύσεται προσφέρειν τὰ δῶρα
τοῦ Θεοῦ αὐτοῦ, and in the 23rd ver.
ἐγγιεῖ is used as an equivalent, cf. Heb.
vii. 19. The word is found only once in
St. Paul, 1 Tim. vi. 3, and there in a
peculiar sense ; but in Heb. it occurs
seven times, and generally in its more
technical sense, vii. 25, x. 1, 22, xi. 6.
It had become so much a technical term
of divine worship that it can be used, as
in x. 1, 22, without an object. Here, as
in vii. 25, it is followed by a dative τῷ
θρόνῳ τῆς χάριτος, the seat of supreme
authority which by Christ's intercession
is now characterised as the source from
which grace is dispensed. Premonitions
of this are found in O.T. ; for although
in Ps. xcvi. (xcvii.) 2 and elsewhere we
find δικαιοσύνη καὶ κρίμα κατόρθωσις
τοῦ θρόνου αὐτοῦ, yet in Isa. xvi. 5 we
read διορθωθήσεται μετ' ἐλέους θρόνος.
Philo encourages men to draw near to
God by representing " the merciful, and
gentle, and compassionate nature of Him
who is invoked, who would always rather
have mercy than punishment" (De Ex-
secr., c. ix). There is also something in
Theophylact's remark : Δύο γὰρ θρόνοι
εἰσὶν, ὁ μὲν νῦν χάριτος, . . . ὁ δὲ τῆς
δευτέρας παρουσίας θρόνος οὐ χάριτος
. . . ἀλλὰ κρίσεως. Similarly Atto :
" Modo tempus est donorum : nemo de
se ipso desperet ". They are to approach μετὰ παρρησίας, for as Philo
says (Quis. Rer. Div. Haer., 4) :
φιλοδεσπότοις ἀναγκαιότατον ἡ παρρησία κτῆμα ; and in c. 5. παρρησία φιλίας
συγγενές. The purpose of the approach
is expressed in two clauses which Bleek
declares to be " ganz synonym ".
This, however, is scarcely correct. As
is apparent from the next verse, the
" obtaining mercy" refers to the pardon
of sins, while the "finding grace " implies assistance given. So Primasius,

βωμεν ἔλεον,¹ καὶ χάριν εὕρωμεν εἰς εὔκαιρον βοήθειαν. V. 1. ᵃπᾶς a ii. 17, et
viii. 3.
γὰρ ἀρχιερεὺς ἐξ ἀνθρώπων λαμβανόμενος, ὑπὲρ ἀνθρώπων καθίσταται
τὰ πρὸς τὸν Θεόν, ἵνα προσφέρῃ δῶρά τε ² καὶ θυσίας ὑπὲρ ἁμαρτιῶν,

¹ T.R. in CᵇDᶜEL ; ἐλεος ℵABC*D*KP. "The exx. of interchange of -ος masc.
Decl. ii., and -ος neut. Decl. iii., have somewhat increased in number [in N.T. Greek]
in comparison with those in the classical language" (Blass, *Gram.*, p. 28, E. Tr.).

² δωρα τε with ℵACDᶜEKLP ; τε omitted by BDᵇ, vg., "ut offerat dona, et sacri-
ficia pro peccatis".

quoted by Westcott "ut misericordiam
consequamur, id est remissionem peccatorum, et gratiam donorum Spiritus
Sancti". ἔλεος and χάρις are, however,
constantly conjoined (*v.* Hort on 1 Pet. i.
2). The close connection of χάριν with
βοήθειαν suggests that ἔλεος is the more
general and comprehensive term, and
that χάρις is becoming already more
associated with particular manifestations
of ἔλεος. There may be ἔλεος, where
there is no χάρις. We first obtain mercy
and then find grace. εὑρίσκειν is everywhere in LXX used with χάριν in this
sense, translating מָצָא. εἰς εὔκαιρον βοήθειαν "for timely help"; assistance in hours of temptation must be
timely or it is useless. For βοήθεια *cf.*
ii. 18 ; and for the whole verse, see
Bishop Wilson's *Maxim* : "The most
dangerous of all temptations is to believe,
that one can avoid or overcome them by
our own strength, and without asking
the help of God".

CHAPTER V.—Ver. 1. Πᾶς γὰρ ἀρχιερεὺς . . . γὰρ introduces the ground of
the encouraging counsel of iv. 16, and
further confirms iv. 15. [But *cf.* Beza :
"Itaque γὰρ non tam est causalis quam
inchoativa, ut loquuntur grammatici" ;
and Westcott : "the γάρ is explanatory
and not strictly argumentative".] The
connection is : Come boldly to the throne
of grace ; let not sin daunt you, for
every high priest is appointed for the
very purpose of offering sacrifices *for sin*
(*cf.* viii. 3). This he must do because he
is appointed by God for this purpose,
and he does it readily and heartily because his own subjection to weakness
gives him sympathy. πᾶς ἀρχιερ.
"Every high priest," primarily, every
high priest known to you, or every ordinary Levitical high priest. There is no
need to extend the reference, as Peirce
does, to "others who were not of that
order". ἐξ ἀνθρώπων λαμβανόμενος,
"being taken from among men," not,
"who is taken from etc.," as if defining

a certain peculiar and exceptional kind
of high priest. It might almost be rendered "since he is taken from among
men" ; for the writer means that all
priesthood proceeds on this foundation,
and it is this circumstance that involves
what is afterwards more fully insisted
upon, that the high priest has sympathy.
For λαμβ. *cf.* Num. xxv. 4, viii. 6. On
the present tense, see below. Grotius
renders "segregare, ut quae ex acervo
desumimus". Being taken from among
men every high priest is also appointed
not for his own sake or to fulfil his own
purposes, but ὑπὲρ ἀνθρώπων καθίσταται,
"is appointed in man's behalf" ; not
with Calvin, "ordinat ea quae ad Deum
pertinent," taking καθ. as middle. The
word is in common use in classical
writers. "The customariness [implied
in λαμβ. and καθ.] applies not to the
action of the individual member of the
class, but to that of the class as a whole".
Burton, *M. and T.*, cxxiv. τὰ πρὸς τὸν
Θεόν, "in things relating to God" ; an
adverbial accusative as in Rom. xv. 17.
See Blass, *Gram.*, p. 94 ; and *cf.* Exod.
xviii. 19, γίνου σὺ τῷ λαῷ τὰ πρὸς τὸν
Θεόν. In all that relates to God the high
priest must mediate for men ; but he is
appointed especially and primarily, ἵνα
προσφέρῃ . . . ἁμαρτιῶν, "that he may
offer both gifts and sacrifices for sins".
Were there no sins there would be no
priest. The fact that we are sinners,
therefore, should not daunt us, or prevent
our using the intercession of the priest.
προσφέρειν, technical term, like our
"offer" ; not so used in the classics.
δῶρά τε καὶ θυσίας, the same combination is found in viii. 3 and ix. 9 with the
same conjunctions. Δῶρα as well as
θυσίαι include all kinds of sacrifices and
offerings. Thus in Lev. i. *passim, cf.*
ver. 3 : ἐὰν ὁλοκαύτωμα τὸ δῶρον αὐτοῦ.
It is best, therefore, to construe ὑπὲρ
ἁμαρτ. with προσφέρειν and not with
θυσίας ; *cf.* ver. 3 and x. 12. So Bleek
and Weiss against Grotius and others ;
e.g., Westcott, who says : "The clause

b ii. 18, et
iv. 15, et
vii. 28.
c vii. 27;
Lev. ix.
et xvi. 3,
etc.
d Exod.
xxviii.; 1 Par. xxiii. 13; 2 Par. xxvi. 16, etc.

2. ᵇμετριοπαθεῖν δυνάμενος τοῖς ἀγνοοῦσι καὶ πλανωμένοις, ἐπεὶ καὶ αὐτὸς περίκειται ἀσθένειαν · 3. ᶜκαὶ διὰ ταύτην¹ ὀφείλει, καθὼς περὶ τοῦ λαοῦ, οὕτω καὶ περὶ ἑαυτοῦ² προσφέρειν ὑπὲρ³ ἁμαρτιῶν. 4. ᵈΚαὶ οὐχ ἑαυτῷ τις λαμβάνει τὴν τιμὴν, ἀλλὰ ὁ καλούμενος⁴

¹ T.R. read by CᶜDᶜEKL ; δι αυτην by ℵABC*D*P, 7, 17, 80.
² T.R. with ℵACDᶜEKLP; αυτου with BD*, 219.
³ υπερ in CᶜDᶜEKL ; περι in ℵABC*D*P and in Levit. xvi. 6 and 15.
⁴ Omit art. with ℵABC*DEK ; insert art. CᵇLP.

ὑπὲρ ἁμ. is to be joined with θυσίας and not with προσφέρῃ as referring to both nouns. The two ideas of eucharistic and expiatory offerings are distinctly marked."

Ver. 2. μετριοπαθεῖν δυνάμενος: "as one who is able to moderate his feeling". The Vulgate is too strong: "qui condolere possit"; Grotius has: "non inclementer affici"; Weizsäcker: "als der billig fühlen kann"; and Peirce: "who can reasonably bear with". As the etymology shows, it means "to be moderate in one's passions". It was opposed by Aristotle to the ἀπάθεια of the Stoics. [Diog. Laert., Arist.: ἔφη δὲ τὸν σοφὸν μὴ εἶναι μὲν ἀπαθῆ μετριοπαθῆ δέ: not without feeling, but feeling in moderation; and Peirce, Tholuck, and Weiss conclude that the word was first formed by the Peripatetics; Tholuck expressly; and Weiss, "stammt aus dem philosophischen Sprachgebrauch". Cf. the chapter of Philo (Leg. Allegor., iii., 45 ; Wendland's ed., vol. i. 142) in which he puts ἀπάθεια first and μετριοπάθ. second; and to the numerous exx. cited by Wetstein and Kypke, add Nemesius, De Natura Hominis, cxix., where the word is defined in relation to grief. Josephus (Ant., xii. 3, 2) remarks upon the striking self-restraint and moderation (μετριοπαθησάντων) of Vespasian and Titus towards the Jews notwithstanding their many conflicts.] If the priest is cordially to plead with God for the sinner, he must bridle his natural disgust at the loathsomeness of sensuality, his impatience at the frequently recurring fall, his hopeless alienation from the hypocrite and the superficial, his indignation at any confession he hears from the penitent. This self-repression he must exercise τοῖς ἀγνοοῦσι καὶ πλανωμένοις: "the ignorant and erring". The single article leads Peirce and others to render as a Hendiadys = τοῖς ἐξ ἀγνοίας πλαν., those who err through ignorance. ἄγνοια is not frequent in LXX, but in Ezek. xlii. 13, and

also in chaps. xliv. and xlvi., it translates אָשָׁם, but in Lev. v. 18 and in Eccles. v. 5 it translates שְׁגָגָה which in Lev. iv. 2 and elsewhere is rendered by ἀκουσίως. A comparison too of the passages in which the word occurs seems to show that by "sins of ignorance" are meant both sins committed unawares or accidentally, and sins into which a man is betrayed by passion. They are opposed to presumptuous sins, sins with a high hand ἐν χειρὶ ὑπερηφανίας, בְּיָד רָמָה (Num. xv. 30), sins which constitute a renunciation of God and for which there is no sacrifice, cf. x. 26. ἐπεὶ καὶ αὐτὸς περίκειται ἀσθένειαν: "since he himself also is compassed with infirmity," giving the reason or ground of μετριοπ. δυναμένος. περίκειμαι, "I lie round," as in Mk. ix. 42, Luke xvii. 2 with περὶ and in Heb. xii. 1 with dative. In Acts xxviii. 20, τὴν ἅλυσιν ταύτην περίκειμαι, it is used passively as here, followed by an accusative according to the rule that verbs which in the active govern a dative of the person with an accusative of the thing, retain the latter in the passive. See Winer, p. 287. and Rutherford's Babrius. The priests, living for the greater part of the year in their own homes, were known to have their weaknesses like other men, and even the high priests were not exempt from the common passions. Their gorgeous robes alone separated them from sinners, but like a garment infirmity clung around them. "How the very sanctity of his office would force on the attention of one who was not a mere puppet priest the contrast between his official and his personal character, as a subject of solemn reflection" (Bruce).

Ver. 3. καὶ δι' αὐτὴν . . . ἁμαρτιῶν "and because of it is bound as for the people, so also for himself to offer for sins". Vaughan recommends the dele-

ὑπὸ τοῦ Θεοῦ, καθάπερ [1] καὶ ὁ [2] ᾿Ααρών. 5. ᵒ οὕτω καὶ ὁ Χριστὸς ᵉ i. 5; Ps.
οὐχ ἑαυτὸν ἐδόξασε γενηθῆναι ἀρχιερέα, ἀλλ᾿ ὁ λαλήσας πρὸς αὐτόν, ii. 7;
"Υἱός μου εἶ σὺ, ἐγὼ σήμερον γεγέννηκά σε". 6. ᶠ καθὼς καὶ ἐν xiii. 33.
ἑτέρῳ λέγει, "Σὺ ἱερεὺς εἰς τὸν αἰῶνα κατὰ τὴν τάξιν Μελχισεδέκ". ᶠ vii. 17;
Joan. viii.
54; Acts
Ps. cx.

[1] καθαπερ in אᶜCᵇDᶜEKLP; καθωσπερ in א*ABD*, 17.
[2] Delete o with אABCD, etc., and in conformity with this writer's usage.

tion of the stop at the end of ver. 2. The law which enjoined that the high priest should on the Day of Atonement sacrifice for himself and his house (ἐξιλάσεται περὶ αὐτοῦ καὶ τοῦ οἴκου αὐτοῦ) before he sacrificed περὶ τοῦ λαοῦ, is given in Lev. xvi. 6, 15.

Ver. 4. καὶ οὐχ ἑαυτῷ τις λαμβάνει τὴν τιμήν "And no one taketh to himself this honourable office." καί introduces a second qualification of the priest, implied in καθίσταται of ver. 1, but now emphasised. An additional reason for trusting in the priest is that he has not assumed the office to gratify his own ambition but to serve God's purpose of restoring men to His fellowship. All genuine priesthood is the carrying out of God's will. The priest must above all else be obedient, in sympathy w th God as well as in sympathy with man. God's appointment also secures that the suitable qualifications will be found in the priest. The office is here called τιμή, best translated by the German "Ehrenamt" or "Ehrenstelle." For τιμή meaning an office see Eurip., Helena, 15; Herodot., ii. 65, παῖς παρὰ πατρὸς ἐκδέκεται τὴν τιμήν; and especially Aristotle, Pol., iii. 10, τιμὰς γὰρ λέγομεν εἶναι τὰς ἀρχάς. Cf. Hor. i. 1, 8 "tergeminis honoribus". Frequently in Josephus τιμή is used of the high priesthood, see Antiq., xii. 2-5, iv. 1, etc.; and the same writer should be consulted for the historical illu-tration of this verse (Antiq., iii. 8-1). In this remarkable passage he represents Moses as saying ἔγωγε . . . ἐμαυτὸν ἂν τῆς τιμῆς ἄξιον ἔκρινα . . . νῦν δ᾿ αὐτὸς ὁ Θεὸς ᾿Ααρῶνα τῆς τιμῆς ταύτης ἄξιον ἔκρινε. The nolo episcopari implied in the words is amply illustrated in the case of Augustine, of John Knox, and especially of Anselm who declared he would rather have been cast on a stack of blazing faggots than set on the archiepiscopal throne, and continued to head his letters "Brother Anselm monk of Bec by choice, Archbishop of Canterbury by violence". On the other hand, see the account of the appointment by his own act (αὐτόχειρ) of the priest king in

Aricia, in Strabo v. 3-12 and elsewhere. ἀλλὰ καλούμενος . . . καθώσπερ καὶ ᾿Ααρών. "but when called by God as in point of fact even Aaron was". If the article is retained before καλ. we must translate "but he that is called," καλούμενος "in diesem amtlichen Sinne nur hier," says Weiss, but see Matt. iv. 21, Gal. i. 15. For Aaron's call, see Exod. xxviii. 1 ff. Schöttgen and Wetstein appositely quote from the Bammidbar Rabbi "Moses said to Korah and his associates:—If my brother Aaron took to himself the priesthood, then ye did well to rebel against him; but in truth God gave it to him, whose is the greatness and the power and the glory. Whosoever, then, rises against Aaron, does he not rise against God?" It is notorious that the contemporary priesthood did not fulfil the description here given.

Ver. 5. οὕτω καὶ ὁ Χριστὸς. . . . "So even the Christ glorified not himself to be made a high priest." ["So hat auch der Christus nicht sich selbst die Herrlichkeit des Hohenpriestertums zugeeignet,' Weizsäcker.] The designation, "the Christ," is introduced, because it might not have seemed so significant a statement if made of "Jesus". It was not personal ambition that moved Christ. He did not come in His own name, nor did He seek to glorify Himself. See John viii. 54; v. 31, 43; xvii. 5, and passim. ἀλλ᾿ ὁ λαλήσας . . . Μελχισεδέκ. "but He [glorified Him to be made a priest] who said, Thou art My Son, I this day have begotten Thee; as also in another place He says, Thou art a priest for ever after the order Melchizedek". The question here is: Why does the writer introduce the quotation from the 2nd Psalm at all? Why does he not directly prove his point by the quotation from the Messianic 110th Psalm? Does he mean that He who said, Thou art my Son, glorified Christ as priest in saying this? Apparently he does, otherwise the καί in καθὼς καὶ ἐν ἑτέρῳ would be unwarranted. By introducing the former of the two quotations and designating

g Matt.   7. ⁸⁹Ὃς ἐν ταῖς ἡμέραις τῆς σαρκὸς αὐτοῦ, δεήσεις τε καὶ ἱκετηρίας
xxvi. 38,
etc., et   πρὸς τὸν δυνάμενον σώζειν αὐτὸν ἐκ θανάτου, μετὰ κραυγῆς ἰσχυρᾶς
xxvii. 46,
50; Marc.
xiv. 33, 36, et xv. 34, 37; Luc. xxii. 42, et xxiii. 46; Joan. xii. 27, et xvii. 1.

God as He that called Christ Son, or
nominated him to the Messianic dignity,
which involved the priesthood, he shows
that the greater and more comprehensive
office of Messiahship was not assumed
by Christ at His own instance and
therefore that the priesthood included in
this was not of His own seeking, but of
God's ordaining; cf. Weiss. Bleek says
the reference to Psalm ii. is made to
lessen the marvel that God should glorify
Christ as priest. Similarly Riehm "dass
Christus in einem so unvergleichlich
innigen Verhältnisse zu Gott steht, dass
seine Berufung zum Hohepriesteramt
nicht befreundlich sein kann;" and
Davidson, "It is by no means meant
that the priesthood of Christ was
involved in His Sonship (Alford), an *a
priori* method of conception wholly
foreign to the Epistle, but merely that
it was suitable in one who was Son,
being indeed possible to none other (see
on i. 3)." Bruce thinks the writer wishes to
teach that Christ's priesthood is coeval
with His Sonship and inherent in it.
κατὰ τὴν τάξιν "after the order;"
among its other meanings τάξις denotes
a class or rank, "ordo quâ dicitur
quispiam senatorii ordinis, vel equestris
ordinis". Thus in Demosthenes, οἰκέτου
τάξιν οὐκ ἐλευθέρου παιδὸς ἔχων, in
Diod. Sic., iii. 6, οἱ περὶ τὰς τῶν θεῶν
θεραπείας διατρίβοντες ἱερεῖς, μεγίστην
καὶ κυριωτάτην τάξιν ἔχοντες. In the
subsequent exposition of the Melch.
priesthood it is chiefly on εἰς τὸν αἰῶνα
that emphasis is laid.

Ver 7. ὃς . . . ἔμαθεν . . . καὶ ἐγένετο.
In these verses the writer shows how
much there was in the call to the
priesthood repugnant to flesh and blood;
how it was through painful obedience,
not by arrogant ambition he became
Priest. The main statement is, He
learned obedience and became perfect
as Saviour. ὃς ἐν τ. ἡμέραις τῆς σαρκὸς
αὐτοῦ "who in the days of His flesh,"
and when therefore He was like His
brethren in capacity for temptation and
suffering; cf. ii. 14. δεήσεις . . .
προσενέγκας "having offered up prayers
and supplications with strong crying
and tears unto him that was able to
save him from death". προσενέγκας
has sometimes been supposed to refer

to the προσφέρειν of ver. 3, and to have a
sacrificial sense. It was such an offering
as became His innocent ἀσθένεια. As
the ordinary high priest prepared himself
for offering for the people by offering
for himself, so, it is thought, Christ was
prepared for the strictly sacrificial or
priestly work by the feeling of His own
weakness. There is truth in this. Weiss'
reason for excluding this reference is
" dass ein Opfern mit starkem Geschrei
und Thränen eine unvollziehbare Vorstellung ist". Cf. Davidson, p. 113, note.
προσφ. is used with δέησιν in later
Greek writers: instances in Bleek.
δεήσεις τε καὶ ἱκετηρίας, these words
are elsewhere combined as in Isocrates,
De Pace, 46; Polybius, iii. 112, 8; cf.
Job. xl. 22. The relation of the two
words is well brought out in a passage
from Philo quoted by Carpzov: γραφὴ
δὲ μηνύσει μου τὴν δέησιν τὴν ἀνθ'
ἱκετηρίας προτείνω. Cf. Eurip., Iph.
Aul., 1216. ἱκετηρία [from ἵκω I come,
ἱκέτης one who comes as a suppliant]
is originally an adjective = fit for sup-
pliants, then an olive branch [sc. ἐλαία,
or ῥάβδος] bound with wool which the
suppliant carried as a symbol of his
prayer. The conjunction of words in
this verse is for emphasis. These supplications were accompanied μετὰ κραυγῆς
ἰσχυρᾶς καὶ δακρύων "with strong crying
and tears," expressing the intensity of
the prayers and so the keenness of the
suffering. The "strong crying" is striking. Schöttgen quotes: "There are
three kinds of prayers, each loftier than
the preceding: prayer, crying, and tears.
Prayer is silent, crying with raised voice,
tears overcome all things." It is to the
scene in Gethsemane reference is made,
and although "tears" are not mentioned
by the evangelists in relating that scene,
they are implied, and this writer might
naturally thus represent the emotion of
our Lord. The prayer was addressed
πρὸς τὸν δυνάμενον σώζειν αὐτὸν ἐκ
θανάτου "to Him that was able to save
Him from death," which implies that the
prayer was that Christ might be saved
from death [" Father if it be possible, let
this cup pass from me"] but also suggests
that the prayer was not formally answered
—else why emphasise that God had power
to answer it? σώζειν ἐκ θανάτου. The

καὶ δακρύων προσενέγκας, καὶ εἰσακουσθεὶς ἀπὸ τῆς εὐλαβείας, 8. h Phil. ii. 6,
etc.
h καίπερ ὢν υἱός, ἔμαθεν ἀφ' ὧν ἔπαθε τὴν ὑπακοήν, 9. i καὶ τελειω- i ii. 10.

prayer recorded in Mark xiv. 36, and the anticipation of Gethsemane alluded to in John xii. 57 [Πάτερ σῶσόν με ἐκ τῆς ὥρας ταύτης] are sufficient to show that it is deliverance from dying that is meant. Milligan, however, says : "Christ is thus represented as praying not that death may be averted, but that He may be saved 'out of it,' when it comes." Westcott thinks the word covers both ideas and that in the first sense the prayer was not granted, that it might be granted in the second. It is preferable to abide by the simple statement that the passion of Christ's prayer to escape death was intensified by the fact that He knew God could deliver Him by twelve legions of angels or otherwise. His absolute faith in the Father's almighty power and infinite resource was the very soul of his trial. καὶ εἰσακουσθεὶς ἀπὸ τῆς εὐλαβείας "and having been heard on account of His godly reverence". εὐλάβεια [from εὖ λαβεῖν to take good hold, or careful hold] denotes the cautious regard which a wise man pays to all the circumstances of an action. Thus Fabius Cunctator was termed εὐλαβής. And in regard to God εὐλάβεια means that reverent submission to His will which caution or prudence dictates. [See Prov. xxviii. 14 and the definitions by Philo. Quis. Rer. Div. Haer., 6.] That ἀπό following εἰσακουσθεὶς means in Biblical Greek "on account of" we have proof in Job xxxv. 12 and Luke xix. 3, as well as from the frequent use of ἀπό in N.T. to denote cause, John xxi. 6; Acts xii. 14, etc. In classical Greek also ἀπό is used for propter, see Aristoph., Knights, l. 767 ὡς ἀπὸ μικρῶν εὔνους αὐτῷ θωπευματίων γεγένησαι. See also the Birds, l. 150 The cautious reverence, or reverent caution—the fear lest He should oppose God or seem to overpersuade Him—which was heard and answered was expressed in the second petition of the prayer in Gethsemane, "Not my will but thine be done". And ἀπό is used in preference to διά, apparently because the source of the particular petition is meant to be indicated, that we may understand that the truest answer to this reverent submission was to give Him the cup to drink and thus to accomplish through Him the faultless will of God. To have removed the cup and saved Him from death would not have answered the εὐλάβεια of the prayer. The meaning

of the clause is further determined by what follows.

Ver. 8. καίπερ ὢν υἱὸς ἔμαθεν ἀφ' ὧν ἔπαθε τὴν ὑπακοήν [having been heard . . .] although He was a son He learned obedience from the things He suffered. The result of his being heard was therefore that he suffered, but in the suffering He learned obedience, perfect unison with the will of God for the salvation of men so that He became a perfected Priest. He learned obedience καίπερ ὢν υἱός : "this is stated to obviate the very idea of assumption on his part" (Davidson). Perhaps, therefore, we should translate, with a reference to ver. 5, "although He was Son". Although Son and therefore possessed of Divine love and in sympathy with the Divine purpose, He had yet to learn that perfect submission which is only acquired by obeying in painful, terrifying circumstances. He made deeper and deeper experience of what obedience is and costs. And the particular obedience [τὴν ὑπακ.] which was required of Him in the days of His flesh was that which at once gave Him perfect entrance into the Divine love and human need. It is when the child is told to do something which pains him, and which he shrinks from, that he learns obedience, learns to submit to another will. And the things which Christ suffered in obeying God's will taught Him perfect submission and at the same time perfect devotedness to man. On this obedience, see Robertson Smith in Expositor for 1881, p. 424. καίπερ is often joined with the participle to emphasise its concessive use [see Burton, 437], as in Diod. Sic., iii. 17, οὗτος ὁ βίος καίπερ ὢν παράδοξος. ἔμαθεν ἀφ' ὧν ἔπαθε, a common form of attraction and also a common proverbial saying, of which Wetstein gives a number of instances; Herodot. i. 207; Æsch., Agam., 177, πάθει μάθος, Demosth., 1232 τοὺς μετὰ τὸ παθεῖν μανθάνοντας. Carpzov also quotes several from Philo, as from the De Somn., ὁ παθὼν ἀκριβῶς ἔμαθεν, and De Profug., 25. ἔμαθον μὲν ὁ ἔπαθον. see also Blass, Gram., p. 299 E. Tr.

Ver. 9. καὶ τελειωθεὶς . . . αἰωνίου "and having [thus] been perfected became to all who obey Him the source [originator] of eternal salvation". τελειωθεὶς (v. ii. 10) having been perfectly equipped with every qualification for the

θεὶς ἐγένετο τοῖς ὑπακούουσιν αὐτῷ πᾶσιν αἴτιος σωτηρίας αἰωνίου.
10. προσαγορευθεὶς ὑπὸ τοῦ Θεοῦ ἀρχιερεὺς κατὰ τὴν τάξιν Μελχισεδέκ.

11. Περὶ οὗ πολὺς ἡμῖν ὁ λόγος καὶ δυσερμήνευτος λέγειν, ἐπεὶ

priestly office by the discipline already
described. Several interpreters (Theodoret, Bleek, Westcott) include in the
word the exaltation of Christ, but
illegitimately. The word must be interpreted by its connection with ἔμαθεν
ὑπακοήν; and here it means the completion of Christ's moral discipline,
which ended in His death. He thus
became αἴτιος σωτηρίας αἰωνίου author,
or cause of eternal salvation, in fulfilment
of the call to an eternal priesthood, ver. 6
εἰς τὸν αἰῶνα and ver. 10. αἴτιος frequently used in a similar sense from
Homer downwards, as in Diod. Sic., iv. 82,
αἴτιος ἐγένετο τῆς σωτηρίας. Aristoph.,
Clouds, 85, οὗτος γὰρ ὁ θεὸς αἴτιός μοι τῶν
κακῶν. Philo, *De Agri.*, 22, π ᾶ σ ι τ ο ῖ ς
ὑ π α κ ο ύ ο υ σ ι ν α ὐ τ ῷ with a reference
to τὴν ὑπακ. of ver. 8. The saved must
pass through an experience similar to the
Saviour's. Their salvation is in learning to
obey. Thus they are harmonised to the
one supreme and perfect will. This is
reversely given in ii. 10.

Ver. 10. προσαγορευθεὶς . . . Μελχισεδέκ "styled by God High Priest
after the order of Melchizedek". "προσαγορεύειν expresses the formal and
solemn ascription of the title to Him
to whom it belongs ('addressed as,'
'styled')" (Westcott). "When the Son
ascended and appeared in the sanctuary
on High, God saluted Him or addressed
Him as an High Priest after the order of
Melchizedek, and, of course, in virtue of
such an address constituted Him such
an High Priest" (Davidson). Originally
called to the priesthood by the words of
Ps. cx., He is now by His resurrection
and ascension declared to be perfectly
consecrated and so installed as High
Priest after the order of Melchizedek.
It may be doubted, however, whether
the full meaning of προσαγορεύειν "address" should here be found. The commoner meaning in writers of the time is
"named" or "called". Thus in Plutarch's
Pericles, iv. 4, Anaxagoras, ὃν Νοῦν προσ-
ηγόρευον, xxvii. 2, λευκὴν ἡμέραν
ἐκείνην προσαγ., xxiv. 6, of Aspasia,
Ἥρα προσαγορεύεται. and viii. 2 of
Pericles himself, Ὀλύμπιον . . . προσ-
αγορευθῆναι. So in Diod. Sic., i. 51,
of the Egyptians, τάφους ἀϊδίους οἴκους
προσαγορεύουσιν. It cannot be certainly

concluded either from the tense or the
context that this "naming" is to be
assigned to the date of the ascension
and not to the original appointment.
The emphasis is on the words ὑπὸ τοῦ
Θεοῦ, not by man but by God has Christ
been named High Priest; and on κατὰ
. . . Μελχ. as warranting αἰωνίου.

The passage v. 11 to vi. 20 is a digression occasioned by the writer's reflection that his argument from the
priesthood of Melchizedek may be too
difficult for his hearers. In order to
stimulate attention he chides and warns
them, pointing out the danger of back-
wardness. He justifies, however, his
delivery of difficult doctrine notwithstanding their sluggishness, and this on
two grounds: (1) because to lay again
the foundations after men have once
known them is useless (vi. 1-8); and (2)
because he cannot but believe that his
readers are after all in scarcely so despe-
rate a condition. They need to have
their hope renewed. This hope they
have every reason to cherish, seeing that
their fathers have already entered into
the enjoyment of it, that God who cannot lie has sworn to the fulfilment of the
promises, and that Jesus has entered the
heavenly world as their forerunner. Ver.
11-14. Complaint of their sluggishness
of mind.

Ver. 11. περὶ οὗ. "Of whom," not,
as Grotius (*cf.* Delitzsch and von Soden)
"De quâ," of which priesthood. It is
simplest to refer the relative to the last
word Μελχισεδέκ; possible to refer it
to ἀρχιερεὺς . . . Μελχ. The former
seems justified by the manner in which
c. vii. resumes οὗτος γὰρ ὁ Μελχ. No
doubt the reference is not barely to Melchizedek, but to Melchizedek as type of
Christ's priesthood. Concerning Melchisedek he has much to say πολὺς ἡμῖν
ὁ λόγος, not exactly equivalent to ἡμῶν
ὁ λόγος, but rather signifying "the exposition which it is incumbent on us to
undertake". [*Cf. Antigone*, 748, ὁ γοῦν
λόγος σοι πᾶς ὑπὲρ κείνης ὅδε.] The
exposition is necessarily of some extent
(c. vii.), although of his whole letter he
finds it possible to say (xiii. 22) διὰ
βραχέων ἐπέστειλα. It is also δυσερμήνευτος "difficult to explain," "hard to
render intelligible." "ininterpretabilis"

νωθροὶ γεγόνατε ταῖς ἀκοαῖς. 12. ᵏ καὶ γὰρ ὀφείλοντες εἶναι διδάσ- k 1 Cor. iii.
καλοι διὰ τὸν χρόνον, πάλιν χρείαν ἔχετε τοῦ διδάσκειν ὑμᾶς, τίνα¹ ᴵ Peter ii.2.
τὰ στοιχεῖα τῆς ἀρχῆς τῶν λογίων τοῦ Θεοῦ· καὶ γεγόνατε χρείαν

¹ τίνα as in Syr., vg., "quae sint elementa". So Origen, Jerome, Augustine,
Cyril. τινὰ Lachmann, WH, Baljon; after Œcumenius and as giving better sense.
"Theory is the guide of practice, practice the life of theory" (Roberts, Clavis
Bibliorum). "The interpreter needs oratio, meditatio, tentatio."

(Vulg.) ; used of dreams in Artemidorus,
τοῖς πολλοῖς δυσερμήνευτοι (Wetstein).
This difficulty, however, arises not wholly
from the nature of the subject, but rather
from the unpreparedness of the readers,
ἐπεὶ νωθροὶ γεγόνατε ταῖς ἀκοαῖς "seeing that you are become dull of hearing". νωθρός = νωθής [see Prom. Vinct.,
62] slow, sluggish ; used by Dionysius
Hal., to denote λίθου φύσιν ἀναίσθητον,
ἀκίνητον. But Plato was said to be
νωθρός in comparison with Aristotle.
Babrius uses the word of the numbed
limbs of the sick lion and of the
"stupid" hopes of the wolf that heard
the nurse threaten to throw the child
to the wolves. ταῖς ἀκοαῖς "in your
sense of hearing." Both in classical and
biblical Greek ἀκοή has three meanings,
"the thing heard," as in John xii. 38;
"the sense of hearing," as in 1 Cor.
xii. 17; and "the ear," as in Mark vii.
35, ἠνοίγησαν αὐτοῦ αἱ ἀκοαί ; cf.
Plummer on Luke, p. 194. Here the
ear stands for intelligent and spiritual
reception of truth. γεγόνατε, "ye are
become," and therefore were not always.
It is not a natural and inherent and
pardonable weakness of understanding
he complains of, but a culpable incapa-
city resulting from past neglect of opportunities.
Ver. 12. καὶ γὰρ ὀφείλοντες. . . .
"For indeed, though in consideration of
the time [since you received Christ] ye
ought to be teachers, ye have need again
that some one teach you the rudiments of
the beginning [the elements] of the
oracles of God."—διὰ τὸν χρόνον, cf.
ii. 3, x. 32 ; how long they had professed Christianity we do not know, but
quite possibly for twenty or thirty years.
Those who had for a time themselves
been Christians were expected to have
made such attainment in knowledge as
to become διδάσκαλοι. This advance
was their duty, ὀφείλοντες. Instead of
thus accumulating Christian knowledge,
they had let slip even the rudiments, so
far at any rate as to allow them to fall
into the background of their mind and
to become inoperative. Their primal need

of instruction had recurred. The need
had again arisen, τοῦ διδάσκειν ὑμᾶς
τινὰ "of some one teaching you," the
genitive following χρείαν, as in ver. 12
and in x. 36. The indefinite pronoun
seems preferable, as the form of the sentence requires an expressed subject to
bring out the contrast to εἶναι διδάσκαλοι, and to ὑμᾶς. τὰ στοιχεῖα . . .
Θεοῦ. The meaning of τῆς ἀρχῆς would
seem to be determined by τῆς ἀρχῆς τ.
Χριστοῦ in vi. 1, where it apparently
denotes the initial stages of a Christian
profession, the stages in which the elements of the Christian faith would
naturally be taught. Here, then, "the
beginning of the oracles of God" would
mean the oracles of God as taught in
the beginning of one's education by these
oracles. This of itself is a strong enough
expression, but to make it stronger τὰ
στοιχεῖα is added, as if he said "the
rudiments of the rudiments," the A B C
of the elements. τῶν λογίων τ. θεοῦ,
"oraculorum Dei, i.e., Evangelii, in quo
maxima et summe necessaria sunt Dei
oracula, quae et sic dicuntur, 1 Peter iv.
11" (Grotius). The "Oracles of God"
sometimes denote the O.T., as in Rom.
iii. 2, Acts vii. 38; but here it is rather
the utterance of God through the Son
(i. 1), the salvation preached by the Lord
(ii. 3) (so Weiss). καὶ γεγόνατε χρείαν
ἔχοντες γάλακτος . . . "and are become such as have need of milk and not
of solid food," "et facti estis quibus lacte
opus sit, non solido cibo" (Vulgate). For
the metaphor, cf. 1 Peter ii. 2; 1 Cor.
iii. 1-3, a strikingly analogous passage,
cf. John xvi. 12, and the Rabbinic term
for young students "Theenekoth"
"Sucklings" (Schoettgen). The same
figure is found in Philo, De Agric., ii.
(Wendland, vol. ii., p. 96) ἐπεὶ δὲ νηπίοις
μέν ἐστι γάλα τροφή, τελείοις δὲ τὰ
ἐκ πυρῶν πέμματα· καὶ ψυχῆς κ.τ.λ.
Abundant illustrations from Greek literature in Wetstein. Instead of becoming
adults, able to stand on their own feet,
select and digest their own food, they
had fallen into spiritual dotage, had
entered a second childhood, and could

l ı Cor. iii
2, et xiv.
20; Eph
iv. 14.

ἔχοντες γάλακτος, καὶ οὐ στερεᾶς τροφῆς. 13. ¹πᾶς γὰρ ὁ μετέχων
γάλακτος, ἄπειρος λόγου δικαιοσύνης· νήπιος γάρ ἐστι· 14. τελείων
δέ ἐστιν ἡ στερεὰ τροφὴ, τῶν διὰ τὴν ἕξιν τὰ αἰσθητήρια γεγυμνα-

only receive the simplest nou.ishment.
Milk represents traditional teaching, that
which has been received and digested by
others, and is suitable for those who
have no teeth of their own and no sufficiently strong powers of digestion.
This teaching is admirably adapted to
the first stage of Christian life, but it
cannot form mature Christians. For this,
στερεὰ τροφή is essential.

Ver. 13. πᾶς γὰρ ... νήπιος γάρ
ἐστι. "For every one who partakes of
milk [as his sole diet] is without experience of the word of righteousness ;
for he is a babe." The reference of
γὰρ is somewhat obscure. It seems intended to substantiate the last clause of
ver. 12 : "Ye cannot receive solid food,
for you have no experience of the word of
righteousness". But he softens the statement by generalising it. Every one that
lives on milk is necessarily unacquainted
with the higher teaching, which is now
λόγος δικ. ἄπειρος having no experience of, ignorant ; as κακότητος ἄπειροι,
Empedocles in Fairbanks, Phil. of
Greece, p. 202. ἄπειρος ἀγρεύειν, Babrius, lxix. 2 ; ἀπ. τοῦ ἀγωνίζεσθαι, An-
tiphon, Jebb, p. 8. λόγου δικαιοσύνης,
with teaching of righteous conduct the
suckling has nothing to do; he cannot
act for himself, but can merely live
and grow; he cannot discern good and
evil, and must take what is given him.
Righteousness is not within the suckling's horizon. He cannot as yet be
taught it; still less can he be a teacher
of it (ver. 12) νήπιος γάρ ἐστι, for he
cannot even speak [νη-έπος=infans], he
is an infant. The infant can neither
understand nor impart teaching regarding a life of which he has no experience,
and whose language he does not know.
Indirectly, this involves that the higher
instruction the writer wished to deliver
was important because of its bearing on
conduct. [Other interpretations abound.
Chrysostom and Theophylact understand
the reference to be either to the Christian
life or to Christ Himself and the know-
edge of His person. Others, as Beza,
Lünemann, and many others, take it as
"a periphrasis for Christianity or the
Gospel, inasmuch as the righteousness
which avails with God is precisely the
contents of the Gospel". Riehm also
thinks that the Gospel is meant, "be-

cause it leads to righteousness ". Westcott understands it of the "teaching
which deals at once with the one source
of righteousness in Christ, and the means
by which man is enabled to be made
partaker of it". The view of Carpzov,
and also that of Bleek, is governed by
the connection of Melchizedek with
righteousness in vii. 2.]

Ver. 14. τελείων δὲ. ... "But solid
food is for the mature, those who, by
reason of their mental habits, have their
senses exercised to discern good and
evil." τέλειος commonly opposed in
classical and Biblical Greek to νήπιος ;
as in Polyb. v. 29, 2, ἐλπίσαντες ὡς
παιδίῳ νηπίῳ χρήσασθαι τῷ Φιλίππῳ,
εὗρον αὐτὸν τέλειον ἄνδρα. Cf. Eph.
iv. 13 ; and Xen., Cyr., viii. 7, 3. They
are here further defined as τῶν ...
κακοῦ. ἕξις [from ἔχω, as habitus from
habeo], a habit of body, or of mind; as
in Plato, Laws (p. 666), τὴν ἐμμανῆ ἕξιν
τῶν νέων. Also, p. 966, Ἀνδραπόδου γάρ
τινα σὺ λέγεις ἕξιν. Aristotle (Nic. Eth.
ii. 5) determines that virtue is neither a
δύναμις nor a πάθος, but a ἕξις, a
faculty being something natural and
innate, while virtue is not. Plutarch
(Moral., 443), following him, defines
ἕξις as ἰσχὺς ... ἐξ ἔθους ἐγγινομένη,
which resembles Quintilian's definition
(x. 1, 1), "firma quaedam facilitas, quae
apud Graecos ἕξις nominatur ". Aristotle
(Categor., viii. 1) distinguishes ἕξις from
διάθεσις, τῷ πολὺ χρονιώτερον εἶναι καὶ
μονιμώτερον, but elsewhere he uses the
words as equivalents. Longinus (xliv. 4)
uses it of faculty. ἕξις, then, is the
habitual or normal condition, the disposition or character; and the expression in the text means that the mature,
by reason of their maturity or mental
habit, have their senses exercised, etc.
αἰσθητήρια: "senses". Bleek quotes
the definition of the Greek lexicographers and of Damascene τὰ ὄργανα
ἢ τὰ μέλη δι᾽ ὧν αἰσθανόμεθα. So
Galen in Wetstein, "organs of sense".
Here the reference is to spiritual faculties
of perception and taste. γεγυμνασμένα
... πρὸς διάκρισιν ..., "exercised so
as to discriminate between good and
evil," i.e., between what is wholesome
and what is hurtful in teaching. [Wet-
stein quotes from Galen, De Dignot.
Puls., ὃς μὲν γὰρ τὸ αἰσθητήριον ἔχει

σμένα ἐχόντων πρὸς διάκρισιν καλοῦ τε καὶ κακοῦ. VI. 1. Διὸ
ἀφέντες τὸν τῆς ἀρχῆς τοῦ Χριστοῦ λόγον, ἐπὶ τὴν τελειότητα φερώ-

γεγυμνασμένον ἱκανῶς οὗτος ἄριστος ἂν
εἴη γνώμων.] The child must eat what
is given to it; the boy is warned what to
eat and what to avoid; as he grows, his
senses are exercised by a various experience, so that when he reaches manhood
he does not need a nurse or a priest to
teach him what is nutritious and what
is poisonous. The first evidence of
maturity which the writer cites is ability
to teach; the second, trained discernment of what is wholesome in doctrine.
The one implies the other. Cf. Isa. vii.
16, πρὶν γνῶναι τὸ παιδίον ἀγαθὸν ἢ
κακόν, and Deut. i. 39. Chrysostom
says οὐ περὶ βίου ὁ λόγος . . . ἀλλὰ
περὶ δογμάτων ὑγιῶν καὶ ὑψηλῶν
διεφθαρμένων τε καὶ ταπεινῶν; the
whole passage should be consulted.

CHAPTER VI.—Ver. 1. Διὸ "wherefore," i.e., because beginnings belong
to a stage which ought long since to
have been left behind (v. 12), ἀφέντες
. . . let us abandon [give up] the
elementary teaching about Christ and
press on to maturity. [Of the use
of ἀφιέναι in similar connections Bleek
gives many instances of which Eurip.,
Androm., 393 may be cited: ἀλλὰ τὴν
ἀρχὴν ἀφεὶς πρὸς τὴν τελευτὴν ὑστέραν
οὖσαν φέρῃ. ἐπὶ τὴν τελειότητα
φερώμεθα is an expression which was
in vogue in the Pythagorean schools.
[Westcott and Weiss press the passive.
"The thought is not primarily of personal effort . . . but of personal surrender to an active influence." But
φέρομαι is used where it is difficult to
discover a passive sense.] It is questioned whether the words are merely the
expression of the teacher's resolution to
advance to a higher stage of instruction,
or are meant as an exhortation to the
readers to advance to perfectness. Davidson advocates the former view, Peake
the latter. It would seem that the author
primarily refers to his own teaching.
The context and the use of λόγον favour
this view. He has been chiding them
for remaining so long "babes," able to
receive only "milk"; let us, he says,
leave this rudimentary teaching and proceed to what is more nutritious. But
with his advance in teaching, their advance in knowledge and growth in character is closely bound up. What the
writer definitely means by τὸν τ. ἀρχῆς
τ. Χριστοῦ λόγον, he explains in his

detailed description of the "foundation,"
which is not again to be laid. It consists
of the teaching that must first be given
to those who seek some knowledge of
Christ. Westcott explains the expression
thus: "the word, the exposition, of the
beginning, the elementary view of the
Christ"; although he probably too nar-
rowly restricts the meaning of "the beginning of Christ" when he explains it as
"the fundamental explanation of the fulfilment of the Messianic promises in Jesus
of Nazareth". Weiss thinks the writer
urges abandonment of the topics with
which he and his readers had been occupied in the Epistle ["also des bisherigen
Inhalts des Briefes".] But this is not
necessarily implied, and indeed is excluded
by the advanced character of much of the
preceding teaching. What was taught
the Hebrews at their first acquaintance
with the Christ must be abandoned, not
as if it had been misleading, but as one
leaves behind school books or foundations: "non quod eorum oblivisci unquam
debeant fideles, sed quia in illis minime
est haerendum". Calvin: as Paul says,
τὰ μὲν ὀπίσω ἐπιλανθανόμενος, Phil. iii.
13. μὴ πάλιν θεμέλιον καταβαλλόμενοι
"not again and again laying a foundation". θεμέλιον possibly a neuter (see
Deissmann, Bibelstudien, 119) as in Acts
xvi. 16; certainly masculine in 2 Tim. ii.
19; Heb. xi. 10; Rev. xxi. 14, 19 twice.
καταβαλλ. the usual word for expressing
the idea of "laying" foundations, as in
Dionys. Hal., iii. 69; Josephus Ant., xv.
11, 3; metaphorically in Eurip., Helena,
164; hence καταβολὴ κόσμου, the foundation of the world. Then follow six particulars in which this foundation consists.
Various arrangements and interpretations
have been offered. Dr. Bruce says: "We
are tempted to adopt another hypothesis,
namely, that the last four are to be regarded as the foundation of the first two,
conceived not as belonging to the foundation, but rather as the superstructure.
On this view we should have to render
'Not laying again a foundation for repentance and faith, consisting in instructions concerning baptisms, laying on of
hands, resurrection, and judgment.' In
favour of this construction is the reading
διδαχήν found in B, and adopted by
Westcott and Hort, which being in opposition with θεμέλιον suggests that the
four things following form the foundation

μεθα· μὴ πάλιν θεμέλιον καταβαλλόμενοι μετανοίας ἀπὸ νεκρῶν ἔργων, καὶ πίστεως ἐπὶ Θεὸν, 2. βαπτισμῶν διδαχῆς,[1] ἐπιθέσεώς τε

[1] T.R. in אACDEKL, vg.; διδαχην in B.

of repentance and faith." But Dr. Bruce returns to the idea that six articles are mentioned as forming the foundation, and Westcott, although adopting the reading **διδαχήν**, makes no use of it. Balfour (*Central Truths*) in an elaborate paper on the passage suggests that only four articles are mentioned, the words, **βαπτισμῶν . . . χειρῶν** being introduced parenthetically, because the writer cannot refrain from pointing out that repentance and faith were respectively taught by two legal rites, baptism and laying on of hands. The probability, however, is, as we shall see, that six fundamentals are intended, and that they are not so non-Christian as is sometimes supposed. These six fundamentals are arranged in three pairs, the first of which is **μετανοίας . . . Θεόν** "repentance from dead works and faith toward God". Repentance and faith are conjoined in Mark i. 15; Acts xx. 21; *cf.* 1 Thess. i. 9. They are found together in Scripture because they are conjoined in life, and are indeed but different aspects of one spiritual act. A man repents because a new belief has found entrance into his mind. Repentance is here characterised as **ἀπὸ νεκρῶν ἔργων.** Many explanations are given. ["Hanc vero phrasin apud scriptores Judaicos mihi nondum occurrisse lubens fateor" (Schoettgen).] The only other place where works are thus designated is ix. 14, where the blood of Christ is said to cleanse the conscience from dead works and thus to fit for the worship of the living God; on which Chrysostom remarks εἴ τις ἥψατο τότε νεκροῦ ἐμιαίνετο· καὶ ἐνταῦθα εἴ τις ἄψαιτο νεκροῦ ἔργου, μολύνεται διὰ τῆς συνειδήσεως, as if sins were called "dead" simply because they defile and unfit for God's worship. [On this view Weiss remarks, "wenigstens etwas Richtiges zu Grunde".] Others think that "dead" here means "deadly" or "death-bringing"; so Peirce; or that it is meant that sins have no strength, are "devoid of life and power"; so Tholuck, Alford; or are "vain and fruitless" (Lünemann). Hofmann says that every work is dead in which there is not inherent any life from God. Similarly Westcott, who says: "There is but one spring of life and all which does not flow from it is

'dead'. All acts of a man in himself, separated from God, are 'dead works'." Davidson thinks that this is "hardly enough," and adds "they seem so called because being sinful they belong to the sphere of that which is separate from the living God, the sphere of death (ii. 14, etc.)". Rather it may be said that dead works are such as have no living connection with the character but are done in mere compliance with the law and therefore accomplish nothing. They are like a dead fleece laid on a wolf, not a part of his life and growing out of him. *Cf.* Bleek and Weiss. Such repentance was especially necessary in Jewish Christians. **καὶ πίστεως ἐπὶ θεόν**, the counterpart of the preceding. The abandonment of formal, external righteousness results from confidence in God as faithful to His promises and furnishing an open way to Himself. What is meant is not only faith in God's existence, which of course had not to be taught to a Jew, but trust in God. Faith is either **εἰς**, **πρός, ἐν**, or **ἐπί** as union, relation, rest, or direction is meant (Vaughan).

Ver. 2. The next pair, **βαπτισμῶν διδαχῆς ἐπιθέσεώς τε χειρῶν** "instruction regarding washings and laying on of hands". "The historical sequence is followed in the enumeration". Some interpreters make all three conditions directly dependent on **θεμέλιον**, "foundation of baptisms, teaching, and laying on of hands". Bengel makes **διδαχῆς** dependent on **βαπτ.** He says: "**βαπτισμοὶ διδαχῆς** erant *baptismi*, quos qui suscipiebant, *doctrinae* sacrae Judaeorum sese addicebant. Itaque adjecto **διδαχῆς** *doctrinae* distinguuntur a lotionibus ceteris leviticis". Similarly Winer (*Gramm.*, p. 240): "If we render **βαπτ. διδ.** *baptisms of doctrine or instruction*, as distinguished from the legal baptisms (washings) of Judaism, we find a support for this designation, as characteristically Christian, in Matt. xxviii. 19, **βαπτίσαντες αὐτούς . . . διδάσκοντες αὐτούς**". It is better to take the words as equivalent to **διδαχῆς περὶ βαπτισμῶν.** In N.T. **βάπτισμα** is regularly used of Christian baptism or of John's baptism, while **βαπτισμός** is used of ceremonial washings as in ix. 10 and Mk. vii. 4. [*Cf.* Blass, *Gramm.*, p. 62. Josephus,

χειρῶν, ἀναστάσεώς τε [1] νεκρῶν, καὶ κρίματος αἰωνίου. 3. ᵃ καὶ ᵃ Acts
τοῦτο ποιήσομεν,[2] ἐάνπερ ἐπιτρέπῃ ὁ Θεός. 4. ᵇ Ἀδύνατον γὰρ xviii. 21;
1 Cor. iv.
19; Jac.
iv. 15.

ᵇ x. 26; Matt. xii. 31, 45; Joan, iv. 10; 2 Peter ii. 20; 1 Joan v. 16

[1] τε in אACDᶜEKL, vg.; omitted in BD gr. P, and rightly rejected by Tr., WH
and Weiss.

[2] T.R. in אBKLN, 17, d, e, f, vg., etc.; ποιησωμεν in ACDEP, Arm. The indicative agrees better with ἐάνπερ, κ.τ.λ.

(*Ant.*, xviii. 5, 2) uses βαπτισμός of John's
baptism.] Probably, therefore, "teaching about washings" would include instruction in the distinction between the
various Jewish washings, John's baptism
and that of Christ (*cf.* Acts xix. 2); and
this would involve instruction in the
cleansing efficacy of the Atonement
made by Christ as well as in the work
of the Holy Spirit. It was very necessary
for a convert from Judaism to understand
the difference between symbolic and real
lustration. The reference of the plural
must, therefore, not be restricted to the
distinction of outward and inward baptism (Grotius), nor of water and spirit
baptism (Reuss) nor of infant and adult
baptism, nor of the threefold immersion
nor, as Primasius, "pro varietate acci-
pientium". ἐπιθέσεώς τε χειρῶν closely
conjoined to the foregoing by τε because the "laying on of hands" was
the accompaniment of baptism in Apostolic times. "As through baptism the
convert became a member of the House
of God, through the laying on of hands
he received endowments fitting him for
service in the house, and an earnest
of his relation to the world to come
(vi. 5)" (Davidson, *cf.* Delitzsch). The
laying on of hands was normally accompanied by prayer. Prayer was the essential element in the transaction, the laying
on of hands designating the person to
whom the prayer was to be answered
and for whom the gift was designed.
Cf. Acts xix. 1-6; viii. 14-17; xiii. 3;
vi. 6; and Lepine's *The Ministers of
Jesus Christ*, p. 141-4. In Apostolic
times baptism apparently meant that the
baptised believed in and gave himself to
Christ, while the laying on of hands
meant that the Holy Ghost was conferred
upon him. In baptism as now administered both these facts are outwardly represented. ἀναστάσεως νεκρῶν καὶ
κρίματος αἰωνίου: "resurrection of
the dead and eternal judgment," "constituting the believer's outlook under
which he was to live" (Davidson). The
genitives depend on διδαχῆς, not on

θεμέλιον, as Vaughan. The phrase ἀνάστασις νεκρῶν naturally includes all the
dead both righteous and unrighteous (see
John v. 29 and Acts xxiv. 15. κρίμα
though properly the result of κρίσις is
not always distinguished from it, see
John ix. 39; Acts xxiv. 25; and *cf.*
Heb. ix. 27). It is "eternal," timeless in
its results. These last-named doctrines,
although not specifically Christian, yet
required to be brought before the notice
of a Jewish convert that he might dis-
entangle the Christian idea from the Jewish Messianic expectation of a resurrection of Israel to the enjoyment of the
Messianic Kingdom, and of a judgment
on the enemies of Israel (*Cf.* Weiss).
Ver. 3. καὶ τοῦτο ποιήσομεν: "and
this will we do," that is, we will go on
to perfection and not attempt again to
lay a foundation. So Theoph.: τὸ ἐπὶ
τὴν τελειότητα φέρεσθαι. And Primasius: "et hoc faciemus, *i.e.*, et ad
majora nos ducemus, et de his omnibus
quae enumeravimus plenissime docebimus
nos, ut non sit iterum necesse ex toto et
a capite ponere fundamentum". Hofmann refers the words to the participial
clause, an interpretation adopted even by
von Soden ["nämlich abermal Funda-
ment Einsenken"] which only creates
superfluous difficulty. The writer, feeling as he does the arduous nature of the
task he undertakes, adds the condition,
ἐάνπερ ἐπιτρέπῃ ὁ Θεός, "if God permit". The addition of περ has the effect
of limiting the condition or of indicating
a *sine qua non*; and may be rendered "if
only," "if at all events," "if at least".
This clause is added not as if the writer
had any doubt of God's willingness, but
because he is conscious that his success
depends wholly on God's will. *Cf.* 1 Cor.
xvi. 7.
Vv. 4-6 give the writer's reason for not
attempting again to lay a foundation.
It is, he says, to attempt an impossibility.
The statement falls into three parts: (1)
A description of a class of persons τοὺς
ἅπαξ φωτισθέντας . . . καὶ παραπεσόντας. (2) The statement of a fact re-

garding these persons ἀδύνατον πάλιν ἀνακαινίζειν εἰς μετάνοιαν. (3) The cause of this fact found in some further characteristics of their career ἀνασταυροῦντας . . . παραδειγματίζοντας.

Ver. 4. First, the description here given of those who have entered upon the Christian life is parallel to the description given in vv. 1, 2 of elementary Christian teaching; although the parallel is not carried out in detail. The picture, though highly coloured, is somewhat vague in outline. " The writer's purpose is not to give information to *us*, but to awaken in the breasts of his first readers sacred memories, and breed godly sorrow over a dead past. Hence he expresses himself in emotional terms such as might be used by recent converts rather than in the colder but more exact style of the historian" (Bruce). ἀδύνατον γὰρ : The γὰρ does not refer to the immediately preceding clause (Delitzsch) but points directly to τοῦτο ποιήσομεν and through these words to ἐπὶ τὴν τελ. φερώμεθα, the sense being "Let us go on to perfection and not attempt to lay again a foundation, *for* this would be vain, seeing that those who have once begun and found entrance to the Christian life, but have fallen away, cannot be renewed again to repentance, cannot make a second beginning. τοὺς ἅπαξ φωτισθέντας, "those who were once enlightened ". τοὺς includes all the participles down to παραπεσόντας, which therefore describe one class of persons; and it is governed by ἀνακαινίζειν. ἅπαξ: " once for all " *semel* (not πότε = quondam) may be taken as remotely modifying the three following participles as well as φωτισθ. Its force is that " once" must be enough; no πάλιν can find place; and it refers back to πάλιν of ver. 1, and forward to πάλιν of ver. 6. φωτισθέντας is used in this absolute way in x. 32 where a comparison with ver. 26 indicates that it is equivalent to τὸ λαβεῖν τὴν ἐπίγνωσιν τῆς ἀληθείας. *Cf.* also 2 Cor. iv. 4 and Eph. i. 18. The source of the enlightenment is τὸ φῶς τὸ ἀληθινὸν ὃ φωτίζει πάντα ἄνθρωπον, the result is repentance and faith, ver. 1. Hatch refers to this passage in support of his contention that the language and imagery of the N.T. are influenced by the Greek mysteries (*Hibbert Lect.*, pp. 295-6). "So early as the time of Justin Martyr we find a name given to baptism which comes straight from the Greek mysteries —the name 'enlightenment' (φωτισμός, φωτίζεσθαι). It came to be the constant

technical term." But as Anrich shows (*Das antike Mysterienwesen*, p. 125) φωτισμός was not one of the technical terms of the mysteries [" Der Ausdruck φωτισμός begegnet in der Mysterienterminologie nie und nirgends ".] The word is of frequent occurrence in the LXX, see esp. Hos. x. 12. φωτίσατε ἑαυτοὺς φῶς γνώσεως [" Ausdruck und Vorstellung sind alttestamentlich "]. Of course it is the fact that φωτισμός was used by Justin and subsequent fathers to denote baptism (*vide* Suicer, s.v.), and several interpret the word here in that sense. So the Syrian versions; Theodoret and Theophylact translate by βάπτισμα and λουτρόν. For the use made of this translation in the Montanist and Novatian controversies see the Church Histories, and Tertullian's *De Pudic.*, c. xx. The translation is, however, an anachronism. [In this connection, the whole of c. vi. of Clement's *Paedag.* may with advantage be read. ἐφωτίσθημεν· τὸ δ' ἐστιν ἐπιγνῶναι τὸν Θεόν. . . . Βαπτιζόμενοι φωτιζόμεθα· φωτιζόμενοι υἱοποιούμεθα· υἱοποιούμενοι τελειούμεθα.]

γευσαμένους τε τῆς δωρεᾶς τῆς ἐπουρανίου, "and tasted the heavenly gift ". γευσαμ. here as elsewhere, to know experimentally; *cf.* ii. 9; Matt. xvi. 29. The heavenly gift, or the gift that comes to us from heaven and partakes of the nature of its source, is according to Chrys. and Œcum : " The forgiveness of sins " ; and so, many moderns, Davidson, Weiss, etc.; others with a slight difference refer it to the result of forgiveness "pacem conscientiae quae consequitur peccatorum remissionem " (Grotius). Some finding that δωρεά is more than once (Acts ii. 38, x. 45) used of the Holy Spirit, conclude that this is here the meaning (Owen, von Soden, etc.); while Bengel is not alone in rendering, " Dei filius, ut exprimitur (ver. 6.) *Christus*, qui per fidem, nec non in sacra ipsius Coena gustatur ". Bleek, considering that this expression is closely joined to the preceding by τε, concludes that what is meant is the gift of enlightenment, or, as Tholuck says, " the δωρεά is just the Christian φῶς objectively taken ". The objection to the first of these interpretations, which has much in its favour, is that it is too restricted : the last is right in emphasising the close connection with φωτισθ., for what is meant apparently is the whole gift of redemption, the new creation, the fulness of life eternal freely bestowed, and

τοὺς ἅπαξ φωτισθέντας, γευσαμένους τε τῆς δωρεᾶς τῆς ἐπουρανίου,
καὶ μετόχους γενηθέντας Πνεύματος Ἁγίου, 5. καὶ καλὸν γευσαμένους

made known as freely bestowed, to the
"enlightened". *Cf.* Rom. v. 15; 2 Cor.
ix. 15. καὶ μετόχους γενηθέντας Πνεύματος Ἁγίου, "and were made partakers
of the Holy Ghost"; a strong expression intended to bring out, as Westcott
remarks, "the fact of a personal character
gained; and that gained in a vital development". The bestowal of the Spirit is
the invariable response to faith. The
believer is πνευματικός. In chap. x. 29,
when the same class of persons is described, one element of their guilt is stated
to be their doing despite to the Spirit of
grace. Grotius and others refer the
words to the extraordinary gifts of the
Spirit; rather·it is the distinctive source
of Christian life that is meant. It is
customary to find a parallel between the
two clauses of ver. 2, βαπτ. διδ. ἐπιθέσ.
τε χειρῶν and the two clauses of this
verse γευσαμ. καὶ μετόχους. There are,
however, objections to this idea.
    Ver. 5. καὶ καλὸν γευσαμένους . . .
"and tasted God's word that it is good".
ῥήματα καλά in LXX (*vide* Josh. xxi. 43)
are the rich and encouraging promises
of God, *cf.* Zech. i. 13, ῥήματα καλὰ
καὶ λόγους παρακλητικούς. Here it
probably means the Gospel in which
all promise is comprehended; *cf.* 1 Pet.
i. 25, ῥῆμα Κυρίου . . . τοῦτο δέ ἐστι
τὸ ῥῆμα τὸ εὐαγγελισθὲν εἰς ὑμᾶς.
Persons then are here described who
have not only heard God's promise, but
have themselves tasted or made trial of
it and found it good They have
experienced that what God proclaims
finds them, in their conscience with its
resistless truth, in their best desires by
quickening and satisfying them. The
change from the genitive, δωρεᾶς, to
the accusative, ῥῆμα, after γευσ. is
variously accounted for. Commonly,
verbs of sense take the accusative of the
nearer, the genitive of the remoter
source of the sensation; but probably
the indiscriminate use of the two cases
in LXX and N.T. arises from the
tendency of the accusative in later
Greek to usurp the place of the other
cases. Yet it is not likely that so
careful a stylist as our author should
have altered the case without a reason.
That reason is best given by Simcox
(*Gram.*, p. 87), "γεύεσθαι in Heb. vi. 4, 5,
has the genitive, where it is merely a
verb of sense, the accusative where it is

used of the recognition of a fact—καλόν
being (as its position shows) a predicate".
With this expression may be compared
Prov. xxxi. 18, ἐγεύσατο ὅτι καλόν ἐστι
τὸ ἐργάζεσθαι. Bengel's idea that the
genitive indicates that a part, while
accusative that the whole was tasted,
may be put aside. Also Hofmann's idea,
approved by Weiss, that the accusative
is employed to avoid an accumulation
of genitives. δυνάμεις τε μέλλοντος αἰῶνος "and [tasted] the powers of the age
to come" [that they were good, for
καλάς may be supplied out of the
καλόν of the preceding clause; or the
predicate indicating the result of the
tasting may be taken for granted]. δυνάμεις is so frequently used of the powers
to work miracle imparted by the Holy
Spirit (see ii. 4, 1 Cor. xii. 28; 2 Cor.
xii. 12; and in the Gospels *passim*) that
this meaning is generally accepted as
appropriate here. See Lünemann. αἰὼν
μέλλων is therefore here used not exactly
as in Matt. xii. 32, Eph. i. 21 where it is
contrasted with this present age or
world, but rather as the temporal
equivalent of the οἰκουμένη ἡ μέλλουσα
of chap. ii. 5, *cf.* also ix. 11, x. i.; and
Bengel's note. It is the Messianic age
begun by the ministry of Christ, but
only consummated in His Second
Advent. A wider reference is sometimes
found in the words, as by Davidson:
"Though the realising of the promises
be yet future, it is not absolutely so;
the world to come projects itself in
many forms into the present life, or
shows its heavenly beauty and order
rising up amidst the chaos of the present.
This it does in the powers of the world
to come, which are like laws of a new
world coming in to cross and by and by
to supersede those of this world. Those
"powers," being mainly still future, are
combined with the good word of promise,
and elevated into a distinct class, corresponding to the third group above, *viz.*:
resurrection and judgment (ver. 2)."
The persons described have so fully
entered into the spirit of the new time
and have so admitted into their life the
powers which Christ brings to bear upon
men, that they can be said to have
"tasted" or experienced the spiritual
forces of the new era.
    Ver. 6. καὶ παραπεσόντας, "and fell
away," *i.e.*, from the condition depicted

Θεοῦ ῥῆμα, 6. δυνάμεις τε μέλλοντος αἰῶνος, καὶ παραπεσόντας,
πάλιν ἀνακαινίζειν εἰς μετάνοιαν, ἀνασταυροῦντας ἑαυτοῖς τὸν υἱὸν

by the preceding participles; " grave
verbum subito occurrens " (Bengel). The
word in classical Greek has the meaning
" fall in with " or " fall upon " ; in Polybius, " to fall away from," " to err,"
followed by τ. ὁδοῦ, τ. ἀληθείας, τ.
καθήκοντος ; also absolutely " to err ".
In the Greek fathers the lapsed are called
οἱ παραπεπτωκότες or οἱ παραπεσόντες.
The full meaning of the word is given in
ὑποστολῆς εἰς ἀπώλειαν of x. 39. The
translation of the A.V. and early English versions " if they shall fall away,"
although accused of dogmatic bias, is
justifiable. It is a hypothesis that is
here introduced. Thus far the writer
has accumulated expressions which present the picture of persons who have
not merely professed the Christian faith
but have enjoyed rich experience of its
peculiar and characteristic influence, but
now a word is introduced which completely alters the picture. They have
enjoyed all these things, but the last
thing to be said of them is that they
have " fallen from " their former state.
The writer describes a condition which
he considers possible. And of persons
realising this possibility he says ἀδύνατον
. . . πάλιν ἀνακαινίζειν εἰς μετάνοιαν,
" it is impossible to renew [them] again
to repentance," "impossible," not "difficult " [as in the Graeco-Latin Codex
Claromontanus, " difficile "]; impossible
not only to a teacher, but to God, for in
every case of renewal it is God who is
the Agent. [Bengel says " hominibus
est impossibile, non Deo," and that
therefore the ministers of God must
leave such persons to Him and wait
for what God may accomplish " per
singulares afflictiones et operationes ".
But cf. x. 26-31.] πάλιν ἀνακαινίζειν,
πάλιν is not pleonastic, but denotes
that those who have once experienced
ἀνακαινισμός cannot again have a like
experience. It suggests that the word
ἀνακαιν. involves, or naturally leads on
to, all that is expressed in the participles
under ἅπαξ from φωτισθέντας to αἰῶνος
of ver. 5. A renewed person is one who
is enlightened, tastes the heavenly gift,
and so on. But as the first stone in the
foundation was μετάνοια (ver. 1), so here
the first manifestation of renewal is in
μετάνοια. The persons described cannot
again be brought to a life-changing repentance—a statement which opens one

of the most important psychological
problems. The reason this writer assigns for the impossibility is given in
the words ἀνασταυροῦντας . . . παραδειγματίζοντας, "crucifying [or " seeing
that they crucify "] to themselves the
Son of God, and putting Him to open
shame ". Edwards understands these
participles as putting a hypothetical
case, and renders "they cannot be renewed after falling away if they persist
in crucifying, etc.". This, however, re-
duces the statement to a vapid truism,
and, although grammatically admissible,
does not agree with the οὐκέτι of the
parallel passage in x. 26. The mitiga-
tion of the severity of the statement is
rather to be sought in the enormity and
therefore rarity of the sin described,
which is equivalent to the deliberate
and insolent rejection of Christ alluded
to in x. 26, 29, and the suicidal blasphemy alluded to in Mk. iii. 29. On
the doctrine of the passage, see Harless,
Ethics, c. 29. In classical and later
Greek the word for "crucify" is not
σταυρόω (of which Stephanus cites only
one example, and that from Polybius),
but ἀνασταυροῦν, so that the ἀνα does
not mean "again" or "afresh," but
refers to the lifting up on the cross, as
in ἀναρτάω or ἀνασκολοπίζω. In the
N.T. no doubt σταυρόω is uniformly
used, but never in this Epistle; and it
was inevitable that a Hellenist would
understand ἀνασταυρ. in its ordinary
meaning. There is no ground therefore
for the translation of the Vulg. " rursum
crucifigentes," although it is so commonly followed. Besides, any crucifixion
by the Hebrews [ἑαυτοῖς] must have been
a fresh crucifixion, and needs no express
indication of that feature of it. The
significance of ἑαυτοῖς seems to be "so
far as they are concerned," not "to
their own judgment" or "to their own
destruction ". The apostate crucifies
Christ on his own account by virtually
confirming the judgment of the actual
crucifiers, declaring that he too has
made trial of Jesus and found Him no
true Messiah but a deceiver, and therefore worthy of death. The greatness of
the guilt in so doing is aggravated by
the fact that apostates thus treat τὸν
υἱὸν τ. Θεοῦ, cf. x. 29. καὶ παραδειγματίζοντας, the verb is found in
Numb. xxv. 4, where it implies ex-

τοῦ Θεοῦ καὶ παραδειγματίζοντας. 7. γῆ γὰρ ἡ πιοῦσα τὸν ἐπ'
αὐτῆς πολλάκις ἐρχόμενον ὑετόν, καὶ τίκτουσα βοτάνην εὔθετον
ἐκείνοις δι' οὓς καὶ γεωργεῖται, μεταλαμβάνει εὐλογίας ἀπὸ τοῦ
Θεοῦ· 8. ἐκφέρουσα δὲ ἀκάνθας καὶ τριβόλους, ἀδόκιμος καὶ κατά-

posing to ignominy or infamy, such as
wa; effected in barbarous times by
exposing the quarters of the executed
criminal, or leaving him hanging in
chains. Archilochus, says Plutarch
(*Moral.*, 520), rendered himself in-
famous, ἑαυτὸν παρεδειγ., by writing
obscene verses. The verb is therefore a
strong expression; "put Him to open
shame" excellently renders it. "This
was the crime the Hebrew Christians
were tempted to commit. A fatal step
it must be when taken; for men who
left the Christian Church and went back
to the synagogue became companions
of persons who thought they did God
service in cursing the name of Jesus"
(Bruce).

Vv. 7 and 8 present an analogy in
nature to the doom of the apostate.
Ver. 7. γῆ γὰρ ἡ πιοῦσα . . . ὑετόν,
"For land which drank in the rain that
cometh oft upon it"; this whole clause
is the subject of vv. 7 and 8; the
subject remains the same, the results are
different. It might almost be rendered,
in order to bring out the emphasis on
γῆ, "For, take the case of land". Such
constructions are well explained by
Green (*Gram.*, 34): "The anarthrous
position of the noun may be regarded as
employed to give a prominence to the
peculiar meaning of the word without
the interference of any other idea, while
the words to which the article is prefixed,
limit by their fuller and more precise
description the general notion of the
anarthrous noun, and thereby introduce
the determinate idea intended." The
comparison of human culture with
agriculture is common. *Cf.* especially
Plut., *De Educ. Puer.*, c. 3; and the
remarkable lines of the *Hecuba*, 590-596.
To make the comparison with the
persons described in vv. 4, 5 apt, the
advantageous conditions of the land are
expressed in ἡ πιοῦσα κ.τ.λ. The
abundant and frequently renewed rain
represents the free and reiterated bestowal
of spiritual impulse; the enlightenment,
the good word of God, the energetic
indwelling of the Holy Spirit, which the
Hebrews had received and which should
have enabled them to bring forth fruit
to God. πιοῦσα, as in Anacreon's

ἡ γῆ μέλαινα πίνει, and Virgil's (*Ecl.*
iii. 3) "sat prata biberunt". Bengel's
note, "non solum in superficie" brings
out the meaning. The aorist expressing
a completed past contrasts with τίκτουσα
and ἐκφέρουσα continuous presents. καὶ
τίκτουσα . . . γεωργεῖται, "and produces herbage meet for those on whose
account also it is tilled". This is one
of the possible results of the natural advantage. τίκτουσα βοτάνη are found in
classic Greek. See examples in Wetstein
and Bleek. εὔθετον originally "con-
veniently situated" and hence "suitable"
"fit" as in Luke ix. 62. ἐκείνοις follows
εὔθετον, not τίκτουσα. The measure of a
field's value is its satisfying the purpose
of those on whose account it is tilled.
δι' οὓς, "for whose sake" or "on whose
account," not, as Calvin, "quorum
opera"; not the labourers, but the
owners are intended or those whom the
owners mean to supply. καὶ γεωργεῖται,
καὶ introduces a consideration which
"brings into relief the naturalness of
the τίκτειν βοτάνην εὔθετον ἐκείνοις"
(Lünemann). Westcott seems to lean
to Schlichting's explanation: "The
laborious culture of the soil seems to
be contrasted with its spontaneous
fruitfulness". *Cf.* the "justissima
tellus" of Vergil, *Georg.* ii. 460. Land
so responding to the outlay put upon
it μεταλαμβάνει εὐλογίας ἀπὸ τοῦ Θεοῦ,
"partakes of a blessing from God".
God's approval is seen in the more and
more abundant yield of the land. The
reality here colours the figure.
Ver. 8. ἐκφέρουσα δὲ . . . "but if
it brings forth thorns and thistles it is
rejected and nigh unto a curse and its
end is burning". The other alternative,
which corresponds to the possible state
of the Hebrews, is here introduced.
With all its advantages, the land may
prove disappointing, may not stand the
sole test (ἀδόκιμος) of land, its production
of a harvest. ἀκάνθας καὶ τριβ. frequently conjoined in LXX, Gen. iii. 17,
Hos. x. viii, and expressive of uselees
and noxious products. [τρίβολος, frequently τριβελής, three pointed, and
originally meaning a caltrop]. ἀδόκιμος
is used under the influence of the
personal reference rather than of the

c Prov. xiv. ρας ἐγγύς, ἧς τὸ τέλος εἰς καῦσιν.   9. Πεπείσμεθα δὲ περὶ ὑμῶν,
31; Matt.
x. 42, et ἀγαπητοί, τὰ κρείττονα¹ καὶ ἐχόμενα σωτηρίας, εἰ καὶ οὕτω λαλοῦ-
xxv. 40;
Marc. ix. μεν.   10. °οὐ γὰρ ἄδικος ὁ Θεὸς ἐπιλαθέσθαι τοῦ ἔργου ὑμῶν, καὶ
41; Joan.
xiii. 20; τοῦ κόπου² τῆς ἀγάπης ἧς ἐνεδείξασθε εἰς τὸ ὄνομα αὐτοῦ, διακονή-
Rom. iii.
4; 1 Thess. i. 3; 2 Thess. i. 6, 7.

¹ κρεισσονα is better authenticated than κρειττονα.
² T.R. in DcE**KL, Copt., Chrys., Thdrt., a gloss from 1 Thess. i. 3; του κοπου
omitted in אABCD*E*P, d, e, f, vg., Basm., Syr., Arm., Aeth.

figure. κατάρας ἐγγύς with a reference to Gen. iii. 18 ἐπικατάρατος ἡ γῆ, and suggested by the εὐλογίας of the previous verse. Wetstein quotes from Aristides the expression κατάρας ἐγγύς, and from the ἐγγύς Chrys. and Theophyl. conclude, rightly, that the curse is not yet in action. ὁ γὰρ ἐγγὺς κατάρας δυνήσεται καὶ μακρὰν γενέσθαι. ἧς τὸ τέλος. What is the antecedent? γῆ, say the Geeek commentaries, Bengel, Riehm, Delitzsch, Lünemann, Alford; κατάρας, say Stuart, Bleek, Weiss, von Soden. The former seems distinctly preferable. Cf. Phil. iii. 19, ὧν τὸ τέλος ἀπώλεια. But here it is εἰς καῦσιν instead of καῦσις "for burning," it serves for nothing else, and is thus contrasted with the land served by the productive land. The burning has with an excess of literality been ascribed to the soil itself, and therefore the example of Sodom and Gomorrah has been adduced. But Grotius is right who finds a metonymy: "de terra dicitur quod proprie iis rebus convenit quae terrae superstant". Reference may be made to Philo, De Agric. c. 4: ἐπικαύσω καὶ τὰς ῥίζας αὐτῶν ἐφιεὶσ᾽ ἄχρι τῶν ὑστάτων τῆς γῆς φλογὸς ῥιπῇ. Cf. John xv. 6. Certainly it points not to a remedial measure, but to a final destructive judgment.

Verses 9-12, sudden transition, characteristic of the author, from searching warning to affectionate encouragement. "Startled almost by his own picture" he hastens to assure the Hebrews that he is convinced it does not represent their present condition. On the contrary he recognises in their loving care of Christ's people a service God cannot overlook and which involves "salvation". They have only to abound in hope as already they are rich in love, and they will no longer be slothful and inanimate but will reproduce in their lives the faith and endurance which have brought others into the enjoyment of the promised and eternal blessing.

Ver. 9. πεπείσμεθα δὲ. . . . "But of you, beloved, we are persuaded things that are better and associated with salvation, though we thus speak." "Alarm at the awful suggestion of his own picture (vv. 4-8) causes a rush of affection into his heart" (Davidson). He hastens to assure them that he does not consider them apostates, although he has described the apostate condition and doom. "It is very like St. Paul's way of closing and softening anything he had said that sounded terrible and dreadful" (Pierce). Cf. 2 Thess. ii. 13; Eph. iv. 20; Gal. v. 10. "The form [πεπείσμεθα] implies that the writer had felt misgivings and overcome them" (Westcott). περὶ ὑμῶν is emphasised, and the unique (in this Epistle) ἀγαπητοί is introduced to reassure them and as the natural expression of his own reaction in their favour. τὰ κρείττονα "things better" than those he has been describing (neither limiting the reference to the condition, although necessarily it is mainly in view, nor to the doom, although the σωτηρίας indicates that it also is in view); and things indeed that so far from being κατάρας ἐγγύς are ἐχόμενα σωτηρίας closely allied to salvation. [Cf. Hamlet's "no relish of salvation in it."] ἐχόμενα = next, from ἔχομαι. I hold myself to, adhere. So locally Mark i. 38, εἰς τὰς ἐχομένας κωμοπόλεις: temporally, Acts xxi. 26, τῇ ἐχομένῃ ἡμέρᾳ, here, as in Herodotus, Plato, and Lucian, "pertaining to," so Herod., i. 120, τὰ τῶν ὀνειράτων ἐχόμενα. εἰ καὶ and καὶ εἰ generally retain in N.T. their distinctive meanings.

Ver. 10. οὐ γὰρ ἄδικος. . . . "For God is not unrighteous to forget your work and the love which ye shewed toward His name in that ye ministered and still do minister to the saints." He recognises in their Christian activities (ἔργου ὑμῶν) and in their practical charities (τῆς ἀγάπης) things that are associated with salvation, because God's justice demands that such service shall

σαντες τοῖς ἁγίοις καὶ διακονοῦντες. 11. ἐπιθυμοῦμεν δὲ ἕκαστον
ὑμῶν τὴν αὐτὴν ἐνδείκνυσθαι σπουδὴν πρὸς τὴν πληροφορίαν τῆς
ἐλπίδος ἄχρι τέλους· 12. ἵνα μὴ νωθροὶ γένησθε, μιμηταὶ δὲ
τῶν διὰ πίστεως καὶ μακροθυμίας κληρονομούντων τὰς ἐπαγγελίας.

not be overlooked. God will bless the field which already has yielded good fruit. He will cherish Christian principle in those that have manifested it. To him that hath shall be given. *Cf.* especially Phil. i. 6. On the doctrinal bearing of the words, see Tholuck in *loc.* It is impossible to think of God looking with indifference upon those who serve Him or affording them no help or encouragement. τῆς ἀγάπης ἧς . . . the love which found expression in personal service (διακονήσαντες) to Christians (ἁγίοις), and of which examples are specified in x. 34, was love εἰς τὸ ὄνομα αὐτοῦ, because it was prompted not by natural relationship or worldly association but by the consideration that they were God's children and people.

Ver 11. ἐπιθυμοῦμεν δὲ . . . You have manifested earnest *love*, cultivate as earnestly your *hope*; that is what I desire. The translation should therefore be "*But we desire*". ἕκαστον ὑμῶν, "each one of you," not merely as Chrysostom interprets πολλὴ ἡ φιλοστοργία· καὶ μεγάλων καὶ μικρῶν ὁμοίως κήδεται, not as Bruce, "The good shepherd goeth after even one straying sheep"; but directly in contrast to the whole body and *general* reputation of the Church addressed. The writer courteously implies that some already showed the zeal demanded; but he desires that each individual, even those whose condition prompted the foregoing warning, should bestir themselves. *Cf.* Bengel's "non modo, ut adhuc fecistis, in communi". τὴν αὐτὴν ἐνδείκνυσθαι σπουδὴν . . . τέλους. The same earnest diligence [σπουδή in exact opposition to νωθροί of v. 11, vi. 12] which had been given to loving ministries, he desires they should now exercise towards a corresponding perfectness of hope—a hope which should only disappear in fruition. πληροφορία "hic non est *certitudo*, sed *impletio* sive *consummatio*, quo sensu πληροφ. habemus, Col. ii. 2, *et* 1 Thess. i. 5, πληροφορεῖν 2 Tim. iv. 5, 17" (Grotius). Alford insists that the subjective sense of the word is uniform in N.T. and therefore translates "the full assurance". But the objective meaning, "completeness," certainly suits Col. ii. 2 πᾶν τὸ

πλοῦτος τ. πληροφορίας τ. συνέσεως and is not unsuitable in Heb. x. 22 and 1 Thess. i. 5, while the verb πληροφορεῖν, at least in some passages, as 2 Tim. iv. 5, has an objective sense. Besides, in the case before us, the one meaning involves the other, for, as Weiss himself says, hope is only then what it ought to be when a full certainty of conviction (eine volle Ueberzeugungsgewissheit) accompanies it. See also Davidson, who says "fulness or full assurance of faith and hope is not anything distinct from faith and hope, lying outside of them and to which they may lead; it is a condition of faith and hope themselves, the perfect condition". ἄχρι τέλους the hope was to be perfect in quality and was also to be continuous "to the end," *i.e.*, until it had accomplished its work and brought them to the enjoyment of what was hoped for. The words attach themselves to ἐνδείκνυσθαι σπουδήν.

Ver. 12. ἵνα μὴ νωθροὶ γένησθε: "that ye become not sluggish," "be not, misses the fine delicacy of the writer" (Alford). "The γένησθε, pointing to the future, stands in no contradiction with γεγόνατε at v. 11. There, the sluggishness of the intellect was spoken of; here, it is sluggishness in the retaining of the Christian hope" (Lünemann). Sluggishness would result if they did not "manifest diligence". μιμηταὶ δὲ τῶν . . . : "but imitators of those who, through faith and patient waiting, are now inheriting the promises". The positive aspect of the conduct that should accompany cultivation of hope. They were not the first who had launched into that apparently shoreless ocean. Others before them had crossed it, and found solid land on the other side. There are many who are fairly described as κληρον. τὰς ἐπαγγελίας. Whether alive or now dead, they have entered on possession of that good thing which they could not see but which God had promised. Alford, apparently following Peirce, denies that κληρονομούντων can mean "who are inheriting," and renders "who are inheritors". To this conclusion he is led, as also Peirce, by the consideration that in c. xi. it is said of

d Gen. xii.
3, et xvii.
4, et xxii.
16, 17;
Ps. cv. 9;
Luc. i. 73.

13. ^d Τῷ γὰρ Ἀβραὰμ ἐπαγγειλάμενος ὁ Θεὸς, ἐπεὶ κατ' οὐδενὸς εἶχε μείζονος ὀμόσαι, ὤμοσε καθ' ἑαυτοῦ, 14. λέγων, "Ἦ μὴν¹ εὐλογῶν εὐλογήσω σε, καὶ πληθύνων πληθυνῶ σε". 15. καὶ οὕτω

¹ T.R. in KL*, al pler and Greek fathers; εἰ μην in אABD*EP, 17, 23, 31, 47*, 71, 137; εἰ μη in CDbLcon, d, e, f., vg., Ambr., Primas. *nisi*. Bleek is of opinion that εἰ μήν is a corrupt form resulting from the mixture of the classical ἦ μήν and the Hebraizing εἰ μή. But Deissmann (*Neue Bibelstud.*, p. 34) adduces examples of εἰ μήν from the Papyri, which prove that it is not a merely Biblical form.

Abraham and the other heroes of faith that they did not receive the promise. But it is also indicated in the same passage that by the coming of Christ the fulness of the promise was fulfilled. It was only "without us" of the Christian period that the patriarchs were imperfect. Those who are presently enjoying the promises attained their present victory and joy, διὰ πίστεως καὶ μακροθυμίας. Necessarily, they first had to believe the promises, but faith had to be followed up by patient waiting. Alford translates μακροθ. by "endurance," but this word rather represents ὑπομονή, while μακροθ. indicates the long-drawn-out patience which is demanded by hope deferred.

Vv. 13-20. Reasons for diligently cultivating hope and exercising patience, thus becoming imitators of those who have patiently waited for the fulfilment of the promises, the reasons being that God has made the failure of the promises impossible, and that already Jesus has passed within the veil as our forerunner.

Ver. 13. Τῷ γὰρ Ἀβραὰμ . . . . "For when God made promise to Abraham, since he could sware by none greater, He sware by Himself, saying, etc." Abraham is introduced because to him was made the fundamental and comprehensive promise (*cf*. Luke i. 73, and Gal. iii.) which involved all that God was ever to bestow. And in Abraham it is seen that the promise is secure, but that only by patient waiting can it be inherited. It is secure because God pledged Himself to perform it. The promise referred to in ἐπαγγειλάμενος seems to be that which was confirmed by an oath, and which is recorded in Gen. xxii. 16-18, κατ' ἐμαυτοῦ ὤμοσα κ.τ.λ. But Westcott prefers to consider that previous promises are referred to, as in Gen. xii. 3, 7, xiii. 14, xv. 5, xvii. 5. The aorist participle ἐπαγγ. admits of either construction. ἐπεὶ κατ' οὐδενὸς . . . ὀμνύω followed by κατά as frequently in classics (Arist., *Frogs*, 94)

and LXX, Isa. xlv. 23, Amos iv. 2, viii. 7, Zeph. i. 5, Matt. xxvi. 63. See references. εἶχε . . . ὀμόσαι, a classical use of ἔχειν from Homer downwards, " to have means or power to do," "to be able ". The greater the Being sworn by, the surer the promise. *Cf*. Longinus, *De Subl*., c. 16, on swearing by those who died at Marathon. ὤμοσε καθ' ἑαυτοῦ, how this oath was given, and how the knowledge of it was conveyed to men, this writer does not say. But it was somehow conveyed to the mind of Abraham that the fulfilment of this promise was bound up with the life of God; that it was so implicated with His purposes that God could as soon cease to be, as neglect the fulfilment of it. Lying as it did at the root of all further development, and marking out as it did the true end for which the world exists, it seemed to be bound up with the very being of God. Paul's way of expressing a similar idea is more congruous to our ways of looking at things, *cf*. 2 Cor. i. 20. *Cf*. Philo's discussion in *De Leg. Allegor*., iii. 72, 3.

Ver. 14. The oath runs εἰ μὴν εὐλογῶν εὐλογήσω σε. . . . "Surely blessing I will bless thee, and multiplying I will multiply thee." "Sentences which denote assurance . . . are in classical Greek introduced by ἦ μήν, which in the Hellenistic and Roman period is sometimes written in the form of εἰ (accent ?) μήν; so in the LXX and in a quotation from it in Heb. vi. 14" (Blass, *Gram*., p. 260); and *cf*. Jannaris, *Hist. Greek Gram*., 2055. μήν is used to strengthen asseveration, suitably therefore in oaths. On the emphatic participle in imitation of the Hebrew absolute infinitive, see Winer, sec. 45, 8, p. 445. The oath here cited was a promise to bless mankind, a promise that through all history God's gracious purpose should run; that, let happen what might, God would redeem and bless the world.

Ver. 15. καὶ οὕτω μακροθυμήσας . . "and thus having patiently waited he

μακροθυμήσας ἐπέτυχε τῆς ἐπαγγελίας. 16. °ἄνθρωποι μὲν ¹ γὰρ e Exod.
κατὰ τοῦ μείζονος ὀμνύουσι, καὶ πάσης αὐτοῖς ἀντιλογίας πέρας εἰς   xxii. 11.
βεβαίωσιν ὁ ὅρκος· 17. ἐν ᾧ περισσότερον βουλόμενος ὁ Θεὸς ἐπι-
δεῖξαι τοῖς κληρονόμοις τῆς ἐπαγγελίας τὸ ἀμετάθετον τῆς βουλῆς

¹ Omit μεν with ℵABD*E*P, 47, d, e, f, vg.; T.R. in CDcE**KL, al pler, Cop.,
Aeth., Chr., Thdrt.

[Abraham] obtained the promise ". οὕτω,
in these circumstances; that is, thus
upheld by a promise and an oath. The
oath warned him of trial. It would not
have been given had the promise been a
trifling one or had it been destined for
immediate fulfilment. μακροθυμήσας,
having *long* kept up his courage and his
hope. Delay followed delay; disappointment followed disappointment. He was
driven out of the promised land, and a
barren wife mocked the hope of the
promised seed, but he waited expectant,
and at length ἐπέτυχε τῆς ἐπαγγελίας,
for although it was true of him, as of
all O.T. saints, that he did *not* obtain
the promise, [μὴ λαβόντες τὰς ἐπαγγελίας, xi. 13; οὐκ ἐκομίσαντο τὴν
ἐπαγγελίαν, xi. 39], but could only
wave his hand to it and salute it
at a distance, yet the initial fulfilment
he did see and was compensated for all
his waiting by seeing the beginnings of
that great history which ran on to the
consummate performance of the promise
in Christ. Bleek and Rendall understand
by ἐπέτυχε . . . "obtained from God a
promise of future blessing," and not the
thing itself. But in this case μακροθυμήσας would be irrelevant. He had not to
wait for the promise, but for its fulfilment.

Ver. 16. ἄνθρωποι γὰρ, κ.τ.λ. "For
men swear by the greater." The procedure of God in confirming His promise
by an oath is justified by human custom,
and the confident hope which God's
oath warrants is justified by the fact
that even a human oath ends debate.
ἄνθρωποι refers back to ὁ Θεός of ver.
13 and forward to ver. 17. τοῦ μείζονος,
him who is greater than the persons
taking the oath, the idea of an oath
being that a higher authority is appealed
to, one of inviolable truth and power
to enforce it. καὶ πάσης αὐτοῖς . . .
"and of all gainsaying among them an
oath is an end for confirmation". "The
oath has two results negative and
positive; it finally stops all contradiction;
and it establishes that which it attests"
(Westcott). On βεβαίωσις as a technical

term, see Deissmann, *Bibl. Studies*,
p. 104. ἀντιλογία is rendered by
"strife" in A.V., and by "dispute" in
R.V.; and this meaning is found in
Exod. xviii. 16; Deut. xix. 17 οἱ δύο
ἄνθρωποι οἷς ἐστιν αὐτοῖς ἡ ἀντιλογία.
But in the other instances of its use
in N.T., Heb. vii. 7, xii. 3; Jud. xi., it
has the meaning of "contradiction" or
"gainsaying". So also in Polybius
xxviii. 7, 4: πρὸς δὲ τὴν ἀντιλογίαν
ἀνίσταντο πολλοί. It is this sense
which suits the context here, as it is
not a *strife* between God and man
which is in question. Besides, εἰς
βεβαίωσιν is more congruous with this
meaning. The meaning is that when
one man disputes the assertion of
another, an oath puts an end to the
contradiction and serves for confirmation. So Davidson, Westcott, Weiss,
etc. πάσης is added not to indicate
the universal deference paid to the oath
(Bleek), but the completeness of its
effect; no room is left for contradiction.
ὁ ὅρκος the generic article, best trans-
la ed "an oath". πέρας an end or
limit, as in Ps. cxix.,96, πάσης συντελείας
εἶδον πέρας; and Ps. cxlv. 3 τῆς μεγαλωσύνης αὐτοῦ οὐκ ἔστι πέρας. εἰς
βεβαίωσιν almost in the technical sense
of a guarantee. See Deissmann's interesting treatment of the word in
Bibelstud., pp. 100-104. On the verse
Calvin remarks: "hic locus docet
aliquem inter Christianos jurisjurandi
usum esse legitimum. Quod observandum est contra homines fanaticos qui
regulam sancte jurandi, quam Deus lege
sua praescripsit, libenter abrogarent."

Ver. 17. ἐν ᾧ περισσότερον. . . .
"Wherefore God, being minded more
abundantly to demonstrate to the heirs
of the promise the immutability of His
purpose, interposed with an oath." ἐν
ᾧ=διὸ (Theoph.), and see Winer, 484. It
m ght be rendered "quae cum ita
sint," or "this being so". The oath
having among men this convincing
power, God disregards the insult implied
in any doubt of His word and conde-
scending to human infirmity confirms

αὐτοῦ, ἐμεσίτευσεν ὅρκῳ, 18. ἵνα διὰ δύο πραγμάτων ἀμεταθέτων,
ἐν οἷς ἀδύνατον ψεύσασθαι Θεόν, ἰσχυρὰν παράκλησιν ἔχωμεν οἱ
καταφυγόντες κρατῆσαι τῆς προκειμένης ἐλπίδος · 19. ἣν ὡς ἄγκυραν

His promise by an oath. περισσότερον neuter adjective for adverb (ii. 1) is to be construed with ἐπιδεῖξαι, the meaning of the comparative being " abundantius quam s ne juramento factum videretur " (Bengel). Carpzov renders by "ex abundanti," and cites Philo, *De Abrahamo* c. 46 where the word of God is said to become an oath, ἕνεκα τοῦ τὴν διάνοιαν ἀκλινῶς καὶ παγίως ἔτι μᾶλλον ἢ πρότερον ἐρηρεῖσθαι. τοῖς κληρονόμοις, not exclusively the O.T. nor exclusively the N.T. heirs, neither Jews nor Gentiles, but all ; see ix. 3, and Gal. iii. 29. τὸ ἀμετάθετον τῆς βουλῆς αὐτοῦ, the unchangeable character of His pu'pose. [ἀμετάθ. 3 Macc. v. 1, 12 ; Polybius with ἐπιβολή, ὁρμή, διάληψις. For use of adjective see Rom. ii. 4, viii. 3 ; 1 Cor. i. 25, etc. Winer, p. 294.] ἐμεσίτευσεν ὅρκῳ, μεσιτεύω, belonging to later Greek, "to act as mediator," but sometimes used transitively "to negotiate," as in Polybius xi. 34, 3. Other examples in Bleek. Here, however, it is used intransitively as in Josephus, *Ant.*, vii. 8, 5. So the margin of A.V. "interposed himself by an oath," improved in R.V. "interposed with an oath ". *Cf.* Josephus *Ant.*, iv. 6, 7; ταῦτα δὲ ὀμνύοντες ἔλεγον καὶ θεὸν μεσίτην ὧν ὑπισχνοῦντο ποιούμενοι. "God descended, as it were, from His own absolute exaltation, in order, so to speak, to look up to Himself after the manner of men and take Himself to witness; and so by a gracious condescension confirm the promise for the sake of its inheritors" (Delitzsch). "He brought in Himself as surety, He mediated or came in between men and Himself, through the oath by Himself" (Davidson).

Ver. 18. The motive of this procedure on God's part has already been indicated in βουλόμενος, but now it is more fully declared. ἵνα διὰ δύο . . . ἐλπίδος " that by two immutable things in which it is impossible for God to lie, we may have a strong encouragement, who fled for refuge to hold fast the hope set before us ". The two immutable things are God's promise and His oath. It is impossible for God to break His promise, impossible also for him to falsify His oath. Both of these were given that even weak men might have strong en-

couragement. The emphasis is on ἰσχυρὰν, no ordinary encouragement. Interpreters are divided as to the construction of κρατῆσαι, Œcumenius, Bleek, Lünemann, and others maintaining its dependence on παράκλησιν, encouragement to hold fast the hope; while others, as Beza, Tholuck, Delitzsch, Weiss, construe it with καταφυγόντες as in A.V. "who have fled for refuge to lay hold upon the hope ". If this latter construction be not adopted, καταφυγ. is left undefined and must be taken in an absolute sense, which is unwarranted. It is the word used in the LXX (Deut. iv. 42, xix. 5 ; Josh. xx. 9) for fleeing from the avenger to the asylum of the cities of refuge. So here Christians are represented as fleeing from the threatened danger and laying hold of that which promises safety. κρατῆσαι (aor. of single act) must therefore be rendered "to lay hold of" and not, as in iv. 14, "hold fast". The former meaning is much more frequent than the latter. τῆς προκειμένης ἐλπίδος, the hope, that is, the object of hope is set before us as the city of refuge was set before the refugee and it is laid hold of by the hope it excites. προκειμ. is used of any object of ambition, "de praemiis laborum ac certaminum" (Wetstein, with examples). *Cf.* Col. i. 5, τὴν ἐλπίδα τὴν ἀποκειμένην ὑμῖν ἐν τοῖς οὐρανοῖς.

Ver. 19. ἣν ὡς ἄγκυραν ἔχομεν . . . "which [hope] we have as an anchor of the soul both sure and steadfast, and entering into that which is within the veil". An anchor was in ancient as well as in modern times the symbol of hope ; see Aristoph., *Knights*, 1224 (1207) λεπτή τις ἐλπίς ἐστ' ἐφ' ἧς ὀχούμεθα. "A slender hope it is at which we ride," and Æsch., *Ag.*, 488 : πολλῶν ῥαγεισῶν ἐλπίδων many hopes being torn away [like the flukes of anchors]. *Cf.* Paley in *loc.* Kypke quotes a saying attributed to Socrates: οὔτε ναῦν ἐξ ἑνὸς ἀγκυρίου οὔτε βίον ἐκ μιᾶς ἐλπίδος ὁρμιστέον. The symbol appears on ancient coins. ἀσφαλῆ τε καὶ βεβαίαν, unfailing and firmly fixed ; negative and positive, it will not betray the confidence reposed in it but will hold firm. ἀσφ. καὶ βεβ., Wisdom, vii. 23. Cebet., *Tab.*, 31. Bleek, Vaughan, Westcott, and

ἔχομεν τῆς ψυχῆς ἀσφαλῆ τε καὶ βεβαίαν, καὶ εἰσερχομένην εἰς τὸ
ἐσώτερον τοῦ καταπετάσματος, 20. ᶠὅπου πρόδρομος ὑπὲρ ἡμῶνᶠ iii. 1, et
iv. 14, et
εἰσῆλθεν Ἰησοῦς, κατὰ τὴν τάξιν Μελχισεδὲκ ἀρχιερεὺς γενόμενος εἰς viii. 1, et
ix. 11.
τὸν αἰῶνα.

others refer these adjectives to ἥν, not
to ἄγκυραν. It seems much more
natural to refer them with Chrys.,
Theoph., etc. to ἄγκυραν. Cf. Vulg.:
"Quam sicut anchoram habemus animæ
tutam ac firmam, et incedentem," and
Weizsäcker "in der wir einen sicheren,
festen Anker der Seele haben, der hinein-
reicht," etc. καὶ εἰσερχομένην . . .
The anchor has its holding ground in
the unseen. Some interpreters who refer the former two adjectives to the
anchor, find so much strangeness or
awkwardness in this term if so applied
that they understand it directly of the
hope itself. But as Davidson and Weiss
show, the εἰσερχ. gives the ground of
the two former adjectives; it is because
the anchor enters into the eternal and
unchangeable world that its shifting or
losing hold is out of the question. (But
cf. also ver. 16). No doubt the figure is
now so moulded to conform to the
reality that the physical reference is
obscure, unless we think of a ship being
warped into a harbour on an anchor
already carried in. Cf. Weiss. That to
which the figure points is obvious. It
is in the very presence of God the anchor
of hope takes hold. The Christian hope
is fixed on things eternal, and is made
sure by God's acceptance of it. [Alford
quotes from Estius: "sicut ancora
navalis non in aquis haeret, sed terram
intrat sub aquis latentem, eique infig-
itur; ita ancora animæ spes nostra non
satis habet in vestibulum pervenisse,
id est, non est contenta bonis terrenis et
visibilibus; sed penetrat usque ad ea,
quae sunt intra velum, videlicet in ipsa
sancta sanctorum; id est, Deum ipsum
et coelestia bona apprehendit, atque in
iis figitur".] τὸ ἐσώτερον τοῦ καταπετάσματος, the holy of holies, the very
presence of God. καταπέτασμα (in non-
biblical Greek παραπέτασμα) is used in
LXX of either of the two veils in the
Temple (מָסָךְ or פָּרֹכֶת, Exod. xxvi.
37; Num. iii. 26; and Exod. xxvi. 31; Lev.
iv. 6) but κάλυμμα, according to Philo,
De Vit. Mes., iii. 5, was the proper
designation of the outer veil, καταπέτ.
being reserved for the inner veil; and in
this sense alone it is used in N.T. as
ix. 3; Matt. xxvii. 51. See Carpzov in

loc. and Kennedy's Sources of N.T.
Greek, 113. τὸ ἐσώτερον τ. κ. is therefore the inmost shrine into which the
Jewish worshipper could not enter but
only the High Priest once a year. For
the expression see Exod. xxvi. 33, etc.
Ver. 20. The holding-ground of the
anchor of hope, the real presence of
God, is further described in the words
ὅπου πρόδρομος ὑπὲρ ἡμῶν εἰσῆλθεν
Ἰησοῦς, "whither as forerunner for us
entered Jesus". ὅποι does not occur
in N.T. or LXX, ὅπου taking its place,
as in English "where" often stands for
"whither"; see Matt. viii. 19, Luke ix.
57, James iii. 4. So, too, occasionally, in
Attic; examples in Bleek. πρόδρομος
as an adjective, "running forward with
headlong speed," see Jebb's note on
Soph., Antig., 107; as a substantive
"scouts" or "advanced guard" of an
army, Herodot., i. 60, and Wisdom xii.
8, ἀπέστειλάς τε προδρόμους τοῦ
στρατοπέδου σου σφῆκας. The more
general meaning is found in Num. xiii.
21, ἡμέραι ἔαρος, πρόδρομοι σταφυλῆς,
Isa. xxviii. 4. The idea may be illustrated by ii. 10, Col. i. 18, 1 Cor. xv. 23.
ὑπὲρ ἡμῶν goes better with πρόδρομος—
which requires further definition—than
with εἰσῆλθεν, although Bleek, Weiss
and others prefer to join it to the verb.
Ἰησοῦς, the human name is used, because it is as man and having passed
through the whole human experience
that Jesus ascends as our forerunner.
His superiority to the Levitical priest
is disclosed in the word πρόδρομος.
When the Levitical High Priest passed
within the veil he went as the representative, not as the forerunner of the
people. Hence indeed the veil. In
Christ the veil is abolished. He enters
God's presence as the herald and
guarantee of our entrance. The ground
of this is given in the concluding clause,
κατὰ τὴν τάξιν . . . αἰῶνα, "having
become [becoming] an High Priest for
ever after the order of Melchizedek".
Jesus carries our hope with Him to the
realities which lie within the veil, because it is as our High Priest who has
made atonement for sin that He is now
at God's right hand. By His death He
secured for us power to enter, to follow
where He has gone before. The parti-

a Gen. xiv.
18, etc.

VII. 1. ᵃ ΟΥΤΟΣ γὰρ ὁ Μελχισεδὲκ, βασιλεὺς Σαλὴμ, ἱερεὺς τοῦ
Θεοῦ τοῦ ὑψίστου, ὁ ¹ συναντήσας Ἀβραὰμ ὑποστρέφοντι ἀπὸ τῆς

¹ T.R. only in C*LP, marked "suspected" by WH; ος in אABC²DEK, 17,
apparently arising from the σ following, " ein für unseren Verf. unmögliches, völlig
unmotivirtes Anakoluth" (Weiss). Alford accepts ος with the anacoluthon.

ciple does not determine the precise
point at which He became High Priest,
before or contemporaneously with His
passing through the veil.

CHAPTER VII. The subject of Christ's
priesthood is resumed; the interpolated
admonition (v. 11-vi. 20) having been
skilfully brought round to a second mention of Melchizedek. The chief reason
for introducing the priesthood of Melchizedek as the type of Christ's priesthood was that it was "for ever". The
Aaronic priesthood was successional, this
single; and in this sense "for ever".
There were, however, other reasons. The
first question with a Jew who was enjoined to trust to Christ's priestly mediation, would be, What are His orders?
He belonged to a tribe "of which Moses
had spoken nothing concerning priesthood". He might or might not be the
true heir to David's throne; but if He
was, did not this very circumstance exclude him from the priestly office? Was
it credible that the nation had been encouraged rigorously to exclude from the
priesthood every interloper, only in order
that at last this rigidly preserved order
should be entirely disregarded? This
writer seizes upon the fact that there
was a greater priest than Aaron mentioned in Scripture—a priest more
worthy to be the type of the Messianic
priesthood, because he was himself a
king, and especially because he belonged to no successional priestly order
but was himself the entire order. This
idea of a priesthood superseding that of
Levi's sons found its way into Scripture
through the hymn (Ps. cx.) which celebrated the dignity (as priest-king) of
Simon the Maccabee. Bickell has shown
that the first four verses of the Psalm are
an acrostic on the name Simon, שׁמעון.
When the Maccabees displaced the
Aaronic priesthood, they found their
justification in the priestly dignity of
Melchizedek, and assumed his style,
calling themselves "priests of the Most
High God". Cf. Charles, Book of
Jubilees, pp. lix. and 191. The chapter
may be divided thus:—

I. Characteristics of Melchizedek, 1-
   10.
   1. In himself as depicted in Scrip-
      ture, 1-3.
   2. In his relation to Levi and his
      line, 4-10.
II. Inadequacy of Levitical priesthood
    in comparison with the Mel-
    chizedek priesthood of Christ,
    11-25.
   1. Levi being provisional, Mel-
      chizedek being permanent,
      11-14.
   2. Official and hereditary: per-
      sonal and eternal, 15-19.
   3. Without oath: with oath,
      therefore final, 20-22.
   4. Plural and successional: sin-
      gular and enduring, 23-25.
III. Summary of the merits of the
     new Melchizedek Priest, Jesus.

Vv. 1-3. Description of Melchizedek as
he appears on the page of Scripture, in
five particulars with their interpretation.
Ver. 1. Οὗτος γὰρ ὁ Μελχισεδὲκ . . .
μένει ἱερεὺς εἰς τὸ διηνεκές. γὰρ closely
connects this passage with the immed
iately preceding words ἀρχ. . . . αἰῶνα
and introduces the explanation of them.
"For this Melchizedek [mentioned in Ps.
cx. and who has just been named as that
priest according to whose order Christ
is called to be Priest] remains a priest
continually." This is the statement on
which he wishes to fix attention. It is
the "for-everness" of the priesthood
which he means especially to insist
upon. The whole order is occupied by
himself. This one man constitutes the
order. He succeeds no one in office and
no one succeeds him. In this sense he
abides a priest for ever. Between the
subject Melchizedek and the verb μένει,
there are insertedfive historical facts taken
from Gen. xiv., with their interpretation.
[On the historicity of Gen. xiv., see
Buchanan Gray in Expositor, May, 1898,
and Driver, Authority and Archaeology,
pp. 45 and 73. See also Beazley's Dawn
of Modern Geography, ii. 189; and esp.,
Boscawen's First of Empires, c. vi.] βασιλεὺς Σαλήμ, the description given in this
verse is taken verbatim [with the needed

κοπῆς τῶν βασιλέων, καὶ εὐλογήσας αὐτόν· 2. ᾧ καὶ δεκάτην ἀπὸ
πάντων ἐμέρισεν Ἀβραάμ· πρῶτον μὲν ἑρμηνευόμενος βασιλεὺς
δικαιοσύνης, ἔπειτα δὲ καὶ βασιλεὺς Σαλήμ, ὅ ἐστι βασιλεὺς εἰρήνης·

grammat cal alterations] from Gen. xiv.
17, 18, 19. Whether Salem stands for
Jerusalem or for Salim in the vale of
Shechem, John iii. 23, has been disputed
from Epiphanius downwards. See Bleek,
who contends that Jerusalem cannot be
meant because Jebus was its old name.
This, however, is now denied, see Moore,
Judges, p. 413, who says that the
common opinion that Jebus was the
native name of the city, has no real
ground in O.T. In the Amarna tablets
Urusalim is used and no trace is found
of any name corresponding to Jebus.
But it is not the locality that is important, but the meaning of Salem. ἱερεὺς . . . "priest of the Most High
God". According to Aristotle (*Pol.*,
iii. 14), the king in heroic times was
general, judge and priest. *Cf.* Virgil
(*Æn.*, iii. 80) "Rex Anius, rex idem
hominum, Phoebique sacerdos," and see
Gardner and Jevon's *Greek Antiq.*, 200,
201. The ideal priesthood is also that
of a king. τοῦ Θεοῦ τοῦ ὑψίστου.
In N.T. "the Most High God" is
found in the mouth of Demoniacs, Mark
v. 7; Luke viii. 28; *cf.* also Acts xvi. 17
and vii. 58, also Luke i. 32, 35, 70, vi.
35. It was a name known alike to the
Canaanites, Phoenicians and Hebrews.
See Fairbairn, *Studies in the Philosophy
of Religion*, p. 317. ὕψιστος was
also a title of Ζεύς, Pind., xi. 2. *Cf.*
also Dalman, *Words of Jesus*, p. 198;
and especially Charles' edition of *Book
of Jubilees*, pp. 191, 213, who shows that
it was the specific title chosen by the
Maccabean priest-kings. ἀπὸ τῆς
κοπῆς "from the slaughter," rather
"overthrow"; "Niederwerfung" (Weizsäcker); "*clades* rather than *caedes*"
(Vaughan) translating in Genesis xiv. 17,
מַהֲכּוֹת, τῶν βασιλέων "the
kings"; well-known from Gen. xiv.,
viz.: Amraphel, Arioch, Chedorlaomer
and Tidal, *i.e.*, Khammurabi, Eriaku,
Kudurlachgumal and Tudchula. But
Boscawen (*First of Empires*, p. 179)
disputes the identification of Amraphel
with Khammurabi. The monuments
show us that these kings were contemporaries two thousand three hundred
years B.C., and furnish many interesting
particulars regarding them; see Driver
in *Authority and Archaeology*, pp. 39-45.

καὶ εὐλογήσας αὐτόν, asserting thus at
once his superiority (ver. 7) and his
priestly authority.

Ver. 2. ᾧ καὶ δεκάτην . . . "to
whom also Abraham divided a tenth of
all" [the spoil]. The startling conclusion
which this act carried with it is specified
in vv. 4-10. The offering of a tithe of
the spoils to the gods was a custom of
antiquity. See Wetstein for examples and
especially Arnold's note on Thucydides,
iii. 50. "Frequently the ἀναθήματα were
of the nature of ἀπάρχαι, or the divine
share of what was won in peace or war.
. . . The colossal statue of Athena
Promachos on the Athenian Acropolis
hill was a votive offering from a tithe of
the booty taken at Marathon" (Gardner
and Jevon's *Greek Ant.*, 181.) For the
O.T. law of tithe see Num. xviii. 21-24;
Lev. xxvii. 30-32. In offering to Melchizedek a tithe Abraham acknowledged
him as priest.

The following clauses ought not to be
in brackets, because they are inserted as
indicating the ground of the main affirmation, μένει εἰς τὸ διηνεκές. The name
and description of Melchizedek already
given are now interpreted, and are so
interpreted as to illustrate the clause
ἀφωμοιωμένος τῷ υἱῷ τοῦ Θεοῦ and
thus prepare for the closing statement.
πρῶτον μὲν ἑρμηνευόμενος . . .
"being first, by interpretation, King of
righteousness and then also King of
Salem, which is King of peace". The
form of the sentence is significant.
[*Cf.* Plutarch, *Timoleon*, iv. 4, τοῦ δὲ
Τιμοφάνους πρῶτον μὲν αὐτῶν κατα-
γελῶντος, ἔπειτα δὲ πρὸς ὀργὴν ἐκφερο-
μένου] "first" by his very name, "then"
by his actual position; probably the
peace of his kingdom is considered as
a consequence of its righteousness.
Righteousness and peace are characteristic properties of the Messianic Kingdom. "In his days shall the righteous
flourish; and abundance of peace so
long as the moon endureth," Ps. lxxii.
7; similarly Isa. ix. 6, 7; Zech. ix. 9; *cf.*
Rom. v. 1; Eph. ii. 4, 15, 17. In Gen.
xiv. 18 the name and title occur together
מַלְכִּי־צֶדֶק מֶלֶךְ שָׁלֵם. The chief
point in this is that the priest is also a
king. ἀπάτωρ, ἀμήτωρ, ἀγενεαλόγητος
"without father, without mother, with-

3. ἀπάτωρ, ἀμήτωρ, ἀγενεαλόγητος· μήτε ἀρχὴν ἡμερῶν, μήτε
ζωῆς τέλος ἔχων· ἀφωμοιωμένος δὲ τῷ υἱῷ τοῦ Θεοῦ, μένει ἱερεὺς
εἰς τὸ διηνεκές.   4. ᵇΘεωρεῖτε δὲ πηλίκος οὗτος, ᾧ καὶ¹ δεκάτην

ᵇ Gen. xiv.
20.

¹ T.R. in ℵACDᶜE**KLP, vg., Syrʳ, Arm.; omit καὶ with BD*E*, d, e, Syrᵇᶜʰ,
Cop. Apparently καὶ has been introduced from verse 2.

out genealogy," that is, he stands in Scripture alone, no mention is made of an illustrious father or mother from whom he could have inherited power and dignity, still less can his priestly office and service be ascribed to his belonging to a priestly family. It is by virtue of his own personality he is what he is; his office derives no sanction from priestly lineage or hereditary rights; and in this respect he is made like to the Son of God. Of course it is not meant that in point of fact he had neither father nor mother, but that as he appears in Scripture he is without father. [τὸ δὲ ἀπάτωρ κ.τ.λ. οὐ διὰ τὸ μὴ ἔχειν αὐτὸν πατέρα ἢ μητέρα, ἀλλὰ διὰ τὸ μὴ ἐν τῇ θείᾳ γραφῇ κατὰ τὸ φανερώτατον ἐπωνομάσθαι. Epiphanius in Wetstein.] On Philo's use of the silence of Scrip. see Siegfried's *Philo.*, p. 179. Philo is quite aware that this kind of interpretation will be said γλισχρολογίαν μᾶλλον ἢ ὠφέλειάν τινα ἐμφαίνειν (*De Somn.*, ii. 45). ἀπάτωρ, Wetstein quotes from Pollux.: ὁ μὴ ἔχων μητέρα, ἀμήτωρ, ὥσπερ ἡ Ἀθηνᾶ· καὶ ἀπάτωρ, ὁ μὴ πατέρα ἔχων, ὡς ὁ Ἥφαιστος. So Apollo was αὐτοφυὴς, ἀμήτωρ. Other examples in Wetstein. In a slightly different sense the word occurs in *Iph. in Taur.*, 863; in Soph, *Elec.*, 1154 we have μήτηρ ἀμήτωρ; and Ion (Eur. *Ion*, 109) says of himself ὡς γὰρ ἀμήτωρ ἀπάτωρ τε γεγώς.

Ver. 3. ἀγενεαλόγητος, resolved in ver. 6 into μὴ γενεαλογούμενος, does not occur in classical nor elsewhere in Biblical Greek. The dependence of Levitical priests on genealogies and their registers is illustrated by Neh. vii. 64. μήτε ἀρχὴν ἡμερῶν ... "having neither beginning of days nor end of life," *i.e.*, again, as he is represented in Scripture. No mention is made of his birth or death, of his inauguration to his office or of his retirement from it. The idea is conveyed that so long as priestly services of that particular type were needed, this man performed them. He is thus the type of a priest who shall in his single person discharge for ever all priestly functions. ἀφωμοιωμένος δὲ τῷ υἱῷ τ. Θεοῦ "but made like

to the Son of God". δὲ attaches this clause to the immediately preceding, "having neither etc.," *but* in this respect made like to the Son of God, see i. 2, ix. 14 and i. 10, 12. "Such a comparison is decisive against attributing these characteristics to Melchisedek in a real sense. They belong to the portrait of him, which was so drawn that he was "made like" the Son of God,—that by the features absent as well as by the positive traits a figure should appear corresponding to the Son of God and suited to suggest Him" (Davidson). μένει ἱερεὺς εἰς τὸ διηνεκές "abideth a priest continually". This statement, directly resting upon the preceding clause, is that towards which the whole sentence (vv. 1, 3) has been tending. It is the permanence of the Melchisedek priesthood on which stress is laid. See below. εἰς τὸ διηνεκές is not precisely "for ever," but "for a continuance," or permanence. Appian (*De Bell. civ.*, i. 4) says of Julius Cæsar that he was created Dictator εἰς τὸ διηνεκές, permanent Dictator. "The permanent character of the priesthood is here described, not its actual duration" (Rendall). It was not destined to be superseded by another. Bruce is not correct in saying: "The variation in expression (εἰς τὸ διηνεκές instead of εἰς τὸν αἰῶνα, vi. 20) is probably made out of regard to style, rather than to convey a different shade of meaning". But he gives the sense well: "If he had had in history, as doubtless he had in fact, a successor in office, we should have said of him, that he *was* the priest of Salem in the days of Abraham. As the case stands, he *is* the priest of Salem."

Vv. 4-10. Superiority of Melchizedek to Levitical priests. The argument is: he was greater than Abraham, the great fountain of the people and of blessing. How much more is he greater than the descendants of Abraham, the Levitical priests?

Ver. 4. Θεωρεῖτε δὲ πηλίκος οὗτος. "But observe how great this man was." His greatness is recognisable in his receiving tithes of Abraham, and in giving him his blessing, *cf.* vv. 1, 2. These

Ἀβραὰμ ἔδωκεν ἐκ τῶν ἀκροθινίων ὁ πατριάρχης. 5. ° καὶ οἱ μὲν c Num.
xviii. 21,
ἐκ τῶν υἱῶν Λευῒ τὴν ἱερατείαν λαμβάνοντες, ἐντολὴν ἔχουσιν ἀπο- 26; Deut.
xviii. 1;
δεκατοῦν τὸν λαὸν κατὰ τὸν νόμον, τουτέστι, τοὺς ἀδελφοὺς αὐτῶν, Josh. xiv.
4; 2 Par.
καίπερ ἐξεληλυθότας ἐκ τῆς ὀσφύος Ἀβραάμ· 6. ᵈ ὁ δὲ μὴ γενεα- xxxi. 5.
d 1 Gen.
xiv.19,20; Rom. iv. 13; Gal. iii. 16.

points are emphasised by several details.
The first evidence of greatness is that
it was no less a man than Abraham
who gave him a tithe of the spoils ᾧ
δεκάτην, κ.τ.λ. Ἀβραὰμ is in emphatic place, but the emphasis is multi-
plied by the position of ὁ πατριάρχης.
It is as if he heard some of his readers
saying, "He must be mistaken, or must
refer to some other Abraham and not the
fountain of all our families and of Levi
and Aaron". He adds ὁ πατρ. to indicate that it is precisely this greatest
of men to whom the people owe even
their being, of whom he says that Melchizedek was greater. ἀκροθινίων
is perhaps chosen also for the purpose
of magnifying the gift. The Greeks
after a victory gathered the spoils in a
heap, θινί, and the top or best part of
the heap, ἄκρον, was presented to the
gods. Cf. Frazer's *Pausanias*, v. 281.

Ver. 5. The significance of this tithing
is perceived when it is considered that,
although the sons of Levi take tithes of
their brethren, this is the result of a mere
legal appointment. Those who pay tithes
are, as well as those who receive them,
sons of Abraham. Paying tithes is in
their case no acknowledgment of personal inferiority, but mere compliance
with law. But Abraham was under no
such law to Melchizedek, and the payment of tithes to him was a tribute to
his personal greatness. καὶ adds a
fresh aspect of the matter. οἱ μὲν ἐκ
τῶν υἱῶν Λευῒ . . . "those of the
sons of Levi who receive the priestly
service have an ordinance to tithe the
people in accordance with the law, that
is, their brethren, although these have
come out of the loins of Abraham".
Not all the tribe of Levi, but only the
family of Aaron received (cf. v. 4)
the ἱερατεία (also in Lk. i. 9), which
Bleek shows to have been used by
classical writers of priestly service,
while ἱερωσύνη was used of the
priestly office. See vv. 11, 12, 24.
ἀποδεκατοῖν, "The best MSS.
make the infinitive of verbs in -όω to
end in -οῖν" (Westcott and Hort, *G.*, *T.*
ii., sec. 410, and cf. Jannaris, *Greek
Gram.*, 851). The verb occurs only in

Biblical Greek, the classical form being
δεκατεύω. κατὰ τὸν νόμον follows
ἀποδεκ. τοὺς ἀδελφοὺς αὐτῶν,
κ.τ.λ. Not their fellow-Levites, although
it is true that the Levites tithed the
people, and the priests tithed the Levites
(Num. xviii. 21-24 and 26-28), but the
words are added in explanation of λαόν
in order to emphasise the fact that the
priests exacted tithes not in recognition
of any personal superiority. Those who
paid tithes were Abraham's descendants
equally with the priests; it was merely
the law which conveyed the right to
tithe their brethren καίπερ ἐξεληλυθότας ἐκ τῆς ὀσφύος Ἀβραάμ.
Ver. 6. In striking contrast, ὁ δὲ
μὴ γενεαλογούμενος . . . "but
he whose genealogy is not counted
from them hath taken tithes of
Abraham, and blessed [see below] him
that hath the promises". γενεαλογέω
is classical Greek, meaning, to trace
ancestry, see Herod. ii. 146. ἐξ
αὐτῶν, not "from the sons of Israel"
(Epiphanius in Bleek), but "from the
sons of Levi," ver. 5; and who therefore
had no claim to tithe appointed by law,
and yet tithed Abraham. καὶ τὸν
ἔχοντα, in Vulgate "qui habebat";
in Weizsäcker "der die Verheissungen
hatte," not "hat"; so Vaughan correctly, "The possessor of". "Him
who owned the promises." Cf. Burton,
124 and 126. εὐλόγηκε, on the perfects of this verse and of this Epistle
(viii. 5, xi. 5, etc.), Mr. J. H. Moulton
asks, "Has anyone noticed the beautiful
parallel in Plato, *Apol.*, 28 c., for the
characteristic perfect in Hebrews, describing what *stands written* in Scripture? ὅσοι ἐν Τροίᾳ τετελευτήκασι (as
is written in the Athenian's 'Bible') is
exactly like Heb. vii. 6, xi. 17, 28" (*Expositor*, April, 1901, p. 280). Vaughan
also says: "The γέγραπται (so to say)
quickens the dead, and gives to the
praeterite of the history the *permanence*
of a *perfect*". Yes; but to translate by
the perfect sacrifices English idiom to
Greek idiom. See Burton, 82, "When
the Perfect Indicative is used of a past
event which is by reason of the context necessarily thought of as separated

λογούμενος ἐξ αὐτῶν, δεδεκάτωκε τὸν [1] Ἀβραάμ, καὶ τὸν ἔχοντα τὰς
ἐπαγγελίας εὐλόγηκε· 7. χωρὶς δὲ πάσης ἀντιλογίας τὸ ἔλαττον
ὑπὸ τοῦ κρείττονος εὐλογεῖται.   8. καὶ ὧδε μὲν δεκάτας ἀποθνήσκοντες ἄνθρωποι λαμβάνουσιν· ἐκεῖ δὲ, μαρτυρούμενος ὅτι ζῇ.
9. καὶ, ὡς ἔπος εἰπεῖν, δι' Ἀβραὰμ καὶ Λευΐ ὁ δεκάτας λαμβάνων
δεδεκάτωται· 10. °ἔτι γὰρ ἐν τῇ ὀσφύϊ τοῦ πατρὸς ἦν, ὅτε συνήν-

e Gen. xiv.
18.

---

[1] τον inserted in ADᵇ, etc., E**KLP, Chr., Thdrt. ; omitted in אBCD*E*, 17, 23,
57, 109.   Bleek omits because " gemäss dem Sprachgebrauche des Verfassers ".

---

from the moment of speaking by an
interval, it is impossible to render it
into English adequately ".   The point
which the writer here brings out is that,
although Abraham had the promises, and
was therefore himself a fountain of blessing to mankind and the person on whom
all succeeding generations depended for
blessing, yet Melchizedek blessed him ;
and as the writer adds :—

Ver. 7. χωρὶς δὲ πάσης ἀντιλογίας
. . . εὐλογεῖται.   " And without any
dispute the less is blessed of the
greater."   Therefore, Abraham is the
less, and Melchizedek the greater.   The
principle [expressed in its widest form
by the neuter] applies where the blessing
carries with it not only the verbal expression of goodwill, but goodwill achieving
actual results.   But man blesses God in
the sense of praising Him, or desiring
that all praise may be His.   So God is
ὁ εὐλογητός, Mk. xiv. 61.   Cf. 2 Cor.
xi. 31, etc.

Ver. 8. Another note of the superiority
of Melchizedek. καὶ ὧδε μὲν δεκάτας
. . . " And here men that die receive
tithes, but there one of whom it is
witnessed that he liveth." ὧδε "here,"
i.e., in this Levitical system with which
we who are Hebrews are familiar, ἐκεῖ,
" there " in that system identified with
that ancient priest. ἀποθνήσκοντες
ἄνθρωποι, "dying men," who therefore as individuals passed away and gave
place to successors, and were in this
respect inferior to Melchizedek, who,
so far as is recorded in Scripture, had
no successor.   Giving to the silence
of Scripture the force of an assertion,
the writer speaks of Melchizedek as
μαρτυρούμενος ὅτι ζῇ, a person
of whom it is witnessed ; note absence
of article.   So Theoph., ὡς μὴ μνημο-
νευομένης τῆς τελευτῆς αὐτοῦ παρὰ τῇ
γραφῇ.   Westcott distinguishes between
the plural of this verse, δεκάτας, appropriate to the manifold tithings under the

Mosaic system and the singular, δεκάτην,
of ver. 4, one special act.

Ver. 9. καὶ ὡς ἔπος εἰπεῖν, " And, I
might almost say," adding a new idea
with a phrase intended to indicate that
it is not to be taken in strictness.   It is
frequent in Philo,see examples in Carpzov
and add Quis rer. div. her., 3.   Adam's
note on Plato, Apol. Soc., 17A, is worth
quoting " ὡς ἔπος εἰπεῖν i. q. paene
dixerim : in good authors hardly ever, if
at all = ut ita dicam.   The phrase is
regularly used to limit the extent or
comprehension of a phrase or word.   It
is generally, but by no means exclusively,
found with οὐδείς and πάντες, οὐδεὶς ὡς
ἔπος εἰπεῖν 'hardly anyone'; πάντες
ὡς ἔ. εἰπ. = nearly everyone."   A significant use occurs in the Republic, p. 341B,
where Socrates asks Thrasymachus
whether in speaking of a " Ruler" he
means τὸν ὡς ἔπος εἰπεῖν ἢ τὸν ἀκριβεῖ
λόγῳ.   The phrase is discussed at great
length by Raphel.   The further idea is,
that " through Abraham even Levi, he
who receives tithes, has paid tithes,"
the explanation being ἔτι γὰρ ἐν τῇ
ὀσφύϊ . . . " for he [Levi] was yet in
the loins of his father [Abraham] when
Melchizedek met him," Isaac not yet
having been begotten.   There was a
tendency in Jewish theology to view
heredity in this realistic manner.   Thus
Schoettgen quotes Ramban on Gen.
v. 2 "God calls the first human
pair Adam [man] because all men
were in them potentially or virtually
[virtualiter]".   And so some of the
Rabbis argued "Eodem peccato, quo
peccavit primus homo, peccavit totus
mundus,quoniam hic erat totus mundus."
Hence Augustine's formula "peccare
in lumbis Adam," and his explanation
"omnes fuimus in illo uno quando
omnes fuimus ille unus" (De Civ. Dei,
xiii. 14).   On Traducianism see Loofs'
Leitfaden, p. 194.

Vv. 11-14.   The imperfection of

τησεν αὐτῷ ὁ Μελχισεδέκ. 11. ¹Εἰ μὲν οὖν τελείωσις διὰ τῆς f ver. 18, 19
Λευϊτικῆς ἱερωσύνης ἦν· ὁ λαὸς γὰρ ἐπ᾽ αὐτῇ ¹ νενομοθέτητο ²· τίς   Gal. ii. 21·
ἔτι χρεία, "κατὰ τὴν τάξιν Μελχισεδέκ" ἕτερον ἀνίστασθαι ἱερέα, καὶ
οὐ "κατὰ τὴν τάξιν Ἀαρὼν" λέγεσθαι; 12. μετατιθεμένης γὰρ τῆς
ἱερωσύνης, ἐξ ἀνάγκης καὶ νόμου μετάθεσις γίνεται. 13. ἐφ᾽ ὃν γὰρ

¹ T.R. in DcE**K, Chrys., Thdrt.; επ αυτης in ℵABCD*E*LP, 17, 31, 37, 46, 73, 118.

² T.R. in DcEKL; νενομοθετηται in ℵABCD*P.

the Levitical priesthood, and by implication of the whole Mosaic system, proved by the necessity of having a priest of another order.

Ver. 11. εἰ μὲν οὖν τελείωσις. . . . "If then there was [or had been] perfecting by means of the Levitical priesthood—for upon it [as a basis] the people have received the law—what further need was there [or would have been] that another priest should arise after the order of Melchisedek and be styled not after the order of Aaron?" εἰ μὲν οὖν introduces a statement of some of the consequences resulting from the introduction of a priest of another order. It argues the failure of the Levitical priesthood to achieve τελείωσις. "Perfection is always a relative word. An institution brings perfection when it effects the purpose for which it was instituted, and produces a result that corresponds to the idea of it. The design of a priesthood is to bring men near to God (ver. 19), and this it effects by removing the obstacle in the way, viz. men's sin, which lying on their conscience impedes their free access to God; compare ix. 9, x. 1, 14 " (Davidson). On the rendering of ἦν see Sonnenschein's Greek Gram., 355, Obs. 3. ὁ λαὸς γὰρ ἐπ᾽ αὐτῆς νενομοθέτηται, the omitted clause is "and we are justified in demanding perfectness from the priesthood," because it is the soul of the entire legislation. All the arrangements of the law, the entire administration of the people, involves the priesthood. If there is failure in the priestly service, the whole system breaks down. It was idle to give a law without providing at the same time for the expiation of its breaches. The covenant was at the first entered into by sacrifice, and could only be maintained by a renewal of sacrifice. The priesthood stood out as the essential part of the Jewish economy. νομοθετεῖν to be a νομοθέτης used in classics sometimes with dative of person, as in LXX,

Exod. xxiv. 12, τὰς ἐντολὰς ἃς ἔγραψα νομοθετῆσαι αὐτοῖς. Sometimes it is followed by accusative of that which is ordained by law. The use of the passive here is peculiar, cf. also viii. 6. The νόμος contained in the word, and expressed separately in ver. 12, is not the bare law contained in commandments, but the whole Mosaic dispensation. τίς ἔτι χρεία, this use of ἔτι is justified by an instance from Sextus Empiricus quoted by Wetstein: τίς ἔτι χρεία ἀποδεικνύναι αὐτά; ἕτερον, not ἄλλον but another of a different kind. ἀνίστασθαι so Acts vii. 18, ἀνέστη βασιλεὺς ἕτερος and cf. the transitive use in Acts ii. 24, 32, iii. 22, 26, vii. 37. καὶ οὐ . . . λέγεσθαι. The negative belongs rather to the description κ. τ. τάξιν ᾽Α. than to the verb and Burton's rule (481) applies. "When a limitation of an infinitive or of its subject is to be negatived rather than the infinitive itself, the negative οὐ is sometimes used instead of μή." λέγεσθαι "be spoken of" or "designated".

Ver. 12. μετατιθεμένης γάρ. . . . "For if the priesthood is changed, there is of necessity a change also of the law". Or, This change of priesthood being made, as it is now being made, a change of the law is also being made. The connection is: What need was there for a new priesthood? It must have been a crying need, for to change the priesthood is to change all. It means nothing short of revolution. Chrysostom rightly τοῦτο δὲ πρὸς τοὺς λέγοντας, τί ἔδει καινῆς διαθήκης;

Ver. 13. This enormous change is in fact being made. ἐφ᾽ ὃν γὰρ λέγεται ταῦτα. . . . "For He with reference to whom this [110th Ps. 4] is said hath partaken of another tribe from which no man hath given attendance at the altar". Here for the first time definitely in this chapter the writer introduces the fulfilment of the Psalm. It was spoken of the Messiah, and He did not belong to the tribe of Levi, but

λέγεται ταῦτα, φυλῆς ἑτέρας μετέσχηκεν, ἀφ' ἧς οὐδεὶς προσέσχηκε
g Esa. xi. 1 ; τῷ θυσιαστηρίῳ · 14. g πρόδηλον γὰρ ὅτι ἐξ Ἰούδα ἀνατέταλκεν ὁ
Matt. i. 2,
etc.; Luc. Κύριος ἡμῶν, εἰς ἣν φυλὴν οὐδὲν περὶ ἱερωσύνης [1] Μωσῆς ἐλάλησε.
iii. 33.
15. Καὶ περισσότερον ἔτι κατάδηλόν ἐστιν, εἰ κατὰ τὴν ὁμοιότητα

---

[1] T.R. in DcKL ; περι ιερεων ουδεν in ℵ*, etc., ABC*D*EP, 17, d, e (de sacerdotibus nihil), arm.

φυλῆς ἑτέρας μετέσχηκεν, has
thrown in his lot with, or become a
member of (cf. ii. 14) a tribe of a different
kind from the Levitical (ver. xi. 11, 12)
being characterised by this, that from it
ἀφ' ἧς issuing from which, not ἐξ, [as in
ver. 14] no one has given attendance at
the altar. [Cf. 1 Tim. iv. 13 ; Acts xx.
28 ; Hdt., ix. 33, γυμνασίοισι ; Thuc., i.
15, τοῖς ναυτικοῖς ; and the equivalent in
1 Cor. ix. 13, οἱ τῷ θυσιαστηρίῳ προσ-
εδρεύοντες.] It is doubtful whether the
perfect μετέσχηκεν can bear the meaning
put upon it by Vaughan : "a striking
suggestion of the identity of Christ in
heaven with Christ upon earth". So
too Weiss. It might seem preferable to
refer it with Burton (88) to the class of
perfects which in the N.T. have an aorist
sense, γέγονα, εἴληφα, ἔσχηκα. So
Weizsäcker "gehörte"; the Vulgate,
however, has "de alia tribu est," and
cf. ἀνατέταλκεν of ver. 14. But the perfects are best accounted for as referring
to the statement of the previous verse.
This great change is being made, for he
of whom the 110th Psalm was spoken
has actually become a member of another
tribe. The result reaches to the change
of priesthood.
Ver. 14. He now proceeds to name
the tribe πρόδηλον γὰρ ὅτι . . . "For
it is evident that out of Judah our
Lord has sprung, concerning which tribe
Moses said nothing about priests".
With πρόδηλον may be compared δήπου
of ii. 16. The facts of our Lord's birth
were so far known that everyone connected Him with Judah. The accounts
of Matthew and Luke were accepted
(cf. Rev. v. 5). This fact of his origin
would naturally militate against His
claims to be Priest ; but this writer here
skilfully reconciles them with Scripture.
Weizsäcker translates by "längst be-
kannt " giving to πρό the temporal
meaning. On Clem., ad Cor., xii., Lightfoot says: "It may be a question in
many passages whether the preposition
denotes *priority in time* or *distinctness*."
Wetstein quotes from Artemidorus καὶ
ἐφάνη πρόδηλον τὸ ὄναρ μετὰ τὴν

ἀπόφασιν and from Polyaenus τί καὶ
χρὴ γράφειν; πρόδηλον γάρ. ἀνατέταλκεν is possibly a reminiscence of
Zech. vi. 12, Ἰδοὺ ἀνὴρ Ἀνατολὴ ὄνομα
αὐτῷ· καὶ ὑποκάτωθεν αὐτοῦ ἀνατελεῖ,
a passage referred to by Philo, see Carpzov in *loc*. εἰς ἣν φυλὴν, "εἰς is applied
to the direction of the thought, as Acts
ii. 25. Δαυὶδ λέγει εἰς αὐτόν, aiming at
Him, E. i. 10, v. 32." Winer, 49, and
so in Dion. Hal., πολλοὶ ἐλέχθησαν εἰς
τοῦτο λόγοι, and cf. our own expression,
"He spoke *to* such and such points ".
Vulg. translates "in qua tribu ". Whatever Moses spoke regarding priests was
spoken with reference to another tribe
and not with reference to Judah.
Vv. 15-19. Imperfection of the Levitical priesthood more abundantly proved
by contrast with the nature of the Melchizedek priest.
Ver. 15. καὶ περισσότερον ἔτι κατάδηλόν ἐστιν. "And more abundantly
still is it evident" [Weizsäcker excellently " Und noch zum Ueberfluss
weiter liegt die Sache klar "]. What
is it that is more abundantly evident ?
Weiss says, It is, that an alteration of
the priesthood has been made. Similarly Vaughan, "And this insufficiency
and consequent supersession of the Levitical priesthood is still more conclusively
proved by the particular designation of
the predicted priest (in Ps. cx. 4) as a
priest, etc.". So too Westcott. But
from the twelfth verse the argument has
been directed to show that there has
been a change of law, and this argument
is continued in ver. 15. This change of
law is evident from the fact that Jesus
belongs to the non-Levitical tribe of
Judah, and yet more superabundantly
evident from the nature of the new priest
who is seen to be no longer "after the
law of a carnal commandment". So
Bleek after Œcumenius, Davidson, Farrar
and others. κατάδηλον, quite evident,
as in Xen., *Mem*., i. 4, 14, οὐ γὰρ πάνυ
σοι κατάδηλον ; Wetstein quotes from
Hippocrates, ἔτι δὲ μᾶλλον κατάδηλον
γίνεται. In πρόδηλον the preposition
has the force of "ob" in "obvious" ; in

Μελχισεδὲκ ἀνίσταται ἱερεὺς ἕτερος, 16. ὃς οὐ κατὰ νόμον ἐντολῆς
σαρκικῆς¹ γέγονεν, ἀλλὰ κατὰ δύναμιν ζωῆς ἀκαταλύτου· 17. ʰ μαρ- ʰ v. 6; Ps.
τυρεῖ² γὰρ, ""Οτι σὺ ἱερεὺς εἰς τὸν αἰῶνα κατὰ τὴν τάξιν Μελχισεδέκ".   cx. 4.

¹ T.R. in CᶜᵒʳʳDᶜEK ; σαρκινης in אABC*D*LP.
² T.R. with CDᶜE**KL ; μαρτυρειται in אABD*E*P.

κατάδηλον the preposition strengthens.
εἰ κατὰ, κ.τ.λ. "if as is the case" or
"since" (cf. ver. 11) "after the likeness
of Melchizedek" the κατὰ τ. ταξιν of
previous verses changed now into κατὰ τ.
ὁμοιότητα, because attention is directed
to the similarity of nature between Melchizedek and this new priest.

Ver. 16.   ὃς οὐ κατὰ νόμον . . .
ἀκαταλύτου, "who has become such
not after the law of a fleshen ordinance
but after the power of an indissoluble
life". This relative clause defines the
"likeness to Melchizedek," and brings
out a double contrast between the new
priest and the Levitical—the Levitical
priesthood is κατὰ νόμον, the other κατὰ
δύναμιν, the one is dependent on what
is σαρκίνη, the other on what belongs
to ζωὴ ἀκαταλύτος. These contrasts
are significant. The Levitical priesthood
rested on law, on a regulation that those
should be priests who were born of
certain parents. This was an outward
νόμος, a thing outside of the men themselves, and moreover it was a νόμος
σαρκίνης ἐντολῆς, regulating the priesthood not in relation to spiritual fitness
but in accordance with fleshly descent.
No matter what the man's nature is nor
how ill-suited and reluctant he is to the
office, he becomes a priest because his
fleshly pedigree is right. The new priest
on the contrary did what He did, not
because any official necessity was laid
upon Him, but because there was a
power in His own nature compelling and
enabling Him, the power of a life which
death did not dissolve. The contrast is
between the official and the personal or
real. All that is merely professional
must be dispossessed by what is real.
Hereditary kings gave way to Cromwell.
The Marshals of France put their batons
in their pockets when Joan of Arc appeared. For the difference between
σάρκινος and σαρκικός see Trench, Synonyms, 257, who quotes the reason assigned by Erasmus for the use of the
former in 2 Cor, iii. 3, "ut materiam
intelligas, non qualitatem". The enactment was σαρκίνη inasmuch as it took
to do only with the flesh. It caused the

priesthood to be implicated with and
dependent on fleshly descent. Opposed
to this was the inherent energy and
potentiality of an indissoluble or indestructible life. The life of the new priest
is indissoluble, not as eternally existing
in the Son, but as existing in Him
Incarnate and fulfilling priestly functions. The term itself "indestructible"
used in place of "eternal," directs the
thought to the death of Jesus which
might naturally seem to have threatened
it with destruction. His survival of
death was needful to the fulfilment of
His functions as priest (see ver. 25).
The meaning and reference of the term
is brought out by the contrast of ver. 28
between "men who have weakness" and
υἱὸν εἰς τὸν αἰῶνα τετελειωμένον. "Unquestionably that which enables the Son
to be Messianic King and High Priest of
men is His rank as Son. But it is true
on the other hand that it is as Son come
in the flesh that He is King and Priest.
And the expression 'hath become priest'
(ver. 16) points to a historical event. It
is, therefore, probable that indissoluble
life is attributed to Him not in general
as the eternal Son, but as the Son made
man."

Ver. 17. That Jesus carries on His
work perennially is proved by Scripture.
"For it is witnessed Thou art a priest
for ever after the order of Melchizedek,"
not merely as in ver. 11, κατὰ τ. τάξιν Μ.,
although this itself involves the perpetuity of the priesthood, but expressly
and emphatically εἰς τὸν αἰῶνα. Vv. 18
and 19 taking up the idea of ver. 16
affirm the negative and positive result of
the superseding of the fleshly ordinance
by the power of an indestructible life.
On the one hand there is an ἀθέτησις
προαγούσης ἐντολῆς, "a setting
aside of a foregoing enactment," that
namely which is referred to in ver. 17,
and on the other hand, there is "a
further bringing in of a better hope".
ἐπεισαγωγὴ κρείττονος ἐλπί-
ίδος, the ἐπί in ἐπεισαγωγὴ balances
προαγούσης, and indicates that the better
hope was introduced over and above all
that had already been done in the same

i Gal. iv. 9.
k iv. 16;
  Joan. i.
  17; Acts
  xiii. 39;
  Rom. iii.
  21, 28, et
  viii. 3;
  Eph. ii.
  18, et iii.
  12; Gal. ii. 16.   1 Ps. cx. 4.

18. ¹Ἀθέτησις μὲν γὰρ γίνεται προαγούσης ἐντολῆς, διὰ τὸ αὐτῆς ἀσθενὲς καὶ ἀνωφελές· 19. ᵏοὐδὲν γὰρ ἐτελείωσεν ὁ νόμος· ἐπεισαγωγὴ δὲ κρείττονος ἐλπίδος, δι᾽ ἧς ἐγγίζομεν τῷ Θεῷ. 20. Καὶ καθ᾽ ὅσον οὐ χωρὶς ὁρκωμοσίας· ¹οἱ μὲν γὰρ χωρὶς ὁρκωμοσίας εἰσὶν ἱερεῖς γεγονότες, 21. ὁ δὲ μετὰ ὁρκωμοσίας, διὰ τοῦ λέγοντος

behalf of bringing men to God. The μὲν . . . δὲ indicate that the sentence must thus be construed, and not as rendered in A.V. The reason of this replacement of the old legal enactment is given in the clause, διὰ τὸ αὐτῆς ἀσθενὲς καὶ ἀνωφελές "on account of its weakness and uselessness". This arrangement depending on the flesh was helpless to achieve the most spiritual of achievements, the union of man with God, the bringing together in true spiritual fellowship of sinful and earthly man with the holy God. So Paul found that arrangements of a mechanical and external nature were ἀσθενῆ καὶ πτωχὰ στοιχεῖα, Gal. iv. 9. "The uselessness (unhelplessness) of the priesthood was proved by its inability to aid men in that ἐγγίζειν τῷ Θεῷ, which is their one want" (Vaughan). The ordinance regulating the priesthood failed to accomplish its object; and indeed this characterised the entire system of which it was a characteristic part. οὐδὲν γὰρ ἐτελείωσεν ὁ νόμος, "for nothing was brought to perfection by the law". The law made beginnings, taught rudiments, gave initial impulses, hinted, foreshadowed, but brought nothing to perfection, did not in itself provide for man's perfect entrance into God's fellowship. Therefore there was introduced that which did achieve in perfect form this reconcilement with God, viz.: a better hope, which is therefore defined as δι᾽ ἧς ἐγγίζομεν τῷ Θεῷ, "by which we draw near to God". The law said (Exod. xix. 21) διαμάρτυραι τῷ λαῷ μήποτε ἐγγίσωσι πρὸς τὸν Θεόν. The "better" hope is that which springs from belief in the indestructible life of Christ and the assurance that that life is still active in the priestly function of intercession. It is the hope that is anchored within the veil fixed in Christ's person and therefore bringing us into God's presence and fellowship.

Vv. 20-22. Another element in the superiority of the covenant established upon the priesthood of Jesus is that in the very manner of the institution of His priesthood it was declared to be permanent. The long parenthesis of ver. 21 being held aside the statement of 20-22 reads thus : " And [introducing a fresh consideration] in proportion as not without an oath [was He made priest] . . . in that proportion better is the covenant of which Jesus has become the surety ". The parenthesis of ver. 21 is inserted to confirm by an appeal to Scripture [Ps. cx. 4] the fact that by the swearing of an oath the Melchizedek priest was appointed, and to indicate the significance of this mode of appointment, viz. : that repentance or change of plan is excluded. That is to say, this priesthood is final, eternal. And the superiority of the priesthood involves the superiority of the covenant based upon it. The oath signifies therefore the transition from a provisional and temporary covenant to that which is eternal. καθ᾽ ὅσον. This form of argument is frequent in Philo, see Quis. Rev. Div. H., 17, etc. οὐ χωρὶς ὁρκωμοσίας, "not without oath-swearing"; the clause may be completed from that which follows, "has he been made priest," as in A.V., although Weiss maintains that this is "sprachwidrig" and that the broken clause "kann natürlich nur aus dem Vorigen ergänzt werden ". But it is most natural and grammatical to complete it from the sentence in which it stands : "As not without an oath, so of a better covenant has Jesus become surety". The parenthesis thus furnishes the needed ground of this statement. He became surety by becoming priest, and as priest he was constituted with an oath. οἱ μὲν γὰρ "For the one [that is, the Levitical priests] εἰσὶν ἱερεῖς γεγονότες "have been made priests" Vaughan renders "are having become priests—are priests having become so ". So Delitzsch, Weiss and von Soden. Westcott says : " The periphrasis marks the possession as well as the impartment of the office ; " and on the "periphrastic conjugation" see Blass, sec. 62; Stephanus Thesaurus s.v. εἰμί, and cf. Acts

πρὸς αὐτόν, "῎Ωμοσε Κύριος καὶ οὐ μεταμεληθήσεται, Σὺ ἱερεὺς εἰς
τὸν αἰῶνα κατὰ τὴν τάξιν Μελχισεδέκ [1]". 22. [m]κατὰ τοσοῦτον [2] m viii. 6.

[1] T.R. in אcADEKLP, d, e, Copt., Syrutr, Aeth. ; om. κατα τ. ταξιν Μελχ. with
א*BC, 17, 80, f, vg., Sah., Basm., Arm.

[2] T.R. אcD³EKL ; τοσουτο with א*ABC, 17, 23, 39, 115. Both forms found in
Attic though τοσουτον is more frequent. See Blass, *Gram.*, p. 36.

xxi. 29, ἦσαν γὰρ προεωρακότες.]. ὁ δὲ
μετὰ ὅρκ. "but the other [the new
priest] with an oath," μετὰ of course not
being instrumental, but " interposito
jurejurando "; where and how this oath
is to be found is next explained, it is δι ὰ
τοῦ λέγοντος . . . "through Him
that saith to him. The Lord sware and
will not repent, Thou art," etc. There
is no call to translate πρὸς αὐτόν
" in reference to Him "; neither is there
any difficulty in referring the words
ὤμοσε . . . μεταμελ. to God. " Though
the words are not directly spoken by
the Lord, they are His by implication.
The oath is His " (Westcott). On the
distinction between μετανοέω and μετα-
μέλομαι see Trench, *Synonyms*, 241. " He
who has *changed his mind* about the
past is in the way to change everything ;
he who has an *after care* may have little
or nothing more than a selfish dread of
the consequences of what he has done."
This, however, does not apply to the
LXX (from which the quotation of this
verse is taken) where both words are
used to translate נחם. *Cf.* 1 Kings xv.
29 and 35. κατὰ τοσοῦτο "by so
much," that is, the superiority of the new
covenant to the old is in the ratio of
eternity to time, of what is permanent
and adequate to what is transitory and
provisional. κρείττονος διαθήκης "of a better covenant " [" id est,
non infirmae et inutilis. Frequens in hac
epistola epitheton,κρείττων, item αἰώνιος,
ἀληθινὸς, δεύτερος, διαφορώτερος,
ἕτερος, ζῶν, καινὸς, μέλλων, νέος,
πρόσφατος, τέλειος " (Bengel)], here
first mentioned in the Epistle, but
whose character and contents and
relation to the " foregoing " covenant
are fully explained in the following
chapter. Here already its " betterness "
is recognisable in this, that it supersedes
the older, and is itself permanent
because perfectly accomplishing the
purposes of a covenant.
Ver. 22. διαθήκη in classical Greek
means a *disposition* (διατίθημι) of one's
goods by will ; frequent in the orators
and sometimes as in Aristoph.,*Birds*, 439,

a covenant. In the LXX it occurs
nearly 280 times and in all but four
passages it is the translation of בְּרִית
"covenant". (See Hatch. *Essays in
Bibl. Greek*, 47.) It is used indifferently
of agreements between men and of
contracts or engagements between God
and man. See Introduction and on ix.
16 and Thayer *s.v.* Of this " better
covenant " Jesus " has become and is "
[γέγονεν] ἔγγυος " surety". ἔγγυος is
explained in the Greek commentators by
ἐγγυητής, which is the commoner of the
two forms, at least in later Greek.
ἔγγυος occurs several times in the
fragments from the second century B.C.
given in Grenfell and Hunt's *Greek
Papyri*, series ii.; also in the fragments
from first century A.D. given in the
Oxyrhynchus Papyri. It is not the exact
equivalent of μεσίτης (found in a similar
connection viii. 6, ix. 15, xii. 24) which
is a more comprehensive term. It has
been questioned why in this place ἔγγυος
is used, and Peirce answers : " I am apt
to think he was led to this by his having
just before used the word ἐγγίζομεν, and
that he did it for the sake of the
paronomasia ". And Bruce says : " There
is literary felicity in the use of the word
as playfully alluding to the foregoing
word ἐγγίζομεν. There is more than
literary felicity, for the two words
probably have the same root, so that we
might render ἔγγυος., *the one who insures
permanently near relations with God*."
More likely he chose the word because
his purpose was not to exhibit Jesus as
negotiating the covenant, but especially
as securing that it should achieve its
end. It has been debated whether it is
meant that Jesus was surety for men to
God, as was held by both Lutheran and
Reformed writers,or with others (Grotius,
Peirce, etc.), that He was surety for God
to men [" His being a surety relates to
His acting in the behalf of God towards
us and to His assuring us of the divine
favour, and to His bestowing the benefits
promised by God " (Peirce)] or, with
Limborch, Baumgarten and Schmid (see
Bleek) that he was surety for both

κρείττονος [1] διαθήκης γέγονεν ἔγγυος Ἰησοῦς. 23. Καὶ οἱ μὲν,
πλείονές εἰσι γεγονότες ἱερεῖς,[2] διὰ τὸ θανάτῳ κωλύεσθαι παρα-
μένειν· 24. ὁ δὲ, διὰ τὸ μένειν αὐτὸν εἰς τὸν αἰῶνα, ἀπαράβατον
ἔχει τὴν ἱερωσύνην· 25. ὅθεν καὶ σώζειν εἰς τὸ παντελὲς δύναται

n ix. 24;
⊦ om. viii.
34; I
Tim. ii. 5;
1 Joan ii.
2.

---

[1] T.R. in אcACcDEKLP; και κρειττονος in א*BC*.
[2] γεγονοτες ante ιερεις with אBLP; post ιερεις in ACDE, 17, d, e.

---

parties. There is no reason to suppose
that the writer particularised in any of
these directions. He merely wished to
express the thought that by the appointment of Jesus to the priestoood, the
covenant based upon this priesthood
was secured against all failure of any of
the ends for which it was established.

Vv. 23-25. Another ground of the
perfectness of the new priesthood is
found in the continued life of the priest,
who ever lives to make intercession and
can therefore save completely, whereas
the Levitical priests were compelled by
death to give place to others.

Ver. 23. καὶ, as above, ver. 20, introducing a new element in the argument. οἱ μὲν, as in ver. 21, the
Levitical priests, πλείονες . . . "have
been made priests many in number,"
not many at one and the same time
[Delitzsch], although that also is true,
but many in succession, as is shown by
the reason assigned διὰ τὸ θανάτῳ
κωλύεσθαι παραμένειν "be-
cause of their being prevented by
death from abiding" "in their office,"
Peirce, as Œcumenius, ἐν τῇ ἱερωσύνῃ
δηλονότι. Others think that remaining
in life is meant. Possibly πλείονες is
used instead of πολλοί, because there is
a latent comparison with the one continuing priest, or with those already
priests; always more and more. He,
on the contrary, ὁ δὲ, by reason of his
abiding for ever ἀπαράβατον ἔχει
τὴν ἱερωσύνην "has his priesthood
inviolable," that is, no other person can
step into it. The form of expression is
similar to that used by Epiphanius of
the Trinity, ἡ δὲ ἀπαράβατον ἔχει τὴν
φύσιν. The meaning of ἀπαράβ. is
contested, some interpreters (Weiss,
etc.) supposing that it signifies "inde-
feasible," or "untransmitted" or "non-
transferable." Indeed, Œcumenius and
Theophylact translate it by ἀδιάδοχον.
But in every instance of its occurrence
given by Stephanus and Wetstein it has
a passive sense, as νόμος, ὅρκος, etc.,
ἀπαράβ., and means unalterable or inviolable. This suits the present passage

perfectly, and returns upon the thought
of ver. 3, that the new priest is sole and
perpetual occupant of the office, giving
place to no successor. ὅθεν, "whence,"
i.e., because of His having this absolute
priesthood; His saving power depends
upon His priesthood. He is able καὶ
σώζειν εἰς τὸ παντελές, "even to save
to the uttermost," not to be referred
merely to time as in Vulgate "in perpetuum," and Chrysostom, οὐ πρὸς τὸ
παρὸν μόνον φησὶν, ἀλλὰ καὶ ἐκεῖ ἐν τῇ
μελλούσῃ ζωῇ. If referred to time, it
might mean either ability to save the
individual eternally, or to save future
generations. Peirce joins it with
δύναται, and renders "whence also he
is perpetually able to save." But the
phrase uniformly means "completely,"
"thoroughly," as in Luke xiii. 11 of
the woman, μὴ δυναμένη ἀνακύψαι εἰς
τὸ παντελές and in the examples cited
by Wetstein. This, as Riehm shows (p.
613, note), includes the idea of perpetuity. The Levitical priests could not
so save: no τελείωσις was achieved by
them; but everything for which the
priesthood existed, everything which is
comprised in the great [ii. 3] and eternal
[v. 9] salvation, the deliverance [ii. 15]
and glory [ii. 10] which belong to it,
are achieved by Christ. The objects of
this saving power are τοὺς προσερχομένους δι' αὐτοῦ τῷ Θεῷ,
"those who through Him approach
God"; "through Him" no longer re-
lying on the mediation of Levitical
priests, but recognising Jesus as the
"new and living way," x. 19-22. This
complete salvation Jesus can accomplish because πάντοτε ζῶν . . . αὐτῶν,
"ever living to intercede on their
behalf". The particular mode in which
His eternal priesthood applies itself to
those who through Him approach God
is that He intercedes for them, thus
effecting their real introduction to God's
presence and their acceptance by Him,
and also the supply of all their need out
of the Divine fulness. ἐντυγχάνειν, "to
meet by chance," "to light upon," takes
as its second meaning, "to converse

τοὺς προσερχομένους δι' αὐτοῦ τῷ Θεῷ, πάντοτε ζῶν εἰς τὸ ἐντυγ- ο iv. 14, 15,
χάνειν ὑπὲρ αὐτῶν. 26. ᵒτοιοῦτος γὰρ ἡμῖν ἔπρεπεν¹ ἀρχιερεύς, et ix. 24; Rom. viii.
ὅσιος, ἄκακος, ἀμίαντος, κεχωρισμένος ἀπὸ τῶν ἁμαρτωλῶν, καὶ 34; 1 Joan ii. 2.

¹ T.R. in ℵCKLP it vg.; insert και before επρεπεν ABDE, Syrutr.

with " (followed by dative), hence "to
entreat one to do something " (Plut.,
Pomp., 55; *Ages.*, 25), and when followed by περί (Polyb., iv. 76, 9) or by
ὑπέρ (Plut., *Cato Maj.*, 9) " to intercede ". (See Liddell and Scott.) It is
not the word itself, but the preposition
following, that gives the idea of *intercession.* The word with a different preposition can be used in the sense of
appealing *against*, as in Rom. xi. 2,
ὡς ἐντυγ. τ. Θεῷ κατὰ τ. Ἰσραήλ, see
also 1 Mac. xi. 25. With ὑπέρ it occurs
in Rom. viii. 27, 34, and with περί in
Acts xxv. 24. Christ, then, treats with
God in our behalf; and He lives for
this. As His life on earth was spent in
the interests of men, so He continues to
spend Himself in this same cause. He
ever lives, and being " the same yesterday, to-day and for ever " (xiii. 8) His
present fulness of life is devoted to
those ends which evoked His energies
while on earth. He secures that the
fulness of Divine resource shall be available for men. " All things are ours."
This intercession is not the same as the
Atoning sacrifice and its presentation
before God, which was accomplished
once for all (ix. 26, x. 18); but it is
based upon the sacrifice which is also
to men the guarantee that His intercession is real, and comprehensive of all
their needs. [*Cf.* Sir Walter Raleigh's
Pilgrimage.]

Vv. 26-28. A summary description of
the Melchizedek ideal priest, drawn in
contrast to the Levitical High Priest,
and realised in the Son who has been
perfected as Priest for ever. Melchizedek
is here dropped, and the priesthood of
the Son is now directly contrasted with
that of the Aaronic High Priest.

Ver. 26. Τοιοῦτος γὰρ . . .
ἀρχιερεύς. "*Such* seems to refer
to the Melchizedek character delineated
in the preceding part of the chapter, or
to all that was said of the nature and
character of the Son from iv. 14 on-
ward. The sense will not differ if it
be supposed to refer to the epithets and
statements that follow, for these but
summarise what went before " (Davidson and others). But it must not be
overlooked that ὅς (ver. 27) is one of

the usual relatives after τοιοῦτος (*cf.*
viii. 1, and Soph., *Antig.*, 691, λόγοις
τοιούτοις οἷς; *cf.* also Longinus, *De
Sublim.*, ix. 2. So that Farrar's statement on chap. viii. 1, "τοιόσδε is pro-
spective, τοιοῦτος is retrospective," is
incorrect), and that the adjectives ὅσιος,
κ.τ.λ. prepare for and give the ground
of the statement made in the relative
clause. The sentence therefore reads:
" So great a high priest as need not
daily, etc., . . . became us," ἡμῖν
ἔπρεπεν, not, as in viii. 1, τοιοῦτον
ἔχομεν ἀρχιερέα (*cf.* iv. 14, 15), because
the writer wishes to draw attention to
the needs of those for whom the priest
was appointed [ἡμῖν emphatic] and his
suitableness to those needs. We, being
what we are, sinful and dependent on
the mediation of others, need a priest in
whom we can wholly trust, because He
Himself is holy, separate from sinners,
without human weakness. Westcott's
distribution of the terms is neat,
although of doubtful validity. " Christ
is personally in Himself *holy*, in relation to men *guileless*, in spite of contact
with a sinful world, *undefiled*. By the
issue of His life He has been *separated
from sinners* in regard to the visible
order, and, in regard to the invisible
world, He has *risen above the heavens*".
ὅσιος frequently in the Psalms, where
it translates חָסִיד] denotes personal
holiness, while ἅγιος and ἱερός express
the idea of consecration. [See Trench,
Synon.] Weiss, however, says: " ὅσιος,
ein Synonym von ἅγιος" (Vulg., Ps. iv.
4, xvi. 10) " bezeichnet die religiöse
Weihe des Gottangehörigen " (Tit. i. 8,
1 Tim. ii. 8). Peirce understands that
here the word means "merciful". But
this is scarcely consistent with N.T. usage.
ἄκακος, "innocent," and frequently with
the idea of inexperience which attaches
to the English word [*cf.* the definition
which Trench, *Synon.*, p. 197, quotes
from Basil; and see also the use of
ἀκακία in Ps. xxxvi. 37, and of ἄκακοι in
Ps. xxiv. 21. Its use in Jer. xi. 19 is
significant, ἐγὼ δὲ ὡς ἀρνίον ἄκακον
ἀγόμενον τοῦ θύεσθαι.] Here the word
seems to point to that entire absence of
evil thought and slightest taint of malice

p v. 3, et ix. ὑψηλότερος τῶν οὐρανῶν γενόμενος · 27. ᵖὃς οὐκ ἔχει καθ᾽ ἡμέραν
12, 28, et
x. 12;   ἀνάγκην, ὥσπερ οἱ ἀρχιερεῖς, πρότερον ὑπὲρ τῶν ἰδίων ἁμαρτιῶν
Lev. ix. 7,
et xvi. 6, θυσίας ἀναφέρειν, ἔπειτα τῶν τοῦ λαοῦ · τοῦτο γὰρ ἐποίησεν ἐφάπαξ,
11.
q ii. 10, et ἑαυτὸν ἀνενέγκας.¹   28. ᑫὁ νόμος γὰρ ἀνθρώπους καθίστησιν
v. 1, 2, 9.
            ἀρχιερεῖς, ἔχοντας ἀσθένειαν · ὁ λόγος δὲ τῆς ὁρκωμοσίας τῆς μετὰ
            τὸν νόμον, υἱὸν εἰς τὸν αἰῶνα τετελειωμένον.

¹ T.R. with BDEKLP; προσενεγκας in אA, 17, 73, 80, Cyr est 93.

which might prompt disregard of human need. ὅσιος denotes His oneness with God, ἄκακος His oneness with His fellow-men. He is not separated from them, or rendered indifferent by any selfishness. Neither has His contact with the world left any soil; He is ἀμίαντος, "stainless," and so fit to appear before God. *Cf.* the stringent laws regarding uncleanness and blemish laid down for the Levitical priests in Lev. xxi. 1, xxii. 9. And as the high priest in Israel was not permitted to go out of the sanctuary nor come near a dead body, though of his father or mother (Lev. xxi. 11, 12), and as the later law enjoined a seven-days' separation of the high priest before the day of Atonement (Schoettgen in *loc.*), so our Lord fulfilled this symbolic isolation by being in heart and life κεχωρισμένος ἀπὸ τῶν ἁμαρτωλῶν. If there is anything in the symbol, then this separation occurred before the sacrifice was made, and as a preparation for it, but almost all modern interpreters (Grotius, Bengel, "separatus est, relicto mundo," Peirce, Tholuck, Bleek, Alford, Davidson, Rendall, von Soden, but not Milligan) refer the separation to His exaltation. " In virtue of His exaltation He is now for evermore withdrawn from all perturbing contact with evil men" (Delitzsch). Being co-ordinate with the previous adjectives, while the ὑψηλότερος γεν. is added by καὶ, it would seem that κεχωρ. refers to the result achieved by His earthly life with all its temptations. By the seclusion of the high priest it was hinted that before entering God's presence the priest must be isolated from the contamination of human intercourse: there must be a period of quarantine; but our High Priest has carried through all the confusion and turmoil and defilement and exasperation of life an absolute immunity from contagion or stain. He was with God throughout, and throughout was separated by an atmosphere of His own from sinners.

καὶ ὑψηλότερος τῶν οὐρανῶν γενόμενος, "and made higher than the heavens," which apparently has a meaning similar to iv. 14, "We have a great High Priest who has passed through the heavens," *cf.* also Eph. iv. 10. It is not "and has been set," but γενόμενος, has by His own career and character attained that dignity. It is by right, as the necessary result of His life, that He is above the heavens. "He is now become, strictly speaking, as to His mode of being, supra-mundane" (Delitzsch). [For the word, *cf.* Lucian, *Nigr.*, 25, ἑαυτὸν ὑψηλότερον λημμάτων παρέχειν, to show himself superior to gains.] ὃς οὐκ ἔχει καθ᾽ ἡμέραν ἀνάγκην... "who does not need daily, like the high priests, to offer sacrifices first for His own sins, then for the people's; for this He did once for all by offering Himself". As shown by the relative, this is the main affirmation to which the preceding clauses lead up. The one offering of Christ is contrasted with the continually repeated offerings of the Levitical high priests; and His Sonship priesthood to which He was instituted by an oath is set over against the service of men who had first to be cleansed from their own defilements before they could sacrifice for the sins of the people. In the words καθ᾽ ἡμέραν, when κατ᾽ ἐνιαυτόν (x. 1) might have been expected, a difficulty has been found. It was on the Day of Atonement, once a year, that the high priest offered first for himself and then for the people, see ix. 7. Accordingly, several interpreters, such as Bleek, Lünemann, Davidson. adopt the idea that the writer blends in one view the ordinary daily sacrifice and the sacrifice of the day of Atonement. Others again, as Hofmann, Delitzsch, Alford, maintain that the position of καθ᾽ ἡμέραν shows that it belongs only to ὃς [Christ], not to οἱ ἀρχιερεῖς, so that the sentence really means: "Who has not need day by day, as the high priests had year by

year ". Weiss renders this interpretation more probable by pointing out that
the words have a reference to πάντοτε
ζῶν εἰς τὸ ἐντυγχάνειν of ver. 25. His
intercession is continuous, from day to
day, but in order to accomplish it He
does not need day by day to purify
Himself and renew His sacrifice. *Cf.*
also the seven days' purification of the
high priest on entering his office, Exod.
xxix. 13-8. θυσίας ἀναφέρειν, a
phrase resulting from the *carrying up* of
the sacrifice to the raised altar, and only
found in Hellenistic, frequently in LXX.
The more usual word in this Epistle
(twenty times and frequently in LXX)
is προσφέρειν. " ἀναφέρειν properly
describes the ministerial action of the
priest, and προσφέρειν the action of the
offerer (Lev. ii. 14, 16, vi. 33, 35), but the
distinction is not observed universally;
thus ἀναφέρειν is used of the people (Lev.
xvii. 5), and προσφέρειν of the priests
(Lev. xxi. 21) " (Westcott). πρότερον
. . . ἔπειτα, as in v. 3, "they must
first offer for themselves, because they
may not approach God sin-stained; they
must also offer for the people, because
they may not introduce a sin-stained
people to God " (Weiss). τοῦτο γὰρ
ἐποίησεν . . . This, *i.e.*, offering for
the sins of the people. But it must be
borne in mind that this writer keeps in
view that Christ also had a preparation
for His priestly ministry in the sinless
temptations and sufferings He endured,
vv. 7-10. The emphasis is on ἐφάπαξ,
in contrast to the καθ' ἡμέραν, and
the ground of the ἐφάπαξ is given in
ἑαυτὸν ἀνενέγκας, an offering
which by the nature of the case could
not be repeated, ix. 27, 28, and which
by its worth rendered repetition superfluous. This difference between the new
priest and the old is based upon their
essential difference of nature, " For the
law appoints as high priests men who
have weakness," which especially gives
the reason, as in v. 3, why they must
sacrifice for themselves. In v. 3 the
weakness is ascribed to the same source
as here; the high priest is ἐξ ἀνθρώπων
λαμβανόμενος. In c. 5, however, the fact
that the high priest is taken from among
men is introduced chiefly for the sake of
illustrating his sympathy: here it is introduced in contrast to υἱόν of the next
clause, which is thus raised to a higher
than human dignity. For had this contrast not been intended, τοὺς would have
been used, and not ἀνθρώπους. The law
only made provision for the appointment

of priests who had human weakness:
the word of the oath (already explained
in vv. 20-22), τῆς μετὰ τὸν νόμον,
" which [oath-swearing] came after the
law," and therefore showed that the
law needed revision and supplementing
[" Debent posteriora in legibus esse per-
fectiora " (Gro ius)]. It might have been
argued that the Law coming after Melchizedek introduced an improved priesthood. It is therefore worth while to point
out that the adoption of the Melchizedek
priesthood as the type of the Messianic
was subsequent to the Law, and consequently superseded it. υἱὸν εἰς τὸν
αἰῶνα τετελειωμένον [appoints],
" a son who has been made perfect for
ever ". υἱὸν, without the article, because attention is called to the nature
of the new priest, as in i. 1. " Son,"
in the fullest sense, as described in i.
1-4, and in contrast to ἀνθρώπους. He
also, though a Son, became man, and
was exposed to human temptations, but
by this experience was " perfected " as
our Priest. *Cf.* vv. 7-10. " For ever
perfected " is directly contrasted with
the sinful yielding to infirmity exhibited
by the Levitical priests, and must therefore be referred to moral perfecting, as
explained in chap. v. This perfectness
of the Son is confirmed and sealed by
His exaltation; He is for ever perfected
in the sense, as Grotius says, " ut nec
morti nec ullis adversis subjaceat ". *Cf.*
ix. 27, 28. The A.V translates " consecrated," which Davidson denounces, with
Alford, as " altogether false ". But this
translation at any rate suggests that it is
perfectness as our priest the writer has
in view; and the use of τελειόω in Lev.
xxi. 10 and other passages cannot be
thus lightly set aside.

CHAPTER VIII.—Vv. 1-6. The idea of
Christ's priesthood, merely suggested in
i. 3, expressly affirmed in ii. 17, has
been from iv. 14 onwards enlarged upon
and illustrated. It has been shown that
Christ is a priest, called by God to this
office and proclaimed by God as High
Priest. The superiority of His orders
as belonging not to the hereditary
Aaronic line, but as being "after the order
of Melchisedek," has also been exhibited.
Passing now from the person and
qualifications of the Priest, the author
proceeds in chap. viii. to illustrate his
greatness from a consideration of the
place of His ministry. It is in heaven
He is seated, a minister of the real
tabernacle, not of that which had been
pitched by Moses as an image and

a i. 3, 13, et
iii. 1, et
iv. 14, et
vi. 20, et
ix. 11, et xii. 2; Eph.i.20; Col. iii. 1.

VIII. 1. ΚΕΦΑΛΑΙΟΝ δὲ ἐπὶ τοῖς λεγομένοις, τοιοῦτον ἔχομεν ἀρχιερέα, ὃς ἐκάθισεν ἐν δεξιᾷ τοῦ θρόνου τῆς μεγαλωσύνης ἐν τοῖς

symbol of it. The priesthood to which God called Him *must* be a heavenly ministry, for were He on earth He would not even be a priest, not to say a High Priest. His ministry, therefore, being in the heaven of eternal realities, is a "better ministry," in accordance with the fact that he is mediating a "better covenant".

Ver. 1. κεφάλαιον ἐπὶ τοῖς λεγομένοις, not, as A.V., "Now of the things which we have spoken this is the sum" (*cf.* Grotius "post tot dicta haec esto summa"), but with Field "Now to crown our present discourse" or with Rendall "Now to crown what we are saying". κεφάλαιον is used to denote either *the sum*, as of numbers added up from below to the *head* of the column where the result is set down, and in this sense it is here understood by Erasmus, Calvin and A.V.; or, *the chief point* as of a cope-stone or capital of a pillar, as in Thucyd., vi. 6. λέγοντες ἄλλα τε πολλὰ καὶ κεφάλαιον, οἱ Συρακόσιοι, κ.τ.λ. Other examples in Field's O.N., to which add Plutarch, *De Educ. Puer.*, 8, ἐν πρῶτον καὶ μέσον καὶ τελευταῖον ἐν τούτοις κεφάλαιον ἀγωγὴ σπουδαία. This latter sense alone satisfies the present passage, and also agrees better with ἐπὶ τοῖς λεγομένοις for ἐπὶ must here be taken in a quasi-local sense, as Vaughan paraphrases "as a capital upon the things which are being said—as a thought (or fact) forming the headstone of the argument—we add this". *Cf.* Luke xvi. 26 καὶ ἐπὶ πᾶσι τούτοις. That λεγομένοις is in the present is manifestly no objection to this rendering. The absence of the article before κεφάλ. does not involve, as Lünemann supposes, that the writer means "a main point" among others, for such words do not in similar situations require the article, *cf.* Demosth.,p. 924, τεκμήριον δὲ τούτου. κεφάλαιον is most easily construed as a nominative absolute (*cf.* Buttmann, p. 381) not, as Bruce, "an accusative in apposition with the following sentence". τοιοῦτον ἔχομεν ἀρχιερέα . . . "so great a High Priest have we as took His seat (or, is set down) on the right hand of the throne of the Majesty in the heavens". τοιοῦτον, not, as Farrar and Rendall, "retrospective,"

although as contrasted with τοιόσδε this is its proper meaning; but here, as frequently in classics [Soph., *Antig.*, 691, λόγοις τοιούτοις οἷς σὺ μὴ τέρψει κλύων, and Demosth., p. 743, followed also by ὥστε] it finds its explanation in ὃς ἐκάθισεν [τοιοῦτον weist natürlich nicht rückwärts sondern vorwärts auf den dasselbe erläuternden Relativsatz. Weiss.] The greatness of the High Priest is manifested by the place where He ministers. His greatness is revealed in his sitting down at the right hand of the Majesty in the heavens. Westcott thinks that the thought of a High Priest who . . . "is King as well as priest is clearly the prominent thought of the sentence". And Moulton on x. 12 says: "The words 'sat down' (Ps. cx. 1), add to the priestly imagery that of kingly state". But undoubtedly Weiss is right in saying "Durch den Relativsatz soll nicht auf die königliche Herrlichkeit Christi hingewiesen werden". The writer means to magnify Christ's priesthood by reminding his readers that it is exercised "in the heavens"; as he says in ix. 24 he has passed εἰς αὐτὸν τὸν οὐρανόν into heaven itself, the very presence of God and eternal reality, the ultimate, highest possible. On the words *cf.* note on i. 3. ἐκάθισεν is considered by Buttmann to be one of those aorists which stand for the perfect (see his instructive remarks on the aversion to the perfect, *Gram.*, p. 198); but this may be doubted, as the sitting is not mentioned as the permanent attitude, but merely as suggesting the exaltation of the High Priest, and the finality of His purification of sins, as in i. 3. Augustine, *De Fide et symbolo*, 7, warns against the suggested anthropomorphism of the words "sitteth at the right hand" and says "*ad dextram* intelligendum est dictum esse, in summa beatitudine, ubi justitia et pax et gaudium est". Here, however, it is rather Christ's *majesty* that is suggested, and as Pearson on this clause of the Creed says, "The belief of Christ's glorious session is most necessary in respect of the immediate consequence which is his most gracious intercession," rather his *availing* intercession. *Cf.* Hooker, Book V., chap. 55.

οὐρανοῖς, 2. ᵇτῶν ἁγίων λειτουργὸς, καὶ τῆς σκηνῆς τῆς ἀληθινῆς, ᵇ ix. 8, 11,
ἣν ἔπηξεν ὁ Κύριος, καὶ ¹ οὐκ ἄνθρωπος. 3. °πᾶς γὰρ ἀρχιερεὺς εἰς ²⁴, et x.
²¹·
τὸ προσφέρειν δῶρά τε καὶ θυσίας καθίσταται· ὅθεν ἀναγκαῖον ἔχειν ᶜ v.1; Eph.
τι καὶ τοῦτον ὃ προσενέγκῃ. 4. εἰ μὲν γὰρ ² ἦν ἐπὶ γῆς, οὐδ' ἂν ἦν
ἱερεύς, ὄντων τῶν ἱερέων ³ τῶν προσφερόντων κατὰ τὸν νόμον τὰ δῶρα,

¹ ADcE**KLP, f, vg., Copt., insert και ; ℵBD*E* 17, d, e, omit και.

² T.R. in DcEKL Syrp, Arm. ; ουν in ℵABD*P, 17, 73, 80, 137, d, e, f, vg.

³ T.R. in DcE**KL Syrutr, Chrys.; ℵABD*E*P, 17, 73, 137, d, e, f, vg. omit των
ιερεων.

Ver. 2. τῶν ἁγίων λειτουργὸς
. . . "a minister of the [true] holy place
and of the true abernacle which the
Lord pitched, not man". τῶν ἁγίων
not = τῶν ἡγιασμένων as Œcumenius
translates, but as in ix. 8, 12, 25; x. 19;
xiii. 11 = ἅγια ἁγίων of ix. 3. In ix.
2, 3, the outer part of the tabernacle is
called ἅγια, the inner ἅγια ἁγίων, but
ver. 8 is conclusive proof that ἅγια without addition was used for the holiest
place. λειτουργὸς cf. note on i. 14.
καὶ τῆς σκηνῆς τῆς ἀληθινῆς, the ideal,
antitypal tabernacle; ἀληθ. used as in
the fourth gospel in contrast not to what
is false, but to what is symbolical. It is
to be taken with ἁγίων as well as with
σκηνῆς. Cf. Bleek; and see ix. 11, τῆς
μείζονος καὶ τελειοτέρας σκηνῆς οὐ χειροποιήτου, which is the equivalent of
the clause added here, ἣν ἔπηξεν ὁ
Κύριος, οὐκ ἄνθρωπος. See also Mark
xiv. 58 and the striking words of Wisdom
ix. 8. In a different sense in Numb.
xxiv. 6, ὡσεὶ σκηναὶ ἃς ἔπηξε Κύριος.
According to the fifth verse, man pitched
a tabernacle which was a shadow of the
true, and the very words in which was
uttered the command so to do, might
have reminded the people that there was
a symbolic and a true tabernacle.
Ver. 3. πᾶς γὰρ ἀρχιερεὺς. . . .
"For every High Priest is appointed for
the offering of gifts and sacrifices, and
therefore it was necessary that this man
also have something to offer". That
Christ is in heaven as a λειτουργός, as
an active minister in holy things, is
proved by the universal law, that every
High Priest is appointed to offer gifts and
sacrifices. Christ is not idle in heaven,
but being there as High Priest He must
be offering something; what that is, He
has told us in vii. 27, but here no emphasis is on the what, but merely on the
fact that He must be offering something,
must be actively ministering in heaven
as a λειτουργός. [Bruce therefore overlooks vii. 27 in his interpretation : "He

is content for the present to throw out
the remark : 'This man must have something to offer,' and to leave his readers
for a while to puzzle over the question,
What is it?"] With ἀναγκαῖον some
have understood ἦν rather than ἐστὶ
"necesse fuit habere quod offerret "
(Beza) followed by Westcott, etc., on the
ground that the reference is to our Lord's
presentation to the Father of His finished
sacrifice. But it is better to give the
word a merely logical and subjective
force; it is a necessary inference that
this man, etc. Behind and beyond this
lies no doubt the reference to Christ's
sacrifice. As the High Priest could not
enter into the Holiest without the blood
of the victim (ix. vii.), so must Jesus
accomplish His priestly office by offering
His own blood (ix. 12). For the words
of the former part of the verse see note
on vi. 1.
Ver. 4. εἰ μὲν οὖν ἐπὶ γῆς . . . "And
indeed if He were on earth He would
not even be a priest, since there are those
who according to law offer the gifts".
μὲν οὖν = et quidem (Devarius, p. 125)
or, it might be rendered "If however,"
see Hermann's Viger, p. 442. Vaughan
says : "The οὖν is (as usual) in accordance with the above statement ; here,
namely, that He must have something to
offer". The apodosis in ver. 6. νυνι δε.
The argument is, given or assumed as
already proved that Christ is our High
Priest, it must be in Heaven He exercises His ministry, for if He were on
earth, He would not even be a priest, not
to say, a High Priest. [As Bleek has it,
"er würde nicht einmal Priester sein,—
geschweige denn Hohe priester ".] He
could not be a priest, because the priestly
office on earth is already filled. The
law [κατὰ νόμον], which can not be
interfered with, regulates all that concerns the earthly priesthood (vii. 12), and
by this law He is excluded from priestly
office, not being of the tribe of Levi
(vii. 14). τὰ δῶρα "the gifts" further

d x. 1;
Exod.
xxv. 40;
Acts vii.
44 ; Col.
ii. 17.

5. ^dοἵτινες ὑποδείγματι καὶ σκιᾷ λατρεύουσι τῶν ἐπουρανίων, καθὼς κεχρημάτισται Μωσῆς μέλλων ἐπιτελεῖν τὴν σκηνήν, "Ὅρα," γάρ φησι, "ποιήσῃς¹ πάντα κατὰ τὸν τύπον τὸν δειχθέντα σοι ἐν τῷ

¹ T.R. in minuscules ; ποιησεις in ℵABDEKLP.

emphasises the rigorous prescriptions of the law. The absence of the article before νόμον does not necessitate though it suggests the translation "according to law ".

Ver. 5. οἵτινες ὑποδείγματι . . . "priests who serve a suggestion and shadow of the heavenly things, even as Moses when about to make the tabernacle was admonished, for 'See,' He says, 'that thou make all things after the pattern shown thee in the Mount'". οἵτινες with its usual classifying and characterising reference, priests distinguished by the fact that they serve a shadow. λατρεύουσιν, originally to work for hire, from λάτρις, a hired servant (Soph., Trach., 70, etc.), but used especially in classics, LXX, and N.T. of service of God. It is followed by the dative of the person served (see reff.) Heb. ix. 14, xii. 28, and xiii. 10 as here οἱ τῇ σκηνῇ λατρεύοντες. ὑποδείγματι, Phrynichus notes, ὑπόδειγμα · οὐδὲ τοῦτο ὀρθῶς λέγεται · παράδειγμα λέγε. To which Rutherford adds, "In Attic ὑποδείκνυμι was never used except in its natural sense of show by implication ; but in Herodotus and Xenophon it signifies to mark out, set a pattern". The meaning of ὑπόδειγμα accordingly is "a sign suggestive of anything," "a delineation," "outline," perhaps "suggestion" would satisfy the present passage. σκιᾷ, "an adumbration of a reality which it does not embody " (Vaughan). A shadow has no substance in itself, no independent existence. It merely gives assurance that there is a reality to cast it, but itself is nothing solid or real. So the tabernacle gave assurance of the existence of a real dwelling of God which itself was not. Cf. x. 1, and Col. ii. 17. τῶν ἐπουρανίων, as in ix. 23 τὰ ὑποδείγματα τῶν ἐν τοῖς οὐρανοῖς . . . αὐτὰ δὲ τὰ ἐπουράνια, heavenly things, in a comprehensive sense. καθὼς κεχρημάτισται . . . καθώς, i.e. the description of the Mosaic tabernacle as a shadow of the heavenly accords with the directions given to Moses in its erection. κεχρημάτισται, χρηματίζω (from χρῆμα) originally means "to transact business," "to advise" or "give answer

to those asking advice " ; hence " to give a response to those who consult an oracle "; then, dropping all reference to a foregoing consultation, it means "to give a divine command " and in passive to be commanded; see Thayer. The perfect tense is explained by Delitzsch thus : "as thou Moses hast received (in our Scriptures) the divine injunction (which we still read there)". But cf. Burton, M. and T., 82. ἐπιτελεῖν, not, to complete what was already begun; but to realise what was determined by God ; cf. Num. xxiii. 23, and Heb. ix. 6; so that it might be rendered "to bring into being ". Ὅρα γάρ φησιν . . . He now cites the authoritative injunction referred to and which determines that the earthly tabernacle was but a copy of the heavenly. γάρ of course belongs to the writer, not to the quotation, and φησιν has for its nominative the Θεός implied in κεχρημάτισται. ποιήσεις. . . . The words are quoted from Exod. xxv. 40 (adding πάντα and substituting δειχθέντα for δεδειγμένον) and are a literal rendering of the Hebrew, so that nothing can be gathered from them regarding N.T. usage. The future indicative being regularly used as a legal imperative (an unclassic usage) it naturally occurs here. κατὰ τὸν τύπον, a stamp or impression (τύπτειν) struck from a die or seal; hence, a figure, draft, sketch, or pattern. How or in what form this was communicated to the mind of Moses we do not know. "In the Mount," i.e., in Sinai where Moses retired for communion with God, he probably pondered the needs of the people to such good purpose that from suggestions received in Egypt, together with his own divinely guided conceptions, he was able to contrive the tabernacle and its ordinances of worship. It is his spiritual insight and his anticipation of his people's wants which give him his unique place in history. And it is both to trifle and to detract from his greatness to say with some of the Rabbis (vide Schoettgen) that models of the Ark and the candlestick and the other equipment descended from heaven, and that Gabriel in a workman's apron showed him how to reproduce the articles shown.

ὄρει ". 6. °νυνὶ δὲ διαφορωτέρας τέτευχε[1] λειτουργίας, ὅσῳ καὶ e vii. 22; 2 Cor. iii. 6. κρείττονός ἐστι διαθήκης μεσίτης, ἥτις ἐπὶ κρείττοσιν ἐπαγγελίαις νενομοθέτηται. 7. Εἰ γὰρ ἡ πρώτη ἐκείνη ἦν ἄμεμπτος, οὐκ ἂν

---

[1] τέτευχε with אcBDcE ; τετυχε with א*AD*KL, 80, 116 ; τετυχηκεν with P, 17. Veitch gives τετυχηκα as the Homeric form, τετυχα Arist. and Demosth. ; τετυχα here and in Diod., "late if correct".

Ver. 6. νυνὶ δὲ ... "But, as it is, He hath obtained a more excellent ministry, by how much He is also mediator of a better covenant, which has been enacted upon better promises." νυνὶ δὲ, i.e., He not being on earth, the δὲ pointing back to μὲν in ver. 4. For νυνὶ δὲ in its *logical* significance, cf. ix. 26; xi. 16; 1 Cor. xiv. 20; Arist. *Ethics*, I. iv. 4. διαφορωτέρας λειτουργίας, more excellent, as what is heavenly or real is more excellent than what is earthly and symbolical. ὅσῳ καὶ κρείττονός ἐστιν διαθήκης μεσίτης, the ministry being a part of the work of mediating the better covenant, it must participate in the superior excellence of that covenant. And the superiority of the covenant consists in this, that it has been legally based on better promises. Had Paul so connected the law and the promises, a quip might have been supposed; but this writer uses νενομ. in its ordinary sense without any allusion to its etymology. What these "better promises" are he shows in vv. 8-12. ἥτις introduces the explanation of the κρείττονος, almost equivalent to "inasmuch as it has been, etc." The μεσίτης (cf. xii. 24) is more comprehensive than the ἔγγυος of vii. 22, although μεσίτης is Hellenistic for the Attic μεσέγγυος, and in *Diod. Sic.* iv. 54 μεσίτης has exactly the sense of ἔγγυος. The full title in 1 Tim. ii. 5 μεσίτης θεοῦ καὶ ἀνθρώπων presents the mediator as one who negotiates for both parties, and is something more than a guarantor. Moses was μεσίτης of the first covenant (Gal. iii. 19; Exod. xx. 19); so that as already intimated in iii. 1, Christ absorbed in His ministry the work of both Moses and Aaron.

Vv. 7-13. A justification of the establishment of a better covenant, on the grounds (1) that the first covenant was not faultless; (2) that Jeremiah had predicted the introduction of a new covenant (a) not like the old, but (b) based upon better promises; and (3) that even in Jeremiah's days the first covenant was antiquated by the very title "new" ascribed to that which was then promised. Ver. 7. εἰ γὰρ ἡ πρώτη ... "For

if that first had been faultless, no place would have been sought for a second." ἡ πρώτη sc. διαθήκη. πρώτη for προτέρα as in Acts i. 1; 1 Cor. xv. 47, and this epistle *passim*. The covenant did not accomplish the purpose for which it was enacted; it did not bring men into spiritual and permanent fellowship with God. *Cf.* vii. 11, 19; Gal. iii. 20. οὐκ ἂν δευτέρας ἐζητεῖτο τόπος. "There would not have been—as we know there *was*—any demand for a second" (Farrar). Probably, however, ἐζητεῖτο refers to God's purpose, [" Inquisivit Deus locum et tempus opportunum" (Herveius)] not to man's craving; although necessarily the two must concur. τόπος is frequently used in the sense of "room" "opportunity" in later Greek, Rom. xv. 23; Luke xiv. 19; and *cf.* especially Rev. xx. 11. τόπος οὐχ εὑρέθη αὐτοῖς. μεμφόμενος γὰρ ... "For finding fault with them He says, Behold, there come days, etc." The γὰρ obviously refers to ἄμεμπτος and justifies it, "For it is with fault finding, etc." But now the object of the blame is slightly changed. "There is a subtle delicacy of language in the insensible shifting of the blame from the covenant to the people. The covenant itself could hardly be said to be faultless, seeing that it failed to bind Israel to their God; but the true cause of failure lay in the character of the people, not in the law, which was holy, righteous and good" (Rendall). This is the simplest construction and agrees with the ascription of blame in ver. 9. Thayer says "it is more correct to supply αὐτήν, *i.e.*, διαθήκην, which the writer wishes to prove was not faultless, and to join αὐτοῖς with λέγει". No doubt this would be more logically consistent, but the question is, What did the writer say? He seems not to distinguish between the covenant and the people who lived under it. The old covenant was faulty because it did not provide for enabling the people to live up to the terms or conditions of it. *It* was faulty inasmuch as it did not sufficiently provide against *their* faultiness. Ἰδού, κ.τ.λ. The quotation which here occupies five verses is taken from

f Jer. xxxi. δευτέρας ἐζητεῖτο τόπος. 8. ¹μεμφόμενος γὰρ αὐτοῖς¹ λέγει, "Ἰδοὺ,
31, etc.
ἡμέραι ἔρχονται, λέγει Κύριος, καὶ συντελέσω ἐπὶ τὸν οἶκον Ἰσραὴλ
καὶ ἐπὶ τὸν οἶκον Ἰούδα διαθήκην καινήν· 9. οὐ κατὰ τὴν διαθήκην
ἣν ἐποίησα τοῖς πατράσιν αὐτῶν, ἐν ἡμέρᾳ ἐπιλαβομένου μου τῆς
χειρὸς αὐτῶν, ἐξαγαγεῖν αὐτοὺς ἐκ γῆς Αἰγύπτου· ὅτι αὐτοὶ οὐκ
g Jer. xxxi. ἐνέμειναν ἐν τῇ διαθήκῃ μου, κἀγὼ ἠμέλησα αὐτῶν, λέγει Κύριος.
33, etc.;
Zach.
viii. 8.　　10. ᵍὅτι αὕτη ἡ διαθήκη ἣν διαθήσομαι τῷ οἴκῳ Ἰσραὴλ μετὰ τὰς

¹ αυτοις with אcBDcEL; αυτους in א*AD*KP, 17, 39, 114, 137, Thdrt., Chrys.

Jeremiah xxxviii. 31-34 in LXX, xxxi. 31-34 A.V. ἡμέραι ἔρχονται is a frequent formula in Jeremiah. καὶ "The ubiquitous Hebrew *and*, serving here the purpose of the ὅτε which might have been expected" (Vaughan). συντελέσω, the LXX has διαθήσομαι, and Augustine (*De Spir. et Lit.* xix.) thinks this word (consummabo) is chosen for the sake of emphasising the sufficiency of the New Covenant. So Delitzsch: "Our author seems here to have purposely selected the συντελέσω to express more clearly the conclusive perfecting power of the new covenant of the gospel." So, too, Weiss, who also calls attention to the fact that it is followed by ἐπὶ as in the expression συντελ. τ. ὀργὴν ἐπὶ . . . But in the face of the occurrence in Jer. xxxiv. 8, (LXX, xli. 8) of the expression συντελέσαι διαθήκην πρὸς . . ., it is precarious to maintain that our author in selecting this word meant more than "complete a covenant". ἐπὶ τὸν οἶκον Ἰσραὴλ καὶ . . ., comprehensive of the whole people of God. Their blameworthy rupture had not severed them from God's grace and faithfulness. διαθήκην καινήν, the expression first occurs in our Lord's institution of the sacrament, τοῦτο τὸ ποτήριον ἡ καινὴ διαθήκη ἐν τ. αἵματί μου, repeated in 1 Cor. xi. 25. In 2 Cor. iii. 6, the καινὴ διαθ. is contrasted with τ. παλαιᾶς διαθ. of ver. 14. The new covenant is also called νέα in xii. 24; καινή properly meaning new in character, νέα young or new in date. As in ver. 7 the condemnation of the old implied a promise of the new; so in ver. xiii., the promise of the new is considered as involving the condemnation of the old. Ver. 9. οὐ κατὰ τὴν διαθήκην "Not according to the covenant which I made with their fathers." These words express negatively wherein the καινότης of the covenant consists. It was not to be a repetition of that which had failed. It was to be framed with a view to avoiding the defects of the old. It must

not be such a covenant as dealt in symbols and externals. That former covenant is further defined in the words ἣν ἐποίησα . . ., a clause which is intended to remind the readers that it was through no lack of power or grace on God's part that the covenant had failed. His intention and power to fulfil His part was put beyond doubt by the deliverance from Egypt. ἐν ἡμέρᾳ ἐπιλαβομένου μου τ. χειρὸς αὐτῶν . . . "sicut nutrix apprehendit manum parvuli, vel qui de fovea per manum attrahit aliquem sive secum ducit" (Herveius). The construction determined by the Hebrew, which, however, has the infinitive not the participle, is, according to Winer (710) "perhaps unusual, but not incorrect." Buttmann, however, (316) condemns it as "a perfectly un-Greek construction" and "nothing more than a thoughtless imitation of the original Hebrew, of which no other similar example is to be found in the N.T." *Cf.* Baruch, ii. 28 ἐν ἡμέρᾳ ἐντειλαμένου σου, κ.τ.λ. *Cf.* Viteau, *Gram.* p. 209-10. On ἐπιλαβ. see ii. 16. ὅτι αὐτοὶ οὐκ ἐνέμειναν "because they continued not in my covenant, and I regarded them not, saith the Lord". Both parties abandoned the covenant and so it became null. Bengel's note on this clause is this: "Correlata, uti ver. 10, ex opposito: *Ero eis in Deum, et illi erunt mihi in populum;* sed ratione inversa: populus fecerat initium tollendi foederis prius: in novo omnia et incipit et perficit Deus". The pronouns are emphatic in both clauses κἀγὼ ἠμέλησα αὐτῶν representing וְאָנֹכִי בָּעַלְתִּי בָם which in A.V. is rendered "although I was an husband to them." Grotius suggests a variant in the Hebrew as giving rise to the translation ἠμέλησα but it seems to be justified by an analogous Arabic expression (see Moses Stuart *in loc.* and Bleek). Ver. 10. ὅτι αὕτη ἡ διαθήκη ἣν διαθήσομαι . . . "For this is

ἡμέρας ἐκείνας, λέγει Κύριος, διδοὺς νόμους μου εἰς τὴν διάνοιαν
αὐτῶν, καὶ ἐπὶ καρδίας αὐτῶν ἐπιγράψω αὐτούς· καὶ ἔσομαι αὐτοῖς
εἰς Θεόν, καὶ αὐτοὶ ἔσονταί μοι εἰς λαόν. 11. ʰ καὶ οὐ μὴ διδάξω- ʰ x. 16;
σιν ἕκαστος τὸν πλησίον¹ αὐτοῦ, καὶ ἕκαστος τὸν ἀδελφὸν αὐτοῦ, 45, 65.
λέγων, Γνῶθι τὸν Κύριον· ὅτι πάντες εἰδήσουσί με, ἀπὸ μικροῦ 27.

Joan. vi.
1 Joan. ii.

¹ T.R. in P, f, vg., Syrp.mg; πολιτην in אABDEKL, d, e, Copt.

the covenant which I will covenant with
the house of Israel after those days, saith
the Lord." The ὅτι justifies the differentiation of this covenant from the Sinai-
tic, and the ascription to it of the term
"new". It also introduces the positive
aspect of the newness of the covenant.
This consists in three particulars. It is
inward or spiritual; it is individual and
therefore universal; it is gracious and
provides forgiveness. μετὰ τὰς ἡμέρας ἐκείνας, i.e., after the days,
spoken of ver. 8, have arrived. διδοὺς
νόμους μου . . . The LXX (vat.)
has διδοὺς δώσω, but this writer omits
δώσω in x. 16 as well as here. The participle cannot be attached either to διαθήσομαι or to ἐπιγράψω without intolerable
harshness. We must, therefore, suppose
that the writer was simply quoting from
the Alexandrian text which omits δώσω
(so also Q = Codex Marchalianus), and
does not concern himself about the ele-
gance or even correct grammar of the
words. See Buttmann, p. 291. νόμους
μου. "The plural occurs again in the
same quotation, x. 16, but not elsewhere
in the N.T.; nor does the plural appear
to be found in any other place of the LXX
as a translation of תּוֹרָה" Westcott.
εἰς τὴν διάνοιαν. "In Aristotle
διάνοια includes all intellect, theoretical
and practical, intuitive and discursive"
(Burnet's Nic. Eth., p. 276). Plato defines
it in Soph. 263 E thus: ὁ μὲν ἐντὸς τῆς
ψυχῆς πρὸς αὐτὴν διάλογος ἄνευ φωνῆς
γιγνόμενος. In N.T. it is sometimes
used for the "mind," as in Eph. iv. 18,
1 Pet. i. 13, 2 Pet. iii. 1; sometimes for
the thoughts produced in the mind, Eph.
ii. 3; sometimes for the inner man generally, as in Luke i. 51, Col. i. 21. And
in this sense here. καὶ ἐπὶ καρδίας
αὐτῶν "and on their heart". καρδίας
may be either genitive singular, or accusative plural, both constructions being found
after γράφειν ἐπί. The meaning is that
God's law, instead of being written on
tables of stone, should under the new
covenant be written on the spirit and
desires of man. "Unde significavit eos
non forinsecus habere, sed ipsam legis

justitiam dilecturos" (Atto). This "better
promise" involves a new spirit, effecting
that man's own will shall concur with the
divine. Cf. 2 Cor. iii. 3. καὶ ἔσομαι
αὐτοῖς . . . "and I will be to them a
God, and they shall be to me a people".
For the distinction between the Hebraistic
construction ἔσομαι εἰς and the legitimate
Greek εἶναι or γένεσθαι εἰς see Buttmann,
p. 150. This of course was the aim of
the old covenant as well, and is expressed
in the original promise, Exod. vi. 7: "I
will take you to myself as my people, and
I shall be to you a God". See also
Jerem. vii. 23. xi. 4. This is the ultimate
statement of the end or aim of all religion.
Ver 11. καὶ οὐ μὴ διδάξωσιν.
. . . "And they shall not teach, each
man his fellow-citizen and each man his
brother, saying, 'Know the Lord,' for all
shall know me from small to great among
them". This second "better" promise
follows on the first as its natural consequence. The inward acceptance of
God's will involves the knowledge of God.
In the new covenant all were to be
"taught of God" (Isa. liv. 13, Jo. vi. 45)
and independent of the instruction of a
privileged class. Under the old covenant,
none but the educated scribe could understand the minutiæ of the law with which
religion was identified. The elaborate
ritual made it impossible for the private
individual to know whether a ram or a
pigeon was the appropriate sacrifice for
his sin, or whether his sin was mortal or
venial. A priest had to be consulted.
Under the new covenant intermediates
were to be abolished. The knowledge of
God was to lie in the heart alongside of
the love of parent or friend, and would
demand for its expression no more external instruction than those primal, instinctive and home-grown affections. οὐ
μὴ διδάξωσιν, "The intensive οὐ·μὴ
(of that which in no wise will or shall
happen) is sometimes—indeed most commonly—joined with the conjunctive aorist, sometimes with the conjunctive
present, sometimes also with the indicative
future". Winer, p. 634, who also discusses Hermann's canon and Dawes'
regarding this form. εἰδήσουσιν, for

Rom. xi.
27. αὐτῶν ἕως μεγάλου αὐτῶν · 12. ¹ὅτι ἵλεως ἔσομαι ταῖς ἀδικίαις
αὐτῶν, καὶ τῶν ἁμαρτιῶν αὐτῶν καὶ τῶν ἀνομιῶν αὐτῶν οὐ μὴ μνησθῶ
ἔτι.'' 13. Ἐν τῷ λέγειν ''Καινὴν,'' πεπαλαίωκε τὴν πρώτην · τὸ δὲ
παλαιούμενον καὶ γηράσκον, ἐγγὺς ἀφανισμοῦ.
a Exod.
xxv. 8.   IX. 1. *ΕΙΧΕ μὲν οὖν καὶ¹ ἡ πρώτη σκηνὴ ² δικαιώματα λατρείας,

---

¹ και in ℵADEKLP, d, e, f, vg., Syrᵖ, Arm.; om. in B, 3, 38, 52, Syrˢᶜʰ, Copt.,
Thphyl.

² σκηνη omitted in ℵABDEKLP, f, vg., and by T., Tr., WH, R.; found in 47,
73, 74, 80, 137, Thdrt.

---

this form of the future Veitch (p. 216)
quotes Homer, Theognis, Herodotus,
Isocrates. **ἀπὸ μικροῦ ἕως μεγάλου**, an expression commonly used in
LXX to denote universality, Gen. xix.
11, where possibly it is equivalent to **ἀπὸ
νεανίσκου ἕως πρεσβυτέρου** of ver. 4 ;
1 Sam. xxx. 19, where it is used of spoils
of war. Gesenius (117, 2) understands
the adjectives as superlatives.
Ver. 12. **ὅτι ἵλεως ἔσομαι ταῖς
ἀδικίαις αὐτῶν** . . . "For I will be
merciful to their iniquities, and their sins
will I remember no more." This third
better promise is united to the former by
ὅτι, showing that the forgiveness of sins
or God's grace is fundamental to any
possible renewal and maintenance of
covenant.
Ver. 13. **ἐν τῷ λέγειν Καινήν.**
"In saying 'New,' He hath antiquated
the first ; and that which is antiquated
and growing old is near extinction [lit.
disappearance]." That is to say, by
speaking in the passage quoted, ver. 8, of
a new covenant, God brands the former
as old. Thus even in Jeremiah's time
the Mosaic covenant was disparaged.
The fact that a new was required showed
that it was insufficient. It was condemned as antiquated. And that which
is antiquated and aged has not much
longer to live. **πεπαλαίωκεν**, the
active is found in LXX, Job. ix. 5 ; xxxii.
15, etc.; the mid. is common, in Plato
and elsewhere in the sense of "growing
old". **ἐγγὺς ἀφανισμοῦ**, cf. ἐγγὺς
κατάρας, vi. 8. **ἀφανισμός**, is suggestive
of utter destruction, abolition ; thus in
Polyb. v. 11, 5 it is joined with ἀπώλεια.
Cf. *Diod. Sic.* v. 32, ἀποκτείνουσιν, ἡ
κατακαίουσιν, ἤ τισιν ἄλλαις τιμωρίαις
ἀφανίζουσι.
CHAPTER IX. Ver. 1-14. The insufficiency of the first covenant is further
illustrated from the character of its
ordinances. For it was not devoid of
elaborate and impressive appointments
and regulations for worship, but these

only pictured their own inefficiency. Especially did the exclusion from the holiest
place of all but the High Priest, who
himself could only enter once a year and
with blood, signify that so long as these
ordinances remained there could be no
perfect approach of the worshipper to
God. But this approach was achieved
by Christ who ministered in the tabernacle
not made with hands, and by His own
blood cleansed the conscience and thus
brought men into true fellowship with God.
CHAPTER IX. Ver. 1. **Εἶχε μὲν
οὖν καὶ ἡ πρώτη** . . . "Even the
first covenant, however, had ordinances
of worship and the holy place suitable to
this world," *i.e.*, as hinted in viii. 2, a
tent pitched by man, constructed with
earthly materials, "of this creation," ver.
11., and thus appealing to sense. Farrar
renders "and its sanctuary—a material
one". **οὖν** is continuative, and might
almost be rendered "to resume". **μὲν**
find its correlative **δὲ** in ver. 6 ; the first
covenant had, indeed, a sanctuary with
elaborate arrangements, but after all it
was only a symbol. That **διαθήκη**, not
σκηνή, is to be understood after **πρώτη**,
is demanded by the context and is now
universally recognised. So Chrysostom,
ἡ πρώτη, τίς ; ἡ διαθήκη. Of the reading σκηνή Calvin says, " nec dubito, quin
aliquis indoctus lector, pro sua inscitia
. . . perperam addiderit." **εἶχε** at first
sight seems to require us to date the
epistle after the destruction of Jerusalem,
but it is quite possible that, as Delitzsch
says, the writer is looking back upon the
old from the platform of the new covenant. "The author in saying *had* merely
looks back from his own historical position to the Mosaic tabernacle and its ordinances, which are everywhere assumed
as the standard of the O.T. things ;
the past 'had' no more implies that the
O.T. ministry had passed away in fact or
even in principle, than the present 'go
in' (ver. 6) implies the reverse" (Davidson.) **δικαιώματα λατρείας. δικ-**

τό τε ἅγιον κοσμικόν· 2. ^bΣκηνὴ γὰρ κατεσκευάσθη, ἡ πρώτη, ἐν b Exod.
ᾗ ἥ τε λυχνία καὶ ἡ τράπεζα καὶ ἡ πρόθεσις τῶν ἄρτων· ἥτις
λέγεται ἅγια¹. 3. μετὰ δὲ τὸ δεύτερον καταπέτασμα σκηνὴ ἡ

xxv. 30,
et xxvi. 1,
etc., et
xxxvi. 1,
etc.; Lev.
xxiv. 5.

¹ Add αγιων AD*E, d, e.

αἰώματα is used, because the writer wishes to draw attention to the fact that the ritual of the first covenant was divinely appointed. He does this because he means to point out (vv. 8, 9) that the Holy Spirit intended these arrangements to be a parable of their own incompetence and transitory nature. κοσμικόν is best illustrated in Rendel Harris' *Teaching of the Apostles*, p. 71 ff. He has collected a number of passages from early Christian writers which show that a "cosmic" mystery or symbol was "a symbol or action wrought upon the stage of this world to illustrate what was doing or to be done on a higher plane". His quotation from Athanasius is especially convincing "Ὥσπερ ἡ ἐκκλησία ὑποτάσσεται τῷ κυρίῳ, οὕτω καὶ αἱ γυναῖκες τοῖς ἀνδράσιν ἐν πᾶσι. ἀπ᾽ αὐτῶν γὰρ τῶν κοσμικῶν, ἐὰν θέλωμεν, καὶ τὰ ἄνω νοοῦμεν. This significant word standing at the close of the sentence sufficiently indicates the incompetence of the whole. The first covenant had its holy place but it was κοσμικόν. For the same reason he goes on to enumerate the articles contained in the ἅγιον. He wishes to bring before us the care with which all its arrangements were made: nothing was haphazard and meaningless. The succeeding verses are indeed the resumption of viii. 5, "See that you make *all* things according to the type shown thee in the mount".

Ver 2. σκηνὴ γὰρ κατεσκευάσθη . . . "For a tent was constructed, the fore-tent, in which were" its appropriate contents. σκηνή, a tent. "Observandum est in primis hanc descriptionem non ad templum sed ad tabernaculum accommodari; quia nimirum noster hic scriptor ea proprie quae Moses secundum exemplar ipsi in monte propositum fabricavit, cum rebus ipsis coelestibus comparat" (Beza). On the construction in which the noun is first conceived indefinitely and is then more clearly defined by the attributive, whose import thus receives special prominence, see Winer, p. 174. ἡ πρώτη, the outer, that into which anyone *first* entered, twice the size of the inner and entered from the east (see Macgregor on Exodus, and appendix by Gillies on construction of tabernacle). Large tents were usually

divided into an outer and an inner, a first and a second. And a tent being windowless, ἡ λυχνία was a necessary article of furniture; the lamp-stand or "candlestick" reminding men that the light of day, the light common to all, was not sufficient to guide to God. *Cf.* Exod. xxv. 31-39; and Zech., c. iv. καὶ ἡ τράπεζα for the making of the table instructions are recorded in Exod. xxv. 23-30, concluding with the injunction "Thou shalt set upon the table showbread before me alway." In Lev. xxiv. 6 it is called "the pure table," because made of "pure" gold. καὶ ἡ πρόθεσις τῶν ἄρτων "and the setting forth of the loaves" called in Exod. xl. 23 (P.) "loaves of the setting forth". In Exod. xxv. 30 the command is given ἐπιθήσεις ἐπὶ τ. τράπεζαν ἄρτους ἐνωπίους ἐναντίον μου, the loaves here being

called לֶחֶם פָּנִים bread of the face or presence. In Lev. xxiv. 5-9 minute instructions for their composition are given and for their "setting forth," and it is added ἔσονται εἰς ἄρτους εἰς ἀνάμνησιν προκείμενα τ. Κυρίου. In 1 Chron. the loaves are called τ. προθέσεως translating

לֶחֶם הַמַּעֲרֶכֶת bread of the row. On the meaning of the "show bread" see Robertson Smith's *Religion of the Semites*, 207 ff. "The table of show bread has its closest parallel in the *lectisternia* of ancient heathenism, when a table laden with meats was spread beside the idol." "But the idea that the gods actually consume the solid food that is deposited at their shrines is too crude to subsist without modification beyond the savage state of society; the ritual may survive, but the sacrificial gifts . . . will come to be the perquisite of the priests". *Cf.* Warde Fowler's *Roman Festivals*, 215-20. ἥτις λέγεται ἅγια. "The qualitative relative directs attention to the features of the place which determine its name as 'Holy'" (Westcott). ἅγια is neuter plural, as in ver. 3. So Theodoret rejecting the reading ἁγία. For this name see Lev. x. 4; Num. iii. 22; but in LXX always with the article, here omitted, possibly, to bring out more prominently the holy character of the place.
Ver. 3. μετὰ δὲ τὸ δεύτερον

c Exod. xvi. λεγομένη ἄγια ἁγίων, 4. °χρυσοῦν ἔχουσα θυμιατήριον, καὶ τὴν
33, et xxv.
10, 21, et κιβωτὸν τῆς διαθήκης περικεκαλυμμένην πάντοθεν χρυσίῳ, ἐν ᾗ
xxvi. 33,
et xxxiv. στάμνος χρυσῆ ἔχουσα τὸ μάννα, καὶ ἡ ῥάβδος Ἀαρὼν ἡ βλαστή-
29 ; Num.
xvii. 10 ;
1 Reg. viii. 9; 2 Par. v. 10.

καταπέτασμα. "And after the
second veil the tent which is called 'Holy
of Holies,'" not, as Westcott, "a tent
[was prepared] which is called," for "when
attributives are placed after with the
article, the article before the substantive
is dropped" (Buttmann, p. 92). The
participle with the article as usual takes
the place of a relative clause. μετὰ in
a local sense [non-classical, Blass, p. 133],
which is here closely akin to the temporal = after the entrant has passed the
second veil. The second veil separated
the Holy place from the Holy of Holies,
and as being the significant veil was
sometimes spoken of without δεύτερον,
simply as τὸ καταπέτασμα, see chap. vi.
19; Mat. xxvii. 51, etc. Instructions for
making and hanging it are given in Exod.
xxvi. 31-35 ; and in ver. 36 the outer veil
is described. The outer veil is sometimes
called καταπέτασμα but more commonly
ἐπίσπαστρον, Exod. xxvi. 36, xxxv. 15
etc. The inner tent was called the ἄγια
ἁγίων, translating קֹדֶשׁ קָדָשִׁים which
in Hebrew idiom is equivalent to a superlative.
Ver. 4. χρυσοῦν ἔχουσα θυμιατήριον. . . . The inner tent is characterised by its furnishings, a golden
altar of incense and the ark of the covenant. θυμιατήριον is rendered both
in A.V. and R.V. by "censer" following
the Vulgate, "aureum habens thuribulum;" Grotius "θυμ: hic non est mensa,
sed impositum mensae batillum;" and
others. In doing so the usage of the
LXX is followed, for in 2 Chron. xxvi. 19,
Ezek. viii. 11, 4 Mac. vii. 11—the only
instances of its occurrence—it renders
מִקְטֶרֶת = censer; while "altar of
incense" is rendered by θυσιαστήριον
θυμιάματος, see Lev. iv. 7, 1 Chron. vii.
49, etc. But Philo (p. 512 A, 668, C),
Josephus Ant., iii. 6, 8, and the versions
of Symmachus and Theodotion in Exod.
xxxi. use θυμιατήριον for "altar of incense". Besides, the form of the word
indicates that it could be used of anything on which incense is offered. It
was, therefore, understood of the "altar"
by Clement Alex. and other fathers; by
Calvin, who says, "quo nomine altare

suffitus vel thymiamatis potius intelligo
quam thuribulum ;" and by most modern
scholars. As has frequently been urged
it is incredible that in describing the furniture of the tabernacle there should be
no mention of the altar of incense. Difficulty has been felt regarding the position
here assigned to it, for in fact it stood
outside the veil ; and the author has been
charged with error. But the change from
ἐν ᾗ of ver. 2 to ἔχουσα is significant,
and indicates that it was not precisely
its local relations he had in view, but
rather its ritual associations, "its close
connection with the ministry of the Holy
of Holies on the day of atonement, of
which he is speaking" (Davidson). The
altar was indeed so strictly connected
with the Sancta Sanctorum that in the
directions originally given for its construction this was brought out (Exod. xxx. 1-6).
"Thou shalt set it before the veil (ἀπέ-
ναντι τ. καταπετάσματος) that is over
the ark of the testimony," and in ver. 10,
"it is most holy (ἅγιον τῶν ἁγίων) to the
Lord". In 1 Kings vi. 20 it is also said
of Solomon that he made the altar of
incense κατὰ πρόσωπον τοῦ δαβὶρ "in
front of the oracle," which brings it
into direct connection with the ark
Cf. also 1 Kings ix. 25. χρυσοῦν,
although made of shittim wood it was
overlaid with gold and is often called
"golden". Here emphasis is laid upon
its golden appearance as being worthy of
its use. καὶ τὴν κιβωτὸν... "and
the ark of the covenant covered all over
with gold". κιβωτός, a box or chest
(in Aristoph. Wasps, 1056, wardrobe) or
ark (a word still used in Scotland, where
the meal-chest is known as the meal-ark).
In LXX and N.T. appropriated to the
chest in the Holy of Holies or to the ark
in which Noah was rescued. For its construction see Exod. xxv. 10. περικεκ.
πάντοθεν χρυσίῳ representing "inside and outside" ἔσωθεν καὶ ἔξωθεν
χρυσώσεις αὐτήν of Exod. xxv. 11.
Here called τῆς διαθήκης because
in it were kept αἱ πλάκες τ. διαθήκης "the tables of the covenant" on
which were written the ten commandments, the sum of the terms to which the
people swore on entering the covenant.
Therefore called in Exod. xxxi. 18 πλάκες

σασα, καὶ αἱ πλάκες τῆς διαθήκης · 5. ᵈ ὑπεράνω δὲ αὐτῆς Χερου- ᵈ Exod.
βὶμ¹ δόξης, κατασκιάζοντα τὸ ἱλαστήριον · περὶ ὧν οὐκ ἔστι νῦν xxv. 18.
λέγειν κατὰ μέρος. 6. ᵉ Τούτων δὲ οὕτω κατεσκευασμένων, εἰς μὲν ᵉ Num.
τὴν πρώτην σκηνὴν διαπαντὸς εἰσίασιν οἱ ἱερεῖς τὰς λατρείας ἐπι- xxviii. 3.

¹ χερουβειν in BDcE ; χερουβειμ AP, 37. The LXX also has the same variants.

μαρτυρίου. These tables were, in LXX, first spoken of as πυξία (τὰ πυξία τὰ λίθινα, Exod. xxiv. 12). They are called πλάκες in Exod. xxxi. 18. Paul also uses this word in contrasting the stone tables of the Law with the σάρκιναι πλάκες of the heart. In 1 Kings viii. 9 it is stated that when Solomon's Temple was dedicated these tables were the sole contents of the ark. In the tabernacle, however, as here described the ark also contained στάμνος χρυσῆ ἔχουσα τὸ μάννα "a golden jar containing manna," as directed in Exod. xvi. 33, 34, Moses said to Aaron λάβε στάμνον χρυσοῦν ἔνα, where it is masculine ; in Aristoph. *Plut.* 545, feminine (see Stephanus, s.v.). Usually it was of earthenware and used for holding wine, honey, etc. τὸ μάννα in Exod. μάν is the form used ; in the other books μάννα. καὶ ἡ ῥάβδος Ἀαρὼν ἡ βλαστήσασα, as related in Num. xvii. 1-10, when the rods of the tribes were laid up before the Lord to determine who were the legitimate priests, ἰδοὺ ἐβλάστησεν ἡ ῥάβδος Ἀαρών. Chrysostom remarks that the contents of the ark were venerable and significant memorials of Israel's rebellion ; the tables of the covenant for the first were broken on account of their sin ; the manna reminding them of their murmuring ; the rod that budded of their jealousy of Aaron.

ὑπεράνω δὲ αὐτῆς χερουβεὶν δόξης . . . "And over it [the ark] Cherubim of glory, overshadowing the mercy-seat" ["obumbrantia propitiatorium" (Vulg.)]. According to Exod. xxv. 18-22, the Cherubim were to be two in number, made of gold, one at each end of the ark, looking towards one another, and overshadowing the mercy seat with their wings [συσκιάζοντες ἐν ταῖς πτέρυξιν αὐτῶν ἐπὶ τοῦ ἱλαστηρίου]. The Cherubim seem to have symbolised, in the manner of the Assyrians and Egyptians, the creatures of God, all that is best in creation, by a combination of excellences found in no single creature. In Ezekiel, i. 10 they have four faces, of a man, a lion, an ox, and an eagle, representing respectively intelligence, strength, steadfastness, rapidity. But *cf.* Davidson, p. 173 and Cheyne's art. in *Encycl. Bibl.*

δόξης, the Cherubim are here called "of glory," probably because closely attached to and, as it were, attendant upon, the place of the manifestation of the divine glory. ["Als *Träger* der Herrlichkeit, in welcher die göttliche Gnadengegenwart sich kund that" (Weiss).] τὸ ἱλαστήριον. In Exod. xxv. 17 Moses is instructed to make a golden cover [כַּפֹּרֶת] to be laid upon the lid of the ark, and this instruction the LXX renders by the words ποιήσεις ἱλαστήριον ἐπίθεμα χρυσίου καθαροῦ. The word ἐπίθεμα alone, without any qualifying adjective, would have been an adequate translation of כַּפֹּרֶת, for both words mean "a cover". But ἐπίθεμα is nowhere else used in the LXX to translate כַּפֹּרֶת, which is regularly translated by ἱλαστήριον, although this word does not express the idea of a material covering. [Philo more than once remarks upon this. In *De Profug.*, 19, in speaking of symbols, he says τῆς ἵλεω δυνάμεως τὸ ἐπίθεμα τῆς κιβωτοῦ, καλεῖ δὲ αὐτὸ ἱλαστήριον. And in *Vit. Mos.* iii. 68, ἧς ἐπίθεμα ὡσανεὶ πῶμα τὸ λεγόμενον ἐν ἱεραῖς βίβλοις ἱλαστήριον.] The reason of this usage is to be found in the fact that this "cover" was sprinkled with blood on the day of atonement, and came, therefore, to be associated with the *covering* of sin. Indeed, the Hebrew word which denotes the material covering is that which is regularly used to express the covering of sin. The original ἐπίθεμα thus became a ἱλαστήριον ἐπίθεμα and finally ἱλαστήριον. (See Deissmann, *Bibelstud.* p. 121-132.) περὶ ὧν . . . μέρος "of which we cannot now speak in detail". ἔστιν, as commonly in classical Greek = ἔξεστι. κατὰ μέρος = one by one. Examples in Wetstein and Bleek (see especially Plato, *Theaet.* 157B, where it is opposed to ἄθροισμα).

Vv. 6-10. Significance of these arrangements. Ver. 6. τούτων δὲ οὕτως κατεσκευασμένων . . . "And after these things had been thus furnished, into the fore-tent, indeed, the priests enter con-

f ver. 25;
Exod.
xxx. 10;
Lev. xvi.
2, 15, 34.

τελοῦντες · 7. ᶠ εἰς δὲ τὴν δευτέραν ἅπαξ τοῦ ἐνιαυτοῦ μόνος ὁ ἀρχιερεύς, οὐ χωρὶς αἵματος, ὁ προσφέρει ὑπὲρ ἑαυτοῦ καὶ τῶν τοῦ

tinually in the performance of their services, but into the inner the High Priest alone once a year not without blood." This is the particular δικαίωμα λατ. (ver. 1) to which he wishes to direct attention, the inaccessible sacredness of the inner chamber, as revealed in the constant openness of the outer-tent, the mysterious closeness of the inner. κατ-εσκευασμένων perfect; the arrangements were made with a view to the abiding service of the first covenant. διαπαντὸς, continuously, opposed to ἅπαξ. ver. 7. εἰσίασιν present tense, as in Homer, Aristoph., Plato, Xenophon. It is not easy to determine whether this present implies the contemporaneous continuance of the services referred to. Tholuck thinks Bleek very "unreasonable" in concluding that it involves that the ark and the services connected with it were extant; but Bleek after reconsideration, finds himself unable to yield the point to "Freund Tholuck". Davidson says, "The present 'go in' does not imply that the Levitical service still continued when this was written; the present is that of the record in Scripture." The Vulgate shows its preference by tendering "introibant". The truth seems to be that although the temple services were yet upheld, the use of the present tense here and in vv. 7, 11, etc., does not involve that. τὰς λατρείας ἐπιτε-λοῦντες, not, as Vulg., "sacrificiorum officia consummantes," for these rather belonged to the court of the priests ; but "performing their services" of trimming the lamp and offering incense; see Edersheim, *The Temple ; Its ministry, etc.*, p. 130-140. ἐπιτελεῖν is used in Herod. and in Diod. Sic., and in Philo, for the accomplishing of religious services but it is not so used in the LXX.

Ver. 7. εἰς δὲ τὴν δευτέραν ἅπαξ τοῦ ἐνιαυτοῦ . . . The law is given in Lev. xvi., both negatively and positively; negatively in ver. 2 μὴ εἰσ-πορευέσθω πᾶσαν ὥραν εἰς τὸ ἅγιον ἐσώτερον τ. καταπετάσματος—promiscuous or continuous, daily entrance was forbidden; and positively, in ver 34 ἅπαξ τοῦ ἐνιαυτοῦ, i.e., one day each year, viz., on the day of Atonement, the tenth of the seventh month the High Priest is to enter. On that day the High Priest was to enter the Holiest at least *thrice*, first with the incense, then with the blood

of the bullock which atoned for his own sins and those of his house, and finally with the blood of the goat for the sins of the people. μόνος ὁ ἀρχιερεύς in contrast with οἱ ἱερεῖς of ver. 6. This point is also emphasised by Philo, *De Mon.*, p. 821 E., where he says that the things inside the veil were hidden from everyone πλὴν ἑνὶ τῷ ἀρχιερεῖ, by Josephus (*Bell. Jud.* v. 5, 7) εἰσῄει ἅπαξ κατ' ἐνιαυτὸν μόνος. See also Lev. xvi. 17. The law was emphasised by the destruction of Nadab and Abhu, Lev. x. 1. The Holiness of the Presence and the difficulty of access was further illustrated and enforced by the demand that sacrifice should open the way οὐ χωρὶς αἵματος. This blood was offered, *i.e.*, sprinkled with the finger on the ἱλαστήριον, first, the blood of the calf to cleanse from his own sins, and then, the blood of the goat to atone for the people's sins. [ἑαυτοῦ is manifestly under the direct government of ὑπὲρ and does not follow ἀγνοημάτων. This word does not occur in Lev. xvi.; on the contrary the strongest words are used, ἀνο-μία, ἁμαρτία, ἀδικία, but *cf.* v. 2.] These three points, then, bring out the impossibility of free access to the Presence; not διαπαντὸς but ἅπαξ τ. ἐνιαυτοῦ; not οἱ ἱερεῖς promiscuously, but μόνος ὁ ἀρχιερεύς; not freely, but οὐ χωρὶς αἵμ-ατος. This was the δικαίωμα λατρείας which could not be neglected under pain of death. What did it signify? τοῦτο δηλοῦντος τ. πνεύματος . . . "*this* the Holy Spirit signifying, that the way into the Holy of Holies has not yet been made manifest, while the fore-tent has still a place". δηλοῦντος, the Holy Spirit is viewed as the author of the ritual and as meaning to teach by every part of it. Vaughan compares 1 Pet. i. 11 and adds, "As there O.T. *prophecy*, so here O.T. *ritual*, is ascribed to the Holy Spirit." τὴν τ. ἁγίων ὁδὸν "the way into the Holiest" as in viii. 2. Access to the Holy of Holies being thus barred was an intimation that the true access to God had not yet been furnished and that therefore worship and fellowship with God (that is, religion) were not yet perfect. [*Cf.* Theoph. ἡ τ. ἁγίων ὁδὸς, τουτέστιν ἡ εἰς τ. οὐρανὸν εἴσοδος. Weiss, "der Weg zum himmlischen Heiligthum '.] So long as the fore-tent (τῆς πρώτης σκηνῆς) has an appointed

λαοῦ ἀγνοημάτων, 8. ᵍτούτο δηλοῦντος τοῦ Πνεύματος τοῦ Ἁγίου, g x., 19, 20;
Joan. xiv.
μήπω πεφανερῶσθαι τὴν τῶν ἁγίων ὁδὸν, ἔτι τῆς πρώτης σκηνῆς 6.
ἐχούσης στάσιν· 9. ʰἥτις παραβολὴ εἰς τὸν καιρὸν τὸν ἐνεστηκότα, h Acts xiii.
39; Gal.
καθ᾽ ὃν¹ δῶρά τε καὶ θυσίαι προσφέρονται, μὴ δυνάμεναι κατὰ συν- iii. 21.
i Lev. xi. 2;
είδησιν τελειῶσαι τὸν λατρεύοντα, 10. ⁱμόνον ἐπὶ βρώμασι καὶ πό- Num.
xix. 7,
μασι καὶ διαφόροις βαπτισμοῖς, καὶ δικαιώμασι² σαρκὸς, ·μέχρι etc.

¹ ον in DᶜEKLP; ην in ℵABD*, 17, 27, 71, 73, 137, f, vg.

² δικαιωμασι in DᶜEKL, f, vg., Syrᴾ; δικαιωματα (sine και) in ℵABP, 6, 17, 27,
31, 73, 137.

place as part of the Divine arrangements
for worship (ἐχούσης στάσιν as in *Polyb.*
v. 5, 3) this signifies that the very Presence of God is inaccessible. The very
object of the division of the Tabernacle
into two rooms, an outer and an inner,
was to impress men with the fact that
the way of access had not actually been
disclosed (πεφανερῶσθαι). Hence the
appropriateness of the rending of the veil
as the symbol that by the perfected work
and sacrifice of Christ the new and living
way (x. 20) was opened.

Ver. 9. ἥτις παραβολὴ εἰς ...
"for this is a parable for the time [then]
present," for the contemporary period.
ἥτις has for its antecedent σκηνῆς. This
is the simplest construction (*Cf.* Winer,
p. 207). That suggested by Primasius
and Vaughan—"Which thing (the fact of
there being a πρώτη σκηνή separate from
the Holy of Holies) was a parable"—is
grammatically admissible. εἰς τ. καιρὸν τὸν ἐνεστηκότα, "for the time
being". In the usual division of time
into past, present and future, the present
was termed ὁ ἐνεστώς. But present to
whom? Several interpreters reply, To
those living under the Christian dispensation. So especially Delitzsch and Alford.
But N.T. usage, and especially the usage
of this Epistle which speaks of the Christian dispensation as "the coming age"
(vi. 5), "the future world" (ii. 5), indicates that "the present time" must refer
to the O.T. period. Besides, the opposition to καιρὸς διορθώσεως points in the
same direction; as also does the clause
under καθ᾽ ἥν. εἰς is here "with reference to". And the meaning is, that the
outer tent which did not itself contain
God's presence, but rather stood barring
access to it, was a parable of the entire
dispensation. In other words, this Tabernacle arrangement was a striking symbol
of the Mosaic economy which could not
of itself effect spiritual approach and
abiding fellowship with God. The Levitical δικαιώματα themselves, on the

ground of which all these arrangements
proceed, emphatically declared their own
inadequacy. Wrapped up in them was
the truth that they could not bring the
worshipper into God's presence. καθ᾽
ἥν δῶρά τε ... "in accordance with
which [parable] are offered both gifts
and sacrifices that cannot perfect him
that doth the service as regards conscience, being only ordinances of the
flesh resting upon meats and drinks
and divers washings, imposed until
a time of rectification". καθ᾽ ἥν-
referring to παραβολὴ; it is in accordance with the parabolic significance of
the Tabernacle and its arrangements, that
gifts and sacrifices were offered which
could only purge the flesh, not the conscience. μὴ δυνάμεναι, Winer's note
(p. 608) is misleading. *Cf.* Jebb's Appendix to Vincent and Dickson's *Modern
Greek*, p. 340. "In later Greek, μή
tended to usurp the place of οὐ," especially with participles. *Cf.* Blass, 255.
κατὰ συνείδησιν τελειῶσαι
means, to give to the worshipper the
consciousness that he is inwardly cleansed
from defilement and is truly in communion with God; to bring conscience finally
into peace.

Ver. 10. μόνον ἐπὶ βρώμασιν
... μόνον evidently introduces the
positive aspect of the virtue of the "gifts
and sacrifices," thus more closely defining
μὴ δυνάμεναι κατὰ συνείδησιν τελειῶσαι
... the gifts and sacrifices are not able
to bring the worshipper into a final rest
as regards conscience, only having effect
so far as regards meats and drinks and
divers washings—ordinances of the flesh,
not of the conscience, imposed until a
time of rectification. The change of
preposition from κατὰ to ἐπὶ need excite
no surprise (*cf.* Aristotle's frequent change
of preposition, *e.g.*, *Eth. Nic.*, iv. 3, 26);
and here there is a slight distinction in
the reference. ἐπὶ has frequently the
meaning "in connection with," "with
regard to" as in Luke xii. 52; John xii.

k iii. 1, et   καιροῦ διορθώσεως ἐπικείμενα.   11. ᵏ Χριστὸς δὲ παραγενόμενος
iv. 14, et
vi. 20, et   ἀρχιερεὺς τῶν μελλόντων ¹ ἀγαθῶν, διὰ τῆς μείζονος καὶ τελειοτέρας
viii. 1.

¹ μελλόντων in אADᶜEKLP, f, vg., Copt., Basm., Syrᴾ·ᵐᵍ ; γενομενων in BD*, d,
e, Syrᴾ text. But the former was more likely to be changed into the latter reading
than *vice versâ*.

16; Acts xxi. 24 [see especially Donald-
son's excellent treatment of this preposition (*Greek Gram.*, p. 518) showing
that with the dative it signifies *absolute
superposition, i.e., rest upon*, or *close to*,
hence addition, subsequence and succession, then " that which is close by us
as a suggesting cause, accompaniment,
motive, or condition". ἐπὶ τοῖς τ. φίλων
ἀγαθοῖς φαιδροὶ γιγνόμεθα, "we are
cheerful on account of the prosperity of
our friends". ὀνομάζοι δὲ πάντα ταῦτα
ἐπὶ ταῖς δόξαις τοῦ μεγάλου ζῴου " but
were to give all these things names from
in accordance with) the opinions of the
great monster" (Plato, *Rep.* 493, c).] The
meaning then is that the virtue (δυνάμεναι)
of the gifts and sacrifices is only in
relation to defilements occasioned by eating and drinking or neglecting the enjoined
purifications. δικαιώματα σαρκὸς
may either be construed as a contemptuous
exclamation appended, or it may be
softened by οὖσαι "which are". μέχρι
καιροῦ διορθώσεως "usque ad
tempus correctionis". διόρθωσις is
a making straight or right; used by
Hippocrates of reducing a fracture, by
Aristotle of repairing roads and houses,
by Polybius of paying debts, of education,
etc. It means, putting things right,
bringing matters into a satisfactory
state, and is thus used of the introduction
of the new covenant, in confirmation of
viii. 8. No term could better express
this writer's view of the characteristic of
Messianic times.

Ver. 11. Χριστὸς δὲ παραγενόμενος... " But Christ having arrived
a High Priest of the good things that were
to be, He, through the greater and more
perfect tabernacle not made with hands,
that is, not of this creation, nor yet
through blood of he-goats and calves, but
through his own blood, entered once for
all into the Holy of Holies, and obtained
eternal redemption." The main thought
of the verse is that Christ has obtained
eternal redemption; the δὲ, therefore,
which introduces it, refers to the inability
of the Levitical gifts and sacrifices to
perfect the worshipper. The greater
efficiency of Christ's ministry results from
its being exercised in a more perfect
tabernacle and with a truer sacrifice.

παραγενόμενος, scarcely, as Vulg.
"assistens" rather "having arrived,"
as in Matt. ii. 1, iii. 1, 13; and frequently
in Luke and Acts. *Cf.* Isa. lxii. 11. Ἰδού
σοι ὁ σωτὴρ παραγίνεται . . . Here it is
in fulfilment of the expectation aroused
by μέχρι. ἀρχιερεὺς τῶν μελ.
"The genitive gives the *subject* of the
high priestly action. *High Priest, concerned about, ministering in, securing and
applying by His ministry* τὰ μέλλ. ἀγαθά.
The genitive here is nearly equivalent to
the accusative τὰ πρὸς τὸν Θεόν in ii.
17" (Vaughan). The good things that
were to be under the new covenant are
specified in viii. 10-12; they surpassed all
expectation, however. "The High
Priest" of the good things coming, is a
notable title. Possibly it is only equivalent to "High Priest of the new
covenant," the contents being used to
stand for the whole dispensation, but
more probably the writer has in view the
slender benefits obtained by the Levitical
High Priest, and contrasts them with the
illimitable good mediated by Christ. διὰ
τῆς . . . σκηνῆς . . . οὐ ταύτης
τῆς κτίσεως. The meaning of διὰ
in ver. 11 favours the understanding of it
here not in a local (Weiss, etc.) but an
instrumental sense, "by means of". It
was because He was High Priest not in the
earthly but the heavenly tabernacle that
He was able to secure these great results.
No doubt διὰ in a similar connection in
iv. 14 and x. 20 is used locally. But this
sense is not so applicable here. Christ is
represented here as the High Priest
ministering in the tabernacle, not passing
through it (*Cf.* Davidson and Westcott).
τῆς μείζονος καὶ τελ. σκηνῆς,
the tabernacle greater and more perfect
than that which has been described in the
preceding verses, and which has itself
been mentioned as the scene of Christ's
ministry, viii. 2. This tabernacle is " not
made with hands" οὐ χειροποιήτου,
as in ver. 24; equivalent to ἣν ἔπηξεν ὁ
Κύριος οὐκ ἄνθρωπος, viii. 2. Our Lord
characterised the temple as χειροποίητον,
Mark xiv. 58. Being of human manu-
facture, viii. 2, it could be only a symbolic
dwelling for God and a symbolic worship
was appropriate. The words οὐ ταύτης τῆς κτίσεως are added in ex-

σκηνῆς, οὐ χειροποιήτου, τουτέστιν, οὐ ταύτης τῆς κτίσεως, 12. ¹ x. 10;
Acts xx.
¹ οὐδὲ δι' αἵματος τράγων καὶ μόσχων, διὰ δὲ τοῦ ἰδίου αἵματος εἰσ- 28; Eph.
i. 7; Col.
ῆλθεν ἐφάπαξ εἰς τὰ ἅγια, αἰωνίαν λύτρωσιν εὑράμενος. 13. ᵐ εἰ i. 14 ¹;
Peter i.
γὰρ τὸ αἷμα ταύρων καὶ τράγων καὶ σποδὸς δαμάλεως ῥαντίζουσα 19; Apoc.
i. 5, et v.
9.

m x. 4; Lev. xvi. 14, 16; Num. xix. 2, 4.

planation, although, as Bleek remarks, they are certainly no clearer than the words they are meant to explain. They are, however, more significant; for they point out that the tabernacle in which Christ ministers does not belong to this world at all, has no place among created things and is thus in striking contrast to the ἅγιον κοσμικόν of ver. 1. It must, however, be acknowledged that Field (*Otium Norv.*, p. 229) has shown reason for believing that we should translate "not of ordinary erection". "By ταύτης I understand *vulgaris, quae vulgo dicitur*"; and κτίσις he sees no occasion to take in any other sense than that in which κτίζειν is commonly applied to a city (3 Esd. iv. 53) or to the tabernacle itself (Lev. xvi. 16). This meaning of ταύτης, though warranted by the LXX cited by Field is, however, rare; and the sense is a little flat, whereas the other interpretation is full of significance.

Ver. 12. οὐδὲ δι' αἵματος τράγων . . . Not only was the place of ministry different, the sacrifice offered also was different. "Not without blood," could the High Priest make his annual entry (ver. 7), but it was with the blood of a calf for himself and of a he-goat for the people. In LXX of Lev. xvi. the τράγος is uniformly called χίμαρος but in Aquila's version τράγος is used in ver. 8 and in Symmachus in vv. 8 and 10. διὰ δὲ τοῦ ἰδίου αἵματος, "So only could He enter *for us*. As the Eternal Son He has a right there; as the High Priest of man, He enters in virtue of the sacrifice of Himself" (Vaughan). ἐφάπαξ, as in vii. 27, in contrast to the ever-recurring annual entrance; and preparing the way for the statement of the last clause, αἰωνίαν λύτρωσιν εὑράμενος. Rutherford (*New Phryn.*, p. 215) says εὑράμην for εὑρόμην represents a common corruption of late Greek, but Veitch seems to think instances of its occurrence in Attic have been tampered with. See Tholuck *in loc.*; and Blass, *G.G.*, p. 45. Probably the aorist participle here expresses the result of the action of the main verb, εἰσῆλθεν. "But it is possible that εἰσῆλθεν is used to describe the whole High Priestly act,

including both the entrance into the holy place and the subsequent offering of the blood, and that εὑράμενος is thus a participle of identical action. In either case it should be translated not *having obtained* as in R.V. but *obtaining* or *and obtained*" (Burton *M. & T.*, 66). [Weiss accurately "Der nachgestellte Participialsatz drückt aus, was in und mit diesem Eingehen geschah".] On the use of the Mid. in N.T. see Thayer, *s.v.* Here it can only mean that Christ obtained salvation by offering Himself. λύτρωσις must, in consistency with the passage, be understood of the deliverance from guilt which enabled the worshipper to enter God's presence. From this flow all other spiritual blessings. It is here termed αἰωνία in contrast to the deliverance achieved by the Levitical High Priest, which had to be repeated year by year. Christ obtained a redemption which was absolute and for ever valid.

Ver. 13. εἰ γὰρ τὸ αἷμα . . . "For if the blood of goats and bulls and an heifer's ashes sprinkling the unclean purify as regards the cleanness of the flesh, how much rather shall the blood of the Christ, who through eternal spirit offered Himself without blemish to God, cleanse your conscience from dead works to serve the living God." The writer thus justifies the affirmation of ver. 12 that by offering His own blood Christ obtained eternal redemption. σποδὸς δαμάλεως, the law of purification with the ashes of the δάμαλις πυρρὰ ἄμωμος is given in Num. xix., where we find the characteristic words of this verse, σποδός, ἄμωμος, ἁγνίζω, ῥαντισμός, καθαρός, but κοινοῦν (not used in LXX) is replaced by ἀκάθαρτος. κεκοινωμένους, "made common," *i.e.*, profane, ceremonially unclean. Defilement was contracted by touching a dead body, or entering into a house in which a corpse was lying, or touching a bone or a tomb; and to enter the Tabernacle while thus defiled was to incur the penalty of being cut off from Israel. The water in which lay the ashes of the burned heifer was therefore provided for purification (ὕδωρ ῥαντισμοῦ) and by using it the worshipper was again rendered fit for entrance to the worship of

n vi. 1;
Luc. i. 74;
 τοὺς κεκοινωμένους ἁγιάζει πρὸς τὴν τῆς σαρκὸς καθαρότητα, 14.
Rom. vi. ⁿ πόσῳ μᾶλλον τὸ αἶμα τοῦ Χριστοῦ, ὃς διὰ πνεύματος αἰωνίου ἑαυ-
13; Eph.
v. 2; Gal. τὸν προσήνεγκεν ἄμωμον τῷ Θεῷ, καθαριεῖ τὴν συνείδησιν ὑμῶν ἀπὸ
i. 4, et ii.
20; Tit.
ii. 14; 1 Peter i. 19, et iii. 18, et iv. 2; 1 Joan. i. 7; Apoc. i. 5.

God. ῥαντίζουσα governs κεκοιν. and is not to be translated as if it were a passive; so Vulg., " aspersus inquinatos sanctificat " (cf. Calvin and Bengel). ἁγιάζει, the meaning is determined by its use in Num. xix., where it signifies the removal of ceremonial defilement: the taking away of that which rendered the person " common " or "profane," and the qualifying him for again worshipping God. This ἁγιασμός extended πρὸς τὴν τῆς σαρκὸς καθαρότητα, " in the direction of" (vi. 11) or "in relation to" (ii. 17, v. 1) (cf. Weiss). The flesh is here opposed to " the conscience" of ver. 14. It was only the flesh that was defiled by attending to the dead; and only the flesh that was cleansed by the prescribed sprinkling. Defilement and cleansing were alike symbolic. It was within a well-defined ceremonial limit these sacrifices and washings availed. What kind of water, no matter how mixed with heifer's ashes, could reach and wash the soul?

Ver. 14. πόσῳ μᾶλλον τὸ αἶμα τοῦ Χριστοῦ. . . . The Levitical sacrifices had their congruous effect, the sacrifice of Christ must also have its appropriate result. The blood offered was not of bulls and goats but of "the Christ;" it was not with another's blood (vicarious, ver. 25) but with His own He entered God's presence. His was not a bodily sacrifice but διὰ πνεύματος αἰωνίου. ὃς διὰ πνεύματος αἰωνίου . . . Θεῷ. This clause is inserted to justify the efficacy of the blood of Christ in cleansing the conscience. It had virtue to cleanse the conscience because it was the blood of one "who through eternal spirit offered Himself blameless to God". How are we to understand διὰ πν. αἰωνίου? Riehm considers it a parellel expression to that of vii. 16, κατὰ δύναμιν ζωῆς ἀκαταλύτου, and that it is here used to bring out the idea that Christ having an eternal spirit was thereby able to perform the whole work of atonement, not merely dying on the cross but passing through that death to present Himself before God. So too Davidson, Weiss and others. This involves that προσήνεγκεν refers not to the cross but to the appearance before God, subsequently to the

death. And it does not account for the absence of the article. It seems more relevant to the passage and more consistent with the purpose of the clause (to show the ground of the efficacy of the blood of Christ) to understand the words as expressing the spiritual nature of the sacrifice which gave it eternal validity. It had superior efficacy to the blood of bulls and goats because it was not of the flesh merely, but was expressive of the spirit. It is the spirit prompting the sacrifice and giving it efficacy, which the writer seeks to indicate. Over against the " ordinances of the flesh" which made the slaughter of animals compulsory and a mere matter of letting material blood, he sets this wholly different sacrifice which was prompted and inspired by spirit and belonged wholly to the sphere of spiritual and eternal things. [Spiritus opponitur conditioni animantum ratione carentium (ver. 13, Bengel); " bezeichnet das Lebensprinzip, in dessen Kraft, von dem beseelt und angetrieben Christus sich opferte " (Kübel)]. It was the spirit underlying and expressed in the sacrifice which gave it all its potency. Spirit is eternal and can alone be efficacious in eternal things. ἑαυτόν. The Levitical High Priest, as stated in ver. 25, entered the holy place ἐν αἵματι ἀλλοτρίῳ, but Christ διὰ τοῦ ἰδίου αἵματος. Also goats and calves were of no great value, but what Christ offered was of infinite value. Two points are brought out by ἑαυτόν. (1) He offered not a vicarious victim; but, as Priest, offered the only true sacrifice, Himself. Therefore His blood had cleansing efficacy. (2) He offered not a cheap animal, but the most precious of sacrifices. προσήνεγκεν, i.e., on the cross; for the clause is an explanation of the value of the blood. Cf. ver. 28. ἄμωμον without blemish, perfect, as required in the Levitical sacrifices, but now with an ethical significance, and therefore possessing an ethical validity. This explains how the blood of Christ should not merely furnish ceremonial cleanness but καθαριεῖ τὴν συνείδησιν ὑμῶν ἀπὸ νεκρῶν ἔργων, a characterisation of sins suggested by the context. Works that defile; as the touching of a dead body defiled the

νεκρῶν ἔργων, εἰς τὸ λατρεύειν Θεῷ ζῶντι ; 15. °Καὶ διὰ τοῦτο δια- ° xii. 24;
θήκης καινῆς μεσίτης ἐστίν, ὅπως θανάτου γενομένου, εἰς ἀπολύτρω- Acts xiii.
σιν τῶν ἐπὶ τῇ πρώτῃ διαθήκῃ παραβάσεων, τὴν ἐπαγγελίαν 39; Rom.
λάβωσιν οἱ κεκλημένοι τῆς αἰωνίου κληρονομίας. ὅπου γὰρ δια- iii. 25, et
θήκη, 16. θάνατον ἀνάγκη φέρεσθαι τοῦ διαθεμένου · 17. ᴾδια- v. 6; 1
                                                                    Tim. ii.
                                                                    5; 1 Peter
                                                                    iii. 18.
                                                                    ᴾ Gal. iii.
                                                                    15.

worshipper. Works from which a man must be cleansed before he can enter God's presence. A pause might be made before ἔργων, from dead—(not bodies but) works. [καθαρίζω, Hellenistic; see Anz. *Subsidia*, 374. In class. καθαίρω is used, as in Herod. i, 44, τὸν αὐτὸς φόνου ἐκάθηρε, and Æsch. *Choeph.* 72.] This cleansing is preparatory to the worship of the living God εἰς τὸ λατρεύειν Θεῷ ζῶντι. The living God, who is all life, can suffer no taint of death in His worshippers. Death moral and physical cannot exist in His presence. λατρεύειν, "ad serviendum, in perpetuum, modo beatissimo et vere sacerdotali" (Bengel).

Ver. 15. καὶ διὰ τοῦτο, "And on this account," that is to say, because, as stated in ver. 14, Christ's blood cleanses the conscience from dead works and thus fits men to draw near to God, διαθήκης καινῆς μεσίτης ἐστίν, "He is mediator of a new covenant". The old covenant with sacrifices which could only cleanse the flesh allowed sins to accumulate. But Christ, as above stated, obtained cleansing from sins, and so laid the essential foundation of a new covenant, viii. 12. ὅπως θανάτου γενομένου . . . "that a death having taken place for deliverance from the transgressions [committed] under the first covenant, those who have been called might receive the promised eternal inheritance". Even under the old covenant this inheritance had been promised. A gospel had been preached to them, and they had been invited, iv. 2. God being during that period the covenant God of the people, this involved eternal good. But until their transgressions were atoned for they could not receive the inheritance. The sacrifices under the old covenant could not atone for sin, therefore a new covenant with a death which could atone was necessary; in order that such a death having taken place and their sins being removed they might receive fulfilment of the promise. The retrospective reference of the death of Christ is here affirmed; as in xi. 40 it is stated that without us, *i.e.*, without the Christian dispensation, the O.T. believers could not be perfected,

The words οἱ κεκλημένοι, therefore, include not only the Hebrews addressed but all who had lived under the O.T. dispensation. ἀπολύτρωσιν . . . παραβάσεων, the genitive is of the object from which redemption is achieved, and ἐπὶ is scarcely "against" as in Vaughan, but rather "in the time of," as in ix. 26, Phil. i. 3.

Ver. 16. ὅπου γὰρ διαθήκη . . . The meaning of these words is doubtful. In the LXX διαθήκη occurs about 280 times and in all but four instances translates בְּרִית, covenant. In classical and Hellenistic Greek, however, it is the common word for "will" or "testament" (see especially *The Oxyrhynchus Papyri*, Grenfell and Hunt, Part I., 105, etc., where the normal meaning of the word appears also from the use of ἀδιάθετος for "intestate" and μεταδιατίθεσθαι for "to alter a will"). Accordingly it has been supposed by several interpreters that the writer, taking advantage of the double meaning of διαθήκη, at this point introduces an argument which applies to it in the sense of "will" or "testament," but not in the sense of "covenant"; as if he said, "where a testamentary disposition of property is made, this comes into force only on the decease of the testator". θάνατον ἀνάγκη φέρεσθαι τοῦ διαθεμένου "it is necessary that the death of him who made the disposition be adduced". On the very common omission of the copula in the third singular indicative see Buttmann, p. 136. φέρεσθαι, "necesse est *afferri* testimonia de morte testatoris" (Wetstein). For passages establishing its use as a term of the courts for the production of evidence, etc., see Field *in loc.* and especially Appian, *De Bell. Civil.* ii. 143, διαθῆκαι δὲ τοῦ Καίσαρος ὤφθησαν φερόμεναι. (See also Elsner *in loc.*) φέρειν is apparently even used for "to register" in the *Oxy. Papyri*, Part II., 244. The reason of this necessity is given in ver. 17. διαθήκη γὰρ ἐπὶ νεκροῖς βεβαία . . . "for a testament is of force with reference to dead people, since it is never of any force when the testator is alive". On this interpretation the

θήκη γὰρ ἐπὶ νεκροῖς βεβαία, ἐπεὶ μὴ ποτε [1] ἰσχύει ὅτε ζῇ ὁ
διαθέμενος. 18. ὅθεν οὐδ' ἡ πρώτη χωρὶς αἵματος ἐγκεκαίνι-
σται. 19. [a]λαληθείσης γὰρ πάσης ἐντολῆς κατὰ νόμον [2] ὑπὸ
Μωϋσέως παντὶ τῷ λαῷ, λαβὼν τὸ αἷμα τῶν μόσχων καὶ τράγων,
μετὰ ὕδατος καὶ ἐρίου κοκκίνου καὶ ὑσσώπου, αὐτό τε τὸ βιβλίον

q Exod.
xxiv. 5, 6;
Lev. xvi.
14, 15, 18.

[1] μη ποτε ℵcADcEKLP ; μη τοτε ℵ*D*.
[2] T.R. in ℵ* ; insert art. with ℵcACD*₂.

words mean that before the inheritance, alluded to in ver. 15, could become the possession of those to whom it had been promised, Christ must die. He is thus represented as a testator. The illustration from the general law relating to wills or testaments extends only to the one point that Christ's people could inherit only on condition of Christ's death. The *reason* of Christ's death receives no illustration. He did not die merely to make room for the heir. The objections to this interpretation are (1) the constant Biblical usage by which, with one doubtful exception in Gal. iii., διαθήκη stands for "covenant," not for "will". On this point see the strong statement of Hatch, *Essays in Bibl. Greek*, p. 48. "There can be little doubt that the word was invariably taken in this sense of "covenant" in the N.T., and especially in a book which is so impregnated with the language of the LXX as the epistle to the Hebrews". (2) His argument regarding covenants receives no help from usages which obtain in connection with testaments which are not covenants. The fact that both could be spoken of under the same name shows that they were related in some way ; but presumably the writer had in view things and not merely words. To adduce the fact that in the case of wills the death of the testator is the condition of validity, is, of course, no proof at all that a death is necessary to make a covenant valid. (3) The argument of ver. 18 is destroyed if we understand vv. 16, 17 of wills ; for in this verse it is the first covenant that is referred to.

But is it possible to retain the meaning "covenant"? Westcott, Rendall, Hatch, Moulton and others think it is possible. To support his argument, proving the necessity of Christ's death, the writer adduces the general law that he who makes a covenant does so at the expense of life. What is meant becomes plain in the 18th verse, for in the covenant there alluded to, the covenanting people were received into covenant through death.

That covenant only became valid ἐπὶ νεκροῖς over the dead bodies of the victims slain as representing the people. Whatever this substitutionary death may have meant, it was *necessary* to the ratification of the covenant. The sacrifices may have been expiatory, indicating that all old debts and obligations were cancelled and that the covenanters entered into this covenant as clean and new men ; or they may have meant that the terms of the covenant were immutable ; or that the people died to the past and became wholly the people of God. In any case the dead victims were necessary, and without them, χωρὶς αἵματος, the covenant was not inaugurated or ratified. Great light has been thrown on this passage by Dr. Trumbull in his *Blood Covenant*, in which he shows the universality of that form of compact and the significance of the blood. The rite of interchanging blood or tasting one another's blood, indicates that the two are bound in one life and must be all in all to one another. On the whole, this interpretation is to be preferred. Certainly it connects much better with what follows. For having shown that by dead victims all covenants are ratified, the writer proceeds ὅθεν οὐδ' ἡ πρώτη χωρὶς αἵματος ἐνκεκαίνισται, "wherefore not even the first,"—although imperfect and temporary—"was inaugurated without blood," *i.e.*, without death. [The perfect here as elsewhere in Hebrews is scarcely distinguishable from the aorist.] Proof that this statement regarding the first covenant is correct he forthwith gives in vv. 19-20.

Ver 19. λαληθείσης γὰρ πάσης ἐντολῆς. . . . "For when Moses had spoken to the people every commandment of the law," this being the needful preliminary, that the people might clearly understand the obligations they assumed on entering the covenant, he then took the blood of the calves and the goats, etc. In Exod. xxiv. 3 ff., an account is given of the inauguration of the first covenant. To that narrative certain

καὶ πάντα τὸν λαὸν ἐρράντισε, 20. ᵣλέγων, "Τοῦτο τὸ αἶμα τῆς
διαθήκης ἧς ἐνετείλατο πρὸς ὑμᾶς ὁ Θεός"· 21. ˢκαὶ τὴν σκηνὴν δὲ
καὶ πάντα τὰ σκεύη τῆς λειτουργίας τῷ αἵματι ὁμοίως ἐρράντισε. 22·ˢ
ᵗκαὶ σχεδὸν ἐν αἵματι πάντα καθαρίζεται κατὰ τὸν νόμον, καὶ χωρὶς

Exod.
xxiv. 8;
Matt.
xxvi. 28.
Exod.
xxix. 36;
Lev. viii.
15, 19, et
xvi. 14.   t Lev. xvii. 11.

additions of no importance are here made. In Exodus no mention is made of goats, only of μοσχάρια. (See Westcott on this discrepancy.) Probably this addition is due to an echo of vv. 12, 13. *Water*, which was added to the blood to prevent coagulation or possibly as a symbol of cleansing; (*cf.* Jo. xix. 34; 1 Jo. v. 6) *scarlet wool*, κόκκινος, so called from κόκκος "the grain or berry of the *ilex coccifera*" used in dyeing (*cf.* Lev. xiv. 4) and the *hyssop* or wild marjoram on which the wool was tied, are all added as associated with sacrifice in general, and all connected with the blood and the sprinkling. ἐράντισεν here takes the place of the κατεσκέδασε of Exodus and the action is not confined to the people as in the original narrative but includes αὐτὸ τὸ βιβλίον, the book itself, that is, even the book in which Moses had written the words of the Lord, the terms of the covenant. Everything connected with the covenant bore the mark of blood, of death. Again, in ver. 20, instead of the ἰδοὺ of the LXX, which literally renders the Hebrew we have τοῦτο τὸ αἷμα κ.τ.λ., a possible echo of our Lord's words in instituting the new covenant, and instead of διέθετο of Exod. xxiv. 8 we have ἐνετείλατο corresponding with the ἐντολή of ver. 19.

Ver. 21. καὶ τὴν σκηνὴν δὲ.... "And he also in like manner sprinkled with the blood the tabernacle and all the instruments of the service". The tabernacle, however, was not yet erected when the covenant was instituted. Delitzsch supposes that a subsequent though kindred transaction is referred to; and colour is given to this supposition by the separation of this verse from ver. 19. But against it is the article in τῷ αἵματι, "the blood," apparently the blood defined in vv. 19 and 20; although it is just possible the writer may have meant "the blood" which formed part of the means of service. Neither was it by Moses but by Aaron the tabernacle and the altar were sprinkled with blood and so cleansed on the day of Atonement. When first erected ἡ σκηνὴ καὶ πάντα τὰ σκεύη αὐτῆς were anointed with oil (Exod. xl. 9) but Josephus records a tradition that it

was consecrated not only with oil but also with blood (*Ant.* iii. 8, 6). It seems that the author adopts this tradition, and ascribes to Moses at the original consecration of the tabernacle the cleansing rites which afterwards were annually performed by Aaron on the day of Atonement.

Ver. 22. καὶ σχεδὸν ἐν αἵματι πάντα ... "And one may almost say that according to the law all things are cleansed with blood, and without blood-shedding is no remission". σχεδὸν qualifies the whole clause and not only πάντα. Whether it qualifies both clauses, as Bleek, Weiss and others suppose, is more doubtful. Westcott and Delitzsch confine its reference to the first clause. ἐν αἵματι "with blood" the usual instrumental ἐν. πάντα, all things, especially, of course, those that were used in God's worship or brought into His tabernacle. Water was used for cleansing from certain pollutions. κατὰ τὸν νόμον, it was not only a contrivance of man but the law of God which enacted that cleansing must be by blood. καὶ χωρὶς αἱματεκχυσίας, "without blood-shedding," a word which occurs only here in Bibl. Greek. See Stephanus s.v. In all the instances cited in Stephanus it means the shedding of blood. Rendall, then, is quite wrong in maintaining (after Tholuck and De Wette) that it means, not the shedding but the outpouring of the blood at the foot of the altar. "The essential idea attached to the one act was destruction of life, of the other devotion of the same life to God. Hence the typical significance of the two acts was also quite distinct; outpouring of blood typified in fact, not physical death, but spiritual martyrdom by the surrender of a living will to God in perfect obedience even unto death". Weiss is strictly accurate in his remark, "αἱμ. kann ohne eine lokale Näherbestimmung nicht die Ausgiessung des Blutes am Altare bezeichnen". The evidence is furnished by Bleek. The words, if not suggested by, inevitably recall our Lord's words (Matt. xxvi. 28) τοῦτο γάρ ἐστιν τὸ αἷμά μου τῆς διαθήκης τὸ περὶ πολλῶν ἐκχυννόμενον

αἱματεκχυσίας οὐ γίνεται ἄφεσις. 23. Ἀνάγκη οὖν τὰ μὲν ὑποδείγματα τῶν ἐν τοῖς οὐρανοῖς τούτοις καθαρίζεσθαι· αὐτὰ δὲ τὰ
ἐπουράνια κρείττοσι θυσίαις παρὰ ταύτας. 24. ᵘοὐ γὰρ εἰς χειρο-
ποίητα ἅγια εἰσῆλθεν ὁ Χριστὸς,[1] ἀντίτυπα τῶν ἀληθινῶν, ἀλλ' εἰς
αὐτὸν τὸν οὐρανόν, νῦν ἐμφανισθῆναι τῷ προσώπῳ τοῦ Θεοῦ ὑπὲρ

u vii. 25;
Rom. viii.
34; 1
Joan. ii. 2.

---

[1] T.R. CcDb,cEKLP; om. o with אAC*D*, 17, 71, 118.

εἰς ἄφεσιν ἁμαρτιῶν. Cleansing was
required of everything connected with
God's worship, because it was stained
through contact with men. And that
this stain was guilt is implied in the use
of ἄφεσις. It is by remission of sin the
stain is removed. And according to the
great law of Lev. xvii. 11, this remission
was attained by the shedding of blood τὸ
γὰρ αἷμα ἀντὶ ψυχῆς ἐξιλάσεται.
ἄφεσις is used absolutely only here and
in Mark iii. 29; elsewhere it is used with
ἁμαρτιῶν or παραπτωμάτων. In Luke
iv. 18 it signifies "release".

Vv. 23-28. The necessity of cleansing
the heavenly sanctuary and the efficiency
and finality of Christ's one sacrifice.

Ver. 23. ἀνάγκη οὖν τὰ μὲν
ὑποδείγματα... "It was necessary,
therefore, that the copies indeed of the
heavenly things be cleansed with these,
but the heavenlies themselves with better
sacrifices than these." ἀνάγκη οὖν,
the οὖν carries to its consequence ver.
22; and the necessity arises from the
injunction of the law there mentioned.
τὰ μὲν ὑποδ. the μὲν ... δὲ show
that the second clause is that to which
attention is to be given, the first clause
introducing it. The statement is almost
equivalent to "As it was necessary ...
so it was necessary" ... The ὑποδείγ.
are the tabernacle and its furnishings, in
accordance with viii. 5; which see. τούτοις, viz., the things mentioned in ver.
19. αὐτὰ δὲ τὰ ἐπουράνια. If the
copies were cleansed by material rites,
realities being spiritual and eternal can
only be cleansed by what is spiritual and
eternal, cf. ver 14. κρείττοσιν
θυσίαις, the plural is suggested by
τούτοις, and states an abstract inference.
But do the "heavenlies" need cleansing?
Bruce says, "I prefer to make no attempt
to assign a theological meaning to the
words. I would rather make them
intelligible to my mind by thinking of the
glory and honour accruing even to heaven
by the entrance there of 'the Lamb of
God'. I believe there is more of poetry
than of theology in the words. For the
writer is a poet as well as a theologian,

and on this account, theological pedants,
however learned, can never succeed in
interpreting satisfactorily this epistle".
But it is scarcely permissible to exclude
at this point of the author's argument
the theological inference that in some
sense and in some relation the heavenlies
need cleansing. The earthly tabernacle,
as God's dwelling, might have been
supposed to be hallowed by His presence
and to need no cleansing, but being also
His meeting-place with men it required
to be cleansed. And so our heavenly
relations with God, and all wherewith
we seek to approach Him, need cleansing. In themselves things heavenly need
no cleansing, but as entered upon by
sinful men they need it. Our eternal
relations with God require purification.

Ver. 24. οὐ γὰρ εἰς χειροποίη-
τα.... The connection, indicated by
γὰρ, is "I say αὐτὰ τὰ ἐπουράνια, for it
is not into a holy place constructed by
man that Christ has entered, but into
heaven itself". Others prefer to connect this verse with κρείττοσιν θυσίαις.
"Better sacrifices" were needed, for
not into, etc. The humanly constructed
tabernacle, being made after the divine
pattern, viii. 5, is here called ἀντίτυπα τῶν ἀληθινῶν. According
to viii. 5 a τύπος of the heavenly realities
was shown to Moses, and what he constructed from that model was an ἀντί-
τυπον, answering to the type. But as
here used with τῶν ἀληθ., ἀντίτυπα (in
agreement with ἅγια) must mean what
we usually speak of as a type, that which
corresponds to and prefigures. In the
only other instance of its occurrence,
1 Pet. iii. 21, it has the converse meaning,
the reality of baptism which corresponds
to or is the antitype of the deluge. The
ἀντίτυπα are contrasted with αὐτὸν
τὸν οὐρανόν, heaven itself [αὐτὸν in
contrast to the mere likeness or copy]
the ultimate reality, the presence of
spiritual and eternal things. "Coelum
in quod Christus ingressus est, non est
ipsum coelum creatum quodcunque fuerit,
sed est coelum in quo Deus est etiam
quando coelum creatum nullum est, ipsa

ἡμῶν· 25. Ϲοὐδ' ἵνα πολλάκις προσφέρῃ ἑαυτὸν, ὥσπερ ὁ ἀρχιερεὺς ⱽ ver. 7;
Exod.
εἰσέρχεται εἰς τὰ ἅγια κατ' ἐνιαυτὸν ἐν αἵματι ἀλλοτρίῳ· 26. ᵂἐπεὶ xxx. 10;
Lev. xvi
ἔδει αὐτὸν πολλάκις παθεῖν ἀπὸ καταβολῆς κόσμου· νῦν¹ δὲ ἅπαξ 2, 34.
ᵂ ı Cor. x.
ἐπὶ συντελείᾳ τῶν αἰώνων, εἰς ἀθέτησιν ἁμαρτίας,² διὰ τῆς θυσίας 11; Eph.
i. 10; Gal.
iv. 4.

¹νυνι in אACP, 37, 39, 47, 73; νυν in DEK.
²T.R. CDcEKL; insert της with אAP, 17, 73.

gloria divina" (Seb. Schmidt in Delitzsch). νῦν ἐμφανισθῆναι . . .
"now to appear openly before the face
of God in our behalf". νῦν "now,"
after His completed work on earth, and
as his present continuous function; in
contrast both to the past ministries, in
which face to face communion was impossible, and to Christ's reappearance to
men, ver. 28. ἐμφανισθῆναι τ.
προσώπῳ τ. θεοῦ. The meaning
of ἐμφανίζω is most clearly seen from
such passages as Exod. xxxiii. 18, Jo.
xiv. 21. In the passive it means "to
be manifest," "to appear openly" or
"clearly," "to show one's self," as in
Mat. xxvii. 53 of the bodies of the saints,
ἐνεφανίσθησαν πολλοῖς. The infinitive
is the infinitive of designed result common in N.T., as in classics, especially
after verbs of motion, cf. Mat. ii. 2, xi. 8,
etc. The aorist may here be used to denote that "the manifestation of Christ, in
whom humanity is shown in its perfect
ideal before the face of God is 'one act
at once'"; but this is doubtful. The
force of ἐμφαν. is strengthened still more
by the emphatic τ. προσώπῳ τ. θεοῦ.
In the earthly sanctuary the law was τὸ
πρόσωπόν μου οὐκ ὀφθήσεται (Exod.
xxxiii. 23) but ἐν νεφέλῃ ὀφθήσομαι ἐπὶ
τ. ἱλαστηρίου (Lev. xvi. 2). In Ps. xlii.
2 we find indeed πότε ἥξω καὶ ὀφθήσομαι τ. προσώπῳ τ. θεοῦ; but this is
the non-literal expression of a poet. In
the present passage the words are not the
loose expression of the ordinary worshipper but are meant to be taken literally.
And the intentionally emphatic character
of the whole phrase is best accounted for
by the fact that the darkness and clouds
of incense in the old sanctuary were
meant as much to veil the unworthiness
of the priest from God as the glory of
God from the priest. Now Christ appears before God face to face with no
intervening cloud. Perfect fellowship is
attained by His perfect and stainless offer
ing of Himself. All is clear between God
and man. For it is ὑπὲρ ἡμῶν "for
us" He enters this presence and fellowship; not that He alone may enjoy it,

but that we may enter into the rest and
blessedness that He has won for us.
Ver. 25. οὐδ' ἵνα πολλάκις....
"Nor yet [did He enter ın] in order to
offer Himself repeatedly," that is, He did
not enter in for a brief stay from which
He was to return to renew His sacrifice.
Westcott holds that the "offering" corresponds with the offering of the victim
upon the altar, not with the bringing of
the blood into the Holy of Holies. He
refers to ver. 14 ἑαυτὸν προσήνεγκεν, to
ver. 28, and also to x. 10. Similarly
Weiss and others. But in ix. 7 προσφέρει
distinctly refers to the bringing in and
application of the blood in the Holy of
Holies, and the context of the present
passage seems decidedly to make for the
same interpretation. The sequence of the
ἵνα clause after εἰσῆλθεν; the analogy
presented in the clause under ὥσπερ; and
the consequence stated under ἐπεὶ (ver. 26)
all combine in favouring this meaning.
The High Priest enters the Holiest annually, but Christ's entering in was of
another kind, not requiring repetition.
The reason for the reiterated entering in
of the High Priest, as well as the possibility of it, is given in the words ἐν
αἵματι ἀλλοτρίῳ. ἐν: "The High
Priest was, as it were, surrounded, envel-
oped, in the life sacrificed and symbolic-
ally communicated" (Westcott). It is
safer to take ἐν in its common instrumental sense: the blood was the instrument which enabled the High Priest to
enter. The reason why the entrance had
to be annually renewed is given in x. 4.
The same contrast between αἷμα ἀλλ-
ότριον and αἷμα ἴδιον is found in ix. 12.
A sacrifice of blood not one's own is
necessarily imperfect, Christ's entrance
to God being διὰ τοῦ ἰδίου αἵματος and
διὰ πνεύματος αἰωνίου had eternal efficacy.
Ver. 26. ἐπεὶ ἔδει αὐτὸν . . .
"Since in that case he must often have
suffered since the creation." If Christ's
one offering of Himself were not eternally
efficacious, if it required periodical
renewal, then this demanded periodical
sacrifice. It was "not without blood"

x Matt. αὐτοῦ πεφανέρωται. 27. καὶ καθ' ὅσον ἀπόκειται τοῖς ἀνθρώποις
xxvi. 28:
Rom. v. ἅπαξ ἀποθανεῖν, μετὰ δὲ τοῦτο κρίσις· 28. ˣοὕτως ¹ ὁ Χριστὸς ἅπαξ
6, 8, 15, et
vi. 10; 1 προσενεχθεὶς εἰς τὸ πολλῶν ἀνενεγκεῖν ἁμαρτίας, ἐκ δευτέρου χωρὶς
Peter iii.
18. ἁμαρτίας ὀφθήσεται τοῖς αὐτὸν ἀπεκδεχομένοις εἰς σωτηρίαν.

¹ Insert καὶ with אACDEKLP.

the entrance was made, and if the entrance required repetition, so must the sacrifice be repeated.. And as sin prevailed ἀπὸ καταβολῆς κόσμου, the παθεῖν must also date from the first. The contrast is with the one offering ἐπὶ συντελείᾳ κ.τ.λ. "If his offering of Himself were not independent of time and valid as a single act, if it were valid only for the generation for whom it is immediately made, then in order to benefit men in the past, He must have suffered often, indeed in each generation of the past" (Davidson). νυνὶ δὲ ἅπαξ... "But now once at the consummation of the ages He has been manifested for sin's abolition by His sacrifice". νυνὶ, "as things are," in contrast to the case supposed in ver. 25, the possibility of His repeated entrance and sacrifice. For the word, see viii. 6. ἅπαξ not πολλάκις, vv. 25, 26; and this, ἐπὶ συντελείᾳ τῶν αἰώνων [for ἐπὶ in this use see Winer, p. 489] at that period of history in which all that has happened since the foundation of the world (ἀπὸ καταβολῆς κόσμου) finds its interpretation and adjustment. If there was to be one sacrifice for all generations, the occurrence of that sacrifice itself marked the period as the consummation. It closes the periods of symbolism, expectation and doubt, suggesting, perhaps, the word πεφανέρωται for Christ's appearance, as that which was dimly foreshadowed, blindly longed for. εἰς ἀθέτησιν τῆς ἁμαρτίας, The object of Christ's appearance, the abolition of sin, made the repetition of His sacrifice unnecessary. In vii. 18 ἀθέτησις is used of permanent displacement, removal, or setting aside, that is, abolition. τῆς ἁμαρτίας of sin, in its most general and comprehensive sense, all sin. This was the great object of Christ's manifestation, the annulling of sin, its total destruction, the counteraction of all its effects. This was to be accomplished διὰ τῆς θυσίας αὐτοῦ "through His sacrifice," the simple subjective genitive. The sentence draws attention not to the nature of the sacrifice, but to its three characteristics, that it was made once for tall, in the consummation, for sin's abolition.

Ver. 27. καὶ καθ' ὅσον ... "And inasmuch as it is reserved for men once to die and, after this, judgment, so, also, Christ, etc." To confirm his statement that Christ's sacrifice was "once for all," he appeals to the normal conditions of human death. To men generally, τοῖς ἀνθρώποις, it is appointed once to die, men are not permitted to return to earth to compensate for neglect or failure, but immediately succeeding upon death, if not in time, yet in consequence, follows judgment. The results of life are entered upon. So Christ died but once and the results will be apparent in His appearing the second time without sin unto salvation. ἀπόκειται "is reserved" as in Longinus' De Subl. ix. 7, ἡμῖν δυσδαιμονοῦσιν ἀπόκειται λιμὴν κακῶν ὁ θάνατος, cf. iii. 5; also Dion. Hal. v. 8, ὅσα τοῖς κακούργοις ἀπόκειται παθεῖν, and especially 2 Tim. iv. 8. What is destined for all men is not simply death, but ἅπαξ ἀποθ. once to die. Cf. the fragment of Sophocles θανεῖν γὰρ οὐκ ἔξεστι τοῖς αὐτοῖσι δίς. μετὰ δὲ τοῦτο κρίσις "after this," but how long, the author does not say. "Man dies once, and the next thing before him is judgment. So Christ died once and the next thing before Him is the Advent" (Vaughan).

Ver. 28. οὕτως. The comparison extends to both terms, the once dying and the judgment. [Cf. Kübel, "die Korrespondenz ist nicht bloss die der gleichen Menschennatur, sondern das, dass mit dem Tod das, was das Leben bedeutet, abgeschlossen, fertig ist"]. The results of the life are settled. And in Christ's case the result is that He appears the second time without sin unto salvation, the sin having been destroyed by His death. ἅπαξ προσενεχθεὶς corresponds to ἅπαξ ἀποθανεῖν of ver. 27. The passive is used to be more in keeping with the universal law expressed in ἀπόκειται of ver. 27. Though the "offering" as we have seen includes both the death and the entrance into the Holiest with the blood, it is the death which is here prominent. εἰς τὸ πολλῶν ἀνενεγκεῖν ἁμαρτίας, "to bear the sins of many". Westcott

X. I. ªΣΚΙΑΝ γὰρ ἔχων ὁ νόμος τῶν μελλόντων ἀγαθῶν, οὐκ   a viii. 5, et
                                                          ix. 9; Col.
αὐτὴν τὴν εἰκόνα τῶν πραγμάτων, κατ' ἐνιαυτὸν ταῖς αὐταῖς θυσίαις [1]   ii. 17.
ἃς προσφέρουσιν εἰς τὸ διηνεκὲς, οὐδέποτέ δύναται [2] τοὺς προσερχο-

[1] ℵP add αυτων.
[2] T.R. in D*, etc., EHKL, d, e, f, vg., Basm., Copt.; δυνανται in ℵACDbP.

says, "the burden which Christ took upon Him and bore to the cross was 'the sins of many' not, primarily, or separately from the sins, the punishment of sins." But in what intelligible sense can sins be borne but by bearing their punishment? In Numbers xiv. 33, *e.g.*, it is said "your sins shall be fed in the wilderness forty years καὶ ἀνοίσουσι τὴν πορνείαν ὑμῶν, where the same verb is used as here to express the idea of suffering punishment for the sins of others. πολλῶν, although it was the death of but one, *cf.* Rom. v. 12-21, but probably only a reminiscence of Isa. lviii. 12. αὐτὸς ἁμαρτίας πολλῶν ἀνήνεγκε. ἐκ δευτέρου . . . a second time He shall appear, ὀφθήσεται, visible to the eye. The word is probably used because appropriate to the appearances after the resurrection, *cf.* Luke xxiv. 34, Acts ix. 17, xiii. 31, 1 Cor. 5, 6, 7, 8 where ὤφθη is regularly used. But on this "second" appearance His object is different. He will come not εἰς τὸ πολ. ἀνεν. ἀμαρτίας, but χωρὶς ἀμ. εἰς σωτηρίαν irrespective of sin, not to be a sin offering but to make those who wait for Him partakers of the great salvation, ii. 3, *cf.* x. 37-39; and ix. 12. τοῖς αὐτὸν ἀπεκδεχομένοις "There may be an illusion to the reappearance of the High Priest after the solemn ceremonial in the Holy of Holies on the day of atonement to the anxiously waiting people" (Vaughan). *Cf.* Luke i. 21. The word is used in 1 Cor. i. 7 and Phil. iii. 20 of the expectation of the second advent, and in 2 Tim. iv. 8 is varied by the beautiful expression "they that have loved His appearing".

CHAPTER X.—Vv. 1-18. *Finality of Christ's one sacrifice.* The law merely presents a shadow of the essential spiritual blessings and does not perfect those who seek God through it. Its sacrifices therefore must be continually repeated and the consciousness of sins is annually revived, for animal blood cannot take sins away. Accordingly, when Christ comes into the world He says, "Sacrifice and offering Thou wouldst not, I am come to do Thy will". He proclaims the uselessness of O.T. sacrifices, that He may clear the ground for "the offering of the body of

Christ". This is the great distinction between Christ and all other priests. They stand daily ministering, He by one offering has perfected those who approach God through Him.

Vv. 1-4. The sacrifices of the law inadequate.

Ver. 1. Σκιὰν γὰρ ἔχων . . . The γὰρ intimates that we have here a further explanation of the finality of Christ's one sacrifice (ix. 28) and therefore of its superiority to the sacrifices of the law. The explanation consists in this that the law had only "a shadow of the good things that were to be, not the very image of the things". Σκιὰν is in the emphatic place, as that characteristic of the law which determines its inadequacy. "A shadow" suggests indefiniteness and unsubstantiality; a mere indication that a reality exists. εἰκών suggests what is in itself substantial and also gives a true representation of that which it images. "The εἰκών brings before us under the conditions of space, as we can understand it, that which is spiritual" (Westcott). So Kübel, etc. The contrast is between a bare intimation that good things were to be given, and an actual presentation of these good things in an apprehensible form. It is *implied* that this latter is given in Christ; but what is asserted is, that the law did not present the coming realities in a form which brought them within the comprehension of the people. [Bleek cites from Cicero, *De Off.*, iii. 17, 69, "nos veri juris germanaeque justitiae solidam et expressam effigiem nullam tenemus, umbra et imaginibus utimur".]

That the law possessed no more than a shadow of the coming good was exhibited in its constantly renewed sacrifices. κατ' ἐνιαυτὸν belongs to ταῖς αὐταῖς θυσίαις, "with the same annually repeated sacrifices," further explained and emphasised by the relative clause, ἃς προσφέρουσιν εἰς τὸ διηνεκὲς, "which they perpetually offer". οὐδέποτε δύναται . . . the law can never with these perpetually renewed offerings perfect the worshippers". "No repetition of the shadow can amount to the substance" (Davidson). The proof is given in the following words, ver. 2: ἐπεὶ οὐκ ἂν ἐπαύ-

μένους τελειῶσαι. 2. ἐπεὶ οὐκ ἂν ἐπαύσαντο προσφερόμεναι, διὰ
τὸ μηδεμίαν ἔχειν ἔτι συνείδησιν ἁμαρτιῶν τοὺς λατρεύοντας, ἅπαξ
κεκαθαρμένους[1]· 3. ἀλλ' ἐν αὐταῖς ἀνάμνησις ἁμαρτιῶν κατ'
ἐνιαυτόν· 4. [b]ἀδύνατον γὰρ αἷμα ταύρων καὶ τράγων ἀφαιρεῖν
ἁμαρτίας. 5. [c]Διὸ εἰσερχόμενος εἰς τὸν κόσμον λέγει, "Θυσίαν καὶ
προσφορὰν οὐκ ἠθέλησας, σῶμα δὲ κατηρτίσω μοι· 6. ὁλοκαυτώματα
καὶ περὶ ἁμαρτίας οὐκ εὐδόκησας[2]· 7. τότε εἶπον, Ἰδοὺ ἥκω· ἐν
κεφαλίδι βιβλίου γέγραπται περὶ ἐμοῦ· τοῦ ποιῆσαι, ὁ Θεὸς, τὸ

b ix. 13;
Lev. xvi.
14; Num.
xix. 4.
c Ps. xl. 6,
7, et l. 8,
etc.; Esa.
i. 11; Jer.
vi. 20;
Amos v.
21.

[1] κεκαθαρισμενους ℵDEHKP, 17, 37, 71.
[2] ηυδοκησας in ACD*HP, 37, 73.

σαντο προσφερόμεναι. The constant
renewal of the yearly round of sacrifices
proves that they were inefficacious, for
had the worshippers once been cleansed
they would have had no longer any consciousness of sins and would therefore
have sought no renewal of sacrifice.
ἐπεὶ, "since," if the O.T. sacrifices had
perfected those who used them. προσφερόμεναι corresponding to προσφέρουσιν, and τοὺς λατρεύοντας to τοὺς
προσερχομένους of previous verse.
ἅπαξ κεκαθ., that is, once delivered from a
sense of guilt, cf. ix. 14, where συνείδησις
is also used in same sense as here, the
consciousness of sin as barring approach
to God. The sinner once cleansed may,
no doubt, be again defiled and experience
a renewed consciousness of guilt. But
in the writer's view this consciousness is
at once absorbed in the consciousness of
his original cleansing. Cf. John xiii. 10.
ἀλλ' ἐν αὐταῖς. ... So far from these
O.T. sacrifices once for all cleansing the
conscience and thus perfecting the worshippers, "by and in them there is a
yearly remembrance of sins," that is, of
sins not yet sufficiently atoned for by any
past sacrifice. Cf. Num. v. 15. θυσία
μνημοσύνου ἀναμιμνήσκουσα ἁμαρτίαν,
and Philo, De Plantat., 25, αἱ θυσίαι
ὑπομιμνήσκουσαι τὰς ἑκάστων ἀγνοίας,
κ.τ.λ. This remembrance of sins is κατ'
ἐνιαυτόν, which is most naturally referred to the annual confession of the
whole people on the day of Atonement.
The remembrance was not of sins previously atoned for but of sins committed
since the previous sacrifice; there was no
perception that any previous atonement
was sufficient for all sin. The underlying ground of this inadequacy being
expressed in ver. 4. ἀδύνατον γὰρ.
... "For it is impossible that the blood
of oxen and goats should take away sins".
This obvious truth needs no proof. There
is no relation between the physical blood

of animals and man's moral offence. Cf.
the Choephori of Æschylus, 70, "all
waters, joining together to cleanse from
blood the polluted hand, may strive in
vain". ἀφαιρεῖν ἁμαρτίας, "to
take away sins", in the sense of removing
their guilt as in Num. xiv. 18, Lev. x. 17,
Rom. xi. 27.

Vv. 5-10. The adequacy of Christ's
sacrifice as fulfilling God's will. διὸ
"wherefore," "such being the ineffectiveness of the sacrifices of the law and the
condition of conscience of those under
them," "when He—that is ὁ Χριστός
ix. 28 to whom alone εἰσερχόμ. is
applicable—comes into the world," referring generally to His incarnate state, not
to His entrance on his public ministry.
λέγει, the words are quoted from Ps.
xl. 6-8 and put in the mouth of Christ
although the whole Psalm cannot be
considered Messianic, cf. ver. 12. In
what sense can λέγει be used of Christ?
It is not meant that He was present in
the psalmist and so uttered what is here
here referred to Him. This idea is
negatived by εἰσερχόμ. It was when
incarnate he used the words. Neither is
it merely meant that by his conduct Christ
showed that these words were a true
expression of his mind. Rather, the
words are considered prophetic, depicting
beforehand the mind of Christ regarding
O.T. sacrifice, and His own mission. In
several O.T. passages God's preference
for obedience is affirmed (1 Sam. xv. 22,
Ps. l. 8, Micah, Isa. i. 11, Hosea, vi. 6)
but this psalm is here selected because the
phrase "a body hast thou prepared for
me" lends itself to the writer's purpose.
In the Psalm indeed, sacrifice is contrasted
with obedience to the will of God. A
body is prepared for Christ that in it He
may obey God. But it is the offering of
this body as a sacrifice in contrast to the
animal sacrifices of the law, which this
writer emphasises (ver. 10). "The con-

θέλημά σου ". 8. Ἀνώτερον λέγων, "Ὅτι θυσίαν καὶ προσφορὰν [1] καὶ ὁλοκαυτώματα καὶ περὶ ἁμαρτίας οὐκ ἠθέλησας οὐδὲ εὐδόκησας"·

[1] θυσιας και προσφορας in א*ACD*P, 17, 23, d, e, f, vg., Sah., Copt.; T.R. in אcDcEKL, Aeth.

trast is between animal offerings and the offering of Himself by the Son. And what is said is that God did not will the former, but willed the other, and that the former are thereby abolished, and the other is established in their room, and as the will of God is effectual. The passage in the epistle is far from saying that the essence or worth of Christ's offering of Himself lies simply in obedience to the will of God. It does not refer to the point wherein lies the intrinsic worth of the Son's offering, or whether it may be resolved into obedience unto God. Its point is quite different. It argues that the Son's offering of Himself is the true and final offering for sin, because it is the sacrifice, which, according to prophecy, God desired to be made" (Davidson).

The writer, in citing Ps. 40, follows the LXX, slightly altering the construction of the last clause by omitting ἠβουλήθην, and thus making τοῦ ποιῆσαι depend upon ἥκω, "I am come to do thy will". *Cf.* ver. 9.

θυσίαν καὶ προσφοράν representing זֶבַח וּמִנְחָה of the Psalm, animal sacrifice and meal offering. *Cf.* Ephes. v. 2. οὐκ ἠθέλησας "thou didst not will," a contrast is intended between this clause and τὸ θέλημά σου of the last clause of ver. 7. σῶμα δὲ κατηρτίσω μοι "but a body didst Thou prepare for me," implying that in this body God's will would be accomplished. *Cf.* ver. 10. The words are the LXX rendering of אָזְנַיִם כָּרִיתָ לִּי, "ears didst Thou dig [or open] for me". The meaning is the same. The opened ear as the medium through which the will of God was received, and the body by which it was accomplished, alike signify obedience to the will of God. ὁλοκαυτώματα καὶ περὶ ἁμαρτίας representing עוֹלָה וַחֲטָאָה of the psalm, whole burnt offering and sin-offering. περὶ ἁμαρτ. occurs frequently in Leviticus to denote sin offering, θυσία being omitted. οὐκ ηὐδόκησας "thou didst not take pleasure in". τότε εἶπον. "Then," that is, when it was apparent that not by animal sacrifices or material offerings could God be propitiated, "I said, Lo! I am come to do Thy will, O God," to accomplish that purpose of Thine which the sacrifices of the O.T. could not accomplish. That this is the correct construction is shown by ver. 9. For construction, *cf.* Burton, *M. and T.*, 397; and Prof. Votaw, *Use of Infin. in N. T.* ἐν κεφαλίδι βιβλίου γέγραπται περὶ ἐμοῦ "in a book [lit. in a roll of a book] it has been written concerning me". κεφαλίς denoting "a little head" was first applied to the end of the stick on which the parchment was rolled, and from which in artistically finished books two *cornua* proceeded. [See Bleek, Rich's *Dict. of Antiq.*, and Hatch's *Concordance*] In the Psalm the phrase is joined with the previous words and might be read, "Lo! I am come, with a roll of a book written for me," in other words, with written instructions regarding the divine will as affecting me. The words can hardly mean that in Scripture predictions have been recorded regarding the writer of the Psalm. This, however, may be the meaning attached to the words as cited in the epistle, although it is quite as natural and legitimate to retain the original meaning and understand the words as a parenthetical explanation that Christ acknowledged as binding *on Him* all that had been written for the instruction of others in the will of God. But the likelihood is that if the writer was not merely transcribing the words as part of his quotation without attaching a definite meaning to them, he meant that the coming of the Messiah to do God's will had been written in the book of God's purpose. (*Cf.* Ps lvi. 9.)

Ver. 8. The significance of the quotation is now explained. "He takes the first away, that he may establish the second." He declares the incompetence of the O.T. sacrifices to satisfy the will of God, in order that he may make room for that sacrifice which is permanently to satisfy God. Ἀνώτερον, "Higher up," here meaning "in the former part of the quotation," corresponding to and contrasted with τότε in ver. 9. λέγων, *i.e.*, Christ, the subject of εἴρηκεν and ἀναιρεῖ. This is necessitated by λέγει in ver. 3. Yet it is not Christ directly, but the mind of Christ uttered by God in Scripture. εἴρηκεν, perfect, as expressing that which

αἵτινες κατὰ τὸν νόμον προσφέρονται· 9. τότε εἴρηκεν, "'Ιδοὺ ἥκω
τοῦ ποιῆσαι, ὁ Θεὸς,[1] τὸ θέλημά σου''.   ἀναιρεῖ τὸ πρῶτον, ἵνα τὸ
δεύτερον στήσῃ· 10. [d] ἐν ᾧ θελήματι ἡγιασμένοι ἐσμὲν οἱ[2] διὰ
τῆς προσφορᾶς τοῦ σώματος τοῦ Ἰησοῦ Χριστοῦ ἐφάπαξ. 11. Καὶ
πᾶς μὲν ἱερεὺς[3] ἔστηκε καθ' ἡμέραν λειτουργῶν, καὶ τὰς αὐτὰς πολλάκις προσφέρων θυσίας, αἵτινες οὐδέποτε δύνανται περιελεῖν ἁμαρ-

d ix. 12.

---

[1] ο θεος omitted in א*ACDEKP, 17, d, e, Sah., Copt.

[2] οι omitted in אACD*E*P, 17, 47, 73.

[3] T.R. in אDEKL, 17, 47, d, e, f, vg.; αρχιερευς in ACP, Syrsch et p, Basm., Arm.

---

permanently fulfils the will of God.
ἀναιρεῖν is used in classic Greek of
the destruction or abolition or repeal of
laws, governments, customs, etc.
Ver. 10. ἐν ᾧ θελήματι . . . "in
which will," that is, in the will which
Christ came to do (ver. 9), "we have been
made fit for God's presence and fellowship by means of the offering of the body
of Jesus Christ once for all". The will
of God which the O.T. sacrifices could
not accomplish was the "sanctification"
of men, that is, the bringing of men into
true fellowship with God. This will has
been accomplished, we have been cleansed
and introduced into God's fellowship
through the offering of the body of Christ.
By the use of the word προσφορᾶς the
writer shows that it was not a mere
general obedience to the will of God he
had in view, but the fulfilment of God's
will in the particular form of yielding
Himself to a sacrificial death. His obedience in order to become an atoning sacrifice took a particular form, the form of
"tasting death for every man". [For a
different view see Bruce in loc. and
Gould's N.T. Theol., p. 169. On the
other hand see Riehm and Macdonell's
Donellan Lectures, p. 49-59.] τοῦ
σώματος 'Ι. Χριστοῦ ἐφάπαξ,
the offering of the body must of course
be taken in connection with ix. 14, διὰ
πνεύματος αἰωνίου and also with the defining words Ἰησοῦ Χριστοῦ. ἐφάπαξ
is added in contrast to the note of inferiority attaching to the O.T. sacrifices,
as given in ver. 1, their need of continual
renewal.
Vv. 11-14. That Christ's one sacrifice
has accomplished its end of bringing men
to God is illustrated by His sitting down
at God's right hand.
Ver. 11. καὶ introduces a new aspect
of the finality of Christ's sacrifice, to wit,
that "whereas every priest stands daily
ministering and often offering the same
sacrifices,—inasmuch as they are such as

never can take sins away—this man having offered one sacrifice for sins for ever
sat down on God's right hand, henceforth
waiting till his enemies be set as a footstool
for his feet. For by one offering He
hath perfected for ever the sanctified."
The argument is in this statement advanced a step. For although the three
points urged in vv. 1-4 are here still in
view, viz., that "the Levitical service
consists of repeated acts (καθ' ἡμέραν,
κατ' ἐνιαυτόν) and these the same (αἱ
αὐταὶ θυσίαι) and essentially ineffective
(οὐδέποτε δύνανται, κ.τ.λ) yet it is
now the action of the priest rather than
the nature of the sacrifice that comes to
the front, and the finality of Christ's
offering is argued from the historical fact
that He was not any longer standing
ministering but had sat down as one who
had quite finished His work. Therefore in
ver. 14 τετελείωκεν εἰς τὸ διηνεκὲς τοὺς
ἁγιαζομένους takes the place of ἡγιασμένοι ἐσμὲν of ver. 10. Nothing further requires to be done to secure in perpetuity the fellowship of man with God.
In the one sacrifice of Christ there is
cleansing which fits men to draw near
to God, to enter into covenant with Him,
and there is also ground laid for their
continuance in that fellowship. The
future (εἰς τὸ διηνεκὲς) is provided for as
well as the past. Limborch quoted by
Bleek says "perficit, i.e., perfecte et plene
a peccatorum reatu liberavit, ita ut in
perpetuum sanctificati sint et ulteriore
aut nova oblatione non indigeant".
"His one offering gathers up into itself
both the sacrifice that inaugurates the
covenant, and all the many sacrifices
offered year by year to maintain it and
to realise it; it reaches the idea which
they strove towards in vain, and by reaching it for ever sets them aside" (Davidson).
In ver. 11 the more expressive περιελεῖν
replaces ἀφαιρεῖν of ver. 4. It means
"to take away something that is all

τίας · 12. °αὐτὸς¹ δὲ μίαν ὑπὲρ ἁμαρτιῶν προσενέγκας θυσίαν εἰς e i. 3, 13, et
τὸ διηνεκὲς ἐκάθισεν ἐν δεξιᾷ τοῦ Θεοῦ, 13. τὸ λοιπὸν ἐκδεχόμενος viii. 1;
ἕως τεθῶσιν οἱ ἐχθροὶ αὐτοῦ ὑποπόδιον τῶν ποδῶν αὐτοῦ. 14. μιᾷ 34; 1 Cor.
γὰρ προσφορᾷ τετελείωκεν εἰς τὸ διηνεκὲς τοὺς ἁγιαζομένους. 15. xv. 25;
Μαρτυρεῖ δὲ ἡμῖν καὶ τὸ Πνεῦμα τὸ Ἅγιον· μετὰ γὰρ τὸ προειρη- iii. 1.
κέναι,² 16. "¹Αὕτη ἡ διαθήκη ἣν διαθήσομαι πρὸς αὐτοὺς μετὰ τὰς f viii. 8;
ἡμέρας ἐκείνας, λέγει Κύριος, διδοὺς νόμους μου ἐπὶ καρδίας αὐτῶν, 31, etc.;
καὶ ἐπὶ τῶν διανοιῶν³ αὐτῶν ἐπιγράψω αὐτούς· 17. καὶ τῶν ἁμαρ- 27.
τιῶν αὐτῶν καὶ τῶν ἀνομιῶν αὐτῶν οὐ μὴ μνησθῶ⁴ ἔτι". 18. Ὅπου g ix. 8, 12;
δὲ ἄφεσις τούτων, οὐκ ἔτι προσφορὰ περὶ ἁμαρτίας. 9, et xiv.
6; Rom.
19. ᵍἜχοντες οὖν, ἀδελφοί, παρρησίαν εἰς τὴν εἴσοδον τῶν ἁγίων v. 2; Eph.
ἐν τῷ αἵματι Ἰησοῦ, 20. ἣν ἐνεκαίνισεν ἡμῖν ὁδὸν πρόσφατον καὶ et iii. 12.

¹ ουτος in NACD*EP, d, e, f, vg.
² ειρηκεναι in NACDEP, it, vg.
³ επι την διανοιαν in NACDgr*P, 17, 47, 73.
⁴ μνησθησομαι in N*ACD*, 17.

round" as δέρματα σωμάτων, a garment, the covering of a letter. In Gen. xli. 42 it is used of Pharaoh taking off his ring. The phrase therefore suggests that man is enwrapped in sin; or if this is to press too hard the etymological meaning, it at least suggests *complete* deliverance. οὗτος *cf.* iii. 3 and viii. 3. εἰς τὸ διηνεκὲς cannot be construed with προσενέγκας but must be taken with ἐκάθισεν. "To say of the Levitical priests that they προσφέρουσιν εἰς τὸ διηνεκὲς (ver. 1) is appropriate; to say of Christ that He προσήνεγκεν εἰς τὸ διην. is almost a self-contradiction" (Vaughan). εἰς τὸ διηνεκὲς ἐκάθισεν balances ἕστηκεν καθ᾽ ἡμέραν, and *cf.* especially i. 3. No doubt the usual position of εἰς τὸ διηνεκὲς is after the word it qualifies, x. 1-14 and vii. 3. τοὺς ἁγιαζ. has no time reference, *cf.* ii. 11.

Vv. 15-18. Proof from Scripture that the one sacrifice of Christ, the mediator of the new covenant is final.

Ver. 15. μαρτυρεῖ δὲ ἡμῖν . . . "And the Holy Spirit also bears witness to us," that is, that the one offering of the Son is final, for under the new covenant there is no further remembrance of sins. ἡμῖν is more naturally construed as a dativus commodi than as the object of μαρτυρεῖ. μετὰ γὰρ τὸ εἰρηκέναι. "For after saying . . ." we expect the apodosis to begin and the sentence to be concluded by an introductory ἔπειτα λέγει or τότε (*cf.* ver. 9), but ver. 17 is not so introduced. The sense, however, is unmistakable. After defining the covenant in its in-

wardness and spirituality (*v.* c. viii. 10), the writer introduces that feature of it which specially serves his present purpose καὶ τῶν ἁμαρτιῶν . . . οὐ μὴ μνησθήσομαι ἔτι, "And I will never any more remember their sins and their transgressions". The conclusion is obvious, "But where there is remission of these, there is no longer offering for sin". For the terms of the new covenant see viii. 8-12. μνησθήσομαι is here used instead of μνησθῶ of LXX and of viii. 12, because the writer emphasises the extension of the forgetting to all futurity.

CHAPS. X. 19—XII. 29. Exhortation to use the access to God opened by Christ and to maintain faith in Him in spite of all temptation to fall away.

CHAP. X. 19-25. Exhortation to draw near to God, to hold fast the Christian hope, and to encourage one another.

Ver. 19. Ἔχοντες οὖν, ἀδελφοί. . . . "Having then, brethren, confidence for the entrance into the holiest by the blood of Jesus, a way which He inaugurated for us fresh and living, through the veil, that is, His flesh." For the form of the sentence *cf.* iv. 14. παρρησίαν εἰς τὴν εἴσοδον, *cf.* iii. 6 and iv. 16 προσερχώμεθα μετὰ παρρησίας, also Eph. iii. 12. ἐν ᾧ ἔχομεν τὴν παρρησίαν καὶ τὴν προσαγωγήν. εἴσοδος may either mean an entrance objectively considered, or the act of entering. Weiss adopts the former meaning, compelled as he supposes by the ὁδὸν which follows in apposition and referring to Jud. i. 24 and Ezek. xxvii. 3. He would therefore

h iv. 14, 16. ζῶσαν, διὰ τοῦ καταπετάσματος, τουτέστι, τῆς σαρκὸς αὐτοῦ, 21.
i Ezech.
xxxvi. 25; ^h καὶ ἱερέα μέγαν ἐπὶ τὸν οἶκον τοῦ Θεοῦ, 22. ⁱ προσερχώμεθα
Eph. ii.
12; Jac. μετὰ ἀληθινῆς καρδίας ἐν πληροφορίᾳ πίστεως, ἐρραντισμένοι τὰς
i. 6.

translate "boldness as regards the entrance". The objection to this interpretation is the meaning put upon εἰς
which more naturally expresses the object
or end towards which the παρρησία is
directed, the entering in, not merely the
object *about which* the παρρησία is exercised. *Cf.* 2 Cor. vii. 10, μετάνοιαν εἰς
σωτηρίαν. But *cf.* Winer on εἰς. The
expression in ix. 8, τὴν τῶν ἁγίων ὁδὸν,
also favours Weiss's interpretation. τῶν
ἁγίων as the Greek commentators remark,
here means "heaven". ἐν τ. αἵματι
Ἰησοῦ, on the whole, it is better to join
these words not with παρρησίαν but with
εἴσοδον. Bleek sees a reference to ix.
25, ὁ ἀρχιερεὺς εἰσέρχεται εἰς τὰ ἅγια ἐν
αἵματι ἀλλοτρίῳ. ἢν ἐνεκαίνισεν
ἡμῖν ὁδὸν . . . "The new and living
way which He inaugurated [or dedicated]
for us." The antecedent of the clause is
εἴσοδον, and this way into the holiest is
here further described as first used by
Christ that it might be used by us. For
ἐγκαινίζειν means to handsel, to take the
first use of a new thing. See Deut. xx.
5. He has entered within the veil as our
πρόδρομος (vi. 19, 20) and has thus
opened a way for us. It is πρόσφατον,
recent, fresh. The lexicographers are
agreed that, originally meaning fresh-
slain and applied to νεκρός, πρόσφατος
came to be used of flowers, oil, snow, misfortune, benefits, in *Sirac.* ix. 10, of a
friend; in Eccles. i. 9 οὐκ ἔστι πᾶν πρόσφατον ὑπὸ τὸν ἥλιον. It was a way
recently opened. Christ was the first who
trod that way. Wetstein, who gives many
examples of the use of the word, cites also
from *Florus*, i. 15, 3, an interesting analogy: "Alter [Decius Mus] quasi monitu
deorum, capite velato, primam ante aciem
diis manibus se devoverit, ut in con-
fertissima se hostium tela jaculatus,
novum ad victoriam iter sanguinis sui
semita aperiret". καὶ ζῶσαν, not as
a way that abides (Chrys., etc.) nor as
leading to life eternal (Grotius, etc.), nor
as a way which consists in fellowship
with a Person (Westcott), but as effective,
actually bringing its followers to their
goal. *Cf.* iv. 12. So Davidson and
Weiss. διὰ τοῦ καταπετάσματος,
a further characteristic of the way, that is,
passed through the veil, that is, His flesh;
which must first be rent before Christ
could pass into the holiest. "This beauti-

ful allegorizing of the veil cannot, of
course, be made part of a consistent and
complete typology. It is not meant for
this. But as the veil stood locally before
the holiest in the Mosaic Tabernacle, the
way into which lay through it, so Christ's
life in the flesh stood between Him and
His entrance before God, and His flesh
had to be rent ere He could enter"
(Davidson).

Ver. 21. καὶ ἱερέα μέγαν. The
opened way into the holiest is not the
only advantage possessed by the Christian,
he has also "a great priest," *cf.* iv. 14
ἔχοντες οὖν ἀρχιερέα μέγαν . . . προσερχώμεθα. Philo (*Leg. ad Gai.*, p. 1035)
calls the High Priest ὁ μέγας ἱερεύς, and
so Lev. xxi. 10, Num. xxxv. 25. But it is
not to the fact that He is High Priest
that this designation here points, but to
His greatness as Son of God and as one
who has passed into the Holy Presence.
Especially is His greatness manifested in
His administration ἐπὶ τὸν οἶκον
τοῦ θεοῦ, over God's house (*cf.* iii. 6)
that is, over those heavenly realities which
replace the house of God on earth, and
necessarily over those for whom the priest
is appointed to minister τὰ πρὸς τὸν θεόν
(v. 1).

Ver. 22. Being thus secure of an acceptable entrance προσερχώμεθα, "let us
keep approaching," that is, to God (vii.
25, xi. 6); a semi-technical term. μετὰ
ἀληθινῆς καρδίας, "with a true
heart" (*cf.* Isa. xxxviii. 3), not with a
merely bodily approach as if all were
external and symbolic, but with that
genuine engagement of the inner man
which constitutes true worship. Chrysostom has χωρὶς ὑποκρίσεως. Davidson
has "with fundamental genuineness";
but it is the genuineness which is elicited
in presence of realities. καρδία is interpreted in 1 Pet. iii. 4, ὁ κρυπτὸς τῆς
καρδίας ἄνθρωπος. It is the inevitable
qualification of one who comes ἐν πληροφορίᾳ πίστεως, "in full assurance of faith," believing not only that
God is (xi. 6) but that a way to His favour
and fellowship is opened by the Great
Priest. To engender this full assurance
has been the aim of the writer throughout the Epistle. ῥεραντισμένοι . . .
λελουσμένοι. These participles express not conditions of approach to God
which are yet to be achieved, but con-

καρδίας ἀπὸ συνειδήσεως πονηρᾶς· 23. ᵏ καὶ λελουμένοι τὸ σῶμα ᵏ iv. 14; 1
ὕδατι καθαρῷ, κατέχωμεν τὴν ὁμολογίαν τῆς ἐλπίδος ἀκλινῆ· πιστὸς Cor. i. 9;
1 Thess.
γὰρ ὁ ἐπαγγειλάμενος· 24. καὶ κατανοῶμεν ἀλλήλους εἰς παροξυσ- v. 24.
1 Rom. xiii.
μὸν ἀγάπης καὶ καλῶν ἔργων, 25. ˡ μὴ ἐγκαταλείποντες τὴν ἐπισυν- 11; 2
Peter iii.
9, 11, 14.

ditions already possessed, "our hearts
sprinkled from an evil conscience and our
body washed with pure water". Both
participles must be construed with προσερχώμεθα. The obvious connection of
"heart" and "body" forbids the attachment of λελουσμένοι to κατέχωμεν. To
connect both participles with κατεχ. is
equally impossible. "προσέρχεσθαι is a
technical liturgical word, and sprinkling
and washing is liturgical acts of preparation" (Delitzsch). Possibly the mention
of sprinkling and washing is an echo of
the injunctions of Exod. xxix. 4, 21, xxx.
20, xl. 30, prescribin g similar preparation
for the priestly functions. Our heart or
inner man by the application of the αἷμα
ῥαντισμοῦ (cf. 1 Pet. i. 2) is delivered
from the consciousness of guilt (ix. 14);
our body by the application of the purifying water of baptism becomes the symbol
of complete purity. "Sprinkled with
that blood which speaketh evermore in
the heavenly sanctuary, and washed with
baptismal water sacramentally impregnated with the same, we are at all times
privileged to approach by a new and living
way the heavenly temple, entering by
faith its inner sanctuary, and there presenting ourselves in the presence of God"
(Delitzsch). Cf. especially Ps. li. 6-7,
and Plutarch, *Isis and Osiris*, c. 80 (p. 383)
where ceremonial purifications are explained on the principle that the Pure and
Undefiled must be worshipped by the pure
in body and soul.

Ver. 23. A second branch of the exhortation is given in the words κατέχωμεν τὴν ὁμολογίαν ... "Let
us hold fast and unbending the confession
of our hope," as in iii. 6. Cf. also vi. 11.
For as yet in this life the fulness of blessing which comes of fellowship with God
is not experienced, the perfected salvation
and the heavenly country (xii. 22-23) are
yet to be reached. But these are the
contents of the Christian hope, and this
hope is confessed and maintained in presence of a commonplace, scoffing and
alluring world. It is to be maintained for
the best of all reasons: πιστὸς γὰρ ὁ
ἐπαγγειλάμενος. The promises of God
are necessarily the ground of hope, v.
vi. 12. These promises cannot fail, because God cannot lie, vi. 18.

Ver. 24. To the exhortation to faith
and hope he adds an exhortation to love:
καὶ κατανοῶμεν ἀλλήλους, "and
let us consider one another," taking into
account and weighing our neighbour's
circumstances and especially his risks, but
this with a view not to exasperating
criticism but εἰς παροξυσμὸν ἀγάπης, "with a view to incite them to love
and good works," acknowledging honest
endeavour and making allowance for imperfection. παροξυσμός is "stimulation"
either to good or evil. In Acts xv. 39 it
is used of angry irritation, as in LXX,
Deut. xxix. 28, Jer. xxxix. 37. So in
medical writers of a *paroxysm*. But frequently in classics the verb is used of
stimulating to good as in Plato, *Epist.* iv.
p. 321 and in Xen. *Cyrop.* 6, 2, 5, τούτους ἐπαινῶν παρώξυνε. Isocrates, *ad
Demon.*, etc. The writer, in vi. 9-10, has
set his readers a good example of this
considerate incitement. In order to fulfil
his injunction they must not neglect
meeting together for Christian worship
and encouragement μὴ ἐγκαταλείποντες
τὴν ἐπισυναγωγὴν ἑαυτῶν. Delitzsch
suggests that the compound word is used
instead of the simple συναγωγή in order
to avoid a word with Judaic associations;
but συναγωγή might rather have suggested the building and formal stated
meetings, while ἐπισυν. ἑαυτῶν denotes
merely the meeting together of Christians.
That these meetings were for mutual
edification is shown by the ἀλλὰ παρα-
καλοῦντες. Some made a practice
of neglecting these meetings, whether
from fear of persecution or from scorn or
from business engagements. Cf. Jude,
18-20, and Moberly's *Minist. Priesthood*,
p. 14. This good custom of meeting together and mutually exhorting one another was to be all the more punctually
and zealously attended to, ὅσῳ βλέπετε ἐγγίζουσαν τὴν ἡμέραν,
"in proportion as ye see the day drawing
near". "The day" is of course the day
of the Lord's return (ix. 28), the day of
days. The Epistle being written in all
probability a year or two before the destruction of Jerusalem, the signs of the
coming day which could be "seen" were
probably the restlessness, forebodings of
coming disaster, and initial collisions with

vi. 4;
Num. xv.
30; Matt.
xii. 31; 2
Peter ii.
20, 21; 1
Joan v. 16.
Ezech.
xxxvi. 5;
Sophon i.
18, et iii.
8.

αγωγὴν ἑαυτῶν, καθὼς ἔθος τισὶν, ἀλλὰ παρακαλοῦντες· καὶ τοσούτῳ μᾶλλον ὅσῳ βλέπετε ἐγγίζουσαν τὴν ἡμέραν. 26. ᵐἙκουσίως γὰρ ἁμαρτανόντων ἡμῶν μετὰ τὸ λαβεῖν ιὴν ἐπίγνωσιν τῆς ἀληθείας, οὐκ ἔτι περὶ ἁμαρτιῶν ἀπολείπεται θυσία· 27. ⁿφοβερὰ δέ τις ἐκδοχὴ κρίσεως, καὶ πυρὸς ζῆλος ἐσθίειν μέλλοντος τοὺς ὑπεναντίους. 28. ᵒἀθετήσας τις νόμον Μωσέως, χωρὶς οἰκτιρμῶν ἐπὶ δυσὶν

o Num. xxxv. 30; Deut. xvii. 6, et xix. 15; Matt. xviii. 16; Joan. viii. 17; 2 Cor. xiii. 1.

the Romans which heralded the great war.

Vv. 26-39. Dreadful result of falling from faith.

Ver. 26. Ἑκουσίως γὰρ ἁμαρτανόντων ἡμῶν.... "For if we go on sinning wilfully after receiving the knowledge of the truth, there no more remains a sacrifice for sins, but a certain dreadful waiting for judgment and a fury of fire which is to devour the adversaries." γὰρ, introducing an additional reason for the preceding exhortation. The emphasis is on ἑκουσίως; and the present tense of ἁμαρτ. must not be overlooked. Cf. τῶν ἀκουσίων ἁμαρτημάτων καταφυγὴν εἶναι τοὺς βωμούς, Thuc. iv. 98. Wilful sin, continued in, means apostasy, repudiation of the covenant. Cf. vi. 6, καὶ παραπεσόντας, and v. 2, τοῖς ἀγνοοῦσιν, and iii. 12. Apostasy can only occur μετὰ τὸ λαβεῖν... a condition which is explained in detail in chap. 6. Without this preceding knowledge of the covenant its wilful repudiation is impossible. Those spoken of in ver. 25, as having abandoned meeting with their fellow Christians, and possibly as having neglected, if not renounced, the confession of their hope, were perhaps alluded to here, as on their way to apostasy. They are warned that they are drifting into an irredeemable condition, for to those who have repudiated and keep repudiating the one sacrifice of Christ, οὐκέτι περὶ ἁμαρτίων ἀπολείπεται θυσία. The only sacrifice has been rejected, and there is no other sacrifice which can atone for the rejection of this sacrifice. "The meaning is not merely that the Jewish sacrifices to which the apostate has returned have in themselves no sin-destroying power, nor even that there is no second sacrifice additional to that of Christ, but further that for a sinner of this kind the very sacrifice of Christ itself has no more atoning or reconciling power" (Delitzsch). That this is the meaning is shown by the positive assertion of what the future does contain, a terrifying prospect of waiting

for inevitable judgment. The expression is not equivalent to φοβερᾶς ἐκδοχὴ κρίσεως, which, as Bleek remarks, would not be so impressive. φοβερός means either "causing fear" or "feeling fear"; "scaring" or "affrighted". Here it is used in the former sense. ἐκδοχὴ occurs elsewhere only in the sense of receiving something or of the acceptation or interpretation of a word; but ver. 13 and ix. 28 guide to the meaning given by the Vulg. expectatis. The τις by leaving the expectation indefinite heightens the terror of it. The imagination is allowed scope. κρίσεως is general, but immediately suggests πυρὸς ζῆλος μέλλοντος, the destined fire; for which see 2 Thess. i. 8-10. "Fiery indignation" very well renders πυρὸς ζῆλος, an anger which expresses itself in fire. The expression is derived from such O.T. phrases as Ps. lxxix. 5 ἐκκαυθήσεται ὡς πῦρ ὁ ζῆλός σου. Cf. Zeph. i. 18 and Deut. iv. 21. This fiery anger is destined to devour the adversaries; as in Isa. xxvi. 11 ζῆλος λήψεται λαὸν ἀπαίδευτον, καὶ νῦν πῦρ τοὺς ὑπεναντίους ἔδεται, and lxiv. 2 κατακαύσει πῦρ τοὺς ὑπεναντίους. Cf. also Isa. xxx. 27 ἡ ὀργὴ τοῦ θυμοῦ ὡς πῦρ ἔδεται, a natural figure used by Homer and others. ὑπεναντίους, see Lightfoot on Col. ii. 14, who shows that it means "direct, close, persistent opposition".

Ver. 28. ἀθετήσας τις νόμον.... "Any one who has set aside Moses' law dies without mercy on the evidence of two or three witnesses," in accordance with the law laid down in Deut. xvii. 6 regarding apostasy; although capital punishment was not restricted to this sin. For ἀθετεῖν cf. 1 Thess. iv. 8; and Isa. xxiv. 16, οὐαὶ τοῖς ἀθετοῦσιν, οἱ ἀθετοῦντες τὸν νόμον, also Ezek. xxii. 26. ἀθέτησις is used absolutely in 1 Sam. xxiv. 12. ἐπὶ... μάρτυσιν, cf. ix. 17; ἀποθνήσκει, perhaps the tense does not carry with it the inference that the law was still being enforced. It may only mean "he dies" according to the law as it stands. χωρὶς οἰκτιρμῶν, to emphasise the inexorableness of the

ἢ τρισὶ μάρτυσιν ἀποθνήσκει· 29. ᵖπόσῳ δοκεῖτε χείρονος ἀξιωθή- ᵖ 1 Cor. xi.
σεται τιμωρίας ὁ τὸν υἱὸν τοῦ Θεοῦ καταπατήσας, καὶ τὸ αἷμα τῆς ²⁹·
διαθήκης κοινὸν ἡγησάμενος ἐν ᾧ ἡγιάσθη, καὶ τὸ πνεῦμα τῆς χάριτος ᑫ Deut.
ἐνυβρίσας; 30. ᑫοἴδαμεν γὰρ τὸν εἰπόντα, "Ἐμοὶ ἐκδίκησις, ἐγὼ xxxii. 35,
ἀνταποδώσω, λέγει Κύριος"· καὶ πάλιν, "Κύριος κρινεῖ τὸν λαὸν xii. 19.
αὐτοῦ". 31. Φοβερὸν τὸ ἐμπεσεῖν εἰς χεῖρας Θεοῦ ζῶντος. 32. ᵣ Gal. iii. 4;
ʳἈναμιμνήσκεσθε δὲ τὰς πρότερον ἡμέρας, ἐν αἷς φωτισθέντες πολλὴν Phil. i.
²⁹, ³⁰,
Col. ii. 1.

law and the inevitable character of the doom. *Cf.* Josephus, c. *Apion*, ii. 30, ὁ νόμος ἀπαραίτητος and Ignatius, *ad Eph.* c. 16.

Ver. 29. πόσῳ δοκεῖτε χείρο-νος. ... "Of how much sorer punishment, think ye, will he be counted worthy, who, etc." The argument of ii. 1-4 and xii. 25. By the parenthetically interjected δοκεῖτε he appeals to their own sense of proportion and fitness; although the judgment alluded to in ἀξιωθήσεται is not theirs but God's. ὁ ... καταπατ-ήσας ... The guilt of the apostate which justifies this sorer punishment is detailed in three particulars. He has trampled on the Son of God. The highest of Beings who has deserved best at his hands is spurned with outrageous scorn. καὶ τὸ αἷμα ... ἡγιάσθη "and has reckoned the blood of the covenant with which he was sanctified, a common thing". "The blood of the covenant" is the blood of Christ (*cf.* ix. 15 ff., xiii. 20); here it is thus designated because repudiation of the covenant is in question. This blood is the purifying agent by which men are fitted for the fellowship and service of God, and so brought within the covenant. *Cf.* ἡγιάσθη with ἁγιάζει of ix. 13 and καθ-αριεῖ of ix. 14. This sole means of purification, the sanctifying virtue of which the supposed apostate has experienced, he now counts κοινὸν, common or unclean. [The Vulg. has "pollutum," the Old Latin "communem". Chrysostom ἀκάθαρτον ἢ τὸ μηδὲν πλέον ἔχον τῶν λοιπῶν; and so Kübel, "which has no more worth than the blood of other men". All these meanings lie close to one another. *Cf.* Mark vii. 2, Acts x. 14. What is "common" is unsanctified, ceremonially unclean.] The third point in the heinousness of the sin of apostasy is τὸ πνεῦμα τῆς χάριτος ἐνυ-βρίσας, "and has insulted the spirit of grace". This seems the direct antithesis to "Moses' law" of ver. 28. The spirit of grace is the distinctive gift of Christian times, and is not only the

Pauline but the universal antithesis to the law. To have blasphemed this gracious Spirit, who brings the assurance of God's presence and pardon, and gifts suited to each believer, is to renounce all part in things spiritual. *Cf.* vi. 4, ii. 4; Eph. iv. 7.

Ver. 30. οἴδαμεν γὰρ τὸν εἰπόντα. ... "For we know Him who said, vengeance is mine, I will repay." The certainty of the punishment spoken of is based upon the righteousness of God. "We know who it is that said"; it is the living God (v. 31). The quotation is from Deut. xxxii. 35 not as in the LXX but as given in Rom. xii. 19 where it is used as an argument for the surrender of private vengeance. In Deut. LXX the words are Ἐν ἡμέρᾳ ἐκδικήσεως ἀντ-αποδώσω. The second quotation, κρινεῖ κύριος ... is from the following verse where the words intimate God's protecting care of His people, using κρινεῖ in the sense common in O.T. Delitzsch thinks that sense may be retained here, but this is less relevant and consistent with the passage. *Cf.* Ecclus. xxvii. 28 ἡ ἐκδίκησις ὡς λέων. and xxviii. 1. φοβερὸν τὸ ἐμπεσεῖν. ... "It is dreadful to fall into the hands of the living God". Where David (2 Sam. xxiv. 14) prefers to do so [ἐμπεσοῦμαι δὴ εἰς χεῖρας κυρίου] it is because he knows his chastisement will be measured and that no unjust advantage will be taken. The dreadfulness of the impenitent's doom arises from the same certainty that absolute justice will be done. As Judge, God is "the living God", who sees and has power to execute just judgment, *cf.* iii. 12, xii. 22, *cf.* xii. 29.

Ver. 32. As in the parallel passage in chap. 6, the writer at ver. 9 suddenly turns from the presentation of the terrifying aspect of apostasy to make appeal to more generous motives, so here he now encourages them to perseverance by reminding them of their praiseworthy past. As Vaughan remarks, the thought is that of Gal. iii. 3. ἀναμιμνήσκε-σθε δὲ τὰς πρότερον ἡμέρας.

s Phil. i. 7, ἄθλησιν ὑπεμείνατε παθημάτων· 33. ᵃτοῦτο μὲν, ὀνειδισμοῖς τε καὶ
et iv. 14.
t Matt. v. θλίψεσι θεατριζόμενοι· τοῦτο δὲ, κοινωνοὶ τῶν οὕτως ἀναστρεφομένων
12, et vi.
20, et xix. γενηθέντες· 34. ᵇκαὶ γὰρ τοῖς δεσμοῖς ¹ μου συνεπαθήσατε, καὶ τὴν
21; Luc.
xii. 33; ἁρπαγὴν τῶν ὑπαρχόντων ὑμῶν μετὰ χαρᾶς προσεδέξασθε, γινώσκοντες
Acts v.
41, et xxi. ἔχειν ἐν ἑαυτοῖς κρείττονα ὕπαρξιν ἐν οὐρανοῖς καὶ μένουσαν. 35.
33; I
1 hess. ii. ᵘμὴ ἀποβάλητε οὖν τὴν παρρησίαν ὑμῶν, ἥτις ἔχει μισθαποδοσίαν
14; I
Tim. vi. 19; Jac. i. 2.   u Matt. x. 32.

¹ T.R. in אDᶜEHKLP, d, e, Aeth.; δεσμιοις AD* f, vg., Syrᵘtr, Copt., Arm.

. . . "But recall the former days, in
which after being enlightened ye endured
much wrestling with sufferings". ἀνα-
μιμ, "remind yourselves," as in 2 Cor.
vii. 15. See Wetstein's examples, where
the genitive not the accusative follows the
verb, and M. Aurelius, v. 31. τὰς πρότερον ἡμ. [as in Thucyd., vi. 9 ἐν τῷ
πρότερον χρόνῳ.] days separated from
the present by some considerable interval,
as is implied in v. 12. They are further
described as ἐν αἷς φωτισθέντες
as in vi. 4; equivalent to "receiving the
knowledge of the truth,"ver. 26. It was
the new light in Christ, shed upon their
relation to God and on their prospects,
which enabled them to endure much
wrestling or conflict with sufferings.
ἄθλησις in the next generation came to
mean "martyrdom," as in *Mart. of S.
Ignatius*, chap. 4. [For the genitive
cf. "certamina divitiarum," Hor. *Epp.*,
i. 5 8.] What these sufferings were
is described in two clauses, they were
partly in their own persons, partly in
their sympathy and voluntary sharing
in the suffering of others, τοῦτο μὲν . . .
θεατριζόμενοι, τοῦτο δὲ κοινωνοὶ . . .
For the distributive formula, "partly," . . .
"partly," see abundant examples from the
classics in Wetstein. See also Plutarch's
Them., v. 4. It may be rendered "as
well by," "as by". θεατριζόμενοι,
"made a spectacle," [ὥσπερ ἐπὶ θεάτρου
παραδειγματιζόμενοι, Theophyl., *cf.* 1
Cor. iv. 9], literally true of the Christians
who were exposed to wild beasts in the
amphitheatre. See Renan's *L'Antéchrist*,
pp. 162 ff., "A la barbarie des supplices
on ajouta la dérision". But here it was
not by lions and leopards and wild bulls
they were attacked, but ὀνειδισμοῖς
τε καὶ θλίψεσιν, "reproaches and
distresses," "opprobriis et tribulationi-
bus" (Vulg.). ὀνειδισμός is frequent
in LXX, and several times in the phrase
λόγοι ὀνειδ. In this Epistle it occurs
again in xi. 26 and xiii. 13, and *cf.* 1 Pet.
iv. 14. Some who have not directly suffered persecution in these forms suffered
by sympathy and by identifying themselves with those who were experiencing
such usage, τῶν οὕτως ἀναστρεφομένων. *Cf.* Phil. iv. 14. Farrar
renders well, "who lived in this condition of things". In what sense they
became κοινωνοί is immediately explained; they sympathised with those
who were imprisoned and welcomed the
violent seizure of their possessions. καὶ
γὰρ, as always, must here be rendered
"For indeed," "for in point of fact,"
proving by more definite instances that
they had become partakers with the persecuted. They had felt for the imprisoned, as was possibly alluded to in
vi. 10, and as they are in xiii. 3 exhorted
still to do. *Cf.* Mat. xxv. 36, which probably formed a large factor in the production of that care for the persecuted
which characterised the early Church.
They had also suffered the loss of their
goods. ἁρπαγήν, the violent and unjust
seizure, as in Mat. xxiii. 25, Luke xi. 39.
ἁρπαγὴ ὑπαρχόντων occurs in Lucian
and Artemidorus. See Stephanus. That
which enables them to take joyfully the
loss of their possessions is their consciousness that they have a possession
which is better and which cannot be
taken away. γινώσκοντες ἔχειν
ἑαυτοὺς [for ὑμᾶς αὐτούς]. If the
true reading is ἑαυτοῖς then the meaning
is easy "knowing that you have for
yourselves". If we read ἑαυτούς, this
may mean, as Davidson, Westcott and
others suppose, "knowing that you have
yourselves a better possession". But
this seems not very congruous with the
writer's usual style. It is more likely that
the writer uses the emphatic "you yourselves" in contrast to those who had
robbed them and now possessed their
goods. So von Soden. Or it may mean
"ye yourselves" in contrast to the possession itself of which they have been
deprived, ye yourselves however stripped
of all earthly goods.
Ver. 35. μὴ ἀποβάλητε οὖν τὴν παρρησίαν . . . "Cast not away, then, your

μεγάλην.   36. ˅ὑπομονῆς γὰρ ἔχετε χρείαν, ἵνα τὸ θέλημα τοῦ ᵛ Luc. xxi.
                                                                     19.
Θεοῦ ποιήσαντες, κομίσησθε τὴν ἐπαγγελίαν.   37. ʷ ῞Ετι γὰρ μικ- ʷ Hab. ii. 3,
                                                                     4; Agg.
ρὸν ὅσον ὅσον, "ὁ ἐρχόμενος ἥξει, καὶ οὐ χρονιεῖ.   38. ὁ δὲ δίκαιος ii. 6; Luc.
                                                                     xviii. 8;
ἐκ πίστεως ¹ ζήσεται· καὶ ἐὰν ὑποστείληται, οὐκ εὐδοκεῖ ἡ ψυχή   Rom. i.
                                                                     17; Gal.
                              iii. 11; 1 Peter i. 6, et ꝩ. 10; 2 Peter iii. 8.

¹ In B of LXX μου follows πιστεως, in A it follows δικαιος. B gives the more
probable reading. In the text of Hebrews T.R. omits μου with DEH**KLP. μου
is inserted after δικαιος in ℵAH*, f, vg., Arm., Clem., Thdrt. Cp. Rom. i. 17, Gal.
iii. 11.

confidence, for it has great recompense
of reward'. The exhortation begun in
ver. 19 is resumed, with now the added
force springing from their remembrance
of what they have already endured and
from their consciousness of a great possession in heaven. A reason for holding
fast their confidence is now found in the
result of so doing. It has great reward.
μισθαποδοσία used in ii. 2 of requital of
sin, here and in xi. 26 of reward. Cf.
Clem. ad Cor. 6, γέρας γενναῖον, and
Wisdom iii. 5. Therefore, μὴ ἀποβάλητε, do not throw it away as a worthless thing you have no further need of.
Retain it, ὑπομονῆς γὰρ ἔχετε χρείαν,
"for ye have need of endurance," of maintaining your hopeful confidence to the
end under all circumstances. Without
endurance the promise which secures to
them the enduring possession cannot be
enjoyed, for before entering upon its enjoyment, the whole will of God concerning them must be done and borne. ἵνα
τὸ θέλημα τ. θεοῦ ποιήσαντες κομίσησθε
τὴν ἐπαγγελίαν, Davidson and Weiss
agree in thinking that "the will of God
is His will that they should hold fast their
confidence". Rather, that accepting all
privation, as they once did (ver. 32) and
recognising all they were called to endure as God's will concerning them, they
should thus endure to the end (cf. iii. 6)
and so receive the promised good (ἐπαγγελία = the thing promised as in vi. 12,
15). κομίσησθε, the verb properly means
to carry off or to recover what is one's
own. See Mat. xxv. 27; 2 Cor. v. 10;
Heb. xi. 13, 19, 39. And their entrance
on the reward of their endurance will not
long be delayed ἔτι γὰρ μικρὸν
ὅσον ὅσον. . . . "For yet a little—
a very little—while and He that cometh
will have come and will not delay."
["Es ist noch ein Kleines, wie sehr, wie
sehr Klein " (Weiss), "noch eine kleine
Zeit, ganz Klein" (Weizsäcker). "Adhuc enim modicum aliquantulum"
(Vulg.). "For yet a little—ever so little
—while" (Hayman)]. The phrase μικ-

ρὸν ὅσον ὅσον is found in Isa. xxvi. 20,
"Go, my people . . . hide thyself for a
very little, till the indignation be over-
past". The double ὅσον is found in
Aristoph. Wasps, 213, where however
Rogers thinks the duplication due to the
drowsiness of the speaker. Literally it
means "a little, how very, how very".
The following words from ὁ ἐρχόμενος
to ἐν αὐτῷ are from Heb. ii. 3-4, with
some slight alterations, the article being
inserted before ἐρχόμενος, οὐ μὴ χρονίσῃ
instead of the less forcible words in
Hebrews, and the two clauses of ver. 4
being transposed. In Habakkuk the conditions are similar. God's people are
crushed under overwhelming odds. And
the question with which Habakkuk opens
his prophecy is ἕως τίνος κεκράξομαι
καὶ οὐ μὴ εἰσακούσεις; The Lord assures him that deliverance will come and
will not delay. By inserting the article,
the writer of Hebrews identifies the deliverer as the Messiah, "the coming
One". Cf. Mat. xi. 3; Luke vii. 19; Jo.
vi. 14. ὁ δὲ δίκαιος. . . . "And the
just sha'l live by faith," i.e., shall survive
these troublous times by believing that
the Lord is at hand. Cf. Jas. v. 7-9.
καὶ ἐὰν ὑποστείληται, "and if he
withdraw himself" or "shrink". The
verb, as Kypke shows, means to shrink
in fear, and it is thus used in Gal. ii. 12.
It is the very opposite of παρρησία.
Accordingly it is thoroughly displeasing
to God, whose purpose it is to bring men
to Himself in confident hope. But the
idea that any of the "Hebrews" can be
in so ignominious and dangerous a position is at once repudiated. ἡμεῖς δὲ. . . .
"But as for us we are not of those who
shrink (literally of shrinking) to perdition
but of faith to the gaining of the soul".
That is, we are not characterised by a
timid abandonment of our confession
(ver. 23) and confidence. Cf. 1 Thess.
v. 5. What such timidity leads to (εἰς
ἀπώλειαν, cf. Acts viii. 20; Rom. ix. 22)
is hopeless perdition. Cf. M. Aurelius
on the δραπέτης, x. 25. ὁ φοβούμενος

μου ἐν αὐτῷ." 39. Ἡμεῖς δὲ οὐκ ἐσμὲν ὑποστολῆς εἰς ἀπώλειαν,
ἀλλὰ πίστεως εἰς περιποίησιν ψυχῆς.

a Rom. viii. 24; 2 Cor. iv. 18.

XI. 1. a῎ΕΣΤΙ δὲ πίστις ἐλπιζομένων ὑπόστασις, πραγμάτων

assurance of things
is Now faith

δραπέτης. But we are of faith whose end is περιποίησις ψυχῆς the acquisition of one's soul. Very similar is Luke xxi. 19, "By your endurance win your souls". See also James v. 20, and 1 Thess. v. 9. Like our word "acquisition" περιποίησις sometimes means the acquiring as in 1 Thess. v. 9 and 2 Thess. ii. 14; sometimes the thing acquired as in Eph. i. 14. [In Isocrates, 2nd Ep., occurs the expression διὰ τὸ περιποιῆσαι τὴν αὐτοῦ ψυχήν (Wetstein)].

CHAPS. XI. 1—XII. 3. That the Hebrews may still further be encouraged to persevere in maintaining faith the writer exhibits in detail its victories in the past history of their people and especially in the life of Jesus. (Cf. Sirach, 44-50.)

Ver. 1. ῎Εστιν δὲ πίστις ἐλπιζομένων ὑπόστασις . . . "Now faith is assurance of things hoped for, proof [manifestation] of things not seen". When ἔστι stands first in a sentence it sometimes means "there exists," as in John v. 2; 1 Cor. xv. 44. But it has not necessarily and always this significance, cf. 1 Tim. vi. 6; Luke viii. 11; Wisdom vii. 1. There is therefore no need to place a comma after πίστις as some have done. The words describe what faith is, although not a strict definition. "Longe falluntur, qui justam fidei definitionem hic poni existimant: neque enim hic de tota fidei natura disserit Apostolus, sed partem elegit suo instituto congruentem, nempe quod cum patientia semper conjuncta sit" (Calvin). ὑπόστασις, literally foundation, that which stands under; hence, the ground on which one builds a hope, naturally gliding into the meaning "assurance," "confidence," as in iii. 14; 2 Cor. ix. 4, xi. 17; Ruth i. 12; Ps. xxxix. 7, ἡ ὑπόστασίς μου παρὰ σοί ἐστιν. ῎Ελεγχος regularly means "proof". See Demosthenes, passim; especially Agt. Androtion, p. 600, ἔλεγχος, ὧν ἂν εἴπῃ τις καὶ τἀληθὲς ὁμοῦ δείξῃ. It seems never to be used in a subjective sense for "conviction," "persuasion"; although here this meaning would suit the context and has been adopted by many. To say with Weiss that the subjective meaning *must* be given to the word that it may correspond with ὑπόστασις is to write the Epistle, not to interpret it. Theophylact renders

the clause φανέρωσις ἀδήλων πραγμάτων. Faith is that which enables us to treat as real the things that are unseen. Hatch gives a different meaning to both clauses: "Faith is the ground of things hoped for, i.e., trust in God, or the conviction that God is good and that He will perform His promises, is the ground for confident hope that the things hoped for will come to pass. . . . So trust in God furnishes to the mind which has it a clear proof that things to which God has testified exist, though they are not visible to the senses." The words thus become a definition of what faith does, not of what it is. Substantially the words mean that faith gives to things future, which as yet are only hoped for, all the reality of actual present existence; and irresistibly convinces us of the reality of things unseen and brings us into their presence. Things future and things unseen must become certainties to the mind if a balanced life is to be lived. Faith mediating between man and the supersensible is the essential link between himself and God, "for in it lay the commendation of the men of old," ἐν ταύτῃ γὰρ ἐμαρτυρήθησαν οἱ πρεσβύτεροι. That is, it was on the ground or their possessing faith that the distinguished men of the O.T. received the commendation of God, being immortalised in Scripture. It might almost be rendered "by faith of this kind," answering to this description. ἐν ταύτῃ has an exact parallel in 1 Tim. v. 10, the widow who is to be placed on the Church register must be ἐν ἔργοις καλοῖς μαρτυρουμένη, well-reported of on the score of good works. οἱ πρεσβύτεροι, those of past generations, men of the O.T. times; as Papias [Euseb., H.E., iii. 39] uses the term to denote the "Fathers of the Church" belonging to the generation preceding his own. The idea that faith is that which God finds pleasure in (x. 38) and is that which truly unites to God under the old dispensations as well as under the new is a Pauline thought, Gal. iii. 6. This general statement of ver. 2 is exhibited in detail in the remainder of the chapter; but first the writer shows the excellence of faith in this, that it is by it that we recognise that there is an unseen world and that out of things unseen this visible world has taken

Conviction not seen *by the For*

ἔλεγχος οὐ βλεπομένων. 2. ἐν ταύτῃ γὰρ ἐμαρτυρήθησαν οἱ πρεσβύτεροι. 3. ᵇΠίστει νοοῦμεν κατηρτίσθαι τοὺς αἰῶνας ῥήματι Θεοῦ,
εἰς τὸ μὴ ἐκ φαινομένων τὰ βλεπόμενα ¹ γεγονέναι. 4. ᶜΠίστει
πλείονα θυσίαν Ἄβελ παρὰ Κάϊν προσήνεγκε τῷ Θεῷ, δι᾽ ἧς ἐμαρτυρήθη εἶναι δίκαιος, μαρτυροῦντος ἐπὶ τοῖς δώροις αὐτοῦ τοῦ Θεοῦ·

ᵇ Gen. i. 1;
Ps.xxxiii.
6; Rom.
iv. 17; 2
Peter iii.
5;
ᶜ xii. 24;
Gen. iv.
4, 10;
Matt.
xxiii. 35.

¹ τὸ βλεπομενον in אAD*E*P, 17, d, e, Copt., Aeth.; T.R. in DcE**KL, f, vg.,
Syrutr, Arm.

rise. This idea is suggested to him because his eye is on *Genesis* from which he culls the succeeding examples and it is natural that he should begin at the beginning. "Before exhibiting how faith is the principle that rules the life of men in relation to God, down through all history, as it is transacted on the stage of the world, the author shows how this stage itself is brought into connection with God by an act of faith" (Davidson). By faith we perceive, with the mental eye νοοῦμεν, *cf.* Rom. i. 20, that the worlds (αἰῶνας, *cf.* i. 2; the visible world existing in time, the temporary manifestation of the unseen is meant, see i. 10, 11) have been framed (κατηρτίσθαι, as in x. 5, σῶμα δὲ κατηρτίσω μοι. In xiii. 21 καταρτίσαι ὑμᾶς, "perfect you" as in Luke vi. 40; 2 Cor. xiii. 11; 1 Thess. iii. 10. The word is perhaps used in the present connection to suggest not a bare calling into existence, but a wise adaptation of part to part and of the whole to its purpose) by God's word, ῥήματι θεοῦ. This is the perception of faith. The word of God is an invisible force which cannot be perceived by sense. The great power which lies at the source of all that is does not itself come into observation; we perceive it only by faith which is (ver. 1) "the evidence of things not seen". The result of this creation by an unseen force, the word of God, is that "what is seen has not come into being out of things which appear". εἰς τὸ . . . γεγονέναι. εἰς τὸ with infinitive, commonly used to express purpose, is sometimes as here used to express result, and we may legitimately translate "so that what is seen, etc." *Cf.* Luke v. 17; Rom. xii. 3; 2 Cor. viii. 6; Gal. iii. 17; 1 Thess. ii. 16. *Cf.* Burton, *M. and T.*, 411. μὴ ἐκ φαινομένων, the Vulgate renders "ex invisibilibus," and the Old Latin "ex non apparentibus" having apparently read ἐκ μὴ φαιν. τὸ βλεπόμενον the singular in place of the plural of T.R. and Vulgate, presents all things visible as unity. Had the visible world been formed out of

materials which were subject to human observation, there would have been no room for faith. Science could have traced it to its origin. Evolution only pushes the statement a stage back. There is still an unseen force that does not submit itself to experimental science, and that is the object of faith. To find in this verse an allusion to the noumenal and phenomenal worlds would be fanciful.

Ver. 4. πίστει πλείονα θυσίαν. . . . "By faith Abel offered to God a more adequate sacrifice than Cain." πλείονα literally "more," but frequently used to express "higher in value" "greater in worth," as in Mat. xii. 41, 42. πλείον Ἰωνᾶ ὧδε, Luke xii. 23; Rev. ii. 19. Does the writer mean that faith prompted Abel to make a richer sacrifice, or that it was richer because offered in faith? Many interpreters prefer the former alternative; ["Der grössere Wert seines Opfers ruhte auf dem Glauben, der Herzenshingabe, die ihn das Beste der Herde wählen liess" (Kübel).] and the choice of the word πλείονα is certainly in favour of this interpretation. δι᾽ ἧς ἐμαρτυρήθη . . . "through which he was certified [or attested] as righteous". It is questioned whether ἧς is the relative of θυσίαν or of πίστει. The succeeding clause which states the ground of the attestation, ἐπὶ τ. δώροις, determines that it refers to θυσίαν. God bore witness ἐπὶ τοῖς δώροις αὐτοῦ, which is explained in Genesis iv. 4 where it says ἐπεῖδεν ὁ θεὸς ἐπὶ Ἄβελ καὶ ἐπὶ τοῖς δώροις αὐτοῦ. God looked favourably on Abel and on his gifts. How this favourable reception of his offering was intimated to Abel we are not told; but by this testimony Abel was pronounced δίκαιος, not "justified" in the Pauline sense but in the general sense "a righteous man"; as in Mat. xxiii. 35 ἀπὸ τοῦ αἵματος Ἄβελ τοῦ δικαίου. But this is not all that faith did for Abel, for καὶ δι᾽ αὐτῆς ἀποθανὼν ἔτι λαλεῖ, "and through the same he, though dead, yet speaks," *i.e.*, speaks notwithstanding

d Gen. v. 24; Eccl. xliv. 16, et xlix. 14.

• Gen. vi. 13; Eccl. xliv. 17; Rom. iii. 22; Phil. iii. 9.

καὶ δι' αὐτῆς ἀποθανὼν ἔτι λαλεῖται. 5. ᵈ Πίστει Ἐνὼχ μετετέθη τοῦ μὴ ἰδεῖν θάνατον, καὶ " οὐχ εὑρίσκετο,¹ διότι μετέθηκεν αὐτὸν ὁ Θεός"· πρὸ γὰρ τῆς μεταθέσεως αὐτοῦ μεμαρτύρηται " εὐηρεστηκέναι τῷ Θεῷ"· 6. χωρὶς δὲ πίστεως ἀδύνατον εὐαρεστῆσαι· πιστεῦσαι γὰρ δεῖ τὸν προσερχόμενον τῷ Θεῷ, ὅτι ἐστὶ, καὶ τοῖς ἐκζητοῦσιν αὐτὸν μισθαποδότης γίνεται. 7. ᵉ Πίστει χρηματισθεὶς Νῶε περὶ

¹ ηυρισκετο in ℵADE.

death. His death was not the end of him as Cain expected it to be. Abel's blood cried for justice. The words of xii. 24 are at once suggested, αἵματι ῥαντισμοῦ κρεῖττον λαλοῦντι παρὰ τὸν Ἄβελ, where the blood of sprinkling is said to speak to better purpose than the blood of Abel. This again takes us back to Gen. iv. 10. "The voice of thy brother's blood cries to me from the ground." The speaking referred to, therefore, is not the continual voice of Abel's example but the voice of his blood crying to God immediately after his death. Cf. Ps. ix. 12 and cxvi. 15. "Precious in the sight of the Lord is the death of His saints." In the case of Abel, then, the excellence of faith was illustrated in two particulars, it prompted him to offer a richer, more acceptable offering, and it found for him a place in God's regard even after his death.

Ver. 5. Πίστει Ἐνὼχ μετετέθη. . . . "By faith Enoch was translated so that he did not see death; and he was not found, because God had translated him. For before his translation he had witness borne to him that he had pleased God well; but without faith it is impossible to please Him well." In the dry catalogue of antediluvian longevities a gem of faith is detected. What lay at the root of Enoch's translation? Faith, because before he was translated he was well-pleasing to God, which implies that he believed in God, or as Chrysostom neatly puts it : πῶς δὲ πίστει μετετέθη ὁ Ἐνὼχ ; ὅτι τῆς μεταθέσεως ἡ εὐαρέστησις αἰτία, τῆς δὲ εὐαρεστήσεως ἡ πίστις. In Ecclus. xliv. 16 he is exhibited as ὑπόδειγμα μετανοίας ταῖς γενεαῖς. μετετέθη "was transferred," removed from one place to another, as in Acts vii. 16, cf. also Gal. i. 6, Jude 4. In Ecclus. lxix. 14 it is represented by ἀνελήφθη ἀπὸ τῆς γῆς. The succeeding clauses imply that his body disappeared. How the tradition arose we have no means of knowing, cf. Suicer, i. 1130, and the Bible Dictionaries. τοῦ μὴ ἰδεῖν may either imply purpose or result. For the former see Mat. ii. 13, Luke ii. 24, Phil. iii. 10; for

the latter, Mat. xxi. 32, Acts vii. 19, Rom. vii. 3, Heb. x. 7. The use of the passive μετετέθη favours the supposition that result is here expressed, and throughout the sentence it is the translation that is prominent rather than the escape from death, which is introduced rather as an explanation of μετετέθη. καὶ οὐχ ηὑρίσκετο. . . . These words are verbatim from the LXX of Gen. v. 24, and are quoted for the sake of bringing out clearly that God was the author of the translation. (Cf. the misquotation in Clem. Ep., chap. 9, οὐχ εὑρέθη αὐτοῦ θάνατος.) God translated him, and this is proved by the fact that preceding the statement of his translation Scripture records that he pleased God well, where the Hebrew has "he walked with God". χωρὶς δὲ πίστεως ἀδύνατον εὐαρεστῆσαι. "But without faith it is impossible to please Him well." The ground of this proposition is given in the following words: πιστεῦσαι γὰρ δεῖ τὸν προσερχόμενον. . . . "For he who cometh to God must believe that He exists and that to those who seek Him He turns out to be a rewarder." To please God one must draw near to Him (τὸν προσερχόμενον in the semi-technical sense usual in the Epistle), and no one can draw near who has not these two beliefs that God is and will reward those who seek Him. So that Enoch's faith, and the faith of every one who approaches God, verifies the description of ver. 1: the unseen must be treated as sufficiently demonstrated, and the hoped for reward must be considered substantial.

Ver. 7. Πίστει χρηματισθεὶς Νῶε. . . . "By faith Noah, on being divinely warned of things not as yet seen, with reverential heed prepared an ark to save his household." Both here and in Mat. ii. 12, 22 χρημ ατ. is translated "warned of God," although "divinely instructed" as in viii. 5 is admissible in all the passages. πίστει must be construed with εὐλαβηθεὶς κατεσκεύασεν and these words must be kept together, although some join εὐλαβηθεὶς with

τῶν μηδέπω βλεπομένων, εὐλαβηθεὶς κατεσκεύασε κιβωτὸν εἰς σωτηρίαν τοῦ οἴκου αὐτοῦ· δι᾽ ἧς κατέκρινε τὸν κόσμον, καὶ τῆς κατὰ
πίστιν δικαιοσύνης ἐγένετο κληρονόμος.   8. ᵗΠίστει καλούμενος ¹ f Gen. xii.
'Αβραὰμ ὑπήκουσεν ἐξελθεῖν εἰς τὸν τόπον ὃν ἤμελλε λαμβάνειν εἰς   1, 4; Acts
vii. 2.

¹ ὁ καλούμενος in AD* 17, Arm., a reading which Calvin censures as "nimio dilutum
ac frigidum".

the preceding words. τ ῶ ν μ η δ έ π ω
β λ ε π, *i.e.*, the flood; *cf.* Gen vi. 14.
ε ὐ λ α β η θ ε ὶ ς here used in preference to
φοβηθεὶς because it is not a timorous
dread of the catastrophe that is signified,
but a commendable caution springing
from regard to God's word. In obedience to this feeling he prepared an ark
[κιβωτὸν used of the ark of the covenant
in ix. 4, and of Noah's ship in Gen. vi. 15,
because it was shaped like a box with a
roof. In Wisdom x. 4 it is spoken of as
"worthless timber," to magnify the salvation accomplished by its means. δι᾽ εὐτε-
λοῦς ξύλου τὸν δίκαιον (Σοφία) κυβ-
ερνήσασα and in Wisdom xiv. 7 it is
ξύλον δι᾽ οὗ γίνεται δικαιοσύνη.] This
ark he built for the saving of his family;
as in Gen. vii. 1 God says to Noah,
εἴσελθε σὺ καὶ πᾶς ὁ οἶκός σου. By
this faith [δι᾽ ἧς] and its manifestation in
preparing the ark, "he condemned the
world"; of which the most obvious
meaning is that Noah's faith threw into
relief the unbelief of those about him.
Cf. Mat. xii. 41. But to this, Weiss objects that in Hebrews κόσμος is not used
to denote the world of men. He therefore concludes that what is meant is that
Noah by building the ark for his own
rescue showed that he considered the
world doomed, thus passing judgment
upon it. Certainly the former meaning
is the more natural and the objection of
Weiss has little weight. A second result
of his faith was that "he entered into
possession of the righteousness which
faith carries with it". The original significance of κληρονόμος is here, as often
elsewhere, left behind. It means little
more than "owner". But no doubt
underneath the word there lies the idea,
familiar to the Jewish mind, that spiritual
blessings are a heritage bestowed by God.
ἡ κατὰ πίστιν δικαιοσύνη is
rendered by Winer (p. 502) "the righteousness which is in consequence of
faith" and he instructively compares Mat.
xix. 3, ἀπολῦσαι τὴν γυναῖκα κατὰ πᾶσαν
αἰτίαν, and Acts iii. 17, κατ᾽ ἄγνοιαν
ἐπράξατε. The first statement in the
history of Noah (Gen. vi. 10) is, Νῶε
ἄνθρωπος δίκαιος, τέλειος ὢν ἐν τῇ γενεᾷ

αὐτοῦ, τῷ θεῷ εὐηρέστησε Νῶε. *Cf.*
Wisdom x. 4. In Genesis the warning
of God is communicated to Noah because
he was already righteous; in Hebrews a
somewhat different aspect is presented,
Noah "became" righteous by building
the ark in faith. He was one of those
who διὰ πίστεως ἠργάσαντο δικαιοσύνην, ver. 33.

From ver. 8 to ver. 22 the faith of the
patriarchs is exhibited, *cf.* Ecclus. xliv. 19.

Ver. 8. Πίστει καλούμενος 'Αβραάμ.
. . . "By faith Abraham on being called
to go out to a place which he was to
receive as an inheritance, obeyed and
went out not knowing whither he was
going." καλούμενος, as in Mark i. 20
and Isa. li. 2, ἐμβλέψατε 'Αβραάμ . . .
ὅτι εἷς ἦν, καὶ ἐκάλεσα αὐτόν. The
present, not κληθείς, expresses the idea
that no sooner was the call given than it
was obeyed ["dass er, so wie der Ruf
an ihn ging, gehorsamte" (Bleek)]. The
same idea is expressed by the immediate
introduction of ὑπήκουσεν, which more
naturally would come at the end of the
clause, and thus allow ἐξελθεῖν (*cf.* Gen.
xii. 1; Acts vii. 2) to follow καλούμενος.
The faith of Abraham appeared in his
promptly abandoning his own country on
God's promise of another, and the strength
of this faith was illustrated by the circumstance that he had no knowledge
where or what that country was. He
went out μὴ ἐπιστάμενος ποῦ ἔρχεται.
The terms of the call (Gen. xii. 1) were
ἔξελθε . . . καὶ δεῦρο εἰς τὴν γῆν, ἣν ἄν
σοι δείξω. It was, therefore, no attractive account of Canaan which induced
him to forsake Mesopotamia, no ordinary
emigrant's motive which moved him, but
mere faith in God's promise. "Even
still the life of faith must be entered on in
ignorance of the way to the inheritance, or
even what the inheritance and rest in each
one's particular case will be, and of the
experiences that the way will bring. This
is true even of ordinary life" (Davidson).
This did not exhaust the faith of Abraham. Further πίστει παρῴκησεν. . . .
"By faith he became a sojourner in a land
[his] by the promise as if it belonged to
another, dwelling in tents, along with

κληρονομίαν, καὶ ἐξῆλθε μὴ ἐπιστάμενος ποῦ ἔρχεται. 9. Πίστει

παρῴκησεν εἰς τὴν γῆν τῆς ἐπαγγελίας ὡς ἀλλοτρίαν, ἐν σκηναῖς
g iii. 4, et
xii. 22, et κατοικήσας μετὰ Ἰσαὰκ καὶ Ἰακὼβ τῶν συγκληρονόμων τῆς ἐπαγ-
xiii. 14;
Apoc.xxi. γελίας τῆς αὐτῆς· 10. ᵍ ἐξεδέχετο γὰρ τὴν τοὺς θεμελίους ἔχουσαν
2.
h Gen. xvii. πόλιν, ἧς τεχνίτης καὶ δημιουργὸς ὁ Θεός.
19, et xxi.
2; Luc. i. 11. ʰ Πίστει καὶ αὐτὴ Σάρρα δύναμιν εἰς καταβολὴν σπέρματος
36; Rom.
iv. 19. ἔλαβε, καὶ παρὰ καιρὸν ἡλικίας ἔτεκεν, ἐπεὶ πιστὸν ἡγήσατο τὸν

Isaac and Jacob, co-heirs with him of the same promise." παρῴκησεν, as in Acts vii. 6, πάροικον ἐν γῇ ἀλλοτρίᾳ, dwelt alongside of the proper inhabitants. *Cf.* Gen. xvii. 8 and *passim.* εἰς in its common pregnant sense, Jo. xxi. 4; Acts viii. 40; Pet. v. 12 and especially Acts vii. 4. He lived in the promised land, ὡς ἀλλοτρίαν, as if it belonged to some other person; neither did he make a permanent settlement in it but dwelt in tents, shifting from place to place, the symbol of what is temporary, see Isa. xxxviii. 12; 2 Cor. v. 4. The presence of his son and grandson must continually have prompted him to settle. They were included in the promise, but they too were compelled to move with him from place to place. But how did this evince faith? It did so by showing that he had given a wider scope and a deeper significance to God's words. He was content to dwell in tents, because he looked for "the city which has the foundations". ἐξεδέχετο γὰρ τὴν . . . πόλιν. "For he expectantly waited for the city." ἐκδέχομαι (Jas. v. 7, ὁ γεωργὸς ἐκδεχ., Acts xvii. 16; 1 Cor. xi. 33) occurs in Soph. *Phil.*, 123, where Jebb says: "The idea of the compound is 'be ready for him,' prepared to deal with him the moment he appears". The city is described as one "that has the foundations" which the tents lacked, and which according to xiii. 14 is by implication not only μέλλουσαν but μένουσαν. In xii. 22 it is called "the city of the living God, the heavenly Jerusalem," and in Gal. iv. 26 ἡ ἄνω Ἱερουσαλήμ. A city was the symbol of a settled condition, as in Ps. cvii. 7, πόλις κατοικητηρίου. *Cf.* the interesting parallel in Philo. *Leg. Alleg.*, iii.-xxvi., p. 103, πόλις δέ ἐστιν ἀγαθὴ καὶ πολλὴ καὶ σφόδρα εὐδαίμων, τὰ γὰρ δῶρα τοῦ θεοῦ μεγάλα καὶ τίμια. It is further described as ἧς τεχνίτης καὶ δημιουργὸς ὁ θεός, "whose constructer and maker is God". τεχνίτης is used of the silversmiths in Acts xix. 24, of God as Maker of the world in Wisdom xiii. 1 and xiv. 2, τεχνίτης δὲ σοφίᾳ κατεσκεύασεν.

Perhaps "artificer" comes nearest to the meaning. δημιουργός, originally one who works for the people, but applied by Plato (*Rep.*, p. 530) to God; and so, very often in Josephus and Philo (see Krebs, *in loc.*). For the use of the title among the Gnostics, see Mansel, *Gnostic Heresies*, p. 19. In Clement, *Ep.*, 20, we have ὁ μέγας δημιουργὸς καὶ δεσπότης τῶν ἁπάντων. In 2 Macc. iv. 1, τῶν κακῶν δημιουργός. "Maker" most adequately translates the word. Wettstein shows that τεχνίτης καὶ δημιουργὸς was not an uncommon combination and aptly compares Cicero (*De Nat. D.*, i. 8) "Opificem aedificatorem mundi". The statement of this verse shows that Abraham and other enlightened O.T. saints (*cf.* chap. iv.) understood that their connection with God, the Eternal One, was their great possession, of which earthly gifts and blessings were but present manifestations.

Ver. 11. Πίστει καὶ αὐτὴ Σάρρα. . . . "By faith Sarah herself also received power to become a mother even when past the age, since she counted Him faithful who had promised." καὶ αὐτὴ Σάρρα is rendered by Vaughan, Sarah "in her place" as [Abraham] in his; she on her part. The reference of αὐτὴ is disputed; it has been understood to mean "Sarah the unfruitful". In D. στεῖρα is added; or, as Chrysostom and Bengel, "vas infirmius," the weaker vessel. Delitzsch thinks that as in Luke xx. 42, xxiv. 15, it merely means "so Sarah likewise". But apparently the reference is to her previous unbelief. By faith she received strength εἰς καταβολὴν σπέρματος, "the act of the husband not of the wife" (see a score of passages in Wetstein), hence Bleek, Farrar and several others prefer to understand the words of "the founding of a family," citing Plato's πρώτη καταβολὴ τῶν ἀνθρώπων. But if εἰς be taken in the same sense as in x. 19, "as regards" or "in connection with" or "with a view to," the difficulty disappears. [*Cf.* Weiss who says the words signify "nicht ein Thun, zu dem sie Kraft empfing, sondern die Beziehung in welcher sie ein Kraft

ἐπαγγειλάμενον. 12. ¹διὸ καὶ ἀφ᾽ ἑνὸς ἐγεννήθησαν, καὶ ταῦτα i Gen. xv.
5, et xxii.
νενεκρωμένου, καθὼς τὰ ἄστρα τοῦ οὐρανοῦ τῷ πλήθει, καὶ ὡσεὶ 17; Rom.
iv. 18.
ἄμμος ἡ παρὰ τὸ χεῖλος τῆς θαλάσσης ἡ ἀναρίθμητος. 13. ᵏΚατὰ k Gen.xxiii.
4, et xlvii.
πίστιν ἀπέθανον οὗτοι πάντες, μὴ λαβόντες ¹ τὰς ἐπαγγελίας, ἀλλὰ 9; 1 Par.
xxix. 15;
πόρρωθεν αὐτὰς ἰδόντες, καὶ πεισθέντες ² καὶ ἀσπασάμενοι, καὶ ὁμο- Ps.xxxix.
12, et
cxix. 19; Joan. viii. 56.

¹ T.R. in אᶜDEKL; μη κομισαμενοι in א*P, 17, 23, 71; μη προσδεξαμενοι in A.
² και πεισθεντες omitted in אADEKLP, and verss.

bedürfte, wenn dasselbe für sie wirksam werden sollte". *Cf.* also Gen. xviii. 12.] Her faith was further illustrated (καὶ = and this indeed) by the circumstance that she was now παρὰ καιρὸν ἡλικίας, the comparative use of παρά frequent in this Epistle. For a woman who in her prime had been barren, to believe that in her decay she could bear a son was a triumph of faith. *Cf.* Gen. xviii. 12-13, ἐγὼ δὲ γεγήρακα. But she had faith in the promise (*cf.* vi. 13-18), "wherefore also there were begotten of one—and him as good as dead—[issue] as the stars of heaven in multitude and as the sand by the seashore innumerable". Probably the καὶ is to be construed with διὸ as in Luke i. 35; Acts x. 29, etc. ἀφ᾽ ἑνὸς, that is, Abraham (*cf.* Isa. li. 2, εἷς ἦν); καὶ ταῦτα, a classical expression, see Xenophon, *Mem.*, ii. 3, and Blass, *Gram.*, p. 248. νενεκρωμένου, "dead" so far as regards the begetting of offspring, *cf.* Rom. iv. 19. καθὼς τὰ ἄστρα, a nominative to ἐγεν. may be supplied, ἔκγονοι or σπέρμα. For the metaphors *cf.* Gen. xxii. 17. ἄστρον is properly a constellation, but used commonly for "a star". χεῖλος found in the classics in same connection. Ver. 13. Not only in life was the faith of the patriarchs manifested, it stood the test of death, κατὰ πίστιν ἀπέθανον οὗτοι πάντες, in keeping with their faith (see Winer, p. 502) these all (that is Abraham, Sarah, Isaac and Jacob) died, and the strength of their faith was seen in this that although they had not received the fulfilment of the promises (ver. 39 and x. 36) they yet had faith enough to see and hail them from afar. As Moses endured because he *saw* the Invisible (ver. 27) so the patriarchs were not daunted by death because they saw the day of Christ (John viii. 56), that is to say, they were so firmly persuaded that God's promise would be fulfilled that it could be said that they *saw* the fulfilment. They hailed them from afar, as those on board ship descry friends on shore and wave a recognition. [Wetstein cites from

Appian, *De Bell. Civ.*, ver. 46, p. 110 where it is said that the soldiers τὸν Καίσαρα πόρρωθεν ὡς αὐτοκράτορα ἠσπάσαντο.] "Such an ἀσπασμός we have in the mouth of the dying Jacob (Gen. xlix. 18): For Thy salvation have I waited, Jehovah" (Delitzsch). This they might have done had they merely believed that the promises would be fulfilled to their descendants, but that their faith extended also to their own enjoyment of God's promise was testified by their confessing that so far as regards the land (τῆς γῆς) of Canaan they were pilgrims and foreigners. This confession was made no doubt by their whole conduct, but as the aorist indicates it was made verbally by Abraham on the occasion of Sarah's death (Gen. xxiii. 4), πάροικος καὶ παρεπίδημος ἐγώ εἰμι μεθ᾽ ὑμῶν, *cf.* xlvii. 9, etc. The article before γῆς, together with the sense of the passage, shows that the land of promise, Canaan, was meant. ἐπὶ γῆς in the same connection is used for "the earth," *cf.* 1 Chron. xxix. 15. Philo (*De Agricult.*, p. 196) refines upon the same idea, παροικεῖν οὐ κατοικεῖν ἤλθομεν· τῷ γὰρ ὄντι πᾶσα μὲν ψυχὴ σοφοῦ πατρίδα μὲν οὐρανὸν, ξένην δὲ γῆν ἔλαχεν. *Cf. De Conf. Ling.*, p. 331. But such a confession implies that those who make it (οἱ γὰρ τοιαῦτα λέγοντες) have not yet found but are in search of a fatherland, πατρίδα ἐπιζητοῦσιν. [*Cf.* Rom. xi. 7, ὃ ἐπιζητεῖ Ἰσραὴλ τοῦτο οὐκ ἐπέτυχεν. Frequent in N.T., to seek, search for. "The ἐπὶ is that of direction, as the ἐκ in ἐκζητεῖν (ver. 6) is that of explanation" (Vaughan).] The acknowledgment, cheerful or sad, that such and such a land is not the home-country makes it manifest (ἐμφανίζουσιν, Jo. xiv. 21, Acts xxiii. 15) that they think of and have in view and are making for a land which they can call their own. ["Si hic peregrinantur, alibi patria est ac fixa sedes" (Calvin).] And that this home-country of their desire is not that from which Abraham and the patriarchs were really derived (Mesopo-

λογήσαντες ὅτι ξένοι καὶ παρεπίδημοί εἰσιν ἐπὶ τῆς γῆς. 14. οἱ γὰρ
τοιαῦτα λέγοντες, ἐμφανίζουσιν ὅτι πατρίδα ἐπιζητοῦσι. 15. καὶ εἰ

1 Exod. iii.
6; Matt.
xxii. 32;
Acts vii.
32.
m Gen.
xxii. 2,
etc.; Eccl.
xliv. 20.
μὲν ἐκείνης ἐμνημόνευον ἀφ᾽ ἧς ἐξῆλθον,[1] εἶχον ἂν καιρὸν ἀνακάμψαι·
16. [1]νυνὶ[2] δὲ κρείττονος ὀρέγονται, τουτέστιν ἐπουρανίου· διὸ οὐκ
ἐπαισχύνεται αὐτοὺς ὁ Θεός, Θεὸς ἐπικαλεῖσθαι αὐτῶν· ἡτοίμασε
γὰρ αὐτοῖς πόλιν. 17. [m]Πίστει προσενήνοχεν Ἀβραὰμ τὸν Ἰσαὰκ
πειραζόμενος, καὶ τὸν μονογενῆ προσέφερεν ὁ τὰς ἐπαγγελίας ἀνα-

---

[1] T.R. in אᶜDᶜE**KL ; εξεβησαν in א*AD*E*P, 17, 73.
[2] T.R. in minusculis; νυν in אADEKLP.

---

tamia) and which they had abandoned, (ἀφ᾽ ἧς ἐξέβησαν) is also evident, because had they cherished fond memories of it they would have had opportunity (εἶχον ἂν καιρὸν, cf. Acts xxiv. 25 ; 1 Macc. xv. 34. The imperfects indicate that this was continuous) to return (ἀνακάμψαι, Mat. ii. 12; Luke x. 6; Acts xviii. 21; frequent in LXX). νῦν δὲ, "but as the case actually stands" (viii. 6, ix. 26 ; 1 Cor. xv. 20, etc.) putting aside this idea that it might be their old home they were seeking, κρείττονος ὀρέγονται, τοῦτ᾽ ἔστιν ἐπουρανίου, it is a better, that is, a heavenly they aspire after. That which in point of fact provoked in the patriarchs the sense of exile was that their hearts were set on a better country and firmer settlement than could be found anywhere, but in heaven. And because they thus proved that they were giving to God credit for meaning by His promises more than the letter indicated, because they measured His promises by the spirit of the promises rather than by the thing promised, He is not ashamed of them, not ashamed to be called their God ; and the proof that He is not ashamed of them is, that He prepared for them a city. The patriarchs showed that they understood that in giving these promises God became their God; therefore God was not ashamed of them, and this showed itself especially in His naming Himself "the God of Abraham, Isaac and Jacob" (Exod. iii. 15). Cf. with this verse, viii. 10 and Mat. xxii. 31, 32. And that He was truly their God He showed by preparing for them a city which should justify the expectations which they had based upon His power and goodness.

Ver. 17. Πίστει προσενήνοχεν Ἀβραάμ. . . . "By faith Abraham when tried offered up Isaac, yea he who had accepted the promises, to whom it had been said, In Isaac shall thy seed be called, offered his only son." The perfect προσενήνοχεν, Blass (Gram., 200) says

"can only be understood as referring to the abiding example offered to us". Similarly Alford, Westcott, Weiss, etc. Surely it is better to have regard to Burton's statement, "The Perfect Indicative is sometimes used in the N.T. of a simple past fact where it is scarcely possible to suppose that the thought of existing result was in the writer's mind". And in Jebb's Appendix to Vincent and Dickson's Gram. of Mod. Greek (p. 327, 8) it is demonstrated that "later Greek shows some clear traces of a tendency to use the Perfect as an Aorist". τὸν is probably here intended not merely to indicate the case of the indeclinable Ἰσαὰκ (Vaughan), cf. vv. 18, 20, but to call attention to the importance of Isaac; and this is further accomplished in the succeeding clause which brings out the full significance of the sacrifice. It was his only son whom Abraham was offering (προσέφερε imperfect in its proper sense of an unfinished transaction) and therefore the sole link between himself and the fulfilment of the promises to which he had given hospitable entertainment (ἀναδεξάμενος, 2 Macc. vi. 19). "The sole link," because, irrespective of any other children Abraham had had or might have, it had been said to him (πρὸς ὃν, denoting Abraham not Isaac), In Isaac shall a seed be named to thee (Gen. xxi. 12); that is to say, it is Isaac and his descendants who shall be known as Abraham's seed. Others are proud to count themselves the descendants of Abraham but the true "seed" (κληθήσεταί σοι σπέρμα, cf. Gal. iii. 16, 29) to whom along with Abraham the promises were given was the race that sprang from Isaac, the heir of the promise. No trial (πειραζόμενος as in Gen. xxii. 1, ὁ Θεὸς ἐπείρασε τὸν Ἀβραὰμ and cf. Gen. xxii. 12) could have been more severe. After long waiting the heir had at last been given, and now after his hope had for several years rooted itself in this one life, he is required to sacrifice

δεξάμενος, 18. ⁿπρὸς ὃν ἐλαλήθη, ""Οτι ἐν 'Ισαὰκ κληθήσεταί σοι
σπέρμα"· 19. λογισάμενος ὅτι καὶ ἐκ νεκρῶν ἐγείρειν¹ δυνατὸς ὁ
Θεός, ὅθεν αὐτὸν καὶ ἐν παραβολῇ ἐκομίσατο. 20. °Πίστει περὶ
μελλόντων εὐλόγησεν² 'Ισαὰκ τὸν 'Ιακὼβ καὶ τὸν 'Ησαῦ. 21. ᵖΠίσ-
τει 'Ιακὼβ ἀποθνήσκων ἕκαστον τῶν υἱῶν 'Ιωσὴφ εὐλόγησε³· καὶ
προσεκύνησεν ἐπὶ τὸ ἄκρον τῆς ῥάβδου αὐτοῦ. 22. �q Πίστει 'Ιωσὴφ
τελευτῶν περὶ τῆς ἐξόδου τῶν υἱῶν 'Ισραὴλ ἐμνημόνευσε, καὶ περὶ τῶν
ὀστέων αὐτοῦ ἐνετείλατο. 23. ʳ Πίστει Μωσῆς γεννηθεὶς ἐκρύβη τρί-
μηνον ὑπὸ τῶν πατέρων αὐτοῦ, διότι εἶδον ἀστεῖον τὸ παιδίον· καὶ
οὐκ ἐφοβήθησαν τὸ διάταγμα⁴ τοῦ βασιλέως. 24. ˢ Πίστει Μωσῆς

n Gen. xxi.
12; Rom.
ix.7; Gal.
iii. 29.
o Gen.
xxvii. 27,
39.
p Gen.
xlvii. 31,
et xlviii.
5, 15, 16,
20.
q Gen. l. 24.
r Exod. i.
16, et ii.
2; Acts
vii. 20.
s Exod. ii.
10,11; Ps.
lxxxiv.10.

¹ εγειρειν in ℵDEKL; εγειραι in AP, 17, 71.   ² ηυλογησεν in A, 17, 37.
³ ηυλογησεν in ADE, 17.   ⁴ δογμα in Avi, 34.

that life and so break his whole connection with the future. No greater test of
his trust in God was possible. He con-
quered because he reckoned (λογισάμενος
"expresses the formation of an opinion by
calculation or *reasoning*, as in Rom. viii.
18; 2 Cor. x. 7" (Vaughan).), that even
from the dead God is able to raise up—a
belief in God's power to do this universally, see John v. 21. This belief enabled
him to deliver his only son to death.
"Whence (ὅθεν, *i.e.*, ἐκ νεκρῶν, although
several commentators, even Weiss, render
it 'wherefore') also he received him
back (ἐκομίσατο, for this meaning see
Gen. xxxviii. 20 and passages in Wetstein) in a figure (ἐν παραβολῇ, not
actually, because Isaac had not been dead,
but virtually because he had been given
up to death. He had passed through the
likeness of death, and his restoration to
Abraham was a likeness of resurrection.
(Whoever wishes to see how a simple expression may be tortured should consult
Alford's long note on this place.)

Ver. 20. Πίστει περὶ μελλόντων. . . .
" By faith Isaac blessed Jacob and Esau
in regard to things future," as is recorded
in the well-known passage, Gen. xxvii.
Isaac thus in his turn exhibited a faith
which could be described as ἐλπιζομένων
ὑπόστασις. "By faith Jacob when dying
(ἀποθνήσκων *cf.* καλούμενος, ver. 8, and
πειραζόμενος, ver. 17: the participle illustrates ver. 13 and also reminds the
reader that Jacob before he died saw his
children's children inheriting the promise
("thy two sons are mine," Gen. xlviii. 5)
blessed each of the sons of Joseph.
ἕκαστον τ. υἱῶν, that is, he gave each an
individual blessing, crossing his hands,
laying his right on the head of Ephraim
the younger, his left on Manasseh, thus

distinguishing between the destiny of the
one and that of the other and so more
abundantly illustrating his faith. καὶ
προσεκύνησεν ἐπὶ τὸ ἄκρον τῆς ῥάβδου
αὐτοῦ, "and worshipped leaning upon
the top of h.s staff". The words are
from the LXX rendering of Gen. xlvii. 31
where after Joseph had sworn to bury his
father in Canaan, "Israel worshipped,
etc.". His exacting this promise from
Joseph was proof of his faith that his
posterity would inherit the land of promise. The LXX translating from an un-
pointed text read הַמַּטֶּה the staff and
not as it is now read הַמִּטָּה the bed,
(as in xlviii. 2). The meaning in either
case is that in extreme bodily weakness,
either unable to leave his bed or if so
only able to stand with the aid of a staff,
his faith was yet untouched by the slightest symptom of decay. "The idea of
προσκυνεῖν is that of *reverence shown in
posture*" (Vaughan). Here Jacob "worshipped" in thankful remembrance of the
promise of God and that his son had
accepted it.

Ver. 22. Similarly Joseph when he in
his turn came to the close of his life
(τελευτῶν, from Gen. l. 16, καὶ ἐτελεύ-
τησεν'Ιωσὴφ)made mention of the exodus
of the children of Israel ("God will surely
visit you and will bring you out of this
land concerning which God
sware to our fathers," Gen. l. 24) and
gave commandment concerning his bones
("ye shall carry up my bones hence with
you," Gen. l. 25. For the fulfilment of
the command see Josh. xxiv. 32).

Vv. 23-31. The writer passes from the
patriarchal age to the times of Moses
and the Judges.

μέγας γενόμενος ἠρνήσατο λέγεσθαι υἱὸς θυγατρὸς Φαραώ, 25.
μᾶλλον ἑλόμενος συγκακουχεῖσθαι τῷ λαῷ τοῦ Θεοῦ, ἢ πρόσκαιρον
ἔχειν ἁμαρτίας ἀπόλαυσιν· 26. μείζονα πλοῦτον ἡγησάμενος τῶν
ἐν Αἰγύπτῳ θησαυρῶν τὸν ὀνειδισμὸν τοῦ Χριστοῦ· ἀπέβλεπε γὰρ
εἰς τὴν μισθαποδοσίαν. 27. ᵗΠίστει κατέλιπεν Αἴγυπτον, μὴ φοβηθεὶς τὸν θυμὸν τοῦ βασιλέως· τὸν γὰρ ἀόρατον ὡς ὁρῶν ἐκαρτέρησε.
28. ᵘΠίστει πεποίηκε τὸ πάσχα καὶ τὴν πρόσχυσιν τοῦ αἵματος,

t Exod. x.
28, 29, et
xii. 31,
etc., et
xiii. 17,
etc.
u Exod. xii.
3, 21, 22.

First the faith of the parents of Moses
(τῶν πατέρων αὐτοῦ, in Stephanus'
Thesaur, several examples are given of
the use of πατέρες for "father and
mother," parents; and consider Eph. vi.
4 and Col. iii. 21) is celebrated. This
faith was shown in their concealing
Moses for three months after his birth
and thus evading the law that male
children were to be killed, called in
Wisd. xi. 7 νηπιοκτόνον διάταγμα. They
did not fear this commandment of the
king. It did not weigh against the
child's beauty which betokened that he
was destined for something great. Their
faith consisted in their confidence that
God had in store for so handsome a child
an exceptional career and would save him
to fulfil his destiny. In Acts vii. 20
Stephen calls him ἀστεῖος τῷ θεῷ, extraordinarily beautiful (*cf*. Jonah iii. 3) or as
Philo, *De Mos*., p. 82, ὄψιν ἀστειοτέραν
ἢ κατ' ἰδιώτην, indicating that he had a
corresponding destiny. Moses himself
when he had grown up (μέγας γενόμενος,
as in Exod. ii. 11 paraphrased by Stephen
(Acts vii. 23) ὡς δὲ ἐπληροῦτο αὐτῷ
τεσσαρακονταετὴς χρόνος.) refused to be
called a son of a daughter of Pharaoh.
The significance and source of this refusal lay in his preferring to suffer ill-
usage with God's people rather than to
have a short-lived enjoyment of sin.
συνκακ., the simple verb in ver. 37, also
xiii. 3 ; the compound here only. τῷ λαῷ
τοῦ θεοῦ, it was because they were God's
people, not solely because they were of
his blood, that Moses threw in his lot
with them. It was this which illustrated
his faith. He believed that God would
fulfil His promise to His people, little
likelihood as at present there seemed to
be of any great future for his race. On
the other hand there was the ἁμαρτίας
ἀπόλαυσις, the enjoyment which was
within his reach if only he committed the
sin of denying his people and renouncing
their future as promised by God. For
"the enjoyment to be reaped from sin"
does not refer to the pleasure of grati-
fying sensual appetite and so forth, but

to the satisfaction of a high ambition
and the gratification of his finer tastes
which he might have had by remaining
in the Egyptian court. Very similarly
Philo interprets the action of Moses, who,
he says, "esteemed the good things of
those who had adopted him, although
more splendid for a season, to be in reality
spurious, but those of his natural parents,
although for a little while less conspicuous, to be true and genuine" (*De
Mose*, p. 86). That which influenced
Moses to make this choice was his estimate of the comparative value of the
outcome of suffering with God's people
and of the happiness offered in Egypt.
μείζονα πλοῦτον . . . εἰς τὴν μισθαποδοσίαν, "since he considered the reproach of the Christ greater riches
than the treasures of Egypt; for he
steadily kept in view the reward". The
reproach or obloquy and disgrace, which
Moses experienced is called "the reproach
of the Christ" because it was on account of his belief in God's saving purpose that he suffered. The expression is
interpreted by our Lord's statement that
Abraham saw his day. It does not
imply that Moses believed that a personal Christ was to come, but only that
God would fulfil that promise which in
point of fact was fulfilled in the coming
of Christ. The writer uses the expression
rather with a view to his readers who were
shrinking from the reproach of Christ
(xiii. 13), than from the point of view of
Moses. Several interpreters (Delitzsch,
etc.) suppose that in virtue of the
mystical union Christ suffered in his
people. But, as Davidson says, "this
mystical union cannot be shown to be
an idea belonging to the Epistle, nor is
this sense pertinent to the connection."
(So Weiss, "die vorstellung liegt un-
serem Briefe fern".) Weiss' own interpretation is ingenious : "The O.T.
church was created by the pre-existent
Messiah to be the people who were
destined to introduce through Him perfect salvation ; therefore each maltreat-
ment of this people was contempt of

ἵνα μὴ ὁ ὀλοθρεύων[1] τὰ πρωτότοκα θίγῃ αὐτῶν. 29. ᵛΠίστει δι- v Exod.xiv.
ἔβησαν τὴν ἐρυθρὰν θάλασσαν ὡς διὰ ξηρᾶς· ἧς πεῖραν λαβόντες οἱ
Αἰγύπτιοι κατεπόθησαν. 30. ᵂΠίστει τὰ τείχη Ἱεριχὼ ἔπεσε,[2] w Jos. vi.
κυκλωθέντα ἐπὶ ἑπτὰ ἡμέρας. 31. ˣΠίστει Ῥαὰβ ἡ πόρνη οὐ συν- x Jos. ii. 1,
ἀπώλετο τοῖς ἀπειθήσασι, δεξαμένη τοὺς κατασκόπους μετ᾽ εἰρήνης.

21, 22.
20.
et vi. 23;
Jac. ii. 25.

[1] ολεθρευων in ADE.   [2] επεσαν in אAD*P, 17, 23, 71.

Him as unable to avenge and deliver
His people". To say that it means
merely "the same reproach that Christ
bore" scarcely satisfies the expression.
The "treasures of Egypt" must be supposed to include all that had been accumulated during centuries of civilisation: ἀπέβλεπεν, he habitually kept in
view the reward. Cf. Xen., Hist., vi. 1, 8
ἡ σὴ πατρὶς εἰς σὲ ἀποβλέπει, also Ps.
xi. 4, Philo, De Opif., p. 4. κατέλιπεν
Αἴγυπτον, "he forsook Egypt," and fled
to Midian. That this flight and not the
Exodus is meant appears from the connection of the clause both with what
precedes and with what follows. It exhibits the result of his choice (ver. 26),
and it alludes to what preceded the
Passover (ver. 28). The word ἐκαρ-
τέρησεν, denoting long continued endurance also suits better this reference.
The only difficulty in the way of accepting this interpretation is found in the
words μὴ φοβηθεὶς τὸν θυμὸν τοῦ βασιλέως, because, according to Exod. ii. 15,
the motive of his flight was fear of the
king. ἐφοβήθη δὲ Μωυσῆς. But what
is in the writer's mind is not Pharaoh's
wrath as cause but as consequence of
Moses' abandonment of Egypt. His
flight showed that he had finally renounced life at court, and in thus indicating by this decisive action that he was
an Israelite, and meant to share with his
people, he braved the king's wrath.
This he was strengthened to do because
he saw an invisible monarch greater than
Pharaoh. Vaughan seems the only interpreter who has precisely hit the
writer's meaning: "the two fears are
different, the one is the fear arising from
the discovery of his slaying the Egyptian,
the other is the fear of Pharaoh's anger
on discovering his flight. He feared and
therefore fled: he feared not, and there
fore fled." Having fled and so cutting
himself off from all immediate opportunity of helping his people, ἐκαρτ-
έρησεν, "he steadfastly bided his
time," because he saw the Invisible,
being thus an eminent illustration of
faith as ἔλεγχος οὐ βλεπομένων. The

aorist gathers the forty years in Midian
into one exhibition of wonderful perseverance in faith. It was the upper
form of the school which disciplined
Moses and wrought him to the mould of
a hero. Another point in his career at
which faith manifested itself was the
Exodus, πεποίηκεν τὸ πάσχα, "he hath
celebrated the Passover". Alford says
the perfect is used on account of the
Passover being "a still enduring Feast".
But it is Moses' celebration of it that the
perfect represents as enduring. The
classical treatment of the question, Has
ποιεῖν a sacrificial meaning in the N.T.?
will be found in Prof. T. K. Abbott's
Essays. ποιεῖν is regularly used of
"keeping" a feast; and this is a classical
usage as well. Cf. Exod. xii. 48, xxiii.
16, xxxiv. 22; 2 Chron. xxxv. 17-19. τὸ
πάσχα originally the paschal lamb,
Exod. xii. 21, καὶ θύσατε τὸ πάσχα,
Mark xiv. 12 τὸ πάσχα ἔθυον, hence the
feast of Passover as in Luke xxii. 1. It
is written φασέκ throughout 2 Chron.
xxx. and xxxv., also in Jer. xxxviii. 8.
καὶ τὴν πρόσχυσιν τοῦ αἵματος, "and
the affusion of the blood" the sprinkling
of the blood on the door posts as commanded in Exod. xii. 7, 22, the object
being that the destroyers of the first-
borns might not touch them. As θιγγάνω
is followed by a genitive in xii. 20 it is
probable that the writer here also meant
it to govern αὐτῶν while πρωτότοκα follows ὀλοθρεύων. So R.V. ὁ ὀλοθρεύων
is taken from Exod. xii. 23. πρωτότοκα,
first-borns of man and also of beasts,
Exod. xii. 12. αὐτῶν is naturally referred to "the people of God," ver. 25.
It was a noteworthy faith which enabled
Moses confidently to promise the people
protection from the general destruction.
On their part also there was the manifestation of a strong faith. διέβησαν
τὴν ἐρυθρὰν θάλασσαν . . .
"they passed through the Red sea as if
on dry land". The nominative must be
taken out of αὐτῶν. διέβησαν, the
usual term for crossing a river or a space.
The Red sea is in Hebrew "the Sea of
[red] weeds". διὰ ξηρᾶς γῆς as in

y Jud. iv. 6, et vi. 11, et xi. 1, et xii. 7, et xiii. 24; 1 Sam. i. 20, et xii. 17, etc., et xiii. 14, et xvii. 45.

32. ʸ Καὶ τί ἔτι λέγω ; ἐπιλείψει γάρ με διηγούμενον ὁ χρόνος περὶ Γεδεὼν, Βαράκ τε καὶ Σαμψὼν καὶ Ἰεφθάε, Δαβίδ τε καὶ Σαμουὴλ

Exod. xiv. 29 ἐπορεύθησαν διὰ ξηρᾶς ἐν μέσῳ τῆς θαλάσσης, also xv. 19; and cf. the various impressions in the Psalms which celebrate the great deliverance. The greatness of the people's faith is accentuated by the fate of the Egyptians, whose attempt to follow was audacity and presumption not faith. ἧς πεῖραν λαβόντες . . . "of which [i.e., of the sea] making trial the Egyptians were swallowed up," Exod. xv. 4 κατεπόθησαν ἐν ἐρυθρᾷ θαλάσσῃ. Another instance of the faith of the people and its effects is found in the fall of the walls of Jericho. The greatness of the faith may be measured by the difficulty we now have in believing that the walls fell without the application of any visible force. God's promise was, πεσεῖται αὐτόματα τὰ τείχη, and believing this promise the people compassed the city seven days. The greatness of their faith was further exhibited in their continuing to compass the city day after day, for in the promise (Josh. vi. 1-5) no mention is made of any delay in its fulfilment and the natural inference would be that the walls would fall on the first day. That none should have felt foolish marching day after day round the solid walls is beyond nature. κυκλωθέντα, see Josh. vi. 6, 14 and for ἐπὶ ἑπτὰ ἡμέρας, Josh. vi. 14. "When applied to time, ἐπί denotes the period over which something extends, as Luke iv. 25, ἐπὶ ἔτη τρία, during three years" (Winer, p. 508). The fall of Jericho and the extermination of its inhabitants suggest the escape of Rahab. ἡ πόρνη, in its strict meaning ("ista meretrix" (Origen), "fornicaria" (Irenaeus), is introduced to emphasise the power of faith; she did not perish along with the disobedient (iii. 18); ἀπειθήσασιν, they knew that the Lord had given the land to Israel (Josh. ii. 9, 10) but did not submit themselves to the acknowledged purpose of Jehovah. Rahab acted upon her belief in this purpose and instead of delivering up the spies as enemies of her country "received them with peace," that is, as friends, risking her life because of her faith.

Vv. 32-40. Summary of the achievements of faith in the times subsequent to Joshua.

Ver. 32. At this point the writer sees that he cannot pursue the method he has been following and give in detail all the signal manifestations of faith, which are recorded in the annals of his people. τί ἔτι λέγω, "what shall I further say?" deliberative subjunctive (cf. Rom. i. 15, etc.) the writer questioning how he is to handle the numberless instances that rise before his mind. He cannot give them all, ἐπιλείψει με γὰρ . . . "for time will fail me if I recount in detail". (Julian, Orat., i. p. 341 B. ἐπιλείψει με τἀκείνου διηγούμενον ὁ χρόνος). ἐπιλείψει με ἡ ἡμέρα is frequent, see many examples in Wetstein. Cf. Virgil, Æn., vi. 121, quid Thesea magnum, quid memorem Alciden? "a favourite device for cutting short a long list" (Page). διηγούμενον means to relate with particularity, see Luke viii. 39, ix. 10; Acts xii. 17; Gen. xxix. 13. On Gideon see Judges vi.-vlii; Barak chronologically earlier, chap. iv, v; Samson, xiii-xvi; Jephthah, who also preceded Samson, xi, xii. Samuel is considered as the first of the prophets as in Acts iii. 24 and xiii. 20. οἵ covers vv. 33, 34, although not every particular cited, while διὰ πίστεως refers to all the verbs to end of 38. This expression supplants the persistent πίστει of vv. 3-31, mainly for euphony. κατηγωνίσαντο βασιλείας, "subdued kingdoms," as is recorded of the Judges and David, who also ἠργάσαντο δικαιοσύνην, which seems to refer to their righteous rule, although the same expression is never used in the LXX except of personal righteousness (Ps. xv. 2) but of David it is thrice said that he was ποιῶν κρίμα καὶ δικαιοσύνην, 2 Sam. viii. 15; 1 Chron. xviii. 14; Jer. xxiii. 5; and of Samuel testimony is borne that he judged righteously, 1 Sam. xii. 3. ἐπέτυχον ἐπαγγελιῶν, "obtained promises" not "the promise" of Messianic salvation (cf. ver. 39) but promises given on special occasions, cf. Josh. xxi. 45; Judges vii. 7, xiii. 5; 1 Kings viii. 56. ἔφραξαν στόματα λεόντων, cf. Daniel vi. 22, ἐνέφραξε τὰ στόματα τῶν λεόντων, also Judges xiv. 5, 6; 2 Sam. xvii. 34, xxiii. 20. ἔσβεσαν δύναμιν πυρός, probably the rescue of Shadrach, Meshach and Abednego was suggested by the allusion to Daniel. δύναμιν is explained by the words of Dan. iii. 22, ἡ κάμινος ἐξεκαύθη ἐκ περισσοῦ. ἔφυ-

καὶ τῶν προφητῶν· 33. ᶻοἳ διὰ πίστεως κατηγωνίσαντο βασιλείας, εἰργάσαντο¹ δικαιοσύνην, ἐπέτυχον ἐπαγγελιῶν, ἔφραξαν στόματα λεόντων, 34. ᵃἔσβεσαν δύναμιν πυρὸς, ἔφυγον στόματα μαχαίρας,² ἐνεδυναμώθησαν ἀπὸ ἀσθενείας, ἐγενήθησαν ἰσχυροὶ ἐν πολέμῳ, παρεμβολὰς ἔκλιναν ἀλλοτρίων· 35. ᵇἔλαβον γυναῖκες³ ἐξ ἀναστάσεως τοὺς νεκροὺς αὐτῶν· ἄλλοι δὲ ἐτυμπανίσθησαν, οὐ προσδεξάμενοι τὴν ἀπολύτρωσιν, ἵνα κρείττονος ἀναστάσεως τύχωσιν· 36. ᶜἕτεροι δὲ ἐμπαιγμῶν καὶ μαστίγων πεῖραν ἔλαβον, ἔτι δὲ δεσ-

z Judic. xiv. 6; 1 Sam. xvii. 34; 2 Sam. viii, 1, et x. 19, et xii. 29 Dan. vi. 22.
a Judic. vii. 21, et xv. 15; 1 Sam. xiv.1,etc., et xx. 1
1 Reg.xix.
1, etc.; 2 Reg. vi. 16, et xx.
7; 1 Par. xxii. 9; Job xlii. 10; Ps. vi. 8, et lxxxix.20, etc.; Esa. xxxviii. 21; Dan. iii. 25.
b 1 Reg. xvii. 23; 2 Reg. iv. 36; 2 Mac. vi. 19, 28, et vii.; Acts xxii. 25. c Jer. xx. 2.

¹ ηργασαντο in א*D* 47*.
² μαχαιρης אAD*; μαχαιρας (more classical) in DᶜEKLP.
³ γυναικας in א*AD*.

γον στόματα μαχαίρης, "escaped the edge of the sword" of which there are many instances recorded, as 1 Sam. xviii. 11; 1 Kings xix. 2; 1 Mac. ii. 28. ἐδυναμώθησαν ἀπὸ ἀσθενείας . . . "out of weakness became strong, waxed mighty in battle, routed the armies of aliens," having in view, possibly, by the deliverance recorded in Judges iv. by Deborah, where παρεμβολή (ver. 16, etc.) is used of the army. Reference may also be made, as von Soden suggests, to the Maccabean deliverances. [παρεμβολή, 1 Macc. iii. 3, 15, 17, etc.; ἀλλοτρ. ii. 7.] On several occasions in Israel's history the three clauses received abundant illustration.
Ver. 35. ἔλαβον γυναῖκες. . . . "Women received their dead by resurrection," as is narrated of the widow of Sarepta, 1 Kings xvii. 17-24, and the Shunamite, 2 Kings iv. 34. ἄλλοι δὲ ἐτυμπανίσθησαν . . . "others were beaten to death". τύμπανον (sc. τύπανον from τύπ. strike) a drum, τυμπανίζω, I beat. From the expression in 2 Mac. vi. 17, 28, ἐπὶ τὸ τύμπανον, it might be supposed that some instrument more elaborate than a rod was meant and Josephus speaks of "a wheel" as being used. But that it was substantially a beating to death is proved by what is said of Eleazar (2 Mac. ii. 30), μέλλων ταῖς πληγαῖς τελευτᾶν, εἶπε. That Eleazar and the seven brethren (2 Mac. vii.) are alluded to is obvious, for it was characteristic of them that they died οὐ προσδεξάμενοι τὴν ἀπολύτρωσιν, not accepting the offered deliverance. Eleazar was shown a way by which he could escape death (2 Mac. vi. 21), and the seven brethren also were first inter-

rogated and would have escaped death had they chosen to eat polluted food. They endured martyrdom, not accepting the escape that was possible, ἵνα κρείττονος ἀναστάσεως τύχωσιν, "that they might obtain a better resurrection," "unto eternal life—'better' than that spoken of in the beginning of the verse, to a life that again ended" (Davidson, Weiss, von Soden). How fully the resurrection was in view of the seven brethren is shown in the saying of the second: "the King of the world shall raise us εἰς αἰώνιον ἀναβίωσιν ζωῆς; of the third who when his hands were cut off declared that he would receive them again from God; of the fourth, who in dying said, "It is good, when put to death by men, to look for hope from God to be raised up again by Him;" and the youngest said of them all, "they are dead under God's covenant of everlasting life".
Ver. 36. ἕτεροι δὲ . . . introducing a different class of victories achieved by faith, although ἐμπαιγμῶν καὶ μαστίγων, "mockings and scourgings" were endured by the martyrs who have just been mentioned (2 Mac. vii. 7 and vii. 1). πεῖραν ἔλαβον, see ver. 29. ἔτι δὲ δεσμῶν . . . "yea, moreover of bonds and prison"; as the examples in Bleek prove, ἔτι δὲ is commonly used to express a climax (cf. Luke xiv. 26); and such imprisonment as was inflicted, e.g., on Jeremiah (xxxviii. 9) was certainly even more to be dreaded than scourging. ἐλιθάσθησαν, "they were stoned," as was Zechariah, son of Johoiada, 2 Chron. xxiv. 20 (Luke xi. 51). There was also a tradition that Jeremiah was stoned at Daphne in Egypt. ἐπρίσθησαν, "they were sawn asunder," a cruel death some-

d 1 Reg.xxi. μῶν καὶ φυλακῆς· 37. ^dἐλιθάσθησαν, ἐπρίσθησαν, ἐπειράσθησαν,¹
13 ; 2 Reg.
i. 8 ; Matt. ἐν φόνῳ μαχαίρας ἀπέθανον· περιῆλθον ἐν μηλωταῖς, ἐν αἰγείοις
iii. 4.
δέρμασιν, ὑστερούμενοι, θλιβόμενοι, κακουχούμενοι· 38. ὧν οὐκ ἦν
ἄξιος ὁ κόσμος· ἐν ἐρημίαις πλανώμενοι καὶ ὄρεσι καὶ σπηλαίοις
e ver. 2.   καὶ ταῖς ὀπαῖς τῆς γῆς. 39. ^eΚαὶ οὗτοι πάντες μαρτυρηθέντες διὰ
τῆς πίστεως, οὐκ ἐκομίσαντο τὴν ἐπαγγελίαν, 40. τοῦ Θεοῦ περὶ
ἡμῶν κρεῖττόν τι προβλεψαμένου, ἵνα μὴ χωρὶς ἡμῶν τελειωθῶσι.

¹ T.R. in ADcEK d, e, f, vg., Copt., Arm. In other MSS. the order varies. "Possibly ἐπειράσθησαν is only a reduplication of ἐπρίσθησαν . . . but it may with at least equal probability be a primitive corruption of some other word" (Hort).

times inflicted on prisoners of war (2 Sam. xii. 31; Amos i. 3, ἔπριζον πρίοσι σιδηροῖς). The reference is probably to Isaiah who according to the *Ascensio Is.* (i. 9, v. 1) was sawn asunder by Manasseh with a wooden saw. *Cf.* Justin, *Trypho*, 120, (πρίονι ξυλίνῳ ἐπρίσατε) and Charles' *Ascension of Isaiah*. Within our own memory some of the followers of the Bâb suffered the same death. ἐπειράσθησαν, "were tempted". Alford says, "I do not see how any appropriate meaning can be given to the mere enduring of temptation, placed as it is between being sawn asunder and dying by the sword". He would therefore either omit the word as a gloss on ἐπρίσθησαν or substitute ἐπρήσθησαν. That is a tempting reading because not only was one of the seven brothers (2 Mac. vi. vii. 5) fried, but those who sought to keep the Sabbath in a cave (2 Mac. vi. 11) were all burned together by order of Philip, Antiochus' governor in Jerusalem. At the same time, the reading, "were tempted" gives quite a good sense, for certainly the most fiendish element in the torture of the seven brothers was the pressure put on each individually to recant. ἐν φόνῳ μαχαίρης ἀπέθανον, "died by swordslaughter," for ἐν φ. μαχ. see Exod. xvii. 13; Num. xxi. 24, etc.; and for ἀπεθ. ἐν see Jer. xi. 22. xxi. 9. Examples of this death abounded in the Maccabean period. περιῆλθον ἐν μηλωταῖς, "they wandered about in sheepskins," (as the mantle of Elijah is called in 2 Kings ii. 8, ἔλαβεν Ἠλιοὺ τὴν μηλωτὴν αὐτοῦ), or even "in goatskins," a still rougher material. This dress they wore not as a professional uniform, but because "destitute," ὑστερούμενοι as in Luke xv. 14. ἤρξατο ὑστερεῖσθαι, Phil. iv. 12 καὶ περισσεύειν καὶ ὑστερεῖσθαι, "hardpressed," θλιβόμενοι, as in 2 Cor. iv. 8 θλιβόμενοι ἀλλ' οὐ στενοχωρούμενοι, κακουχούμενοι, "maltreated," see ver.

25. ὧν οὐκ ἦν ἄξιος ὁ κόσμος, "of whom the world was not worthy". "The world drove them out, thinking them unworthy to live in it, while in truth it was unworthy to have them living in it" (Davidson). Vaughan aptly compares Acts xxii. 22. After this parenthetical remark the description is closed with ·another participial clause, ἐπὶ ἐρημίαις πλανώμενοι . . ." "wandering over deserts and mountains, and in caves and in the holes of the earth," verified 1 Kings xviii. 4; 2 Macc. v. 27 where it is related of Judas and nine others, ἀναχωρήσας εἰς τὴν ἔρημον, θηρίων τρόπον ἐν τοῖς ὄρεσι διέζη. *Cf.* also 2 Mac. x. 6, ἐν τοῖς ὄρεσι καὶ ἐν τοῖς σπηλαίοις θηρίων τρόπον ἦσαν νεμόμενοι. In the *Ascensio Isaiae*, ii. 7, 12, Isaiah and his companions are said to have spent two years among the mountains naked and eating only herbage.

Ver. 39. καὶ οὗτοι πάντες, "And these all," that is, those who have been named in this chapter, "although they had witness borne to them through their faith," as has been recorded (ver. 2-38), "did not receive the promise," that is, as already said in ver. 13, they only foresaw that it would be fulfilled and died in that faith. But this failure to obtain the fulfilment of the promise was not due to any slackness on the part of God nor to any defect in their faith; there was a good reason for it, and that reason was that "God had in view some better thing for us, that without us they should not be perfected". The κρεῖττόν τι is that which this Epistle has made it its business to expound, the perfecting (τελειωθῶσιν) of God's people by full communion with Him mediated by the perfect revelation (i. 1) of the Son and His perfect covenant (viii. 7-13), and His better sacrifice (ix. 23). And the perfecting of the people of God under the O.T. is said to have been impossible, not as might have

XII. I. ^aΤΟΙΓΑΡΟΥΝ καὶ ἡμεῖς τοσοῦτον ἔχοντες περικείμενον ^a x. 36;
ἡμῖν νέφος μαρτύρων, ὄγκον ἀποθέμενοι πάντα καὶ τὴν εὐπερίστατον   Rom. vi. 4, et xii. 12; I Cor. ix. 24; 2

Cor. vii. I; Eph. iv. 22; Phil. iii. 13, 14; Col. iii. 8; I Peter ii. I, et iv. 2.

been expected "apart from the Son," but χωρὶς ἡμῶν, because the writer has in view the history of the Church, the relation of the people of God in former times to the same people in Messianic times.

CHAPTER XII.—Ver. I. Τοιγαροῦν καὶ ἡμεῖς. . . . "Wherefore, as we have so great a cloud of witnesses encompassing us, let us likewise lay aside every encumbrance and sin that clings so close and run with endurance the race that is set before us, looking to the leader and perfecter of faith, even Jesus, who for the joy set before him endured a cross despising shame and has sat down at the right hand of the throne of God." τοιγαροῦν, "wherefore then" more formal and emphatic than the usual, διὰ τοῦτο, διὸ, ὅθεν, οὖν. καὶ ἡμεῖς, we in our turn, we as well as they, and with the added advantage of having so many testimonies to the good results of faith. νέφος used frequently in Homer and elsewhere, as "nubes" in Latin and "cloud" in English to suggest a vast multitude. μαρτύρων, "witnesses," persons who by their actions have testified to the worth of faith. The cloud of witnesses are those named and suggested in chap. xi.; persons whose lives witnessed to the work and triumph of faith, and whose faith was witnessed to by Scripture, cf. xi. 2, 4, 5. This cloud is περικείμενον, because, as the writer has just shown, look where they will into their history his Hebrew readers see such examples of faith. It is impossible to take μάρτυρες as equivalent to θεαταί. If the idea of "spectator" is present at all, which is very doubtful, it is only introduced by the words τρέχωμεν . . . ἀγῶνα. The idea is not that they are running in presence of spectators and must therefore run well; but that their people's history being filled with examples of much-enduring but triumphant faith, they also must approve their lineage by showing a like persistence of faith. ὄγκον ἀποθέμενοι πάντα, ὄγκος, a mass or weight or burden (= φόρτος), hence a swelling or superfluous flesh [cf. especially Longinus, iii. 9, κακοὶ δὲ ὄγκοι καὶ ἐπὶ σωμάτων καὶ λόγων. and from Hippocrates in Wettstein, καὶ γὰρ δρόμοι ταχεῖς, καὶ γυμνάσια τοιαῦτα, σαρκῶν ὄγκον καθαίρει.] The allusion therefore

is to the training preparatory to a race by which an encumbering superfluity of flesh is reduced. The Christian runner must rid himself even of innocent things which might retard him. And all that does not help, hinders. It is by running he learns what these things are. So long as he stands he does not feel that they are burdensome and hampering. καὶ τὴν εὐπερίστατον ἁμαρτίαν. Of the difficult word εὐπερ. Chrysostom gives two interpretations; "which is easily avoided," and "which easily encompasses or surrounds us". In the sense of "avoid" the verb περιΐστάσθαι occurs in 2 Tim. ii. 16 and Tit. iii. 9, but it is scarcely credible that in the present context such an epithet could be applied to sin. The second interpretation has been generally accepted ["circumstans nos peccatum" (Vulg.); "qui nous enveloppe si aisément"; "die Sünde, die immer zur Hand ist" (Weizsäcker)]. This meaning suits the context and the action enjoined in ἀποθέμενοι, suggesting, as it does, the trailing garment that encumbers the runner. The article τὴν does not point to some particular sin, but to that which characterises all sin, the tenacity with which it clings to a man. We might suppose from the word itself that it alluded to sin as an enemy encompassing from well-chosen points of vantage, but this does not suit the figure of the race nor the ἀποθέμενοι. [Porphyry, de Abstin., says γυμνοὶ δὲ καὶ ἀχίτωνες ἐπὶ τὸ στάδιον ἀναβαίνωμεν ἐπὶ τὰ τῆς ψυχῆς Ὀλύμπια ἀγωνισόμενοι. "Ut cursores vestimenta non solum abjiciunt, nudique currunt, verum etiam crebris exercitationibus, ne corpus nimis obesum et ineptum reddatur, efficiunt: ita et vos omnia impedimenta in studio virtutis, et tarditatem vestram crebris meditationibus vincite" (Wetstein).] δι᾽ ὑπομονῆς, after the negative preparation comes the positive demand for endurance, cf. x. 36. τρέχωμεν . . . ἀγῶνα, as in Herod. viii. 102, πολλοὺς ἀγῶνας δραμέονται οἱ Ἕλληνες. προκείμενον, [frequent with ἀγών, as in Arrian's Epict., iii. 25, οὐ γὰρ ὑπὲρ πάλης καὶ παγκρατίου ὁ ἀγὼν πρόκειται. Cf. Orestes of Eurip., 845, and Ignatius to Eph., c. 17. τοῦ προκειμένου ζῆν.] appointed, lying before us as our destined

b i. 3, 13, et ἁμαρτίαν, δι' ὑπομονῆς τρέχωμεν τὸν προκείμενον ἡμῖν ἀγῶνα· 2.
ii. 10, et
viii. 1; ᵇἀφορῶντες εἰς τὸν τῆς πίστεως ἀρχηγὸν καὶ τελειωτὴν Ἰησοῦν, ὃς
Luc.xxiv.
26, 46; ἀντὶ τῆς προκειμένης αὐτῷ χαρᾶς, ὑπέμεινε σταυρὸν, αἰσχύνης κατα-
Acts iii.
15, et v. φρονήσας, ἐν δεξιᾷ τε τοῦ θρόνου τοῦ Θεοῦ ἐκάθισεν.¹   3. ἀναλογί-
31; Phil.
ii. 8, etc.;σασθε γὰρ τὸν τοιαύτην ὑπομεμενηκότα ὑπὸ τῶν ἁμαρτωλῶν εἰς
1 Peter i.
3. αὐτὸν² ἀντιλογίαν, ἵνα μὴ κάμητε ταῖς ψυχαῖς ὑμῶν ἐκλυόμενοι.
c 1 Cor. x.
13.   4. ᶜΟὔπω μέχρις αἵματος ἀντικατέστητε πρὸς τὴν ἁμαρτίαν

¹ κεκαθικεν in אADEKLP.

² εις εαυτον AP Vulg.; εις εαυτους א*D*E*. ["Looks like the conceit which some reader wrote upon his margin" (Davidson).]

trial. This let us run, not waiting for a pleasanter, easier course, but accepting that which is appointed and recognising the difficulties as constituent parts of the race. Success depends on the condition attached ἀφορῶντες . . . Ἰησοῦν, fixing our gaze on Him who sets us the example (ἀρχηγὸν) of faith, and exhibits it in its perfect form (τελειωτής), who leads us in faith and in whom faith finds its perfect embodiment. ἀρχηγός properly means one to whom anything owes its origin (cf. ii. 10), but here it rather indicates one who takes the lead or sets the example most worth following. Jesus is the ἀρχηγὸς τῆς πίστεως because he is its τελειωτής. In Him alone do we see absolute dependence on God, implicit trust, what it is, what it costs, and what it results in. (Hence the human name Ἰησοῦν.) On Him therefore must the gaze be fixed if the runner is to endure, for in Him the reasonableness, the beauty, and the reward of a life of faith are seen. Faith manifested itself in Jesus, especially in His endurance of the cross in virtue of His faith in the resulting joy beyond. ὃς ἀντὶ τῆς προκειμένης αὐτῷ χαρᾶς . . . ἀντί here as in ver. 16 denotes the price paid, or reward offered, "in consideration of". There was a joy set before Jesus, which nerved Him to endure. This joy was the sitting in the place of achieved victory and power, not a selfish joy, but the consciousness of salvation wrought for men, of power won which he could use in their interests. This hope or confident expectation so animated Him that He endured the utmost of human suffering and shame. The shame is mentioned αἰσχύνης καταφρονήσας, because His despising of it manifests a mind fixed on the glory that was to follow and filled with it.

Ver. 3. ἀναλογίσασθε γὰρ. . . . The reason for fixing the gaze on Jesus is given. That reason being found in the τοιαύτην. This so great contumely and opposition endured by Jesus the Hebrews are to consider, "to bring into analogy, think of by comparing" with their own and so renew their hopeful endurance. τὸν . . . ἀντιλογίαν, "Him who has endured at the hands of sinners such contradiction against Himself." The desire on the part of several interpreters to put a stronger meaning into ἀντιλογία —although quite unsupported by usage— reveals a feeling that verbal abuse or contradiction was a much less severe trial than such as are enumerated in chap. xi. But not only was it this ἀντιλογία which brought Christ to the cross and formed the αἰσχύνη of it, but it was the repudiation of His claims throughout His life which formed the chief element in His trial. It was predicted (Luke ii. 34) that He would be a σημεῖον ἀντιλεγόμενον, full of significance misinterpreted, full of God rejected. It was precisely this general rejection and contempt from which the Hebrews were themselves suffering. They were finding how hard it was to maintain a solitary faith contradicted and scorned by public sentiment. Think then, says this writer, of Him who has endured at the hands of sinners so much more painful contradiction "against Himself". ἵνα μὴ κάμητε . . . "that ye wax not weary, fainting in your souls". ψυχαῖς may be construed either with κάμητε or with ἐκλυόμενοι; better with the latter. [Polybius, xx. 4, 7, speaking of the demoralisation of the Boeotians says that giving themselves up to eating and drinking, οὐ μόνον τοῖς σώμασιν ἐξελύθησαν ἀλλὰ καὶ ταῖς ψυχαῖς.]

Ver. 4. Οὔπω μέχρις αἵματος . . . "Not yet unto blood have ye resisted in your contest with sin." Bengel says: "a cursu venit ad pugilatum". Cf. 1 Cor. ix. 24-27. But this is doubtful.

ἀνταγωνιζόμενοι, 5. ^dκαὶ ἐκλέλησθε τῆς παρακλήσεως, ἥτις ὑμῖν d Job v. 17
Prov. iii.
ὡς υἱοῖς διαλέγεται· "Υἱέ μου, μὴ ὀλιγώρει παιδείας Κυρίου, μηδὲ 11, 12;
Apoc. iii.
ἐκλύου ὑπ' αὐτοῦ ἐλεγχόμενος. 6. ὃν γὰρ ἀγαπᾷ Κύριος παιδεύει· 19.
μαστιγοῖ δὲ πάντα υἱὸν ὃν παραδέχεται." 7. Εἰ¹ παιδείαν ὑπομένετε, ὡς υἱοῖς ὑμῖν προσφέρεται ὁ Θεός· τίς γάρ ἐστιν

¹ ει in minusculis; εις in ℵADKLP, Vulg.

μέχρις αἵματος [Theoph., ἄχρι θανάτου, cf. Rev. xii. 11.] Does this mean,
Ye have not yet become a martyr church,
suffering death in Christ's cause ; or does
it mean, Ye have not yet resisted sin in
deadly earnest ? The interpretation is
determined by the connection. Jesus
endured the ἀντιλογία of sinners even to
blood, the death of the cross ; the Hebrews have not yet been called so to
suffer in their conflict, a conflict which
every day summons them to fresh resistance against the sin of failure of faith
and apostasy. "'Sin' is not here put
for sinners, nor is it sin in their persecutors ; it is sin in themselves, the sin of
unbelief, which is here regarded as their
true antagonist, though of course the ex-
cesses of their persecutors gave it its
power against them" (Davidson and
Weiss).

Vv. 5-17. The Hebrews are reminded
that their sufferings are tokens of God's
fatherly love and care.

Ver. 5. καὶ ἐκλέλησθε. . . . "And
ye have clean forgotten the exhortation,
which speaks to you as to sons, My Son,
etc.". καὶ introduces a fresh consideration. Calvin, Bleek and others treat the
clause as an interrogation, needlessly.
The παράκλησις is cited from Prov. iii.
11, and includes vv. 5 and 6. The only
divergence from the LXX is the insertion
of μου after υἱέ. But Bleek calls attention to the fact that the Hebrew of the last
clause stands, according to the present
punctuation, וּכְאָב אֶת־בֵּן יִרְצֶה =
and as a father the son in whom he
delights. The LXX instead of כְאָב
have read כָאַב the Piel of כָאַב to
feel pain, and so to cause pain; certainly a better sense. In the Book of
Proverbs the speaker identifies himself
with wisdom, and here the words are
justifiably viewed as Divine. ὀλιγώρει
is classical, meaning "make light of,"
"neglect," "despise". παιδεία is discipline, or correction, or the entire training and education of childhood and

youth. And it is here urged that by the
trials and difficulties of life God trains
His children ; that to view sufferings in
separation from God and to be oblivious
of God's design in them is disastrous ;
and that despondency and failure of faith
under suffering are inappropriate, for
trials are not evidence of God's displea-
sure, but on the contrary tokens of His
love, the uniform discipline to which
every son must be subjected, ὃν γὰρ
ἀγαπᾷ . . . the emphasis falling on
ἀγαπᾷ. ὃν παραδέχεται, "whom
He takes to Him as a veritable son,
receives in his heart and cherishes"
(Alford). The word is similarly used in
Polybius, xxxviii. 1, 8. [The same passage from Proverbs is cited by Philo (De
Cong. Erud. gratia, p 544) who adds,
οὕτως ἄρα ἡ ἐπίπληξις καὶ νουθεσία
καλὸν νενόμισται, ὥστε δι' αὐτῆς ἡ πρὸς
θεὸν ὁμολογία συγγένεια γίνεται· τί γὰρ
οἰκειότερον υἱῷ πατρὸς ἢ υἱοῦ πατρί;
Cf. Menander's ὁ μὴ δαρεὶς ἄνθρωπος οὐ
παιδεύεται, and Seneca's De Providentia
where the same comparison is elaborated,
and the great principle laid down "non
quid, sed quemadmodum feras, interest".]

Ver. 7. The inference from the passage cited is obvious, εἰς παιδείαν
ὑπομένετε, "it is for training ye are
enduring (are called to endure), as sons
God is dealing with you". [προσφέρεται
is common ; as in Xenophon, οὐ γὰρ
ὡς φίλοι προσεφέροντο ἡμῖν; and in
Josephus, ὡς πολεμίοις προσεφέροντο.]
Their sufferings are evidence that God
considers them His sons and treats them
as such ; for what son is there whom
his father does not correct? τίς γὰρ
υἱός . . . similar in form to Matt. vii.
9, τίς ἐστιν ἐξ ὑμῶν ἄνθρωπος;—εἰ δὲ
χωρίς. . . . Whereas did they receive
no such treatment, were they free from
that discipline of which all (God's children) have become partakers (as illustrated in chap. xi.) then in this case they
are bastards and not sons ; their freedom
from the discipline which God uniformly
accords His children would prove that
they were not genuine sons.

υἱὸς ὃν οὐ παιδεύει πατήρ; 8. εἰ δὲ χωρίς ἐστε παιδείας, ἧς

Num. xvi. μέτοχοι γεγόνασι πάντες, ἄρα νόθοι ἐστὲ καὶ οὐχ υἱοί. 9. °εἶτα
22, et
xxvii. 16; τοὺς μὲν τῆς σαρκὸς ἡμῶν πατέρας εἴχομεν παιδευτὰς, καὶ ἐνετρε-
Eccl. xii.
1, 7; Esa. πόμεθα · οὐ πολλῷ μᾶλλον ὑποταγησόμεθα, τῷ πατρὶ τῶν πνευμάτων,
lviii. 16,
Zach. xii. καὶ ζήσομεν; 10. οἱ μὲν γὰρ πρὸς ὀλίγας ἡμέρας, κατὰ τὸ δοκοῦν
1.
       αὐτοῖς, ἐπαίδευον· ὁ δὲ ἐπὶ τὸ συμφέρον, εἰς τὸ μεταλαβεῖν τῆς

       ἁγιότητος αὐτοῦ. 11. πᾶσα δὲ[1] παιδεία πρὸς μὲν τὸ παρὸν οὐ

       δοκεῖ χαρᾶς εἶναι, ἀλλὰ λύπης · ὕστερον δὲ καρπὸν εἰρηνικὸν τοῖς

[1] WH read μεν with א*P, 17, 21, d; δε is found in אcADcKL, f, Vulg., etc.
["None of the particles are satisfactory, though δέ was sure to be introduced"
(Hort).]

Ver. 9. With εἶτα a fresh phase of
the argument is introduced. [Raphel *in
loc.* is of opinion that εἶτα here as frequently in the classics is "nota inter-
rogantis cum vehementia et quasi indig-
natione quadam"; but it gives a better
construction if we take it in the sense of
"further" as in 1 Cor. xii. 5, 7, and
Mark iv. 28, πρῶτον χόρτον, εἶτα στάχυν,
εἶτα πλήρης σῖτος.] The argument is,
"the fathers of our flesh we used to
have as trainers, and we had them in
reverence; shall we not much rather be
subject to the Father of our spirits and
live?" The article before πνευμάτων
makes it probable that there is no reference to angels but only an antithesis to
τῆς σαρκὸς ἡμῶν. The position of the
two words σαρκός and πνευμάτων confirms this. καὶ ζήσομεν is unexpected, and is inserted to balance καὶ
ἐνετρεπόμεθα [on this verb see Anz. p.
269] in the rhythm of the sentence.
The thought is that only by subjection
to the Father of our spirit can we have
life. Delitzsch maintains that this verse
strongly favours the theory of Creationism
and quotes Hugo de S. Victore, "Nota
diligenter hanc authoritatem, per quam
manifeste probatur, quod animae non
sunt ex traduce sicut caro". It is safer
to say with Davidson, "It is as a spirit,
or on his spiritual side, that man enters
into close relation with God; and this
leads to the conception that God is more
especially the Author of man's spirit, or
Author of man on his spiritual side,
and to designations such as those in
Num. xvi. 22". Modern science scouts
Creationism; although if Wallace's idea
of the evolution of man be accepted it
might find encouragement.
Ver. 10. οἱ μὲν γάρ. . . . The
reasonableness of the appeal of ver. 9 is
further illustrated by a comparison of
the character and end in the earthly and

heavenly fathers' discipline respectively.
The earthly fathers exercised discipline
for a few days in accordance with what
commended itself to their judgment as
proper; a judgment which could not be
infallible and must sometimes have hindered rather than helped true growth;
but the heavenly Father uses discipline
with a view to our profit that we may
partake of his holiness. Two notes of
imperfection characterise the discipline
of the fathers of our flesh. (1) It is
πρὸς ὀλίγας ἡμέρας, "for a few
days," *i.e.*, during the brief period of
youth. It must cease when manhood is
attained, whether or not it has attained
its end. (2) It is κατὰ τὸ δοκοῦν
αὐτοῖς, subject to misconception both
of the end to be reached and the means
by which it can be attained. In contrast
to this second feature the discipline of
the Father of our spirit is without fail
ἐπὶ τὸ συμφέρον, "for our advantage,"
which is defined in εἰς τὸ μεταλαβ-
εῖν τῆς ἁγιότητος αὐτοῦ, "that
we may partake of His holiness," in
which the contrast to the incomplete
Ver. 11. πᾶσα δὲ παιδεία. . . .
Another encouragement to endure chastening: if it is allowed to do its work
righteousness will result. "Now all
chastisement for the present indeed
seems matter not of joy but of grief,
afterwards however it yields, to those
who are disciplined by it, the peaceable
fruit of righteousness". [πᾶσα, as
Chrys. says, τουτέστι καὶ ἡ ἀνθρωπίνη
καὶ ἡ πνευματική.] πρὸς τὸ παρόν,
see Thucyd., ii. 22. οὐ δοκεῖ . . .
λύπης, Chrys. καλῶς εἶπεν· οὐ δοκεῖ.
οὐδὲ γάρ ἐστι λύπης ἡ παιδεία, ἀλλὰ
μόνον δοκεῖ, see Bleek. Chastisement
is here viewed as an opportunity for
cultivating faith and endurance and to
those who use the opportunity and are
exercised and trained by it, δι' αὐτῆς

δι᾽ αὐτῆς γεγυμνασμένοις ἀποδίδωσι δικαιοσύνης. 12. ᶠΔιὸ "τὰς ᶠEsa, xxxv.
3.
παρειμένας χεῖρας καὶ τὰ παραλελυμένα γόνατα ἀνορθώσατε"· 13. g Matt. v.
8; Rom.
καὶ "τροχιὰς ὀρθὰς ποιήσατε ¹ τοῖς ποσὶν ὑμῶν," ἵνα μὴ τὸ χωλὸν xii. 28; 2
Tim.ii.22.
ἐκτραπῇ, ἰαθῇ δὲ μᾶλλον. 14. ᵍΕἰρήνην διώκετε μετὰ πάντων, καὶ h iii. 12;
Deut.
τὸν ἁγιασμὸν, οὗ χωρὶς οὐδεὶς ὄψεται τὸν Κύριον· 15. ʰἐπισκοποῦν- xxix. 18;
Acts xvii.
13; 2 Cor. vi.; 1 Gal. v. 12.

¹ ποιησατε in אᶜADKL ; ποιειτε in א*P, 17.

γεγυμνασμένοις, it necessarily
yields, renders as the harvest due, ἀποδίδωσιν, as its fruit increased righteousness of life. But why "peaceful"
εἰρηνικὸν? Probably because the result of the conflict (γεγυμνασμένοις) and
victory is peace in God and peace of conscience. It is a peace which can only
be attained by those who have used their
trials as a discipline and have emerged
victorious from the conflict.

Ver. 12. διὸ τὰς παρειμένας
... "Wherefore" introducing the immediate application of this encouraging
view of trials, "lift up" to renew the
conflict, "the nerveless hands" fallen to
your side and "the paralysed knees".
ἀνορθώσατε seems at first sight more appropriate to χεῖρας than to γόνατα
(Vaughan) but it is here used in the
general sense of "restore," "renew the
life of"; as in Soph., O.T., 46-51, ἀσφ-
αλείᾳ τήνδ᾽ ἀνόρθωσον πόλιν. It might
be rendered "revive". Probably the
writer had in his mind Isa. xxxv. 3,
ἰσχύσατε, χεῖρες ἀνειμέναι καὶ γόνατα
παραλελυμένα. In Sir. xxv. 23 the woman that does not increase the happiness
of her husband is χεῖρες παρειμέναι καὶ
γόνατα παραλελυμένα, in other words,
makes him despair and cease from all
effort. So here, the hands hang down
in listless consciousness of defeat. καὶ
τροχιὰς ὀρθὰς ... "and make
straight paths for your feet, that that
which is lame be not turned out of the
way but rather be healed". The words
are quoted from Prov. iv. 26, ὀρθὰς
τροχιὰς ποίει σοῖς ποσί, and if ποιήσατε is retained they form a hexameter
line. The whole verse forms an admonition to the healthier portion of the church
to make no deviation from the straight
course set before them by the example of
Christ, and thus they would offer no
temptation to the weaker members [τὸ
χωλὸν, the lame and limping] to be turned
quite out of the way, but would rather
be an encouragement to them and so
afford them an opportunity of being
healed of their infirmity. [A number of

interpreters take ἐκτραπῇ in the sense of
"dislocated". Thus Davidson, "The
words 'turned out of the way' mean in
medical writers 'dislocated,' and this
gives a more vigorous sense and forms a
better opposition to 'be healed'. Inconsistency and vacillation in the general
body of the church would create a way
so difficult for the lame, that their lame-
ness would become dislocation, and they
would perish from the way; on the other
hand, the habit of going in a plain path
would restore them to soundness." This
is inviting, but there is much against it.
(1) The medical use of ἐκτρέπομαι is
rare (see Stephanus) and not likely to
occur here. (2) When used in a general
sense ἰαθῇ is an appropriate antithesis;
thus in Niceph. Call. (see Stephanus)
occur the words Ἰωάννῃ τῷ Ἱεροσολύμων
πατριάρχῃ τὴν ἀκοὴν ἐκτραπεῖσαν ἰᾶ-
ται. (3) The passage in Proverbs from
which the former part of the verse is cited
goes on thus: "Turn not aside to the
right hand nor to the left".] Immediately after these words follows a clause
which guides to the interpretation of
εἰρήνην διώκετε μετὰ πάντων,
"God will make thy ways straight and
will guide thy goings in peace"; and a
considerable part of the counsels given
in the context in Proverbs concerns the
maintenance of peaceful relations with
others. The circumstances of the Hebrews were fitted to excite a quarrelsome
spirit, and a feeling of alienation towards
those weak members who left the straight
path. They must not suffer them to be
alienated but must restore them to the
unity of the faith, and in endeavouring
to reclaim them must use the methods of
peace not of anger or disputation. καὶ
τὸν ἁγιασμὸν ... "and the consecration without which no one shall see
the Lord". The ἁγιασμός which this
Epistle has explained is a drawing near
to God with cleansed conscience (x. 14,
22), a true acceptance of Christ's sacrifice as bringing the worshipper into fellowship with God.
Ver. 15. ἐπισκοποῦντες μή

Gen. xxv.
33; Eph.
v. 3; Col.
iii. 5; 1
Thess. iv.
3.
k Gen.
xxvii. 34,
etc.

τες μή τις ὑστερῶν ἀπὸ τῆς χάριτος τοῦ Θεοῦ · μή τις ῥίζα πικρίας
ἄνω φύουσα ἐνοχλῇ, καὶ διὰ ταύτης[1] μιανθῶσι πολλοί[2] · 16. ἱ μή
τις πόρνος, ἢ βέβηλος, ὡς Ἡσαῦ, ὃς ἀντὶ βρώσεως μιᾶς ἀπέδοτο[3] τὰ
πρωτοτόκια αὐτοῦ. 17. ᵏ ἴστε γὰρ ὅτι καὶ μετέπειτα θέλων κληρο-

[1] T.R. in אDKL; δι' αυτης AP, 17, 47.
[2] T.R. in DKLP; οι πολλοι in אA, 17, 47.
[3] T.R. אDKLP, 17; απεδετο AC.

τις ὑστερῶν... "watching" "taking the oversight" (thoroughly scrutinising as in the case of sick persons," Chrys.) addressed not to the teachers or rulers but to all. The object of this supervision is to prevent the defection of any one of their number. "As if they were travelling together on some long journey, in a large company, he says, Take heed that no man be left behind; I do not seek this only, that ye may arrive yourselves, but also that ye should look diligently after the others" (Chrys.), and cf. M. Arnold's In Rugby Chapel. μή τις ὑστερῶν... may be construed either by supplying ᾖ, or by supposing a break at θεοῦ (so Davidson), or by carrying on the τις ὑστερῶν to ἐνοχλῇ. The simplest seems to be the first: "lest any be failing (= fail) of the grace of God," i.e., lest he never reach the blessings which the grace of God offers. Cf. iv. 1. Another contingency to be guarded against by careful watching is expressed in μή τις ῥίζα πικρίας... words borrowed from Deut. xxix. 18, μή τίς ἐστιν ἐν ὑμῖν ῥίζα ἄνω φύουσα ἐν χολῇ καὶ πικρίᾳ, "lest any root of bitterness springing up trouble you". As in Deuteronomy so here the bitter root which might spring up and bring forth its poisonous fruit among them, was one of their own members who might lead them astray or introduce evil practises and so the whole community [οἱ πολλοί] might be defiled [μιανθῶσιν], i.e., rendered unfit for that approach to God and fellowship with Him to which they were urged in the preceding verse. A little leaven leaveneth the whole lump, Gal. v. 9, where also it is a person that is referred to. Ver. 16. μή τις πόρνος... specific forms in which roots of bitterness might appear among them. πόρνος is to be taken in its literal sense and not as signifying departure from God [but cf. Weiss]. Neither is it to be applied to Esau, in spite of the passages adduced by Wetstein to show that he was commonly considered a fornicator, and of

Philo's interpretation of "hairy" as "intemperate and libidinous"; v. Delitzsch. From xiii. 4 it appears that fornication was one of the dangers to which these Hebrews were exposed. ἢ βέβηλος ὡς Ἡσαῦ, a profanity which was especially betrayed in his bartering for a single meal [ἀντὶ βρώσεως μιᾶς] his own rights of primogeniture. Esau lightly parting with his religious privileges and his patrimony for a present gratification is an appropriate warning to those who day by day were tempted to win comfort and escape suffering by parting with their hope in Christ. The warning is pointed by the fate of Esau. ἴστε γὰρ ὅτι καὶ μετέπειτα... "for ye know that even though he was afterwards desirous to inherit the blessing he was rejected, though he sought it with tears; for he found no place of repentance". "The term 'repentance' is here used not strictly of mere change of mind, but of a change of mind undoing the effects of a former state of mind" (Davidson). In other words, his bargain was irrevocable. The words must be interpreted by the narrative in Genesis (xxvii. 1-41), where we read that some time after the sale of the birthright (μετέπειτα) Esau sought the blessing with tears (xxvii. 38, ἀνεβόησε φωνῇ Ἡσαῦ καὶ ἔκλαυσεν) but found his act was unalterable. The lesson written on Esau's life as on that of all who miss opportunities is that the past is irreparable, and however much they may desire to recall and alter it, that cannot be. It was this which the writer wished to enforce. If now, through any temptation or pressure, you let go the benefits you have in Christ, you are committing yourselves to an act you cannot recall. It must also be observed that the author is confining his attention to the one act of Esau, not pronouncing on his whole life and ultimate destiny. [μετανοίας τόπον. So Pliny, Ep., x. 97, "poenitentiae locus;" and Ulpian, Digest., xl. Tit. 7, "poenitentiae haeredis is locum non esse" (Wetstein)].

νομῆσαι τὴν εὐλογίαν, ἀπεδοκιμάσθη· μετανοίας γὰρ τόπον οὐχ [1] Exod. xix. 10, etc., et xx. 19; Deut. v. 22.
εὗρε, καίπερ μετὰ δακρύων ἐκζητήσας αὐτήν.

18. [1]Οὐ γὰρ προσεληλύθατε ψηλαφωμένῳ ὄρει,[1] καὶ κεκαυμένῳ [m] Exod.xx. 19; Deut. v. 5, 24, et xviii. 16.
πυρὶ, καὶ γνόφῳ, καὶ σκότῳ, καὶ θυέλλῃ, 19. [m]καὶ σάλπιγγος ἤχῳ,
καὶ φωνῇ ῥημάτων, ἧς οἱ ἀκούσαντες παρῃτήσαντο μὴ προστεθῆναι

[1] T.R. Dgr KL, 37, 116; omit ορει א AC, 17, 47, f, Vulg., Cod., Opt., Syr. Pesch.

Vv. 18-29. In this paragraph we have the climax of the Epistle. Its doctrine and its exhortation alike culminate here. The great aim of the writer has been to persuade the Hebrews to hearken to the word spoken by God in Christ (i. 1, ii. 1-4). This aim he still seeks to attain by bringing before his readers in one closing picture the contrast between the old dispensation and the new. The old was characterised by material, sensible transitory manifestations; the new by what is supersensible and eternally stable. The old also rather emphasised the inaccessible nature of God, His unapproachable holiness, His awful majesty, and taught men that they could not come near; the new brings men into the very presence of God, and though He be "Judge of all" yet is He surrounded with the spirits of perfected men. But as the writer seeks to quicken his readers to a more zealous faith He shows also the awful consequences of refusing Him that speaketh from heaven. Not the fire and smoke of Sinai threaten now to consume the disobedient, but "our God is a consuming fire"; not a symbolic and material element threatened, but the very Eternal and All-pervading Himself. And, returning to the idea with which he commenced the Epistle and so making its unity obvious, the writer contrasts the voice that shook the earth with the infinitely more terrible voice that shakes the heavens also, that terminates time and brings in eternal things.

Ver. 18. Οὐ γὰρ προσεληλύθατε... "For ye have not approached," assigning a further reason for the previous exhortation. Your fathers drew near [Deut. iv. 11, προσήλθετε καὶ ἔστητε ὑπὸ τὸ ὄρος] to hear God's word. The word is used in its general sense, and the idea of drawing near as an accepted worshipper is not intended. ψηλαφωμένῳ... As MS. authority removes ὄρει, the construction is doubtful. The R.V. renders "the mount that might be touched," indicating that "the mount" is not in the text. This is justified by the antithetic clause, ver. 22, ἀλλὰ προσε-

ληλύθατε Σιὼν ὄρει, which already was in his mind. Others translate "ye are not come to a palpable and kindled fire," which is grammatically possible, but open to the objection that "a palpable fire," a fire that can be touched is precisely what this fire was not, and it is an awkward mode of expressing a "material" fire. A third rendering is "Ye are not come to that which can be touched and is kindled with fire". κεκαυμένῳ πυρὶ, "that burned with fire" is in agreement with Deut. iv. 11, τὸ ὄρος ἐκαίετο πυρὶ ἕως τοῦ οὐρανοῦ· σκότος, γνόφος, θύελλα; see also Deut. v. 22, 23, ix. 15; Exod. xix. 18. The "gloom and mist and tempest (or hurricane) and the blast of trumpet (Exod. xix. 16, φωνὴ τῆς σάλπιγγος ἤχει μέγα) and voice of words" (Deut. iv. 12, ἐλάλησε Κύριος πρὸς ὑμᾶς ἐκ μέσου τοῦ πυρὸς φωνὴν ῥημάτων) are enumerated to accentuate the material and terrifying character of the revelation on which the O.T. dispensation was founded. The regularly recurrent καὶ gives emphasis to this enumeration; all the features of the manifestation were of the same character. The article is omitted before each particular, because each is introduced not for its own sake but for the general effect. From ἧς to ἔντρομος (ver. 21) describes the terror induced by these manifestations, (1) first in the people (οἱ ἀκούσαντες) who begged that not a word more should be added to them (προστεθῆναι suggested by Deut. v. 25 and xviii. 16, οὐ προσθήσομεν ἀκοῦσαι τὴν φωνὴν Κυρίου, "we will not any more hear, etc.,") for they could not endure that which was being commanded, "If even a beast touch the mountain it shall be stoned" (Exod. xix. 12, 13); and (2) also in Moses, for, so terrifying was the appearance that Moses said, "I am extremely afraid (Deut. ix. 9) and tremble". (ἔκφοβός εἰμι was uttered by Moses when God's anger was roused by the people's idolatry; Stephen (Acts vii. 32) uses ἔντρομος γενόμενος of Moses at the burning bush.)

n Exod.xix. αὐτοῖς λόγον· 20. ᵑοὐκ ἔφερον γὰρ τὸ διαστελλόμενον, ''Κἂν θηρίον
13.   θίγῃ τοῦ ὅρους, λιθοβοληθήσεται, ἢ βολίδι κατατοξευθήσεται¹''·
o Gal. iv.
26; Apoc. 21. καὶ, οὕτω φοβερὸν ἦν τὸ φανταζόμενον, Μωσῆς εἶπεν, ''Ἔκφοβός
iii. 12, et
xxi. 2, 10. εἰμι καὶ ἔντρομος·'' 22. ᵒἀλλὰ προσεληλύθατε Σιὼν ὅρει, καὶ πόλει

¹ This clause occurs in none of the uncials—the sole authority is ''nonnulli
minusculi''.

Ver. 22. The Christian standing and
attainment are now described in contrast
with the Jewish. Ye are brought into
the fellowship of eternal realities. ἀλλὰ προσεληλύθατε, "but ye have
drawn near" (already you have entered
into your eternal relation to the unseen)
to Σιὼν ὅρει, "in the twenty-three passages in the LXX where the two words
are combined the order is uniformly ὅρος
Σιὼν and not Σιὼν ὅρος. Evidently here
the 'Zion mountain' is mentally contrasted with another, the 'Sinai mountain'. And thus the omission of ὅρει in
the revised text of ver. 18 is virtually
supplied" (Vaughan). The ideal Zion
is the place of God's manifestation of
His presence (Ps. ix. 11, lxxvi. 2) but
also of His people's abode (Ps. cxlvi. 10;
Isa. i. 27 and passim). It is therefore
impossible to find another particular of
the enumeration in πόλει θεοῦ ζῶντος Ἰερουσαλὴμ ἐπουρανίῳ, as
if the latter were "the transcendent
sphere of God's existence where He is
manifested only to Himself," and the
latter "the place where His people
gather and where He is manifested to
them". (Cf. Isa. lx. 14, κληθήσῃ πόλις
Κυρίου, Σιών); the mount and the city
are viewed together as the meeting-place
of God and His people, where the "living God" manifests fully His eternal
fulness and sufficiency. It is "the heavenly Jerusalem" (cf. Gal. iv. 26, ἡ ἄνω
Ἰερουσαλήμ and Rev. xxi. 2, ἡ πόλις ἡ
μέλλουσα [καὶ μένουσα], xiii. 14) as being
not the earthly and made with hands
but the ultimate reality [cf. the beautiful
description in Philo, De Som., ii. 38, and
the Republic, ix. p. 592, where after
declaring that no such city as he has
been describing exists on earth Plato
goes on to say, Ἀλλ' ἐν οὐρανῷ ἴσως
παράδειγμα ἀνάκειται τῷ βουλομένῳ
ὁρᾶν καὶ ὁρῶντι ἑαυτὸν κατοικίζειν.
Also the fine passage in Seneca, De Otio,
chap. 31, on the two Republics.] καὶ
μυριάσιν ἀγγέλων, and to myriads
of angels, the usual accompaniment of
God's glory and ministers of His will, as
in Deut. xxxii. 2; Rev. v. 11; and Dan.

vii. 10, μύριαι μυριάδες παρειστήκεισαν
αὐτῷ. The construction of the following
words is much debated. (1) πανηγύρει
καὶ ἐκκλησ. may be construed in apposition with μυρ. ἀγγέλων, to myriads of
angels, a festal gathering and assembly
of the first-born enrolled in heaven; or,
(2) a new particular may be introduced
with καὶ ἐκκλησ.; or, (3) a new particular may be introduced with πανηγύρει, "to myriads of angels, to a festal
gathernig and assembly of the first-born."
On the whole, the first seems preferable.
For although angels are not elsewhere
called the "first-born" of God, they are
called "sons of God" (Job. i. 6, ii. 1,
xxxviii. 7; Gen. vi. 2, 4; Ps. lxxxix. 6)
and the designation is here appropriate
to denote those who are the pristine inhabitants of heaven. Cf. the first choir
of Angelicals in the "Dream of Geron-
tius," who sing:—

"To us His elder race He gave
    To battle and to win,
Without the chastisement of pain,
    Without the soil of sin";

and Augustine in De Civ. Dei, x. 7, "cum
angelis sumus una civitas Dei . . . cujus
pars in nobis peregrinatur, pars in illis
opitulatur". πανήγυρις, meaning a
festal gathering of the whole people, and
ἐκκλησία meaning the assembly of all
enrolled citizens, seem much more applicable to angels. They are enrolled as
citizens (ἀπογεγ. see the Fayûm and
Oxyrhynchus Papyri, passim) in heaven,
and welcome the younger sons now introduced. The myriads of angels which
on Sinai had made their presence known
in thunders and smoke and tempest, terrifying the people, appear now in the
familiar form of a well-ordered community
in the peaceable guise of citizens rejoicing
over additions to their ranks (Luke xv.
10). καὶ κριτῇ θεῷ πάντων,
"and to a Judge who is God of all," and
by whose judgment you must therefore
stand or fall (cf. x. 27, 30, 31). Among
the realities to which they had been
introduced this could not be omitted. He
who is God of all living is the ultimate

Θεοῦ ζῶντος, Ἱερουσαλὴμ ἐπουρανίῳ, καὶ μυριάσιν ἀγγέλων, 23. p Luc. x. 20.
[p] πανηγύρει καὶ ἐκκλησίᾳ πρωτοτόκων ἐν οὐρανοῖς ἀπογεγραμμένων, q viii. 6, et ix. 15, et
καὶ κριτῇ Θεῷ πάντων, καὶ πνεύμασι δικαίων τετελειωμένων, 24. x. 22, et xi. 4;
[q] καὶ διαθήκης νέας μεσίτῃ Ἰησοῦ, καὶ αἵματι ῥαντισμοῦ κρείττονα[1] Gen. iv. 10; Exod.
λαλοῦντι παρὰ τὸν[2] Ἄβελ. 25. [r] Βλέπετε μὴ παραιτήσησθε τὸν xxiv. 8; 1 Tim. ii. 5;
λαλοῦντα. εἰ γὰρ ἐκεῖνοι οὐκ ἔφυγον,[3] τὸν ἐπὶ τῆς γῆς παραιτη- 1 Peter i. 2.
σάμενοι χρηματίζοντα, πολλῷ μᾶλλον ἡμεῖς οἱ τὸν ἀπ᾽ οὐρανῶν r ii. 3, et x. 28.

[1] T.R. 17, 47; **κρειττον** ℵACDKLMP, d, f, Vulg.

[2] T.R. in ℵACDKMP, d, f, Vulg.; **παρα το** in L, b, 106, 108.

[3] T.R. ℵcDcKLM, Thdrt.; **εξεφυγον** in ℵ*ACP, 17, 57, 118, Chr. 419.

reality, and the Hebrews have been brought near not only to His city with its original inhabitants, but to Himself; and to Himself as allotting without appeal each soul to its destiny. **καὶ πνεύμασι . . .** "and to spirits of just men made perfect," "spirits," as in 1 Pet. iii. 19, of those who have departed this life and not yet been clothed with their resurrection body. **δικαίων τετελειωμένων** is largely illustrated by Wetstein who quotes many examples of "justi perfecti" from the Talmud. It is perhaps more relevant to refer to xi. 4 and to the whole strain of the Epistle whose aim it is to perfect the righteousness of the Hebrews, see chap. vi. Of course O.T. and N.T. saints are referred to. But as without us, *i.e.*, without sharing in our advantages, they could not be perfected, xi. 40, there is at once introduced the recent covenant (**νέας** "new in time," not, as usual, **καίνης** "fresh in quality,") because the idea first in the writer's mind is not the opposition to the old but the recent origin of the new. (But *cf.* Col. iii. 9; 1 Cor. v. 7). It is remarkable that the Mediator of this covenant is here called by his human name "Jesus". The reason probably is that already there is in the writer's mind the great instrument of mediation, **αἵματι ῥαντισμοῦ**, "blood of sprinkling". In mediating the old covenant Moses, **λαβὼν τὸ αἷμα κατεσκέδασε τοῦ λαοῦ**, Exod. xxiv. 8. [**αἷμα ῥαντισμοῦ**, however, does not occur in LXX, though **ὕδωρ ῥαντισμοῦ** is found four times in *Numbers*]. But in ix. 19 this writer replaces **κατεσκέδασε** with the more significant **ἐράντισεν**; *cf.* ix. 13. In 1 Pet. i. 2 we have **ῥαντισμὸν αἵματος Ἰησοῦ Χριστοῦ**. The "blood of sprinkling" is therefore the blood by which the new covenant is established, see xiii. 20, **αἵματι διαθήκης αἰωνίου**, this blood having the power to cleanse the conscience, ix. 14, x. 22. It cleanses because it speaks better than Abel's, **κρεῖττον λαλοῦντι παρὰ τὸν Ἄβελ** for while that of Abel cried for vengeance [Gen. iv. 10, **φωνὴ αἵματος τοῦ ἀδελφοῦ σου βοᾷ πρός με ἐκ τῆς γῆς**] that of Jesus is a message of salvation, the **κρεῖττόν τι** of xi. 40. But it may be adverbial. "Ille flagitabat ultionem, hic impetrat remissionem" (Erasmus).

Ver. 25-29. A final appeal. The readers are warned against being deaf to God's final revelation, for if even the revelation at Sinai could not with impunity be disregarded, much less can the revelation which has reached them and which discloses to them things eternal and God in His essential majesty.

Ver. 25. **βλέπετε** (in the same sense and in a similar connection in iii. 12) **μὴ παραιτήσησθε**, "See that you refuse not"—as those mentioned in ver. 19 did—**τὸν λαλοῦντα**, "Him that speaketh," *i.e.*, God as in i. 1 and the close of this verse; "for if those did not escape (punishment) when they refused Him that made to them divine communications on earth, how much less shall we who turn away from Him who does so from heaven"? The argument is the same as in ii. 3. Those who at Sinai begged to be excused from hearing did so in terror of the manifestations of God's presence. But this is taken both as itself rooted in ignorance of God and aversion, and also as the first manifestation of a refusal to listen which in the history of Israel was often repeated. Punishment followed both in the Sinai generation, iii. 7-19, and in after times. The speaking **ἐπὶ γῆς**, *i.e.*, at Sinai (and through the prophets? i. 1) is contrasted with speaking **ἀπ᾽ οὐρανῶν**, which can only mean speaking from the midst of and in terms of eternal reality, without those earthly

§ ver. 19;
Agg. ii. 6,
7.
t Ps. cii. 26;
Matt.
xxiv. 35;
2 Peter
iii. 10.
u 1 Peter ii.
5.
v Deut. iv.
24, et ix.
3.

ἀποστρεφόμενοι, 26. *οὗ ἡ φωνὴ τὴν γῆν ἐσάλευσε τότε, νῦν δὲ ἐπήγγελται, λέγων, ""Ετι ἅπαξ ἐγὼ σείω οὐ μόνον τὴν γῆν, ἀλλὰ καὶ τὸν οὐρανόν". 27. ᵗΤὸ δὲ, ""Ετι ἅπαξ," δηλοῖ τῶν σαλευομένων τὴν μετάθεσιν, ὡς πεποιημένων, ἵνα μείνῃ τὰ μὴ σαλευόμενα. 28. ᵘδιὸ βασιλείαν ἀσάλευτον παραλαμβάνοντες, ἔχωμεν χάριν, δι᾽ ἧς ᵛλατρεύωμεν εὐαρέστως τῷ Θεῷ μετὰ αἰδοῦς καὶ εὐλαβείας.[1] 29. ᵛκαὶ γὰρ "ὁ Θεὸς ἡμῶν πῦρ καταναλίσκον".

[1] T.R. is only supported by KL, Chrys.; ευλαβειας και δεους in ℵ*ACD*, 17, 71, 73.

symbols which characterised the old revelations, vv. 18, 19. The revelation in the Son is a revelation of the essential Divine nature in terms that are eternally true and valid. *Cf.* ix. 14, διὰ πνεύματος αἰωνίου. The difference between the two revelations is disclosed in their results or accompaniments; of the former, τότε, it is said ἡ φωνὴ τὴν γῆν ἐσάλευσεν, "the voice shook the earth," even that symbolic and earthly manifestation was well fitted to convey just impressions of God's holiness; [ἔδωκε φωνὴν αὐτοῦ, ἐσαλεύθη ἡ γῆ Ps. xlvi. 5, also Ps. xviii. 7 and in Ps. lxviii. 8, γῆ ἐσείσθη ; Jud. v. 4, 5, sometimes as in Ps. cxiv. 7 more explicitly ἀπὸ προσώπου Κυρίου ἐσαλεύθη ἡ γῆ.] The expression sets forth not only the majesty of God who speaks, but also the effects that follow in agitation and alteration [*cf.* the *Antigone* line 163, τὰ μὲν δὴ πόλεος θεοὶ πολλῷ σάλῳ σείσαντες]. νῦν δὲ ἐπήγγελται, "But now he has promised"—the passive used in middle sense as in Rom. iv. 21—the promise is in Hag. ii. 6, 7, where under this strong figure the new order of things introduced by the rebuilding of the temple is announced. (*Cf.* Sir. xvi. 18, 19) λέγων, Ἔτι ἅπαξ . . . saying, "Yet once (or, Once more) I will shake not only the earth but also the heaven". And what the writer especially sees in this promise is declared expressly in ver. 27, τὸ δὲ Ἔτι ἅπαξ δηλοῖ . . . "the expression 'once more' indicates the removal of what has been shaken as of what has been made (created), that what is not shaken may abide". The ἅπαξ indicates the finality of this predicted manifestation of God—only once more was he to reveal Himself. This revelation has made known to us and put us in possession of that which is eternal, so that when all present forms of existence pass away (*cf.* i. 11, 12), what is essential and eternal may still be retained. Underlying the interpretation which the writer gives to ἅπαξ is the belief that some

time things temporal must give place to things eternal; else he could not have argued that the final "shaking" was to be equivalent to a removal, (μετάθεσις, change of place in xi. 5; but in vii. 12 removal, displacement; and so here) or destruction of the heavens and the earth. The words ὡς πεποιημένων show that he considered that all that had been made might or would be destroyed, as in i. 10, "the works of God's hands shall perish". (*Cf.* γένεσις φθορᾶς ἀρχή]. ἵνα is dependent on μετάθεσιν, transitory things are removed that the things that are eternal may appear in their abiding value. διὸ, seeing that these perishable things must pass away "let us who are receiving a kingdom (a realm in which we shall be as kings, Luke xii. 32, xxii. 29; Rev. i. 6) that is immovable and inalienable have grace" (iv. 16, xii. 15). Many interpreters (Weiss, Westcott, Weizsäcker, Peake) render ἔχωμεν χάριν as in Luke xvii. 9; 1 Tim. i. 12, "let us feel and express thankfulness" which is a very suitable inference to draw from " our receiving an immovable kingdom" and is relevant also to the following clause. But as χάρις is used by this writer in iv. 16 of God's helping favour, and as the τις ὑστερῶν ἀπὸ τῆς χάριτος τοῦ θεοῦ of ver. 15 is still in view, it seems simpler and more adequate to render as A.V. It is God's grace, δι᾽ ἧς λατρεύωμεν . . . "by means of which we may acceptably serve God [λατρεύωμεν as in ix. 14, possibly in a broader sense than mere worship] with reverence (v. 7) and fear ". An additional or recapitulating reason is given in the closing words, " For indeed our God is a consuming fire," words derived from Deut. iv. 24. The fire and smoke which manifested His presence at Sinai (ver. 18) were but symbols of that consuming holiness that destroys all persistent inexcusable evil. It is God Himself who is the fire with which you have to do, not a mere physical, material, quenchable fire.

XIII. 1. ^aἩ ΦΙΛΑΔΕΛΦΙΑ μενέτω.   ^bτῆς φιλοξενίας μὴ ἐπι-   a Rom. xii.
10; Eph.
λανθάνεσθε·   2. διὰ ταύτης γὰρ ἔλαθόν τινες ξενίσαντες ἀγγέλους·   iv. 2, 3; 1
Peter i.
3. ^cμιμνήσκεσθε τῶν δεσμίων, ὡς συνδεδεμένοι· τῶν κακουχουμένων,¹   22, et ii.
17, et iii.
ὡς καὶ αὐτοὶ ὄντες ἐν σώματι.   4. τίμιος ὁ γάμος ἐν πᾶσι, καὶ ἡ   8, et iv. 8.
b Gen.xviii.
1, et xix.

1; Rom. xii. 13; 1 Peter iv. 9.   c Matt. xxv. 36; Rom. xii. 15; Col. iv. 18; 1 Peter iii. 8.

¹ κακοχουμ. in D^cKLMP.

CHAPTER XIII. In this chapter we find exhortations apparently springing out of a desire to arrest symptoms of a tendency to hide their Christian profession disowning their teachers and fellow Christians and resenting the shame and hardship incident to the following of Christ.

Vv. 1-6. Exhortations to social manifestations of their Christianity. Ἡ φιλαδελφία μενέτω. "Let love of the brethren continue"; it existed (vi. 10) and so, as Chrys. says, he does not write Γίνεσθε φιλάδελφοι, ἀλλὰ, μενέτω ἡ φιλ. In the general decay of their faith tendencies to disown Christian fellowship had become apparent, x. 24, 25. This might also lead to a failure to recognise the wants of Christians coming from a distance, therefore hospitality is urged; not as a duty they did not already practise, but, gently, as that which they might omit through forgetfulness and as that which might bring them a message from God: τῆς φιλοξενίας μὴ ἐπιλανθάνεσθε, "Entertainment of strangers do not neglect; for thus some have entertained angels unawares," as in Gen. xviii.-19; Jud. vi. 11-24, xiii. 2-23 [For testimonies to the hospitality of Christians Bleek refers to Lucian, De Morte Peregrin., chap. 16 and to the 49th Epistle of Julian, On the hospitality of the East see Palgrave's Essays, p. 246-7.] ἔλαθόν τινες ξενίσαντες though a common classical idiom, occurs nowhere else in the N.T. Some of their fellow Christians might be in even more needy circumstances and therefore

Ver. 3. μιμνήσκεσθε (ii. 6) τῶν δεσμίων (x. 34), "Be mindful of those in bonds" (Matt. xxv. 36). This also they had already done (x. 34). The motive now urged is contained in the words ὡς συνδεδεμένοι, "as having been bound with them," as fellow-prisoners. The ὡς ἐν σώματι of the next clause might invite the interpretation, "for we also are bound as well as they," and colour might be given to this by the Epistle to Diognetus, chap. 6. χριστια-

νοὶ κατέχονται μὲν ὡς ἐν φρουρᾷ τῷ κόσμῳ; but more likely the expression is merely a strong way of saying that all the members of Christ's body suffer with each, 1 Cor. xii. 26. τῶν κακουχουμένων, "the maltreated," cf. xi. 37; you must be mindful of these "as being yourselves also in the body," i.e., not emancipated spirits, and therefore liable to similar ill-usage and capable of sympathy. [A striking illustration of the manner in which the early Christians obeyed these admonitions may be found in the Apology of Aristides: ξένον ἐὰν ἴδωσιν, ὑπὸ στέγην εἰσάγουσι καὶ χαίρουσιν ἐπ' αὐτῷ ὡς ἐπὶ ἀδελφῷ ἀληθινῷ· οὐ γὰρ κατὰ σάρκα ἀδελφοὺς ἑαυτοὺς καλοῦσιν, ἀλλὰ κατὰ ψυχήν. The Syriac Apology adds "If they hear that any of their number is imprisoned or oppressed for the name of their Messiah, all of them provide for his needs". Accordingly in the Martyrdom of Perpetua we read that two deacons were appointed to visit her and relieve the severity of her imprisonment.] It is interesting to find that Philo claims for Moses a φιλαδελφία towards strangers, enjoining sympathy, ὡς ἐν διαιρετοῖς μέρεσιν ἔν ζῶον, as being all one living creature though in diverse parts; and in De Spec. Legg. 30 he has ὡς ἐν τοῖς ἑτέρων σώμασιν αὐτοὶ κακούμενοι. Westcott gives from early Christian documents a collection of interesting prayers for those suffering imprisonment.

Ver. 4. τίμιος ὁ γάμος ἐν πᾶσιν. "Is ἔστω or ἐστί to be supplied?" Probably the former, as in ver. 5, "Let marriage be held in honour among all". As a natural result of holding marriage in honour, its ideal sanctity will be violated neither by the married nor by the unmarried. Therefore the καὶ links the two clauses closely together and has some inferential force, "and thus let the bed be undefiled" [μιαίνειν τὴν κοίτην occurs in Plutarch to denote the violation of conjugal relations. Used with γυναῖκα in Ezek. xviii. 6, xxiii. 17]. The next clause shows in what sense the

Exod.
xxiii. 8;   κοίτη ἀμίαντος · πόρνους δὲ καὶ μοιχοὺς κρινεῖ ὁ Θεός.   5. ^d ἀφιλάρ-

Deut.xvi.
19, et   γυρος ὁ τρόπος · ἀρκούμενοι τοῖς παροῦσιν.   αὐτὸς γὰρ εἴρηκεν,

xxxi.6,8;   "Οὐ μή σε ἀνῶ, οὐδ᾽ οὐ μή σε ἐγκαταλίπω ¹ " ·   6. ^e ὥστε θαρροῦντας
Jos. i. 5;

1 Par.   ἡμᾶς λέγειν, "Κύριος ἐμοὶ βοηθός, καὶ οὐ φοβηθήσομαι τί ποιήσει
xxviii.20;

Prov. xv.   μοι ἄνθρωπος".   7. ^f Μνημονεύετε τῶν ἡγουμένων ὑμῶν, οἵτινες ἐλά-
16; Matt.

vi. 25, 34. λησαν ὑμῖν τὸν λόγον τοῦ Θεοῦ· ὧν ἀναθεωροῦντες τὴν ἔκβασιν τῆς
Phil. iv.

11; 1Tim. ἀναστροφῆς, μιμεῖσθε τὴν πίστιν.
vi. 6, etc.

e Ps. lvi. 4,   8. Ἰησοῦς Χριστὸς χθὲς ² καὶ σήμερον ὁ αὐτός, καὶ εἰς τοὺς
11, et

cxviii. 6. αἰῶνας.   9. ^g διδαχαῖς ποικίλαις καὶ ξέναις μὴ περιφέρεσθε ³ ·
f ver. 17.

g Jer. xxix.

8; Matt. xxiv. 4; Joan. vi. 27; Rom. xiv. 17, et xvi. 17; Eph. iv. 14, et v. 6; Col. ii. 8, 16;
2 Thess. ii. 2; 1 Tim. iv. 3; 1 Joan.iv.1.

---

¹ εγκαταλειπω in אACDᶜKLMP, 17.

² εχθες in אAC*D*M ; χθες in C³DᶜKL.

³ T.R. in KL, 47; παραφερεσθε in אACDMP, 17, 23, 37, 73.

---

words are to be taken. William Penn's saying must also be kept in view : "If a man pays his tailor but debauches his wife, is he a current moralist?" For marriage as a preventative against vice, *cf.* 1 Cor. vii. and 1 Thess. iv. 4. Weiss gathers from the insertion of this injunction that the writer is not guided in his choice of precepts by the condition of those to whom he is writing but by "theoretical reflection". But in the face of xii. 16, this seems an unwarranted inference. πόρνους . . . ὁ θεός. Fornicators may escape human condemnation, but God (in emphatic position) will judge them.

Ver. 5. As in Eph. v. 5 and elsewhere impurity and covetousness are combined, so here the precepts of ver. 4 lead on to a warning against love of money: ἀφιλάργυρος ὁ τρόπος, "let your turn of mind [disposition] be free from love of money, content with what you have". [ὁ τρόπος frequently in classical writers in this sense, as Demosthenes, p. 683, αἰσχροκερδὴς ὁ τρόπος αὐτοῦ ἐστιν. Other examples in Kypke. ἀρκεῖσθαι τοῖς παροῦσι was also commonly used to denote contentment with what one has. Examples in Raphel and Wetstein.] This contentment has the firm foundation of God's promise ; αὐτὸς γὰρ εἴρηκεν, "for Himself hath said," *i.e.*, God. Οὐ μή σε ἀνῶ. . . . The quotation is from Deut. xxxi. 5, where however the third person is used. Similar promises, similarly expressed, occur in Gen. xxviii. 15 ; Deut. xxxi. 8; Josh. i. 5 ; 1 Chron. xxviii. 20. Philo (*De Conf. Ling.*, chap. 32, not 33 as in Bleek and Davidson) gives

the quotation literatim as in the text here. ὥστε θαρροῦντας ἡμᾶς λέγειν, "so that we boldly say, The Lord is my helper, I will not fear". In Prov. i. 21 wisdom at the gates of the city θαρροῦσα λέγει. The words quoted under λέγειν are from Ps. cxviii. 6, the first word Κύριος and the last ἄνθρωπος being brought into strong contrast.

Vv. 7-16. The Hebrews are exhorted to keep in remembrance their former leaders, to abide steadfastly by their teaching, to rid themselves of the ideas of Judaism, to bear the shame attaching to the faith of Christ, to persevere in good works. Μνημονεύετε τῶν ἡγουμένων ὑμῶν . . . "Have in remembrance them who had the rule over you, especially as they are those who spoke to you the word of God". μνήμον. might be used, as in xi. 22 and Gal. ii. x, τῶν πτωχῶν μνήμ., of keeping living persons in mind (and so Rendall) but what follows makes it more likely that it here refers to the past. These deceased leading men were the persons alluded to in ii. 3 and iv. 2, who first "spoke" the word of the gospel to the Hebrews and who were now no longer present. The word ἡγούμενοι, occurring also in vv. 17 and 24 and in Acts xv. 22 (and *cf.* Sir. xxx. 18, οἱ ἡγούμενοι ἐκκλησίας) is a general term for leading and influential men in whom some undefined authority was vested. Official status was not yet defined and official titles were not yet universal. The chief reason why they are to be held in remembrance is given in the clause under οἵτινες, "for they are they who". But an additional reason is

καλὸν γὰρ χάριτι βεβαιοῦσθαι τὴν καρδίαν, οὐ βρώμασιν, ἐν οἷς οὐκ
ὠφελήθησαν οἱ περιπατήσαντες.[1]　　　 10. Ἔχομεν θυσιαστήριον, ἐξ
οὗ φαγεῖν οὐκ ἔχουσιν ἐξουσίαν οἱ τῇ σκηνῇ λατρεύοντες.　 11. ὧν
γὰρ εἰσφέρεται ζώων τὸ αἷμα περὶ ἁμαρτίας εἰς τὰ ἅγια διὰ τοῦ
ἀρχιερέως, τούτων τὰ σώματα κατακαίεται ἔξω τῆς παρεμβολῆς·
12. διὸ καὶ Ἰησοῦς, ἵνα ἁγιάσῃ διὰ τοῦ ἰδίου αἵματος τὸν λαόν,
ἔξω τῆς πύλης ἔπαθε. 13. τοίνυν ἐξερχώμεθα πρὸς αὐτὸν ἔξω τῆς
παρεμβολῆς, τὸν ὀνειδισμὸν αὐτοῦ φέροντες. 14. οὐ γὰρ ἔχομεν

h Exod.
xxix. 14;
Lev. iv.
12, 21, et
vi. 30, et
xvi. 27;
Num.xix.
3.
i Joan. xix.
17, 18.
k xi. 10, 16;
Mich. ii.
10; Phil.
iii. 20.

[1] περιπατουντες in ℵ*AD*.

suggested in the following clause, ὧν
ἀναθεωροῦντες . . . "whose faith
ımitate as you closely consider the issue
of their manner of life". ὧν follows
ἀναστροφῆς. ἀναθεωρέω in Theophrastus
and Diodorus Siculus is explicitly contrasted with the simple verb to denote a
keener and more careful observation.
We cannot therefore render, as naturally
we might, "look back upon". ἔκβασιν,
in 1 Cor. x. 18 has the meaning "escape";
but in Wisd. ii. xvii., as here, it denotes
the end of life with a distinct reference to
the manner of it, as illustrating the man's
relation to God. The leading men
among the Hebrew Christians had,
whether by martyrdom (as Weiss, etc.)
or not, sealed their teaching and exhibited
a faith worthy of imitation. Ver. 8 gives
force both to ver. 7 and to ver. 9. Imitate
their faith, for the object of faith has not
changed nor passed away. Ἰησοῦς
Χριστὸς ἐχθὲς . . . "Jesus Christ
yesterday and to-day is the same, yea
and for ever." ὁ αὐτὸς exactly as in
Plutarch's *Pericles*, xv. 2, where in describing the influence of success upon
Pericles it is said οὐκέθ' ὁ αὐτὸς ἦν, he
was no longer the same. ἐχθὲς is the
proper Attic form, χθές the old Ionic, see
Rutherford's *New Phryn.*, 370. "Yesterday and to-day," in the past and in the
present Jesus Christ is the same, and He
will never be different. Therefore, διδαχαῖς ποικίλαις καὶ ξέναις
μὴ παραφέρεσθε. "Be not carried
away by teachings various and unheard
of, and foreign." παραφερ. is used
in Diodorus and Plutarch of being swept
away by a river in flood; *cf.* παραρυῶμεν
of ii. 1. The teachings against which the
Hebrews are here warned are such constructions of Old Testament institutions
and practises as tended to loosen their
attachment to Christ as the sole mediator of the New Covenant. These teachings were "various," inasmuch as they
laid stress now on one aspect, now on

another of the old economy ["bald in
der Schriftgelehrsamkeit, bald in pein-
licher Gesetzeserfüllung, bald im Op-
ferkult, bald in den Opfermahlzeiten"
(Weiss)]. They were ξέναι both as being
novel and as being irreconcileable with
pure Christian truth. καλὸν γὰρ χάριτι.
. . . "For it is good that by grace the
heart be confirmed, not by meats." The
present wavering unsatisfactory condition of the Hebrews is to be exchanged
for one of confidence and steadfastness
not by listening to teachings about meats
which after all cannot nourish the heart,
but by approaching the throne where grace
reigns and from which it is dispensed,
iv. 16. From the following verse (ver.
10) in which sacrificial food is expressly
mentioned, it would appear that the reference in οὐ βρώμασιν is not to asceticism
nor to the distinction of clean and unclean meats, but to sacrificial meals.
These are condemned by experiment as
useless, ἐν οἷς οὐκ ὠφελήθησαν
. . . "which were of no avail to those
who had recourse to them" (Moffatt).
Cf. the ἀσθενὲς καὶ ἀνωφελὲς of vii. 18.
Sacrificial meals are also shown to be
irreconcileable (ξέναι) with the Christian
approach to God, for our (the Christian)
altar is one from which neither worshippers nor priests have any right to eat.
The point he wishes to make is, that in
connection with the Christian sacrifice
there is no sacrificial meal. As in the
case of the great sacrifice of the Day of
Atonement the High Priest carried the
blood into the Holy of Holies, while the
carcase was not eaten but burned outside
the camp; so the Christian altar is not
one from which food is dispensed to priest
and worshipper. οἱ τῇ σκηνῇ λατρεύοντες refers to the Christian worshippers. The figure introduced in θυσιαστήριον is continued in these words. To
refer them to the O.T. priests is to shatter
the argument. Literally the words mean
"they who serve the tabernacle," that is,

¹Lev. vii. ὧδε μένουσαν πόλιν, ἀλλὰ τὴν μέλλουσαν ἐπιζητοῦμεν.　15. ¹Δι'
12; Ps. l.
23, et li. αὐτοῦ οὖν ἀναφέρωμεν θυσίαν αἰνέσεως διαπαντὸς τῷ Θεῷ, τουτέστι,
19; Ose.
xiv. 2; καρπὸν χειλέων ὁμολογούντων τῷ ὀνόματι αὐτοῦ.　16. ᵐτῆς δὲ εὐ-
Eph. v.
20: 1 ποιΐας καὶ κοινωνίας μὴ ἐπιλανθάνεσθε· τοιαύταις γὰρ θυσίαις
Peter ii.5.
m 2 Cor. ix. εὐαρεστεῖται ὁ Θεός.
12; Phil.
iv. 18.　17. ⁿΠείθεσθε τοῖς ἡγουμένοις ὑμῶν, καὶ ὑπείκετε· αὐτοὶ γὰρ
n ver. 7;
Ezech. ἀγρυπνοῦσιν ὑπὲρ τῶν ψυχῶν ὑμῶν, ὡς λόγον ἀποδώσοντες· ἵνα μετὰ
iii. 18, et
xxxiii. 2,
8; Phil. ii. 29; 1 Thess. v. 12; 1 Tim. v. 17; 1 Peter v. 5.

the priests, cf. viii. 5. The peculiarity, he says, of our Christian sacrifice is that it is not eaten. Then follows in support of this statement an analogy from the O.T. ritual, ὧν γὰρ εἰσφέρεται ζώων. . . . "For the bodies of those animals, whose blood is brought into the holy place by the High Priest as an offering for sin, are burned outside the camp." Cf. Lev. iv. 12, 21. In conformity with this type (διὸ καὶ Ἰησοῦς) Jesus, that He by His own blood might purify the people from their sin, suffered outside the gate. "The burning of the victim was not intended to sublimate but to get rid of it. The body plays no part in the atoning act, and has in fact no significance after the blood has been drained from it. The life, and therefore the atoning energy, resides in the blood and in the blood alone. On the writer's scheme, then, no function is left for the body of Jesus. It is 'through his own blood,' that he must 'sanctify the people'. It is thus inevitable that while the writer fully recognises the fact of the Resurrection of Christ (ver. 20), he can assign no place to it in his argument or attach to it any theological significance" (Peake). The suffering ἔξω τῆς πύλης is equivalent to the αἰσχύνη of xii. 2; the ignominy of the malefactor's death was an essential element in the suffering. The utmost that man inflicts upon criminals he bore. He was made to feel that he was outcast and condemned. But it is this which wins all men to Him. τοίνυν ἐξερχώμεθα πρὸς αὐτὸν . . . "let us therefore go out to him outside the camp bearing his reproach". Cf. xi. 26. Do not shrink from abandoning your old associations and being branded as outcasts and traitors and robbed of your privileges as Jews. This is the reproach of Christ, in bearing which you come nearer to Him. And the surrender of your privileges need not cost you too much regret, "for we have not here (on earth) an abiding city, but seek for that

which is to be," that which has the foundations, xi. 10, the heavenly Jerusalem, xii. 22. That which is spiritual and eternal satisfies the ambition and fills the heart. Cf. Mark iii. 35; Phil. iii. 20. The want of recognition and settlement on earth may therefore well be borne.

Ver. 15. δι' αὐτοῦ οὖν ἀναφέρωμεν. Going without the camp as believers in the virtue of Christ's atoning sacrifice, and bearing His shame as those who seek to be identified with Him, we are brought near to God and are disposed to offer Him a sacrifice of praise (Lev. vii. 2 ff.). The δι' αὐτοῦ is in the emphatic position; "through Him" and not through any Levitical device. And this Christian sacrifice is not periodic, but being spiritual is also continual (διαπαντὸς). That there may be no mistake regarding the material of the sacrifice of praise, an explanation is added: τοῦτ' ἔστιν καρπὸν χειλέων, "that is to say, the fruit of lips (cf. Hos. xiv. 3) celebrating His name". Thayer gives this translation, supposing that ὁμολογ. is here used in the sense of ἐξομολογέω, Ps. xlv. 17, etc.; cf. also 1 Esdr. ix. 8. But the sacrifice of praise which can be rendered with the lips is not enough. "Be not forgetful of beneficence and charity for with such sacrifices God is well pleased."

Vv. 17-End. The conclusion of the Epistle.

Ver. 17. "Obey your rulers and submit; for they watch for your souls, knowing they are to give account, that they may do this with joy not with lamentation—for this would be profitless to you."

Having exhorted the Hebrews to keep in mind their former rulers and adhere to their teaching, the writer now admonishes them, probably in view of a certain mutinous and separatist spirit (x. 25) encouraged by their reception of strange doctrines, to obey their present leaders, and yield themselves trustfully (ὑπείκετε)

χαρᾶς τοῦτο ποιῶσι, καὶ μὴ στενάζοντες· ἀλυσιτελὲς γὰρ ὑμῖν
τοῦτο. 18. Προσεύχεσθε περὶ ἡμῶν· πεποίθαμεν γὰρ, ὅτι καλὴν

to their teaching—an admonition which,
as Weiss remarks, shows that these
teachers held the same views as the
writer. The reasonableness of this injunction is confirmed by the responsibility of the rulers and their anxious
discharge of it. They watch, like wake-
ful shepherds (ἀγρυπνοῦσιν), or those
who are nursing a critical case, in the
interest of your souls (ὑπὲρ τῶν ψυχῶν
ὑμῶν) to which they may sometimes seem
to sacrifice your other interests. They
do this under the constant pressure of a
consciousness that they must one day
render to the Chief Shepherd (ver. 20) an
account of the care they have taken of
His sheep (ὡς λόγον ἀποδώσοντες).
Obey them, then, that they may discharge their responsibility and peform
these kindly offices for you (τοῦτο referring not to λόγον ἀποδώσοντες as
Vaughan, etc., which would require a
much stronger expression than ἀλυσι-
τελές, but to ἀγρυπνοῦσιν) joyfully and
not with groaning (στενάζοντες, the
groaning with which one resumes a
thankless task, and with which he con-
templates unappreciated and even opposed work). And even for your own
sakes you should make the work of your
rulers easy and joyful, for otherwise it
cannot profit you. Your unwillingness
to listen to them means that you are out
of sympathy with their teaching and that
it can do you no good (ἀλυσιτελὲς γὰρ
ὑμῖν τοῦτο).

Ver. 18. προσεύχεσθε περὶ ἡμῶν.
. . . Both the next clause and the next
verse seem to indicate that by ἡμῶν the
writer chiefly, if not exclusively, meant
himself; the next clause, for he could
not vouch for the conscience of any
other person; the next verse because one
principal object or result of their prayer
was his restoration to them. Request
for prayer is common in the Epistles,
1 Thess. v. 25; 2 Thess. iii. 1; Rom. xv.
30; Eph. vi. 18; Col. iv. 3. The reason
here annexed is peculiar. "The allusion
to his purity of conduct, and strong assertion of his consciousness of it, in
regard to them and all things, when he
is petitioning for their prayers, implies
that some suspicions may have attached
to him in the minds of some of them.
These suspicions would naturally refer
to his great freedom in regard to Jewish
practises" (Davidson). But notwithstanding ver. 23 it may be that he was

under arrest and shortly to be tried and
naturally adds to his request for prayer a
protestation of his innocence of all civil
offence. [καλῶς ἀναστραφῆναι occurs
in *Perg. Inscrip.*, v. Deissmann, p. 194,
E. Tr.] The writer was conscious of a
readiness and purpose to live and conduct himself rightly in all circumstances.
This gives him confidence and will lend
confidence to their prayers. He is more
urgent in this request (περισσοτέρως
παρακαλῶ) because he is desirous to be
quickly restored to them; implying that
he in some sense belonged to them and
that the termination of his present exile
from them would be acceptable to them
as well as to him. [The verb ἀποκαθ.
first occurs in Xenophon, see Anz. p.
338.]

While asking their prayers for himself
the writer prays for them: ὁ δὲ θεὸς
τῆς εἰρήνης. . . . He prays to the
God of peace (*cf.* 1 Thess. v. 23; 2 Thess.
iii. 16; Rom. xv. 33, xvi. 20; 2 Cor. xiii.
11; Phil. iv. 9) because this attribute of
God carries in it the guarantee that a
termination shall be put to all misunderstanding, disturbance, and inability to do
His will. His love of peace is shown in
nothing more than in His concluding an
eternal covenant with men. This covenant was sealed when "our Lord Jesus,"
having laid down his life for the sheep,
was brought up from the dead in virtue
of the perfect and accepted sacrifice (ἐν
αἵματι, διαθήκης). Elsewhere in the
Epistle the blood is spoken of as giving
entrance to the presence of God, here as
delivering from that which prevented
that entrance. As Vaughan says: "The
arrival in the heavenly presence for us
in virtue of the atoning blood is here
viewed in its *start* from the grave. . .
It was in virtue of the availing sacrifice
that Christ either left the tomb or re-
entered heaven." ἐν αἵματι διαθήκης is therefore more naturally connected with ἀναγαγών than with τὸν
ποιμένα, although the two connections
are closely related. It was as the Great
Shepherd that Jesus gave His life for the
sheep and by this act established for ever
His claim to be the Shepherd of His
people. It is this claim also that guarantees that He will lose none but will
raise them up at the last day (*cf.* John
xv.). [It is probable that the phrasing
of this verse was influenced by Zech. ix.
7, σὺ ἐν αἵματι διαθήκης σου ἐξαπέ-

συνείδησιν ἔχομεν, ἐν πᾶσι καλῶς θέλοντες ἀναστρέφεσθαι · 19. περισσοτέρως δὲ παρακαλῶ τοῦτο ποιῆσαι, ἵνα τάχιον ἀποκατασταθῶ ὑμῖν.

o Esa. xiv.
11;
Ezech.
xxxiv. 23;
Zach. ix.
11; Joan.
x. 11;
Acts ii.
24;
1 Peter ii.
25. et v. 4.
p 2 Cor. iii.
5; Phil.
ii. 13.

20. °Ὁ δὲ Θεὸς τῆς εἰρήνης, ὁ ἀναγαγὼν ἐκ νεκρῶν τὸν ποιμένα τῶν προβάτων τὸν μέγαν ἐν αἵματι διαθήκης αἰωνίου, τὸν Κύριον ἡμῶν Ἰησοῦν, 21. Ρκαταρτίσαι ὑμᾶς ἐν παντὶ ἔργῳ¹ ἀγαθῷ, εἰς τὸ ποιῆσαι τὸ θέλημα αὐτοῦ, ποιῶν² ἐν ὑμῖν τὸ εὐάρεστον ἐνώπιον αὐτοῦ διὰ Ἰησοῦ Χριστοῦ · ᾧ ἡ δόξα εἰς τοὺς αἰῶνας τῶν αἰώνων. ἀμήν.

22. Παρακαλῶ δὲ ὑμᾶς, ἀδελφοί, ἀνέχεσθε τοῦ λόγου τῆς παρακλήσεως · καὶ γὰρ διὰ βραχέων ἐπέστειλα ὑμῖν. 23. Γινώσκετε τὸν ἀδελφὸν Τιμόθεον³ ἀπολελυμένον, μεθ' οὗ, ἐὰν τάχιον ἔρχηται,

¹ אּD*, d, f, vg. omit εργω; CDcKMP, Syrsch, Arm., Aeth. insert εργω. A has εργω και λογω αγαθω.

² א*AC*, 17* read αντω ποιων; 71 reads αντος ποιων. T.R. is found in אcCbDKMP. [WH say that "there can be little doubt that αὐτὸς ποιῶν is the true reading".]

³ ημων is found in אACD*M, 17, 37, 47, 71, vg.

στειλας δεσμίους σου ἐκ λάκκου οὐκ ἔχοντος ὕδωρ, and by Isa. lxiii. 11, ποῦ ὁ ἀναβιβάσας ἐκ τῆς θαλάσσης τὸν ποιμένα τῶν προβάτων.] The prayer follows, καταρτίσαι ὑμᾶς, "perfectly equip you" (cf. xi. 3) ἐν παντὶ ἔργῳ ἀγαθῷ, "in every good work," that is, enabling you to do every good work and so equipping you εἰς τὸ ποιῆσαι τὸ θέλημα αὐτοῦ, "for the doing of His will," "doing in you that which is well pleasing in His sight through Jesus Christ" (cf. Phil. ii. 13). The words διὰ Ἰησοῦ Χριστοῦ are apparently attached not exclusively to τὸ εὐάρεστον κ.τ.λ., but to the whole clause and especially to καταρτίσαι; it is through Jesus, now reigning as Christ, that all grace is bestowed on His people. The doxology may be to the God of peace to whom the prayer is addressed, more probably it is to Jesus Christ, last-named and the great figure who has been before the mind throughout the Epistle.

Ver. 22. The writer adds, in closing, a request that the Hebrews would take in good part his "word of exhortation"—a request which implies that they were in an irritable state of mind, if not against the writer, then because their own conscience was uneasy. As a reason for their bearing with his exhortation he urges its brevity "for indeed (καὶ γὰρ) I have written (ἐπέστειλα as in Acts xv. 20) to you with brevity" (διὰ βραχέων, cf. δι' ὀλίγων ἔγραψα, 1 Pet. v. 12). To them it might seem that he had said too

much; his own feeling was that he had been severely cramped by the limits of a letter.

Ver. 23. γινώσκετε τὸν ἀδελφὸν ἡμῶν. . . . "Know that our brother Timothy has been released" (ἀπολελυμένον, for example of this use of the participle, see Winer, sec. 45, 4 b). Evidently Timothy had been under arrest; where, when, or why is not known. The information is given because it would interest these Hebrew Christians, who were therefore friends of his, not Judaizers. μεθ' οὗ . . . "with whom, if he come soon, I will see you". He takes for granted that Timothy would at once go to them; and he speaks as one who is himself free or is immediately to be free to determine his own movements. [τάχειον, = θᾶττον, a comparative in the sense of a positive; a classical usage; and cf. John xiii. 27, ὃ ποιεῖς ποίησον τάχιον.] The usual greetings are added. Epistolary form required this (see the Egyptian papyri) but in view of what the writer has said regarding the rulers, and in view of the πάντας here expressed, it may be supposed that the formula was here filled with significant contents. Who was to convey the salutations? Or, in other words, who was directly to receive the letter? Probably one or two of the leading men representing the Church. This would account for the πάντας. The greetings were not on the writer's part only. οἱ ἀπὸ τῆς Ἰταλίας, "they of Italy" joined

ὄψομαι ὑμᾶς.　24. Ἀσπάσασθε πάντας τοὺς ἡγουμένους ὑμῶν, καὶ
πάντας τοὺς ἁγίους.　ἀσπάζονται ὑμᾶς οἱ ἀπὸ τῆς Ἰταλίας.　25.
ἡ χάρις μετὰ πάντων ὑμῶν.　ἀμήν.

　　Πρὸς Ἑβραίους ἐγράφη ἀπὸ τῆς Ἰταλίας διὰ Τιμοθέου.

in them. The form of expression is that which is ordinarily used to denote natives of a place, as in Luke xxiii. 50; John i. 44, xi. 1; Acts xvii. 13, etc. Winer says (p. 785): "a critical argument as to the place at which the Epistle was written should never have been founded on these words". Vaughan is certainly wrong in saying that the more natural suggestion of the words would be that the writer is himself in Italy and speaks of the Italian Christians surrounding him. The more natural suggestion, on the contrary, is that the writer is absent from Italy and is writing to it and that therefore the native Italians who happen to be with him join him in the salutations he sends to their compatriots.

The Epistle closes with one of the usual formulae, " Grace be with you all ".

THE GENERAL EPISTLE OF JAMES

INTRODUCTION.

I. AUTHORSHIP AND DATE.—§ 1. *External Data.* That parts, at all events, of this Epistle were known and cited by very early Church writers seems certain. It is, however, precarious to build too much upon the fact that similarities of thought and expression are found between this Epistle and other early writings. Such similarities do not necessarily prove anything more than that the thought-movements of the times were exercising the minds of many thinkers and writers. If, that is to say, it is found that various writings belonging to the early ages of Christianity contain thoughts, words, and even sentences which are also seen to occur in this Epistle, it would be arbitrary to assume that this fact necessarily proved the influence of the latter upon the former, or *vice-versa*; and it would, moreover, be dangerous to use this assumption as a basis upon which to found conclusions regarding the date and authorship of the Epistle. We are far from denying that the similarities referred to *may* denote indebtedness on the part of the writer of our Epistle to the writings in question, or *vice versa*—as, for example, in the case of *Sirach*— but in such cases there must be no doubt as to whether the particular writing is earlier or later than our Epistle. A concrete example will make our meaning clear. Some writers regard the similarity of language between the *Testaments of the Twelve Patriarchs* and *St. James* as evidence that the latter influenced the former, and this is regarded as evidence in favour of an early date of our Epistle. Thus Lightfoot (*Galatians,* p. 320, note), says that the language of the writer of the *Testaments* on the subject of the law of God is " formed on the model of the Epistle of St. James," and he refers to Ewald, who makes a similar remark; again, on p. 221, note, he says in reference to this pseudepigraph: " On the whole, however, the language in the moral and didactic portions takes its colour from the Epistle of St. James ". So, too, Mayor (*The Epistle of St. James,* p. iv.) speaks of the writer of this work as one " who seems to have been much influenced by the teaching and example of St. James," and a large number of quotations are given to prove this contention.

Now, Charles, who may justly be claimed as our leading authority on all that concerns the *Pseudepigrapha*, has shown conclusively in his edition of the *Testaments* (1908) that this work was written originally in Hebrew in 109-106 B.C.; the Jewish additions he regards as belonging to the years 70-40 B.C., and in its Greek form it appeared "at the latest" in 50 A.D.; the thirty Christian interpolations (approximately) belong probably to different dates, but scarcely any of these come into consideration in the present connection (see pp. l.-lxv.); instances of St. *James* probably utilising the *Testaments* are given on p. xc. Or, to mention another instance, the similarities between St. *James* and the *Epistle to the Corinthians* of Clement of Rome are likewise pointed to as a proof of the early date of St. *James*, because Clement (end of first century and beginning of second century) was influenced by it; but the most striking part of this similarity is the way in which each deals with the subject of faith and works. This subject was, however, one of the fundamental causes of difference between Jews and Christians at all times (indeed, the minds of thinking Jews were exercised by it *before* the Christian era), and it is dealt with in a number of other works of various dates—*Testaments of the Twelve Patriarchs, Testament of Abraham, Apoc. of Baruch*, 2 (4) *Esdras, Book of Enoch*, and often in the later Jewish literature;—therefore it is difficult to see why St. *James* necessarily influenced Clement on a subject which was so much in evidence in a large variety of writings; and the statement of Mayor, that "the fact that Clement balances the teaching of St. Paul by that of St. James is sufficient proof of the authority he ascribes to the latter" (p. lii.), seems a little too strong, especially as St. James is not mentioned by name in Clement. Similarities are also found between St. *James* and pseudo-Clement, the *Didache*, the *Epistle of Barnabas*, the *Epistles of Ignatius*, Hermas, Justin Martyr, the *Epistle to Diognetus*, Irenæus, Theophilus, Tertullian, Clement of Alexandria, and the Clementine Homilies; all these authorities, ranging from the first century to the former half of the third, are often pointed to as showing their recognition of our Epistle, because they show the marks of its influence upon them. The possibility of such indebtedness is not denied, but in the majority of cases it cannot be said that the similarities *prove* it; nor do they necessarily prove the canonicity, and still less the authorship of our Epistle, especially as not in one single instance is the Epistle mentioned by name in the authorities mentioned above. The earliest writer, as far as is known, who refers to the Epistle definitely as Scripture, and as having been written by St. James, is Origen

(d. 254 A.D.). His testimony is as follows : In his commentary on
St. John xix. 6 he refers to our Epistle in the words, . . , ὡς ἐν τῇ
φερομένῃ Ἰακώβου ἐπιστολῇ ἀνέγνωμεν, a phrase which obviously suggests doubt as to its authorship, though apparently it is quoted as
Scripture. On the other hand, passages from our Epistle are quoted
as the words of "James the Apostle" on at least five occasions ; and
besides this, there are a number of cases in which direct quotations
from it are clearly regarded as Scripture. This is, moreover,
definitely asserted in his *Comm. in Ep. ad Rom.*, iv. 1, and in
Hom. in Lev., ii. 4. On four occasions St. James is mentioned by
name, once as the " brother of the Lord " Further, quotations, more
or less distinct, from our Epistle are found in the *Constitutiones
Apostolicae* (fourth century, but containing earlier material), and in
Lactantius (c. 300 A.D.). The next important writer who gives direct
evidence on the subject is Eusebius (c. 270-340 A.D.). In speaking of
the Catholic Epistles, and **after** referring to the martyrdom of James
the Just, he says : " The first of the Epistles styled Catholic is said
to be his. But I must remark that it is held to be spurious (νοθεύεται).
Certainly not many old writers have mentioned it, nor yet the Epistle
of Jude, which is also one of the Epistles called Catholic. But
nevertheless we know that these have been publicly used with the rest
in most churches " (*H.E.*, ii. 23). Then, again, in enumerating the list
of New Testament books (*H.E.*, iii. 25), he says : " Among the contro-
verted books (ἀντιλεγόμενα), which are nevertheless well known and
recognised by many (γνωρίμων ὅμως τοῖς πολλοῖς), we class the Epistle
circulated under the name of James ". In spite of this, however,
Eusebius prefaces a quotation from the Epistle (v. 13) with the
words, λέγει γοῦν ὁ ἱερὸς Ἀπόστολος (*Comm. in Ps.* i.), and later
on in the same work he refers to another passage from the Epistle
(iv 2) as Scripture (. . . τῆς γραφῆς λεγούσης . . .). At the same time
it will be wise not to build too much upon these last two references.
In a case like this, where the writer would, if anything, be biassed
in favour of ascribing Apostolic authorship to the Epistle, a passage
which casts doubt upon its genuineness is really more weighty
evidence than one in the opposite direction ; moreover, a book which
went by a certain name might well be quoted by Eusebius in accordance with the common acceptation, without his adding, each time
he mentioned it, his doubts concerning the correctness as to its title.
Upon the whole, the evidence of Eusebius, though uncertain, seems
to point to our Epistle as being genuine Scripture, but not as having
been written by St. James. This uncertain testimony is repeated
by Jerome (born c. 330-350 A.D.), who says in his *De Viris*

Illustr., ii.: " Jacobus qui appellatur frater Domini . . . unam tantum scripsit epistolam, quae de septem Catholicis est, quae et ipsa ab alio quodam sub nomine ejus edita asseritur, licet paulatim tempore procedente obtinuerit auctoritatem" (quoted by Westcott, *Canon of the N.T.*, p. 452); elsewhere, however, Jerome quotes from the Epistle as from Scripture. This evidence, therefore, runs on somewhat the same lines as that of Eusebius; and when it is remembered that these two writers stand out as the two greatest authorities of antiquity on the subject of the Canon, it must be conceded that their witness ought almost to be regarded as final. It is worth recalling that recently Jerome's *status* as a reliable witness has been greatly strengthened by the discovery of a gospel-fragment[1] which in the MS. in which it has been discovered forms a part of the Longer Ending of the canonical Gospel of St. Mark. " Writing against the Pelagians in 415-416 (*C. Pelag.*, ii. 15), Jerome quoted a passage which 'in some copies [of the Latin Gospels] and especially in Greek codices' followed immediately after St. Mark xvi. 14 [the words are then given]; hitherto Jerome's statement has been entirely without support; now at length it has been recovered in the Greek. . . ."[2] Three other facts of importance must be recorded regarding the external *data* as to authorship; they concern the question of canonicity, and therefore indirectly that of authorship. The Muratorian Fragment, which " may be regarded on the whole as a summary of the opinion of the Western Church on the Canon shortly after the middle of the second century" (Westcott, *op. cit.*, p. 212), omits *St. James* in its list of canonical writings. Secondly, our Epistle is not included in the Syriac version of the N.T. brought to the Syrian Church by Palūt, bishop of Edessa, at the beginning of the third century; " the *Catholic Epistles* and the *Apocalypse* formed no part of the old Syriac version. In the Peshitta this defect is partially supplied by a translation of James, 1 Peter and 1 John, in agreement with the usage of Antioch as represented by Chrysostom" (Burkitt in *Encycl. Bibl.* iv. col. 5004); Prof. Burkitt quotes *Addai*, 46: " The Law and the Prophets and the Gospel . . . and the Epistles of Paul . . . and the Acts of the Twelve Apostles— these writings shall ye read in the Churches of Christ, and besides these ye shall read nothing else "; and adds, " Neither in Aphraates nor in the genuine works of Ephraim are there any quotations from the Apocalypse or the Catholic Epistles." And thirdly, our Epistle

---

[1] See the *Biblical World*, pp. 138 ff. (1908).

[2] Swete in the *Guardian*, 1st April, 1908; see also Swete, *Zwei neue Evangelienfragmente*, p. 9 (1908); Gregory, *Das Freer-Logion*, pp. 25 ff. (1908).

does not figure in the "Cheltenham List". The first time that the Epistle appears to have been officially recognised as canonical was at the council of Carthage 397 A.D.[1]

The balance of the historical evidence of the first three and a half centuries is thus distinctly against St. James having been the author of this Epistle. If we had external evidence alone to go upon we should assuredly be compelled to follow what seems to have been the opinion of Origen, Eusebius, and Jerome; that is to say that, while on the whole regarding the Epistle as canonical, it is difficult to believe that St. James can have been the author.

If the Epistle was written by St. James, it is almost universally granted that it must have been the St. James who presided at the council of Jerusalem—"James the Lord's brother"—who was the author (see § 2 below), the claims of any other of this name being too inconsiderable to be seriously thought of; but in this case it is difficult to account for the fact that doubt was thrown upon the canonicity of the Epistle for so long, and still more difficult is it to account for the fact that the name of St. James was not connected with it from the beginning. The position of authority which the Apostle held in the early Church (Acts xii. 17; Gal. i. 18, 19), the important fact of his having already inspired an Epistle (Acts xv. 19, 20), and the traditions concerning him in later times (see Josephus, *Antiq.* xx. ix. 1; Eusebius, *H.E.* II. 23), all lead to the supposition that if the Epistle had really been written by him it would have been accepted as genuine and canonical from the first, in which case the doubtful expressions of Origen, Eusebius, and Jerome, and the adverse testimony of the Old Syriac Version and the Muratorian Fragment would have been impossible.

On the other hand, it must be allowed that there are strong *a priori* arguments in favour of St. James' authorship. The position held by him in the early Church compels one to expect writings from him; the head of the mother-Church of Christendom would, of all people, be the most obvious one from whom one would look for communications of one kind or another to daughter-churches. Still more within the natural order of things would be an Epistle of a general character—something in the form of an encyclical—addressed not to any particular local Church, but to the whole body of believers; the fact that this one is addressed to the Dispersion only strengthens the argument, because, in the earliest days, the nucleus of the

---

[1] It was also accepted by the somewhat earlier but much less important Council of Laodicea, about 363 A.D.

Christian congregations was formed by those who were Jews by race.
Secondly, there is the analogy of the Epistle inspired by him at the
Council of Jerusalem , this fact proves that the Apostle recognised
it to be within his province to inspire—if nothing more—communications to distant Churches , this particular epistle was addressed to
Gentiles, whose conversion lay more particularly within the province
of St. Paul, the more reason, therefore, that Jewish converts should
also be written to by the head of the Church of Jerusalem, the city
which these had always looked upon as their " Mother ".   And then,
thirdly, although, as we have already seen, the early patristic evidence
is not in favour of St. James' authorship, we are bound to recognise
the fact that there was a tradition as early as the beginning of the
third century which brought the name of St. James into connexion
with this Epistle.

It is fully realised—and the point needs emphasis—that weighty
arguments can be adduced against both sets of considerations mentioned above ; it is just the most perplexing thing regarding. this
Epistle that whether an early or a late date be contended for, whether
the authorship of St. James be insisted on, or that of some other,
unknown, writer, no *conclusive* argument can be put forth on either
side ; nothing has yet been said on either side which has forced conviction on the other.   It must be allowed, further, that the objections
raised against the contentions on either side are, in almost every
instance, strong, and are not to be brushed aside offhand.   Considerations of space forbid even an enumeration of the many arguments which are urged on either side, recourse must be had to the
more comprehensive Commentaries for this ; but the fact is certainly
noteworthy that, no matter how strong the arguments put forth on
either side, valid objections can be urged against one and all ; either
position taken up seems so strong from one point of view, and is yet
so weakened from another point of view.   The one positive conclusion to be drawn from this seems to be the paradoxical one that both
are right ; that is to say, that an Epistle, which is embodied in our
present one, was originally written by St. James, and that to it were
added subsequently other elements.   This is a procedure which could
be paralleled by other examples, spurious additions made to authentic documents, in perfect good faith, being not unknown—*e.g.*, the
Longer Ending of St. Mark's Gospel.   Proof for this contention is as
little forthcoming as for the various other theories that have been
suggested, but it would at least account for the conflicting evidence
of Origen, Eusebius and Jerome ; and when we come to deal with
the internal evidence of the Epistle, it will be seen to account for

more than one perplexing feature. It is at best a *faute de mieux* and, for the present, does not profess to be anything more.

§ 2. *Internal Data.*—The writer of the Epistle calls himself James, and in addressing the " twelve tribes of the Dispersion " shows himself to have been a man of more than ordinary authority. According to the evidence of the New Testament, there was only one James who occupied a position of authority such as is implied in this Epistle, namely, " James, the Lord's brother "; thus in Gal. i. 18, 19, St. Paul tells of how after the three years' retirement which followed after his conversion, he went and saw St. Peter and " James the Lord's brother "; in Acts xii. 17 we read that when St. Peter had been released from prison he said to his friends: " Tell these things unto James, and to the brethren "; again, in Gal. ii. 9 St. Paul recounts the action of " James, and Cephas, and John, who were reputed to be pillars," and who, on seeing that grace had been given to him, offered to him and Barnabas the right hand of fellowship, " that we should go unto the Gentiles, and they unto the circumcision "; and further, in the same passage, ver. 12, the mention of certain men " who came from James " marks him out as a leader. Then, and perhaps most important of all, there is the account in Acts xv. 4-29 of the council at Jerusalem, at which the leading part is taken by St. James.[1] Once more, in Acts xxi. 18 the position of importance which St. James occupied is again clearly seen in that when St. Paul and his companions had returned to Jerusalem after their missionary journey they were first received, apparently informally, by the brethren, and then on the following day " they went unto James, and all the elders were present "; these words plainly imply something in the nature of an official, formal reception. Lastly, in 1 Cor. xv. 7, St. Paul speaks of the special appearance of our Lord after His resurrection to St. James. It is certainly worth particular notice that among these references to St. James the most important are supplied directly or indirectly by St. Paul; this fact should of itself be sufficient to show the improbability of any conscious antagonism between the teaching on the subject of faith and works as contained respectively in the Pauline Epistles and that of St. James—assuming the latter to be authentic. At all events, the leading position held by St. James which these passages reveal, makes it in the highest degree probable that the James mentioned in the opening verse of our Epistle is to be identified with " James the Lord's brother ".

[1] Note how his very words in Acts xv. 20 are incorporated in the letter which he sent (verse 29).

The next point in the internal evidence to emphasise is the similarity to be observed between the letter inspired by St. James, together with his speech, at the council of Jerusalem, and certain parts of the Epistle which bears his name. The most important of these are as follows :—

(i.) The salutation, χαίρειν, Acts xv. 23, Jas. i. 1 ; this form is found elsewhere in the New Testament only in Acts xxiii. 26.

(ii.) The words, τὸ καλὸν ὄνομα τὸ ἐπικληθὲν ἐφ' ὑμᾶς, in Jas. ii. 7, which can only be paralleled in the New Testament by those in Acts xv. 17 : ἐφ' οὓς ἐπικέκληται τὸ ὄνομα μου ἐπ' αὐτούς.

(iii.) The occurrence of the word ὄνομα in a specially pregnant sense, Jas. ii. 7, v. 10, 14, and Acts xv. 14, 26 ; this is not used elsewhere in the New Testament in quite the same sense.

(iv.) The pointed allusions to the Old Testament, which are characteristic of St. James' speech, viz., Acts xv. 14, 16-18, 21, also play an important part in the Epistle, or at least in certain parts of it.

(v.) The affectionate term ἀδελφός, which occurs so often in the Epistle (i. 2, 9, 16, 19 ; ii. 5, 15 ; iii. 1 ; iv. 11 ; v. 7, 9, 10, I2, 19), is also found in Acts xv. 13, 23 ; especially noticeable is the verbal identity between Jas. ii. 5, ἀκούσατε ἀδελφοί μου, and Acts xv. 13, ἄνδρες ἀδελφοὶ ἀκούσατέ μου.

(vi.) Other verbal coincidences are : ἐπισκέπτεσθαι, Jas. i. 27, Acts xv. 14 ; τηρεῖν and διατηρεῖν, Jas. i. 27, Acts xv. 29 ; ἐπιστρέφειν, Jas. v. 19, 20, Acts xv. 19 ; ἀγαπητός, Jas. i. 16, 19, ii. 5, Acts xv. 25. In some of these cases too much stress must not be laid upon the similarities ; but it is certainly striking that in the rather restricted scope which the short passage in Acts offers there should, nevertheless, be so many points of similarity with portions of the Epistle. The fact almost compels us to recognise the same mind at work in each, though this does not necessarily apply to the whole of the Epistle ascribed to St. James.

Further internal evidence as to authorship is afforded by indications which point to the writer as having been a Jew. And the first point that strikes one here is the copious use of the O.T. which is characteristic of the writer. There are, it is true, only five *direct* verbal quotations, viz., i. 11 from Isa. xl. 7 ; ii. 8 from Lev. xix. 18 ; ii. 11 from Exod. xx. 13.14 ; ii. 23 from Gen. xv. 6 ; iv. 6 from Prov. iii. 34 ; but the atmosphere of the O.T. is a constituent element of the Epistle ; for over and above the O.T. events which are mentioned, there is an abundance of clear references to it, which shows that the mind of the writer was saturated with the spirit of the ancient

Scriptures. Some of the most obvious of these references are the
following: i. 10, see Ps. cii. 4-11; ii. 21, see Gen. xxii. 9-12; ii. 23,
see Isa. xli. 8, 2 Chron. xx. 7; ii. 25, see Josh. ii. 1 ff.; iii. 6, see
Prov. xvi. 27; iii. 9, see Gen. i. 26; iv. 6, see Job xxii. 29; v. 2,
see Job xiii. 28; v. 11, see Job i. 21-22, ii. 10; v. 17-18, see 1 Kings
xvii. 1, xviii. 41-45. Further, there is the use of the specifically
Israelite name for God, "Jehovah Sabaoth" (v. 4), and the references to Law (*Torah*) in ii. 8-12, iv. 11; this use of νόμος, *i.e.*,
without the article, is in accordance with the extended use of the
word *Torah* among the Jews, meaning as it does, not only the Law
given on Mount Sinai, not only the whole of the Pentateuch, but
also the entire body of religious precepts in general (see especially ii.
12, where right speaking and acting in general are included under
proper *Torah*-observance). The reference to γέεννα in iii. 6, is also
a distinct mark of Jewish authorship; and the way in which the
prophets are spoken of in v. 10 points in the same direction. It is
to be observed that the use of the O.T. is wide, all three of the
great divisions of the Jewish Canon—Law, Prophets, and Writings—
being represented.

But what speaks still more for Jewish authorship is the accumulation of many small points indicative of Hebrew methods of thought,
expression, and phraseology; examples of this abound in the Epistle,
indeed its "Hebraic" colouring is one of its most pronounced
characteristics. While it will not be necessary to give exhaustive
lists, some examples of the different categories of the small points
just referred to must be offered.

(i.) There are a number of instances in which the Greek is
reminiscent of Hebrew phraseology; it is not meant by this to imply
that a Hebrew text was the original form of such passages and
phrases, but only that the Greek form of the expression of thought
seems to be moulded from a Hebrew pattern, *i.e.*, that the mind of
the writer was accustomed to express itself after the manner of one
to whom Hebrew ways of thinking were very familiar, and who in
writing Greek, therefore, almost unconsciously reverted to the
Hebrew mode. The point of what has been said will perhaps
be best realised when it is seen how naturally, in a number of
instances, a Hebrew equivalent of the Greek suggests itself, *e.g.*:
ii. 7 . . . τὸ καλὸν ὄ ομα τὸ ἐπικληθὲν ἐφ' ὑμᾶς, it will be seen
that the Hebrew equivalent of this sounds more natural:
את־השם הטוב אשר נקרא עליכם . . . ; iii., 18 . . . ἐν εἰρήνῃ
σπείρεται τοῖς ποιοῦσιν εἰρήνην, although there is no fault to find with
the Greek, a Hebrew equivalent suggests itself almost spontaneously:

בשלום יזרע לעשׂי השלום . . . ; the same may be said of the following : i. 12, . . . τὸν στέφανον τῆς ζωῆς, עטרת החיים ; i. 19 . . . βραδὺς εἰς τὸ λαλῆσαι βραδὺς εἰς ὀργήν, קשׁה לדבר וקשׁה לכעוס; ii. 12, οὕτως λαλεῖτε καὶ οὕτως ποιεῖτε, כן דברו וכן עשׂו; ii. 23, ἐλογίσθη αὐτῷ εἰς δικαιοσύνην, תחשׁב־לו לצדקה ; iii. 18, καρπὸς δικαιοσύνης, פרי הצדקה ; iv. 10, ταπεινώθητε ἐνώπιον Κυρίου, השׁפלו לפני יהוה ; iv. 13, ἄγε νῦν οἱ λέγοντες . . . , v. 1, ἄγε νῦν οἱ πλούσιοι, for this mode of address cf. Am. vi. 1, הוי השׁאננים בציון ; v. 3 ὁ ἰὸς αὐτῶν εἰς μαρτύριον ὑμῖν ἔσται, והיתה הלאתם בכם לעדות ; v. 8, στηρίξατε τὰς καρδίας ὑμῶν, אמצו לבבכם ; v. 10, 14, ἐν ὀνόματι Κυρίου, בשׁם יהוה ; v. 17, προσηύξατο τοῦ μὴ βρέξαι, לבלתי היות מטר . . . It is not suggested that in these, as well as in a number of other cases, the Greek is a translation from the Hebrew ; but it will not be denied that the form of the Greek does suggest the Hebrew idiom, and therefore that the writer was a Jew.[1]

(ii.) Secondly, the well-known predilection for assonance on the part of Hebrew writers appears in this Epistle, and is further illustrative of the " Hebraic" colouring of it ; this is noticeable both in the repetition of the same words or roots, as well as in the tendency to alliteration ; so marked a feature of the Epistle is this that it is met with in almost every verse, and therefore only a few examples need be given : i. 4, ἔργον τέλειον ἐχέτω ἵνα ἦτε τέλειοι. i. 13, μηδεὶς πειραζόμενος λεγέτω ὅτι ἀπὸ Θεοῦ πειράζομαι· ὁ γὰρ Θεὸς ἀπείραστός ἐστιν κακῶν. i. 19, . . . βραδὺς εἰς τὸ λαλῆσαι βραδὺς εἰς ὀργήν. iii. 6, καὶ φλογίζουσα τὸν τροχὸν τῆς γενέσεως καὶ φλογιζομένη ὑπὸ τῆς γεέννης. iii. 7, πᾶσα γὰρ φύσις . . . δαμάζεται . . . τῇ φύσει. iii. 18, . . . ἐν εἰρήνῃ σπείρεται τοῖς ποιοῦσιν εἰρήνην iv. 8, ἐγγίσατε τῷ Θεῷ καὶ ἐγγίσει ὑμῖν. iv. 11. μὴ καταλαλεῖτε ἀλλήλων ἀδελφοί· ὁ καταλαλῶν ἀδελφοῦ ἢ κρίνων τὸν ἀδελφὸν αὐτοῦ καταλαλεῖ νόμου καὶ κρίνει νόμον· εἰ δὲ νόμον κρίνεις οὐκ εἶ ποιητὴς νόμου ἀλλὰ κριτής . . . v. 7-8, μακροθυμήσατε οὖν ἀδελφοί . . .

---

[1] We are not forgetting Deissmann's very true words : " We have come to recognise that we had greatly over-estimated the number of Hebraisms and Aramaisms in the Bible. Many features that are non-Attic and bear some resemblance to the Semitic and were therefore regarded as Semiticisms, belong really to the great class of international vulgarisms, and are found in vulgar papyri and inscriptions as well as in the Bible " (*The Philology of the Greek Bible*, pp. 62 f., 1908) ; but it is not the language so much as the mode of thought, which, when expressed in Hebrew, is so often reminiscent of O. T. phraseology, to which we refer.

μακροθυμῶν ἐπ᾽ αὐτῷ ἕως λάβῃ πρόϊμον καὶ ὄψιμον. μακροθυμήσατε
καὶ ὑμεῖς . . . The following are some good instances of alliteration:
i. 2, πᾶσαν χαρὰν ἡγήσασθε ὅταν πειρασμοῖς περιπέσητε ποικίλοις. iii. 5
μικρὸν μέλος ἐστὶν καὶ μεγάλα αὐχεῖ. iii. 8, τὴν δὲ γλῶσσαν οὐδεὶς
δαμάσαι δύναται. iv. 8, καθαρίσατε χεῖρας . . . ἁγνίσατε καρδίας. How
thoroughly in the Hebrew fashion this repetition of words and
alliterative tendency is may be seen by observing a few examples,
taken quite at random, from the O.T., e.g., Am. vi. 7, 13; Isa. ix. 5;
Nah. i. 2; Ps. cxix. 13, cxxii. 6, etc., etc.

(iii.) Instances of pleonastic phraseology in the Epistle must also
be regarded as witnessing to Jewish authorship; among such are the
following: i. 8, ἀνὴρ δίψυχος, corresponding to the Hebrew אִישׁ;
the same is seen in i. 12, μακάριος ἀνὴρ ὅς . . . Cf. Ps. i. 1,
אַשְׁרֵי הָאִישׁ אֲשֶׁר; i. 19, ἔστω δὲ πᾶς ἄνθρωπος; i. 7, μὴ γὰρ οἰέσθω
ὁ ἄνθρωπος ἐκεῖνος . . . ; i. 23, οὗτος ἔοικεν ἀνδρὶ κατανοοῦντι . . . ;
ii. 2, ἀνὴρ χρυσοδακτύλιος. Suggestive of Hebrew phraseology, again
are such passages as iii. 7, τῶν ἵππων τοὺς χαλινοὺς εἰς τὰ στόματα
βάλλομεν εἰς τὸ πείθεσθαι αὐτοὺς ἡμῖν; iv. 2, οὐκ ἔχετε διὰ
τὸ μὴ αἰτεῖσθαι ὑμᾶς. Reminiscent of Hebrew thought are
also the words in i. 15, ἡ ἐπιθυμία συλλαβοῦσα τίκτει ἁμαρτίαν; for the
similar idea see Ps. vii. 14, *Behold he travaileth with iniquity, yea
he hath conceived mischief, and brought forth falsehood;* so, too,
the words in ii. 7, βλασφημοῦσιν τὸ ὄνομα . . . ; here, moreover, the
omission of the preposition should be noticed; then also, in v. 7, the
familiar πρόϊμον καὶ ὄψιμον (cf. Jer. v., 24, גֶּשֶׁם יוֹרֶה וּמַלְקוֹשׁ), and
in v. 17, the regular Hebraism προσευχῇ προσηύξατο (תְּפִלָּה הִתְפַּלֵּל)·

(iv.) The Hebraic character of the Epistle is further illustrated
by a certain terse and forcible way of putting things, reminding one
often of the prophetic style, e.g., ii. 3, *Sit thou here in a good place,*
and in the same verse, *Stand thou there;* iv. 2 ff., *Ye lust and
have not; ye kill, and covet, and cannot obtain; ye fight and war;
ye have not because ye ask not. . . . Ye adulteresses, know ye not
that the friendship of the world is enmity against God?* iv. 7, *Be
subject, therefore, unto God; but resist the devil.* v. 1, *Go to now,
ye rich, weep and howl for your miseries which are coming upon
you.* Then, again, the way in which vivid pictures are presented in
few but pregnant words is also illustrative of the same prophetic
style, e.g., in i. 6, the picture of the man who doubts; in ii. 2, of
the rich man and the poor man entering the synagogue; and in v.
4, of the defrauded labourers. Under this heading must also be
mentioned the distinctive way in which the writer of the Epistle

frames many of his sentences; generally speaking they are short and simple, which points, perhaps, to a natural habit of forming them on the Hebrew or Aramaic pattern; indirect statement is never expressed by the infinitive, but only by ὅτι with the indicative; the simple structure will be seen from the following instances: i. 3, γινώσκοντες ὅτι . . . κατεργάζεται ὑπομονήν. i. 7, μὴ γὰρ οἰέσθω . . . ὅτι λήμψεται . . . ii. 20, θέλεις δὲ γνῶναι . . . ὅτι ἡ πίστις χωρὶς τῶν ἔργων ἀργή ἐστιν; ii. 24, ὁρᾶτε ὅτι ἐξ ἔργων δικαιοῦται ἄνθρωπος. ii. 19, σὺ πιστεύεις ὅτι εἷς θεός ἐστιν. ii. 22, βλέπεις ὅτι ἡ πίστις συνήργει . . . iii., 1, . . . εἰδότες ὅτι μεῖζον κρίμα λημψόμεθα. iv. 5, δοκεῖτε ὅτι κενῶς ἡ γραφὴ λέγει . . . ; v. 11, . . . εἴδετε ὅτι πολύσπλαγχνός ἐστιν ὁ Κύριος. This fact of there being no subordination of sentences, but only co-ordination is very suggestive of the simple Hebrew construction of sentences. Mention should also be made of the entire absence of the optative mood in the Epistle. On the other hand, we have instances of the prophetic perfect, in v. 2, σέσηπεν and γέγονεν, in v. 3, κατίωται; and also of the gnomic aorist, e.g., i. 2, ἀνέτειλεν, where the Hebrew idiom is imitated, see Isa. xl., 7, . . . יבש חציר נבל ציץ. Further, the extended use of the word ποιεῖν is extremely suggestive of Hebrew usage, e.g., ii. 13, ἡ γὰρ κρίσις ἀνέλεος τῷ μὴ ποιήσαντι ἔλεος, the phrase sounds more natural in Hebrew: . . . לאשר לא־עשה חסד; i. 22, γίνεσθε δὲ ποιηταὶ λόγου, Hebrew: והיו עשי הדבר, cf. i. 25; ii. 8, καλῶς ποιεῖτε, Hebrew: לעשות תיטיבו, cf. ii. 19; iii. 12, μὴ δύναται συκῆ ἐλαίας ποιῆσαι, Hebrew: היוכל עץ התאנה לעשות זיתים; iii. 18, τοῖς ποιοῦσιν εἰρήνην Hebrew: לעשי שלום; iv. 13, . . . καὶ ποιήσομεν ἐκεῖ ἐνιαυτὸν . . . . Hebrew: ונעשה שם שנה . . . And, once more, the extended use of διδόναι in v. 18, is also in accordance with the Hebrew idiom. Lastly, there are a few other minor points which seem to betray greater familiarity with Hebrew than with Greek idiom; among these are; *the use of the genitive of quality*, e.g., i. 15, ἀκροατὴς ἐπιλησμονῆς, ii. 4, κριταὶ διαλογισμῶν πονηρῶν, iii. 6, κόσμος τῆς ἀδικίας (See Vorst, *Hebr.* . . . pp. 244 ff.); *the lax use of number*, e.g., ii. 15, ἐὰν ἀδελφὸς ἢ ἀδελφὴ γυμνοὶ ὑπάρχωσιν . . . ; iii. 14, εἰ ἐριθίαν ἔχετε ἐν τῇ καρδίᾳ ὑμῶν . . . ; iii. 10, ἐκ τοῦ αὐτοῦ στόματος ἐξέρχεται εὐλογία καὶ κατάρα; *the use of the article is inconsistent;* and *the disregard of cases is, in some instances, irregular*, e.g., iii. 9, καταρώμεθα τοὺς ἀνθρώπους (acc. instead of dat.), v. 6, κατεδικάσατε τὸν δίκαιον (acc. instead of gen.) cf. Mayor *in loc*. While allowing due weight to "international vulgarisms," one cannot help feeling that many of these features point to a Jewish atmosphere of thought, and a Jewish mode of expression.

From all that has been said, therefore, it must be clear that the author of our Epistle was a Jew; as far as it goes, this evidence is in the direction of favouring the authorship of St. James; though it is, of course, far from being in any sense conclusive.   But while the internal evidence, so far, speaks distinctly in favour of St. James being the writer of the Epistle, there are some other weighty considerations which point in the opposite direction.   Firstly, one might reasonably have expected in an Epistle written by St. James that the fact of his having been the brother of the Lord would have been specially mentioned; this, one might think, would have been insisted on for its own sake, quite apart from the authority and prestige which the mention of it would have conferred upon the writer.   Though the fact would have been well known in his immediate surroundings, or even throughout Palestine, and would therefore not have necessitated mention in an Epistle addressed to Palestinian congregations, it was different when, as in the present case, the scattered churches of the Dispersion were being written to; the more authoritative the name of the person who addressed them, the more effective would be the influence of the Epistle upon them.   The occurrence of the Lord's name in the opening verse of the Epistle—" a servant of God and of the Lord Jesus Christ "—offered a natural and obvious opportunity for the mention of the writer's close tie to Him.   In reply to this it may well be said that after the resurrection of Christ, and the consequent proclamation of His Divinity to all the world, there would be a natural and very seemly hesitation, on the part of those who were His relations after the flesh, to assert this tie; but this argument is to some extent weakened by the words in John xix. 25-27, which were written later than our Epistle (on the assumption of St. James authorship): " But there were standing by the Cross of Jesus His mother and His mother's sister, Mary the wife of Clopas, and Mary Magdalene.   When Jesus therefore saw His mother, and the disciple standing by whom He loved, He saith unto His mother . . . "; if St. John could record thus distinctly the relationship between our Lord and the Blessed Virgin so long after, there does not seem sufficient reason why St. James should not have referred to his own relationship with our Lord.   Apart, however, from the non-mention of this relationship, one might, at any rate, have expected a reference to apostleship in the opening verse of the Epistle; for that St. James was regarded as an apostle in the early Church is clear from 1 Cor. xv. 7, Acts xv. 22, Gal. ii. 8, 9.   A second reason for questioning the authorship of St. James is the absence of any references to the great outstanding events connected with our Lord's Person—His manner of life on earth, His sufferings and death, His resurrection and ascension. There are special reasons for expecting to find such references in this Epistle—assuming it to have been written by St. James. It is almost impossible to believe that one who had known Christ, and had been an eye-witness of His doings and a hearer of His teaching, should maintain such absolute silence on these things when addressing a letter to fellow-believers which touches otherwise on such a large variety of subjects. If there was one thing of paramount importance in the early days of Christianity it was that the fact of Christ's resurrection should be proclaimed; one has but to remember how often reference is made to this in the Acts—about twenty-five times—how it is mentioned or implied in all the Pauline Epistles, in the Epistle to the Hebrews, as well as in 1 Peter and 1 and 2 John, to realise the conviction and practice of the other apostles in this; and yet St. James, to whom had been vouchsafed a special manifestation of the risen Lord, can write an Epistle to Jewish-Christians who were scattered abroad without the slightest reference, implicit or explicit, to this cardinal tenet of the faith! The fact of the Epistle being addressed to the Dispersion makes this omission all the more strange; for on the assumption that St. James wrote it, *i.e.*, that it was probably the earliest in date of all the books of the New Testament, there must have been many among those addressed who would require strengthening in their belief, or who would possibly have heard of the resurrection for the first time from a " pillar " of the Church, supposing it had been mentioned; and, therefore, one might reasonably have expected to have found it occupying a central position in the Epistle. It is fully realised that to argue from omissions is not always safe; it is, however, impossible not to be struck by the omissions referred to if the Epistle was written by St. James. On the assumption of a late date, at all events for the bulk of the Epistle, when the main tenets of the faith, such as the resurrection, were regarded as " first principles " and were meant rather for " babes " in faith (*cf.* Heb. vi. 1 and context), these omissions would not cause surprise; but they would be very difficult to account for on the assumption of St. James' authorship, which would imply a date prior to c. 63 A.D. for its composition. In reply to this it may well be urged that in Acts xv. we have an instance of an Epistle written in the earliest ages of Christianity in which no references to the cardinal tenets of the faith are found; but in an Epistle like this (Acts xv. 23 ff.), written for one specific purpose, and therefore of small scope, such references cannot well be expected. The possibility is conceivable that a similar letter, though addressed to a different class of hearers, may have constituted the original form of the Epistle that now bears the name of St. James; in this case the absence of the references spoken of above would be quite comprehensible.

Another omission which is likewise difficult to account for on the assumption of the authorship of St. James, is that of any direct reference to Christ as the Messiah of Old Testament prophecy. For a Jew writing to Jewish-Christians in the earliest ages of Christianity such an omission is incomprehensible. The insistence on the Messiahship of our Lord would be the first step in the propagation of the faith among Jews; and if an Epistle of this length and comprehensive character in the subjects touched upon had been written by St. James he could scarcely have omitted some reference, though but a passing one, to the Messiah Whom he had seen and known. The question as to whether our Lord was the promised Messiah or not was one which was naturally surging in the minds of Jews in those early days; the question, "Art Thou He that should come?" perplexed the minds of many others long after the time of the Baptist; for Jews it was all-important, for everything depended upon it. The fact, therefore, that the Messiahship of Jesus is taken for granted in the Epistle (see i. 1, ii. 1) proves that these Jews of the Dispersion regarded this truth as axiomatic; and this would be almost impossible to understand among Jews of the *Dispersion* in the earliest ages of Christianity, if the conditions of the time are taken into consideration; the only way whereby this could be brought within the bounds of probability would be to restrict the meaning of *Dispersion*, but this would be arbitrary and without justification, seeing that in our Epistle the word is used without qualification, and, therefore, evidently intended to mean what was ordinarily understood by it.

A further objection urged against the authorship of St. James is the improbability of one in such a humble walk in life as a Galilæan peasant, the son of Mary and Joseph, being able to pen an Epistle of this kind in Greek. The writer of the Epistle displays a considerable knowledge of the Greek *Wisdom* literature, of various N.T. books, and of other Greek writings. It may be said in reply that opportunities for learning Greek were not wanting in Palestine, and the fact of humble birth was certainly no hindrance to the acquiring of knowledge among the Jews. But in a case like this, in which proof either for or against is not forthcoming, one must to a large extent be guided by a balance of probabilities. As far as our knowledge goes there was really nothing to induce St. James to learn Greek; there is no evidence for supposing that he extended his evangelistic efforts beyond the confines of Palestine; on the contrary, the evidence is in the other direction; as overseer of the Church in Jerusalem his activity must have been almost, if not altogether, exercised among those of his own race. Moreover, it is certain that the Palestinian Jewish teachers altogether discouraged everything that tended to the spread and influence of the Greek spirit, for they rightly (from their point of view) regarded it as a menace to orthodox Judaism (see Bergmann, *Jüdische Apologetik im neutestamentlichen Zeitalter*, p. 80, etc.); and for a Jew to go to heathen assemblies to learn was, to say the least, improbable in Palestine. As an apostle of the circumcision (Gal. ii. 9) in Palestine the various dialects of the Palestinian vernacular were amply sufficient for St. James' purposes. It must also be confessed that, even granting that St. James knew Greek, the large acquaintance with some of the Pauline Epistles which the writer of our Epistle shows is against the authorship of St. James; for how was St. James to gain such an intimate know-ledge of these without having them before him? It is certain that in those early days there were not many copies of them, and what-ever copies there were would be needed outside of Palestine rather than inside; nor is it quite clear why St. James should have required them at all. These Epistles must have been treasured by the Churches addressed as their special possession; copies of them are not likely to have been circulated generally until they had become authoritative documents in the Church at large, and this can scarcely have been the case until close upon the end of the first century at the earliest. The two Epistles that come into considera-tion are *Romans*, written from Corinth in c. 58 A.D., and *Galatians*, probably slightly earlier, perhaps from Antioch (or Ephesus?); these are the earliest dates that can be assigned to them, and as St. James was martyred probably in 63 A.D., there certainly does not appear to have been sufficient time for them to have reached that stage of importance in the eyes of Christians generally for copies to have been circulated outside of the particular congrega-tions addressed. This argument does not appeal, of course, to those who hold that St. Paul was indebted to St. James' Epistle. On the other hand, the analogy of the letter inspired by St. James in Acts xv. suggests the possibility that something of the same kind may have been repeated; but in this case we should look for some-thing more homogeneous than the Epistle (in its entirety) which at present bears his name.

Turning now more specifically to the question of *date*, we have, firstly, the entire absence of any reference to the destruction of Jerusalem. This can either imply that the Epistle was written some time before that event, or else some considerable time after. It is an argument which is conclusive neither for an early nor for a late date, and can only be used to emphasise the correctness of a result, concerning the date, reached on other grounds. There is, however, one consideration which suggests (though it certainly cannot be said to amount to proof) an early date; the words in v. 7-9, especially "stablish your hearts, for the coming of the Lord is at hand," are, in view of such a passage as Mark xiii. 14-37—see especially verses 28 ff.—more natural from one who was writing before the Fall of Jerusalem. Again, the silence in our Epistle regarding the great controversy on the question of the admission of Gentiles into the Church may well be used as an argument in favour of an early date, though it may also imply the opposite. Silence on this subject, which clearly agitated the Church to such an extent as to shake the very pillars (*cf.* Gal. ii 11 ff.) can only be satisfactorily explained on one of two hypotheses ; either the Epistle was written before this controversy arose, or else it was not written until so long after that there was no occasion to refer to it. It is, therefore, an argument which can be used both in favour of an early and a late date, and is thus, like that just referred to, inconclusive. But see further on this below. In the next place, the *data* to be gathered from the Epistle as to the *order and constitution of the Church* are important in seeking to fix an approximate date. The meeting-place for worship of the Jewish-Christians to whom the Epistle is addressed is called the "Synagogue" ; from this it has been argued that the Epistle was written at a time when Christian and Jewish places of worship had not yet become differentiated ; if, it is said, the Epistle had been written, say, during the first half of the second century, such place of meeting would have been termed ἐκκλησία. In reply to this, how- ever, it can be urged that συναγωγή is used of a distinctively Chris- tian assembly, *e.g.*, by Hermas in *Mand.*, xi. 9. Again, in iii. 1 mention is made of "many teachers," and in v. 14 of the "elders (or presbyters) of the Church" (τῆς ἐκκλησίας) ; that no reference is made to "bishops" or "deacons" points to an undeveloped consti- tution of the Church, and therefore to an early date for the Epistle ; moreover, the expression "many teachers" may imply a time when regular church officers for this purpose had not yet been ordained. But, on the other hand, it can be argued that the existence of "elders of the Church" does point to an organised system, and that the "many teachers" is better understood at a time when the number of Christians had greatly increased. Here, again, the argument on either side is inconclusive. Once more, *the condition of the Churches* to which the Epistle is addressed has not unnaturally been pointed to as not suggestive of the very early years of Christianity ; the earnestness and zeal which one might expect in those of the first generation of Christians is conspicuously lacking among those addressed ; the impression gained as to the characteristics of these is disappointing—the unbridled tongue, worldliness, quarrelling, jealousy, a mercenary spirit, despising of the poor, flattering the rich, lust, and an entire absence of the wisdom that is from above, with the virtues which this brings in its train. This argument is extremely well answered by Mayor (pp. cxxviii. ff.), who gives a number of examples showing that a similar state of morals was exhibited in other newly-formed Christian communities ; but his answer is not conclusive, for some of the examples cited—Ananias and Sapphira, Simon—are so obviously exceptional ; others, such as the murmuring of Hellenistic Jews against the Hebrews because their widows were neglected in the daily ministration, and the jealousy between Jews and Gentiles mentioned in Acts xv., and the case of those who had not heard "whether there be any Holy Ghost," are not, strictly speaking, analogous. Moreover, a difference must be made between recently converted Jews and those among the Gentiles who became Christians ; among the former there had always been a previous training in moral discipline, which was not the case with the Gentiles ; the characteristics, therefore, alluded to above, which are spoken of in reference to Jewish-Christians sound stranger than if Gentile-Christians were in question. If, on the other hand, the Epistle—or those parts of it which come into consideration in this connection—was written after Christianity had been established for two or three generations, the conditions described would be more comprehensible.

The conditions just referred to must, in part, have been the cause of the predominantly *ethical character of the Epistle ;* morals rather than religion sound the dominant note, and for an Epistle like this to have been written during the Apostolic age, when religious fervour was so pronounced, is certainly a little difficult of explanation. The attempts to solve this problem which have been made only bring into relief the incongruousness of the need of such a tone in an Epistle written in the middle (or shortly after the middle) of the first century ; for it differs utterly in this respect from other Apostolic writings. It is, of course, true to say that "no Apostolic writing fails to exhibit the moral interest as the consistent aim of all doctrine and instruction; the appeal for conduct corresponding to the new teaching is the regular conclusion of all doctrinal exposition ";[1] but the Apostles, as the same writer truly observes, always start from "the new revelation of the nature of man's dependence on God and God's work in man, which was contained in the Life, the Death, the Resurrection of the Lord Jesus,"[2] and this is just what is left aside—or perhaps, more correctly, taken for granted—in our Epistle; but in an Apostolic writing we legitimately look for the foundation-truths to be at least as prominent as the ethical standard which is based upon them. The argument based on this fact speaks for a late date. Next, a subject already dealt with, namely, the *Judaic tone* of the Epistle, is sometimes put forward in favour of an early date; but this characteristic could be used in support of any date from 200 B.C.-200 A.D., to give the narrowest margin; the argument, therefore, is wholly inconclusive. More to the point is that based upon the mention of the *Diaspora*. For the "twelve tribes of the Dispersion" to be addressed presupposes a widely-spread Christianity, such as would require many years to permit it to have developed itself, so that the use of the phrase in reference to Jewish-Christians almost compels one to postulate a late date for the bulk of the Epistle. The only reply forthcoming to refute this contention is to restrict the meaning of the term "Dispersion"; but, as already pointed out above, the Epistle gives us no authority for this, and what the Jews meant by the twelve tribes of the Dispersion is so well known that this reply ought scarcely to be considered. Then, on the other hand, the absence of all reference to the Temple and its worship has been used as an argument that the Temple no more existed, and that therefore the Epistle must at any rate be later than the year 70 A.D. This argument, however, seems quite inconclusive, for, unless for some specific purpose, why should it be mentioned in an Epistle to Jewish-Christians?

Finally, it is worth inquiring whether the silence of the Epistle concerning the two great distinctive marks of Judaism—*viz.*, Circumcision and the Sabbath—throws any light upon the question of date. The opinion had been directly expressed by St. James that circumcision was unnecessary for Gentile-Christians (Acts xv. 19, *cf*. xv. 5); on the other hand, Jewish-Christians would, of course, have been circumcised, in the first generation; but there must have arisen at an early stage the question as to whether the children of Jewish-Christians should be circumcised or not; it can hardly be doubted

[1] Parry, *A Discussion of the General Epistle of St. James*, p. 93.
[2] *Ibid.*

that the congregations in the Dispersion to whom our Epistle was addressed comprised a certain number of Gentile- as well as Jewish-Christians, and the latter must have known that the former were not circumcised, neither they nor their children, and therefore the question must have arisen as to which was the right course; it was a subject with which St. Paul had had to deal (1 Cor. vii. 18); as soon as the two classes of Christians began to associate, it must have become necessary to have some uniformity in this matter; it concerned the children more especially. On the assumption of an early date for the Epistle one might almost have a right to expect some reference to the question on account of its importance in the eyes of Jews, whereas on the assumption of a late date, when the usage of non-circumcision had been in vogue for some time, the silence on the subject would be natural. It is, perhaps, worth while pointing out that the question was probably to some extent complicated by the fact that baptism, as well as circumcision, was practised among the Jews, as regards proselytes, both before and after the founding of Christianity; during the first centuries of Christianity it became a burning question among the Rabbis whether circumcision without baptism was sufficient; some maintained that baptism alone sufficed. These were things concerning which the scattered congregations of the Dispersion must, in these early years of the planting of the faith, have needed guidance. As regards the Sabbath, some authoritative expression of opinion would also seem to have been demanded if the Epistle were of early date; those who had only comparatively recently become Christians might be expected to have required some guidance as to the observance of the Sabbath and the Lord's Day; even if both were observed, as was probably the case among the early Jewish-Christians, questions as to the relative importance of each can scarcely have been wanting when one remembers the punctiliousness in all that concerns observances which is so characteristic of the Jew. The silence on these two subjects is, of course, inconclusive as to date; all that can be said is that, assuming an early date for the Epistle, some reference to them might reasonably be expected, while if it were written about 125-130 A.D. this silence would be natural.

The net result, then, of these considerations as to authorship and date appears to be as follows: A great deal is to be said in favour of St. James' authorship, and, therefore, in favour of an early date; at least as much is to be said in favour of a late date (say the first or second quarter of the second century), and, therefore, against the authorship of St. James. Against every argument adduced in favour of either view serious objections can be urged; but then these objections, again, can for the most part be upset by counter-arguments. In view of such a perplexing state of affairs it is extremely difficult, perhaps impossible, to reach a satisfactory conclusion ; one thing is quite clear, and that is, that the advocates of either contention have a great deal to urge in support of their position, and that, therefore, dogmatic assertion regarding either is precarious, and belittling of the adversaries' arguments uncalled for. Any conclusion reached must, for the present, be tentative ; and, therefore, the view here held is provisional—the view, that is to say, that the name of St. James attaching to the Epistle is authentic, but that, in the first instance, the Epistle was a great deal shorter than as we now possess it ; sections being added from time to time, probably excerpts from other writings, or adaptations of these. Indeed, it is possible that we have here something in the shape of text and commentary, the latter being enlarged as time went on. If one remembers how, on an infinitely larger scale, of course, the comments of the words of Scripture by degrees became the *Mishna*, the comments on these the *Gemara*, and how ultimately the ponderous mass known as the *Talmud* came into being, the possibility of this intensely Jewish Epistle having grown by a process of comments, which ultimately came to be regarded as part of the Epistle itself, will be realised. One or two tentative examples of the supposed process will be given in III. on the analysis of the Epistle. This view does not profess to be anything more than theory, it is probably incapable of proof ; but it has, at least, the merit of justifying the position both of those who advocate an early as well as those who believe in a late date for the Epistle.

II. LITERARY CHARACTERISTICS.—These have to a large extent been already dealt with ; but a brief reference to three other points is demanded on account of their special importance.

(i.) One of the most striking features of the Epistle is the extended acquaintance with the *Wisdom* literature which it exhibits. Many instances of this will be found in the Commentary, here it must suffice to indicate by references some of the more important and striking examples ; the following passages should be compared together : i. 5, Sir. i. 1, 26, Wisd. vi. 14, vii. 14, 15 ; i. 8, Sir. i. 28, ii. 12, v. 9 : i. 12, Wisd. v. 16 ; i. 13, Sir. xv. 11-15 (especially in the Hebrew original), xv. 20 ; i. 19, Sir. v. 11 (the words " and let thy life be sincere," which are inserted by A.V., are found neither in the Hebrew nor the Greek ; their absence makes the agreement between the words in Jas. and this passage closer), i. 29, iv. 29, v. 13 ; i. 27, Sir. vii. 34-36, *cf.* iv. 10 ; ii. 6, Wisd. ii. 10 (in the Greek) ; iii. 2,

Sir. xiv. 1, **xix.** 16, xxv. 8, xxxvii. 18; **iii. 5, 6,** Sir. v. 13, 14, viii. 3
xxviii. 11; **iii. 8,** Sir. xxviii. 16-18; **iii. 10,** Sir. xxviii. 12 (see also
context); **iii. 13, 17,** Wisd. vii. 22-24; **v. 4,** Sir. iv. 1-6, xxxiv. 22;
v. 7, Sir. vi. 19; **v. 16,** Sir. iv. 26; **v. 17,** Sir. xlviii. 3 (*cf.* context).
These are very far from being exhaustive, and only two books of the
Wisdom literature have been referred to, whereas points of contact
are to be found in several others. This knowledge and sympathy
with the *Wisdom* literature suggest a Hellenistic rather than a Palestinian Jew.

(ii.) A second literary characteristic, and one which is further
indicative of Hebraic colouring (see above), is to be found in the
large number of parallelisms which the Epistle contains. This well-
known Hebrew literary characteristic appears sometimes more clearly
than at others in the Epistle, but a few of the most obvious examples
are the following :—

i. 9, 10ª. *Let the brother of low degree glory in his high estate ;*
And the rich in that he is made low.

i. 15. *Then the lust, having conceived, beareth sin ;*
And the sin, being full-grown, bringeth forth death.

i. 17. *Every good gift and every perfect boon is from above,*
Coming down from the Father of lights,
With Whom can be no variation,
Nor shadow that is cast by turning.

i. 19, 20. *But let every man be swift to hear, slow to speak, slow*
to wrath ;
For the wrath of man worketh not the righteousness of
God.

i. 22. *Be ye doers of the word, and not hearers only,*
Deluding your own selves.

iii. 11, 12. *Doth the fountain send forth from the same opening*
sweet and bitter water ?
Can a fig tree, my brethren, yield olives, or a vine figs ?

See, further, iv. 7, 10, v. 4, 5, 9. This, too, is in the style of much of
the *Wisdom* literature, and reminds one often of the Book of Proverbs
especially.

(iii.) Lastly, one cannot fail to be struck by the number of words
—a large number when the shortness of the Epistle is considered—
which are either ἄπ. λεγ. in the New Testament, or very rarely found,
outside the Epistle, in the Septuagint or New Testament; this denotes a knowledge of Greek literature and of the Greek language
generally, which is very noticeable ; attention is drawn to such words

in the Commentary whenever they occur. For other literary characteristics see I. § 2.

III. ANALYSIS OF THE EPISTLE.—The vast majority of commentators are agreed that no consistent scheme is presented in this Epistle, but that it contains rather a number of unconnected sayings which are for the most part independent of one another. The analysis of the Epistle shows the correctness of this view in the main.[1] In some cases it is possible that a thought-connection of a secondary character exists which is not at once apparent; by a thought-connection of a secondary character is meant, when in two succeeding sections a subordinate, not the main, thought of the earlier is taken up and dealt with in the later; an example may be seen in the two sections i. 2-4, i. 5-8; the main thought in the former is the being joyful in temptations, the subject of patience is a subordinate thought, and still more so, that of lacking in nothing; but it is this last which is taken up in the succeeding section and attached to the thought of lacking in wisdom; so that, although it is perfectly true to say there is no genuine connection between these two sections, yet there is a secondary connection. It is improbable that the two sections come from the same writer, because they are lacking in real mental sequence; and yet a semblance of sequence is apparent; if both came from the same writer one would either expect a genuine sequence of thought if the two were intended to be connected, or else a clear indication of each being self-contained. As they stand, it looks as though the former were a text, and the latter a comment upon it, very much like the similar process which occurs incessantly in the *Mishna*.[2] The next section, i. 9-11, deals with the subject of rich and poor; it stands in an isolated position here, but is intimately connected with the later section, ii. 1-13. With i. 12-16 we have another instance of what looks like text and comment; the subject is that of temptation, and comes most naturally after i. 4; the text is contained in ver. 12, the following verses then comment on the nature of temptation. This is an instructive instance illustrative of the theory of the authorship of the Epistle here tentatively advocated (see above); for on comparing the simple, straightforward character of ver. 12 with the intricate chain of thought in the two following verses, it is almost impossible to postulate identity of authorship.

---

[1] Parry's attempt to show that the Epistle is "a very careful and logical exposition of a single theme" (*op. cit.* p. 6) is ingenious, but much too artificial to carry conviction.

[2] Catch-words, it would seem, played their part in the formation and grouping of sections.

i. 17 belongs to the preceding, possibly (see IV. § 1), and i. 18 seems to be a comment on the " Father of lights ". i. 19ᵇ-20 forms an isolated saying. A self-contained section on the subject of practical r eligion follows in i. 21-25, to which vv. 26, 27 form an addition. ii. 1-13 has already been referred to ; it is followed by a section (ii. 14-26) of deep interest on the subject of faith and works, to which iii. 13-18 belong, according to the subjec t-matter. iii. 1-12 is a self-contained passage dealing with the subject of self-control as regards the tongue. If these first three chapters show a want of homogeneity, the last two do so in an even more pronounced way ; the various sections are clearly divided off, showing no connection with each other, the whole forming a collection of extracts, apparently ; thus, iv. 1-10 contains warnings and exhortations concerning the practical religious life ; iv. 11, 12 is a short section on the need of observing the second great commandment of the Law ; iv. 13-17 lays stress on the uncertainty and fleeting character of earthly life; v. 1-11 is an eschatological section, and extremely practical ; v. 12, which prohibits swearing, is almost a quotation from the Sermon on the Mount ; v. 13-18 gives directions concerning the visitation of the sick ; and the abrupt ending v. 19, 20 speaks of the reward of those who convert sinners from their evil ways.

It will thus be seen that the Epistle is for the most part a collection of independent sections ; some of these were evidently originally intended to be comments on the Apostle's words, possibly added by one or more of the elders of the churches addressed for the benefit of the members ; others seem to be wholly independent, and not to have had anything to do with the Epistle in the first instance. The various elements of which the Epistle is now composed have to a large extent become so intermingled that the attempt to differentiate between them seems hopeless. But, generally speaking, we should look for the simplest, most direct and straightforward parts as being those which would be the most likely words of the Apostle ; so that such parts as i. 13-16 and ii. 14-26 can hardly be regarded as from the same hand as, *e.g.*, ii. 1-13 (in the main).

IV. Some Jewish Doctrines Considered.—As is often mentioned in the notes, there are some points of Jewish theology which figure rather prominently in this Epistle ; there are above all two subjects, specifically Jewish, which play an important part, and therefore a brief consideration of these will not be out of place here :—

(i.) *The Jewish doctrine of the Yetser hara'*.—Speculations as to the origin of sin were rife among Jewish thinkers at all times ; the perplexity which is so plainly apparent in the words of St. Paul

(Rom. vii. 22-23), *For I delight in the law of God after the inward man; but I see a different law in my members, warring against the law of my mind, and bringing me into captivity under the law of sin which is in my members*, had been felt by many long before his day. The origin of the existence of the "law of sin in the members," which asserted itself in spite of the ardent desire of men to be free from its power, was the great problem which had to be solved. The result was the theory, based upon the observed facts of experience, that within man, as part of his created being, there were two tendencies: the tendency towards good, *Yetser ha-tob* (יצר הטוב), and the tendency towards evil, *Yetser hara'* (יצר הרע). But whence originated these two tendencies? If they both formed part of man's nature from the beginning, it followed that their creation was due to God; there was, of course, no difficulty about ascribing the creation of the good tendency to Him, but that He should have created anything evil was obviously a difficulty. The varying thoughts and speculations on the subject will perhaps best be seen by giving a few illustrations as examples. In Sir. xv. 14, 15, we have these interesting words, according to the Greek Version: "He made man from the beginning, and left him in the power of his will" (ἐν χειρὶ διαβουλίου αὐτοῦ); "if thou willest, thou wilt observe the commandments, and to exhibit faithfulness is a matter of thy good pleasure" (καὶ πίστιν ποιῆσαι εὐδοκίας); the significance of these words is only realised when they are read in the Hebrew, *viz.*, "God [this is the reading of the Syriac and Latin as well] created man from the beginning; and He delivered him into the hand of him who took him for a prey (חותפו); and He gave him over into the power of his will (יצרו)"; here it is clear that the second clause is an explanatory gloss (it is wanting in the Greek), the object being to indicate that to be in the power of the *Yetser* (which is here clearly used in reference to the *evil* tendency) is equivalent to being in the power of Satan. This is important as showing that the evil tendency is not ascribed to divine creation, but that over against the good which God created in man there is an opposition of evil which is due to the activity of Satan. This thought of opposing tendencies is apparent elsewhere in the same book, *e.g.*, xxxiii. 15: "Good is set against evil, and life against death; so is the godly against the sinner. So look upon all the works of the Most High; there are two and two, one against another" (the Hebrew of these verses is not extant); here the writer comes perilously near ascribing the creation of evil to God; but in another passage the question is left

open, xxxvii. 3 : " O evil tendency (יצר רע), why wast thou made to
fill the earth with thy deceit?" It is, at all events, rot directly
ascribed to God ; these pathetic words remind one of those of St.
Paul in Rom. vii. 24.   The same hesitation to assert that God
created evil is observable in a curious passage from the pseudepigraph called *The Life of Adam and Eve (Apocalpyse of Moses)*,
§ 19 ;[1] this describes the origin of evil, and tells of how in the
garden of Eden Satan took the form of an angel, but spoke "through
the mouth of the Serpent," and aroused within Eve the desire to
eat of the fruit of the tree that stood in the middle of the garden ;
first of all, however, we are told that he made her swear that she
would give of the fruit to Adam as well ; then the text goes on :
"When he (*i.e.*, the Serpent) had, then, made me swear, he came
and ascended up into it (*i.e.*, the tree).   But in the fruit which he
gave me to eat he placed the poison of his malice, namely, of his
lust ; for lust is the beginning of all sin.   And he [other authorities
read " I "] bent down the bough to the earth, then I took of the fruit
and ate."   Here the origin of evil *in man* is satisfactorily accounted
for ; its existence in Satan is taken for granted, and no attempt is
made to follow it up further back.   Noticeable here, too, is the way in
which lust is brought into connection with the origin of sin ; this is
an idea which seems to have been widely prevalent in Jewish circles,
the lust of Satan towards Eve being described as the beginning of
sin in the world (See *Sanhedrin*, 59 *b* ; *Sotah*, 9 *b* ; *Jebamoth*, 103 *b* ;
Abodah Zara, 22 *b* ; *Bereshith Rabba*, c. 18, 19) ; so that it is very
interesting to read in our Epistle, after i., 13, 14 (which will be
referred to presently), in which the impulse to sin in man is dealt
with, the words : " . . . when he is drawn away by his own lust,
and enticed.   Then the lust, when it hath conceived, beareth sin ;
and the sin, when it is full grown, bringeth forth death".   This
thought of a relationship between sin and death is graphically
illustrated in the *Jerusalem Targum* to Gen. iii. 6, where it is
said that at the moment in which Eve succumbed to temptation
she caught sight of Sammael, the angel of death.   Other theories
as to the origin of sin were that it was brought into existence
by man, *e.g.*, Enoch xcviii. 4, " Sin has not been sent upon the
earth, but man himself has created it," this is the teaching, apparently, in Jas. i. 14 ; in ch. lxxxv. of the same book it is taught that
fallen angels were the originators of sin (*cf. Bereshith Rabba*,
c. 24 ; *Yalkut Shim. Beresh.*, 42).   None of these theories was,

---

[1] The two works run parallel to a large extent.

however, satisfactory; none really gave the answer to the problem
that was constantly presenting itself; if, for a moment, the contention was put forth that man himself originated sin, a very
little thought showed that this, too, was untenable, for the very
nature of the "evil tendency" forbade the idea that man could
have created it.   Therefore, at a very early period, comparatively
speaking, the teaching which afterwards became crystallised in
Rabbinical writings, must have been put forth,—the logical, if
dangerous, doctrine, that God, as the Creator of all things, must
have also created the *Yetser hara'*, the "evil tendency"; thus in
Bereshith Rabba, c. 27, it is definitely stated that God created the
Yetser hara'; in *Yalkut Shim. Beresh.*, 44-47, the Almighty is made
to say : "I grieve that I created man of earthly substance; for had I
created him of heavenly substance he would not have rebelled
against me"; again *ibid.* 61 : "It repenteth me that I created the
Yetser hara' in man, for had I not done this he would not have rebelled
against me"; and in *Kiddushin*, 30*b*, we read: "I created an evil
tendency (*Yetser ra'*).   I created for him (*i.e.*, for man, in order to
counteract this) the Law as a means of healing.   If ye occupy
yourselves with the Law, ye will not fall into the power of it (*i.e.*,
the *Yetser ra'*).   Once more, according to *Bammidbar Rabba*, c. 22,
we are told of how God created the good and the evil tendencies :
the former was placed in man's right side, the latter in his left side.
In other passages it is pointed out that the *Yetser tob* is Wisdom
and Knowledge of the Law (Weber, *Jüdische Theologie*, p. 218).
The danger of such a doctrine is obvious, a danger which could not
be more vividly illustrated than in the words of St. Paul, Rom. vii.
15-24 : " . . . but if what I would not, that I do, I consent unto the
Law that it is good.   So now it is no more I that do it, but sin which
dwelleth in me. . . . but if what I would not, that I do, it is no more
I that do it, but sin which dwelleth in me, . . . "; that teaching like
this, taken with the belief that the *evil tendency* was created by God,
would be perverted was almost inevitable; it was the existence of
such perversions which must have called forth the words in i. 13 f.
of our Epistle : "Let no man say when he is tempted, I am tempted
of God; for God cannot be tempted with evil, and He Himself
tempteth no man . . . "; then, possibly, the words in verse 17 of
the same chapter, "Every good gift and every perfect boon is from
above . . . " refer to the *Yetser ha-tob*, and are intended to exclude
the belief that the *Yetser hara'*, whereby men were tempted, came
from God.

    (ii.) *The Jewish Doctrine of Works.*—There are, according to

Rabbinical teaching, two categories of good works : i. *Mitzvôth*
(מצורת) lit. " commandments " ; these consist in observances of the
Torah ; ii. Works of love, of which the most important is almsgiving,
indeed so high does this stand that it has the technical name of צדקה
(" righteousness ") ; these two categories comprise the whole body
of מעשים טובים (" good works "), the former representing man's
duty to God, the latter His duty to His fellow-creatures ; *cf.* Matt.
xxii. 36-40, " . . . Thou shalt love the Lord thy God . . . thy neighbour as thyself.   On these two commandments hangeth the whole
law and the prophets."   According to Jewish teaching, there are
certain works of obligation ; good works done over and above these
are of free-will, and by these justification in the sight of God is attainable.   There are two classes of men, those who do a sufficient
number of good works to be justified in the sight of God—these are the
צדיקים,   " the righteous "—and those who do not—these are the
רשעים,   " the wicked " ; these two are differentiated on earth, for it
is said in *Sanhedrin*, 47 *a*, that a רשע may not be buried by the side
of a צדיק.   But besides these two classes, there is an intermediate
one, the " ones between " (בינונים), who are half good and half
bad ; these can, by adding one good work, become reckoned among
the " righteous " on the Day of Atonement (*Rôsh hashshana*, 16 *b*).
The צדיקים—the " righteous "—were regarded as being in a state of
זכות (*Zecûth*), which meant that their accumulation of good works
was great enough to enable them to stand justified in the sight of God.
In addition to this there was also the doctrine of זכות אבות
(" merit of the fathers "), according to which the works of super-
erogation of departed ancestors went to the account of their descendants.   The being in a state of *Zecûth* entitled a man, *per se*, to
what was technically known as מתן שכר, lit. " the gift of reward "
(*cf. Debarim rabba*, c. 2) ; and this applied to earthly reward as well
as to reward hereafter.   So that good works demanded reward from
God ; thus it is said in *Yalkut Shim. Beresh.*, 109, that it is by right
that a man is rewarded with the good things in the Garden of Eden,
because he has won them for himself.   Justification by faith comes
only so far into consideration in that it is reckoned among the
מעשים טובים (" good works "), which, like all others, goes to swell
the list of a man's מצורת, *cf.* Jas. ii. 24, " Ye see that by works a
man is justified and not only by faith ".

There is, at bottom, an intimate connection between the doctrine of the good and evil " tendency," dealt with above, and the doctrine of works ; for it was by man's free-will that the good tendency was put into action which resulted in the accomplishment of good works ; and it was by man's free-will that the evil tendency was resisted, and this constituted *per se* a *mitzvah* ; *cf. Kiddushin,* 39 b, 40 a, where it is taught that the desire to do a *mitzvah* (*i.e.,* the calling of the good *Yetser* into action) is reckoned as though it were actually accomplished ; and the temptation to do a sinful act (*i.e.,* the motion of the evil *Yetser*) if resisted likewise constitutes a *mitzvah*. It was, perhaps, almost inevitable that the danger would arise of taking merit for good deeds, *i.e.,* for exercising the good tendency, while repudiating responsibility for the often involuntary assertion of the evil tendency ; that, however, the danger did arise does not admit of doubt ; it was *naïvely* illogical, for while the exercise of the good tendency, resulting in good works, was regarded as solely due to human initiative—such a thing as " prevenient grace " did not come into account, *cf.* Eph. ii. 8-10—the evil tendency came to be looked upon as a human misfortune, and not of the nature of guilt in man, *cf.* Jas. i. 13, where this is combated.

These facts should be taken into consideration in seeking to realise the significance of some passages in our Epistle ; thus, in i. 2-4, 12, we have Jewish teaching pure and simple, and the fact goes to substantiate the opinion that these verses, at all events, must be very early ; one could not conceive them in the mouth of St. Paul, *cf.* 1 Cor. x. 13, Rom. ii. 4, whose teaching on this subject, though *apparently* more developed, is really fully in accordance with that of Christ ;[1] on the other hand, we have in ii. 10 (" For whosoever shall keep the whole law, and yet stumble in one point, he is become guilty of all ") a principle which is certainly not that of normal Jewish teaching. On the very important section, ii. 14-26, see the notes in the Commentary, and what has been said above. Lastly, in v. 19, 20, we have again a thought which is especially Jewish ; that a man should be able to " cover a multitude of sins " by virtue of his good deed is directly anti-Christian, because it makes the forgiveness of sins a matter which a man can effect, and thus wholly antagonistic to the doctrines of Grace and Atonement. On the word "to cover," the English equivalent for the Hebrew כפר, see *Church and Synagogue,* April 1908, pp. 43-45.

---

[1] As an example of this see the writer's article, " The Parable of the Labourers in the Vineyard," in the *Expositor,* April, 1908.

V. The Apparatus Criticus.—The following are the authorities, together with their abbreviations, which have been utilised :—

1. Uncials :—

א Cod. Sinaiticus (iv. cen.).

ב Cod. Patiriensis (v. cen.), containing only iv. 14-v. 20.

A Cod. Alexandrinus (v. cen.).

B Cod. Vaticanus (iv. cen.).

C Cod. Ephraemi (v. cen.), wanting from Jas. iv. 3 to the end.

K_2 Cod. Mosquensis (ix. cen.), cited as K.

L_2 Cod. Angelicus Romanus (ix. cen.), cited as L.

P_2 Cod. Porfirianus (ix. cen.), cited as P; much illegible in Jas. ii. 13-21.

2. Cursives :—

Cited by their numbers, but only when they offer readings of interest ; curss = the consensus of a number of cursives.

3. Versions :—

The Old Latin :—

m the pseudo-Augustinian *Speculum* (viii. or ix. cen.).

ff Cod. Corbeiensis (vi. cen.).

s Frag. Vindobonensia (vi. cen.); wanting in v. 11-20.

The Vulgate :—

The two most important MSS. are :—

Vulg^A Cod. Amiatinus (viii. cen.).

Vulg^F Cod. Fuldensis (vi. cen.).

Latt = the consensus of the Latin versions.

The Syriac Versions :—

Pesh = Peshiṭtâ (belongs to the first half of the v. cen.).

Syr^{lee} = A Syriac Lectionary written in the dialect most probably used by our Lord (vi. cen.). Of Jas. it contains only i. 1-12.

Syr^{hk} = The Harklean Syriac (vii. cen.).

Syrr = the consensus of the Syriac versions.

The Armenian Version (v. cen.).*
The Coptic (Bohairic) *Version* (vi.-vii. cen.).*
The Ethiopic Version (iv. cen.).*
The Sahidic Version (iii. cen.).*

4. Church Fathers:—

Cyr = Cyril of Alexandria (v. cen.).
Dam = John Damascene (viii. cen.).
Did = Didymus of Alexandria (iv. cen.).
Oec = Oecumenius (xi. cen.).
Orig = Origen (iii. cen.).
Thl = Theophylact (xi. cen.).

5. Printed Editions:—

rec = Textus Receptus.
Ti = Tischendorf.
Treg = Tregelles.
WH = Westcott and Hort.
W = Weiss.

The Greek text used in the following pages is that published by Nestle, 1907.

VI. Literature.—The following selected list of Commentaries, etc., only takes account of the more recent works; for a full bibliography recourse must be had to Mayor's enumeration:—

Pfleiderer, *Urchristenthum*, 1887.
Beyschlag, *Der Brief des Jacobus*, 1888.
Plummer, *St. James*, in the "Expositor's Bible," 1891.
Weiss, *Die Katholischen Briefe* . . . 1892.
Spitta, *Der Brief des Jakobus*, 1898.
   „   *Zur Geschichte und Litteratur des Urchristenthums*, ii., 1896.
Von Soden, *Hand-Commentar* . . . 1899.
Parry, *A Discussion of the General Epistle of St. James*, 1903.
Grafe, *Die Stellung und Bedeutung des Jakobusbriefes in der Entwickelung des Urchristenthums*, 1904.
Knowling, *The Epistle of St. James*, in the "Westminster Commentaries," 1904.
Carr, *The Epistle of St. James*, in the "Cambridge Greek Testament for Schools and Colleges," 1905.

---

* These dates refer to the century in which the versions were probably first made, not to any extant MSS. of them.

Mayor, *The Epistle of St. James*, 1906.

Patrick, *James, the Lord's Brother*, 1906.

See also the *Introductions* of Salmon, Scrivener, Weiss, Zahn, Holtzmann, and Gregory.

The following is a selection of some valuable articles:—

Adeney, in the *Critical Review*, July, 1896.

Brückner, in the *Zeitschrift für wissenschaftliche Theologie*, 1874.

Cone, in *Encycl. Bibl.* art. "James (Epistle)".

Fulford, in Hastings' *Dict. of Christ and the Gospels*, art. "James".

Moffatt, in the *Expos. Times*, xiii. pp. 201-206, "The Righteousness of the Scribes and Pharisees".

Mayor, in Hastings' *Dict. of the Bible*, artt. "James," "James, General Epistle of".

Sieffert, in Herzog's *Realencyclopädie*, art. "Jacobus".

Simcox, in *The Journal of Theological Studies*, July, 1901.

Von Soden, in *Jahrbücher für protestantische Theologie*, 1884.

Weiss, in the *Neue Kirchliche Zeitschrift*, May, June, 1904.

But perhaps of the greatest help of all are the many side-lights to be gathered from the study of such works as the following:—

Bergmann, *Jüdische Apologetik im neutestamentlichen Zeitalter*, 1908.

Bousset, *Die Religion des Judenthums im neutestamentlichen Zeitalter*, 1903.[1]

Büchler, *Der galiläische 'Am-ha'Areṣ des zweiten Jahrhunderts*, 1906.

Charles, *The Testaments of the Twelve Patriarchs*, 1908.

„ *The Book of Enoch*, 1893.

Dalman, *Die Worte Jesu*, 1898.

Deissmann, *Bibelstudien*, 1895.

„ *Neue Bibelstudien*, 1897.

Fiebig's series of *Ausgewählte Mischnatractate*, 1905, etc.

Friedländer, *Die religiösen Bewegungen innerhalb des Judenthums im Zeitalter Jesu*, 1905.

Harnack, *The Mission and Expansion of Christianity in the First Three Centuries* (Engl. trans. by Moffatt) 1908.

Holtzmann, *Neutestamentliche Zeitgeschichte*, 1906.

---

[1] A new edition of this book has appeared.

Resch, *Agrapha*, 1906.

Schürer, *History of the Jewish People in the Time of Jesus Christ* (Engl. trans. by Macpherson, Taylor, and Christie), 1890, etc. [1]

Smend, *Die Weisheit des Jesus-Sirach*, 1906.

Taylor's edition of *Pirqe Aboth*, "Sayings of the Jewish Fathers," 1897.

Weber, *Jüdische Theologie auf Grund des Talmud und verwandter Schriften*, 1897.

The Talmudical works of Wünsche, Bacher, Strack, Fiebig, etc.

[1] A new edition of this work has appeared.

ΙΑΚΩΒΟΥ.[1]

I. 1. **ᵃΙΑΚΩΒΟΣ** Θεοῦ καὶ Κυρίου Ἰησοῦ Χριστοῦ[2] ᵇδοῦλος ταῖς a Acts xii.
δώδεκα ᶜφυλαῖς ταῖς ἐν τῇ ᵈδιασπορᾷ[3] ᵉχαίρειν.
17; cf.
Matt. xiii.
55.
b Rom. i. 1;

Phil. i. 1; Tit. i. 1; 2 Pet. i. 1; Jude i.; cf. 1 Pet. ii. 16; 2 Tim. ii. 24. ᶜLukᵉ xxii. 30; Acts
xxvi. 17; cf. Matt. xix. 28.   d Deut. xxxii. 26; 1 Pet. i. 1; John vii. 35; cf. Acts ii. 5-11, viii.
1, xv. 23, xxiii. 6.   e 2 Macc. ix. 19; Acts xv. 23.

[1] Inscr. + επιστολη BKP, curss., om. ℵ επιστολη καθολικη του αγιου αποστολου
ιακωβου L, Epistola Catholica beati Jacobi Apostoli Vulg. (Epistulae Catholicae
Vulgᴬ), επ. του απ. ιακωβου Pesh.

[2] דמרן Pesh., Syrᶫᵉᶜ.   [3] Add דישראל להלין Syrᶫᵉᶜ.

CHAPTER I.—Ver. 1. Ἰάκωβος: A very common name among Palestinian Jews, though its occurrence does not seem to be so frequent in pre-Christian times. Some noted Jewish Rabbis of this name lived in the earliest centuries of Christianity, notably Jacob ben Korshai, a "Tanna" (i.e., "teacher" of the Oral Law) of the second century. The English form of the name comes from the Italian Giacomo. Θεοῦ καὶ Κυρίου Ἰησοῦ Χριστοῦ: Only Κυρίου here can refer to Christ; in Gal. i. 1 the differentiation is made still more complete . . . διὰ Ἰησοῦ Χριστοῦ καὶ θεοῦ πατρὸς τοῦ ἐγείραντος αὐτὸν ἐκ νεκρῶν. On the other hand, in John xx. 28, we have ὁ Κύριός μου καὶ ὁ Θεός μου. But the disjunctive use of καὶ in the words before us does not imply a withholding of the divine title from our Lord, for the usage of Κύριος in the N.T., especially without the article, when connected with Χριστός, is in favour of its being regarded as a divine title, see e.g., 1 Cor. i. 1-3, etc. Hellenistic Jews used Κύριος as a name for God; the non-use of the article gains in significance when it is remembered that ὁ Κύριος, "Dominus," was a title given to the early Roman Emperors in order to express their deity, cf. Acts xxv. 26, where Festus refers to Nero as ὁ Κύριος. The Palestinian Syriac Lectionary (containing, as generally conceded, the dialect which our Lord spoke), as well as the Peshittâ, read "Our Lord," the expression used in the Peshittâ in Matt. viii. 25, Κύριε, σῶσον, ἀπολλύμεθα, and in xx. 33, Κύριε, ἵνα ἀνοιγῶσιν οἱ ὀφθαλμοὶ ἡμῶν; both instances of divine power being exercised. Χριστοῦ: the use of this title, applied to Jesus without further comment, speaks against an early date for the Epistle; in a letter written to Jews during the apostolic age it is inconceivable that the Messiah should be referred to in this connection without some justification; Jewish beliefs concerning the Messiah were such as to make it impossible for them to accept Jesus as the Messiah without some teaching on the subject; this would be the more required in the case of Jews of the Dispersion who could not have had the same opportunities of learning the truths of Christianity as Palestinian Jews. The way in which the title is here applied to our Lord implies that the truth taught was already generally accepted. The absence of the article also points to a late date. δοῦλος: Generally speaking, to the Jew δοῦλος (עֶבֶד), when used in reference to God, meant a *worshipper*, and when used with reference to men a *slave;* as the latter sense is out of the question here, δοῦλος must be understood as meaning worshipper, in which case the deity of our Lord would appear to be distinctly implied. ταῖς δώδεκα φυλαῖς ἐν τῇ διασπορᾷ: the "twelve tribes" was merely a synonym for the Jewish race (ἔθνος Ἰουδαίων), but there was a real

f Phil. iii. 1; cf.
Matt. v. 12.
g 1 Pet. i. 6.
h Rom. v. 4; 1 Pet. i. 7.

2. Πᾶσαν χαρὰν ⁱ ἡγήσασθε, ἀδελφοί μου, ὅταν ᵍ πειρασμοῖς ¹ περιπέσητε ποικίλοις, 3. γινώσκοντες ὅτι τὸ ʰ δοκίμιον ² ὑμῶν ³ τῆς

¹ Add סגיאא Pesh.   ² δοκιμον 28ᵃ.   ³ Om. Syrlec.

distinction between the Jews of the Dispersion and the Palestinian Jews. The latter were for the most part peasants or artisans, while the former, congregated almost wholly in cities, were practically all traders (cf. iv. 13). In each case there was a restricted circle of the learned. The connection of the Diaspora-Jews with Palestine became less and less close, until at last it consisted of little more than the payment of the annual Temple dues; with very many one visit in a lifetime to Jerusalem sufficed, and this was of course entirely discontinued after the Destruction, when the head-quarters of Jewry became centred in the Rabbinical academy of Jabne. From the present point of view, it is very important to bear in mind, above all, two points of difference between Palestinian and Diaspora-Jews, (1) Language, (2) Religion. (1) Among the former, Aramaic had displaced Hebrew; Aramaic was the language of everyday life, as well as of religion (hence the need of the Methurgeman to translate the Hebrew Scriptures in the Synagogues); among the latter Greek was spoken. It is not necessary to insist upon the obvious fact that this difference of language brought with it a corresponding difference of mental atmosphere; the Jew remained a Jew, but his way of thinking became modified. (2) Their contact with other peoples brought to the Diaspora-Jews a larger outlook upon the world; at the same time, they could not fail to see the immeasurable superiority of their faith over the heathen cults practised by others. This resulted on their laying greater stress on the essentials of their faith; the ethical side of their religion received greater emphasis, the spirituality of belief became more realised, and it therefore followed of necessity that universalistic ideas grew, so that proselytism became, at one time, a great characteristic among the Diaspora-Jews; Judaism contained a message to all peoples, it was felt; and thus the particularistic character of Palestinian Judaism found no place among the Diaspora-Jews. But, at the same time, the Bible of these Jews, which exercised an immense influence upon their thought and literature, was Hebraic in essence though clothed in Greek garb; hence that extraordinarily interesting phenomenon, the Hellenistic Jew. In view of what has been said it is interesting to note that two outstanding characteristics of the Epistle before us are: Hebraic thought and diction expressed in Greek form, and the emphasis laid on ethics rather than on doctrine. The meaning of διασπορά is quite unambiguous, and there is no justification for restricting it to the Eastern Dispersion; it includes the Jews of Italy, Macedonia, Greece, Asia Minor and, above all, Egypt, as well as of Asia. For further details see Esther iii. 8, viii. 9, ix. 30, x. 1; Acts ii. 9-11; Syb. Orac., iii. 271; Josephus, Antiq. XIV., vii. 12; Contra Ap., i. 22, etc., etc. χαίρειν: Cf. Acts xv. 23, xxiii. 26, the only other occurrences of this form of salutation in the N.T. "Historically there is probably no ellipsis even in the epistolary χαίρειν" (Moulton, Grammar of N.T. Greek (1), p. 180). It is of interest to note that in the Epistle inspired by St. James (Acts xv. 23) this form of salutation is used; it would, however, be precarious to draw deductions as to authorship from this, for the use of the infinitive for the imperative is quite common in Hellenistic Greek; as Moulton says: "We have every reason to expect it in the N.T., and its rarity there is the only matter of surprise" (Ibid.). The Peshittâ and Syrlec have the Jewish form, Shalôm.

Ver. 2. Πᾶσαν χαρὰν: Cf. Phil. ii. 29, μετὰ πάσης χαρᾶς: the rendering in Syrlec, which is rather a paraphrase than a translation, catches the meaning admirably: בכל חדוא הוו חאדין אחי, "With all joy be rejoicing my brethren." ἡγήσασθε: the writer is not to be understood as meaning that these trials are joyful in themselves, but that as a means to beneficial results they are to be rejoiced in; it is the same thought as that contained in Heb. xii. 11: πᾶσα μὲν παιδεία πρὸς μὲν τὸ παρὸν οὐ δοκεῖ χαρᾶς εἶναι ἀλλὰ λύπης, ὕστερον δὲ καρπὸν εἰρηνικὸν τοῖς δι' αὐτῆς γεγυμνασμένοις ἀποδίδωσιν δικαιοσύνης.

πίστεως[1] [1]κατεργάζεται [k]ὑπομονήν.   4. ἡ δὲ[2] ὑπομονὴ ἔργον [i] Rom. v. 3;
cf. Luke
τέλειον ἐχέτω,[3] ἵνα ἦτε [l]τέλειοι καὶ [m]ὁλόκληροι, ἐν μηδενὶ λειπό-   xxi. 19.
[k] Luke viii.
15; Rom
ii. 7; Heb. x. 36; 2 Pet. i. 6; 2 Thess. i. 4.   [l] Cf. iii. 2; Matt. v. 48.   [m] Thess. v. 23.

[1] Om. της πιστεως B[3] (hab B[1]), 81, ff, Syr[hk].   [2] Om. Vulg[A].

[3] Some lat. MSS. read *habet* others *habeat*.

ἀδελφοί μου: this term of address was originally Jewish; in Hebrew, אָח is used, in the first instance, of those born of the same mother, *e.g.*, Gen. iv. 2, etc.; then in a wider sense of a relative, *e.g.*, Gen. xiv. 12, etc.; and in the still more extended meaning of kinship generally, *e.g.*, of tribal membership, Num. xvi. 10; as belonging to the same people, *e.g.*, Exod. ii. 11; Lev. xix. 7, and even of a stranger (גֵּר) sojourning among the people, Lev. xix. 34; it is also used of those who have made a covenant together, Am. i. 9; and, generally, of friends, 2 Sam. i. 26, etc.; in its widest sense it was taken over by the Christian communities, whose members were both friends and bound by the same covenant (*cf.* the origin of the Hebrew word for "covenant," בְּרִית, from the Assryo-Babylonian *Biritu* which means "a fetter"). This mode of address occurs frequently in this Epistle, sometimes the simple ἀδελφοί without μου (iv. 11, v. 7, 9, 10), sometimes with the addition of ἀγαπητοί (i. 16, 19, ii. 5). πειρασμοῖς: in vv. 12 ff. πειρασμός obviously means allurement to wrong-doing, and this would appear to be the most natural meaning here on account of the way in which temptation is analysed, though the sense of external trials, in the shape of calamity, would of course not be excluded; "it may be that the effect of external conditions upon character should be included in the term" (Parry). It is true that the exhortation to look upon temptations with joy is scarcely compatible with the prayer, "Lead us not into temptation" (Matt. vi. 13; Luke, xi. 4) or with the words, "Pray that ye enter not into temptation" (Matt. xxvi. 41; Luke xxii. 40; see too Mark xiv. 38; Luke xxii. 46; Rev. iii. 10); but, as is evident from a number of indications in this Epistle, the writer's Judaism is stronger than his Christianity, and owing to the Jewish doctrines of free-will and works, a Jew would regard temptation in a less serious light than a Christian (see Introduction § iv.). Most pointedly does Parry remark: "There is a true joy for the warrior when he meets face to face the foe whom he has been directed to subjugate, in a warfare that trains hand and eye and steels the nerve and tempers the will . . . "; this is precisely the Jewish standpoint; while the Christian, realising his sinfulness and inherent weakness, and grounded in a spirit of humility, reiterates the words which he has been taught in the Lord's Prayer. This passage is one of the many in the Epistle which makes it so difficult to believe that it can all have been written by St. James.—περιπέσητε: the connection in which this word stands in the few passages of the N.T. which contain it supports the idea that in πειρασμοῖς external trials are included (Luke x. 30; Acts xxvii. 41).—ποικίλοις: Cf. 1 Pet. i. 6., ἐν ποικίλοις πειρασμοῖς, Pesh. adds πολλοῖς, *cf.* 3 Macc. ii. 6, ποικίλαις καὶ πολλαῖς δοκιμάσας τιμωρίαις.

Ver. 3. γινώσκοντες: "recognising"; this seems to be the force of the word γιγνώσκω in Hellenistic Greek (see Lightfoot, *Ep. to the Galatians*, p. 171); if so, it comes very appositely after ἡγήσασθε.—τὸ δοκίμιον ὑμῶν τῆς πίστεως: according to instances of the use of the word δοκίμιον given by Deissmann (*Neue Bibelstudien*, pp. 187 ff.) it means "pure" or "genuine"; it is the neuter of the adjective used as a substantive, followed by a genitive; the phrase would thus mean: "That which is genuine in your faith worketh . . . "; this meaning of δοκίμιον makes 1 Pet. i. 7 clearer and more significant; *cf.* Prov. xxvii. 21 (Sept.); Sir. ii. 1 ff. On πίστις see ver. 6.—κατεργάζεται: emphatic form of ἐργάζεται, "accomplishes".—ὑπομονήν: the word here means "the frame of mind which endures," as distinct from the act of enduring which is the meaning of the word in 2 Cor. i. 6, vi. 4. Philo calls ὑπομονή the queen of virtues (see Mayor, *in loc.*), it is one which has probably been nowhere more fully exemplified than in the history of the Jewish race.

Ver. 4. ἡ δὲ ὑπομονὴ ἔργον τέλειον ἐχέτω: "But let endurance have its perfect result"; the possibility

n 1 Kgs. iii. μ.ενοι.   **5.** Εἰ δέ τις ὑμῶν ⁿλείπεται σοφίας, °αἰτείτω παρὰ τοῦ
9, xi. 12;
Prov. ii. ʿΘεοῦ ¹ πᾶσιν ᑫἁπλῶς καὶ μὴ ʳὀνειδίζοντος, καὶ δοθήσεται
3-6.
Matt. vii.
7.   p Sir. i. 1, 26, xxxix. 6; Wisd. vi. 14, 22, vii. 13; cf. Job xxxii. 8; Prov. viii. 17, xxviii. 5.
q Rom. xii. 8.   r Sir.xli. 22.

¹ του Θεου του διδοντος A.

of losing heart is contemplated, which
would result in something being lacking;
the words recall what is said in the
Testaments of the Twelve Patriarchs, Jos.
ii. 7. "For endurance (μακροθυμία) is a
mighty charm, and patience (ὑπομονή)
giveth many good things". *Cf.* Rom. v.
3.—ἵνα ἦτε τέλειοι: *Cf.* Matt. v.
48, xix. 21; see Lightfoot's note on the
meaning of this word in Phil. iii. 15,
"the τέλειοι are in fact the same with
πνευματικοί" (*Ep. to the Philippians*, p.
153). That in the passage before us it
does not mean perfect in the literal sense
is clear from the words which occur in iii.
2 (assuming that the same writer wrote
both passages), πολλὰ πταίομεν ἅπαντες. "The word τέλειος is often used
by later writers of the baptised" (Mayor).
—ὁλόκληροι: *Cf.* Wisd. xv. 3; in its
root-meaning ὁλόκληρος implies the "entire lot or destiny," so that the underlying idea regarding a man who is ὁλόκληρος means one who fulfils his lot;
here it would mean 'those who fully
attain to their high calling'. — ἐν
μηδενὶ λειπόμενοι: this is merely
explanatory of ὁλόκληροι.

Ver. 5. There is no thought-connection between this verse and what has preceded, it is only by supplying something
artificially that any connection can be
made to exist, and for this there is no
warrant in the text as it stands (see
Introduction III.). In ver. 4 ὑπομονή
has as its full result the making perfect of
men, so that they are lacking in nothing;
when, therefore, the next verse goes on
to contemplate a lacking of wisdom,
there is clearly the commencement of a
new one. The occurrence of λειπόμενοι
and λείπεται, which is regarded by some
as a proof of connection between the two
verses, denotes nothing in view of the
fact that the subject-matter is so different;
moreover, there is a distinct difference in
the sense in which this word is used in
these two verses; coming behindhand in
what one ought to attain to is quite different from not being in possession of the
great gift of wisdom; this difference is
well brought out by the Vulgate rendering: " . . . in nullo *deficientes*. Si quis
autem vestrum *indiget* sapientia . . . "—

εἰ δέ τις ὑμῶν λείπεται σοφίας
Cf. iii. 13-17; the position assigned to
Wisdom by the Jews, and especially by
Hellenistic Jews, was so exalted that a
short consideration of the subject seems
called for, the more so by reason of the
prominence it assumes in this Epistle.
It is probable that the more advanced
ideas of Wisdom came originally from
Babylon; for, according to the Babylonian cosmology, Wisdom existed in
primeval ages before the creation of the
world; it dwelt with Ea, the god of
Wisdom, in the depths of the sea (*cf.*
Prov. viii. 22-30); Ea the creator was
therefore guided by Wisdom in his creative work (see Jeremias, *Das alte Testament im Lichte des alten Orients*, pp. 29,
80); in Biblical literature Wisdom became the all-discerning intelligence of
God in His work of Creation; as it was
needed by God Himself, how much more
by men! Hence the constant insistence
on its need which is so characteristic of
the book of Proverbs. This laid the
foundation for the extensive *Ḥokmah* (or
Wisdom) literature of the Hellenistic
Jews, which exercised also a great influence upon the Jews of later times. Under
the influence of Greek philosophy Wisdom became not only a divine agency,
but also assumed a personal character
(Wisd. vii. 22-30). According to the
Jerusalem Targum to Gen. i. 1 Wisdom
was the princip e whereby God created
the world. Generally speaking, in the
later Jewish literature Wisdom refers to
worldly knowledge as distinct from religious knowledge which is all comprised
under the term *Torah* ("Law"); and
therefore Wisdom, unlike the *Torah*, was
not regarded as the exclusive possession
of the Jews, though these had it in more
abundant measure, *e.g.*, it is said in
Kiddushin, 49 *b*: "Ten measures of wisdom came down from heaven, and nine of
them fell to the lot of the Holy Land".
On the other hand, Wisdom and the
Torah are often identified.—αἰτείτω:
for the prayer for Wisdom, *cf.* Prov.
ii. 3 *f.*; Wisd. vii. 7, ix. 4; Sir. i. 10,
li. 13; in the Epistle of Barnabas xxi. 5,
it says: ὁ Θεὸς δῴη ὑμῖν σοφίαν . . .
ὑπομονὴν — παρὰ τοῦ διδόντος
θεοῦ πᾶσιν ἁπλῶς: there is an in-

αὐτῷ. 6. ᵃαἰτείτω δὲ ἐν πίστει, μηδὲν ᵗδιακρινόμενος· ὁ γὰρ | [s] Mark xi.
24; 1 Tim.
διακρινόμενος ἔοικεν ᵘκλύδωνι ² θαλάσσης ³ ἀνεμιζομένῳ καὶ ῥιπιζο- | ii. 8; cf.
Heb. x.
μένῳ ³. 7. μὴ γὰρ οἰέσθω ὁ ἄνθρωπος ἐκεῖνος ὅτι λήμψεταί ⁴ τι ⁵ | 22.
t Cf. ii. 4;
Matt. xxi

21. u Luke viii. 24; Eph. iv. 14; cf. Matt. xi. 7; Isa. lvii. 20.

¹ Autem, ff, Vulgꟳ. ² Add et s. ³⁻³ Transp., Pesh.
⁴ λήψεται KLP, curss. ⁵ Om. אᵃ, 36, s.

teresting parallel to this thought in the
opening treatise of the Talmud, *Berachoth*, 58 *b* : "Blessed art Thou, O Lord
our God, King of the universe, Who hast
imparted of Thy wisdom to flesh and
blood"; the point of the words "flesh
and blood" is that the reference is to
Gentiles as well as Jews, corresponding
thus to the πᾶσιν in the words before us.
The force of ἁπλῶς lies in its sense of
"singleness of aim," the aim being the
imparting of benefit without requiring
anything in return; the thought is the
same as that which underlies Isa. lv. 1,
*Ho, every one that thirsteth . . . come,
buy wine and milk without money and
without price, i.e.*, it is to be had for the
asking.—μὴ ὀνειδίζοντος: the addition of this is very striking; it is intended
to encourage boldness in making petition
to God; many might be deterred, owing
to a sense of unworthiness, from approaching God, fearing lest He should resent
presumption. The three words which
express the method of Divine giving—
πᾶσιν, ἁπλῶς, μὴ ὀνειδίζοντος—must
take away all scruple and fear; *cf.* Heb.
iv. 16, *Let us therefore draw near with
boldness unto the throne of grace. . . .*—
καὶ δοθήσεται αὐτῷ: *Cf.* Matt. vii. 7.
Ver. 6. ἐν πίστει: πίστις, as used
in this Epistle, refers to the state of mind
in which a man not only believes in the
existence of God, but in which His
ethical character is apprehended and the
evidence of His good-will towards man
is acknowledged; it is a belief in the
beneficent activity, as well as in the personality, of God; it includes reliance on
God and the expectation that what is
asked for will be granted by Him. The
word here does not connote faith in the
sense of a body of doctrine. This idea of
faith is not specifically Christian; it was,
and is, precisely that of the Jews; with
these אֱמוּנָה (*Emûnah*) is just that
perfect trust in God which is expressed
in what is called the "Creed of Maimon-
ides," or the "Thirteen principles of
faith"; it is there said: "I believe with
perfect faith that the Creator, blessed be
His name, is the Author and Guide of
everything that has been created, and that

He alone has made, does make, and will
make all things". In Talmudical literature, which, in this as in so much else,
embodies much ancient material, the
Rabbis constantly insist on the need of
faith as being that which is "perfect
trust in God"; the *mĕchûsarê 'amanah,
i.e.*, "those who are lacking in faith,"
(*cf.* Matt. vi. 30, ὀλιγόπιστοι =
קְטַנֵּי אֱמוּנָה) are held up to rebuke;
it is said in *Soṭah*, ix. 12 that the disappearance of "men of faith" will bring about
the downfall of the world. Faith therefore, in the sense in which it is used in
this Epistle, was the characteristic mark
of the Jew as well as of the Christian.
In reference to αἰτείτω δὲ ἐν πίστει
Knowling draws attention to Hermas,
Mand., ix. 6, 7; Sim. v. 4, 3.—μηδὲν
διακρινόμενος: διακρίνεσθαι means
to be in a critical state of mind, which is
obviously the antithesis to that of him
who has faith; it excludes faith *ipso facto*;
Cf. Matt. xxi. 21, *If ye have faith and
doubt not* (μὴ διακριθῆτε) . . .; Aphraates quotes as a saying of our Lord's:
"Doubt not, that ye sink not into the
world, as Simon, when he doubted, began
to sink into the sea".—ἔοικεν κλύ-
δωνι θαλάσσης: a very vivid picture; the instability of a billow, changing
from moment to moment, is a wonder-
fully apt symbol of a mind that cannot
fix itself in belief. ἔοικεν occurs only
here and in ver. 23 in the N.T., κλύδων
only elsewhere in Luke viii. 24.—ἀνε-
μιζομένῳ: a number of verbs are used
in this Epistle ending in -ιζω, *viz.*,
ὀνειδίζω, ῥιπίζω, παραλογίζομαι, φλογ-
ίζω, ἐγγίζω, καθαρίζω, ἁγνίζω, ἀφανίζω,
θησαυρίζω, θερίζω, στηρίζω, μακαρίζω;
the word before us is one of the sixteen used in the Epistle which do not
occur elsewhere in the N.T., nor in
the Septuagint.—ῥιπιζομένῳ: from
ῥιπίς a "fan"; it occurs here only in the
N.T., but *cf.* Dan. ii. 35 (Septuagint),
καὶ ἐρρίπισεν αὐτὰ ὁ ἄνεμος; the word
is not used in Theodotion's version.
With the verse before us *cf.* Eph. iv. 14.
. . . κλυδωνιζόμενοι καὶ περιφερόμενοι
παντὶ ἀνέμῳ τῆς διδασκαλίας.
Ver. 7. μὴ γὰρ οἰέσθω, etc.: γὰρ

v *Cf.* iv. 8; παρὰ τοῦ Κυρίου,[1] 8. ἀνὴρ[2] ^vδίψυχος, ^wἀκατάστατος ἐν πάσαις
Sir. i. 28,
v. 9, 10.; ταῖς ὁδοῖς αὐτοῦ. 9. ^xΚαυχάσθω δὲ ὁ[3] ἀδελφὸς ὁ ταπεινὸς ἐν τῷ
cf. 1 Kgs.
xviii. 21;
Ps. cxix. 113 (Heb.); Sir. ii. 12; Matt. vi. 24. w 2 Pet. ii. 14; *cf.* iii. 16. x *Cf.* ii. 13, iii.
14, iv. 6.

[1] With comma, Ti., Weiss; with stop, Treg.; without punctuation, WH.
[2] Add γαρ 33. [3] Om. B, 65, Arm, WH in brackets.

almost in the sense of διὰ τοῦτο. The verb occurs very rarely, see John xxi. 25; Phil. i. 17. There is a ring of contempt in the passage at the idea of a man with halting faith expecting his prayer to be answered. ἄνθρωπος is used here in reference to men in general; ἀνήρ in the next verse is more specific; in this Epistle ἀνήρ occurs usually with some qualifying word.—τοῦ Κυρίου: obviously in reference to God the Father on account of the τοῦ διδ. Θεοῦ above.

Ver. 8. δίψυχος: Although this word is not found in either the Septuagint or elsewhere in the N.T. (excepting in iv. 8) its occurrence is not rare otherwise; Clement of Rome, quoting what he calls ὁ προφητικὸς λόγος, says: ταλαίπωροί εἰσιν οἱ δίψυχοι, οἱ διστάζοντες τῇ καρδίᾳ . . . (Resch, *Agrapha*, p. 325 [2nd ed.]); the word occurs a number of times in Hermas, *e.g.*, *Mand.*, ix. 1, 5, 6, 7; xi. 13; so too in Barn., xix. 5, and in Did., iv. 4, as well as in other ancient Christian writings and in Philo. The frame of mind of the ἀνὴρ δίψυχος is equivalent to a "double heart," see Sir. i. 25, μὴ προσέλθῃς αὐτῷ (*i.e.*, the fear of the Lord) ἐν καρδίᾳ δισσῇ; this is precisely the equivalent of the Hebrew לֵב וָלֵב in Ps. xii. 3, which the Septuagint unfortunately translates literally, ἐν καρδίᾳ καὶ ἐν καρδίᾳ. In Enoch xci. 4 we have: "Draw not nigh to uprightness with a double heart, and associate not with those of a double heart"; as the Greek version of this work is not extant it is impossible to say for certain how "double heart" was rendered. On the construction here see Mayor.—ἀκατάστατος ἐν πάσαις ταῖς ὁδοῖς αὐτοῦ: this is severe, and reads as if the writer had some particular person in mind. The double-hearted man is certainly one who is quite unreliable. Ἀκατάστατος, which occurs only here and in iii. 8 (but see critical note) in the N.T., is found in the Septuagint, though very rarely; in Isa. liv. 11 we have Ταπεινὴ καὶ ἀκατάστατος οὐ παρεκλήθης, where the Hebrew

for ἀκατάστ. (סֹעֲרָה) means "stormtossed". In the verse before us the word seems to mean unreliability, the man who does not trust God cannot be trusted by men; this probably is what must have been in the mind of the writer.—ἐν πάσαις, etc.: a Hebrew expression for the course of a man's life in the sense of his "manner of life" (ἀναστροφή, see iii. 13) see Prov. iii. 1, ἐν πάσαις ὁδοῖς σου γνώριζε αὐτήν (Hebrew αὐτόν), ἵνα ὀρθοτομῇ τὰς ὁδούς σου. The sense of the expression is certainly different from ἐν ταῖς πορείαις αὐτοῦ in ver. 11 which refers to the days of a man's life.

Vv. 9-11. An entirely new subject is now started, which has no connection with what has preceded; such a connection can only be maintained by supplying mental links artificially, for which the text gives no warrant. Vv. 9-11 deal with the subject of rich and poor; they may be interpreted in two ways; on the one hand, one may paraphrase thus: Let the brother who is "humble," *i.e.*, belonging to the lower classes and therefore of necessity (in those days) poor, glory in the exaltation which as a Christian he partakes of; but let him who was rich glory in the fact that, owing to his having embraced Christianity, he is humiliated (*cf.* 1 Cor. iv. 10-13), "let the rich brother glory in his humiliation as a Christian" (Mayor)—taking ταπείνωσις, however, as having the sense of self-abasement which the rich man feels on becoming a Christian. This interpretation has its difficulties, for it is the rich man, not merely his riches, who "passes away"; so, too, in ver. 11; moreover, if it is a question of Christianity, ὕψει and ταπεινώσει cannot well *both* refer to it, since they are placed in contrast; this seems to have been felt by an ancient scribe who altered ταπεινώσει to πίστει in the cursive 137 (see critical note above), thinking, no doubt, of ii. 5, οὐχ ὁ θεὸς ἐξελέξατο τοὺς πτωχοὺς τῷ κόσμῳ πλουσίους ἐν πίστει . . . It seems wiser to take the words as they stand, and to

ὕψει αὐτοῦ, 10. ὁ δὲ ˣπλούσιος ἐν τῇ ᵃταπεινώσει[1] αὐτοῦ, ὅτι y Matt.
ὡς ᵇἄνθος χόρτου ᵇ ᶜπαρελεύσεται. 11. ἀνέτειλεν γὰρ ὁ ἥλιος z Jer. ix.23.

xxiii. 12.
a Cf. Heb.
x. 34.

b—b Isa. xl. 6, 7 ; 1 Pet. i. 24 ; cf. Ps. cii. 4, 11 ; Job xiv. 2.   c Cf. 1 Cor. vii. 31.

[1] πιστει 137.

seek to interpret them without reading in something that is not there, especially as the writer (or writers) of this Epistle is not as a rule ambiguous in what he says; in fact, one of the characteristics of the Epistle is the straightforward, transparent way in which things are put. Regarded from this point of view, these verses simply contain a wholesome piece of advice to men to do their duty in that state of life unto which it shall please God to call them; if the poor man becomes wealthy, there is nothing to be ashamed of, he is to be congratulated; if the rich man loses his wealth, he needs comfort,—after all, there is something to be thankful for in escaping the temptations and dangers to which the rich are subject; and, as the writer points out later on in ii. 1 ff., the rich *are* oppressors and cruel,—a fact which (it is well worth remembering) was far more true in those days than in these.

Ver. 9. καυχάσθω: it is noticeable that this word is only used in the Pauline Epistles, with the exception in this verse and in iii. 14, iv. 16; it is used, generally, in a good sense, as here and iii. 14, though not in iv. 16.—ὁ ἀδελφός: see note on ver. 2.—ταπεινός: cf. Luke i. 52, refers to the outward condition of a man, and corresponds to the Hebrew דַּל and עָנִי, which like ταπεινός, can refer both to outward condition and character; the latter is the meaning attaching to ταπ. in iv. 6. In Sir. xi. 1 we read: σοφία ταπεινοῦ ἀνύψωσεν κεφαλήν, καὶ ἐν μέσῳ μεγιστάνων καθίσει αὐτόν. Cf. Sir. x. 31 (Hebrew).

Ver. 10. ὁ πλούσιος: equally a "brother"; cf. the whole section ii. 1-13 below.—ὡς ἄνθος χόρτου...: these words, together with ἐξήρανεν τὸν χόρτον, etc., in the next verse, are adapted from the Sept. of Isa. xl. 5-8, . . . καὶ εἶπα τί βοήσω; Πᾶσα σὰρξ χόρτος, καὶ πᾶσα δόξα ἀνθρώπου ὡς ἄνθος χόρτου· ἐξηράνθη ὁ χόρτος καὶ ὁ ἄνθος ἐξέπεσεν, τὸ δὲ ῥῆμα τοῦ Θεοῦ ἡμῶν μένει εἰς τὸν αἰῶνα, which differs somewhat from the Hebrew. It is an interesting instance of the loose way in which scriptural texts were made use of without regard to their original meaning; the prophet refers to πᾶσα σάρξ, whereas in the

verse before us the writer makes the words refer exclusively to the rich, cf. the words at the end of the next verse, οὕτως καὶ ὁ πλούσιος ἐν ταῖς πορείαις αὐτοῦ μαρανθήσεται. To the precise Western mind this rather free use of Scripture (many examples of it occur in the Gospels) is sometimes apt to cause surprise; but it is well to remember that this inexactness is characteristic of the oriental, and does not strike him as inexact; what he wants in these cases is a verbal point of attachment which will illustrate the subject under discussion; what the words originally refer to is, to him, immaterial, as that does not come into consideration. χόρτος in its original sense means "an enclosure" in which cattle feed, then it came to mean the grass, etc., contained in the enclosure, cf. Matt. vi. 31.—παρελεύσεται: equally true of rich and poor, cf. Mark xiii. 31 for the transient character of all things, see also iv. 14 of this Epistle.

Ver. 11. ἀνέτειλεν: the "gnomic" aorist, i.e., expressive of what always happens; it gives a "more vivid statement of general truths, by employing a distinct case or several distinct cases in the past to represent (as it were) all possible cases, and implying that what has occurred is likely to occur again under similar circumstances" (Moulton, p. 135, quoting Goodwin); he adds, "the gnomic aorist . . . need not have been denied by Winer for Jas. i. 11 and 1 Pet. i, 24". The R.V. gives the present, in accordance with the English idiom, but clearly the Greek way is the more exact; the same applies to Hebrew, though this particular verb does not occur in the corresponding passage in either the Septuagint or the Massoretic text; an example may, however, be seen in Nah. iii. 17. ὁ ἥλιος ἀνέτειλεν, καὶ ἀφήλατο, καὶ οὐκ ἔγνω τὸν τόπον αὐτῆς (see R.V.).—σὺν τῷ καύσωνι: the east wind which came from the Syrian desert, it was a hot wind which parched the vegetation and blighted the foliage of the trees; the Hebrew name רוּחַ הַקָּדִים "the wind of the east," or simply קָדִים, expresses the quarter whence it comes,

d Matt. xx.
12; Luke
xii. 55.
e Quoted
from Isa.
xl. 7
f—f Quoted
from Dan.
xii. 12.
g Cf. v. 11.; 1 Pet. iii. 14; Prov. iii. 11.

σὺν τῷ ᵈκαύσωνι¹ καὶ ἐξήρανεν τὸν χόρτον, ²καὶ τὸ ἄνθος
αὐτοῦ,³ ᵉἐξέπεσεν² καὶ ἡ εὐπρέπεια τοῦ προσώπου αὐτοῦ⁴ ἀπώ-
λετο· ²οὕτως καὶ ὁ πλούσιος ἐν ταῖς πορείαις⁵ αὐτοῦ⁶ μαρανθή-
σεται.² 12. ᶠᵍΜακάριος ἀνὴρ⁷ ὃς ὑπομένει ᶠ⁸ πειρασμόν, ὅτι

¹ Add Suo ff.
²—² Syrᵈᵉᶜ om. και το ανθος αυτου εξεπεσεν, and ουτως και . . . μαρανθησεται.
³ Om. 69.   ⁴ Om. B.   ⁵ ποριαις אA, 40, 89, 97, Thl.; in actu ff.
⁶ εαυτου C¹(vid).   ⁷ ανθρωπος A, 70ª, 104.
⁸ υπομενη 13, m, υπομεινη 13ª, sustinuerit, ff.

the Greek καύσων, "burner," describes its character, see Hos. xiii. 15;
Ezek. xvii. 10; it became especially
dangerous when it developed into a
storm, on account of its great violence,
see Isa. xxvii. 8; Jer. xviii. 17; Ezek.
xxvii. 26.—ἐξέπεσεν: the equivalent
Hebrew word is נָבֵל, which like the
cognate root in other Semitic languages,
contains the idea of dying, cf. Isa. xxiv.
4, xxvi. 19.—εὐπρέπεια τοῦ προσώπου αὐτοῦ: pleonastic; προσ. is
used mostly in reference to persons, e.g.,
in Sir. it occurs twenty-eight times, and
only in two instances to things other than
persons, viz., xxxviii. 8, καὶ εἰρήνη παρ'
αὐτοῦ ἐστιν ἐπὶ προσώπου τῆς γῆς [He-
brew marg., however reads מִפְּנֵי אָדָם,
xl. 6 . . . ἀπὸ προσώπου πολέμου
[Hebrew text, however, מִפְּנֵי רוּדָף].
εὐπρέπεια does not occur elsewhere in
the N.T.; see Sir. xlvii. 10, its only
occurrence in that book.—ἐν ταῖς
πορείαις αὐτοῦ: see above ver. 8.
—μαρανθήσεται: only here in N.T.
Vv. 12 ff. The section vv. 12-16 is
wholly unconnected with what immediately precedes; it takes up the thread
which was interrupted at i. 4. In i. 2-4
the brethren are bidden to rejoice when
they fall into temptations because the
purifying of their faith which this results
in engenders ὑπομονήν, and if ὑπομονή
holds sway unimpeded they will be lacking in nothing. But it is, of course, a
prime condition here that those who are
tempted should not succumb; the rejoicing is obviously only in place in so
far as temptation, by being resisted,
strengthens character; therefore the
writer goes on to speak (ver. 12) of the
blessedness of the man who fulfils this
first condition, who endures (ὃς ὑπομένει)
temptation, for he shall receive the crown
of life, the reward of those in whom

ὑπομονή has had its perfect work. It is
this intimate connection between i. 2-4
and i. 12 ff. which induces one to hazard
the conjecture that they were not originally
separated by the intervening verses, which
deal with entirely different subjects, and
which therefore interrupt the thought-
connection clearly existing between the
two passages just mentioned.—In ver. 13
the occurrence of the words: "Let no
man say when he is tempted, I am
tempted of God," show that this view
was actually held, indeed the belief was
very widely prevalent and had been for
long previously, e.g., in Sir. xv. 11 ff. it is
said: "Say not thou, It is through the
Lord that I fell away; for thou shalt not
do the things that he hateth. Say not
thou, It is he that caused me to err; for
he hath no need of a sinful man. . . .
He himself made man from the beginning, and left him in the hand of his own
counsel . . ."; to say, with some commentators, that there is no reference here
to any definite philosophical teaching,
and that the words only express a natural
human tendency to shift the blame for
evil-doing in a man from himself to God,
is an extraordinary position to take up;
the tendency to shift blame is certainly
natural and human, but it is not natural
to shift it on to God; either on to fellow-
men, or on to Satan, but not on to God!
But besides this, nobody conversant with
the teaching of Judaism during the centuries immediately preceding the commencement of the Christian era, and
onwards, could for a moment fail to see
what the writer of the Epistle is referring
to; a writer who in a number of respects
shows himself so thoroughly au fait with
the thought-tendencies of his time (i. 5,
iii. 13-18, ii. 14-26, ver. 19-20 besides the
passage before us) was not likely to have
been ignorant of the fact that among all
the thoughtful men of his day the great
question of the origin of evil was being

δόκιμος ʰ γενόμενος λήμψεται τὸν στέφανον τῆς ¹ ζωῆς, ὃν ᵏ ἐπηγγεί- λατο ¹ τοῖς ¹ ἀγαπῶσιν αὐτόν.

13. ᵐ Μηδεὶς πειραζόμενος λεγέτω ὅτι ἀπὸ ² Θεοῦ πειράζομαι ³ · ὁ γὰρ Θεὸς ἀπείραστός ἐστιν κακῶν, πειράζει δὲ αὐτὸς οὐδένα.ᵐ

h Rom. xvi·
10.
i Rev. ii.10;
cf. Wisd.
iv. 2, v.
16; 1 Cor.
ix. 25.
k See ii. 5
cf.; Matt.

x. 22, xix. 28, 29.   l 1 Cor.ii. 9.   m—m Cf. Sir. xv. 11, 12, 20.

¹ Add ο κυριος KLP, Syrʰᵏ., Thl., Oec., etc., rec. + κυριος C, 4, 13⁽ᵛⁱᵈ⁾, 117, + ο θεος Syrˡᵉᶜ, Pesh., Vulg., Copt., Aeth.

² υπο ℵ 69.   ³ Tentatur ƒƒ, Vulg.

constantly speculated upon. The words with which this section concludes—" Be not deceived, my beloved brethren "— show that there was a danger of those to whom the Epistle was addressed being led astray by a false teaching, which was as incompatible with the true Jewish doctrine of God as it was with the Christian; indeed, on this point, Jewish and Christian teaching were identical. The subject referred to in this section, vv. 12-16, is dealt with more fully in the Introduction IV., § 1, which see.

Ver. 12. **Μακάριος ἀνήρ**: this pleonastic use of **ἀνήρ** is Hebraic; cf. Ps. i. 1, where the expression אַשְׁרֵי הָאִישׁ ("O, the blessedness of the man . . .") is rendered **μακάριος ἀνήρ** by the Septuagint.—**ὑπομένει**: carries on the thought of **ὑπομονή** in ver. 4; the absence of all reference to divine grace entirely accords with the Jewish doctrine of works, and is one of the many indications in this Epistle that the writer (or writers) had as yet only imperfectly assimilated Christian doctrine, see further Introduction IV., § 2.—**πειρασμόν**: see note on i. 2.—**δόκιμος γενόμενος**: for δοκ. see note on i. 2; cf. Luther's rendering: "nachdem er bewähret ist," which contains the idea of something being preserved, i.e., the genuine part, after the dross (as it were) has been purged away.—**τὸν στέφανον τῆς ζωῆς**: Wisdom and the Law (Torah) are said to be an ornament of grace to the head (Prov. i. 9), and Wisdom "shall deliver unto thee a crown of glory" (Prov. iv. 9); in Pirqe Aboth vi. 7 this is said of the Torah, of which it is also said in the same section, "She is a tree of life to them that lay hold upon her" (Prov. iii. 18); in Sir. xv. 6 it is said that a wise man shall "inherit joy, and a crown of gladness (there is no mention of a crown in the Hebrew), and an everlasting name," cf. xxxii. (xxxv.) 2. In the Test. of the Twelve Patriarchs, Lev. iv. 1, we read· "Be followers of his com-

passion, therefore, with a good mind, that ye also may wear crowns of glory"; cf. Asc. of Isaiah, vii. 22, viii. 26, ix. 10-13. The Hebrew עֲטָרָה is used both in a literal and figurative sense (for the latter see, e.g., Job xix. 9) it is probably in a figurative sense that the word is here used.—**ὃν ἐπηγγ. τοῖς ἀγαπ. αὐτόν**: the insertion of ὁ Θεός or ὁ Κύριος is found only in authorities of secondary value. The words **λήμψεται τὸν στέφανον τῆς ζωῆς ὅν . . .**, introduced by **ὅτι** (cf. in next verse **ὅτι ἀπὸ θεοῦ** . . .) refer perhaps to a saying of our Lord's which has not been preserved elsewhere; the thought seems to be present in such passages as 2 Tim. ii. 5, iv. 8; 1 Pet. v. 4; Rev. ii. 10, iii. 11, iv. 4, vi. 2; cf. 1 Cor. ix. 25, which makes it all the more probable that the words were based ultimately on some actual "Logion" of Christ (cf. Matt. xix. 28; Luke xxii. 30; cf. too, the following words which occur in the Acta Philippi: . . . **μακάριός ἐστιν ὁ ἔχων τὸ ἑαυτοῦ ἔνδυμα λαμπρόν· αὐτὸς γάρ ἐστιν ὁ λαμβάνων τὸν στέφανον τῆς χαρᾶς ἐπὶ τῆς κεφαλῆς αὐτοῦ**, see Resch, Agrapha(²), p. 280). Against this it might be urged that mention would probably have been made of the fact if the words were actually those of our Lord, in the same way in which this is done in Acts xx. 35, where St. Paul directly specifies his authority in quoting a saying of Christ. There is an interesting passage in the History of Barlaam and Josaphat, quoted by James in "The Revelation of Peter," p. 59, which runs: "And as he was entering into the gate, others met him, all radiant with light, having crowns in their hands which shone with unspeakable beauty, and such as mortal eyes never beheld; and when Josaphat asked: 'Whose are the exceeding bright crowns of glory which I see?' 'One,' they said, 'is thine'".

Ver. 13. **Μηδεὶς πειραζόμενος λεγέτω**: In view of the specific doc-

n Matt. v. 14. ἕκαστος δὲ πειράζεται¹ ὑπὸ τῆς ἰδίας ⁿ ἐπιθυμίας ἐξελκόμενος καὶ
28.
o 2 Pet. ii. °δελεαζόμενος· 15. ᵖεἶτα ἡ² ἐπιθυμία συλλαβοῦσα τίκτει ἁμαρτίαν,
14, 18.
p—p Cf. Ps. ἡ δὲ ἁμαρτία ᵖ ἀποτελεσθεῖσα ἀποκύει³ ᑫθάνατον.
vii. 14.
q Cf. Rom.
v. 12.

¹ Om. s.   ² Om. C.   ³ ἀποκυεῖ WH.

---

trine which is being combated in these verses, it is probable that the verb πει-ράζω is here used in the restricted sense of temptation to lust, and not in the more general sense (πειρασμοῖς ποικί-λοις) in which πειρασμός is used in i. 2. This view obtains support from the re-peated mention of ἐπιθυμία in vv. 14, 15. The tendency to a sin which was so closely connected with the nature, the lower nature, of man (cf. Rom. vii. 23) would, on this very account, be regarded by many as in the last instance referable to the Creator of man; that this belief was held will be seen from the authorities cited in the Introduction IV., § 1. On this view πειραζόμενος refers to tempta-tion of a special kind, ἐπιθυμία; cf. Matt. v. 28, πᾶς ὁ βλέπων γυναῖκα πρὸς τὸ ἐπιθυμῆσαι . . . ; 1 Pet. ii. 11, Ἀγαπητοί, παρακαλῶ . . . ἀπέχεσθαι τῶν σαρκικῶν ἐπιθυμιῶν αἵτινες στρα-τεύονται κατὰ τῆς ψυχῆς; iv. 2-3 . . . εἰς τὸ μηκέτι ἀνθρώπων ἐπιθυμίαις ἀλλὰ θελήματι Θεοῦ. . . .—ὅτι: Cf. the par-allel use of בְּ in Hebrew.—ἀπεί-ραστός ἐστι κακῶν: "Untempt-able of evil"; see Mayor's very inter-esting note on ἀπείραστος; the word does not occur elsewhere in N.T., nor in the Septuagint. If the interpretation of this passage given above be correct, the meaning here would seem to be that it is inconceivable that the idea should come into the mind of God to tempt men to lust; the "untemptableness" has per-haps a two-fold application: God cannot be tempted to do evil Himself, nor can He be tempted with the wish to tempt men. The word in its essence is really an insistence upon one of the fundamental beliefs concerning the Jewish doctrine of God, viz., His attribute of Holiness and ethical purity; the teaching of many centuries is summed up in the third of the "Thirteen Principles" of Maimon-ides: "I believe with perfect faith that the Creator, blessed be His name, is not a body, and that He is free from all the accidents of matter, and that He has not any form whatsoever". The Peshittâ rendering of this clause, from which one might have looked for something sug-gestive, is very disappointing and en-tirely loses the force of the Greek.—πειράζει, etc., see Introduction IV., § 1.

Ver. 14. ἕκαστος δὲ πειράζε-ται ὑπὸ τῆς ἰδίας ἐπιθυμίας: according to this the evil originates in man himself, which would be the case more especially with the sin of lust; with regard to temptation to sin of an-other character see 1 Thess. iii. 5, . . . μή πως ἐπείρασεν ὑμᾶς ὁ πειράζων, who is doubtlessly to be identified with Satan. —ἐξελκόμενος καὶ δελεαζόμε-νος: describes the method of the work-ing of ἐπιθυμία, the first effect of which is "to draw the man out of his original repose, the second to allure him to a definite bait" (Mayor). ἐξελκ. is in its original meaning used of fishing, δελεαζ. of hunting, and then of the wiles of the harlot; both the participles might be transferred, from their literal use in appli-cation to hunting or fishing, to a meta-phorical use of alluring to sensual sin, and thus desire entices the man from his self-restraint as with the wiles of a harlot, a metaphor maintained by the words which follow, 'conceived,' 'bear-eth,' 'bringeth forth'; cf. 2 Pet. ii. 14, 18, where the same verb is found, and Philo, Quod omn. prob. lib., 22, 'driven by passion or enticed by pleasure'" (Knowling).

Ver. 15. εἶτα: continuing the des-cription of the method of the working of ἐπιθυμία.—ἡ ἐπιθυμία συλλαβοῦ-σα τίκτει ἁμαρτίαν: With this idea of personification, cf. Zech. v. 5-11, where the woman "sitting in the midst of the ephah" is the personification of Wickedness; and for the metaphor see Ps. vii. 15 (Sept.), ἰδοὺ ὠδίνησεν ἀνομίαν, συνέλαβεν πόνον καὶ ἔτεκεν ἀδικίαν. Since ἐπιθυμία is represented as the parent of ἁμαρτία it can hardly be re-garded as other than sinful itself; indeed, this seems to be taught in the Targum of Jonathan (a Targum which had received general recognition in Babylonia as early as the third century A.D., and whose ele-ments therefore go back to a much earlier time) in the paraphrase of Isa. lxii. 10,

16. Μὴ [1] [r] πλανᾶσθε, ἀδελφοί μου ἀγαπητοί. 17. [s] Πᾶσα [t] δόσις [r] 1 Cor. vi.
ἀγαθὴ καὶ πᾶν δώρημα [u] τέλειον [v] ἄνωθέν ἐστιν [2] καταβαῖνον [3] ἀπὸ [4] 9; cf.
Eph. v. 6.
s Ps. lxxxv.
12; Tobit

iv. 19; John iii. 27; 1 Cor. iv. 7.   t Matt. vii. 11; Phil. iv. 15.   u Eccles. iii. 14.   v Cf.
iii. 15, 17; John iii. 3.

[1] μηδὲ 13.   [2] Om. ff, εστιν, WH.

[3] καταβαινων A, 13; κατερχομενον 27[a].   [4] παρα K, curss.

where it says that the *imagination* of sin
is sinful, *cf.* Jer. Targ. i. to Deut. xxiii.
11; this is evidently the idea in the words
before us.—ἀποτελεσθεῖσα : this
word does not occur elsewhere in the
N.T., and only very rarely in the Septuagint, *cf.* 1 Esdras, v. 7, ἀπεκώλυσαν τοῦ
ἀποτελεσθῆναι (A reads ἐπιτελεσθ.) τὴν
οἰκοδομήν; 2 Macc. xv. 39. . . οἶνος
ὕδατι συνκερασθεὶς ἤδη καὶ ἐπιτερπῆ
τὴν χάριν ἀποτελεῖ . . .; it refers here
to sin in its full completeness, Vulg., *cum
consummatum fuerit.* The passage recalls Rom. vi. 28, τὰ γὰρ ὀψώνια τῆς
ἁμαρτίας θάνατος. Mayor quotes the
appropriate passage from Hermas, *Mand.*,
iv. 2. ἡ ἐνθύμησις αὕτη Θεοῦ δούλῳ
ἁμαρτία μεγάλη· ἐὰν δέ τις ἐργάσηται
τὸ ἔργον τὸ πονηρὸν τοῦτο, θάνατον
ἑαυτῷ κατεργάζεται. Just as ἐπιθυμία
and θάνατος belong together, and the
latter testifies to the existence of the
former, so πίστις and ἔργα belong together, and the latter proves the existence
of the former; see ii. 22, ἐκ τῶν ἔργων ἡ
πίστις ἐτελειώθη.—ἀποκύει: only here
and in ver. 18 in the N.T., it only occurs
once in the Septuagint, 4 Macc. xv. 17, ὦ
μόνη γύναι τὴν εὐσέβειαν ὁλόκληρον ἀπο-
κνήσασα.—θάνατον: in *Tanchuma,
Bereshith*, 8, it is taught that Adam's sin
was the means of death entering into the
world, so that all generations to the end
of time are subject to death; this teaching is, of course, found in both early and
late Jewish literature; but it probably is
not this to which reference is made in the
passage before us. In seeking to realise
what the writer meant by death here one
recalls, in the first place, such passages
as Rom. v. 21: *As sin reigned in death,
even so might grace reign through righteousness unto eternal life through Jesus
Christ our Lord; cf.* vi. 21, vii. 24; John
v. 24: *He that heareth my word, and
believeth him that sent me, hath eternal
life, and cometh not into judgement, but
hath passed out of death into life; cf.* viii.
51, 52; 1 John iii. 14: *We know that we
have passed from death unto life:* see
also Rom. vii. 24; 2 Cor. i. 9, 10; 2 Tim.
i. 10; and Jas. v. 20, . . . *shall save a
soul from death . . .;* it seems clear that

in passages like these death is not used
in its literal sense, and probably what
underlies the use of the word is that which
is more explicitly expressed in Rev. ii. 11,
*He that overcometh shall not be hurt of
the second death;* xx. 6 . . . *Over these
the second death hath no power;* xxi. 8,
*But for the fearful, and unbelieving, and
abominable, and murderers, and fornicators . . . their part shall be in the lake
that burneth with fire and brimstone;
which is the second death.* But there is
another set of passages in which death is
used in its literal sense; these should be
noted, for it is possible that they may
throw light on the use of θάνατος in the
verse before us:—Matt. xvi. 28, *Verily I
say unto you, there be some of them that
stand here, which shall in no wise taste of
death, till they see the Son of Man coming
in his Kingdom,* almost the identical
words occur in Mark ix. 1; Luke ix. 27;
the belief in the near advent of Christ
witnessed to by such passages as 1 Cor.
xi. 26; 2 Thess. ii. 1, etc., shows that the
possibility of not dying, in the literal
sense of the word, was entertained; for
those who were living would know that
when Christ, who had overcome death,
should be among them again, there could
be no question of death. The belief in
the abolition of death when the Messiah
should come was held by Jews as well as
by Christians, see *e.g., Bereshith Rabba,*
chap. 26, *Wajjikra Rabba,* chap. 30.
The possibility may therefore be entertained that the writer of this Epistle is
contemplating death in its literal sense,
which those Christians will not escape
in whom ἐπιθυμία holds sway, but which
they are able to escape if they remain
faithful until the return of Christ; that
this is expected in the near future is clear
from v. 7, *Be patient, therefore, brethren,
until the coming of the Lord . . . stablish
your hearts; for the coming of the Lord is at
hand.*—μὴ πλανᾶσθε: *i.e.,* as regards
the false teaching concerning the cause
of sin in their hearts. The affectionate
ending, "My beloved brethren" witnesses
to the earnestness of the writer's feelings.

Ver. 17. The following saying of R.
Chaninah (first century, A.D.) is preserved:

w Job xxv. τοῦ πατρὸς τῶν *φώτων, παρ' ᾧ οὐκ ἔνι [1] ˣπαραλλαγὴ ἢ τροπῆς [2]
3; cf. 1
John i. 5. ʸἀποσκίασμα.[3] 18. ᶻβουληθεὶς [4] ᵃἀπεκύησεν ἡμᾶς λόγῳ ἀληθείας,ᵃ
x Mal. iii.
6; cf. εἰς τὸ εἶναι ᵇἡμᾶς ᶜἀπαρχήν τινα τῶν αὐτοῦ [5] κτισμάτων.
Num. xiii.
19.
y Wisd. vii. 18.   z John iii. 3; cf. Phil. ii. 13.   a—a John i. 13; 1 Pet. i. 23.   b Cf. Eph.
i. 12.   c Jer. ii. 3; Rev. xiv. 4; Rom. viii. 19-23.

[1] ἐστιν ℵP, 36.   [2] Modicum obumbrationis ff.
[3] αποσκιασματος ℵB.   [4] Add enim, Vulg., pr. αυτος γαρ 40.
[5] εαυτου ℵ³ACP, 105; WH altern. reading.

א"ר חנינא אין דבר רע יורד
מלמעלה: ("R. Chaninah said, 'No
evil thing cometh down from above'".).
On the possible connection between this
verse and the preceding section, see
Introduction IV., § 1.—πᾶσα δόσις
ἀγαθὴ καὶ πᾶν δώρημα τέλειον:
Mayor remarks on this: "It will be observed that the words make a hexameter
line, with a short syllable lengthened by
the metrical stress. I think Ewald is
right in considering it to be a quotation
from some Hellenistic poem. . . . The
authority of a familiar line would add
persuasion to the writer's words, and account for the somewhat subtle distinction
between δοσ. ἀγ. and δω. τελ.". In Theodotion's version of Daniel ii. 6, occur the
words: . . . δόματα καὶ δωρεὰς . . ,
which represent מתנן and נבזבה
in the corresponding Aramaic (the Septuagint has another reading); the distinction
between these two is perhaps that the
former refers to gifts in the ordinary
sense, while the latter is a gift given in
return for something done, i.e., a reward;
but it cannot be said that the Greek reflects this distinction, though it is worthy
of note that Philo makes a special distinction between them, "inasmuch as the
latter noun is much stronger than the
former, and contains the idea of greatness and perfection which is lacking in
the former; Philo, De Cherub., 25; and
so De Leg. Alleg., iii. 70, where he applies to the latter noun the same epithet
'perfect' as in the Greek of the verse
before us" (Knowling).—ἄνωθέν ἐστιν: it is a question whether one should
read: "Every good gift . . . from above
comes down from . .," so the Peshiṭtâ;
or "Every good gift . . . is from above,
coming down from . . ."; Mayor thinks
that on the whole "the rhythm and balance of the sentence is better preserved
by separating ἐστι from καταβαῖνον".—
ἀπὸ τοῦ πατρὸς τῶν φώτων:

Cf. on the one hand, Sir. xliii. 9, Κάλλος
οὐρανοῦ, δόξα ἄστρων, κόσμος φωτίζων,
ἐν ὑψίστοις Κύριος; and, on the other 1
John i. 5, ὁ Θεὸς φῶς ἐστιν καὶ σκοτία
ἐν αὐτῷ οὐκ ἐστιν οὐδεμία. There can
be no doubt that in the passage before
us this double meaning of light, literal
and spiritual, is meant.—παραλλαγή:
only here in the N.T., and in 4 Kings ix, 20
(Septuagint); it is rendered שוחלפא
in the Peshiṭtâ, a word which is used variously of "change," "caprice," and even
"apostasy" (see Brockelmann, Lex. Syr.,
s.v.). In Greek, according to Mayor, the
word may be taken "to express the contrast between the natural sun, which varies
its position in the sky from hour to hour
and month to month, and the eternal
source of all light".—τροπῆς ἀποσκί-
ασμα: neither of these words is found
elsewhere in the N.T., and the latter
does not occur in the Septuagint either;
the former is used in the Septuagint of
the movements of the heavenly bodies,
Deut. xxxiii. 14: καὶ καθ' ὥραν γενημ-
άτων ἡλίου τροπῶν . . .; cf. Job xxxviii.
33. The meaning of the latter part of
the verse before us is well brought out
by Luther: "Bei welchem ist keine Ver-
änderung noch Wechsel des Lichts und
Finsterniss". If, as hinted above, there
is a connection between this verse and
the section i. 5-8, the meaning may perhaps be expressed thus: When, in answer
to prayer, God promises the gift of wisdom, it is certain to be given, for He does
not change; cf. for the thought, Rom. xi.
29, ἀμεταμέλητα γὰρτὰ χαρίσματα καὶ
ἡ κλῆσις τοῦ Θεοῦ.

Ver. 18. Again we have a verse without any connection between what precedes or follows; the words ἴστε, ἀδελφοί μου ἀγαπητοί of ver. 19 seem to
belong to ver. 18. As we have seen,
ver. 17 most probably contains a quotation; the possibility of ver. 18 being also a
loose quotation, from some other author,
should not be lost sight of; it would ex-

19. ¹Ἴστε,² ἀδελφοί μου ἀγαπητοί.¹ Ἔστω δὲ³ πᾶς ἄνθρωπος d Sir. v. 11
ταχὺς εἰς τὸ ᵃἀκοῦσαι, βραδὺς εἰς τὸ ᵉλαλῆσαι, βραδὺς εἰς ᶠὀργήν·
20. ᵍὀργὴ γὰρ ἀνδρὸς δικαιοσύνην Θεοῦ οὐκ ἐργάζεται.ᵍ⁴ 21.
διὸ⁵ ʰἀποθέμενοι πᾶσαν ᶦῥυπαρίαν καὶ περισσείαν⁶ ᵏκακίας ἐν⁷

Sir. v. 11
Eccles. v.
1.
e Cf. iii. 2;
Prov. x.
19, xvii.
27;
Eccles. v.
2; Sir. i.

29, iv. 29, v. 13.   f Prov. xiv. 29; cf. Eccles. vii. 9; Eph. iv. 26.   g—g Col. iii. 8.   h Eph.
iv. 22; Col. iii. 8; 1 Pet. ii. 1; cf. Acts xv. 9; Heb. xii. 1.   i Rev. xxii. 11.   k Tit. iii. 3.

^{1—1} και νυν αδελφοι ημων AethP; εστε αδελφοι ημων και Aethr.

² ωστε KLᵃP, Syrʰᵏ, Thl., Oec., etc.; ιστω א¹ rec. |אבנר] Pesh.; add δε A.

³ και εστω A, 13; om. δε KLP², Syrʰᵏ, Pesh., Arm., Thl., Oec., etc., rec.

⁴ ου κατεργ. C*KᵃLP, Thl., Oec., etc., rec.; cf. v. 3.

⁵ Pr. et ff.   ⁶ περισσευμα A, 13, 68.   ⁷ εμ א.

plain, as in the case of ver. 17, the abrupt way in which it is introduced; the ἴστε, taken as an indicative, might well imply that the writer is referring his readers to some well-known writing, much in the same way as St. Paul does in Acts xvii. 28, ἐν αὐτῷ γὰρ ζῶμεν καὶ κινούμεθα καὶ ἐσμέν, ὡς καί τινες τῶν καθ' ὑμᾶς ποιητῶν εἰρήκασιν· "τοῦ γὰρ καὶ γένος ἐσμέν". For the general thought of the verse cf. 1 John iii. 9.—βουληθεὶς ἀπεκύησεν ἡμᾶς λόγῳ ἀληθείας: this is strongly suggestive of an advanced belief in the doctrine of Grace, cf. John xv. 16. οὐχ ὑμεῖς με ἐξελέξασθε, ἀλλ' ἐγὼ ἐξελεξάμην ὑμᾶς. The rare word ἀπεκύησεν is, strictly speaking, only used of the mother. "It seems clear that the phrase has particular reference to the creation of man, κατ' εἰκόνα ἡμετέραν καὶ καθ' ὁμοίωσιν. This was the truth about man which God's will realised in the creation by an act, a λόγος, which was the expression at once of God's will and man's nature" (Parry). —ἀπαρχήν τινα τῶν αὐτοῦ κτισμάτων: ἀπαρχή = תְּרוּמָה used in reference to the Torah in She-moth Rabba, chap. 33; see further below; the picture would be very familiar to Jews; just as the new fruits which ripen first herald the new season, so those men who are begotten λόγῳ ἀληθείας proclaim a new order of things in the world of spiritual growth; they are in advance of other men, in the same way that the first-fruits are in advance of the other fruits of the season. Rendel Harris illustrates this very pointedly from actual life of the present day in the East: "When one's soul desires the vintage or the fruitage of the returning summer, chronological advantage is everything. The trees that are a fortnight to the fore are the talk and delight of the town" (Present Day

Papers, May, 1901, "The Elements of a Progressive Church").

Vv. 19-20. Another isolated saying, strongly reminiscent of the Wisdom literature; the frequent recurrence (see below) of words of this import suggests that here again the writer is recalling to the minds of his hearers familiar sayings.

Ver. 19. ταχὺς εἰς τὸ ἀκοῦσαι βραδὺς εἰς τὸ λαλῆσαι: Cf. Sir. v. 11, γίνου ταχὺς ἐν ἀκροάσει σου, καὶ ἐν μακροθυμίᾳ φθέγγου ἀπόκρισιν; see iv. 29, xx. 7. A similar precept is quoted in Qoheleth Rabba, v. 5 (Wünsche): "Speech for a shekel, silence for two; it it is like a precious stone"; cf. Taylor's ed. of Pirqe Aboth, p. 25.—βραδὺς εἰς ὀργήν: Cf. Eccles. vii. 10 (R.V. 9), μὴ σπεύσῃς ἐν πνεύματί σου τοῦ θυμοῦσθαι, ὅτι θυμὸς ἐν κόλπῳ ἀφρόνων ἀναπαύσεται; see, too, Prov. xvi. 32. Margoliouth (Expos. Times, Dec. 1893) quotes a saying which, according to Mohammedan writers, was spoken by Christ: "Asked by some how to win Paradise, He said: 'Speak not at all'. They said: 'We cannot do this'. He said then: 'Only say what is good'." It must be remembered that the Arabs are the most foul-mouthed people on earth.

Ver. 20. ὀργὴ γὰρ, etc.: Man's wrath is rarely, if ever, justifiable; even "just indignation" is too often intermixed with other elements; and frequently the premisses on which it is founded are at fault. Man, unlike God, never knows all the circumstances of the case. On the subject of anger, see Matt. v. 21, 22, and cf. the Expositor, July, 1905, pp. 28 ff.

Vv. 21-25 form a self-contained section. By putting away all impurity the "implanted word" can influence the heart; but it is necessary not only to hear the word but also to act in accordance with it.

Ver. 21. ἀποθέμενοι: used in

l iii. 13; *cf.* πραΰτητι [1] δέξασθε τὸν ᵐ ἔμφυτον λόγον τὸν ⁿ δυνάμενον [2] σῶσαι τὰς
Ps. xxv.
9. ψυχὰς ὑμῶν.ⁿ [3] 22. γίνεσθε δὲ ᵒποιηταὶ λόγου,[4] καὶ μὴ ἀκροαταὶ
m Wisd.
xii. 10.
n—n Acts xiii. 26; Rom. i. 16; 1 Cor. xv. 2; Eph. i. 13; 2 Tim. iii. 15; Heb. ii. 3.   o Matt. vii.
26; Rom. ii. 13.

[1] Add σοφιας P, add καρδιας Thl., πραυτητι Weiss.
[2] Qui potestis *ff*.   [3] ημων Lᵃ.
[4] νομου C², 38ᵃ, 73, 83, Aeth., Thl.

Heb. xii. 1 of putting off every weight preparatory to "running the race that is set before us"; the metaphor is taken from the divesting oneself of clothes.— ῥυπαρία: not elsewhere in the N.T. or Septuagint; the Syriac has מנפולא which is the same word used in Ezek. xliv. 6 for the Hebrew תועבה "abomination," meaning that which is abhorrent to God; usually it has reference to idolatrous practices, but it occurs a number of times in the later literature in reference to unchastity, this more especially in Proverbs. The adjective is used in Zech. iii. 4 of garments, and *cf.* Rev. xxii. 11, where the meaning is "filthy". The word before us, therefore, probably means "filthiness" in the sense of lustful impurity.—περισσείαν κακίας: not merely "excess" in the sense of the A.V. "superfluity" and the R.V. "overflowing," because κακία in the smallest measure is already excess. The phrase seems to mean simply "manifold wickedness"; this has to be got out of the way first before the "implanted word" can be received.—ἐν πραΰτητι: this must refer to the meekness which *is* the natural result of true repentance. *Cf.* Matt. iv. 17, *Repent ye, for the Kingdom of Heaven is at hand.*—τὸν ἔμφυτον λόγον: ἔμφυτος occurs only here in the N.T.; in Wisd. xii. 10 we have, οὐκ ἀγνοῶν ὅτι πονηρὰ ἡ γένεσις αὐτῶν καὶ ἔμφυτος ἡ κακία αὐτῶν. Mayor holds that the expression must be understood as "the rooted word," *i.e.,* a word whose property it is to root itself like a seed in the heart, *cf.* Matt. xiii. 21, οὐκ ἔχει δὲ ῥίζαν ἐν ἑαυτῷ; and Matt. xv. 13, πᾶσα φυτεία ἣν οὐκ ἐφύτευσεν ὁ πατήρ μου ὁ οὐράνιος ἐκριζωθήσεται; and *cf.* iv. Esdr. ix. 31, "Ecce enim semino in vobis legem meam, et faciet in vobis fructum et glorificabimini in eo per saeculum". The meaning "rooted word" agrees admirably with the rest of the verse, and seems to give the best sense, see further below. — τὸν δυνάμενον σῶσαι τὰς ψυχὰς ὑμῶν: *Cf.* 1 Pet. i. 9., τὸ τέλος τῆς πίστεως σωτηρίαν ψυχῶν. The words before us leave the impression that those to whom they were addressed could not yet be called Christians; πᾶσαν ῥυπαρίαν καὶ περισσείαν κακίας, which they are enjoined to put off, implies a state far removed from even a moderate Christian ideal; and the "rooted word,' which is able to save their souls, has evidently not been received yet. On the subject of the "rooted word" being able to save souls, see further under ver. 22.

Ver. 22. γίνεσθε: perhaps best expressed by the German "Werdet," though Luther does not render it so.—ποιηταὶ λόγου, καὶ, etc.: Taylor quotes an appropriate passage from the Babylonian Talmud: "On Exod. xxiv. 7 which ends (lit.), *We will do and we will hear*, it is written (*Shabbath*, 88a) that "when Israel put *we will do* before *we will hear*, there came sixty myriads of ministering angels, and attached to each Israelite two crowns, one corresponding to *we will do*, and the other to *we will hear;* and when they sinned there came down a hundred and twenty myriads of destroying angels and tore them off" (quoted by Mayor, p. 67). The duty of doing as well as hearing is frequently insisted upon in Jewish writings. See, further, Matt. vii. 24, etc. As to the precise meaning to be attached to λόγος opinions differ; but the mention twice made of *hearing* the word makes it fairly certain that in the first instance— whatever further meaning it connoted—reference is being made to the reading of the Scriptures in the synagogue; further, the mention, also twice made, of the *doing* of the word makes it a matter of practical certainty that the reference is to the *Torah*, the Law; the fact that Jews are being addressed only emphasises this. For the attitude of the Jews towards the *Torah* during the centuries immediately preceding Christianity and onwards, see Oesterley and Box, *The Religion and Worship of the Synagogue*, pp. 135-151; here it must suffice to say that it was regarded as the final revelation of God for all time, that it was the means of salvation, and that its practice was the

μόνον¹ ᵖπαραλογιζόμενοι ἑαυτούς²· 23. ᑫὅτι³ εἰ τις ʳἀκροατὴς ᵖCol. ii. 4.
λόγου⁴ ἐστὶν καὶ οὐ ʳποιητής,ᑫ οὗτος ἔοικεν ἀνδρὶ κατανοοῦντι⁵ τὸ   q–q Cf. ii.
                                                                       14-20;
                                                                       Matt. vii.
                                                                       24-27;
                                     Luke vi. 46-49.   r Rom. ii. 13.

¹ μονον ακροαται ℵACKLP, Oec., Ti.   ² Aliter consiliantes ff.
³ Om. A, 13.   ⁴ νομου 83.   ⁵ κατανουντες (sic) ℵ¹.

highest expression of loyalty towards
God. Jews who had from childhood been
taught to regard the *Torah* in this light
would have found it very difficult to dis-
card the time-honoured veneration accorded to it, and there was no need to do
so, seeing the place that Christ Himself
had given to it (Matt. v. 17-18, vii. 12,
xii. 5, xix. 17, xxiii. 3; Luke x. 26, xvi.
17, 29), and provided that its teaching in
general was regarded as preparatory to
the embracing of Christianity. The intensely practical writer of this passage
realised that those to whom he was writing must be drawn gently and gradually,
without unduly severing them from their
earlier belief, which, after all, contained
so much which was identical with the
new faith. The *Torah*, which had been
rooted in their hearts and which was to
them, in the most literal sense, the word
of God, was the point of attachment between Judaism and Christianity; it was
utilised by the writer in order to bring
them to Christ, the "Word" of God in a
newer, higher sense. All that he says
here about the λόγος was actually the
teaching of the Jews concerning the
Torah, the revealed word of God; and
all that he says was also equally true,
only in a much higher sense, of the teaching of Christ, the "Word" of God,—
this latter, higher conception of the
"Word of God," the מימרא, was one
with which Hellenistic Jews were quite
familiar;—what has been said can be
illustrated thus:—

In ver. 18 it is said, "Of his own will
he brought us forth by the *word* of
truth"; the Jews taught that they were
the children of God by virtue of the *Torah*.
In ver. 21 it is said, "Wherefore putting
away all filthiness . . . receive the rooted
word"; according to Jewish ideas, purity
and the *Torah* were inseparable, it was
an ancient Jewish belief that the *Torah*
was the means whereby lust was annihil-
ated in a man. In the same verse, the
expression ἔμφυτος λόγος can have a
two-fold meaning in reference to the
Torah; either it contains an allusion to
the belief that the *Torah* was implanted,
like Wisdom, in God Himself from the
very beginning, hence the expression

רֵאשִׁית ("beginning") used of the
Torah; or else the writer is referring to
the teaching of the *Torah* which was
implanted, and therefore rooted, in every
Jew from the earliest years. Once more,
it is said that this word is able to save
souls. Among the Jews it was an
axiom that the *Torah* was the means of
salvation; to give but one quotation
illustrative of this ancient belief, in
Wajjikra Rabba, 29 it is written:

אין אורח חיים אלא תורה

("*Torah* is the only way that leadeth
to life"). And finally, as already remarked, the necessity of being doers as
well as hearers of the *Torah* is a commonplace in Jewish literature. For many
illustrations showing the correctness of
what has been said, see Weber, *Jüdische
Theologie* (2nd Ed.), pp. 14-38, Bousset,
Die Religion des Judenthums (1st Ed.),
pp. 87-120, the various editions of *Midra-
shim* translated by Wünsche in "Biblio-
theca Rabbinica," and the handy collection
being issued under the editorship of Fiebig, entitled "Ausgewählte Mischnatractate". It will have been noticed that all
that the writer of this passage says about
λόγος as applicable to the Law, or *Torah*,
is equally applicable, only in a much higher
sense, to Christ; this will be obvious and
need not be proved by quotations. But
it is interesting to observe that apparently
precisely the same thing was done by
our Lord Himself, as recorded by St.
John in the fourth Gospel; He adapted
Jewish teaching on the *Torah* and applied it to Himself; for details of this,
see Oesterley and Box, *op. cit.*, pp. 139 ff.
It will be noticed that in our Epistle the
writer presently goes on to substitute
νόμος (*Torah*) translated by Wünsche in "Biblio-
very significant; the "perfect law of
liberty," and the "royal law," both refer
to the *Torah* as perfected by the "King
of the Jews".—παραλογιζόμενοι
ἑαυτούς: *i.e.*, deceiving the heart, as
it is expressed in ver. 26; the rebuke
shows the intimate knowledge on the
part of the writer of the spiritual state of
those to whom he is writing.

Ver. 23. οὗτος ἔοικεν ἀνδρὶ.
ἐν ἐσόπτρῳ: With the thought here

s 1 Cor.
xiii. 12; 2
Cor. iii. 8.
t 1 Pet. i. 12.
u Cf. ii. 12;
John viii.
32; Rom.
viii. 2 ;
Gal. v. 1.
v–v Rom.
ii. 13.
w Luke xi.
28; John
xiii. 17.   x Cf. Heb. iv. 1.   y iii. 2, 3.   z iii. 6; Ps. xxxiv. 13 (14 in Heb.); Ps. cxli. 3.

πρόσωπον τῆς γενέσεως [1] αὐτοῦ ἐν ˢἐσόπτρῳ · 24. κατενόησεν γὰρ [2] ἑαυτὸν καὶ ἀπελήλυθεν, καὶ εὐθέως ἐπελάθετο ὁποῖος ἦν. 25. ὁ δὲ ᵗπαρακύψας εἰς νόμον τέλειον τὸν τῆς ᵘἐλευθερίας καὶ παραμείνας,[3] οὐκ [4] ᵛἀκροατὴς ἐπιλησμονῆς γενόμενος ἀλλὰ ποιητὴς ᵛ ἔργου, οὗτος ʷμακάριος [5] ἐν τῇ ποιήσει αὐτοῦ [5] ἔσται. 26. Εἴ [6] τις ˣδοκεῖ θρη- σκὸς εἶναι,[7] μὴ ʸχαλιναγωγῶν [8] ᶻγλῶσσαν ἑαυτοῦ [9] ἀλλὰ ἀπατῶν

[1] Om. της γενεσεως Pesh., et al.   [2] Om. ff.
[3] Add εν αυτω Vulg. (om. Vulgᶠ), Pesh., Syrʰᵏ, Arm.
[4] Pr. ουτος KLP, Pesh., Arm., Thl., Oec., rec.
[5]—[5] In operibus suis ff.   [6] Add δε CP, Pesh., latt., Copt., Treg.
[7] Add εν υμιν KL, curss., Thl., Oec., rec.
[8] χαλινων B.   [9] αυτου ℵACKL, Oec., Ti., Treg., WH (altern. reading).

contained, cf. Pseudo-Cyprian in De duo-bus mont., chap. 13 : "Ita me in vobis videte, quomodo quis vestrum se videt in aquam aut in speculum" (Resch., op. cit., p. 35), cf. 1 Cor. xiii. 12; 2 Cor. iii. 18.— τὸ πρόσωπον τῆς γενέσεως αὐ-τοῦ: Cf. Jud. xii. 18, πάσας τὰς ἡμέ-ρας τῆς γενέσεως, "all the days of the natural life," γεν. being used of unen-during existence; if this is the meaning here, it is used "to contrast the reflexion in the mirror of the face which belongs to this transitory life, with the reflexion, as seen in the Word, of the character which is being here moulded for eternity" (Mayor). In ver. 24, "forgetteth what manner of man he was" makes it improbable that the reference is to the "natural face," because a man would probably have some idea as to what his features were like. If πρόσωπον is here used in the sense of "personality" (as in Sir. iv. 22, 27, vii. 6, x. 5, xlii. 1, etc.) then the reference would perhaps be to a man looking into his conscience, i.e., "the personality at its birth," before he had become sin-stained; this being what he was origin-ally meant to be. The Peshiṭṭa simplifies the matter by omitting τῆς γενέσεως, and is followed in this by some minor author-ities.—ἐσόπτρῳ: Cf. Sir. xii. 11 . . . καὶ ἔσῃ αὐτῷ ὡς ἐκμεμαχὼς ἔσοπτρον; and Wisd. vii. 26.

Ver. 24. κατενόησεν . . . ἀπε-λήλυθεν: gnomic aorists, see note on ἀνέτειλεν, ver. 11.

Ver. 25. παρακύψας: in Sir. xiv. 20 ff. we read, Μακάριος ἀνὴρ ὃς ἐν σοφίᾳ τελευτήσει . . . ὁ παρακύπτων διὰ τῶν θυρίδων αὐτῆς. The word means literally to "peep into" with the idea of eagerness and concentration, see Gen.

xxvi. 8; Mayor says that the παρὰ "seems to imply the bending of the upper part of the body horizontally"; if this is so the word would be used very appropriately of a man poring over a roll of the Torah. —εἰς νόμον τέλειον . . . : see above ver. 22.—οὐκ ἀκροατὴς ἐπι-λησμονῆς, etc.: Cf. with this what is quoted as a saying of our Lord in the Doctrina Addaei : "Thus did the Lord command us, that that which we preach before the people by word we should practise in deed in the sight of all" (Resch., op. cit., p. 285). — ἐπιλη-σμονῆς : does not occur elsewhere in the N.T., and only very rarely in the Septuagint; see Sir. xi. 27, κάκωσις ὥρας ἐπιλησμονὴν ποιεῖ τρυφῆς.— ἐν τῇ ποιήσει αὐτοῦ: only here in the N.T., cf. Sir. xix. 18 (20 in Greek), πᾶσα σοφία φόβος Κυρίου, καὶ ἐν πάσῃ σοφίᾳ ποίησις νόμου ; and li. 19, καὶ ἐν ποιήσει μου (Bᵃᵇ read λιμοῦ) διηκριβασάμην (this clause does not exist in the Hebrew, and is probably a doublet); cf. Sir. xvi. 26.

Vv. 26, 27. Although these verses are organically connected with the preceding section, they are self-contained, and deal with another aspect of religion. While the earlier verses, 19b-25, emphasise the need of doing as well as hearing, these speak of self-control in the matter of the tongue. At the same time it must be confessed that these verses would stand at least equally as well before iii. 1 ff.— δοκεῖ: the danger of regarding the ap-pearance of religion as sufficient was the greater inasmuch as it was characteristic of a certain type of "religious" Jew, cf. Matt. vi. 1, 2, 5, 16; it must not, how-ever, be supposed that this represented the normal type; the fact that the need of

καρδίαν ἑαυτοῦ,[1] τούτου[2] μάταιος ἡ ᵃθρησκεία.[3] 27. θρησκεία[4] a Acts xxvi.
καθαρὰ καὶ ἀμίαντος παρὰ τῷ[5] ᵇΘεῷ καὶ[6] πατρὶ[7] αὕτη ἐστίν, ᶜἐπι- b iii. 9;
σκέπτεσθαι ᵈὀρφανοὺς καὶ χήρας[d] ἐν τῇ θλίψει αὐτῶν, ᵉἄσπιλον
ἑαυτὸν[8] ᶠτηρεῖν ἀπὸ[9] τοῦ κόσμου.

II. 1. ᾿ΑΔΕΛΦΟΙ μου, μὴ ἐν ᵃπροσωπολημψίαις[10] ἔχετε τὴν ᵇπί-

Eph. v.
20; 1 Cor.
xv. 24;
Col. ii. 2.
c Sir. vii.
35; Matt.
xxv. 36.
d—d Job

xxxi. 17-18; Isa. i. 17; Sir. iv. 10; 2 Macc. iii. 10, viii. 28, 30.   e Cf. 2 Pet. iii. 14.   f 1 Tim
v. 22; 1 John v. 18; Rom. xii. 2.   a Deut. i. 17, x. 17; Prov. xxiv. 23; 2 Cor. v. 16; 1 Pet
i. 17; Jude 16.   b Mark xi. 22.

¹ αυτου ℵACKL, Oec., Ti., Treg., WH (altern. reading).

² του ℵ¹.   ³ θρησκια ℵ Ti.

⁴ θρησκια ℵ Ti., add γαρ A, 70, 83, 123, Pesh.; add δε Syrʰᵏ, latt., Copt.; add
autem ff.

⁵ Om. τω ℵ¹C²KL, curss., 40, 73, 99, Ti.

⁶ Om. και 99, 126, a, ff, Pesh., Aeth.   ⁷ Pr. τω A; om. ff.

⁸ σεαυτον A, Aeth.   ⁹ εκ CP.   ¹⁰ -ληψιαις KLP, curss.

reality in religion is so frequently insisted upon by the early Rabbis shows that their teaching in this respect was the same as that of this writer.—θρησκός: Hatch, as quoted by Mayor, describes θρησκεία as "religion in its external aspect, as worship or as one mode of worship contrasted with another"; this agrees exactly with what has just been said. θρησκός does not occur elsewhere in the N.T. nor in the Septuagint. — χαλιναγωγῶν: (B reads χαλινῶν). Not found elsewhere in the N.T. or in the Septuagint; χαλινός is used in Ps. xxxi. (Heb. xxxii.) 9 in the Septuagint, as well as in the versions of Aquila and Quinta; for the thought cf. Ps. xxxviii. (Heb. xxxix.) 2, cxl. (Heb. cxli.) 3, though the word is not used in either of these last two passages. Mayor quotes the interesting passage from Hermas, Mand., xii. 1. ἐνδεδυμένος τὴν ἐπιθυμίαν τὴν ἀγαθὴν μισήσεις τὴν πονηρὰν ἐπιθυμίαν καὶ χαλιναγωγήσεις αὐτήν.—γλῶσσαν ἑαυτοῦ; the reference is to the threefold misuse of the tongue, slander, swearing and impure speaking; see Eph. v. 3-6.

Ver. 27. θρησκεία καθαρὰ . . . αὕτη ἐστίν . . .: As illustrating this, Dr. Taylor (Expos. Times, xvi. 334) quotes the Ποίμανδρος of Hermes Trismegistos: καὶ τοῦτό ἐστιν ὁ θεός, τὸ πᾶν . . . τοῦτον τὸν λόγον, ὦ τέκνον, προσκύνει καὶ θρήσκευε. θρησκεία δὲ τοῦ Θεοῦ μία ἐστί, μὴ εἶναι κακόν. Cf. too, the following from the Testaments of the Twelve Patriarchs, Jos. iv. 6: "The Lord willeth not that those who reverence Him should be in uncleanness, nor doth He take pleasure in them that commit adultery, but in those that approach Him with a pure

heart and undefiled lips".—ἐπισκέπτεσθαι ὀρφανοὺς καὶ . . . αὐτῶν: this was reckoned among the גמילות חסדים "practice of kindnesses," which are constantly urged in Rabbinical writings, e.g., Nedarim, 39b, 40a; Ket., 50a; Sanh., 19b. Cf. too, Sir. iv. 10, γίνου ὀρφανοῖς ὡς πατήρ, καὶ ἀντὶ ἀνδρὸς τῇ μητρὶ αὐτῶν. In the Apoc. of Peter, § 15, occur these words: οὗτοι δὲ ἦσαν οἱ πλουτοῦντες καὶ τῷ πλούτῳ αὐτῶν πεποιθότες καὶ μὴ ἐλεήσαντες ὀρφανοὺς καὶ χήρας, ἀλλ᾿ ἀμελήσαντες τῆς ἐντολῆς τοῦ Θεοῦ. Cf. also the Apoc. of Paul, § 35.

CHAPTER II.—Vv. 1-13 take up again the subject of the rich and poor which was commenced in i. 9-11.

Ver. 1. μὴ . . . ἔχετε: the imperative, which is also found in all the versions, seems more natural and more in accordance with the style of the Epistle than the interrogative form adopted by WH. — ἐν προσωπολημψίαις: the plural form is due to Semitic usage, like ἐξ αἱμάτων in John i. 13; cf. Rom. ii. 11; Eph. vi. 9; Col. iii. 25.—τὴν πίστιν τοῦ Κυρίου . . .: the mention of the "faith of Christ" is brought in in a way which shows that this was a matter with which the readers were well acquainted. The phrase must evidently mean the new religion which Christ gave to the world, i.e., the Christian faith.—τῆς δόξης: the intensely Jewish character of this Epistle makes it reasonably certain that the familiar Jewish conception of the Shekinah is what the writer is here referring to. The Shekinah (from the root שכן "to dwell")

c 1 Cor. ii. στιν τοῦ Κυρίου ἡμῶν Ἰησοῦ Χριστοῦ [1] τῆς ᵉδόξης.[2]　2. ἐὰν γὰρ [3]
8; *cf.*
Acts vii. εἰσέλθῃ εἰς ᵈσυναγωγὴν [4] ὑμῶν ἀνὴρ χρυσοδακτύλιος ἐν ἐσθῆτι °λαμ-
2.
d Acts vi.
9, etc.; Heb. x.25.　　　e Luke xxiii. 11.

[1] Χριστου, WH (altern. reading).

[2] Pesh. places της δοξης after πιστιν, so too 69, 73, *a, c*; it is om. by 13, Sah.;
and rendered "honeris" by *ff*, though the Vulg. reads "gloriae". WH read της
δοξης;

[3] Autem *ff*.　　　[4] Pr. την א³AKLP, curss., Thl., Oec., rec.

enoted the visible presence of God
dwelling among men. There are several
references to it in the N.T. other than in
this passage, Matt. ix. 7; Luke ii. 9;
Acts vii. 2; Rom. ix. 4; *cf.* Heb. ix. 5;
so, too, in the Targums, *e.g.*, in Targ.
Onkelos to Num. vi. 25 ff. the "face (in
the sense of appearance or presence) of
the Lord" is spoken of as the *Shekinah*.
A more materialistic conception is found
in the Talmud, where the *Shekinah* appears in its relationship with men as one
person dealing with another; *e.g.*, in *Sota*,
3*b*, it is said that before Israel sinned
the *Shekinah* dwelt with every man sever-
ally, but that after they sinned it was
taken away; *cf. Sota*, 17*a*, where it is
said : "Man and wife, if they be deserving, have the *Shekinah* between them";
so, too, *Pirqe Aboth.*, iii. 3 : "Rabbi
Chananiah ben Teradyon [he lived in the
second century, A.D.] said, Two that sit
together and are occupied in words of
Torah have the *Shekinah* among them"
(*cf.* Matt. xviii. 20); see further Oesterley
and Box, *Op. cit.*, pp. 191-194. The *Shekinah* was thus used by Jews as an indirect expression in place of God, the
localised presence of the Deity. "In the
identification of the *Shekinah* and cognate
conceptions with the incarnate Christ, 'a
use is made of these ideas,' as Dalman
says, 'which is at variance with their
primary application'. It marks a specifically Christian development, though
the way had certainly been prepared
by hypostatising tendencies" (Box, in
Hastings' DCG., ii. 622*a*). That Christ
was often identified with the Divine *Shekinah* may be seen from the examples
given by Friedländer, *Patristische und Tal-
mudische Studien*, pp. 62 ff. If our interpretation of δόξα here is correct, it will
follow, in the first place, that the meaning of the phrase . . . Ἰησοῦ Χριστοῦ
τῆς δόξης is free from ambiguity, *viz.*,
". . . Have faith in our Lord Jesus
Christ, the *Shekinah*" (literally "the
glory"); this is precisely the same
thought that is contained in the words,

". . . who being the effulgence of his
glory . . . (Heb. i. 2-3). And, in the
second place, this rendering shows that
the words are an expression of the Divinity
of our Lord; *cf.* Bengel's note : "τῆς
δόξης : est appositio, ut ipse Christus
dicatur ἡ δόξα". [Since writing the
above the present writer finds that Mayor,
p. 78, refers to Mr. Bassett's comment
on this verse, where the same interpretation is given, together with a number of
O.T. quotations; it seems scarcely possible to doubt that this interpretation is
the correct one.]

Ver. 2. εἰς συναγωγὴν ὑμῶν:
as the Epistle is addressed to the twelve
tribes of the Dispersion no particular
synagogue can be meant here; it is a
general direction that is being given.
In the N.T. the word is always used of a
Jewish place of worship; but it is used
of a *Christian* place of worship by Hermas, *Mand.*, xi. 9. . . . εἰς συναγωγὴν
ἀνδρῶν δικαίων . . . καὶ ἔντευξις γένηται πρὸς τὸν Θεὸν τῆς συναγωγῆς τῶν
ἀνδρῶν ἐκείνων. Harnack (*Expansion
. . .* i. 60) says : "I know one early Christian fragment, hitherto unpublished, which
contains the expression: Χριστιανοί τε
καὶ Ἰουδαῖοι Χριστὸν ὁμολογοῦντες".
This latter may well refer to a place of
worship in which converted Gentiles and
Jewish-Christians met together. And this
is probably the sense in which we must
understand the use of the word in the
verse before us. The Jewish name for
the synagogue was בית הכנסת
("house of assembly"); according to
Shabbath, 32*a*, the more popular designation was the Aramaic name בית עמא
("house of the people"); Hellenistic
Jews used the term προσευχή = οἶκος
προσευχῆς as well as συναγωγή.—ἀνὴρ
χρυσοδακτύλιος, etc.: *Cf.* Sir. xi.
2, μὴ αἰνέσῃς ἄνδρα ἐν κάλλει αὐτοῦ, καὶ
μὴ βδελύξῃ ἄνθρωπον ἐν ὁράσει αὐτοῦ.
For ἀνήρ see note on ver. 7. χρυσοδακτύλιος does not occur elsewhere in
the N.T. nor in the Septuagint; *cf.* Luke

πρᾷ, εἰσέλθῃ δὲ καὶ[1] πτωχὸς ἐν ῥυπαρᾷ ἐσθῆτι, 3. [2]ἐπιβλέψητε δὲ[2] f Luke i. 48.
ἐπὶ τὸν φοροῦντα τὴν ἐσθῆτα τὴν [g]λαμπρὰν καὶ εἴπητε[3]· σὺ κάθου   g Luke xxiii. 11.
ὧδε καλῶς, καὶ τῷ πτωχῷ εἴπητε· σὺ στῆθι ἐκεῖ[4] ἢ κάθου[5] ὑπὸ[6]   h iii. 17; cf. Rom. xiv. 1.
τὸ ὑποπόδιόν[7] μου,[8] 4. οὐ[9] [h]διεκρίθητε ἐν ἑαυτοῖς καὶ ἐγένεσθε i Matt. xv. 19.
κριταὶ διαλογισμῶν [1]πονηρῶν; 5. Ἀκούσατε, ἀδελφοί μου ἀγαπητοί· k Eph. i. 4;
οὐχ ὁ Θεὸς [k]ἐξελέξατο τοὺς πτωχοὺς τῷ κόσμῳ[10] πλουσίους ἐν [1]πίστει   1 Cor. i. 27, 28; cf. Job xxxiv. 19.

1 Prov. iii. 7; Luke xii. 21; 2 Cor. viii. 9; Rev. ii. 9.

[1] δε και is rendered "autem" by ff.
[2] και επιβλ. ℵAKL, Oec., Ti., Treg., rec.   [3] Add αυτω KLP, Vulg., Oec.
[4] Pon post καθου 2°B, ff, WH marg.
[5] Pr. ωδε ℵC²KLP, curss., Thl., Oec., rec.
[6] επι B³P, 13, 29, 69, a, c, d, Pesh., Arm., Sah.
[7] Add των ποδων A, 13, Vulg., Syrr., Aeth.   [8] Eorum s.
[9] Pr. και KLP, a, Thl., Oec., rec. B¹, ff, WH marg. do not make it interrogative
[10] του κοσμου A²C²KLP, a, Pesh.; του κοσμου τουτου Aeth., Oec.; εν τω κοσμω τουτω 29, Vulg.; pr. εν 27, 43, 64, om. 113.

xv. 22. λαμπρᾷ, probably in reference to the fine white garment worn by wealthy Jews.—πτωχὸς ἐν ῥυπαρᾷ ἐσθῆτι: ῥυπαρός occurs elsewhere in the N.T. only in Rev. xxii. 11 (cf. 1 Pet. iii. 21) and very rarely in the Septuagint, see Zech. iii. 3, 4; in the Apoc. of Peter we have, in § 15, . . . γυναῖκες καὶ ἄνδρες ῥάκη ῥυπαρὰ ἐνδεδυμένοι . . .—There is nothing decisive to show whether the rich man or the poor man (presumably not regular worshippers), who are thus described as entering the Synagogue, were Christians or otherwise; on the assumption of an early date for the Epistle they might have been either; but if the Epistle be regarded as belonging to the first half of the second century non-Christians are probably those referred to; but it would be futile to attempt to speak definitely here, for a good case can be made out for any class of worshipper.

Ver. 3. ἐπιβλέψητε: "look upon with admiration," the exact force of the word is conditioned by the context; it quite expresses the Hebrew פָּנָה אֶל, the meaning of which varies according to the context, e.g., in Ps. xxv. 16 (Sept. xxiv. 16) it is "to look graciously," in Deut. ix. 27, "to look sternly".—σὺ κάθου ὧδε καλῶς: the reference is to the kind of seat rather than to its position; chairs, or something corresponding to these, were provided for the elders and scribes (cf. Matt. xxiii. 6; Mark xii. 39; Luke xi. 43), and would no doubt have been offered to persons of rank who might enter, while the poorer men would sit on the floor,

which is indeed clearly implied by the words ὑπὸ τὸ ὑποπόδιόν μου. The official who directed people to their seats was called the חַזָּן (Chazzan) i.e., the man who "had charge"; we read of the existence of this official in the Synagogue within the Temple precincts in Jerusalem (Yoma, vii. 1).

Ver. 4. οὐ διεκρίθητε ἐν ἑαυτοῖς: "Are ye not divided among yourselves"? The Peshittâ uses the word אתפלג, the same as that used in Luke xi. 17. "Every Kingdom divided against itself." The reference in the verse before us might be to the class distinctions which were thus being made, and which would have the effect of engendering envy and strife, and thus divisions.—κριταί: the Peshittâ has the interesting rendering מפרשנא (instead of the usual word for "judge" דינא), which comes from the root meaning "to divide".—διαλογισμῶν πονηρῶν: Cf. Matt. xv. 19, ἐκ τῆς καρδίας ἔρχονται διαλογισμοὶ πονηροί: genitive of quality, "judges with evil surmisings," viz., of breaking up the unity of the worshippers by differentiating between their worldly status; the writer is very modern! διαλογισμοί is generally used in a bad sense, cf. Luke v. 21, 22; Rom. i. 21.

Ver. 5. Ἀκούσατε, ἀδελφοί μου ἀγαπητοί: This expression, which one would expect to hear rather in a vigorous address, reveals the writer as one who was also an impassioned speaker;

m Matt.   καὶ ^mκληρονόμους τῆς ⁿβασιλείας ¹ἧς ^oἐπηγγείλατο ² τοῖς ἀγαπῶ-
xxv. 34.
n Matt.v.3; σιν ^pαὐτόν; 6. ὑμεῖς δὲ ^qἠτιμάσατε τὸν πτωχόν.   οὐχ ³ οἱ πλούσιοι
Luke vi.
20, xii. 32.
o i. 12.   p Exod. xx. 6; 1 Cor. ii. 9; cf. Prov. viii. 17; 2 Tim. iv. 8.   q v. 6; 1 Cor. xi. 22.

¹ ἐπαγγελίας ℵ*A (cf. Heb. vi. 17).
² Pr. ο θεος Pesh.   ³ ουχι AC¹, a, c, 69, 180.

cf. in the same spirit, the frequent ἀδελφοί, and especially, ἄγε νῦν, iv. 13, v. i.—ἐξελέξατο: a very significant term in the mouth of a Jew when addressing Jews; cf. Deut. xiv. 1-2, Υἱοί ἐστε Κυρίου τοῦ θεοῦ ὑμῶν . . . ὅτι λαὸς ἅγιος εἶ Κυρίῳ τῷ Θεῷ σου, καὶ σὲ ἐξελέξατο Κύριος ὁ θεός σου γενέσθαι σε αὐτῷ λαὸν περιούσιον . . . cf. Acts. xiii. 17; 1 Cor. i. 27. There is an interesting saying in Chag. 9b where it is said that poverty is the quality most befitting Israel as the chosen people.—πτωχοὺς τῷ κόσμῳ: i.e., poor in the estimation of the world; the reading τοῦ κόσμου or ἐν τῷ κόσμῳ τούτῳ loses this point; cf. Matt. x. 9; Luke vi. 20.—πλουσίους ἐν πίστει: "Oblique predicate" (Mayor). In the Testaments of the Twelve Patriarchs, Gad. vii. 6 we read: "For the poor man, if, free from envy, he pleaseth the Lord in all things, is blessed beyond all men" (the Greek text reads πλουτεῖ which Charles holds to be due to a corruption in the original Hebrew text which reads יֶאְשָׁ֯ר = μακαρισ-τός ἐστι). See, for the teaching of our Lord, Matt. vi. 19; Luke xii. 21. Πίστις is used here rather in the sense of trust than in the way in which it is used in ii. 1.—κληρονόμους τῆς βασιλείας: the Kingdom must refer to that of the Messiah, see v. 7-9, and Matt. xxv. 35, δεῦτε οἱ εὐλογημένοι τοῦ πατρός μου κληρονομήσατε τὴν ἡτοιμασμένην ὑμῖν βασιλείαν ἀπὸ καταβολῆς κόσμου, but not Matt. v. 3 which treats of a different subject. It is of importance to remember that the Messianic Kingdom to which reference is made in this verse was originally, among the Jews, differentiated from the "future life" which is apparently referred to in i. 12, . . . λήμψεται τὸν στέφανον τῆς ζωῆς, ὃν ἐπηγγείλατο τοῖς ἀγαπῶσιν αὐτόν. There was a distinction, fundamentally present, though later on confused, in Jewish theology, between the "Kingdom of Heaven" over which God reigns, and that of the Kingdom of Israel over which the Messiah should reign. An integral part of the Messianic hope was the doctrine of a resurrection (cf. Isa. xxiv. 10; Dan. xii. 2). This first assumed definite form, apparently, under the impulse of the idea that those who had suffered martyrdom for the Law (Torah) were worthy to share in the future glories of Israel. In the crudest form of the doctrine the resurrection was confined to the Holy Land—those buried elsewhere would have to burrow through the ground to Palestine—and to Israelites. And the trumpet-blast which was to be the signal for the ingathering of the exiles would also arouse the sleeping dead (cf. Berachoth, 15b, 4 Esdras iv. 23 ff.; 1 Cor. xv. 52; 1 Thess. iv. 16). According to the older view, the Kingdom was to follow the resurrection and judgment; but the later and more widely held view was that a temporary Messianic Kingdom would be established on the earth, and that this would be followed by the Last Judgment and the Resurrection which would close the Messianic Era. This was to be followed by a new heaven and a new earth. In the eschatological development which took place during the first century B.C. Paradise came to be regarded as the abode of the righteous and elect in an intermediate state; from there they will pass to the Messianic Kingdom, and then, after the final judgment they enter heaven and eternal life. In our Epistle there are some reflections of these various conceptions and beliefs, but they have entered into a simpler and more spiritual phase. That the reference in the verse before us is to the Messianic Kingdom seems indubitable both on account of the mention of the "Lord Jesus Christ" (Messiah) with which the section opens, showing that the thought of our Lord was in the mind of the writer, and because of the mention of the "Kingdom," and also on account of the direct mention of the coming of the Messiah as Judge, later on in v. 7-9. And if this is so then we may perhaps see in the words ὁ θεὸς ἐξελέξατο a reference to Christ.

Ver. 6.   ἠτιμάσατε: Cf., though in an entirely different connection, Sir. x. 23, οὐ δίκαιον ἀτιμάσαι πτωχὸν συνετόν (δίκαιον is absent in the Hebrew);

ʳ καταδυναστεύουσιν ὑμῶν,¹ καὶ αὐτοὶ² ˢἕλκουσιν ὑμᾶς εἰς ᵗκριτήρια ; r Wisd. ii.
10.
7. οὐκ³ αὐτοὶ ᵘβλασφημοῦσιν τὸ καλὸν ᵛὄνομα τὸ ἐπικληθὲν⁴ ἐφ' s Acts xvi.
19.
t Acts viii.

3, xiii. 50, xvii. 6, xviii. 11.   u 1 Tim. vi. 1; 1 Pet. iv. 14; cf. Acts xiii. 45.   v Acts xv. 17;
cf. Jer. vii. 10; Mal. i. 11.

¹ ὑμας א¹A, 19, 20, 65, Ti.   ² αυτοι και s.
³ και A, c, 13, Syrhᵏ, Aeth.   ⁴ επικεκληθεν C¹.

the R.V. "dishonoured" accurately represents the Greek, but the equivalent
Hebrew word would be better rendered
"despised" which is what the A.V. has.
"Dishonouring" would imply the withholding of a right, "despising" would
be rather the contempt accorded to the
man because he was poor. There can
be little doubt that it is the former which
is intended here, but the idea of the latter
must also have been present.—οὐχ οἱ
πλούσιοι καταδυναστεύουσιν
ὑμῶν : the rich here probably refer to
wealthy Jews, though it does not follow
that "there could have been no question
of rich Jews if the city and the temple
had fallen" (Knowling), for the Epistle
was addressed to Jews of the Dispersion,
the bulk of whom were not affected, as
far as their worldly belongings were concerned, by the Fall of Jerusalem. On
the other hand, the possibility of the
reference being to rich Jewish-Christians,
or Gentile-Christians, cannot be dismissed off-hand, for on the assumption
of a late date for the Epistle it is more
likely that these would be meant. The
writer is taxing his hearers both with bad
treatment accorded to the poor, as well
as pusillanimity with regard to the rich.
The word καταδυν. only occurs once
elsewhere in the N.T., Acts x. 38, . . .
πάντας τοὺς καταδυναστευομένους ὑπὸ
τοῦ διαβόλου; but fairly frequently in
the Septuagint, e.g., Am. viii. 4; Wisd.
ii. 10, xi. 14. The accusative ὑμᾶς,
which is the reading of א¹A, etc., is in
accordance with the frequent usage of
the Septuagint, where καταδυν. often
takes an accusative instead of the genitive.—αὐτοί: "The pronoun αὐτὸς is
used in the nominative, not only with the
meaning 'self' when attached to a subject, as in classical Greek, but also when
itself standing for the subject, with a less
amount of emphasis, which we might
render 'he for his part,' or 'it was he
who,' as in the next clause; it is disputed
whether it does not in some cases lose
its emphatic force altogether, as in Luke
xix. 2, xxiv. 31" (Mayor). ἕλκουσιν:
See Matt. x. 7, 18. Cf. Acts xvi. 19,

. . . ἐπιλαβόμενοι τὸν Παῦλον καὶ τὸν
Σίλαν εἵλκυσαν εἰς τὴν ἀγορὰν ἐπὶ τοὺς
ἄρχοντας.—κριτήρια : Cf. 1 Cor. vi 2,
4, either Jewish (cf. the Peshiṭṭâ rendering
בית דינא) tribunals or Gentile ones.
Ver. 7. βλασφημοῦσιν : for the
force of the word cf. Sir. iii. 16, ὡς
βλάσφημος ὁ ἐγκαταλιπὼν (the Greek
is certainly wrong here, the Hebrew has
בוזה, "he that despiseth") πατέρα.
Cf. Rom. ii. 24, τὸ ὄνομα τοῦ θεοῦ δι'
ὑμᾶς βλασφημεῖται ἐν τοῖς ἔθνεσιν (Isa.
lii. 5) ; the word in the N.T. is sometimes
general in its application, of evil speaking
with regard to men (in the Apoc. of Peter
the phrase, οἱ βλασφημοῦντες τὴν ὁδὸν
τῆς δικαιοσύνης occurs twice, 7, 13) ; at
other times, specifically with reference to
God or our Lord.—τὸ καλὸν ὄνομα
τὸ ἐπικληθὲν ἐφ' ὑμᾶς : the name
here (especially in view of καλόν) must be
"Jesus" (Saviour), for the Jews would not
be likely to have blasphemed the name of
"Christ" (Messiah) ; in Acts iv. 10-12 it is
also the name of "Jesus," concerning which
St. Peter says: Neither is there any other
name under heaven, that is given among
men, wherein we must be saved. τὸ ἐπικλ.
ἐφ' ὑμ. is a Hebraism, in Am. ix. 12 we
have: אשר נקרא שמי עליהם
which the R.V. renders (incorrectly) :
"which are called by my name," it
should be : "Over whom my name was
called," as rendered by the Septuagint,
excepting that it repeats itself unnecessarily, ἐφ' οὓς ἐπικέκληται τὸ ὄνομά μου
ἐπ' αὐτούς. The Peshiṭṭâ, too, has,
שמא טבא דאתקרי so that the
R.V. rendering here is incorrect, though
the margin has "which was called
upon you". The idea which the phrase
expresses is very ancient; a possession
was known by the name of the possessor (originally always a god), this
was the name which was pronounced
over, or concerning, the land; in the
same way, a slave was known under the
name of his master, it was the name
under whose protection he stood. And

w Matt. xxii. ὑμᾶς; 8. εἰ μέντοι νόμον τελεῖτε ᵂ βασιλικὸν¹ κατὰ τὴν ˣ γραφήν·
38; John
xiii. 34; ʸἀγαπήσεις τὸν πλησίον σου ὡς σεαυτόν,²ʸ καλῶς ποιεῖτε.
cf. Gal.
vi. 2.   9. εἰ δὲ ᶻπροσωπολημπτεῖτε,³ ἁμαρτίαν ἐργάζεσθε, ἐλεγχόμενοι ὑπὸ
x Cf. ii. 23.
y—y Quoted
from Lev. xix. 18; cf. Rom. xiii. 9.   z Deut. i. 17.

¹ βασιλικον τελειτε C, Syrʰᵏ; τον βασ. P.
² ως σαυτον B; ως εαυτον 4, 25, 28, 31, 36, Thl.; ως εαυτους a.
³ -ληπτειτε KLP.

so also different peoples were ranged
under the names of special gods; this
usage was the same among the Israelites,
who stood under the protection of Jahwe
—the name and the bearer were of course
not differentiated. This, too, is the meaning here; it does not mean the name
that they bore, or were called by, but the
name under whose protection they stood,
and to which they belonged. Parallel to
it was the marking of cattle to denote
ownership. (See, in reference to what
has been said, Deut. xxviii. 10; 2 Sam.
xii. 28; Jer. vii. 10). In the passage before us there is not *necessarily* any reference to Baptism, though it is extremely
probable that this is so; Mayor quotes
Hermas, *Sim.* ix. 16, πρὶν φορέσαι τὸν
ἄνθρωπον τὸ ὄνομα τοῦ Υἱοῦ τοῦ Θεοῦ
νεκρός ἐστιν· ὅταν δὲ λάβῃ τὴν σφραγῖδα (baptism) ἀποτίθεται τὴν νέκρωσιν
καὶ. ἀναλαμβάνει τὴν ζωήν. Resch (*op
cit.* p. 193) quotes a very interesting passage from Agathangelus, chap. 73, in
which these words occur: . . . καὶ εἰπὼν
ὅτι τὸ ὄνομά μου ἐπικέκληται ἐφ' ὑμᾶς,
καὶ ὑμεῖς ἐστὲ ναὸς τῆς θεότητός μου.
In the passage before us, the omission
of all mention of the name, which would
have come in very naturally, betrays
Jewish usage; as Taylor truly remarks
(*Pirqe Aboth.*, p. 66): "A feeling of
reverence leads the Jews to avoid, as far
as possible, all mention of the Names of
God. This feeling is manifested . . . in
their post-canonical literature, even with
regard to less sacred, and not incom-
municable Divine names. In the Talmud
and Midrash, and (with the exception of
the Prayer Books) in the Rabbinic writings generally, it is the custom to abstain
from using the Biblical names of God,
excepting in citations from the Bible;
and even when *Elohim* is necessarily
brought in, it is often intentionally mis-
spelt . . ." It should be noted that this
phrase only occurs once elsewhere in the
N.T., and there in a quotation from the
O.T., quoted by St. James in Acts xv.
17.

Ver. 8. μέντοι: "nevertheless"
there is a duty due to all men, even the
rich are to be regarded as "neighbours,"
for the precept of the Law, "Thou shalt
love thy neighbour as thyself" (Lev. xix.
18), applies to all men.—νόμον βασιλικόν: "There is no difficulty in the
anarthrous νόμος being used (as below, iv.
11) for the law of Christ or of Moses on
the same principle that βασιλεύς could be
used for the King of Persia, but the addition of an anarthrous epithet should not
have been passed over without comment,
as it has been by the editors generally"
(Mayor). The reference is to the *Torah*,
as is obvious from the quotation from
Lev. xix. 18, and therefore βασιλικόν—if
this was the original reading—must refer
to God, not (in the first instance) to
Christ; the Peshittâ reads: "the law of
God".—τελεῖτε: in Rom. ii. 27 we
have the phrase νόμον τελεῖτε.—τὴν
γραφήν: cf. 1 Cor. xv. 3 κατὰ τὰς
γραφάς. On a papyrus belonging to the
beginning of the Christian era, the phrase
κατὰ τὴν γραφήν is used in a legal sense
in reference to a contract, *i.e.*, something
that is binding (Deissmann, *Neue Bibelst.*,
p. 78). When used in reference to the
Torah, as here, it was of particular significance to Jews who, as the "people of
God" were bound by the Covenant.—
καλῶς ποιεῖτε: Cf. Acts xv. 29; 2
Pet. i. 19.

Ver. 9. προσωπολημπτεῖτε:
see note on ii. 1; the word does not occur
elsewhere in the N.T. nor in the Septuagint; cf. Lev. xix. 15; Deut. xvi. 19.—
ἁμαρτίαν ἐργάζεσθε: the strength
of the expression is intended to remind
his hearers that it is wilful, conscious
sin of which they will be guilty, if they
have this respect for persons on account
of their wealth. It is well to bear in
mind that the conception of sin among the
Jews was not so deep as it became in the
light of Christian teaching.—ἐλεγχόμενοι: *i.e.*, by the words in Lev. xix. 15.,
μὴ θαυμάσῃς πρόσωπον δυνάστου.—
παραβάται: the verb παραβαίνω

τοῦ νόμου ὡς παραβάται. 10. ὅστις¹ γὰρ² ὅλον τὸν νόμον τηρήσῃ,³ a iii. 2; 2
ᵃπταίσῃ ⁴ δὲ ἐν ᵇ ἑνί, γέγονεν πάντων ᶜ ἔνοχος. 11. ὁ γὰρ εἰπών⁵· Pet. i. 10;
ᵈ⁶μὴ μοιχεύσῃς,⁷ εἶπεν καί· μὴ φονεύσῃς ᵈ⁶. εἰ δὲ οὐ ⁸μοι- Jude 24.
χεύεις, φονεύεις⁸ δέ, γέγονας⁹ παραβάτης¹⁰ νόμου. 12. οὕτως 19.
λαλεῖτε καὶ οὕτως ποιεῖτε ὡς διὰ νόμου ᵉ ἐλευθερίας μέλλοντες κρίνε-

b Matt. v.
19.
c Mark iii.
29; Gal.
iii. 10.
d—d Quoted
from
Exod. xx.
e i. 25.

13, 14; cf. Deut. v. 17, 18.

¹ Qui ff.   ² Autem Vulg.

³ τηρησει KLP; πληρωσει A, *a*, *c*, 63, 69, Syrʰᵏ; πληρωσας τηρησει 13; τελεσει 66, 73.

⁴ πταισει KLP.   ⁵ ειπας A.   ⁶—⁶ Transp. C, 69, Syrʰᵏ, Arm., Thl.

⁷ μοιχευσεις L.   ⁸—⁸ Transp. 15, 70, Arm.; -σεις K, Thl.; -σης LP.

⁹ εγενου AB.   ¹⁰ αποστατης A.

precisely expresses the Hebrew עבר "to cross over"; cf. Rom. ii. 25, 27; Gal. ii. 18; Heb. ii. 2, ix. 15, and see Matt. xv. 2, 3. To cross over the line which marks the "way" is to become a transgressor.

Ver. 10. τηρήσῃ: τηρεῖν is used here with a force precisely corresponding to the Hebrew שָׁמַר when used in reference to the Law, or a statute, the Sabbath, etc.; the idea is that of guarding something against violation.—πταί-ίσῃ δὲ ἐν ἑνί: πταίειν = the Hebrew כשל, "to stumble over" something; the picture is that of a παραβάτης stumbling over the border which marks the way; cf. the oft-used expression in Jewish writings of making a "hedge" or "fence" around the Torah, e.g., Pirqe Aboth., i. 1. With the verse before us cf. Sir. xxxvii. 12, . . . ὃν ἂν ἐπιγνῷς συντηροῦντα ἐντολάς . . . καὶ ἐὰν πταί-ίσῃς συναλγήσει σοι, and ver. 15 καὶ ἐπὶ πᾶσι τούτοις δεήθητι Ὑψίστου ἵνα εὐθύνῃ ἐν ἀληθείᾳ τὴν ὁδόν σου.— ἐν ἑνί: used in a pregnant sense, "in one matter" or "in any single point".— γέγονεν πάντων ἔνοχος: While there are a certain number of passages in Rabbinical writings which are in agreement with this teaching (e.g., Bemidbar Rabb., ix. on Num. v. 14; Shabbath, 70b; Pesikta, 50a; Horaioth, 8b; quoted by Mayor), there can be no doubt that the predominant teaching was in accordance with the passage quoted by Taylor (in Mayor, op. cit., p. 89) from Shemoth Rabb. xxv. end: "The Sabbath weighs against all the precepts"; as Taylor goes on to say: "If they kept it, they were to be reckoned as having done all; if they profaned it, as having broken all".

Rashi teaches the same principle. This is quite in accordance with the Jewish teaching regarding the accumulation of מצות ("commandments," i.e., observances of the Law); a man was regarded as "righteous" or "evil" according to the relative number of מצות or evil deeds laid to his account; the good were balanced against the bad; according as to which of the two preponderated, so was the man reckoned as among the righteous or the wicked (see the writer's article in the Expositor, April, 1908, "The Parable of the Labourers in the Vineyard").— πάντων is equivalent to all the precepts of the Torah. For ἔνοχος cf. Matt. xxvi. 66; 1 Cor. xi. 27; Gal. iii. 10; see also Deut. xxvii. 26, and Resch, op. cit., p. 47.

Ver. 11. μὴ μοιχεύσῃς, etc.: for the order of the seventh commandment preceding the sixth, cf. the Septuagint (Exod. xx. 13, 14), and Luke xviii. 20; Rom. xiii. 9. With this mention of adultery and murder together should be compared §§ 9, 10 of the Apoc. of Peter; in the former section the punishment of adulterers is described, in the latter that of murderers, while in § 11 mention is made of the children who were the victims of murder. Possibly it is nothing more than a coincidence, but the fact is worth drawing attention to that in the Apoc. of Peter (or, more strictly, in the extant remains of this) the punishment is described only of those who had been guilty of evil speaking (blasphemy), adultery, murder, and the wealthy who had not had pity upon widows and orphans. These are the sins upon which special stress is laid in our Epistle; other sins receive only incidental mention.

Ver. 12. οὕτως λαλεῖτε καὶ οὕτως ποιεῖτε: When one thinks of

f–f Job σθαι. 13. ᶠἡ γὰρ¹ κρίσις ἀνέλεος² τῷ μὴ ποιήσαντι ἔλεος³·
xxii. 6-11;
Prov. xxi. ᵍκατακαυχᾶται⁴ ἔλεος⁵ κρίσεως.ᶠ
13; Ezek.
xxxv. 11;   14. Τί τὸ⁶ ʰὄφελος, ἀδελφοί μου, ἐὰν πίστιν λέγῃ τις⁷ ἔχειν
Matt. v.
7, vi. 15,
xviii. 29, 34, 35, xxv. 45, 46; Mark xi. 26; Luke vi. 38, xvi. 35; *cf.* Rom.i.31. g i. 9; iii. 14.
h 1 Cor. xv. 32.

¹ Autem *ff.*   ² ανιλεως L, *a*, Chrys., Thl., rec., non miserebitur, *ff.*   ³ ελεον K

⁴ κατακαυχασθω A, 13, 27, *a*, Copt.; κατακαυχατε B; κατακαυχασθε C² ras,
Pesh., + δε ℵ³A, 13, + autem, Vulg., *a*, *ff*, Syrr., Oec.

⁵ ελεον CKL, Oec.   ⁶ Om. το BC¹, Arm., Tregmg; WH.

⁷ τις λεγη AC, Tregmg.

the teaching of our Lord in such passages as Matt. v. 22, 28, where sinful feelings and thoughts are reckoned as equally wicked with sinful words and acts, it is a little difficult to get away from the impression that in the verse before us the teaching is somewhat inadequate from the Christian, though not from the Jewish, point of view.—δ ι ὰ ν ό μ ο υ ἐ λ ε υ θ-ε ρ ί α ς : See above i. 22, 25, and *cf.* John vii. 32-36.—μ έ λ λ ο ν τ ε ς κ ρ ί ν ε-σ θ α ι : *cf.* ver. 7, 8, and especially ver. 9, ἰδοὺ ὁ κριτὴς πρὸ τῶν θυρῶν ἔστηκεν.

Ver. 13. ἡ γὰρ κρίσις ἀνέλεος, etc.: *Cf.* Matt. v. 7, vii. 1, xviii. 28 ff., xxv. 41 ff. For the form ἀνέλεος see Mayor, *in loc.* The teaching occurs often in Jewish writings, *e.g.*, Sir. xxviii. 1, 2, ὁ ἐκδικῶν παρὰ Κυρίου εὑρήσει ἐκδίκησιν, καὶ τὰς ἁμαρτίας αὐτοῦ διαστηριῶν διαστηρίσει. ἄφες ἀδίκημα τῷ πλησίον σου, καὶ τότε δεηθέντος σου αἱ ἁμαρτίαι σου λυθήσονται. *Test. of the Twelve Patriarchs*, Zeb. viii. 1-3 : " Have, therefore, yourselves also, my children, compassion towards every man with mercy, that the Lord also may have compassion and mercy upon you. Because also in the last days God will send His compassion on the earth, and wheresoever He findeth bowels of mercy He dwelleth in him. For in the degree in which a man hath compassion upon his neighbours, in the same degree hath the Lord also upon him " (Charles); *cf.* also vi. 4-6. *Shabbath*, 127*b*: " He who thus judges others will thus himself be judged". *Ibid.*, 151*b* : " He that hath mercy on his neighbours will receive mercy from heaven ; and he that hath not mercy on his neighbours will not receive mercy from heaven ". *Cf.* also the following from Ephraem Syrus, *Opp.*, I. 30ℝ (quoted by Resch. *op. cit.*, p. 197): καὶ μακάριοι οἱ ἐλεήσαντες, ὅτι ἐκεῖ ἐλεηθήσονται· καὶ οὐαὶ τοῖς μὴ ἐλεήσασιν, ὅτι οὐκ ἐλεηθήσονται.—π ο ι ή σ α ν τ ι : this use

of ποιεῖν is common in the Septuagint and corresponds to the Hebrew עָשָׂה; it is often used with חֶסֶד ("kindness").—κ α τ α κ α υ χ ᾶ τ α ι : "triumphs over ".

Vv. 14-26. On this section see Introduction IV., § 2. There are a few points worth drawing attention to, in connection with the subject treated of in these verses, before we come to deal with the passage in detail : (1) π ί σ τ ι ς here means nothing more than belief in the unity of God, *cf.* ver. 20 τ ὰ δ α ι μ ό ν ι α π ι σ τ ε ύ ο υ σ ι ν . . . ; this is a very restricted use of the word, both according to Hebrew and Greek usage. The Hebrew אֱמוּנָה means primarily "faithfulness," "steadfastness," "reliability," and is used in reference to God quite as much as in reference to men. This is also the force of the verb אָמַן ; it is only in the Hiph'al that the meaning "to believe in," in the sense of "to trust," arises. The use of πίστις in the Septuagint varies ; mostly it corresponds to אֱמוּנָה, but not infrequently this latter is rendered ἀλήθεια, *e.g.*, Psa. lxxxviii. (lxxxix.) 34, 50, xcvii. (xcviii.) 3, though in each of these cases Aquila and Quinta render πίστις. In Sir. xli. 16, πίστις is the rendering of the Hebrew אֱמֶת ("truth"), while in xlv. 4, xlvi. 15 it corresponds to אֱמוּנָה in the sense of "reliability". In Sir. xxxvii. 26 the Greek is obviously corrupt, πίστις stands there for the Hebrew כָּבוּד ("glory"), which is clearly more correct. But the most interesting passage on the subject in Sir. from our present point of view is xv. 15 : ἐὰν θέλῃς, συντηρήσεις ἐντολάς, καὶ πίστιν ποιῆσαι εὐδοκίας ; of which the Hebrew is : אם תחפץ תשמר מצוה ואמונה לעשות רצונו (" If it be thy will thou dost observe the

ἔργα δὲ μὴ ¹ἔχῃ; μὴ δύναται ἡ πίστις ¹ σῶσαι αὐτόν; 15. ἐὰν ²i i. 23;
Matt. vii.
21; cf.
xxi. 29.

¹ Add sola, ff; add sine operibus, Sah.
² Add δε ACDKL, curss., Vulg., rec.

commandment, and it is faithfulness to do His good pleasure"; the context shows that it is a question here of man's free-will). Here πίστις is used in a distinctly higher sense than in the passage of our Epistle under consideration. In so far, therefore, as πίστις is used in the restricted sense, as something which demons as well as men possess, it is clear that the subject is different from that treated by St. Paul in Romans; and therefore the comparison so often made between the two Epistles on this point is not à propos. (2) That which gave the occasion for this section seems to have been the fact that, in the mind of the writer, some of the Jewish converts had gone from one extreme to another on the subject of *works*. Too much stress had been laid upon the efficacy of works in their Jewish belief; when they became Christians they were in danger of losing some of the excellences of their earlier faith by a mistaken supposition that works, not being efficacious *per se* (which so far was right) were therefore altogether unnecessary, and that the mere fact of believing in the unity of God was sufficient. Regarded from this point of view, there can, again, be no question of a conflict with Pauline teaching as such. The point of controversy was one which must have agitated every centre in which Jews and Jewish-Christians were found. In this connection it is important to remember that the "faith of Abraham" was a subject which was one of the commonplaces of theological discussion both in Rabbinical circles as well as in the Hellenistic School of Alexandria; regarding the former, see the interesting passage from the Midrashic work, *Mechilta*, quoted by Box in Hastings' *D.C.G.*, ii. 568*b*. The error of running from one extreme into another, in matters of doctrine, is one of those things too common to human nature for the similarity of language between this Epistle and St. Paul's writings in dealing with the subject of faith and works to denote antagonism between the two writers. (3) The passage as a whole betrays a very strong Jewish standpoint; while it would be too much to say that it could not have been written by a Christian, it is certainly difficult to understand

how, *e.g.*, ver. 25 could have come from the pen of a Christian. (4) It is necessary to emphasise the fact that this passage cannot be properly understood without some idea of the subject of the Jewish doctrine of works which has always played a supremely important part in Judaism; for this, reference must be made to IV., § 2 of the Introduction, where various authorities are quoted.

Ver. 14. τί τὸ ὄφελος: B stands almost alone in omitting τό here; in I Cor. xv. 32, the only other place in the N.T. where the phrase occurs τό is inserted. A somewhat similar phrase occurs in Sir. xli. 14, . . . τίς ὠφελία ἐν ἀμφοτέροις; the abruptness of the words betrays the preacher.—ἀδελφοί μου: a characteristic mode of address in this Epistle. With ἀδελφός *cf.* חבר in Rabbinical literature. — ἔργα : = the Hebrew מצות (literally " command; ments," *i.e.*, fulfilling of commandments): see Introduction IV., § 2.—πίστις. *i.e.*, as expressed in the *Shema'* (Deut. vi, 4 ff.): " Hear O Israel, the Lord our God, the Lord is One . . ."; this was the fundamental tenet of the Jewish faith, and that it is this to which reference is made, and not the Christian faith, is obvious from ver. 19 which contains the essence of the *Shema'*.—σῶσαι: the belief in the efficacy of works among the Jews has always been very strong; the following quotations express the traditional teaching of Judaism on the subject: " He that does a good work in this world, in the world to come his good work goes before him;" *Sota*, 3*b*, in *Kethuboth*, 67*b* we have the following: " When Mar Ukba lay a-dying, he asked for his account; it amounted to 7000 Zuzim (*i.e.*, this was the sum-total of his almsgiving). Then he cried out: 'The way is far, and the provision is small' (*i.e.*, he did not think that this sum would be sufficient to ensure his justification in the sight of God, and thus gain him salvation); so he gave away half of his fortune, in order to make himself quite secure." Again, concerning a righteous man who died in the odour of sanctity, it is said, in *Tanchuma, Wayyakel*, i.: " How much alms did he give, how much did he study the *Torah*, how many *Mitzvoth* (*i.e.*

k Luke iii. ἀδελφὸς ἢ ἀδελφὴ γυμνοὶ ᵏ ὑπάρχωσιν καὶ λειπόμενοι ¹ τῆς ἐφη-
11; cf.
Lev. xxv. μέρου τροφῆς, 16. ¹εἴπῃ² δέ³ τις⁴ αὐτοῖς ἐξ ὑμῶν· ὑπάγετε⁵ ἐν
35; Job
xxii. 6,
xxxi. 19, 20.   l—l 1 John iii. 17, 18.

¹ Add ωσιν ALP, m, Thl., Oec., rec.   ² ειπει ℵ¹.

³ και ειπη A, 13, a.   ⁴ τι ℵ¹.   ⁵ υπαγε C¹ vid, 63.

'commandments,' see above) did he fulfil! He will rest among the righteous."
It is also said in *Baba Bathra* 10a, that
God placed the poor on earth in order to
save rich men from Hell; the idea, of
course, being that opportunities for doing
Mitzvoth were thus provided. In a
curious passage in the *Testament of
Abraham*, chap. xvi., it is said that Thanatos met Abraham and told him that he
welcomed the righteous with a pleasant
look and with a salutation of peace, but
the sinners he confronted with an angry
and dark countenance; and he said that
the good deeds of Abraham had become
a crown upon his (Thanatos') head.
In *Wisdom*, iv. 1 we have, . . . ἀθανασία
γάρ ἐστιν ἐν μνήμῃ αὐτῆς (ἀρετῆς),
ὅτι καὶ παρὰ Θεῷ γινώσκεται καὶ παρὰ
ἀνθρώποις. Cf. Enoch ciii. 1-4.
Ver. 15. In accordance with the very
practical nature of the writer, he now
proceeds to give an illustration of his
thesis which is bound to appeal; he must
have been a telling preacher.—ἐὰν: the
addition of δέ is fairly well attested, but
the reading of Bℵ where it is omitted is
to be preferred.—ἀδελφή: the specific
mention of "sister" here is noteworthy;
it is the one point in this passage which
suggests distinctively Christian influence.
This is apparently the only place in the
Bible in which "sister" is mentioned in
this special connection.—γυμνοί: Cf.
Test. of the Twelve Patriarchs, Zeb. vii.
1-3; "I saw a man in distress through
nakedness in winter-time, and had compassion upon him, and stole away a garment secretly from my father's house
(another reading is 'my house'), and
gave it to him who was in distress. Do
you, therefore, my children, from that
which God bestoweth on you, show compassion and mercy without hesitation to
all men, and give to every man with a
good heart. And if you have not the
wherewithal to give to him that needeth,
have compassion for him in bowels of
mercy" (Charles). Of course it is not
literal nakedness that is meant in the
passage before us; in the case of men
the Hebrew עָרוּם (= γυμνός), is also
often used in a literal sense, is also fre-

quently used in reference to one who was
not wearing a כְּתֹנֶת (= χιτών) and thus
appeared only in סְדִינִים, "under-gar-
ments," see Am. ii. 6; Isa. xx. 2 f.; Job
xxii. 6, xxiv. 7-10. In the case of women,
the reference is likewise to the כְּתֹנֶת,
though in this case the garment was both
longer and fuller than that of men; at
the same time, it is improbable that the
"sister" would have appeared without a
veil, unless, indeed, we are dealing with a
venue which is altogether more Western;
this is a possibility which cannot be
wholly excluded.—λειπόμενοι: must
be taken with ὑπάρχωσιν as the addition
of ὦσιν is poorly attested.—ἐφημέρου
τροφῆς: "the food for the day"; the
words express the dire necessity of those
in want. Cf. Matt. vi. 11, Τὸν ἄρτον
ἡμῶν τὸν ἐπιούσιον δὸς ἡμῖν σήμερον,
and Nestle's note on ἐπιούσιος in Hastings' *D.C.G.*, ii. 58a. ἐφήμερος does not
occur elsewhere in the N.T. or the Septuagint.

Ver. 16. ὑπάγετε, θερμαίνεσθε,
χορτάζεσθε: these words do not
seem to be spoken in irony; this is clear
from the τί τὸ ὄφελος. They are spoken
in all seriousness, and it is quite possible
that those whom the writer is addressing
were acting upon a mistaken application
of Christ's words in Matt. vi. 25 ff., *Be not
anxious for your life, what ye shall eat,
or what ye shall drink ; nor yet for your
body, what ye shall put on. . . . Be not
therefore anxious, saying, What shall we
eat? or, What shall we drink? or,
Wherewithal shall we be clothed? For
after all these things do the Gentiles
seek ; for your Heavenly Father knoweth
that ye have need of all these things.* It
was entirely in accordance with their idea
of πίστις that these people should leave
to their Heavenly Father what, according
to both Jewish and Christian teaching,
it was *their* duty to do.—μὴ δῶτε δέ:
"The plural is often used after an indefinite singular" (Mayor).—τὰ ἐπι-
τήδεια τοῦ σώματος: only here in
the N.T., but often found in classical
writers; Mayor gives instances.—τί τὸ
ὄφελος: in the earlier passage in which

εἰρήνῃ, θερμαίνεσθε καὶ χορτάζεσθε, μὴ δῶτε¹ δὲ αὐτοῖς² τὰ ἐπι-
τήδεια³ τοῦ σώματος, τί τὸ⁴ ὄφελος; ¹ 17. οὕτως καὶ ἡ πίστις,
ἐὰν μὴ ἔχῃ ἔργα,⁵ νεκρά ἐστιν καθ᾽ ἑαυτήν. 18. ἀλλ᾽ ἐρεῖ ᵐτις ˙
⁶σὺ πίστιν ἔχεις,⁷ κἀγὼ ἔργα ἔχω⁶˙⁸ δεῖξόν μοι τὴν πίστιν σου⁹
χωρὶς¹⁰ τῶν ἔργων,¹¹ ¹²κἀγώ σοι ⁿδείξω¹³ ἐκ τῶν ἔργων μου¹⁴ τὴν
•πίστιν.¹⁵ ¹² 19. ᵖσὺ¹⁶ πιστεύεις ὅτι¹⁷ εἷς ἐστιν¹⁸ ὁ Θεός.¹⁷ καλῶς

l—l 1 John iii, 17, 18.
m Rom. ix. 19.
n iii. 13.
o Gal. v. 6 cf. Matt. vii. 16, 17.
p 1 Cor. viii. 6.

¹ Dederit ff. ² ei s. ³ Alimentum ff.
⁴ Om. το BC¹, Arm., Tregmg, WH. ⁵ εργα εχη L, Arm., Thl., Oec..
⁶—⁶ Tu operam habes ego fidem habeo ff. ⁷ εχεις; WH (altern. reading).
⁸ εχω, Weiss; εχω. WH. ⁹ Om. 68, ff. ¹⁰ εκ KL, m., Thl., rec.
¹¹ Add σου CKL, a, Aeth., Thl., rec.
¹²—¹² Et ego tibi de operibus fidem ff.
¹³ δειξω σοι ACKL, Syrr., Thl., Oec. Tregmg. ¹⁴ Om. Latt. (hab s), Syrhk.
¹⁵ Add μου AKLP, m Vulg., Syrr., Copt., Aeth., Thl., Oec., rec. ¹⁶ Om. s.
¹⁷—¹⁷ εις Θεος εστιν ; B, 69, a, c, Thl., Tregmg, WH ; εις ο Θεος εστιν ; C Syrhk,
Weiss, WH (altern. reading) ; ο Θεος εις εστιν K²L, Did., Oec.
¹⁸ Om. ff.

this phrase occurs there is no question of irony, it is a direct fallacy which is being combated; in this verse, too, the writer is correcting a mistaken idea, this comes out clearly in the next verse.

Ver. 17. οὕτως καὶ ἡ πίστις . . .: just as faith without works is dead, so this spurious, quiescent charity, which is content to leave all to God without any attempt at individual effort, is worthless. —καθ᾽ ἑαυτήν: the Vulgate in semet-ipsa brings out the force of this; such faith is, in its very essence, dead; cf. the Peshiṭtâ.

Ver. 18.—ἀλλ᾽ ἐρεῖ τις: these words, together with the argumentative form of the verses that follow, imply that a well-known subject of controversy is being dealt with. Ἀλλ᾽ ἐρεῖ τις is a regular argumentative phrase, used of an objection. "Instead of the future the optative with ἄν would be more common in classical Greek, but the latter form is rather avoided by the Hellenistic writers, occurring only eight times in the N.T.,—thrice in Luke, five times in Acts" (Mayor).—ἔχεις: the interrogative here suggested by WH does not commend itself, as the essence of the argument is the setting-up of two opposing and definite standpoints.—κἀγὼ: In the N.T. καί "often coalesces with ἐγώ (and its oblique cases), ἐκεῖ, ἐκεῖθεν, ἐκεῖνος, and ἄν; but there are many exceptions, and especially where there is distinct co-ordination of ἐγώ with another pronoun or a substantive. There is much division of evidence" (WH, The N.T. in Greek,

II. App., p. 145).—δεῖξόν μοι τὴν πίστιν σου . . .: πίστις is not used quite consistently by the writer; faith which requires works to prove its existence is not the same thing which is spoken of in the next verse as the possession of demons; the difference is graphically illustrated in the account of the Gadarene demoniac; in Luke viii. 28 the words, What have I to do with thee, Jesus, thou Son of the Most High God, express a purely intellectual form of faith, which is a very different thing from the attitude of mind implied in the words which describe the whilom demoniac, as, sitting, clothed and in his right mind, at the feet of Jesus (ver. 35).—With the whole verse cf. Rom. iii. 28, iv. 6.

Ver. 19. σὺ πιστεύεις ὅτι εἷς ἐστιν ὁ Θεός: Cf. Mark xii. 29, 1 Cor. viii. 4, 6; Eph. iv. 6. The reading varies, see critical note above; the interrogative is unsuitable, see note on ἔχεις in the preceding verse. Somewhat striking is the fact that the regular and universally accepted formula (whether Hebrew or Greek) among the Jews is not adhered to; the Septuagint of Deut. vi. 4, which corresponds strictly to the original, runs: Κύριος ὁ θεὸς ἡμῶν Κύριος εἷς ἐστιν, and this is also the exact wording in Mark xii. 29, The stress laid on Κύριος (= יְהוָֹה) in the original is very pointed, the reason being the desire to emphasise the name of Jahwe as the God of Israel (note the omission of the article before Κύριος) ; it sounded a particularistic note. The elimination of Κύριος in the verse

q 1 Cor. x. ποιεῖς· καὶ τὰ ᵍ δαιμόνια ʳ πιστεύουσιν καὶ φρίσσουσιν. 20. θέλεις
20.
r Matt. viii. δὲ γνῶναι, ὦ ἄνθρωπε ˢ κενέ, ὅτι ἡ πίστις ᵗ χωρὶς τῶν ἔργων ἀργή ¹
28, 29;
Mk. v. 2
—7; Luke iv. 33, 34; Acts xvi. 16, 17, xix. 15.   s Judg. ix. 4 (Sept.); 1 Cor. xv. 36; cf.
Matt. v. 22.   t Rom. iii. 28.

¹νεκρα ℵAC²KLP, Vulg., Pesh., Syrʰᵏ, Copt., Arm., Aeth., Oec., rec.; vacua ff.

before us, and the emphatic position of ὁ Θεός,, is most likely intentional, and points to a universalistic tendency, such as is known to have been a distinctive characteristic of Hellenistic Judaism. To Jews of all kinds belief in the unity of God formed the basis of faith; this unity is expressed in what is called the *Shema* (Deut. vi. 4 ff.), *i.e.*, "Hear," from the opening word of the passage referred to; strictly speaking, it includes Deut. vi. 4-9, xi. 13-21; Num. xv. 37-41, though originally it consisted of the one verse, Deut. vi. 4. From the time of the Exile, according to *Berachoth*, i. 1, the recitation of the *Shema* every morning and evening became the solemn duty of all true Jews. To the present day it is the confession of faith which every Jew breathes upon his death-bed. It is said of Rabbi Akiba, who suffered the martyr's death, that he breathed out at the last the word "One" in reference to the belief in the Unity of God as contained in the *Shema* (*Ber.*, 61b). A few instances may be given from Jewish literature in order to show the great importance of and honour attaching to the *Shema*: "They cool the flames of Gehinnom for him who reads the *Shema*" (*Ber.*, 15b); "Whoever reads the *Shema* upon his couch is as one that defends himself with a two-edged sword" (*Meg.*, 3a); it is said in *Ber.*, i. § 2, that to him who goes on reading the *Shema* after the prescribed time no harm will come; in *Suk.*, 42a, it is commanded that a father must teach his son to read the *Shema* as soon as he begins to speak. The very parchment on which the *Shema* is written is efficacious in keeping demons at a distance.—The single personality of God is frequently insisted upon in the O.T., Targums, and later Jewish literature; in the latter this fundamental article was sometimes believed to be impugned by Christian teaching concerning God, and we therefore find passages in which this latter is combated (see, on this, Oesterley and Box, *op. cit.*, p. 155); in the Targums all anthropomorphisms are avoided, since they were considered derogatory to the Divine Personality. We must suppose that it was owing to this intense jealousy

wherewith the doctrine of the Unity of God was guarded that in the passage before us there are no qualifying words regarding the Godhead of Christ; when St. Paul (1 Cor. viii. 6) enunciates the same doctrine, ἀλλ' ἡμῖν εἷς θεὸς ὁ πατήρ, he is careful to add, καὶ εἷς Κύριος Ἰησοῦς Χριστός. Such an addition might well have been expected in the verse before us; its omission must perhaps be accounted for owing to the very pronounced Judaistic character of the writer.—καλῶς ποιεῖς: it is impossible to believe that there is anything ironical about these words; as far as it went this belief was absolutely right; the context, which is sometimes interpreted as showing the irony of these words, only emphasises the inadequacy of the belief by itself.—τὰ δαιμόνια πιστεύουσιν καὶ φρίσσουσιν: one is, of course, reminded of the passage, Luke viii. 26 ff. (= Matt. viii. 28 ff.), already alluded to above: δέομαί σου, μή με βασανίσῃς, or, more graphically, in the parallel passage, ἔκραξαν λέγοντες, τί ἡμῖν καὶ σοί, υἱὲ τοῦ Θεοῦ; ἦλθες ὧδε πρὸ καιροῦ βασανίσαι ἡμᾶς; cf. Acts xix. 15; 1 Thess. ii. 18. On demons see the writer's article in Hastings' *D.C.G.*. i. 438 ff.—Mayor gives some interesting reminiscences of these words in other early Christian writings, *e.g.*, Justin, *Trypho*, 49, etc.—φρίσσουσιν: ἅπ. λέγ. in the N.T.; literally "to bristle," cf. Job iv. 35; the very materialistic ideas concerning evil spirits which is so characteristic of Jewish Demonology would account for an expression which is not, strictly speaking, applicable to immaterial beings. One of the classes of demons comprised the שעירים ("hairy ones"), in reference to these the word φρίσσουσιν would be extremely appropriate (see further, on Jewish beliefs concerning demons, the writer's articles in the *Expositor*, April, June, August, 1907).

Ver. 20. The words of this and the following verses, to the end of ver. 23, belong to the argument commenced by a supposed speaker—ἀλλ' ἐρεῖ τις—; it is all represented as being conducted by

ἐστιν; 21. Ἀβραὰμ ὁ πατὴρ ἡμῶν οὐκ ἐξ ἔργων ἐδικαιώθη, u Gen. xxii.
ἀνενέγκας Ἰσαὰκ τὸν υἱὸν αὐτοῦ ἐπὶ τὸ ᵘθυσιαστήριον; 9-12. v Heb. xi.
22. βλέπεις ὅτι ἡ πίστις ᵛσυνήργει¹ τοῖς ἔργοις αὐτοῦ, καὶ ἐκ τῶν 17.

¹ συνεργει א¹A, Ti., Treg., communicat ff.

one man addressing another, the second person singular being used; with the ὁρᾶτε of ver. 24 the writer of the Epistle again speaks in his own name, and, as it were, sums up the previous argument.—Θέλεις δὲ γνῶναι: "Dost thou desire to know," i.e., by an incontrovertible fact; the writer then, like a skilful disputant, altogether demolishes the position of his adversary by presenting something which was on all hands regarded as axiomatic. As remarked above, the question of Abraham's faith was a subject which was one of the commonplaces of theological discussion in the Rabbinical schools as well as among Hellenistic-Jews; this is represented as having been forgotten, or at all events, as not having been taken into account, so that the adversary, on being confronted with this fact, must confess that his argument is refuted by something that he himself accepts. It is this which gives the point to ὦ ἄνθρωπε κενέ. For κενέ the Peshittâ has הלשא "feeble," in its primary sense, but also "ignorant," which admirably expresses what the writer evidently intends. Both Mayor and Knowling speak of κενός as being equivalent to Raca (Matt. v. 22), but the two words are derived from different roots, the former from a Grk. root meaning "to be empty," the latter from a Hebr. one meaning "to spit" [see the writer's article in the Expositor, July, 1905, pp. 28 ff.]; κενός has nothing to do with Raca.—ἀργή: the reading νεκρά is strongly attested; the Corbey MS. makes a pun by reading "vacua," after having written "o homo vacue". Ἀργή is not so strong as νεκρά; cf. Matt. xii. 36, πᾶν ῥῆμα ἀργόν.

Ver. 21. Ἀβραὰμ ὁ πατὴρ ἡμῶν: A stereotyped phrase in Jewish literature.—οὐκ ἐξ ἔργων ἐδικαιώθη: the writer is referring to the well-known Jewish doctrine of זכות (Zecûth), on this subject see Introduction IV., § 2.—ἀνενέγκας Ἰσαὰκ . . .: on this subject an example of Jewish haggadic treatment may be of interest: "When Abraham finally held the knife over his beloved son, Isaac seemed doomed, and the angels of heaven shed tears which fell upon Isaac's eyes,

causing him blindness in later life. But their prayer was heard. The Lord sent Michael the archangel to tell Abraham not to sacrifice his son, and the dew of life was poured on Isaac to revive him. The ram to be offered in his place had stood there ready, prepared from the beginning of Creation (Aboth, v. 6). Abraham had given proof that he served God not only from fear, but also out of love, and the promise was given that, whenever the 'Aḳedah [= the "binding," i.e., of Isaac] chapter was read on New Year's day, on which occasion the ram's horn is always blown, the descendants of Abraham should be redeemed from the power of Satan, of sin, and of oppression, owing to the merit of him whose ashes lay before God as though he had been sacrificed and consumed," Pesiḳ. R., § 40 (quoted in Jewish Encycl., i. 87a). It is interesting to notice that even in the Talmud (e.g., Ta'anit, 4a) the attempted sacrifice of Isaac is regarded also from a very different point of view, such words as those of Jer. xix. 5; Mic. vi. 7, being explained as referring to this event (see further Proceedings of the Soc. of Bibl. Arch., xxiv. pp. 235 ff.).

Ver. 22. βλέπεις . . .: as these words are the deduction drawn from what precedes, it is better to take them in the form of a statement, and not as interrogative.—ἡ πίστις συνήργει: this implies a certain modification, with regard to πίστις, of the earlier position taken up by the writer, for in ver. 21 he says: "Was not Abraham our father justified by works?" no mention being made of faith; while here faith is accorded an equal place with works; cf. Gal. v. 6, πίστις δι' ἀγάπης ἐνεργουμένη, concerning which words Lightfoot says that they "bridge over the gulf which seems to separate the language of St. Paul and St. James. Both assert a principle of practical energy, as opposed to a barren, inactive theory". On συνήργει see Test. of the Twelve Patriarchs, Gad., iv. 7, "But the spirit of love worketh together with the law of God . . ." (Charles).—καὶ ἐκ τῶν ἔργων ἡ πίστις ἐτελειώθη: it is obvious that "faith" is used here in the highest sense, not merely as an attitude of mind,

w Cf. 1 Thess. i. 3; John vi. 28, 29
x iv. 5, Gal. iii. 8; 1 Tim. v.18;
1 Pet. ii. 6.
z 2 Chron. xx. 7; Isa. xli. 8; cf. Wisd. vii. 27.

ἔργων ᵂ ἡ πίστις ἐτελειώθη,[1] 23. καὶ ἐπληρώθη ἡ ˣγραφὴ ἡ λέγουσα· ʸἐπίστευσεν δὲ[2] Ἀβραὰμ τῷ Θεῷ,[3] καὶ ἐλογί-σθη αὐτῷ εἰς δικαιοσύνην,ʸ καὶ ᶻφίλος[4] Θεοῦ ἐκλήθη. 24.

y–y Quoted from Gen. xv. 6; cf. 1 Macc. ii. 52; Rom. iv. 3; Gal. iii. 6·

[1] ετελειωθη ; Treg. [2] Om. δε L, latt. (hab s).
[3] Domino ff. [4] δουλος 69.

---

but as a God-given possession. It must, however, be further remarked that if the Judaism of the Jewish-Christian writer of this part of the Epistle had been somewhat less strong, the words under consideration would probably have been put a little differently; for according to the purely Christian idea of faith, works, while being an indispensable proof of its existence, could not be said to perfect it, any more than the preaching of the faith could be said to perfect the preacher's belief; though works are the result and outcome of faith, they belong, nevertheless, to a different category.

Ver. 23. There is some little looseness in the way the O.T. is used in these verses; in ver. 21 mention is made of the *work* of offering up Isaac, whereby, it is said (ver. 22), faith is perfected; then it goes straight on (ver. 23) to say that the Scripture was fulfilled which saith, "Abraham believed . . "; this reads as though the quotation were intended to refer to the offering up of Isaac,—the proof of perfected faith; but as a matter of fact the quotation refers to Abraham's belief in Jehovah's promise to the effect that the seed of Abraham was to be as numerous as the stars of heaven. In the O.T., that is to say, there is no connection between the quotation from Gen. xv. 6 and the offering-up of Isaac. This manipulation of Scripture is strongly characteristic of Jewish methods of exegesis.—ἐπίστ-ευσεν δὲ Ἀβραὰμ . . .: the N.T. = Septuagint, which differs from the Hebrew in reading τῷ Θεῷ instead of τῷ κυρίῳ,, and the passive ἐλογίσθη for the active. Faith, according to Jewish teaching, was a good deed which was bound to bring its reward; it was one of those things which *demanded* a reward; the phrase זְכוּת אֱמוּנָה ("the merit of faith, *i.e.*, "trustfulness") occurs in *Beresh. Rabba*, chap. 74, where it is parallel to זְכוּת תּוֹרָה ("the merit of [keeping] the Law"); merit, that is to say, is *acquired* by trusting God, just as merit is *acquired* by observing the pre-

cepts of the *Torah;* the man who has acquired sufficient merit is in a state of *Zecûth, i.e.,* in that state of righteousness, attained by good works, wherein he is in a position to *claim* his reward from God. Very pointed, in this connection, are the reiterated words of Christ in Matt. vi. 5, 16, "Verily, I say unto you, they have received their reward".—φίλος θεοῦ: Cf. 2 Chron. xx. 7; Isa. xli. 8; Dan. iii. 35 (Septuagint); in Sir. vi. 17 the Septuagint reads: ὁ φοβοί με ος Κύριον εὐθύ-νει φιλίαν αὐτοῦ, ὅτι κατ' αὐτὸν οὕτως καὶ ὁ πλησίον αὐτοῦ; the Hebrew has: "For as He Himself is, so is His friend, and [as is His Name, so are His works" ("works" must refer, most likely, to the "friend," not to God); the Syriac runs: "They that fear God show genuine friendship, for as He Himself is, so are His friends, and as is His Name, so are His works". In the *Book of Jubilees,* xix. 9, it says in reference to Abraham: "For he was found faithful (believing), and was written down upon the heavenly tablets as the friend of God"; this is repeated in xxx. 20, but from what is said in the next verse it is clear that all those who keep the covenant can be inscribed as "friends" upon these tablets. Deissmann (*Bibelstudien*, pp. 159 f.) points out that at the court of the Ptolemies φίλος was the title of honour of the highest of the royal officials. In *Wisd.* vii. 27 the "friends of God" is an expression for the "righteous". The phrase φίλος Θεοῦ, therefore, while in the first instance probably general in its application, became restricted, so that finally, as among the Arabs, "the friend of God," *Khalil Allah,* or simply *El Khalil,* became synonymous with Abraham. Irenæus, iv. 16, iv. 34, 4, refers to Abraham as "the friend of God," but he does not mention our Epistle; if a reference to this was intended it is the earliest trace of an acquaintance with it. See, further, an interesting note of Nestle's in the *Expository Times,* xv. pp. 46 f.; cf. Gen. xviii. 17 where the Septuagint

ὁρᾶτε ὅτι[1] ἐξ ἔργων [a]δικαιοῦται ἄνθρωπος καὶ οὐκ ἐκ πίστεως μόνον.[2a] a—a Heb.
xi. 33.
25. ὁμοίως[3] δὲ[4] καὶ [b]Ῥαὰβ ἡ πόρνη οὐκ ἐξ ἔργων [c]ἐδικαιώθη, b—b Josh.
ii. 4, xv.
ὑποδεξαμένη τοὺς ἀγγέλους[5] καὶ ἑτέρᾳ[6] ὁδῷ ἐκβαλοῦσα[7 b]; 26. 6, 17.
c 2 Macc.
ὥσπερ γὰρ[8] τὸ σῶμα [e]χωρὶς πνεύματος νεκρόν ἐστιν, οὕτως καὶ[9] ἡ i. 10;
Acts xiii.
πίστις χωρὶς ἔργων[10 f] νεκρά ἐστιν. 1; 1 Cor.
xi. 34;
III. 1. Μὴ πολλοὶ [a]διδάσκαλοι γίνεσθε, ἀδελφοί μου, εἰδότες Heb. xi.
31.
d Cf. Luke
x. 38, and see 1 Kgs. viii. 46.   e ii. 10.   f ii. 17.   a Cf. i. 19; Matt. xxiii. 8; Rom. ii.
20, 21; 1 Cor. xi. 31; 1 Tim. i. 7.

[1] τοινυν KL, Oec.   [2] μονον; Treg.

[3] ουτως C, Pesh., Copt., Arm., Aeth.   [4] Om. C, ff, Pesh., Copt., Arm.

[5] κατασκοπους CKmgL, Pesh., Arm., exploratores ex XII. tribus filiorum israhel ff.

[6] Pr. per ff, pr. ex s.   [7] Pr. eos ff.

[8] Om. B, Pesh., Arm., Aeth., WH (placed in mg.), autem ff, Orig.

[9] Om. ff.   [10] Pr. των ACKLP, Thl., Oec., Tregmg.

reads, οὐ μὴ κρύψω ἀπὸ Ἀβραὰμ τοῦ
παιδός μου ἃ ἐγὼ ποιῶ, which is quoted
by Philo with τοῦ φίλου μου instead of
τοῦ π. μου. In the MS., 69 φίλος in
the verse before us is rendered δοῦλος
(see critical note above).

Ver. 24. ὁρᾶτε: The argument between the two supposed disputants having
been brought to a close, the writer addresses his hearers again, and sums up in
his own words.—μόνον: the writer, by
using this word, allows more importance
to faith than he has yet done; there is
not necessarily any inconsistency in this,
the exigencies of argument on controversial topics sometimes require special
stress to be laid on one point of view to
the partial exclusion of another in order
to balance the one-sided view of an opponent.

Ver. 25. Ῥαὰβ ἡ πόρνη: It must
probably have been the position already
accorded to Rahab in Jewish tradition
that induced the writer to cite an example
like this. In Mechilta, 64b, it is said
that the harlot Rahab asked for forgiveness of her sins from God, pleading on
her own behalf the good works she had
done in releasing the messengers. The
attempts which have been made to explain away the force of πόρνη are futile.

Ver. 26. πνεύματος: Spitta's suggested reading, κινήματος, is very ingenious, but quite unnecessary; רוּחַ is
often used of "breath," and the Greek
equivalent, πνεῦμα, is also used in the
same way in the Septuagint.

CHAPTER III.—Vv. 1-18 form a self-
contained section; the subject dealt with
is the bridling of the tongue, see above
i. 19, 26, 27.

Ver. 1. Μὴ πολλοὶ διδάσκαλοι
γίνεσθε: the Peshittâ reads : " Let
there not be many teachers among you";
both the Greek version, which implies
that the " teachers " belonged to the congregation of the faithful, as well as the
Syriac, which implies that "teachers" from
outside were welcomed,—cf. Pseud-Clem.,
De Virginitate, i. 11 . . . quod dicit Scriptura, "Ne multi inter vos sint doctores,
fratres, neque omnes sitis prophetae . . ."
(Resch., op. cit., p. 186),—bear witness to
what we know from other sources to have
been the actual facts of the case. It is
the greatest mistake to suppose that
διδάσκαλοι here is equivalent to Rabbis
in the technical sense. In the Jewish
" Houses of Learning " (i.e., the Synagogues, for these were not exclusively
places of worship) whether in Palestine
or in the Dispersion (but more so in the
latter), there was very little restriction in
the matter of teachers; almost anyone
would be listened to who desired to be
heard. We have an example of this in
the case of our Lord Himself, who found
no difficulty in entering into Synagogues
and teaching (Matt. xii. 9 ff., xiii. 54;
Mark i. 39; Luke vi. 14 ff., etc., etc.),
although His presence there must have
been very distasteful to the Jewish
authorities, and although on some occasions the ordinary hearers altogether dis-
sented from what He taught (e.g., John
vi. 59-66); the same is true of St. Peter,
St. John, and above all of St. Paul. In
the case of St. Paul (or his disciples)
we have an extremely interesting instance (preserved in the Babylonian
Talmud, Meg., 26a) of an attempt, a
successful attempt, made on one occasion to stop his teaching; it is said

b ii. 10. ὅτι μεῖζον κρίμα λημψόμεθα.[1] 2. πολλὰ γὰρ [2] πταίομεν [b]ἅπαντες·
c—c i. 19;
Sir. xiv. [c]εἴ τις ἐν λόγῳ οὐ πταίει,[3] [d]οὗτος [4] [a]τέλειος ἀνήρ,[c] δυνατὸς [5] [f]χαλιν-
1, xix. 16,
xxv. 8, αγωγῆσαι καὶ ὅλον τὸ σῶμα. 3. εἰ δὲ [6] τῶν ἵππων τοὺς [g]χαλινοὺς
xxxvi. 18.
d Matt. xii. εἰς τὰ στόματα [7] βάλλομεν εἰς [8] τὸ πείθεσθαι αὐτοὺς ἡμῖν,[9] καὶ ὅλον
37.
e i. 4.
f i. 26. g Ps. xxxii. 9; xxxix. 9.

[1] λήψομεθα KLP, curss., sumitis Vulg. (accipiemus ff).
[2] Autem ff. [3] Non erat ff. [4] Add erit ff.
[5] δυναμενος א, curss., Cyr., Thl.; add τε Cvid.
[6] ειδε γαρ א (om. γαρ א[3]); ιδε CP, curss., Syrhk, Arm., Sah., Thl.; הַאְ גִיר Pesh.
[7] το στομα A, curss., Pesh., Syrhk, Arm.
[8] προς AKLP, curss., Thl., Oec., rec.
[9] ημιν αυτους AC, curss., Tregmg; om. ημιν ff.

that the Synagogue of the Alexandrians (mentioned in Acts vi. 9), which was called "the Synagogue of those of Tarsus," *i.e.*, the followers of St. Paul, was bought up by a Tannaite ("teacher") and used for private purposes (see Bergmann, *Jüdische Apologetik im neutestamentl. Zeitalter*, p. 9). Like the Athenians (Acts xvii. 21), many inquiring Jews were always ready to hear some new thing, and welcomed into their houses of learning teachers of all kinds (*cf.* Acts xv. 24; 1 Tim. i. 6, 7). The following would not have been said unless there had been great danger of Jews being influenced by the doctrines condemned: "All Israelites have their part in the world to come, . . . but the following (Israelites) have no part therein,—he who denies that the Resurrection is a doctrine the foundation of which is in the Bible, he who denies the divine origin of the *Torah*, and (he who is) an Epicurean" (*Sanh.*, xi. 1; quoted by Bergmann, *op. cit.*, p. 9). The custom of Jews, and especially of Hellenistic Jews, of permitting teachers of various kinds to enter their Synagogues and expound their views, was not likely to have been abrogated when they became Christians, which was in itself a sign of greater liberal-mindedness. The διδάσκαλοι, therefore, in the verse before us, must, it is held, be interpreted in the sense of what has been said. The whole passage is exceedingly interesting as throwing detailed light upon the methods of controversy in these Diaspora Synagogues; feeling seems to have run high, as was natural, mutual abuse was evidently poured forth without stint, judging from the stern words of rebuke which the writer has to use (ver. 6). On the διδάσκαλοι in the early Church see Harnack, *Expansion* . . . i. pp. 416-461.—ειδο-

τες ὅτι μεῖζον κρίμα λημψόμεθα: *Cf. Pirqe Aboth*, i. 18. "Whoso multiplies words occasions sin"; i. 12. "Abtalion said, Ye wise, be guarded in your words; perchance ye may incur the debt of exile, and be exiled to the place of evil waters; and the disciples that come after you may drink and die, and the Name of Heaven be profaned"; Taylor comments thus on these words: "Scholars must take heed to their doctrine, lest they pass over into the realm of heresy, and inoculate their disciples with deadly error. The penalty of untruth is untruth, to imbibe which is death". λημψόμεθα: the writer does not often associate himself with his hearers as he does here; the first person plural is only rarely found in the Epistle (*cf.* πταίομεν in the next verse).

Ver. 2. πταίομεν: see note above on this word ii. 10.—εἴ τις ἐν λόγῳ οὐ πταίει: *Cf.* Sir. xix. 16, τίς οὐχ ἥμαρτεν ἐν τῇ γλώσσῃ αὐτοῦ;—τέλειος: see note on i. 4.—ἀνήρ: see note on i. 12.—χαλιναγωγῆσαι: see note on i. 26.—καὶ ὅλον τὸ σῶμα: it is quite possible that these words are meant literally; the exaggerated gesticulation of an Oriental in the excitement of debate is proverbial; that the reference here is to even more than this is also quite within the bounds of possibility, *cf.* John xviii. 22; Acts xxiii. 2, 3.

Ver. 3. εἰ δὲ: this is the best attested reading, but see Mayor's admirable note in favour of the reading ἴδε γάρ.—τῶν ἵππων: "The genitive is here put in an emphatic place to mark the comparison. It belongs both to χαλινούς and to στόματα, probably more to the former as distinguishing it from the human bridle, so we have ἄχρι τῶν χαλινῶν τῶν ἵππων, Apoc. xiv. 20, ἐπὶ

τὸ σῶμα αὐτῶν μετάγομεν.[1] 4. ἰδοὺ[2] καὶ τὰ πλοῖα, τηλικαῦτα[3] h Acts
ὄντα καὶ ὑπὸ ἀνέμων σκληρῶν[4] ἐλαυνόμενα, μετάγεται ὑπὸ ἐλαχίστου i Acts xiv.5.
[h] πηδαλίου[5] ὅπου[6] ἡ[1] ὁρμὴ[7] τοῦ εὐθύνοντος βούλεται[8][5]· 5. οὔ- 4; lxxiii.
τως[9] καὶ ἡ γλῶσσα μικρὸν μέλος ἐστὶν καὶ[10] μεγάλα[k] αὐχεῖ.[10] ἰδοὺ xxviii. 10.
ἡλίκον[11] πῦρ ἡλίκην ὕλην ἀνάπτει· 6. καὶ[12] ἡ γλῶσσα[13][1] πῦρ,[14] ὁ Prov. xvi.
27; Sir.
viii. 8; cf. Prov. xii. 18, xv. 1, 2

xxvii. 40.
k Ps. xii. 3,
8, 9; Sir.
l Cf. i. 26;

[1] μεταγομεν αυτων A, 13.   [2] ειδε 24.   [3] Pr. τα B.

[4] Pr. tam ff; σκληρων ανεμων AL, curss.

[5]—[5] Et ubicumque diriguntur volumptate eorum qui eas gubernant ff.

[6] Add αν ACKLP, curss., Thl., Oec., Tregmg, rec.

[7] Om. η ορμη s.   [8] βουληται ACKR; βουληθη 13.

[9] ωσαυτως A, 5.   [10]—[10] μεγαλαυχει אC²KL, curss., Thl., Oec.

[11] ολιγον A¹C²KL, curss., Syrr., Sah., Copt., Arm., Aeth., pusillum ff.

[12] Om. א¹.   [13] Ti. punctuates thus: αναπτει η γλωσσα,.

[14] Weiss punctuates: πυρ.

τὸν χαλινὸν τοῦ ἵππου, Zech. xiv. 20.
Cf. Ps. xxxii. 9" (Mayor). Knowling
draws attention to Philo who "speaks of
the easy way in which the horse, the most
spirited of animals, is led when bridled,
De Mundi Opif., p. 19E".—καὶ ὅλον
τὸ σῶμα...: Cf. what was said in the
preceding verse.

Ver. 4. τηλικαῦτα: Cf. 2 Cor.
i. 10; Heb. ii. 3; Rev. xvi. 18, the only
other N.T. passages in which the word
occurs.—πηδαλίου: only elsewhere
in N.T. in Acts xxvii. 40.—ὁρμή: only
elsewhere in the N.T. in Acts xiv. 5, used
there, however, in the sense of a rush of
people. The graphic picture in this verse
gives the impression that the writer gives
the result of personal observation.

Ver. 5. ἡ γλῶσσα...; For this
idea of the independent action of a member of the body taken as though personality were attached to it see Matt. v. 29,
30, xv. 19; it is quite in the Hebrew style,
cf. in the O.T. the same thing in connection with anthropomorphic expressions.
Moffatt (Expository Times, xiv. p. 568)
draws attention to Plutarch's essay, De
Garrulitate, 10, where the union of
similar nautical and igneous metaphors
(as in Jas. iii. 4-6) is found; "the
moralist speaks first of speech as beyond
control once it is uttered, like a ship
which has broken loose from its anchorage.
But in the following sentence, he comes
nearer to the idea of James by quoting from
a fragment of Euripides these lines :—

Μικροῦ γὰρ ἐκ λαμπτῆρος Ἰδαῖον λέπας
Πρήσειεν ἄν τις· καὶ πρὸς ἄνδρ' εἰπὼν
ἕνα,
Πύθοιντ' ἂν ἀστοὶ πάντες."—

καὶ μεγάλα αὐχεῖ: ἅπ. λεγ. in
N.T.; the same would apply to the alternative reading (see critical note above)
μεγαλαυχεῖ. In Sir. xlviii. 18 we have,
καὶ ἐμεγαλαύχησεν ὑπερηφανίᾳ αὐτοῦ.
Mayor most truly remarks: "There is no
idea of vain boasting, the whole argument
turns upon the reality of the power which
the tongue possesses"; this fully bears
out what has been implied above, that this
section has for its object the attempt to
pacify the bitterness which had arisen
in certain Synagogues of the Diaspora
owing to controversies aroused by the
harangues of various "teachers".—ἰδοὺ
ἡλίκον πῦρ ἡλίκην ὕλην ἀνά-
πτει: at the risk of being charged with
fancifulness the surmise may be permitted as to whether this picture was not
suggested by the sight of an excited audience in some place of meeting; when an
Eastern audience has been aroused to a
high pitch, the noise of tongues, and
gesticulation of the arms occasioned by
the discussion following upon the oration
which has been delivered, might most
aptly be compared to a forest fire; the
tongue of one speaker has set ablaze all
the inflammable material which controversy brings into being. The possibility
that the writer had something of this kind
in his mind should not be altogether excluded.—ἀνάπτει occurs in the N.T. elsewhere only in Luke xii. 49; Taylor
(quoted by Mayor) says: "On fires
kindled by the tongue see Midr. Rabb.
on Lev. (xiv. 2) xvi. where the words are
almost the same as those in St. James,
quanta incendia lingua excitat!"

Ver. 6. See critical note above for
suggested differences in punctuation.—

m Matt. xv. κόσμος τῆς ἀδικίας,¹ ἡ γλῶσσα καθίσταται ἐν τοῖς μέλεσιν ἡμῶν,
11, 18, 19;
cf. xii. 36, ἡ ² ᵐ σπιλοῦσα ὅλον τὸ σῶμα καὶ φλογίζουσα τὸν ⁿ τροχὸν τῆς γενέ-
37; Jude
23.
n Ps. lxxvii. 18 (Heb.); Eccles. xii. 6.

¹ Add ουτως P, curss., Thl., Oec., rec.; add ουτως και L, 106.   ² και ℵ¹, Ti.

καὶ ἡ γλῶσσα πῦρ: this metaphor
was familiar to Jews, see Prov. xvi. 27,
. . . And in his lips there is as a scorch-
ing fire; the whole of the passage Sir.
xxviii. 8-12 is very à propos, especially ver.
11, ἔρις κατασπευδομένη ἐκκαίει πῦρ,
καὶ μάχη κατασπεύδουσα ἐκχέει αἷμα.
Knowing refers to Psalms of Sol. xii. 2-
4, where the same metaphor is graphically
presented, but the reference is to slander,
not to the fire engendered by public controversy; ver. 2 runs: "Very apt are the
words of the tongue of a malicious man,
like fire in a threshing-floor that burns
up the straw" (the text in the second
half of the verse is corrupt, but the
general meaning is clear enough).—καὶ
ἡ γλῶσσα πῦρ, ὁ κόσμος τῆς
ἀδικίας . . . τῆς γεέννης: Carr
has a very helpful note on this difficult
verse, he says: "a consideration of the
structure of the sentence, the poetical
form in which the thoughts are cast, also
throws light on the meaning. From this
it appears that the first thought is resumed
and expounded in the last two lines,
while the centre doublet contains a parallelism in itself. The effect is that of an
underground flame concealed for a while,
then breaking out afresh. Thus φλογίζουσα and φλογιζομένη refer to πῦρ, and
σπιλοῦσα to κόσμος, though grammatically these participles are in agreement
with γλῶσσα."—ὁ κόσμος τῆς ἀδικίας: This expression is an extremely
difficult one, and a large variety of interpretations have been suggested; the real
crux is, of course, the meaning of κόσμος.
In this Epistle κόσμος is always used in
a bad sense, i. 27, ii. 5, iv. 4. In the
Septuagint ὁ κόσμος is several times the
rendering of the Hebrew צָבָא, "host"
(of heaven, i.e., the stars, etc.), see Gen.
ii. 1; Deut. iv. 19, xvii. 3; there is no Hebrew word which corresponds to κόσμος,
properly speaking; and it would therefore
be no matter of surprise if a Jew with
a knowledge of Hebrew should use κόσμος
in a loose sense. In the N.T. αἰών is
often used in the same sense as κόσμος,
e.g., Matt. xii. 32; Mark iv. 19; Eph. i.
21, of this world; here again it is mostly
in an evil sense in which it is referred to,
whether as αἰών or κόσμος. It is, therefore, possible that κόσμος might be used
in the sense of αἰών, by a Jew, but as
referring to a sphere not on this earth.
Schegg (quoted by Mayor) interprets the
phrase, "the sphere or domain of iniquity," and though this is not the natural
meaning of κόσμος, this cannot be urged
as an insuperable objection to his interpretation; we are dealing with the work
of an Oriental, and a Jew, in an age long
ago, and we must not therefore look for
strict accuracy. If κόσμος may be regarded as being used in the sense of αἰών,
which is applicable to this world or to the
world to come, then Schegg's "domain
of iniquity" might refer to a sphere in the
next world. When it is further noticed
that the tongue is called "fire," and that
this fire has been kindled by ἡ γέεννα, the
place of burning, it becomes possible to
regard the words ὁ κόσμος τῆς ἀδικίας
as a symbolic expression of Gehenna (see
further below, under τῆς γεέννης).—
καθίσταται: "is set," i.e., "is consti
tuted". Mayor says: "It is opposed to
ὑπάρχω, because it implies a sort of
adaptation or development as contrasted
with the natural or original state; to
γίγνομαι, because it implies something
of fixity".—ἡ σπιλοῦσα: σπίλος
means a "stain," cf. Jude 23.—φλογίζουσα: ἅπ. λεγ. in N.T., cf. Wisd. iii.
28.—τὸν τροχὸν τῆς γενέσεως.
"the wheel of nature," i.e., the whole
circle of innate passions; the meaning
is that this wrong use of the tongue engenders jealousy, and faction, and every
vile deed, cf. ver. 16. For the different
interpretations of the phrase see Mayor.—
φλογιζομένη ὑπὸ τῆς γεέννης:
In Jewish theology two ideas regarding
the fate of the wicked hereafter existed,
at one time, concurrently; according to
the one, Hades (Sheol) was the place to
which the spirits of all men, good as well
as bad, went after death; at the resurrection, the good men arose and dwelt in
glory, while the wicked remained in
Sheol. According to a more developed
belief, the place of the departed was not
the same for the good and the bad; the
former went to a place of rest, and awaited
the final resurrection, while the latter
went to a place of torment; after the

σεως¹ καὶ °φλογιζομένη ὑπὸ τῆς ᴾγεέννης. 7. πᾶσα γὰρ² φύσις ο Luke xvi.
θηρίων τε καὶ πετεινῶν ἑρπετῶν τε³ καὶ ἐναλίων δαμάζεται καὶ ᴾ Matt. v.
δεδάμασται⁴ τῇ φύσει⁵ τῇ ἀνθρωπίνῃ, 8. τὴν δὲ⁶ γλῶσσαν οὐδεὶς ⁷ ᵠ Ps. cxl. 3;
δαμάσαι δύναται ἀνθρώπων⁷ᶜ ἀκατάστατον⁸ κακόν, μεστὴ ἰοῦ ᵠθα- 11; cf. Sir.
νατηφόρου. 9. ἐν αὐτῇ εὐλογοῦμεν τὸν Κύριον⁹ καὶ πατέρα, καὶ ἐν 17-23.
αὐτῇ καταρώμεθα τοὺς ἀνθρώπους τοὺς ᴿκαθ᾽ ὁμοίωσιν Θεοῦ ᴿ ʳ—ʳ Quoted
from Gen.
i. 27.

¹ Add ημων א, 7, 25, 68, Vulg., Pesh., Aeth.; γεεννης Thl., Oec.   ² Autem *ff*.
³ Om. A, curss., Arm.   ⁴ Om. και δεδαμασται, Pesh.
⁵ Add autem *ff*.   ⁶ Om. *ff*.
⁷ δυναται δαμ. ανθρ. אAKP, 69, 133, *a*, *c*, Treg^mg, Ti.; δυν. ανθρ. δαμ. L, curss.,
Arm., Copt., Thl., Oec.
⁸ ακατασχετον CKL, curss., Pesh., Cyr., Dam., Thl., Oec., rec.
⁹ Θεον KL, curss., Vulg., Syr^hk, Epiph., Thl., Oec.

resurrection the good enter into eternal bliss, the wicked into eternal woe, but whether these latter continue in the same place in which they had hitherto been, or whether it is a different place of torment, is not clear. A realistic conception of the place of torment arose when the "Valley of Hinnom" (גי־הנם = ἡ γέεννα), was pointed out as the place in which the spirits of the wicked suffered; but very soon this conception became spiritualised, and there arose the belief that the Valley of Hinnom was only the *type* of what actually existed in the next world. The fire which burned in the Valley of Hinnom was likewise transferred to the next world; hence the phrases: γέεννα τοῦ πυρός, κάμινος τοῦ πυρός, etc. Cf. iv. Esdr. vii. 36; Rev. ix. 1, etc.

Vv. 7, 8. These verses, are, of course, not to be taken literally; their exaggerative character rather reminds one of the orator carried away by his subject. But it must be remembered that to the Oriental the language of exaggeration is quite normal. Moreover, this enumeration of various classes of animals was familiar from the O.T., and would be uttered as stereotyped phrases often are, it being well understood that the words are not to be taken *au pied de la lettre*; *e.g.*, a very familiar passage from the *Torah* runs: καὶ ὁ τρόμος ὑμῶν καὶ ὁ φόβος ἔσται ἐπὶ πᾶσιν τοῖς θηρίοις τῆς γῆς καὶ ἐπὶ πάντα τὰ ὄρνεα τοῦ οὐρανοῦ καὶ ἐπὶ πάντα τὰ κινούμενα ἐπὶ τῆς γῆς καὶ πάντας τοὺς ἰχθύας τῆς θαλάσσης (Gen. ix. 2); and one who shows so much familiarity with the Wisdom literature would be well acquainted with what tra-

dition had imputed to Solomon: ἐλάλησε περὶ τῶν κτηνῶν καὶ περὶ τῶν. πετεινῶν καὶ περὶ τῶν ἑρπετῶν καὶ περὶ τῶν ἰχθύων (1 Kings iv. 33), *cf.* Gen. i. 26 (i. 27 is quoted in the next verse); Deut. iv. 17, 18; Acts x. 12.

Ver. 9. ἐν αὐτῇ: this is Hebrew usage, *cf.* εἰ πατάξομεν ἐν μαχαίρῃ, Luke xxii. 49; ἀποκτεῖναι ἐν ῥομφαίᾳ, Rev. vi. 8.—εὐλογοῦμεν: this use is Hellenistic. Both in speaking and writing the Jews always added the words ברוך הוא ("Blessed [be] He") after the name of God; *cf.* Mark xiv. 61, where ὁ εὐλογητός is used in reference to God. —τὸν Κύριον καὶ πατέρα: the reading Κύριον can scarcely be right; Θεόν is not, it is true, well attested (see critical note), but it is required on account of the καθ᾽ ὁμοίωσιν Θεοῦ; neither the combination τὸν θεὸν καὶ πατέρα nor τὸν Κύριον καὶ πατέρα is in accordance with ordinary Jewish usage; the exact phrase does not occur in the Bible elsewhere, the nearest approach being Tobit xiii. 4, . . . καὶ Θεὸς αὐτὸς πατὴρ ἡμῶν εἰς πάντας τοὺς αἰῶνας. *Cf.* Isa. lxiii. 16, σὺ Κύριε πατὴρ ἡμῶν, and 1 Chron. xxix. 10, εὐλογητὸς εἶ, Κύριε, ὁ Θεὸς Ἰσραὴλ, ὁ Πατὴρ ἡμῶν. Although the Jews frequently speak of God as "Father," it is usually in a different combination, probably the most usual being "Our Father" alone, or "Our Father and King"; in the great prayer called the "Shemôneh 'Esreh" ("Eighteen" [Nineteen] Blessings), which was formulated in its final form about the year 110 A.D., each of the forty-four petitions which it contains begins with the words: *Abinu Malkênu* * ("Our Father, our King").

* To be distinguished from the "Abinu Malkênu" prayer used in the penitential portion of the Jewish Liturgy.

s—з *Cf.* Sir. γεγονότας· 10. · ᵇἐκ τοῦ αὐτοῦ στόματος ἐξέρχεται εὐλογία καὶ
xxviii. 12.
κατάρα.ᵃ οὐ χρή, ἀδελφοί μου, ταῦτα οὕτως γενέσθαι. 11. μήτι
t Heb. xi. ἡ πηγὴ ἐκ τῆς αὐτῆς ᵗὀπῆς βρύει τὸ γλυκὺ καὶ τὸ πικρόν; 12. μὴ
38.
δύναται, ἀδελφοί μου, συκῆ ἐλαίας ποιῆσαι ἢ ἄμπελος σῦκα; ¹οὔτε
ἁλυκὸν γλυκὺ¹ ποιῆσαι ὕδωρ.
u Gal. vi. 4.
v ii. 18. 13. Τίς ² ᵘσοφὸς καὶ ἐπιστήμων ἐν ὑμῖν; ᵛδειξάτω ἐκ τῆς καλῆς

¹—¹ ουτως ουτε αλυκον γλυκυ C², latt., Pesh.; ουτως ουδεμια πηγη αλυκον και
γλυκυKL, curss., Thl., Oec., rec.

² Om. K, curss.; pr. ει 7, curss.

Πατήρ is always used in reference to God
in order to emphasise the divine love;
and in the passage before us a contrast is
undoubtedly implied between the love of
the Father towards all His children, and
the mutual hatred among these latter.—
καταρώμεθα: this word shows that the
special sin of the tongue which is here
referred to is not slander or backbiting
or lying, but personal abuse, such as
results from loss of temper in heated controversy. *Cf.* Rom. xii. 13, εὐλογεῖτε καὶ
μὴ καταρᾶσθε, and see the very appropriate passage in the *Test. of the Twelve
Patriarchs*, Benj. vi. 5, ἡ ἀγαθὴ διάνοια
οὐκ ἔχει δύο γλώσσας εὐλογίας καὶ
κατάρας.—τοὺς καθ᾽ ὁμοίωσιν
Θεοῦ γεγονότας: quoted, apparently from memory, from Gen. i. 26,
where the Septuagint reads, κατ᾽ εἰκόνα
ἡμετέραν καὶ καθ᾽ ὁμοίωσιν; the Hebrew
דְּמוּת (ὁμοίωσις) is synonymous with
צֶלֶם (εἰκών). The belief that men are
made in the material likeness of God is
taught both in Biblical and post-Biblical
Jewish literature; philosophers like Philo
would naturally seek to modify this. An
interesting passage which reminds one
of this verse is quoted by Knowling from
Bereshith, R. xxiv., Rabbi Akiba (born in
the middle of the first century A.D.), in
commenting on Gen. ix. 6, said: "Whoso
sheddeth blood, it is reckoned to him as
if he diminished *the likeness*"; then referring presently to Lev. xix. 18 (*Thou
shalt not take vengeance, nor bear any
grudge against the children of thy people,
but thou shalt love thy neighbour as thyself*), he continues, "Do not say: 'after
that I am despised, let my neighbour also
be despised'. R. Tanchuma said, 'If
you do so, understand that you despise
him of whom it was written, *in the likeness of God made He him*'." The lesson
is that he who curses him who was made
in the image of God implicitly curses the
prototype as well.

Ver. 10. ἐκ τοῦ αὐτοῦ στόμα-
τος: This incongruity is often rebuked
in Jewish literature; it was the more
needed because in earlier days it was not
regarded as reprehensible, *cf.* Prov. xi.
26, xxiv. 24, xxvi. 2, xxx. 10, etc.—
εὐλογία καὶ κατάρα: this does not
imply a combination of blessing and cursing, as though such a combination were
condemned, while either by itself were
allowable (Mayor); it simply means that
the mouth which blesses God when uttering prayer, curses men at some other
times, *e.g.*, during embittered controversy.—οὐ χρή: ἅπ. λεγ. in N.T.
Ver. 11. μήτι ἡ πηγή . . . τὸ
πικρόν: these words show that the
writer is thinking of the real source
whence both good and evil words come;
cf. Matt. xii. 34, 35: *Ye offspring of
vipers, how can ye, being evil, speak good
things? for out of the abundance of the
heart the mouth speaketh* . . . ; *cf.* ἐν τῇ
καρδίᾳ ὑμῶν below; βρύει does not occur
elsewhere in the N.T. or the Septuagint;
and ὀπή is only found elsewhere in the
N.T. in Heb. xi. 38, *cf.* Exod. xxxiii. 22;
πικρόν is only used here and in ver. 14
in the N.T.; *cf.* Sir. iv. 6, . . . κατα-
ρωμένου γάρ σε ἐν πικρίᾳ ψυχῆς αὐτοῦ.
Ver. 12. With the whole verse *cf.*
Matt. vii. 16, 17; for the use of ποιεῖν
see Matt. iii. 10, πᾶν δένδρον μὴ ποιοῦν
καρπόν . . . ; ἁλυκόν does not occur
elsewhere in the N.T. or Septuagint,
though in Num. iii. 12, Deut. iii. 17,
etc., we have the phrase ἡ θάλασσα ἡ
ἁλυκή = the Dead Sea. "There is great
harshness in the construction μὴ δύναται
ποιῆσαι; οὔτε ποιῆσαι. If the government of δύναται is continued, we ought
to have ἤ for οὔτε followed by a question; otherwise we should have expected
an entirely independent clause, reading
ποιήσει for ποιῆσαι" (Mayor).
Ver. 13. Τίς σοφὸς καὶ ἐπιστήμων ἐν ὑμῖν: The writer's appeal

ʷ ἀναστροφῆς τὰ ἔργα αὐτοῦ ἐν ˣπραΰτητι σοφίας. 14. ʸεἰ δὲ¹
ˣζῆλον πικρὸν ἔχετε καὶ ªἐριθείαν² ἐν τῇ καρδίᾳ³ ὑμῶν,ʸ μὴ κατα-
καυχᾶσθε⁴ ⁵καὶ ψεύδεσθε κατὰ τῆς ἀληθείας.⁵ 15. οὐκ ἔστιν αὕτη
ἡ σοφία ᵇἄνωθεν κατερχομένη, ἀλλὰ⁶ ᶜἐπίγειος, ᵈψυχική, δαιμονι-
ώδης· 16. ὅπου γὰρ⁷ ᵉζῆλος καὶ ᶠἐριθεία,⁸ ἐκεῖ⁹ ᵍἀκαταστασία

w Gal. i. 13
cf. 1 Pet.
ii. 12.
x i. 21.
y—y iii. 16;
Eph. iv.
31; Rom.
xiii. 13;
Acts v.17.
z 1 Cor. iii.
3.

a Gal. v. 20.   b i. 17, iii. 17.   c Cf. 1 Cor. ii. 6, 7.   d 1 Cor. ii. 14.   e Acts v. 13; Rom.
xiii. 13; 1 Cor. iii. 3.   f Gal. v. 20.   g 1 Cor. xiv. 33.

---

¹ Add αρα AP, curss.   ² ερειθιαν B¹; ερειθειαν A, εριθιαν 13, 101, WH.
³ ταις καρδιαις ℵ, curss., Latt., Syrr., Copt., Arm.   ⁴ καυχασθε A, curss.
⁵—⁵ της αγηθ. και ψευδ. ℵ¹, Ti.; κατα της αληθ. και ψευδ. ℵ³, Pesh.
⁶ αλλ ACKLP.   ⁷ Autem ff.
⁸ εριθεια B¹; ερειθεια B²; εριθια 13, 101, WH; ερεις C; ερις P.
⁹ + και ℵA, curss., Weiss.

---

to the self-respect of his hearers. σοφός
and ἐπιστήμων (the latter does not occur
elsewhere in the N.T.) are connected in
Deut. i. 13, where in reference to judges
it is said, δότε αὐτοῖς ἄνδρας σοφοὺς καὶ
ἐπιστήμονας καὶ συνετούς, cf. Deut. iv.
6; Isa. v. 21.—ἐκ τῆς καλῆς ἀναστροφῆς: Cf. 1 Pet. ii. 12. ἀναστροφή is literally a "turning back,"
but later connotes "manner of life". Cf.
a quotation from an inscription from Perga-
mos (belonging to the second century
B.C.) given by Deissmann, in which it is
said concerning one of the royal officials:
ἐν πᾶσιν κα[ιροῖς ἀμέμπτως καὶ ἀδ]εῶς
ἀναστρεφόμενος (op. cit., p. 83).—ἐν
πραΰτητι σοφίας: cf. with the
whole of this verse Sir. iii. 17, 18,
Τέκνον, ἐν πραΰτητι τὰ ἔργα σου διέ-
ξαγε, καὶ ὑπὸ ἀνθρώπου δεκτοῦ ἀγα-
πηθήσῃ. Ὅσῳ μέγας εἶ, τοσούτῳ ταπεινοῦ σεαυτόν, καὶ ἔναντι Κυρίου εὑρήσεις
χάριν. The pride of knowledge is always
a subtle evil, cf. 1 Cor. viii. 1.
Ver. 14. εἰ δὲ ζῆλον πικρὸν
ἔχετε καὶ ἐριθείαν ἐν τῇ καρδίᾳ ὑμῶν: This makes it quite clear
that what has been referred to all along
is controversial strife; the bitter use of
the tongue which the writer has been
reprobating is the personal abuse which
had been heaped upon one another by
the partisans of rival schools of thought.
ζῆλον is mostly used in a bad sense in
the N.T., though the opposite is sometimes the case (e.g., 2 Cor. xi. 2; Gal. i.
14); the intensity of feeling which had
been aroused among those to whom the
Epistle was addressed is seen by the
words ζῆλον πικρόν, with the latter word
in an emphatic position; they form a striking contrast to πραΰτητι σοφίας. The
word ἐριθείαν, derived from ἔριθος "a

hireling," means "party-spirit".—μὴ
κατακαυχᾶσθε: the malicious tri-
umphing at the least point of vantage
gained by one party was just the thing
calculated to embitter the other side; this
was a real "lying against the truth,"
because such petty triumphs are often
gained at the expense of truth.
Ver. 15. οὐκ ἔστιν αὕτη ἡ σοφία ἄνωθεν κατερχομένη: The
wisdom referred to,—acute argumentl
subtle distinctions, clever controversia
methods which took small account of
truth so long as a temporary point was
gained, skilful dialectics, bitter sarcasms,
the more enjoyed and triumphed in
if the poisonous shaft came home and
rankled in the breast of the opponent,—
in short, all those tricks of the unscrupulous controversialist which are none
the less contemptible for being clever,—
this was wisdom of a certain kind; but,
as expressed by the writer of the Epistle
with such extraordinary accuracy, it was
earthly (ἐπίγειος) as opposed to the wisdom which came down from above, it
was human (ψυχική, i.e., the domain
wherein all that is essentially human
holds sway) in that it pandered to self-
esteem, and it was demoniacal (δαιμονιώδης) in that it raised up the "very
devil" in the hearts of both opposer and
opposed. Nowhere is the keen knowledge of human nature, which is so characteristic of the writer, more strikingly
displayed than in these vv. 15, 16.
Ver. 16. πᾶν φαῦλον πρᾶγμα:
this sums up the matter; cf. John iii. 20,
πᾶς γὰρ ὁ φαῦλα πράσσων μισεῖ τὸ
φῶς, and with this one might compare
again the words in our Epistle, i. 17,
πᾶσα δόσις ἀγαθή . . . ἄνωθέν ἐστιν
καταβαῖνον ἀπὸ τοῦ πατρὸς τῶν φώτων.

h i. 17.
i 1 Cor. ii.
6, 7.
k Cf. iv. 8;
2 Cor. vii.
11; Phil.
v. 8; 1
Tim. v.
22; 1 Pet.
iii. 2; 1
Jn. iii. 3.

καὶ πᾶν φαῦλον πρᾶγμα.   17. ἡ δὲ ᵸἄνωθεν¹ ᶦσοφία πρῶτον μὲν
ᵏἁγνή ἐστιν, ἔπειτα ᶦεἰρηνική, ᵐἐπιεικής, εὐπειθής,² μεστὴ ⁿἐλέους,
καὶ καρπῶν ἀγαθῶν, ᵒἀδιάκριτος, ᵖἀνυπόκριτος.³   18. ᑫκαρπὸς⁴ δὲ
δικαιοσύνης⁵ ἐν ʳεἰρήνῃ σπείρεται τοῖς ποιοῦσιν εἰρήνην.

IV. 1. ΠΟΘΕΝ⁶ ᵃπόλεμοι καὶ πόθεν⁷ μάχαι ἐν ὑμῖν; οὐκ ἐντεῦ-

l Heb. xii. 11.   m Phil. iv. 5.   n Gal. v. 22; cf. Luke vi. 36.   o ii. 4; cf. 2 Cor. v. 16.
p Rom. xii. 9.   q Is. xxxii. 17; Am. vi. 12; Gal. vi. 8; Phil. i. 11; Heb. xii. 11.   r Matt. v. 9.
a 2 Tim. ii. 23; Tit. iii. 9.

¹ Dei ff.   ² + Bonis consentiens Vulg. (om. Vulgᴬ).
³ Pr. καὶ KL, curss., Thl., Oec., rec.; pr. inreprehensibilis ff.
⁴ Pr. ο ℵ.   ⁵ Pr. τῆς K, Oec.   ⁶ Pr. et s.
⁷ Om. KL, curss., Vulg., rec.

Ver. 17. ἡ δὲ ἄνωθεν σοφία:
the divine character of wisdom is beautifully expressed in Wisd. vii. 25, ἀτμὶς
γάρ ἐστιν τῆς τοῦ Θεοῦ δυνάμεως, καὶ
ἀπόρροια τῆς τοῦ παντοκράτορος δόξης
εἰλικρινής.—ἁγνή: in Wisd. ix. 10, the
prayer is uttered that God would send
forth wisdom "out of the holy heavens
. . ."; of that which is thus holy the
first characteristic would be purity, the
two ideas are inseparable; it is also possible that in the mind of the writer there
was the thought of the contrast between
purity and the sin which he knew some
of his hearers to be guilty of (see above,
the notes on i. 12 ff., iv. 3, 4).—εἰρην-
ική; only elsewhere in the N.T. in
Heb. xii. 11; cf. Prov. iii. 17, where it is
said of wisdom that "all her paths are
peace". The word is evidently chosen
to emphasise the strife referred to in an
earlier verse.—ἐπιεικής: the word is
meant as a contrast to unfair, unreasonable argument, cf. Pss. of Sol. v. 14.—
εὐπειθής: this word, again, implies a
contrast to the unbending attitude of self-
centred controversialists; it does not occur elsewhere in the N.T.—μεστὴ
ἐλέους καὶ καρπῶν ἀγαθῶν: the
exact reverse of the cursing and bitterness
of which some had already been con-
victed; in Wisd. vii. 22, 23, wisdom is
spoken of as having a spirit which is:
φιλάγαθον . . . φιλάνθρωπων.—ἀδι-
άκριτος: Cf. διακρίνομαι above (i. 6,
ii. 4) which, as Mayor points out, makes
it probable that we must understand the
adjective here in the sense of "single-
minded"; perhaps one might say that
here it means almost "generous," in contrast to the unfair imputations which
might be made in acrimonious discussion; the word occurs here only in the
N.T.—ἀνυπόκριτος: Cf. 1 Pet. i.

22; "genuine," as contrasted with the
spurious "earthly" wisdom.

Ver. 18. The keynote of this verse is
peace, as contrasted with the jealousy,
faction and confusion mentioned above;
peace and righteousness belong together,
they are the result of true wisdom, the
wisdom that is from above; on the other
hand, strife and "every vile deed" belong
together, and they are the result of the
wisdom that is "earthly, ψυχική, demoniacal".

CHAPTER IV.—Vv. 1 ff. These verses
reveal an appalling state of moral depravity in these Diaspora congregations;
strife, self-indulgence, lust, murder, covetousness, adultery, envy, pride and slander
are rife; the conception of the nature of
prayer seems to have been altogether
wrong among these people, and they appear to be given over wholly to a life of
pleasure. It must have been terrible for
the writer to contemplate such a sink of
iniquity. On the assumption, therefore,
of unity of authorship for this Epistle, it
is absolutely incomprehensible how, in
view of such an awful state of affairs, the
writer could commence his Epistle with
the words: "Count it all joy, my brethren,
when ye fall into manifold temptations".
It is held by some that the writer is, in
part, using figurative language; thus,
Mayor and Knowling do not think that
the adultery referred to is meant literally;
but in view of the mention of the "pleasures that war in your members," and of
the injunctions "Cleanse your hands,"
"Purify your hearts," it is difficult to believe that the writer is speaking figuratively. Is one to regard the words in
ii. 11 ("For he that saith, Do not commit
adultery, said also Do not kill . . .") as
figurative also? And i. 14, 15? Cf.
Acts xv. 20, 29. Moreover, it is one of

θεν, ἐκ τῶν ᵇ ἡδονῶν ὑμῶν ᵒτῶν στρατευομένων ἐν τοῖς μέλεσιν ὑμῶν ᵒ; b iv. 3

2. ἐπιθυμεῖτε καὶ οὐκ ἔχετε¹· ᵈ φονεύετε² καὶ ᵉζηλοῦτε, καὶ οὐ δύνασθε ἐπιτυχεῖν· μάχεσθε καὶ πολεμεῖτε. οὐκ ἔχετε³ διὰ τὸ μὴ

Luke viii. 14; 2 Pet. ii. 13.
c—c Rom. vii. 23; 1 Pet. ii. 11;
d v. 6. e 1 Cor. xii. 31.

cf. Rom. vi. 13.

¹ Habebitis *ff.* ² φονεύετε. καὶ WH (altern. reading); φθονεῖτε καὶ Erasmus.

³ καὶ οὐκ εχ. ℵP, curss., Latt., Syrr., Arm., Aeth., Thl., Oec., Ti.; add δε rec. [From here to end of Ep. C is wanting.]

the characteristics of the writer that he speaks straight to the point. It is true that in the O.T. adultery is sometimes used in a figurative sense, meaning unfaithfulness to Jahwe; but it is well to remember that such a use is quite exceptional; out of the thirty-one passages in which adultery is spoken of, in only five is a figurative sense found. In the N.T. there are only two possible cases of a figurative use apart from the verse before us (Matt. xii. 39 = xvi. 4, Mark viii. 38). The word "to commit fornication" (זנה) occurs oftener, in the O.T., in a figurative sense; but in comparison with the vastly larger instances of a literal sense, the former must be regarded as exceptional. But even granting that this particular word is figuratively used, there is still a terrible list of other sins, the meaning of which cannot be explained away; these are more than sufficient to bear witness to the truly awful moral condition of those to whom the Epistle is addressed. On the assumption of an early date for our Epistle, the low state of morals here depicted is extremely difficult to account for. In a community which had recently received and accepted the new faith, with its very high ideals, one would naturally look for some signs of new-born zeal, some conception of the meaning of Christianity, some reflex of the example of the Founder; religious strife, owing to a mistaken zeal, one can understand; isolated cases of moral delinquency are almost to be expected; but the collective wickedness of a new-born Christian community,—this would be quite incomprehensible; and it is clear from the verses before us that the writer is not singling out exceptions. In a second or third generation the community living among heathen surroundings might conceivably become so contaminated as to have lost its genuinely Christian character; with the lapse of years there is an inevitable tendency to deteriorate, until a new spirit of discipline is infused. It seems more in accordance with known facts, and with common-

sense, to regard the people to whom this Epistle (or part of it) was addressed as those who had deteriorated from the high ideal set by their fathers and grandfathers, and to see in the writer one who sought to inspire a new sense of discipline and morals into the hearts of his Jewish-Christian brethren. — Vv. 1-10 form a self-contained whole, dealing with the general state of moral depravity in the community (presumably the writer has more particularly one community in view), and ending with a call to repentance. Vv. 11, 12 form another independent section, belonging in substance to ii. 1-13. Vv. 13-17 form again a separate section without any reference to what precedes or follows.

Ver. 1. πόλεμοι καὶ μάχαι: the former refers to the permanent state of enmity, which every now and then breaks out into the latter; like war and battles. — ἐν ὑμῖν: comprehensive. — ἐντεῦθεν: lays special stress on the place of origin, which is seen in the following words: ἐκ τῶν ἡδονῶν ὑμῶν: ἡδοναί is sometimes used of the lusts of the flesh, *e.g.*, in the *Letter of Aristeas* (Swete, *Intro. to O.T. in Greek*, p. 567), in answer to the question: "Why do not the majority of men take possession of virtue"? it is said: "Ὅτι φυσικῶς ἅπαντες ἀκρατεῖς καὶ ἐπὶ τὰς ἡδονὰς τρεπόμενοι γεγόνασιν. Cf. 4 Macc. vi. 35; Luke viii. 14; Tit. iii. 3; 2 Pet. ii. 13.—τῶν στρατευομένων ἐν τοῖς μέλεσιν ὑμῶν: the same thought is found in 1 Pet. ii. 11, παρακαλῶ ἀπέχεσθαι τῶν σαρκικῶν ἐπιθυμιῶν αἵτινες στρατεύονται κατὰ τῆς ψυχῆς, *cf.* Rom. vii. 23; 1 Cor. ix. 7.

Vv. 2, 3. ἐπιθυμεῖτε καὶ οὐκ ἔχετε . . . : It must be confessed that these verses are very difficult to understand; we have, on the one hand, lusting and coveting, murdering and fighting; and, on the other hand, praying. Murdering and fighting are the means used in order to obtain that which is coveted; yet in the same breath it is said that the reason why the coveted things are not

f Prov. i. αἰτεῖσθαι ὑμᾶς· 3. ᵗ αἰτεῖτε καὶ οὐ λαμβάνετε, διότι κακῶς ᵍ αἰτεῖ-
28.
g Rom.viii. σθε, ἵνα ἐν ταῖς ʰ ἡδοναῖς ὑμῶν δαπανήσητε.¹ 4. ¹ μοιχαλίδες,² οὐκ
26; cf. 1
Jn. v. 14. οἴδατε ὅτι ἡ φιλία τοῦ ᵏ κόσμου ³ ¹ ἔχθρα τοῦ Θεοῦ ἐστιν⁴; ᵐ ὃς ἐὰν ⁵
h Matt. vii.
7.   οὖν ⁶ βουληθῇ φίλος εἶναι τοῦ κόσμου, ἐχθρὸς ⁷ τοῦ Θεοῦ καθίσταται.ᵐ
i Matt. xii.
39.   5. ἢ δοκεῖτε ὅτι κενῶς ἡ ⁿ γραφὴ λέγει· πρὸς φθόνον ⁸ ἐπιποθεῖ τὸ
k Matt. vi.
24; Luke
vi. 26; 1 Jn. ii. 15.   l Rom. viii. 7; Eph. ii. 15.   m—m Jn. xv. 19: xvii. 14; Gal. i. 10.
n ii. 23.

¹ καταδαπανησητε א¹; δαπανησετε B, Weiss.

² Pr. μοιχοι και א³KLP, curss.; μοιχοι Latt. (exc. ff), Pesh., Copt., Aeth., Arm.

³ του κοσμου τουτου א, 68, Vulg., Pesh., Arm., Aeth.

⁴ εστιν τω Θεω א, Copt., Ti.

⁵ Om. ος א; ος αν א³AKL, curss., Thl., Oec., Treg.

⁶ Om. L, curss.   ⁷ εχθρα א¹, 7.   ⁸ λεγει προς φθ. A, curss., Arm.

obtained is because they are not asked for! Is it intended to be understood that this lust (in the sense, of course, of desiring) and covetousness are not gratified only because they had not been prayed for, or not properly prayed for? This is what the words mean as they stand; but çan it ever be justifiable to pray for what is evil? There is something extraordinarily incongruous in the whole passage, which defies explanation if the words are to be taken in their obvious meaning. Only one thing seems clear, and that is a moral condition which is hopelessly chaotic.—Carr says that "these two verses are among the examples of poetical form in this Epistle"; perhaps this gives the key to the solution of the problem. It may be that we have in the whole of these verses 1-10 a string of quotations, not very skilfully strung together—a kind of "Stromateis"—taken from a variety of authorities, in order to make this protest against a disgraceful state of affairs more emphatic and authoritative.—**φονεύετε**: the reading **φθονεῖτε** cannot be entertained if any regard is to be paid to MS. authority; even if accepted it would not really simplify matters much.—**ζηλοῦτε**: refers rather to persons, **ἐπιθυμεῖτε** to things.
Ver. 3. **αἰτεῖτε … αἰτεῖσθε**: There does not seem to be any difference in meaning between the active and middle here: "If the middle is really the stronger word, we can understand its being brought in just where an effect of contrast can be secured, while in ordinary passages the active would carry as much weight as was needed" (Moulton, op. cit., p. 160); cf. Mark vi. 22-25, x. 35-38; 1 John v. 15.—**δαπανήσητε**: Cf. Luke xv. 14, 30; Acts xxi. 24.

Ver. 4. **μοιχαλίδες**: the weight of evidence is strongly in favour of this reading as against **μοιχοὶ καὶ μοιχαλίδες**. The depraved state of morals to which the whole section bears witness must in part at least have been due to the wickedness and co-operation of the women, so that there is nothing strange in their being specifically mentioned in connection with that form of sin with which they would be more particularly associated.—**οὐκ οἴδατε … καθίσταται**: what seems to be in the mind of the writer is John. xv. 18 ff. … εἰ ἐκ τοῦ κόσμου ἦτε, ὁ κόσμος ἂν τὸ ἴδιον ἐφίλει· ὅτι δὲ ἐκ τοῦ κόσμου ἂν οὐκ ἐστέ, ἀλλ' ἐγὼ ἐξελεξάμην ὑμᾶς ἐκ τοῦ κόσμου, διὰ τοῦτο μισεῖ ὑμᾶς ὁ κόσμος …—**καθίσταται**: "is constituted"; cf. the Vulgate constituitur.
Ver. 5. **ἡ γραφὴ λέγει πρὸς φθόνον …**: this attributing of personality to Scripture is paralleled, as Lightfoot points out (Gal. iii. 8), by the not uncommon Jewish formula of reference מה ראה "Quid vidit". According to Lightfoot the singular **γραφὴ** in the N.T. "always means a particular passage of Scripture; where the reference is clearly to the sacred writings as a whole, as in the expressions, 'searching the Scriptures,' 'learned in the Scriptures,' etc., the plural **γραφαί** is universally found, e.g., Acts xvii. 11, xviii. 24, 28. … Ἡ γραφὴ is most frequently used in introducing a particular quotation, and in the very few instances where the quotation is not actually given, it is for the most part easy to fix the passage referred to. The biblical usage is followed also by the earliest fathers. The transition from the 'Scriptures' to the

ᵒπνεῦμα ὃ ᴾκατῴκισεν¹ ἐν ἡμῖν²; 6. μείζονα δὲ �q δίδωσιν χάριν �q · o Gal. v. 17·
³διὸ λέγει· �qὁ Θεὸς ⁴ὑπερηφάνοις ἀντιτάσσεται,⁵ ταπεινοῖς
δὲ δίδωσιν χάριν.�q ³　7. ὑποτάγητε οὖν ⁶ τῷ Θεῷ· ἀντίστητε δὲ⁷

p Cf. Gen.
vi. 5, viii.
21; Num.
xi. 29.
q–q Quoted from

Prov. iii. 34(Sept.); cf. Matt. xiii. 12; Job xxii. 29; Ps. cxxxviii. 6; Prov. xxix. 23; Matt. xxiii.
12. Luke i. 52; 1 Pet. v. 5.

¹ κατωκησεν KLP, curss., Latt., Syrr., Copt., Thl., Oec., rec.
² ημιν, Ti., vobis ƒƒ.　　³—³ Om. LP, curss.　　⁴ Add κυριος 5, 16.
⁵ αντιτασσετε B.　　⁶ Om. ουν ƒƒ.
⁷ Om. δε KLP, curss., Thl., Oec., rec.

'Scripture' is analogous to the transition from τὰ βιβλία to the 'Bible'" (ibid., pp. 147 f.). In the present instance the "Scripture" is nowhere to be found in the O.T.; it is, however, reflected in some Pauline passages, Gal. v. 17, 21, and cf. Rom. viii. 6, 8; 1 Cor. iii. 16: ἡ γὰρ σὰρξ ἐπιθυμεῖ κατὰ τοῦ πνεύματος, τὸ δὲ πνεῦμα κατὰ τῆς σαρκός (Gal. v. 17); τὸ πνεῦμα τοῦ Θεοῦ οἰκεῖ ἐν ὑμῖν (1 Cor. iii. 16). It is difficult not to see a Pauline influence in our passage; and what is certainly noteworthy is the fact that the two Agrapha which the Epistle contains (i. 12 and the one before us) are both closely connected with St. Paul, i. 12 = 2 Tim. iv. 8; iv. 5 = Gal. v. 17. But that which is conclusive against the "Scripture" here referring to the O.T. is the fact that the doctrine of the Spirit is not found there in the developed form in which it is represented here; the pronounced personality of the Spirit as here used is never found in the O.T. The reference here must be to the N.T., and this is one of the many indications which point to the late date of our Epistle, or parts of it. As early a document as the Epistle of Polycarp (110 A.D.) refers once to the N.T. quotations as "Scripture"; and in the Epistle of Barnabas (about 98 A.D. according to Lightfoot, but regarded as later by most scholars) a N.T. quotation is prefaced by the formula "It is written".—πρὸς φθόνον ἐπιποθεῖ . . .: on this very difficult text see, for a variety of interpretations, Mayor's elaborate note; the best rendering seems to be that of the R.V. margin: "That Spirit which he made to dwell in us yearneth for us even unto jealous envy". The words witness to the truth that the third Person of the Holy Trinity abides in our hearts striving to acquire the same love for Him on our part which He bears for us. It is a most striking passage which tells of the love of the Holy Spirit, as (in one sense) dis-

tinct from that of the Father or that of the Son; in connection with it should be read Rom. viii. 26-28; Eph. iv. 30; 1 Thess. v. 19.

Ver. 6. μείζονα δὲ δίδωσιν χάριν: these words further emphasise the developed doctrine of the Spirit referred to above; they point to the nature of divine grace, which is almost illimitable. These verses, 5, 6, witness in a striking way to the Christian doctrine of grace, and herein breathe a different spirit from that found in most of the Epistle.—ὁ Θεὸς . . . χάριν: Cf. Sir. x. 7, 12, 18; Pss. of Sol. ii. 25, iv. 28; the quotation is also found in 1 Pet. v. 5; taken with the preceding it teaches the divinity of the Holy Spirit. Ephrem Syrus quotes this as a saying of Christ's (Opp. iii. 93 E., ed. Assemani; quoted by Resch, op. cit., p. 199).

Ver. 7. ὑποτάγητε οὖν τῷ Θεῷ: Cf. Heb. xii. 9, οὐ πολὺ μᾶλλον ὑποταγησόμεθα τῷ πατρὶ τῶν πνευμάτων καὶ ζήσομεν. It is not a question of subjection either to God or the devil, but rather one of the choice between self-will and God's will; it is the proud spirit that has to be curbed.—ἀντίστητε δὲ τῷ διαβόλῳ, καὶ φεύξεται ἀφ' ὑμῶν: the two ideas contained in these words are very Jewish; in the first place, the withstanding of the devil is represented as being within the competence of man; the more specifically Christian way of putting the matter is best seen by comparing the words before us with the two following passages: Luke x. 17, Ὑπέστρεψαν δὲ . . . λέγοντες· κύριε, καὶ τὰ δαιμόνια ὑποτάσσεται ἡμῖν ἐν τῷ ὀνόματί σου. And the passage in 1 Pet. v. 6 ff. which is parallel to the one before us, is prefaced by the words, "Casting all your anxiety upon Him, because He careth for you," and followed by the words, "And the God of all grace . . . shall Himself perfect, stablish, strengthen you". The

r Eph. vi. τῷ ᵗδιαβόλῳ, καὶ φεύξεται¹ ἀφ' ὑμῶν· 8. ᵉἐγγίσατε τῷ Θεῷ,² καὶ
11, 12; 1
Pet. v. 8, ἐγγίσει³ ὑμῖν. ᵗκαθαρίσατε χεῖρας, ἁμαρτωλοί, καὶ ᵘἁγνίσατε
9.
s 2 Chron.
xv. 2; Zech. i. 3; Luke xv. 30; cf. Lam. iii. 57.   t Isa. i. 16.   u Jer. iv. 14; 1 Pet. i. 22·
1 Jn. iii. 8.

¹ φευξετε B¹ (-ται B²).
² D(omi)no s Vulgʳ; ad dominum ff; add et ipse ff.
³ εγγιει Treg., Ti.

difference between the Jewish and Christian doctrines of grace and free-will here cannot fail to be observed. It is useless to cite the words, " Be subject unto God," as indicating divine assistance in withstanding the devil, because the subject of thought in either passage is quite independent; the meaning is not that ability to withstand the devil is the result of being subject to God; but two courses of action are enjoined, in each of which man is represented as able to take the initiative.—In the second place, the representation of Satan (the devil) here is altogether Jewish; the Hebrew root from which "Satan" comes (שׂטם) means "to oppose," or "to act as an adversary"; the idea is very clearly brought out in Num. xxii. 22, where the noun is used: *And the Angel of Jahwe placed himself in the way for an adversary* (literally "for a Satan"). This is precisely the picture represented in the words before us; the ancient Hebrew idea of something in the way is to some extent present in the Greek ὁ διάβολος, from διαβάλλω "to throw across," *i.e.*, the pathway is impeded (*cf.* Eph. iv. 27, vi. 11). Jewish demonology was full of intensely materialistic conceptions; the presence of demons in various guise, or else invisible, was always feared; primarily it was bodily harm that they did; the idea of spiritual evil, as in the passage before us, was later, though both conceptions existed side by side. The words under consideration are possibly an inexact quotation from *Test. of the Twelve Patriarchs*, Naphth. viii. 4, "If ye work that which is good my children . . . and the devil shall flee from you". Knowling quotes an interesting parallel in Hermas, *Mand.*, xii. 5, 2, where in connection with the devil it is said, "If ye resist him he will be vanquished, and will flee from you disgraced".

Ver. 8. ἐγγίσατε τῷ θεῷ, καὶ ἐγγίσει ὑμῖν: here, again, we have what to Christian ears sounds rather like a reversal of the order of things; we should expect the order to be that expressed in such words as, " Ye did not choose me, but I chose you " (John xv. 16). The words before us seem to be a quotation (inexact) from Hos. xii. 6 (Sept.), . . . ἐγγίζε πρὸς τὸν θεόν σου διὰ παντός. The Hebrew phrase אֶל־נָגַשׁ is a technical term for approaching God for the purpose of worship, *e.g.*, Exod. xix. 22; Jer. xxx. 21; Ezek. xliv. 13. There is an extraordinary passage in *Test. of the Twelve Patriarchs*, Dan. vi. 1, 2 which runs, "And now, fear the Lord, my children, and beware of Satan and his spirits. Draw near unto God and to the angel that intercedeth for you, for he is a mediator between God and man" (the latter part here is not a Christian interpolation).—καθαρίσατε χεῖρας: *Cf.* Ps. xxiv. 4, ἀθῷος χερσὶ καὶ καθαρὸς τῇ καρδίᾳ . . .; in Hos. i. 16 we have, λούσασθε, καθαροὶ γένεσθε, and in Sir. xxxviii. 10, ἀπόστησον πλημμελίαν καὶ εὔθυνον χεῖρας, καὶ ἀπὸ πάσης ἁμαρτίας καθάρισον καρδίαν. In each case it is a metaphorical use of language which otherwise expressed the literal ritual washing; the former, taken from the latter, was in use at least as early as exilic times.—ἁμαρτωλοί: the close connection with this word and the δίψυχοι which follows almost immediately recalls the language in Sir. v. 9, . . . οὕτως ὁ ἁμαρτωλὸς ὁ δίγλωσσος.—ἁγνίσατε καρδίας: the thought of these, as well as of the preceding words, is an adaptation of Ps. lxxii. (lxxiii.) 13, Ἄρα ματαίως ἐδικαίωσα τὴν καρδίαν μου, καὶ ἐνιψάμην ἐν ἀθῴοις τὰς χεῖράς μου. The verb ἁγνίζω (הִתְקַדֵּשׁ) means originally to sanctify oneself preparatory to appearing before the Lord by separating oneself from everything that might cause uncleanness; the idea of separating oneself is still present in the passage before us, because mourning implied temporary withdrawal from the world and its doings. Mayor quotes in connection with this verse, Hermas, *Mand.*, ix. 7, καθάρισον τὴν καρδίαν σου ἀπὸ τῆς διψυχίας.—δίψυχοι: *Cf.* Hos. x. 2,

καρδίας,¹ ᵛδίψυχοι. 9. ταλαιπωρήσατε καὶ ² ᵂπενθήσατε³ καὶ⁴ᵛ i. 18.
κλαύσατε⁵· ὁ γέλως ὑμῶν εἰς πένθος μετατραπήτω⁶ καὶ ἡ χαρὰ ˣ Wisd.
εἰς ˣκατήφειαν. 10. ᵞταπεινώθητε⁷ ἐνώπιον Κυρίου⁸ καὶ ὑψώσει ᵞ 1 Pet. v.
ὑμᾶς.

11. Μὴ ᶻκαταλαλεῖτε ⁹ἀλλήλων, ἀδελφοί·⁹ ¹⁰ ὁ καταλαλῶν ἀδελφοῦ ἢ ¹¹ ᵃκρίνων τὸν ἀδελφὸν αὐτοῦ καταλαλεῖ νόμου καὶ κρίνει νόμον·

w Matt.v.4.
x Wisd.
xvii. 4.
y 1 Pet. v.
6.
z 1 Pet. ii.
1; Eph.
iv. 31.
a Matt. vii.
1.

---

¹ Add vestra *ff*. ² Om. *ff*. ³ Miseri *ff*.
⁴ Om. Ti. ⁵ Om. και κλαυσατε 15, curss., Pesh.
⁶ μεταστραφητω ℵAKL, curss., Oec., Ti., Treg., WH (altern. reading).
⁷ Add ουν ℵ, 56. ⁸Pr. του D, curss., Weiss.
⁹—⁹ αδελφοι μου αλληλων A, curss. ¹⁰ Frater. *ff*. ¹¹ και KL, curss., rec. et *ff*.

---

and in addition to the passages referred to above, i. 8, *cf*. Barnabas xix. 5, οὐ μὴ διψυχήσῃς, πότερον ἔσται ἢ οὔ, and the identical words in Did. iv. 4.

Ver. 9. ταλαιπωρήσατε: ἅπ. λεγ. in N.T. *cf*. Mic. ii. 4; Jer. iv. 13; "undergo hardship"; it was a recognised tenet in Jewish theology that self-inflicted punishment of any kind was a means of reconciliation, *e.g.*, in *Mechilta*, 76a, the words of Ps. lxxxix. 32 (33 in Heb.), *I will visit their transgression with the rod, and their iniquity with stripes*, are interpreted to mean that the pain suffered under liberal chastisement is one of the means of reconciliation with God; for instances of how chastisement has reconciled men to God, see *Baba mezia*, 84 *a b*.—πενθήσατε καὶ κλαύσατε: these words are found together in 2 Esdras xviii. 9 (= Neh. viii. 9); and in Luke vi. 25 we have, οὐαὶ ὑμῖν οἱ γελῶντες νῦν, ὅτι πενθήσετε καὶ κλαύσετε. Repentance (תשובה) was, according to Jewish teaching, also in itself another of the means of reconciliation.—ὁ γέλως ὑμῶν εἰς πένθος μετατραπήτω: μετατραπ. ἅπ. λεγ. in N.T.; *cf*. Am. viii. 10, καὶ μεταστρέψω τὰς ἑορτὰς ὑμῶν εἰς πένθος.—καὶ ἡ χαρὰ εἰς κατήφειαν: *Cf*. Jer. xvi. 9; Prov. xiv. 13; the words express the contrast between the loud unseemly gaiety of the pleasure-seeker, and the subdued mien and downcast look of the penitent. κατήφειαν occurs only here in the N.T.; it is often found in Philo.

Ver 10. ταπεινώθητε ἐνώπιον Κυρίου καὶ ὑψώσει ὑμᾶς: *Cf*. Sir. ii. 17, οἱ φοβούμενοι Κύριον ἑτοιμάσουσι καρδίας αὐτῶν καὶ ἐνώπιον αὐτοῦ ταπεινώσουσι τὰς ψυχὰς αὐτῶν, and *cf*. iii. 18; in the *Test. of the Twelve Patriarchs*, Jos. xviii. 1, we read, "If ye also, therefore, walk in the commandments of

the Lord, my children, He will exalt you there (*i.e.*, on high), and will bless you with good things for ever and ever". Although the actual word is not mentioned in these vv. 7-10, it is obvious that they constitute a call to repentance. Both as establishing a proper relationship towards God, and as a means of bringing about that relationship, the need of repentance had always been greatly insisted on by Jewish teachers; in *Pirqe Aboth, e.g.*, iv. 15, it is said, "Repentance and good works are as a shield against punishment"; and Taylor quotes *Berachoth*, 17a, "It was a commonplace in the mouth of Raba that, The perfection of wisdom is repentance," *cf*. *Bereshith Rabba*, lxv.; *Nedarim*, 32b, etc., etc.

Vv. 11, 12. The subject of these verses, speaking against and judging others, is the same as that of the section ii. 1-13; they follow on quite naturally after vv. 12, 13 of that chapter, while they have nothing to do with the context in which they now stand. They constitute a weaving together of several quotations, much after the style of the section which precedes.

Ver. 11. Μὴ καταλαλεῖτε ἀλλήλων, ἀδελφοί, etc.: this speaking against one another must be taken together with the judging of one another; it is a question of deciding who is and who is not observing the *Torah*; some of the brethren were evidently arrogating to themselves the right of settling what did and what did not constitute obedience to the *Torah*, and those who, according to the idea of the former, were not keeping the *Torah*, were denounced and spoken against. Difficulties of this kind were bound to be constantly arising in a community of Jewish-Christians; if unnumbered differences of opinion with regard to legal observances was characteristic,

b 1 Macc. εἰ δὲ νόμον κρίνεις, οὐκ εἶ ¹ ᵇποιητὴς νόμου ἀλλὰ κριτής. 12. εἰς
  ii. 67;
  Rom. ii. ἐστιν ᶜνομοθέτης ² καὶ ᵈκριτής,³ ὁ δυνάμενος σῶσαι καὶ ᵉἀπολέσαι·
  13.
c Is. xxxiii. σὺ δὲ ⁴ τίς εἶ, ὁ κρίνων ⁵ τὸν ᶠπλησίον ⁶ ;
  22.
d Matt. vii. 13. ᵍἌγε ⁷ νῦν οἱ λέγοντες· ʰσήμερον ἢ ⁸ αὔριον πορευσόμεθα ⁹
  1.
e Matt. x. εἰς τήνδε τὴν πόλιν καὶ ⁱποιήσομεν ¹⁰ ἐκεῖ ¹¹ ἐνιαυτὸν ¹² καὶ ᵏἐμπορευ-
  28.
f Rom. ii. 1,
  xiv. 4.   g v. i.   h Prov. xxvii. 1; Luke xii. 18-20.   i Matt. xx. 12.   k 2 Pet. ii. 3.

¹ ουκετι KP, curss.   ² Pr. ο ℵAKL, curss., Ti., Treg., WH mg.

³ Om. και κριτης KL, curss., rec.   ⁴ Om. δε Sah., Arm., Oec., rec.

⁵ ος κρινεις KL, curss., rec.

⁶ ετερον KL, curss., rec.; add οτι ουκ εν ανθρωπω αλλ εν Θεω τα διαβηματα
ανθρωπου κατευθυνεται K, curss.

⁷ Jam ff.   ⁸ και AKLP, curss., Cyr., Thl., Oec., rec.

⁹ πορευσωμεθα AKL, curss., Thl.   ¹⁰ ποιησωμεν ℵAKL, curss., Treg.

¹¹ Om. A, 13, Cyr.   ¹² Add ενα AKL, curss., Syrr., Arm., Cyr., Thl., Oec., rec.

as we know it to have been, of Rabbin-
ism, it was the most natural thing in the
world for Jewish-Christians to differ upon
the extent to which they held the *Torah*
to be binding. The writer of the Epistle
is finding fault on two counts; firstly,
the fact of the brethren speaking against
one another at all, and secondly, their
presuming to decide what was and what
was not *Torah* - observance. — καταλαλεῖ νόμου καὶ κρίνει νόμον :
the reason why speaking against and
judging a brother is equivalent to doing
the same to the Law is because the Law
has been misinterpreted and misapplied ;
the Law had, in fact, been maligned ; it
had been made out to be something that
it was not. It is not a general principle,
therefore, which is being laid down here,
viz. : that speaking against a brother or
judging a brother is always necessarily
speaking against and judging the Law ;
these things are breaches of the Law, but
not necessarily for that reason denunciation of it ; the point here, as already remarked, is a maligning of the Law by
making it out to be something that it was
not. It is not a general principle, but a
specific case, which is referred to here.—
εἰ δὲ νόμον κρίνεις, οὐκ εἶ ποιητὴς . . . κριτής: here again it is a
specific case which is referred to; as a
general principle the statement would be
contrary to fact, for it is possible to give
a judgment upon the Law, in the sense of
criticising it, or even to denounce it, and
yet obey it ; the Rabbis were constantly
discussing and giving their judgments on
points of the Law, and were nevertheless
earnest observers of its precepts. When
a man misinterpreted the Law, and then

acted upon that misinterpretation, and denounced others who did not do likewise,
then he was truly not a doer of the Law,
but a judge,—and a very bad one too.

Ver. 12. εἰς ἐστιν νομοθέτης
καὶ κριτής; the words are intended
to show the arrogant impertinence of
those who were judging their neighbours
on a misinterpretation of the Law. The
word νομοθέτης does not occur elsewhere
in the N.T., though νομοθετέω and νομο-
θεσία do; *cf.* Ps. xxvii. 11.—ὁ δυνάμενος σῶσαι καὶ ἀπολέσαι:
Cf. Matt. x. 28, τὸν δυνάμενον καὶ ψυχὴν
καὶ σῶμα ἀπολέσαι ἐν γεέννη, and Luke
vi. 9.—σὺ δὲ τίς εἶ ὁ κρίνων τὸν
πλησίον: we find very similar words
in Rom. xiv. 4, σὺ τίς εἶ ὁ κρίνων ἀλ-
λότριον οἰκέτην; In *Pirqe Aboth*, i. 7,
we read, "Judge every man in the scale
of merit," *i.e.*, Give every man the benefit of the doubt (Taylor) ; *cf. Shabbath*,
127b, "He who thus judges others will
thus himself be judged".

Vv. 13-17 form an independent section
entirely unconnected with what precedes
or follows. The section is very interesting as giving a picture of the commercial
Diaspora-Jew. The Jews of the Dispersion had, from the outset, to give up agricultural pursuits ; since for the most part
they congregated in the cities it was
commerce in which they engaged chiefly.
A good instance of the *Diaspora*-Jew
going from city to city occurs in Josephus,
Antiq., xii. 2-5 (160-185), though the
period dealt with is far anterior to that
of our Epistle. Egypt was, of course,
the greatest centre of attraction, and
many wealthy Jews were to be numbered
among the large Jewish population of

σόμεθα¹ καὶ κερδήσομεν². 14. οἵτινες οὐκ ἐπίστασθε³ τῆς ¹αὔ- 1—1 i. 10;
ριον⁴· ποία⁵ ἡ⁶ ζωὴ ὑμῶν⁷; ἀτμὶς γάρ ἐστε⁸ ἡ⁹ πρὸς ὀλίγον
φαινομένη, ἔπειτα καὶ¹⁰ ἀφανιζομένη.¹ 15. ἀντὶ τοῦ λέγειν ὑμᾶς·

Job vii. 7;
Ps.xxxix.
6, 12; cii.
3: Luke
xii. 20; 1
Cor. vii.
31.

¹ εμπορευσωμεθα KL, curss.   ²κερδησωμεν KL, curss.   ³επισταται P, 68.

⁴ το της αυρ. אKL, curss., Latt., Pesh., Sah., Copt., Thl., Oec., Treg., Ti.; τα της
αυρ. AP, 7, 13, 69, 106, a, c, Syrʰᵏ, Tregᵐᵍ, WH (altern. reading).

⁵ Add γαρ א³AKLP, curss., Tregᵐᵍ (WH altern. reading); add autem ff.

⁶ Om. B.   ⁷ ημων 13, 69, Syrʰᵏ, Thl.; ff runs on without the interrogative.

⁸ Om. ατμις γαρ εστε א; om. γαρ A, Vulg., Copt.; momentum enim est ff.
Vulg., Copt., Thl. read εστιν; AKP, curss. read εσται.

⁹ Om. η BP, WH.

¹⁰ Pr. δε LPב, curss.; δε Sah., Thl., Oec.; om. 36, 38, 69, Syrʰᵏ, Copt.

Alexandria; Philo speaks of Jewish ship-owners and merchants in this city (*In Flaccum*, viii.). When such Jews embraced Christianity there would be, obviously, no reason for them to give up their calling. It must, however, be confessed that both this section and the following read far more naturally as addressed to Jews than to Jewish-Christians. Ver. 13.—Ἄγε: this expression of disapproval occurs only here and in v. 1 in the N.T.; although it is used here and there in the Septuagint, it is the rendering of different Hebrew words; one may compare, though it is not the equivalent of ἄγε, the Aramaic expression of disapproval יא לכן ("Ah you!" literally "Woe unto you"). Ἄγε is used with either a singular or a plural subject, *cf.* Jud. xix. 6; 2 Kings iv. 24.—σήμερον ἢ αὔριον πορευσόμεθα: *Cf.* Prov. xxvii. 1, μὴ καυχῶ τὰ εἰς αὔριον, οὐ γὰρ γινώσκεις τί τέξεται ἡ ἐπιοῦσα. There is a Rabbinical saying, in *Sanhed.*, 100b, which runs: "Care not for the morrow, for ye know not what a day may bring forth. Perhaps he may not be [alive] on the morrow, and so have cared for a world that does not exist for him" (quoted by Edersheim, *Life and Times*, ii. 539); *cf.* Luke xii. 16 ff.; xiii. 32, 33.—ἐμπορευσόμεθα: 2 Pet. ii. 3 is the only other passage in the N.T. in which this word occurs; it means primarily "to travel," then to travel for the purpose of trading, and finally "to trade" simply.—κερδήσομεν: a rare form; "the Attic is κερδανῶ, with aorist ἐκέρδανα, Ion. and late Attic κερδήσομαι, aorist ἐκέρδησα; the latter occurs often in the N.T." (Mayor). Ver. 14. οἵτινες οὐκ ἐπίστα-

σθε τὸ τῆς αὔριον: "Ye are they that know not . . ."; it is the contrast between the ignorance of men, with the consequent incertitude of all that the morrow may bring forth, and the knowledge of God in accordance with Whose will (*cf.* ἐὰν ὁ κύριος θελήσῃ in the next verse) all things come to pass.—ποία ἡ ζωὴ ὑμῶν; "Of what kind is your life"? The reference here is not to the life of the wicked, but to the uncertainty of human life in general; the thought of the ungodly being cut off is, it is true, often expressed in the Bible, but that is not what is here referred to; it is evidently not conscious sin, but thoughtlessness which the writer is rebuking here.—ἀτμὶς γάρ ἐστε: the reading ἐστε, in preference to ἐστι or ἔσται, makes the address more personal; ἀτμὶς is often used for "smoke," *e.g.*, Acts ii. 17; *cf.* Ps. cii. 3 (4), ἐξέλιπον ὡσεὶ καπνὸς αἱ ἡμέραι μου; the word only occurs here in the N.T., in Acts ii. 19 it is a quotation from Joel ii. 30 (Sept.) iii. 3 (Heb.). In Job vii. 7 we have μνήσθητι ὅτι πνεῦμά μου ἡ ζωή, *cf.* Wisd. ii. 4; the rendering "breath" instead of "vapour" does not commend itself on account of the former being invisible, and the point of the words is that man does *appear* for a little time (πρὸς ὀλίγον φαινομένη) and then disappears, *cf.* Wisd. xvi. 6.—ἀφανιζομένη: the word occurs, though in a different connection, in Sir. xlv. 26.

Ver. 15. ἀντὶ τοῦ λέγειν ὑμᾶς: "A classical writer would rather have said δέον λέγειν or οἵτινες βέλτιον ἂν εἶπον" (Mayor).—ἐὰν ὁ κύριος θελήσῃ: *Cf. Berachoth*, 17a, "It is revealed and known before Thee that our will is to do Thy will" (quoted by Taylor,

m Acts
xviii. 21;
cf. Dan.
v 23.
n Rom. i.
30; 2
Tim. iii.
2; 1 Jn.
ii. 16.
o 1 Cor. v. 6; cf. 2 Cor. vii. 4.

ἐὰν ὁ Κύριος ᵐθελήσῃ,¹ καὶ ζήσομεν² καὶ³ ποιήσομεν⁴ τοῦτο ἢ ἐκεῖνο.⁵ 16. νῦν δὲ καυχᾶσθε⁶ ἐν ταῖς ⁿἀλαζονίαις⁷ ὑμῶν· πᾶσα⁸ ᵒκαύχησις τοιαύτη πονηρά ἐστιν. 17. ᵖεἰδότι οὖν⁹ καλὸν ποιεῖν καὶ μὴ ποιοῦντι,¹⁰ ἁμαρτία αὐτῷ¹¹ ἐστιν.ᵖ

p—p Luke xii. 47, 48; Jn. ix. 41, xv. 22; Rom. xiv. 23; 2 Pet. ii. 21; cf. Rom. i. 20, 21, 32, ii. 17, 18, 23; 1 Tim. i. 13.

¹ θελη BP, 69, a, d, Tregmg, WH.

²ζησωμεν KL⅂, curss., Cyr., Thl., Oec.; pr. si Vulg. (om. s Vulgᴀ).

³Om. Vulg., Pesh., Sah., Copt., Arm., Aeth, Cyr.

⁴ποιησωμεν KL⅂, curss., Thl., Oec.   ⁵ Totum comma deest s.

⁶κατακαυχασθε ℵ, 7.   ⁷ αλαζονειαις B³K, Treg., Weiss; superbia ff.

⁸απασα ℵ.   ⁹ Scientibus autem ff.   ¹⁰ Facientibus ff.   ¹¹ Illis ff.

op. cit., p. 29); cf. John vii. 17, ἐάν τις θέλῃ τὸ θέλημα αὐτοῦ ποιεῖν, γνώσεται . . . In the Hebrew commentary on a curious little work called The Book of the Alphabet of Ben Sira there occur the words **גזר שם אם**, i.e., "If the Name (= God) wills"; and it is said that this formula should never be omitted when a man is about to undertake anything. This passage occurs in the comment on the eleventh proverb of the "Alphabet," which runs : "The bride enters the bridal chamber and, nevertheless, knows not what will befall her". The formula, "If the Name wills," is, according to Ginsberg, of Mohammedan origin, "for the use of formulas was introduced to the Jews by the Mohammedans". The formula is, of course, not Ben Sira's, as it forms no part of the work ascribed to him; the commentary in which it occurs belongs to about the year 1000 probably (see Jewish Encycl., ii. 678 f.). Cf., further, Acts xviii. 21, τοῦ θεοῦ θέλοντος, 1 Cor. iv. 19, ἐὰν ὁ κύριος θελήσῃ; and in Pirqe Aboth, ii. 4 occur the words of Rabban Gamliel (middle of third century A.D.), "Do His will as if it were thy will, that He may do thy will as if it were His will. Annul thy will before His will, that He may annul the will of others before thy will" (Taylor). —καὶ ζήσομεν καὶ . . . both life and action depend upon God's will.

Ver. 16. νῦν δὲ: "but now," i.e., as things are; cf. 1 Cor. xiv. 6, νῦν δὲ, ἀδελφοί, ἐὰν ἔλθω . . .—καυχᾶσθε ἐν ταῖς ἀλαζονίαις ὑμῶν: those vauntings were, of course, not on account of following out their own will in despite of the divine will, but because of the thoughtlessness which did not take God's will into account, and therefore boasted of the ability of following one's own bent. Both are bad, but conscious opposition to the will of God would, of the two, be worse. Ἀλαζονίαις comes from ἀλαζών which is literally a "wanderer," then it comes to mean one who makes pretensions. Cf. Prov. xxvii. 1, μὴ καυχῶ τὰ εἰς αὔριον, οὐ γὰρ γινώσκεις τί τέξεται ἡ ἐπιοῦσα: the word occurs only here and in 1 John ii. 16 (ἡ ἀλαζονεία τοῦ βίου) in the N.T.—πᾶσα καύχησις τοιαύτη . . . : boasting of this kind must be evil because it forgets God, and unduly exalts self.

Ver. 17. Although this verse may be regarded as standing independent of what has preceded, and as being in the form of a more or less inexact quotation, it is quite permissible to take it with what has gone before. Those to whom the words have been addressed had, to some extent, erred through thoughtlessness; now that things have been made quite plain to them, they are in a position to know how to act; if, therefore, in spite of knowing now how to act aright, the proper course is neglected, then it is sinful. This seems to be the point of the words of this verse.—The words are perhaps an echo of Luke xii. 47, ἐκεῖνος δὲ ὁ δοῦλος ὁ γνοὺς τὸ θέλημα τοῦ κυρίου αὐτοῦ καὶ μὴ ἑτοιμάσας ἢ ποιήσας πρὸς τὸ θέλημα αὐτοῦ δαρήσεται πολλάς. With καλὸν ποιεῖν cf. Gal. vi. 9, τὸ δὲ καλὸν ποιοῦντες μὴ ἐνκακῶμεν.—ἁμαρτία αὐτῷ ἐστιν: for the converse of this, namely, doing what is wrong in ignorance—in which case it is excusable—see Acts iii. 17, "And now, brethren, I wot that in ignorance ye did it, as did also your rulers"; 1 Tim. i 13, ". . . howbeit, I obtained mercy, because I did it ignorantly in unbelief".—It is, however, quite possible that we have in these words the enunciation of the principle that sins of omission

V. 1. ᵃἌΓΕ νῦν οἱ ᵇπλούσιοι, κλαύσατε¹ ὀλολύζοντες ἐπὶ ταῖς

a iv. 13.
b Am. vi. 1;
Prov. xi.
28; Luke vi. 24; 1 Tim. vi. 9.

¹ κλαυσονται 13.

are as sinful as those of commission; when our Lord says, ". . . these things ought ye to have done, and not to have left the other undone" (Matt. xxiii. 23), it is clear that the sins of omission are regarded as wilful sin equally with those of commission, *cf.* Matt. xxv. 41-45. There is always a tendency to reckon the things which are left undone as less serious than actually committed sin; this was certainly, though not wholly so, in Judaism. It is exceptional when we read, for example, in 1 Sam. xii. 23, "God forbid that I should sin against the Lord in ceasing to pray for you"; as a rule sins of omission are regarded as venial, according to the Jewish doctrine, and are not punishable. The conception of sin according to Rabbinical ideas is well seen in what is called the '*Al Chêt* (*i.e.*, "For the sin," from the opening words of each sentence in the great *Widdui* ["Confession"] said on *Yom Kippur* ["the Day of Atonement"]); in the long list of sins here, mention is made only of committed sins. In the Jerusalem Talmud (*Yoma*, viii. 6) it is said that the Day of Atonement brings atonement, even without repentance, for sins of omission; in *Pesikta*, 7*b* the words in Zeph. i. 12, "I will search Jerusalem with candles, and I will punish the men . . .," are commented on by saying, "not by daylight, nor with the torch, but with candles, so as not to detect venial sins," among these being, of course, included sins of omission. Although this is, in the main, the traditional teaching, there are some exceptions to be found, *e.g.*, *Shabbath*, 54*b*; "'Whosoever is in a position to prevent sins being committed by the members of his household, but refrains from doing so, becomes liable for their sins.' The same rule applies to the govenour of a town, or even of a whole country" (see *Jewish Encycl.*, xi. 378). Having regard to the very Jewish character of our Epistle, it is quite possible that in the verse before us the reference is to this subject of sins of omission.

Chapter V.—Chap. V. contains five distinct sections; of great interest is the fact that the first two—1-6, 7-11—deal respectively with Jewish and Christian Eschatology; this subject will be dealt with presently; ver. 12 is a short section

containing an adaptation of some words from the "Sermon on the Mount"; 13-18 deals with the subject of the visitation of the sick in the early Church; while vv. 19, 20 bring the Epistle to an abrupt termination with a very pronounced utterance upon the Jewish doctrine of works. Each of these sections is self-contained, and it would be impossible to have a clearer or more pointed illustration than this chapter offers of the "patchwork" character of our Epistle.

It will not be necessary, in dealing with the very large subject of Jewish Eschatology, to do more than indicate very briefly its connection with the section vv. 1-6 of this chapter; at the same time, a slight reference to its leading ideas is essential, as some of these are referred in this passage; one of these is the punishment about to overtake the wicked —who are often identified with the *rich* —in the "last days". Jewish Eschatology, or the "Doctrine of the last things," is based on the teaching of the O.T. prophets regarding the "Day of the Lord," or, as the phrase runs, "the last day," or "last time"; another formula which occurs frequently is "in those days". "By the time of the New Testament period Judaism was in possession of most, if not all, of its eschatological ideas. These had been developed during the two eventful centuries that immediately preceded the rise of Christianity. It was these centuries which saw the rise of the *Apocalyptic Movement* with its vast eschatological developments that were essentially bound up with the doctrine of a future life, and a belief in a judgment after death, with rewards and punishments" (Oesterley and Box, *op. cit.*, p. 211). The four outstanding subjects that the doctrine of the last things comprises are: (1) The signs of the approach of the "Messianic Era"—this latter took the place of the "Day of the Lord" in the development of eschatological thought, (2) the actual advent of the Messiah, together with the great events that should then come to pass, *viz.*, the ingathering of Israel and the resurrection of the dead; (3) The judgment upon the wicked; (4) The blessedness of the righteous (*Cf.* the writer's *The Doctrine of the Last Things*). In

c Rom. iii. ᶜταλαιπωρίαις ὑμῶν ταῖς ἐπερχομέναις.¹ 2. ὁ πλοῦτος ὑμῶν ᵈσέ-
16.
d Matt. vi.
19, 20.

¹ Add υμιν ℵ, 5, 8, 25, Vulg., Pesh., Copt., Arm., Aeth.

the passage before us (vv. 1-6) three of the above are referred to, *viz.*, the Messianic Era; the punishment of the wicked, and (implicitly) the blessedness of the righteous. In ver. 3 the phrase ἐν ἐσχάταις ἡμέραις points indubitably to the times of the Messiah; the language is that of *Jewish* Eschatology based on prophetic teaching (*cf.* Isa. ii. 2; Mic. iv. 1; Hos. iii. 5; Joel iii. 1; Am. viii. 11, ix. 11; Zech. viii. 23). In vv. 1, 3 the punishment of the wicked is referred in the words, κλαύσατε ὀλολύζοντες ἐπὶ ταῖς ταλαιπωρίαις ὑμῶν ταῖς ἐπερχομέναις : . . .καὶ ὁ ἰὸς αὐτῶν . . . φάγεται τὰς σάρκας ὑμῶν ὡς πῦρ; as illustrating this *cf. Book of Enoch* xcvi. 8, "Woe unto you mighty who violently oppress the righteous, for the day of your destruction will come; in that time many happy days will come for the righteous, then shall ye be condemned"; xciv. 7, 8, 9, "Woe to those that build their houses with sin . . . ; and those who acquire gold and silver will perish in judgment suddenly. Woe to you, ye rich, for ye have trusted in your riches. . . . Ye have committed blasphemy and unrighteousness, and have become ready for the day of slaughter and the day of darkness and the day of the great judgment"; xcv. 7, "Woe to you sinners, for ye persecute the righteous . . .; xcvi, 4, "Woe unto you, ye sinners, for your riches make you appear like the righteous . . . and this word shall be a testimony against you"; many other similar quotations could be given, the striking resemblance in thought and language with our passage cannot fail to be observed; see further below, ver. 1. And lastly, in ver. 6, there is an implicit reference to the happiness of the righteous, in the words, κατεδικάσατε, ἐφονεύσατε τὸν δίκαιον· οὐκ ἀντιτάσσεται ὑμῖν; that is to say, the righteous can afford to suffer such ill-treatment because he knows that the time of essedness is coming for him; this is also frequently referred to in the Book of Enoch, *e.g.*, xcvi. 1, "Be hopeful, ye righteous; for suddenly will the sinners perish before you, and ye will have lordship over them according to your desires; 3, Wherefore, fear not, ye that suffer; for healing will be your portion". The non-mention in our passage of the actual

advent of the Messiah by name was characteristic of Jewish usage at certain periods, and is significant here. On the other hand, the section comprising vv. 7-11 is wholly Christian; the utterly different tone and language of this, as compared with the section vv.1-6, cannot be accounted for by saying that the one is addressed to the wicked, the other to the righteous; because in the latter there is a distinct reference to those who are in danger of being judged on account of murmuring against one another (ver. 9). But there are one or two points whereby the respectively Jewish and Christian form of Eschatology may be clearly discerned. (1) The language on which Jewish eschatological ideas are based is that of the prophets; the section vv. 1-6 is steeped in O.T. phraseology; on the other hand, the actual references to the Advent in vv. 7-11 are in N.T. language; the O.T. references in this section have nothing to do with the Advent. (2) It is characteristic of Jewish Eschatology that, generally speaking, there is indefiniteness as to when the Messianic Era will be inaugurated; it differs herein somewhat from the prophetical teaching, owing, as a matter of fact, to the rise of apocalyptic conceptions: on the other hand, the Christian, like the prophetical, view of the Advent is that it will take place in the very near future (". . . behold the judge standeth at the door "). (3) In Jewish pre-Christian eschatological literature the Messianic Era is frequently depicted without any reference to the personality of the Messiah; on the other hand, in the N.T., it is the rule that when the second Advent is referred to Christ is mentioned under the titles of the "Son of Man " or the "Lord " (*cf.* Matt. x. 23, xiii. 41, 42, xvi. 27, 28, xix. 28, xxv. 31-33, etc., Phil. iv. 5, ὁ κύριος ἐγγύς, 1 Cor. xvi. 22, μαρὰν ἀθά, and see *Didache*, x. 6, εἴ τις ἅγιός ἐστιν, ἐρχέσθω· εἴ τις οὐκ ἐστί, μετανοείτω· μαρὰν ἀθά. ἀμήν). (4) Besides there being no reference to the personality of the Messiah in the Jewish eschatological section there is the further contrast between it and the Christian section that in the latter the distinctively Christian expression ἡ παρουσία τοῦ κυρίου twice occurs; against this the Jewish section

·σηπεν, καὶ τὰ °ἱμάτια ὑμῶν ᶠσητόβρωτα γέγονεν· 3. ὁ χρυσὸς
ὑμῶν ¹ καὶ ὁ ἄργυρος ᵍ κατίωται,¹ καὶ ὁ ἰὸς αὐτῶν εἰς μαρτύριον ὑμῖν

e Cf. ii. 2.
f Bar.vi.12;
Job xiii.
28.
g Sir.xii.11.

¹—¹ κατιωται και ο αργυρος A꠱, 13.

makes use of the distinctively Jewish title for God, the "Lord of Sabaoth".

It is thus difficult to resist the conclusion that we have here, in the section vv. 1-6, a passage which did not originally belong to the Epistle at all, but was taken or adapted from some Jewish eschatological work; it will be generally acknowledged that this section has absolutely nothing specifically Christian about it. That the writer (compiler?) should have incorporated this in his Epistle is quite natural, seeing that he was writing to Jews; equally as natural is it that he should, as a Christian writing to (Jewish-) Christians, add the developed Christian form of the same subject, interspersing it with O.T. references for the sake of his hearers [see further, *Bk. of Jubilees*, i. 29, v. 12, xxiii. 26-30; *Enoch*, x. 13, xvi. 1; *Ass. of Moses*, i. 18, x. 13; *Test. of the Twelve Patriarchs*, Reuben, vi. 8; *Apoc. Bar.* xxvii. 15, xxix. 8, lvi. 2; 4 *Esdr.* ix. 5].

Ver. 1. Ἄγε νῦν: See above iv. 13. —κλαύσατε ὀλολύζοντες ἐπὶ ταῖς ταλαιπωρίαις ὑμῶν ταῖς ἐπερχομέναις: according to the original prophetic conception these "miseries" which were to overtake the wicked, were to come to pass in the "Day of the Lord," *i.e.*, during the Messianic Era; this belief became extended during the development of ideas which took place during the two centuries preceding the Christian Era. Whatever the reasons were which brought about the belief, it is certain that the expression "those days" came to be applied to a certain period which was immediately to *precede* the coming of the Messiah; without doubt a number of prophetical passages were regarded as suggesting this (see below). The descriptions given of these "days," which are to foretell the advent of the Messiah, belong to apocalyptic conceptions; in their general outline the "signs" of these times are identical. Prophetical passages such as the following laid the foundation : "The iniquity of Ephraim is bound up; his sin is laid up in store. The sorrows of a travailing woman shall come upon him . . ."; then, on the other hand, "I will ransom them from the power of the

grave; I will redeem them from death . . ." (Hos. xiii. 12-14); again, ". . . The day of thy watchmen, even thy visitation, is come; now shall be their perplexity. Trust ye not in a friend, put ye not confidence in a guide . . . for the son dishonoureth the father, the daughter riseth up against her mother . . . a man's enemies are the men of his own house" (Mic. vii. 4-6); another characteristic which played a great part in the later apocalypse is contained in Joel ii. 10 ff., "the earth quaketh before them; the heavens tremble; the sun and the moon are darkened, and the stars withdraw their shining. . . . *Cf.* Zech. xiv. 6 ff.; Dan. xii. 1, etc., etc. Throughout the immense domain of apocalyptic literature these themes are developed to an enormous extent; they are familiar to us from the Gospels, Matt. xxiv., xxv.; Mark xiii. 14-27; Luke xxi. 9-19. In Jewish literature references to them also occur with frequency; this period is called the time of "travail," and more specifically, the "birth-pangs," or "sufferings" of the Messiah—*Cheble ha-Meshiach*, or *Cheblo shel Mashiach*, see *Pesikta rab.*, xxi. 34; *Shabbath*, 118*a*; *Sanhedrin*, 96*b*, 97*a*, etc., etc. See further Oesterley, *The Doctrine of the Last Things*, chap. vii. The great diffusion and immense popularity which the apocalyptic literature enjoyed makes it certain that the writer of our Epistle was familiar with the subject; the "miseries," therefore, referred to in the passage before us may quite possibly have reference to the sufferings which were to take place in the time of travail preceding the actual coming of the Messiah.—ὀλολύζοντες: only here in the N.T., but fairly frequent in the Septuagint, Isa. xiii. 6; Joel i. 5, 13; Jer. iv. 8, etc.; in the first of these passages the connection is the same as here, . . . ἐγγὺς γὰρ ἡμέρα κυρίου, and see Luke vi. 24, "Woe unto you rich . . .," which is strongly reminiscent of the verse before us.

Ver. 2. The use of the Hebraic prophetic perfects in this passage is another mark of Jewish authorship. ὁ πλοῦτος ὑμῶν: this cannot refer to wealth in the abstract because this would be out of harmony with the rest of the verse which

h *Cf.* Prov. ἔσται ¹ καὶ φάγεται ² τὰς σάρκας ὑμῶν ὡς ³ h πῦρ.⁴ ¹ ἐθησαυρί-
xvi. 27.
i Rom. ii. 5; σατε ⁵ ἐν k ἐσχάταις ἡμέραις.⁶   4. ἰδοὺ ⁷ ὁ ¹ μισθὸς ⁸ τῶν ἐργατῶν
cf. Mic.
vi. 10;   τῶν ἀμησάντων τὰς m χώρας ὑμῶν ὁ ἀφυστερημένος ⁹ ἀφ᾽ ὑμῶν ¹⁰
Matt. vi.
19.
k *Cf.* v. 8, 9.   1 Lev. xix. 13; Job xxiv. 10, 11; Jer. xxii. 13; Sir. iv. 1, xxxiv. 22.   m *Cf.*
Luke xxi. 21.

¹ Om. *s.*   ² φαινετε אֹ¹.   ³ Pr. ο ιος ΑΡℶ, curss.

⁴ Add o Aeth., Thl.   ⁵ Add vobis iram Vulg. (om. *s*, om. iram VulgF).

⁶ ημεραις εσχαταις A.   ⁷ Pr. et *ff.*   ⁸ Mercedes *ff.*

⁹ απεστερημενος AB³P, curss.; αποστερημενος KL; quod abnegastis *ff.*

¹⁰ Om. αφ υμων *ff.*

---

speaks of literal destruction; we have
here precisely the same idea, as to actual
destruction, as that which occurs in the
eschatological passage *Enoch*, xcviii. 1
ff., where in reference to foolish men
"in royalty, and in grandeur, and in
power, and in silver and in gold, and in
purple . . .," it says that "they will perish thereby together with their possessions and with all their glory and their
splendour".—σέσηπεν: ἅπ. λεγ. in
N.T., *cf.* Sir. xiv. 19, πᾶν ἔργον σηπόμε.
νον ἐκλείπει.—σητόβρωτα: ἅπ. λεγ·
in N.T., *cf.* Job xiii. 28, παλαιοῦται
ὥσπερ ἱμάτιον σητόβρωτον; Sir. xlii. 13,
ἀπὸ γὰρ ἱματίων ἐκπορεύεται σής. For
the form of the word *cf.* σκωληκόβρωτος
in Acts xii. 23.

Ver. 3. κατίωται: in Sir. xii. 11
we have καὶ γνώσῃ ὅτι οὐκ εἰς τέλος
κατίωσεν in reference to a mirror; the
Hebrew, which is followed by the Syriac,
is corrupt, but evidently read חֶלְאָה,
which is the same word used in the preceding verse (ἰοῦται); the Hebrew word
may perhaps be used in the sense of
"filth" (see Oxford Hebrew Lexicon,
s.v.), and possibly this more general
term is what was originally intended in
the verse before us, since gold cannot
strictly be said to rust. The word occurs
in one other passage *viz.*, in Sir., xxix.
10, but unfortunately the Hebrew for this
is wanting. The force of the κατα is intensive.—ὁ ἰός: used in iii. 8 of the
poison of the tongue, in a figurative sense;
the meaning "rust" is secondary.—εἰς
μαρτύριον ὑμῖν ἔσται: this metaphor is quite in the Hebrew style; עֵד
(= μαρτύριον), though generally used of
persons, is in a fair number of instances
used of inanimate things in the O.T.; *cf.*
in the N.T. Mark vi. 11; Luke ix. 5.—
φάγεται: a Hellenistic form, unclassical, *cf.* Sir. xxxiii, 23 (Sept.) πᾶν βρῶμα
φάγεται κοιλία, *cf.* xi. 19, xlv. 21 (Sept.).

—τὰς σάρκας ὑμῶν: "The plural
σάρκες is used for the fleshy parts of the
body both in classical and later writers
. . . while the singular σάρξ is used for
the whole body" (Mayor); in the Septuagint we meet with a similar phrase in
a number of cases, *e.g.*, Mic. iii. 3.
. . . κατέφαγον τὰς σάρκας τοῦ λαοῦ
μου; 2 Kings ix. 36; in these and other
instances the Hebrew בָּשָׂר (= σάρξ)
is always in the singular (unlike "blood,"
which is often used in the plural).—ὡς
πῦρ: this comparison must probably
have been suggested by the fact that fire,
in a literal sense, often figures in apocalyptic pictures, *cf.*, *e.g.*, *Enoch*, cii. 1,
"And in those days when He brings a
grievous fire upon you, whither will ye
flee, and where will ye find deliverance?" xcviii. 3, where mention is made
of "the furnace of fire," x. 13, "the abyss
of fire"; this idea arose originally because "Gehenna" was conceived of as
the place of torment, and a fire in the
literal sense was constantly burning in
the valley of Hinnom; the fire in the place
of torment is referred to in Matt. xxv. 41
τὸ πῦρ τὸ αἰώνιον, Mark ix. 44 ὅπου ὁ
σκώληξ αὐτῶν οὐ τελευτᾷ καὶ τὸ πῦρ οὐ
σβέννυται, Jude 7 πυρὸς αἰωνίου . . .
See Carr's interesting note on ὡς πῦρ.
ἐθησαυρίσατε.—ἐν ἐσχάταις ἡμέραις: see prefatory note to this chapter.
Ver. 4. ἰδοὺ: this interjection, though
good Attic, is used by some N.T. writers
with a frequency which is unclassical,
(Mayor) *e.g.*, in this short Epistle it occurs
six times, while on the other hand St. Paul
uses it only nine times (once in a quotation) in the whole of his writings; its
frequent occurrence is a mark of Jewish
authorship, as Jews were accustomed to
the constant use of an equivalent interjection (הִנֵּה) in their own tongue.
—ὁ μισθὸς τῶν ἐργατῶν: μισθός
occurs several times in Sir. in the sense

κράζει,[1] καὶ αἱ [n]βοαὶ τῶν θερισάντων εἰς τὰ ὦτα Κυρίου [o]σα-[n] Deut.
xxiv. 14,
βαὼθ εἰσελήλυθαν.[2] 5. [p]ἐτρυφήσατε ἐπὶ τῆς γῆς καὶ[3] [q]ἐσπατα- 15; Is.v.9;
Job xxxi.
λήσατε, [r]ἐθρέψατε τὰς καρδίας ὑμῶν ἐν[4] ἡμέρᾳ[5] [s]σφαγῆς. 38-40; cf.
Exod. ii.
23.

[o] Rom. ix. 29; Rev. xviii. 5.   [p] Cf. Job xxi. 13; Luke xvi. 19, 25; 2 Pet. ii. 13.   [q] Am. vi.
(Sept.); cf. 1 Tim. v. 6.   [r] Luke xxi. 34.   [s] Quoted from Jer. xii. 3; cf. 1 Sam. ix. 12, 13.
Ezek. xxxiv. 3.

[1] Clamabunt ff.

[2] εισεληλυθασιν ℵKL, curss.; εισεληλυθεν A; εισεληλυθεισαν ⊐.

[3] Om. και A, 73, Copt.   [4] ως εν ℵ[3]AKL⊐, curss.   [5] ημεραις A.

of reward, but not in that of wages due; in the same book ἐργάτης occurs twice (xix. 1, xl. 18), but in neither case with the meaning "agricultural labourer," which is its usual meaning in the N.T., cf. Matt. ix. 37, but on the other hand Luke. x 7, ἄξιος ὁ ἐργάτης τοῦ μισθοῦ αὐτοῦ.— τῶν ἀμησάντων: ἅπ. λεγ. in N.T.; whatever difference of meaning there may have been originally between ἀμᾶν and θερίζειν they are used as synonyms in the Septuagint, and the same is true, according to Mayor, of classical Greek. —τὰς χώρας ὑμῶν: often, as here, used in the restricted sense of "fields," cf. for the variety of meaning which it can bear the three instances of its occurrence in Sir. x. xliii. 3, xlvii. 17; for its meaning of "fields," both in singular and plural, see Luke xii. 16, xxi. 21; John iv. 35.—ὁ ἀφυστερημένος ἀφ' ὑμῶν: "which is kept back by you," "on your part," or as Mayor renders as an alternative, "comes too late from you"; the ἀφ' ὑμῶν is not really required, it is omitted by ff. The withholding of wages due was evidently a sin of frequent occurrence, see Lev. xix. 13; Deut. xxiv. 14, 15; Job xxiv. 10; Mic. iii. 10; Jer. xxii. 13; Prov. iii. 27, 28; Mal. iii. 5; Sir. xxxi. (xxxiv.) 22; Tob. iv. 14.—ἀφυστ. only here in N.T.— κράζει: a thoroughly Hebraic idea which occurs several times in the O.T., cf. for the "crying out" of inanimate things, Gen. iv. 10; Job xxiv. 12; Ps. lxxxiv. 2; Prov. viii. 1; Lam. ii. 18; Hab. ii. 11.—αἱ βοαί: only here in N.T., cf. Exod. xi. 23.—εἰς τὰ ὦτα κυρίου σαβαώθ: quoted from Isa. v. 9; one of the many marks in this section, vv. 1-6, which suggest that it did rot originally belong to the N.T.; it is certainly extraordinary that the usual Septu-

agint rendering, Κύριος παντοκράτωρ or ὁ Κύριος τῶν δυνάμεων, is not used here; though it is true σαβαώθ is sometimes transliterated, it is nevertheless exceptional. "Jahwe Sabaoth" was the ancient Israelite name of Jehovah as war-god.

Ver. 5. ἐτρυφήσατε: ἅπ. λεγ. in N.T.; it occurs in Sir. xiv. 4 for the Hebrew ברע,* which means "to revel," followed by ב. Luther translates: Ihr habt wohlgelebet, "Ye have lived well"; but the German word "schwelgen" so exactly describes the Greek that one wonders why he did not adopt it; the English "to revel" comes nearest to it, and this is the R.V. rendering of the word in the Sir. passage referred to. τρυφᾶν with its compounds is used in a good as well as in a bad sense; for the former see Ps. xxxvii. 4, 11; Isa. lv. 2, lxvi. 11; Neh. ix. 25.—ἐπὶ τῆς γῆς: the contrast is between their enjoyment of the good things of the earth and what their lot is to be hereafter; cf. Luke xvi. 25, "Remember that thou in thy lifetime receivedst thy good things, and Lazarus in like manner evil things; but now he is comforted, and thou art in anguish".—ἐσπαταλήσατε: only elsewhere in N.T. in 1 Tim. v. 6; it occurs in Ezek. xvi. 49 of the women of Jerusalem who are compared to those of Sodom; see also Sir. xxi. 15; the compound κατασπ. occurs in Am. vi. 4; Prov. xxix. 21; neither the word itself nor its compound is used in a good sense, expressing as it does the living of a life of wanton self-indulgence.—ἐθρέψατε τὰς καρδίας ὑμῶν: this use of καρδία is thoroughly Hebraic, לב being used in a very wide sense in Hebrew, cf. Ps. civ. 15, ". . . and bread

---

*This is not biblical Hebrew, which would be התענג (Isa. lxvi. 11), or
התעון (Neh. ix. 25); ברע occurs in the Targums, but means there "to shout
for joy".

t Hos. i. 6
(Sept.).
u Luke xxi.
19; Heb.
x. 36.
v 1 Thess.
ii. 19.
w Matt.
xxi. 33.
x Sir. vi. 19.

6. κατεδικάσατε,¹ ἐφονεύσατε τὸν δίκαιον ᵛ· οὐκ ᵗἀντιτάσσεται
ὑμῖν.³

7. ᵘΜακροθυμήσατε οὖν,⁴ ἀδελφοί, ἕως τῆς ᵛπαρουσίας τοῦ
Κυρίου. ἰδοὺ ὁ ᵂγεωργὸς ˣἐκδέχεται τὸν τίμιον καρπὸν τῆς γῆς

¹ Add et ff.   ² δικαιον. WH.   ³ υμιν ; WHmg.   ⁴ Om. ουν s.

that strengtheneth man's heart" (לבב
which does not differ from לב in meaning), cf. Jud. xix. 5.—ἐν ἡμέρᾳ σφαγῆς : there is something extremely significant in this quotation from Jer. xii. 3,
because Jeremiah uses this expression
(יום הרגה) as the day of judgment;
and not only so, but this prophet had also
coined a new word for Gehenna, viz.,
"Geharêgah" = "the valley of slaughter" (Jer. vii. 32. xix. 6). These expressions—"day of slaughter" and "valley
of slaughter " — belong to Jeremiah
(Enoch, xvi. 1 quotes the expression καὶ
ἀπὸ ἡμέρας καιροῦ σφαγῆς), and in using
the words "day of slaughter" the writer
of our Epistle is undoubtedly giving them
the meaning that they had originally;
the passage before us probably means
that these luxurious livers will be revel-
ling in self-indulgence on the very day
of judgment, cf. our Lord's words in
Luke xvii. 27 ff., "They ate, they drank
. . . and the flood came and destroyed
them all . . . after the same manner
shall it be in the day that the Son of
man is revealed". The tense ἐθρέψατε
is in accordance with Hebrew usage of
regarding a thing in the future as having
already taken place; it is wholly in the
prophetic style.

Ver. 6. κατεδικάσατε, ἐφονεύσατε τὸν δίκαιον: this expresses
what must often have taken place; the
prophetical books often refer to like
things; there is no reason for regarding
this as some specific case of judicial
murder. Cf. Am. ii. 6, 7, v. 12; Wisd. ii.
10 ff. The antithesis between the צדיק
("righteous ") and רשע ("wicked ") is
a commonplace in Jewish theology.—
οὐκ ἀντιτάσσεται ὑμῖν : the
statement of fact here, instead of the
interrogative as read by some authorities,
is more natural, and more in accordance
with the prophetical style which is so
characteristic of this whole passage. This
picture of patient acquiescence in ill-
treatment is really a very vivid touch, for
it shows, on the one hand, that the

down-trodden realised the futility of
resistance; on the other, that their hopes
were centred on the time to come.

With the whole of this section cf.
the words in The first book of Clement,
which is called The Testament of our
Lord Jesus Christ, 12 : "The harvest is
come, that the guilty may be reaped and
the Judge appear suddenly and confront
them with their works".

Vv. 7-11. The section 7-11 is a Christian adaptation of the earlier Jewish conception of the Messianic Era; in place
of αἱ ἐσχάται ἡμέραι there is ἡ παρουσία
τοῦ Κυρίου, the one a specifically Jewish, the other a specifically Christian expression; the two expressions, which represent, as it were, the titles of Jewish
and Christian Eschatology respectively,
are sufficient to show the difference of
venue regarding these two sections. It
is characteristic of one type of apocalyptic literature that the central figure
of the Messiah is not mentioned, while
another type lays great emphasis on the
Messianic Personality; vv. 1-6 represents
the former of these; that it contains no
trace of Christian interpolation is the
more remarkable in that it is utilised by a
Jewish-Christian writer and is incorporated in Christian literature. The fact is
additional evidence in favour of its being
a quotation,—one of several which our
Epistle contains. It is christianised by
the addition to it of vv. 7-11, which,
though interspersed with O.T. reminiscences, is specifically Christian. A
similar christianising of Jewish material
by adding to it is found, though on a
much smaller scale, in Rev. xxii. 20,
Ἀμὴν ἔρχου κύριε Ἰησοῦ, which forms a
response to the preceding ναί, ἔρχομαι
ταχύ. Dr. Schiller-Szinessy (in Encycl.
Brit., art. "Midrash") discovered that
the Hebrew equivalent of the words Ἀμήν
ἔρχου (= אמן בא) indicated acros-
tically a primitive hymn, which still appears in all the Jewish prayer books, and
is known from its opening words as 'Ἐκ
Kelohenu ("There is none like our God");
see Singer's The Authorised Daily Prayer

ʸ μακροθυμῶν ἐπ᾽ αὐτῷ¹ ἕως² λάβῃ³ ᶻπρόϊμον⁴ καὶ ὄψιμον.⁵ y Sir. xviii.
8. μακροθυμήσατε⁶ καὶ ὑμεῖς, ªστηρίξατε τὰς καρδίας ὑμῶν, ὅτι ἡ
ᵇπαρουσία τοῦ Κυρίου ἤγγικεν. 9. μὴ στενάζετε, ἀδελφοί,⁷ κατ z Deut. xi.

11; Luke
viii. 15,
xviii. 17.
14; Job
xxix. 23

Jer. v. 24; Joel ii. 23; Zech. x. 1.   a 1 Thess. ii. 16, iii. 13.   b Heb. x. 25; 1 Pet. iv. 7
cf. Rom. xiii. 11.

¹ αυτον KL, curss., Thl.; om. Vulg., Arm.
² Add αν אP⸆, 13, rec.; add ου curss.
³ Add νετον AKLP, curss., Pesh., rec.; add καρπον א³ (καρπον τον א¹), Copt.
⁴ πρωιμον B³KL, curss.   ⁵ Add fructum ff.   ⁶ Add ουν אL, 9.
⁷ Add μου A⸆, 13, pon post; αλληλων אL, Syrr., Thl., Oec., Ti.; om. K, 15, 16.

Book, p. 167). This hymn consists of five verses of four lines each; the first word of each line in the first verse begins with א, of the second verse with מ, of the third with נ, of the fourth with ב, and of the fifth with א, thus making a four-fold repetition of the formula אמן בא (= "Amen, Come"). This formula is the short title of the hymn referred to and " is actually written instead of the hymn in the place where it is to be used after the Additional Service for the New Year, and again towards the conclusion of the additional service for the eighth day of Solemn Assembly . . ., at the end of the Feast of Tabernacles" (Taylor, *The Teaching of the Twelve Apostles*, pp. 78 ff., and see Box in *Church and Synagogue*, iii., pp. 41 ff.). The formula "Amen Bo" belonged to Jewish Eschatology, and possibly took its origin from the phrase עולם הבא (= "The age to come," a common expression for the Messianic Era); it is christianised by the Jewish-Christian writer in the Apocalypse by the addition of κύριε Ἰησοῦ, just as in the passage before us the second, obviously Christian, section vv. 7-11, is added on to the former, quite as obviously Jewish, in order to make the whole Christian.

Ver. 7. Μακροθυμήσατε οὖν: the verb, as well as the adjective, is used both of God and man, *e.g.*, Rom. ii. 4; 2 Cor. vi. 6; it expresses the attitude of mind which is content to wait; when used of God it refers to His long-suffering towards men (*e.g.*, Sir. xviii. 11); it is possible that in the present connection this is also implied in view of ver. 9.— Perhaps οὖν was added in order to join it on to the preceding section; it is omitted by the OL MS. *s*.—ἕως τῆς παρουσίας τοῦ Κυρίου: see above, introductory words to this section. Πα-

ρουσία does not occur in the Septuagint, being (with τοῦ Κυρίου) specifically Christian; but with τοῦ Θεοῦ, instead of τοῦ Κυρίου, it occurs in *Test. of the Twelve Patriarchs*, Jud. xxii. 2, ἕως παρουσίας τοῦ Θεοῦ τῆς δικαιοσύνης (the words are omitted in the Armenian Version).—ὁ γεωργός: *Cf.* Sir. vi. 18; *Test. of the Twelve Patriarchs*, Issach. v. 3 ff.—καρπόν: used in the sense of "produce of the soil".—ἕως λάβῃ: the context shows that the subject must be "the earth," not "the fruit," for the simple reason that the fruit is not in existence when the "former" rains descend; the great importance of the "former" rains (called both יורה and מורה) was that they moistened the earth (commencing about the month of October) after it had been hardened by the blazing summer sun, and thus enabled it to receive the seed; without the "former" rains to moisten the earth one might as well sow seed on rocks. The subject might possibly be "the husbandman" as he may be said in a certain sense to receive the rain, but the most obvious subject, and that upon which the meaning of the verse most naturally depends, is the earth.—πρόϊμον καὶ ὄψιμον: *Cf.* Deut. xi. 14, and often, יורה ומלקוש Ver. 8. στηρίξατε τὰς καρδίας: a Hebrew idiom, סעד לב; in the O.T. mostly of strengthening the body with food.—ἡ παρουσία τοῦ Κυρίου ἤγγικεν: see above; *cf.* Matt. iii. 2; Luke xxi. 28; Phil. iv. 6; 1 Pet. iv. 7; 1 Cor. xv. 52; 1 Thess. iv. 15; 1 John i. 18.

Ver. 9. μὴ στενάζετε: "A strengthened expression for μὴ καταλαλεῖτε iv. 11" (Carr); it refers to the inward feeling of grudge against another. The word shows that it is not only the righteous who are addressed in this section.—

ᶜ 2 (4) Esdr.
viii. 18;
ἀλλήλων ἵνα μὴ κριθῆτε¹ · ἰδοὺ ὁ ᵒκριτὴς πρὸ τῶν ᵈθυρῶν² ἔστηκεν.³

cf. 1 Pet.
iv.5; Rev.
10. ᵉὑπόδειγμα⁴ λάβετε,⁵ ἀδελφοί,⁶ τῆς κακοπαθείας⁷ καὶ τῆς

xxii. 12.
d Matt.
ᶠμακροθυμίας⁸ τοὺς ᵍπροφήτας, οἳ ʰἐλάλησαν ἐν⁹ τῷ¹⁰ ὀνόματι

xxiv. 33;
Mark xiii.
Κυρίου.¹¹ 11. ἰδοὺ ¹μακαρίζομεν τοὺς ᵏἱπομείναν-

29; *cf.* 1
Cor. iv. 5.
τας¹¹² · τὴν ὑπομονὴν ¹᾽Ιὼβ ἠκούσατε, καὶ τὸ τέλος¹³ Κυρίου εἴδετε,¹⁴

e John xiii.
15; Heb.
ὅτι ᵐπολύσπλαγχνός¹⁵ ἐστιν ὁ Κύριος¹⁶ καὶ ⁿοἰκ-

iv. 11; 2
Pet. ii. 6.
τίρμων ᵐ 12. Πρὸ πάντων δέ,¹⁷ ἀδελφοί ᵒμου,¹⁸ μὴ ὀμνύετε, μήτε

f Col. i. 11.
g Matt. v.
12.
τὸν οὐρανὸν μήτε τὴν γῆν μήτε ἄλλον τινὰ ὅρκον · ἤτω δὲ¹⁹ ὑμῶν τὸ

h 2 Pet. i. 21.   i—i *Cf.* Dan. xii. 12. See Matt. v. 10.   k Matt. x. 22; Col. i. 11.
l Job i. 21, 22, ii. 10.   m—m Ps. ciii. 8, cxi. 4; *cf.* Num. xiv. 18.   n Luke vi. 36.   o—o Matt.
v. 34-37; *cf.* Mal. iii. 5; Heb. vi. 16.

¹ κατακριθητε ⊐·   ² Januam *ff.*   ³ Stat *ff.*   ⁴ Add δε ⊐·

⁵ λαβετε . . . και της μακροθυμιας εχετε (lectio ex duabus confusa) ⊐; om.
λαβετε A, 13, Aeth.

⁶ Add μου אKL, 13, rec.   ⁷ κακοπαθιας B¹P, WH; καλοκαγαθιας א.

⁸ Add εχετε א³A, 13, Aeth.   ⁹ Om. εν AKL⊐, curss.

¹⁰ Om.τω א, Chrys.   ¹¹ Pr. του ⊐.

¹² υπομενοντας KL ⊐, curss., Copt., Arm., Aeth., Thl., Oec., rec.

¹³ ελεος 27, 29.   ¹⁴ ιδετε AB³LP, curss.   ¹⁵ πολυευσπλαγχνος curss., Thl.

¹⁶ Om. ο Κυριος KL, curss.; om. ο B, WHmg, Weiss.

¹⁷ ουν א¹; om. K, curss.   ¹⁸ Om. μου ⊐.

¹⁹ Add ο λογος א*, 8, Copt., Aeth.

ὁ κριτὴς πρὸ τῶν θυρῶν ἔστη-
κεν : *Cf.* Rev. iii. 20. For the idea of
the Judge standing at the door see Matt.
xxiv. 33, . . . γινώσκετε ὅτι ἐγγύς ἐστιν
ἐπὶ θύραις, xxv. 10 ff. (the parable of the
Ten Virgins). In its origin the idea
is antique; *cf.* the following from the
Mishna (*Ab.* iv. 16) : "This world is as
if it were a vestibule to the future world;
prepare thyself in the vestibule, that thou
mayest enter the reception-room"; this
saying is one of Jacob of Korsha's who
lived in the second century A.D.—ἔστηκεν : for the tense see above.
Ver. 10. ὑπόδειγμα : *Cf.* Sir. xliv.
16 and especially John xiii. 15, ὑπόδ.
ἔδωκα ὑμῖν . . . of our Lord.—τῆς
κακοπαθείας : ἅπ. λεγ. in N.T. *cf.* 4
Macc. ix. 8. It means "endurance" rather
than the R.V. "suffering"; this goes
better with μακροθυμίας, "patience".
The rendering "endurance" has support
from the papyri, see Deissmann, *Neue
Bibelst.*, pp. 91 f.—ἐν τῷ ὀνόματι:
although this use of the phrase is paralleled by its use in the papyri (see Deissmann, *Bibelst.*, pp. 143-5: *Neue Bibelst.*,
pp. 25, 26), it is more probable that in this
case it comes through the Septuagint
from the Hebrew בשם; *cf.* above ii. 7.

Ver. 11. μακαρίζομεν : *Cf.* 4
Macc. xviii. 13, used in reference to
Daniel.—᾽Ιώβ : Job occupies a high
place of honour in post-biblical Jewish
literature, *cf.* the pseudepigraphic work
"The Testament of Job".—τὸ τέλος
Κυρίου : the final purpose of Jehovah
with regard to Job; it could not refer to
Christ, for the whole passage is dealing
with O.T. examples.—πολύσπλαγχ-
νος : ἅπ. λεγ. in N.T.—οἰκτίρμων:
only elsewhere in N.T. in Luke vi. 36;
cf. Sir. ii. 11 and often in the Septuagint.

Ver. 12. Πρὸ πάντων . . .: The
most natural way of understanding these
words would be to take them in connection with something that immediately
preceded, but as there is not the remotest
connection between this verse and the
section that has gone just before, this is impossible here; the verse must be regarded
as the fragment of some larger piece; it
is not the only instance in this Epistle of
a quotation which has been incorporated,
only in this case the fragmentary character is more than usually evident. That
it is not a quotation from the Gospel, as
we now have it (Matt. v. 33-37), must be
obvious, for if it were this, it would
unquestionably approximate more closely

[p] ναὶ ναὶ, καὶ τὸ οὒ οὔ, ἵνα μὴ ὑπὸ κρίσιν[1] πέσητε.° 13. [q] Κακοπαθεῖ
τις ἐν[2] ὑμῖν; προσευχέσθω· εὐθυμεῖ τις; [r] ψαλλέτω. 14. ἀσθενεῖ[3]
τις ἐν ὑμῖν; προσκαλεσάσθω τοὺς [s] πρεσβυτέρους τῆς ἐκκλησίας,[4]
καὶ προσευξάσθωσαν ἐπ' αὐτὸν[5] [t] ἀλείψαντες[6] ἐλαίῳ ἐν ὀνόματι τοῦ

p 2 Cor. i. 17, 18.
q Ps. l. 15.
r Rom. xv. 9; 1 Cor. xiv. 15; Eph. v. 19; Col. iii. 16.
s Acts xi. 30.
t Mark vi. 13; *cf.* xvi. 18.

[1] εις υποκρισιν KLPב, curss., rec. (ed. Steph.). [2] Ex *ff*.
[3] Pr. et *ff*. [4] Om. της εκκλησιας *ff*. [5] αυτους א[1].
[6] Add αυτον אAKL, curss., Treg.

to the original; on the other hand, its general similarity to the Gospel passage proves that there must be a relationship of some kind between the two. Probably both trace their origin to a saying of our Lord's which became modified in transmission, assuming various forms while retaining the essential point. An example of a similar kind can be seen by comparing together Matt. x. 26; Luke viii. 17 and the fourth of the New Oxyrhynchus Sayings: Λέγει Ἰησοῦς Πᾶν τὸ μὴ ἔμπροσθεν τῆς ὄψεώς σου καὶ τὸ κεκρυμμένον ἀπὸ σοῦ ἀποκαλυφθήσεται. οὐ γάρ ἐστιν κρυπτὸν ὃ οὐ φανερὸν γενήσεται καὶ τεθαμμένον ὃ οὐκ ἐγερθήσεται (Grenfell and Hunt's restoration). In any case the verse before us must originally have been preceded by a context which contained various precepts of which this was regarded as the most important, on account of the words πρὸ πάντων.—μὴ ὀμνύετε . . .: this was a precept enjoined by many of the more devout Jews; Pharisees avoided oaths as much as possible, the Essenes never swore; a very good pre-Christian example of the same precept is contained in Sir. xxiii. 9-11, Ὅρκῳ μὴ ἐθίσῃς τὸ στόμα σου, καὶ ὀνομασίᾳ τοῦ ἁγίου μὴ συνεθισθῇς . . . ἀνὴρ πολύορκος πλησθήσεται ἀνομίας . . .—ἤτω: *Cf.* 1 Cor. xvi. 22, the only other occurrence of this form in the N.T.

Ver. 13. κακοπαθεῖ: See note on v. 10; it refers perhaps rather to mental worry or distress, while ἀσθενεῖ refers to some specific bodily ailment.—εὐθυμεῖ; only found elsewhere in Acts xxvii. 22, 25 in the N.T.—ψαλλέτω: refers both to playing on a stringed instrument (Sir. ix. 4) and to singing (Eph. v. 19), and is also used of singing with the spirit (1 Cor. xiv. 15).

Ver. 14. ἀσθενεῖ . . . προσκαλεσάσθω, etc.: *Cf.* Sir. xxxviii. 14, καὶ γὰρ αὐτοὶ Κυρίου δεηθήσονται, ἵνα εὐοδώσῃ αὐτοῖς ἀνάπαυσιν καὶ ἴασιν χάριν ἐμβιώσεως. In regard to the practice of primitive Christianity in the matter of caring for the sick Harnack says: "Even from the fragments of our extant literature, although that literature was not written with any such intention, we can still recognise the careful attention paid to works of mercy. At the outset we meet with directions everywhere to care for sick people, 1 Thess. v. 14. . . . In the prayer of the Church, preserved in the first epistle of Clement, supplications are expressly offered for those who are sick in soul and body (1 Clem. lix., τοὺς ἀσθενεῖς ἴασαι . . . ἐξανάστησον τοὺς ἀσθενοῦντας, παρακάλεσον τοὺς ὀλιγοψυχοῦντας). . . . Epistle of Polycarp, vi. 1; Justin Martyr, lxvii. . . ."; he also quotes Lactantius, *Div. Inst.*, vi. 12: "Aegros quoque quibus defuerit qui adsistat, curandos fovendosque suscipere summae humanitatis et magnae operationis est" (*Expansion* . . . i. 147 f. first English ed.). A like care was characteristic of the Rabbis, who declared it to be a duty incumbent upon every Jew to visit and relieve the sick whether they were Jews or Gentiles (*Git.*, 61 *a*, *Soṭah*, 14 *a*); "the *Haberim*, or *Ḥasidic* associations, made the performance of this duty a special obligation" (*Jewish Encycl.*, xi. 327).—τοὺς πρεσβυτέρους τῆς ἐκκλησίας: both the words "presbyters" (= "priest") and "ecclesia" were taken over from the Jews, being the Greek equivalents for זקנים and קהל. While, however, the word πρεσβύτερος was, without question, in the Christian Church taken over from the זקן in the Jewish Church, it is well to recall the extended use which attached to it according to the evidence of the papyri. The phrase ὁ πρεσβύτερος τῆς κώμης occurs on a papyrus belonging to the time of the Ptolemies, and is evidently an official title of some kind; οἱ πρεσβύτεροι is found together with ἱερεῖς of an idola-

u *Cf.* Acts **Κυρίου.**¹ 15. **καὶ ἡ εὐχὴ** ² **τῆς** ᵘ**πίστεως** ᵛ**σώσει τὸν κάμνοντα, καὶ**
ix. 40,
xxviii. 8, **ἐγερεῖ αὐτὸν ὁ Κύριος· κἂν ἁμαρτίας ᾖ** ³ ʷ**πεποιηκώς, ἀφεθήσεται** ⁴
and see
Matt.ix.2.
v Matt. ix. 21, 22.   w Is. xxxiii. 24; Mark ii. 5; Luke v. 20; *cf.* i Jn. v. 16.

¹ Om. τοῦ Κυρίου BA, Orig., Tregᵐ ; ῑῡ χ̄ῡ ϵ. WH place it in brackets.

² προσευχη P, curss.   ³ ην ב.   ⁴ αφεθησονται P, 7.

trous worship (c. 40 B.C.); and in the
second century A.D. οἱ πρεσβύτεροι
occurs in reference to "elders" of villages
in Egypt. The Septuagint translators
were therefore probably using in this case
a word which had a well-known technical
sense. Deissmann believes it possible,
therefore, that the Christian congregations of Asia Minor got the title of πρεσβύτερος from the minor officials who
were so called, and not necessarily from
the Jewish prototype (*Op. cit.*, pp. 153
f.). This might well be the case in various centres, though not all (as for example, Babylonia), of the Diaspora, but
not in Palestine. It is, of course, an
open question as to whether our Epistle
was written from Palestine or not; see,
further, Deissmann (*Neue Bibelst.* pp.
60 ff.). As regards ἐκκλησία, Harnack
remarks that "originally it was beyond
question a collective term (*i.e.*, קָהָל) ;
it was the most solemn expression of the
Jews for their worship as a collective
body, and as such it was taken over by
the Christians. But ere long it was applied to the individual communities, and
then again to the general meeting for
worship. . . . Its acquisition rendered
the capture of the term 'synagogue' a
superfluity, and once the inner cleavage
had taken place, the very neglect of the
latter title served to distinguish Christians
sharply from Judaism and its religious
gatherings even in terminology. . . .
Most important of all, however, was
the fact that ἐκκλησία was conceived of,
in the first instance, not simply as an
earthly but as a heavenly and transcen-
dental entity" (*op. cit.*, pp. 11 ff.);
"קָהָל (usually rendered ἐκκλησία in
LXX) denotes the community in relation
to God, and consequently is more sacred
than the profaner עֵדָה (regularly translated by συναγωγή in the LXX). . . .
Among the Jews ἐκκλησία lagged far
behind συναγωγή in practical use, and
this was all in favour of the Christians
and their adoption of the term" (*ibid.*).
In the verse before us it is the combination of these two terms, οἱ πρεσβύτεροι
τῆς ἐκκλησίας which points to a de-

veloped organisation among the communities of the Diaspora, and therefore
to a late date for this part of the Epistle.
—ἀλείψαντες ἐλαίῳ: a common
Jewish usage, see Isa. i. 6; Mark vi.
13; Luke x. 34. As oil was believed to
have the effect of curing bodily sickness, so it became customary to use it
preparatory to Baptism, possibly with the
idea of its healing, sacramentally, the
disease of sin; that it was joined to
Baptism as an integral part of the sacrament is certain. Prayer was, of course,
an indispensable accompaniment.— ἐν
ὀνόματι . . .: *Cf.* Mark xvi. 17;
Luke x. 17; Acts iii. 6, 16, iv. 10, xvi.
18; and on the formula, the note above,
ii. 17.

Ver. 15. ἡ εὐχὴ τῆς πίστεως:
Cf. Matt. xxi. 22.—σώσει: for this
sense *cf.* Matt. ix. 22; Mark v. 23; John
xi. 12.—κάμνοντα: in this sense only
here in the N.T., though it is used in a
somewhat similar sense in Hebrew xii. 3.
—ἐγερεῖ: it seems most natural to take
this as referring to the sick man being
raised up from his bed of sickness, though
the use of κάμνειν in Heb. xii. 3 suggests
the possibility of spiritual comfort being
also included.—ὁ Κύριος: this must
probably refer to Christ, though the O.T.
reference in the context would justify the
contention that Jahwe is meant.—κἂν:
Cf. Mark xvi. 18; Luke xiii. 9, as showing that this does not necessarily mean
"even if". —ἁμαρτίας ᾖ πεποιηκώς ἀφεθήσεται αὐτῷ: *Cf.* Sir.
xxxviii. 9, 10, Τέκνον, ἐν ἀρρωστήματί
σου μὴ παράβλεπε, ἀλλ' εὖξαι Κυρίῳ,
καὶ αὐτὸς ἰάσεταί σε· ἀπόστησον πλημμελίαν καὶ εὔθυνον χεῖρας, καὶ ἀπὸ
πάσης ἁμαρτίας καθάρισον καρδίαν;
The Jewish belief on this subject
may be illustrated by the following:
in *Test. of the Twelve Patriarchs*,
Simeon, ii. 11 ff., because Simeon
continued wrathful against Reuben, he
says, "But the Lord restrained me, and
withheld from me the power of my
hands; for my right hand was half
withered for seven days"; in Gad. v. 9 ff.
the patriarch confesses that owing to his
hatred against Joseph God brought upon

αὐτῷ. 16. ˣ ἐξομολογεῖσθε οὖν ¹ ἀλλήλοις τὰς ἁμαρτίας,² καὶ προσ- x Sir. iv. 26.
εύχεσθε ³ ὑπὲρ ἀλλήλων, ὅπως ʸ ἰαθῆτε.⁴ πολὺ ἰσχύει δέησις δικαίου   y Matt. xiii.
ˣ ἐνεργουμένη. 17. ᵃ Ἡλείας ⁵ ἄνθρωπος ἦν ὁμοιοπαθὴς ἡμῖν, καὶ   15; Luke iv. 18;
προσευχῇ ᵇ προσηύξατο τοῦ μὴ βρέξαι, καὶ οὐκ ἔβρεξεν ἐπὶ τῆς γῆς   Heb. xii. 13.
ἐνιαυτοὺς ᶜτρεῖς καὶ μῆνας ἕξ· 18. καὶ ⁶ πάλιν ᵈ προσηύξατο, καὶ ὁ   z 2 Cor. i.6; 1 Tim. ii. 1; cf.
οὐρανὸς ἱἐτὸν ἔδωκεν ⁷ καὶ ἡ γῆ ἐβλάστησεν τὸν καρπὸν αὐτῆς.   Gen.xviii. 23-32; Jn. ix. 31; Acts viii.

24; 1 Pet. iii. 12.   a 1 Kgs. xvii. 1, xviii. 1; Acts xiv. 15.   b Cf. Sir. xlviii. 2, 3, Luke xxii.
15; Rev. xi. 6.   c Luke iv. 25.   d 1 Kgs. xviii. 42, 45; 2 (4) Esdr. vii. 39.

¹ Om. L, curss., ff, Arm., Aeth.; δε 107, Pesh.

² τα παραπτωματα KL, curss., Pesh., Orig., Thl., Oec.; add υμων L, 69, a, c, ff, Vulg., Syrr., Copt., Aeth.

³ ευχεσθε אKLP, curss., Thl., Oec., Treg., Ti., WH (altern. reading).

⁴ Ut remittatur vobis ff.   ⁵ Ηλιας אAB³KLP, curss.

⁶ Sed ff.   ⁷ εδωκεν υετον A, 13, 73, Latt., Treg., Ti., WHmg,; εδ. τον υετ. א.

him a disease of the liver, "and had not the prayers of Jacob my father succoured me, it had hardly failed but my spirit had departed". That sin brings disease was, likewise in the later Jewish literature, an article of faith, indeed here one finds specified what are the particular sicknesses that particular sins bring in their train. According to Rabbinical teaching there are four signs by means of which it is possible to recognise the sin of which a man has been guilty: dropsy is the sign that the sin of fornication has been committed, jaundice that of unquenchable hatred, poverty and humiliation that of pride, liver complaint (?) (אסכרה) that of back-biting. In Shabbath, 55 a, it says: "No death without sin, no chastisement without evil-doing", and in Nedarim, 41 a it says: "No recovery without forgiveness". Leprosy may be due to one of eleven sins, but most probably to that of an evil tongue (see Weber, Jüdische Theologie, pp. 245 f.).

Ver. 16. ἐξομολογεῖσθε . . . ἁμαρτίας: see critical note above. Confession of sins has always played an important part in Judaism; the O.T. word for confession of sins is תודה,* the later term, which denotes more particularly the liturgical form of confession, is וידוי. Private as well as public confession was enjoined, and many forms of confession, both general and particular, exist, among others one for the sick; it was the duty of the Rabbis to urge the sick person to confess his sins. Confession is regarded as a meritorious act:

according to Sanhedrin, 103 a, it has the effect of enabling the worst sinners to inherit everlasting life (see, among other authorities, Hamburger's Realencycl. des Judent, article "Sündenbekenntniss".). For the custom of the early Church cf. Didache, iv. 14, xiv. 1.—προσεύχεσθε ὑπὲρ ἀλλήλων: the need of intercessory prayer is strongly emphasised in O.T., N.T. and the later Jewish literature, see above and the next note.—πολὺ ἰσχύει δέησις δικαίου ἐνεργουμένη: one is reminded of the well-known instance of Rabbi Johanan ben Zakkai (end of first century, A.D.) who, when in need of the prayers of a righteous man on behalf of his sick child, said, "Although I am greater in learning than Chaninah, he is more efficacious in prayer; I am, indeed, the Prince, but he is the steward who has constant access to the King" (Berachoth, 34 b). A curious saying of Rabbi Isaac is contained in Jebamoth, 64 a: "The prayer of the righteous is comparable to a pitchfork; as the pitchfork changes the position of the wheat so the prayer changes the disposition of God from wrath to mercy" (quoted in Jewish Encycl., x. 169). With δικαίου cf. δίκαιον in ver. 6. On ἐνεργουμένη see Mayor's elaborate note.

Ver. 17. Ἡλείας: Elijah plays an immense part in the later Jewish literature, see Hamburger, op. cit., article "Elias". With his mention here cf. Sir. xlviii. 1 ff.—προσευχῇ προσηύξατο: Hebraism cf. Luke xxii. 15; John iii. 29, etc., etc.

Ver. 18. With this and the preceding

* This word is sometimes used as meaning praise given to God by the act of confession of sins, cf. Ryle, Ezra . . ., p. 132.

e--e Cf. Gal. 19. **Ἀδελφοί μου,[1] ἐάν τις ἐν ὑμῖν πλανηθῇ ἀπὸ τῆς[2] ἀληθείας καὶ
vi. τ.
f Matt. [f] ἐπιστρέψῃ τις αὐτόν,* 20. γινώσκετε ὅτι[3] ὁ [f] ἐπιστρέψας ἁμαρτωλὸν
xviii. 15.
g Ps. li. 13 ἐκ πλάνης ὁδοῦ αὐτοῦ[4] [h] σώσει[5] [16] ψυχὴν αὐτοῦ ἐκ θανάτου[6] καὶ
(15 in
Heb .); [k] κ α λ ύ ψ ε ι[7] πλῆθος ἁμαρτιῶν.[8]
Mal. ii. 6;
cf. Prov.
xi. 30. h Rom. xi. 14; cf. xiii. 9.　　i Acts xxvii. 37.　　k Cf. Prov. x. 12; 1 Pet. iv. 8, and
see Ps. xxxii. 1, lxxxv. 2; Rom. iv. 7.

[1] Om. L, curss., Did., Oec., rec.　　[2] Add οδου της ℵ, 5, Pesh., Copt.

[3] γινωσκετω οτι ℵAKLP, Treg., Ti., WHmg; om. ff, Sah.

[4] Om. ff.　　[5] Salvat ff, Orig.; salvavit Vulgᵣ.

[6]—[6] την ψυχην A, 73, Arm.; om. αυτου KL, curss., Sah., Orig., Thl., Oec., Treg.;.
pon αυτου post θαν. B, ff, Aeth., Weiss, WHmg.

[7] καλυπτει Vulg., Orig., Dam.　　[8] Peccati ff; add αμην 40.

Subscr. ιακωβου B; επιστολη ιακωβου ℵ; ιακωβου επιστολη A, 40, 67, 177;
ιακωβου αποστολου επιστολη καθολικη P, 63; τελος του αγιου αποστολου ιακωβου
επιστολη καθολικη L; τελος της επιστολης του αγιου αποστολου ιακωβου τοι
αδελφοθεου 38; explicit epistola Jacobi filii Zaebedei ff; most MSS. have no subscr.

verse cf. Taʻanith, 24 b, where we are told of how Rabbi Chaninah, on being caught in a shower of rain, prayed: "Master of the Universe, the whole world is pleased, while Chaninah alone is annoyed"; then the rain immediately ceased. On arriving home he prayed: "Master of the Universe, shall all the world be grieved while Chaninah enjoys his comfort?" Whereupon the rain came down again (see *Jewish Encycl.*, vi. 215).

Ver. 19. πλανηθῇ: "The passive aorist is used with a middle force in classical writers, as well as in the LXX, Deut. xxxii. 1; Ps. cxix. 176; Ezek. xxxiv. 4" (Mayor). — ἀπὸ τῆς ἀληθείας: Cf. Mark xii. 14, . . . ἐπ' ἀληθείας τὴν ὁδὸν τοῦ θεοῦ διδάσκεις, this seems to be the way in which ἀλήθεια is here used, cf. John iii. 21, v. 33; viii. 32.—ἐπιστρέψῃ: excepting here (and in the next verse) and Luke i. 16, 17 this word is always used intransitively in the N.T. (cf. however Acts xxvi. 18).

Ver. 20. γινώσκετε: taking this as an indicative one may regard the words that follow as a quotation, a course which commends itself owing to the comparatively large number of quotations with which the Epistle abounds; at the same time it must be remembered that the weight of MS. evidence is in favour of γινωσκέτω. — καλύψει . . . (Hebrew כפר) cf. 1 Pet. iv. 8, one of the strongest of the many marks of Jewish authorship which the Epistle contains; according to Jewish doctrine good works balance evil ones; the good work of converting a sinner is reckoned here as one of the most efficacious in obliterating evil deeds; on the whole subject see Introduction IV., § 2.